Spanish Colonial Lives

Documents from the
Spanish Colonial Archives of New Mexico, 1705–1774

Spanish Colonial Lives

**Documents from the
Spanish Colonial Archives of New Mexico,
1705–1774**

A Companion in Part to
The Spanish Archives of New Mexico
by Ralph Emerson Twitchell

**Linda Tigges, Editor
J. Richard Salazar, Translator**

SANTA FE

© 2013 by Linda Tigges
All Rights Reserved.

No part of this book may be reproduced in any form or by any electronic or mechanical means including information storage and retrieval systems without permission in writing from the publisher, except by a reviewer who may quote brief passages in a review.

Sunstone books may be purchased for educational, business, or sales promotional use. For information please write: Special Markets Department, Sunstone Press, P.O. Box 2321, Santa Fe, New Mexico 87504-2321.

Book and Cover design › Vicki Ahl
Body typeface › Minion Pro
Printed on acid-free paper

Library of Congress Cataloging-in-Publication Data

Spanish colonial lives : documents from the Spanish colonial archives of New Mexico, 1705-1774 : a companion in part to the Spanish archives of New Mexico by Ralph Emerson Twitchell / Linda Tigges, editor ; J. Richard Salazar, translator.
  pages cm
 Includes bibliographical references and index.
  ISBN 978-0-86534-970-4 (hardcover : alk. paper) -- ISBN 978-0-86534-971-1 (softcover : alk. paper)
  1. New Mexico--History--To 1848. 2. New Mexico--History--To 1848--Sources. 3. New Mexico--History--To 1848--Biography. I. Tigges, Linda. II. Salazar, J. Richard, Translator. III. Twitchell, Ralph Emerson, 1859-1925. Spanish archives of New Mexico.
 F799.S694 2013
 978.9'01--dc23
                    2013035300

WWW.SUNSTONEPRESS.COM
SUNSTONE PRESS / POST OFFICE BOX 2321 / SANTA FE, NM 87504-2321 /USA
(505) 988-4418 / ORDERS ONLY (800) 243-5644 / FAX (505) 988-1025

CONTENTS

List of Illustrations 7
Appendix: Maps 7
Abbreviations in Text and Notes 7
Preface 9
Historical Introduction 12

DOCUMENTS

1. Colony in Danger of Demise; Cabildo Begs Viceroy for Soldiers and Provisions 33
2. New Mexicans Cut Out of Trading Market; Bandos Written to Limit Outsiders from Trading. . . 41
3. Governor Peñuela to the Viceroy: Presidio Soldiers Have Retaken Stolen Livestock near Albuquerque, More Guns and Horses Requested 57
4. Gambling in Santa Cruz Ends with Settler Pledging Saddle for Debt 61
5. Albuquerque Endangered by Indian Attacks; Settlers Demand Return of Presidio Soldiers 79
6. Baptism of Apaches Required 84
7. Bartolomé Garduño Delivers Mail to Mexico City, including a Wolf Skin, Piñon Nuts, and a Residencia Report; Accused of Illegal Behavior 91
8. Soldiers Flee Kingdom; Search by Presidio Soldiers Proves Futile 106
9. Escort Attacked by Apaches on Camino Real; Governor Holds Council of War 125
10. Deserter Found but Weapons and Horses Traded Away 149
11. Fight at Chimayó; Brother Defends Sister with Costly Results 160
12. Mother Petitions for Return of Son from the Royal Mines of Chihuahua 182
13. Sergeant Killed in Indian Attack; Widow Petitions for Death Benefits 185
14. Knives, Daggers, Carbines, Pistols, and Swords Prohibited in Towns by Viceroy and Governor 196
15. Religious Procession Takes Place at Santa Fe Parroquia; Edict of Faith Read 202
16. Treacherous Road Hazards Ordered Removed to Forestall Apache Attacks 214
17. Trip to Salt Lakes Announced for Santa Cruz, Taos, and Residents of the Tewa Jurisdiction . . 218
18. Knife Fight Results in Murder; Fugitive Claims Church Sanctuary, Pardoned for Moqui Campaign 221
19. Apprentice Contract for Ten-Year-Old Written by Tailor and Father for All Eventualities 235
20. Clash at Church Door between Governor Bustamante and Reverendo Padre Guerrero 240
21. Horse Trade for Young Apache Male Complicated When Mare Shot with Musket Ball 251
22. Sanctuary Claimed by Soldier after Threatening Sergeant; Accused Discharged from Presidio 261
23. Albuquerque Dispute over New Acequia; Injuries Feared for Family 295
24. Soldier Wounded When Bullet from Presidio Salvo Ricochets off Cemetery Monument 309
25. Pedro García Jurado Disciplined by Albuquerque Priest for Braided Hair 320
26. Silk Skirts Traded and Returned as False; Trader Complains 349
27. Accusations of Illegal Trading Exchanged by Northern New Mexico Officials; Governor Punishes Both 368
28. Albuquerque Ranchers Refuse Governor's Orders to Pull Livestock Back to Settlement 403
29. Meeting of Albuquerque Residents Held; Governor Prohibits Exports of Goods 408
30. Forty-Two Albuquerque Settlers Request Repeal of Trade Prohibitions 414
31. Pawnee Boy, Son of Family Servant , Identified in Animal Theft 421
32. Attack on Alcalde Mayor of Laguna; Wounded with Own Sword 431
33. Fuenclara Neighbors Trade Insults in Acequia Dispute 437
34. Parents Apply for Priesthood for Son and Are Investigated for Purity of Blood 449
35. Santa Fe Acequias to Be Cleaned as Mandated by Governor 461

36. Settlers Fear Moths, Plead for Sale of Wool 465
37. Salvador Martínez, Son of Former Governor Felix Martínez, Asks Viceroy for Appointment as Albuquerque Squadron Leader 470
38. Salvador Martínez and Soldiers, Stuck in Mexico City without Funds, Ask Viceroy for Help . . 478
39. Mexican Inquisition Investigates Bárbara García for Casting a Spell on Her Lover; Reference Made to Scandalous Priests 483
40. Deal Made between Traders Falls Apart; Blacksmith Petitions Governor Vélez Cachupín 491
41. Santa Cruz Rancher Registers Brand and Venta for Livestock 510
42. Taos Settlers Stall Building Fences Ordered by Governor Cachupín 515
43. Governor Marín del Valle Tightens Regulation of Trade Fairs; Retaliation by Indians Feared . 524
44. Royal Roads in Santa Fe to Be Unblocked; Offending Property Owners Listed 536
45. Bernardo Miera y Pacheco Petitions Governor to Repair Cannon; Villages Elders Express Doubt; Blacksmith Tomás de Sena Submits Bid 544
46. Presidio Drummer Esteban Rodríguez Reinstated as Requested by Soldiers 554
47. Drums, Leg Irons, Guns, Cannons, and Other Weapons Inventoried by Governor Cachupín . 558
48. Dead Mule and Horses Cause Dispute between Santa Cruz Trader and San Juan Indian; Why Money Is Better Than Barter 563
49. Return of Chinese Colcha with Silk Border Disputed by Santa Fe Residents 577
50. Chihuahua/Santa Fe Merchant Toribio Ortiz Sues for Seven Hides from Chama Trader 584
51. Relicario Stolen or Lost on Return from El Paso; Owner Accuses Soldier 610
52. Atrisco Family Members Dispute Entrances and Exits to Property 635
53. Flood Damages Visited by Governor and Local Worthies; Emergency Procedures Initiated . . . 645
54. Cadaver Found under Tree by Young Herder; Results in Inquest 649

Glossary 655
Appendix: Maps 658
Bibliography 665
Index 679

List of Illustrations

1. Felipe V, king of Spain, 1700–1724, 1724–1746 34
2. Tenth duke of Albuquerque and Marqués of Cuéllar, Francisco V Fernández de la Cueva Enríquez y Fernández de la Cueva, viceroy of New Spain, 1702–1710 37
3. Early New Mexico wooden stirrups with bindings. 63
4. First duke of Linares and Marqués of Valdefuentes, Gernando de Alencastre Noroña y Silva, viceroy from 1710 to 1716 97
5. Saddle used by presidio soldiers in the eighteenth century 153
6. Officer's pistol, made in Madrid in 1703 and found in Durango, México 197
7. Nuestra Señora de la Soledad (Our Lady of Solitude), ca. 1830, from northern New Mexico . . . 204
8. Second marqués of Casa Fuerte, Juan de Acuña, viceroy from 1722 to 1734 242
9. Corpus Christi procession on San Francisco Street, Santa Fe, New Mexico, ca. 1880 243
10. Late seventeenth-century, early eighteenth-century cup-hilt broadsword 264
11. Belduque, eighteenth century. 370
12. Fifth count of Fuenclara, Pedro Cebrián y Agustín, viceroy from 1742 to 1746. 433
13. *Cavador*, or digging hoe 462
14. First count of Revillagigedo, Juan Francisco de Güemes y Horcasitas, viceroy from 1746 to 1755. 479
15. Copy of petition for registration with brand and *marca* (*venta*) shown in the margin 512–513
16. St. Raphael, by Bernardo Miera y Pacheco, 1780. 545
17. Four-pounder Spanish light swivel cannon 549
18. Colonial lance. 559
19. *Escopeta*, an eighteenth-century smoothbore, muzzle-loading musket or carbine 559
20. Late eighteenth- or early nineteenth-century *mantón de Manila*, or embroidered silk shawl . . 578
21. Eighteenth-century Agnus Dei *relicario* medallion in gold frame 612

Appendix: Maps

1. 1767 Urrutia map 658
2. 1779 Miera y Pacheco map 659
3. Central and Northern New Spain in the Eighteenth Century 660
4. General Locations of Roving Indian Tribes in the Early and Mid-Eighteenth Century 661
5. New Mexico in the Early and Mid-Eighteenth Century, Upper Río Grande 662
6. New Mexico in the Early and Mid-Eighteenth Century, Lower Río Grande 663
7. Borderland Presidios in the Mid-Eighteenth Century 664

Abbreviations in Text and Notes

AGN: Archivo General de la Nación
SANM: Spanish Archives of New Mexico
NMGS: New Mexico Genealogical Society

The Journals of don Diego de Vargas

ASA: A Settling of Accounts
BOB: Blood on the Boulders
BFA: By Force of Arms
RBC: Remote Beyond Compare
RCR: To the Royal Crown Restored
TDC: That Disturbances Cease

PREFACE

Research on postrevolt Spanish Colonial New Mexico revealed that not many translated archival documents addressed the day-to-day life of New Mexicans. Many of the wills, land grants, and other transactions were translated in the 1930s by the Works Progress Administration (WPA). These were supplemented by the works of the Bandeliers, the Flints, John Kessell and Rick Hendricks, Alfred Barnaby Thomas, and others, mostly about military or mission history. This meant that for many subjects relating to the daily lives of the colonists, the same translated material was used over and over again, or else bits and pieces were extracted from longer documents with no chance to review the overall context and with no Spanish transcription to which the reader could refer.

Working with J. Richard Salazar, former director of the Archival Services Division at the New Mexico State Records Center and Archives, we found that the untranslated Spanish Colonial documents in New Mexico, California, Mexico City, and elsewhere were a rich source of information. These documents include mandates of the governors, petitions, lawsuits, and complaints from the settlers which, in addition to their historic significance, were interesting to read. Of particular interest were the interrogatories, similar to police and court investigations of witnesses and suspects, and in some cases similar to contemporary legal depositions. Some of these documents provided the words of people who were charged by or were bringing charges against someone else for civil and criminal violations of the law. Others were contracts, descriptions of events, councils of war, and governors' mandates and orders, all of which is good and useful stuff.

With the encouragement of publisher James Smith, Richard and I selected documents written mostly during the early and mid-eighteenth century, after the death of don Diego de Vargas and before don Juan Bautista de Anza became governor, although some are a bit later. In terms of subject matter, the general criteria for selection were that the documents reflect something about the everyday lives of the New Mexicans, have historical significance, and tell a good story. For the early period, 1705–1725, most of the documents are from the Spanish Archives of New Mexico (SANM II), the second volume of the compilation prepared by Ralph Emerson Twitchell. Later in the century, the documents are from a broader range of sources, including several from the Pinart Collection at the Bancroft Library at the University of California at Berkeley, many of which were taken from New Mexico in the later nineteenth century.

In regard to the editorial policy, the translations are intended to reflect the style and feeling of the writer or speaker. In many cases the reader is looking at a transcript, or something close to it, of the testimony of a person speaking to or being questioned by a local official or the governor. The investigations were often thorough, with the officials asking the same questions of several witnesses and suspects, often getting similar but slightly different answers. In response, the New Mexicans used everyday words, often rambled on, and sometimes added rhetorical flourishes they thought appropriate for the occasion. Even when some of the settlers were presenting a written petition or agreement, they appear to have written as they spoke, New Mexico at that time being a society where the character of communication was oral, and many people were illiterate, or nearly so. At the risk of being repetitious, nearly all of this language is included in the following documents.

To help the reader have a better sense of the document, we included a synopsis of each one and, in a couple of complicated cases, a procedural outline. Generally, notes from the editor are provided, giving the context or emphasizing points that might otherwise be overlooked. In a few cases where procedural phrases were repeated and did not contribute to understanding the document, the information is found only in the transcript. For some of the more difficult documents, where the testimony was emotionally charged, convoluted, or just plain muddled, explanatory language is included to assist in the reader's understanding.

To further provide a context for the documents, biographical notes and notes on words, place names, and other matters have been added. The biographical notes are provided for nearly all the persons mentioned, excluding witnesses who did not played a part in the discussion. For names that are repeated, the biographical footnote is provided only the first time the name is mentioned. All names and other key words are included in the index. In preparing the biographical notes, we relied on information from Alfred Barnaby Thomas, the Kessell and Hendricks volumes on don Diego de Vargas, the Fray Angélico Chávez book on *Origins of New Mexico Families*, as well as material written by Charles Cutter, Jim Norris, Eleanor Barrett, José Esquibel, Stanley Hordes, and others. Especially useful for the biographical notes were the materials published by the New Mexico Genealogical Society and the Hispanic Genealogical Research Center. These notes are intended to provide background rather than genealogical information, which can be found elsewhere.

Unless otherwise noted at the end of each document, the final version of the transcriptions and translations were made by J. Richard Salazar, sometimes with the assistance of Linda Tigges. Our general practice was to transcribe the documents as they were written, but to spell out abbreviations. The transcriptions are available following each translation. In regard to the translations, the style of the translations is intended to reflect the way of speaking and writing of the time, in some cases using Spanish word order. Proper names are spelled in a consistent way, usually following Fray Angélico Chávez's *Origins of New Mexico Families* or the translations of the Vargas papers by Kessell and Hendricks. Spanish words are provided when they reflected common usage or have a meaning that could not be easily translated. In most cases, the English translation is provided in brackets, a footnote, or the glossary. In an effort to assist the reader, punctuation and paragraphs have been added, and names are shown in brackets to clarify antecedents.

Our appreciation goes to those people, including James Clois Smith, Jr. of Sunstone Press, who showed an interest in Spanish Colonial documents and who supported our efforts to transcribe and translate them. We also thank the persons who helped to review the documents that were produced. Not many people are familiar with the archaic Spanish of eighteenth-century New Spain, and we are grateful for the help of Rick Hendricks, Gerald Gonzales, Stan Hordes, Rob Martinez, Cordelia Thomas Snow, Nancy Brown Martinez, Henrietta Christmas, and Robin Farwell Gavin for their assistance, comments, and corrections. Thanks also goes to those who reviewed portions of the book, including Elinore Barrett, Harry Moul, Rick Hendricks, and Malcolm Ebright, as well as the staff of the New Mexico State Archives, the State Library in Santa Fe, and the Center for Southwest Studies at the University of New Mexico in Albuquerque. Special thanks goes to Tom Ireland, Paul Lewis, and Margaret Moore Booker, who helped put together the final product.

HISTORICAL INTRODUCTION

"Bring back my son so that he is not lost in the mines of Chihuahua!" said María de Quiros when asking the governor's permission for her godfather, Francisco Casados, to leave the province and bring back her son, who had been taken away by his grandfather.[1]

At least, that is the translation of her petition to the governor. We will never know the exact language she used, but we do know when she pleaded her case, and to whom, and what words the presidio scribe wrote down, just as we know many other things about the lives of Spanish Colonial New Mexicans from the documents they left behind, some of which are included in the collection of translations and transcriptions that follows.

This historical introduction describes the Spanish and Pueblo settlements where these stories took place, as well as the military system their inhabitants lived under. It also deals with the jurisdiction and duties of Spanish officials at the provincial and local levels, including the administration of civilian and military justice, and interactions between the Spanish settlers, the settled Pueblo Indians, and the often hostile nomadic Indians. Finally, there is a discussion of the legal and illegal trade in which nearly all of them were involved.

Demographics and Settlement Locations

It is relatively easy to estimate the numbers of settlers who returned to the colony after the Pueblo Revolt of 1680, because most of the colonists came as organized, documented groups. Following the successful 1692 *entrada*, don Diego de Vargas returned in December 1693 with seventy families. The census made in El Paso before they left listed 959 individuals.[2] In June of 1694, a second group, led by Fray Francisco Farfán and Captain Cristóbal Velasco,[3] arrived in Santa Fe with 335 people, and in late 1694 Juan Páez Hurtado led a group of 41 so-called families consisting of about 90 people.[4] In addition, Vargas originally brought along some 100 soldiers, along with about 18 Franciscans.[5] Adding all these numbers, by 1710 or so there would have been approximately 1,500 settlers in the colony, not including those who remained behind at El Paso. At the time, the number of Pueblo Indians was estimated to be nearly 7,000, not including those at Zuni or Hopi.[6]

In spite of the hazards of the frontier, including deadly diseases[7] and hostile Indians, the number of settlers in New Mexico increased over time. Ross Frank, an economic historian, estimates that in 1740 the number of settlers in the colony was around 3,000, compared to 6,000 Pueblo Indians, whose numbers had been reduced but still surpassed those of the settlers. He calculates that the population of Spanish colonists and Pueblo Indians eventually became equal, but not until the 1780s, when there were an estimated 8,000 to 9,000 in each group.[8]

The colonists first settled at Santa Fe and then further north at the town of Santa Cruz, founded by Vargas. Others settled to the south along the Río Grande at locations including the villa of Albuquerque, founded in 1706, and the old settlement of Atrisco, on the west side of the river. With the eventual increase in numbers and the subsequent need for more land for crops and pastures for their herds, the settlers expanded to the north, to Santa Fe and Santa Cruz and the Taos area, including places like Puesto de Chama, Embudo, and La Soledad. They also scattered east and west of the Río Grande, for example, to Belén Tomé, and along the Río Puerco. The 1750 census lists thirty settlements between Taos and El Paso. The Menchero map of 1745 shows six additional place names, and the Miera y Pacheco map of 1779 (Map 2, Appendix) shows eighty-six places, although many of them appear to have been plazas of a single extended family or settlements with only a few people.[9]

Given this information for the early 1700s, it seems that there were not many settlers in the colony given the size of the province, and that those few people were widely scattered over a large area. Even so, many if not most of them surely knew each other, and, considering the vast amount of intermarriage among family groups, many were related. At the very least, two people were likely to know somebody they both knew, as happens in small towns and rural areas today. These connections are seen in the documents, making the quarrels more personal and sometimes leaving old grievances to be settled. On the other hand, the connections also meant that when settlers were, for example, threatened by an unpopular decision from governor, they would unite, hire a scribe to write a petition in the proper form, and send it off with their all their signatures and marks, or have it signed by somebody they knew.[10]

Military Aspects of the Colony

Overriding all of the local ambitions and controversies was the constant threat of war—continuous, ongoing raids and campaigns that required that every adult male be a soldier at the presidio or with the militia, and that both men and women be prepared for an Indian attack. The colonists and the Pueblos were surrounded by hostile Indian tribes: the Apaches, Navajos, Utes, Pawnees, and later the Comanches, and they had many things that these Indians wanted, including their livestock, goods, and themselves. Life on the frontier meant Indian attacks, counterattacks, full military campaigns, and expeditions, which could result in death or crippling for some, widowhood for women, or, if captured, slavery for them and their children. Such conditions generated fears that were always present.

The best evidence of the extent of the ongoing military aspect of the settlement is found in a list of the thirty-three most important campaigns and expeditions occurring between 1705 and 1769. Note that conflicts were recorded with at least seven tribes and that the attacks came from all directions, not just at the more distant locations like Zuni, but also in places much closer to home: the Sandía Mountains, Santa Clara, and Galisteo (see Maps 4 and 5, Appendix).

1705, May. Cuervo y Valdés expedition against Navajo raiders.[11]
1705, June. Cuervo y Valdés led a campaign against the Gila Apaches.[12]
1705, July. Revolt of Zuni.[13]
1705, August–September. Roque Madrid led a campaign against the Navajos.[14]
1706. Cuervo y Valdés led a campaign against the Hopis.[15]
1706. Ulibarrí expedition to El Cuartelejo.[16]
1711. Juan Páez Hurtado pursued Apaches.[17]
1713. Governor Peñuela approved two campaigns against the Navajos at Santa Clara and Jemez.[18]
1714. Valverde chased Faraón Apaches eastward from the Sandía Mountains.[19]
1715. Juan Páez Hurtado expedition against the Faraón Apaches in eastern New Mexico to the Canadian River.[20]
1716. Felix Martínez led a campaign against the Moqui (Hopi) pueblos.[21]
1716. Campaign from Taos against the Utes and Comanches.[22]
1719. Valverde expedition against the Utes and Comanches from Taos to the Arkansas River.[23]
1720. Villasur expedition against the Comanches and Pawnees.[24]
1724. Utes attacked Jemez; Comanches attacked La Jicarilla.[25]
1724. Bustamante expedition against Faraón Apaches in the Ladrón and Sandía Mountains.[26]
1724. Comanches defeated Apaches in a nine-day battle.[27]
1731. Cruzat y Góngora held council of war for a campaign against the Faraón Apaches.[28]
1734. Juan Páez Hurtado led campaign against the Faraón Apaches.[29]
1736. Juan Páez Hurtado led campaign against the Utes near Chama.[30]
1741–1742. Mendoza campaign against the Comanches to the east.[31]
1746. Comanches attacked Pecos.[32]
1746–1747. Codallos expedition beyond Abiquiu against Utes and Comanches.[33]
1747. Sáenz de Garvisu campaign in the Gila near the Ladrón and Magdalena Mountains.[34]
1747. Comanche raid on Abiquiu.[35]
1748. Comanches attacked Pecos and Chama.[36]
1748. Codallos defended Pecos against another attack.[37]
1749. Comanche assault on Galisteo.[38]
1750. Utes and Apaches united in an attack on the Comanches.[39]
1751. Comanche attack on Galisteo; Cachupín campaigns to the east.[40]
1756–1760. Bernardo de Miera y Pacheco led three campaigns against the Comanches.[41]
1767–1768. Mendiñueta campaigned against the Comanches.[42]
1769. Comanche attack on Pecos.[43]

Protection of the colonists based on a military organization was established by don Diego de Vargas as part of the Reconquest. It was a change from the prerevolt *encomienda/estancia* system, in which, at least in theory, military defense was provided in exchange for tribute from the Indians. The *encomenderos*, who maintained their own weapons and horses, served in campaigns against Indians raiders and performed escort duties to protect the trade caravans and traveling officials. In time of need, their efforts were supplemented by other colonists and Pueblo Indian auxiliaries.[44]

In New Mexico after the Reconquest, the military system was reorganized with the presidio system, serving as the basis for the defense of the colonies. The presidios had existed in New Spain since after the sixteenth-century conquest. In the 1550s, the Spanish established garrisons and eventually presidios along the highways and trade routes and provided escorts for the caravans and other travelers in the conquered areas. Additional solders and presidios were added as Spanish occupation moved north and confronted the increasingly hostile Indians. By the 1720s, there were twenty-three presidios on the northern frontier, all of them, except Santa Fe, along the border between Nueva Viscaya and New Mexico (see Map 7, Appendix).[45] Though the presidios were established and garrisoned by the early 1700s, there was no effective system for coordinating or governing them.[46] The governors and officers were generally independent, allowing the less scrupulous to use the presidios as a source of profit. Ranching and commercial operations could be supported by using the soldiers for labor, and the presidio supply caravans could be used to transport goods the officials wished to trade. In addition, the lack of oversight meant that the governors, who were in charge of purchasing supplies for the soldiers, enriched themselves with inflated prices and inadequate supplies.

By the second decade of the eighteenth century, the corruption and ineffectiveness of the northern presidios came to the attention of the cost- and efficiency-conscious viceroy, Marqués de Casa Fuerte,[47] who mounted a full-scale investigation. In 1724 he sent Brigadier Pedro Rivera north to identify cost-cutting measures and investigate claims of abuse and fraud. The attention of the viceroy was particularly drawn to New Mexico because of the disaster of the Villasur expedition[48] in 1720 and the charges and countercharges of fraud and corruption received by the viceroy from both presidio captain and interim governor Felix Martínez and his successor, Governor Flores Mogollón. Charges were also made by the colonists against Mogollón's successors, the governors Valverde and Bustamante.[49]

Leaving Mexico City on November 21, 1724, Rivera spent over three and a half years visiting the twenty-three northern frontier presidios.[50] In 1726 he spent the summer in Santa Fe, meeting with Governor Bustamante, interviewing former governors Felix Martínez and Valverde, and analyzing the situation at the presidio.[51] By 1728 Rivera was back in Mexico City and had written recommendations that were adopted as the *Reglamento de 1729*.[52] For the colonists, some of his recommendations must have been discouraging, especially the reduction in the number of soldiers from 100 to 80. In defending himself, Rivera said he dismissed 20 people on the Santa Fe payroll because "they were receiving wages as *alcaldes mayores, alfereces reales, ayudantes, capitanes de campaña*, and *reformados* without actually doing anything."[53] Rivera also supported his case by pointing out that other frontier presidios had only 30 to 50 men.[54] He provided a pay scale for the presidio, with the paid positions limited to the governor; a *teniente*, or lieutenant; an *alférez*, or standard bearer; a sergeant; and the regular soldiers, who probably included the *cabos*, or corporals.[55] The alcaldes mayores, ayudantes, *clarinero*, and *tambor* (bugler and drummer) were not to be included on the public payroll.[56]

Military Aspects: The Governor as Captain General

As spelled out in the 1681 *Recopilación de leyes de los reynos de las Indias*, commonly known as the Laws of the Indies, the governors were appointed for three- to five-year terms, although sometimes they stayed for only two years or were reappointed, for example, Governor Bustamante, who served from 1724 to 1731.[57] The governor's responsibilities were a combination of the executive, judicial, and military as suggested by his titles of *gobernador* and *capitán general*. As captain general, he was in charge of initiating and leading military campaigns, establishing garrisons of soldiers in the pueblos and settlements when needed, and buying supplies for the soldiers. The governor was then paid back from the presidio payroll account in Mexico City through an agent to whom the soldiers gave their power of attorney.[58] As an executive, the governor wrote *bandos*, or orders, for example, prohibiting the soldiers from gambling or from selling presidio horses. The governor also granted licenses for such things as animal brands, trading, or leaving the province.

The governor was, of course, responsible for carrying out the policies of the king and viceroy as set forth in the Laws of the Indies. This could be a challenge, because the laws were generally written to apply to all of Spain's American dominions. One of the laws that directly affected New Mexico was the policy of the Spanish Crown toward the Indians, which provided that both the settled and roving Indians be treated with "courtesy," limiting the governor to defensive action against them except in certain cases where a "just war" was warranted.[59] This was restated by the viceroy in 1706, when the Duke of Albuquerque sent instructions to the Santa Fe *cabildo*, or town council, elaborating on the meaning of a just war, stating that the governor "shall maintain and preserve all that is acquired by defensive arms, refraining from the offensive and endeavoring by the most gentle measures that his prudence and zeal in the service of both majesties may suggest, to bring peace obedience and submission to them [the hostile Indians]."[60] Regarding the treatment of friendly and even indifferent Indians, the 1729 *Reglamento* used the words, *con agrado y buen modo*, "with affability and courtesy."[61]

Because of the policy of just war, the governors were expected to justify any military action by showing that the Indians had initiated hostilities or had acted against the Church or local authorities. As a result, especially in the early years after the Reconquest, before ordering an expedition of any size, the governors would call a *junta de guerra*, or council of war. The purpose of the council was to gather information and listen to the opinions of the alcaldes and other respected persons.[62] In later years, as the attacks of the hostile Indians increased, the juntas were called less often, the need for the campaigns being obvious.

One private and often troublesome matter for governors was how to reimburse themselves for the expense of acquiring the office without generating too many complaints. In the early years of the eighteenth century, governors purchased their office outright, but after the second decade, they paid an initial purchase price in addition to a kind of income tax on the first year's salary and on subsequent income, the sum total of which could be onerous.[63] As stated above, one method of recouping costs was charging inflated prices on the supplies that they bought for the soldiers and presidio with an extra charge added for expenses.[64] In an attempt to limit this, government officials including Governor don Diego de Vargas, Lieutenant Governor Juan Páez Hurtado, Brigadier Rivera, and others prepared a presidio supply price list that included military goods such as swords, muskets, and horses, and also chocolate, tobacco, and plain and fancy fabric of all kinds, including Chinese silk.[65] A second method used by the governors for recovering the costs of office was to take advantage of their position by establishing stock-raising operations, as Governor Valverde did.[66]

A third method of recouping expenses was to engage in trade. The governors collected goods from the Pueblo Indians, settlers, and roving Indians, and sold them to their agents to the south. In addition, by the 1730s, governors, and sometimes local merchants, were involved in the collection of tithes, a procedure that gave the collector an edge on trading.[67] Earlier, the Franciscans had the authority to collect the tithe rental, but there are no records that they did so, the colony perhaps being considered too poor. In 1732, however, after wresting jurisdiction of New Mexico from the Franciscans, the bishop of Durango began collecting the tithe, asking for 10 percent of the value of goods sold by the settlers as well as of the increase in livestock. In addition to the tithe, an amount equal to about one-third of what was collected was charged by the collector, usually the governor. The tithe was usually paid in goods. The collector was responsible for gathering the tithe goods, transporting them to the markets in the south for sale, and then delivering the money to the church in Durango. The collector could then keep the remainder, probably using that amount to pay creditors and for buying goods for future trade. Records from 1732 to 1734 and 1744 to 1767 (data for the interceding years are missing) show that four of the collectors were governors: don Joachín Codallos, Vélez Cachupín, Marín del Valle, and Portillo de Urrisola.

As a way of evaluating the governors' effectiveness and keeping a check on their money-making schemes, the Laws of the Indies established the *residencia*, an evaluation of the outgoing governor's conduct by the incoming governor, with the results set forth in a written report. The report, often consisting of several hundred folios, could include anything from a list of documents in the archives at the *casas reales* to questions asked by the viceregal agents of officials of the military, pueblo leaders, and the alcaldes In some cases, mostly those in the early part of the century, the testimony in the residencia could be vindictive, with charges, not always substantiated, of scandal and corruption.[68] Generally, after the late 1730s, the residencia became more form than content, officials repeating each other's answers and claiming that they knew of no wrong committed by the governor.[69]

Military Aspects: Soldiers of the Presidio and the Militia

Among other things, Brigadier Rivera's 1729 *Reglamento* spelled out the duties of the soldiers. Whether their number was 100 or 80, as in the years after 1729, their duties were numerous and, given the size of the New Mexico province, probably exceeded more than what they could possibly accomplish. Their immediate duty was protection of the settlers and the Pueblo Indians, although only a portion of the soldiers were directly involved in this. The documents show that in the early years, where there were 100 soldiers assigned to the Santa Fe presidio, only 40 to 70 soldiers were assigned to a campaign at any one time.[70] The lack of presidio soldiers in a campaign was made up by the local militias and by large numbers of Pueblo auxiliaries.[71] For example, in a 1704 muster by don Diego de Vargas, there were 27 soldiers and militia and at least 120 Indian auxiliaries.[72] In a 1714 campaign against the Faraón Apaches in the Sandías, there were 50 presidials, 20 militia, and 150 Pueblo auxiliaries.[73]

One of the other tasks of the presidio soldiers was providing couriers and escorts. The *Reglamento*, apparently trying to lower costs, stated that escorts were only to be used for couriers going to and from El Paso, protection of the governor's trade caravans (which came twice a year), visitations by the governor to the pueblos, and trips by religious personnel.[74] Soldiers were also assigned to act as sentries for the presidio in Santa Fe, including the guardhouse, which at times housed both the armory and prisoners accused of crimes. In addition, presidio soldiers served as a kind of police and emergency-response team for the Santa Fe civilians—for example, for the 1767 flood of the city.[75] A related duty of the soldiers at Santa Fe was participation in religious and civic events, including firing off salutes and circling the plaza on horseback with flags or emblems in ritual processions.[76] Perhaps most onerous of all, in terms of numbers of soldiers and time spent, was guarding the presidio horse herds, which could number from 500 to 2,000, in various assigned pastures. This task was not a favorite of the soldiers, being both tedious and dangerous, and officers used horse-herd guarding assignments as punishment. To prevent abuses, the *Reglamento* stated that the maximum length of time for a horse-herd assignment was fifteen days.[77]

Finally, the soldiers were responsible for maintaining their own equipment and uniforms, which they purchased from the supplies bought by the governor's agent.[78] The 1729 *Reglamento* stated that each New Mexican soldier was to be paid 400 pesos plus six pounds of power. From this they would pay for a uniform, lance, sword, musket, *cuero* (leather jacket), and other equipment, with the cost of goods based on government price list.[79] We know from the soldiers' wills and other documents that soldiers purchased equipment like saddles, bridles, and sometimes horses beyond that provided by the presidio.

As an illustration, a soldier's list of equipment was found in Manuel Vigil's will of March 1732, in which he said that he had been a soldier for about twenty years. "On account of this illness which has come upon me, and by order of the governor and captain general, Don Gervasio Cruzat y Gongora, I delivered four horses, saddle, arquebus and case, leather jacket, sword, a shield, lance, powder pouches; all the aforesaid I delivered by order of the aforesaid; and I request that my accounts be liquidated so that if I owe anything to my enlistment, I order it be paid, and if my enlistment owes me anything, I order it be collected."[80] Given the equipment the soldiers had to purchase, the low pay, and the fixed prices for goods, it is no wonder that many, if not most, of the presidio soldiers were usually in debt and tried to find ways, some legal and some not, of adding to their presidio incomes. The documents show soldiers asking for land grants, raising crops and livestock, and bartering their goods at the trade fairs, as well as illegal gambling, unlicensed trading, and the theft and sale of presidio horses and equipment.

As suggested above, the presidio soldiers were supported by the settler militia, who were commanded by a militia captain appointed by the governor and sometimes served under the same officers as the presidio soldiers.[81] Members of the militia were expected to respond immediately to a call for arms at the times and places ordered by the alcaldes and governors, and were to be properly armed and provisioned with items that they provided themselves.[82] In addition, the militia soldiers had to have horses available, usually three to five each, for a raid or expedition. They were also supposed to be responsible for maintenance of their horses and for guarding them against Indian theft. As seen from the documents, this latter requirement was a problem, especially for the Albuquerque militia, who had the burden of providing pastures for the horses of both the settlers and the squadron of presidio soldiers, and it was often a cause of complaint.[83]

The documents show that the number of settler militiamen accompanying the presidio soldiers on a campaign could be as many as fifty, as, for example, in the 1736 expedition against the Utes, where there were thirty-six presidials and seventy Pueblo Indians. More often the militia numbered ten to twenty persons.[84]

Civil Government: The Governor

After the Reconquest, civil political power in the province was held by three positions: the governors, the cabildo members (called *regidores*), and the alcaldes mayores. In other cities in New Spain, the cabildo and the governor shared political power, the one acting as a check on the other, with the cabildo sometimes the dominant power. In the first two decades of the eighteenth century, the documents show that the governor and the Santa Fe cabildo did work together in administering the colony. A certain protocol was followed, with the petitions from the settlers submitted to the cabildo members, who sent them on to the governor, who then responded back to the cabildo and, when appropriate, to the viceroy.[85] However, as discussed in the section on the cabildo below, the power of the cabildo eroded until by 1725, the political control of the province was in the hands of the governor and his appointees, the alcaldes mayores.[86]

The governors were guided by regulations set forth in the Laws of the Indies, to some extent by the 1729 military regulations prepared by Brigadier Pedro de Rivera, and by the residencia, the written review of the governor made by his successor. In addition, the governors were always under the watchful eye of the viceroy and his staff, and, ultimately, that of the king, who appointed the governors and who could recall them at will. On a local level, residents, soldiers, Indians, and religious could and did petition the viceroy and, less frequently, the king about their complaints with the governor. If this did not satisfy the complaints to their liking, the colonists could always wait until a new governor was appointed and try out their petition on him. For example, in 1736 Albuquerque settlers effectively used this strategy to have what they saw as onerous trade restrictions on wool and other items removed.[87]

As the chief provincial executive, the governors prepared mandates and orders, sending them to the alcaldes to be proclaimed in the jurisdictions. Sometimes they handed down orders prohibiting certain behavior such as gambling or carrying arms in towns. They also mandated that certain things be done, such as attending church, clearing the roads, or responding when the town crier beat the drum. At other times announcements were sent from Spain or Mexico City to be read locally, such as those about a royal marriage or the birth of an heir to the Spanish throne.

An important and sometimes hazardous responsibility of the governor was licensing, scheduling, and policing, sometimes in person, the often turbulent trading fairs. The governor could set prices for trade goods and establish conditions of sale. Anther duty was being in charge of public works projects, for example, repairing government buildings and maintaining such roads as there were. The governor scheduled visits and authorized escorts to the salt lakes in the Salinas Basin, gave notice for trade caravans to the south, and managed the delivery of official correspondence and other mail to El Paso, Mexico City, and elsewhere. Anyone wishing to travel outside the province needed his approval. He authorized land grants and was required to make at least one visitation to each pueblo during his tenure. The governor also attended and cooperated, or was supposed to cooperate (see Doc. 20), in the organization of religious rituals. In addition, he was concerned with the economic viability of the colony in the province's and his own interest.

As set forth below in more detail, the governor acted as the final judge for the soldiers, the Pueblo Indians, and the settlers. In practice this meant that most cases, excluding those of the Indians, were investigated and heard by the alcaldes prior to the governor's review of the investigation and his determination of the sentence. In the case of Indians, the law stated that the case was to go immediately to the governor. In all cases, the governor's decision could be, and sometimes was, appealed to the Audiencia of Guadalajara or to the viceroy.

Civil Government: The Cabildo

As stated above, in the first few decades of the eighteenth century, the governor was assisted in his duties and advised by the cabildo, as had been the case in the prerevolt colony. Under Spanish law, there was to be a cabildo for every chartered *villa*, the official name for a town granted a municipal charter by the king.[88] The two other villas in northern New Mexico, besides Santa Fe, were Santa Cruz and Albuquerque, though there is no evidence that either of the latter two had a cabildo, relying instead on the alcaldes mayores. The Santa Fe cabildo, reconstituted after the Reconquest, had four to six members, called *regidores*. It had judicial duties relating to Santa Fe, and two members were appointed as magistrates called *alcaldes ordinarios*, who were agents of the cabildo charged with hearing both criminal and civil cases. It addition, the cabildo had police authority over the community. Petitions by Santa Fe residents were first addressed to its members, and then to the governor. Members were supposed to be able to read and write and have some position in the community. Members of the cabildo served without pay.[89]

In Santa Fe, the cabildo disappeared after the Bustamante administration in the 1720s. Marc Simmons and Ted J. Warner both state that the demise of the cabildo in New Mexico was related to the members taking sides in the dispute between governors Felix Martínez and Flores Mogollón. According to Warner's account of the conflict, Mogollón had abolished the Santa Fe cabildo, and his successor, Martínez, reestablished it. Then the next governor, Antonio Valverde, abolished it again, so disgusted with its behavior that he sent the members, including the venerable Juan Páez Hurtado, to Mexico City in chains.[90] When requested by the viceroy to reappoint the cabildo, Bustamante did not do so,[91] apparently ending it for once and for all until its reappearance in the Mexican period as the *ayuntamiento*.[92]

Civil Government: Alcaldes Mayores

With the cabildo no longer active, and even before then, the role of maintaining the colony on a local level depended on the alcaldes, officially called *alcaldes mayores y capitanes de guerra*.[93] They were appointed by the governor with the qualification that they could read and write and had their residence outside the district, or *jurisdicción*, to which they were assigned. Although the number of districts is not exactly known for the first part of the eighteenth century, by the last quarter of the century, there were at least six and probably seven jurisdictions, called *alcaldías*, as shown on the Miera y Pacheco map of 1779.[94] The alcaldías, which included both Indian pueblos and Spanish settlements, were Santa Fe, Santa Cruz de la Cañada, Albuquerque, Taos, Los Queres, Sandía, and Laguna. In addition, Pecos and Galisteo made up one alcaldía.

The duties of the alcaldes were extensive and, for a conscientious official, must have been difficult. They were, in effect, the governors' men on the ground, having daily contact with the settlers and with the Puebloan and other Indians. Like the governors, the alcaldes had a military role, being charged with organizing and leading the militia, reporting raids and attacks, and often leading counterattacks. In some cases, they held appointments in the regular army.[95] Also, like the governors, they had judicial and police responsibilities. Within their jurisdiction, they received and investigated complaints and petitions on boundaries, exits and entries to properties, water use, and local disputes. They could arrest people who violated the law. Generally, they sent legal cases on to the governor, but sometimes the alcaldes handed down a sentence themselves. In addition, the alcalde often had the unenviable task of carrying out the punishment imposed by the governors.

The alcalde also notarized local documents such as wills and deeds, investigated the ownership of land for prospective land grants, and was responsible for proclaiming and distributing the *bandos* (orders), *autos* (a judicial or administrative decree), *reales cédulas* (royal orders), and other official orders sent by the governor. When an alcalde received the original document from the governor, he wrote a statement of receipt, signing it with his rubric,[96] and then sent the document on to the next alcalde on the list, who did the same thing, until all the specified alcaldes had signed off, and the document was sent to the archives at the casas reales in Santa Fe. Because of these signed receipts (of which there are a great many), we know the names of the alcaldes and their jurisdiction, and that they could, in fact, read and write, although some were more practiced than others.

One of the alcalde's more hazardous duties, aside from being a part of a military campaign, was acting as the governor's representative in meetings and negotiations with the hostile Indians who wished to trade. The alcalde was responsible for ensuring that all trading with the Indians was done with a license at a licensed trade fair and that trading did not include prohibited goods. When the trade fairs occurred, the alcalde opened the fair, enforced the governor's regulations for prices, goods, and behavior, and generally tried to keep the peace among groups that, at other times, were avowed enemies of the Spanish and each other.[97]

For all this and for other unnamed duties that the alcaldes performed, they received no pay, though they could collect fees based, at least in theory, on an officially approved fee schedule. An example from a 1765 criminal case exacted fees for thirteen various aspects of the proceedings, including the original declaration by the defendant, testimony of each witness, ratification of witness statements, and sentencing. However, in a case like that of Document 11, involving an attack by one settler on another, the fees depended on the time spent by each official.[98] The alcalde could appoint a *teniente*, or lieutenant alcalde, to help them.

Marc Simmons suggests that the settlers filled the position for the prestige and because of the economic possibilities of the job, such as local patronage, collecting fees for their services, and exacting tribute from and otherwise exploiting the Indians and sometimes the settlers. They could also use their position to their own advantage in trading at and sometimes outside the trade fairs.[99]

Civil Government: Judiciary

The numerous criminal and civil cases in the archives show the governor and alcaldes working with angry and demanding settlers, soldiers, and Pueblo Indians. The legal cases include testimony and accusations, and as such are often emotional, rambling, and full of contradictory and sometimes incomprehensible remarks. Nevertheless, as a study by Charles Cutter shows, there was, in fact, a defined judicial process extending from the accusation and arrest to the sentencing. This process, he suggests, was intended to provide compromise, avoid vendettas and feuds, and preserve harmony within the hard-pressed colony. With so few colonists, every person counted, and getting along with each other was essential.

The judicial process began with an accusation, usually in the form of a petition to the governor, with the alcalde then assigned to carry out fact-finding that could include an examination of the site, especially where boundaries or water rights were involved, and discussions with neighbors and other witnesses. In the case of an assault in a criminal complaint, the alcalde would request a physical examination by a surgeon or master barber of the aggrieved person and would examine any weapons. In many cases, the investigation was carried out by a *juez receptor*, a temporary presiding judge in charge of collecting evidence and sometimes fees for the judicial process. Once collected, the evidence was provided to the alcalde or the governor, who was also given the power to examine cases and witnesses.[100] A variety of people, including the accused and accuser, witnesses, and persons knowing the accused or accuser, were required to give testimony. In most cases, the accused had an opportunity to challenge the accuser and the accuser to respond to that, and so on, back and forth in a sometimes lengthy process that Cutter calls the *correo*.[101] The testimony was written down by a scribe in what appears to be a verbatim transcript or something close to it. For criminal complaints, the accused could be kept in the presidio guardhouse during the investigation or placed under house arrest in their or someone else's house. In one case, the accused were kept in the town stocks.[102] In some cases, the property of the accused, and sometimes the accuser, would be sequestered, giving the officials assurance that court costs would be paid.[103] Legally, accused persons could take sanctuary in a church, where they could be interrogated but not made to leave, although sometimes they were.[104]

After the testimony was heard, the governor, and occasionally the alcalde, would hand down a determination for civil suits or a sentence for crimes, both of which would, often as not, include a shared solution requiring both parties to pay a fine or carry out some remediation. Remediation was often used in civil matters such as disputes about water rights or property boundaries. For example, for cattle caught wandering onto someone else's property, the sentence could be repairing damages to the neighboring property, an *acequia* (irrigation ditch), or wall. At other times, the sentence was making adobes for repairing the roof of a public building such as the casas reales. These kinds of solutions support Cutter's view that the aim of the judiciary was to "find justice and restore social harmony" rather than punishment, and that the alcaldes and governors were allowed flexibility to do so.[105]

In criminal cases, there were more punitive sentences. For habitual bad behavior or acts considered immoral, such as adultery, the sentence might include banishment, often temporary, and usually not often outside the province. A severe sentence, such as 200 lashes, was not uncommon, although it is not clear how many times it was fully imposed. Persons were sometimes sentenced to the stocks in the plaza.[106] Other sentences were work repairing public buildings, or for especially heinous crimes, being sent to the mines or cotton mills (*obrajes*) to the south.[107] The accused were sometimes held in the presidio guardhouse. A term in the local jail was used as a threat and sometimes imposed, though the resources of most communities were not always adequate to provide a secure prison. There are few cases of capital punishment, although whipping and working in the mines or obrajes might amount to that. Race was a consideration in sentencing. Penalties for the Spanish were different, often involving fines or, for soldiers, loss of rank. For Indians, blacks, and mestizos, the punishment tended to be whipping or work. Banishment might be imposed upon anyone.[108]

Trade: Background and Regulation

In spite of, or maybe because of, poverty in New Mexico, many New Mexicans, Puebloans, and members of at least five Indian tribes (Apache groups, Navajos, Utes, Pawnees, and especially Comanches) were involved in trade. In addition, the traders included the governors and merchants from El Paso, Chihuahua, and areas farther south.

The documents describe these merchants, who, trading with the Spanish, Puebloans, and roving Indians, traveled up and down the Camino Real moving their goods in escorted caravans. We know about them from complaints in the documents about deals gone bad between traders and from accusations of illegal trading made by other settlers and sometimes by their trading partners. We also find the merchants' names in the wills of those who, when they found themselves in New Mexico and ailing, tried to put their affairs in order by including a list of debts and goods owed in their wills. Examples are Toribio Ortiz, Juan García de la Mora, Diego Torres, Juan José Moreno, Bernardo Miera y Pacheco, and many others. In addition, the tithe records give us the names of tithe collectors such as don Joseph de Roybal, don Joseph Bustamante (Governor Domingo de Bustamante's brother), don Juan Antonio Unanue, and don Juan Joseph Moreno.[109]

As stated above, all trade in New Mexico was under the purview of the governor, who was responsible for its regulation and encouragement in order to demonstrate the financial viability of the settlements to the Spanish Crown, with the preferred outcome that the colony would become less dependent on the royal treasury. Costs had been cut as a result of the 1729 recommendations of Brigadier Pedro de Rivera, described above, but the colony still remained a financial burden on the Spanish government.

One often used method of the governors for management of trade in New Mexico was the enactment of mandates. When, in the early 1700s, it appeared that the El Paso and Chihuahua merchants were cutting out the New Mexicans and trading directly with the Indians, the governors adopted laws stating that only New Mexico residents were allowed to trade in the province.[110] Later, when the New Mexicans, desperate for trade, started selling their breeding stock and basic goods, the governors ordered that such animals and goods could not be sold until the reserves were built up, the reserves providing an excess that could be traded outside the province.[111] In an attempt to reduce fights and retaliations among the Spanish officials, Spanish traders, and Indian traders resulting from misunderstandings, drunkenness, and outright cheating by all of them, the governors required licenses for trading and mandated that trading with the hostile Indians had to take place at licensed trade fairs as enforced by the alcaldes and, sometimes, the presence of the governor.[112] Finally, the governors set prices and mandated strict prohibitions and severe punishments for the sale by soldiers of presidio weapons, horses, and military equipment.[113]

Trade: Patterns, Goods, and Locations

The concept of a trade triangle is useful in understanding the interaction of the various trade groups and trade patterns in New Mexico.[114] The nomadic Indians are at the apex of the triangle, since they controlled the most valuable goods—buffalo hides, animal skins, and human captives. From the apex, the legs of the triangle extend to the Spanish settlements and the pueblos, trade going back and forth between all three points. At the bottom, a line can be drawn vertically from the triangle to the south, representing a trade corridor between the New Mexicans and the southern merchants. Generally, most of the goods accumulated by the New Mexican trade triangle and sold outside the colony were funneled along this north–south route. By the 1740s, and perhaps earlier, the nomadic Indians, mostly the Comanches, established a second trading corridor, this time east–west. The connection was with the French, the Texas settlers, and some of the Indian tribes to the east.

The trade triangle, like most generalities, has complications. One complication was the ongoing conflict between the Spanish colonists and Pueblo Indians, on one hand, and the nomadic Indians, on the other. As has been stated, the Indian tribes that had the most valuable resources— hides, captives, and later, horses—were also the tribes that were raiding the colonists and the Puebloans. Collectively, the nomadic tribes had greater numbers and, in many cases, better firearms and other weapons. The situation was volatile at the best, but trade was so important to the colonists and the Pueblos that they traded horses and other livestock, food, knives, and other goods with Indians, even the Comanches, who would sometimes leave a trading fair and make a raid on the nearby pueblos such as Galisteo or Pecos or somewhere in the colony. The situation was made more turbulent over time by the increasing size of the flocks of sheep, which proved to be a great temptation to the roving Indians.

The second complication was that nearly all trade was by barter, not cash. This situation led to misunderstanding and grievances because, of course, barter hardly ever comes out even. For example, the trade price agreed upon for one mule might be ten hides and a little more, such as a *fanega*[115] of wheat, or a silk skirt and a pair of pants, with some of the goods at the brother-in-law's house, which he would deliver when he could. The settlers, alcaldes, and governors understood the importance of written agreements, and written contracts or receipts are frequently mentioned. But even when a written IOU or other documents existed, trading deals were difficult to keep track of and easy to misrepresent, resulting in bad feelings, accusations, and petitions to the alcalde and the governor.

A third trade complication had to do with the contracts made to New Mexican merchants or, more often, to the governors for the collection of church tithes for the bishop of Durango. The collector's fee, about one-third the total tithe, could be used to pay creditors and to buy goods for future trading, giving the tithe collector an advantage over the settlers. The tithe-collection process hurt the economy of the colony, especially when the governor held the contract, because it took 13 percent (10 percent for the tithe plus the 3 percent payment for the collector) of much-needed goods outside the colony, with no return. That is, the payment for the goods stayed at Durango with the bishop or was used by the collector-merchants to buy goods in the south. If the collector was a trader who lived in New Mexico, at least some of the profits might stay in the province. In the case of the governor or outside collectors, however, all of the goods and money would leave the province for the Durango church, creditors in the south, or the governor's own account, located elsewhere in New Spain.

Leaving aside trade complications and looking at the location of trade centers and goods exchanged, it helps to return to the concept of the trade triangle and trade corridors. The apex of the triangle, where the most valuable goods originated, was at

Taos, Pecos, and Picuris, especially in the early years.[116] Geographically, these locations were at the border between the nomadic Indians and the Spanish and Puebloans, which could and sometimes did operate as a neutral ground for both. Other locations associated with trade, probably mostly unlicensed and therefore illicit, included Quemado, Ojo Caliente, Las Trampas, Truchas, Chimayó, and Puesto de Chama.[117] The goods flowed south from northern New Mexico, from Pecos and Galisteo on the east and from the pueblos on the west down the trade corridor of the Camino Real. The traders and their goods converged at Albuquerque, or at Sevilleta in later years, making up a caravan that traveled on to El Paso, Parral, the mining country around Chihuahua, Durango, or farther south to Mexico City and elsewhere.

The specific goods generated from within the trade triangle came from a variety of sources. First, from the non-Christian Indians at the peak of the triangle came the valuable items of buffalo robes, tanned deerskin, and other hides and pelts, tallow and dried meat, and captives. Later in the period, the Comanches provided guns, most often from the French; and horses, sometimes from Texas, and sometimes stolen from the New Mexican settlers and, to their disgust, traded back to them.[118] In later years, after the Comanches started breeding their own horses, the horses came from their *rancherías*. From a second point of the triangle, the pueblos, came wool and cotton textiles, usually described as coarsely woven, including blankets and mantas as well as stockings and other woven products. In addition, the Puebloans provided maize, piñon nuts and other food products, pottery, and worked leather goods.

From the third point on the triangle came the goods from the New Mexican settlers, including items made of iron or other metals such as tools, knives and awls, copper pots, and bridles and bits, as well as worked leather goods. The climate of New Mexico being hospitable to the grape, the settlers produced wine and brandy as well as a locally grown tobacco, called *punche*. After the 1740s and 1750s, the settlers also traded sheep on the hoof and wool, sometimes woven.[119] (For example, in 1744 Fray Miguel de Menchero stated that in the villa of Albuquerque and the village of Atrisco, 100 families were employed in weaving hose and blankets.)[120] Sometimes the New Mexicans traded horses and other livestock, finer fabrics, and trinkets like mirrors and buttons. Like the unsettled Indians and the Puebloans, the Spanish also traded captives.[121] While somewhat later than this period, tithe data from church records is relevant, showing that in 1796 and 1797, goods collected from the colonists to meet the tithing requirement were sheep, horses, yearling calves, cotton, wool, spun cloth, onions, chile, beans, vegetables, corn, and wheat.[122]

In return for the goods from New Mexico, the southern merchants sent north along the trade corridor manufactured goods associated with the military, for example, weapons, horses and mules, riding gear, and clothes. Ingots of iron were especially valued because the settlers could make knives and tools from them to trade.[123] Also, merchants from the south sent chocolate, sugar, indigo, and manufactured and imported luxury goods like hats, porcelain china, jewelry, and silk and other fine fabrics.[124]

An indication of the kind of goods that came to New Mexico in the early years is found in a 1710 payroll document for the workers at the reconstruction of the church of San Miguel in Santa Fe. For example, the document states that Domingo Romero, a day laborer, earned 8 pesos a month and his food. In terms of pay for all his work, he was providing the following items, which altogether totaled 61 pesos: one greatcoat lined with flannel and silk valued at 25 pesos, one measure of corn, a shawl valued at 2 pesos, some Brussels hose valued at 3 pesos, some shoes, a measure and a half of corn, a pack of cards, a buffalo hide, four buffalo hides for Romero's father-in-law (payment for a debt?), and a large needle.[125]

An important aspect of trade in New Mexico was the ransom or trade of captured human beings. Historians state that trading or ransoming of captives had been carried out by the Indians prior the arrival of the Spanish.[126] This was accelerated after the arrival of the Spanish because of the labor needs of the mines in Nueva Vizcaya and to an extent by those of the settlers. Though enslavement of the Indians, including the barter of Indians captured by others, was prohibited under the Spanish laws of 1542, the capture of slaves under certain conditions of war was accepted.[127] The 1681 Laws of the Indies prohibited the buying and selling of Indian slaves, and went on to prohibit their sale through the fiction of ransom, or *rescate*. However, the concept of selling the prisoners captured in a "just war" remained.[128]

The New Mexican governors did not prohibit the trade of captives, probably realizing that, given the high profits from the trade and the long tradition of ransoming, it would have been carried on illegally anyway. They did restrict the trading of captives to the licensed trade fairs and tried to set the prices.[129] The Franciscans forbade the friars from participating in such trade, even though some of them saw it as acceptable if done for the sake of making Christians of the heathen captives. In 1700 and 1701, Santa Fe mission records stated that buying captives from Apaches and other tribes was "forbidden by church and civil law."[130] In 1738 the friars were directed to abstain from attending trade fairs or from acquiring *piezas* (Indians) to sell.[131]

For the colonists, the trading of captives at the trade or ransom fairs or the outright purchase of slaves had three aspects. The first aspect was the intent to ransom Spanish women and children who had been captured by the Indians so that they could be sent back to their families. A second aspect or purpose for paying the "ransom" for Indian captives at the trade fairs was their use as labor in the homes and ranches of the settlers.[132] These Indians were to be brought up as Christians and, at least in theory, released upon adulthood, remaining in service until their ransom was paid off. Some of the Indians stayed with their Spanish families, while others became part of the population of Genízaros, many of whom lived together in frontier settlements.[133] These settlements were frequently on the frontiers between the settled Spanish and Pueblos and the nomadic Plains Indians, for example, Abiquiu, where they were provided a community grant; Plaza de Jarales, of the Tomé grant; Ojo Caliente; San Miguel de Bado; Sabinal; Belén; and Las Nutrias.[134] The third aspect of paying the ransom, or more often, the outright purchase of slaves, was for resale as labor in mines and workshops to the south,[135] for which there was a constant demand, generating high prices. Altogether, the business of ransoming or buying captives supported a raiding/trading syndrome, continuing because the trade was so lucrative. Over time, the ransoming of Indian captives for use as servants in New Mexican homes, the use of Genízaro settlements as frontier buffers again the hostile Indians, and the outright buying and selling of Indian slaves became part of the frontier culture of New Spain.

Another kind of trade was the buying and selling of land. There are a large number of documents having to do with land grants and transactions from the post-Reconquest period. Many of the land grants were made by the governors in response to petitions by individuals with the claim that the parcel of land was originally owned by the petitioners or their families who lived there before the Reconquest. Other petitioners claimed they deserved the land on the basis of military service, or because all the good land had been used up and the grant was needed for the petitioner's large family. These private grants, unlike those made before the 1680 revolt, were for small parcels and could be sold by the owner, and then resold again, providing the settler with the potential for economic improvement.[136]

In the 1720s, once the initial settlement period had taken place and much of the fertile and well-watered land was in private ownership or occupied by the pueblos, the settlers began to petition for lands in outlying areas such as along Río Puerco and in the areas of Truchas, Embudo, Ojo Caliente, and Taos, and petitioned the governor for a land grant in those locations.[137] In some cases, however, once the land was granted, the settlers had to retreat because of Indians raids, and the land was sold and resettled in later times.

Conclusion

In looking at the documents in this book as a whole, three themes stand out: the need for protection of the colony and the pueblos from the raids of the hostile Indians; the necessity for trade by the colonists and Puebloans with each other and with those same hostile Indians; and the need for cooperation between the Spanish and the Puebloans in military campaigns, trade, and daily life.

After the Reconquest, it became clear that the old mercantilist/encomendero system of exploitation was no longer workable. Given the scarce resources of New Mexico and increasing raids by the hostile tribes, the Spanish and the Pueblo people had to learn to work together and to jointly arrive at some kind of accommodation with the hostile Indians who threatened to overcome the colony. Military leadership was important, as Governors Cachupín and Anza showed, but given the superior numbers, horses, and equipment of the hostile tribes, it was not enough. Trade was important for economic reasons but also as an alternative to war, trade sometimes being an effective method of accommodating the Indians and limiting their raids. Most of the governors made every effort to control excesses by limiting trading to certain locations where it could be more easily controlled. Regulations for prices and procedures were established, so that the roving Indians would have no reason for offense. Although the situation was unstable and the raiding continued, the alternative of not trading with the hostile Indians was unacceptable. At the very least, an embargo on Indian trade was probably unenforceable, and at the worst would have resulted in retaliation through increased raiding and war that would have been destructive to both the Spanish and Puebloan settlements.

In spite of the precariousness of life on the frontier, neither the colonists nor the governors, viceroys, or Spanish Crown ever gave up on New Mexico. As shown in the documents, the colonists lived their lives, planning their children's future, celebrating religious events, traveling here and there, arguing and compromising with their neighbors and relatives, and generally carrying on as best they could.

Death Data from New Mexico Mission Documents[138]

1699, November. Father Garaycoechea buried 30 children.
1719. Nambe, 2 adults and 21 children died of smallpox.
1728, December. Jemez, 109 Indians died of *sarampión* (measles).
1729. Acoma, many died of sarampión during December 1728 and January 1729.
1733. Jémez (Fray Juan del Pino), smallpox epidemic during June and July.
1733. Santa Ana, smallpox epidemic.
1733. Santa Fe, many deaths in May and June, no cause given.
1736. Santa Fe, 38 deaths in November, no cause given.
1737. Santa Fe, 67 deaths in October and November, no cause given.
1737. Santa Cruz, many children died, no cause given.
1738. Pecos, smallpox epidemic.
1747. Zuni, 200 Indians died of smallpox, number not accurate since many were not reported.
1747. Santa Fe, 68 deaths July to September, no cause given.
1747. Pecos, epidemic in August, disease not given.

Notes

1. See Doc. 12.
2. Kessell and Hendricks, RCR: 17.
3. Kessell, Kiva: 267; Kessell and Hendricks, RCR: 245-49.
4. Colligan, Hurtado: 21. This information is from the master rolls, although, according to Colligan, some of the people may have been counted twice or may not have gone to New Mexico at all.
5. Kessell, Kiva: 255.
6. Barrett, Settlement: 116; Hackett, Historical Documents 3: 373-76.
7. The population of New Mexico for the settlers and especially the Pueblo Indians, was heavily impacted by infectious diseases. Notes taken by Fray Angélico Chavez from his review of the church death records show that smallpox and measles continued to be a scourge throughout the eighteenth century (see "Death Data from New Mexico Mission Documents," above). Smallpox, measles, and other infectious diseases continued to reduce the Spanish and Indian population through the first part of the twentieth century (Chávez, Archives: 233-39; Greenfield, History of Public Health: 7).
8. Frank, Settler to Citizen: 48, 49.
9. Olmstead, Censuses: unnumbered table of contents.
10. For example, see Doc. 30.
11. Hendricks and Wilson, Navajos: 1-4.
12. Ibid.: 3.
13. Flagler, "Defensive Policy": 463.
14. Jones, *Pueblo Warriors*: 71; Hendricks and Wilson, *Navajos*: 2-5.
15. Flagler, "Defensive Policy": 464.
16. Thomas, *After Coronado*: 16-21.
17. Kessell, *Kiva*: 361-62.
18. Jones, *Pueblo Warriors*: 79-80
19. Thomas, *After Coronado*: 23.
20. Ibid.: 22-25.

21. Jones, *Pueblo Warriors*: 94-95.
22. Thomas, *After Coronado*: 27.
23. Ibid.: 26-33.
24. Ibid.: 133-36.
25. John, *Storms*: 253.
26. Jones, *Pueblo Warriors*: 103; John, *Storms*: 267-68; SANM II 3#29.
27. Hämäläinen, *Comanche Empire*: 35.
28. SANM II #362.
29. SANM II #395.
30. Jones, *Pueblo Warriors*: 115.
31. SANM II #443.
32. Kessell, *Kiva*: 372.
33. Thomas, *Plains Indians*: 17.
34. Kessell, *Kiva*: 375; Jones, *Pueblo Warriors*: 118.
35. Thomas, *Plains Indians*: 27.
36. Kessell, *Kiva*: 374.
37. Thomas, *Plains Indians*: 17.
38. Kessell, *Kiva*: 380.
39. Thomas, *Plains Indians*: 29-30.
40. Kessell, *Kiva*: 383.
41. Ibid.: 386.
42. Thomas, *Plains Indians*: 39.
43. Kessell, *Kiva*: 395.
44. Warner, "Felix Martinez": 19.
45. Moorhead, *Presidio*: 31-33.
46. Ibid.: 36.
47. See the illustration in Doc. 20.
48. In 1720 an expedition led by don Pedro Villasur was attacked in the area of what is now southeastern Nebraska. Over thirty presidio soldiers killed by Pawnee Indians, apparently armed with French weapons and possibly accompanied by the French (Norris, *Year Eighty*: 86).
49. The most thorough discussion of this controversy is found in Warner ("Felix Martinez").
50. Naylor and Polzer, *Pedro de Rivera*: 10.
51. Jones, *Pueblo Warriors*: 103-5.
52. The title of the regulations begins, "Reglamento para Todos los Presidios de las Provincias internas de esta Governación," but the document is generally referred to as the *Reglamento de 1729*.
53. Naylor and Polzer, *Pedro de Rivera*: 150-51. An *alférez real* was an ensign or a royal standard bearer; *ayudante* an aide-de-camp; *capitán de campaña* a captain for the duration of the campaign; and *reformado* a retired soldier, though it could mean a person in the reserves.
54. Ibid.: 146-56.
55. Ibid.: 245.
56. Ibid.: 245, 246, 261.
57. Tyler, *Indian Cause*: 59. Simmons points out that for much of the later eighteenth century, the governors served five-year terms (Simmons, *Spanish Government*: 56-57).
58. The purchase of soldier's supplies began with approval of funds by the viceroy. The governor would ask the soldiers to sign a power-of-attorney document that gave him the right to spend the money. He would then contract with a paymaster, or *aviador*, often located in Mexico City or Chihuahua, for the purchase and delivery of supplies from the south to New Mexico. Once there, the supplies would be distributed to the soldiers. Based on a price list, with a certain amount added for expenses, the supplies would be credited against the salary owed to the soldiers. An ongoing complaint was that the price of the goods and the expense costs were inflated, with the soldier often forced into debt. According to John Baxter, in some cases, the governors would buy or extract the supplies locally, supplying the soldiers and then paying themselves with the soldiers' payroll (Warner, "Felix Martinez": 13-15; John Baxter, personal communication, January 13, 2013).
59. Book III, Law 65, Title 4 of the 1681 Laws of the Indies states, "Kind, gentle methods shall be used to attempt to bring rebellious Indians to peace" (Tyler, *Indian Cause*: 41; Naylor and Polzer, *Pedro de Rivera*: 237).
60. As translated in Twitchell, *Spanish Archives* 2: 138-39.
61. The relevant paragraphs state, "Sec. 41. The Governors and commanders will not wage war against any nation of gentile Indians who continue to be friendly or against groups that remain indifferent. Nor will they be permitted to bother them for any reason. Rather, they should try to gain their friendship with affability and courtesy. The love that they show them will help in their subjugations. Sec. 42. The governors and commanders are prohibited from helping any nation of gentile Indians in waging war against another nation that has good relations with our troops, except in the case of a nation that attacks our provinces. Then it would be necessary to render such aid" (Naylor and Polzer, *Pedro de Rivera*: 257).

62. See Doc. 9.
63. Cutter, *Legal Culture*: 58. For example, in 1707 Governor Peñuela paid a purchase price of 4,000 pesos and one-third of all profits from the office (Warner, "Felix Martinez": 35).
64. Naylor and Polzer (*Pedro de Rivera*: 12). There is an extensive discussion in Warner ("Felix Martinez").
65. Warner, "Felix Martinez": 48-49; Naylor and Polzer, *Pedro de Rivera*: 282-86.
66. Kessell et al., *ASA*: 208-9.
67. The information on tithe rentals comes from Frank, "Settler to Citizen": 62-64, 167-76, 439-45.
68. Scholes, "Royal Treasury": 87.
69. See, for example, the "Residencia de el General don Henrique de Olavide y Michelena, Gubernador de este Reyno de la Nueva Mexico," *Pinard Collection*, P-E 47, Bancroft Collection, University of California, Berkeley.
70. Jones, *Pueblo Warriors*: 91-118.
71. For a detailed discussion see Jones, *Pueblo Warriors*; and Carter, *Indian Alliances*.
72. Jones, *Pueblo Warriors*: 66-67.
73. Ibid.: 86-87.
74. Naylor and Polzer, *Pedro de Rivera*: 270-72.
75. See Doc. 53.
76. See Docs. 16, 20, and 24.
77. Naylor and Polzer, *Pedro de Rivera*: 270-72.
78. Warner, "Felix Martinez": 15.
79. Naylor and Polzer, *Pedro de Rivera*: 245, 282-87; Moorhead, *Presidio*: 41.
80. SANM I #1220, WPA translation.
81. Jones, *Pueblo Warriors*: 171-73.
82. Ibid.: 114, 170, 173.
83. For example, Doc. 5.
84. Jones, *Pueblo Warriors*: 91-118.
85. For example, Doc. 2.
86. See Cutter, *Legal Culture*: 69-75; and Simmons, *Spanish Government*: 194-95.
87. See Doc. 29.
88. Except in the charter communities, the word *villa* can also and usually does mean a town.
89. Simmons, *Spanish Government*: 193-95; Cutter, *Legal Culture*: 93-96.
90. See SANM II #407; Simmons, *Spanish Government*: 194-95; Warner, "Felix Martinez": 118 n3.
91. Some clues as to the demise of the cabildo are found in SANM II #407, in what appears to be the draft of a letter written by Governor Bustamante to Brigadier Rivera during his inspection. Because the document is so sketchy, a translation of the document has not been published at this time. There is some suggestion that the letter is the governor's draft copy. In his summary of the document, Twitchell calls it a "blotter of a letter" (Twitchell, *Spanish Archives*: 208).
92. Warner, "Felix Martinez":120-21; Simmons, *Spanish Government*: 195-96.
93. See Cutter, *Legal Culture*: 82-92; Simmons, *Spanish Government*: 170-75.
94. See Map 2.
95. Cutter, *Legal Culture*: 91-92.
96. A rubric is a unique mark or flourish added to a signature.
97. See Doc. 27.
98. Cutter, *Legal Culture*: 90-92.
99. Simmons, *Spanish Government*: 174.
100. Ibid.: 162-63; Cutter, *Legal Culture*: 99.
101. Cutter, *Legal Culture*: 128.
102. See Doc. 32.
103. See Doc. 11.
104. Simmons, *Spanish Government*: 179; West, "Asylum": 373; Cutter, *Legal Culture*: 129; see also Docs. 18 and 22.
105. Cutter, *Legal Culture*: 132.
106. For example, see SANM II #432.
107. SANM II #477 records an Indian man being sentenced to five years of hard labor at the obraje of the alcalde of Socorro del Sur, south of El Paso.
108. Cutter, *Legal Culture*: 140-41.
109. Frank, *Settler to Citizen*: 147.
110. See Doc. 2.
111. As the number of sheep increased, the trade embargo was lifted, only to be invoked again in the 1770s as drought and Indian raids decreased the size of the herds (Baxter, *Las Carneradas*: 51-52; SANM II #697).
112. Thomas, *Plains Indians*: 31-32. The conflicts were not always between the Spanish and Indians, but sometimes among the Spanish themselves. For example, a fight occurred in 1726 at Taos between the alcalde

Manuel Tenorio de Alba and his men, and some of the Spanish traders. The traders were incensed when Tenorio bought two captives for his own customers, Brigadier Pedro de Rivera and Fray Antonio Gabaldón, before opening the trade fair. The traders retaliated by ignoring the prices fixed by Tenorio de Alba and started trading on their own, resulting in the fracas between the two parties (Kessell, *Kiva*: 367-68). Another example occurred in 1725, when Governor Bustamante brought proceedings against traders who had caused trouble with the "heathen" Indians at Pecos (SANM II #340a).

113. For the above paragraph, see Doc. 43 as an example.
114. The concept of trade triangles is based on the work of Philip Curtis on trade patterns in the West Indies and elsewhere (Curtis, *Cross Cultural Trade*).
115. A fanega is equal to about 1.5 to 2.5 bushels. Put differently, based on the fanega bins at the Museum of International Folk Art, one fanega is the amount of grain that fills a bin of about 18 inches by 8 inches by 9 inches.
116. Jones, *Pueblo Warriors*: 142.
117. Brugge, *Captives*: 120.
118. Works, "Trading Places": 276.
119. The New Mexicans also did some weaving. For example, in the 1768 will of Miguel Lucero, an Albuquerque alcalde, his inventory of goods includes a loom and woven material (SANM I #454, WPA translation).
120. Hackett, *Historical Documents*: 400.
121. See Works, "Trading Places": 271-74; Foote, "Spanish-Indian Trade": 22; Cutter, *Legal Culture*: 166; John, *Storms*: 317-21; and Thomas, *After Coronado*: 2.
122. Frank, "Settler to Citizen": 454.
123. See Doc. 40 for the case brought by blacksmith Salvador García against Juan García de la Mora.
124. Snow, "Chihuahua": 139.
125. Kubler, *San Miguel*: 27.
126. Kessell, *Kiva*: 12; Brugge, *Captives*: 31.
127. Tyler, *Indian Cause*: 95.
128. Brugge, *Captives*: 123-25.
129. For example, Governor Marín del Valle's order in Doc. 43.
130. Chávez, *Archives*: 21-22.
131. Kessell, *Kiva*: 307.
132. For a discussion of ransoming, see Jones, "Rescue": 129-48.
133. Historians define Genízaros as Indians from various locations who had lost their tribal identity, though not quite gaining an identity as Spanish.
134. Chávez, "Genízaros": 99; Ebright and Hendricks, *Witches*: 30.
135. See Doc. 6.
136. Jenkins, "Taos": 85-114; Jenkins, "Tewa": 113-34; Ebright, *Land Grants*: 22-24.
137. Baxter, *Las Carneradas*: 24; Jenkins, "Taos": 98-99; SANM II #604.
138. Greenfield, *History of Public Health*: 7, based on Chávez, *Archives*: 231-40.

1

COLONY IN DANGER OF DEMISE; CABILDO BEGS VICEROY FOR SOLDIERS AND SUPPLIES
May 8, 1705. Source: SANM II #114.

Synopsis and editor's notes: With the leader of the Reconquest, don Diego de Vargas, recently dead, and the situation of the reestablished colony dire, the members of the Santa Fe *cabildo* urged the new governor to ask the viceroy and the *audiencia* in Mexico City for help. Governor Cuervo y Valdés took office in Santa Fe on March 10, 1705, with the following petition of the cabildo presented to him on May 8, less than two months later. The cabildo complained of an epidemic of illness among the settlers and the unexpected Apache and Navajo raids, and listed their need for clothes, farming equipment, guns, gunpowder, and horses. The petition apparently had some effect. The viceroy responded on February 28, 1706, promising guns, gunpowder, and thirty additional soldiers. Not content to wait for the viceroy's supplies, Governor Cuervo led expeditions against the Navajos and Apaches in June and July of 1705 with equipment partly purchased with his own money (John, *Storms*: 226-27; Flagler, "Defensive Policy": 89-104).

The Santa Fe cabildo, formally the *cabildo*, *justicia*, and *regimiento*, had been part of the colony since the seventeenth century. In many towns of New Spain, and certainly in Mexico City, the cabildo played a dominant role in the government of the town and adjacent areas. Having a cabildo was one of the privileges given by the king to a town that was designated as a *villa*, or chartered town. The cabildo was a municipal body with judicial and executive authority, and, in Santa Fe, police authority. The proper procedure, as can be seen here, was for its members to work with the governor, in this case making a written request that was formally received by the governor. The governor then added his own thoughts and sent it sent on to the viceroy. Unfortunately, in New Mexico as elsewhere in New Spain, the governor and cabildo did not always get along. In the second decade of the century, the relationship was acrimonious; in one case, Governor Valverde sent members to Mexico City in chains. By the later 1720s, the cabildo ceased to exist. Though Santa Cruz and Albuquerque were also granted villa status, neither Vargas nor Cuervo y Valdés had a cabildo put in place, the alcaldes mayores and governors taking on its responsibilities (see Cutter, *Legal Culture*: 93-96; Doc. 27).

Governor and Captain General

[We] the cabildo, justicia, and regimiento of this villa of Santa Fe, the principal town of this kingdom and provinces of New Mexico, appear before you in all of the proper form which is given to us in the name of all of the residents to whom we refer, and say that upon your honor [Governor Francisco Cuervo y Valdés] entering your governorship and assuming control of it, you ordered that a general muster of the residents be held of the weapons belonging to his majesty [Felipe V] which are held by a number of residents and of the people who are capable of bearing them when needed for the defense of this kingdom, their families, and their households. Having done this, with the greatest zeal in the royal service, your honor found that most of the said arms that belong to his majesty are broken[1] and in a state of ill repair, because this kingdom does not have an armorer[2] employed by his majesty who can repair and put them right. There are numerous individuals who do not have arms, who are destitute and very poor.

Felipe V, king of Spain, 1700–1724, 1724–1746.
Image from Los governantes de México, Vol. 1, by Manuel Rivera (México, 1872).

In attending to this, we are aware that your honor is very eager to send a notice by courier to the court and city of México informing his excellency, the viceroy [the Duke of Albuquerque] and other ministers, of your arrival and your taking of possession. On behalf of the said citizens, we are asking you to inform his honor and the royal *junta*[3] of the extreme poverty, hunger, and nakedness in which they live, unable to acquire any type of relief. On some occasions when going for a load of wood to the mountains, which are very near to this said villa, there have been some deaths caused by the Apaches, and as such the said citizens are very limited in doing what they have to do and thus they cannot accomplish much. This is more so at this time because the past years have been so terrible with much illness, as was seen in the past year of 1704,[4] and because of the continuing war against the enemy Apache nations who surround us. In particular the bellicose and widespread Navajo nations have arisen again, which we have experienced for the first time since this kingdom was conquered in [16]80 (which was found as it was upon your arrival). Their continuous invasions and ambushes have caused numerous deaths and robberies each and every day and will become worse due to their immediacy in the heavily wooded and high country which surrounds our settlements.

This will continue even though your honor has taken every measure and provided escorts and the presidial soldiers. But regardless of these, the residents cannot subsist with a modicum of comfort amidst such war because they are lacking everything. Even though they cannot control this, they may be able to at least accomplish part of it if they are assisted by the zealous ministers which make up the imperial audiencia[5] and by his excellency, the *príncipe*, whose assistance, even though it might be small, can provide us with a few iron plowshares, hoes, and spades [*hierra de rexas, coas y azadones*], which are all badly needed, and without which the cultivation and the working of the lands are limited. Also needed is cloth such as baize, cotton, campeche cloth,[6] and thread [*vayeta, manta, campeche, y hilos*] so that the residents can dress themselves and rid themselves of so much nakedness, along with harsh necessities caused by all of the referred-to reasons, as well as a certain number of horses which up to now his excellency has seen fit to provide and which shall remain in charge of your honor and by the succeeding governors. These horses shall be held with the royal horse herd of this said royal presidio, under the guard and garrison by the soldiers so that on the occasion of need for the royal service, they are readily available.

We also petition for munitions of gunpowder and balls [*polvora y valas*], which up until the year past of 1703 his majesty provided for us, but are now not available to us. Now all of the residents are found without munitions or means to purchase them, as your honor is aware because of the muster that has been held, thus they are exposed to the occurrence of risks as has happened.

Lacking all of this aid, it is certain that this settlement will neither be able to prosper nor be maintained. If no aid is given, we will be forced to leave and look for another place outside of this kingdom. Because of this we petition and seek that your honor is willing to send out this account, as it is done for the benefit of all the residents, and which is what we await from your honor's good zeal, swearing in our best and proper form that this, our petition, is not done in malice, but for what is necessary, etc.

Juan de Uribarrí (rubric)[7]
Antonio de Valverde Cossio (rubric)[8] Diego Arias de Quiros (rubric)[9]
Antonio de Aguilera Ysasi (rubric)[10]
Antonio Montoya (rubric)[11] Antonio Lucero de Godoy (rubric)[12]

Before me,
Cristóbal de Góngora (rubric)[13]
Secretary of the cabildo

Presentation

At the villa of Santa Fe, the principal town of this kingdom and province of New Mexico, on the 8th of May, 1705, the cabildo, justicia, and regimiento of this said villa presented this written document before me, General Francisco Cuervo y Valdez, caballero of the Order of Santiago, governor and captain general of this kingdom and province of New Mexico, castellan of the forces and presidios for his majesty.

Decree

Having seen the said written justification and representation which was made by the said cabildo, justicia, and regimiento in favor of the residents of this kingdom by which reason and upon whom I legitimately favored the solicitation of their aid in order to remedy their extreme and numerous needs, which I am aware that they are suffering, and by which I am touched. Because I am in charge of this kingdom as governor and captain general, it [the request of the cabildo] cannot be left without my making legitimate and just representation to his excellency, the viceroy, Duke of Albuquerque. This is so that his grandness [*su grandeza*] upon his review of this document which, with my representation and information, he will receive as has been provided with my representation and information, will provide the aid that the said cabildo asks for on behalf of the said residents along with the other measures that his excellency will provide for the maintenance and conservation of this kingdom and aid to its inhabitants. So that it is valid, I approved, ordered, and signed it with my secretary of government and war.

Francisco Cuervo y Valdés (rubric)
before me,
Alfonso Rael de Aguilar (rubric)[14]
Secretary of government and war

Tenth duke of Albuquerque and Marqués of Cuéllar, Francisco V Fernández de la Cueva Enríquez y Fernández de la Cueva, viceroy of New Spain, 1702–1710. Image from *Los governantes de México,* Vol. 1, by Manuel Rivera (México, 1872).

ORIGINAL DOCUMENT

Señor Governador y Capitan General

El Cabildo, Justizia y Reximento de esta Villa de Santa Fee cavezera de este Reyno y Provinzias de la Nueba Mexico ante Vuestra Señoria paresemos en forma de derecho qual nos convenga en nombre de toda la vezindad de quien hablamos y dezimos que abiendo entrado Vuestra Señoria a su govierno y tomado possezion de el se sirvio de acordar y mandar pasar muestra general alos vezinos tanto de las armas de Su Magestad que en su poder tienen quantos de las personas que pueden tomarlas en la ocasion para defensa de dicho Reyno, sus casas y familias y aviendolo assi executado con puntal zelo al Real Servizio a reconocido Vuestra Señoria por la resena la mayor parte de las dichas armas de quenta de Su Magestad quebradas y echadas a perder por no aber en este Reyno armero de Su Magestad que las compongan y alinen y ai muchos sin ellas destitados y pobres y atendiendo a hallarse Vuestra Señoria prompto para despachar correo a la Corte y Ciudad de Mexico dando al Excellentisimo Señor Virrey y Señores ministros quenta de su llegada y possesion pedimos a Vuestra Señoria en nombre de dicha vezindad cuya parte hazemos ynforme a Su Excellenzia y la Real Junta la mucha pobreza, ambre y desnudes con que se hallan ymposibilitados para adquirir algun alivio y pocas vezes que abiendo salido al monte como estan ynmediato a esta dicha Villa a traer una poca de lena lo an muerto los dichos Apaches y asi se hallan oprimidos y sin poder adelantar su travajo y mucho mas oy que an sido los años de atras pasados teribles y muy enfermos como se bido el de setecientos y quatro y la continua guerra de los enemigos contra de Naciones Apacha que la sircumbalan mayormente abiendose sublebado de nuebo las Naciones de la belicosa y dilatada aquienes llaman Navajoes y de quien se a experimentado desde primera vez que se conquisto este dicho Reyno antes de el año de ochenta (abiendolo asi allado en su entrada) con continuadas ymbaciones y emboscadas causando muertes y rovos cada dia y se aguardan mayores por lo ynmediato que esta de aspera y encumbrada serrania a nuestras poblaciones aun en medio de estar dadas por Vuestra Señoria todas las providencias y escoltas nesesarias con los presidiales empero aunque no ubiese de por medio dicho guerra presisamente no pudieron subsistir estos vezinos en mediana comodidad faltandoles en todo y aunque este no le consigan podran alo menos que en parte los ateindan tan zelosos ministros como componen la ynperial audienzia y Su Excellentisimo Principe de quienes el socorro aunque sea un poco hierro de rexas, coas y azadones de que en el todo se careze y atrasa la ynopia el cultivo y labranza de las tierras y asi mismo un socorro de pano, vayeta, mantas, campeches, hilo para que se vistan y rediman tanta desnudez y asperas nesesidades causadas de las razones referidas y tambien una porcion de cavallos la que Su Excellenzia fuese servido de librar y que esta se conserve en poder de Vuestra Señoria y los otros Señores Governadores que adelante fueren en el cuerpo dela cavallada de este Real Presidio debajo dela escolta y guarnizion de sus soldados para que en las ocasiones de el Real Zervizio tengan el prompto la providenzia pidiendo y representando se restituyan las municiones de polvora y valas que asta el año pasado de setezientos y tres tenia consedidas Su Magestad y abiendose oy dado de mano a su providenzia se hallan todos lo vezinos sin municiones ni caudal para poderlas comprar expuesto ala contingencia y riesgo de el acudente como se esta experimentado y aun Su Señoria le consta por la dicha muestra que tiene pasada y reconosida pues faltando este socorro tenemos por muy sierto que esta vezindad no se a de poder mantener ni subsistir pues no alla medio para su alivio y esta clamando por salirse a buscarlo fuera de el Reyno, por tanto a Vuestra Señoria pedimos y suplicamos se sirva de asi executarlo pues depende de dicho ynforme el bien por toda la dicha vezindad que asi lo esperamos de su buen zelo de Vuestra Señoria jurando en toda forma de derecho este nuestro pedimento no ser de malicia y en lo necessario, ut supra.

Juan de Uribarri (rubric)
Antonio de Balverde Cossio (rubric)
Diego Arias de Quiros (rubric)
Antonio de Aguilera Ysasy (rubric)
Antonio Montoya (rubric)
Antonio Lusero de Godoy (rubric)
Ante mi

Xptobal de Gongora (rubric)
Secretario de Cabildo

Presentazion

En la Villa de Santa Fee cavezera de este Reyno y Provinzias dela Nueva Mexico en ocho dias del mes de Mayo de mill y setezientos y cinco años: El Cavildo, Justizia y Regimento desta dicha Villa presento esta escritura y representazion ante mi el General Francisco Cuervo y Valdés, Cavallero del Orden de Santiago, Governador y Capitan General deste Reyno y Provincias dela Nueva Mexico, Castellano de Sus Fuerzas y Presidios por Su Magestad.

Auto

Por mi vista y lo justificado de dicha escriptura y representazion que hase dicho Cabildo, Justizia y Reximento, a favor de la vezindad deste Reyno por la parte y aquien lexitimamente le yntumbe el solizitar sus alivios, remediar sus estremos y las demasias nesesidades las cuales me consta estan padeciendo y por lo que ami toca, y estar a mi cargo este Reyno como Governador y Capitan General de el no abra omision el hazer la justa y lexitima representazion que el Excellentisimo Virrey Duque de Alburquerque para que Su Grandeza con vista de este escripto de que hase remission con lo a el proveydo y con dicha mi representazion e ynforme mande dar el socorro que dicho Cavildo pide para dichos vezinos y las demas Providenzias que Su Excellencia fuere servido para la mantenzion y conservazion de este Reyno y alivio de sus avitadores y para que asi conste asi lo provey, mande y firme con me Secretario de Governazion y Guerra.

Francisco Cuervo y Valdes (rubric)
Ante mi
Alphonsso Rael de Aguilar (rubric)
Secretario de Governazion y Guerra

Notes

1. In regard to broken weapons, things were not much better fifty years later. See Doc. 45.
2. There may not have been an armorer at the presidio in 1705, though in 1692 Francisco Lucero de Godoy accompanied Vargas as captain of artillery and armorer and served him for seven years, according to a charge made about back pay in May of 1701. Also, in 1703, upon his return to the colony as governor, Vargas stated that all weapons not in working order "be given to the armorer to be repaired and made serviceable." However, no name is provided (Kessell and Hendricks, *BFA*: 319-20 n6; Kessell et al., *ASA*: 42, 203).

3. The term *junta* could have meant the *real junta de guerra*, or royal war council; or the *junta de hacienda*, or royal treasury council (Tyler, *Indian Cause*: 319, 327).
4. This illness may be that described on March 28, 1793, as affecting Captain Alfonso Rael de Aguilar and Diego Velasco, later resulting in the death of Vargas (Kessell et al., *ASA*: 221).
5. The audiencia was the highest royal court of appeals within New Spain, also serving as a council of state to the viceroy (Tyler, *Indian Cause*: 319).
6. In this context, campeche appears to be cloth, probably cotton, colored violet, dark blue, or black, from the dye of the logwood tree that grew (and still grows) in Campeche Bay in the Yucatán (Cámara, "Logwood": 324-29).
7. A *rubric* is a flourish added to a signature. Juan de Uribarrí (aka Ulibarrí), born in San Luis Potosí, New Spain, became the *alcalde mayor* and captain of the El Paso presidio in 1699. By 1702 he was in New Mexico and married to Juana Hurtado, a stepsister of Martín Hurtado, first alcalde of Albuquerque. By 1709 he was alcalde of Santa Cruz. He died in Mexico City in 1716 (NMGS, *Aquí*: 54; Kessell et al., *BOB*: 46-47).
8. Antonio de Valverde Cossio, originally from Santander, Spain, came to New Mexico with Vargas in 1693 and served as captain-for-life of the El Paso presidio and later as the alcalde mayor of the area. He served as governor of New Mexico from 1717 to 1722. He died in 1728, the owner of a large farming, livestock, winegrowing, and brandy-making operation near El Paso (Kessell et al., *Accounts*: 258).
9. Captain Diego Arias de Quiros was from Asturia, Spain, arriving in El Paso at least by 1687, where he was presidio captain. In 1694 he was in New Mexico, serving as royal *alférez* of Santa Fe. He received a grant of land east of the Governor's Palace, marrying María Gómez Robledo in 1714. He survived the 1720 attack on the Villasur expedition and went on to become alcalde mayor and *alcalde ordinario* of Santa Fe in the 1720s (Kessell et al., *BOB*: 35; Thomas Chávez, *Moment*: 151-52; SANM II #44).
10. Captain Antonio Aguilera de Ysasi was a native of Mexico City, coming to New Mexico in 1694 with the Farfán-Velasco expedition. He was a member of the Santa Fe cabildo by 1697. He also served as *alguacil mayor*, or chief constable, from at least 1703 to 1705 (Kessell and Hendricks, *RCR*: 324 n52; SANM II #137b; Esquibel, "Residents": 68).
11. [Juan] Antonio [Sotomayor] Montoya was part of a muster at the El Paso presidio in 1692–1683, coming to that presidio as a convict. He was born in Mexico City, and his family arrived in New Mexico in 1677. He returned to New Mexico in 1693, becoming a member of the cabildo by 1703. Two of his daughters married members of the Durán y Chávez family (Kessell and Hendricks, *RCR*: 78 n23; Chávez, *Origins*: 199, 234; SANM II #94a).
12. Antonio Lucero de Godoy was an adjutant at the El Paso presidio in the 1689s and 1690s. Though many of his family were killed in 1680, he came to New Mexico in 1693, serving as captain at the presidio, and a member of the cabildo by 1703. He died in 1712. An ancestor of his, Pedro Lucero de Godoy, was in New Mexico in 1616. Antonio's descendants lived near Santa Fe and had extensive holdings near Taos (Kessell and Hendricks, *BFA*: 487 n61; Kessell et al., *BOB*: 1167 n29; SANM II #53 and #95a; Barrett, *Settlement*: 101, 192, 199, 210).
13. According to Esquibel, Cristóbal de Góngora was the great-grandson of Bartolomé Góngora, from Andalusia, Spain, who was the author of several books and gained the favor of several viceroys. Chávez states that Cristóbal was the son of a wax worker from Mexico City who came to New Mexico with his family in 1693 with the Farfán-Velasco expedition. Cristóbal was a presidio soldier and clerk of the cabildo in Santa Fe, serving as a notary from 1701 to 1711. In 1714 he was a notary in El Paso (Chávez, *Origins*: 188; Kessell et al., *BOB*: 671 n28; Esquibel, "Residents": 55, 67).
14. Alfonso (aka Alonso) Rael de Aguilar I was a native of Lorca, Spain. He served as the secretary of government and lieutenant general for Vargas by 1692 and later for Governor Cuervo. He was also alcalde of Santa Fe, a "protector" of the Indians, and acted as a *juez comisión*, or an acting magistrate, as well as sergeant major and a captain. He married Josepha García de Noriega, an aunt or great-aunt of Luis García de Noriega of Albuquerque. Alfonso died in 1735. His son also signed his name as Alonso (Chávez, *Origins*: 263; Kessell and Hendricks, *BFA*: 203 n8l; Simmons, *Spanish Government*: 86; see also Cutter, *Protector*).

2

NEW MEXICANS CUT OUT OF TRADING MARKET; BANDOS WRITTEN TO LIMIT OUTSIDERS FROM TRADING
June 9, 1704, to August 25, 1705.
Sources: SANM II #117 and #118.

Synopsis and editor's notes: The following documents describe the efforts of Lieutenant Governor Juan Páez Hurtado, the cabildo, and Governor Francisco Cuervo y Valdés to establish and manage the New Mexican trading economy by adopting regulations preventing outside traders from cutting out New Mexicans from the newly opened Indian trading markets. In the first document it appears that outsiders from New Spain were bringing their horses and mules north and trading them (or having them traded by New Mexicans acting as a front) to the nomadic Indians. The Indians paid a higher price for the horses and mules than offered by the New Mexicans at least partly because the horses from the south were of better quality and more variety. The result was that the goods received from the Indians went with the outside merchants to the south, leaving the New Mexicans without basic needs and items which they could trade themselves. The policies of the governors and cabildos were intended to keep the wealth that resulted from the Indian trade in the colony. In effect, these laws created an embargo on the sale of the horses and mules from outside the colony, which, as might have been expected, and as shown in some of the following documents, created illegal trading, a kind of black market that operated outside the governor's powers of enforcement.

These early mandates also established prices for the trade goods, following a policy set by the previous governor, don Diego de Vargas. One reason for this price fixing was to keep the settlers from cheating and undercutting each other and the Indians at the trade fairs, which caused bad feelings and resulted in fights, raids, and reprisals. With the battles and deaths resulting from the Reconquest and the 1696 revolt at Santa Cruz looming in the background, the governors and cabildo were making every effort to keep the uneasy peace that had been established.

SANM II #117

Bandos #1 and #2. The 1703 Vargas bando and the June 9, 1704, Hurtado readoption

Captain Juan Páez Hurtado,[1] lieutenant governor and captain general of this kingdom and province of New Mexico for the Marqués de la Nava de Brazinas, now deceased, former governor and captain general of this said kingdom for his majesty, etc.[2]

Inasmuch as the illustrious cabildo, justicia, and regimiento of this villa of Santa Fe, before me, requested on this day of this date, that without hesitation the bando [Bando #1][3] ordered by the Marqués de la Nava de Brazinas, now deceased, governor and captain general that he was of this kingdom, be readopted, in which was contained the mandate that no entry be permitted [to outsiders] into the pueblos of Taos and Pecos, where the heathen Apache Indians hold their ransom [*rescate*][4] and trade fairs. This is because the residents [working with the outsiders] take numerous excellent horses to them and the Apaches give for them a higher price than is customary, and thus devaluate the amount that is customary in the kingdom.

For this reason, the residents are not to be permitted to acquire horses or mules from outside of the province and claim that they were always theirs.[5] The alcaldes mayores[6] of the said pueblos of Taos and Pecos are to make sure that the residents who want to gain from the said trade fairs are actual settlers of this kingdom, and if not, they are to become settlers of the kingdom, and they, the settlers, are to be the only ones who can participate in the trade fairs, and no one else. Recognizing that their [the cabildo's] request is justifiable, I immediately order [Bando #2] that no others from outside the province are to partake in the trade fairs, nor are they to give their horses or mules to the alcaldes mayores or to any of the residents of this said kingdom under penalty of their losing whatever they had acquired at the trade fair. The vecinos who acquire them are to be banished to the frontiers of this kingdom for the period of one year. The alcaldes mayores are to lose their positions as such, which will be done immediately.

In order to fulfill this mandate, I order that this be made public in this said villa [Santa Fe] at the sound of the military instruments with the assistance of the said illustrious cabildo along with the aid of the secretary of government and war, who will testify to the publication of such, and who will make copies of this to remit to the alcalde mayor of the new villa of Santa Cruz[7] so that the same is carried out at that place. The amount of goods that is obtained from this [the enforcement of this order] is to be given, from the inception, to the poor who are in the most in need, who are to be noted and a list drawn up by the illustrious cabildo, who is to obey and corroborate everything that is ordered by the said bando which was promulgated at the order of the said Marqués, now deceased. Also I order the said alcaldes mayores to make sure that no one gives more than one horse for a *pieza*[8] of two Apaches which are brought for sale. Also, with regards to buffalo and elk hides, the most which should be given [for the sale of two Apaches] should be no more than eighteen piezas.

So that this is valid, I signed it at this villa of Santa Fe with the secretary of government and war on the 9th of June, 1704.

Juan Páez Hurtado (rubric)
At the order of the lieutenant general
Alfonso Rael de Aguilar (rubric)
Secretary of government and war

    I, the captain Alfonso Rael de Aguilar, secretary of government and war of this kingdom, in compliance with and in obedience to the order that I was given, on this day of the said date, at the sound of the military instruments and by the voice of the drummer, Sebastián,[9] black, and with the assistance of the illustrious cabildo, and before a large crowd which was gathered, publicized the said bando.

Alfonso Rael de Aguilar (rubric)
Secretary of government and war

Bando #3. June 1, 1705. Petition by the Cabildo for readoption of the Vargas/Páez Hurtado bando

Villa of Santa Fe
June 1, 1705

    Governor and Captain General

    [We] the cabildo, justicia, and regimiento of this villa before your honor, appear in all the proper right which we have and say that we present and duplicate the petition[10] which we presented before the predecessor of your honor, the Marqués of the Nava de Brazinas, governor and captain general, who was of this kingdom, and his lieutenant governor, Juan Páez Hurtado, on the previous year. The petition was made in order to control and end the entry of persons from outside the province from trading with either the heathen Indians, or with those recently converted, due to the numerous atrocities [at the trade fairs] and to the large numbers of horses [brought in from the outside]. This is prejudicial to these poor residents, who are found deserted due to the numerous casualties caused by the widespread wars which are spread throughout the country. [The lack of horses in New Mexico] is also due to the small supply of grain available from the previous years due to the high temperatures and scarcity of rain and the infestation of insects, which brought numerous illnesses[11] with no relief or improvement, reasons which were taken into consideration and were of great concern to the said Marqués de la Nava de Brazinas [don Diego de Vargas] and the Captain Juan Páez Hurtado. This concern prompted the above mentioned [Vargas] to bring forth an order [Bando #1] which totally disallowed foreign residents from participating in trade fairs or exchange, or to enter into contracts, imposing upon them the penalties which are indicated in his mandate; and secondly, under no less zeal, ordering through a royal bando [Bando #2], which was to be made public on the 9th day of June of the previous year of 1704, in which was repeated and corroborated that which was ordered by the said Marqués (deceased) in which was shown the established rate and price which should be given for the value of commercial goods. It adds that the original residents and the alcalde mayor or any person who obtains animals from foreigners with the pretense of selling them [as their own] or exchanging them for goods is to be banished for the period of one year to the frontiers of this said kingdom. All of which is to be done for the benefit of the residents as well as for the service of his majesty and for the best subsistence of such, for the advancement and propagation of Our Holy Catholic Faith, and for protection against those who wish to enter into this said kingdom.

To which we say that it is because of our duty and for the best consequences which follow for our benefit and to which your honor should attend with much zeal, desire, and great application for the good of the royal service for which it is well stated, ordering that it remain as such and as provided shall be safeguarded and complied with according to the order and bando as stated and duplicated. As such it refers to all of the horses which have been brought in during the present year to the places with the best trade goods and which should be excluded from the pueblos of the native Indians of Taos and Pecos so that the trade fairs, contracts, and commercial sales are celebrated and executed with the Spanish residents of this kingdom as was customarily done before the general uprising of the year of [16]80, which is generally known and publicized, and done in no other way. Also, the rest of the residents who brought clothing or any other type of goods to sell at the rate that is allowed in the kingdom, without altering the prices, shall be made aware of the penalties that your honor will impose upon those who sell [illegally] as well as on those who purchase. Also those residents who come from outside the province and are involved with those residents of this kingdom and villa and who continue to take out the goods which they had brought shall be made aware of the reparations which can be imposed, one with the other, of that which has been stated in the order of the Marqués.

Of your honor we ask that you act in favor of these residents, revalidating, confirming, and amplifying that which was provided by his predecessors so that as such we shall receive all of the relief and good which is solicited, ordering that this be made known along with the other petitions, orders, and bandos to the referred-to residents and to the alcaldes mayores of the jurisdictions of the Villa Nueva de Santa Cruz and Bernalillo, pueblos of Pecos and Taos, swearing by all form that this is the petition of the royal cabildo which we present to your honor, and for what is necessary, etc.

Juan de Uribarrí (rubric)
Diego Arias de Quiros (rubric)
Antonio de Aguilera Ysasy (rubric)
Antonio Lucero de Godoy (rubric)
By order of the cabildo, justicia, and regimiento
Xptobal de Góngora (rubric)
Secretary of the cabildo

Bando #3. June 1, 1705. Bando mandated by Governor Cuervo y Valdés

Presentation

At the villa of Santa Fe on the 1st of June, 1705, before me, General don Francisco Cuervo y Valdés, knight of the Order of Santiago, governor and captain general of this kingdom and of the provinces of New Mexico and castellan of the forces and presidios for his majesty, etc. was presented by the cabildo, justicia, and regimiento[12] of this villa of Santa Fe, headquarters of this kingdom and provinces of New Mexico, with the instruments and orders [Bando #1] referred to and duplicated within it as dictated by the Marqués de la Nava de Brazinas, my predecessor, who may be in the Holy Glory, and which was retained by his lieutenant general and captain, Juan Páez Hurtado. These bandos I order to be executed, observed, complied with, and safeguarded as they are contained, being that they are for the good and benefit of the residents of this kingdom and which were preserved by the said illustrious cabildo as indicated in their petition.

So that they have the effect that is indicated and which is asked for, I order [Bando #3] all the strangers who have come into this kingdom with a large number of horses in order to participate in the trade fairs and dealings with the gentile Apaches who customarily arrive on an annual basis at the pueblos of Taos and Pecos to return to the *puestos* [settlements] of Bernalillo and La Cañada, settlements of the Spanish, with their horses, prohibiting them, as I shall prohibit them, not to enter into the referred pueblos and the frontiers. This is due to the excessive and bad consequences which result from them taking advantage of the goods which the said Apaches bring with them, which could benefit the residents of this kingdom. The residents are always ready and eager to acquire them because that is all that is offered by the royal service of his majesty, being that they are not given anything else except what they can acquire from the said Apaches in the trade fairs, dealings, and contracts which they carry on with them. I cannot prohibit the said strangers from doing what they do and what they can do as far as their dealings, trade fairs, and contracts with the said residents of this kingdom. This I can permit and do permit them to do, but I do not permit it with the Apaches, as has been said.

If they want to do this they will have to come and settle and become residents of this [kingdom]. In order to uphold all of this as is stated in the said document presented by the said illustrious cabildo, I impose the penalty of their [the outsiders] losing their said horses which I will apply to the expenses of war, justice, and for the informer. As for that which can be gained by the said cabildo, justicia, and regimiento, it is seen that a number of persons have come into this kingdom with goods of clothing and other merchandise in order to sell them for more value than what is known and what is the custom, altering and raising their prices, which is bad, improper, and an inconvenience to the residents. In order to correct this matter, I order those who have brought said goods and merchandise with them not to sell them at a higher price nor add more value than has been the custom. For this, I impose the penalty of their losing their merchandise and goods, which I will apply in the same manner as has been expressed. As for the residents who have purchased them, they are to be banished to one of the frontiers of this kingdom for one year. If they are soldiers belonging to this royal presidio, they are to be banished to guard the horse herd for one year.

In order to execute and comply with all of that which is referred to, and so that the strangers and other persons, who are the ones who have brought in the merchandise, understand what is meant by this order and decree, I order that it be made public at this villa with the solemnity of the military instruments and in loud and intelligible voices, with the assistance of the said illustrious cabildo and that of my secretary of government and war, who is to impose the certification of its publication, and once this done he shall submit a copy to the alcaldes mayores of the jurisdictions of La Cañada and Bernalillo so that they each make it known to the public. So that it is known for all time, it is to be placed into the archives of this government, where it shall be returned along with this order and the attachments. I also order the alcaldes mayores of Taos and Pecos not to allow strangers into their jurisdictions, and in case there is found some disobeying what is ordered because of some confusion or abstruse reason and they pretend not to understand all that is ordered by me in this decree, you are to continue the case until it reaches a state of sentencing, and once this is done it shall be submitted to me in order for me to execute it according to the law and their right.

This order is not to be disobeyed by anyone for any reason and is to be executed to its fullest. If, to the contrary, a just charge is to be given, I will punish those to the fullest extent, declaring them unfaithful to his majesty. So that they all understand, it shall be made known to them and explained to them individually by my secretary of government and war, and shall be placed as a proceeding so that it is known by everyone. I thus approved, ordered, and signed it with my secretary of government and war, etc.

Francisco Cuervo y Valdés (rubric)
before me
Alfonso Rael de Aguilar (rubric)
Secretary of government and war

Publication

At this villa of Santa Fe on the 8th of June, 1705, I, Captain Alfonso Rael de Aguilar, secretary of government and war, in compliance with and in obedience of what the said governor has ordered regarding the above decree which was made public in a loud and intelligible voice before a large number of people in the plaza of this Villa by Sebastián Rodríguez, drummer, with the assistance of the illustrious cabildo, justicia, and regimiento, I placed it as a proceeding, and so that it would take effect, I certified and signed it.

Alfonso Rael de Aguilar (rubric)
Secretary of government and war

Notification[13]

Continuing, on the said day, month, and year, I, the present secretary of government and war, in execution of what was mandated by the said governor and captain general by the order aforementioned which I gave notice of and read to General Juan de Uribarrí, alcalde mayor and war captain of the pueblo of Pecos and its jurisdiction, and he having heard it, stated that he would obey it, and promptly and with undivided attention would execute that which was ordered, and he signed it before me, to which I certify, etc.

Juan de Uribarrí (rubric)
Alfonso Rael de Aguilar (rubric)
Secretary of government and war

Notification

Continuing, on the said day, month, and year, I, the present secretary of government and war, by virtue and in execution of that which was mandated by the order aforementioned which I gave notice of and read personally to Captain don Felix Martínez,[14] alcalde mayor of the jurisdiction of Taos and Picuris, and he having heard it stated that he would obey it, and promptly and with undivided attention would execute that which was ordered, and he signed it before me, to which I certify, etc.

Felix Martínez (rubric)

SANM II #118

Bando #4. August 25, 1705. Bando initiated by Governor Cuervo y Valdez

General don Francisco Cuervo y Valdés, knight of the Order of Santiago, official judge and acting treasurer of the royal treasury of the city of Guadalajara in the kingdom of Galicia, governor and captain general of this kingdom of New Mexico and its provinces, and castellan of the forces and presidios for his majesty, etc.

Whereas, I have received a notice regarding the grave damages and extortions which are continuously being committed in the pueblos of Pecos, Taos, and Picuris and other frontiers and defensive places within this kingdom with the assistance of the residents of this kingdom in the said pueblos, and also by those who come into the said pueblos from the outside to commercially deal with the friendly infidel Indians, which is customarily done at the ransom fairs which are celebrated every year. In particular, I have received notice of the extortions carried out on the governors of the said pueblos and by the rest of the Indians who live within them, and which have been reported by their alcaldes mayores, and for other motives, reasons and causes which I have been experiencing, everything being a disservice to our majesty, and I have [received notice of] the grave damages which are received by the said Indians of the said pueblos, to whom I need to be attentive according to the obligation of my office.

By virtue of this, I order expressly by this order [Bando #4][15] that no resident of the said referred places, regardless of their status, quality, or condition, whatever it may be, shall dare to go to the said pueblos for any reason, nor under any pretense, valid or invalid, without my express license, under penalty of losing their lives and being traitors to the King, losing their goods, which upon being confiscated I will apply, from this time forward, half to the treasury of his majesty and the other half for the expenses which were incurred. The same punishment will be given to those who at the present time are found in the said pueblos, and who are to leave from them immediately, taking with them the horses which they have, everything being done according to the royal laws of the newly conquered and settled places. This order is done at the request of and written by the cabildo, justicia, and regimiento of this villa of Santa Fe, headquarters of this kingdom and province of New Mexico. The decree and bando which was promulgated by me, and previously approved by my predecessors, having been read, and so that it is complied with, I order to be sent to the said alcaldes mayores of the said pueblos of Pecos and Taos, where it is to be publicized, obeyed, made known, guarded, complied with, and enforced, under penalty of two hundred pesos which are to be applied in the same manner and for the interest and betterment of the native Indians of the said pueblos, leaving a copy at their casas reales. The said original order is to be returned along with any proceedings which are created during its execution. It is done at this said Villa of Santa Fe on the 25th of August, 1705, and I signed it with the secretary of government and war, etc.

    Francisco Cuervo y Valdés (rubric)
  By order of the governor and captain general
    Alfonso Rael de Aguilar (rubric)
    Secretary of government and war

At this pueblo of Nuestra Señora de Los Ángeles de Porciúncula[16] on the 29th of August, 1705, I, General Juan Uribarrí, in compliance with and obedience to that which was ordered by General don Francisco Cuervo y Valdés, knight of the Order of Santiago, governor and captain general of this kingdom of New Mexico, having arrived at this place as its alcalde mayor and captain general, and making the contents known to them, notified the individuals Juan Francisco and Salvador Montoya, residents of this said kingdom, who upon having heard and understanding the order, obeyed it, and within twenty-four hours after getting their horse herds rounded up, left, taking their horses with them. Having taken the testimony, word for word, of what was stated in the said order, it was left at the casas reales with their governor, don Felipe. I submitted the said order to the governor and captain general, there being present, besides the above said, the corporal of the squadron, Bartolomé Sánchez, who signed it along with me as assisting witness on the said day, etc.

        Juan de Uribarrí (rubric)
        assisting witness
        Bartolomé Sánchez

ORIGINAL DOCUMENTS

SANM II #117

Yo Capitan Juan Paez Hurtado, Theniente de Governador y Capitan General de este Reino y Provinzias de la Nueva Mexico, por el Marquez de la Naba de Brazinas ya difunto, Governador y Capitan General que fue deste dicho Reino por Su Magestad, ut supra.

Por quanto el Illustrisimo Cavildo, Justizia y Reximiento de esta Villa de Santa Fee ante mi hiso representazion oy dia de la fecha suplicandome que sin embargo del bando que de orden del Señor Marques de la Naba de Brazinas ya difunto, Governador y Capitan General que fue deste disho Reino a pedimento de el dicho Illustrisimo Cabildo y en el consta la provision para fuera entren a los Pueblos de los Thaos y Pecos a los rescattes que los Yndios gentiles Apaches a hazer sus ferias y que dichos vezinos traen numero de cavallos y ser de buena calidad dandoles dichos Apaches mas de lo que ese ussa y costumbre ymponiendolos a que los dichos generos tengan valor desfrutando este Reino y que asi mismo el que no permita que ninguno de los vezinos deste dicho Reino cojan ningunas vestias caballares ni mulares de los de tierra fuera con el pretexto de que son suyas, ni tampoco los Alcaldes Mayores de dichos Pueblos de Taos y Pecos y si dichos vezinos quierense gosar de dichos rescates y ferias se bengan a poblar a este dicho Reyno y que solamente puedan hazer dichos rescates los vezinos deste dicho Reyno y no otros: y reconoziendo ser su representazion justa por el presente mando que ninguno de los dichos vezinos de tierra fuera entren a dichos rescattes ni tampoco den las dichas sus vestias cavallares y mulares alos dichos Alcaldes Mayores ni ninguno de los vezinos deste dicho Reyno debaxo de la pena de perdimiento de las dichas a lo que con ellas hubieren rescatado: y a los dichos vezinos que las cojiesen destierrados a las fronteras de este dicho Reyno por el tiempo de un año: y a los Alcaldes Mayores depribasion de ofizio que se executara prontamente: para cuyo complimento mando se publique en esta dicha Villa con asistenzia del dicho Illustrisimo Cabildo y a son de los ynstrumentos militares y con la del Secretario de Governazion y Guerra quien pondra la fee de su publicazion y sacara otro con este y se remita a la Villa Nueva de Santa Cruz a su Alcalde Mayor para que asi mismo se haga la misma diligencia y la dicha pena ympuesta aplico desde luego para los pobres mas nezesitados que para ello dara y hara lista el dicho Illustrisimo Cabildo reyterando y corrobarando en el todo el dicho Bando promulgado de orden de dicho Señor Marques ya difunto y asi mismo mando a dichos Alcaldes Mayores no consientan que den mas que tan solamente un cavallo por una pieza de dos Apaches los que traen a vender: y en quanto de los cueros de Sibolo y antas por lo mas que se pudiere dar bajando de diez y ocho piezas y para que asi conste lo firme en esta Villa de Santa Fee con el Secretario de Governazion y Guerra en nueve dias del mes de Junio de mill y setezientos y quatro años.

Juan Paez Hurtado (rubric)
Por mando del Señor Theniente General
Alphonso Rael de Aguilar (rubric)
Secretario de Governazion y Guerra

Yo el Capitan Alphonso Rael de Aguilar, Secretario de Governazion y Guerra deste Reyno en cumplimento y obedezimento de lo que por el dicho Vando seme ordena se publico oy dia de la fecha a son de los instrumentos militares y por vos de Sebastian, Negro, tambor y con assistencia del Illustrisimo Cabildo hallandose mucho concurso de gente a dicha publicazion y para que conste doy fee y lo firme en esta Villa de Santa Fee en nuebe dias del mes de Junio de mill setezientos y quatro años.

Alphonso Rael de Aguilar (rubric)
Secretario de Governazion y Guerra

Villa de Santa Fee y
Junio 1 de 1705

Señor Gobernador y Capitan General

El Cabildo, Justizia y Reximento de esta Villa de Santa Fee ante Vuestra Merzed paresemos en toda forma de derecho qual convenga y decimos que hasemos representazion y reproduccion de los pedimentos que ante los antecessores de VSsa.

El Señor Marquez de la Naba de Brazinas, Governador y Capitan General que fue de este Reyno y su Theniente de Governador Joan Paez Hurtado hisimos el año pasado para el afecto y reparo de que no entren vezinos de la tierra fuera a rescatar con los Yndios Ynfieles ni los recien reduzidos con los copiosos trosos y partidas de caballadas por ser en perjuizio desta pobre vezindad que tan deseriodada se halla a causa de aber de subrisuir y cargar los accidentes continuos de la guerra esterelidado de el paiz y rigoroso temple con mas la ynopia de grano que los años de atras an ocasionado la sequedad y la napestas mucha enfermedad y ningun reparo y alivio rasones que en las representaciones adjuntas notificaron a los dichos Señores Marques de la Naba de Brazinas y Capitan Juan Paez Hurtado el primero a prover un auto en que totalmente priva a los vezinos foraneos de poder selebrar rescate, cambio ni otro contrato ynponiendo para ellos las penas que constan al trangesor de su mandato y el segundo con no menor zelo ordenando en un Real Bando que mando publicar el dia nuebe de Junio de el año proximo pasado de mil setecientos y quatro en que repite y corrovora lo mandado por el dicho Marques (difunto) pone tasa descriminada y precio fue de lo que se deve dar por valor de los generos comercianos y anade que el vezino originario y asistente de el Reyno Alcalde Mayor o persona tomare de las dichas vestias de los foraneos con pretexto de compra o cambalache sea desterrado por un año a una de las fronteras deste dicho Reyno que todo lo expresado es en beneficio de esta besindad y mas en servicio de Su Magestad para la mejor subsistenzia de ella adelantamiento y propagacion de nuestra Santa Fee Catolica y alentor a los que quisieran entrar a dicho Reyno en donde digo de nuestra obligazion y demas buenas consequenzias que se siguen de su logro a que atendera VSSa. con su mucho zelo buen deseo y gran applicazion al bien de el Real zervizio en que tanto se espresa y en pocos meses emos experimentado ordenado se estte en el todo alo proveydo se guarde y complase contexto de auto y bandos expresados y reproducidos y que se refieren con sus cavalladas los que an benido el presente año al paraje de mayor comodidad y retirado de los Pueblos de los Yndios naturales de Taos y Pecos y que sus rescates y tratos y comerzio lo selebren tengan y executen con los vezinos Españoles de este Reyno como acostumbravan aser antes dela sublevassion general de el año de ochenta como es savido y muy publico y no de otra forma y asi mismo el que los demas vezinos que traxeren generos de alguna ropa o mercansias bender al corriente de el Reyno sin alterar precios ynponiendo las penas que VSSa. estimare concertir enlos que benden como en los que compran entendiendose esta pension tanto con los vezinos de la tierra fuera quanto con los deste Reyno y Villa de el reparo que pueden hazer los unos y los otros tengan presente lo expresado en el auto de dicho Señor Marques y bulban a sacar los generos que ubiesen traydo, a VSSa. pedimos se sirva de proveer a favor de esta vezindad rebalidando, confirmando y amplificando lo proveydo por sus antecessores que en ello reziviremos todos el alivio y bien que se zolicita mandando se notifique este y los demas pedimentos autos y bandos alos referidos vezinos y a los Alcaldes Mayores de las jurisdiziones de la Villa Nueba de Santa Cruz y Bernalillo, Pueblos de Pecos y Thaos jurando en toda forma este nuestro pedimento el Real Cavildo en VSSa. ymploramos y en lo nessesario, ut supra.

      Juan de Uribarri (rubric)
     Diego Arias de Quiros (rubric)
Antonio de Aguilera Ysasy (rubric) Antonio Montoya (rubric)
     Antonio Lucero de Godoy (rubric)
   Por mando del Cavildo, Justizia y Reximento
      Xptobal de Gongora (rubric)
      Secretario del Cabildo

Presentazion

En la Villa de Santa Fee en primero dia del mes de Junio de mill y setezientos y cinco años ante mi el General Dn. Francisco Cuervo y Valdés, Cavallero del Orden de Santiago, Governador y Capitan General de este Reino y Provinzias dela Nueva Mexico y Castellano de Sus Fuerzas y Presidios por Su Magestad, ut supra. La presento el Cavildo, Justizia y Regimento desta Villa de Santa Fee, cavesera deste Reyno y Provinzias dela Nueba Mexico con los ynstrumentos y ordenes que en ella refieren y reproduzen que fueron dadas por el Marques de la Naba de Brazinas mi antezessor que Santa Gloria gose y reserbada por Su Theniente General y Capitan Juan Paez Hurtado las quales mando se executen obserben, cumplan y guarden como en ellas se contienen por ser en bien y utilidad de los vezinos deste Reyno y su conservazion como dicho Illustrisimo Cavildo le refiere en el dicho su escripto: y para que tengan el efecto que se pretende y solizita, ordeno a los dichos forasteres que han entrado a este Reino con numero cresido de cavallada a haser sus ferias y cambalaches con los Yndios Apaches gentiles que acostumbran benir todos los años a los Pueblos de Thaos y Pecos se retiren a los Puestos de Bernalillo y La Cañada poblaziones de Españoles con dichas sus cavalladas prohiviendoles como les prohivo que no entren a los referidos Pueblos y fronteras por las malas y permiziossas consequenzias que de ello se siguen y ser como lo es en desfrutar los generos que dichos Apaches traen y que estos los peuden gosar la vezindad deste Reyno por rason de estar siempre promptos ya parejados los para todo quanto se ofrese en el Real Servizio de Su Magestad y no tener otro alivio sino es el que pueder adquirir con dichos Apaches en las ferias, tratos y comerzio que con ellos se tiene; y no les prohivo a los dichos faroneos el que puedan hazer y hagan sus tratos, ferias y contratos con los dichos vezinos deste Reyno pues esto solamente seles deve permitir y permito y no con los dichos Apaches como dicho es: pues si quesieren tenerlos se bengan a poblar y avezindar este Reyno y no de otra suerte y para la devida observanzia de lo referido y delo demas que en dichos ynstrumentos se expressa presentados con el escripto por dicho Illustrisimo Cavildo les ympongo la pena de perdimento de las dichas sus cavalladas y desde luego la aplico para gastos de guerra, Justizia y denunciador: y por lo que toca al punto que dicho Cavildo, Justizia y Regimento representa de que an entrado algunas personas a este Reyno con generos de ropa y mercanzias para benderlas a mas balor de lo que es visto y costumbre alterando y subiendo los prezios de cuya mala y ympostura se sigue la yncombenenzia a dicha vezindad y para el reparo que esta materia deve tener, mando a los dichos que hubieren traydo dichos generos y mercadurias no las bendan a mas prezio ni balor de el que se astilado: y para ello les ymponga la pena de perdimento de las dichas sus mercadurias y generos lo qual aplico en la misma forma que ba expresada: y los vezinos que las comprasen desterrados a una de las fronteras deste Reyno por el tiempo de un año: y si fueren soldados de este Real Presidio desterados por el tiempo de un año de la guardia de la cavallada: y para la devida execuzion y cumplimiento de todo lo referido y que esten enterados los dichos forasteros y demas personas que habla este orden y auto y son los que han traydo dichas mercanzias mando se publique en esta Villa con la solemnidad de los ynstrumentos militares en altos y yntelegibles vozes con asistenzia del dicho Illustrisimo Cavildo y con la de mi Secretario de Governazion y Guerra quien pondra la fee de su publicazion y fecha esta deligenzia se remita a los Alcaldes Mayores de las jurisdiziones de La Cañada y Bernalillo para que cada uno en la suya lo haga publicar poniendolo por deligenzia y conste de ella en todo tiempo en el archivo desta Governazion a donde debolvesen este orden y autos con los demas que ban adjuntos. Y asi mismo mando alos Alcaldes Mayores de Thaos y Pecos no consientan en dichas sus jurisdiziones a los dichos forasteros y en casso de que en ellos ayga alguna ynobedenzia yendo yncontra viniendo en alguna manera que sea con confusas y metafisicar rasones y pretenden confundir con ellas lo que por este auto por mi ordenado y mandado seles haga la caussa o caussas sigiendola hasta estar en estado de sentenzia y estandolo me haran remision de ellas para darsela segun la ley del derecho: no disimulando por ningunos respectos cossa alguna yebando asi a executar todo lo referido: y al lo contrario sele hara el justo cargo castigandolos con todo rigor de derecho: y declarandolos por malos miembros de Su Magestad y para que esten entendidos los suso dichos se les hara notorio y yntimara mi Secretario de Governazion y Guerra a cada uno de por si y en sus personas: poniendolo por diligenzia y para que conste asi a los unos como a los otros, asi lo probey, mande y firme con mi Secretario de Governazion y Guerra, ut supra.

      Francisco Cuervo y Valdés (rubric)
      Ante mi
      Alphonso Rael de Aguilar (rubric)
      Secretario de Governazion y Guerra

Publicazion
En la Villa de Santa Fee en ocho dias del mes de Junio de mill setezientos y cinco años yo el Capitan Alphonso Rael de Aguilar Secretario de Governazion y Guerra en cumplimento y obedezimento delo que dicho Señor ordena y manda en el auto de esta otra parte, el qual se publico en altas y yntelijibles vozes por Sevastian Rodriquez, tambor, hallandose mucho concursio de gente en la plaza desta Villa y con asistencia del Illustrisimo Cavildo, Justizia y Regimento y para que conste lo puse por diligenzia de que doy fee y lo firme.

      Alphonso Rael de Aguilar (rubric)
      Secretario de Governazion y Guerra

Notificazion
Luego yncontinenti en dicho dia, mes y año yo el presente Secretario de Governazion y Guerra y en execuzion delo mandado por dicho Señor Governador y Capitan General por el auto dela buelta el qual ley y notifique al General Juan de Uribarri en su presencia, Alcalde Mayor y Capitan Aguerra del Pueblo de Pecos y su jurisdizion y haviendolo oydo dijo que lo obedezia y obedeze y executara prompto y devidamente el que se le ordena y lo firmo ante mi de que doi fee, ut supra.

Juan de Uribarri (rubric)
Alphonso Rael de Aguilar (rubric)
Secretario de Governazion y Guerra

Notificazion
Luego yncontinenti en dicho día, mes y año yo el presente Secretario de Governazion y Guerra en virtud y en execuzion delo mandado por el auto dela buelta el qual ley y notifique al Capitan don Feliz Martinez Alcalde Mayor dela jurisdizion de Thaos y Picuris en su persona y haviendolo oydo dijo que lo obedezia y obedecio y executara prompto y devidamente el que se le ordena y lo firmo ante mi que doy fee, ut supra.
Phelix Martinez (rubric)

SANM II #118

1705

El General don Francisco Cuervo y Valdes, Caballero del Orden de Santiago, Juez Oficial y Tessorero Factor de la Real Hacienda Caxa de la Cuidad de Guadalajara en el Reyno de la Galizia, Governador y Capital General deste Reyno de la Nueva Mexico y Sus Provinzias, Castellano de Sus Fuerzas y Presidios por Su Magestad, ut supra.

Por quanto a mi notizia a llegado los gravisimos y yncombenientes danos menoscullos y extorciones que se siguen asen y executan en los Pueblos de Pecos, Thaos y Picuris y demas destas fronteras y antemurales con la assistencia y morada que hasen en dichos Pueblos los vezinosdeste Reyno y los que de fuera del entran a comerciar con los Indios ynfieles amigos, como an acostumbrado en los Rescates que se celebran cada un año y por particulares que las que he tenido, delos Governadores de los dichos Pueblos y de los demas Yndios sus havitadores ynclinaziones y relazion que me han hecho sus Alcaldes Mayores y otros motivos, razones y causas que estoy experimentando, todo hecho en deservicio de Vuestra Magestad, grave perjuicios que resiven los dichos Yndios de los referidos Pueblos aquienes debo atender según la obligazion de mi empleo, en Virtud de lo qual mando expresamente por este mi orden que ningun vezino de las referidas de qualesquiera estado, calidad o condizion que sean, se atreva a pasar a los dichos Pueblos a efecto ninguno ni con pretexto balido ni ynbalido, sin expresa licenzia mia, pena de la vida, y traidor a el Rey con perdimiento de bienes que confiscados los aplico desde hora para siempre por mitad Camara de Su Magestad y gastos de quien yso la misma pena comprehendo a los que al presente se hallara en dichos Pueblos quienes luego an de salir de ellos; retirando las cavalladas que tubieren, por ser conforme a Leyes Reales de nuebas conquistas y poblaciones; autos que sean seguido en virtud de pedimento y reproduccion del Cabildo, Justizia y Reximiento desta Villa de Santa Fe, cavesera deste Reyno y Provinzia de la Nueba

Mexico, y oido lo probeydo por los ilioness mis antessesores, decretos y vando que de mi orden se a promulgado y para que tenga ili cumplimiento este dicho orden mando a los dichos Alcaldes Mayores de las referidos Pueblos de Pecos y Thaos lo publiquen, yntimen y hagan notorio haziendole guarden y cumplir y ynbiolablemente, pena de doscientos pesos que aplico en la misma forma y de los intereses y belaciones de los Yndios naturales de los dichos Pueblos, dejando copia en las Casas Reales de ellos desde dicho orden que an de devolver con las diligencias que en su execusion obraren; y es fecho en esta dicha Villa de Santa Fee en veinte y cinco dias del mes de Agosto de mill setecientos y cinco años y lo firme con el Secretario de Governazion y Guerra, ut supra.

Francisco Cuervo y Valdes (rubric)
Por mando del Señor Governador y Capitan General
Alphonso Rael de Aguilar (rubric)
Secretario de Governazion y Guerra

En este Pueblo de Nuestra Señora de los Angeles de Porsiuncula en veynte y demá dem del mes de Agosto de mil sietecientos y sinco años yo el General Joan Uribarri en cumplimiento y obedecimiento de lo ordenado por el Señor General don Francisco Cuerbo y Valdes, Caballero del Orden de Santiago, Gobernador y Capitan General deste Reyno dela Nueba Mexico abiendo llegado a el como su Alcalde Mayor y Capitan General hize notorio su contexto y lo notifique en las personas de Joan Francisco y Salvador Montoya vecinos de dicho Reyno quienes abiendolo oydo y entendido obedecieron y a las veynte y quatro horas que llego su caballada se salieron y retiraron del demáso su caballada y abiendo sacado testimonio ala letra de dicho auto y en donde lo dexo en estas Casas Reales a su Gobernador don Felipe y hago demáso de este dicho auto a dicho Governador y Capitan General demás ose presentedemás de los dichos el Cavo de Esquadra Bartolome Sanchez que lo firmo juntamente con migo como testigo de asistencia en dicho dia, ut supra.

Juan de Urribari (rubric)
Testigo de Asistencia
Bartholome Sanchez (rubric)

Notes

1. Juan Páez Hurtado was born in Seville, Spain, in 1663. He was in El Paso as an *alférez* in 1692 and was *justicia mayor* in El Paso in 1693. In 1695 he led a group of settlers to New Mexico. After the death of Vargas in 1704, he was acting governor until 1705, also serving in the same post in 1718 and 1724, and was lieutenant governor in 1731–1736. In 1739 he was alcalde mayor of Santa Fe. He died in 1742 (Kessell and Hendricks, *BFA*: 300-301 n3).
2. Vargas died on April 8, 1704 (Kessell et al., *ASA*: 262).
3. This first bando was written in November of 1703 as shown in the translation in Kessell and Hendricks (*ASA*: 206-7). The 1703 bando apparently overrode the earlier permission given by Governor Cubero and the

cabildo allowing buffalo robes, buckskins, and piñon nuts to be sent to Sonora and Vizcaya for exchange for sheep, horses, and mules.
4. As stated in the introduction, the trade fairs were often called *rescates*, or ransom fairs, because, at least initially, much of the trading had to do with the ransoming of captives taken by the Indians. The practice of ransoming captives had been established prior to European contact but was continued in an increased form after European contact.
5. In an undocumented case, Fernando Ocaranza states that during the governorship of Antonio Valverde (1719–1720), some settlers traded with the Indians outside an officially opened trade fair, storing the hides and skins in their houses. Upon learning of this, Cristóbal Torres confiscated the goods under the direction of General Juan Páez Hurtado (Ocaranza, *Establecimientos*: 186-90).
6. According to Charles Cutter, the *alcaldías* were geographic administrative units presided over by the alcaldes mayores. New Mexico generally had eight alcaldías, which he suggests existed from the seventeenth century and were probably based on geography and numbers of people. In most cases the alcaldía was supposed to be reached with a day's journey by the alcalde, who was required to live outside it (Cutter, *Legal Culture*: 83). The boundaries of the alcaldías in 1779 are shown on the Miera y Pacheco map (Map 2, Appendix).
7. Santa Cruz was founded by Vargas as a villa but was decimated by the revolt of 1696. Governor Cuervo y Valdez claimed to have resettled the villa in 1706. Its formal name was La Villa Nueva de Santa Cruz de la Cañada (Simmons, *Albuquerque*: 45; Twitchell, *Spanish Archives*, 2: 122; AGN, *Reales Cédulas*, L35, E25, f1 2).
8. *Pieza* has multiple meanings. Here the first use of the word has to do with the Apache captives, while the second relates to the number of goods, in this case, eighteen hides. It can also mean a monetary value, as in *piezas de oro*, or gold coins. Indian captives are discussed further in the introduction.
9. According to Fray Angélico Chávez, Sebastián Rodríguez was in New Spain in 1689, when he petitioned for a marriage contract. In another document from 1692, he stated that he was fifty years old and been official drummer of the garrison at El Paso for seven years. By 1697, in a third document, he stated that he was a drummer of the Santa Fe garrison and had been born in San Pablo de Luanda in Portuguese Guinea on the African west coast. The last mention of him was in 1706. By 1716 the drummer for the Santa Fe presidio was Esteban Rodríguez, probably his son, who is mentioned in another document below (Chávez, "Drummer": 131-38; Doc. 46). While Rodríguez was one of the few Negros named, blacks were certainly not unknown in New Mexico in the early eighteenth century. A partly preserved mandate by Governor Cuervo y Valdez from1706 states that "all those residents of this said kingdom of any quality [class] that are found having in their service any Indians of the nation, mulattos or blacks, shall send them to the parochial church at this said villa [Santa Fe] at the hours that are designated by the Reverend Father Guardian so that he can teach them the Christian doctrine" (SANM II #121, editor's translation).
10. This is probably the petition from the cabildo in Kessell et al. (*ASA*: 206). That petition is dated November 26, 1703.
11. This is a reference to the illness, probably dysentery, from which many settlers died, including Governor Vargas (see Doc. 1).
12. Note that in this document, the governor is careful to attend to a certain protocol regarding the cabildo, following their lead in certain matters and showing his cooperation. This pattern changed with later governors, particularly with Governor Bustamante in the 1720s.
13. This notification language identifies the three most important trade centers of the time: Pecos, Taos, and Picuris.
14. Felix Martínez [Torrelaguna] was born in Galicia, Spain, and was recruited by Vargas, becoming his *ayudante*, or aide-de camp, in 1694. Martínez was commander of the El Paso presidio in 1695 and captain of the Santa Fe presidio in 1704, being appointed captain-for-life by Viceroy Linares in 1711. He was interim governor by 1715. He was involved in controversies involving complaints by presidio soldiers and with his successor, Governor Marqués de la Peñuela. The investigations by the viceroy lasted until the mid-1720s (Chávez, *Origins*: 226; Warner, "Felix Martínez": 31, 45, 56, 61, 90-91).
15. This third bando was mandated by Governor Cuervo on August 25, 1705, almost three months after the second bando, translated above. In this one, Cuervo, sounding annoyed, ordered that no settler whether from inside or outside the province should dare go to the Indian pueblos of Pecos, Taos, or Picuris for any reason without a license from him, and if they did their goods would be confiscated. There was a slight shift apparent here, in that he seems to be allowing outsiders to trade, but only if they have a license from the governor. As can be seen in other documents, the next step in the attempt to keep Indian trading under control was to mandate that licensed trade fairs be the only places that trade with the Indians could take place. Mandates regarding trade fairs and trade goods continued throughout the century (see SANM II #115, #320, and #403; and Docs. 40 and 43).
16. The patroness of Pecos was Our Lady of the Angels of Porciúncula, the name sometimes given to the pueblo (Kessell et al., *BOB*: 400).

3

GOVERNOR PEÑUELA TO THE VICEROY: PRESIDIO SOLDIERS HAVE RETAKEN STOLEN LIVESTOCK NEAR ALBUQUERQUE, MORE GUNS AND HORSES REQUESTED
May 31, 1708. Source: AGN PI L36 E2, 179-80.

Synopsis and editor's notes: After 100 head of cattle had been stolen by the Apaches, Governor Peñuela ordered pursuit of the Indians by Captain Felix Martínez. Martínez took thirty soldiers from the Santa Fe presidio and Albuquerque garrison, sixty Indian auxiliaries, and some settlers from the Albuquerque militia, and pursued and killed a number of Indians, returning with much of the stolen livestock. In this document, Governor Peñuela writes to the viceroy about the victory, though he does not mention Martínez. The marginal notations were provided by the viceroy's fiscal officer (Warner, "Felix Martinez": 37-38).

José Chacón, Marqués de la Peñuela, was a member of Andalusian nobility and a member of the Order of Santiago. As such he was the only hereditary marqués to serve as governor of New Mexico, since Vargas was not granted his title until after his first term as the governor. The last sentence of the document, convoluted but gracefully flattering, reflects Peñuela's courtly upbringing (Flagler, "Defensive Policy": 455).

[Marginal note]
To the fiscal officer
with the following information.
(rubric of fiscal officer without name)
That cattle that were stolen by the
enemy from the residents of Albuquerque
along with the equipment from the presidial soldiers.
Expenses for war and peace are requested.

[Marginal note]
Responded to on this 8th day.
México, June 18, 1708.
(rubric of fiscal officer without name)

Your most excellent sir

Sir: Having received written notice dated January the 12th from the alcalde mayor of the Villa of Albuquerque in which he informed me that the Apaches from a distant nation had taken all the cattle belonging to those residents, we left at once with the entire company and their captain and at the distance of forty leagues from this jurisdiction. At the Sierra de Los Ladrones[1] we engaged them in battle, and fortunately retook from them all of the animals with the exception of seven cattle which they had killed with their arrows. Upon fleeing, they took with them some of the horses that they had stolen, but we were not able to follow them because of the heavy snow that had fallen. Such a pleasant surprise could not have occurred except that during the month of December there was received by this company some four hundred horses and one hundred mules[2] with which it [the presidio] was equipped, as well as the fact that everyone was able to keep their livelihoods.

This humble submission is due to the complete confidence that I owe to your excellency for providing us with that which is left over in other places such as the Real de Minas de San Joseph de Parral[3] from benefits provided for war and peace. This government should be provided with that which is needed in order to keep the Indians friendly, which is a necessity in this province keeping the unfruitfulness from the described understanding of your excellency, weighing my shortcomings before God, and that in this employment, there is no satisfaction that can be considered for those inevitable expenses whom everyone seeks without being able to obtain any recourse other than from your excellency, whom most excellent person Our Lord should keep for many years, which is something I wish for, and which should hopefully be granted. Villa of Santa Fe, April 4, 1708.

Your most excellent sir
I kiss the hand of your excellency
Your most humble servant
Marqués de la Peñuela [1707–1712] (rubric)
[To the]
Most Excellent Duke of Albuquerque

ORIGINAL DOCUMENT

Mexico y Mayo 31 de 1708

                    Excellentisimo Señor

Al fiscal con
los antecedentes (rubric)
Que quitaron los
enemigos los reses que
les habian robado a los de
Alburquerque y que
equipo a los presidiales.
Pide gastos de pas y guerra.

Respondido oy dia de
la fecha. Mexico y
Junio 18 de 1708 Años.
(rubric)

                    Señor

Haviendo tenido papel de dose de Henero del Alcalde Mayor de la Villa de Alburquerque en que me participa que los Apaches desta dilatisima nacion se avian llevado todo el ganado mayor de la vecindad con este aviso hise salir toda la compania con su Capitan y a quarenta leguas de distancia de dicha xurisdizion en la Sierra de Los Ladrones tubieron estos armas, la felizidad de haver restaurado todo el ganado menos siete reses que avian flechado dejando tambien alguna cavallada que avian urtado se pusieron dichos enemigos en huyda, no los siguieron por la mucha nieve que les cayo (Cuyo buen supresso no se ubiera podido lograr si no me ubieran entrado por el mes de Diziembre quatrocientos cavallos y cien bestias mulares con las que le e equipado esta Compañía de suerte que pueden servir todos su emplazas.) Que este mi rendimiento con toda confianza de que le de dever a Vuestra Excellencia que de lo que sobra en otros parages como en el Real de Minas de San Joseph de Parral de lo que tiene asignado para paz y guerra. Se de a este govierno lo que fuere servido pues para tener a los Yndios amigos se nesesita desta Providencia tener por ociosso en la discrepta comprehension de Vuestra Excellensia el ponderarle mi cortedad de mi

Dios y que en este empleo no ai ningunos cumplimentos para costear estos gastos tan ynescusables pues todos piden sin tener yo otro recurso que el de Vuestra Excellensia cuya excellentisima persona guarde Nuestro Señor en su mayor grandesa los anos que deseo y e menester. Villa de Santa Fee y Abril 4 de 1708 anos.

Excellentisimo Señor
Beso la mano de Vuestra Excellensia
Su mas Rendido
El Marques de la Penuela (rubric)

[To]
Excellentisimo Señor Duque de Alburquerque

Translated by J. Richard Salazar, Linda Tigges, and Rob Martinez

Notes

1. La Sierra de los Ladrones, literally, mountain of thieves, was named because it was believed to have been a refuge of alleged Navajo and Apache horse thieves. It is located south of Las Nutrias and Sevilleta and northwest of Socorro (Kessell and Hendricks, *BFA*: 625 n31).
2. Military regulations required each soldier to have a certain number of horses, ranging from five to twelve, with some mules for support. Mules cost much more than horses, so that if each of the 100 presidio soldiers had had one mule, they were well equipped indeed. In regard to the price of horses and mules, in 1701, when Vargas was accused of padding the prices of presidio goods, the complaint states his price was 20 pesos for a horse, 25 pesos for a packhorse, and 40 pesos for a mule; that is, one mule was worth two horses. While the price of the animals was considered too high by the settlers, the cost differential between horses and mules was not disputed (Tigges, "Pastures": 241-44; Kessell et al., *ASA*: 38-39).
3. By this time, the mines at Parral had been in decline for many years. It may be that this resulted in a surplus of military goods and supplies available for use elsewhere.

4

GAMBLING IN SANTA CRUZ ENDS WITH SETTLER PLEDGING SADDLE FOR DEBT
November 25, 1711 to October 19, 1712. Source: SANM II #168.

Synopsis and editor's notes: Here we see several men gathered at the house of Francisco Rivera: Baltazar Trujillo, Miguel Tenorio de Alba, and Juan Archibeque. Juan de Mestas may also have been there, or least some of his tobacco was. Francisco Rivera and Baltazar Trujillo gambled for some skins; Rivera lost, and unable to pay, left his saddle as a pledge. Sometime later, Rivera, having paid his debt, went to retrieve his saddle, but finding that it had been damaged, demanded payment for it. Trujillo refused to pay, so Rivera took his complaint to the alcalde, Roque Madrid. While he was at it, Rivera made a second complaint about not getting paid four pesos for some work he had done for a certain Juan Trujillo, who appears to have been Baltazar's father. The cases went from the alcalde to the lieutenant governor, Juan Páez Hurtado, and then to the governor, the Marqués de Peñuela. But the governor required additional information, and the case was returned to Páez Hurtado, who asked to hear more testimony from Rivera and Trujillo. At that time, Hurtado ordered Juan Trujillo to pay the four pesos to Rivera and asked for testimony from Miguel Tenorio de Alba. When the case returned to the governor, Rivera urged the governor to act, saying that he wished to leave the kingdom with anyone who was going. There was no final determination by the governor, probably because the two parties arrived at some agreement and Rivera withdrew his complaint and left the province, or else that portion of the document is lost.

Gambling was a continuing problem in New Mexico and New Spain, as evidenced by the number of orders prohibiting it. The *Recopilación de leyes de los reynos de las Indias* (Law of the Indies) provided that gambling with dice and cards for more than ten pesos *de oro* (of gold) a day was prohibited, as were other games of chance involving the same amount. In 1702 Vargas ordered that soldiers caught gambling would lose their active duty post and retirement privileges. Citizens caught gambling would spend one month in jail and one month working on the church, and debts incurred from gambling would be cancelled. In 1707 Governor Peñuela mandated a similar prohibition. In 1729 Brigadier Rivera included a provision in the recently adopted military regulations that stated: "Because the losses the soldiers incur in gambling ruin them in such a way that they cannot carry out their duties, the captains and commanders of the presidios will not tolerate or permit solders to gamble at games of chance with anything they have, including horses and family jewels." Subsequent governors and officials followed suit in 1737, 1741, 1746, 1749, 1768, and 1778. In 1732 Governor Cruzat y Góngora also prohibited gambling in the pueblos. Notes of colonial burials prepared by Fray Angélico Chávez show that gambling and violence could sometimes be combined, stating that in 1798, a New Mexican called El Torero or El Toreador was killed by an accidental gun blast while playing a game called *el torderito* (Chávez, *Archives*: 235; Kessell et al., *TDC*: 194 n202; Kessell et al., *ASA*: 201-2; Naylor and Polzer, *Pedro de Rivera*: 59; SANM II #91, #134, #366, #438, #504, #602, and #913).

Though Rivera and Trujillo were surely aware that gambling was illegal, Rivera still went to the alcalde and governor asking for payment for his ruined saddle. In doing so, Rivera, in particular, seems to talk around the gambling, generally referring to it as *rifara*, which literally means raffle, and Trujillo calls it entertainment. As the biographical footnotes suggest, the men meeting at Rivera's house were all adults and were among the respected members of the community.

Jesus, Mary, and Joseph, Villa of Santa Fe
Year of 1711–12

Demand by Francisco de Rivera,[1] resident of Villa Nueva de Santa Cruz, against Baltazar Trujillo[2] for having pledged an item to him for a debt which was returned abused.

Alcalde mayor and war captain

Francisco de Rivera, resident of the new villa de Santa Cruz, appears before your honor in his most proper form, which he has according to his right, and says: It has been a little more than three years since I made a bet during an *apuesta de juego* [betting game] with Baltazar Trujillo, also a resident of this jurisdiction, and for the amount that I lost and was owing to him, I pledged to him a good riding saddle.[3] But because he did not want anything else, he insisted that I pay him with hides. But he has hung onto the saddle until now, apparently satisfied to hold onto it for what I owe to him. Not being content with what I gave him to hold, because he was not assured of the money with the said item, his household members have been using the saddle to the point where it has been abused and torn, and a stirrup has been broken. He has given it back to me in this condition knowing full well that the laws do not allow him to do this, as they state that items that are pawned are not to be used without the authority of the owner or of the royal justice, which was never allowed. He should have been satisfied with holding it; using it thus makes a double payment, being that it has been devalued by its use.

For all of this, I argue in my favor and ask and petition your majesty that he attend to my petition and order that my item be returned to me as I gave it to him and not in the manner which it is in. Also, I should receive four pesos which Juan Trujillo[4] has owed me for over two years for personal work which I performed for him, for which I ask for mercy to receive in my best and proper form according to my petition which is not done in malice but according to what is necessary, etc.

Francisco de Rivera (rubric)

Early New Mexico wooden stirrups with bindings. Photo by Wyatt Davis. Image courtesy of the Palace of the Governors, Photo Archives, Santa Fe, Neg. No. 55882.

Presentation

At the villa de Santa Cruz, on the 25th of November, 1711, the above was presented to me and upon my review took it as was presented according to his right and order that Baltazar Trujillo and Juan Trujillo respond to it according to the law. And so that it is valid, I approved, ordered, and signed it as presiding judge with my assisting witnesses, etc.

Roque Madrid (rubric)

assisting witnesses
Juan de Atienza (rubric)
Miguel de Quintana (rubric)

Alcalde mayor and war captain

[I] Baltazar Trujillo, resident of this jurisdiction from the puesto of Pojoaque, appear before your honor in the best and proper form to which I am entitled and am allowed and say, sir, that it has been more than four years when I was traveling, I do not remember where, that I arrived at the house of Francisco de Rivera, who appears before your honor demanding a saddle which he left as a pledged item for six hides. At this time, I was persuaded and asked a number of times by several individuals to play *rifara*[5] for a bundle of tobacco[6] which I had, and on which I did play. The said Francisco de Rivera, having been overwhelmed by what he had lost for the tobacco in playing rifara, and not being able to pay what he had lost, persuaded me to play with him for two hides. I did not want to do it, but upon his insistence, I committed myself and told him to continue playing for hides, in which case, if I would lose, I would put up as many as forty hides, which if I lost I would deliver to him. Upon winning the six [hides] which he had put up, I told him to pay up or continue playing. At which time he brought up the rifara for the tobacco and continued playing for additional hides, which he lost and which he could not pay. Thus he had to give up the riding saddle which is mentioned, but which was not as new as he says it was, and which I did not want to accept, but which he left as a pledged item, and then he left from here and went on his way.

All of this [complaint] I take as a malicious act, being that so much time has elapsed and his insistence that the saddle was new. During this time, I had left it where he had left it and had even forgotten about it to the point where it could have gotten rotten. He also says that he had satisfied his debt by giving me on my account one-half of a fanega of wheat and four small hides, which should have been full hides and not the equivalent of twelve pesos, which is what the six [hides] amount to, but which I in all honesty was forced to take. In reality, if I had used it [saddle] I would have noticed that the stirrup were broken. It is also true that it has been over a year that the item was pledged, and as such I am not obligated to pay any expenses.

In all of this, as in anything, your honor should determine that which is done in justice, for whom I ask and petition that your honor approve this, and I swear in proper form that this petition is not done in malice but according to what is necessary, etc.

Baltazar Trujillo (rubric)

Presentation

At the villa of Santa Cruz on the 27th of November, 1711, before me, the *maestre de campo* [field commander], Roque Madrid,[7] alcalde mayor and war captain of the said villa and its jurisdiction, the above was presented by the stated and upon being reviewed by me took it as was presented and order that Francisco de Rivera respond to it within the time allowed by the law. So that it is valid, I signed it on the said day, month, and year acting as presiding judge, along with my assisting witnesses, etc.

Roque Madrid (rubric)

assisting witnesses:
Juan de Atienza (rubric)
Miguel de Quintana (rubric)

Alcalde mayor and war captain

[I] Francisco de Rivera, resident of this jurisdiction, appear according to my royal right, which is allowed to me and respond to that stated by Baltazar Trujillo which is lacking the truth, being that he has never played at rifara for any tobacco with me, and it was only on one certain occasion that I was dealing with a bunch of tobacco, which was with Juan de Mestas.[8] However, before the rifara was opened, I paid him [Mestas] for the tobacco. As for this crime of not paying expenses, I did not have to pay anything other than having to resist what he says in his statement, being that it is not given that I persuaded him to gamble because I could not pay for the tobacco, as he argues, and which has to be proven being that he is a minor and as such is not capable of having done it.[9] He [Trujillo] says to others that it was because of the game in which he could put up as many as forty hides and which he considered to be entertainment. Because of the [value of the] items and being that I had lost so much, I gave him my saddle, with the understanding and knowledge that he was not to use it. I can prove what I have stated by the Captain Miguel Tenorio de Alba,[10] being that he [Tenorio de Alba] was present and knew that I would give him [Trujillo] the satisfaction for the said [debt], as was stated, choosing from the excess that he would give from that which was the bet, given the proof of my good faith and the understanding I have regarding the matter. Having full knowledge of how this issue is, I could in no way receive a sentence from any royal justice, nor how it could be that he would pay me for the hides, when he has negated to pay me the six pesos[11] for the others for which I gambled, being that the item [the saddle] which during the interim had been turned over to him, of which Captain Miguel Tenorio de Alba has physical knowledge. He [Romero] cannot account for what he says about the saddle, saying that it was not as I say it was, when it is true that he can be accused for what happened to it, that a stirrup was broken, or how it could possibly have gotten rotten, as it was stuck in a corner. I can prove his malicious intent when he says that the [small] hides were not equivalent to what I owed him. I say that he does not agree with this, and I say that it more than satisfies it, being that he still owes me the said six pesos, as I gave him a note when I sent them [the items] to him, saying that if he was not content with them, I would make them good in some other way. As he did not do this, it meant that he was satisfied. For this proof, I ask that he produce it [the note], but he thinks he is so smart regarding the last issue, that he says that because it has been over a year since the item was pawned, he is not obligated to pay any remainder, which he does, being that the circumstances are as I have said, and that if he should not be satisfied with such, he should cite to me the book, chapter, and page where this law is found.

For all of this, I ask and petition that our honor be pleased to attend to my matter as well as to order that Juan pay me the four pesos, which he admits that he owes to me for my personal work,[12] which included [the production of] four *varas*[13] of *sallal* [sackcloth] for which he now says that he will give me a fanega of corn, which does not pay for the amount that is owed to me for my work, and could not possibly be enough for anyone to do it and cannot be provided [elsewhere] because it [cloth] cannot be found in the kingdom at the present time. All this being left for the sake of justice, he says that I should go see the presiding judge, who could say that it could be done for a lesser price. I swear in my proper right that this, my petition, is not done in malice, and I seek royal aid for what is necessary, etc.

Francisco de Rivera (rubric)

Presentation

On the 5th of December, 1711, at this villa of Santa Cruz, before me, the maestre de campo, Roque Madrid, alcalde mayor and war captain of this said villa, the above stated presented it to me and upon my review ordered that Baltazar Trujillo respond to it within the term of the law. So that it is valid, I signed it as presiding judge, along with my assisting witnesses on the said day, month, and year, etc.

Roque Madrid (rubric)

assisting witnesses:
Juan de Atienza (rubric)
Miguel de Quintana (rubric)

Alcalde mayor and war captain

[I] Baltazar Trujillo, resident of this jurisdiction, appear before your honor in my best form according to the right which I have and say, sir, in response to the points which are argued by Francisco de Rivera in which he states that I am wrong, I say to this that I am right, and if he did not understand it, that is something else. What I say is that when I played rifara for a bundle of tobacco, those who were included in this rifara game were myself, Captain Miguel Tenorio de Alba, and Juan de Archibeque.[14] This was played by all four of us, I or one of the others actually starting it. As to what he says that I am of a minor age, I can recognize malicious intent, as he stated at the time of the said rifara, in order to persuade me to partake, [which] was because he had the intention of taking it [the tobacco] without it costing him anything. From that time on, he had no intention of paying a thing. All of this is proof of my truthfulness.

As for that which he states that he left me the saddle under the conditions which he refers to, the proof shall be found by what he says that he would give me an ox and I would pay him the difference. I was in no need of an ox, and in no way was the deal made. As to what he says that, according to his knowledge a royal justice could not sentence him for anything, I say that he thus recognizes his malicious intent and therefore he left me the saddle with a bad intention. As for the six pesos which he demands, he needs to come up with the proof regarding the charges. In regard to the four hides which I took, I did it to get out from under the length of time that it had taken him to pay them. As to the point where he tells me to show him the chapter and pages where the law states that in the passing of time nothing is to be paid [for expenses], I say that the law states what it is found to state and has been found, and that if there is nothing in the law, then one will only know what it will be according to their own needs [or situation], and more so for material goods.

As corrupt as he is, I find him at fault for everything that he did at the time that he pledged what he did. I ask and petition your majesty that you be served to prove through justice what you will, and I am prepared to obey everything that is reasonable as to what I believe, and if maliciousness is found on my part I am prepared to be sentenced. I swear to God and to the sign of the Holy Cross and to my proper right that this, my written document, is not done in malice but according to what is necessary, etc.

      Baltazar Trujillo (rubric)

Act of Submission

  At the villa of Santa Cruz on the 9th of December, 1711, before me, the maestre de campo, Roque Madrid, alcalde mayor of the said villa and of its jurisdiction, presented that which is herein contained and by me reviewed and took it as was presented and attending to the allegations of both parties I submit these proceedings to the lord Marqués, or governor and captain general of this kingdom, so that upon his review he will approve and order what he thinks is right. So that it is valid, I signed it as presiding judge, along with my assisting witnesses on this said day, etc.

      Roque Madrid (rubric)

assisting witnesses:
Juan de Atienza (rubric)
Miguel de Quintana (rubric)

Decree

  At the villa of Santa Fe, headquarters of this kingdom and provinces of New Mexico, on the 23rd of August, 1712, I, Admiral don Joseph Chacon Medina Salazar y Villaseñor, caballero of the order of Santiago, Marquez de la Peñuela, the governor and captain general of this said kingdom and castellan of his forces for his majesty, having received these proceedings from the maestre de campo, Roque Madrid, alcalde mayor and war captain of the new villa de Santa Cruz and its jurisdiction of La Cañada, for their satisfaction, I order my lieutenant general, don Juan Páez Hurtado, to continue with them, finish them and conclude a sentence according to what he finds according to his judgment, and whom I expect to comply with to the end, as he always has, with his obligation, safeguarding justice according to what he finds, sealing justice, and concluding everything according to their rights, and so that it is valid I approved, ordered, and signed it with my secretary of government and war.

      Márquez de la Peñuela (rubric)
      before me
      Cristóbal de Góngora (rubric)
      Secretary of government and war

At the villa of Santa Fe on the 25th of August, 1712, I, General Juan Páez Hurtado, lieutenant governor and captain general of this kingdom, in compliance with the above proceedings, upon having seen the allegations of the parties, and having failed to see the statement of Captain Miguel Tenorio, I ordered the maestre de campo, Roque Madrid, alcalde mayor of the Villa Nueva de Santa Cruz, to receive it and once it is received, to return the proceedings so that I can review them. As for the four pesos that Juan Trujillo owes to the said Francisco de Rivera, I order him to pay them, as it was owed to him for personal work which was to his satisfaction. Also, the alcalde mayor is first of all to put aside the expenses for this entire procedure. So that all of the above is valid, I signed it along with the secretary of government and war on the said day.

Juan Páez Hurtado (rubric)
before me
Cristóbal de Góngora (rubric)
Secretary of government and war

Proceedings

At the Villa Nueva de Santa Cruz on the 1st of September, 1712, I, the *maestre de campo*, Roque Madrid, having received the proceedings given to me by the lieutenant general don Juan Páez Hurtado, who ordered me to take the statement of Captain Juan [Miguel] Tenorio de Alba, who is cited in them and which will conclude these proceedings, placing them in a state of sentencing. By virtue of this, I, the said war captain, made him appear before me to receive his sworn statement which he made to God, Our Lord, and a sign of the Cross under which he promised to tell the truth as to what he knew about the case.

He was asked if he knew about the claims which were brought by one against the other. He said that it was true that he was present at the time that the matter of the disagreement over the six hides was brought up by Baltazar Trujillo, and it occurred in the following manner. It happened that Juan de Mestas proposed to gamble for a bundle of tobacco. Among those who were involved was Francisco de Rivera, who, before the gambling took place, purchased the tobacco from Juan de Mestas for one hide, and he [Mestas] took it and was totally satisfied. After this took place, he [Rivera] continued to gamble with the said Trujillo until he lost six hides, and after which he attempted to pay him off by letting him have two cows. Seeing that he had lost the hides, and that Trujillo would not take the cows, he tried to persuade Trujillo, in various ways, to forget about the hides, which Trujillo would not do. He [Rivera] told Baltazar to go easy on him, saying that he would sell an ox to your honor and would be given whatever was paid along with a plowshare in order to satisfy [Trujillo]. However, Trujillo could not be convinced, and as a last resort [Rivera] left him the saddle as a pledged item until he had satisfied the [debt of] six hides. The forty [hides] which he [Trujillo said he could] put up for gambling, he [Tenorio de Alba] never saw. This he says is what he knows regarding the sworn statement which he has made and which he affirmed and ratified, having nothing else to say or delete and said that he was thirty-eight years of age, more or less. So that it is valid, he signed it with me and my assisting witnesses on the said day.

Roque Madrid (rubric)
Miguel Tenorio de Alba (rubric)

assisting witnesses:
Bartolomé Lovato (rubric)
Juan de Atienza (rubric)

Act of Submission

At the Villa Nueva de Santa Cruz on the 1st of September, 1712, I, the maestre de campo, Roque Madrid, alcalde mayor and war Captain of the said villa and of its jurisdiction, having received the statement of Captain Miguel Tenorio de Alba, cited by the parties, submit these proceedings to the lieutenant general, who is aware of them, so that upon his review he will determine what to do. So that it is valid, I signed it with my assisting witnesses on the said day.

Roque Madrid (rubric)
Miguel Tenorio de Alba (rubric)

assisting witnesses:
Bartolomé Lovato (rubric)
Juan de Atienza (rubric)

Presented on the 19th of October of 1712, Villa of Santa Fe, before the governor and captain general.

Governor and captain general

[I] Francisco de Rivera, resident of the Villa Nueva de Santa Cruz, appear before your honor according to what my royal right permits and say that according to what I have presented in writing to the general don Juan Páez Hurtado, petitioning him to act upon some proceedings that the admiral Marqués de la Peñuela was pleased to submit to him to act upon and who has verbally responded to me saying that the referred to proceedings are found in the possession of your honor. I say that, being about to leave to go outside the kingdom with anyone who is about to leave, petition and ask your honor, with all your kindness, to feel sorry for me in what I seek regarding this issue, which is to be done for the sake of justice, which is what I expect to acquire from your greatness, and I swear in my proper right that this my petition is not done in malice, but for what is necessary, etc.
Francisco de Rivera (rubric)

Having been reviewed by me, I took it as it was presented and ordered that Baltazar Trujillo appear before me to settle with this party within the period of two days and that this be taken care of according to this decree by Captain Jazinto Sánchez, alcalde mayor of Villa Nueva de Santa Cruz and its jurisdiction of La Cañada. I thus approved and rubricated it before the secretary of government and war on the 19th of October, 1712.

(the rubric of Juan Páez Hurtado)
Roque de Pinto (rubric)
Secretary of government and war

[Editor's note: The final determination of the case is not provided, perhaps because there was a compromise, because Rivera was planning to leave for the province, or else because it is missing from the document.]

ORIGINAL DOCUMENT

Jesus, Maria y Joseph, Villa de Santa Fee
Año de 1711

Demanda puesta por Francisco de Rivera vezino de la Villa Nueva de Santa Cruz a Baltazar Truxillo por averle empenado una prenda y bolversela maltratada.

Señor Alcalde Mayor y Capitan Aguerra

Francisco de Rivera vesino de la Villa Nueva de Santa Cruz ante Vuestra Señoria paresco en cuanto aya lugar en derecho y mi fabor combenga y digo que abia poco mas de tres años que cause doze pesos de apuesta de juego a Baltazar Truxillo asi mesmo vezino de esta jurisdission por cuia cantidad le di en prenda una silla gineta echiza buena y por que esto abia de ser en gamusas y no querer el contenido otra cosa ninguna me he detenido asta la presente que lo tengo satisfecho y no contento con tener asegurado el dinero con una prenda como la referida a estado la gente de su casa usando de ella de forma que la an maltratado y aun rompido y quebrado un estribo desta suerte mela enbiaba y reconosiendo que las lelles reconosen que so uso de las prendas aun que sea en materia lisita sin boluntad de su dueño o actoridad de la Real Justizia sino siendolo esta de bien aberme pagado de su mano con el usso de ella que

es doble paga por desmereser en su balor y despues apersibir la paga de su enpeno por todo lo cual y lo mas que alegar puedo ami fabor, a Vuestra Magestad pido y suplico se sirba en justizia de atender ami relazion mandando seme buelba mi prenda segun la entrege y de no balor de forma que you puedo sacar otra tal como tambien cuatro pesos que Juan Truxillo me debe ba para dos años de mi trabajo personal que en ello resebire merced seguro en toda forma de derecho esta mi petision no ser de malisia y en lo necesario, ut supra.
      Francisco de Rivera (rubric)

Presentazion
En la Villa de Santa Cruz en este y biente and sinco dias del mes de Nobiembre de mil setesientos y honse años la presento el contenido y por mi vista la ube por presentada en cuanto a lugar en derecho y mando a Baltazar Truxillo y a Juan Truxillo respondan en testimonio de la lei y para que conste, lo provei mande y firme como Juez receptor con los testigos de mi assistencia, ut supra.
      Roque Madrid (rubric)
testigo de assistencia testigo de asssistencia
Juan de Atienza (rubric) Miguel de Quintana (rubric)

    Señor Alcalde Mayor y Capitan Aguerra

Baltazar Truxillo vesino de esta jurisdiction en el Puesto de Pojoaque paresco ante Vuestra Señoria en la mas bastante forma que aia lugar en derecho y al mio combenga y digo Señor que abra tiempo de mas de cuatro años que llendo de camino no se para onde llego a mi casa Francisco de Rivera quien ante Vuestra Señoria me demanda una silla que me dejo por prenda de sies gamusas que causo el aberme persuadido munchas veses con las tantas partias a que rifara un manojo de tabaco el cual ube de rifar y abiendolo cargado dicho Francisco de Rivera se armo con lo que perdio en la dicha rifa del tabaco y despues o por no pagar dicha rifa me possio a que gugasemos que yo rompido poniendome delante como dose gamusas y yo a no querer jugar asta que fue tanta su partia que le dije que siguiria contra la gamusas poniendole yo para el dicho que yo cuarenta gamusas a que silas ganava selas llebara y abiendole yo ganado seis no quiso pasar adelante sino que parase el guego y me pagase las seis pues fue su prinsipio la rifa del tabaco que yo abia rifado a que se armo con dichas gamusas tanto que me ubo de largar una silla gineta como dise pero no tan Nueva sin querer yo admiterla mas a la dejo por prenda y se fue en lo que conosco obro con malisia pues alcabo de tanto tiempo me pide lo nuebo de la silla que aberla yo dexado donde la dexo no abiera momoria de tal silla por que se ubiere podrido y en lo que dise que me tiene satisfecho lo que es que dio por mi cuenta media fanega de trigo y cuatro gamusillas siendo que abian de ser gamusas y no equibale a dose pesos que montan las seis que es berdad que me servi de ellas en algunas ocasiones en berdad que si eso le ubiera echo y la ubiere allado que los estribos no estaban quebrados tambien es berdad como tambien el que en pasando de enpeno una prenda año y dias no esta obligado el que la tiene a pagar menos cabos y asi en esto como en todo lo demas determinara Vuestra Señnoria lo que fuere en justizia por todo lo cual a Vuestra Señoria pido y suplico se sirva de prober esta y juro en debida forma esta mi petision no ser de malisia y en lo nesesario, ut supra.

Baltazar Truxillo (rubric)

Presentazion

En la Villa de Santa Cruz en beinte y siete dias del mes de Nobiembre de mil setesientos y honse años ante mi el Maestre de Campo Roque Madrid Alcalde Maior y Capitan Aguerra de dicho Villa y su jurisdizion la presento el contenido y por mi vista la ube por presentada y mando a Francisco de Rivera responda en termino de la lei y para que conste la firme en dicho dia mes y año actuando como Jues Receptor con los testigos de mi asistensia, ut supra.

Roque Madrid (rubric)

testigo de asistenzia testigo de asistenzia
Juan de Atienza (rubric) Miguel de Quintana (rubric)

Señor Alcalde Mayor y Capitan Aguerra

Fransico de Rivera vesino de esta jurisdizion paresco en cuanto el Real derecho me remite y digo respondiendo ala de Baltazar Truxillo que dize mal y falta ala berdad por que con migo no a rifado ningun tabaco quien en una cierta occasion fue con un manojo fue Juan de Mestas a quien antes que lo rifara por el futuro contingente page a su contento y habiendo causado este delito no tube que pagar ni para que resistirme como el dicho dize en la susa y siendo esto assi no es dable que le porfiara a jusgar por no pagar como me argulie y caso que ubiera sido prueba que es menor de edad o no capas para no aberlo echo o quedo acostumbrado pero dize a otros a fuego como tambien el que me pusso las cuarenta gamusas que dize que es entretenimiento si use la lista y con repetida y suplicarle entrege mi silla de bajo del conosimiento y albertensia que no abia de usar al ella. Y lo pruebo con el Capitan Miguel Tenorio de dicha quien se aio presente y sabe que le daba en satisfasion del referida esta con buen escojido con tal que me diera la demasia ocunarexa prueba de mi legalidad anu con el conosimiento que tengo de que sobre materia y el visto como lo esta no me podia recaer sentensia de la Real Justissia ni como me abia de pagar las gamusas cuando se a negado a pagarme seis pesos de otras que yo rife estando una prenda delante interin se entregaban de que tiene fisico conosimiento dicho Capitan Miguel Tenorio de Alba ni tan poco satisfaze el que diga que la silla no estaba como digo en la anterior

cuando es berdad que acusado de ella y quebrado un estribo ni como se abia de podrir arimada a un rincon prueba que su malisiosa proposision en cuanto a que dize que no equibatean las gamusas alo que le restaba digo que repunia por que lo tengo mas que satisfecho tanto por deberme todabia los referidos seis pesos cuanto por aberle dado un papel cuando se las enbie en que le digo que si no se alla contento con ellas satisfare de otro modo que lo quede es pues por entonses no les puso defecto las aio sufisientes y para prueba a esto pido aga demostrasion del y pues se alla (tan perito) en el ultimo punto que dize que en pasando año y dia de enpeno una prenda no esta obligado a satisfaser menos cabos el que la tiene siendo con las sircumstansias que esta digo que quedare satisfecho con tal que me site el thomo, capitulo y foxas donde se alla esa lei por todo lo cual a Vuestra Señoria pido y suplico se sirba de atender ami relasion como tambien a mandar que Juan me satisfaga los cuatro pesos que confiesa me debe de mi trabajo personal que entonses abia de ser con cuatro varas de sallal y ahora dise dara una fanega de maiz que no equibaje al montuo ni mi persona se abia de ocupar en trabajar a ninguno por lo que no he menester ni en el Reino tiene coriente y siendo esto tan de justizia dise que balla a aber ala Real Justissia que pareze modo de menos presio y juro en toda forma de derecho esta mi petision no ser de malisia al Real ausilio imploro y en lo nesesario ut supra.
Francisco de Rivera (rubric)

Presentazion
En sinco dias del mes de Disiembre de mil setesientos y onse años en esta Villa de Santa Cruz ante mi el Maestre de Campo Roque Madrid Alcalde Mallor y Capitan Aguerra desta dicha Villa la presento el contenido por mi vista la ube por presentada y mando a Baltazar Truxillo responda en termino de la lei y para que conste lo firme como Juez receptor con los testigos de asistensia en dicho dia mes y año, ut supra.
       Roque Madrid (rubric)
testigo de asistensis testigo de asistensia
Juan de Atienza (rubric) Miguel de Quintana (rubric)

       Señor Alcalde Mayor y Capitan Aguerra

Baltasar Truxillo vesino desta jurisdizion ante Vuestra Señoria paresco en la mas bastante forma que aia lugar en derecho y al mio combenga y digo Señor respondiendo a los puntos que a su parte alega Francisco de Rivera en que dise no digo bien, digo a este punto que bien digo y que sino lo entendio es otra cosa que lo que digo es que rife un manojo de tabaco y lo rifo, Su Merse, y el Capitan Miguel Tenorio de Alva y Juan de Archibeque con que entre los cuatro lo rifamos y asi lo propio es desir yo que lo rife o que otro de los dichos lo diga supuesto que fue entre los cuatro, y en cuanto a que dise ser yo menor de edad puede reconoser su malisia pues dijo en la occasion dela dicha

rifa persuadiendome a ello que queria ber si selo llebaba sin que le costara nada y pues le dolio entonses desde luego fue su intension no pagar nada prueba de mi berdad y en cuanto a lo que dise que me dejo la silla con las condisiones que refiere dara la prueba en cuanto a que dise me daba un buei y que le pagara la demasia no nesesitaba yo de tal buei ni menos se iso tal trato, y en cuanto a que dise por su buen conosimiento que por materia inlisita no le podia recaer sentensia de la Real Justisia, digo que entonses se conose mas bien su malisia pues me dejo la dicha silla con mala intension y en cuanto a otros seis pesos que me demanda dara la prueba en cuanto a la cuenta de las cuatro gamusas que las resebi tales cuales por salir de su dilasion y en cuanto a que dise le muestre el capitulo y foxas donde se alla la lei que dise que en pasando no se pagan menos la bos digo que en la lei declara sopla allara y eso si ubiera otra no ubiera quien supliera al proximo su nesesidad y mas en prendas de materia tan coruptible como es lo allo culpable por todo lo cual y el tiempo de su enpeno, a Vuestra Magestad pido y suplico se sirva de prober en justizia que me ayo apersibido a obedeser en todo lo que fuere rason de ella que asi lo creo y si en mi se reconose malisia se sentenzie y juro en toda forma de derecho por Dios y por la Señal de la Santa Cruz este mi escrito no ser de ella y en lo nesesario, ut supra.
Baltazar Truxillo (rubric)

Auto de Remizion
En la Villa de Santa Cruz en nueve dias del mes de Disiembre de mil setesientos y onse años ante mi el Maestre de Campo Roque Madrid Alcalde Maior de dicha Villa y su jurisdision la presento el contenido y por mi vistra la hube por presentada y atendiendo alos alegatosde un y otra parte ago remision destos autos al Señor Marques Governador y Capitan General deste Reino para que con su vista provei y mande lo que fuere servido y para que conste lo firme como Juez Reseptor con los testigos de mi assistensia en dicho dia, ut supra.
    Roque Madrid (rubric)
Testigo de asistensia testigo de asistensia
Juan de Atienza (rubric) Miguel de Quintana (rubric)

Autto
En la Villa de Santa Fee cavesera de este Reyno y Provincias de la Nueva Mexico en veinte y tres dias del mes de Agosto de mill setecientos y doze años yo el Almirante Dn. Joseph Chacon Medina Salazar y Villaseñor Cavallero del Orden de Santiago, Marques dela Peñuela Governador y Capitan General deste dicho Reyno y Castellano de Sus Fuerzas y Presidios por Su Magestad aviendome hecho remission de estos autos el Maestre de Campo Roque Madrid Alcalde Mayor y Capitan Aguerra de la Villa Nueva de Santa Cruz y su jurisdision de la Cañada para la mayor satisfacion de ellos ordeno ami Theniente General Dn. Juan Páez Hurtado los siga y fenesca y sentensie segun

allare por su naturaleza de quien espero cumplira en el todo (como siempre) con su obligazion guardandole justisia a quien la hubiere dejando el juicio serrado y concluyo en toda forma y conforme a derecho e para que conste asi lo probey mande y firme con mi Secretario de Governazion y Guerra.

El Marquez de la Peñuela (rubric)

Ante mi

Cristobal de Gongora (rubric)

Secretario de Governazion y Guerra

En la Villa de Santa Fee en beinte y sinco dias del mes de Agosto de mill setecientos y doze años yo el General Juan Paez Hurtado Theniente de Governador y Capitan General de este Reyno en cumplimiento del auto de la buelta aviendo reconosido el alegato de las partes y hechar menos la declarazion del Capitan Miguel Tenorio, ordeno a el Maestre de Campo Roque Madrid Alcalde Mayor de la Villa Nueva de Santa Cruz la resiva y fecha me debuelba los autos para en su vista para ver lo que convenga y por lo que mira a los quatro pesos de Juan Truxillo que deve a el dicho Francisco de Rivera selos hara pagar por ser de trabajo personal a su satisfazion, y asi mismo hara en primer lugar dicho Alcalde Mayor que aparten las costas prosesales y por que de todo lo referido conste lo firme con el Secretario de Governazion y Guerra en dicho dia.

Juan Paez Hurtado (rubric)

Ante mi

Xptobal de Gongora (rubric)

Secretario de Governazion y Guerra

Auto

En la Villa de Santa Cruz en primer dia de el mes de Septiembre de mill seteceintos y doze yo el Maestre de Campo Roque Madrid haviendome enterado del auto expedido por el Theniente General Dn. Joan Paez Hurtado quien me ordena reziva la declarazion del Capitan Juan Tenorio de Alba sitado en estos autos que con ella se concluse poniendose en estado de sentensia en cuia virtud hize parecer ante mi al dicho Capitan Aguerra le rezivi juramento que iso por Dios Nuestro Señor y una Señal de Cruz devajo de cuio cargo prometio dezir verdad en lo que supiere al caso tocante y preguntado que los puntos de una y otra peticion dijo que es verdad haverse hallado presente en la occasion que fue causo del delito de las seis gamusas a Baltazar Truxillo y que fue en la forma siguiente que haviendo dispuesto rifar un manojo de tabaco Juan de Mestas fue uno de los que jugaron en la rifa Francisco de Rivera que antes de la execusion de dicha rifa satisfizo en su presencia a Juan de Mestas con una gamuza que a su satisfacion cojio que no estubo negatibo ala satisfacion que despues de esto prosiguio jugando con dicho Truxillo hasta tanto que perdio seis gamusas que al presente llevaria a alguilar dos bacas y viendose con las gamusas perdidas y que no

avia conseguido el alguilar las dos bacas le suplico le fiase las gamusas con repetidas ynstancias y no queriendo condesender a su ruego le dijo ajuste monos Señor Baltazar le dara a Vuestra Majestad un buei y me dara la demasia o una rexa en la misma conformidad que por ninguno de estos medios lo consiguio y por ultimo le ubo de dejar la silla en satisfacion del enpeno hasta tanto que satisfueiese las seis gamusas que de las quarenta que dize le puso efectivas a jugar no las vido que esto es la verdad y lo que save de vajo del juramento que fecho tiene en que se afirmo y ratifico que no tiene que anadir ni quitar que es de edad de treinta y ocho años poco mas o menos y para que conste lo firmo con migo y los de mi asistensia en dicho dia.
      Roque Madrid (rubric)
     Miguel Thenoria de Alba (rubric)
   testigo de asistenzia testigo de asistenzia
   Bartholome Lovato (rubric) Juan de Atienza (rubric)

Auto de Remizion
En la Villa Nueva de Santa Cruz en primer dia del mes de Septiembre del a8ño de mil setecientos y doze yo el Maestre de Campo Roque Madrid Alcalde Maior y Capitan Aguerra de dicha Villa y su jurisdizion aviendo rezivido la declarazion del Capitan Miguel Tenorio de Alba sitado de las partes hago remision de los autos al Señor Theniente General quien tiene conosimiento de ellos para que con su bista determine lo que combenga y para que conste lo firme con los de mi asistensia en dicho dia.
Roque de Madrid (rubric)
Miguel Tenorio de Alba (rubric)
testigo de asistenzia testigo de asistenzia
Bartholome Lobato (rubric) Juan de Atienza (rubric)

Presentado en 19 de Octubre
de 1712 y Villa de Santa Fee ante el
Señor Governador y Capitan General

     Señor Governador y Capitan General

Francisco de Rivera vesino de la Villa Nueva de Santa Cruz ante Vuestra Señoria paresco en cuanto el Real derecho me permite y digo que por cuanto tengo presentado escripto al General Dn. Juan Paez Hurtado suplicandole se sirbiesse de decretar sobre unos autos que el Señor Almirante Marquez dela Peñuela fue servido de someter a su jusgado y aberme respondido berbar que assi los referidos auttos como el excripto se allan en el de Vuestra Señoria y yo proximo a salir a la tierra afuera con los primeros que lo executasen, a Vuestra Señoria pido y suplico con el debido rendimiento se sirba de tener comiserasion de mi determinado sobre este punto lo que fuese ser sido en

justissia que espero alcansar de su grandeza y juro en toda forma de derecho esta mi peticion no ser de malisia y en lo nesesario ut supra.
Francisco de Rivera (rubric)

Y vista por mi la ube por presentada y mande que Baltasar Trujillo comparesca ante mi ajustarse con esta parte dentro de segundo dia y que lo requiera con este auto el Capitan Jazinto Sanchez Alcalde Maior de la Villa Nueva de Santa Cruz y jurisdizion de la Cañada; asi lo provey y rubrique ante el Secretario de Governazion y Guerra en diez y nueve de Octubre de mill setezientos y doze.
(The rubric of Juan Paez Hurtado)
Roque de Pintto (rubric)
Secretario de Governazion y Guerra

Notes

1. This appears to be Francisco [Afán] Rivera [de Betanzos], who came to New Mexico from Mexico City in 1694, when he was nineteen, with his father, Andrés de Betanzos; and his brother in 1694 with the Farfán-Velasco expedition. His father was a stonemason. Francisco was a merchant and one of the original settlers of Santa Cruz, of which he was an alcalde in 1705 (Chávez, *Origins*: 148, 266; Kessell and Hendricks, *RCR*: 247).
2. Baltazar Trujillo was a native New Mexican who returned with the Reconquest. He was born in 1673. His parents were Juan Trujillo and Elvira Sánchez Jiménez. At the time this document was written, he was thirty-nine. This probably means that when Rivera referred to him as a minor, he was insulting him. In a document of around 1715, Baltazar is listed as a captain. In 1715 he was named in a lawsuit by Pojoaque Pueblo, claiming that he was occupying land that they had purchased from Miguel Tenorio de Alba. He also owned land in the Taos area by 1725 and was accused by the Taos Indians of encroaching on their land (Christmas and Rau, *Pojoaque*: 14-18; SANM I #7; Chávez, *Origins*: 297; Ebright, "Advocates": 311-12; Jenkins, "Taos": 92-94; Jenkins, "Tewa": 119).
3. The Spanish word used for the saddle was *gineta*, also spelled *jineta*. A gineta saddle was like a jockey's saddle, allowing the rider to ride with the knees bent and stirrups high. The term *jinete* can mean a cowboy or rodeo rider, or at least someone skilled at riding. According to Wikipedia (accessed May 10, 2013), that term came from the Berber *zenata*. The Berbers used light-horse tactics, later adopted by the Spanish.
4. This Juan de Trujillo is most likely a soldier who was in New Mexico purchasing land in Pojoaque in 1701. His wife was Elvira Sánchez Jiménez, whom he married in 1695, and Baltazar Trujillo was his son. His daughter was María Trujillo, who married Juan de Mestas Peralta. He purchased land in Santa Cruz in 1701, which was revalidated in 1713 (Chávez, *Origins*: 296-97; Christmas and Rau, *Pojoaque*: 5, 9, 13-14; SANM I #1136).
5. As stated above, the word that Rivera most often uses for gambling is *rifara*, which ordinarily means a gambling game or sometimes a raffle. It is not known whether he is referring to a game of which we now know little, or whether he wants to avoid using the term *jugar*, the usual term for gambling. It seems likely that they were gambling with dice.
6. Among the varieties of tobacco grown in the New World, *Nicotiana rustica*, locally called *punche*, was grown and cultivated in New Mexico by both the Spanish and Indians. For smoking, five or six leaves were bundled together and wrapped in a corn husk. There was no Crown monopoly on tobacco until 1766, when the viceroy, the Marqués de Croix, mandated that tobacco grown in New Mexico be prohibited and that a duty be placed on the tobacco imported from Mexico (Kinnaird, "Tobacco": 329-39; Kessell and Hendricks, *BFA*: 305 n19).
7. Roque Madrid was born in New Mexico in 1644, the son of Francisco II de Madrid and the grandson of Francisco I de Madrid, who arrived in 1603. Roque owned land along the Santa Fe River near Agua Fría. In 1685 he was the head of the El Paso presidio, serving as sergeant major and captain. He fought in many campaigns with Vargas. He settled in Santa Cruz and was alcalde there between 1699 and 1707 (Barrett, *Settlement*: 101-2, 210; Kessell et al., *BOB*: 211 n43).
8. Juan de Mesta [Peralta] returned to Santa Fe in 1693 and was listed in the presidio muster of 1697. By 1710 he was living in Pojoaque. In 1699 he was the recipient of a grant below the pueblo of Pojoaque named San Bue-

naventura, made by Governor Rodríguez Cubero. He revalidated in the grant in 1713 (Kessell et al., *TDC*: 128; Chávez, *Origins*: 219; SANM I #735; Barrett, *Settlement*: 101; SANM I #1136).

9. The language here is very difficult, with Rivera's anger and frustration making him nearly incoherent. It may reflect Rivera's despair at being brought before Roque Madrid and being challenged by Trujillo, while trying to avoid the fact that, given the governors' orders against gambling, he should not have been playing rifara at all. The statement about Trujillo being under age means his word cannot be taken as such, but must be proven by other evidence. However, Trujillo later states that he is not a minor, a statement supported by other documentation. See note 2, above.

10. Miguel Tenorio de Alba was a native of New Mexico and one of the first settlers of Santa Cruz. In 1697 he was listed as a blacksmith and was a cabildo scribe and a secretary of government and war to the governor. He and his wife, Agustina Romero, baptized a son, Cayetano, in Santa Cruz in 1711. In 1718 he was alcalde and war captain for Santa Cruz, and in 1719 for Taos Pueblo. He was killed while serving in the Villasur campaign in 1720 (Kessell et al., *BOB*: 570 n52; SANM II #236; NMGS, *Santa Cruz*: 1).

11. The 6 pesos may refer to the saddle's loss of value. That is, because of the damage, the gambling debt paid by Rivera was too much, and 6 pesos were owed to him.

12. These items were probably part of Rivera's merchandise.

13. In this case, the word *vara* is a Castilian yard of about 33 inches, or .838 meters (Hadley et al., *Presidio*: 534).

14. Juan de Archibeque was born in Bayonne, France, in 1671, as Jean l'Archeveque. He accompanied the La Salle Expedition in 1684 but fled after the murder of La Salle. He and another survivor of the expedition, Jacques Grolet (later called Gurulé), lived with the Indians for two years, eventually meeting Spanish troops, then they were sent to the mines in Mexico and then to Spain. Archibeque was in New Mexico by 1694, having come with the Farfán-Velasco expedition. He married Antonia Gutiérrez in 1694 and upon her death married doña Manuela de Roybal, daughter of don Santiago Roybal, captain and high sheriff of the Holy Office of the Inquisition. In 1720 he was killed on the Villasur expedition (Kessell et al., *RCR*: 341-42 n135; Esquibel, "Residents": 68; Thomas Chávez, *Moment*: 159).

5

ALBUQUERQUE ENDANGERED BY INDIAN ATTACKS; SETTLERS DEMAND RETURN OF PRESIDIO SOLDIERS
October 15, 1712. Source: SANM II #181.

Synopsis and editor's notes: In 1706, having founded the villa of Albuquerque and been apprised of ongoing Indian raids, Governor Francisco Cuervo y Valdez assigned ten presidio soldiers to the villa, naming Martín Hurtado the captain of the squadron with the title *justicias mayor* and *capitán de guerra*. The next governor, the Marqués de la Peñuela (1707–1712), removed the soldiers. This resulted in a 1708 petition to the cabildo from two representatives of the people of Albuquerque, Fernando Durán y Chávez and Baltazar Romero, asking that the troops be returned. This request was forwarded to the governor and denied. Then, in the following 1712 document, fourteen Albuquerque residents, most of them first founders of Albuquerque or related to first founders, again sent a petition to the new governor, Juan Ignacio Flores Mogollón, asking for a return of the garrison. This time the petition was approved.

The reason for Peñuela's withdrawal of the squadron may have been his belief that consolidation of the presidio forces in Santa Fe would be more effective in counteracting the attacks occurring in the province. Governor Vélez Cachupín, writing about requests from Albuquerque for more protection in 1754, agreed with this position, stating, "I have tried to accustom them [the people of Albuquerque] to the idea that each one should take care of the defense of his own hacienda. The number of settlers in that area is sufficient to do so; besides, they are well trained and experienced in war. I wished them to do this because of the great difficulty the presidio meets in providing the escorts which each jurisdiction wishes. One should always keep the presidio as a unit, otherwise its strength, which is the main thing, is weakened when it is necessary to attend immediately to any area threatened. When such a threat occurs, one can quickly oppose the enemy by calling the militia together until the troops arrive" (SANM I #1205, Twitchell translation; Thomas, *Plains Indians*: 143; Greenleaf, "Founding of Albuquerque": 7; Twitchell, *Spanish Archives* II: 351-53; NMGS, *Aquí*: vii–viii; Flagler, "Chacón": 473).

This document also shows the way in which the residents could unite and persistently and successfully petition successive governors for their demands.

Villa of Santa Fe and October 15 of 1712
Before the Governor and Captain General[1]

The inhabitants of this villa of San Felipe de Albuquerque, appearing before your lordship unanimously and thereby speaking with one voice, in solidarity, now say that as it happened in the year one thousand seven hundred and six, we settled in said villa as ordered by the lord governor don Francisco Cuervo, the predecessor of your honor. By virtue of said governor having placed an *escolta* [detachment or escort] of ten soldiers with their captain for our safety, and having given an account of this to his excellency [written] by said people [of Albuquerque] with a resolution from general meeting, it served his excellency to grant and confer as certain a detachment upon this villa, which order was mandated for placement in the government archive, and this was done. The lord Marqués de la Peñuela, who was [the next] governor of this kingdom, withdrew the said guard, for which reason we now find ourselves so accosted by the enemy Apaches—such that we are not safe in our homes nor our persons. All this is stemming from having withdrawn the said detachment during all the time the said lord Marqués governed, so they stole from us many horses and cattle, and they have done so with such boldness that they ride throughout this vicinity in daylight, having recognized that we do not have the forces needed to protect our animals.

We ask and plea to you in name of his majesty, may God guard him, that it please you to provide us said detachment, for through them we will receive our major relief and yours, which come from safeguarding the orders of his majesty as his loyal vassals. And we swear in the required form that our petition is not malicious, but is to attain justice, and what is necessary, and so forth.

Cristóbal Jaramillo (rubric)[2]
At the request of Joachín Sedillo[3]
[Signed by] Francisco de la Candelaria (rubric)

Francisco de la Candelaria (rubric)[4]
Luis García (rubric)[6]
At the request of Felisiano de la Candelaria
[Signed by] Francisco de la Candelaria (rubric)

At the request of Juan de Torres[9]
[Signed by] Francisco de la Candelaria (rubric)

At the request of Juan Vallejo[11]
[Signed by] Francisco de la Candelaria (rubric)
At the request of Antoni[o] Varela
[Signed by] Francisco de la Candelaria (rubric)

Juan Varela (rubric)[5]
Gerónimo Jaramillo[7] (rubric)
At the request of Cristóbal Barela[8]
[Signed by] Francisco de la Candelaria (rubric)

At the request of Cristóbal García[10]
[Signed by] Francisco de la Candelaria (rubric)

Pedro López (rubric)[12]

[Marginal entry] Station the detachment which these parties ask for being informed two days ago through the alcalde mayor of that jurisdiction that the Apache Indians were carrying out some thefts of horses and cattle, I quickly sent six soldiers, and I will

dispatch a complement of ten more now and always when necessary for their greater safety, and if they inform me, I will give them prompt assistance.
[rubric of the governor]

ORIGINAL DOCUMENT

Villa de Santa Fee y Octubre 15 de 1712
Numero 291

Ante
Señor Governador y Capitan General

Los vezinos de esta Villa de el Señor San Phelipe de Alburquerque, parezenos ante Vuestra Señoria unanimes y conformes todos a voz de uno, y cada uno de por si, *in solidum* y dezimos que por quanto el año de mil setezientos I seis, nos poblamos en esta dicha Villa por orden de el Señor Governador Don Francisco Cuerbo antesesor de Vuestra Señoria, en virtud de habernos puesto dicho General una escolta de diez señores soldados con su Capitan para nuestro resguardo, y abiendo dado quenta a su Excelencia de dicho poblazion con resoluzion de junta general se sirvio su Excelencia dar por azertada y confirmar esta dicha Villa con ecolta cuio mandamiento para en el del archivo de govierno, y esto seyo puesto. El Señor Marques de la Peñuela Governador que fue de este Reino nos retiro dicha escolta, por cuia causa nos hallamos oi tan acosados de los enemigos Apaches – que no tenemos segaros nuestras haziendas ni personas, todo originiado de havernos quitado la dicha escolta, todo el tiempo que a governado sobre dicho Señor Marques, llebandonos quantas caballos y reses an podido con tanta osadia que se pasean de dia por todos estos contornos con el conozimiento de no tener nosotros fuerzas para operarles por lo que. Vuestra Señoria pedimos y suplicamos en nombre de su Magestad que Dios guarde se sirba de proveernos la dicha escluta, que en ellos reziveremos nuesttro maior alivio y Vuestra es el guardar los ordenes de su Magestad como su leal basallo. Y juramos en devida forma no ser malizioso nuestro pedimento, sino es por alcanzar Justizia. Y en lo necesario etc.

Christobal Jaramillo (rubric)
Aruego de Joachin Sedillo
Francisco de la Candelaria (rubric)
Francisco de la Candelaria (rubric)   Juan Barela (rubric)
Luis Garcia (rubric)   Geronimo Jaramillo (rubric)
Aruego de Felisiano de la Candelaria   Aruego de Christobal Barela
Francisco de la Candelaria (rubric)   Francisco de la Candelaria (rubric)
Aruego de Juan de Tores   Aruego de Christobal Garcia
Francisco de la Candelaria (rubric)   Francisco de la Candelaria [rubic]

Aruego de Juan Ballejo
Francisco de la Candelaria
Francisco de la Candelaria (rubric)

Pedro Lopez (rubric)
Aruego de Antoni[o] Barela

[Marginal entry] Pondrase la escolta que piden estas partes y con la noticia que abra dos ndi y medio el Alcalde maior de aquella Jurisdizion de que azian algunas robos de ndioss y reses los ndios apaches despache luego seis soldados y enviare cunplimento a la excolta de diez y siempre que sea necesario para su resguardo mas y se me de noticia dare pronta providenzia (rubric)

Translated and transcribed by Gerald Gonzales and Linda Tigges

Notes

1. Governor Flores Mogollón had just been installed as the new governor. He served from October 1712 to 1715.
2. Cristóbal [Varela] Jaramillo I, who is here signing for Joachín Sedillo, was part of an El Paso military muster in 1680 and was in Bernalillo by 1697. He was married to Casilda López Sedillo, sister to Joachín. His daughter, María de la Rosa, was married to Diego de Torres; a second daughter, Francisca, was married to Antonio Lucero de Godoy; and a son, Cristóbal II, was married to Inés González Bas. In 1704 Cristóbal and his brother Juan Francisco petitioned for lands on the west side of the river. Gerónimo Jaramillo was his son. In 1739 he is listed as a petitioner for the Tomé grant (Kessell and Hendricks, *RCR*: 89 n70; *BOB*: 151, 1173-74 n109-10; Alexander (*Cottonwoods*: 329).
3. Joachín Sedillo (Rico de Reyes, also spelled Cedillo) was born in prerevolt New Mexico. He returned by 1695. In 1716 he received a grant of 22,000 acres west of the Río Grande and south of Isleta Pueblo. It eventually became part of Rancho San Clemente (Chávez, *Origins*: 285; Alexander, *Cottonwoods*: 8).
4. Francisco [de la] Candelaria and his brother Feliciano (aka Felix) were born in the Río Abajo prior to the 1680 revolt, returning with their mother by 1696. Their family is the subject of an article by Francisco Sisneros, "Anna de Sandoval": 79-87.
5. Juan Varela [Jaramillo], a brother of Cristóbal who, was born in New Mexico. He married Isabel López Sedillo, a sister to the wife of Cristóbal I, and a sister to Joachín Sedillo. Juan was a petitioner for the Tomé grant in 1739 (Kessell et al., *BOB*: 1173-74 n110; Alexander, *Cottonwoods*: 328).
6. Captain Luis García [de Noriega] was the son of Captain Alonso García de Noriega II, who in 1680 was one of the leaders of the refugees traveling to El Paso and who returned with the Reconquest. Alonso was killed by an Apache in 1696. An ancestor, Alonso García de Noriega I, was in New Mexico by 1636. Luis was listed in a military muster at Bernalillo in 1704. Sometime after that, he and two brothers received the San Antonio grant near Albuquerque from Governor Peñuela. As stated above, in 1715 he was the alcalde of Albuquerque. When he died in 1746, because of the large size of his estate and because he had children from two marriages, his will was contested in several lengthy probate cases. His daughter Rosalia married Salvador Martínez (Kessell et al., *ASA*: 222; SANM I #341; SANM II #484; Chávez, *Origins*: 181; Barrett, *Settlement*: 139).
7. Gerónimo Jaramillo was a son of Cristóbal Varela Jaramillo I and Casilda Cedillo Rico de Rojas. He married Gertrudis Silva, who had a daughter, Casilda, who married Antonio Vallejo. In 1734, he was the alcalde of Bernalillo and Albuquerque (Chávez, *Origins*: 199; NMGS, *Aquí*: 403, 405, 425, 462, 465-66; SANM I #87, #178, WPA translations).
8. This is could be Cristóbal Varela Jaramillo II. However, given that the surname Varela is used, not Jaramillo, it is more likely to be Cristóbal Varela de Losada, who was living in Bernalillo in 1699. This would make him the son of Diego Valera Losada, a prerevolt occupant of the Isleta jurisdiction, and at one time the adjutant general of New Mexico (Chávez, *Origins*: 305; Kessell el al., *BOB*: 453 n89).
9. Juan de Torres is on the presidio list of 1697. According to Chávez, he was a native of Zacatecas and was living

in Albuquerque by 1710. It is not known whether he was related to Diego Torres (Kessell and Hendricks, *RCR*: 128; Chávez, *Origins*: 295).

10. This is Cristóbal García I, who stated later in the document that he was one of the first founders of Albuquerque. He may be the Cristóbal García, husband of Isabel Romero, whose child, Cristóbal II, was baptized in Albuquerque in 1708. Alternatively, another baptismal record hints that he could be Tomás Cristóbal García de Noriega, of whom there is no doubt that he was a first founder. This name appears in the baptismal records as Cristóbal, partially erased, with the name "Tomás" written over it (NMGS, *Aquí*: 21, 249).

11. A Juan Vallejo was in New Mexico by 1716, marrying Angelina Varela Jaramillo, but it is not known if this is the person referenced in this document. Both a Juan Vallejo *el grande* and Juan Vallejo the younger are listed as petitioners for the Tomé grant in 1739 (Alexander, *Cottonwoods*: 328; Chávez, *Origins*: 303).

12. This is probably Pedro López de Castillo, who arrived in New Mexico in 1697 as an alférez (Kessell et al., *BOB*: 1167 n67, 1174 n114). It is not Pedro López Gallardo.

6

BAPTISM OF APACHES REQUIRED
September 26, 1714. Source SANM II #212.

Synopsis and editor's notes: In 1714 Governor Flores Mogollón carried out Spanish law by requiring that all Apaches bought at trade fairs be baptized before being taken out of the kingdom. Though the law prohibited slavery, there was an exception for those captured in a just war; the campaigns against the Apaches were probably considered in this way. Mogollón's concern was the risk of losing their souls if they died before being taken into the Christian faith through the sacrament of baptism. Citing his previous experience with the baptism of recently arrived Negro slaves, probably when he was governor of the province of Nuevo León, he stated that the Indians were first to be anointed with baptismal water by the trader. Then, after being purchased, they were to be anointed with the Holy Oil, completing the process of bringing them into the Catholic Church. Because Mogollón insisted on notifying all the districts in the province that had slaves, we have a list of their locations and the names of their alcaldes. This and an earlier 1706 document from Governor Cuervo y Valdez show that the governors considered the spiritual welfare of all persons in their province to be their responsibility. In the 1706 document, Governor Cuervo ordered that all the Indians, Negros, and mulattos were to be instructed in the Christian doctrine.

Dn. Juan Ygnacio Flores Mogollón, governor and captain general of this kingdom and provinces of New Mexico and castellan of the forces and presidios for his majesty, etc.

Being that I have been notified that the Apaches who are purchased at the trade fairs, be they old or young, by the residents of this kingdom and by other foreigners who purchase them to take them to faraway places to sell them, take them without being baptized, which is the most important thing imposed by the king, our lord, whom God may guard. This, taking them to sell, is tolerated and permitted, but the concern is the risk given to these souls without being baptized. I have recently been informed that there have been cases where along the roadways some youngsters have fallen from their horses and have been killed. The same thing has happened from carts that have left this kingdom. Just today, we have learned that on the previous day, the twenty-fifth of the present month, the Apaches killed two young boys when they went for wood with the sons of Miguel Coca.[1] Another one [at a different time] was killed, and one was taken alive. I have had the experience that at the ports of the Indies[2] of this kingdom the ships come in with huge numbers of negros and upon reaching the docks, men from all religions from the city board the said ships and very freely anoint them with the waters of the Holy Baptism. This is done to the old and to the young. Once this is done, they then hand them over to the owners who have purchased them, who are to instruct them in their doctrine so that at a later date they are given the oils.[3]

I order all of the residents of this kingdom that once they have heard or have been notified of this decree, they proceed to take all of the Apaches that they have to the Reverend Padre Ministro so that they are baptized, the consequence being that none of them leave the kingdom without being baptized. This is to include everyone, old and young, and is left to the discretion of the said Reverend Padres according to what has been taught. I have seen this done at the ports of the ocean with the huge numbers of negroes, as I have stated, and this needs to be done under the penalty of losing the said Apaches who are left without being baptized, and they [purchasers] are not to be permitted to deal for them if it is known that they have not been baptized due to their omission or lack of responsibility. I pray and hope that God may guard all of the said Reverend Padre Ministros. I personally ask and request that I be informed which residents in their district have them and to have them baptized immediately. If they refuse to have this done, they are to notify me as to why it is not done as a service to God, our Lord, which shall be reported to his majesty, the King, our lord.

This decree is to be published at this villa, in the customary places, so that all of the inhabitants are notified of it, and is to be sent to all of the jurisdictions of this kingdom, with all of the alcaldes mayores placing at the bottom of the page their acknowledgment, with the last one who receives it returning it to this secretariat, where it will be forever found. This is done on the twenty-sixth of September, 1714. I signed it along with don Joseph Manuel Golthomey[4] due to the absence of my secretary of government and war.

Don Juan Ygnacio
Flores Mogollón (rubric)
At the order of the governor and captain general
don Joseph Manuel Giltomey (rubric)

Published at the sound of the military instruments at the customary places by the voice of Esteban Rodríguez, drummer, on the day of this date, to which I certify and I signed it.

don Joseph Manuel Giltomey (rubric)

At the Villa Nueva de Santa Cruz on the 28th of September, 1714, I, the alcalde mayor and war captain of the said villa, Sebastián Martín,[5] in fulfillment of the decree of the previous page expedited by the governor and captain general of this kingdom, who is don Juan Ignacio Flores Mogollón, I ordered the settlers of this jurisdiction to gather together and to whom I made known the said decree, and which upon being heard and understood, all who were present in unison stated that they would comply with it. And so that it is valid I signed it on the said day, to which I certify, etc.

Sebastián Martín (rubric)

At this Pueblo of San Geronimo de Taos on the 30th of September, 1714, I, Lieutenant to the alcalde mayor of the said pueblo, in compliance and in obedience to the above decree, I made it known to the natives of this jurisdiction through their interpreter, and its contents was understood. And so that it is valid I signed it on the said day, month, and year.

Juan de Pineda[6] (rubric)

In this jurisdiction of the Keres, Cochiti, Santo Domingo, and San Felipe on the 3rd of October, 1714, I, Captain Antonio Baca,[7] lieutenant to the alcalde mayor of the said jurisdiction, in compliance with and in obedience to the decree above issued by the general don Juan Ygnacio Flores Mogollón, governor and captain general of this kingdom and provinces of New Mexico and castellan of his forces and presidios, made it known to them through their interpreter, and so that it is valid I signed it at this pueblo of San Felipe on the said day.

Antonio Baca (rubric)

In compliance with and in obedience to the above decree, found on the first page of this document and issued by the general don Juan Ygnacio Flores Mogollón, governor and captain general of this kingdom and provinces of New Mexico, castellan of his forces and presidios for his majesty, I, Tiburcio de Ortega,[8] alcalde mayor and war captain of the places of Jémez, Zia, and Santa Ana, made it known to them through their interpreters, who were well versed in the Castilian and in their own mother languages. And so that it is valid I signed it on the 4th of October, 1714.

Tiburcio de Ortega (rubric)

In compliance with and in obedience to the decree above issued by his excellency, don Juan Ygnacio Flores Mogollón, governor and captain general of this kingdom and provinces of New Mexico and castellan of his forces and presidios for the King, our lord, I, Pedro de Chaves,[9] alcalde mayor and war captain of the pueblo of San Agustín de la Isleta, made it known to the said Indians through interpreters versed in the Castilian and in their own language. And so that it is valid I signed it on the 5th of October, 1714, etc.

Pedro de Chaves (rubric)

In compliance with and in obedience to this royal decree issued by the governor don Juan Ygnacio Flores Mogollón, captain general of this kingdom and provinces of New Mexico and castellan of his forces and presidios for the King our lord, I, Captain Antonio de Uribarrí, alcalde mayor of the pueblos of Acoma, La Laguna, and Zuni, made it known to them that which was stated in this royal decree through their faithful and loyal interpreters. And so that it is valid I signed it on the 6th of October, etc.

Antonio de Urribarí[10] (rubric)

ORIGINAL DOCUMENT

Don Juan Ygnacio Flores Mogollon, Governador y Capitan General deste Reyno y Provincias dela Nueva Mexico y Castellano de Sus Fuerzas y Presidios por Su Magestad, ut supra.

Por quanto tengo notizia que los Apaches que se compran en los rescates grandes y pequenos por los vezinos deste Reyno y de otros estantes foraneos que sacan a distintas partes a vender salen sin baptisarse que es fin principal por que el Rey, Nuestro Senor, que Dios Guarde, permite y tolera este trato y el riesgo con que salen estas almas, pues estoy ynformado a caesido en los caminos caer los muchachos delas vestias y matarse, como assi mismo subsedio en los carros que salieron de este Reyno, y oy se avisto en dos muchachos que mataron los Apaches ayer veinte y cinco del corriente que havian ydo por lena con los hijos de Miguel Coca, y al uno mataron y al otro llevaron vivo, y teniendo experiensia en que en los puertos de las Yndias deste Reyno entran los navios con armasones de Negros y luego que llegan a el puerto pasan de todas las relixiones dela cuidad abordo de dichos navios y subcondicione les hechan el agua del Santo Baptismo asi a los grandes como a los pequenos y despues pasan alos duenos que los compran, quienes los ynstruyen en la doctrina para que despues les pongan los olios; mando a todos los vezinos del Reyno que luego que oygan o tengan notizia deste vando passen a llevar todos los Apaches con que se allasen alos Reverendos Padres Ministros para que los Baptisen con apersevimiento de que no dejare salir ninguno del Reyno que no supiere este Baptizado siendo pequeno y siendo grande si le paresiere azerlo a dichos Reverendos Padres segun lo que se practica y e visto se executa en los puertos del mar con las armasones de Negros que llevo referido pena de perdimento de dichos Apaches que se reconosieren yr sin Baptismo y de no permitirles puedan tratar en ellos por su omision

 Y descuydo, y ruego y encargo en nombre de Su Magestad que Dios Guarde a todos los referidos Reverendos Padres Ministros, y dela mia pido y suplico zelen el saver que vezinos en su distrito los tienen y agan los Baptisen luego; y de si renunzia meden notizia pues tan del servizio de Dios Nuestro Senor y que constantas veras en cargas Su Magestad el Rey Nuestro Senor y este Vando se publicara en esta Villa en las partes acostumbradas para que llegue a notizia de todos sus moradores y pasara a todas las jurisdiciones deste Reyno poniendo cada Alcalde Mayor en la suya al pie su cumplimiento y el ultimo que la reziviere lo devolvera a esta Secretaria para que en todo tiempo conste donde es fecho en veinte y seis de Septiembre de mill setecientos y catorze y lo firme con Dn. Joseph Manuel Gilthomey por ausiensia de mi Secretario de Governazion y Guerra =

     Dn. Juan Ygnacio
    Flores Mogollon (rubric)
 Por mando del Senor Governador y Capitan General
   Dn. Joseph Manuel Gilthomey (rubric)

Publicase a son delos ynstrumentos militares en las partes acostumbradas por vos de Esteban Rodriguez, tambor, oy dia dela fecha de que doi fee y lo firme.
    Don Joseph Manuel Gilthomey (rubric)

En la Villa Nueba de Santa Cruz en veinte y ocho dias del mes de Septiembre de setecientos y catorze anos, yo el Alcalde Maior y Capitan Aguerra de dicha Villa Sebastian Martin en cumplimiento del auto dela buelta expedido por el Senor Governador y Capitan General de este Reyno que lo es el Senor Dn. Juan Ignacio Flores Mogollon, mande juntar a los moradores de dicha jurisdicion a quienes les ize notorio dicho Bando que oido y entendido dixeron todos juntos estaban prontos a su cumplimiento y para que conste lo firme en dicho dia de que doi fee, ut supra.
    Sebastian Martin (rubric)

En este Pueblo de San Geronimo de los Taos en treynta dias del mes de Septiembre de mil y setesientos y catorze anos yo el Teniente de Alcalde Mayor de dicho Pueblo en cumplimiento y obedesimiento del auto dela buelta les yse notorio a todos los naturales desta jurisdision por ynterprete que lo entendieron y para que conste lo firme en dicho dia, mes y ano =
    Juan de Pineda (rubric)

En esta jurisdission delos Queres, Cochiti, Santo Domingo y San Felipe en tres dias del mes de Octubre de mill setesientos y quatorze y el Teniente de Alcalde Mayor de dicha jurisdision en cumplimiento y obedezimiento del auto arriba despedido por el Senor General Dn. Juan Ygnacio Flores Mogollon, Governador y Capitan General de este Reyno y Provincias dela Nueva Mexico y Castellano de Sus Fuerzas y Presidios, yo el Capitan Antonio Baca yse notorio por ynterprete y para que conste lo firme en este Pueblo de San Felipe en dicho dia.
      Antonio Baca (rubric)

En cumplimiento y obedesimiento del Bando dela primera foxa deste pliego espedido por el Senor General Dn. Juan Ygnacio Flores Mogollon, Governador y Capitan General de este Reyno y Provincias dela Nueba Mexico, Castellano de Sus Fuerzas y Presidios por Su Magestad, yo Tiburcio de Ortega, Alcalde Mayor y Capitan Aguerra delos Puestos de Jemes, Sia y Santa Ana di a entender su contenido a dicho Yndios por ynterpretes berzados en lengua Castellana y la suia maternal y para que conste lo firme en quatro de Octubre de mil zetesientos y catorze anos.
      Tiburcio de Ortega (rubric)

En cumplimiento y obedsimiento del Bando espedido de ariba por Su Excellencia Dn. Juan Ygnacio Flores Mogollon, Governador y Capitan General de este Reyno y Probinsias dela Nueva Mexico y Castellano de Sus Fuerzas y Presidios por el Rey Nuestro Senor, yo Pedro de Chabes, Alcalde Maior y Capitan Aguerra del Pueblo de San Agustin dela Isleta di a entender de su contenido a dichos Yndios por ynterpretes bersados en lengua Castellana y a sulla maternal y para que conste lo firme en sinco de Octubre de mil setesientos y catorse anos, ut supra.
      Pedro de Chabes (rubric)

En cumplimiento y obedesimiento deste Real Bando expedido por el Senor Gobernador Dn. Juan Ygnasio Flores Mogollon, Capitan General deste Reino y Probincias dela Nueba Mexico y Castellano de Sus Fuerzas y Presidios por el Rey Nuestro Senor, yo el Capitan Antonio de Urribari, Alcalde Mayor de los Pueblos de Acoma, La Laguna y Zuni les yse entender lo que en este Real Bando es contenido por medio de sus ynterpretes fieles y legales y para que asi conste de su deligensia lo firme en seis dias de Octubre, ut supra.
      Antonio de Uribarri (rubric)

Notes

1. Miguel [de la Vega y] Coca was the son of Cristóbal de la Vega and Mariana Coca, and was born in Mexico City around 1673. He arrived in New Mexico by 1697 or earlier. In 1699, after his first wife, Manuela Medina, died, he married María Montoya. In 1725 he was listed as the Santa Fe alcalde, and from 1727 to 1731 he was the alcalde mayor of Taos and Picuris. He prepared his will in 1752 and died some time before 1759 (Kessell et al., *BOB*: 671 n23; SANM I #405, #652, #1084 ; Chávez, *Origins*: 307-8.
2. Mogollón was probably citing his experience as governor of Nueva León, which is bordered on the east by the Gulf of Mexico. He was originally from Seville, Spain (Warner, "Felix Martinez": 61; Kessell, *Kiva*: 312).
3. In this context, "given the oils" means the act of anointing with oil, the part of baptism bringing the subject into the Christian faith. By the sixteenth century, phrases like "I deny the holy oil that was used to baptize me" were considered blasphemous and subject to punishment (Rawlings, *Spanish Inquisition*: 117).
4. Don Joseph Manuel Giltomey [or Gil Tomé] was a native of the Philippines and the son of Juan Giltomey and Antonia Flores. He was in New Mexico by 1696 and in 1706 was granted uncultivated land on the south side of the Santa Fe River by Governor Cuervo y Valdez. In 1713 he was an *ayudante* at the presidio. In 1715, he was given permission to go to El Paso to seek a cure for his ailments. He married Isabel Olivas and lived in Santa Cruz, where he was a notary. He died in 1727 (Chávez, *Origins*:186; Christmas and Rau, "Una Lista": 196; SANM I #1136;
Kessell, *RBC*: 297 n5; Kessell et al., *BOB*: 568-69 n43).
5. Captain Sebastián Martín [Serrano] was born around 1671 in San Luis Potosí to Pedro Martín Serrano de Salazar and Juana de Argüello, returning to New Mexico in 1693 with his parents to resettle their land in the La Cañada area. He was a presidio soldier in 1697 and in 1714 was the alcalde of Santa Cruz. In 1712 Martín revalidated a grant near Picuris made by Governor Vargas. He was granted extensive lands north of San Juan. The settlement took its name from a chapel that he built called Nuestra Señora de la Soledad. His wife was María Luján. He gained fame in the area as an Indian fighter (Kessell and Hendricks, *RCR*: 80 n32; Kessell et al., *TDC*: 129; SANM I #1136; Chávez, *Origins*: 223-24; also see also 16).
6. Juan de [la Mora] Piñeda (aka Piñeda de Guzmán) came to New Mexico from Sombrerete, arriving at least by 1695. For a short time in 1714, he was a sergeant at the presidio. Piñeda was married to Clara de Chávez, and between 1715 and 1720, he was the alcalde mayor of Taos. He died in 1727, having purchased land in Santa Fe in 1716 and 1722 (Chávez, *Origins*: 258; SANM I #168 and #682; Christmas and Rau, "Una Lista": 200).
7. This Antonio Baca was the son of Manuel Baca, who returned to Santa Fe in 1693 with his wife, María de Salazar. Antonio married María de Aragón in 1706. From 1715 to 1716 he was an alférez with the presidio (Chávez, *Origins*: 141; Christmas and Rau, "Una Lista": 196).
8. Tiburcio Ortega was born in New Mexico in 1755 and was a refugee in El Paso as a scribe, married to Margarita Otón. He was a protector of the Indians in El Paso between 1692 and 1712. In 1693, while still in El Paso, he was the secretary of the cabildo and also alguacil mayor. Also in El Paso, he was a notary for the friars. In 1694 he is shown as a member of the cabildo in Santa Fe. In 1711 he was imprisoned by Lieutenant Governor Valverde for opposing the exploitation of the Indians (Kessell and Hendricks, *BFA*: 487 n63; Kessell and Hendricks, *RCR*: 382, 564).
9. See Doc. 7.
10. Antonio Ulibarrí (aka Uribarrí) was the brother or maybe half or stepbrother of Juan de Ulibarrí, whose name is included in so many early documents. Antonio was married to María Durán y Chaves in 1711. He was the alcalde for the Laguna jurisdiction in 1714. In 1715 he presented a petition to the presidio stating that as an alcalde he was unable to continue to be responsible for his military arms and horses as well as for keeping the book of soldiers and accounts. In 1745 he was alcalde of Santa Fe. In 1750 he was appointed by Governor Cruzat y Góngora to defend an Indian from Tesuque Pueblo in a legal case (Chavez, *Origins*: 299-300; Christmas and Rau, "Una Lista": 198; SANM I #339; Norris, *Year Eighty*: 136).

7

BARTOLOMÉ GARDUÑO DELIVERS MAIL TO MEXICO CITY, INCLUDING A WOLF SKIN, PIÑON NUTS, AND A RESIDENCIA REPORT; ACCUSED OF ILLEGAL BEHAVIOR
March 1713– July 4, 1715. Source: SANM II #190.

Synopsis and editor's notes: In 1713 Fray Juan de Tagle asked Bartolomé Garduño to deliver the *residencia* of former governor Cuervo y Valdez to Mexico City. Governor Juan Ygnacio Flores Mogollón then asked him to take along several other documents. Pedro de Chaves provided the military escort to El Paso for Garduño as well as for the former captain of the Santa Fe presidio, Felix Martínez. Martinez was traveling to Mexico City to plead his case before the viceroy for retaining his post as captain of the Santa Fe presidio. When Garduño left El Paso for Mexico City, he took one of the soldiers from the escort, Carlos López, along with him. He claimed that he needed López because he felt ill, and that permission had been given for doing this. In the governor's opinion, however, López did not have permission to leave the province. However, when Garduño and López returned to New Mexico, the governor took no action against them. At about the same time, a third presidio soldier, Bernardino Fernández, went to Mexico to deliver a prisoner. He also returned, but not until two years later, and no action was taken (Warner, *Felix Martinez*: 71).

In July of 1715, when these three soldiers, Garduño, López, and Fernández, as well as settlers Cristóbal Arellano and Ramón García Jurado, left the kingdom without notice or permission, Governor Mogollón belatedly ordered an investigation of the 1713 activities of Garduño and López. The following document is a record of that investigation.

A second document of June 1715 (Doc. 8) describes the search for the five soldiers in the Albuquerque area, where most of the fugitives lived.

Jesus, Mary, and Joseph, Villa of Santa Fe, New Mexico

Year of 1715

Criminal case against Bartolomé Garduño[1] for having gone to the city of México to take the mail in the past year of 1713, and for having taken with him to the said city, without permission, the soldier Carlos López,[2] along with other issues which are included in these proceedings [of July, 1715].

[Exhibit 1, used in the following proceedings]

    Governor and Captain General don Juan Ygnacio Flores Mogollón

My dear sir and master. I received what your honor sent to me and I am most happy that you keep yourself in perfect health, and I present to you that which I have so that your honor can make use of it; also my dear sir, when the residencia of the General don Francisco Cuervo (may he be in heaven) was concluded, your honor favored me by being able to name the person who would deliver the said residencia to Mexico City, for which he would be paid three hundred and fifty pesos. As such, I informed your honor that I had chosen Sergeant Bartolomé Garduño, whom I thought was the best person for the job, and who would be one to return immediately, being that he had no other business other than the residencia, which was all that I requested. I ask God to safeguard your honor for many years. San Ildefonso, June 1715.
    My dear sir
I kiss the hand of your honor, as I am your servant and your chaplain
    Fray Juan de Tagle[3] (rubric)

[Exhibit 2, used in the following proceedings]

My dear sir. On this occasion I submit with Bartolomé Sánchez Garduño the proceedings of the residencia which your majesty took of my father,[4] who may be in heaven, and which I find conforms to the accounting which was given by the assessor and through which remuneration of this favor is provided. I will be forever grateful and happy to be of service in whatever is needed by your majesty, whose life may God guard for many years. México, November 28, 1714.
    I kiss the hand of your majesty
    our most sincere servant
    Alfonso Luis Cuervo y Valdés (rubric)

[Exhibit 3, used in the following proceedings]

[To] Governor don Juan Ygnacio Flores Mogollón

    I, the capitán de compañía, Bartolomé Garduño, say that I received the following papers and items[5] from my governor and captain general, don Juan Ygnacio Flores Mogollón, who dispatched me to Mexico City.[6]

1 – A stack of papers one-half of a vara in length and three fingers in height addressed to the *licenciado* don Francisco Flores Mogollón, alcalde mayor of Quantitlán, who is in the service of his majesty _____

2 – Two confidential papers addressed to the said, wrapped in hides, one containing some skins of a wolf and the other containing piñon nuts _____

1 – A stack of papers a vara long addressed to General don Antonio Valverde,[7] captain of the presidio of El Paso, who is in the service of his majesty _____

1 – A confidential letter for don Juan Cortes from the king _____

2 – Letters to El Parral, one for don Juan Felipe de Orosco and the other one for don Martín de Miquelena _____

2 – Letters to Zacatecas, one for don Martín Berdugo,[8] treasurer of that office, and the other one wrapped for one don Juan Callexas _____

Total, 9 items

These are all of the said papers and wrapped items which I have received and have on my person and which God willing I will turn over and bring back an answer or a receipt of having been given to them. So that it is valid forever, I signed this at this villa of Santa Fe, New Mexico on the 9th of March 1713.

                  Bartolomé Garduño (rubric)

[Proceedings of 1715]

Consists of seven pages.
            The judge is the governor and captain general,
            don Juan Ygnacio Flores Mogollón

Beginning of the proceedings brought forth against Bartolomé Garduño and Carlos López, soldier of this presidio

At the villa of Santa Fe, New Mexico, on the 4th of May, 1713, I, don Juan Ygnacio Flores Mogollón, governor and captain general of this kingdom and provinces of New Mexico for his majesty, say that I dispatched, on the 10th of March past, an escort to the presidio of El Paso, convoying the persons of don Felix Martínez[9] and Bartolomé Garduño. The said Garduño, a soldier of this presidio, was granted permission through influence which he had with Reverend Custodio Fray Juan de Tagle to proceed to Mexico City, with the assurance that he would return within six months, and with whom were submitted the proceedings of the residencia of General don Francisco Cuerbo de Valdés, along with some letters which are noted by a receipt that he left signed, and which is held in the office of the secretary [of the cabildo].

The corporal of the said escort was don Pedro de Chaves,[10] by whom it was made known that he returned minus one soldier who had gone with him by the name of

Carlos López, and whom I made to appear before me to see why this was done without my order. He, Chaves, answered that the said Bartolomé Garduño, on the day that he left from the presidio of El Paso, told him that he had an order from me for that purpose, and that he believed him indisputably, and which order he allowed without telling his lieutenant general, don Antonio Balverde, captain of the royal presidio of El Paso.

Considering the sincerity with which he executed what he did, I will not file the charges which correspond to this on the said corporal don Pedro de Chaves, but will file them against the said Bartolomé Garduño for the malice and falseness which he used in deceiving the said corporal. Accordingly, I also file the same charges against the soldier Carlos López, who should not have gone on such a long trip without having written authorization from me. I order that, once they return to this presidio, they are to be held prisoners in the royal guardhouse in order to receive their confessions and hear them according to justice if they had anything to say and to castigate them for such a bad deed and for disobedience and to warn the others, so that they know that they are to comply with their obligations. I thus approved, ordered, and signed it with my secretary of government and war.

don Juan Ygnacio
Flores Mogollón (rubric)
by order of the governor and captain general
Roque de Pinto[11] (rubric)
Secretary of government and war

Statement of Corporal don Pedro de Chaves

At the villa of Santa, New Mexico, on the 1st of July, 1715, I, don Juan Ygnacio Flores Mogollón, governor and captain general of these provinces for his majesty, say that having initiated the proceedings on the 4th of May of the prior year of 1713 against Bartolomé Garduño and Carlos López, for the said Garduño having taken the said Carlos López with him without my permission or the permission of his corporal, which notice was given to me by don Pedro de Chaves, corporal of the escort, the proceedings have not been followed until now. It being most important that they are carried out against both of them,[12] I ordered that the said don Pedro de Chaves appear before me, and upon being present, I received his sworn statement which he made before God and to the sign of the Cross, promising to tell the truth.

Chaves was asked if the notification which he gave to me was true, and if it is contained in that which was read to him at the beginning of the proceeding. He said that it was true that on the day Bartolomé Garduño left from El Paso, he [Garduño] took Carlos López from the escort of which this declarant was the corporal. Garduño was asked how he could take the soldier from the squadron. Garduño answered that he had the right to take him, being that he was the captain of the campaign, and he [Chaves] in all sincerity was persuaded that it could be possible, although at the head of the proceedings, it is seen where he [Garduño] told him [Chaves] that he had a verbal order from him [Chaves] which allowed Garduño to take López. But he was

misinformed, because Garduño was not told that he could take him [López], and there was no one present to verify this, as this [discussion] occurred in the street.¹³ In order to better assure all this, he [Chaves] said that he had a letter from his majesty [the viceroy] that he [Chaves] brought with him, and upon turning it over to the governor, all of his companions from the escort said that they came [back to Santa Fe] without López.¹⁴ Chaves said that this was the truth regarding his sworn statement which he has made, and which he affirmed and ratified, and he said that he was thirty-eight years of age and he signed it along with me and my secretary of government and war.
      don Juan Ygnacio Flores Mogollón (rubric)
      Pedro de Chaves (rubric)
    by order of the governor and captain general
      Roque de Pinto (rubric)
      Secretary of government and war

Statement of the Corporal Lorenzo Rodríguez¹⁵

 At the villa of Santa Fe, New Mexico, on the 2nd of July, 1715, I, said governor and captain general, in order to continue with the investigation of this case, made appear before me the corporal of the squadron, Lorenzo Rodríguez, from whom upon being present I received his sworn statement which he made to God, Our Lord, and to the sign of the Cross, regarding the charges, to which he promised to tell the truth as to what he was asked.

 He was asked if on the 10th of March of the previous year of 1713, he went as one of the soldiers on the escort in which don Pedro de Chaves was the corporal, to the royal presidio of El Paso, convoying don Felix Martínez and Bartolomé Garduño, who were going to Mexico City. He said that he was with the escort as one of the soldiers, as the question asks. He was asked if he knew if the said Bartolomé Garduño had taken along with him a soldier who was with the said escort by the name of Carlos López without my permission or that of his corporal, don Pedro de Chaves. He said that he knew that Bartolomé Garduño had taken Carlos López with him, as they returned to this villa [Santa Fe] without him, but he does not know if the corporal had allowed Garduño to take him. He said that all of his companions from the escort knew this, which included Ramón de Medina,¹⁶ Pedro Segura,¹⁷ and the others.¹⁸ He does not know, or has not heard, if Carlos López had my permission to go with the said Garduño. He said that everything that he has stated is the truth regarding the sworn statement which he has made and which he affirmed and ratified. He said that he was thirty-five years of age, and he signed it along with me, the said governor, and with my secretary of government and war.
      don Juan Ygnacio Flores Mogollón (rubric)
      Lorenzo Rodríguez (rubric)
    by order of the governor and captain general
      Roque de Pinto (rubric)
      Secretary of government and war

Statement of Ramón de Medina

    Continuing, I, said governor and captain general, in order to proceed with the investigation of this cause, made to appear before me Ramón de Medina, a soldier of this presidio, and one of those who escorted don Felix Martínez and Bartolomé Garduño when they left for Mexico in March of the prior year of 1713, for which the corporal was don Pedro de Chaves. Upon being present, I received his [Medina's] sworn statement which he made to God, Our Lord, and to the sign of the Cross, promising to tell the truth regarding whatever he was asked. He was asked if he went on the escort which is expressed above. He said that he was one of the soldiers on the said escort of which don Pedro de Chaves was the corporal. He was asked if the said Bartolomé Garduño took along with him the soldier Carlos López without my permission or that of Corporal don Pedro de Chaves. He said that he knew that the said Garduño had taken along with him the said soldier Carlos López, but he does not know if he had permission or not, and that he had heard the said Bartolomé Garduño tell Corporal don Pedro de Chaves that he was taking the soldier Carlos López with him because he was not feeling well, and that if his illness got him down, it was a must that the papers which he had under order of the governor got delivered. He said that don Pedro de Chaves told him that if he had been given such an order, to take him. He said that he had heard a number of soldiers say that he, Garduño, had told the same thing to General don Antonio Valverde [the El Paso presidio commander]. He said that the said Bartolomé Garduño had wanted to take him, the declarant, to Mexico, but he would not go because he was ill. He said that what he has stated is the truth regarding the sworn statement which he has made and which he affirmed and ratified, saying that he was twenty-three years of age, more or less. He did not sign because he did not know how; I, the said governor signed it, along with my secretary of government and war.

        don Juan Ygnacio Flores Mogollón (rubric)
    by order of the governor and captain general
            Roque de Pinto (rubric)
        Secretary of government and war

    At the villa of Santa Fe, New Mexico, on the 4th of July 1715, I, don Juan Ygnasio Flores Mogollón, governor and captain general of these provinces of New Mexico for his majesty, say that on the 6th of June of this year there was presented to me by General don Antonio Valverde, from his excellency, Duke of Linares of this New Spain, a dispatch dated the 6th of November of the prior year of 1714, at the request of Bartolomé Garduño, Carlos López, and Bernardino Fernández,[19] who falsely state that I had sent them on a business trip. At the bottom of the dispatch I have given my response so that your excellency, upon your review, will be informed of the truth and of the motive which I had for having made the above proceedings against the said Bartolomé Garduño and Carlos López, who, even though they returned to the kingdom, did not appear before me. Nor did I look for them, attending to the dispatch which was presented to me. Even though it was done with evil intent, it came to being as it was as honestly executed, and with the malice done, I had to do what I did.

First duke of Linares and Marqués of Valdefuentes, Gernando de Alencastre Noroña y Silva, viceroy from 1710 to 1716. Image from *Los governantes de México*, by Manuel Rivera, Vol. 1 (México, 1872).

Notwithstanding not having carried out proceedings against them, I was given notice that they had fled on the 24th of June [1715], taking along two others.[20] Because it is very unlikely that they will come up with new falsities to present to his excellency, I ordered that on the 1st of July [1715] there appear before me don Pedro de Chaves to explain the notice which he had given to me regarding the truth of the initial proceedings, which until the present day have been left in that uncompleted status. I also called upon two other companions who went on the escort so that the initial complaint would be complete, and so that it is for all time recorded. He [Garduño] did not go on business that I had given to him, but rather to take the mail, earning 350 pesos. I order that the letter [of 1715; see Exhibit 1] of Reverend Father Fray Juan de Tagle, who was the one who paid him for taking the residencia to don Francisco Cuerbo, and that [letter] was brought forth [by Garduño] when he returned and turned over to Juan García de la Riva,[21] who is the one who brought it to me along with the letter from don Alfonso Luis Cuerbo de Valdez [Exhibit 2], to be included with these proceedings. Also, since he did not bring, nor have I been given, the response to the numerous letters which he received and took according to his receipt, I order that it [the receipt, Exhibit 3] also be kept with these [proceedings], in case I need to submit them to his excellency so that he is aware of the intention of the said Bartolomé Garduño and Carlos López. I thus approved, ordered, and signed it, along with my secretary of government and war.

        don Juan Ygnacio Flores Mogollón (rubric)
        by order of the governor and captain general
        Roque de Pinto (rubric)
        Secretary of government and war

ORIGINAL DOCUMENT

        Jesus, Maria y Joseph Villa de Santa Fee de la Nueva Mexico

        Año de 1715

Causa criminal contra Bartolome Garduño por aver ydo de correo a la Cuidad de Mexico por Marzo del año pasado de 1713, y averse llebado sin lizensia a dicha Cuidad al soldado Carlos Lopez y todo lo que en estos autos constan.

        Juez el Governador y Capitan General Don Juan Ygnazio Flores Mogollon

Consta de 7 foxas

        Señor Governador y Capitan General Don Juan Ygnazio Flores Mogollon

Muy Señor y Dueño Mio. Recibi el de Vuestra Señoria y me alegro se mantenga en perfecta salud a cuya obstansia ofresco la que al presente gozo para que fuere Vuestra Señoria serbido ocuparla y Muy Señor Mio quando se concluio la residenzia de el General Don Francisco Cuerbo (que este en gloria) se sirbio Vuestra Señoria de favorecerme en que yo nombrase ala persona que avia de llebar dicha residenzia ala Cuidad de Mexico que por su trabaxo sele senalaba tresientos y sinquenta pesos y en la ocassion suplique a Vuestra Señoria que pues lo dejava ami elecion fuesse a llebar dicha residenzia el Sargento Bartolome Garduño quien me parecia era muy al proposito y que volviera con toda brevedad pues no llebaba otro negozio que lo de

dicha residenzia es quanto seme ofresse y pedir a Dios me guarde a Vuestra Señoria muchos años. San Yldefonso y Junio de 1715.
      Muy Señor Mio
   Beso la Mano de Vuestra Señoria Su Mu Servidor y
   Seguro Capellan Fray Juan de Tagle (rubric)

Señor Mio, en esta ocasion remito con Bartholome Sanchez Garduño los autos de la Residenzia que Vuestra Magestad tomo ami Padre y Señor que Santa Gloria aia para siendo servido se conforme con la sentensia que el Asesor dio que en remunersion de este favor viviere perpetuamente agradesido y sirviese en quanto se ofresiere a Vuestra Majestad cuia vida guarde Nuestro Señor muchos años. Mexico y Nobiembre 28 de 1714 años.
     Beso la mano de Vuestra Majestad
      Su muy seguro servidor
    Alphonso Luis Cuerbo y Valdes (rubric)

  [To] Señor Governador Don Juan Ygnazio Flores Mogollon

Digo yo el Capitan de Campaña Bartolome Garduño que rezevi de mi Governador y Capitan General Don Juan Ygnazio Flores Mogollon quien me despacho ala Cuidad de Mexico los pliegos siguientes _____

1 – Pliego de media vara de largo y tres dedos de alto rotulado al Lizenciado Don Francisco Flores Mogollon Alcalde Mayor de Quantitlan que es del servizio de Su Majestad. _____
2 – Dos pliegos senzillos rotulados al dicho con dos enboltorios de gamusa el uno con unos pellejos de lobo merino y el otro unos pinones _____
1 – Un pliego de una bara de largo rotulado al General Don Antonio Balverde Capitan de Presidio del Passo del servizio de Su Majestad _____
1 – Una carta sensilla a Don Juan Cortes del Rey _____
2 – Cartas para el Parral la una a Don Juan Phelipe de Orosco y la otra a Don Martin de Miquelena _____
2 – Cartas para Zacatecas la una a Don Martin Berdugo tesorero de aquella caxa y la otra con un enboltorito a Don Juan Callexas _____
[Total] 9

Todos los referidos pliegos y enboltorios he rrezivido y tengo en mi poder los quales llevandome Dios con bien entregare y traire repuesta o resivo de averlos dado y para que conste siempre lo firme en esta Villa de Santa Fee de la Nueva Mexico en nueve de Marzo de mill setezientos y treze años. =
     Bartolome Garduño (rubric)

Auto cavesa de proseso contra Bartolome Garduño y Carlos Lopez soldado de este Presidio

En la Villa de Santa Fee de la Nueva Mexico en quatro de Mayo de mill setezientos y treze años yo Don Juan Ygnazio Flores Mogollon Governador y Capitan General deste Reino y Provinzias de la Nueva Mexico por Su Majestad. Digo que haviendo despachado el dia diez de Marzo pasado deste año excolta al Presidio del Paso conboyando las personas de Don Felix Martinez y Bartolome Garduño y dicho Garduño soldado de este Presidio a quien conzedi lizensia por ynflujo y empeno de el Reverendo Custodio Frai Juan de Tagle para pasar ala Cuidad de Mexico asegurandome bolviera dentro de seis meses y con el remiti unos autos de residenzia del General Don Francisco Cuerbo de Valdez y otras cartas que constan por resivo que dejo firmado y para en esta Secretaria y de Cavo de dicha excolta yva Don Pedro de Chaves y aviendo sabido que dicho Cavo trajo menos un soldado de los que yban en dicha excolta llamado Carlos Lopez le hize pareser ante mi para que diese rason donde lo dejava y como lo executo sin orden mio, que respondio que dicho Bartholome Garduño el dia que salio del Presidio del Paso le dijo lo llevava con orden que tenia mio para ello y que el lo creyo indisputable, y lo permitio sin aver dado parte de averlo executado ami Theniente General Don Antonio Balverde Capitan del Real Presidio del Paso y considerando la sensilles con que lo executo condeseo de azertar no le ago el cargo que le corresponde a dicho Cavo Don Pedro de Chaves; y selo ago a dicho Bartholome Garduño por la malizia y falsedad con que obro en enganar a dicho Cavo y asi mismo le ago el cargo al soldado Carlos Lopez pues no devio seguir viaje tan delatado sin ber orden firmado de mi mano y mando que luego que se redusgan a este Presidio sean presos en el Cuerpo de Guardia para reziverles sus confesiones y oirlos en justizia si la tubiesen y castigar semejante maldad y enovedienzia para escarmiento de los demas y que sepan como an de cumplir con su obligazion, asi lo provei, mande y firme con mi Secretario de Governazion y Guerra =

Don Juan Ygnazio
Flores Mogollon (rubric)
Por mando del Señor Governador y Capitan General
Roque de Pintto (rubric)
Secretario de Governazion y Guerra

Declarazion del Cavo don Pedro de Chaves

En la Villa de Santa Fee de la Nueva Mexico en primero de Jullio de mill setezientos y quinze años yo Don Juan Ygnasio Flores Mogollon Governador y Capitan General de estas Provinzias por Su Majestad digo que por quanto hize auto caveza de proceso el dia quatro de Mayo del año pasado de mill setezientos y treze que es el de la buelta, contra Bartolome Garduño y Carlos Lopez por averse llevado dicho Garduño sin lizensia mia ni de su Cavo a dicho Carlos Lopez cuya notizia me dio Don Pedro de Chaves Cavo de excolta y quadarse en este estado dicha caveza de proceso asta oy, siendo preziso seguirla contra los dos mande campareziese ante mi dicho Don Pedro de Chaves quien estando presente le rezevi juramento que hizo por Dios Nuestro Señor y la Señal de la Cruz so cargo de el prometio dezir verdad y siendo preguntado si es zierto la notizia que me dio y consta en dicha caveza de proceso la qual le fue leyda? Dijo que es cierto que el dia que salio del Paso Bartolome Garduño se llevo a Carlos Lopez soldado de la excolta de que yva de Cavo este declarante, quien aviendo tenido la notizia paso a reconvenirle a dicho Bartholome Garduño que como se llevava el soldado de su Esquadra y le respondio puedo llevarlo este y el que ami me pareziere que para eso soi Capitan de Campaña y el con senzilles se persuadio a que podria ser asi y que aunque consta en la caveza de prozeso la notizia que me dio de que le avia dicho Garduño que tenia orden berbal mio para llevarlo se equiboco pues no le dijo que esto no fue en presenzia de naide suio que le encontro en la calle y alli selo dijo; y que para mas asegurarlo le dijo llevara Vuestra Majestad una carta para mi Governador la qual trajo y me entrego y que el averselo llevado lo diran todos los companeros de la excolta pues se bino sin el y que esto es la verdad so cargo del juramento que fecho tiene lleva en que se afirmo y ratifico y dijo ser de hedad de treinta y ocho años y lo firmo con migo y mi Secretario de Governazion y Guerra.

     Don Juan Ygnazio
     Flores Mogollon (rubric)
     Pedro de Chaves (rubric)
   Por mando del Señor Governador y Capitan General
     Roque de Pintto (rubric)
     Secretario de Governazion y Guerra

Declarazion del Cavo Lorenzo Rodriguez

En la Villa de Santa Fee de la Nueva Mexico en dos dias del mes de Jullio de mill setezientos y quinze años yo dicho Governador y Capitan General hize parezer ante mi para mas averiguazion en esta causa al Cavo de Esquadra Lorenzo Rodriguez al cual estando presente le rezevi juramento que hizo por Dios Nuestro Señor y la Señal de la Cruz so cargo del qual prometio dezir verdad en lo que fuere preguntado y siendolo si el dia diez de Marzo del año pasado de mil setezientos y treze salio como uno de los soldados en la excolta que yva de Cavo Don Pedro de Chaves al Real Presidio del Paso comboyando a Don Felix Martinez y Bartholome Garduño que yvan para Mexico? Dijo que yva en la excolta como uno delos soldados, como la pregunta refiere. Preguntado si save que dicho Bartholome Garduño se llevo con sigo un soldado de dicha excolta llamado Carlos Lopez sin lizenzia mia ni de su

Cavo Don Pedro de Chaves? Dijo que save que selo llevo con sigo dicho Bartholome Garduño a Carlos Lopez pues se bolvieron sin el a esta Villa pero que no save si el Cavo le reconvino dicho Cavo a Garduño sobre la llevada y que esto lo saven los demas companeros de la excolta como son Ramon de Medina, Pedro Segura y los demas, y que no save ni a oido dezir que llevase lizensia mia para yr en compania del dicho Garduño, Carlos Lopez; y que todo lo que lleva declarado es la verdad so cargo del juramento que fecho tiene en que se afirmo y ratifico y dijo ser de hedad de treinta y sinco años y lo firmo con migo dicho Governador y mi Secretario de Governazion y Guerra =

Lorenzo Rodriguez (rubric)
Don Juan Ygnasio
Flores Mogollon (rubric)
Por mando del Señor Governador y Capitan General
Roque de Pintto (rubric)
Secretario de Governazion y Guerra

Declarazion de Ramon de Medina

Y luego yncontinenti yo dicho Governador y Capitan General para mas averiguazion en este causa hize parecer ante mi a Ramon de Medina, soldado de este Presidio y uno delos que fueron excoltando a Don Felix Martinez y Bartholome Garduño quando salieron para Mexico por Marzo del año pasado de mill setezientos y treze en que yva de Cavo Don Pedro de Chaves al qual estando presente le resevi juramento que hizo por Dios Nuestro Señor y la Señal de la Cruz so cargo del qual prometio dezir verdad en lo que fuese preguntado y siendolo si fue en la excolta que arriva se expressa? Dijo fue como uno de los soldados en dicha excolta y de Cavo yva Don Pedro de Chaves. Preguntado se el dicho Bartholome Garduño se llevo consigo al soldado Carlos Lopez sin lizensia mia ni de dicho Cavo Don Pedro de Chaves? Dijo que save que dicho Garduño selo llevo consigo a dicho soldado Carlos Lopez que no save si fue con lizensia o sin ella y que oyo este declarante dezir a dicho Bartholome Garduño al Cavo Don Pedro de Chaves yo melo llevo con migo al soldado Carlos Lopez por que boi enfermo y si me apuran los males sera preziso el que cruze estos pliegos que traigo orden del Señor Governador; y dicho Don Pedro de Chaves dijo pues si Usted trae essa orden llevelo; y que oio dezir a algunos soldados le avia dicho lo mismo el dicho Garduño al General Don Antonio Balverde; y que el dicho Bartholome Garduño quiso llevar a este declarante a Mexico y se excuso diziendo estava enfermo y que la que lleva dicho es la verdad so cargo del juramento que fecho lleva en que se afirmo y ratifico y dijo ser de hedad de veinte y tres años poco mas o menos no firmo por no saver firmelo yo dicho Governador con mi Secretario de Governazion y Guerra =

Don Juan Ygnasio
Flores Mogollon (rubric)

Por mando del Señor Governador y Capitan General
Roque de Pintto (rubric)
Secretario de Governazion y Guerra

En la Villa de Santa Fee de la Nueva Mexico en quatro de Julio de mill setezientos y quinse años yo Don Juan Ygnacio Flores Mogollon Governador y Capitan General destas Provincias de la Nueva Mexico por Su Majestad. Digo que por quanto el dia seis de Junio pasado de este año seme presento un despacho por el General Don Antonio Balverde del Excellentisimo Señor Duque de Linares Virrey desta Nueva Espana su fecha de seis de Noviembre del año pasado de setezientos y catorze ganado a pedimento de Bartholome Garduño, Carlos Lopez y Bernardino Fernandez, y dezir estos con falsedad que yo los avia despachado a un negocio sobre que al pie del despacho di la repuesta para que Su Excellensia en vista de ella quedase enterado de la verdad y del motivo que tube para averles echo auto cavesa de prozeso al dicho Bartholome Garduño y Carlos Lopez quienes aunque entraron en el Reino no se pusieron en mi presenzia ni yo hize buscarlos atendiendo al despacho que seme presento pues aunque fue ganado con siniestro ynforme le binere como tal asta que enterado su execusion de mi verdad y su malizia me mandase lo que devia executar, y no obstante no haviendo echo deligenzia contra ellos tube notizia se huyeron el dia veinte y quatro de Junio, llevandose otros dos, y por que es mui dable buelvan con nuevas falsedades a representar a Su Excellensia mande el dia primero de Julio compareziese Don Pedro de Chaves y declarase la notizia que me dio sobre que conforme la caveza de proseso que asta el referido dia se avia quedado en aquel estado; y otros dos companeros de dicha excolta para que estubiese la cavesa en plenaria, y para que en todo tiempo conste no aver ydo a negosio mio, sino de correo ganando trezientos y cinquenta pesos. Mando se acomule a estos autos el papel del Reverendo Padre Frai Juan de Tagle quien selos pago por llevar la residenzia de Don Francisco Cuerbo la qual trajo a ora quando bino y entrego a Juan Garcia dela Riva quien mela trajo con carta de Don Alphonso Luis Cuerbo de Valdes, la qual mando se acomule a estos autos, y por quanto no trajo ni yo la e tenido repuesta de muchas cartas que quando la llevo le entregue y constan por su recivo se acomule este tambien por si nezesario fuese remitir los autos a Su Excellensia para que quede entendido del mal prozeder del dicho Bartholome Garduño y Carlos Lopez asi lo provei, mande y firme con mi Secretario de Governazion y Guerra.

Don JuanYgnasio
Flores Mogollon (rubric)
Por mando del Señor Governador y Capitan General
Roque de Pintto (rubric)
Secretario de Governazion y Guerra

Notes

1. According to Chávez, Captain Bartolomé Garduño was originally from Querétaro, Mexico, arriving in New Mexico after the Reconquest (Chávez, *Origins*: 185). By 1696 he is named as a witness in a land grant (SANM I #2). He was also listed as *segundo capitán de guerra* of the presidio in a 1712–1719 inventory, having previously been captain of the company (Christmas and Rau, "Una Lista": 197).
2. Carlos López, born around 1680, was a son of Nicolás López and Ana Luján, both natives of the Río Abajo district. He was a soldier at the El Paso Presidio and was one of the 100 soldiers allotted to the Santa Fe presidio in 1697, remaining a soldier up until 1718. In 1698 he married María Gonzales Apodaca, and in 1701 he and his brother Juan received a grant in the Pojoaque area. Eventually, he sold some of his land to Catarina Durán, widow of Pasquel Trujillo, named in SANM II #239f, below. He married Juana de Sedillo, daughter of Joaquín Sedillo and María Barba, in 1716. His mother may have been a cook at the governor's palace in 1712 (Kessell et al., *BOB*: 1167 n65; *RCR*: 127, 192 n171; Christmas and Rau, "Una Lista": 198; SANM I #1227; Christmas and Rau, *Pojoaque*: 10, 69-70).
3. Fray Juan de Tagle ministered to San Ildefonso for twenty-five years (1701–1726), also ministering to Santa Clara. He was vice-*custos* of the Holy Office of the Inquisition in 1704–1706 and *comisario* in 1720 (Norris, *Year Eighty*: 24, 50, 58, 63; Kessell and Hendricks, *RCR*: 28 n12; see also Doc. 15).
4. Governor Francisco Cuervo y Valdez.
5. This listing of the items suggests several questions: Why is the residencia that he was supposed to be delivering not mentioned in the list? Were the piñon nuts and the wolf skin included as a gift, or as trading items for Garduño and López, or payment for a debt? Was he responsible for delivering the items addressed to persons in Parral, Zacatecas, and Quantitlán, or if he did not, who did?
6. In effect, though Garduño was hired to deliver a specific item, he was acting as a courier or a kind of mailman for the presidio. At that time, the mail could go by a supply caravan, a special courier, or, as in this case, a courier going with a group of travelers accompanied by an escort (see Kessell and Hendricks, *RCR*: 202 n5). It has been estimated that the average day's travel for a courier was forty-five miles (Bloom, *New Mexico*: 16). Of related interest is a document from 1712, written by Governor Peñuela, stating that the viceroy had ordered that no mail be sent at the expense of the royal treasury unless it was of importance to the royal service. Peñuela, showing a certain independence, then stated that he was sending the mandate to the alcaldes at royal expense (SANM II #176). Also of interest, though over sixty years later, is a 1778 order from Viceroy Croix providing penalties for breaking open the mail, referring to mailbags with padlocks and reinforcements. No hides or wolf skins are mentioned (SANM II #730a).
7. See Doc. 1.
8. Martín Verdugo de Haro y Ávila held the office of royal treasurer for the city of Zacatecas (Kessell and Hendricks, *RCR*: 469 n2).
9. Felix Martínez had been appointed captain of the presidio for life by the viceroy but was dismissed from that position in October of 1712 by Governor Mogollón. He stayed in Santa Fe until March of 1713, when he left for Mexico City with the escort described in this document (Warner, "Felix Martinez": 61, 70).
10. Pedro [Durán] y Chaves was the son of Fernando Durán y Chávez II, a prerevolt settler who returned in 1693 with his family. Fernando and his family lived in Bernalillo and then Atrisco. Pedro was a squadron leader of the militia, alcalde mayor of Zuni, Acoma, and Laguna, and is listed as a presidio soldier in 1697. The referred-to escort is also discussed in Doc. 9. Though the original Spanish document uses the name Pedro de Chaves, Fray Angelico Chávez includes this same person as part of the Durán y Chávez family. To avoid confusion, the name Pedro de Chaves has been used in the English translation (Payne, "Lessons": 397, 398; Kessell et al., *TDC*: 298; Chávez, *Origins*: 160-61).
11. Don Roque de Pinto was given the rank of captain in December 1714. On May 31, 1715, he resigned, stating that he could not fulfill his responsibilities because of ailments for which there was no cure (Christmas and Rau, "Una Lista": 195-96).
12. See Doc. 8.
13. It appears that Garduño and Chaves talked about Garduño taking López with him in a conversation in the street. Here Chaves is saying that at that time he did not give Garduño permission to take López.
14. This is the escort described in Doc. 9.
15. Lorenzo Rodríguez, from Zacatecas, is shown in the 1697 list of presidio soldiers and also in the 1710–1712 presidio list of soldiers. In 1720 then–Corporal Rodríguez was killed in the Villasur expedition (Kessell and Hendricks, *RCR*: 188-89; Christmas, *Military Records*: 46).
16. Román de Medina was born in Zacatecas, the son of Santa Fe presidial soldier Diego de Medina. Román is shown in 1712 as transferring land in Santa Fe. He is also listed as soldier in the 1712–1717 presidio records. In 1720 Medina was killed in the Villasur expedition (SANM II #940; Christmas and Rau, "Una Lista": 200; Christmas, *Military Records*: 46).

17. Pedro Segura was from Zacatecas and is shown on the 1697 list of soldiers. He was killed with the Villasur expedition in 1720 (Kessell et al., *TDC*: 191 n154; Christmas and Rau, "Una Lista": 200; Christmas, *Military Records*: 46).
18. All three of these soldiers—Rodríguez, Medina, and Segura—were killed in the Villasur expedition of 1720. At least Rodríguez and Segura may have known each other since 1697, when they were the 1697 presidio list.
19. Bernardino Fernández was a soldier with the Santa Fe presidio in 1697. In 1713 he disappeared for two years while escorting a prisoner to Mexico City. The prisoner escaped, and Fernández did not return to Santa Fe until sometime later. It appears that he was in the Mexico City area at the same time as Garduño and López and could have returned with them (Christmas and Rau, "Una Lista": 197; Kessell et al., *TDC*: 127;SANM II #187).
20. See Doc. 8.
21. Juan García de la Riva was the son of Captain Miguel de la Riva from Mexico City. In 1708 Juan was *alcalde ordinario de segundo voto*, an examining justice, and in 1716 a member of the Santa Fe cabildo as *alcalde ordinario de primer voto* (Kessell and Hendricks, *RCR*: 318 n31; Cutter, *Legal Culture*: 95-96; SANM II #137b).

8

SOLDIERS FLEE KINGDOM; SEARCH BY PRESIDIO SOLDIERS PROVES FUTILE
June 25–29, 1715. Source: SANM II 223.

Synopsis and editor's notes: This second document from the summer of 1715 reports that after the three soldiers and two other New Mexicans left the kingdom, the presidio soldiers and Albuquerque officials were ordered to search for them and to question their relatives and other presidio soldiers, asking where the five men had gone and why. Though nobody questioned admitted to knowing anything much, their testimony provides some clues: Martín Hurtado said that as far as he knew, the men went to the pueblos, though he did not say which ones. He did say that when Fernández came around, he stayed with Arellano, and Garduño stayed with Ramón García. When questioned, Arellano's wife said that he told her they were going to look for pots, and García Jurado's wife said that he told her that he wanted some lengths of cloth. She said that he did not take anything, not even a tortilla, and just the clothes he was wearing. This information suggested that they went on a trading expedition to the pueblos that may not have been sanctioned had they asked for permission. After all, ten years or so before, Cristóbal de Arellano had been a soldier in Zuni country and would have been familiar with the area. He was later the alcalde mayor at the Zia pueblos. From other records we know that they returned, that they were not punished, and that they later held responsible positions.

Note that horses provided a key element of this investigation, since the fugitives needed horses for any kind of travel and did not seem to have any of their own, nor did they take any from the royal horse herd, at least according to the testimony of the horse herd guards. No one who was questioned admitted knowing anything more about the horses than they did about anything else, and the investigation was stymied.

Year of 1715

Criminal cause against Bartolomé Garduño,[1] Cristóbal de Arellano,[2] Bernardino Fernández,[3] Carlos López, and Ramón García Jurado[4] for having fled as fugitives from this kingdom of New Mexico without permission from their governor and captain general, etc.

Governor and Captain General

Sir, I inform your honor that on the day of San Juan, which was yesterday [June 24, 1715], about twelve o'clock noon, I received secret information that five men had fled from this villa, who were Bartolomé García, Carlos López, Bernardino Fernández, Cristóbal de Arellano, and Ramón García Jurado. Upon receiving the said notice I took action as quickly as I could to make sure that this was true, and looking for the said subjects, I was unable to locate any of them. Upon ascertaining that they had indeed fled, I left with all of the residents [of Albuquerque] to follow them up to where the horse herd was being guarded. On asking those who were there if they knew anything, there was no one who knew anything. From there I left accompanied by the corporal in charge, along with the other soldiers, in their pursuit going as far as Los Esteros de San Pablo,[5] following their tracks. Not being able to proceed any further, we turned back because, for one, we did not want to leave the horse herd at the risk of the Apaches and also because the residents who were spread out along the road in different places had very tired horses and as such were at the risk of the Apaches. Also, many of them had no arms, and some were without saddles. Therefore, your honor shall do as he sees best. This is all that I have to offer to your honor, whose life may God guard for many years. Albuquerque, June 25, 1715.

I kiss the hand of your honor
your most obedient servant
Luis García[6] (rubric)

To don Juan Ignacio Flores Mogollón, whom God may guard for many years, governor and captain general of this kingdom and provinces of New Mexico, castellan of the forces and presidios for his majesty at the villa of Santa Fe.

Governor and Captain General

Sir: Your honor should already know, because of what has been written to you by the alcalde mayor Luis García, that five men have fled, and it is badly felt by me that this could not be remedied because we received word late. Even though I felt that we should have followed them, I did not dare do it because I noticed that the horses of my companions were not in shape to catch up to them, and the end result would be that the horses would end up being hurt without any benefit. Also this settlement would have been left unprotected at a time that is very risky, being that at the present time there are rumors of an invasion, and if the invasion does occur at this villa, your honor should file charges against me being that this escort is here in order to safeguard it from the enemy, and only by the order of your honor could I leave it. This is all that I have to inform your honor, whose life may God guard for many years. Alburquerque, June 25, 1715.

I kiss the hand of your honor
your most obedient servant
Alonso García[7] (rubric)

To don Juan Ignacio Flores Mogollón, whom may God guard for many years, governor and captain general of this kingdom and provinces of New Mexico, castellan of his forces and presidios for his majesty, in the villa of Santa Fe.

At the villa of Santa Fe, New Mexico, on the 26th of June, 1715, I, don Juan Ignacio Flores Mogollón, governor and captain general of this kingdom and provinces of New Mexico and castellan of his forces and presidios for his majesty, say that having just received two letters, one from Captain Luis García, alcalde mayor of the villa of Alburquerque, and another one from the corporal of the escort, Alonso García, by which I am informed that on the 24th of the present month, Bartolomé Garduño, Bernardino Fernández, Carlos López, Cristóbal de Arellano, and Ramón García Jurado had fled from there without permission, and having followed them up to Los Esteros de San Pablo, they were unable to catch up to them as they fled the kingdom. I order that these documents be incorporated at the beginning of these proceedings, and I order that Sergeant Major don Alfonso Rael de Aguilar, along with the captain of the campaign and royal alférez, Eusebio and don Alonso Rael de Aguilar,[8] all from this villa, proceed immediately to that of Alburquerque and inquire as to how their escape was made possible, who aided them, and who provided the horses. For this, I give him the power and the faculty which is required. Also, I order my secretary of government and war that the testimony of everyone be written regarding the cause which the said has so that the originals can be included with these proceedings, and sent by mail to his majesty, the most excellent viceroy, so that he will do as he sees best and remedy the cause for this kingdom. I thus approve, order, and sign it with my secretary of government and war.

Don Juan Ignacio Flores Mogollón (rubric)
at the order of the governor and captain general
Roque de Pinto (rubric)
Secretary of government and war

Proceedings at the villa of San Felipe de Alburquerque on the 27th of June, 1715. I, Sergeant Major don Alfonso Rael de Aguilar, *juez de comisión*[9] in this case, and in order to follow this and argue for the truth to find out who assisted those fugitives and criminals and gave them the required assistance to be able to flee, I order that the corporal of the squadron, Francisco García, be questioned and asked if the said criminals had some horses in with the royal horse herd. Also to be questioned are Captain

Martín Hurtado,[10] father-in-law of Ramón García, the wife of Cristóbal de Arellano, Graciano Romero, and any other persons who could know anything, as required to get to the truth. So that it is valid, I signed it with my said witnesses, acting as presiding judge, due to the lack of a public or royal scribe, there not being one in this kingdom.

                Alfonso Rael de Aguilar (rubric)
                Alonso Rael de Aguilar (rubric)
                Eusebio de Aguilar (rubric)

Statement of Captain Martín Hurtado

At the villa of San Felipe de Alburquerque on the said day, month, and year, I, Sergeant Major don Alphonso Rael de Aguilar, juez de comisión in this cause in continuation of the proceedings performed by me, made appear before me Captain Martín Hurtado, resident of this said villa, who upon being present, received his sworn statement which he made to God, Our Lord, and to the sign of the Cross, under which he promised to tell the truth about everything he knew and in what he was asked as follows.

He was asked if he knew on what day and hour his son-in-law, Ramón García Jurado, Cristóbal de Arellano, Carlos López, Bernardino Fernández, and Bartolomé Garduño left from this said villa. He said that he had gotten notice that they left on the feast day of San Juan at about the hour of four o'clock in the afternoon, and that as far as his memory serves him, he was notified by Cristóbal Jaramillo, and that the said Jaramillo told him that the alcalde mayor had told him that everyone was to follow them. He then mounted his horse and went to catch up to the alcalde mayor and encountered him at the *paraje* of Los Gómez,[11] as they were returning from having followed the said fugitives, and then asked him [the alcalde mayor] if he was to continue following them [and said that] he would gladly go along so that he could return his son-in-law. The alcalde mayor told him that they had gone as far as the Esteros de San Pablo and had returned with their horses being very tired. This was his answer.

He was asked to state and declare the truth being that his son-in-law would have told him about his trip, secretly and in confidence, and he [may have] agreed not to say anything. He said that it had been quite a few days that they had spoken and that they were not close because he [Ramón García Jurado] had gambled away everything that he had, including his buttons, and that he had reprimanded him.[12] This was his answer.

He was asked if he knew where the said Ramón García and the others who fled with him had their horses. He stated that his son-in-law did not have a single horse because the one that he had he had gambled away. As for the others, he did not know where they had them. This was his answer.

He was asked if he knew in what homes the fugitives had been lodged. He said that what he knew was that Bartolomé Garduño, for a few days before they left, had been at the home of his son-in-law, Ramón García. This was his answer.

He was asked how he knows that the few days before they left the said Garduño was at the house of his son-in-law, and where did they spend their time during this time. He said that as far as he was told they went to the pueblos. He also said that when Bernardino Fernández came around, he spent time at the home of Arellano. As for Carlos López, he really does not know where he spent his time and where he was lodged. This was his answer.

He was asked if he knew or had been told where the fugitives had the horses and who had aided them for their trip. He said that he knows nothing regarding the question, because he has not gone anywhere in over three months. This was his answer.

He was asked how it is that he can say that he has not been anywhere in over three months, being that he has already declared that Cristóbal Jaramillo gave him the notice that the alcalde mayor had gone out to follow the fugitives. Where was it that you were when the said alcalde mayor gave the order to the residents to follow them? He said that he was at his home, and that he had just gotten there from irrigating his wheat. This was his answer.

He said that everything he has stated is the truth regarding his sworn statement which he has made and which he affirmed and ratified. He said that he was forty-five years of age, and he signed it along with me and my assisting witnesses acting as juez de comisión.

Alfonso Rael de Aguilar (rubric)
Martín Hurtado (rubric)
Alonso Rael de Aguilar (rubric)
Eusebio Rael de Aguilar (rubric)

Statement of the Corporal Francisco García[13]

Continuing, on the said day, month, and year, I, the said juez de comisión, in order to continue with the investigation of this cause made appear before me Corporal Francisco García, a soldier of the presidial castle of the villa of Santa Fe, from whom, upon being present, received his sworn statement which he made to God, Our Lord, and to the sign of the Cross under his proper right and to which he promised to tell the truth as to everything that he knew and what he was asked. He was asked if he knew on what day and what hour Cristóbal de Arellano, Ramón García Jurado, Carlos López, Bartolomé Garduño, and Bernardino Fernández fled from this Villa, and where they were going on their trip. He said that on the feast day of San Juan, the alcalde mayor had informed him that they had fled, but he did not know where they were going or what their intentions were. This was his answer.

He was asked where the said fugitives had their horses, and if he knew what person assisted and provided for them in order to flee. He said that he did not know where they had them, nor did he know who provided for them and assisted them. This was his answer.

He was asked in what homes in the said villa they had stopped at and who had lodged them. He said that Bartolomé Garduño had been at the house of Ramón García and Bernardino Fernández at the home of Cristóbal de Arellano. He had only seen them a few times, as they always would go and stay eight to ten days and then return, but this he knew only from word of mouth, as he always cared for their horses. Carlos López, on the day that he arrived, stopped shortly at the home of this declarant, but he did not see him anymore, as he left the following day. This was his answer.

He was asked to state the truth, and not to deny anything, if the said fugitives had left their horses with the royal horse herd, and as the corporal that he is, he should have definitely known if the horses were kept and taken from there. He said that they never left their horses with those of the royal horse herd, that he does not deny it, and that it was the truth. Even though he was asked other questions, he stated that he did not know anything else other than what he has stated, which is the truth, and what he knows about the sworn statement which he has made which he affirmed and ratified. He said he was forty years of age and did not sign because he did not know how. I, the said juez de comisión, signed it along with my assisting witnesses acting as juez de comisión due to the lack of a public or royal scribe.

Alfonso Rael de Aguilar (rubric)
Alonso Rael de Aguilar (rubric)
Eusebio de Aguilar (rubric)

Statement of doña Bernardina Hurtado[14]

At the villa of San Felipe de Alburquerque on the 28th of June, 1715, I, the said juez de comisión, in order to continue with the investigation of this cause made appear before me, doña Bernardina Hurtado, legitimate wife of Ramón García Jurado, from whom I took her sworn statement which she made to God, Our Lord, and to the sign of the Cross, under which she promised to tell the truth in everything that she knew and was asked. She was asked what motive and reasons her husband could have had for having fled, leaving without permission from the said governor and captain general. She said that he had never told her anything. This was her answer.

She was asked to say and declare the truth precisely, being that she was his wife and he should have told her why they were fleeing along with the motives for doing it. She said that he never confided in her because he did not want her telling her mother and father, who he was mad at. This was her answer.

She was asked if for the trip she had prepared any food or washed his clothes, which would have been a sign for making a trip. She said that for a sign of fleeing he had asked her to make him some lengths of cloth for the festive day of San Juan, but she did not think anything of it because it was a festive day. As for the clothes, he did not have anything other than what he was wearing. This was her answer.

She was asked if at the time of his departure, upon mounting his horse, what it was that her husband told her. She said that he did not say much other than, "good-bye my daughter" [adios hija]. This was her answer.

She was asked how long Bartolomé Garduño had stayed at her home. She said that he had never stayed for any length of time. When he came from outside the kingdom, he left immediately and returned within a few days and left once more, which was something he always did.[15] This was her answer.

Although other questions were asked over and over regarding the case, she said that she did not know anything other than what she has said and stated which was the truth regarding the sworn statement which she has made, and which she affirmed and ratified. She said she was twenty-three years of age and did not sign because she did not know how. I, the said juez de comisión, signed it along with my assisting witnesses acting as juez de comisión due to the lack of a public or royal scribe.

Alfonso Rael de Aguilar (rubric)
Alonso Rael de Aguilar (rubric)
Eusebio de Aguilar (rubric)

Statement of Graziana Romero[16]

Continuing, on the said day, month, and year, I, said juez de comisión, in order to continue with the investigation of this cause made appear before me Graziana Romero, legitimate wife of Cristóbal de Arellano, from whom I received her sworn statement which she made to God, Our Lord, and the sign of the Cross, under her proper right, and she promised to tell the truth regarding everything that she knew and what she was asked. She was asked what the reasons and the motives were for her husband to have fled and left without permission from the señor governor. She said that she did not know anything. This was her answer.

She was asked to tell the truth, being that she was his wife, he should have told her why he was fleeing. She said that she does not know anything, and that he told her nothing about this. This was her answer.

She was asked if for doing and executing his leaving, she should have definitely prepared food for him and washed his clothes. She said that she did not prepare food for him, not even one tortilla, and that he did not take any clothes at all other than what he was wearing. This was her answer.

She was asked if on the day that he left, what reasons he gave when he left. He told her that he was going to find some *ollas* [pot or kettle used in cooking].

This was her answer. She was asked how long had Bernardino Fernández stayed at her home. She said that he always stayed there when he was around, usually two or three days, then he would leave. Although she was asked other questions over and over regarding the said subject, she said that she did not know anything else other than what she has stated. She said she was thirty-three years of age and did not sign because she did not know how; I, said juez de comisión, signed it along with my assisting witnesses due to the lack of a public or royal scribe, acting as juez de comisión.

Alfonso Rael de Aguilar (rubric)
Alonso Rael de Aguilar (rubric)
Eusebio de Aguilar (rubric)

Statement of Captain Cristóbal Jaramillo[17]

Continuing, on the said day, month, and year, I, said juez de comisión, in order to continue with the investigation of this cause, made appear before me Captain Cristóbal Jaramillo, resident of this said villa of San Felipe de Alburquerque, who upon being present, received his sworn statement which he made to God, Our Lord, and to the sign of the Cross, under which he promised to tell the truth in everything that he knew and was asked. He was asked if he knew that Cristóbal de Arellano, Ramón García, Bernardino Fernández, Carlos López, and Bartolomé Garduño had fled from this said villa and for what reason. He said that he did not know anything; that the alcalde mayor of this villa, Luis García, had told him how they had gone as fugitives and they were following them. This was his answer.

He was asked who gave Captain Martín Hurtado the information that they had fled as fugitives and that the alcalde mayor had been in pursuit. He said that this declarant gave the said Hurtado the information and that they left together and they met up with the alcalde mayor along with others who went with him to pursue the fugitives. This was his answer.

He was asked if he knew at whose home the said fugitives had stayed. He said that he had heard that they came and went and that he does not know anything else. This was his answer.

He was asked if he knew where the said fugitives kept their horses; if they were with the royal horse herd. He said that he did not know anything, and although he was asked other questions, over and over, regarding the case, he said that he did not know anything else other than what he has stated, which is the truth and is what he knows regarding the sworn statement which he has made and which he affirmed and ratified after it was read back to him. He said that he was fifty years of age and did not sign because he did not know how; I, said juez de comisión, signed it along with my assisting witnesses acting as juez de comisión due to the lack of a public or royal scribe.

     Alfonso Rael de Aguilar (rubric)
     Alonso Rael de Aguilar (rubric)
     Eusebio de Aguilar (rubric)

Statement of Sebastián de Salas[18]

Continuing, on the said day, month, and year, I, said juez de comisión, in order to continue with the investigation of this cause, made appear before me Sebastián de Salas, resident of this said villa, from whom upon being present received his sworn statement which he made to God, Our Lord, and to the sign of the Cross, under which he promised to tell the truth in everything that he knew and what he was asked. He was asked if he knows or has heard at what place Bernardino Fernández, Carlos López, Bartolomé Garduño, Cristóbal Arellano, and Ramón García, kept their horses, and who aided and supplied them so that they could leave the kingdom without the permission of the governor and captain general. He said that he does not know a thing regarding the question. This was his answer.

He was asked if he knew at what homes the fugitives had stayed. He said that at times he saw Bernardino Fernández at the home of Cristóbal de Arellano, and Bartolomé Garduño at the home of Ramón García, and he knows that they went and came, but did not see them stay for any length of time. Even though he was asked other questions, over and over again regarding the cause, he said that he did not know anything else other than what he has answered, which is the truth regarding the sworn statement which he has made and which he affirmed and ratified. He said that he was forty-five years of age and did not sign because he did not know how. I, said juez de comisión, signed it along with my assisting witnesses, acting as juez de comisión.

Alfonso Rael de Aguilar (rubric)
Alonso Rael de Aguilar (rubric)
Eusebio de Aguilar (rubric)

Statement of Juan de Dios Martínez[19]

Continuing, on the said day, month, and year, I, said juez de comisión, in order to continue the investigation of this cause made appear before me Juan de Dios Martínez, soldier in the presidial castle of the villa of Santa Fe, who upon being present, took his sworn statement which he made to God, Our Lord, and the sign of the Cross, under which he promised to tell the truth in everything that he knew and what he was asked. He was asked how many horses Bernardino Fernández, Carlos López, Bartolomé Garduño, Ramón García, and Cristóbal de Arellano had with the royal horse herd, and at that time that they fled, what person or soldiers gave them to them. He said that they did not have a single horse in with the royal horse herd and that he did not see anyone give them any. This was his answer.

He was asked if he had heard where they kept the horses, who gave them to them, and who aided them in fleeing. He said that did not know where the horses were kept or who gave them to them. This was his answer.

He was asked if he knew at what homes in this said villa the fugitives stayed. He said that he had seen Bernardino Fernández at the home of Cristóbal de Arellano, Bartolomé Sánchez [Garduño] at the home of Ramón García, and Carlos López, when he returned from outside the kingdom, stayed at the home of Corporal Francisco García, but once he left he never saw him again. Although he was asked other questions regarding the issue, he said that he did not know anything else other what he has said, which is the truth and what he knows regarding the sworn statement that he has made and which he affirmed and ratified once it was read back to him. He said he was thirty-four years of age and he signed it along with me and my assisting witnesses acting as juez de comisión due to the lack of a scribe.

Alfonso Rael de Aguilar (rubric)
Juan de Dios Martínez (rubric)
Alonso Rael de Aguilar (rubric)
Eusebio de Aguilar (rubric)

Submittal of the proceedings

    At the villa of San Felipe de Alburquerque on the 29th of June, 1715, I, Sergeant Major don Alfonso Rael de Aguilar, in this case by virtue of the order of don Juan Ignacio Flores Mogollón, governor and captain general of this kingdom of New Mexico for his majesty, having followed this cause and the proceedings which are herein contained, I submit them to his honor so that upon his review he can determine that which is the most convenient.[20] As such I approved, ordered, and signed it with my assisting witnesses acting along with me as juez de comisión due to the lack of a public or royal scribe.

                      Alfonso Rael de Aguilar (rubric)
                      Alonso Rael de Aguilar (rubric)
                      Eusebio de Aguilar (rubric)

    It is found in twelve pages including this one and I rubricated it (rubric).

ORIGINAL DOCUMENT

Año de 1715

Causa criminal contra Bartholome Garduno, Xptobal de Arellano,
Bernarding Fernandez, Carlos Lopez y Ramon Garcia Jurado
Sobre
Haverse ydo fujitivos deste Reyno de la Nueva Mexico sin lizensia
de su Governador y Capitan General, ut supra

Señor Governador y Capitan General

Señor: Doi noticia a Vuestra Señoria como el dia de San Juan que fue ayer como alas dose del dia tuve notisia secretamente de que se yban juidos de esta Villa sinco hombres que fueron Bartolome Garduno, Carlos Lopez, Bernardino Fernandez, y Xptobal de Arellano y Ramon Garcia Jurado, y con dicha notisia passe luego a toda diligensia a saver lo sierto y buscando a los dichos sujetos no halle ninguno y conosiendo ser sierta su juida sali con todos los mas delos vesinos en su seguimiento asta llegar ala guardia de la cavallada y preguntando por ellos no huvo quien diera razon y de alli Sali con el Cavo Principal y demas soldados en su seguimiento y fuimos hasta Los Esteros de San

Pablo sobre sus rastros y no pudiendo pasar mas adelante nos bolvimos lo uno por no dexar la cavallada a riesgo de los Apaches y lo otro por que los mas de los vesinos se quedavan senbrados por el camino con las bestias cansadas y quedavan aresgados de los Apaches y tanvien por que munchos yban sin armas y algunos sin silla, assi Vuestra Señoria dispondra lo que fuere servido; es cuanto se ofrese desir a Vuestra Señoria, cuya vida Guarde Dios muchos años, Alburquerque, Junio 25 de 1715.

                      Beso la mano de Su Señoria,
                           Su Mayor Servidor
                            Luis Garcia (rubric)

[To]

Al Señor Don Juan Ignacio Flores Mogollon Guarde Dios Muchos Años, Governador y Capitan General deste Reino y Provincias dela Nueva Mexico, Castellano de Sus Fuerzas y Presidios por Su Majestad. En la Villa de Santa Fee.

                    Señor Governador y Capitan General

Señor, ya Vuestra Señoria sabra por la que le escrive el Alcalde Mayor Luis Garcia como se han juido esos sinco hombres y es sentido muncho el no haverlo podido remediar que no fue posible por que tuvimos la notisia tarde y aunque mi animo era seguirlo en forma no me atrevi por que vi que no estavan los cavallos de los companeros para poderlos alcansar y que lo que se sacava de seguirlos era muncha perdida de cavallos y sin provecho, y que quedava desamparada esta poblason en tiempo tan aresgado como es el presente pues andan voses de alsamiento y si susedra alguna ynvasion en esta Villa me haria Vuestra Señoria el cargo pues es estar aqui esta escolta es a fin de resguardarla de los enemigos y solo con orden de Vuestra Señoria pudiera desanpararla; es cuanto se ofrese desir a Vuestra Señoria, cuya vida Guarde Dios muchos años. Alburquerque y Junio 25 de 1715.

                      Beso la mano de Vuestra Señoria,
                           Su Mayor Servidor
                           Alonso Garcia (rubric)

[To]

    Al Señor Don Juan Ignacio Flores Mogollon Guarde Dios muchos años, Governador y Capitan General de este Reino y Provincias dela Nueva Mexico, Castellano de Sus Fuerzas y Presidios por Su Magestad en la Villa de Santa Fee

    En la Villa de Santa Fee dela Nueva Mexico en veinte y seis dias del mes de Junio de mill setezientos y quinze años, yo Don Juan Ignacio Flores Mogollon

Governador y Capitan General de este Reyno y Provincias dela Nueva Mexico y Castellano de Sus Fuerzas y Presidios por Su Magestad: Digo que por quanto acavo de recivir dos papeles del Capitan Luis Garcia, Alcalde Maior de la Villa de Alburquerque el uno, y el otro del Cavo dela Escolta Alonso Garcia, en que me notizian averse huido sin lizenzia el dia veinte y quatro del corriente Bartholome Garduno, Bernardino Fernandez, Carlos Lopez, Xptoval de Arellano, y Ramon Garcia Jurado; quien haviendolos seguido asta los Esteros de San Pablo no los pudieron alcansar que yvan fuera del Reino cuyos papeles mando se acomule a este auto cavesa de proceso y mando salga luego de esta Villa el Sargento Maior Don Alfonso Rael de Aguilar con el Capitan de Campana y Alferez Real, Don Alonso Rael y Eusebio Rael, ala de Alburquerque a ynquirir como executaron esta fuga; quienes la fomentaron para ella y dieron cavallos; que para todo le doy el poder y facultad que se require; y asi mismo mando ami Secretario de Governazion y Guerra aga sacar ala letra testimonio de las caussas que los referidos tienen para unir con este auto, los originales y azer correo de Su Magestad al Excellentisimo Señor Virrey para que de las providenzias que convengan con la brevedad que requiere el remedio que nezesita poner en este Reino, asi lo provei mande y firme con mi Secretario de Governazion y Guerra =
    Don Juan Ignacio
    Flores Mogollon (rubric)
Por mando del Señor Governador y Capitan General
    Roque de Pinto (rubric)
    Secretario de Governazion y Guerra

Autos

En la Villa de San Phelipe de Alburquerque en veynte y siete dias del mes de Junio de mil setezientos y quinze años yo el Sargento Mayor Don Alfonso Rael de Aguilar, Juez de Comision en esta caussa y para seguirla y aberiguar la verdad quien los fomento alos fujitivos y reos en ella con el avio nezesario fueron hazer desta fuga mando se exsamine al Cavo de Esquadra Francisco Garcia y sele pregunte que si dichos reos tenian algunos cavallos en el Real de la Cavallada y asi mismo al Capitan Martin Hurtado suegro de Ramon Garcia y ala muger de Xptobal de Arellano, Granciana Romero, y alas demas personas que reconozia de por comunmente y ser nezessario hasta yndagar la verdad, y para que conste lo firme con los testigos ynfrascriptos de mi assistenzia acutuando como Juez Rezeptor a falta de Scribano Publico y Real que no lo ay en este Reyno =
    Alphonso Rael de Aguilar (rubric)
    Alonso Rael de Aguilar (rubric)
    Eusebio de Aguilar (rubric)

Declarazion del Capitan Martin Hurtado

En la Villa de San Phelipe de Alburquerque en dicho dia mes y año yo el Sargento Mayor Don Alphonso Rael de Aguilar Juez de Comision en esta caussa en seguimiento del auto por mi proveydo hize parezer ante mi al Capitan Martin Hurtado vezino de esta dicha Villa al qual estando presente le rezevi juramento que hizo por Dios Nuestro Señor y una Señal de Cruz de bajo de cuyo cargo prometio de dezir verdad en todo quanto supiere y le fuere preguntado y haviendolo sido; si save que dia y a que ora se fueron de esta dicha Villa su yerno Ramon Garcia Jurado, Xptobal de Arellano, Carlos Lopez, Bernardino Fernandez y Bartolome Garduno. Dijo que el dia de San Juan tubo la notizia como alas quatro de la tarde, y que Xptobal de Jaramillo le dio dicha notizia en su memoria de este declarante, y que el dicho Jaramillo le dijo que el Alcalde Maior avia dicho que todos los siguiessen y luego monto a cavallo y fue en siguimiento de su Alcalde Mayor y lo encontro en el Paraje de los Gomez que ya benia de buelta de seguir a dichos fuxitivos y le dijo que si determinaba bolverlos a seguir yria muy gustosso por tal de bolver a su yerno a lo qual respondio que havian llegado hasta los Esteros de San Pablo y que llegaron con los cavallos cansados y esto responde _____

Preguntado diga y declare la verdad pues siendo su yerno le havia de comunicar su viaje y hazer en toda confianza de guardarle secreto. Dijo que havia muchos dias que no se comunicaban con este declarante y estaban de quiebra por occasion de haber jugado quanto tenia hasta los botones y que este declarante lo reprimendio, y esto responde _____

Preguntado que donde tenia los cavallos el dicho Ramon Garcia y los demas que con el hizieron fuga. Dijo que el dicho su yerno no tenia ningun cavallo por que uno que tenia lo havia jugado y que los demas que se huyeron no save donde los tenian y esto responde _____

Preguntado que en que cassas los havian ospedado a los dichos fujitivos. Dijo que lo que save es que Bartholome Garduno los pocos dias que salian benia a esta Villa paraba en cassa de Ramon Garcia su yerno, y esto responde _____

Preguntado que como dize que los pocos dias que salian benir a esta Villa paraba en casa de su yerno el dicho Garduno; pues todo el tiempo que aqui vinieron donde estubieron. Dijo se yban a los Pueblos segun tubo notizia y que Bernardino Fernandez paraba quando benia en cassa de Arellano y Carlos Lopez no save justamente donde paraba y se ospedaba, y esto responde _____

Preguntado si save o tubo notizia a donde tenian los cavallos dichos fujitivos y quien los avio para executar dicho viaje. Dijo que save nada de lo que la pregunta refiere por que no a salido de fuera mas aya de tres meses, y esto responde _____

Preguntado como dise que amas de tres meses que no sale de su cassa pues tiene ya declarado que Xptobal Xaramillo le dio la notizia de que el Alcalde Maior salio en seguimiento de dichos fujitivos; pues donde se hallava quando el dicho Alcalde Mayor dio orden que todos los vezinos los siguieran. Dijo que estava en su cassa y que havia benido de regar su trigo, y esto responde _____

Y que todo lo que tiene dicho es la verdad por el juramento que fecho tiene en que se afirmo y ratifico y dijo ser de hedad de quarenta y zinco años y lo firmo con migo y los testigos de mi asistenzia actuando como Juez Rezeptor =

Alphonso Rael de Aguilar (rubric)
Martin Hurtado (rubric)
Alonso Rael de Aguilar (rubric)
Eusevio Rael de Aguilar (rubric)

Declarazion del Cavo Francisco Garcia

Luego yncontinenti en dicho dia, mes y año yo dicho Juez de Comision para la aberiguazion de esta caussa hize parecer ante mi al Cavo Francisco Garcia soldado del Castillo Presidial de la Villa de Santa Fee al qual estando presente le rezivi juramento que hizo por Dios Nuestro Señor y una Senal de Cruz en forma de derecho debajo de cuyo cargo prometio de dezir verdad en todo quanto supiere y le fuere preguntado y haviandolo sido, si sabe que dia y a que hora se huyeron y hizieron fuga de esta dicha Villa Xptobal de Arellano, Ramon Garcia Jurado, Carlos Lopez, Bartholome Garduno y Bernardino Fernandez y para donde hera su yntenzion hazer su viaje. Dijo que el dia de San Juan supo por el Alcalde Maior que se havian huydo y que no save para donde ni con que yntenzion y esto responde _____

Preguntado donde tenian los cavallos los dichos fujitivos y si save que persona los fomento y avio para hazer dicho fuga. Dijo que no save donde los tenian, ni tampoco save quien los avio y fomento y responde _____

Preguntado en que cassas de esta dicha Villa havian parado y los havian ospedado. Dijo que Bartholome Garduno parava en cassa de Ramon Garcia, Bernardino Fernandez en la cassa de Xptobal de Arellano, y muy pocas vezes los vido por que siempre yban y se estaban ocho y diez dias y venian, y luego se yban y esto lo oyo dezir por que este declarante se estaba cuydando su cavallada y Carlos Lopez el dia que llego paro en su cassa deste declarante y no lo bolvio a ver mas, por que otro dia se fue, y esto responde _____

Preguntado diga y declare la verdad y no la niegue si los dichos fujitivos tenian sus cavallos en el Real dela cavallada y como Cavo que es prezissamente devia saver los cavallos que entran y sacan, y asi diga lo que save en esta pregunta. Dijo que nunca metieron sus cavallos en el Real de la cavallada, pues no lo negara sino que dijera la verdad y aunque sele hizieron otras preguntas y rrepreguntas alas tocantes dijo que no save mas que lo que tiene dicho y declarado que es la verdad y lo que save por el juramento que fecho tiene en que se afirmo y ratifico y dijo ser de hedad quarenta años y no firmo por no saver firmelo yo dicho Juez de Comision con los testigos de mi asistenzia actuando ante mi como Juez Rezeptor a falta de Scribano Publico y Real =

Alphonso Rael de Aguilar (rubric)
Alonso Rael de Aguilar (rubric)
Eusebio de Aguilar (rubric)

Declarazion de Dna. Bernardina Hurtado

En la Villa de San Phelipe de Alburquerque en veynte y ocho dias del mes de Junio de mill setezientos y quinse años yo dicho Juez de Comision para la aberiguazion desta caussa hize parecer ante mi a Dna. Bernardina Hurtado muger legitima de Ramon Garcia Jurado ala qual estando presente le resevi juramento que hizo por Dios Nuestro Señor y una Señal de Cruz de bajo de cuyo cargo prometio de dezir verdad en todo quanto supiere y le fuere preguntado y haviendola sido que motivo y que caussas tubo el dicho su marido para haver hecho fuga y haverse ydo sin lizenzia del Señor Governador y Capitan General. Dijo que no lo save por que nunca le comunico nada y esto responde _____

Preguntada, diga y declare la verdad pues siendo su muger presisamente le avia de comunicar dicha fuga y los motivos que tenia para hazerlo. Dijo que nunca hiso confianza de ella el dicho su marido por ocasion de que no selo dijiera esta declarante a su madre y a su padre con quien estava enojado el dicho su marido y esto responde _____

Preguntada que si para hazer el viaje presisamente le havia de hazer bastimento y labarle la rropa y para esto le havia de dezir como hera para hazer dicha fuga. Dijo que para haser dicha fuga le mando hazer unos panos para el dia de San Juan discuvriendo esta declarante que por ser dia festivo la mandava hazer y que la rropa no tenia mas que lo que tenia en el cuerpo y responde _____

Preguntada que al tiempo de la partenzia y de suvir a cavallo que rasones le dijo y comunico el dicho su marido. Dijo que no le dijo cossa alguna sino es que se despidio diziendole adios hija, y esto responde _____

Preguntada quanto tiempo estubo en su cassa Bartholome Garduno. Dijo que nunca estubo de asiento por que luego que vino de tierra afuera se fue y de alli a unos dias vino y se bolbio a yr y desta manera andava y esto responde _____

Y anque se le hizieron otras preguntas y rrepreguntas al caso tocante dijo que no save mas de lo que tiene dicho y declarado que es la verdad por el juramento que fecho tiene en que se afirma y ratifico y que es de hedad de veynte y tres años y que no firmo por no saver firmelo yo dicho Juez con los testigos de mi asistenzia actuando ante mi como Juez Rezeptor a falta de Scribano Publico y Real =

    Alphonso Rael de Aguilar (rubric)
    Alonso Rael de Aguilar (rubric)
    Eusevio de Aguilar (rubric)

Declarazion de Graziana Romero

Luego yncontinenti en dicho dia, mes y año yo dicho Juez de Comision para la aberiguazion desta caussa hize parezer ante mi a Graziano Romero muger legitima de Xptobal de Arellano ala qual estando presente le rezevi juramento que hizo por Dios Nuestro Señor y una Senal de Cruz en forma de derecho de bajo de cuyo cargo prometio dezir verdad en todo quanto supiere y le fuere preguntado y haviendola sido que caussas y motivos tubo el dicho su marido para haver hecho fuga y haversse ydo sin lizensia del Señor Governador. Dijo que no save nada, esto responde _____

Preguntada diga y declare la verdad pues siendo su muger selo havia de comunicar como queria hazer dicha fuga. Dijo que no save nada y nunca le comunico nada de esto, y responde _____

Preguntada que para hazer y executar dicha fuga presisamente le avia de hazer bastimento y componerle y laberle su rropa. Dijo que no le hiso bastimento ni una tortilla y que no llevo ninguna ropa sino es la que tenia y responde _____

Preguntada que el dia que se fue el dicho su marido que razones de dijo quando se despidio. Dijo que se yba a buscar unas ollas y esto responde _____

Preguntada quanto tiempo estubo en su cassa de esta declarante Bernardino Fernandez. Dijo que siempre estubo de levante por que estaria dos o tres dias y se alargo mucho y aunque sele hizieron otras preguntas y rrepreguntas al casso tocantes dijo que no save mas delo que tiene dicho y declarado y que es de hedad de treynta y tres años y no firmo por no saver firmelo yo dicho Juez de Comision con los testigos ynfrascriptos de mi asistenzia a falta de Scribano Publico y Real actuando como Juez Rezeptor.

    Alphonso Rael de Aguilar (rubric)
    Alonso Rael de Aguilar (rubric)
    Eusevio de Aguilar (rubric)

Declarazion del Capitan Xptobal Jaramillo

Luego yncontinenti en dicho dia, mes y año yo dicho Juez de Comision para la aberiguazion de esta caussa hize parezer ante mi al Capitan Xptobal Jaramillo vezino de esta dicha Villa de San Phelipe de Alburquerque del qual estando presente le rezevi juramento que hizo por Dios Nuestro Señor y una Senal de Cruz debajo de cuyo cargo prometio dezir verdad en todo quanto supiere y le fuere preguntado y haviendolo sido si save que dia se fueron y hizieron fuga de esta dicha Villa Xptobal de Arellano, Ramon Garcia, Bernardino Fernandez, Carlos Lopez y Bartholome Garduno a que oras y por que caussa. Dijo que no save nada que el Alcalde Mayor desta Villa Luis Garcia le dio la notizia como se havian ydo fujitivos los susso dichos y que los yba seguiendo y esto responde _____

Preguntado que persona le dio la notizia al Capitan Martin Hurtado como dichos fuxitivos se yban y dicho Alcalde Mayor yba en su seguimento. Dijo que este declarante le dio dicha notizia a dicho Hurtado y salieron juntos y lo encontraron en el camino a dicho Alcalde Mayor con los demas que en su compania havian ydo a seguir a dichos fujitivos, y esto responde _____

Preguntado si save en que cassa paravan los dichos fujitivos. Dijo que oyo dezir que yban y benian y no save otra cosa y responde _____

Preguntado si save donde tenian dichos fujitivos sus cavallos si los tenian en el Real de la cavallada. Dijo que no supo nada y aunque sele hizieron otras preguntas y rrepreguntas al caso tocantes dijo que no save mas delo que tiene dicho y declarado que es la verdad y lo que save por el juramento que fecho tiene en que se afirmo y ratifico haviendole leydo esta su dicha y declarazion y dijo ser de hedad de cinquenta años y no firmo por no saver firmelo yo dicho Juez de Comision con los testigos de mi asistenzia actuando ante mi como Juez Rezeptor a falta de Scribano Publico y Real.

      Alphonos Rael de Aguilar (rubric)
      Alonso Rael de Aguilar (rubric)
      Eusevio de Aguilar (rubric)

Declarazion de Sevastian de Salas

 Luego incontinente en dicho dia mes y año yo dicho Juez de Comision para la aberiguazion de esta caussa hize parezer ante mi a Sevastian de Salas vezino de esta dicha Villa al qual estando presente le resevi juramento que hizo por Dios Nuestro Señor y una Señal de Cruz de bajo de cuyo cargo prometio de dezir verdad en todo quanto supiere y le fuere preguntado y haviendole sido si save o a oydo de dezir en que paraje tenian los cavallos Bernardino Fernandez, Carlos Lopez, Bartholome Garduno, Xptobal Arellano y Ramon Garcia y que persona los avio y fomento para que executaran la fuga sin lizensia del Señor Governador y Capitan General haviendose ydo a tierra fuera. Dijo que no save cossa de lo que la pregunta refiere y responde _____

 Preguntado si save en que cassas pararon los dichos fujitivos. Dijo que algunas vezes vido a Bernardino Fernandez en la cassa de Xptobal de Arellano y a Bartholome Garduno en la cassa de Ramon Garcia y que supo que yban y benian y no los vio estar de asiento y aunque sele hizieron otras preguntas y rrepreguntas tocante a esta caussa dijo que no save mas de lo que tiene dicho que es la verdad por el juramento que fecho tiene en que se afirmo y ratifico y dijo ser de hedad de quarenta y zinco años y no firmo por no saver firmelo yo dicho Juez con los testigos de mi asistenzia actuando como Juez Rezeptor.

      Alphonso Rael de Aguilar (rubric)
      Alonso Rael de Aguilar (rubric)
      Eusevio de Aguilar (rubric)

Declarazion de Juan de Dios Martinez

 Luego yncontinenti en dicho dia, mes y año yo dicho Juez de Comision para la aberiguazion de esta caussa hize parezer ante mi a Juan de Dios Martinez soldado del Castillo Presidial de la Villa de Santa Fee al qual estando presente le rezevi un juramento que hizo por Dios Nuestro Señor y una Señal de Cruz de bajo de cuyo cargo prometio de dezir verdad en todo quanto supiere y le fuere preguntado y haviendole sido si save quantos cavallos tenian en el Real de la cavallada Bernardino Fernandez, Carlos Lopez, Bartholome Garduno, Ramon Garcia y Xptobal de Arellano y quando hizieron la fuga que persona o soldados los entrego. Dijo que no tenian los susso dichos ningun cavallo en el Real de la cavallada y que no les conozio ninguno y esto responde _____

Preguntado o a oydo dezir donde las tenian las cavalgaduras, quien se las dio y fomento para executar dicha fuga. Dijo que no lo save donde tenian sus cavallos ni quien selas dio y esto responde _____

Preguntado si save en que cassa de esta dicha Villa pararon los dicho fujitivos. Dijo que Bernardino Fernandez lo vio en cassa de Xptobal de Arellano, Bartolome Sanchez (Garduno) en la cassa de Ramon Garcia y a Carlos Lopez quando vino de tierra fuera paro en cassa del Cavo Francisco Garcia y que luego se fue y no lo vio nunca despues y aunque sele hizieron otras preguntas tocantes a esta materia dijo que no save mas de lo que tiene dicho que es la verdad y lo que save por el juramento que fecho tiene en que se afirmo y ratifico haviendole leydo este su dicho y declarazion y dijo ser de hedad de treynta y quatro años y lo firmo con migo y los testigos de mi asistenzia actuando ante mi como Juez Rezeptor a falta de Scribano =

    Alphonos Rael de Aguilar (rubric)
    Alonso Rael de Aguilar (rubric)
    Eusevio de Aguilar (rubric)

Auto de Remission

En la Villa de San Phelipe de Alburquerque en veynte y nueve dias del mes de Junio de mill setezientos y quinze años yo el Sargento Mayor Don Alphonso Rael de Aguilar Juez de Comision en esta caussa en virtud de orden del Señor Don Juan Ignacio Flores Mogollon Governador y Capitan General deste Reyno de la Nueva Mexico por Su Magestad, haviendo seguido esta caussa y hechas las deligencias que en ella constan hago remission a Su Señoria para que en su vista determine lo que hallare por combenynte, asi lo provey mande y firme con los testigos de mi asistenzia actuando ante mi como Juez Rezeptor a falta de Escribano Publico y Real =

    Alphonso Rael de Aguilar (rubric)
    Alonso Rael de Aguilar (rubric)
    Eusevio de Aguilar(rubric)

Ba en doze foxas
con esta y lo rubrique (rubric)

Notes

1. For Bartolomé Garduño and Carlos López, see Doc. 7.
2. Cristóbal de Arellano was born in Aguascalientes, New Spain, and was in New Mexico as a presidio soldier in 1697. In 1702 he was stationed in the Acoma and Zuni country, and by 1704 he was alcalde mayor and captain at San Ildefonso Pueblo. In July 1714, he was appointed captain of the campaign, taking the place of Bartolomé Garduño, who had resigned. In 1716, a year after this document was written, he was alcalde

mayor at Santa Ana, Jémez, and Zia Pueblos. His knowledge of the pueblos suggests that the group may have gone to one of them (Kessell et al., *BOB*: 566-67 n38; *TDC*: 129; Christmas and Rau, "Una Lista": 195-96).
3. As stated in Doc. 7, in 1713 Bernardino Fernández disappeared in New Spain while escorting a prisoner to Mexico City. The prisoner was Miguel Luján, who had been found guilty of killing his wife, Catalina de Valdés, and who escaped to take sanctuary in a church in New Spain. Since this is approximately the same time that Garduño and López were spending time in the south, it is possible that a connection between the three soldiers might have been taken place at that time (SANM II #187).
4. Ramón García Jurado's father was José García Jurado, from Mexico City, who came with his parents to New Mexico in 1693. José held many positions in New Mexico, including *procurador general* (attorney) for the Santa Fe cabildo and alguacil mayor, chief constable. Ramón was alférez real in the Moqui campaign in 1716. In 1723 he went to Mexico City to protest actions of Governors Valverde and Bustamante. He was alcalde of Bernalillo and other nearby pueblos in 1732 when he was accused of mistreating the Indians, and was banished to Zuni Pueblo for two years. In a document from 1744, he called himself *procurador de Albuquerque* (Chávez, *Origins*: 183-84; Cutter, *Protector*: 46, 75; *Legal Culture*: 101; Kessell et al., *BOB*: 111 n52, 218, 1160 n6).
5. The location of Los Esteros de San Pablo is not known at this time. It could be the marshy area south of Albuquerque, perhaps near or an alternative name for Los Esteros de Mejía, in what was the Atrisco area (Barrett, *Settlement*: 212, map 8). It is not shown on either of the Menchero or Miera y Pacheco maps.
6. See Doc. 5.
7. This is probably Alonso García de Noriega III, a son of Alonso II and brother to Luis García (Chávez, *Origins*: 181).
8. Two sons of Alfonso Rael de Aguilar I were Alonso and Eusebio. Alonso was made alférez of the Santa Fe presidio in 1713. He is probably best known for stabbing another soldier in 1715, as translated in Doc. 18. Alonzo served as a soldier, marrying Isabel Durán y Chávez, a sister to the Pedro Durán y Chávez mentioned in Docs. 7 and 9. According to Chávez, Eusebio was an alférez in 1716 and a guard at Laguna Pueblo in 1720 (Christmas and Rau, "Una Lista": 197; Kessell et al., *BOB*: 1172 n106; Chávez, *Origins*: 263).
9. The *juez de comisión* was a temporary appointee of the governor. The appointee could act as a magistrate and assist with the legal processing (Cutter, *Legal Culture*: 99).
10. See Doc. 9.
11. The Paraje de Gómez is not found on the Menchero or Miera y Pacheco map (Map 2, Appendix). It could be the site of the prerevolt estancia of Francisco Gómez Robledo on the Camino Real east of the Río Grande, near Atrisco (Barrett, *Settlement*: 212, map 8).
12. A prohibition of gambling was frequently mandated by the governors, for example, Vargas in 1702 and Peñuela in 1707, and many others after this time. Apparently, it was frequently ignored (see Doc. 4).
13. See Doc. 9.
14. Bernardina Hurtado was the daughter of Martín Hurtado and Catalina Varela Jaramillo and the second wife of Ramón García Jurado (Chávez, *Origins*: 197).
15. This behavior sounds unusual, but Garduño may have been regularly hired as a courier and used the García Jurado residence as a place to stay between trips. Doc. 7 describes him as a *reformado*, which usually means a retired soldier.
16. Graziana Romero was the daughter of Francisco Romero de Pedraza and Francisca Romero de Salas. Francisco Romero was an alcalde of Santo Domingo in 1664 and a notary for the cabildo in 1686. He and his family returned to New Mexico in 1693. From 1696 to 1704, he was a member of the cabildo (Chávez, *Origins*: 271; Scholes et al., *Domínguez de Mendoza*: 221 n32).
17. See Doc. 4.
18. Sebastián de Salas was from Seville, Spain, and a member of the Farfán-Velasco expedition of 1694. At one time he owned land in Pojoaque and Santa Cruz (Chávez, *Origins*: 278; SANM I #678, #927).
19. Juan de Dios Martínez, from Mexico City, is listed as a presidio soldier in a muster of 1704. He is apparently a different person than Juan de Dios Sandoval Martínez (Chávez, *Origins*: 227; Kessell et al., *ASA*: 222).
20. There is no indication of Governor Mogollón's decision regarding this matter. However, on July 1, 1715, a few days after the governor received the reports about the fugitive soldiers, he initiated proceedings regarding the irregular behavior of Garduño and López that took place earlier, in May of 1713. In that document, the governor says that he did not file charges at that time but would do so when the soldiers were returned to the presidio. There is, however, no document showing that he did so (Doc. 7).

9

ESCORT ATTACKED BY APACHES ON CAMINO REAL; GOVERNOR HOLDS COUNCIL OF WAR
August 2–9, 1713. Source: SANM II #198.

Synopsis and editor's notes: In the summer of 1713, after leaving the military escort at El Paso, Bartolomé Garduño and Carlos López, probably along with Felix Martínez, continued on to Mexico City (see Doc. 7). At the same time a caravan returned to Santa Fe under the same military escort of Pedro de Chávez. At the *paraje* or watering hole of El Muerto, part way through the Jornada del Muerto going north, the group was harassed by Apaches, and some horses and donkeys were killed and injured. This was nothing new for the site. Don Antonio de Valverde, the general at the El Paso presidio, had earlier sent a warning about depredations of the hostile Indians at El Muerto. Even before the 1680 revolt, there had been problems. Records show that on June 24, 1671, Apaches attacked the retinue of incoming governor don Juan Miranda at the Paraje de Muerto, killing four people and escaping with a drove of government mules (Scholes et al., *Domínguez de Mendoza*: 25, 142).

Because of the history of Indian attacks at the site, Governor Mogollón interviewed several witnesses about the 1713 Indian attack, including Pedro de Chávez and a traveler with the caravan, Juan de Archibeque. Each of the witnesses said that the Indians killed and injured some animals and then left. Having received the testimony, Mogollón then called a council of war (*junta de guerra*) of military officials and other respected persons, asking them if a campaign should be mounted against the Apaches. The first soldier to speak was for it, with the others against it, though several of the younger men, who had apparently traveled through the area, qualified their remarks by saying that those who spoke against war with the Apaches should go on a trip through the area. Note that Frenchman Juan de Archibeque, having returned to the colony under guard in 1694, was now considered worthy of being asked to participate in a council of war.

Jesus, Mary, and Joseph, Villa of Santa Fe
New Mexico
Year of 1713

Testimony of statements which were received from different corporals who went on escorts from this royal presidio to that of El Paso along with a council of war, with the originals being submitted to his excellency the Duke of Linares, viceroy of this New Spain, in eight pages.

At this villa of Santa Fe in New Mexico on the 2nd day of August, 1713, I, don Juan Ygnacio Flores Mogollón, governor and captain general of this kingdom and provinces of New Mexico for his majesty, say that, having received notice that on various occasions when trips have been made to the royal presidio of El Paso, there have been times when horses have been killed by the enemy Apaches at the Paraje del Muerto[1] and at Peñuelas. For this reason I order that statements be taken from the corporals who have been in charge of the said escorts.

In addition, I have received a letter from General don Antonio de Valverde dated the 16th of July in which he touches on the risks of such by the Apaches who are supposedly at peace. This letter reads as follows: "Two days after [Captain Cristóbal] Arellano[2] got here [to El Paso], there arrived at this presidio the alférez Castrillón,[3] who this day proceeds to return on his trip and carries this to your honor, which within a short time should be received by your honor, and tells you about the care that should be taken and what should be done about this matter; and if your honor does not come up with a way to scare those Apaches at El Muerto, they will do something malicious. That is the place where they usually commit their bad deeds, and, if nothing is done, they will continue doing them. They continue to do this and continue to say that they are at peace. Your honor should resolve this matter whichever way is best done."

Upon receiving their [the corporals'] statements, I shall prove what has been occurring regarding this matter. I thus approved, ordered, and signed this with my secretary of government and war.

        don Juan Ygnacio Flores Mogollón
   by order of the governor and captain general
              Roque de Pinto
       Secretary of government and war

Statement of Alférez Salvador de Santistevan[4]

At the said villa on the said day, month, and year, I, said governor and captain general, in order to receive the statements which have been ordered by me to be taken from the corporals in charge of the escorts that have gone to the royal presidio of El Paso, made appear before me Salvador Santistevan, alférez of this company of this presidial castle, from whom I received his sworn statement which he made to God, Our Lord, and the sign of the Cross, and to which he promised to tell the truth.

He was asked what happened in the month of March of this year at the Paraje del Muerto with the Apaches when they were escorting the residents of this said presidio from the presidio of El Paso. He said that being at the spring of the said El Muerto watering the horses in the late afternoon, and upon preparing to leave, about thirty Apaches, more or less, came upon them to try to take the horses from them and they [the Apaches] killed a horse and a burro and wounded three mares with their arrows, although those did not die. The escort was then placed in a state of defense along with several of the residents, who were Francisco Lorenzo de Casados,[5] a captain; Juan de Archibeque;[6] and Agustín Luján.[7] Francisco Casados fired his arquebus[8] [early musket] at an Apache with a type of *perdigones* [bird-shot], which appeared to have hit his face according to the gestures which he made by shaking his body. Then after having taken the horses out onto flat land, he got his soldiers and the residents ready to stay alert all night to guard the camp and the horses, making sure that the Apaches did not try to take them, being that they were quite numerous.

In the morning, upon continuing their journey very alertly, they saw on a small hill at La Laguna a large number of Apaches yelling at them. That same night it had rained so much, they could not follow them, nor could the Apaches get close to them due to the heavy mud in which the horses would get stuck. Continuing on their trip, the Apaches kept following them at a distance to see if they could possibly steal their horses until they reached Paraje de Felipe Romero,[9] which was some forty leagues from the Aguaje del Muerto. Once they reached the said Paraje in the morning, they no longer saw them. This he says is the truth about what happened regarding the sworn statement which he has made, and upon his statement being read back to him he affirmed and ratified it. He stated that he was thirty-five years of age and did not sign it because he did not know how; I, said governor, signed it with my secretary of government and war.

don Juan Ygnacio Flores Mogollón
as per the order of the governor

Roque de Pinto
Secretary of government and war

Statement of Agustín Luján

At the villa of Santa Fe on the 3rd of August, 1713, I, said governor and captain general, made appear before me Agustín Luján, a resident of this villa, who is cited by the alférez Salvador de Santistevan in his statement, from whom I received his sworn statement, which he made to God, Our Lord, and the sign of the Cross, and he promised to tell the truth about what he was asked, and he was read the statement made by the said Alférez Santistevan.

He said that he was with the said alférez and the others whom he named at the Aguaje del Muerto watering the horses, and upon finishing, the Apaches, who were about twenty more or less, came upon them, and they shot and killed with their arrows one horse and one burro on the spot, and wounded three horses which belonged to a resident, of which one died the following day. The alférez then placed everyone on the defense and took the horses out into the flatland. Afterwards it rained heavily and he ordered everyone to take much care at the camp and with the horses, making sure that they [the Apaches] did not come upon them that night.

The next morning they left, and at the hill, which is called Las Espías,[10] which is immediately next to the lakes, they saw that the entire hill was full of Apaches, and when the day was dawning they heard much shouting. Continuing with their journey, this witness noticed that they [the Apaches] stopped following them during the day and traveled by night with bad intentions until when they were close to the place of Felipe Romero. Luján said that on the afternoon that the Apaches came upon them at the spring, Francisco Lorenzo Casados fired his arquebus with some type of bird-shot which appeared to him to have hit an Apache according to the gesture he made as he placed his hand on his face. This he says is the truth regarding his sworn statement that he has made which he affirmed and ratified. He said that he was fifty years of age. He did not sign because he did not know how; I, said governor, signed it with my secretary of government and war.

don Juan Ygnacio Flores Mogollón
by the order of the governor and captain general
Roque de Pinto
Secretary of government and war

Statement of Juan de Archibeque

At the said villa on the said day, month, and year, I, said governor, made appear before me Juan de Archibeque, resident of the this villa, from whom I received his sworn statement which he made to God, Our Lord, and the sign of the Cross. He promised to tell the truth as to what he was asked, which was, if he had come into this kingdom during the month of March, of this year from the royal presidio of El Paso with the escort which was headed by the alférez Salvador de Santistevan, and what happened at the Paraje del Muerto. He said that he came into this kingdom from the said presidio of El Paso with the escort and that from Peñuelas three residents and three soldiers went ahead of the others to see if there was water at the Aguaje del Muerto, which they did in fact find, and made smoke signals so that the people from the camp would take the horses to drink, which in fact they did. After the horses were done drinking, the Apaches came upon them and killed one horse and a donkey with their arrows as well as wounding three mares, one of which died. The alférez then placed the soldiers as well as the residents on the defense, and Captain Francisco Lorenzo de Casados fired his arquebus with a type of bird-shot, which, according to the gestures made by an Apache, appeared to have hit him.

After they took the horses out in the flat land it began to rain heavily until nighttime came and it got dark, at which time Alférez Santistevan ordered all the residents and the soldiers to be with great vigilance and care because he was afraid that the Apaches would attack the camp. About midnight they heard an Apache coming to the camp, but upon getting close his horse stumbled in a gopher hole [*tusera*] and he fell and fled. All that night and for the following two days the horses were left without grazing, and as such the thirty-three horses were quite tired. This he says is the truth regarding his sworn statement which he has made, which he affirmed and ratified upon his statement being read back to him. He added that five or six mornings later they found some tracks left by the Apaches which circled the horses. He said that he was forty-three years of age and he signed with me, the said governor, and my secretary of government and war.

don Juan Ygnacio Flores Mogollón

Juan de Archibeque

by order of the governor and captain general

Roque de Pinto

Secretary of government and war

Statement of Captain Francisco Lorenzo de Casados

At this said villa on the said day, month, and year, I, said governor and captain general, made appear before me Captain Francisco Lorenzo de Casados, from whom he received his sworn statement which he made to God, Our Lord, and the sign of the Cross, promising to tell the truth in what he was asked. Being read the statement of the Alférez Salvador de Santistevan, who cited him in his statement, Casados said that he came into this kingdom in the escort which was headed by the corporal, Alférez Salvador de Santistevan, in the month of March. And that from the Sitio de Peñuelas the said declarant along with three soldiers and two residents went to the Paraje and Aguaje del Muerto in order to find out if there was water for the horses, and having found that there was, they made smoke signals so that they could take the horses to drink, which they did. After they had finished, upon getting ready to leave, about twelve Apaches came upon them, with others that could be seen afoot at a distance, and with their arrows, they killed a horse, a burro, and wounded three mares, one which later died, and attempted to break up the horses. The soldiers and residents were placed on the defensive in order to take the horses onto the flat land. At the same time he saw that an Apache pointed his bow at him to fire an arrow at him, at which time he fired his arquebus with a type of bird-shot which appeared to have hit him. After they had gone onto flatter lands, where it started to rain heavily until it became night time, the alférez Santistevan ordered that all the residents and soldiers be on the alert with great care because he was afraid the Apaches would come into the camp. About midnight an Apache came to check the camp and being close his horse stumbled, throwing the Apache, who then fled, and upon fleeing they heard loud yelling.

In the morning they saw numerous Apaches in the small hill known as Las Espías, and that night the horses were left without grazing, and during the following days the thirty-three horses were very tired. Afterwards, every night they [the Indians] encircled them with smoke and in the morning tracks could be seen around the horses, which meant that they came with the intention to steal the horses. This he says is the truth regarding the sworn statement which he has made, and he affirmed and ratified it, and said that he was forty-six years of age, and he signed it with me, the said governor, and my secretary of government and war.

don Juan Ygnacio Flores Mogollón
Francisco Lorenzo Casados
by order of the governor and captain general
Roque de Pinto
Secretary of government and war

Statement of don Pedro de Chávez[11]

At this villa of Santa Fe on the 4th of August, 1713, I, said governor and captain general, made appear before me don Pedro Durán y Chávez, corporal of the squadron of the company of this presidial castle, who went as escort and escorted those who left in March with Captain don Felix Martínez and Bartolomé Garduño,[12] who were taking the mail to the City of Mexico.[13] I received a sworn statement from him that he made to God, Our Lord, and the sign of the Cross, to which he promised to tell the truth in what he was asked and to tell what happened during his trip from this presidio to that of El Paso and on his return from that one to this one. He said that he left from this presidio for that of El Paso on the 8th of March of this same year escorting Captain don Felix Martínez and Bartolomé Garduño, who were going to the city of México, and that from this villa down to the said presidio of El Paso the trip went without any problem. However, on their return, which was in the month of April, at the Aguaje and Paraje del Muerto, upon watering their horses with two soldiers at guard and three as lookouts on a hill, two Apaches approached through an arroyo upon the horses and killed three mules and a horse with their arrows. He then sent the rest of the soldiers to follow them, and, coming upon them, they followed them to the top of a ridge where they left them and then took the horses to better ground and continued across. The Apaches, who appeared to be about six, began to yell and send out alarming sounds behind the camp for over a league. Upon being followed by this declarant, after finding their tracks, the Apaches fled, and after that they were never seen again. This he says is the truth regarding the sworn statement which he has made and which he affirmed and ratified, saying that he was thirty-five years of age, and he signed it with me, the said governor, and my secretary of government and war.

don Juan Ygnacio Flores Mogollón

Pedro de Chávez
by order of the governor and captain general
Roque de Pinto
Secretary of government and war

Statement of don Antonio Castrillón

At the villa of Santa Fe, New Mexico, on the 5th of August, 1713, I, the said governor and captain general, made appear before me the alférez don Antonio Álvarez Castrillón, who on this day arrived at this presidio as corporal of the escort which came from the royal presidio of El Paso, from whom I received his sworn statement, which he made to God, Our Lord, and the sign of the Cross regarding what he was asked, to which he promised to tell the truth. He was asked what happened to him with the Apaches on his way from the presidio of El Paso and from this one [presidio] to that of El Paso. He said that upon leaving this presidio [of Santa Fe] as corporal of the escort for that of El Paso on the 18th of this past April of this year, at the paraje which is known as El Bosque Grande de Los Alamos,[14] he met the corporal of the squadron, who was coming with his escort from El Paso, Pedro de Chávez, who told him that at the Paraje del Muerto, among the cottonwoods, some enemy Apaches had come upon him and killed five horses, and having resisted them, the Apaches began to throw stones at them so that the soldiers would follow them to the top of a mesa, where according to the corporal was where the rest of the Apaches were.

Then the corporal told him that they retreated in order to get to better land on which to travel, and that they then continued their trip with much diligence, being that the Apaches were without shame and more were continuing to gather at the said paraje and in the sierra. This declarant then proceeded on his trip and decided not to stop at the said paraje because he had with him numerous mules and horses, and he went directly across for more than thirty leagues without water, but did not encounter any Apaches and only a few tracks.

He said that he left from the presidio of El Paso for this one [the presidio at Santa Fe] on the 16th of the past July under the escort of General don Antonio de Valverde, who added more soldiers to the ten which he had for his escort. This was due to the fact that Sergeant Domingo Misquia[15] had just arrived at that presidio from this one [Santa Fe] and told him that the Apaches were everywhere. He said that one morning while at breakfast with his companions at the Paraje and Aguaje de Peñuela, at about eight in the morning an Apache was daring enough to go running into the horse herd of the said sergeant and killed a horse with his arrows, and was able to flee without being able to be caught by the sergeant or his companions. With this information, the general told this declarant to proceed with all vigilance and care.

Leaving on their trip and reaching the paraje which is called El Perrillo,[16] he made camp, and that night he felt that the enemy Apaches were trying to surround the camp. Knowing that they [Indians] had been sensed, they left through the upper side [of the camp] to the Camino Real, where they placed a wooden cross which they had painted black, and along with it they left a hide and a bagful of *piñole de mescale*,[17] and on the ground they drew other crosses around the said cross. In the morning this declarant and his other companions saw this and from their experiences recognized it as a sign of peace, and they placed a bagful of *biscochos* [biscuits] and some *tavaco* [tobacco] and continued their trip, taking the cross and other items with them to see if they [the Apaches] would come to speak with them. They then left slowly from the camp, and the said Apaches never got close to them, but the companions, who were at a distance behind them with the horses, said that five Apaches were following them. He then told them not to get too far behind, but to let them [Apaches] come to them. They [the Apaches] never caught up to them but were seen spying on them, so that under the sign of peace they hurriedly continued their trip and doubled their time. But the Apaches did the same, always following behind until they reached the Aguaje de Fray Cristóbal,[18] where they encircled the horses, but they, the Apaches, could not do anything, and when they were sensed, they retreated and were never seen again. When they are at peace they always make smoke signals, but on this occasion they did not. This he said is the truth about what happened regarding his sworn statement, which he has made and which he affirmed and ratified and signed it with me, the said governor, and my secretary of government and war.

don Juan Ygnacio Flores Mogollón
don Antonio Álvarez Castrillón
by order of the governor and captain general
Roque de Pinto
Secretary of government and war

Decree

In the villa of Santa Fe on the 7th of August, 1713, I, don Juan Ygnacio Flores Mogollón, governor and captain general of these provinces for his majesty, having seen the statements made by the corporals of the escorts, ordered the adjutant, Cristóbal de Góngora,[19] to cite for tomorrow at eight in the morning all of the corporals, officials, and some residents in order to hold a council of war regarding this matter. I thus approved, ordered, and signed this with my secretary of government and war.

don Juan Ygnacio Flores Mogollón
by order of the governor and captain general
Roque de Pinto
Secretary of government and war

Council of War

In fulfillment of the decree approved by me and the summons made by the adjutant Cristóbal de Góngora so that the said corporals, active and retired, of this presidio along with some of the residents who have gathered on this the 8th of the present month in this castle for a council of war, and in fulfillment of this the following were present. General don Juan Páez Hurtado,[20] lieutenant general and former captain general and retired captain, who has had active status; the actual captain, Cristóbal de la Serna;[21] the lieutenant of the company, Francisco Montes Vigil;[22] active Alférez Salvador de Santistevan; interim Sergeant Juan de la Mora Pineda;[23] active officials, Field Marshal Roque Madrid;[24] retired Captain don Alonso Rael de Aguilar;[25] Adjutant General of the Kingdom Joseph Domínguez;[26] retired Captain

Tomás [elsewhere referred to as Thomas] Olguín;[27] retired Alférez and War Captain Martín Hurtado;[28] retired Alférez don Antonio Álvarez Castrillón; actual Royal Alférez don Alonso Rael de Aguilar; the captain of the campaign Pedro Luján;[29] the corporal of the squadron and war Captain don Pedro Durán y Chávez; the corporal of the squadron Francisco García;[30] the corporal of the squadron Lázaro Durán;[31] the corporal of the squadron Antonio Tafoya.[32] The residents were: Captain Juan García de la Riva;[33] the ordinary alcalde Captain Antonio Montoya;[34] Captain Francisco Lorenzo de Casados; Captain Juan de Archibeque; and Corporal Mateo Trujillo.[35]

All of the above were to give me in writing their thoughts of what should be done, making them aware of the part of the letter from the general don Antonio de Valverde, captain of the royal presidio of El Paso, which is found in the first proceedings as provided by me along with statements of the corporals of the escorts. So that they were made aware, the orders of our majesty, whom God may guard, were [included] as well as the two orders of his excellency the Duke of Alburquerque, viceroy who was of this New Spain, the dates of one of them being the 23rd of December, 1707, and the other one the 7th of July, 1708.[36]

Being made aware of everything contained in them, they began to present their thoughts as best as they could in the following manner. The corporal of the squadron, Antonio Tafoya, having seen the decrees and orders of his excellency, was of the opinion of finding the enemy and punishing them. He did not sign because he did not know how. The corporal of the squadron, Lázaro Durán, said that having seen the decree and orders, it would not be a good thing to make war, and that the order of his majesty should be observed. He did not sign because he did not know how. The corporal of the squadron, Francisco García, understanding what is contained in the orders and decrees, stated that the war should not be started, and the orders of his majesty should be observed. He did not sign because he did not know how. The corporal of the squadron and war captain, don Pedro Durán y Chaves, understanding the said decree and orders, said that in his experience it has been more than one year that the Apaches entered into the pueblo of Ysleta and the villa of Alburquerque in peace; and even though at different times three or four horses have been lost, it is his opinion that war not be started for this reason, and also because we have the orders of his majesty, and he signed it.

The captain of the campaign, Pedro Luján, said that it was his feeling that there was not sufficient reason to go into war due to reasons expressed in the decrees and that the order of the superior government should be observed. He did not sign. Royal alférez don Alonso Rael de Aguilar was of the opinion that the war should not be started, observing that which was ordered by his majesty, and he signed it. The retired alférez don Antonio Castrillón, understanding the decrees and orders, said that they should be observed as orders and mandates of our lord the king, and should remain at peace knowing the malice of the Apaches and that he has to be more familiar with decrees of his excellency the viceroy. He recognizes the malice and zeal with which the Apaches can execute their bad deeds, but that a defensive war is not sufficient to contain them, and he signed it. The retired alférez Cristóbal de Torres, understanding the decrees and orders, was of the opinion that it was not a good thing to start a war due to the orders of his majesty, and he signed it.

The retired alférez and war captain, Martín Hurtado, understanding the reason for the council, said that in the year of 1705, when the villa of Alburquerque was founded, he was the alcalde mayor. Since that time, the Indians had been in and out of peace, and the Apaches even to this day, even though they have left the area, continue to come and have taken some horses and livestock. Upon being followed by our escorts, even though we were not able to overtake them, we were able to get back some mares and a horse, but he feels that it is not necessary to go to war, since we have the orders of his majesty. It is his opinion that his excellency, the viceroy, be advised of this, and he signed it. The retired captain Thomas Olguín, being informed of the decrees and orders, stated that because of the numerous robberies and deaths which the Apaches have committed, they should be punished with arms, but being that we have the orders of his majesty, he feels that it should be suspended and that notice of everything be given to his excellency, the viceroy of this New Spain, so that his excellency can determine how to contain the Apaches from committing their murders and robberies, and he signed it. The adjutant general of the kingdom, Joseph Domínguez, understanding the decrees and orders according to the experiences which he has over numerous years of service, is of the same opinion and agrees with everything that is stated by Captain Thomas Olguín, and he signed it.

The retired captain don Alonso Rael de Aguilar says that he feels the same as what is stated by adjutant general Joseph Domínguez and captain Thomas Olguín, and he signed it. Field Marshal Roque Madrid, understanding the reason for the council, said that he was convinced and agreed with the opinion given by retired alférez don Antonio Álvarez Castrillón, and he signed it. The interim sergeant of the company, Juan de la Mora Pineda, understanding the decrees and orders, said that he agreed with the opinion of retired captain Thomas Olguín, and he signed it. Alférez of the company Salvador de Santistevan was of the opinion that they should go after the Apaches, otherwise they would not be contained, and that according to that which was ordered by his majesty, an account should be given his excellency, the viceroy, before it is determined what should be done. He did not sign. Lieutenant of the company Francisco Montes Vigil said that, understanding the decrees and orders, it should be left up to that which was ordered by the king, our lord, and that he agrees with the opinion of retired captain Thomas Olguín due to the great experience which he has and which he has been in under his military command. He is of the opinion that his excellency be informed of the condition of this kingdom and of the atrocities which the residents experience at all hours by the robberies which are committed, and being that they are not punished, is partly due to the crown, and he signed it.

The actual captain of the company Cristóbal de la Serna said that it was his opinion to hold off, for now, the soldiers' pursuit of the enemy, in order to obey, as it should be, the orders of the King, our lord, and to give an account of everything to his excellency, the viceroy. In the interim, the escorts which go and come to the presidio of El Paso should not be less than twenty men, since those of ten or twelve which have been going have been surrounded. He is also of the opinion that some of the members of the council and some residents should go on the trips. He signed it. General don Juan Páez Hurtado, being aware of the decrees and orders, said that he agreed in everything stated by captain Thomas Olguín, and in that which was stated by the actual captain Cristóbal de la Serna regarding the idea that the escorts should be of twenty men when they go escorting the residents who are loaded with goods. When escorting the mail,[37] which travels very rapidly, ten men are sufficient. Also, captain Cristóbal de la Serna and some of the other military personnel of the council should go along. He signed it. Captain Juan García de la Riva, ordinary alcalde and resident of this said villa, understanding the decrees and orders, said that he was in agreement with opinions of General don Juan Páez Hurtado, Captain Cristóbal de la Serna, Captain Thomas Olguín, and the other military personal, and he signed it. Captain Antonio Montoya, resident of this villa, and understanding the reason for the council, stated that he was in agreement with the opinion of Captain Thomas Olguín and Captain Cristóbal de la Serna and his thinking about the reinforcement of the escorts, and he signed it.

Captain Francisco Lorenzo de Casados, resident of this villa, understanding the decrees of the matter and the orders, said that he agreed with the opinion of captain Cristóbal de la Serna, and he signed it. Captain Juan de Archibeque, resident of this villa, said that upon observing the orders of the superior government and orders of his majesty, it is his opinion that the war against the Apaches be suspended for now until his excellency the viceroy of this New Spain is informed. He stated that his highest consideration is to contain them with arms in order to obtain the peace, being that they do not admit to their insults and robberies which are committed at any occasion throughout the whole kingdom and to all the residents, but that he expects that through the great dignity of his excellency, he will approve orders enough to contain and punish them. He signed it. Corporal Mateo Trujillo, resident of this villa, understanding the reason for this council, said that he was in agreement with the opinion of adjutant general Joseph Domínguez and captain Thomas Olguín, and he signed it.

I, the said governor, having seen, on one part, the opinions which are given, first giving an account to his excellency following the lines of that which was determined and which leaves it up to his excellency to make a determination, order that these decrees and those opinions of the council be sent in writing to his excellency the Duke of Linares, viceroy of this New Spain, who upon his review will order to carry out that which is most convenient, leaving a copy of all of the proceedings with the secretary of this government due to the risks and contingencies of the road. For this it shall be posted by his majesty in order to comply with his royal service.

He signed it with all of those of the council who knew how at this villa of Santa Fe, New Mexico, along with those who assisted me, on the 8th of August, 1713.

    don Juan Ygnacio Flores Mogollón
    Juan Páez Hurtado
    Cristóbal de la Serna
    Francisco Montes Vigil
    Joseph Domínguez
    Juan de la Mora Pineda

Roque Madrid
Alfonso Rael de Aguilar
Thomas Olguín
Martín Hurtado
Cristóbal Torres
Don Antonio Álvarez Castrillón
Alonso Rael de Aguilar
Pedro de Chávez
Juan García de la Riva
Antonio Montoya
Francisco Lorenzo de Casados
Juan de Archibeque
Mateo Trujillo

By order of the governor and captain general
Roque de Pinto
Secretary of government and war

It is in agreement with the original by which I, the present secretary, in fulfillment of that which was ordered by the governor, compiled the present testimony, and [it] is corrected and inserted, in the presence of adjutant Cristóbal de Góngora and don Joseph de Giltomey, on this present common paper because the sealed kind is not found in these provinces, and [it] is done at this villa of Santa Fe on the 9th of August, 1713. In testimony of the truth, I place my signature and my usual rubric.
　　　　by Roque de Pinto (rubric)
　　　　Cristóbal de Góngora (rubric)
　　　　Joseph María Giltomey (rubric)

ORIGINAL DOCUMENT

Jesus, Maria y Joseph, Villa de Santa Fee de la
Nueva Mexico
Año de 1713

Testimonio de unas declaraziones que selas rezivimos a diferentes Cavos que fueron de excoltas desde este Real Presidio al del Paso y Junta de Guerra que originales se remitieron al Exmo. Señor Duque de Linares Virrey de esta Nueva Espana en ocho foxas.

En la Villa de Santa Fee dela Nueva Mexico en dos dias del mes de Agosto de mill setecientos y treze años yo Dn. Juan Ygnacio Flores Mogollon Governador y Capitan General deste Reyno y Provincias dela Nuevo Mexico por Su Majestad, digo que por quanto tengo notisia que en distintas veces que an ydo y venido al Real Presidio del Passo an experimentado matansa de vestias que an executado los Apaches enemigos en el Paraje del Muerto y Peñuelas, mando se resivan declaraciones alos Cavos que an sido de dichas escoltas y juntamente con la carta que rezevi del General Dn. Antonio de Valverde su fecha de dies y seis de Jullio en que toca un capitulo sobre los desahogos de dichos con el seguro dela paz cuyo tenor de dicho capitulo es el siguiente. A los dos dias de haver benido Arellano, arivio a este Presidio el Alferez Castrillon quien sale oy en prosecusion de su viaje obligarme llegue ala presencia de Vuestra Señoria sin contra tiempo ninguno, va encargados del cuidado y del que deve hazer en esse medio y si Vuestra Señnoria no da probidencia que a essos Apaches del Muerto seles de una espantada temo executen alguna maldad que es donde acostumbran executarle y como a dar no llevan una rosiada los conseden muy sobre si y muy pagados de que nos tienen enganados con sus pages palladas. Vuestra Señoria resolvera en esta materia lo que fuere muy servido. Y resividas que sean dichas declaraciones probehere lo que convenga en esta materia assi lo pronuncie, mande y firme con mi Secretario de Governazion y Guerra. Dn. Juan Ygnacio Flores Mogollon. Por mandado del Señor Governador y Capitan General, Roque de Pinto, Secretario de Governazion y Guerra.

Declarazion del Alferez Salvador de Santistevan
En dicha Villa en dicho dia mes y año yo dicho Governador y Capitan General para las declaraciones que he mandado se rezivan a los Cavos de las escoltas que an ido al Real Presidio del Passo hize parezer ante mi a Salvador de Santistevan, Alferez, dela Compania deste Castillo Presidial a quien rezevi juramento que hiso por Dios Nuestro Señor y la Senal de la Cruz so cargo del qual prometio desir verdad. Y preguntado que les subsedio en el mes de Marzo de esta año viniendo escolteando los vezinos deste dicho Presidio del Passo a esta Villa en el Paraje del Muerto con los Apaches. Dixo que estando a dar agua al Aguaje de dicho Muerto ala cavallada sobre tarde al salir, despues de aver venido seles alojaron como treinta yndios poco mas o menos a querer quitar la cavallada y les flecharon un cavallo y un burro que murieron alli y tres yeguas que hirieron aunque no murieron y puesta en defensa su escolta con algunos vezinos que fueron Francisco Lorenzo de Cassados y Juan de Archibeque y Agustin Luxan. Francisco Casados tiro un arcabuzaso que estava con perdigones y parese yrio un Apache en la cara segun la demostrasion que le vieron hazer de sacudirse el rostro y que haviendo sacado alo llano su cavallada pusso en orden la gente y vezinos para que velasen el Real y cavallada toda la noche reselandose no diessen en el los Apaches por los muchos que se juntaron. Y por la manana seguiendo su viaje con el mismo cuydado vieron en un serrito de La Laguna bieron muchos Apaches que gritavan. Y como aquella noche avia llovido mucho no pudieron ni la escolta seguirlos, ni los Apaches

asercarse por el mucho lodo en que se atascavan las vestias; y que dichos Apaches lo vinieron siempre siguiendo ala vistas aver si podian hurtar alguna cavallada asta el Paraje de Phelipe Romero, que abra de distancia desde el Aguaje del Muerto quarenta leguas. Que haviendo llegado a dicho Paraxe por la manana no los volvieron a ver mas. Y que esto es la verdad y lo que passo so cargo del juramento que llevo fecho en que se afirmo y ratifico siendole leyda esta su declarazion, declaro ser de edad de treynta y cinco años, no firmo por no saver firmelo yo dicho Governador con mi Secretario de Governazion y Guerra = Dn. Juan Ygnacio Flores Mogollon = Por mandado del Señor Governador y Capitan General, Roque de Pinto, Secretario de Governazion y Guerra =

Declarazion de Agustin Lujan

En la Villa de Santa Fee en tres dias del mes de Agosto de mill setecientos y treze años yo dicho Governador y Capitan General hize parezer ante mi a Agustin Lujan vecino desta Villa a quien zita en su declarazion el Alferez Salvador de Santisteban aquien rezevi juramento que hizo por Dios Nuestro Señor y la Señnal de la Cruz so cargo del qual prometio dezir verdad en loque le fuere preguntado, y siendole leyda la declarazion de dicho Alferez Santisteban. Dixo que estando este declarante con dicho Alferez y los demas que expressa a el Aguaje del Muerto a dar agua ala cavallada; y despues de aver venido saliendo les dieron sobre la cavallada los Apaches que le parese seran como veinte poco mas o menos, y hirieron y flecharon un cavallo y un burro que murieron alli y tres yeguas de un vezino que tambien flecharon y la una de ellas murio el dia siguiente, y dicho Alferez puso ala gente en defensa asta que saco la cavallada a un llano; y despues llovio mucho y mando todos estubiesen con mucho cuydado en el Real y cavallada temiendose no se alojasen aquella noche, y por la manana salieron y en el Serro que llaman de Las Espias que esta ynmediato alas lagunas bieron estaba todo el Serro lleno de Apaches y que quando iba aclarando el dia oieron muchos gritos y prosiguiendo el viaje reconosio este testigo de dia paravan y de noche caminavan siguiendolos con danada yntencion asta serca del de Phelipe Romero y que Francisco Lorenzo Casados la tarde que se alojaron a el aguaje los dichos Apaches le tiro un arcabuzasso; y que le parese lo hirio segun la demostracion que hizo el Apache de ponerse la mano en la cara, y que esto es la verdad so cargo del juramento que lleva fecho en que se afirmo y ratifico, declara ser de edad de cinquenta años, no firmo por no saver, firmelo yo dicho Governador con mi Secretario de Governazion y Guerra = Dn. Juan Ygnacio Flores Mogollon = Por mandado del Señnor Governador y Capitan General, Roque de Pinto, Secretario de Governazion y Guerra =

Declarazion de Juan de Archibeque

En dicha Villa en dicho dia, mes y año yo dicho Governador hize parecer ante mi a Juan de Archibeque vezino de esta Villa a quien rezivi juramento que hizo por Dios Nuestro Señor y la Senal de la Cruz so cargo del qual prometio dezir verdad en loque fuere preguntado y siendolo si por el mes de Marzo pasado de este año entro a este

Reyno desde el Real Presidio del Passo en la escolta que venia de Cavo el Alferez Salvador de Santisteban y que en el Paraje del Muerto que subsedio? Dixo, que entro a este Reyno desde dicho Presidio del Passo en la referida escolta y que desde Peñuelas se adelantaron tres vecinos y tres soldados a reconoser si avia agua en el Aguaje del Muerto como con efecto la allaron y despues hizieron humada para que la gente del Real llevase la cavallada a vever como con efecto la executaron y despues de aver venido la cavallada dieron los Apaches sobre ella y les flecharon y mataron un cavallo y un burro y hirieron tres yeguas que una de ellas se murio y dicho Alferez pusso los soldados en defensa los soldados como tambien los vezinos y el Capitan Francisco Lorenso de Casados le tiro a un Apache un arcabuzasso que oyo dezir tenia perdigones y valas y que segun las demostraciones que hizo el Apache le pareze lo hirio y despues que sacaron la cavallada al llano enpesso a llover copiosamente asta que serro la noche que mando el Alferez Santisteban todos los vesinos y soldados estubiesen con gran vejilansia y cuydado por que se reselava diera aquella noche los Apaches en el Real y como a media noche sentieron benia un Apache a reconoser el Real y tropesso el cavallo en una tusera y cayo desde donde se fue huyendo y como toda aquella noche estubo la cavallada sin dejarla comer en majadas el dia siguiente y otro despues; seles quedaron asi alos soldados como a los vezinos como treinta y tres vestias cansadas y que esta es la verdad so cargo del juramento que lleva fecho en que se afirmo y ratifico siendole leyda esta su declarazion y solo anade que sinco o seis mananas despues se reconosia unos rastros de Apaches alrededor dela cavallada, declaro ser de edad de quarenta y tres años y lo firmo con migo dicho Governador y mi Secretario de Governazion y Guerra = Dn. Juan Ygnacio Flores Mogollon = Juan de Archibeque = Por mandado del Governador y Capitan General, Roque de Pinto Secretario de Governazion y Guerra =

Declarazion del Capitan Francisco Lorenzo de Casados
En esta dicha Villa en dicho dia, mes y año yo dicho Governador y Capitan General hize parezer ante mi al Capitan Francisco Lorenzo de Cassados aquien rezevi juramento que hizo por Dios Nuestro Señor y la Senal dela Cruz so cargo del qual prometio dizer verdad en lo que fuese preguntado y siendole leyda la declarazion del Alferez Salvador de Santisteban quien lo zita en su declarazion, dixo que entro a este Reyno en la escolta de que venia de Cavo el Alferez Salvador de Santisteban por el mes de Marzo y que desde el Sitio de Peñuelas se adelanto este declarante con tres soldados y dos vezinos al Paraxe y Aguaje del Muerto para avisar al Real para que entrase la cavallada a vever y haviendola allado hizieron umada para que llegase la cavallada a vever como con efecto la llevaron y despues que vevio al salir se alojaron como doze Apaches sin otros que vio apie que los doze de acavallo se alojaron ala cavallada y flecharon y mataron un cavallo y un burro y hirieron tres yeguas, que uno de ellas murio y que dichos Apaches asian rostro a querer cortar la cavallada y puestos en defensa los soldados y vezinos para sacar la cavallada a mejor tierra este declarante vido que un Apache le apuntava con un flecha a quien le tiro un arcabusaso con vala y perdigon que le parese lo hirio, y despues que salieron a tierra mas llana donde les empeso a llover copiosamente asta

que serro la noche que mando el Alferez Santisteban que todos los vezinos y soldados estubiesen con gran cuydado por que reselava diesen los Apaches en el Real y como a media noche vino un Apache a reconoser y ya que estava serca tropezo el cavallo y cayo y el dicho Apache se fue huyendo y al romper el dicho oyeron gran griteria; por la manana vieron muchos Apaches en el Serrito que llaman De Las Espias y como aquella noche estubo la cavallada en majada y como los dias siguientes sele quedaron cansadas mas de treinta vestias y despues todas las noches los sercavan de humos y por la manana se bian rostros al rededor dela cavallada que se dava a entender benian con yntencion de hurtar cavalladas y que esto es la verdad so cargo del juramento que lleve fecho en que se afirmo y ratifico y que es de edad de quarenta y seis años y lo firmo con migo dicho Governador y mi Secretario de Governazion y Guerra = Dn. Juan Ygnacio Flores Mogollon = Francisco Lorenzo Cassados = Por mandado del Señor Governador y Capitan General, Roque de Pinto, Secretario de Governazion y Guerra =

Declarazion de Dn. Pedro de Chavez

En la Villa de Santa Fee en quatro dias del mes de Agosto de mill setecientos y treze años yo dicho Governador y Capitan General hize parezer ante mi a Dn. Pedro Duran y Chavez, Cavo de Esquadra dela Compania deste Castillo Presidial quien fue escoltando la escolta que salio por Marso con el Capitan Dn. Felix Martinez y Bartolome Garduño que yba de correo ala Ciudad de Mexico a quien rezivi juramento que hizo por Dios Nuestro Señnor y la Señal de la Cruz so cargo del qual prometio dezir verdad en lo que fuere preguntado y siendolo que le susedio en el viaje desde este Presidio a el del Passo y de buelta de aquel asta este; dixo que salio deste Presidio para el del Passo el dia ocho de Marzo passado deste año escolteando al Capitan Dn. Felix Martinez y Bartolome Garduño que yban ala Ciudad de Mexico y que desde esta Villa asta dicho Presidio del Passo fueron sin contra tiempo alguno y que de buelta que fue por el mes de Abril en el Aguaje y Paraje del Muerto estando a dar agua ala cavallada estando dos soldados de posta y tres de sentinela en un serro se alojaron por un arroyo dos Apaches ala cavallada flecharon y mataron tres mulas y un cavallo y este declarante mando alos demas soldados lo siguiessen y dieron sobre ellos y se subieron ala sierra donde los dexaron y saliendo con la cavallada a mejorarse de tierras y se fueron crusando y los Apaches que serian como seis gritandoles y dando alaridos de tras del Real mas de una legua, y asi que este declarante le asia rostro se yban huyendo los Apaches y que alli se quedaron y no los volvio a ver mas y que esto es la verdad so cargo del juramento que lleva fecho y que se afirmo y ratifico y que es de edad de treinta y cinco años, y lo firmo con migo dicho Governador y mi Secretario de Governazion y Guerra = Dn. Juan Ygnacio Flores Mogollon = Pedro de Chaves = Por mandado del Señnor Governador y Capitan General = Roque de Pinto, Secretario de Governazion y Guerra =

Declarazion de Dn. Antonio Castrillon

En la Villa de Santa Fe de la Nueva Mexico en cinco dias del mes de Agosto de mill setezientos y treze años yo dicho Governador y Capitan General hize parezer ante mi a el Alferez Dn. Antonio Alvarez Castrillon quien entro oy en este Presidio de Cavo de escolta que viene del Real Presidio del Passo aquien rezivi juramento que hizo por Dios Nuestro Señor y la Senal de la Cruz so cargo del qual prometio dezir verdad en lo que fuere preguntado y siendolo que le passo con los Apaches desde dicho Presidio del Paso asta esta Villa y desde este a el del Passo; dixo que haviendo salido deste Presidio de Cavo de escolta para el del Passo el dia diez y ocho de Abril passado de este año en el Paraje que llaman El Bosque Grande de Los Alamos encontro al Cavo de esquadra Pedro de Chaves que venia del Passo con escolta y le dixo a este declarante como en el Paraje del Muerto en los alamos le avian salido los Apaches enemigos y le mataron cinco cavallos y que aviandolos resistido dichos Apaches tiraron a empenarlos para que subieran tras de ellos a una mesa donde dicho Cavo le dixo avia discurrido estava la fuersa de dicho Apaches y que dicho Cavo le dixo solo trato de retirarse para mejorarse de tierra y que fuesse este declarante y demas companeros con cuydado por que dichos Apaches estavan muy desvergonzados y se yban juntando muchos en dicho Paraje y sierra y siguiendo este declarante en viaje no resolvio a llegar a dicho Paraje por haver muchada mulada y cavallada y cruso de cargo mas de treinta leguas sin agua y no encontro ningunos Apaches solo algunos rostros y que salio del Presidio del Passo para este el dia diez y seis de Jullio proximo pasado en escolta del General Dn. Antonio Valverde resuelbo agregarle otros soldados mas delos diez que traia de su escolta por rason de que acava de llegar el Sargento Domingo de Mesquia aquel Presidio quien salio de este y le havia dicho estaban los Apaches muy sobresi, pues estando almorsando el y sus companeros en el Paraje y Aguaje de Peñuela como alas ocho del dia tubo un Apache el atrevimiento de meterse corriendo a cavallo de entrarse en la cavallada de dicho Sargento flechando y mato un cavallo saliendose dicho Apache huyendo sin poder darle alcanse dicho Sargento ni demas de sus companeros y con esta notisia le prebino dicho General a este declarante viniesse con toda vexilensia y cuydado y saliendo en prosecusion de su vieje y llegando a el Paraje que llaman del Perrillo sento el Real y sentio aquella noche andavan los enemigos Apaches sercando el Real y reconosiendo avian sido sentidos se fueron por el lado de arriva a el Camino Real y en el pusieron una cruz de madera que avia de dichos enemigos tenido de negro y con ella pusieron una gamusa y una talega de pinole de mescale y en suelo pintaron otras cruzes al rededor de dicha cruz que por la manana vido este declarante y demas sus companeros y conosiendo por las experiensias que le asisten ser senal de paz les puso otra cruz una talega con viscocho y un poco de tavaco y siguio su viaje trayendose la cruz y demas por ver si llegavan a hablar fue poco a poco con el Real y dichos Apaches nose asercaron y solo le dixeron los companeros que venian algo atras con la cavallada los venian sinco Apaches siguiendo a que les dio por orden no se alejaran sino que los dejaran llegar que nunca llegaron a el Real sino alo largo espiando para darle devajo de pas motivo para que se apresurare este declarante y demas companeros y doblaron las jornadas que los Apaches asian lo mismo viniendo siempre alo largo asta el Aguaje de Fray Xptobal que le rodearon la cavallada y no pudieron dichos Apaches aser nada por aver sido sentidos y se retiraron y que no los volvio a ver mas y que siempre que vienen de paz vienen haziendo humos y en esta occasion no los hizieron y que esto es la verdad y lo que paso so cargo del juramento que lleva fecho en que se afirmo y ratifico y lo firmo con migo dicho Governador y mi Secretario de Governazion y Guerra = Dn. Juan Ygnacio Flores Mogollon = Dn. Antonio Alvarez Castrillon = Por mandado del Señor Governador y Capitan General ante mi Roque de Pinto Secretario de Governazion y Guerra =

Auto
En la Villa de Santa Fee en siete dias del mes de Agosto de mill setecientos y treze años yo Dn. Juan Ygnacio Flores Mogollon Governador y Capitan General destas Provincias por Su Majestad haviendo visto las declaraciones hechas por los Cavos de las escoltas mando a el Ayudante Xptobal de Gongora zite para manana ocho del corriente a todos los Cavos y oficiales y algunos vezinos para hazer junta de guerra sobre esta materia, asi lo probei, mande y firme con mi Secretario de Governazion y Guerra = Dn. Juan Ygnacio Flores Mogollon = Por mandado del Señor Governador ante mi Roque de Pinto Secretario de Governazion y Guerra =

Junta de Guerra
En cumplimiento del auto por mi probeydo y zitacion hecha por el Ayudante Xptobal de Gongora para que dichos los Cavos unicos y reformados deste Presidio con algunos vezinos dela Villa concurriesen oy, ocho del corriente en este Castillo para la Junta de Guerra y en su obedecimiento se allaron el General Dn. Juan Paez Hurtado, Theniente General de Governador y Capitan General que asido y Capitan reformado con exersicio, el Capitan actual Xptobal de la Serna, el Theniente dela Compania Francisco Montes Vixil, el Alferez vivo Salvador de Santisteban, el Sargento ynterim Juan de la Mora Pineda, oficiales vivos: el Maestro de Campo Roque Madrid, el Capitan reformado Dn. Alonso Rael de Aguilar, el Ayudante General del Reyno Joseph Dominguez, el Capitan reformado Tomas Olguin, el Alferez reformado y Capitan Aguerra Martin Hurtado, el Alferez reformado Dn. Antonio Alvarez Castrillon, el Alferez Real actual Dn. Alonso Rael de Aguilar, el Capitan de campaña Pedro Lujan, el Cavo de esquadra y Capitan Aguerra Dn. Pedro Duran y Chavez, el Cavo de esquadra Francisco Garcia, el Cavo de esquadra Lazaro Duran, el Cavo de esquadra Antonio Tafoya y de vezinos el Capitan Juan Garcia dela Rivas, Alcalde Ordinario el Capitan Antonio Montoya, el Capitan Francisco Lorenzo de Cassados, el Capitan Juan de Archibeque y el Cavo Mateo Trujillo; aquienes para que cada uno me de su parezer por escripto les hize notorio el capitulo de carta del General Dn. Antonio de Valverde, Capitan del Real Presidio del Passo, que esta en el primer auto por mi probeydo y las declaraciones de

los Cavos de escolta que constan en estos autos y assi mismo para que tubiessen presentes las ordenes de Su Majestad, que Dios Guarde, dos mandamientos del Excellentisimo Duque de Alburquerque, Virrey que fue desta Nueba Espana la fecha el uno de veinte y tres de Diziembre de setecientos y siete y el otro de siete de Julio de setecientos y ocho y entendidos del contenido de todos empesaron a dar su parezer por el mas moderno en la manera siguiente = El Cavo de escuadra Antonio Tafoya teniendo presente los autos y mandamientos de Su Excellencia fue de parezer se devia buscar a el enemigo para castigarlo y no firmo por que dixo no saber = El Cavo de escuadra Lazaro Duran dixo teniendo presentes los referidos autos y mandamientos que no combenia azer la guerra por observar lo mandado por Su Majestad, no firmo por que dixo no saver = El Cavo de escuadra Francisco Garcia entendido del contenido delos mandamientos y autos dixo no deverse romper la guerra observando las ordenes de Su Majestad, no firmo por que dixo no saver = El Cavo de escuadra y Capitan Aguerra Dn. Pedro Duran y Chaves enterado de dichos autos y mandamientos dixo que tiene experiensia que amas de un año entran de paz los Apaches en el Pueblo de la Ysleta y Villa de Alburquerque y aunque an faltado en distintas ocasiones tres y quatro vestias no es de sentirse rompa la guerra por este motivo y por tener presentes los ordenes de Su Majestad y lo firmo = El Capitan de campaña Pedro Lujan dixo ser de sentir de no ser bastante caussa para hazerles la guerra los motivos expresados en los autos y que se deve observar lo mandado por le Superior Govierno y no firmo = El Alferez Real Dn. Alonso Rael de Aguilar fue de parezer no combenia romper la guerra areglandose a lo mandado por Su Majestad y lo firmo = El Alferez reformado Dn. Antonio Castrillon entendido delos autos y mandamientos dixo, se deven observar estos como ordenes y mandatos del Rey Nuestro Señor, y que es de pas por conosiendo la veleydad y malicia de los Apaches se deve ynformar con los autos al Excellentisimo Señor Virrey, pues conose de su malisia y rezela que siempre que coji Apaches puedan an de executar sus maldades, y que no es bastante la guerra defensiva para contenerlos y los firmo = El Alferez reformado Xptobal de Torres entendido delos autos y mandamientos fue de parezer no combenia romper la guerra en cumplimento delo mandado por Su Majestad y lo firmo = El Alferez reformado y Capitan Aguerra Martin Hurtado entendido del fin a que se ase la junta dixo que el año de setecientos y cinco se fundo la Villa de Alburquerque y fue de Alcalde Mayor a ella y que en todo este tiempo an entrado y salido de paz los yndios Apaches asta oy aunque al yrse suelen llevarse y an faltado algunas vestias y ganado que se an llevado y aviendolos seguido en distintas ocasiones con su escolta en una de ellas les quito vestias y un cavallo aunque no los pudo alcansar y que es de sentir no deverse romper la guerra por estos motivos por tener presentes las ordenes de Su Majestad pero que es de parezer se ve dar quenta al Excellentisimo Virrey y lo firmo = El Capitan reformado Thomas Olguin entendido de los autos y mandamientos dixo que segun los muchos rovos y muertes que los Apaches an executado se deven castigar con las armas pero que teniendo presente las ordenes de Su Majestad es de sentir se suspenda y de notisia de todo al Excellentisimo Señor Virrey desta Nueva Espana para que Su Excellencia determine el poder contenerlos pues resela que siempre que los Apaches puedan executar sus muertes y rovos y lo firmo = El Ayudante General del Reyno Joseph Dominguez entendido delos autos y mandamientos segun las experensias que le asisten de tantos años de servicio es del mismo dictamen y sigue en todo el parezer del Capitan Thomas Olguin y lo firmo = El Capitan reformado Dn. Alonso Rael de Aguilar dixo que su pareser era el mismo que los que tenian dados el Ayudante General Joseph Dominguez y Capitan Thomas Olguin y lo firmo = El Maestro de Campo Roque Madrid entendido el fin dela junta dixo se areglava y siguia en todo el parezer del Alferez reformado Dn. Antonio Alvarez Castrillon y lo firmo = El Sargento interino de la Compania Juan dela Mora Pineda entendido delos autos y mandamientos dixo seguia en todo el parezer del Capitan reformado Thomas Olguin y lo firmo = El Alferez dela Compania Salvador de Santistevan que su sentir es dever darsela a los Apaches por que de dicho modo no se contendran y que areglandose alo mandado por Su Majestad se de quenta al Excellentisimo Señor Virrey antes que determinara lo que fuere servido y no firmo = El Theniente dela Compania Francisco Montes Vixil dijo que entendido delos autos y mandamientos se deve estar alo mandado por el Rey Nuestro Señor y que sigue en todo el parezer del Capitan reformado Thomas Olguin por las grandes experiensias que le asisten y aver militado devajo de su mano, y que es de sentir se represente a Su Excellencia el bien deste Reino y los atrasos que sus vezinos experimentan a todas oras en los rovos que executan que viendo que no se castigan lo padese el credito de las coronas y lo firmo = El Capitan actual de la Compania Xptobal dela Serna dixo ser su pareser suspender por ahora el que las armas sigan a el enemigo por observar como deve los ordenes del Rey Nuestro Señor y que se de quenta de todo al Excellentisimo Señor Virrey y que en el interin se refuersen las escoltas que ban y vienen al Presidio del Passo y ninguna vaxe de veinte hombres, pues ala de diez o doze que an ydo se avian arojado y deste mismo sentir ymbose fueron algunos dela junta y vezinos y lo firmo = El General Dn. Juan Paez Hurtado entendido de los autos y mandamientos dixo se conforma en todo y por todo con el parezer del Capitan Thomas Olguin y que en lo representado por el Capitan actual Xptobal dela Serna sobre que las escoltas sean del numero de veinte hombres esto se entienda quando salgan escolteando alos vezinos que ban con cargas y que yendo escoltiando un correo que ba ala lixera es bastante escoltarla de diez hombres, y del mismo sentir ymbose fue el Capitan Xptobal dela Serna y otros dichos muchos militares dela junta y la firmo = El Capitan Juan Garcia de la Riva, Alcalde Ordinario y vezino desta dicha Villa entendido de los autos y mandamientos dixo se conformaba en todo con los parezeres del General Dn. Juan Paez, Capitan Xptobal dela Serna y Capitan Thomas Olguin y demas militares y lo firmo = El Capitan Antonio Montoya vezino desta Villa entendido del contenido dela junta dixo se conformaba en todo con el parezer del Capitan Thomas Olguin y del Capitan Xptobal dela Serna en lo que mira al refuerzo de las escoltas y lo firmo = El Capitan Francisco Lorenzo de Cassados vezino desta Villa entendido delos autos dela materia y mandamientos dixo seguia en todo el pareser del Capitan Xptobal dela Serna y lo firmo = El Capitan Juan de Archibeque vezino desta Villa dixo que observando los mandamientos del Superior Govierno y ordenes de Su Majestad es de sentir se suspenda por aora el aserles guerra alos Apaches asta dar quenta al Excellentisimo Virrey desta Nueba Espana poniendo en su alta consideracion qual presiso es contenerlos con las armas pues con el seguro de la paz, ellos no omiten sus ynsultos y rovos siempre que hallan occasion en que lo padeze generalmente todo el Reyno y vezindad y que espera de la gran venignidad de Su Excellencia probera las ordenes combenientes para contenerlos y castigarlos y lo firmo = El Cavo Matheo Trujillo vezino desta Villa entendido del fin dela junta dixo seguia en todo los parecer del Ayudante General Joseph Dominguez y Capitan Thomas Olguin y lo firmo = Yo dicho Governador haviendo visto la una parte de los pareceres que se desixen a dar quenta primero a Su Excellencia siguiendo el mismo dictamen y qual presiso es la brevedad del que Su Excellencia determinare, mando se remitan estos autos y junta ala letra al Excellentisimo Señor Duque de Linares Virrey desta Nueva Espana quien con su vista mandara execute lo que tubiere por mas combeniente quedando testimonio de todos los autos en la Secretaria desta Governazion por los riesgos y contingensias del camino y para ello salga posta de Su Majestad por combenir asi a Su Real Servicio y lo firme con todos los que supieron en la junta en esta Villa de Santa Fee dela Nueba Mexico y la de mi assistencia en ocho de Agosto de mill setecientos y treze años = Dn. Juan Ygnacio Flores Mogollon = Juan Paez Hurtado = Xptobal dela Serna = Francisco Montes Vixil = Joseph Dominguez = Juan dela Mora Pineda = Roque Madrid = Alfonso Rael de Aguilar = Thomas Olguin = Martin Hurtado = Xptobal Torres = Dn. Antonio Alvarez Castrillon = Alonso Rael de Aguilar = Pedro de Chavez = Juan Garcia dela Rivas = Antonio Montoya = Francisco Lorenzo de Cassados = Juan de Archibeque = Matheo Truxillo = Por mandado del Señor Governador y Capitan General, Roque de Pinto, Secretario de Governazion y Guerra =

Concuerda con su original de donde yo el presente Secretario en cumplimiento delo mandado por el Señor Governador saque el presente testimonio y ba corrrejido y consertado y se allaron presentes el Ayudante Xptobal de Gongora y Dn. Joseph de Giltomey y en el presente papel comun por que el sellado no corre en estas provincias que es fecho en esta Villa de Santa Fee en nueve de Agosto de mil setezientos y treze años = En testimonio de verdad hago mi firma y rubrica acostumbrada.

          Por Roque de Pinto (rubric)
          Xptobal de Gongora (rubric)
          Joseph Maria Giltomey (rubric)

Notes

1. The locations of the *parajes*, *aguajes*, *sitios*, and other places cited in these documents are shown on Maps 5 and 6, Appendix, based on the Menchero and Miera y Pacheco historic maps and the Camino Real study maps (National Park Service, *Camino Real*; Wheat, *Mapping*, 1: 84, 119). Generally they refer to stopping places with water holes. The paraje of El Muerto and the sitio of Peñuelas were on the Jornado del Muerto on the east bank of the Río Grande; El Muerto was about 30 km north of Peñuelas. All sites were on the east bank of the Río Grande (Kessell and Hendricks, *BFA*: 478 n16, n17).
2. See Doc. 8.
3. Don Antonio Álvarez Castrillón was in New Mexico by 1696 and an alférez in 1707. In 1715 he was granted permission to leave the kingdom (Christmas and Rau, "Una Lista": 196; SANM I #2; Chávez, *Origins*: 351).
4. Salvador de Santistevan was born in Mexico City and was in Santa Fe by 1695. In 1697 he is on the list of presidio soldiers. In 1714 he was the alférez of Santa Fe. On the 1723 presidio muster, he is shown as an ayudante, or aide-de-camp, with all his arms and seven horses. According to Chávez, he owned land on the west bank of the Río Grande, across from Santa Cruz (Kessell and Hendricks, *RCR*: 191 n163; Christmas, *Military Records*: 49; Chávez, *Origins*: 284).
5. Francisco Lorenzo Casados was a convict, or *forzado*, born in Cadiz. He was in New Mexico by 1694, having come with the Farfán-Velasco expedition. In 1715 he was a militia captain. He was buried in El Paso in 1729. His son, Francisco Joseph de Casados, a resident of Santa Fe, was married to María de Archibeque, one of the daughters of Juan de Archibeque (Chávez, *Origins*: 137; Kessell et al., *TDC*: 341 n133, Esquibel, "Mexico City": 69).
6. See Doc. 4.
7. Agustín Luján was part of the muster at the El Paso garrison in 1681. He was a presidio soldier by 1697, marrying María Luisa Maese, sister-in-law of Martín Hurtado, in 1701 (Kessell and Hendricks, *BFA*: 83 n44; Kessell et al., *TDC*: 127; Chávez, *Origins*: 213).
8. The word *arquebus*, or *harquebus*, applies to a variety of guns, but it generally means an early smoothbore matchlock with a stock resembling that of a rifle. Its range was about 650 feet, or 200 meters. It was originally fired from a support. It was superseded by the *fusil* and other guns by the seventeenth century, though a gun called an arquebus was still being used in the early eighteenth century in New Mexico (*Online Encyclopedia Britannica*, accessed March 22, 2013).
9. This was the abandoned estancia of Felipe Romero [de Pedraza], San Antonio de Sevilleta, near the pueblo of Sevilleta on the east side of the Río del Norte (Barrett, *Settlement*: 156-60).
10. Cerro de las Espías, literally, "hill of spies."
11. See Doc. 7.
12. See Doc. 7.
13. See Doc. 7.
14. This could be one of the cottonwood groves near Tomé, or more likely, the Bosque Grande de doña Luisa [Montoya de Trujillo], north of Albuquerque (Barrett, *Settlement*: 12, 212).
15. Sergeant Domingo Mizquia was the son of Captain Lázaro de Mizquia, a soldier at El Paso in 1705, and María Lucero de Godoy. Lázaro first arrived in New Mexico in 1677 as part of an escort for convicts. In 1694 he was a member of the El Paso cabildo. In 1717 he was a sergeant at the Santa Fe presidio (Chávez, *Origins*: 375; Kessell and Hendricks, *RCR*: 77 n16; Kessell et al., *BOB* 1: 37; SANM II #281; Scholes et al., *Domínguez de Mendoza*: 45, 244).
16. According to Kessell and Hendricks, the El Perrillo watering hole was named in 1598 by the Oñate expedition when a dog with muddy paws found the spring for the travelers. Its location is somewhat confused by the language in this document, but in the 1693 campaign dairy of Vargas, he lists the parajes in order, as follows: "I am directing them to the outpost of San Diego, coming by way of the river road, to leave alone the water holes fed by rainwater that may be in the outposts of El Perrillo, Las Peñuelas, and El Muerto, which is the camino real the wagons and carts must take" (Kessell and Hendricks, *BFA*: 478 n15; *RCR*: 381).
17. Today *piñole de mescale* usually means ground, parched corn mixed with sugar and water served as a drink, but since here it comes in a bag, the term may refer to just the corn.
18. Aguaje de Fray Cristóbal was the north end of the Jornado del Muerto, providing access to the river. It was south of Socorro and the pueblo of Senucu and the place where, in 1680, the two groups of refuges under Otermín and Alonso García joined together (Kessell and Hendricks, *BFA*: 478 n118; Hackett, *Historical Documents*: 27-28).
19. Cristóbal de Góngora was the son of Juan de Góngora and Petronilla de la Cuera from Mexico City. Coming to New Mexico by 1710, Cristóbal married Inez de Aspeitia Chávez (Chávez, *Origins*: 188, 359).
20. See Doc. 15.
21. Cristóbal de la Serna was the son of Felipe de la Serna, who returned to New Mexico with the Reconquest. Cristóbal was in El Paso in 1694, and there he married Josefa Madrid, the daughter of Roque Madrid. In 1706 he was a squad leader and then a captain with the Santa Fe presidio, leading expeditions against the

Navajos, Utes, and Comanches. In 1710 he received a large land grant south of Taos Pueblo. He died in 1720 as a member of the Villasur expedition (Kessell et al., *TDC*: 184 n14; Jenkins, "Taos": 91).

22. Francisco [Montes] Vigil was from Zacatecas. In 1696 he worked with Juan Páez Hurtado in recruiting settlers for New Mexico. After Alameda Pueblo was abandoned by the Tewas in 1708, he was given a grant for it. Presidio records show that he was promoted to lieutenant in 1713, but he requested a discharge in 1715 due to serious injuries. However, in the muster of June 18, 1723, he is listed as a soldier with all his weapons and seven horses. In 1732 his son, Manuel Vigil, also a soldier, stated that his father had left him a piece of land in La Cañada and a large room with a patio (Kessell et al., *BOB*: 561 n22; *TDC*: 229 n1; Christmas and Rau, "Una Lista": 195; Christmas, *Military Records*: 49; SANM I #1220).

23. According to Chávez, Juan de la Mora Pineda was a native of Sombrete and was in New Mexico by 1695. In 1708 he was married to Clara de Chaves, a natural daughter of don Fernando Durán y Chaves. He was alcalde mayor of Taos between 1715 and 1729 (Chávez, *Origins*: 161, 258).

24. See Doc. 4.

25. See Doc. 1.

26. This could be José Domínguez de Mendoza, a natural son of either Tomé II or Antonio Domínguez de Mendoza and Ana Velasco, an Indian woman who served as a cook and laundress at the governor's palace. José returned with the Reconquest, having previously married Juana López Sambrano in 1682. In 1692 he was an alférez, in 1700 an adjutant, in 1705 a captain, and by 1707 an ayudante, or aide-de-camp. He owned land along the Río Grande near Tomé/Fuenclara (Chávez, *Origins*: 169-70; Kessell et al., *TDC*: 99, 100, 285; Barrett, *Settlement*: 145, 147, 148-55, 212; Chávez, "Mission Records": 160-61; Scholes et al., *Domínguez de Mendoza*: 414 n211).

27. Thomas López Olguín or Holguín was the son of Captain Juan López Olguín II, who was born in New Mexico and returned in 1697. Juan's name is carved on Inscription Rock at El Morro. Tomás was at the Santa Fe presidio at least by 1692, and a captain by 1706. He served as second-in-command with the 1716 Hopi campaign and was alcalde of Santa Cruz at that time. He was killed with the Villasur expedition in 1720. An ancestor, Juan I López Holguín, was in New Mexico in 1600 and was one of founders of Santa Fe (Kessell and Hendricks, *RCR*: 178-79 n45; *TDC*: 100-101; Barrett, *Settlement*: 77, 145, 192).

28. Martín Hurtado was a son of Andrés Hurtado and Bernardina Salas. Andrés, a prerevolt *encomendero*, was an alcalde at Santa Ana in 1661. Martín was a soldier with the El Paso presidio until 1697, returning to New Mexico to be one of the founders of Albuquerque. Governor Cuervo y Valdez selected him to be the first alcalde of Albuquerque, from 1606 to 1722, as well as captain of the military squad (Barrett, *Settlement*: 59, 139, 178; Kessell and Hendricks, *BFA* 2: 171 n16; Chávez, *Origins*: 197; Simmons, *Albuquerque*: 88).

29. Captain Pedro Luján was the son of Captain Juan Luis Luján, who returned with the Reconquest at least by 1693. He was a campaign captain by 1713 and, as part of the governor's staff, took part in the Hopi campaign of 1716. He married Francisca Martín de Salazar in 1691; their daughter, Isabel, married Juan Lucero de Godoy in 1703. His ancestor, Juan Luján, came from the Canary Islands to New Mexico in 1600 (Kessell and Hendricks, *RCR*: 175 n29; Barrett, *Settlement*: 113-14).

30. This could be Francisco García de Noriega, a son of Lázaro García Noriega and Nicolosa Varela, who were killed in 1680. His grandfather was Alonso García de Noriega, a prerevolt lieutenant governor of the Río Abajo. Francisco was one of the 100 soldiers at the presidio in 1697 and was later granted land in the Río Grande bosque near Bernalillo. A Francisco García is listed as a soldier in a presidio document from 1712 to 1719 (Kessell and Hendricks, *RCR*: 128, 187 n115; *TDC*: 187; Christmas, *Military Records*: 49; Chávez, *Origins*: 181-82; Christmas and Rau, "Una Lista": 197).

31. Both Kessell et al. and Chávez state that there were two people named Lázaro Durán, both living around the same time and both associated with Santa Cruz. A soldier, Lázaro Durán, is listed in a presidio document as being replaced on January 4, 1719, by another soldier, but no other information is given (Chávez, *Origins*: 170-71; Kessell et al., *BOB*: 1176 n128, 1177 n146; Christmas and Rau, "Una Lista": 200). Lázaro Durán also appears in Doc. 18.

32. Antonio Tafoya [Altamirano] was from Michoacán and was serving with the presidio in New Mexico by 1697. He married the widow of Antonio García de Noriega in 1695, María Luisa Godines, not retiring until 1747 (Kessell et al., *TDC*: 127, 186 n101). He also appears in Doc. 24.

33. Born in Mexico City, Captain Juan García de la Riva was the son of Miguel García de la Riva, a weaver, who arrived in New Mexico with his family in 1694 with the Farfán-Velasco expedition. Juan was an alcalde ordinario in Santa Fe in 1708 and an officer of the Holy Office of the Inquisition. A document from July 3, 1716, states that de la Riva was alcalde of Santa Cruz and "the jurisdiction of the Teguas" (Chávez, *Origins*: 183; Esquibel, "Residents": 68; See also Doc. 7).

34. There were two captains named Antonio Montoya. It is likely that this is the Antonio Montoya who came with Vargas in 1693, having married María Hurtado earlier in El Paso. In 1716 he took part in the Moqui (Hopi) campaign with the Santa Fe militia. He died sometime before 1725. Or it could be the Antonio Montoya, son of Diego Montoya, who came to New Mexico in 1693 and married Bernarda Baca in 1707. In 1736 he was the alcalde of Santa Fe (Chávez, *Origins*: 235-36; NMGS, *Aquí*:17).

35. Mateo Trujillo was a native of New Mexico and part of the El Paso presidio in 1681. He was with the Santa Fe presidio by 1697. He received a land grant near Santa Clara in 1700 and owned land in Santa Fe (Kessell et al., *TDC*: 189 n141; see also Jenkins, "Tewa").
36. These two documents exist in the Spanish Archives of New Mexico as SANM II #136 and #143. A discussion of this matter is also included in Twitchell's translation of SANM #124, a document from July 30, 1706 in which the viceroy responds to concerns raised by Governor Cuervo y Valdez and the Santa Fe cabildo. Relevant to this matter is a statement by the viceroy stating that "the said governor shall maintain and preserve all that is required by defensive war, refraining from offensive [war] and endeavouring, by the most gentle measures that his prudence and zeal in the service of both Majesties may suggest, to bring peace, obedience and submission to them" (Twitchell, *Spanish Archives*, 2: 138-39). This concept of a "just war" is also discussed in Pagden (*Lords*: 94-96). It is set forth in the *Recopilación de leyes de los reynos de las Indias, Concerning War* (Lib. 3, Título 4, Leyes 8-10), which begins by stating, "Kind, gentle methods shall be used to attempt to bring rebellious Indians to peace" (Kessell and Hendricks, *BFA*: 222; Tyler, *Spanish Laws*: 41d).
37. For additional information on the mail, see Doc. 7.

10

DESERTER FOUND BUT WEAPONS AND HORSES TRADED AWAY
October 29 to November 16, 1713. Source: SANM II #200.

Synopsis and editor's notes: In this document, the presidio soldiers were charged with tracking down Pedro López Gallardo, who seemed to have had a hard time obeying military orders. He was first assigned to serve with a military escort going to the salt fields in the Salinas. He failed to appear in time to join the escort, and when he did show up at the presidio was sent to guard the horse herds, which was probably considered a punishment. Then he was assigned to go with an escort to El Paso but asked for permission to visit his wife in La Cañada before he went. Failing to return, a soldier was sent to bring him back, but his wife said he had left for the Río Abajo without his weapons. Governor Flores Mogollon then sent troops to find him and bring him to the guardhouse in Santa Fe, which they did. When López was asked about the loss of the presidio horses and weapons that had been assigned to him, he explained that he had loaned them, traded them, and given them away. The governor told him that he would be removed from the military if he continued this behavior, but his immediate punishment was to join the next two campaigns at his own expense.

If the punishment here seems light, it must be noted that in 1713, there were few Hispanic settlers in New Mexico and no more than 100 soldiers, who were far outnumbered by the Apaches and other hostile Indians that continually raided the province. Debilitating punishment or removal from the province would have meant one less active adult male. Each soldier was important and of value whatever his effectiveness and behavior.

Jesus, Mary, and Joseph, Villa of Santa Fe, year of 1713
Criminal cause against Pedro López,[1] soldier of this presidio for having fled.

At this villa of Santa Fe, New Mexico, on the 30th of October, 1713, I, don Juan Ygnacio Flórez Mogollón, governor and captain general of these provinces for his majesty, have received notice from the lieutenant of the company of this royal presidio, Francisco Montes Vigil,[2] who had assigned the soldier Pedro López the role of serving with the escort[3] that leaves for El Paso.

López was found attending to the royal horse herd, which he had to do because of his failure to appear to go on the escort that left for the Salinas because he had gone into hiding at La Cañada [Santa Cruz]. Since he had neglected to do this, he had been given the duty of guarding the horse herd. He then had been enlisted by the interim Sergeant Juan de la Mora Pineda[4] to go on the escort which was to go to El Paso. Before he was to leave on the trip, he was given permission to go to La Cañada, where his wife lived, to prepare for the trip.

However, [since López] failed to return from there on time, Dimas Jirón,[5] a soldier from this presidio, was ordered to go there to bring him back. He [Jirón], however, returned without bringing him back, saying that he was not at his home. Realizing that this was the result of disobedience and desertion, and so that a similar bad deed does not go without punishment and as an example to the others so that they remain to fulfill their obligation in the royal service, I order that this decree be placed at the head of this proceeding and that a statement be taken from his *compañero* [friend, or possibly godfather], Dimas Jirón, and also that notice be given to the alcaldes mayores of the various jurisdictions so that they can apprehend him, if he is not in sacred refuge,[6] and bring him as a prisoner to this *real cuerpo de guardia* [royal guardhouse].[7] I thus approved, ordered, and signed it with my secretary of government and war.

don Juan Ygnacio
Flórez Mogollón (rubric)
at the order of the governor and captain general
Roque de Pinto (rubric)
Secretary of government and war

At this villa on the said day, month, and year, I, said governor and captain general, by virtue of the decree at the head of these proceedings, made to appear before me Dimas Jirón, a soldier of this presidio, from whom I received his sworn statement, which he made before God and to the sign of the Holy Cross, and to which he promised to tell the truth about everything that he knew and what he was asked. He was asked if on the 27th of this present month he was given the order by Lieutenant Francisco Montes Vigil to proceed to La Cañada in search of Pedro López and to bring him back with him. He said that in compliance with the order which had been given to him, he left on that same day for La Cañada, where Pedro López has his family, and upon reaching his home, he asked his wife, Sebastiana Martín, for him. She informed him that on Tuesday, in the afternoon, her husband had been there. He had arrived without his arms, and she proceeded to ask him where he had left them. He told her that he had left them at the home of Sergeant Pineda. She said that on that night he left again, telling her that if anyone from the presidio came to look for him, she was to say that he had gone to the Río Abajo.[8] This is what he [Jirón] told his lieutenant and that this is the truth regarding the sworn statement which he has made and which he affirmed and ratified, saying that he is twenty-three years of age, and that there is no relationship [with anyone involved]. He signed it along with me and my secretary of government and war.

dn. Juan Ygnacio
Flórez Mogollón (rubric)
Dimas Jirón (rubric)
at the order of the governor and captain general
Roque de Pinto (rubric)
Secretary of government and war

At this villa of Santa Fe, New Mexico, on the 29th of October, 1713, the lieutenant of this presidia castle brought before me the soldier Pedro López, whom I ordered to be turned over to the corporal of the guard of this said castle and be placed in fetters [*par del grillos*], which he proceeded to execute. So that it is valid I ordered that this be placed into the proceedings, which I signed along with my secretary of government and war.

don Juan Ygnacio
Flórez Mogollón (rubric)
at the order of the governor and captain general
Roque de Pinto (rubric)
Secretary of government and war

At the villa of Santa Fe, New Mexico, on the 2nd of November, 1713, I, the said governor and captain general, ordered that Pedro López, a soldier in this presidio and a prisoner, be brought before me in order to take his confession, and from whom I received his sworn statement which he made to God, Our Lord, and to the sign of the Cross, in which he promised to tell the truth regarding everything which he was asked. He was asked if the lieutenant of this company had placed and held him guarding the royal horse herd for not having obeyed the order which he gave him to go with the escort to the Salinas when the residents went for salt headed by Alférez Cristóbal de Torres,[9] who was the corporal in command. He responded, saying that it was true that he was placed to guard the royal horse herd for not having complied with the order which had been given to him. He was asked what his motive was for not having obeyed the order given to him. He said that upon having gone to his home in order to prepare food for his trip, his horse had gotten away from him with the saddle on and did not return within three days, which was the reason for not going on the trip, and for which reason he was placed to guard the horse herd.

He was asked if Sergeant Juan de la Mora Pineda went to get him from the horse herd, ordering that he had been named to go with the escort which was leaving for El Paso. He was also asked if the lieutenant of the company had given him permission to go to his home, and what the motive was for not returning as he was ordered, but rather fled. He said that it was true that the sergeant went to get him from where he was with the horse herd and brought him back to this villa, but he did not tell him that he was to go with escort to El Paso, and that the lieutenant of the company did give him permission to go to his home for two days. He was asked that upon agreeing to his confession that he had been given permission to go home, why did he not comply with the order of returning after two days, not even having returned in eleven days. Even though his partner [Pineda] went to try to bring him back, he returned without him, saying that his wife told him that he had been there two days before, and that López had arrived without his arms, and upon her asking him where he had left them, he responded by saying that he had left them at the home of Sergeant Pineda. He said that he had left from there the following morning, leaving instructions for his wife to say that if anyone from the presidio went looking for him to tell them that he had gone to the Río Abajo and that he had left his arms at the home of the sergeant. He said that he had told her this so that she would not be worried, saying that he had left and had been in hiding all of this time because he was afraid that he would be punished by the corporals for not having complied with their orders.

He was asked what had become of the sword [*espada*], the arquebus, and the horses which had been given to him, which were eight in all. He stated that he had loaned the arquebus to Carlos López[10] when he went to El Paso, and that he [Carlos] had given him a blunderbuss [*trabuco*],[11] which is the one which he now has; the sword he loaned to Francisco Velásquez;[12] and that of the eight horses[13] which had been given to him, he has two, and as for the other ones, he traded two for one, another one he leased out, and the others he bartered. He was asked if he is aware of the crime which he has committed by confessing that he had on two different occasions disobeyed the orders which had been given to him. He said that he well knows what he has done, but that he had done it because of the fear he had that the corporals would stick him with their *cuchillos* [knives]. He also said that he remembers lending another horse to Carlos López. He said that everything which he has stated is the truth regarding the sworn statement, which he has made and which he affirmed and ratified and that he is forty years of age, more or less, and he signed it with me and my secretary of government and war.

don Juan Ygnacio
Flores Mogollón (rubric)
Pedro López (rubric)
At the order of the governor before me
Roque de Pinto (rubric)
Secretary of government and war

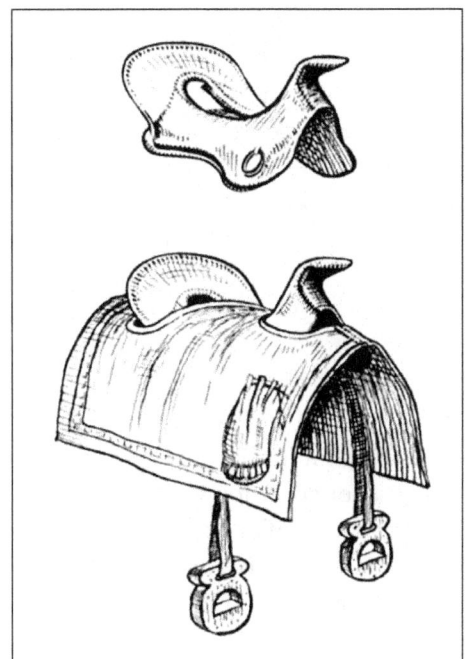

The saddle used by presidio soldiers had a hardwood tree and a rawhide cover. A large leather covering was placed over the bow and cantle, and a smaller pad sometimes held saddle bags. Brinkerhoff and Faulk, *Lancers*: 77, Plate 13. Image courtesy of the Arizona Historical Society, Tempe.

At the villa of Santa Fe, New Mexico, on the 7th of November, 1713, I, said governor and captain general, made to be brought before me Pedro López, a soldier of the this presidio and a prisoner, so that he can in effect ratify the confession which he has made in the preceding page, which was read to him word by word by the present secretary. He said that he affirms and ratifies it once, twice, and three times, and that if it was necessary he would swear to the same thing once more. He signed it along with me and my secretary of government and war.

don Juan Ygnacio
Flórez Mogollón (rubric)
Pedro López (rubric)
at the order of the governor before me
Roque de Pinto (rubric)
Secretary of government and war

At the villa of Santa Fe on the 16th of November, 1713, I, don Juan Ygnacio Flores Mogollón, governor and captain general of these provinces for his majesty, having seen the ratification by Pedro López, criminal in this cause and prisoner in the royal guardhouse, appear in the court room of my jurisdiction, wearing my *sombrero gordo* [large hat],[14] with my *vara* [cane] of captaincy general, in all my seriousness and the justful respect which I am warranted by this case. I declare upon the said Pedro López, for now, my definitive sentence which I declare upon him for what he did, warning him that if in the future he would again do what he did, he will be charged as follows: that he not be allowed to be employed as a presidial soldier; also, I condemn him as I have stated, that he is to join the next two campaigns which I order at his own expense. This sentence shall be made known to the said Pedro López by my secretary of government and war, certifying that he performed it, and so that it is valid I pronounced, ordered, and signed it with my secretary of government and war.

don Juan Ygnacio [Roybal][15]
Flores Mogollón (rubric)
at the order of the governor before me
Roque de Pinto (rubric)
Secretary of government and war

Continuing, I, the present secretary in compliance with that which was ordered by the señor governor, went to the royal guardhouse of this presidial castle and within it I read and notified the sentence which was given, and understanding it, he said that he would consent to it and obey it, and he signed it in the presence of Captain Ygnacio de Roybal and Corporal Ramón García Jurado,[16] who also signed it, to which I certify.

Pedro López (rubric)
Ygnacio de Roybal (rubric) Ramón García Jurado (rubric)
Roque de Pinto (rubric)
Secretary of government and war

ORIGINAL DOCUMENT

Jesus, Maria y Joseph, Villa de Santa Fee, año de 1713

Causa criminal contra Pedro Lopez soldado de este Presidio por haver hecho fuga.

En 3 fojas

En la Villa de Santa Fee dela Nueba Mexico en treinta dias del mes de Octubre de mill setezientos y treze años yo Dn. Juan Ygnacio Florez Mogollon, Governador y Capitan General destas Provinzias por Su Magestad haviendome dado notizia el Theniente de la Compania deste Real Presidio Francisco Montes Vijil como aviendo senalado para la escolta que sale para El Paso al soldado Pedro Lopez quien se allava en el Real con la cavallada detenido por aver faltado al nombramiento que de el se hizo en la escolta que salio para las salinas quedandose escondido en La Canada sin executar el viaje por cuio delito ussando de considerazion lo avia puesto en dicha cavallada y haviendolo alistado como ba referido para la escolta de El Paso que dio orden el Sargento ynterino Juan de la Mora Pineda lo traspasso para que se previenesse para el viaje y le conzedio lisenzia pasase en el ynterim a La Canada donde tiene su mujer y que biendo que

tardava despacho a Dimas Jiron, soldado de este Presidio para que lo traxese quien bolvio sin el diziendo no estaba en su casa de donde se conoze la ynobedienzia y fuga y para que semejante maldad no se quede sin castigo y sirva de exemplar para contener alos demas y que cumplan con su obligazion en el Real Servizio mando sirva este auto de caveza de prozeso y sele reziva su declarazion a dicho companero Dimas Jiron y se de notizia a los Alcaldes Maiores de las jurisdiziones para que lo aprehendan no estando efuxiado en sagrado y lo remitan preso a este Real Cuerpo de Guardia, asi lo provei, mande y firme con mi Secretario de Governazion y Guerra.
    Dn. Juan Ygnacio
    Florez Mogollon (rubric)
 Por mandado del Señor Governador y Capitan General
    Roque de Pinto (rubric)
    Secretario de Governazion y Guerra

En la Villa de Santa Fee dela Nueba Mexico en treinta dias del mes de Octubre de mill setezientos y treze años yo Dn. Juan Ygnacio Florez Mogollon, Governador y Capitan General desta Provinzias por Su Magestad haviendome dado notizia el Theniente de la Compania deste Real Presidio Francisco Montes Vijil como aviendo senalado para la escolta que sale para El Paso al soldado Pedro Lopez quien se allava en el Real con la cavallada detenido por aver faltado al nombramiento que de el se hizo en la escolta que salio para las salinas quedandose escondido en La Canada sin executar el viaje por cuio delito ussando de considerazion lo avia puesto en dicha cavallada y haviendolo alistado como ba referido para la escolta al Sargento ynterino Juan de la Mora Pineda lo traspasso para que se previenesse para el viaje y le conzedio lizenzia pasase en el ynterin a La Canada donde tiene su mujer y biendo que tardava despacho a Dimas Jiron, soldado de este Presidio para que lo traxera quien bolvio sin el diziendo no estaba en su casa de donde se conoze la ynoveddienzia y fuga y para que semejante maldad no se quede sin castigo y sirva de exemplar para contener alos demas y que cumplan con su obligazion en el Real Servizio mando sirva este auto de caveza de prozeso y sele reziva su declarazion a dicho companero Dimas Jiron y se de notizia a los Alcalde Maiores delas jurisdiziones para que lo aprehendan no estando efuxiado en sagrado y lo remitan preso a este Real Cuerpo de Guardia, asi lo provei, mande y firme con mi Secretario de Governazion y Guerra.
    Dn. Juan Ygnacio
    Florez Mogollon (rubric)
 Por mandado del Señor Governador y Capitan General
    Roque de Pinto (rubric)
    Secretario de Governazion y Guerra

En esta dicha Villa en dicho dia, mes y año yo dicho Governador y Capitan General en virtud del auto cavesa de prozeso hize parezer ante mi a Dimas Jiron, soldado de este Presidio a quien rezivi juramento que hizo por Dios Nuestro Señor y la Señal de la Cruz so cargo del qual prometio dezir verdad en lo que supiese y le fuere preguntado y siendolo si el dia veinte y siete deste presente mes le dio orden su Theniente Francisco Montes Vijil para que pasase a La Canada en busca de Pedro Lopez y lo trajese asi consigo; dijo que cumpliendo con el orden que sele avia dado salio dicho dia a La Canada donde tiene su familia dicho Pedro Lopez y llegando a su casa pregunto por el a su mujer Sevastiana Martin quien le respondio que el Martes en la tarde avia estado su marido alli que llego sin armas y preguntandole donde las avia dexado le respondio que en casa del Sargento Pineda, y que aquella noche bolvio a irse y dexo dicho a dicha su mujer que si le binieran a buscar del Presidio algun companero dijese avia ydo al Rio Abajo y que esta notizia dio a su Theniente y que es la verdad so cargo del juramento que fecho lleva en que se afirmo y ratifico y que es de edad de veinte y tres años, que no le tacan las generales y lo firmo con migo y mi Secretario de Governazion y Guerra.

Dn. Juan Ygnacio
Florez Mogollon (rubric)
Dimas Giron (rubric)
Por mandado del Señor Governador y Capitan General
Roque de Pinto (rubric)
Secretario de Governazion y Guerra

En la Villa de Santa Fee de la Nueva Mexico en veinte y nueve de Octubre de mill setecientos y treze el Theniente dela Compania deste Castillo Presidial trajo ami prezenzia al soldado Pedro Lopez aquien mande lo entregase al Cavo de la Guardia deste dicho Castillo y le echasen un par de grillos quien lo executo asi y para que conste lo mande poner por dilixenzia que firme con mi Secretario de Governazion y Guerra.

Dn. Juan Ygnacio
Florez Mogollon (rubric)
Por mandado del Señor Governador y Capitan General
Roque de Pinto (rubric)
Secretario de Governazion y Guerra

En la Villa de Santa Fee dela Nueva Mexico en dos dias del mes de Noviembre de mill setezientos y treze años yo dicho Governador y Capitan General hize traer ami prezenzia a Pedro Lopez soldado deste Presidio y preso para efecto de rezevirle su confesion aquien rezevi juramento que hizo por Dios Nuestro Señor y la Señal de la Cruz so cargo del qual prometio dezir verdad en lo que fuere preguntado y siendolo si el Theniente desta Compania lo puso detenido en el Real de la Cavallada por no aver ovedezido la orden que le avia dado de yr de escolta a las salinas quando fueron los vezinos por sal y de Cavo el Alferez Xptobal de Torres? Dijo que es zierto lo puso en la cavallada dicho Theniente por no aver cumplido con la que sele avia mandado de yr alas salinas. Preguntado que motivo tubo para faltar a cumplir con la orden que sele avia dado? Dixo que aviendo ydo a su casa a prevenirse de bastimento sele huyo el cavallo ensillado y no paresio en tres dias por cuia razon se quedo sin azer el viaje y que por la misma en castigo lo avian puesto en la cavallada. Preguntado si el Sargento Juan de la Mora Pineda fue ala cavallada a sacarlo dandole orden estava nombrado para la escolta que sale al Paso y si lo trajo a esta Villa y el Theniente dela Compania le dio por dias lizenzia para que fuese a su casa y no bolvio que que motivo tubo por aver faltado ala orden y echo fuga? Dixo que es verdad que el Sargento fue por el ala cavallada y lo trajo a esta Villa pero que no dijo que estava nombrado para la escolta del Paso y que el Theniente dela Compania le dio lizenzia para yr por dos dias a su casa. Preguntado que si confiessa ser zierto averle dado lizenzia por dos dias falto del orden y cumplimiento de su obligazion no pareziendo en onze dias y aunque se despacho al companero Dimas Jiron que lo trajese bolvio sin el diziendo que su mujer la avia dicho avia estado alli dos dias antes su marido que avia llegado sin las armas y que preguntandole donde las avia dexado le dijo a su mujer que en casa del Sargento Pineda y que se avia buelto a salir por la manana dejando prevenida a su mujer que si fueran a buscarlo del Presidio dijera avia ydo al Rio Abajo. Dijo que es verdad previno su mujer dijese avia ido al Rio Abajo y que avia dexado las armas en casa del Sargento que esto le dijo por que no tubiese pesadumbre pero que el averse retirado y escondido este tiempo fue de medio de que no lo castiguen los Cavos por no aver cumplido con lo que sele mandava. Preguntado que que a echo la espada, arcabuz y cavallos que sele an dado que son ocho? Dixo que el arcabuz lo presto a Carlos Lopez que fue al Paso quien le dejo un trabuco que es el que tiene ay y la espada la presto a Francisco Velasquez y que de los ocho cavallos que sele an dado tiene dos por que los damas troco dos por uno y otro dio por alquile de otro y los demas los canvalacho. Preguntado que si no save el delito en que a yncurrido en aver confesado a faltado en dos ocasiones alas ordenes que sele an dado? Dixo que bien conoze a yncurrido en el pero que a sido de temor no le acuchillen los Cavos y que se aquerda tiene prestado otro cavallo a Carlos Lopez y que todo lo que lleva dicho es la verdad so cargo del juramento que lleva fecho en que se afirmo y ratifico y que es de edad de quarenta años poco mas o menos y lo firmo con migo y mi Secretario de Governazion y Guerra.

    Dn. Juan Ygnacio
   Florez Mogollon (rubric)
    Pedro Lopez (rubric)
 Por mandado del Señor Governador
     Ante mi
   Roque de Pinto (rubric)
 Secretario de Governazion y Guerra

En la Villa de Santa Fee de la Nueba Mexico en siete uel del mes de Noviembre de ue setezientos y treze años yo dicho Governador y Capitan General hize traer ami prezenzia a Pedro Lopez soldado de este Presidio y presso para efecto de que se ratificase en su uelveio que tiene fecho en la foxa uelveioe a quien se le uel de berbum adverbum el presente Secretario y dijo que en ella se afirma y ratifica una, dos y tres bezes y que si uelveio fuere lo uelve a jurar de nuevo y lo firmo con migo y mi Secretario de Governazion y Guerra.

     Dn. Juan Ygnacio
     Florez Mogollon (rubric)
     Pedro Lopez (rubric)
   Por mandado del Señor Governador
      Ante mi
     Roque de Pinto (rubric)
   Secretario de Governazion y Guerra

En la Villa de Santa Fee en dies y seis de Noviembre de mill setezientos y treze años yo Dn. Juan Ygnacio Florez Mogollon Governador y Capitan General destas Provinzias por Su Magestad haviendo visto la ratificazion de Pedro Lopez reo en esta caussa presso en el Real Cuerpo de Guardia haziendo audienza en la sala de mi juzgado con sombrero gordo baston de Capitan General usando de toda con mi serazion y por justos respectos que a ello me mueben fallo atento a los meritos dela causa que devo declaro a dicho Pedro Lopez como por la presente mi sentenzia difinitiva le declaro por asuelto aperziviendole para en lo adelante que si bolviere a reinsidir en otra le cargare esta; y asi mismo declaro no dever tener plaza de soldado presidario y solo le condeno usando como llevo dicho en dos campanas que a de azer a su costa las primeras que se ofrezieren de orden mio y esta mi sentenzia sela ara notorio a dicho Pedro Lopez mi Secretario de Governazion y Guerra poniendo la fee de averlo executado asi y para que conste asi lo pronunzie, mande y firme con dicho mi Secretario de Governazion y Guerra.

     Dn. Juan Ygnacio
     Flores Mogollon (rubric)
   Por mandado del Señor Governador
      Ante mi
     Roque de Pinto (rubric)
   Secretario de Governazion y Guerra

Y luego yncontinenti yo el presente Secretario en cumplimiento delo mandado por el Señor Governador vaje al Real Cuerpo de Guardia deste Castillo Presidial y en el le ley y notifique la sentenzia dada y entendido dixo la ovedeze y consiente y lo firmo estando presente el Capitan Ygnazio de Roybal y el Cavo Ramon Garcia Jurado quienes lo firmaron de que doy fee.

Pedro Lopez (rubric)
Ygnacio de Roybal (rubric)
Ramon Garcia Jurado (rubric)
Roque de Pinto (rubric)
Secretario de Governazion y Guerra

Notes

1. This soldier was Pedro López Gallardo, from Querétaro, who in 1694 married Sebastiana Martín, daughter of Domingo Martín, a prerevolt settler. In 1710 he was in Santa Fe working as a clerk for the reconstruction of the San Miguel church and was also hired, along with Bernardino Sena, to collect alms to finance the reconstruction. In March 1711, he and his wife baptized a son, Gerónimo, in Santa Cruz. In 1693 a soldier named Pedro López deserted along with ten other soldiers and settlers and 118 horses, but it is not known whether this is the same person. The presidio records show that on November 16, 1713, a Pedro López was replaced as a presidio soldier by Gerónimo Ortega (Kessell and Hendricks, *RCR*: 455; Kessell et al., *BOB*: 1161 n17; Christmas and Rau, "Una Lista": 200; Kubler, *San Miguel*: 23; NMGS, *Santa Cruz* 1: 1).
2. See Doc. 9.
3. This could well have been the escort that included Bartolomé Garduño, Carlos López, and Felix Martínez cited in Doc. 9.
4. See Doc. 9.
5. Dimas [Girón de Tejeda] was from Mexico City, the son of Tomás Jirón, who was claimed to be a native New Mexican. Dimas was in New Mexico by 1697, and, having settled in Santa Cruz by 1695, was a presidio soldier by 1716. Presidio records show that on January 17, 1719, he was replaced as a soldier by Joseph Trujillo (Kessell et al., *BOB*: 644 n20, 1152; Christmas and Rau, "Una Lista": 198).
6. See the discussion of sanctuary in Doc. 18.
7. When the palace was robbed by Isidro Sánchez in 1720, the guardhouse was on the south side of the palace, or the north side of the plaza, with a second-story balcony nearby (SANM II #320; personal communication, Cordelia T. Snow, July 17, 2012).
8. The Río Abajo is usually considered to be to south of Santa Fe, and including the Bernalillo and Albuquerque area.
9. Cristóbal de Torres was born in New Mexico around 1660 and was a soldier at the El Paso presidio in 1681, and was still there on inactive duty in 1700. In 1698 he was acting as a courier to New Spain. In 1710 he was an alférez in Albuquerque and by 1719 was the alcalde of Santa Cruz and had received a land grant in the Chama area. His wife was Angela Leyba, and Diego de Torres, mentioned below, was their son A note in the presidio documents records that on January 22, 1716, Alférez Cristóbal Torres stated that due to his serious injuries, he could not continue as a soldier. Then–acting governor Felix Martínez replaced him with Alférez don Ramón García de Luna (Kessell and Hendricks, *RCR*: 175 n31; *TDC*: 422; Chaves, *Origins*: 294-95; Christmas and Rau, "Una Lista": 196).
10. This same Carlos López appears in document Doc, 7with Bartolomé Garduño. He may have been a relation of this Pedro López, but no documentation has been found showing this is the case. He was the son of Nicolás López and a native New Mexican, born in the Río Abajo area.
11. The word *trabuco* can also mean fireworks (Velásquez, *Dictionary*).
12. Francisco Velásquez was listed as a soldier in the presidio list of 1712–1719 and was present at a muster on March 20, 1713. In 1733 he was named in a claim from a Pecos Indian, Miguel Jaehi, who stated that Francisco Velásquez, a presidio soldier, had purchased a door from him in exchange for a bridle bit but had not paid him in twelve years (Christmas and Rau, "Una Lista"; Christmas, *Military Records*: 52; Kessell, *Kiva*: 322).
13. At this time, this may have been standard issue of horses per soldier. The presidio records for 1723 show that the number of horses held per soldier ranged from five to eight (Christmas, *Military Records*: 49-50).
14. A *sombrero gordo* may have been a hat worn for ceremonial purposes. A hat referred to in the 1727 will of Antonio Vallejos as a "high silk hat" may be similar (SANM I #82, WPA translation).
15. See Doc. 16.
16. See Doc. 8.

11

FIGHT AT CHIMAYÓ; BROTHER DEFENDS SISTER WITH COSTLY RESULTS
July 27 to September 13, 1715. Source: SANM II #228.

Synopsis and editor's notes: The criminal proceedings against Diego Martín [Moraga] began with Joseph Vásquez testifying that he had stopped at the house of Diego Martín to get a light for his *cigarro* and following that, stopped at the house of Cristóbal Martín. Vásquez said that at Diego Martín's house, he saw Diego's sister and spoke to her, and then, traveling on, he dropped his cigarro (or his light) and got off his horse. Martín appeared and hit him on the head with the handle of a *coa* [shovel], and the two men tangled, with Martín biting Vásquez's finger. However, in later testimony, Diego Martín said that when Vásquez got off his horse at Diego's house, he went to a room behind the Martín house and that Diego's sister had motioned that Vásquez was there. Martín pointed out that Vásquez had previously been ordered not to go to his house. In regard to the fight, Martín said that Vásquez was trying to put out his eye with a finger. Hearing this and other testimony from bystanders, the alcalde, Joseph Trujillo, referred the case to Governor Mogollón. The governor assessed Martín court costs and ordered Vásquez to live with his wife in Santa Fe and not go to the Martín house.

The case is an example of the care and detail that went into investigations of misconduct, especially those before Governor Flores Mogollón. As pointed out in the introduction, while New Mexico was a frontier colony, efforts were made to follow legal procedures. The sense is that disruptions of the peace were not acceptable, and when such violations occurred, both parties were at fault. The punishments were intended to keep the peace and not allow feuds or reprisals to start.

Because the proceedings were so detailed, they are outlined below.

1. Alcalde Joseph Trujillo was notified of a dispute between Diego Martín and Joseph Vásquez.
2. A surgeon went to the house of Joseph Vasquez to look at his wounds.
3. The surgeon gave testimony before Alcalde Joseph Trujillo.
4. Vásquez gave testimony.
5. The alcalde went to the house of Diego Martín and sequestered goods for the court costs.
6. Testimony was heard from a neighbor and Martín.
7. Martín was taken to the Santa Fe guard house.
8. In Santa Fe, the governor asked for testimony from another neighbor and requested the alcalde to ask Vásquez if he wished to press charges.

9. Vásquez said he did not wish to press charges because of the court costs.
10. Testimony was heard from another neighbor.
11. The master barber (not the surgeon mentioned above) declared that the wounds of Vásquez were healed.
12. The governor ordered Vásquez not to go to the house of Martín and to live with his wife in Santa Fe or be banished from the kingdom.
13. The governor ordered Martín to pay for the medical and court costs.
14. Vásquez said that he would go to Santa Fe after he had harvested his crops.

Villa of Santa Fe of New Mexico
Year of 1715

Criminal proceedings against Diego Martín Moraga,[1] resident of La Cañada, for having inflicted injuries upon Joseph Vásquez.[2]

This contains twelve pages including receipts.

Proceedings

In the new villa of Santa Cruz on the 27th of the month of July of 1715, I, the retired alférez Joseph Trujillo,[3] alcalde mayor and war captain of the said villa and of its jurisdiction, was notified by Lieutenant Alcalde Mayor Joseph Madrid[4] that the brother of Joseph Vásquez had notified him of a dispute that occurred at the puesto de Chimayó between Diego Martín and Joseph Vásquez, and that said Diego Martín had seriously wounded the said Joseph Vásquez. Madrid stated that the trouble had occurred on the 24th of the present month.

I then went to the home of Joseph Vásquez to attend to the obligations of my duty with the surgeon[5] Francisco Xavier Romero[6] and Protector General[7] Juan de Atienza,[8] along with my lieutenant, to see what the extent of the injuries were that were inflicted upon Joseph Vásquez. So that this is all valid, I signed it as presiding judge, along with the said protector and with Joseph Madrid, who acted as assistants, on the said day, etc.

      Joseph Trujillo (rubric)
      Assisting witness
      Juan de Atienza (rubric)

Statement of Francisco Xavier Romero

At this puesto of Chimayó on the said day, month, and year, I, the said alcalde mayor, requested that in fulfillment of my obligations, the said Francisco Xavier Romero should report what he has seen and observed regarding the injuries which the said Joseph Vásquez has received and to declare under oath the extent of what they are;

which he did to God our Lord and to the sign of the Holy Cross, promising to tell the truth as to everything that he knows and understands.

He was asked what his thoughts were of the injuries which he had seen and which were inflicted upon the person of Joseph Vásquez, who is a resident of this Puesto de Chimayó, and to make his statement.

Vásquez stated that as far as he knows, the two wounds which he has are dangerous because they are below the crown of the head, and according to his knowledge could not be caused by teeth, as is the one which he has on the finger of his right hand, which is very close to being cancerous [*canser*],[9] this is what he answers.

He was asked what type of instrument could have caused such a wound and to make his statement.

He stated that the one on the head was caused by a *palo* [cudgel or pole], and that the one on the hand or the finger was by a bite, according to what the wound tells him; this was his answer.

He was asked what the size of the wound was, to state and declare.

He stated that the wound on the head was two fingers wide and one inch in length; this was his answer.

He stated that he did not know anything else and that he confirmed it once, twice, and three times, and that he is fifty-six years old, more or less, and does not testify as to the generalities. He did not sign because he did not know how. I, the alcalde mayor as presiding judge, along with the protector, signed it, being that there were no others who assisted, etc.

      Before me as presiding judge
      Joseph Trujillo (rubric)
       assisting witness
      Juan de Atienza (rubric)

Proceedings

I, the said alcalde mayor, order that the said Francisco Xavier Romero is to assist in the healing process of the said injured, and is to be paid for his services. The Holy Sacraments were given to the injured person as they are usually ordered. So that it is valid, I, the said alcalde mayor, signed it along with the protector, on the said day, month, and year, etc.

      before me as presiding judge
      Joseph Trujillo (rubric)

Statement of Joseph Vásquez

Continuing, on the said day, month, and year, I, the said alcalde mayor, received the sworn statement of Joseph Vásquez, which he made before God, Our Lord, and the sign of the Holy Cross, in which he promised to tell the truth in what he knew and in what he was asked.

He was asked what had happened, why it happened, what it was done with, and what the occasion was, he was to respond.

He said that the truth was, that upon coming to his house, being at the house of Diego Martín, and having a cigarro on his person, he had stopped at the house of Cristóbal Martín[10] to ask for a light in order to light his cigarro, and during that time a young boy came out of the said house, and he asked the boy for a light. At the same time, he looked up and saw the sister of Diego Martín and spoke to her, telling her good afternoon, to which the lady returned the greetings. The young boy gave him the light and he left to continue on the road to go to his house. Upon beginning to light the cigarro, he dropped it, and he got off the horse to get the light, and at the same time he heard some footsteps behind him, and when he turned to look, Diego Martín hit him, and he saw a coa flying forward, but he did not feel it. Then he went for the stick or the iron tool, and at the same time, turning his right hand in order to grab him, Martín got Vásquez and bit his finger, which is the one which is injured. He said there were no others around at the time other than Antonio Martín[11] and María Barba, relatives of the said Diego Martín. All this he says is the truth, and that he feels that the reason that he has stated is all that there is, and he ratified it once, twice, and three times. He said that he was related through the part of the wife of Diego Martín and that he was twenty-four years of age, more or less. He did not sign because he did not know how. I, the said alcalde mayor, and the protector who assisted me, along with Juan de Aragón and Lieutenant Joseph Madrid, signed it on the said day, month, and year, etc.

        Before me as presiding judge
        Joseph Trujillo (rubric)
        assisting witness
        Juan de Atienza (rubric)

Sequestration

Continuing, on the said day, month, and year, I, the alcalde mayor, went to the house of Diego Martín and inquiring about the goods which he has, was shown the following.

First of all, a reddish-colored horse, a riding saddle, a bridle, some stirrups, an arquebus and an *adarga* [shield], two corn fields, and a wheat field, which were left under the care of Lieutenant Joseph Madrid, leaving the planted fields under the care of the wife of Diego Martín, with the understanding that they are to be sequestered until the decision of the superior government.[12] So that it is valid, I signed it as presiding judge, along with the protector, Juan de Aragón, and the lieutenant, on the said day, month, and year, etc.

        Before me as presiding judge
        Joseph Trujillo (rubric)
        assisting witness
        Juan de Atienza (rubric)

Statement of María Barba

At the new villa of Santa Cruz on the 23rd of July of 1715, I, the retired Alférez Joseph Trujillo, alcalde mayor and war captain of the said villa and of its jurisdiction, ordered to appear before me María Barba Luján, who was cited in the statement of Joseph Vásquez. Upon being present, I took her sworn statement in her full right, which she made for God, Our Lord, and for the sign of the Holy Cross, and promised to tell the truth in what she knew and what she was asked.

She was asked what she knew about the incident that Diego Martín had with Joseph Vásquez, also if she knew why it happened, at whose house it happened, if she knew what had come of it, and what other persons had seen it. She was to say and declare.

She said that all she knew was that after the incident occurred, she was summoned to get help by a young son of Fernando Martín, saying that his mother needed her so that she could help cure the said Joseph Vásquez, but that at that time she could not go. Later on, the mother of the said young boy again went to summon her, and that at that time, at the pleadings of the young man's mother, she went to assist. She said that she was able to stop the blood that ran from his head and that the wound on the head was measured at five points [stitches], and that she assisted with an injury on a finger on one of his hands, saying that it was in bad shape, but does not remember which hand. She stated that she did not see any other person, nor did she see where the incident had occurred. She said that she did not know anything else and confirmed it once, twice, and three times and said that she was forty years of age, more or less, and that she was related to the said Diego Martín. She did not sign, saying that she did not know how, and I, the said alcalde mayor, signed it, along with my assisting witnesses, acting as presiding judge, on the said day, month, and year, etc.

    Before me acting as presiding judge
    Joseph Trujillo (rubric)
    assisting witness
    Juan de Atienza (rubric)

Statement of Diego Martín

Continuing, on the said day, month, and year, I, the said alcalde mayor, having ordered to appear before me Antonio Martín, cited in the statement of Joseph Vásquez, but not finding him in this jurisdiction, nor any other persons who were present at the time of the incident of the herein mentioned as is stated, I ordered to appear before me Diego Martín. Upon being present I received his sworn statement under his full right, which I made to God, Our Lord, and to the sign of the Cross, and to which he promised to tell the truth in whatever he knew and in what he was asked.

He was asked if he knew the reason for being held prisoner. He was to say and declare. He said that he did, and that this was his answer. He was asked what the reasons were for having injured the Joseph Vásquez so seriously, and what brought about the fight with the said Joseph Vásquez, and what other persons were present and was to say and declare.

He said that upon all of his family leaving from the house for other places, and his sister Josefa being left alone in the house, and while he was irrigating his chile field, he noticed that his sister was making gestures with her head in different directions and towards where he was, and upon seeing these gestures, he suspected that something was wrong. Thus he went to his house. Upon getting there, he saw and recognized the said Joseph Vásquez and noticed that he was leaving from a room which has not been roofed and was behind the main door of the house. At which time he went after the said Joseph Vásquez without the intention of attacking him, but rather to ask him what he was looking for and to remind him that he was not to be at this house, as he had already been ordered by the justice, and he [Martín] had also told him that he was not to go to his house. Upon seeing him leave from the unroofed part of the house, he noticed that the said Joseph Vásquez leaned over to pick up some rocks, and it was at that point that Martín hit him on the head with the handle of the coa. This he says is the truth and is what he answers.

He was asked how he can say that he hit him with the coa, when they were face to face, when the said Joseph Vásquez stated that upon being hit he turned his hand to grab whomever hit him, at which time he bit the finger of his right hand, he said and declared.

Martín stated that what Vásquez says is not true, because at that time they went at each other as if wrestling, and that Vásquez was attempting to poke Martín's eyes out with his fingers. It is true that Martín did bite his finger at that time and that during the time that they were wrestling the said Joseph Vásquez said that they should stop. At which point they let go of each other and each one went to their houses; he went to his house, and the injured person went to the house of Fernando Martín.[13] He stated that it was his jealousy of the honor of his sister which motivated the act. He said that this is the truth regarding his sworn statement, which he has made and which he ratified once, twice, and three times, and says that he is twenty-three years old, more or less, and that he is related to the injured person through his wife. He did not sign because he said that he did not know how; I, the said alcalde mayor, signed it as presiding judge with my assistants in the said new villa on the said day, month, and year, etc.

Before me as presiding judge
Joseph Trujillo (rubric)
assisting witnesses
Miguel Martín (rubric)
Juan de Atienza (rubric)

Proceedings
Continuing, on the said day, month, and year, I, the said alcalde mayor, took the said person of Diego Martín before the don Juan Ignacio Flores Mogollón, governor and captain general of this kingdom, along with the proceedings done by me. There

being lacking [in the proceedings] the person of Antonio Martín, who, as he is in this villa of Santa Fe, is one of the ones cited by the said Joseph Vásquez, and in consideration of that which is required by this supreme government, he is to be brought forth to hear what he knows without further hesitation due to the poor security which there is in this jurisdiction because of the lack of a jail and prison [*carsel y prisiones*]. I thus took him before the presence of the said governor so that his honor can determine what needs to be done. I thus approved and ordered this acting as presiding judge on the said day, month, and year.

                        Before me as presiding judge
                        Joseph Trujillo (rubric)
                           assisting witnesses
                        Miguel Martín (rubric)
                        Juan de Atienza (rubric)

    These proceedings consist of four written pages, and so that it is valid I signed it with my assistants.

                        Before me as presiding judge
                        Joseph Trujillo (rubric)

Proceedings

    In this villa of Santa Fe of New Mexico on the 30th day of July of the year 1715, I, don Juan Ignacio Flores Mogollón, governor and captain general of this kingdom and province of New Mexico for his majesty, having seen these proceedings which were submitted to me by the alcalde mayor of the new villa of Santa Cruz and of the jurisdiction of La Cañada, Joseph Trujillo, along with the paper in which he tells me that he is bringing the prisoner, Diego Martín, the offender in the case, and which I order the corporal of the guardhouse to receive him, the said Diego Martín, as a prisoner with all the diligence and custody. The corporal being present, he stated that he has received him and that he will keep him under the guard and custody that is necessary. In the said proceedings it is not stated in the declaration of Joseph Vásquez, the injured person, whether he is going to lodge a complaint against the said Diego Martín or if he will pardon him. I order that the originals be sent back to the said alcalde mayor so that he can execute this matter, and also to receive the statement of Antonio Martín, who today is to be found in that jurisdiction and upon doing this he is to return them. I thus approved, ordered, and signed it with my secretary of government and war.

                      Juan Ignacio Flores Mogollón (rubric)
               by order of the governor and captain general
                          Roque de Pinto (rubric)
                        Secretary of government and war

At this new villa of Santa Cruz on the last day of the month of July of the present year of 1715, in fulfillment and in obedience to the proceedings above expedited by don Juan Ignacio Flores Mogollón, governor and captain general of this kingdom of New Mexico and of its provinces for the king, our honor, I, the retired alférez Joseph Trujillo, alcalde mayor and war captain of the said villa and of its jurisdiction, went to the puesto de Chimayó to the house where Joseph Vásquez, the person who was injured by the said Diego Martín, is staying, along his wife and his brother, Antonio Vásquez. I asked if due to the wounds and injuries which he had received they were going to prosecute in a civil or criminal manner the said Martín, or if they were willing to forgive the individual who caused the injuries. The said Joseph Vásquez answered and stated that they would not file charges and would forgive the person who injured him because he is so poor that he does not have enough to pay for the care which is being given to him by the order of the royal justice. The same answer and reasons were given by his wife and his brother. So that it is valid, I, the said alcalde mayor, signed it as presiding judge with my assisting witnesses on the said day, etc.
before me as presiding judge

                    Joseph Trujillo (rubric)
                        assisting witnesses
                    Miguel Martín (rubric)
                    Juan de Atienza (rubric)

    Continuing, at the said puesto de Chimayó on the said day, month, and year, I, the said alcalde mayor and war captain, made appear before me Antonio Martín, and being in my presence received his sworn statement which he made before God, Our Lord, and to the Sign of the Holy Cross and promised to tell the truth in everything that he knew and what he was asked.
    He was asked if he was around when the fight or disturbance occurred between Diego Martín and Joseph Vásquez and if he knew the reason or the motive for the said action and if there were other persons present, he was asked to state and say.
    He stated that he was not present nor much less does he know the reasons they had for the act, nor does he know anything else regarding what he is asked about the pending case. This he said is the truth to what he swears and states, this is his answer.
    He was asked where he was on the day of the disturbance by the said Diego Martín and Joseph Vásquez, this he was asked to answer.
    He said that he was working on his garden about two arquebus shots away and does not know anything else, and if there were any other questions regarding the case, he does not know anything else other than what he has already stated. He ratified this once, twice, and three times, and that in the generalities of the law, his daughter is the wife of Joseph Vásquez, and on the part of Diego Martín, he is his nephew by blood,

and that he is sixty years old, more or less. He did not sign because he said that he did not know how. So I, the said alcalde mayor, signed it as acting presiding judge with my assistants on the said day, month, and year, etc.

Before me as presiding judge
Joseph Trujillo (rubric)
assisting witnesses
Miguel Martín (rubric)
Juan de Atienza (rubric)

I, the alcalde mayor, Joseph Trujillo, submit these proceedings to don Juan Ignacio Flores Mogollón according to the order of his honor so that upon his review he will decide what is to be determined, and so that it is valid I signed it at this Puesto de Chimayó on the 31st of July, 1715, along with my assistants, etc.

Before me as presiding judge
Joseph Trujillo (rubric)
assisting witnesses
Miguel Martín (rubric)
Juan de Atienza (rubric)

Proceedings and statement of his health

At this Villa of Santa Fe of New Mexico on the 2nd day of the month of September of 1715, I, don Juan Ignacio Flores Mogollón, governor and captain general of this kingdom and provinces of New Mexico for his majesty, it being brought to my attention that Joseph Vásquez is found healed of his injuries, I ordered him to appear before me along with the master barber, Antonio Durán de Armijo. Upon being present, I ordered the said master barber to check his wounds, and upon having done it, I received his sworn statement which he made before God, Our Lord, and the sign of the Holy Cross, in which he promised to tell the truth in whatever he was asked. He was asked if the said Joseph Vásquez is now found healthy and without the fear of death from the injuries which were inflicted by Diego Martín. He stated that upon having examined him and according to his knowledge, the said Joseph Vásquez is now healthy and free of the injuries and without any visible lesions, and that this is the truth. He signed it with me, the said governor, along with secretary of government and war.

Juan Ignacio Flores Mogollón (rubric)
by order of the señor governor and captain general
Roque de Pinto (rubric)
Secretary of government and war

Continuing, I, the said governor and captain general, having seen the statement of health given by Antonio Durán de Armijo in which he assures me that Joseph Vásquez is in good health, I order him to come to this villa to live along with his wife so as to keep him from ever going into the house of Diego Martín. If he does not comply with this order he will be banished from this kingdom. Being that Francisco Xavier Romero says that he cured him in twenty-three days, the cost for which is two rams for doing this, I order that from the goods which Diego Martín has, he shall pay the said Francisco Romero the two rams and two reales for each day that he took care of him. I also sentence the said Diego Martín the sum of six pesos to be applied for the construction of this holy church. He shall also pay all of the costs incurred, personal and professional, which are to be appraised by Sergeant Major don Alfonso Rael de Aguilar, and once everything has been paid, the sequestered goods are to be returned, and he is to be released from prison, and he is ordered never to have any more problems with the said Joseph Vásquez. At the foot of these proceedings and upon his being notified, the appraisal of the expenses are to be noted so that it will forever be known. I thus approved, ordered, and signed this with my secretary of government and war. Also, I order that Joseph Vásquez be paid eight pesos, which is the salary for a month.

Juan Ignacio Flores Mogollón (rubric)
by order of the governor and captain general
Roque de Pinto (rubric)
Secretary of government and war

Notification of Joseph Vásquez

I, the present secretary of government and war, in compliance with the preceding order of the governor and captain general, notified and read to Joseph Vásquez personally that which was ordered, and upon having heard and being understood, he said that he would obey and that he would be able come to Santa Fe once he harvested his crops. This is what I give as his response, which was done in the presence of [witnesses] Corporal Juan Ruiz Cordero and Juan de Ledesma. He did not sign because he did not know how. I signed it on the said day, month, and year.

Roque de Pinto (rubric)
Secretary of government and war

Appraisal of the expenses

In the villa of Santa Fe on the 10th of September, 1715, I, Sergeant Major don Alfonso Rael de Aguilar, in execution and in compliance of the order above approved by the governor and captain general, don Juan Ignacio Flores Mogollón, in which he ordered me to make an appraisal of the expenses, both personal and professional, which were brought forth in this case, are as follows.

First of all, four pesos and one-half to the governor for having acted in this case.	4 pesos 4 reales
Also, for Captain Roque de Pinto, secretary of government and war, I appraise three pesos.	3 pesos
Also, for Captain Joseph Trujillo, alcalde mayor of the new villa of Santa Cruz, for all that he did, as well as for personal expenses which he incurred in the case, nine pesos.	9 pesos
For Juan de Atienza, I allow him for having written the case along with the said alcalde mayor, four pesos.	4 pesos
Also, five pesos and six reales for twenty-three days which Francisco Xavier Romero took in curing the said Joseph Vásquez at two reales for each day as allowed by the order of the general, along with two rams which the said Francisco Xavier used in his commission, which at two pesos each, comes out to be what needs to be paid to the said Francisco Xavier.	9 pesos 6 reales
Also, two reales for the paper which was used in this case.	0 pesos 2 reales
For everything, the sum amounts to thirty pesos and four reales, and so that it is valid, I signed it on the said day, month, and year.	total 30 pesos 4 reales

Alfonso Rael de Aguilar (rubric)

I, the present secretary of government and war, in compliance with the order of the governor and captain general, went down to the guardhouse of this presidio and at that place read to and notified Diego Martín, prisoner and criminal in these proceedings, who, having heard and understanding what I read to him, said that he would obey and comply with the order. He then turned over to me the amount due for the expenses so that I would distribute them and included a receipt to be placed with the proceedings. He did not sign because he did not know how; the secretary signed them on the 10th day of September, 1715.

Roque de Pinto (rubric)
Secretary of government and war

I, Captain Juan García de la Riva, say that I received from Diego Martín, resident of La Cañada, the six pesos which he was fined for the construction of the holy church. Being that General Juan Páez Hurtado, who is in charge of the said construction, is not in the villa, I kept the payment until he returns. It being the truth, I signed it at this said villa of Santa Fe on the 3rd of September, 1715.

Juan García de la Riva (rubric)

I, Joseph Trujillo, alcalde mayor of the new villa of Santa Cruz and the jurisdiction of La Cañada, say that I received from Diego Martín nine pesos for my payment regarding the criminal case that was filed against the said, and which I was in charge of, and I also received four pesos for the payment that was due to Juan de Atenzia for having written the proceedings. Villa of Santa Fe, New Mexico, September 13, 1715.

        Joseph Trujillo (rubric)

 The total is 13 pesos.

ORIGINAL DOCUMENT

     Villa de Santa Fee de la Nueva Mexico
       Año de 1715

Causa criminal contra Diego Martin Moraga vezino dela jurisdizion dela Cañada por haver dado unas heridas a Joseph Vasquez

Consta de 12 fojas con los recivos.

Autos
En la Villa Nueva de Santa Cruz en beinte y siete dias del mes de Julio de mil setesientos y quinse años yo el Alferes reformado Joseph Truxillo Alcalde Mayor y Capitan Aguerra de dicha Villa y su jurisdizion abiendo sido abisado por el Teniente de Alcalde Mallor Joseph Madrid como en el Puesto de Chimayó se ofrecio una pendensia entre Diego Martin y Joseph Basques y que el dicho Diego Martin abia mal erido al dicho Joseph Basques y que al dicho Teniente le abiso un hermano del dicho Joseph Basques disiendole abian erido al dicho su hermano y que parase aberlo en compania del Alcalde Mallor si estaba en la jurisdizion que luego paso a mi casa dicho Teniente y me abiso disiendome lo que abia pasado el dia beinte y cuatro del coriente y pasando ala casa de dicho Joseph Basques alas diligencias de mi obligacion con el sirujano Francisco Xabiel Romero y del Protector General Juan de Atienza y de mi dicho Teniente di fee delas eridas de dicho Joseph Basques y para que asi conste lo firme como Juez receptor con dicho Protector y Joseph Madrid por de asistensia en dicho ut supra. Ante mi como Juez receptor.
        Joseph Truxillo (rubric)
       Testigo de asistencia
      Juan de Atienza (rubric)

Declaracion de Francisco Xabiel Romero

  En este Puesto de Chimayó en dicho dia mes y año yo dicho Alcalde Mallor yse para cumplimento de mi cargo que el dicho Francisco Xabiel Romero declarase lo que tiene reconocido y visto de las eridas con que se halla Joseph Basques asiendo antes el juramento acostumbrado que asi lo yso por Dios Nuestro Señor y la Senal de la Santa Cruz y prometio desir verdad en todo lo que entiende y sabe. _____

  Preguntado que siente de las eridas que vistas y reconosidas tiene en la persona de Joseph Basques vesino que es deste dicho Puesto de Chimayó, diga y declare. _____

  Dixo que por lo que conose ber las dos eridas que vistas tiene son peligrosas por que la tiene abajo de la mollera alla en su consiencia tener lastimadas las comesuras y que selo ensena la esperensia de no poder partir con los dientes dicha erida unos mas y es y que la que tiene en la mano derecha en el dedo que le sia y alminique y que esta mui sercana a canser y esto responde. _____

  Preguntado si reconose con que ynstrumento se dieron dicha erida, diga y declare. _____

  Dixo que el de la cabesa fue palo y que la de la mano o dedo fue mordida segun le dixo la dicha erida y esto responde._____

  Preguntado que tanto es lo abierto de dichas eridas, diga y declare. _____

  Dixo tener la erida de la cabesa dos dedos de ancho y de largo una pulgada y esto responde. _____

  Preguntado si sabe otra cosa a este caso tocante diga y declare. _____

  Dixo no saber mas que lo que tiene dicho a que se ratifico por una, dos y tres veses y que es de edad de sincuenta y seis años poco mas o menos y que en las generales no testa aca y no firmo por no saber firmelo yo dicho Alcalde Mallor como Juez receptor y el Protector y mi Teniente por no aber otros de asistencia en dicho ut supra.

Ante mi como Juez receptor
Joseph Truxillo (rubric)
Testigo de asistencia
Juan de Atienza (rubric)

Auto

Hordeno yo dicho Alcalde Mallor a dicho Francisco Xabiel Romero asista ala curasion de dicho erido a quien se las sitara su trabajo y prosigiera dandole antes los Santos Sacramentos segun ordena y para que conste lo firme yo dicho Alcalde Mayor y el Protector en dicho dia mes y año ut supra.

Ante me como Juez receptor
Joseph Truxillo (rubric)

Declaracion de Joseph Basques

Y luego yncontinente en dicho dia mes y año yo dicho Alcalde Mallor le resivi juramento a Joseph Basques y conosimiento lo yso por Dios Nuestro Señor y la Senal de la Santa Cruz y prometio desir verdad en lo que supiere y le fuere preguntado. _____

Preguntado quien le dio y por que le isieron y con que le ysieron y en que lugar y que fue la ocasion diga y declare. _____

Dixo que es berdad que biniendo para su casa y estando antes la de Diego Martin y trallendo un sigaro en la mano llego ala casa de Cristobal Martin a pedir una lumbre para asender su sigaro y que a este tiempo salio un muchacho de la dicha casa y sela pidio y que alsando los ojos asi arriba bide ala hermana del dicho Diego Martin y le dio las buenas tardes y que la mujer delas retorno y que dandole la lumbre el muchacho se despidio y fuese yiendo el camino para su casa y que al yr a ensender su sigaro sele callo la lumbre y que al baxarse a cojerla sintio pasos por de tras y que al boltear la cara le dio el dicho Diego Martin el golpe que si lo bido fue saltar una coa para adelante pero que no sintio y se fue con el palo o con el fiero y que a este tiempo boltiendo la mano derecha a quererlo coxer le cogio con los dientes de un dedo que es el que tiene mordido y que no abia mas personas que Antonio Martin y María Barba parientes del dicho Diego Martin que no abia otras personas y que es la berdad que no siente en su consiencia aber mas motibo que el que tiene declarado a que se ratifico por una, dos y tres beses y que le toca por partes de la mujer del dicho Diego Martin y que es de edad de beinte y cuatro años poco mas o menos y no firmo por desir no saber firmelo yo dicho Alcalde Mallor y dicho Protector de asistencia con mas Juan de Aragon y el Teniente Joseph Madrid en dicho dia mes y año ut supra.

      Ante mi como Juez receptor
      Joseph Truxillo (rubric)
      Testigo de asistensia
      Juan de Atienza (rubric)

Embargo

Y luebo yncontenenti en dicho dia mes y año pase yo dicho Alcalde Mallor ala casa de Diego Martin y asiendo ynquesision de sus bienes fueron manifestados los siguientes. _____

Primeramente un caballo rosillo, una silla gineta, un freno y unas espuelas, un arcabus y una adarga, dos milpas de mais, una de trigo, la cual queda en deposito en la persona del Teniente Joseph Madrid e dejo las simenteras que quedan en cargo de la muger del dicho Diego Martin con la adbertencia de que se embargan asta la determinacion del Superior Gobierno y para que conste lo firme como Juez receptor y el dicho Protector y Juan de Aragon y el Teniente en dicho dia ut supra.

      Ante mi como Juez receptor
      Joseph Truxillo (rubric)
      Testigo de asistencia
      Juan de Atienza (rubric)

Declarasion de Maria Barba

En la Villa Nueba de Santa Cruz en beinte y nuebe dias del mes de Julio del año de mil setesientos y quinse años yo el Alferez Reformado Joseph Truxillo Alcalde Mallor y Capitan Aguerra de dicha Villa y su jurisdizion mande pareser ante mi a Maria Barba Luxan sitada en la declarasion de Joseph Basques y estando presente le resevi juramento en toda forma de derecho que lo yso por Dios Nuestro Señor y la Señal de la Santa Cruz y prometio desir verdad en todo lo que supiere y le fuere preguntado. _____

Preguntado que sabe del pleyto que tiene Diego Martin con Joseph Basques y si sabe por que fue y en casa de quien y si bido con que le yso y quien otras personas lo bieron diga y declare. _____

Dixo que lo que sabe es solo que despues que ya abia pasado la pendencia la fue a llamar un muchacho hijo de Fernando Martin disiendo le llamaba su madre para que fuera a curar al dicho Joseph Basques y que entonses le dijo al muchacho que no podia yr y que despues fue la madre de dicho muchacho por ella y que entonses fue a los ruegos que le yso la dicha y que le curo estacandole la sangre que de la erida de la cabesa le coria y que en dicha erida de la cabesa le dio sinco puntadas y que en un dedo de una mano le bido y curo y que dicho dedo se lo bido pasado y que no se acuerda en cual delas dos manos fue que no bido otras personas y que no bido donde fue el plieto ni sabia otra cosa que lo que tiene dicho en que se ratifico por una, dos y tres beses y que es de edad de cuarenta años poco mas o menos y que en las generales le toca el dicho Diego Martin y no firmo por desir no saber firmelo yo dicho Alcalde Mallor y los de asistensia auctuando como Juez receptor en dicho dia, mes y año ut supra.

Ante mi como Juez receptor
Joseph Truxillo (rubric)
Testigo de asistencia
Juan de Atienza (rubric)

Declarasion de Diego Martin

Y luego yncontinenti en dicho dia, mes y año yo dicho Alcalde Mallor abiendo mandado pareser ante mi a Antonio Martin sitado en la declarasion de Joseph Basques y no allandose en esta jurisdision ni otras personas que presentes se allasen en el dicho pleito de los contenidos segun lo declarado mande pareser ante mi a Diego Martin y estando presente le resibi juramento en toda forma de derecho que lo yso por Dios Nuestro Señor y la señal de la Santa Cruz y prometio decir berdad en todo lo que supiere y le fuere preguntado. _____

Preguntado si sabe la causa de su prision diga y declare. _____

Dixo que si y esto responde. _____

Preguntado por que occasion yrio alebosamente a Joseph Basques y con que le yrio y por que fue la pendensia que con el dicho Joseph Basques tubo y que otras personas abia delante diga y declare. Dixo que es berdad que abiendo salido toda la gente de su casa afuera y estando sola su hermana Josefa sola en la casa y no abiendo otra persona en ella y que estando este declarante regando su guerta de chile bido que la dicha su hermana estaba bolteando la cara para todas partes y por a donde estaba el dicho declarante y quien biendo estas demostraciones le causo malisia y que entonses se fue para su casa y que al yr llegando bido y conosio al dicho Joseph Basques que yba saliendo de un cuarto que esta por techar que cae ala espalda dela puerta principal de su casa y que entonses se fue para el dicho Joseph Basques sin yntension de aserle mal sino a desirle y preguntarle que buscaba y con yntension de requirirle que no le fuese a su casa pues ya selo tenian mandado por justicia y que este declarante tambien dise selo tenia ya dicho no llegase a su casa y que en la occasion que lo aio saliendo del destechado cuarto al llarlo bido se abalanso el dicho Josef Basques a coger piedras y que entonses le dio con el cabo de la coa en la cabesa y que esto es la berdad y esto responde._____

Preguntado como dise que le dio el golpe con dicha coa cara a cara cuando dise el dicho Joseph Basques que al golpe bolteo la mano para coger a quien le dio y que entonses le mordio el dedo de la mano derecha diga y declare. _____

Dixo que falta a la berdad en lo que dise por que luego se agararon los dos como luchando y que biendo este declarante le tiraba a sacar los ojos con los dedos defendiendose es berdad que le mordio entonses el dedo y que en la lucha en que estaban le dijo el dicho Joseph Basques que se acabara aquello y que entonses se soltaron y cada uno se fue a su casa el dicho declarante para la suia y el herido para la casa de Fernando Martin y dise este declarante que el selo de la honra de su dicha hermana que es la sulla le motibo a el echo que es la berdad so cargo del juramento que fecho tiene a que se ratifico por una, dos y tres beses y que es de edad de beinte y tres años poco mas o menos y que le toca el erido por partes de la muger deste declarante y no firmo por desir no saber firmelo yo dicho Alcalde Mallor actctuando como Juez receptor con los de asisstensia en dicha Villa Nueba en dicho dia, mes y año ut supra.

Ante me como Juez receptor
Joseph Truxillo (rubric)
Testigo de asistencia
Miguel Martin (rubric)
Juan de Atienza (rubric)

Auto
Y luego yncontinente en dicho dia, mes y año yo dicho Alcalde Mallor teniendo por combeniente pase la persona de Diego Martin a la presencia del Señor don Juan Ignacio Flores Mogollon Governador y Capitan General auctual deste Reyno con las diligencias por mi echas y faltando en ellas la persona de Antonio Martin por allarse en esa Villa de Santa Fee aquien sita la de el dicho Joseph Basques y considerandose

alla en el Supremo Juisio deste Reyno se solisitara para oirle en juisio no lo dilato mas por la poca seguridad que ai en esta jurisdizion de carsel y prisiones lo remito ala presensia de dicho Señor para que Su Señoria determine lo mas que combenga asi lo probei y mande auctuando como Juez receptor en dicho dia, mes y año ut supra.

Ante mi como Juez receptor
Joseph Truxillo (rubric)
Testigo de asistencia
Juan de Atienza (rubric)
Miguel Martin (rubric)

Costar estos auctos de cuatro foxas escritas y para que conste lo firme y los de asistencia.

Ante mi como Juez receptor
Joseph Truxillo (rubric)

Auto
En la Villa de Santa Fee dela Nueva Mexico en treinta dias del mes de Julio de mil setecientos y quinze años yo don Juan Ignacio Flores Mogollon Governador y Capitan General deste Reino y Provincias dela Nueva Mexico por SM., haviendo visto estos autos que me remite el Alcalde Mayor dela Villa Nueba de Santa Cruz y jurisdizion dela Cañada Joseph Truxillo, con el papel que escribe en que me dize remite preso a Diego Martin reo, en ellos, el que le mando al Cavo dela Guardia lo reziva por preso al dicho Diego Martin con toda guardia y custodia y estando presente dicho Cavo digo tenerlo resevido y que lo tendra con la guardia y custodia nezesaria; y por quanto en dichos autos no consta en su declarazion de Joseph Vasques el erido si se querella del dicho Diego Martin o lo perdona mando que originales se remitan estos autos a dicho Alcalde Mayor para que ejecute esta diligencia y le reziva asi mismo la declarazion a Antonio Martin que se alla oy en aquella jurisdizion y fecho melo devoluera asi lo provey, mande y firme con mi Secretario de Governazion y Guerra.

Juan Ignacio Flores Mogollon (rubric)
Por mando del Governador y Capitan General
Roque de Pinto (rubric)
Secretario de Governazion y Guerra

En la Villa Nueva de Santa Cruz en el postrero dia del mes de Julio del presente año de mil setecientos y quinse años en cumplimiento y obedesimiento del aucto de ariba espedido por el Señor don Juan Ignacio Flores Mogollon Governador y Capitan General deste Reyno dela Nueba Mexico y sus Probincias por el Rey Nuestro Señor yo el Alferez Reformado Joseph Truxillo Alcalde Mallor y Capitan Aguerra de dicha

Villa y su jurisdizion pase al Puesto de Chimayó ala casa donde se alla la persona de Joseph Basques quien se alla lastimado dela persona de Diego Martin quien yrio a dicho Joseph Basques y estando presente dicho herido y juntamente su esposa y Antonio Basques hermano de dicho herido aquienes pregunte si del agrabio y heridas que tiene su parte secrellan sivil y criminalmente digan en esta materia lo que sienten y si perdonan al causante de dichas heridas a que respondio el dicho Joseph Basques que no secrella y que perdona el dano de sus heridas y que si solo pide se mire que es pobre y no tiene con que pagar la cura que sele esta asiendo de horden dela Real Justicia y la mesma rason dan su esposa y hermano y para que asi conste la firme yo dicho Alcalde Mallor auctuando como Juez receptor con los testigos de asistencia en dicho ut supra.

          Ante mi como Juez receptor
          Joseph Truxillo (rubric)
          Testigo de asistencia
          Miguel Martin (rubric)
          Juan de Atienza (rubric)

    Luego yncontinente en dicho Puesto de Chimayó en dicho dia mes y año yo dicho Alcalde Mallor y Capitan Aguerra mande pareser ante mi a Antonio Martin y estando presente le resevi juramento el cual hizo en toda forma de derecho por Dios Nuestro Señor y la Senal de la Santa Cruz y prometio desir berdad en todo lo que supiere y fuese preguntado. _____

    Preguntado si se allo en el disgusto o pendencia que tubo Diego Martin con Joseph Basques y que rasones tubieron o el motibo por que se origino dicha pendensia y si abia otras personas alo dicho presentes diga y declare. _____

    Dixo no aberse allado presente y que menos no sabe las rasones que tubieron ni el motibo de dicha pendensia ni otra cosa alguna delo que sele pregunta al caso tocante y que es la berdad la que jura y declara y esto responde. _____

    Preguntado donde se allaba el dia de la pendensia de los dichos Diego Martin y Joseph Basques diga y declare. _____

    Dixo se allaba en su guerta trabaxando cosa de dos tiros de arcabus y que no sabe otra cosa y aunque sele ysieron otras preguntas y repreguntas al caso tocante dixo no saber mas que lo que referido lleba a que se ratifico por una, dos y tres beses y que en las generales de la ley le toca la muger del dicho Joseph Basques como que es su hija y por partes de Diego Martin es su sobrino carnal y que es de edad de sesenta años poco mas o menos y no firmo por desir no saber firmelo yo dicho Alcalde Mayor auctuando como Juez receptor y los de asistencia en dicho dia mes y año ut supra.

          Ante mi como Juez receptor
          Joseph Truxillo (rubric)
          Testigo de asistencia
          Miguel Martin (rubric)
          Juan de Atienza (rubric)

Remito yo el Alcalde Mallor Joseph Truxillo estos auctos ala presensia del Señor don Juan Ignacio Flores Mogollon adjuntos ala hordenasion de Su Señoria para que en bista de ellos determine lo que combenga y para que conste lo firme en este Puesto de Chimayó en treinta y uno de Julio del año de mill setesientos y quinse años y los de asistensia ut supra.

Ante mi como Juez receptor
Joseph Truxillo (rubric)
Testigo de asistensia
Miguel Martin (rubric)
Juan de Atienza (rubric)

Auto y fee de Sanidad
En la Villa de Santa Fee dela Nueva Mexico en dos dias del mes de Septiembre de mill setezientos y quinse años yo don Juan Ignacio Flores Mogollon Governador y Capitan General de este Reino y Provincias dela Nueva Mexico por SM., haviendo llegado ami notizia que Joseph Vasquez se allava sano de sus heridas le mande comparezer ante mi con el Maestre de Barbero Antonio Duran de Armijo y estando presente le mande al dicho Maestro de Barvero le reconociere las eridas y aviendolo ejecutado le rezevi juramento que hizo por Dios Nuestro Señor y la Señal de la Santa Cruz so cargo del qual prometio dezir verdad en lo que fuere preguntado; y siendolo que si el dicho Joseph Varquez se halla ya sano y sin peligro de muerte de las eridas que le dio Diego Martin, dijo que haviendolo visto y reconosido a su leal saver y entender esta ya bueno y libre delas eridas el dicho Joseph Vasquez y sin peligro de muerte ni quedar sin lesion alguna y que esta es la verdad y lo firmo con migo dicho Governador y mi Secretario de Governazion y Guerra.

Juan Ignacio Flores Mogollon (rubric)
Antonio Duran de Armijo (rubric)
Roque de Pinto (rubric)
Secretario de Governazion y Guerra

Y luego yncontinenti yo dicho Governador y Capitan General haviendo visto la fee de Sanidad dada por Antonio Duran de Armijo en que asegura estar en el todo bueno Joseph Vasquez mando sele notifique se benga a bivir a esta Villa con su mujer para quitar la ocasion de que buelva a entrar en la casa de Diego Martin con aperzevimiento que de no ejecutarlo luego saldra desterrado del Reino; y por quanto confiesa haverlo curado veinte y tres dias Francisco Xabier Romero y haver gastado con el dos carneros mando que de los vienes encargados que tiene el dicho Diego Martin sele pague al dicho Francisco Romero los dos carneros y a razon de dos reales por dia dela curazion y sentenzio al dicho Diego Martin en seis pesos para la fabrica de esta Santa Yglesia y que pague las costas prozesales y personales y las taze el Sargento Mayor don Alfonso Real de Aguilar y satisfecho todo lo referido sele alze el embargo de sus bienes y sea suelto de la prision adviertiendole no buelva a tener mas cuestion con el dicho Joseph Vasquez y al pie de este auto y notificado se pondra la tazasion de costas para que siempre conste asi lo provei, mande y firme con mi Secretario de Governazion y Guerra. Asi mismo mando sele pagen ocho pesos al dicho Joseph Vasquez salario de un mes.

Juan Ignacio Flores Mogollon (rubric)
Por mando del Señor Governador y Capitan General
Roque de Pinto (rubric)
Secretario de Governazion y Guerra

Notificacion a Joseph Vasquez
Yo el presente Secretario de Governazion y Guerra en cumplimento del auto antezedente del Señor Governador y Capitan General le lei y notifique a Joseph Vasquez en su persona lo que consta que aviendolo oydo y entendido dijo lo obedeze y que podra benirse a esta Villa luego que alze su cosecha y esto dio por su respuesta presente el Cavo Juan Ruiz Cordero y Juan de Ledesma y no firmo por no saber firmelo yo en dicho dia, mes y año.

Roque de Pinto (rubric)
Secretario de Governazion y Guerra

Tazasion de costas

En la Villa de Santa Fee en diez dias de el mes de Septiembre de mill setezientos quinze años yo el Sargento Mayor don Alfonso Rael de Aguilar en execusion y cumplimiento del auto de ariba probeyido por el Señor Governador y Captian General don Juan Ignacio Flores Mogollon en que me manda haga tassasiones de las costas que se an causado en esta causa azi personales como prosesales las quales son en la manera siguiente.

Primeramente quatro pesos y medio al Señor Governador por lo actuado en esta causa.	0oo4 pesos 4 reales
Mas al Capitan don Roque de Pinto Secretario de Governazion y Guerra la tasso tres pesos.	0oo3 pesos
Mas le tasso al Capitan Joseph Truxillo Alcalde Mayor dela Villa Nueba de Santa Cruz por lo actuado y demas dilixencias personales que en esta causa tiene Echa, nuebe pesos.	0oo9 pesos
A Juan de Atienza le tasso por aver escrito esta caussa con dicho Alcalde Mayor cuatro pesos.	0oo4 pesos

Mas cinco pesos y seis reales por veinte y tres dias que Francisco Xavier Romero estubo curando al dicho Joseph Basques a dos reales por cada un dia senalado por el auto de dicho Señor General con mas dos carneros que el dicho Francisco Xabier gasto en su comicion que a dos pesos cada uno   0oo9 pesos 6 reales
ymporta uno y otro lo que se a de pagar al dicho Francisco Xabier.   0oo0 pesos 2 reales

Mas dos reales del papel que se a gastado en esta causa.

Que por todas suman y montan treinta pesos y quatro reales y que para   0o30 pesos 4 reales
que asi conste lo firme en dicho dia mes y año.

Alphonso Rael de Aguilar (rubric)

Yo el presente Secretario de Governazion y Guerra en cumplimento del auto del Señor Governador y Capitan General baje al Cuerpo de Guardia deste Presidio y en el le lei y notifique a Diego Martin preso y reo en estos autos quien aviendolo oydo y entendido dijo lo ovedeze y consiente y que examine y me entrega las costas para que yo las reparta y ponga recivo en los autos y no firmo por no saver firmelo el presente Secretario en diez de Septiembre de mill setezientos y quinze.

Roque de Pinto (rubric)
Secretario de Governazion y Guerra

Digo yo el Capitan Juan Garcia de la Rivas que rezevi de Diego Martin vesino de La Cañada zeis pesos en que fue multado los quales son para la fabrica dela Santa Yglesia y por no allarse en esta Villa el General Juan Paes Hurtado quien corre en dicha fabrica los apersevi asta que el dicho benga y por zer verdad lo firme en esta dicha Villa de Santa Fee en tres de Zetiembre de mil zetesientos y quinse años.

Juan Garcia de la Riva (rubric)

Digo yo Joseph Truxillo Alcalde Mayor de la Villa Nueva de Santa Cruz y jurisdizion dela Cañada que recivi de Diego Martin nueve pesos de los derechos dela causa criminal que contra el dicho e seguido y asi mismo recivi quatro pesos delos derechos que tocavan de dicha causa a Juan de Atienza por averlas escripto. Villa de Santa Fee de la Nueva Mexico y Septiembre 13 de 1715.

Joseph Truxillo (rubric)

Son 13 pesos

Notes

1. Diego Martín Moraga was the son of Cristóbal Martín Serrano and Antonia Moraga, a family who had land in Chimayó. He married Manuela de Vargas in 1714. His mother and other members of the family were involved in several disputes in the area regarding hexing, land boundaries, and slander. He also had a brother, Cristóbal, who is probably the person mentioned in the document (Jenkins, "Women": 340-43; Chávez, *Origins*: 224-25). When this case was heard, the authorities would have been familiar with the family. The high cost of the proceedings charge to Martín could be a result of the family's continuing disruptive behavior.
2. This person cannot be identified with any certainty at this time. A Joseph Vásquez, a maker of carts [*carretas*], lived in Santa Fe in 1709, and in 1715, when twenty-four years old, lived at Santa Cruz with his wife Francisca de Torres. However, it is unlikely that this is the Vásquez in question, who was, as stated below, married to a Martín. In the 1697 livestock distribution, there is a José Vásquez, married to a Juana, but no other information is given (Chávez, *Origins*: 309; Kessell et al., *BOB*: 1154, 1176 n132).
3. Captain Joseph Trujillo is on a 1697 list of soldiers and was one of the eight soldiers assigned to the Santa Cruz garrison in 1701. In 1700–1701, he was granted land near San Ildefonso and Santa Cruz, which were validated in 1713. His parents, Cristóbal Trujillo and María de Manzanares, were prerevolt settlers. In 1706 Joseph was appointed temporary alcalde at Pecos while Juan de Ulibarrí was on campaign. Joseph was an alcalde of Santa Cruz in 1715. His name is on Inscription Rock at El Morro(Kessell et al., *TDC*: 128; Kessell, *Kiva*: 505; Chávez, *Origins*: 297; SANM I #72, #1136).
4. This Joseph Madrid is probably the son of Roque Madrid and Juana López. Roque was a prerevolt settler who returned to New Mexico and served with Vargas and later in a variety of military expeditions. In 1696, during the Pueblo uprising, Joseph was a reserve adjutant (Chávez, *Origins*: 218; Kessell et al., *BOB*: 804-5, 956 n43).
5. The term *surgeon*, or *cirujano*, has a different meaning from that of master barber, used later in the document when referring to Antonio Durán de Armijo. Note that the surgeon inspected the wounds, but the master barber was used to determine that they had healed. *Cirujano* seems to denote a higher status and perhaps more extensive training.
6. Francisco Xavier Romero was a native of Mexico City, arriving in Santa Fe in 1694. He married María de la Cruz and later moved to Chimayó, where he was a shoemaker and practiced medicine. In 1732 he and Pasquala Padilla attended the baptism of a child in Santa Cruz (Chávez, *Origins*: 273; NMGS, *New Mexico Baptisms*: 23).
7. The Protector of the Indians was appointed by the governor to provide aid and defense for the Pueblo Indians and to represent their legal rights and privileges, allowing them access to the Spanish legal system. The person in that position generally acted upon the request of the Indians and did not have authority over them (Cutter, *Protector*: ix–x, 1-3).
8. Juan de Atienza came to New Mexico from Puebla in 1694 with the Farfán-Velasco expedition. His father, José, had the title of the alguacil mayor of the Holy Office of the Inquisition in New Mexico. Juan de Atienza was the alcalde mayor of Santa Cruz in the earlier 1700s and served as protector of the Indians from 1713 to 1716. He was the last active appointee to this position. It is not clear why he was part of this investigation unless one of the people involved was an Indian, or perhaps because he was a former alcalde (Cutter, *Protector*: 53-57; Esquibel, "Mexico City": 67).
9. *Canser* probably means septic or infected.
10. Cristóbal Martín was probably the brother of Diego Martín, the husband of María Montoya, and the son of Cristóbal Martín Serrano and Antonia Moraga, who returned to New Mexico in 1693. However, he could also be the elder Cristóbal Martín Serrano. All of the Martíns mentioned in this document were probably part of the Martín Serrano clan and descendants of Luis Martín Serrano, a prerevolt settler (Chávez, *Origins*: 222-226; see also Doc. 27).
11. Antonio Martín [Serrano] was the son of either Luis II or Apolinario Martín Serrano. He and María Barba were married in 1698 after Antonio's first wife, Inés de Ledesma, died. In 1703 he stated that he was born in the puesto of Chimayó. He was probably an uncle of the Diego Martín mentioned here. María Barba was the daughter of Esteban Barba and María Luján. In 1717 she returned to El Paso (Chávez, *Origins*: 222; Kessell and Hendricks, *RCR*: 327 n61; Kessell et al., *BOB*: 1162 n23; *TDC*: 187-88).
12. The term "superior government" is often used as a kind of flattering term to refer to the next higher level of government, usually the governor's office.
13. Fernando (aka Hernando) Martín (Serrano), the son of Luis Martín and Antonia de Miranda, and was born at La Cañada. He was a soldier at El Paso when he married María Montaño in 1685 (Kessell et al., *BOB*: 960 n70)

12

MOTHER PETITIONS FOR RETURN OF SON FROM THE ROYAL MINES OF CHIHUAHUA
October 31, 1715. Source: SANM II #239d.

Synopsis and editor's note: In this document, María de Quiros authorized her godfather, Francisco Lorenzo Casados, or his son, Francisco Joseph Casados, if the father was not available, to travel to the mines of Chihuahua or of Santa Rosa Cusihuiriáchic, to bring back her son, Juan [Durán] de Armijo. According to María, Juan was taken there by his grandfather, José de Quiros, who would not allow him to return to New Mexico. It is not known with any certainty whether the son returned to New Mexico, since his brothers, who were in New Mexico, had very similar names. He may be the Juan Durán de Armijo who had a son, José Antonio, who served as a blacksmith's apprentice in Taos (Chávez, *Origins*, 137).

It should be noted that once María de Quiros gave the authorization, the governor would have had to give approval for any trip to Chihuahua, since his permission was required for travelers who wanted to go outside the colony. As an example, a surviving 1732 notice from Governor Cruzat y Góngora provides the date that residents may leave under escort from Albuquerque to the south, ordering that, "No one is to leave the province without my express permission. For all of this, the said alcaldes mayores are to submit a list of all who intend to go, so that upon reviewing it, permission is granted for them to leave" (SANM II #377).

The royal mine of Cusihuiriáchic, on the edge of the Parral mining zone near Chihuahua, was established during the seventeenth century at a time when the more important silver strikes were made with the last big bonanza occurring in 1686. At one time, Chihuahua was the administrative center of the area, a parish seat, and the largest Spanish settlement in the region. In the period after the revolt of 1680 and before the Reconquest, many former and future New Mexico residents lived in the area, for example, Pedro Durán y Chávez and Nicolás Lucero de Godoy. It may be that José de Quiros knew the area from that time (West, *Mining*: 7, 12-14). For a list of former and future New Mexico residents living at Cusihuiriáchic, see Kessell and Hendricks (*BFA*: 119 n64).

[Marginal note]
Authority given
by the barber's wife

On the 31st of October, 1715, at the villa of Santa Fe, headquarters of this kingdom and provinces of New Mexico. Before me Captain Juan García de la Riva, alguacil mayor [high sheriff] of the Holy Office [Inquisition] and alcalde ordinario of this villa, acting before me as presiding judge with my assisting witnesses due to the lack of a public or royal scribe, which there is none in this kingdom, appeared María de Quiros,[1] legitimate wife of the sergeant of the militia, Antonio Durán de Armijo,[2] whom I know. She stated that she gave her complete authority in everything that is required, first of all to her godfather, Francisco Lorenzo Casados, and secondly to his son, Francisco Joseph de Casados,[3] with the understanding that if one cannot act, the other one can.

She states that she is married to the said sergeant [Antonio Durán de Armijo] but that at the present time he is not at this Villa of Santa Fe, because he has been ordered by Governor and Captain General don Juan Ygnacio Flores Mogollón to go to the jurisdiction of La Cañada to heal his injuries, for which reason he, the sergeant, cannot do what is required. Because of this the said María de Quiros is left without the aid of her husband to support and provide for her and thus is left to authorize the above to bring back a legitimate son of hers by the name of Juan Durán de Armijo, who is found either in the royal mining towns of Chihuahua or of Cusihuiriáchic with his grandfather, Joseph de Quiros, who is not permitting him to return to this kingdom. For this reason, she gives her full authority, with full and general administration, for them to bring him back so that he is not lost in the said royal mining towns, so that they are at no time disallowed from doing this, in order that they can appear before the justices of his majesty with full rigor and right and order her son, Juan de Armijo, to be brought back to this kingdom, and so that his grandfather, Joseph de Quiros, cannot stop them.

She did not sign it because she did not know how. However, so that the authority she gave is allowed, it was signed with her full consent by one of the witnesses who was present. Those who were present as witnesses were Francisco Rendón, Juan Ruis Cordero, and Antonio López, along with myself and my two assisting witnesses. It was done on common paper because the sealed kind is not found in this kingdom, to which I certify.

Corrected between the lines near the word Joseph[4]

ORIGINAL DOCUMENT

Poder que otorgo la mujer de el barbero

En la Villa de Santa Fe cavesera de este Reyno y Provincias de la Nueva Mexico en treinta y uno de Octubre de mill setesientos quinze años. Ante mi el Capitan Juan

Garcia de la Riva Alguasil Mayor del Santo Oficio y Alcalde Ordinario desta Villa, actuando ante mi como Juez Rezeptor con los ynfrascriptos testigos de mi asistenzia por no haver Escribano publico ni Real en este Reyno, parecio María de Quiros, muger legitima del Sargento de Milisia Antonio Duran de Armijo a quien doy fee conosco y dixo que da su poder cumplido que en bastante se requiere y es nessesario en primer lugar al Capitan Francisco Lorenso Casados, su compadre, y en segundo lugar a su hijo Francisco Joseph de Casados con la facultad delo que el uno pueda pues pueda segir el otro. Y por quanto es casada con el suso dicho Sargento quien al presente no se alla en esta Villa de Santa Fee por aver salido de alla de orden del Señor Governador y Capitan General Dn. Juan Ygnacio Flores Mogollon ala jurisdision de La Cañada a curar unas heridas y por essa causa no lo ase el dicho Sargento por allarse sin tener la dicha Maria de Quiros sin tener quien en ausencia de dicho su espose la socorra y fomente aze representasion que da dicho poder a los suso dichos para que le traigan a un hijo suy lexitimo llamado Juan Duran de Armijo el qual anda asi a los Reales de minas de 'Chiguagua o Cusihuiriáchic'[5] con su abuelo Joseph de Quiros quien le embarasa la entrada a este Reyno por cuya razon da el poder referido con libre y general administrasion para que lo triagan y no se bea el dicho su hijo perdido en dichos Reales de minas y para que en ningun tiempo le pongan el embaraso para todo lo qual puedan pareser y parescan ante las justisias de Su Magestad para que con todo rigor y apremio le manden al dicho su hijo Juan de Armijo se benga y lo traigan a este dicho Reyno y el dicho su abuelo Joseph de Quiros no lo ympida y para que conste de su otorgamiento no firmo por que dixo no saber, firmelo uno delos testigos que presentes se allaron a su otorgamiento que lo fueron Francisco Rendon, Juan Ruis Cordero y Antonio Lopez con migo y los dicho testigos de mi asistensia y en el presente papel comun por que el sellado no corre en este Reyno de que doi fee = enmendado Joseph Valga = entre [renglones]

Notes

1. María de Quiros came to New Mexico with her father, José de Quiros, in 1695 from Sombrerete (see Map 3, Appendix). In the same year, she married Antonio Durán de Armijo. In 1705 José de Quiros left for the mines of Chihuahua with his grandson (Chávez, *Origins*: 136, 263; Kessell et al., *BOB*: 558 n14).
2. Antonio Durán de Armijo was born in Zacatecas, coming to New Mexico in 1695, where he was known as a notary and a master barber, a term used for a person with some medical experience. He was a master sergeant at the presidio by 1716. He and María de Quiros are known to have had three children, one of whom was Juan Durán de Armijo. In 1742 he, a widower, married Bárbara Montoya, widow of Diego Romero, a landowner in the Taos area. When he died in 1748, his will stated that he owned land in Taos and Las Trampas (Chávez, *Origins*: 136-37; Jenkins, "Taos": 97; see also Docs. 13, 19, and 24).
3. Francisco Joseph de Casados, a resident of Santa Fe, was married to María Bárbara de Archibeque, one of the daughters of Juan de Archibeque. His father was Francisco Lorenzo Casados, from Cadiz (Chávez, *Origins*: 137).
4. The words "de Chihuahua y Cusihuiriáchic" were an amendment and were written between the lines. See the transcription.
5. These words were an amendment, written above the line.

13

SERGEANT KILLED IN INDIAN ATTACK; WIDOW PETITIONS FOR DEATH BENEFITS
November 2, 1715. Source: SANM II #239f.

Synopsis and editor's notes: In 1715 Antonia Durán wrote to Governor Juan Ignacio Flores Mogollón, asking that money be paid to her from the soldiers' insurance fund because of the death of her husband, Sergeant Pasqual Trujillo. She stated that because he was killed in the province of Nueva Vizcaya, rather than New Mexico, some soldiers were saying that the money should not be paid. In her carefully-written request, she pointed out that such money had been recently paid from the fund for the death of three other presidio soldiers. The governor agreed with her and asked Captain Felix Martínez to collect the money and to adjust the amount, including the presidio salary owing to her husband and subtracting the presidio debts. This was done, with the result that not much money was left. In this case, Mogollón also acted as a kind of probate judge, reviewing the items that were in her husband's estate and those that belonged to her. At first he set up a guardianship for the children, but then changed his mind and ruled that no guardian was required.

The clarity of the petition, and the fact that she had it written at all, suggests that Antonia Durán was a capable and able person. Unfortunately, when all the accounting was done, there were 745 pesos owed to the governor and 41 to Feliz Martinez, probably for "company store" military supplies. The result was that the money that came to her and her nine children was only 286 pesos. Her husband's salary for two months and twenty-three days was only a little over 97 pesos.

Petition by Antonia Durán, widow of the Sergeant Pasqual Trujillo,[1] in which she asks that the governor and captain general order that each soldier pay ten pesos for every soldier who died [while on active duty] and that the said governor order that they are paid by the auditor of this presidio, don Felix Martínez,[2] who executed it.

Year of 1715

Villa of Santa Fe, New Mexico

Contained in four pages

Governor and Captain General

At this villa of Santa Fe, New Mexico, on the 2nd of November, 1715, this was presented by the below stated to the governor and captain general.

[I] Antonia Durán, resident of this villa of Santa Fe, and widow of Pasqual Trujillo, former sergeant of this presidial castle, appear before your honor in the best form which is given to me by my right, and I say that I received a written agreement from the soldiers of this presidia castle on the third of November of the past year of 1712, which was approved by Sergeant Major don Alfonso Rael de Aguilar, the alcalde ordinario, in which they obligated themselves and agreed by their own right to pay ten pesos, each one, which are to be paid by General Martínez. In regard to this, my husband, with the permission of your honor, left on a trip to the city of México and upon returning from his trip he was killed by the barbaric Indians in the kingdom of Viscaya, for which reason and due to their obligation, by the written agreement which they all agreed to, all of the soldiers are obligated to pay the ten pesos. I have been notified that some of them do not want to pay because they say that my husband did not die in the service of the king, our lord. This is malicious, improper, unfounded, and unreasonable.

First of all, as I have stated, my husband left this kingdom with the written permission of your honor, drawing the salary which his majesty has allowed the soldiers of this presidio according to their rank, and his was that of sergeant, a position he held, with the salary which he drew, and under which he lost his life. Secondly, it is publicly well known that my husband lost his life being a loyal vassal [*vasallo*] defending our Holy Catholic faith against the barbaric Indians who invade the kingdom of Vizcaya. He tried to protect and save the lives of the soldiers and the residents who came with the rear guard when they were attacked by the said barbaric [Indians]. He was with the front guard in the company of others, and upon receiving word that they [the rear guard] had been attacked, he went to their aid, as a good vassal should, in order to assist them and defend the faith of God to fight the enemy, which was how he lost his life, along with the others. Thirdly, there is no clause in the written agreement which is contrary to this, and in fact, it states that for every soldier and his companion who dies, they are obligated to pay the said ten pesos, not finding any obscure reason or law by which they claim not having to pay, particularly when my husband had paid for the soldiers who had been killed, namely Matías Lobato,[3] Juan Antonio Ramos,[4] and Gregorio Ramírez.[5] For those above named, there had not been any opposition as some have shown against my husband.[6] For which reason I make it well known to his honor, so that he will attend to the said obligation of the written agreement, being that my said husband died in the royal service, and so that he will order that the said ten pesos are paid to me by all of the soldiers, which is what I argue for and is in my favor.

Of your honor I ask and petition in all sincerity that you be pleased to order that I be granted what I ask for, which is what I expect with great justification from your honor, from whom I request the royal assistance which is done for justice, and I swear in due form that it is done for the best, etc.
       Antonia Durán (rubric)

Being reviewed by me, don Juan Ygnacio Flores Mogollón, governor and captain general of this kingdom and province of New Mexico for his majesty, I took it as it was presented, and agreeing to the fact that what the party states is true, I order Captain don Felix Martínez, the actual auditor of this presidio, that he charge the account of every soldier the ten pesos which they are obligated to pay, so that they cannot ignore their obligation to the agreement which they made, and which they were charged for in the deaths of those mentioned in this written document. He is also to adjust the account of the deceased including the salary up to the time that he died. He was killed while he held the position of sergeant of this company, having left with my permission, and was not a deserter of the royal service, in which case if he had been, he would not be covered by the agreement which they have made. In addition to that stated, he shall deduct from the amount that which is owed to me up to the 16th of June and adjust the account of his salary up to that said day. He is also to deduct everything which the said captain had supplied for him and shall liquidate what remains as his pay, making sure that the account is clear and distinct at the bottom of these proceedings, and which are to be made known to General don Juan Páez Hurtado, alcalde ordinario, to whom I give full commission as required and as needed, so that in my name the account is fully liquidated, and he is to sign it along with the captain. As such I approved, ordered, and signed it along with my secretary of government and war in the villa of Santa Fe, New Mexico, on the 2nd of November, 1715.
      don Juan Ygnacio Flores Mogollón (rubric)
          before me
       Roque de Pinto (rubric)
     Secretary of government and war

In this villa of Santa Fe on the 4th of November, 1715, I, General Juan Páez Hurtado, alcalde ordinario of this said villa, in fulfillment of the above decree, came to the house and residence of Captain don Felix Martínez, captain-for-life of this royal presidio, who upon his being present, I notified him of the said decree, and who upon having heard and understanding it, said that he had heard it, will obey it and comply fully with that which is ordered. So that it is safeguarded, I, said alcalde ordinario, fully explained the petition of Antonia Durán, widow of Sergeant Pasqual Trujillo, and the decree provided for her along with her response. So that it is valid I signed it as presiding judge with my assisting witnesses, who signed along with me and the said Captain don Felix Martínez, who, because the petition is done for justice, granted the request as was asked for.

Juan Páez Hurtado (rubric)
Presiding judge
assisting witness
Miguel Tenorio de Alba (rubric)
Antonio Durán de Armijo (rubric)

At this villa of Santa Fe on the 5th of November, 1715, I, General Juan Páez Hurtado, alcalde ordinario of it, by virtue of my commission proceeded to make the adjustment of the account of Sergeant Pasqual Trujillo in the following manner.

First of all, he remained owing to the governor seven hundred forty-five pesos as can be seen by the note which was submitted by the said [General Hurtado] to Captain don Felix and was deducted from his honor's book. 745 –
Item, he owed ten pesos which was paid by the said captain to the deceased
   Gregorio Ramires. 010 –
Item, he owed another ten pesos which were paid for the same reason to the
   deceased Juan Antonio Ramos. 010 –
Item, he owed according to the book of Captain don Felix forty-one pesos for
   what he had provided to him. 041 –
The total for all of this amounts to 806 pesos
What the said Sergeant Pasqual Trujillo is to receive amounts to nine hundred
   and ninety[7] pesos from the agreement of the soldiers 990 –
Item, his salary for two months and twenty-three days, from July 16 until the
   7th of September 97 pesos and 6 reales 097-6 –
The two separate accounts amount to 1087-6 –
Deducted from the total are eight hundred and six pesos 806 –
After the deductions there is left for the widow two hundred and eighty-one
   pesos and six reales 281-6 –

So that the adjustment of debts which I have made by virtue of the commission given to me as presiding judge is valid, I signed it along with the captain and my assisting witnesses on the said day.

Juan Páez Hurtado (rubric)
Felix Martínez (rubric)
assisting witnesses
Miguel Tenorio de Alba (rubric)
Antonio Durán de Armijo (rubric)

At this villa of Santa Fe, New Mexico, on the 19th of November, 1715, I, don Juan Ygnacio Flores Mogollón, governor and captain general of this kingdom and provinces of New Mexico for his majesty, having seen the above account and from it know that there is owed to the widow two hundred and eighty-one pesos and six reales from which Captain don Félix Martínez is to pay eight [pesos] to General Juan Páez Hurtado for having gone through it and figured out the said account. From the two hundred and seventy-three pesos and six reales which remain he is to divide the amount into two promissory notes, each one in the amount of one hundred thirty-six pesos and seven reales, one being for the said widow, Antonia Durán, and the other one for Captain Joseph Trujillo,[8] whom I appoint as guardian for the minor children of Sergeant Pasqual Trujillo, deceased, and of the said widow, Antonia Durán, his wife. The said widow is to inform me of the other goods which they had, which ones belonged to her, and the ones which they shared, separating those which belong to the said minors. For this I had her, Antonia Durán, appear before me, and from whom upon being present received her sworn statement, which she made to God, Our Lord, and to the sign of the Cross, to which she promised to tell the truth about whatever she was asked, stating which goods were left by her husband. She said that there were two branded horses with the brand of his majesty which were left at the presidio of El Paso when he went to Mexico, three hundred breeding lambs, thirty-six rams, and two oxen. These she says are the goods which her husband left, along with the children, who are Juan, Domingo, Francisco, María, Josepha, Andrés, Bernardo, Antonio, and Pasqual Trujillo. To the said Juan Trujillo, who is on his own, his father, Sergeant Pasqual Trujillo, left him everything that was due to him and belonged to him except that he has part of the house in which the family lives.

Although she has stated that he left three hundred and thirty-six sheep, it is well known and public knowledge that they belong to the declarant, who upon finding herself in need, was given the major number of them by her brother, so that she could sustain herself, and I inform the governor of this so that she can keep what is hers.

I, the governor, being made aware of this, approve that she, the said Antonia Durán, keep them as hers. There being no other goods which belong to the minor children, other than the one hundred thirty-six pesos and seven reales, even though the promissory note is made in favor of Captain Joseph Trujillo, I order Captain don Félix Martínez to pay it to the said Antonia Durán, but that each one of the minor children should be given the amount of twelve pesos, more or less, and the court finds that no guardian is required.[9] The house in which they live, being somewhat large, I order that the widow be notified that she is not to sell it at any time without special permission and the consent of her children. I thus approved, ordered, and signed it with my secretary of government and war.

            don Juan Ygnacio Flores Mogollón (rubric)
                        before me,
                    Roque de Pinto (rubric)
            Secretary of government and war

Notification

     Continuing on, I, the present secretary of government and war in fulfillment of the preceding decree of the governor and captain general, read and notified Antonia Durán, widow of Sergeant Pasqual Trujillo, in her proper person, whom I know, who upon having heard and understood everything said that she would obey and agree to it and that she would not sell the house now, or at any time, unless it was with the special consent of her children. She did not sign because she did not know how.[10]

               Roque de Pinto (rubric)
               Secretary of government and war

ORIGINAL DOCUMENT

Petizion de Antonia Duran buida del Sargento Pasqual Trujillo en que pide al Señor Governador y Capitan General la mande pagar diez pesos que cada soldado esta obligado a pagar al soldado que muriere que dicho Señor Governador mando los pagase el Capitan Dn. Feliz Martinez aveador deste Presidio quien lo executo.

               Año de 1715
     Villa de Santa Fee de la Nueba Mexico

Consta de 4 fojas

             Governador y Capitan General

En esta Villa de Santa Fee de la Nueva Mexico en 2 de Noviembre de 1715 la presento la contenida ante el Señor Governador y Capitan General

Antonia Duran vezina desta Villa de Santa Fee y viuda de Pascual Truxillo Sargento que fue deste Castillo Presidial, paresco ante Vuestra Señoria en la mejor forma que el derecho me consede y digo, que aviendo zelebrado escritura de compromiso los soldados de esta Castillo Presidial el dia tres de Noviembre del pasado año de mill setecientos doze la qual passo ante el Sargento Mayor Dn. Alfonso Rael de Aguilar, Alcalde Ordinario obligandose en forma y conforme a derecho a pagar diez pesos cada uno por el General Martinez y por que aviendo salido el dicho mi marido con lisensia de Vuestra Señoria para la Cuidad de Mexico de buelta de dicho su biaje en el camino lo mataron los Yndios barbaros en el Reyno de la Vizcaya; por cuya razon y de dicha obligazion y por dicha escriptura hizieron dever pagar los dichos diez pesos cada uno de dichos soldados; y por que a llegado ami notizia que algunos de ellos an dicho que no quieren pagarlos por dizir que el dicho mi marido no murio en servizio del Rey Nuestro Señor, cuya proposision es malisiosa, baga y sin ningun fundamento y fuera de toda razon; lo primero que como llevo dicho salio deste Reyno el dicho mi marido con lisensia que por escrito dio Vuestra Señoria y ganando el sueldo que Su Magestad tiene consignado alos soldados de este Presidio como uno de los de su dotasion y con el exercicio de Sargento, con que mientras esta ligado en dicha Plaza y gosando de dicho sueldo y en ellas pierde la vida muere en servicio de Su Magestad; lo segundo que el dicho mi marido perdio la vida peleando como es publico y notorio en defensa de Nuestra Santa Fee Catholica y como buen vassallo contra los Yndios varvaros que ymbaden el Reyno de la Vizcaya y pudo librarse y no peligrar la vida por razon de que viniendo caminando con una tropa de soldados y vezinos a estos les salieron dichos varbaros que venian de retaguardia y el dicho mi marido de manguardia en compania de otros que aviendo llegado a su notizia de que estavan peleando fue cin resolucion y como buen vasallo a faboreserlos diciendo publicamente que yba a defender la fee de Dios peleando con los enemigos con esfuerzo a donde perdio la vida con los demas que alli yban; lo terzero no obsta en dicha escriptura de obligazion y compromiso clausela que se oponga sino que llanamente dize que por el soldado y companero que muriere se obligan a pagar dichos diez pesos no allando razon ni justizia de que pretendan no querer pagarlos con razones metafisicas, mayormente aviendo pagado el dicho mi marido por los soldados que an muerto como son Matias Lobato, Juan Antonio Ramos y Gregorio Ramirez, y para estos no ubo oposicion ni contradizion alguna y solamente la tienen algunos en el dicho mi marido, cuyas razones pongo en la gran comprehension de Vuestra Señoria para que atendiendo a la dicha obligazion y escriptura de compromisso y de la aver muerto el dicho mi marido en el Real Servicio sea de servir Vuestra Señoria justizia mediante de mandar seme paguen los dichos diez pesos cada uno de dichos soldados por tanto y lo demas que alegar puedo y ay a mi favor.

A Vuestra Señoria pido y suplico con todo rendimiento sea muy servido de mandar hazer como llevo pedido que assi lo espero de la gran justificazion de Vuestra Señoria en quien ymploro el Real Auxilio pues es de justizia la qual pido y juro en forma y en lo nessesario, ut supra.

      Antonia Duran (rubric)

Y vista por mi Dn. Juan Ygnacio Florez Mogollon Governador y Capitan General deste Reino y Provinzias dela Nueva Mexico por Su Majestad la ube por presentada y por constarme ser zierto todo lo que esta parte representa, mando al Capitan Dn. Felix Martinez Aveador actual deste Presidio cargue ala quenta de cada soldado los diez pesos en que son obligados pues no tienen chanzelada la obligazion y compromiso que hizieron como a cargado las de los difuntos que menziona este escripto y le ajuste la quenta al difunto del sueldo debengado asta el dia en que fallezio; pues lo mataron teniendo actualmente plaza de Sargento desta Compania y aver salido con lizenzia mia pues solo no llevando la que fuera aver desertado del Real Servizio en ese caso no deviera ser comprehendido en el compromiso que tienen fecho; y anotandole lo referido resayara del monte lo que consta averme quedado deviendo asta dies y seis de Junio que se le ajuste la quenta y tiene anonado su sueldo asta dicho dia y tamvien revajara todo lo que dicho Capitan ubiere suplido a esta parte y lo que le sobrara liquido le pagara poniendo la quenta con toda claridad y distinzion al pie de esta auto que se ara notorio el General Dn. Juan Paez Hurtado Alcalde Ordinario a quien doy toda la comision que se requiere y es nesessaria para que en mi nombre se alle ala liquidazion de dicha quenta que firmara con dicho Capitan, asi lo provei, mande y firme con mi Secretario de Governazion y Guerra en la Villa de Santa Fee de la Nueva Mexico en dos de Noviembre de mill setezientos y quinze años.

    Dn. Juan Ygnacio Flores Mogollon (rubric)
    Ante mi
    Roque de Pintto (rubric)
    Secretario de Governazion y Guerra

En esta Villa de Santa Fee en quatro dias del mes de Nobiembre de mill setecientos y quinze años yo el General Juan Paez Hurtado, Alcalde Ordinario de dicha Villa, en cumplimiento del auto de arriba vine a la casa y morada del Capitan Dn. Felix Martinez, Capitan Vitalico deste Real Presidio a quien estando presente le ise notorio el auto zitado que haviendolo oido y entendido dixo, que lo oye y obedese y que dara entero cumplimiento como se le ordena y que para su resguardo yo dicho Alcalde Ordinario le di testimonio dela petizion de Antonia Duran, viuda del Sargento Pasqual Truxillo y del auto a ella proveido y su respuesta y para que conste lo firme como Juez Rezeptor con testigos de asistenzia que lo firmaron con migo y el dicho Capitan Dn. Felix Martinez a quien por ser de justizia su pedimento doy el testimonio que pide =

    Juan Paez Hurtado (rubric)
    Juez receptor
    testigo de assistencia
    Miguel Tenorio de Alba (rubric)
    Antonio Duran de Armijo (rubric)

En esta Villa de Santa Fee en sinco dias del mes de Noviembre de mill setecientos y quinze años, yo el General Juan Paez Hurtado, Alcalde Ordinario de alla en virtud de comission pase a el ajuste de quentas del Sargento Pascual Truxillo en la forma siguiente

Primeramente quedo debiendo a el Señor Governador setecientos qua
   renta y sinco pesos como consta de la memoria que dicho Señor remitio
   a el Capitan Dn. Felix, y se saco del libro de Su Señnoria   745 –
Yten, deve dies pesos que pago dicho Capitan a el difunto Gregorio
   Ramires   010 -
Yten, deve otros dies pesos que pago por lo mismo a el difunto Juan
   Antonio Ramos   010 -
Yten, deve en el libro del Capitan Dn. Felix quarenta y un pesos que le a
   Suplido   041 -
Cuyas por todas montan   806 pesos

Lo que a de aver el dicho Sargento Pascual Truxillo son nobesientos y
   nobenta pesos del compromiso delos soldados   990 –
Yten, a de aver del sueldo de dos meses y beinte y tres dias desde 16 de
   Julio hasta 7 de Septiembre, 97 pesos y 6 reales   097-6
Cuyas dos partidas montan   1087-6
Que rebajados ochocientos y seis pesos   806 –
   Del cargo sele restan ala viuda dosientos y ochenta y un pesos y seis reales   281-6

Y para que conste de dicho ajuste de quentas que en virtud de comision hize actuando como Juez receptor con testigos de asistenzia la firme con el dicho Capitan y testigos en dicho dia =

Juan Paez Hurtado (rubric)
Juez receptor
Phelix Martinez (rubric)
testigo de assistenzia
Miguel Tenorio de Alba (rubric)
Antonio Duran de Armijo (rubric)

En esta Villa de Santa Fee de la Nueva Mexico en diez y nueve dias del mes de Noviembre de mill setezientos y quinse años yo Dn. Juan Ygnacio Flores Mogollon, Governador y Capitan General deste Reino y Provinzias de la Nuevo Mexico por Su Magestad haviendo visto la quenta antezedente y que de ella consta deversele ala buida docientos y ochenta y un pesos y seis reales mando que de ellos pague el Capitan Dn. Felix Martinez los ocho al General Juan Paez Hurtado por lo actuando y travajado en dicha quenta y que de los dozientos y setenta y tres pesos y seis reales restantes haga dos vales cada uno de ziento y treinta y seis pesos y siete reales, el uno a favor de la dicha buida Antonia Duran y el otro a favor del Capitan Joseph Truxillo aquien nombro por tutor de los hijos menores del Sargento Pasqual Truxillo, difunto, y dela dicha Antonia Duran, su mujer que fue; y constandome tener la dicha buida otros vienes y para saver los que son y separarlos que le pertenezieren alos dichos menores mande comparezer ante mi ala dicha Antonia Duran ala qual estando presente le rezevi juramento que hizo por Dios Nuestro Señor y la Señal de la Cruz so cargo del qual prometio dezir verdad en lo que fuere preguntado y siendolo que que vienes dejo el dicho su marido; dijo que la casa en que vive, dos cavallos errados con el hiero de Su Magestad, que dejo en el Presidio del Paso quando fue a Mexico, trezientas ovejas de vientre, treinta y seis borregos machos y hembras, dos bueyes; que estos son los vienes que el dicho su marido dejo y los hijos que son Juan, Domingo, Francisco, María, Josepha, Andres, Bernardo, Antonio y Pasqual Trujillo, y que el dicho Juan Trujillo por estar emanzipado le entrego su padre el Sargento Pasqual Trujillo toda la parte que le tocava y pertenezia exzepto tiene parte en la casa de bivienda, y que aunque lleva declarado aver dejado las trescientas y treinta y seis borregos es publico y notorio son de la declarante pues hallandose nezesitada le remitio mayor porzion que la referida su hermano, para que se socorrase y que asi me suplica ami dicho Governador la tenga presente para ampararla en lo que es suyo que haviendola oydo yo dicho Governador siendo publico ser las ovejas de la dicha Antonia Duran desde luego selas aplico por suyas y no haviendo otros vienes que pertenescan alos menores que son los ciento y treinta y seis pesos y siete reales aunque el vale esta echo a favor del Capitan Joseph Trujillo mando al Capitan Dn. Feliz Martinez los pague a la dicha Antonia Duran pues le corresponde a cada menor como a doze pesos poco mas o menos y para esta corte no nezesitan de tutor y la casa de bivienda que es de alguna entidad, mando se le notifique a la dicha biuda no la benda a ora ni en ningun tiempo sin expesial gusto y consentimiento de sus hijos, asi lo provei, mande y firme con mi Secretario de Governazion y Guerra =

     Dn. Juan Ygnacio
     Flores Mogollon (rubric)
     Ante mi,
     Roque de Pintto (rubric)
   Secretario de Governazion y Guerra

Notificazion
Y luego yncontinenti yo el presente Secretario de Governazion y Guerra en cumplimiento del auto antezedente del Señor Governador y Capitan General lo ley y notifique a Antonia Duran buida del Sargento Pascual Truxillo en su persona que conosco quien aviendolo oydo y entendido dijo lo ovedeze y consiente y que no bendera la casa a ora ni en ningun tiempo si no fuese con expezial consentimiento de sus hijos y no firmo por no saver doi fee =
     Roque de Pintto (rubric)
Secretario de Governazion y Guerra

Notes

1. Antonia de Tapia Durán and her husband, Pascual Trujillo were a part of an El Paso muster of 1692, with Pascual claiming to be a native of New Mexico. In 1692 they were living at the pueblo of Isleta with an extended household, which included Francisco and Feliciano Candelaria, sons of Ana de Sandoval y Manzanares, two of Albuquerque's first founders. Pascual's aunt was Ana de Sandoval y Manzanares. Antonia and Pascual were in Santa Fe in 1694. By 1713 Pasqual had purchased land in Santa Cruz and was holding the rank of sergeant. Pascual may have been the son of Cristóbal Trujillo, who married the sister of Ana de Sandoval, but this is not certain. On December 12, 1715, after the death of Trujillo, Francisco Tamaris, (later killed by Alonso Real de Aguilar) took his place at the presidio (NMGS, *Aquí*: 123-25; Chávez, O*rigins*: 163, 298; Kessell and Hendricks, *RCR*: 60-61, 93 n96; SANM I #932; Christmas and Rau, "Una Lista": 197; Doc. 18).
2. See Doc. 2.
3. Matías Lobato was on the 1697 list of presidio soldiers. He lived in Santa Cruz in 1705 and died in 1715 (Kessell et al., *TDC*: 128; Chávez, *Origins*: 206; see also SANM II #239a).
4. Juan Antonio Ramos, a native of Salvatierra, was in New Mexico by 1694. In 1705 he was banished to Santa Cruz. He replaced Juan Luján Romero at the presidio on August 23, 1714, and was killed less than one year later on August 21, 1715 (Kessell et al., *BOB* 2: 1168-69 n79; Christmas and Rau, "Una Lista": 199).
5. Gregorio Ramírez, born in Zacatecas, came to New Mexico in 1696 and was on the 1697 list of presidio soldiers. He died in 1715 (Kessell and Hendricks, *RCR*: 546 n22; *BOB*: 1164 n40; *TDC*: 128; Chávez, *Origins*: 264).
6. She appears to be referring to SANM II #239e, a petition by María Canseco, widow of Juan Antonio Ramos, for adjustment of his debts. This petition was approved by Governor Felix Martínez on October 22, 1715.
7. Full strength for the presidio at this time was 100 soldiers. Not counting her deceased husband, there would have been 99, each paying 10 pesos.
8. See Doc. 11.
9. Mogollón seems to have reversed his earlier decision appointing Captain Joseph Trujillo as a guardian.
10. This appears to be a contradiction, since the original petition was signed and rubricated by her.

14

KNIVES, DAGGERS, CARBINES, PISTOLS, AND SWORDS PROHIBITED IN TOWNS BY VICEROY AND GOVERNOR
December 14–24, 1715. Source: SANM II #236.

Synopsis and editor's notes: In this document, Governor Felix Martínez repeats a royal order from the king and the viceroy, the duke of Linares, that prohibited carrying certain weapons, including knives, daggers, carbines, pistols, and swords, in settled places. Martínez points out a similar order had been made by Governor Vargas and stated that such weapons had been used in a recent fight among soldiers, probably referring to the murder of Francisco Tamaris by Alonso Rael de Aguilar (SANM II #239j and Doc. 18).

Because the original order was sent out from Spain under the signature of King Philip V, it is difficult to know if anyone in New Mexico had the types of daggers and swords named by the king, though most New Mexicans probably had some kind of sword or gun. As the reader may recall, a similar prohibition having to do with carrying arms in towns was ordered by Wyatt Earp and other sheriffs of the American West, probably for similar reasons, and perhaps with similarly uneven results.

[Marginal note]
Bando promulgated at this villa
and other jurisdictions, which
ordered that knives not be
allowed to be carried within settlements.

I, don Felix Martínez, captain-for-life of the royal presidio of this villa of Santa Fe, *regidor* for life of its *ayuntamiento*,[1] governor and captain general of this kingdom, castellan of the forces and presidios for his majesty, etc.

Whereas, the royal *cédula* [royal decree] of his majesty [Philip V], ordered by the most excellent viceroy of New Spain [Duke de Linares] and by the ministers of his royal audiencia of the court and of the city of México, as were promulgated through his royal bandos, which were ordered to be complied with and which prohibited, without exception of any person, but everyone in general, of any status, from carrying within any settled places, be they cities, villas, or any community, knives on their sashes, daggers, carbines, pistols, large swords which are of a certain length, or narrow-bladed swords,[2] imposing penalties upon those who do not comply with the royal mandates. In reference to the fact that at this villa of Santa Fe, my predecessor, Marqués de la Nava de Brazinas [don Diego de Vargas], promulgated a bando the previous year of 1704, which provided with the prescribed penalty that no person be excluded from being prohibited from carrying the above mentioned arms, nor that with the passing of time it be forgotten, and so that it is not, it should be brought up periodically. Only recently, due to its lack of being observed, an occurrence took place in which a soldier had the courage to stab his sergeant.[3]

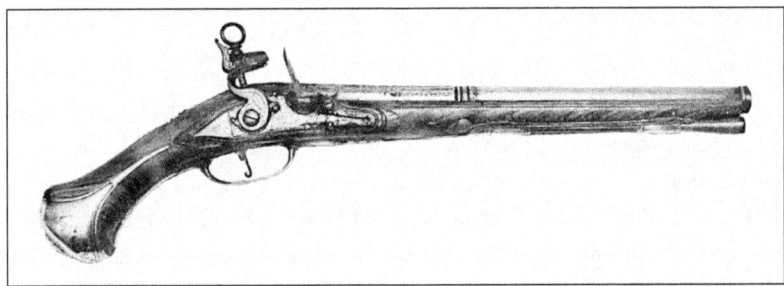

Officer's pistol, made in Madrid in 1703 and found in Durango, México. It is a .62 caliber smoothbore with a 12½-inch barrel. Brinkerhoff and Faulk, *Lancers*: 75, Plate 11. Image courtesy of the Arizona Historical Society, Tempe.

In order to remedy these terrible, unwarranted occurrences in the future, I order that in all of the settlements of this kingdom of New Mexico, no one in any settlement be permitted to carry any of the arms mentioned in this bando, under penalty, if they are soldiers, of the loss of their position [*puesto*]; if they are officials, of diminution of their rank and loss of those positions. If they are soldiers who have been reduced in their duties due to their capabilities because of injuries, they are to remain without compensation until they are evaluated as to what they owe to his majesty, and they are to be banished to guard the royal horse herd for as long as it is required for them to pay back what they owe. I will give to the denouncer those arms which belonged to those who were guilty of the royal mandates. For the resident who does not fulfill what is herein ordered, I condemn him to two hundred lashes and to be sold to an ore crusher[4] for four years. If he is a nobleman, he will be fined one hundred pesos, which I will apply in thirds for the construction of the church of this villa, for the expenses of the judge, and for the denouncer, along with more than two years of banishment to the frontiers of this kingdom.

This said bando I order to be published at the corners of the public plaza of this villa to the sound of the military instruments with the assistance of the illustrious cabildo, which my secretary of government and war will certify, along with all of the military corporals, who will place their certification of publication upon this. Once this is carried out, the bando is to be submitted to the alcalde mayor of the new villa de Santa Cruz, and the same shall be done by submitting it to the alcalde mayor of the villa de San Felipe de Alburquerque, so that each one, for whatever it is worth to him, will have it published in their jurisdictions. Once it is executed, they will submit it back to this superior government so that it remains with the secretary.

Done at this villa of Santa Fe on the 14th of December, 1715.
Felix Martínez (rubric)
by order of the governor and captain general
Miguel Tenorio de Alba[5] (rubric)
Secretary of government and war

Publication

I, Captain Miguel Tenorio de Alba, secretary of government and war, by virtue of that which was ordered in this royal bando by Captain don Felix Martínez, who is permanently captain-for-life from this royal presidio, governor and captain general of this kingdom, published it at this villa of Santa Fe to the sound of the military instruments at the gate of the guardhouse and all other accustomed places by the voice of Esteban Rodríguez,[6] drummer, before a large number of people along with those of the illustrious cabildo and military personal, to which I certify.

Miguel Tenorio de Alba (rubric)

At the new villa of Santa Cruz on the 19th of December, 1715, I, the retired alférez, Joseph Trujillo, alcalde mayor and war captain of this said villa and of its jurisdiction, in fulfillment and in obedience of the aforesaid decree, promulgated by the governor and captain general don Felix Martínez, made it known to all of the residents of my jurisdiction, who upon having heard and understood it, stated that as loyal vassals of his majesty would obey it. So that it is valid I signed it acting as presiding judge with those who assisted me on the said day, month, and year, etc.

before me as presiding judge
Joseph Trujillo (rubric)
Assisting witnesses
Joseph de Atienza (rubric)
Juan de Atienza (rubric)

At this villa of San Felipe de Alburquerque on the 24th of December, 1715, I, Captain Martín Hurtado, alcalde mayor and war captain of this said villa and of its jurisdiction, in compliance with and obedience to the above decree promulgated by the governor and captain general don Felix Martínez, made it known to the residents of this jurisdiction, who having heard and understood it, said that as loyal vassals of his majesty, they would obey it. So that it is valid, I signed it on the said day, month, and year, acting as presiding judge, with my two assisting witnesses who were Juan de Dios Martínez and José de Silva.

before me as presiding judge
Martín Hurtado (rubric)
assisting witness
José de Silva (rubric)
Juan de Dios Martín (rubric)

ORIGINAL DOCUMENT

Vando que se promulgo en esta Villa
y demas jurisdisiones sobre que
no traigan en poblado cuchillos

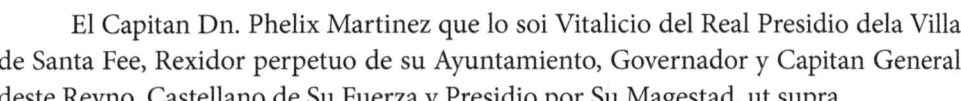

El Capitan Dn. Phelix Martinez que lo soi Vitalicio del Real Presidio dela Villa de Santa Fee, Rexidor perpetuo de su Ayuntamiento, Governador y Capitan General deste Reyno, Castellano de Su Fuerza y Presidio por Su Magestad, ut supra.

Por quanto por Real Zedula de Su Magestad ordenadas por los Excellentisimos Señores Vireyes dela Nueba Espana y Señores Ministros de Su Real Audienzia de la Corte y Ciudad de Mexico por su mandado promulgadas en sus Reales Vandos mandando en su cumplimiento y prohibiendo sin exeptcion personas sino a todas en general de qualesquier estado que sean no puedan traer en poblado en las ciudades, villas y lugares armas ofensibas como son cuchillos en zinta, panales, almaradas, carabinas, pistoletes, espadas largas demas de marca ni de agujas ynponiendo las penas a los ynobedientes a sus Reales mandates, y en atencion a que en esta Villa de Santa Fee mi antesesor el Marques de la Nava de Brazinas promulgo bando el pasado año de setecientos y quatro en que se proibe salas penas en el contenidas ninguna persona sea osada a traer en poblado las armas ariba mencionadas con el trascurso del tiempo sean olbidado por haverlo reiterado los que le susedieron y aora nuebamente por su ynobserbancia haverse sedido el que un soldado tubiese el atrevimiento de darle una punalada a su Sargento y para remediar en lo de adelante tan pernidosas malas y ditestables consequencias mando a todos las poblasones de este Reino dela Nueba Mexico ninguno sea osado a traer en poblado ninguna de las armas mensionadas en este bando de bajo de la pena si fuere soldado de privacion de sus puestos a los oficiales y degradacion de sus honores y reformados de sus plazas y a los soldados raios de darlos por inabiles para el ministerio de soldados en que se mantendran hasta tanto que devenguen lo que constare dever a Su Magestad desterrados en la guardia de la Real cavallada todo el tiempo que nesesitaren para cumplir dicha deuda aplicando como desde luego aplico al denunciador las armas de los transgresores a los Reales mandates y al vesino que incurriese en lo aqui mandado si fuere plebeio le condeno desde a ora en pena de doscientos azotes y vendido a un mortero por quatro años, y si fuere noble en pena de cien pesos que aplico por tercias partes para la fabrica de la yglesia de esta Villa, gastos de Justicia y denunziante con mas de dos años de destierro a las fronteras de este Reino, y dicho Vando mando se publique en la plaza publica desta Villa en sus esquinas al zon de los ynstrumentos militares con asistanzia de Su Ylustre Cavildo que sitara para ello mi Secretario de Governazion y Guerra con todos los cavos militares y pondra la fee de su publicazion y fecho lo remitira ala Villa Nueba de Santa Cruz a su Alcalde Mayor, y este ara la misma remission a el Alcalde Mayor de la Villa de San Phelipe de Alburquerque para que cada uno, por lo que le toca lo agan publicar en sus jurisdiciones para que conste de averlo asi executado, y fecho lo remitan a este superior govierno para que conste en su secretaria, fecho en esta Villa de Santa Fee en catorze dias del mes de Diciembre de mill setesientos y quinze años.

      Phelix Martinez (rubric)
   Por mando del Señor Governador y Capitan General
      Miguel Thenoria de Alva (rubric)
      Secretario de Governazion y Guerra

Publicazion
Yo el Capitan Miguel Tenorio de Alba Secretario de Governazion y Guerra en virtud de lo mandado en este Real Bando por el Señor Capitan Dn. Felix Martinez que los es Vitalicio de este Real Presidio, Governador y Capitan General deste Reyno se publico en esta Villa de Santa Fee al son de los ynstrumentos militares en la puerta del Cuerpo de Guardia y demas partes acostumbradas y por voz de Esteban Rodriguez, tambor, hallandose mucho conserto de gente a su publicacion el Ylustrisimo Cavildo y señores militares, de que doy fee.

      Miguel Tenorio
      de Alba (rubric)

En la Villa Nueba de Santa Cruz en dies y nuebe dias del mes de Disiembre de mill setesientos y quinse años yo el Alferes Reformado Joseph Truxillo Alcalde Mayor y Capitan Aguerra de dicha Villa y su jurisdision en cumplimiento y obedesimiento del aucto dela buelta espedido por el Señor Governador y Capitan General Dn. Felix Martines le ise notorio alos vesinos desta mi jurisdision quienes le olleron y entendieron y como leales basallos de Su Magestad le obedesieron y para que conste lo firme autuando como Jues Reseptor con los de asistensia en dicho dia mes y año ut supra =

      Ante mi como Jues Reseptor
      Joseph Truxillo (rubric)
      de asistensia
      Joseph de Atienza (rubric)
      Juan de Atienza (rubric)

En esta Villa de San Felipe de Alburquerque en veinte y cuatro dias del mes de Disiembre de mil setesientos y quinse años yo el Capitan Martin Hurtado Alcalde Maior y Capitan Aguerra desta dicha Villa y su jurisdision en cumplimiento y obedesimiento del auto dela buelta espedido por el Señor Governador y Capitan General Dn. Felis Martines lo yse publicar a los vesinos de esta jurisdision quienes lo olleron y entendieron y dieron el obedesimiento como leales vasallos de Su Magestad y para que conste lo firme en dicho dia mes y año atuando como Jues Reseptor con dos testigos de mi asistensia que lo fueron Juan de Dios Martines y Jose de Silva.

    Ante mi como Jues Reseptor
    Martin Hurtado (rubric)
    testigo de asistensia
    Jose de Silva (rubric)
    Juan de Dios Martin (rubric)

Notes

1. The term *ayuntamiento* was rarely used in Santa Fe at this time. Martínez may have been thinking of the town councils in other parts of New Spain.
2. More precisely, the Spanish reads *cuchillos en zinta* (knives in their sashes); *puñales,* (dagger); *almarada* (dagger with an triangular used for stabbing, or a bayonet); *carabinas* (carbines); *pistoletes* (small pistols); *espadas largas de más de marca* (long swords usually measured at more than ¾ of an inch); and *agujas* (swords with narrow, needlelike blades (personal communication, Rick Hendricks, state historian, November 1, 2011).
3. Martínez may be referring to the December 1715 murder of Sergeant Tamaris by Alonso Real de Aguilar. See Doc. 18 and SANM II #239j.
4. Martínez is probably referring to work in the mines in New Spain rather than in New Mexico. As background, Ruth Pike states that there was a shortage of labor in New Spain at this time due to the diseases that killed so many Indians and the high price of black slaves. Because of this, for a variety of crimes labor on projects considered in the interest of the state was often used as a punishment. The interest of the state could include anything that helped develop the economy, including labor in mines and factories and in the infamous textile mills, the *obrajes* (Pike, "Penal Servitude": 22-24. On the obrajes in New Spain, see Greenleaf, "Obraje": 227-50).
5. See Doc. 4.
6. Esteban Rodríguez followed his father, Sebastián Rodríguez (Doc. 2) as presidio drummer by 1716. Esteban was also the town crier by 1732 (Chávez, *Origins*: 270).

15

RELIGIOUS PROCESSION TAKES PLACE AT SANTA FE PARROQUIA; EDICT OF FAITH READ
June 16, 1716. Source: AGN Inq. L552, Exp. 5 DF.

Synopsis and editor's notes: This document, written by Fray Joseph Narváez Valverde, comes from the files of the Holy Office of the Inquisition and was apparently written to show his superiors that the Edict of Anathema had been read and proper procedures followed. The detailed description shows the important personages of Santa Fe escorting the religious dignitaries to the church, hearing the service, and then proceeding back to the *convento*. The place of each person in the procession is noted as well as the location and seating in the church.

That the reading of the edict was accompanied by such an imposing procession shows the importance of the event to the church officials (see also Doc. 20). A similar document from 1626 describes the reception of Fray Alonso de Benavides as comisario of the Holy Office for New Mexico, his entrance into Santa Fe, and a high mass that included reading the edicts of faith (see "Plans for Benavides' Reception" and "Entrance of Benavides into Santa Fe," following this document). After the Reconquest, edicts of faith were proclaimed throughout the colony at least as early as 1706, when Comisario Fray Juan Álvarez ordered them read and proscribed conduct investigated. For example, Governor Felix Martínez ordered the publication of the edicts of faith in 1716. The edicts continued to be read, or at least were expected to be read, at least up until 1751, when a priest was charged with neglecting to proclaim them. The content of the edicts read at San Ildefonso and Santa Fe is not known.

Inquisition historian Helen Rawlings gives several examples of edicts of faith. They deal with such matters as "inviting people to identify Lutherans and Judaizers within their midst, solicitation by confessors or other clerics of women and of others in the act of confession, and persons showing signs of 'diverse heresies'" (see "Edict of Faith," following this document).

According to Rawlings and Henry Lea, since the early sixteenth century, inquisitors had been appointed by the Vatican to search out religious deviance, calling upon the inhabitants to come forth with any suspicion of others' heresy under pain of prosecution by the Inquisition Tribunal. Both historians, as well as Richard Greenleaf, agree that the reach of the Inquisition was much diminished in Spain by 1700 and continued to decline thereafter. However, as shown by the Abiquiu witchcraft trials, the Inquisition was still a force in New Mexico through the mid-eighteenth century (Martinez, "Toledo"; Ebright and Hendricks, *Witches*; Hodge et al., *Benavides' Revised Memorial*: 26-129; Rawlings, *Spanish Inquisition*: 29-31, 62, 102-3, 118, 126; Norris, *Year Eighty*: 63; Lea, *Inquisition*: 91-98; Greenleaf, "Inquisition": 20, 31, 42-48).

[Marginal note]
Testimony of the
publication of the
General Edict

1716

    I, Fray Joseph Narváez Valverde,[1] lay religious of the Order of St. Francis, notary of the Holy Office [of the Inquisition] of this Villa of Santa Fe in the kingdom of New Mexico, say that Reverendo Padre Comisario[2] of the Holy Office [of the Inquisition] Fray Juan Tagle,[3] having just finished publishing the edict of faith and letter of anathema, has come from the Mission of San Ildefonso to this villa of Santa Fe on the second day of the month of June. Today he went to the royal palace of the governor and captain general of the kingdom, who is don Felix Martínez,[4] accompanied by the alguacil mayor of the Holy Office, Captain Juan García de la Riva and don Mateo de la Peña,[5] who the said Reverendo Padre Comisario chose to carry the standard bearing the arms of the Holy Tribunal, and I, said notary public, going with them and all with the insignias of the Holy Tribunal. Said governor ordered the company of the royal presidio to present themselves, and upon our arrival and departure, they fired a salute. From the doors of the palace, the said governor, accompanied by his lieutenant general, received the said Reverendo Padre Comisario with every civility and politeness. Entering inside in each other's company, the Reverendo Padre Comisario informed him, the governor, that the edicts of the faith would be published the seventh day of the month of June, so that he might assist in honoring this with his soldiers and others. To which the governor responded by offering himself without reservation so that all could be best accomplished.

    From here, with the same companions, said Reverendo Padre Comisario went to the houses of the illustrious cabildo, regimiento, and justicia members, who, upon receiving him, made the same welcoming demonstrations, which were expanded upon in other ways by alcalde Francisco Lorenzo Casado,[6] who had previously met with the Reverendo Padre Comisario, Fray Joseph Antonio Guerrero,[7] the minister of the *parrochia* and *convento*[8] of Nuestra Padre San Francisco of said villa of Santa Fe, and for his part, offered all that would be needed by his party for the observances. The Reverendo Padre Comisario had some days before sent his documents and the orders of the Holy Office to the villas and settlements of San Felipe de Alburquerque, the new villa of Santa Cruz, Bernalillo, Cañada de Chimayó, and Nuestra Señora de la

Soledad of Río Arriba,⁹ admonishing the residents and inhabitants to be at the church and villa of Santa Fe on the assigned day. He ordered that on Thursday, the fourth of said month of June, I, said notary, go forth, as I did, being accompanied by the men of the illustrious cabildo, soldiers of the royal presidio, and other honored persons of this said villa, taking the written order of said Reverendo Padre Comisario, which at the sounding of the military instruments I read at the four customary principal corners of the most important streets of this villa.

Nuestra Señora de la Soledad (Our Lady of Solitude), ca. 1830, from northern New Mexico, attributed to "Molleno." Tempera and gesso on a pine panel, 39 by 28 cm.
Mather, *Colonial Frontiers*: 33. File No. FA.1979.64-77.
Image courtesy of the Museum of International Folk Art, Santa Fe.

On Sunday, the seventh, the governor and captain general, don Feliz Martínez, accompanied by his royal presidio soldiers, all on horseback, came to the convento of Our Father St. Francis, where the Reverendo Padre Comisario and other ministers were waiting. Taking forth the Reverendo Padre Comisario, the governor organized the procession in the best manner that could be done despite the impoverishment of this kingdom, with the ministers who were present going forth with their insignias. All in this form, first the company marched by horseback, and then I, said notary, was accompanied by one of the most principal residents, followed by Padre Predicador[10]

Fray Carlos Delgado,[11] who bears the title of notary of the Holy Tribunal for the city of Querétaro. Immediately following after was Reverendo Padre Fray Francisco Antonio Páez,[12] comisario of the Holy Office of the jurisdiction of El Paso, who is also presently the priest of the *custodia*[13] of Pecos Pueblo. Each of them was accompanied by one of the principal residents, being Captain don Mateo de la Peña, who carried the standard with the arms of the Holy Office. Accompanying him was the regidor Salvador Montoya[14] and Captain Ygnacio de Roybal,[15] who was the former alcalde ordinario of the said villa. Following him was the alguacil mayor with the staff of the Holy Office; Captain Juan García de la Riva, current alcalde ordinario; and then in their midst the lieutenant general don Juan Páez Hurtado[16] and don Francisco Lorenzo Casado, alcalde ordinario; and from El Paso, the Reverendo Padre Comisario of the Holy Office, with the governor and captain general escorting him on his right side.

Having passed through the customary streets, they arrived at the door of the church, where the missionary priests were waiting, who had come from their jurisdictions for this event; and with them was the Reverendo Padre Custodio and *juez eclesiástico ordinario* of this kingdom, Fray Antonio Camargo.[17] They all welcomed said Reverendo Padre Comisario and the Reverendo Padre Custodio, accompanying them so as to place them in the seating at the high altar, with a seat [*silla*] and cushion [*almohada*] for the Reverendo Padre Comisario on the "gospel" [*evangelico*] side, and next to him was a bench on which were seated the rest of the ministers and in their accustomed places, the governor and the illustrious cabildo.[18]

The Mass then began, which was sung by the notary, Padre Predicador Fray Carlos Delgado. When the reading of the gospel ended, the said notary of the Holy Office arose and read the Edicts of the Faith in a clear, loud, and understandable voice, which, this being concluded, the sermon was given by Padre Predicador Fray Juan Mingues.[19]

Because that in this kingdom the inhabitants find themselves surrounded by heathen enemies and they travel along the roads at grave risk to their lives, it is necessary for these persons who come from the villas and said jurisdictions to return there to protect their houses, families, and holy places of worship, it being for some of them long distances of twenty-five and more leagues. In order that they be informed in all this [the Edicts], being so far away and little versed in such events, and serving them as a reminder of their heavy obligations, the Reverendo Padre Comisario deemed it worthwhile that, even though the letter of anathema had been published on six sequential days, on this same day he had the said letter read again after the Apostles Creed was recited, so that the referred-to persons would see the fearsome and affectionate ceremonies of our Holy Mother the Church. Then this was carried out, which having been finished, the Mass continued, and then being concluded, the said Reverendo Padre Predicador returned to take forth the said Reverendo Padre Comisario and the officials, so that they then mounted and went out on horseback in the same order as before, circulating through the customary streets until bringing said Reverendo Padre Comisario and ministers to the governor and cabildo. In their presence, they, in particular and in common, gave thanks in the name of the most Holy Tribunal for the good manner in everything they had done and for the Catholic observances, which they had carried out accompanied by such a Holy Act. Though the assigned days had already passed, the said Reverendo Padre Comisario remained at said convento so that on Sunday the fourteenth of June he would read the letter of anathema, choosing Sunday, a holy feast day for the entire congregation because of the greater attendance. Afterwards, he stayed until the sixteenth, when he returned to his mission.

All of which I certify as truthful, as I have indicated, and so that it is clear to their lordships of the most Holy Tribunal, I provided these statements which I signed with my name in this convento of St. Francis in the Villa of Santa Fe, on the eighteen day of the month of June of 1716.

In testimony of the truth of this I affix my signature and customary rubric.
Fray Joseph Narváez Valverde (rubric)
Notario of the Holy Office

ORIGINAL DOCUMENT

Testimonio
Publicasion
del Edicto
General
1716

Digo yo fray Joseph Navaiz Balverde Religioso laico, de la obrevancia de Nuestro Padre San Francisco, Notario del Santo Oficio de esta Villa de Santa Fe del Reyno de la Nueva Mexico: Como haviendo acabado el Reverendo, Padre Commissario del Santo Oficio Fray Juan Tagle el publicar Los Edictos de fe, i carta de Anathema, bino desa Mission de San Ildefonso [a]desta Villa de Santa Fe el dia dos del mes de Junio y este dia pasó a el Real Palaciodel Governador y Capitan General deste Reino, que lo es don Feliz Martinez acompañado de el Alguacil Mayor del Santo Oficio el Capitan Juan Garcia de la Rivas i de don Matheo de la Peña a quien eligio dicho Reverendo Padre Commisario para que llevase el estandarte con las armas del Santo Tribunal yendo yo dicho Notario Publico juntamente i todos con los insignios del Santo Tribunal i dicho Governador mando tender la compaña del Real Presidio quien a la llegada i salida hizo salvo; salio dicho Governador a las puertas del Palacio acompañado de su Theniente General en donde con toda urbanidad i politica recibio a dicho Reverendo Padre Commissario acompañados i entrado dentro, le dio a entender como se publicaban los edictos de fe el dia siete de dicho mes de Junio para que con sus soldados i demas assistiese a condecorrar tan santo acto a que respondio ofresiendose en un todo para quanto fuese del maior facimiento; de aqui paso con el mismo acompañamiento dicho Reverendo Padre Commisario a las casas del ylustre Cabildo, Justicia i Regimiento quienes hizieron al recibimiento las mesmas demostraciones ampliandose en otras por el Alcalde Ordinario Francisco Lorenso Casado; y haviendo antes visto al Reverendo Padre Guardian e ministro de la parrochia y convento de Nuestro Padre San Francisco de dicha Villa de Santa Fe Fray Joseph Antonio Guerrero ofrecio todo quanto estuviera de su Parte para la celebracion. Y haviendo dias antes embiado el Reverendo Padre Commisario sus escritos i ordenes del Santo Oficio a las villas i poblasones De San Phelipe de Alburquerque, de Santa Cruz de la villa neuva, Bernalillo, Cañada de Chimayo i Nuestra Señora de la Soledad de Rio Arriba sitando a sus vesinos i moradores para que se hallasen el asignado dia en la iglesia i Villa de Santa Fe ordenó dicho Reverendo Padre Commisario que el jueves quatro de dicho mes de junio saliese yo dicho notorio como sali acomparañdose los señores del yllustre cabildo, soldados de Real Presidio i otras personas condecorados de esta dicha Villa llevando escrito el orden de dicho Reverendo Padre Commissario que a son de los instrumentos los militares ley en las quatro esquinos mas principales de los calles acustumbaradas de esta dicha Villa y el dia domingo siete vino a el Convento de Nuestro Padre San Francisco en donde esperava el Reverendo Padre Commisario i demas ministros el Governador y Capitan General Don Feliz Martinez acompañado de su Real Presidio todos acaballo i sacando de dicho Convento a dicho Reverendo Padre Commisario se ordeno el paseo con el mejor facimiento que cabe en la pobresa de este Reino yendo los ministros que se hallaron con sus ynsignios en esta forma la compañia marchando a caballo primero i luego yo dicho notario acompañado de uño de los vesinos mas principales seguiole el Padre Predicador fray Carlos Delgado quien tiene Titulo de Notario de ese Santo Tribunal para la Cuidad de Queretaro immediatamente El Reverendo Padre fray Francisco Antonio Paez Commisario del Santo Officio de la jurisdicion Del Passo, quese halla oi ministro en esta Custodia del Pueblo de Pecos, acompañando a cada uno, uno de los principales vecinos siguiole el Capitan don Matheo de la Peña que llevava el estandarte con las Armas del santo officio acompañandole el Regidor Salbador Montoya i el Capitan Ygnacio de Roival alcalde ordinario que ha sido de esta dicha Villa, luego le seguio el Alguacil mayor con la vara del Santo Officio, el Capitan Juan Garcia de la Riva actual alcalde ordinario llevandole en medio el Theniente General don Juan Paez Hurtado i el Alcalde Ordinario Don Francisco Lorenzo Casado y del Paso el Reverendo Padre Commisaro del Santo Oficio llevandole al lado desecho el Governador y Capitan General i haviendo paseado las calles acostumbradas legados a la Puerta de la yglesia estavan esperando los Religiosos Misioneros, que para tal acto binieron de sus jurisdiciones, i con ellos el Reverendo Padre Custodio y Jues Eclesiastico Ordinario de este Reyno, Fray Antonio Camargo quienes resivieron a dicho Reverendo Padre Commisario i acompañados hasta ponerlos en el aciento que hera en el altar maior para el Reverendo Padre Commisario una silla i almoada al lado del evangelio a quien seguia una Banca que se sentaron los demas Ministros y en sus lugares acostumbrados el Governador i ylustre Cabildo se principio la Missa que canto el Padre Predicador fray Carlos Delgado notario i al tiempo de acabarse el evangelio subiyo dicho Notario del Santo Officio i ley en vos clara, alta e inteligible los edictos de la fe los quales concluidos predicó el sermon el Padre Predicador Fray Juan Mingues. y porque en este Reyno se hallan sus moradores sercados de enemigo ynfieles i se andan los caminos con grave riesgo de las vidas, i ser preciso que las personas que asistieron de las Villas e jurisdiciones dichos se bolvieren para el resguardo sus casas, familias, e Santos templos, i aver a algunas la distancia de beinte i cincos i mas leguas, para que fuesen enterados en todo, i que como tan retirados i poco versados en ver tales actos les sirviese de recuerdo a su mala obligacion, tomo a bien el Reverendo Padre Commissario el que aunque la carta de Anathema se havia de publicar dentro de seis dias siguientes como se hizo, dicha carta en este mesmo dia, acabado el credo se leyese; Para que los referidos viesen las Ceremonias de Nuestra Santa Madre yglesia tan temorosas i tiernas, assi se executo la qual acabada se prosiguio La Missa i concluida dichos Reverendos Padres Predicadores bolvieron a sacar a dicho Reverendo Padre Commisario i oficiales asta que se paso acaballo i con el mismo orden antesedente se rodearon las calles acostumbradas asta traer al convento Governador e comun a dicho Reverendo Padre Commisario e ministros en suya presencia les dio en particular e en comun las gracias, en nombre de tan Santo Tribunal para lo bien que lo hizieron, e demostraciones Catholicas con que se solisitaron condecorar tan Santo Acto quedandose dicho Reverendo Padre Commisario en dicho convento para que el Domingo catorse de Junio se leyese la carta de Anathema pasados ya los dias asignados eligiendos el Domingo por el mayor concurso en dia de fiesta, i despues se detubo hasta el dia diez i seis que se bolvio su Mision. Todo lo qual zertifico sea asi verdad como lo llebo refelido y para que conste a los Señores de tan Santo Tribunal di el presente que firme de mi nombre en este convento de Nuestro Padre San Francisco de la Villa de Santa Fe en diez y seis dias del mes de Junio de mill setecientos i diez i seis años.

En testimonio de verdad hago mi firma i rubrica acostumbrada

Fray Joseph Narbaiz Valverde (rubric)

Notario del Santo Officio

This transcription and translation were prepared by Gerald Gonzales and Linda Tigges.

Supplemental Information

"Plans for Benavides' Reception in Santa Fe as Commissary of the Holy Office. Santo Domingo, January 6, 1626"; and "Entrance of Benavides into Santa Fe, January 24-25, 1626." Documents VI and VII (Hodge et al., *Benavides' Revised Memorial*).

Document VI

Plans for Benavides' Reception in Santa Fe as Commissary of the Holy Office.
Santo Domingo, January 6, 1616.

At the aforesaid town, convent, day, month, and year. Since there has never been a commissary of the Holy Office in these provinces and since this is the first time that the Holy Office has appointed one in the person of the said father commissary, Fray Alonso de Benavides, in order to accord him the treatment befitting his office, he was instructed to settle the matters of the Holy Office with the proper care, above all in a new land such as this where they are not acquainted with them. He wrote a letter in his own hand and bearing his own signature to Admiral Don Felipe Sotelo Osorio, who had just arrived in the same supply train as governor and captain general of these provinces. He wrote likewise another one in his own hand and signature to the cabildo of the city of Santa Fe, headquarters of the Spaniards who serve in these frontiers, notifying them that the inquisitors, Doctor Juan Gutiérrez Flores, Licenciado Gonzalo Mecía Lobo, doctor Don Francisco Bazán y Albornoz, apostolic inquisitors in the New Spain, had honored him with the appointment as first commissary of the Holy Office in these provinces in order that he should read and publish there the edits of our holy Catholic father and take charge of all the matters pertaining to the Holy Office in the same manner as is done by the other commissaries of the Holy Office in the posts assigned to them. The said father commissary felt that this brought great honor to the said gentleman as well as to the cabildo and other Spaniards, for since they were the ones who planted the faith in this land, helping with their arms the Franciscan friars who were preaching the gospel, they too would have this bulwark of our holy Catholic faith: the tribunal of the holy office which defends it. Since the celebration day of the conversion of Saint Paul was so near, the 25th of this month of January, on which day the glorious saint is honored as the general patron on account of the marvelous things he has done in this region, it seemed to the father commissary that on this day the holy edicts should be read in the church of the said city, and the said father commissary accepted in the name of the Holy Office. To these letters and suggestions both the said governor and the cabildo replied, expressing pleasure at being so honored, saying that they would always be grateful and obedient to the Holy Office. They asked the father commissary to make this entrance into the said city on the 24th day of the said month, the day before that of the conversion of Saint Paul, in order that they might receive him as its general ecclesiastical judge by apostolic authority as are received all the other custodians in this land, and also to demonstrate their pleasure and joy in receiving him as a commissary of the Holy Office, to whom from then on they submitted with special inclination and humility. Wherefore, the said father commissary arranged his entrance of the said day, which I certify.

Fr. Alonso de Benavides, Commissary. (rubric)
Given before me, Fr. Pedro de Hortega, notary. (rubric)

Document VII

Entrance of Benavides into Santa Fe, January 24-25, 1616

On January 24, 1626, Father Fray Alonso de Benavides, commissary of the Holy Office in these provinces of New Mexico, having left the town and convent of Santo Domingo the preceding day to make his first entrance in the said villa as commissary of the Holy Office, which now and for the first time was established in these provinces, said that for this function it was necessary to make the proclamation in the said villa that very day and to appoint the officials who were to do it, inasmuch as the edicts of our holy Catholic father were to be read and proclaimed with the usual solemnity on the following day. Thus he appointed Captain Manuel Correa Falcón well born and of good reputation, to the office of alguacil mayor of the Holy Office; likewise he named the sargento mayor of these provinces, Francisco Gómez, to carry the standard of the our holy Catholic faith with the arms and emblem of the Holy Office. He, too, was of good repute and one of the best qualified in these provinces.

The father commissary accompanied by them and by me, the present notary, Fray Pedro de Hortega, and by all the friars of this custodia, on the said 24th of this January, entered the said city. At the outskirts of the city there came to welcome him the governor, alcaldes, cabildo and all the other people, properly arranged on horseback in war array. The governor with his pennant and the others welcomed him with much courtesy and affection, firing salvos with their harquebuses and artillery, placing him in the position of honor. He was likewise received in the church with the solemnity with which the friars usually welcome their prelates for the first time, for the said father commissary also held this office, and with even greater honors, saying that since they had planted our holy Catholic faith in these provinces among so many barbarous nations, as friars of St. Francis, faithful sons of the holy Roman church, they were also planting the tribunal of the Holy Office, since it was a friar of St. Francis whom the holy office was sending with such honor for this purpose. On this and other occasions, they displayed the affection and obedience they hold for the holy tribunal.

When the said governor, alcaldes, and cabildo had accompanied the said father commissary to his cell and left him there, they in the same manner accompanied the alguacil mayor through the principal streets, announcing, as is customary, that on the following day, the edicts of our holy Catholic faith would be read and published in the parish church of the city, and that no one should fail to be present. Every time they made the announcement they made a salvo with the harquebuses and bugles. On that night, quite a stormy one, they lighted their luminaries and celebrated as much as they could. On the next day, the 25th of the month, day of the conversion of Saint Paul, at the time of high mass, the said governor, alcaldes, cabildo and all the other people and the harquebusiers came to the cell of the said father commissary to accompany him to the church. This they did, the banner of our holy Catholic faith being carried before them in the hands of the said sargento mayor, accompanied by the captains. Behind him came the alguacil mayor, accompanied by the friars, and I, the said notary, with the most prominent friars of this custodia. The said father commissary walked between the present governor and his predecessor, who was there at the time.[20]

In this order, we entered the church up to the place of the father commissary, which was on the side of the gospel at the main altar. He had a kneeling chair with a cushion, and opposite him, on the other side, a platform covered with a carpet where I, the present notary, at and also the alguacil mayor and the sargento mayor, who carried the banner. The said governor took his seat at the transept of the church, and high mass began. It was sung by Father Fray Ascensio de Zárate, the former vice custodian, two prominent guardians acting as deacons. The gospel being finished, I, the said notary, rose; flanked by the standard of father and the alguacil mayor, I received the edicts from the hands of the father commissary, mounted the pulpit, and read them in a loud and intelligible voice to that all might hear them. I returned them to the said father commissary at his place. Then began the sermon by Father Fray Alonso de Estremera, teacher of theology. He delivered a great sermon. During the mass, at the appropriate time, *pax*[21] was given, first to the father commissary and then to the governor. After mass the same official again accompanied the father commissary to his cell in the same order as before. At this cell the governor, alcaldes, and cabildo once more offered themselves to him, acknowledging them as commissary of the Holy Office, and saying that in the discharge of his office, they would serve and aid him in everything as faithful Christians of the church and the holy tribunal. The father commissary replied with very kind words for all, to which I testify, which met with general applause.

     Fr. Alonso de Benavides, Commissary. (rubric)
     Fr. Pedro de Hortega, notary. (rubric)

Edict of Faith: Diverse Heresies, ca. 1590 (adapted by Helen Rawlings)

  If anyone has said that they do not believe in Paradise or Glory for the good nor Hell for the bad; of it anyone has made blasphemous statements, such as "I don't believe, I deny, I refuse" against God, the Virgin Mary, her virginity and purity or the saints in Heaven; or if anyone knows of somebody who has invoked the devil, using spells to provoke responses, mixing the holy with the profane; or if anybody has been a witch or a wizard; if anyone knows of any cleric or friar who has married or any unordained priest who has delivered the sacraments; if anybody has heard of a confessor who has made a pass at a women during confession, provoking her into dishonest behavior; if anybody knows of anybody who has married for a second or third time while his first wife or her first husband was still alive; if anybody knows of anyone who has practiced fornication, usury, or believes that perjury is not a sin; if anyone has abused or mistreated a holy image; if anyone has express disbelief in the articles of faith; if anyone has been excommunicated for a year or more; if any has despised or held the laws of the Holy Mother Church in disrespect . . . [may they declare it]. Source: Miguel Jiménez Monteserin, *Introducción a la Inquisición Española: Documentos básicos para el estudio del Santo Oficio*, translated by Helen Rawlings (Madrid: Editora Nacional), as found in Rawlings, *Spanish Inquisition*: 118.

Notes

1. Fray Joseph Narváez Valverde was a lay brother in New Mexico from 1694 to 1706. His duties included acting as a surgeon, notary, and ecclesiastical secretary (Norris, *Year Eighty*: 50; Kessell et al., *TDC*: 551 n51).
2. *Comisario* was a title given by the Franciscans to friars who were agents with delegated authority who led

groups of their brethren into unorganized territories (Kessell and Hendricks, *BFA*: 248 n2; Scholes, "Church and State": 164).
3. Fray Juan [Gonzales] Tagle was a native of Santander, Spain, professing his vows in 1695. He appeared in New Mexico in 1699 as a missionary priest, serving at San Ildefonso from 1701 to 1726. He held the vice-custos office in 1704–1706 and around 1710. He was the custos and commissary of the Inquisition by 1720 (Norris, *Year Eighty*: 58; Kessell et al., *TDC*: 328 n12; see also Doc. 7).
4. Norris points out that Felix Martínez, perhaps needing support for his self-appointed position of acting governor, hoped to gain the backing of the Franciscans and the Inquisition by ordering the alcaldes mayores and their lieutenants of the villas and towns to post the edict of faith, requiring at least one person from each family to attend (Norris, *Year Eighty*: 84; SANM II #269a).
5. No information could be found on Don Mateo de la Peña, but he could have been a brother or relation of Baltazar de la Peña or Fray Juan de la Peña (Kessell and Hendricks, *RCR*: 551 n50; Kessell et al., *TDC*: 166-78).
6. See Doc. 11.
7. Fray José Antonio Guerrero was from Mexico City, professed his faith in 1692, and arrived in New Mexico in 1699. He was vice-custos in 1724–1727 and 1731–1733 (Norris, *Year Eighty*: 51, 67, 90; Chávez, *Archives*: 10).
8. At this time, the term *convento* was used to mean a religious community, not just a residential facility (personal communication, Rick Hendricks, April 13, 2012).
9. The settlement of Nuestra Señora de la Soledad del Río Arriba was a large grant made to Sebastián Martín Serrano on land held before the revolt by his family. Martín Serrano moved to the area from Santa Cruz around 1705 and was made alcalde of the Santa Cruz jurisdiction in 1714. The settlement took its name from a chapel built by Martín Serrano and was also referred to as La Soledad, Río Arriba, or Las Soledad del Río Arriba. In 1744 the settlement, between Embudo and San Juan was shown by Fray Miguel de Menchero as having forty families in the "hacienda and ranches of Nuestra Señora de la Soledad." The 1750 Spanish census listed residents of Nuestra Señora del Río de Norte Arriba, including the large families of Captain Sebastián Martín and Captain don Juan Joseph Lovato. The settlement was abandoned or partly abandoned around 1750 because of Indian depredations but reestablished in 1751 along with Abiquiu and Chama. A 1752 census of Governor Cachupín showed a population of 140 people at La Soledad del Río Arriba. In 1760 Bishop Tamarón mentioned a settlement named Río Arriba near Chama. In 1763 Santiago Lucero [de Godoy] purchased the property. His wife was Bárbara Martín, a granddaughter of Sebastián Serrano Martín. The name Soledad appears on maps for many years after the purchase by Lucero. It is shown in the Miera y Pacheco map of 1778 with a symbol indicating a chapel. The 1779 Miera y Pacheco map (Map 2, Appendix) showed it as Soledad/Río Arriba. In the 1816 census, the villages of Embudo, Joya, Canoa, and Plaza de Los Ángeles were shown in the area, but neither Soledad nor Los Luceros. The name Soledad appeared on the 1841 Arrowsmith map, but the Gregg map of 1844 showed only Los Luceros.
There is some question about the location of La Soledad del Río Arriba. J. Richard Salazar, whose family is from that area, says that at one time the village of Alcalde, which is across the river from Chamita, was called Río Arriba, one of the names used for Soledad. He suggest that both settlements were in the Serrano Martín grant and that Alcalde may be a name with recalls Sebastián Serrano Martín or some later alcalde (SANM I #369 and #1129; Sze, "Los Luceros": 27-28; Adams, *Tamarón*: 97; Eidenbach, *Atlas*: 53, 57, 84, 87; Olmstead, *Censuses*: 30, 33, 150, 151, 154, 159; Jones, *Los Paisanos*: 123-24; Thomas, *Plains Indians*: 120-21; also Docs. 42 and 27; J. Richard Salazar, personal communication, Jan. 25, 2012).
10. *Predicador* means preacher.
11. Fray Carlos [José] Delgado was born in Andalusia, Spain, and came to New Spain to Querétaro with the Propaganda Fide in 1708 (the Propaganda Fide had been formed in 1622 to provide specialized instruction for missionaries). He was in New Mexico by 1710, staying there until 1747. He was noted for his work among the Hopis and Navajos, also serving at Jémez, Taos, Isleta, and El Paso. In 1748 he brought seventy families of Tewa and Hopi Indians to Sandía Pueblo. He had also served as comisario of the Inquisition for New Mexico. John Kessell called him the outstanding Franciscan to serve in New Mexico in the eighteenth century (Norris, *Year Eighty*: 21-22, 66-67, 104; Kessell, *Kiva*: 307, 334, 539 n8; Simmons, *Albuquerque*: 105).
12. Fray Francisco Antonio Páez is not found either in Norris or Chávez.
13. A *custodia* was a semi-independent area subject to the general control of the province of which it formed a part, headed by a custodian, or custos, who exercised certain administrative powers as prelate. Generally a custodia was a transitional stage, not yet sufficient in membership and size to have provincial status. New Mexico was in the custody of St. Paul, or the Custodia de San Pablo del Nuevo Mexico (Norris, *Year Eighty*: 11; Gutiérrez, *Corn Mothers*: 98).
14. Salvador Montoya was the son of Diego Montoya, who came to New Mexico in 1693, eventually settling in the Río Abajo area. Salvador married a sister of Juan García de la Riva. While this document states that in 1716 he was an alcalde mayor of Pecos, Kessell's list of alcaldes for Pecos for that year shows Alphonse Rael de Aguilar as alcalde. Montoya was a member of the cabildo Santa Fe in 1715 (Chávez, *Origins*: 183, 236; Kessell, *Kiva*: 505; SANM II #221).
15. Captain Ignacio de Roybal [y Torrado] came from Galacia, Spain, arriving in New Mexico by 1694, when he married Francisca Gómez Robledo. In 1698 he was granted a house and lands by Governor Cubero (SANM

I #1136). In 1704 he was captain and justicia mayor of the Tewas of the San Ildefonso jurisdiction, serving as the notary for San Ildefonso, Santa Cruz, and Pojoaque between 1715 and 1721. He served as an alguacil mayor, or chief constable, of the Holy Office. He may have served as an accountant, given the statement in the 1714 will of Antonio Godines that Roybal was owed "for his book of accounts" (Kessell et al., *BOB*: 952 n1; SANM I #305).

16. See Doc. 9.
17. Fray Antonio Camargo was a native of Santander, Spain, professing his vows in Mexico City in 1697 and arriving in New Mexico in 1699. He served in Tesuque, Bernalillo, San Felipe, Nambe, and San Ildefonso. He was custos in 1709–1717 (Kessell et al., *TDC*: 443 n130; Chávez, *Origins*: 244; Norris, *Year Eighty*: 84-85, 89-90, 109).
18. Whether or not an official was entitled to a cushion could be a point of controversy. Ritual, ceremony, and custom could indicate levels of political power. In an example from 1620, church officials in Mexico City complained about the seating of the viceroy, stating that he should not sit on a cushion when seated in the audiencia because it made him higher than the others (Coneque, *Image*: 119). Being allowed to sit on a chair rather than a bench was also a sign of political power. In this document, the comisario has a seat (*silla*) and a cushion (*almohada*), while the others, including the governor, sit on a bench.
19. Fray Juan Mingues was born in Mexico City in 1677, professing his vows in 1694. In 1705 he accompanied Governor Francisco Cuervo y Valdés to New Mexico. According to Juan Candelaria's remembrances many years later, he become the first Franciscan friar for the new villa of Albuquerque, later residing in the palace in Santa Fe and serving as chaplain to the presidio. He died with the Villasur expedition in 1720 (NMGS, *Aquí*: 527-30; Candelaria, "Information": 274; Norris, *Year Eighty*: 86).
20. The incumbent governor was Felipe de Sotelo Osorio, who came in the same train with Benavides. Juan de Eulate's term had expired in 1625.
21. This is the blessing, "God be with you!"

16

TREACHEROUS ROAD HAZARDS ORDERED REMOVED TO FORESTALL APACHE ATTACKS
April 16, 1716. Source: SANM II #260.

Synopsis and editor's notes: In this document, Governor Felix Martínez orders alcaldes Salvador Montoya and Juan García de la Riva and the alcalde of Taos and Picuris to cut back the trees and bushes along the roads to discourage Apache ambushes.

Keeping roads and passageways open was an ongoing problem in New Mexico. In 1703 there were complaints when one of the settlers in Chimayó closed a portion of the Camino Real and planted crops on it. In 1753 Governor Cachupín ordered the Taos settlers to unblock certain passages at Taos, and in 1756 Governor Marín del Valle ordered the residents of Santa Fe to remove their gardens and fences from the city roads (Docs. 42, 44). Then, much later, in 1861, the Territorial Legislature adopted a law stating that the justices of the peace should "see that no person obstructs the roads that lead to different parts of this Territory with wagons, nor carts, nor timber, nor by making excavations, nor in any other manner that may obstruct the mail, or any person passing" (Kessell et al., *ASA*: 181-88; Chávez Collection #15; *Law of the Territory of New Mexico, 1861*, Article LVI, Chapter XCVI, Section 1).

Captain don Felix Martínez, captain-for-life of the royal presidio of the villa of Santa Fe, lifetime regidor of its ayuntamiento, governor and captain general of the kingdom and its provinces, castellan of the forces and presidios for his majesty, etc.

Being that his majesty (whom God may guard) has declared through his royal ordinances that all of the governors, *corregidores*,[1] alcaldes mayors, and other officials, each one within his district, ensure that the roads be repaired and cleared so that they are safe for traveling. As this kingdom is under my custody, and that the roads from Pecos to this villa, the one from this said villa to the pueblo of Tesuque, and the one from Taos and Picuris are heavily wooded and winding, to the point where with complete confidence our common enemy, the Apaches, at their will can rob and kill our majesty's vassals. In order to avoid this danger, I order the adjutant Salvador Montoya,[2] alcalde mayor of the pueblo of Pecos, to order that the Indians from that pueblo cut down the trees along the road from Arroyo Hondo up to the said pueblo, cutting down the trees all the way to the ground, and to remove them from the road to the edge of the forest, where, as they become dry, they are to be burned, leaving the road more visible. In the same manner, Captain Juan García de la Riva³ is to do the same from the top of this villa up to the pueblo of Tesuque, cutting down the tree trunks that may be found in the said road. The alcalde mayor of Taos and Picuris is to do the same, using all of the Indians from his jurisdiction who are needed with their axes [*hachas*].

This order is to be given to those above by my secretary of government and war as is ordered at this villa of Santa Fe on this the 16th of April, 1716.

Felix Martínez (rubric)
by order of the governor and captain general
Miguel Tenorio de Alva (rubric)
Secretary of government and war

[Marginal note]
Notification which I,
Miguel Tenorio de Alva,
secretary of government
and war, gave to those who
are mentioned in this decree.

In compliance with the order which was given to me in this decree by the governor and captain general, I proceeded to the house and home of the captains Juan García de la Riva and Salvador Montoya, and whom, upon their being present, notified them of the above decree word by word, and having heard it, they said that they would obey it as loyal vassals of his majesty and that in compliance with it, they would execute the clearing of the roads as each one is ordered. So that it is valid, they signed it along with me the said secretary of government and war, on the said day, the 16th of April.⁴

Juan García de la Riva (rubric)
Salvador Montoya (rubric)
Miguel Tenorio de Alva (rubric)
Secretary of government and war

ORIGINAL DOCUMENT

El Capitan Dn. Phelix Martinez que lo soi Bitalico de el Reino, Presidio dela Villa de Santa Fee, Rejidor perpetuo de su Ayuntamiento, Governador y Capitan General deste Reino y Provinzias dela Nueva Mexico y Castellano de Sus Fuerzas y Presidios por Su Magestad, ut supra.

Por quanto Su Magestad (Dios le Guarde) tiene dispuesto por sus Reales Ordinanzias que todos los governadores, correjidores, alcalde maiores y demas justicias, cada uno en su distrito, haga que se limpien y compongan los caminos para que con seguridad se trajinen y estando a mi cuidado el govierno de este Reino y que los caminos de Pecos asta la Villa, y el de dicha Villa a el Pueblo de Tezuque y el de Taos y Picuris son mui montosos y barrancosos, donde, con toda seguridad se puede emboscar el comun enemigo Apache y a su salvo executar muertes y robos en los basallos de Su Magestad, para ebitar este dano mando al Ayudante Salvador Montoya, Alcalde Maior de el Pueblo de Pecos haga que los Hindios de el desmonten el camino desde el Aroio Hondo asta dicho Pueblo, cortando los arboles a rais de el suelo y desbiandolos de el camino alas orillas de el monte para en estando secos pegarles fuego, y que quede mas escombrado el camino, y lo mismo executar el Capitan Juan Garcia de la Ribas, desde el alto de esta Villa asta el Pueblo de Tezeque cortando los troncones que hubiere en el dicho camino; y el Alcalde Mayor de Taos y Picuris executen lo mismo, sacando para esto de sus jurisdiziones los Hindios que le parezieren nesesarios con hachas; y este horden lo hara notorio alos contenidos mi Secretario de Governazion y Guerra que es fecho en esta Villa de Santa Fee en dies y seis dias del mes de Abril de mil setecientos y dies y seis anos.

Phelix Martinez (rubric)
Por mando del Senor Governador y Capitan General
Miguel Thenorio de Alva (rubric)
Secretario de Governazion y Guerra

[Marginal note]
Notoridad que yo Miguel Thenorio de Alva,
Secretario de Governazion y Guerra hize
a los contenidos en este auto.

[Marginal note]
Obedezimiento

En cumplimiento de lo que seme ordena en esta auto por el Señor Governador y Capitan General pase ala casa y morada de los Capitanes Juan Garcia de la Ribas y Salvador Montoya aquienes estando presentes les hize notorio el auto de la vuelta de berbo ad berbum que haviendolo oído dijeron que lo obedecen como leales vasallos de Su Magestad y que en su cumplimiento pondrán luego por execucion la limpia de caminos cada uno lo que le toca y para que conste lo firmaron con migo dicho Secretario de Governazion y Guerra en dicho dia diez y seis de Abril =

        Juan Garcia de la Riva (rubric)
        Salvador Montoya (rubric)
        Miguel Thenorio de Alva (rubric)
        Secretario de Governazion y Guerra

Notes

1. Usually called *regidores*. They were members of the cabildo.
2. See Doc. 16.
3. See Doc. 9.
4. This short paragraph gives an example of how the documents got from the governor to each alcalde for their signatures. In this case, the secretary, Tenorio de Alva, on the same day that the governor wrote the order, rode to the house of each of the two alcaldes and, in person, notified them of the order and had them sign it.

17

TRIP TO SALT LAKES ANNOUNCED FOR SANTA CRUZ, TAOS, AND RESIDENTS OF THE TEWA[1] JURISDICTION
July 3–8, 1716. Source: SANM II #252.

Synopsis and editor's notes: In the summer of 1716, Governor Felix Martínez scheduled a trip to the salt lakes in the Salinas, south of Glorieta Mesa and east of the Sandía/Manzano mountain group for the people of Santa Cruz and the Tewas of Taos. He stated that he had been informed that it had been a long time since anyone had gone there. His order is one of many from the eighteenth century, when the governors regularly scheduled escorted trips to the area. Another example is the order of June 1, 1730 when Governor Juan Domingo Bustamante announced that the presidio escort would leave Galisteo for the salt lakes on June 9. Governors Olavide y Micheleña and Gaspar Domingo Mendoza gave similar orders in 1738 and 1740.

The salt lakes, sources of high-quality surface salt, had been mined since precontact times. The Tompiro pueblos of Gran Quivira and Abo were located nearby, perhaps because of their proximity to the lakes. The Spanish were mining salt there by 1630, with the Parral silver mining districts sending salt caravans north by 1650. In the seventeenth century, the revenues from salt appear to have been a monopoly of the governor, but the monopoly was discontinued after the return of the Spanish in the eighteenth century. A trip to the salt lakes could be dangerous without or even with a military escort. In his comments on colonial death records, Fray Angélico Chávez found that in 1708 a Nambe Pueblo Indian was killed by an Apache while guiding soldiers who had gone to collect salt for Governor Peñuela (SANM II #435; #357; #426; Kraemer, "Salt Trade": 24-28; Chávez, *Archives*: 233).

Bando promulgated at the order of the governor and captain general don Felix Martinez.

I, Captain don Felix Martínez,[2] being as I am appointed for life general for the royal presidio of the villa of Santa Fe, regidor of its ayuntamiento, governor and captain general of this kingdom and provinces of New Mexico, and castellan of the forces and presidios for his majesty, etc.

It has been brought to my attention on various and different occasions that I need to send a detachment to the Salinas to bring salt, as it is lacking in the entire kingdom because it has been a long time since anyone has gone to the said Salinas, which indeed is a fact. At the present time, I order the alcalde mayor of the Villa of Santa Cruz and the jurisdiction of the Teguas [Tewas] to inform the residents and the Indians of his jurisdiction that on the 20th of the present month an escort is to leave from this said villa. Thus I am informing the residents of the jurisdiction so that if anyone is interested in going or in sending someone, they can do so. This order is to be made known by the lieutenant to the alcalde mayor of the pueblo of San Gerónimo de Taos so that if the natives are interested in going, they can plan on doing so on that particular day. So that it is valid, I signed it at the villa of Santa Fe on the 8th of July, 1716, along with my secretary of government and war.

     Felix Martínez (rubric)
 at the order of the governor and captain general
    Miguel Tenorio de Alba (rubric)
    Secretary of government and war

[Marginal note] In compliance with the order which was given by the governor and captain general, I proceeded to inform the residents and Indians of my said jurisdiction in order to assure that it was carried out. I thus signed it at the said villa of Santa Cruz on the 10th of July, 1716.
    [Juan] García de la Riva (rubric)

ORIGINAL DOCUMENT

Vandos que se promulgaron de Orden del Señor Governador y Capitan General Dn. Felix Martinez

El Capitan Dn. Phelix Martinez que lo soi Bitalizio del Real Presidio dela Villa de Santa Fee, Regidor de Su Ayuntamiento Governador y Capitan General deste Reyno y Provincias dela Nueba Mexico y Castellano de Sus Fuerzas y Presidios por Su Magestad, ut supra.

En cumplimiento del auto que parese del Señor Governador y Capitan General pase aser notorio a los vesinos y Yndios de dicha mi jurisdision para que conste de aserle asi ejecutado. Lo firme en dicha Villa de Santa Cruz en tres de Julio de mil setesientos y dies y seis años.
Garcia de la Riva (rubric)

Por quanto se me an echo barias y diferentes representaziones para que despachaze alas Salinas a traer sal por allarse falto de ella todo el Reino por haver muchos dias que no se va a dichas Salinas y por constarme ser zierto, por el presente mando al Alcalde Maior dela Villa de Santa Cruz y jurisdizion de los Teguas haveze a todos

los bezinos y Yndios de dicha su jurisdision como el dia veinte del coriente sale de esta Villa la escolta que tengo senalada para los besinos de ella para que si alguno quiziere yr o imbiarlo puede azerlo y este orden lo mostrara el Theniente de Alcalde Maior del Pueblo de San Geronimo de Thaos para que si sus naturales quiezieran yr lo puedan executar para dicho dia y para que conste lo firme en esta Villa de Santa Fee en ocho de Julio de mil setezientos y dies y seis años con mi Secretario de Governazion y Guerra.
Phelix Martinez (rubric)
Por mando del Señor Governador y Capitan General
Miguel Thenorio de Alva
Secretario de Governazion y Guerra
(Alva's rubric)

Notes

1. The 1779 Miera y Pacheco map (Map 2, Appendix) shows the *alcaldía* of Santa Cruz including areas both east and west of the Río Grande from the Tesuque, Chama, and Picuris drainages north to the Río Trampas (Eidenbach, *Atlas*: 55).
2. Information on Felix Martínez is included in Doc. 2. Note that at this time Martínez had again claimed this appointment as captain-for-life, granted to him in 1711 by Viceroy Linares and later rescinded by Governor Flores de Mogollón. On September 30, 1716, Martínez was directed to turn the government over to Captain Valverde (Warner, "Felix Martinez": 45, 107).

18

*KNIFE FIGHT RESULTS IN MURDER; FUGITIVE CLAIMS
CHURCH SANCTUARY, PARDONED
FOR MOQUI CAMPAIGN*
August 1 to November 4, 1716. Source: SANM II #256a.

Synopsis and editor's notes: In 1716 Governor Felix Martínez, about to begin a campaign in the province of Moqui (Hopi), declared an amnesty for all persons under sanctuary in any church in the province if they joined the campaign. One of those people, (perhaps the only one) was Alonso Rael de Aguilar II, the son of the well-known soldier-settler Alfonso Rael de Aguilar. In December of 1715, Alonso Rael de Aguilar had killed Sergeant Francisco Tamaris in a knife fight that also involved his brother, Eusebio Rael de Aguilar. Another document, SANM II #239j, shows that Alonso originally took sanctuary in Santa Fe in December 15, 1715, with the church surrounded by fourteen soldiers. However, in May of 1715 when Juan Páez Hurtado searched the church, he found that Alonso had escaped, apparently to another church sanctuary. Messengers were sent to the alcaldes of four jurisdictions, but no one admitted to seeing him. Now, in this case, Alonso Rael de Aguilar petitioned for amnesty, provided his version of the fight, and agreed to join the campaign against the Moquis (Chávez, *Origins*: 292; West, "Asylum": 130-31; Cutter, *Legal Culture*: 129; SANM II #239j).

The right of church sanctuary extended from medieval times, with the church and state often differing on the extent of protection it provided. In New Mexico, the first record of sanctuary is for no less than Governor Pedro Peralta in Santa Fe in 1613. In Santa Fe in 1697–1700, both Governor Vargas and Juan Páez Hurtado claimed sanctuary during the administration of Governor Cubero. In 1701 Fray Francisco Farfán sent orders to fourteen missions stating that excommunication would be incurred by lay people not honoring ecclesiastical immunity, perhaps referring to the Vargas and Hurtado sanctuary. Eliza Howard West's article on the right of asylum provides an extensive discussion of thirty-two recorded cases of sanctuary in New Mexico in the eighteenth century, primarily in Santa Fe, Albuquerque, and Santa Cruz. An intriguing circular from 1769 by Viceroy Marqués de Croix to New Mexico states that a royal order had been sent providing the means for extracting a guilty person from sacred places. However, only the cover letter is extant (Chávez, *Archives*: 21; West, "Asylum": 148-49; Kessell et al., *BOB*: 223 n97; Kessell et al., *TDC*: 155, 318; SANM II #646).

Under the name of the king, Our Lord, and his royal word, a public notice[1] was presented for the term of eight days at the royal guardhouse of this said villa of Santa Fe. So that everyone is informed, I order my secretary of government and war to make it public at the four corners of the principal plaza under the sound of the military instruments. Once this is done, he is to submit it to the alcalde mayor, or to his lieutenant, of the new villa of Santa Cruz so that it is made public at that place, and once it is done he is to certify that it was executed as ordered. From there, it is to be submitted to San Felipe de Alburquerque so that the alcalde mayor at that place will do the same. Upon it being done, it is to be submitted to my secretary so that he can place it into the archives under his command. So that it is valid, I signed it at this said villa of Santa Fe on the 1st of August, 1716, with my secretary of government and war. Don Felix Martínez.

at the order of
the governor and captain general
Miguel Tenorio de Alba[2]
Secretary of government and war.

Publication

In fulfillment of that which the governor and captain general has ordered me to do in the above proceedings, I went to the royal guardhouse of this villa and the other places indicated and pronounced the said royal bando before a large group of persons. So that it is valid, I signed it on the 1st of September [he may have meant August], 1716.

Miguel Tenorio de Alva
Secretary of government and war

Publication

At the villa of Santa Cruz on the 2nd of August, 1716, I, Alférez Cristóbal de Torres,[3] the lieutenant to the alcalde mayor and war captain of the said villa and of its jurisdiction, due to the absence of Captain Juan García de la Riva,[4] alcalde mayor, made public the bando above provided by the governor and captain general, don Felix Martínez, on this day of this date in the plaza of the said villa, and having read it, was taken to be understood by everyone. So that it is valid, I signed it at the said villa of Santa Cruz on the said day, month, and year, acting as presiding judge along with my assisting witnesses.

Cristóbal de Torres

Assisting witnesses
Francisco de Rivera
Juan de Atienza

At the villa of San Felipe de Albuquerque on the 4th of August of 1716, I, the captain and alcalde mayor and war captain, having seen the royal bando provided by the governor, don Felix Martínez, made it publicly known to the residents and settlers, and so that it is known that it was carried out as ordered, I signed it on the said day.
Antonio Gutiérrez[5]

Governor and captain general

[I] the captain of the company of this presidial castle of the villa of Santa Fe, Alonso Rael de Aguilar,[6] appear before your honor at this royal guardhouse where I present myself by virtue of the royal bando of amnesty, which was ordered to be promulgated by your honor on the first of the current month. It reads that everyone who is found under sanctuary in the sacred presence of the churches of this kingdom, for whatever crimes they may have committed except for that of *cessa magestatis*,[7] should present themselves at the royal guardhouse and, under the name of his majesty (whom God may guard), will be pardoned by joining the campaign, which your honor will personally lead and execute under his great zeal and application to the faraway province of Moqui, to reduce to our Holy Catholic faith the native apostates of that and other nations which are found there.

I [Alonso Real de Aguilar] am one of those who is under sanctuary in one of the churches for having inflicted a wound upon Sergeant Francisco de Tamaris,[8] now deceased. The reason for this was motivated by the fact that when the royal alférez, Eusebio Rael de Aguilar, my brother, had ordered the said sergeant to take a letter to the pueblo of Santo Domingo, he [Eusebio] was told that the horse that he [the sergeant] was on did not belong to him [the sergeant] but was owned by Joseph Luján.[9] The sergeant responded that he [Eusebio] should take it [himself] either on foot or on horseback. This was what my brother told me. I then proceeded to go to the sergeant, and I gave him the letter telling him to take it, and if the horse belonged to Joseph Luján, I would bring him [Luján] two others, if he needed them, being that they were under my care and that I had received them from the regidor, Salvador Montoya,[10] who owed them to the said Luján. Having said this to the said sergeant, he said that he would ask my brother if it was done as a request, to which Eusebio responded that it was not a request, that it was an order, no matter whose horses they were. He [the sergeant] then asked for a second and third time if it was a request. Saying that he [Eusebio] would punish with his sword [*espada*] those who did not have manners, and that if he [the sergeant] would get mad, he would make him take it on foot or on horseback. To which I told him to report immediately to me and to which he responded by coming at me furiously, at which time some persons who were around stepped in and stopped him.

I then proceeded to go to the royal guardhouse, telling the sergeant that he had a beautiful *gerenga* [profanity not translated], not saying anything else to him, at which time he became furious once more and with his sword drawn attempted to strike me, against which I could have defended myself with my sword in its sheath, but, while attempting to draw it, Martín de Valenzuela[11] caught my arm while attempting to draw it, and I lost it.

Seeing myself totally at a loss because the said sergeant viciously came at me swinging his sword trying to kill me, I very carefully positioned myself with the best defense which I could, and suddenly realizing that I had a knife [*cuchillo*], I threw it at him and stabbed him with it in order to contain him from his violence, my intent being only to defend myself. Disregarding the fact that I am the captain of the campaign, he should know that he is under my orders as is implied by the title and rank which I have.

In due solemnity and as is necessary, I present this petition to your honor and by which I ask and request that he be pleased to add it to the proceedings of the case which has been carried out against me and that it remain there for all time for whatever is done against me for the sake of justice and for whatever charges are brought forth. Before anything else, a testimony should be brought forth regarding the royal bando of amnesty, and, in the same manner should be added to the proceedings of the case, as it is the only thing that can be of value to me. The royal sanctuary is the main thing for my defense, as I have stated, finding myself at this royal guardhouse, where I very anxiously and readily await the execution of the campaign to the province of Moqui and all the others of the royal service.

For this reason I petition and ask your honor that he be pleased to release me from this royal guardhouse in order to gain the amnesty which has been promulgated by the royal bando issued by your honor, and to order that this be done as I have requested, which is for the sake of justice and the royal assistance which I seek from your honor, I swear in due form that it is not done in malice but through what is necessary, etc.

Alonso de Aguilar

Presentation
At the villa of Santa Fe on the 3rd of August, 1716, before me, Captain don Felix Martínez, governor and captain general of this kingdom and province of New Mexico and castellan of the forces for his majesty.

Proceedings
It was presented as submitted by him [Alonso Rael de Aguilar], and upon my review I left it as it was presented and left the amnesty secure through the royal word, and so that he can be given whatever he requires for said campaign, I grant him

permission to freely leave the royal guardhouse. I inform him and order him from this day forth not to carry a knife in any settlement, and once he returns from the campaign he is to appear before me so that I can declare him absolved for the crime he committed.

I order my secretary that this petition and the title of captain of the campaign be added to these proceedings, and once the campaign is carried out, he [the secretary] is to inform him of the cited bando. These proceedings are to be made known to the corporal of the guard, Juan Ruiz Cordero,[12] so he will release him to go to his home, and he is also to inform the petitioner of this, carrying out the notice as is ordered. I thus approved, ordered, and signed it, along with my secretary of government and war on the said day.

don Felix Martínez
before me Miguel Tenorio de Alva
Secretary of government and war

I, the said secretary of government and war, certify that [regarding the above order] I have personally notified the captain of the campaign, don Alonso Rael de Aguilar, who is in the royal guardhouse of this villa of Santa Fe, with the corporal of the squadron of the forces, Juan Ruiz Cordero, also being present. So that it is valid, I signed it on the 3rd of August, 1716.

Miguel Tenorio de Alva
Secretary of government and war

Don Juan Ygnacio Flores Mogollón,[13] governor and captain general of this kingdom and provinces of New Mexico and castellan of the forces and presidios for the king, Our Lord, etc.

Being there is a vacancy in one of the two positions of captain of the campaign of this presidio because a criminal complaint has been brought against Captain Cristóbal de Arellano,[14] who was the one who held it, I order that it be annotated as executed. The secretary of his majesty, whom God may guard, having given approval for a person of excellent quality, merits, and service to be able to hold the position in the royal service, and being that these and other good qualities which are required and are found in the person of the royal ensign, Alonso Rael de Aguilar, who in this royal presidio has served his majesty for almost ten years with the approval of its officials, having relinquished the obligation of the functions for the present, in the name of the king, Our Lord, I nominate, name, and designate as captain of the campaign the said Ensign Alonso Rael de Aguilar so that as such he can enjoy it and perform it, bringing the accustomed insignia, immediately acquiring the position. I order the captain of this presidio that he have as such a captain of the campaign and that the lieutenant, alferez, sergeant, and other active officials as well as those who are retired [or on reserve] from this company of this said presidio to accept, obey, and respect him.

For this position, I grant all of the graces, privileges, and exemptions which his majesty has conceded to this position under whose royal name I declare them and grant them. So that it is valid, I order that the present title and rank of captain of the campaign be dispatched as signed by my name and sealed with the seal of my arms and making certain that my secretary of government and war enters all of this into the book under his charge as done in this villa of Santa Fe, New Mexico on the 3rd of April, 1715, on the present common paper, as the sealed type is not found here. This is to be made public at the *plaza de armas*[15] so that everyone knows about it.

      Don Juan Ygnacio Flores Mogollón
    by order of the governor and captain general
        Roque de Pintto
      Secretary of government and war

On the said day I performed the order and it was made known public at this plaza de armas.

I, the captain of the campaign of this presidial body of the villa of Santa Fe, appear before your honor in the best form which by right I am given. I say that I have appeared before the royal guardhouse by virtue of the royal bando of amnesty, which order was promulgated by your honor, who has issued the written proceedings which I presented ordering the corporal of the guard of the said royal guardhouse to allow me to leave from there so that I would have sufficient time to prepare for the campaign to the province of Moqui, which your honor is awaiting to carry out, and for which I have been given amnesty from the case which is being carried out against me. By this order of your honor, I am to be provided with my weapons and horses, your honor seeing that they are given to me so that I can carry out the said campaign and everything else that is to be done for the service of his majesty. As such, I ask and petition your honor that he be pleased to order that which I ask for is done, and as such I await from his great justification that which I ask for in justice and swear in due form, etc.

        Alonso Rael de Aguilar

Presentation
Villa of Santa Fe, New Mexico, August 8th, 1716.

The herein named presented it to me, Captain don Felix Martínez, which I am for life, of this royal presidio, governor and captain general of this kingdom and provinces of New Mexico and castellan of the forces and presidios for his majesty.

Proceedings

It being reviewed by me, I took it as was presented and ordered my lieutenant general in the case, which was followed against the petitioner, to give him the arms and horses which are to be provided for him so that he can carry out the campaign to the province of Moqui as has been ordered, and so that it is valid, I ordered that it be placed with the proceedings, and I signed it with my secretary of government and war. On the said day, month, and year.

don Felix Martínez
before me Miguel Tenorio de Alva
Secretary of government and war

At this villa of Santa Fe on the 12th of August, 1716, I, General Juan Páez Hurtado, lieutenant to the governor and captain general of this kingdom, in fulfillment of the above decree turned over to the captain of the campaign, Alonso Rael de Aguilar, the younger, all of the goods which are included in the inventory above. As for the horses which are to be included, but which are not in the inventory and which were five by order of the sergeant of the campaign of this presidio, Lázaro Durán, I, turned them over to the said captain so that along with the other items which he has received he can acknowledge their receipt at the bottom of this order which I signed on this said day.

Juan Páez Hurtado

I, the captain of the campaign, don Alonso Rael de Aguilar, say that I received from the lieutenant general Juan Páez Hurtado all of the items which his honor had allowed me and are included in these proceedings along with my horses which by his order were being held with the horses of the royal presidio, and so that it is known that I have received them, I signed it at this villa of Santa Fe on the 14th of August, 1716. Alonso Rael de Aguilar

Declaratory Decree

At the villa of Santa Fe on the 4th of November, 1716, I, Captain don Felix Martínez, being as I am for life, of this presidio of the villa of Santa Fe, regidor of the ayuntamiento,[16] governor and captain general of this kingdom and province of New Mexico and castellan of his forces and presidios for his majesty, say that the captain of the campaign, Alonso Rael de Aguilar, presented himself at the royal guardhouse of this said villa of Santa Fe on the 3rd of August of the present year. By virtue of the bando promulgated on the first of the said month of August, he committed himself to carry out, along with me, the campaign to the province of Moqui at his own expense, including his arms and horses, which commitment he fulfilled, always being prompt to do whatever was ordered by me, including the excursions and functions which were carried out in the said campaign, I hereby, in the name of the king, Our Lord, declare him to be free and absolved of the punishment which corresponded to the crime of having caused the death of Sergeant Francisco García Carnero [also known as Francisco de Tamaris], and he can freely travel in and out of this kingdom. This amnesty is given to him under the right which I have by the authority given to me by my employment. So that it is valid, I signed it with my secretary of government and war on this said day.

Don Felix Martínez
before me Miguel Tenorio de Alva
Secretary of government and war

ORIGINAL DOCUMENT

Nombre del Rey Nuestro Señor de bajo de cuyo seguro Real palabra se presentaron en el Real Cuerpo de Guardia de esta dicha Villa de Santa Fee dentro del termino de ocho dias y para que venga a notizia de todos ordeno a mi Secretario de Governazion y Guerra lo haga publicar en su plaza principal en las quatro esquinas al son de los instrumentos militares y hecha su publicazion lo remita ala Villa Nueva de Santa Cruz a su Alcalde Mayor o Theniente para que en ella lo publique poniendo la fee de averlo asi executado y de alli lo remita ala de San Felipe de Alburquerque para que su Alcalde Mayor asi lo aga y fecho lo remita a dicho mi Secretario para que conste en el archibo de su cargo y para que conste lo firme en dicha Villa de Santa Fee en primero de Agosto de mill setecientos y diez y seis años con mi Secretario de Governazion y Guerra = Dn. Felix Martinez = Por mando del Señor Governador y Capitan General Miguel Tenorio de Alba, Secretario de Governazion y Guerra =

Publicazion = En cumplimiento delo que el Señor Governador y Capitan General me ordena por el auto dela foja anterior pase a el Cuerpo de Guardia de esta Villa y de mas partes zitadas y promulgue dicho Real Vando con numeroso concurso de gente y para que conste lo firme en primero de Septiembre de mill setecientos y dies y seis años = Miguel Tenoria de Alva, Secretario de Governazion y Guerra. _____

Publicazion = En la Villa Nueba de Santa Cruz en dos dias del mes de Agosto de mill setecientos y diez y seis años yo el Alferez Xptobal de Torres, Theniente de Alcalde Mayor y Capitan Aguerra de dicha Villa y su jurisdiction por ausiencia del Capitan Juan Garcia de la Rivas Alcalde Mayor hize notorio el Vando de ariva probeido por el Señor Governador y Capitan General Dn. Felix Martinez oy dia dela fecha en la plaza de dicha Villa asiendo leer y yntimar para que venga a notizia de todos y para que conste lo firme en dicha Villa de Santa Cruz en dicho dia, mes y año autuando ante mi como juez receptor con los ynfrascriptos testigos de mi asistenzia = Xptobal de Torres = testigo de asistenzia Francisco de Rivera = testigo de asistenzia Juan de Atienza _____

En la Villa de San Felipe de Alburquerque en quatro dias del mes de Agosto del año de mill setecientos y diez y seis, yo el Capitan y Alcalde Mayor y Capitan Aguerra aviendo visto el Real Vando probeydo por el Señor Governador Dn. Felix Martinez lo hize notorio en esta dicha Villa en junta de todos los vezinos y moradores y para que conste de tal obedesimiento lo firme en dicho dia = Antonio Gutierrez _____

Señor Governador y Capitan General = El Capitan de la compania deste Castillo Presidial dela Villa de Santa Fee Alonso Rael de Aguilar paresco ante Vuestra Señoria en este Cuerpo de Guardia en donde me presento en virtud del Real Vando de yndulto mandado promulgado por Vuestra Señoria el dia primero del presente mes dela fecha cuya expresion es a que todos los que se allasen efuxiados en el sagrado dela yglesias de este Reino por qualesquiera delictos que ayan cometido menos el de *cessa magestatis* que se presenten en dicho Real Cuerpo de Guardia que en nombre de Su Magestad (que Dios guarde) sele perdonan aziendo la campaña que Vuestra Señoria en persona con su gran zelo y aplicazion al Real Servizio se alla proximo a executar ala delatada Provinzia de Moqui a reducir al gremio de Nuestra Santa Fee Catholica a los naturales apostatas de ella y de mas naziones que en ella se allan de los sub traidos de este Reyno; y siendo yo uno delos efuxiados en una de dichas yglesias por ocacion de aver dado un herida al Sargento Francisco de Tamaris, (aka Francisco Garcia Carnero) ya difunto, cuyo casual hecho fue motivado de que aviandole mandado el suso dicho al Alferez Rael Eusebio Rael de Aguilar, mi hermano, llevase una carta al Pueblo de Santo Domingo, le repondio que el cavallo en que andava no era suyo sino es de Joseph Lujan; y dicho Sargento le respondio que dicha carta sela avia de llevar apie o acavallo, cuya razon me dio mi hermano y luego fui aver a dicho Sargento dandosela yo de que dicho cavallo era del dicho Joseph Lujan y lo avia ymbiado a traer dela cavallada con otros dos para entregarselos por estar de mi quenta por averlos rezivido del Rexidor Salvador Montoya quien selos devia a dicho Lujan y aviendole dado esta razon al suso dicho Sargento respondio que sele yba a tomar requesta por mi hermano le dixe que no era tomarle requesta sino es solamente satisfaserla de quien eran dichos cavallos y volvio Segunda y terzera ves que si era requesta que con la espada que tenia castigaria desvergonsados y que la carta si se enfadava sela aria llevar apie o acavallo alo qual le dixe que se reportara y contuberia viniendose luego para mi con grande ympeni y furia a cuyo tiempo se pusieron de por medio algunas personas que alli se allaron y entonses viniendome yo para el Cuerpo de Guardia dixe que era muy linda geringa (no ablando ya con el) alo qual volvio con grande colera con la espada desnuda dandome de cuchilladas que repare con la espada enbaynada y queriendola desembaynar para defenderme no pude y a este tiempo me agaro la espada de la guarnicion Martín de Valenzuela y me tiro el brazo por cuyo motivo la solte y viendome en el todo perdido por reconozer que dicho Sargento me queria matar me fue presiso ponerme en defensa con la mayor diligenzia que pude porque se vino para mi con gran violenzia y coraje tirandome de estacadas, y por que no me matara me acorde del cuchillo que traia y le di con el para contenerlo de su violenzia no siendo el animo mas que defenderme; no atendiendo a que me allava del Capitan de Campania y devia de estar sujeto debajo de mis ordenes como consta del titulo y patente que con la solemnidad en derecho nesesaria ago presentazion a Vuestra Señoria a quien con todo rendimiento pido sea muy servido de mandar se acomule a los autos y caussa que contra ami se hubiere seguido y conste en ella en todo tiempo para quanto seme pueda azer ni parar por juicio lo que seme pueda azer de cargo y ante todas cosas de que se saque un testimonio del dicho Real Bando de yndulto y dela misma forma se acomule a dicha caussa por ser unicamente lo que me puede valer y hazer mayor fuerza ami defensa de bajo de cuyo Real amparo como llevo dicho me presento en este dicho Cuerpo de Guardia a donde estoy muy prompto conciega y rendida obedenzia a executar dicha campaña a la Provincia de Moqui y todas las demas del Real Servizio por tanto, a Vuestra Señria pido y suplico sea muy servido de averme por presentado en este Real Cuerpo de Guardia y de que goze del yndulto mandado promulgar por dicho Real Vando por Vuestra Señoria y de mandar azerlo que llevo pedido pues es de justizia y el real auxilio en Vuestra Señoria ymploro y juro en forma no ser de malisia y en lo nesesario, ut supra. Alonso de Aguilar _____

Presentazion
En la Villa de Santa Fee en tres il del mes de Agosto del año de il setecientos y diez y seis ante mi el Capitan Dn. Felix Martinez, Governador y Capitan General desta Reyno y Porvinzia de la Nueva Mexico y Castellano de Sus Fuerzas por Su Magestad.

Auto
La presento el contenido y por mi vista la ube por presentada y por admitido a el yndulto devajo del seguro y palabra Real y para que pueda aviarse delo nesesario para dicha campaña le doy licenzia para que salga libremente del Real Cuerpo de Guardia y le apercibo y mando no cargue cuchillo en lo de adelante en poblado ninguno y de buelta de la campaña parecera ante mi para declararlo por absuelto del delicto cometido y mando ami Secretario que esta peticion y el titulo del Capitan de Campaña lo acomule alos autos y executado como llevo dicho la campaña le de testimonio del zitado vando y este auto sele ara notorio al Cavo de la Guardia Juan Ruiz Cordero para

que lo dexe yr a su cassa y juntamente lo ara al suplicante poniendo la fee de aviso asi executado y para que conste asi lo probey, mande y firme con mi Secretario de Governazion y Guerra en dicho dia =
Dn. Felix Martinez = Ante mi, Miguel Tenorio de Alva = Secretario de Governazion y Guerra = _____

Yo el presente Secretario de Governazion y Guerra doy fee aver hecho notorio el auto de ariva al Capitan de Campaña Alonso Real de Aguilar en su persona en el Cuerpo de Guardia desta Villa de Santa Fee estando presente el Cavo de Esquadra de la fuerza Juan Ruiz Cordero y para que conste lo firme en tres dias del mes de Agosto del año de mill setecientos y diez = Miguel Tenoria de Alva = Secretario de Governazion y Guerra. ___

Don Juan Ygnacio Flores Mogollon Governador y Capitan General deste Reyno y Provincias dela Nueba Mexico y Castellano de Sus Fuerzas y Presidios por el Rey Nuestro Señor, ut supra _____

Por quanto se alla vaca una delas dos plazas de Capitan de Campañ deste Presidio por averlo seguido caussa criminal al Capitan Xptobal de Arellano quien la obtenia y mando sele anotase como se executo y combiniendo al Secretario de Su Magestad que Dios Guarde el probeerla en persona de calidad, meritos y servicios para que se puedan ofrezer en el Real Servizio y por que estas y las demas buenas partes que se desian requieren y nesesitan concurren y se allan en la del Alferez Real Alonso Real de Aguilar quien es este Real Presidio a servido a Su Magestad serca de diez años con aprobasion de los oficiales de el aviendo desamparado su obligazion en las funciones que se an ofresido por el presente en nombre del Rey Nuestro Señor le elijo, nombro y senalo por Capitan de Campaña al dicho Alferez Alonso Real de Aguilar para que como tal lo usse y exerze trayendo la ynsignia acostumbrada y entrando desde luego a su possezion y mando al Capitan deste Presidio le aya y tenga por tal Capitan de Campaña y al Theniente, Alferez y Sargento y demas oficiales vivos y reformados de la Compania deste dicho Presidio le acaten, ovedescan y respeten por cuyo empleo le consedo todas las gracias, prevellexios y esepciones que Su Magestad tiene consedidas por razon deste empleo en cuyo Real nombre selas declaro y consedo y para que conste le mande despachar el presente titulo y patente de Capitan de Campaña firmado de mi nombre y sellado con el sello de mis armas y refrendado de mi Secretario de Governazion y Guerra quien tomara la razon en el libro de su cargo que es fecho en esta Villa de Santa Fee de la Nueva Mexico en tres dias del mes de Abril de mill setesientos y quinze años y en el presente papel comun por no correr el sellado; y se ara notorio en esta Plaza de Armas para el conozimiento de los unos y los otros = Dn. Juan

Ygnacio Flores Mogollon = Por mandado del Señor Governador y Capitan General, Roque de Pintto, Secretario de Governazion y Guerra ___

En dicho dia tome la razon y se hizo notorio en esta Plaza de Armas _____

El Capitan de Campaña de este Cuerpo Presidial de la Villa de Santa Fee paresco ante Vuestra Señoria en la mejor forma que el derecho me consede y digo que aviendome presentado en el Real Cuerpo de Guardia en virtud del Real Vando de yndulto mandado promulgar por Vuestra Señoria quien fue servido de probeer auto al escipto que presente mandando al Cavo de la Guardia de dicho Real Cuerpo de Guardia saliesse de el para tener tiempo bastante para que me aviase para poder azer la campaña a la Provinzia de Moqui que Vuestra Señoria se alla proximo a executar a donde soy yndulto por la caussa que contra mi se a seguido, y por que de orden de Vuestra Señoria se embargaron mis armas y cavallos por lo qual se a de servir Vuestra Señoria de mandar seme vuelban y entrieguen para que pueda executar dicha campaña y todas las demas que se ofrecieron en servicio de Su Magestad, por tanto a Vuestra Señoria pido y suplico sea muy servido de mandar azer como lo pido que assi lo espero de su grande justificazion pido justizia y juro en forma ut supra = Alonso Rael de Aguilar _____

Presentazion
Villa de Santa Fee de la Nueva Mexico y Agosto ocho de mill setecientos y diez y seis años = La presento el contenido ante mi el Capitan Dn. Felix Martinez que lo soy Vitalico deste Real Presidio, Governador y Capitan General de este Reyno y Provinzias dela Nueva Mexico y Castellano de Sus Fuerzas y Presidios por Su Magestad _____

Auto
Y por mi vista la ube por presentada y mando ami Theniente General Juez en la caussa que siguio contra el suplicante le entriegue las armas y cavallos que le tubiese embargados para que pueda azer la campaña ala Provinzia de Moqui como se ofrese y para que conste mande se acomule alos autos y lo firme con mi Secretario de Governazion y Guerra = En dicho dia mes y año = Dn. Felix Martinez = Ante mi Miguel Tenoria de Alva = Secretario de Governazion y Guerra _____

En esta Villa de Santa Fee en doze dias del mes de Agosto de mill setesientos y diez y seis años yo el General Juan Paez Hurtado, Theniente de Governador y Capitan General deste Reino en cumplimiento del auto de ariva entregue a el Capitan de Campaña Alonso Rael de Aguilar, el moso, todos los vienes que constan en el ynbentario desta cavesa y por lo que mira a los cavallos embargados que no constan en dicho ynbentario y fueron sinco de orden al Sargento de la Campaña de este Presidio Lazaro Duran selos entriegue a dicho Capitan para que de los demas vienes que tiene rezividos de su rezivo al pie deste obedecimiento que firme en dicho dia = Juan Paez Hurtado _____

Digo yo el Capitan de Campaña Dn. Alonso Rael de Aguilar que rezivi del Señor Theniente General Juan Paez Hurtado todos los vienes que Su Merced me tenia embargados y constan en estos autos con mas los cavallos que de su orden estavan detenidos en la cavallada deste Real Presidio y para que conste de averlos rezivido lo firme en esta Villa de Santa Fee en catorze dias del mes de Agosto de mill setecientos y diez y seis años = Alonso Rael de Aguilar _____

Auto Declaratorio
En la Villa de Santa Fee en quatro dias del mes de Noviembre de mill setecientos y diez y seis años yo el Capitan Dn. Felix Martinez que lo soy Vitalico de este Presidio de la Villa de Santa Fee, Rexidor de Su Ayuntamiento, Governador y Capitan General de este Reino y Provincias dela Nueba Mexico y Castellano de Sus Fuerzas y Presidios por Su Magestad digo que haviendo presentado en el Real Cuerpo de Guardia de esta dicha Villa de Santa Fee el Capitan de Campaña Alonso Rael de Aguilar el dia tres de Agosto de el presente and de la fecha en virtud del vando promulgado en primero del dicho mes de Agosto ofresiendose aser la campaña en mi compania ala Provinzia de Moqui a su costa con armas y cavallos la cual executo estando prompto a todo quanto por mi le fue ordenado, asi en las tales como en las demas corredurias y funciones que en dicha campaña se ofrecieron por lo que le devo declarar y declaro por libre y absuelto de la pena quele correspondia a el delicto de aver dado muerte a el Sargento Francisco Garcia Carnero (aka Francisco de Tarmaris), en nombre del Rey, Nuestro Señor, y que pueda andar libremente assi en este Reyno como fuera de el y dicho yndulto le concedo usando de la regalia de mi empleo y para que conste lo firme con mi Secretario de Governazion y Guerra en dicho dia = Dn. Felix Martinez = Ante mi Miguel Tenorio de Alva, Secretario de Governazion y Guerra.

Notes

1. As is stated later in this document, the notice was for an amnesty for persons who had taken church sanctuary if they joined the campaign to the province of Moqui [Hopi].
2. See Doc. 4.
3. See Doc. 10.
4. See Doc 9.

5. Although there are two persons identified as Antonio Gutiérrez in this period, this is most likely Captain Gutiérrez, the leader of the auxiliary soldiers for Isleta Pueblo. In 1716 he was granted lands between the Río Puerco and Río Grande at an area called Sitio de Gutiérrez (Chávez, *Origins*: 186; Alexander, *Cottonwoods*: 8).
6. See Doc. 1.
7. *Cessa magestatis* is a Latin term referring to crimes against the sovereign, i.e., treason.
8. Francisco Tamaris, also known as García Carnero, was a native of El Valle de San Bartolomé in New Spain and was in New Mexico by 1693. As stated in the document, in 1715 he was a sergeant of the Santa Fe presidio. He was killed in December of 1715 (Chávez, *Origins*: 292; West, "Asylum": 130-31; Cutter, *Legal Culture*: 129; see also SANM II #239j for the legal proceedings regarding the murder).
9. Joseph Luján may have been the son of Corporal Juan Luján and María Martín and the grandson of Domingo Luján who returned to resettle in New Mexico. A José Luján appeared in 1703 in don Diego Vargas's campaign journal and was listed in June 28, 1723, in a presidio muster (Christmas, *Military Records*: 49; Chávez, *Origins*: 212; Kessell et al., *ASA*: 220).
10. See Doc. 15.
11. Martín de Valenzuela and his wife, Inés, were living in Pojoaque in 1703. A report of 1717 shows that he joined the presidio on April 12, 1717, replacing Joseph Fernandes (Kessell et al., *BOB*: 1169 n83; Christmas and Rau, "Una Lista": 201).
12. Juan Ruiz Cordero was a native New Mexican, returning with his wife, María Carrillo Terrazas, in 1694 as part of the Farfán-Velasco expedition. In 1716 he was made an ayudante to General Felix Martínez (Chávez, *Origins*: 277; Kessell and Hendricks, *RCR*: 294).
13. Don Juan Ygnacio Flores Mogollón was the previous governor. This is apparently the original appointment of Alonso, made in 1715.
14. Cristóbal Arellano was one of the soldiers who had fled the colony with Bartolomé Garduño and three others in 1715 (also see Doc. 8). Apparently that case had not yet been resolved.
15. The plazas of the chartered villas and other towns were often used as military parade grounds and the locations of military musters. Because of that, they were often referred to as *plazas de armas*.
16. Governor Martínez is referring to the cabildo.

19

APPRENTICE CONTRACT FOR TEN-YEAR-OLD WRITTEN BY TAILOR AND FATHER FOR ALL EVENTUALITIES
October 1721. Source: SANM II #312.

Synopsis and editor's notes: In October of 1721, a contract with master tailor Vicente de Armijo of El Paso was made for ten-year-old Salvador Manuel de la Cruz y Armijo by his father, Vicente de Armijo. The contract was for ten years. Both of the adult parties made an effort to forestall all the problems that could possibly occur, including bad food, incomplete training, improper behavior by the boy or the tailor, and breach of contract. The contract is one of the few existing known from this period. Much later, in 1804, an apprenticeship was mentioned in the will of Manuel Mares, where he stated, "I declare to my son Juan de Jesús, I have placed him in the office of blacksmith with Manuel Sena for the term of five years, of which he only lacks 1½ years, and the said Sena takes the responsibility to send him home well trained and well dressed" (SANM I #604, WPA translation). Later still, the Territorial Laws of 1851 provided extensive regulations for "masters, servants, and apprentices" dealing with many of the concerns about abusive treatment that Armijo discussed in this contract for his son (*Territorial Laws of New Mexico*, Article XXXV, Chapter LXXVI, Act of July 30, 1851).

Year of 1721

Document of the party Joseph Garzía,[1] master tailor for the obligation to give instruction to a young son of Vicente Armijo.[2]

Let know whoever sees this written instrument, that in this villa of Santa Fe, capital of this kingdom of the New Mexico, on the 21st day of the present month of October 1721, there appeared before me, the captain Francisco Bueno de Bohorques y Corcuera,[3] alcalde mayor and war captain of this villa, in my capacity as presiding judge, and the assisting witnesses acting before me because of the lack of a public or royal notary anywhere in this kingdom, namely Joseph Garzía, master tailor [*sastre*][4] and inhabitant of the jurisdiction of El Paso del Río de Norte and resident of said villa, and Vicente de Armijo, inhabitant of said villa. Vicente de Armijo says that he has a son who presently is ten years old named Salvador Manuel de la Cruz y Armijo.[5] In order that he, the father, will not lose the opportunity to comply with a father's obligation to give him learning, he endeavors to place him in an occupation. The boy, liking the occupation of tailor and finding that he is talented since he already knows how to read and write, he, the father, surrenders him to said Joseph Garzía for the time of four years. This is so that during these years the boy will serve him and advance in his work through the tailor's obligation to maintain, clothe, advise, correct, and punish him and teach him the said trade of tailor in such a manner that the boy remains skilled enough so that another teacher in any other place can give him the letter of attainment.

That being so, he, Garzía, will not ask the boy for anything else during his four-year apprenticeship, nor will he thereafter ask or demand a single thing for the boy's services. But if the agreement is not fulfilled within the apprenticeship and by the completion of the four years, teaching him what the said teacher knows about his occupation and which a good tradesman is required to know, then the father retains the right to request and demand in a formal judicial proceeding, or apart from one, whatever else seems fitting and just. And in the same way he, the said Joseph Garzía, is obliged not to remove said boy outside the jurisdiction of El Paso, but in case of some unforeseen happenstance or if he, the tailor, voluntarily leaves that jurisdiction for another place, he, notwithstanding, is obligated to give the boy training and complete the four years. And in case he does not, because of some other just reason, he is obligated to surrender the boy to a person whom he designates. The said Vicente de Armijo is pledging to pay the fee of 50 pesos according to the agreement that we have made.

Both Armijo and Garzía remain subject to the penalty for whoever departs from this document, including the additional costs and whatever else the justice, by mandate, might sentence them to thusly: Garzía is to pay for the time that the boy would have served, and in the same way, the said Vicente de Armijo remains under the same obligation so that if he [Armijo] or a person he designates should take the boy before the remaining four years is completed, then he, the father, is obligated to pay the fee for that which the boy would have learned in said time, if there is no proof of mistreatment amounting to not clothing or feeding him. All of which the said Joseph Garzía having heard, Garzía said that he is content with that, which by means of this agreement, he obligates himself in full and for all of it so that the time of four years having been completed, if it serves the will of God, our Lord, to give them life for that long, he will fully convey to said boy the trade of tailor to the satisfaction of whatever master tailor knows it. And for that he, Garzía, will not request or demand anything else unless the boy leaves or is removed from the tailor's house before completing the four years without a very just reason. In that instance, the tailor retains the right to ask for whatever completes the time remaining. Thus in this way, as in everything else contained in this document, they, Garzía and Armijo, remain obligated to the agreement between the two by virtue of which they obligated themselves to its completion.

The said parties renounce the invocation of those laws that favor them, and they submit themselves to the tribunal of royal justice that every part of the jurisdiction has, so that in this way the agreement will be fulfilled. For which object they obligate themselves with their persons and the goods they have or acquire. So they swore and signed this with me, the alcalde mayor, the said Joseph Garzía, and, at the request of said Vicente de Armijo, because of his not knowing how to write, one of the instrumental witnesses who was present signed for him, and they were Antonio Durán de Armijo,[6] Manuel Tenorio,[7] and Gregorio Garduño,[8] whom I swear I know, as well as knowing said parties.

At the request of Vicente de Armijo
Antonio Durán de Armijo (rubric)
Joseph Garzía (rubric)
Witness: Joseph Manuel Chirinos (rubric)

Done before me, Francisco José Bueno de Bohorques Corcuera,
Jues Receptor (rubric)
Assisting witness,
Diego Arias de Quiros (rubric)

ORIGINAL DOCUMENT

Año de 1726
Escriptura que otorgo Joseph Garzia Maestro de Sastre de Obligasion de darle enzeñado a Visente de Armijo un muchacho hijo sullo—

Sepan quantos esta carta de escriptura Vieran como en este villa de Santa Fe cavezera de este Reyno de la nueve Mexico en el dia veinte uno del prezente mes de Octubre de mill setecientos y veynte años paresieron ante mi el Capitan Don Francisco Bueno de Bohorques y Corcuera Alcalde Maior y Capitan Aguerra de dicha villa y los testigos de mi assistenzia actuando ante mi como juez Receptor a falta de ecrivano publico y Real que no lo ay en este Reyno es a saver Joseph Garzia Maestre de Sastre y vezino de la jurisdizion del passo del Rio del norte y residente en dicha villa, y Vizente de Armijo vezino de dicha villa el qual dijo que tiene un hijo que presente se allo de hedad de dies años llamado Salvador Manuel de la Cruz y Armijo el qual porque no se le pierda cumpliendo con la obligazion de padre en darle enzeñanza trato de ponerlo a ofizio y siendolo de gusto de dicho muchacho el de sastre y allando abilidad en el que lla save leer y escrivir se lo entriega a dicho Joseph Garzia por el tiempo de quatro años para que en ellos ze sirva y aproveche de su travajo con obligazion de que lo a de mantener y bestir sugetar correxir y castigar y enzeñarle dicho oficio de sastre de manera que quede abil para que otro maestro en qualquier parte le pueda dar carta de esamen y que Siendo asi no le pidira a dicho muchacho durante el plaso de los dichos quarto años ni tanpoco le demandara ni pedirá cossa alguna por su zervisio pero que no cumpliendo con lo tratado de darzelo enseñado dentro del plasso y cumplido de los quatro años a todo aquello que dicho maestro de sastre save en su ofizio y que require saver un buen ofisial; [que] queda el derecho a salvo para pedir y demandar en juyzio y fuera del lo que mas le combenga y fuere de justicia como asi mismo sea de obligo el dicho de Joseph Garcia a que no sacara a dicho muchacho de la jurisdizion del paso para a fuera en cazo de que por alguna asidente repentivo o boluntario salga de aquella jurisdicion para otra parte si no que este obligado a dejar lo enseñado y cumplir los quatro años y en caso de no por algun otro que zea justo este obligado a entregarlo a la persona que nombraze y el dicho Vicente de Armijo afianzando la multa de sinquenta pesos en que segun trato que tenemos echo quedan de pena para el que ze saliere fuera de esta escriptura con mas las costas y lo que por derecho mandado de la justizia fuere condenado a pagar por el tiempo que se ubiere zervido del muchacho como asi mismo queda en la misma obligacion el dicho Vicente de Armijo si por si o por la persona que nombrase fuere quitado el muchacho antes de tiempo cumplidos los quatro años queda obligado a la paga de la multa y de lo que se ubiere aprendido en dicho tiempo sino es que zea con probanza de mal trata suma desnudes o anbre todo lo qual oydo por el dicho Joseph Garzia dijo que es contento que por esta escriptura ze obligo a ello en todo y por todo y que cumplido el tiempo de los quatro años si Dios nuestro Señor es zervido de darselos de vida dara echo oficial de sastre a dicho muchacho a satisfazion de qualquier maestro que lo entienda y que por ello no pedirá ni demandara cossa alguna si no es que ze lo quiten o el se salga de su cassa antes de cumplir los quatro años sin motivos muy justos que entonzes le queda el derecho a salvo para pedir la enseñanza o que lo cumpla el tiempo que le faltare y que asi en esto como en todo demas que contiene esta escriptura queda obligado por zer trato entre los dos en cuya birtud se obligan a su cumplimiento y renunsian los dichos otorgantes las leyes que pueden ablar a su favor y ze someten al fuero de la justizia Real de qualquier parte de la jurisdizion que sea para que asi ze lo aga cumplir para lo qual se obligan con sus personas y vienes avidos y por aber y asi la otorgaron y firmo conmigo dicho Alcalde Maior el dicho Joseph Garzia y a su ruego del dicho Visente de Armiojo por nos saver; uno de los testigos ystrumentales que lo fueron; y prezentes se allaron Antonio Duran de Armijo, Manuel Thenorio y Gregorio Garduño a quienes doy fee conosco y a dichos otorgantes

      Arruego Vicente de Armijo
      Antonio de Armijo
      Joseph Garzia testigo
      Joseph Manuel Chirinos

Paso ante mi Francisco Jose Bueno De Bohorques Corcuera
Testigo de Assistenca
Jues Receptor = Diego Arias de Quiros

Transcribed and translated by Gerald Gonzales and Linda Tigges

Notes

1. Joseph Garzía was described as a master tailor in a 1739 Santa Fe deed. However, his will of the same year does not mention his occupation; the only reference to his trade was a pair of scissors (SANM I #329, #355, WPA translations).
2. Vicente (Durán de) Armijo was a son of José de Armijo and Catalina Durán, who came from Zacatecas with their family in 1695. In 1703 he was granted land by Vargas south of the river in Santa Fe. A person of this name worked on the restoration of San Miguel Chapel in 1710, though this may have been another Armijo. His will of 1743 suggests that he was a trader with his possessions including such items as wall tapestries made of skins, knives and awls, buffalo hides and other skins, three brass mortars, and piñon. The will stated that doña Francisca, the daughter or granddaughter of Alonso Rael de Aguilar, owed him for a pound of sweet chocolate (Chávez, *Origins*: 137-38; SANM #1136; SANM I #26, WPA translations).
3. Don Francisco Bueno de Bohorques y Corcuera is found listed in the presidio records for 1714 as a *cabo*, or corporal, asking for a license to leave to New Mexico to look for a cure for a kick in his leg by a horse (Christmas and Rau, "Una Lista": 197). He apparently returned by 1718, because he was listed as an alcalde of Santa Fe in two documents: SANM I #170 and SANM II #317a.
4. The occupation of tailor was a relatively common one. Among the settlers that came with the Velasco-Farfán group in 1695, eight were listed as tailors (Kessell and Hendricks, *RCR*: 293-95). García was a master tailor [*maestre de sastre*], implying that he was also teacher.
5. According to Chávez, Vicente had three sons, all named Salvador; the person named here is the third one. There are several persons of this name in the documents, though none are listed as being a tailor. It may be the boy did not return from El Paso, or did not finish his apprenticeship. Or he could be the Manuel Durán de Armijo who died in El Paso in 1747. Less likely is the Salvador Manuel de la Cruz Armijo who was married in Santa Fe in 1735 and died in1761 at the age of forty-five, too young to be the tailor's apprentice if the date is correct (Chávez, *Origins*: 137-38).
6. This was Vicente's brother, both sons of José de Armijo, from Sombrete (Chávez, *Origins*: 136; see Doc. 12).
7. Manuel [López] Tenorio [de Alba] was an adopted son of Miguel Tenorio de Alba of Santa Cruz. His parents were apparently Alfonso Salazar y López and Luisa Gómez de Arellano. Manuel married Francisca Vega y Coca in 1721 and was an alcalde of Pecos, 1725-1738. He was made a captain in 1732 (Chávez, *Origins*: 293; Kessell, *Kiva*: 505; Christmas and Rau, "Una Lista": 78).
8. Gregorio Garduño was the son of Bartolomé Garduño, a military sergeant, originally from Querétaro, who appears in Docs. 7 and 8. In 1720 Gregorio married Juana Sedillo, a daughter of Juan Sedillo Rico de Rojas and a granddaughter of Joaquín Sedillo, a prerevolt New Mexican. In 1743 he was a witness for Vicente's will (Chávez, *Origins*: 185, 285; SANM I #26, WPA translation).

20

CLASH AT CHURCH DOOR BETWEEN GOVERNOR BUSTAMANTE AND REVERENDO PADRE GUERRERO
June 14–23, 1727. Source: SANM II #343a.

Synopsis and editor's notes: In 1727 a change in ritual procedure by the governor and the reverendo padre disrupted the celebration of Corpus Christi. Shortly thereafter, perhaps anticipating an attack by the Franciscans, Governor Juan Domingo Bustamante set down an account of the affair. According to the governor, Reverendo Padre Fray Joseph Antonio Guerrero did not come out of the church to meet the governor, as was usual at this celebration, but instead sent two assistants. Governor Bustamante deemed this a sign of disrespect and retaliated the next day by not going with the soldiers who performed a procession around the plaza, firing their guns and going up to the door of the church. Instead, Bustamante went up to the church by himself. In response to this breach of procedure, two friars came out of the church to meet him, dressed in the vestments that they usually wore inside for the mass. Then the Reverendo Padre came to the door of the church and said that he was stopping the procession until the governor went with them in the procession in the regular way. Governor Bustamante said that he refused, and he and the friar spoke angrily. Then the Reverendo, carrying the Divine Host, went up to the altar along with Governor Bustamante and his men, a very unusual circumstance which was shocking to the congregation.

Juan Domingo de Bustamante, nephew and son-in-law of the previous governor, don Antonio Valverde de Cosio, was governor from 1722 to 1730. He previously had been lieutenant governor of the El Paso presidio. In many ways, Bustamante marks a new generation of leadership in that he was not one of the officers of Vargas, nor was he of that generation. In writing about Bustamante, both John Kessell and Jim Norris note the antagonism between the governor and the Franciscans. Kessell states that in 1731 Fray Pedro Antonio Esquer of the Pecos mission called Governor Bustamante "an irreverent ogre without a single redeeming grace." Norris suggests that the animosity came about because of Bustamante's support of the bishop of Durango rather than the missions of the Franciscans, and because of his lack of support for Franciscans in their efforts to regain missionary control of the Hopis from the Jesuits. Governor Bustamante, however, must not have been entirely antireligious; in 1725 he built, at his own expense, the church at the Mission of San Francisco de Nambe. The beam from the choir loft gave his name as responsible for construction of the church. When the church collapsed in the early 1900s, Santa Fe artist Gerald Cassidy collected the beam for his house in Santa Fe, where it can still be seen (Kessell, *Kiva*: 324; Chávez, *Origins*: 150; Norris, *Year Eighty*: 88-89; Kessell, *Missions*: 66-71).

On the surface, the disturbance appears to have been just a matter of precedence. However, as stated by Alejandro Cañeque in his book on New Spain in the seventeenth and eighteenth centuries, at this time public ritual was an acknowledgment of power. Any change in the ritual reflected a shift of power and political relationships, and was thus significant. Of interest is a similar but reversed situation that took place some forty years later in 1768, when Governor Mendiñueta complained to the viceroy about the refusal of the clergy to honor him on feast days (Cañeque, *Living Image*: 120-43; SANM I #634).

The day of Corpus Christi, the Feast of the Holy Eucharist, was celebrated on the first Sunday after Pentecost (which comes the seventh Sunday after Easter), Pentecost commemorating the descent of the Holy Spirit. The Corpus Christi festival was held in honor of the Real Presence of the body (*corpus*) of Jesus Christ appearing in the Eucharist, or the bread and wine of the Holy Communion. Originating as a festival in the mid-1200s, by the fifteenth century it became a principal feast of the church and, by the sixteenth century, was celebrated throughout the New World. The 1551 Council of Trent characterized the feast as a "triumph over heresy" that conveyed status to the religious and civic leaders who took part in or watched the procession. Persons who refused to participate were condemned. A special receptacle, the monstrance, containing the divine host—that is, the bread become manifest as the flesh of Christ—was carried as part of the procession. The monstrance was eventually returned to the church escorted by members of the city's ecclesiastical and municipal officials and accompanied by salvos fired by the military.

Mention of the Corpus Christi festival was also made in 1716, when Governor Felix Martínez ordered the pueblos to send a total of 220 men with their axes to cut wood to be placed along the procession route. They were to dig holes for the posts, probably for shelters or *ramadas* and provide the foliage to cover them. Each pueblo was to provide flowers for decoration. In addition, the pueblos were also to assign dancers to be in the procession ahead of the Blessed Sacrament or Divine Host. Historian and translator J. Richard Salazar recalls watching the Corpus Christi procession as a child, when a banner representing the body of Christ would be taken from the cathedral and paraded around the plaza accompanied by citizens marching on both sides and escorted by young girls, all dressed in white (*Merriam Webster Unabridged Dictionary of the English Language*, 1986; Katzew, *Contested Visions*: 139-41; Dean, *Inka Bodies*: 7-11; *Encyclopedia Britannica*, 15th edition, 3: 648; SANM II #251; J. Richard Salazar, personal communication, March 19, 2013).

General don Juan Domingo de Bustamante, governor and captain general of this kingdom and provinces of New Mexico, castellan of the forces and frontiers for his majesty, etc.[1] It has been customary at this villa of Santa Fe that on feast days the custodian of the church and other religious of the convent have met the governor and captain general at the door of the church with their holy water sprinkler [*isopo de aqua bendita*], and the priests who are in charge of the church have always been observed to personally go out with the Holy community, as has been done with those who have preceded me, as well as with myself. However, on the eleventh of the present month of June, upon having gone to vespers on the day of Corpus Christi, the Reverendo Padre Guardian and Vice Custodian Fray Joseph Antonio Guerrero,[2] who is the custodian of the church as well as vice-custodian of the friars, would not go out as is the custom, but it was done by two other religious, causing great scandal due to the obvious disrespect which he [the Reverendo Padre Guardian] showed to a royal authority in front of the people. What he caused does not need to be made public [outside of Santa Fe] due to the thinking of the inhabitants of this kingdom, particularly because the majority of them are Indians, who due to their ignorance will see it as a total lack of respect.

Second marqués of Casa Fuerte, Juan de Acuña, viceroy at the time of this document from 1722 to 1734. Image from *Los governantes de México,* by Manuel Rivera, Vol. 1 (México, 1872).

Because of this and because it was a prudent thing to do in order to avoid further disrespect, on the following day I decided to go to the low mass, leaving the company of soldiers, along with the officers of this presidial castle in the plaza de armas. [This was done] so that there they would receive the Blessed Sacrament and would perform their usual salvos, duties to the flag, and other military functions, which included firing their arms in reverence to the Divine Majesty, and from this said plaza they would march, accompanying the procession, up to the door of the church, where they would place themselves in formation and repeat the salvos.

However, before the procession left,[3] being that I had not joined it because of what had happened, there appeared before me, because of the order of the priest and vice-custodian [Guerrero], two religious individuals dressed wearing their albs[4] and vestments, crossing the public plaza coming to the palace to tell me to go with the procession to attend the veneration. What was I to think upon seeing the two priests all dressed in their sacred vestments [outside the church]? But in order to avoid further scandal, which was indeed caused by seeing them in such a manner, I proceeded to go to the church. Upon arriving with the procession at the door, the said vice-custodian stood, carrying the host of the Venerated Christ [*Cuerpo de Xpto Sacramentado*][5] in his hands telling me not to go beyond that point until I ordered the firing of arms and the hoisting of the flag to be performed at the usual place. I told him that the soldiers were at their proper place where they were obligated to be. But without regard to what I answered him, he would not continue the procession. At which time I continued to hold to my commitment and told him that it was not up to him to remand the order of where the arms had to be, that the soldiers were already in place with their orders which I had given them and that they knew their obligations. He then asked me if I did not recognize him as an ecclesiastical judge. I told him that I did, asking if he recognized me as governor and captain general of this kingdom. He did not answer me and turned around and returned to the altar, and I, my secretary, alcalde mayor, and the others who accompanied me went along with him, [he] carrying the divine host up to the altar, where we left him at his throne. All of this caused extreme bewilderment among the people, voices shouting, and crying of women, because of the scandal of having seen the host of the Venerated God disturbed.

Corpus Christi procession on San Francisco Street, Santa Fe, New Mexico, ca. 1880.
Photographer unknown.
Image courtesy of the Palace of the Governors, Photo Archives, Santa Fe, Neg. No. 074178.

Shortly after having returned to the palace, the two religious once again came to me to try to persuade me to send for the arms, which I did not do because I already had them at the said plaza as I have stated, leaving sufficient guards at the church to guard the Blessed Sacrament. With all my due respect, I told the priest to tell the vice-custodian that the scandal was already done, that I did not want to add any more to the matter, and, to avoid further disturbance, I would not go, nor did I go. At eleven o'clock the procession began, and the company performed their obligation in the prescribed manner with love and devotion to the Divine Majesty, as was seen.

Being that I am accountable according to regulations which I have to observe during functions, and as a requirement and verification of the truth, it is a necessity that the alcalde mayor of this villa add at the bottom of this report his certification and true testimony of what I have stated and as to what happened as he saw it, without giving his interpretation, along with the issues that the vice-custodian brought up before the said alcalde mayor and Salvador de Santistevan.[6] This he is to do as a sworn statement regarding what happened according to my right in order to avoid scandal and other problems which can create disturbances in this kingdom, which I must preserve. This order is to be given by my secretary of government and war to the alcalde mayor.

I thus decreed, ordered and signed it at this said villa on the 14th of June, 1728.

Don Juan Domingo de Bustamante

At this said villa on the said day, month, and year, I, the present secretary of government and war, in compliance with the order, made the above order known to Captain Diego Arias, alcalde mayor of the said villa. So that it is valid, I signed it and placed it as being carried out.

Antonio de Gruciaga[7]
Secretary of government and war

I, Captain Diego Arias de Quiros, alcalde mayor and war captain of this villa of Santa Fe, headquarters of this kingdom of New Mexico, certify that I faithfully give my testimony as to what I know and according to my right I am obligated to do regarding the above proceedings which are brought forth by the general don Juan Domingo de Bustamante, governor and captain general of this said kingdom. Everything that he has stated is the absolute truth being that I was present on the day of the vespers as well as being at high mass on the day of Corpus, and also being there at the time that the procession began, before the said governor went there, along with the time that the two religious came to the palace of his honor dressed in the manner in which they were, which caused bewilderment to everyone due to all of the excessive behavior. It was public knowledge and well known by everyone that the said governor acted with all prudence in his palace as well as at the church, where he was in complete reverence to the Divine Majesty of our Sacred God.

I also saw that about eleven o' clock the procession, of which I was a part, began, and the soldiers, lieutenant to the captain, alférez, and the rest of the officials received it with all due diligence and respect, discharging their arquebuses, raising the flag and lowering it to the ground three times, lined up in a file in formation in the best order that I have ever seen since I begin assisting in this kingdom and villa forty years ago. I swear before God, Our Lord, that I have never seen such a solemnity as this one with all its brilliance and elegance as the one of this day. The altar which was set up at this royal presidio was adorned with such beauty. The said governor having beautified it with hangings of brocades, numerous wax candles with various odors, and praise for the occasion of the day as presented by one of the military personal. The said company then marched behind the procession, and before they reached the church they went ahead and placed themselves at formation at the door so that the custodian carrying the host of the Venerated Christ could enter the church, and they then did their royal salvos as was done years before, as had been arranged for such a revered feast day. On the eighth day, at the cemetery,[8] the company assisted and in their military formation performed the accustomed salvos for the said saint. I also certify that it has been a custom that the governors, the prelate [*prelado*],[9] other religious and the said custodian all get together at the door of the church for the entire week. It is also true that disrespect was shown during the vespers,[10] which can be proven because the said vice-custodian told him in so many words that he had been shown disrespect and as such he also knew how to do the same.

All of the above I certify in accordance with the petition of the governor and captain general of this kingdom, and I signed it at this Villa of Santa Fe on the 27th acting as presiding judge with two assisting witnesses being that there is no public or royal scribe in this kingdom and on this paper since the sealed kind is not found here, to which I certify.

Diego Arias de Quiros

Witnesses
Francisco Casados
Manuel Tenorio de Alba

At this villa of Santa Fe, headquarters of this kingdom of New Mexico, on the 21st of June, 1727, I, the said alcalde mayor, in attending to that which the governor and captain general of this kingdom ordered regarding the sworn statement which is to be received from Salvador Santistevan, made him appear before me to receive the statement which he made to God, Our Lord, and to the sign of the Cross, swearing to tell the truth in whatever he was asked.

He, Santistevan, was asked what were the questions that the Reverend Father Fray Joseph Antonio Guerrero, guardian of this convent and vice-custodian, asked him following the high mass on the day of Corpus. He said that while the declarant was in the company of Captain Diego Arias, alcalde mayor of this villa, standing to the side of the main door of the church, the said Reverend Padre Vice-custodian stopped and asked where the arms [soldiers with weapons] were and if it was not a custom that they came to the door of the church on these days. The declarant responded saying that it was true that it was a custom for this to happen, but that the governor had determined that all the arms, except for the four soldiers which he had assigned to guard the Blessed Sacrament, would remain garrisoned at the plaza de armas to his satisfaction, and that it would be there where they would receive the Divine Majesty [the host] and where they would do the salvos, fire their arquebuses, humble themselves before the flag, and make a complete turn while following the host of the Venerated Christ, all being at formation, and for the second time fire their arquebuses. This was all to be done at the plaza de armas, and then they would follow the procession marching at the rear up to the door of the church. Once there the God of the heavens and earth would enter [the church], all of which would then be concluded. Before the beginning of the high mass, he [Salvador Santistevan] had been sent to assist to make sure that everything was done, and it was at this time that he [the priest] stated that the governor had been very disrespectful to him, not having gone out to receive him when he went to do the *visita*, and that he also knew how to be disrespectful. The declarant also stated that in the thirty years, more or less, that he has been in this kingdom, he truthfully has never seen the presidial company in such order, having seen the salvos which were perfectly done at the plaza de armas in reverence to the Blessed Sacrament. He said that everything which he has declared in his sworn statement is the truth, and being read back to him, he affirmed and ratified it. He said that he was more than forty-six years of age. He did not sign it because he did not know how; I, the said alcalde mayor, signed it along with my assisting witnesses, acting as I have stated.

Diego Arias de Quiros

Witness Francisco el Casados
Witness Manuel Tenorio de Alva

    This copy concurs with its original from where I copied it at the order of Governor don Juan Domingo de Bustamante, governor and captain general of this kingdom of New Mexico, and it is truly corrected and amended. Having seen me make the copy were the witnesses Francisco Joseph de Casados[11] and Manuel Tenorio de Alva, who assisted me, and with whom it was authorized, and I signed it at this villa of Santa Fe on the 23rd of June, 1727, acting as presiding judge due to the lack of a public or royal scribe, which there is none in this kingdom, and on this paper being that the sealed kind is not available.
    I place my usual signature in testimony to the truth.

Diego Arias de Quiros (rubric)

Witness Miguel Enríquez (rubric)
Witness Manuel Tenorio de Alba (rubric)

ORIGINAL DOCUMENT

El General Don Juan Domingo de Bustamante Governador y Capitan General deste Reino deste Reino y Provinsias dela Nueva Mexico Castellano de Sus Fuerzas y fronteras por Su Magestad, ut supra. Por quanto he sido costumbre en esta Villa de Santa Fee que en los dias de stado han resevido el guardian y demas religiosos deste conbento en comunidad al Governador y Capitan General en la puerta dela yglesia con el isopo del agua bendita y las beses que se han allado en dicho conbento los Reverendos Padres Custodios, lo han observado dignandose salir en persona con la Santa comunidad asi con todos mis antesesores como con migo y el dia onse del presente mes de Junio habiendo pasado a bisperas del dia del Corpus el Reberendo Padre Guardian y Visecustodio Fray Joseph Antonio Guerrero no se digno salir como se hacostumbra en comunidad y solo lo ysieron dos relijiosos causando con este expreso escandalo por el evidente desayre que de pensado me hiso desatendiendo ala hautoridad Real que represento y por aver sido en acto publico y la nota que causo quita dela publisidad y ser materiales muchos delos avitadores desde Reino y la mas parte de ellos Yndios quienes biendo esta desafreso consideran en su ygnoransia menos respecto que obstengo y baliendome de acto prudente y escusar otro desaire maior tube por mejor yr el dia siguiente a misa resada dejando prevenida la compania de soldados con todos los oficiales deste Castillo Presidial en la Plaza de Armas para que en ella resivieran al Santisimo Sacramento y le isieran la salvas acostumbradas abatiendo bandera en toda forma y politica militar con estruendo de piese suelos de fuego que disparar en culto, reverente ala Divina Magestad y desde dicha plasa en marcha aconpanaran la prosession asta la puerta de la yglesia en donde puestos en fila ysieron salva y antes de salir la prosession acausa de no haver ido yo por lo espresado pasaron de orden de dicho Padre Visecustodio dos religiosos revestidos con alvas y admaticas pasando la plaza publica asta este Palacio aque yo fuese ala prosesion y atendiendo ala benerasion que devia tener biendo dos saserdottes revestidos con vestidurias sacras y hoviendo no pasara retro maior escandolo pues no causo poco el ber los benir de dicha forma pase ala yglesia y saliendo con la prosesion en la puerta se paro dicho Visecustodio con el cuerpo de Xpto Sacramentado en las manos disiendo no pasava adelante de aquel puesto asta que yo mandara binieran alli las armas y abatieran la vandera al oria propuesta: respondi que las harmas estaban en su lugar en donde arian la hobligasion y sin enbargo de mi respuesta presistio a no proseguir la prosesion yiendo yo sin tenasidad y continuasia le dije que lo que proponia no era acto aquel lugar de su difinision ni su paternidad ni yo lo havianos de disolver que las armas estavan en su lugar aprontadas con hordenes que me tocavan dar y que cada uno savia su hobligasion: y a esto dijo que sino le conosia por Juez Eclesiastico; dijele que si, y anadi que si ami no me tenia o conozia por Governador y Capitan General deste Reino, a que no respondio y se bolvio para el altar y yo mi Secretario, Alcalde Mayor y demas acompanados pasamos con Su Divina Magestad asta dicho altar donde lo dejamos en su trono y a esta acsion causo el estremo de boses llanto de mujeres con escandolo de aver bisto rebolver a un Dios Sacramentado y aviendome buelto a este Palacio despues de un rato bolvieron los dichos dos relijiosos a persuadirme inbiara las armas lo qual no execute por tenerlas en dicha plasa como llevo dicho y deje en la iglesia las guardias suficientes al Señor Sacramentado y con todo respecto deje a dicho padre dijeran al Visecustodio que ya el escandolo estaba echo y no queria dar mas cuerpo a esta materia y que asi no pasava ni pase adelante por escusar disturbios y alas onse del dia salio la prosesion hiso esta compania su hobligasion en la forma prevenida con esmero y Reverensia a tan Divina Magestad como se vido y por que me toca dar cuenta en donde combenga para el areglamento que devo observar en estas funsiones es nesesario para su berificassion y berdad el que el Alcalde Mayor desta Villa al pie de estte requerimiento me de sertificasion y berdadero testimonio delo que llevo referido y paso pues se hallo presente como lo bido sin interpretasion alguna como tanbien las rasones que dicho Visecustodio dijo a dicho Alcalde Mayor y a Salbador de Santistevan hara las diga de bajo de juramento segun y como fueron por convenir asi a mi derecho y evitar escandalos y otros perjuicios que perturben este Reino que devo atender a su maior conservasion y este auto ara saber mi Secretario de Governazion y Guerra a dicho Alcalde Mayor asi lo decrete mande y firme en dicha Villa a catorse dias del mes de Junio de mill setesientos y beinte y ocho años = Don Juan Domingo de Bustamante.

En dicha Villa dia mes y año yo el presente Secretario de Governazion y Guerra en cumplimiento de lo mandado ise saver el auto de arriva al Capitan Diego Arias Alcalde Maior de dicha Villa y para que conste lo firme y puse por diligensia. Antonio de Gruciaga Secretario de Governazion y Guerra =

El Capitan Diego Arias de Quiros Alcalde Mayor y Capitan Aguerra desta Villa de Santa Fee capital de este Reyno dela Nueva Mexico zertifico doi fee y verdadero testimonio en quanto puedo y por derecho devo como todo lo que el auto antesedente mensiona el Señor General Don Juan Domingo de Bustamante Governador y Capitan General deste dicho Reino es sierto y verdad todo lo que expresa por constarme haverlo bisto por haver estado presente asi el dia de las bisperas como en misa maior el dia del Corpus y quando salio la presesion y antes de ir dicho Señor ni venir a los dos Religiosos al Palacio de Su Señoria revestidos en la forma y manera que sita causando admirasion a todos este exceso y supo de publico y notorio que dicho Señor Governador se porto con toda prudensia asi en su Palacio como en la yglesia donde estubo con toda Reverensia ala Divina Magestad de Dios Sacramentado y tanbien bido como a las onse del dia salio la prosesion que aconpane y la resivieron los soldados, Theniente de Capitan, Alferez y demas ofisiales con todo esmero y respecto asiendo salva disparando los arcabuses y tremoleando la Real bandera por tres beses rindiendo la por el suelo, puesta la fila en tan buena horden que en quarenta años que ha que asisto en este Reino y Villa juro por Dios Nuestro Señor no haver visto esta funsion con el lusimiento y culto que el dia sitado y el altar que se puso en este Real Presidio

adornado con toda asea poniendo dicho Señor todo esmero en colgaduras de brocatos lasos muchas luses de sera y olores, y una loa a el intento del dia que represento un militar y la sitada paso en marcha de tras de la prosesion y antes que llegara a la iglesia se adelanto y puestos en fila al entrar la Custodia con el cuerpo de Cristo Sacramentado ysieron salva Real verdad y como las antesedientes arreglado todo ablas ordenes que tubo siempre prevenidas para tan Reverente funsion y el dia de su otava que se iso en el simenterio de dicho Santo asisto en fila militar la dicho cocmpania asiendo la salva acostumbrada asi mesmo sertifico aver sido costumbre aver resevido alos Señores Governadores el Prelado y Religiosos y el mismo Custodio todos en comunidad en la puerta de la iglesia todos los dias de tabla y es sierto fue desaire manifiesto en las vísperas y se prueva por aver dicho me a mi dicho Visecustodio después de todo lo presedido estas palabras ami me an echo tambien desaires yo tambien los se aser todo lo qual por ser sierto y la verdad lo sertifico a pedimento del Señor Governador y Capitan General deste Reino y lo firme en esta Villa de Santa Fee en beinte y siete actuando como Juez receptor con dos testigos de assistensia por no haver Escribano Publico ni Real en este Reino y en este papel por no averlo ni correr el sellado, de que doi fee =
      Diego Arias de Quiros =

testigo testigo
Francisco Casados = Manuel Tenorio de Alba =

En la Villa de Santa Fee capital deste Reino de la Nueva Mexico en beinte y un dias del mes de Junio de mill setesientos y beinte y siete años yo dicho Alcalde Maior en atension alo que el Señor Governador y Capitan General deste Reino manda sobre que sele resiva juramento a Salvador Santistevan para lo qual lo ise pareser ante mi quien estando presente le resevi juramento que iso por Dios Nuestro Señor y la Señal de la Cruz so cargo del qual prometio deseñor berdad delo que le preguntara y siendolo que rasones fueron las que el dia del Corpus despues de misa maior le dijo el Reverendo Padre Fray Joseph Antonio Guerrero guardian deste conbento y Visecustodio segun y como fueron dijo que estando el declarante en compania del Capitan Diego Arias Alcalde Maior desta Villa parados a un lado dela puerta principal dela yglesia llego dicho Reverendo Padre Visecustodio donde estaban y les pregunto disiendoles Señores se a acostumbrado el que las armas bengan a la puerta de la yglesia estos dias? Respondio el declarante es berdad se a acostumbrado pero el Señor Governador tiene determinado el que las armas todas menos quatro soldados que estos los dedico a la guardia del Santisimo Sacramento y que los demas se quedaron guarnisiendo la Plasa de Armas para su maior justimento y que en ella resivieran a el enbocar en dicha Plaza su Divina Magestad sele isiera salva disparando los arcabuses y tremoleando la bandera y en horden se fuesen bolteando el rostro al Señr Sacramentado todos destocados y disparando por segunda ves y abatiendo la bandera y se iso por toda la Plaza de Armas y luego fue siguiendo la prosesion por de tras en marcha asta la puerta de la yglesia y en ella a el entrar el Señor del sielo y tierra se tremoleara y dieron carga serada y esto se executo por que desde antes dela misa maior me mando como ayudante se dispusiera y a esto dijo que los Alcaldes Maiores le avian echo muchos desaires no saliendole a resivir quando fue ala visita y que el tambien savia aser desaires y tambien dise el que declara que en treinte años mas o menos que a que entro a este Reino asegura con toda berdad no haver visto con tanta horden ylusimiento ala Compania Presidial aser las salvas que vido en la Plaza de Armas en culto reverante al Santisimo Sacramento y que todo lo que lleva dicho es la berdad so cargo del juramento que fecho tiene en que siendoselo leido en el se afirmo y ratifico, dijo ser de edad de mas de quarenta y seis años, no firmo por no saver, firmelo yo dicho Alcalde Mayor con los testigos de mi asistensia ynfrascriptos actuando como dicho es.

       Diego Arias de Quiros =

testigo testigo
Manuel Tenorio de Alva = Francisco de Casados =
Enmendado = hiso = vale

Este traslado concuerda con su original de donde lo saque de horden del Señor Governador Don Juan Domingo de Bustamante Governador y Capitan General deste Reino dela Nueva Mexico ba sierto y berdadero correjido y consertado y a saber sacar fueron testigos Francisco Joseph de Casados y Manuel Tenorio de Alva que lo fueron de mi asistensia con quienes lo autorise y firme en esta Villa de Santa Fee en beinte y tres dias del mes de Junio de mill setesientos y beinte y siete años actuando como Jues Receptor a falta de Escribano Publico o Real que no lo ai en este Reino y en este papel por no correr el sellado = Ago mi firma acostumbrada en testimonio de verdad.

       Diego Arias de Quiros (rubric)

testigo testigo
Miguel Enriquez (rubric) Manuel Thenorio de Alba (rubric)

Notes

1. The viceroy at this time was the Marqués de Casa Fuerte, 1722–1734.
2. Fray Joseph Antonio Guerrero was a *criollo*, that is, born of Spanish parents, in Mexico City, who also took his vows in 1692. In 1701 as custos [or head of the custody] for the New Mexico region, he ordered his brother Franciscans to keep away from civil lawsuits and not write letters to Mexico City complaining about the governor, but to bring their complaints to the custos and to say out of Santa Fe unless specifically ordered to be here. He served in New Mexico until 1743 (Norris, *Year Eighty*: 45-46, 67, 109). Guerrero also appears in Docs. 15 and 25.
3. The procession would have left the church to go around the plaza.
4. An alb was a full-length, long-sleeved tunic, usually gathered at the waist, and white (*Webster's Dictionary*, 1986).
5. This probably means that the vice-custodian was carrying the monstrance to show to the congregation.
6. See Doc. 9.
7. Antonio de Gruciaga was secretary of government and war at least by 1727 (SANM I #84). To date, nothing more is known about him.
8. See Doc. 24, where another presidio salvo is mentioned.
9. A *prelado* is a church official of superior rank (*Webster's Dictionary*, 1986).
10. *Vespers* is a religious service said before nightfall (*Webster's Dictionary*, 1986).
11. In Doc. 12, from 1715, Casados was named as one of two men who had been given the power of attorney from María de Quiros from the mines of Chihuahua. If, in fact, he made the journey, he had returned by 1728.

21

HORSE TRADE FOR YOUNG APACHE MALE COMPLICATED WHEN MARE SHOT WITH MUSKET BALL
August 3–September 8, 1731. Source: SANM II #363.

*ynopsis and editor's note*: This somewhat complicated document really includes two cases, with a third more minor case intertwined with the second. The paragraphs of the original have been rearranged to address each case separately.

The first case begins when Miguel Martínez de Sandoval sent a petition to the governor, stating that in 1728 he went outside the province to find some horses to bring back to New Mexico and sell. On his return with the horses, he met Joseph de Chávez, the under-age son of Nicolás de Chávez. Joseph told Miguel that he had an overworked male mule, or *macho*,[1] that he would sell to Miguel for two horses. Miguel agreed and, upon taking possession of the animals, fed it so that it regained its strength. When Miguel's son went on a military campaign, possibly that of 1728 to the Moquis ordered by General Bustamante,[2] the son took along the animal. During the campaign, Nicolás de Chávez took the macho away from him, saying that his son did not have the authority to sell the mule. In this document, Miguel petitioned for the mule's return. Antonio Pacheco and Pedro Marcial Rael, who supported Miguel, said that they had heard a resident of the Río Abajo, Juan Gallegos, tell Miguel that it was all right to buy the horses from Joseph, and that Joseph's father had given him permission to sell. Alcalde Gonzales Bas ordered the father, Nicolás de Chávez, to return the macho to Miguel.

In the second case, which also includes a third, Miguel stated that Juan de Chávez (not the son of Nicolás, who had a son of the same name) owed him a horse and a mare for killing his, Miguel's, mare. Juan de Chávez sidestepped the issue and stated that in 1727 he sold Miguel a young male Apache for fifteen mares and a colt that Miguel was to bring back from outside the kingdom. When Miguel returned, he asked Juan if he would accept some silk skirts instead, and Juan agreed to a deal of the silk skirts as well as two horses for the Apache. Juan de Chávez took the horses, and presumably the silk skirts, giving one horse to his son André. This seems to have satisfied Miguel. In what really is a third case, Chávez then admitted that he killed a mare of Miguel's because the mare got in with some of his horses and caused a problem. When the son of Miguel came to get the mare and found it dead, Chávez said he would compensate for the loss by giving Miguel a pair of cloth pants, some silk stockings that Miguel owed someone else, and five pesos that Miguel would have to collect from the soldier Francisco Herrera. Apparently Miguel was satisfied with this. There is no judgment by the alcalde on this case, probably because the parties agreed to compromise or because it has been lost.

The document shows how the lack of money and the use of barter complicated the trading system. In the third case, the complaint was resolved by a complicated payment for the dead mare, including some cloth pants, silk stockings, and five pesos that had to be collected from a third party that owed them to the person from whom the petitioner was collecting. Of additional interest is the value of the young Apache male: fifteen mares and a colt or silk skirts and two horses. Note that in another one of the transactions, the proposed value of a macho is twice that of the horse, about the same as that noted in other documents. The sale of the Apache is an example, similar to that discussed by Governor Mogollón in Document 6, of a straight-across financial transaction, since Juan de Chávez already owned the boy. There is no discussion of rescate, or ransoming. Finally, this document is one of several in which silk items are part of the trade, as in Documents 26 and 49.

[Marginal note]
Villa of Santa Fe
August 3, 1731
This part
presents the information
that he offers.

Demand of Miguel Martínez de Sandoval,[3] resident of the Villa of Santa Fe, against Joseph de Chávez[4] regarding the loan of two horses.
Villa of Santa Fe, August 3, 1731

This party presents the information which he offers

Governor and captain general (rubric)

[First case]

[I] Miguel Martínez de Sandoval, resident of the Villa of Santa Fe, appear before you and humbly present myself at the feet of your honor in the best form which I have according to my right and say that, in the year of twenty-eight [1728], I left this area and went outside the kingdom hoping to find a better way of life to sustain my obligations. On my said trip I tried to find some horses which I could bring back. Upon doing this, I encountered a resident of the Río Abajo by the name of Joseph de Chávez, son of Nicolás de Chávez,[5] whose animals had gone astray, who also had left [this area]. The said Joseph de Chávez approached me and told me that he had a macho, which he had overworked because he did not have any horses, and asked me if I would give him two horses for the said macho. I told him that I did not want to do it because he was under age; to which he [Joseph de Chávez] said that his father had given him the approval to do what was needed in case of an unexpected opportunity.

With this resolved, I made up my mind to give him the two horses for the said macho. Having had it for a while in this kingdom, and after having fed it corn [*mais*] so that the macho would regain its strength and be of value to me, it happened that General don Juan Domingo de Bustamante, who was governor of the kingdom at the time, ordered a campaign to be carried out, in which a son of mine was ordered to participate, and who took the macho with him. During this campaign the father, Nicolás, of the said Joseph de Chávez also participated and took the macho away from my son, saying his son was under age and as such he could not have made the deal. Since then, I have tried various times to get my two horses back, which he has not wanted to do, always seeming to be involved in other things. I therefore humbly ask and petition your honor that you correct this through justice, which is what I seek and hope to accomplish by having my horses returned to me, being that I am a poor individual hindered by my poor eyesight.

[Second case]

There is also another individual from the Río Abajo who owes me a horse and a mare, being that he killed my mare with a musket ball. This person is another Juan de Chávez,[6] but is not the son of the said Nicolás. All of this places me in need, which is the reason I beg and plead for the petition for which I humbly seek. I hope that your honor will feel sorry for me and assist me for these reasons, and order that everything be paid. If additional information is needed, I will promptly provide it, and I swear in my best form this document is not done in malice but according to what is necessary, etc.

    Miguel Martínez de Sandoval (rubric)

[First case]

At the villa of Santa Fe, on the 4th of August, 1731, before me, Captain Diego Arias de Quiros, alcalde mayor and war captain of this said villa, there appeared Miguel Martínez de Sandoval, resident of this said villa, and whom I swear that I know. In order to comply with that [petition] which was approved by the said governor and captain general on the 3rd of the present month, and according to the information which was provided as given by the said Miguel Martínez de Sandoval, the said alcalde, Antonio Pacheco,[7] was made to appear before me, from whom I received his sworn statement which he made to God, Our Lord, and to the sign of the Holy Cross, in which he promised to tell the truth as to what he knew and what he was asked.

He [Pacheco] was asked if he knew Joseph Chávez, the son of Nicolás Chávez, residents of the Río Abajo. He stated that he did know him. He was asked if he was present at the time of the exchange of the macho for the horses. He said that he had been, and that the circumstance was that the said Miguel Martínez de Sandoval did not want to give him the horses, but that at the same time another resident of the said Río Abajo named Juan Gallegos,[8] who had gone with him on the trip outside the kingdom, told the said Miguel Martínez de Sandoval that it would be fine for him to give the two horses for the macho, being that he [Juan Gallegos], knew that the father of Joseph de Chávez had given him the authority to do whatever was necessary for whatever was offered. This he says is the truth of his sworn statement, which he has made and which he affirmed and ratified. He said that he was thirty-five years of age, more or less. He did not sign because he did not know how. I, the said alcalde mayor, signed it with my assisting witnesses acting as presiding judge, to which I certify.

    Juan Manuel Chirinos (rubric)
    Diego Arias de Quiros (rubric)

Continuing, on the said day, month, and year, in order to proceed with the said information, I made appear before me, as alcalde mayor, the person of Pedro Marsial Rael,[9] from whom I received his sworn statement which he made to God, Our Lord, and to the sign of the Holy Cross regarding the charges, to which he promised to tell the truth in everything that he knew and what he was asked. He was asked if he was present at the time that Joseph de Chávez, son of Nicolás de Chávez, made his trade. He stated that he was present at the time that the trade was made, and that the said Miguel de Sandoval did not want to make the exchange with the said Joseph de Chávez because he was under age, but that Juan Gallegos told the said Miguel de Sandoval that it was fine to go ahead and make the trade with the said Joseph de Chávez being that in front of him [Gallegos], his father, Nicolás de Chávez, had told him that in case of finding something worthwhile, he had the full power to place everything on his account. This, he says, is what he knows regarding his sworn statement, which he has made and he affirmed and ratified it, saying that he was twenty-two years of age, more or less. He did not sign because he said he did not know how; I, said alcalde mayor signed it along with my assisting witnesses acting as presiding judge, to which I certify.

    Juan Manuel Chirinos (rubric)
    Joseph de Reano (rubric)
    Diego Arias de Quiros (rubric)

At this villa of San Felipe de Alburquerque on the 8th of September, 1731, by virtue of the proceedings expedited by the governor and captain general and by Captain Diego Arias de Quiros, alcalde mayor of the villa of Santa Fe, I ordered that Captain

Juan Gonzales, alcalde mayor and war captain of this said villa, to order that all of the above stated be continued, and upon having understood everything he [Nicolás de Chávez] was ordered to return the said macho above mentioned and after he had returned it continue with the order of the governor, which is to represent and argue his right, which he was satisfied with, on the said day, month, and year. So that it is valid he signed it with me and my two assisting witnesses, etc.

Before me as presiding judge

       Juan Gonzales Bas[10] (rubric)

       Juan Chávez (rubric)

assisting witness:
Joseph de Quintana (rubric)
Martín Hurtado (rubric)

[Second case]

[Marginal note]
Villa of Santa Fe
August 4, 1731
The alcalde of the Villa
of Alburquerque
is to continue the investigation regarding
that which is contained
in this petition.

  At this villa of San Felipe de Albuquerque on the 7th of August, 1731, I, Captain Juan Gonzales Bas, alcalde mayor and war captain of this villa and of its jurisdiction, made to appear before me Juan de Chávez [not the son of Nicholas de Chávez], against whom a demand is made for a horse and a mare.

  He says in his sworn statement, which I took from him before God, Our Lord, and the Holy Cross, that he does not owe him [Sandoval] any horses. That in the year of twenty-seven (1727), he, Juan de Chávez, sold to Miguel de Sandoval a young Apache male for the price of fifteen mares and a colt which he [Sandoval] was to have brought back to him from outside the kingdom. Upon his return, he called upon Chávez to give him what he had brought back, and upon seeing what he had brought, the said Sandoval asked him if he wanted to go for something other than the mares, which included some silk skirts [or petticoats] which he, Chávez, liked, and it was agreed that he would take them along with two horses in lieu of the fifteen mares, and they were satisfied. Of the two horses, one was given to Chávez immediately, and the other one was given to his son Andrés.

[Third case]

As for the mare[11] that he [Sandoval] makes the case that she had been killed by a musket ball by Chávez, he [Chávez] admits to having done it because the mare was wild and was always around two horses that he had, and the horses wanted to take the mare, and that was the reason for having killed it. After the mare was killed, the son of Miguel, Andrés de Sandoval,[12] came to collect her, and it was with him that he [Chávez] dealt and adjusted things for his satisfaction for killing the said mare, giving Andrés a pair of cloth pants, some silk stockings that Miguel de Sandoval owed to the witness, along with five pesos that Sandoval was to receive from the soldier Francisco de Herrera,[13] who owed them to Chávez. All of this was given to the said Andrés de Sandoval in payment for the mare, and he left satisfied, the grayish, untamed mare not being worth that much. If he, Miguel de Sandoval, is not satisfied with what he, Chávez, has given to him, then he should return everything that he [Chávez] had given to the said Andrés de Sandoval, and he will pay him with a mare that would be [similar to the one killed], untamed and wild. This is what Juan de Chávez said, and which he affirmed and ratified regarding his sworn statement which he has made, and he signed it along with me and my assisting witnesses, acting as presiding judge due to the lack of a public scribe on the said day, month, and year, etc.

       Juan Gonzales Bas (rubric)
       Juan Chávez (rubric)

assisting witness:
Joseph de Quintana (rubric)
Martín Hurtado (rubric)

[Editor's note: This was apparently the end of the case. No final statement was made by the governor, or else the final statement is lost.]

ORIGINAL DOCUMENT

Villa de Santa Fee y
agosto 3 de 1731
esta parte
presente la informasion
que ofreses

Miguel Martinez de Sandoval vezino de la Villa de Santa Fee paresco postrado a los pies de Vuestra Senoria en la mas bastante forma que aya lugar en derecho y al mio conbenga y digo que el ano de veinte y ocho sali a la tierra fuera con mi bista a buscar mi bida para mantener mis obligaciones y en dicho mi biaje busque unos cavallos para

traer y en este entonses se vido desabiado de bestias un hijo de un vezino del Rio Abajo que abia salido tambien y me llego a ber este dicho que el qual se llama Joseph de Chavez hijo de Nicolas de Chavez y me intimo el dicho Joseph de Chavez la nezesidad que le asistia de bestias que tenia un macho y lo via fatigado por no tener mas bestias que si yo le queria azer el bien de darle dos cavallos por el dicho macho alo qual le respondi que no queria por conoserlo por hijo de familia a esto no falto quien me dixera que su padre le avia dado facultad en caso de que se viera desaviado y con esta resolusion me determine a darle los dos cavallos por el dicho macho y teniendolo ya por mi en este Reyno y abiendolo mantenido con mais para que bolviera y pudiera zervirme se ofrezio una campana que executo el General Dn. Juan Domingo de Bustamante estando Governador de este dicho Reyno fuese apersevido para dicha campana un hijo mio quien llevo dicho macho y en este entonces fue tambien su padre de dicho Joseph de Chavez quien le quito al dicho mi hijo el macho disiendo que su hijo hera hijo de familia y que no podia dar cosa por parte ninguna a lo qual he solisitado por algunas bezes me envie mis dos cavallos y nunca a querido size a propasado en algunas cosas y atendiendo yo alo muy piadoso de Vuestra Señoria justificara en justizia que es la que pido y espero alcansar en virtud de que se me buelban mis caballos que soy un pobre impedido de la vista; como tambien otro vezino de dicho Rio Abajo me esta debiendo un cavallo y una llegua que la qual llegua me la mato de un pelotaso que el qual es otro Juan de Chavez que no es el hijo de dicho Nicolas todo esto me haze mucha falta por todo lo qual pido y suplico rendidamente. A Vuestra Señoria se duela de mi y que me asiste bastante razon y mande se me pague todo lo dicho y prometo informazion estoy pronto a darla y juro en devida forma no ser de malisia este mi escripto y en lo nezesario, ut supra.
      Miguel Martinez de Sandoval (rubric)

En la Villa de Santa Fee en quatro dias del mes de Agosto de mill setezientos y treinta y un años paresio ante mi el Capitan Diego Arias de Quiros, Alcalde Mayor y Capitan Aguerra de dicha Villa parecio Miguel Martinez de Sandoval vezino de dicha Villa aquien doy fee, conosco y para cumplir con lo probeido por el Senor Governador y Capitan General de tres del corriente de dicho mes para la informasion que ofrese dicho Miguel Martinez de Sandoval para dicho efecto yse pareser ante mi dicho Alcalde Antonio Pacheco aquien le resivi juramento que yso por Dios Nuestro Senor y la Señal de la Santa Cruz desir berdad de lo que supiere y le fuere preguntado. Preguntado que si conose a Joseph de Chavez hijo de Nicolas de Chavez vesinos de el Rio Abajo? Dijo que si los conose. Preguntado que si se hallo presente este testigo ala feria del macho por los dos cavallos? Dijo que si y con sircustansia que dicho Miguel Martin de Sandoval no se los queria dar y en la occasion se allo presente otro vezino de dicho Rio Abajo llamado Juan Gallegos que salieron justos para tierra fuera le dijo a dicho Miguel Martin de Sandoval que bien podia darle los dos cavallos por el macho por que le costava a dicho Juan Gallegos el que su padre de dicho Joseph de Chavez le avia

dado facultad para todo lo que sele ofreziese y que esta es la berdad por el juramento que fecho tiene en que se afirmo y ratifico y dijo zer de hedad de treinta y sinco años poco mas o menos, no firmo por no saber firmelo yo dicho Alcalde Mayor con los testigos de mi asistenzia actuando como Juez receptor doy fee.
    Juan Manuel Chirinos (rubric)
    Diego Arias de Quiros (rubric)

Yncontinente en dicho mes y ano para proseguir con dicha ynformazion yse pareser ante mi dicho Alcalde Mayor a Pedro Marsial Rael al qual le resivi juramento que yso por Dios Nuestro Senor y la Señal de la Santa Cruz so cargo del cual prometio de desir berdad en todo lo que supiere y le fuere preguntado. Preguntado que si se hallo presente al trato que hiso Joseph de Chabez hijo de Nicolas de Chavez? Dijo que si se abia allado en dicho trato y canbalache y que dicho Miguel de Sandoval no queria azer canbalache con dicho Joseph de Chabes por ser hijo de familia a que le dijo Juan Gallegos a dicho Miguel de Sandoval que bien podia azer el canbalache con dicho Joseph de Chabes por que delante de el le avia dicho su padre Nicolas de Chabes que si se ayaba desabiado o en algun otro aprieto que le dava facultad para que usara de todo lo que llevava a su cargo. Que esto es lo que save por el juramento que fecho tiene en que se afirmo y ratifico y que es de hedad de veinte y dos años poco mas o menos; no firmo por que dijo no saber, firmelo yo dicho Alcalde Maior con los testigos ynfrascriptos de mi asistenzia actuando como Juez Rezeptor, doi fee.
    Juan Manuel Chirinos (rubric)
    Joseph de Riano (rubric)
    Diego Arias de Quiros (rubric)

Villa de Santa Fee y Agosto 4 de 1731.
El Alcalde [de] la Villa de Alburquerque haga averiguazion sobre lo contenido en esta petizion.

En esta Villa de San Felipe de Alburquerque en siete dias del mes de Agosto de mill setecientos y treinta y un años yo el Capitan Joan Gonzales Baz Alcalde Mayor y Capitan Aguerra desta dicha Villa y su jurisdizion yse pareser ante mi a Juan de Chavez contra quien demanda essa parte un cavallo y una llegua y dise que de bajo de juramento que le resivi por Dios Nuestro Senor y la Santa Cruz que no dio tal caballo que el ano de veinte y siete le bendio Juan de Chavez a Miguel de Sandoval un Apachuelo por presio de quinse lleguas y un potro que le avia de aver traido de tierra afuera y aviendo benido el dicho Miguel de afuera lo llamo a entriego y estandose ojastando le dijo dicho Miguel que si queria en lugar de las lleguas cuia pollera del Apache a que aviendo la bisto se conpusieron en darle la pollera y dos cavallos por las quinse lleguas y quedaron ojastados y delos dos cavallos el uno le entrego luego y el otro selo libro en su hijo Andres a quien se resivio y dise el declarante quien lo llevo toca ala llegua que le ase el cargo que mato de un pelotaso que es verdad que lo mato reportarle mal sino por que era una llegua mestena a mui sinvatora la cual se avia juntado en dos cavallos que el tenia los cuales respondia cojer por lo mucho que la llegua traia y que en tonses la mato y despues de muerta la llegua bino su ijo del dicho Miguel de Sandoval a cobrarla como ser ijo que es Andres de Sandoval en quien tubo trato y ajuste de para a satisfaccion de la dicha llegua dio un corte de calsones de pano en todo recaudo unas medias de seda que esto se lo devia al declarante Miguel de Sandoval y demas desto sinco pesos que le dio en poder del soldado Francisco de Errera quien lo resibio luego y los aporciono el dicho Andres de Sandoval y se quedo satisfecho la llegua no baliendo tanto y sierto no haver bastante que seme buelbale dicho y dare la llegua conforme era la talla regiega y mui simarona y esto respondio en que se afirmo y ratifico so cargo de juramento que fecho tiene y lo firmo con migo y los testigos de mi assistenzia autuando como Jues Rezeptor a falta de escribano publico en dicho dia mes y aóo ut supra.

      Juan Chabes (rubric)
      Juan Gonzales Bas (rubric)

Testigo de asistenzia
Joseph de Quintana (rubric)
Martin Hurtado (rubric)

En esta Villa de San Phelipe de Alburquerque en ocho dias del mes de Septiembre de mill setecientos treinta y un años en virtud del auto de ariba espedido del Senor Governador y Capitan General y del Capitan Diego Arias de Quiros Alcalde Mayor dela Villa de Santa Fee mande compareser ante mi el Capitan Juan Gonzales Alcalde Mayor y Capitan Aguerra desta dicha Villa aquien le mande continar todo lo ariva expreso y aviendolo entendido se conforma entregar el dicho macho ariba mencionado y que despues de entregado procure el recurso del Señor Governador a representar y alegar de su derecho y en esto se conformo en dicho dia, mes y año y para que asi conste lo firmo con migo y dos testigos de mi asistenzia ut supra.

      Ante mi como Jues Reseptor
      Nicolas de Chaves (rubric)
      Juan Gonzales Bas (rubric)

Testigo de asistenzia:
Joseph de Quintana (rubric)
Juan de Dios de Bergara (rubric)

[Back page]

Año de 1731
Demanda de Miguel Martines de Sandoval vesino de la Villa de Santa Fee contra Joseph de Chavez sobre el prestame de dos caballos.

Notes

1. A *macho* is a male mule. A *mula* is a female.
2. SANM II #352.
3. Miguel de [Dios] Martínez de Sandoval (aka Sandoval Martínez) came to New Mexico with his parents with the Farfán-Velasco expedition in 1694. His father, Juan de Dios Sandoval de Martínez, lived for some time in Santa Cruz. Miguel's wife was Lucía Gómez Robledo. Miguel was a soldier with the Santa Fe presidio by 1697 and a presidio captain by 1714, though on April 16, 1714, he presented a petition for his resignation to the governor, due to his many ailments (Chávez, *Origins*: 282; Kessell and Hendricks, *RCR*: 319 n33; *TDC*: 129; Christmas and Rau, "Una Lista": 200).
4. As stated in the document, Joseph de Chávez was the son of Nicolás de Chávez and the grandson of don Fernando Durán y Chávez, a prerevolt settler. A land-conveyance document of 1734 notes Joseph as being a settler of the Río Puerco, Atrisco area (Chávez, *Origins*: 160-63; SANM I #178).
5. Nicolás de Chávez was a son of don Fernando Durán y Chávez, who owned land in the Atrisco area; at least part of the land was purchased from Diego Vásquez Borrego (Chávez, *Origins*: 163; NMGS, *Aquí*: 151).
6. Nicolás did have a son named Juan, but apparently not this one. This Juan de Chávez could have been the son of Bernardo or of Antonio Durán y Chávez, both sons of don Fernando (Chávez, *Origins*: 161-62).
7. It is unclear of what jurisdiction Antonio Pacheco was the alcalde, though it was not Santa Fe. An undated will for Antonio states that he was a blacksmith and gives a description of his equipment. In 1734 an Antonio Pacheco, husband of Felipa Romero, was buried at the Military Chapel of La Castrense. The alcalde mayor of Santa Fe who signed the document was Antonio Ulibarrí, who was in the position from 1734 to 1737 and 1742 to 1749, which dates the will to that period (SANM I #1222, WPA translation; Gallegos and Esquibel, "Alcaldes": 216-17; Christmas et al., *New Mexico Burials*: 14).
8. This may be Juan Antonio Gallegos, the son of Antonio Gallegos II, who was living in Bernalillo in 1699 and later died when serving as a sergeant in Bernalillo in 1715. Antonio Gallegos I was in New Mexico prior to 1680. A 1761 will for Juan Gallegos states that he was a squadron corporal and gives an extensive list of goods, including a variety of clothing and one cow "in the woods of the villa with its calf" (Chávez, *Origins*: 179; SANM I, #358, WPA translation).
9. Pedro Marcial Rael was a son of Alonso Rael de Aguilar. He was killed by Comanches in 1771 (NMGS, *Aquí*: 152, 170).
10. Juan Gonzales Bas II, was the son of Juan Gonzales Bas I and Nicolasa Zaldivar Jorge. Juan returned to New Mexico with the family, settling in Bernalillo and Albuquerque. He was a captain by 1710, alcalde mayor of Albuquerque in 1712, and served in many administrative positions, including lieutenant governor. His wife was María López del Castillo; he also had a son named Juan (Barrett, *Conquest*: 176; Chávez, *Origins*: 189; Kessell et al., *BOB*: 1173 n109).
11. Apparently the mare was not one of the two horses traded above, but another horse that got mixed in with the horses of Chávez.
12. A 1758 document states that Andrés de Sandoval was one of many heirs of his mother, Lucía Gómez Robledo. He is listed in a November 18, 1790, presidio muster as having six horses and a macho (SANM I #861; Christmas, *Military Records*: 216).
13. Francisco Herrera is listed in a June 18, 1723, muster as a soldier with all his weapons and seven horses, and without a lance. A note in the 1741 presidio power-of-attorney document stated that Juan Herrera was "leaving with pleasure his father Francisco Herrera," though it is not known what this meant (Christmas, *Military Records*: 50, 54).

22

SANCTUARY CLAIMED BY SOLDIER AFTER THREATENING SERGEANT; ACCUSED DISCHARGED FROM PRESIDIO

September 28, 1731–January 16, 1732. Source: SANM II #363c.

Synopsis and editor's notes: In 1731, when on duty with a presidio squadron in the Sandía Mountains, Ysidro Sánchez found himself in trouble when he reached for his arquebus in an angry response to an accusation by his corporal, Lorenzo Trujillo. When the sergeant pulled out his sword and other soldiers in the squadron tried to grab Sánchez, Sánchez fled with several soldiers, including Corporal Trujillo, in pursuit. He stopped when the soldiers caught up with him, but then fled again when the corporal hit him several times. Sánchez took sanctuary in the Isleta church until the corporal talked him into leaving. After a thorough investigation, including hearing testimony from all of the soldiers, Governor Cruzat y Góngora ordered Sánchez to leave the army, with any other punishment considered already executed.

The squadron was probably in the Sandía Mountains to carry out the reprisals against the Faraón Apaches, discussed in a June 15–18, 1731, council of war called by Governor Cruzat y Góngora (SANM II #378). The Faraón Apaches had been making raids on the area since at least the second decade of the century. According to Oakah Jones, the raids of the Faraón Apaches had occurred with increasing frequency in the 1730s, when the Spanish began selling the Apaches that they captured to the "friendly tribes of the kingdom," probably the Pueblos. One result of this was that later, in 1732, Cruzat y Góngora ordered this practice stopped, with fines levied against any Spanish settlers selling an Apache to the Puebloans, and with whipping for the Indians purchasing the Apaches (Jones, *Pueblo Warriors*: 111).

Isidro Sánchez [Bañales] appears several times in the documents of the Spanish Archives. In 1720, when he was twenty years old, he was charged with stealing goods from the palace of the governors. By 1723 Sánchez was listed as a soldier with the presidio. A native of Zacatecas, he married Teresa Varela Jaramillo in Albuquerque in 1725. Sánchez was apparently educated or at least literate, acting as a witness in several court cases. In 1740 he was a legal counsel for a controversial case in Albuquerque involving the ownership of some sheep. The alcalde of Albuquerque, Joseph Baca, was so annoyed by his behavior that he wrote what amounted to a restraining order. Baca stated that Isidro was creating disturbances and fomenting litigation and ordering him to stop acting as the local lawyer, though he later used Isidro as a witness. Attorney and historian Malcolm Ebright has another point of view, seeing him as a people's lawyer. In 1744 Isidro was a citizen of Fuenclara/Tomé (SANM II #307, #459a, #463; Christmas, *Military Records*: 50; Cutter, *Legal Culture*: 101; Ebright, "Advocates": 318).

One reason that the case is of interest is the detailed procedures that Governor Cruzat y Góngora required, involving testimony from all of the soldiers. As with a contemporary police investigation, there is much repetition, but with each testimony, new detail is added. The procedures are listed below.

1. The governor makes a statement of alleged offense.
2. He sends the case to the lieutenant general of the presidio, Antonio Velarde.
3. Velarde has Sergeant Trujillo, the accused, Isidro Sánchez, and two others testify.
4. Velarde has all the persons sign a ratification of their testimony.
5. Velarde sends the written testimony and ratifications to the governor.
6. The governor asks for more testimony, which is taken this time by Diego Arias de Quiros, the new lieutenant general.
7. Five more soldiers give testimony, probably the rest of the squadron.
8. All of these soldiers sign a ratification of their testimony.
9. Velarde sends the information back to the governor.
10. The governor hands down the sentence.

Year of 1731
Criminal case against Isidro Sánchez, soldier of this royal presidio, accused of pulling [*echado mano*] his arquebus on his corporal, Lorenzo Trujillo[1]

In the villa of Santa Fe, on the 28th of September, 1731, I, Colonel don Gervasio Cruzat y Cruzat y Góngora, governor and captain general of this kingdom of New Mexico for his majesty, etc. say that Isidro Sánchez, a soldier of the cavalry company of the royal presidio of this said Villa of Santa Fe, is a prisoner within the guardhouse of the royal palace, accused of the crime of pulling his arquebus on his corporal, Lorenzo Trujillo, on an occasion when the said corporal was in charge of a squadron that was on duty to reconnoiter the mountains of Sandía.[2] Due to the fact that I find myself involved in matters relating to duties of his majesty, and not available for duties involving the royal justice, and so that this case is not forgotten, I commit this case to my lieutenant general don Antonio Pérez Velarde,[3] so that he can act on it. Upon it being ready for a sentence to be handed down, he shall return it to this superior government. I thus approved this, ordered, and signed it with the assisting witnesses below signed due to the lack of a public or royal scribe, of which there are none in this kingdom.

don Gervasio Cruzat y Cruzat y Góngora (rubric)
Gaspar Bitton (rubric)
Juan Antonio de Unanue (rubric)

Decree

In the villa of Santa Fe on the 20th of October, 1731, I, don Antonio Pérez Velarde, lieutenant general of this kingdom, say that I have been given the commitment to continue this case by the governor and captain general so that I can continue it against Isidro Sánchez, soldier of this presidial castle and prisoner in the royal guardhouse, for the crime which is expressed by the order which is provided by the governor. So that I know how to argue for the truth and in order to proceed against the said Isidro Sánchez, I need to order and did order the declaration of the said Lorenzo Trujillo be received, so that he can state and declare the motives and reasons which the said Isidro Sánchez had for pulling out his arquebus, the place where they were, and all the other circumstances which caused him to commit such a terrible crime. Upon receiving his said declaration, I will proceed with the rest of the proceedings as required. I thus approved, ordered, and signed it with my assisting witnesses, acting as presiding judge due to the lack of a public or royal scribe.

Antonio Pérez Velarde (rubric)
Felipe Tafoya (rubric)
Alfonso de Aguilar (rubric)

Statement of Corporal Lorenzo Trujillo

In the villa of Santa Fe on the 24th of October, 1731, I, the said lieutenant general, by virtue of the prior proceedings approved by me, caused to appear before me the corporal Lorenzo Trujillo, who upon being present, gave his sworn statement which he made to God, Our Lord, and to the sign of the Cross, under which he promised to tell the truth about everything that he knew and about which he was asked. He said that, upon having left on a campaign which was ordered by the said governor, and being at the Ojo de Juan Luján[4] when they were getting ready to leave, Isidro Sánchez said that they could steal his food, but that they should not steal his ammunition. To this, the said declarant said that no one would steal it, that all of the soldiers from this villa had ammunition to spare. Then, the said Isidro, upon his horse, came to him where he was afoot and told me that he spoke the truth, but even if they had it [the ammunition], they would steal other things. Then this declarant answered that no one had taken it and then attempted to mount his horse, but while he [Trujillo] was attempting to mount his horse, he, [Sánchez, tried to] pull out his arquebus, at which time he [Trujillo] pulled out his sword [*espada*] and swung at him. Simultaneously, Sánchez continued trying to pull out his arquebus, but he could not do it because it was wrapped up in a cloth and tied up with a leather strap. Upon seeing that he could not pull out the arquebus, he attempted to throw it at Trujillo, but the declarant snatched it from his hands, and then he called the other soldiers for them to grab Sánchez, but they could not do it because they were afoot, and he [Sánchez] fled, going in the direction of Abo.[5]

He [Trujillo] followed him, taking along with him Baltazar de Abeytia[6] and Joachín de Anaya,[7] and catching up to him, this declarant asked him if he knew what he had committed. He answered that he well knew what he had done. Then this declarant tried to hit him with the sword three blows in order to castigate him and to end the matter, but he, Sánchez, fled on his horse and went to Isleta,[8] at which time the declarant went back to take care of his troops. This, he says, is what happened and is what he knows concerning his sworn statement which he has made which he has affirmed and ratified upon his statement being read back to him. He said that his age was thirty-eight. He did not sign it because he did not know how; I, said lieutenant general, signed it with my assisting witnesses.

Antonio Pérez Velarde (rubric)

Felipe Tafoya (rubric)

Alfonso de Aguilar (rubric)

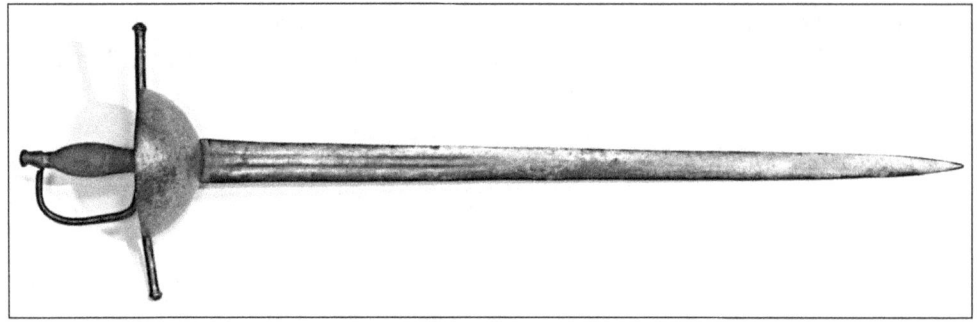

Late seventeenth-century, early eighteenth-century cup-hilt broadsword (*espada ancha*), length 32 inches, blade 26 inches. Photo by Blair Clark. Palace of the Governors Artifact No. 9985/45. Image courtesy of the Palace of the Governors, Photo Archives, Santa Fe.

Statement which he took from Isidro Sánchez, offender

In this villa of Santa Fe on the 25th of October, 1731, I, the said lieutenant general, say that upon hearing the statement given by the corporal Lorenzo Trujillo, from which is learned that the said Isidro Sánchez pulled his arquebus, along with everything else that is stated. In order to proceed against the said Isidro Sánchez, offender in this case, [I] decided to order and did order that his confession be made and upon that being done, to continue with the proceedings which are to follow. I thus approve order and sign it with my assisting witnesses acting as presiding judge due to the lack of a public or royal scribe.

Antonio Pérez Velarde (rubric)

Felipe Tafoya (rubric)

Alfonso de Aguilar (rubric)

Confession of Isidro Sánchez, offender in this case

In this villa of Santa Fe on the said day, month, and year, I, the said lieutenant general by virtue of the said proceedings approved by me, made Isidro Sánchez to appear for this case. Upon being received, he gave his sworn statement, which he made according to his right, under which charge he promised to tell the truth as to everything that he knew and what he was asked, as far as what his name was, how old he was, what his occupation was, where he was from, and his marital status. He said that his name is Isidro Sánchez, that he is thirty-one years of age, that his occupation was to serve the king, our majesty, in this royal presidio, and that he is a native of the Ciudad de Zacatecas, and that his marital status is that he is married; this is what he answered.

He was asked if he knew the reason why he was a prisoner. He said that until now he has not committed any crime for him to be in prison. He was asked to state and declare the truth regarding the reason for these proceedings, what reasons he had for doing what he did against the corporal Lorenzo Trujillo while they were on a campaign and were at the Paraje del Ojo de Juan Luján, and what he, Trujillo, said concerning the stealing of his munitions, and the other reasons why he pulled his arquebus and tried to use it, but he could not do it because it was wrapped in a cloth and tied with a leather strap.

Sánchez said that it was all false, that he did not pull his arquebus. What did happen was that he said that someone had stolen his gunpowder, and the corporal answered him saying that he never had it, that he was a liar, which he repeated numerous times. Sánchez said that Trujillo then mounted his horse and came at him, trying to hit him with his sword; and he, being afraid, fled from there and was quickly followed for about three leagues. Upon seeing that the corporal had stopped, he also stopped, and shortly was joined by Baltazar de Abeytia, who told him to return. He answered him that he would remain there, as he was fleeing from the corporal, and he told him [Abeytia] to tell him [the corporal] that everything should come to an end. Baltazar then left him and went back to report to the corporal, who then came to where Sánchez was and told him to give himself up as a prisoner. Sánchez said that he obeyed him and turned over the reins to him, and he, the corporal, took him with his arms crossed to where Abeytia was and turned the reins over to him so that he could take him. Then, after obeying everything he was asked to do, he, Trujillo, hit him numerous times and mistreated him badly to the point where he was sore for numerous days.

Upon being treated so cruelly, after having given himself up under false pretenses, Sánchez said that he once again fled and went to take refuge within the sacredness of the Holy Church,[9] recognizing the fact that he would always be discriminated against for having committed a grave crime, for which he would be treated without justice, [the corporal] being full of lies, he [Sánchez] having been told that everything was fine. As such he realized that he would be safe within the sacredness of the church and that he would not be lacking in anything, though it was told to him that he would have to fulfill his obligation by caring for the horse herd which belonged to the royal presidio, where he would be taken and placed into custody as a prisoner. This he says is the truth as to what happened and was stated by him in his sworn confession which he affirmed and ratified upon it being read back to him. He signed it along with me, acting as presiding judge, and my assisting witnesses due to the lack of a public or royal scribe, etc.

Antonio Pérez Velarde (rubric)

Isidro Sánchez Bañales (rubric)

Felipe Tafoya (rubric)

Alfonso de Aguilar (rubric)

Decree

In the villa of Santa Fe on the 26th of October, 1731, I, said lieutenant general, say that I have seen the confession that Isidro Sánchez, the offender and prisoner in this case, has made, including the denial of what transpired involving the pulling of his arquebus, and have taken the statement of what had occurred from the corporal Lorenzo Trujillo. In order to learn more and to determine the truth, I decided to order and did order that statements be taken from Joachín de Anaya and Baltazar de Abeytia, soldiers in this presidial castle, who were both cited in the statement by the said corporal. In this way, they can say and state if the said Isidro Sánchez pulled his arquebus and attempted to shoot Trujillo, and I can see if Trujillo's said statement is valid and correct as made against the said offender. So that it is valid I approved, ordered, and signed it with my assisting witnesses, acting as presiding judge and due to the lack of a pubic or royal scribe, etc.

Antonio Pérez Velarde (rubric)

Felipe Tafoya (rubric)

Alfonso de Aguilar (rubric)

Statement of Joachín de Anaya

In the villa of Santa Fe on the said day, month, and year, I, the said lieutenant general, by virtue of the aforesaid proceedings approved by me, made appear before me Joachín de Anaya, soldier in this presidio, who upon being before me, made his sworn statement before God, Our Lord, and to the sign of Cross, under which he promised to tell the truth in everything that he knew and was asked of him.

Having heard the proceedings of what was stated, he said that, being at Ojo de Juan Luján, he found himself under a cedar tree some distance from where the said corporal was and did not see or hear the noise or disturbance which took place. He could only presume what the said corporal had done. He then mounted his horse and seeing that the said Isidro fled and the corporal went after him, he followed them for about a league and one-half, where the said corporal took his horse and gave his to him [Trujillo], and Trujillo returned back to the royal camp where the other soldiers were with orders to send five soldiers to go catch up to said corporal. This, he said, is what he saw and nothing else, and is the truth regarding the sworn statement which he has made, and he affirmed and ratified. He said that he was thirty-five years of age and he did not sign because he did not know how. I, the said lieutenant general, signed it along with my assisting witnesses acting as presiding judge due to lack of a public or royal scribe, etc.

Antonio Pérez Velarde (rubric)

Felipe Tafoya (rubric)

Alfonso de Aguilar (rubric)

Statement of Baltazar de Abeytia

In this villa of Santa Fe on the said day, month, and year, I, the lieutenant general, in order to continue the prosecution of this case and by virtue of the proceedings approved by me in this case, made appear before me Baltazar de Abeytia, soldier in this presidial palace, who upon being present, gave his sworn statement which he made to God, Our Lord, and to the sign of the Cross, under which he promised to tell the truth about everything that he knew and what he was asked, and having heard the proceedings of the said, he stated what he knew as follows.

He said that what he knew and saw was that the corporal Lorenzo Trujillo and Isidro Sánchez had a dispute about someone having stolen gunpowder which belonged to Sánchez, and the corporal had hit him a few blows, and Sánchez told him that there was no reason for him to have hit him, and the said Isidro fled. The said corporal asked him, Abeytia, for his horse, which he gave to him, and the said corporal went after Isidro. He, the said declarant, also went after him and caught up to the corporal and then proceeded to catch up to the said Isidro, where he asked him where he was going, telling him that he would fix everything with the corporal. He [Abeytia] went back to where the corporal was and asked him to fix everything and end the whole thing.

The said corporal told him that he would not fix anything, and he, Abeytia, then went back to where Isidro was and took the reins of his horse, taking him as such to the said corporal. Upon arriving where the corporal was, he was told to take him, the said Isidro, always with his arms crossed. Then for the second time, the corporal poked him with his sword, and the said Isidro told him, "See how passionate you are with me." Then he fled again, being afraid of how he would be treated, seeing how terribly mad he, the corporal, was, and then went to seek refuge in the sacredness of the church of Ysleta. This is what he answered. He was then asked if he saw that the said Isidro Sánchez pulled out his arquebus to fire at the said corporal. He said that he did not, because Sánchez had it wrapped with a cloth that covered the gunlock [*llave*], and what he saw was another soldier carrying it. He said that this, his sworn statement which he has made, was the truth, and he affirmed and ratified it upon his statement being read back to him. He said he was twenty-two years of age, and he signed it with me, the said lieutenant, along with my assisting witnesses.

Antonio Pérez Velarde (rubric)

Baltazar de Abeytia (rubric)

Felipe Tafoya (rubric)

Alfonso de Aguilar (rubric)

Decree

    In the villa of Santa Fe on the 20th of October, 1731, I, the said lieutenant general, having heard the statements of Joachín de Anaya and Baltazar de Abeytia, who were cited by the corporal Lorenzo Trujillo in his statement, I ordered and did order that they appear before me and their statements be read to them so that they can identify them as their own and to see if they have anything to add or delete, and so that these statements can be ratified as such. As such I approved, ordered, and signed it with my assisting witnesses.

Antonio Pérez Velarde (rubric)

Felipe Tafoya (rubric)

Alfonso de Aguilar (rubric)

Ratification by Lorenzo Trujillo

    In this villa of Santa Fe on the said day, month, and year, I, the said lieutenant general, by virtue of the above proceedings approved by me, made to appear before me the corporal Lorenzo Trujillo, who, upon being present, I received his sworn statement which he made under his proper right and he promised to tell the truth in everything that he knew and was asked. Having read to him a statement which he has made in these proceedings, he said that it was his and that he affirms and ratifies it once, twice, and three times and any other times which may be required, and that he does not have anything to add or delete other than what he has said and stated, because it is the truth concerning the sworn statement which he has made, and he says that his age is as said in his statement. He did not sign because he did not know how. I, said lieutenant, signed it along with my assisting witnesses, acting as presiding judge due to the lack of a scribe.

Antonio Pérez Velarde (rubric)

Felipe Tafoya (rubric)

Alfonso de Aguilar (rubric)

[Editor's note: The decrees, ratifications, and statements for Lorenzo Trujillo, Isidro Sánchez, Joachín Anaya, and Baltazar de Abeytia use exactly the same language as that above and are not included in the translation, though they are included in the transcription.]

Decree regarding the blame and the charges

In the villa of Santa Fe on the 29th of October, 1731, I, said lieutenant general, say that having followed this criminal case against Isidro Sánchez, soldier of this presidial castle, notwithstanding the denial which he made in his confession, I charge him to be at fault for having taken out his arquebus and trying to load it in order to fire it at the corporal Lorenzo Trujillo, but was not able to do so because it was wrapped up in a cloth and tied, along with everything else as the case reveals and charge him as such. He is to respond to this within the period of three days, and as such he is to be notified of these proceedings and is to be given copies of everything. So that it is valid, I signed it with my assisting witnesses acting as presiding judge due to the lack of a scribe. It is attested to that the arquebus has not been turned in.

      Antonio Pérez Velarde (rubric)
      Felipe Tafoya (rubric)
      Alfonso de Aguilar (rubric)

Notification

In continuing, I, said lieutenant general by virtue of that which was ordered by the above proceedings, so that the offender in this case Isidro Sánchez is notified, I read and notified him personally and gave him copies of these proceedings in this criminal case, and he having understood its contents said that he has heard everything. He signed it along with me the said lieutenant and my assisting witnesses, acting as presiding judge due to the lack of a public or royal scribe.

      Antonio Pérez Velarde (rubric)
      Isidro Sánchez Bañales (rubric)
      Felipe Tafoya (rubric)
      Alfonso de Aguilar (rubric)

Statement by Isidro Sánchez

      Lieutenant General

[I] Isidro Sánchez Bañales, soldier in this presidial castle and prisoner in this royal guardhouse because of what the corporal Lorenzo Trujillo has against me, I affirm everything in the confession and ratification which I have made in this case, which is in my favor. And I say that justice prevailing, your majesty should absolve me and turn me free from prison [*prizion*], where I am at, because he has not given me nor committed me to any cause for my being in prison regarding that which the corporal states that I pulled out my arquebus and proceeded to try to shoot him, which I could not do because it was wrapped in a cloth and tied with a leather strap.

His accusation is illicit, false, and wrong, because not even in my smallest imagination could I have possibly done that. If I had intended to do that, I would have prepared the arquebus, taking off the wrappings without any hesitation, in order to do what was intended. Because of this, it is seen that the said corporal with his fear of me and his slander, showing his implacable enmity as he did from the very beginning of the dispute, not only with his offensive words but also with his actions, as he showed in his poisonous rage by stabbing me not once, but by continuing it a second time.

From which because this cruelty, I fled, and he followed me, and once he stopped, I tried to gain his friendship by waiting for him to cool his temper, for which reason I waited for Baltazar de Abeytia, when he told me that he would fix everything with the corporal. Then going back to where he was, they begin to talk, and then the corporal came to where I was at, telling me to give myself up as his prisoner, which I did, and taking the reins from my horse and giving them to him. He then gave some furious blows as I was with my arms crossed, as has been stated by the witnesses who were cited by the said corporal. Recognizing that he could not control his hot temper and poisonous passion [*colerica y enconada passion*], I once again fled, being afraid of him, and went to seek refuge in the sacredness of the church at Isleta, recognizing that I would be incriminated for this and would have to experience what I am presently going through. The corporal then proceeded to have me come out from the sanctuary under the assurance that he would not cause me any more harm or damage.

At this time, lieutenant general, I urge your highest consideration be given this issue, because in the case that I committed the crime of which the corporal accuses me, when he got me out of the church under the pretense of not causing me any more hurt, it can be seen that in all ways I am found innocent, particularly of having committed the crime which he wrongly accused me. Of your majesty, I ask and petition that you be well pleased to release me free from the prison which I am in and that you administer the zealous justice which I ask for, and I swear by my right that this is not done in malice, protesting the costs, and in whatever is necessary, etc.

Isidro Sánchez Bañales (rubric)

In the villa of Santa Fe on the 30th of October, 1731, before me, don Antonio Pérez Velarde, lieutenant general of this kingdom, he who wrote it, presented it to me; and seen by me, I took it as presented, and I ordered it and did order that it be incorporated with the proceedings. As such I approved, ordered, and signed it with my assisting witnesses acting as presiding judge due to the lack of public or royal scribe.

Antonio Pérez Velarde (rubric)
Felipe Tafoya (rubric)
Alfonso de Aguilar (rubric)

Order to Submit [to the governor]

In the villa of Santa Fe on the said day, month, and year, I, said lieutenant general, say that having finalized this cause against Isidro Sánchez, which I have conducted by virtue of the commission of the colonel don Gervasio Cruzat y Cruzat y Góngora, governor and captain general of this kingdom for his majesty, I state that it is concluded, and it is in the stage of sentencing, and for its pronouncement I make and did make its submission to his honor so that upon his review and according to the merits of the case he could determine and hand down what he sees is best, as he always does. I thus approved, ordered, and signed it with my assisting witnesses acting as presiding judge due to the lack of a public or royal scribe.

      Antonio Pérez Velarde (rubric)
       Felipe Tafoya (rubric)
      Alfonso de Aguilar (rubric)

[Decree by the governor]

In this villa of Santa Fe, on the 17th of November, I, Colonel don Gervasio Cruzat y Góngora, governor and captain general of this kingdom of New Mexico for his majesty, upon review of the submission of the proceedings which were given to me by my lieutenant general don Antonio Pérez Velarde, and this case requiring more proof for its best justification, I order and did order that don Diego Arias de Quiros,[10] who has acquired the post of lieutenant general, continue it and receive new information [and] examine in the best juridical form the soldiers Francisco Velasques,[11] Joseph Jaramillo,[12] Joachín Sánchez,[13] Miguel de Ribera,[14] and Gerónimo de Ortega,[15] who were present in the case, as was stated in his declaration by Lorenzo Trujillo. I thus approved, ordered, and signed it with my assisting witnesses acting as presiding judge due to the lack of a public or royal scribe, which there is none in this kingdom.

   don Gervasio Cruzat y Cruzat y Góngora (rubric)
      Gaspar de Bitton (rubric)
     Juan Antonio de Unanue (rubric)

[Decree by the lieutenant governor]

In this capital, villa of Santa Fe on the 26th of November, 1731, I, Captain Diego Arias de Quiros, lieutenant general, in fulfillment of the proceedings above expedited by the colonel don Gervasio Cruzat y Góngora, governor and captain general of this kingdom, I went to gather information about the criminal case which is being carried out against Isidro Sánchez, soldier of this royal presidio, for having lost his respect for his corporal Lorenzo Trujillo, as is evidenced on the back of the first page. So that it is valid I signed it with my assisting witnesses acting as presiding judge due to the lack of a public or royal scribe, which there is none in this kingdom.

      Diego Arias de Quiros (rubric)
      Juan Manuel Chirinos (rubric)
      Juan Joseph Lovato (rubric)

Statement of Miguel de Rivera

Continuing, on the said day, month, and year, in order to continue with this business, I, captain Diego Arias de Quiros, lieutenant general, made appear before me Miguel de Rivera, soldier in this royal presidio, who upon being present, gave his sworn statement which he made to God, Our Lord, and the sign of the Holy Cross, regarding the case, and promised to tell the truth in everything that he knew and what he was asked.

He was asked if he was present at the paraje, which is known as the Ojo de Juan Luján, where the said Isidro Sánchez pulled out his arquebus to fire at Corporal Lorenzo Trujillo. He said that he was not present at the time because he had gone down to the spring to fill his *guaje*[16] with water. By time he got to where his companions were, an order was received by them from the said corporal Lorenzo Trujillo for a squad to get some horses ready in order to follow the said Isidro Sánchez, he being one of the ones who went after him. But they could not catch up to him, so they returned to the camp. He was then asked over and over again various questions, but he stated that he did not know anything else other than what he had said under the oath which he had made, and he affirmed and ratified it. He said that he was thirty-four years of age, more or less. He did not sign because he did not know how. I signed it with my assisting witnesses acting as presiding judge due to the lack of a public or royal scribe of which there is none in this kingdom.

    Diego Arias de Quiros (rubric)
    Juan Manuel Chirinos (rubric)
    Juan Joseph Lovato (rubric)

Statement of Joseph de Jaramillo

Continuing, on the said day, month, and year, I, said lieutenant general, in prosecution of these proceedings, made appear before me Joseph Jaramillo, soldier in this royal presidio, from whom upon being present I received his sworn statement which he made to God, Our Lord, and to the sign of the Holy Cross, under which he promised to tell the truth as to what he knew and about what was asked.

He was asked if he was present at the Paraje del Ojo de Juan Luján, which is where the said corporal Lorenzo Trujillo states that the said Isidro Sánchez pulled out his arquebus to fire at him. He stated that he had heard that the said Isidro Sánchez had said that they had stolen his munitions, to which the said corporal answered that no one would have taken them, that he had never taken them with him, telling him that he was a liar. He [Jaramillo] said that he did not see anything else as he, the said declarant, had begun to pack up a load behind a cedar tree. Upon finishing this, he heard a disturbance and came out from behind the tree and saw Francisco Velasques with the arquebus belonging to Isidro Sánchez in his hand, and the said corporal and some others running after the said Isidro Sánchez. He was then asked if he heard or saw anything else regarding this matter. He stated that he did not, that this was the truth about what he saw and that he does not know anything else regarding the charges of this sworn statement which he has made, which he affirmed and ratified and stated that he was twenty-two years of age, more or less. He did not sign because he did not know how. I signed it with my assisting witnesses acting as presiding judge due to the lack of a public or royal scribe, which there is none in this kingdom.

     Diego Arias de Quiros (rubric)
     Juan Manuel Chirinos (rubric)
     Juan Joseph Lovato (rubric)

Statement of Joachín Sánchez

 Continuing, I, said lieutenant general in prosecution of these proceedings, made appear before me Joachín Sánchez, who being present I received his sworn statement which he made to God, Our Lord, and to the sign of the Holy Cross, under which he promised to tell the truth as to what he knew and was asked.

 He was asked if he was present at the Paraje de el Ojo de Juan Luján, which is where the corporal Lorenzo Trujillo states that the said Isidro Sánchez pulled out his arquebus to fire at him. He stated that he did not know or see anything, and that he was at a distance from the camp at the spring. When he left from there, he saw that they were riding after the said Isidro Sánchez, and he followed them trying to catch him, but they could not do so. This is what he knows under the sworn statement which he has made and which he affirmed and ratified. He said that he was thirty-eight years of age, more or less, and he signed it with me and my assisting witnesses, acting as presiding judge due to the lack of a public or royal scribe, which there is none in this kingdom.

     Diego Arias de Quiros (rubric)
     Juan Manuel Chirinos (rubric)
     Juan Joseph Lovato (rubric)

Statement of Francisco Velasques

 In this villa of Santa Fe, capital of this kingdom of New Mexico, on the 6th of December, 1731, I, Captain Diego Arias de Quiros, lieutenant general of this said kingdom, in order to continue with these proceedings which are being conducted against Isidro Sánchez, soldier of this royal presidio, for having lost the respect [*perdido el respecto*] to the corporal of the squad, Lorenzo Trujillo, according to his declaration, which starts on the back of page one, made to appear before me Francisco Velasques, soldier of this royal presidio, who upon being present received his sworn statement which he made to God, Our Lord, and the sign of the Holy Cross, under which he promised to tell the truth about everything that he knew and what he was asked.

He was asked if he was present at the paraje which is known as El Ojo de Juan Luján, which is where the said corporal Lorenzo Trujillo states that the said Isidro Sánchez pulled out his arquebus in order to use it on him. He said that what he had seen was that as he was packing his load along with the offender in order to get ready to go on their trip, the offender, Isidro Sánchez, told him that someone had stolen his gunpowder, and that from there the said Isidro Sánchez went and told the corporal, who responded by telling him that no one would have stolen his gunpowder, that he probably never had packed it. The said Isidro then told him that upon them leaving [the presidio] they had passed muster with everything. The corporal then told him that he knew that he never had it and pulled his sword and attempted to strike him with it, from which he, Isidro, fled, and upon doing this he dropped his arquebus from his carrying case and he hurriedly went to pick it up in order to defend himself from the sword blows, which were struck by the corporal, and upon one of the strikes, he knocked it to the ground. At that point I, said declarant, took the arquebus, and saw that it was wrapped with two cloths and tied with a strong string. The said offender was then taken for a second time, and the corporal begin to try to strike him once more, at which time the said Isidro fled, and they were not able to catch him.

He said that since the beginning of the campaign, he had seen that the said Isidro had his flask [*frasco*] full of gunpowder. He was then asked if he knew or heard that when the said offender took refuge in the church, he knew or heard the reasons that were given for him to come out from the church. He said that the said corporal had gone after the said Isidro Sánchez and that the corporal had told him to come out of the church to fulfill his obligation, that everything that had happened would be forgotten, and for him to come out under full security.

This he said is the truth about all that he knows and saw under the sworn statement, which he has made, which he affirmed and ratified. He said he was forty years of age, more or less. He did not sign because he did not know how; I, said lieutenant general, signed it with my assisting witnesses acting as presiding judge due to the lack of a public or royal scribe, which there is none in this kingdom.

    Diego Arias de Quiros (rubric)
    Juan Manuel Chirinos (rubric)
    Juan Joseph Lovato (rubric)

Statement of Gerónimo de Ortega

In this capital and villa of Santa Fe of this kingdom of New Mexico on the 29th of December, 1731, I, Captain Diego Arias de Quiros, lieutenant general of this said kingdom, in order to prosecute this cause against Isidro Sánchez, soldier of this royal presidio, made appear before me Gerónimo Ortega, soldier of this said presidio, from whom, being before me, I received his sworn statement which he made to God, Our Lord, and the sign of the Holy Cross, under which he promised to tell the truth as to everything that he knew and was asked.

He was asked if he was present at the paraje, which is known as the Ojo de Juan

Luján, when the corporal of the squadron, Lorenzo Trujillo, went to reconnoiter the land. The said declarant said that his horse was saddled, and upon being ready to leave from the paraje, he heard that the said Isidro Sánchez had told his corporal that someone had stolen his gunpowder and that the said corporal answered him saying that all the soldiers had sufficient munitions, that no one would steal it, and that he probably did not take it with him. Isidro then answered that whoever took it could have done it if they did not have any; that he could have given them some if they did not have any. The corporal then answered him saying that no one would have taken it, that they were all men of good character and of what age was he,[17] that he, the said Isidro Sánchez, would be full of lies. At which time, the said corporal mounted his horse and the said Isidro told him, sir corporal, what you state is wrong; at which point the said corporal pulled his sword and went after the said Isidro Sánchez.

After the said declarant had mounted his horse, he heard the said corporal say, "All for the king."[18] Some others then mounted their horses, and he saw that Francisco Velasques had in his hands the arquebus belonging to the said Isidro Sánchez wrapped in the manner that he uses all the time. They then went after the said Isidro Sánchez, but they could not catch him, and they then returned to camp. Ortega was then asked a few other questions to which he answered that he did not know anything else other than what he has stated, which is the truth, regarding the sworn statement which he has made, which he affirmed and ratified. He said he was forty years of age. He did not sign because he did not know how. I, said lieutenant general, signed it with my assisting witnesses acting as presiding judge due to the lack of a public or royal scribe, which there is none in this kingdom.

Diego Arias de Quiros (rubric)
Juan Manuel Chirinos (rubric)
Juan Joseph Lovato (rubric)

Decree

In this villa of Santa Fe, capital of this said kingdom, on the said day, month, and year, I, said lieutenant general, in order to prosecute this cause, ordered and did order for the witnesses who have given their declarations in the proceedings that have been expedited by the colonel don Gervasio Cruzat y Cruzat y Góngora to have their statements ratified. I thus approved, ordered, and signed it with my assisting witnesses acting as presiding judge due to the lack of a public or royal scribe, which there is none in this kingdom.

Diego Arias de Quiros (rubric)
Juan Manuel Chirinos (rubric)
Juan Joseph Lovato (rubric)

[Editor's note: The decrees and ratifications of statements by Miguel de Rivera, Joseph

Jaramillo, Joachín Sánchez, and Francisco Velasques use exactly the same language and are not included here in the translation, though they are included in the transcription.]

Decree of Submission

In this capital, villa of Santa Fe, in this kingdom of New Mexico, on the 7th of January, 1732, I, Captain Diego Arias de Quiros, lieutenant general of the said kingdom, say that I have examined in juridical form the witnesses cited in the order issued by the colonel don Gervasio Cruzat y Cruzat y Góngora, governor and captain general of this said kingdom for his majesty, in order to make final this case which has been followed against Isidro Sánchez, which has been concluded and is now in the state of sentencing. For its pronouncement, I have made and did make submission to his honor so that, upon his review and according to the merits of this said cause, he can determine and do what he thinks, which, as always, is for the best. As such I approved, ordered, and signed it along with my assisting witnesses, acting as presiding judge due to the lack of a public or royal scribe.

                Diego Arias de Quiros (rubric)
                Juan Manuel Chirinos (rubric)
                Juan Joseph Lovato (rubric)

Sentence

In this criminal case which has been conducted against Isidro Sánchez, soldier in the cavalry company of this royal presidio of the villa of Santa Fe for the escape which he committed, abandoning his camp during a campaign, and for the action which he took in pulling out his arquebus on his corporal Lorenzo Trujillo, as is brought forth in his statement and his escape being proven, and having examined the motives which he had for this and having seen the proceedings, along with everything else which has been brought forth, I find that the acts and merits of the case which have been brought forth as to having come out from the sanctuary of the church of the pueblo of Isleta under the word of the corporal Lorenzo Trujillo, and for the time which he suffered while in prison,[19] I should order and did order that his employment as a soldier be abolished and that testimony of this sentence be made known so that upon being seen it is executed. I thus judge, pronounce, and order. I signed it with my assisting witnesses due to the lack of a public or royal scribe, which there is none in this kingdom. It is done on common paper, there being none which is sealed.

            Don Gervasio Cruzat y Cruzat y Góngora (rubric)
                      Gaspar Bitton (rubric)
                  Juan Antonio de Unanue (rubric)

Pronouncement

The sentence being given and pronounced as written by me, Colonel don Gervasio Cruzat y Cruzat y Góngora, governor and captain general of this kingdom of New Mexico, having made a public audience before my tribunal in this villa of Santa Fe on the 16th of January, 1732, I signed it with my assisting witnesses due to the lack of public or royal scribe, which there is none in this kingdom.

   don Gervasio Cruzat y Cruzat y Góngora (rubric)
   Gaspar Bitton (rubric)
   Juan Antonio de Unanue (rubric)

ORIGINAL DOCUMENT

Año de 1731

Causa criminal fulminada contra Isidro Sanchez, soldado de este Real Presidio sobre haver sido acusado por haver echado mano de su escopeta contra el Cavo Lorenzo Truxillo.

En la Villa de Santa Fee en veinte y ocho dias del mes de Septiembre de mil setecientos y treinta y un años yo el Coronel Dn. Gervasio Cruzat y Cruzat y Góngora, Governador y Capitan General de este Reino dela Nueva Mexico por Su Majestad ut supra, por quanto se halla preso en el Cuerpo de Guardia de este Real Palacio Isidro Sanchez soldado de la Compania de Acavallos de este Real Presidio de dicha Villa de Santa Fee, acusado del crimen de agresor por haver hechado mano a su escopeta contra el Cabo Lorenzo Trujillo en occasion que dicho Cavo estaba mandando la esquadra que se hallava en campaña a recorrer la Sierra de Sandia y por hallarme ocupado en dependencias del servicio de Su Majestad y no pare el curso de su Real Justicia, cometto esta causa a mi Theniente General Dn. Antonio Perez Velarde para que la actue y estando en estado de sentencia la debuelba a este Superior Gobierno, assi lo provei, mande y firme con los testigos ynfranscriptos de mi asistencia a falta de Escribano Publico y Real que no lo ay en este Reino.

   Don Gervasio Cruzat y Cruzat y Gongora (rubric)
   Gaspar Bitton (rubric) Juan Antonio de Unanue (rubric)

Auto

En la Villa de Santa Fee en veynte dias del mes de Octubre de mill setezientos y treinta y un años yo Dn. Antonio Perez Velarde, Theniente General de este Reino, digo que haviendome cometido el conozimiento de esta causa el Señor Governador y Capitan General, para que la siga contra Isidro Sanchez, preso en el Real Cuerpo de Guardia y soldado de este Castillo Presidial por el delito que expressa el auto preveydo por

dicho Señor Governador y para saver y aberiguar la verdad y prozeder contra el dicho Isidro Sanchez, devia de mandar y mando se reziva la declarazion al dicho Lorenzo Trujillo y diga y declare los motivos y causas que el dicho Isidro Sanchez tubo para hechar mano al arcabuz, en que paraje, y todas las zircumstancias que prezedieron para que ejecutara tan exseciable delicto y en vista de dicha declarazion prozeder en las demas deligencias que convienen, asi lo provey, mande y firme con los testigos de mi asistensia actuando por Rezeptoria a falta de escribano Publico y Real.
      Don Antonio Perez Velarde (rubric)
      Alphonso de Aguilar (rubric)
      Felipe Tafoya (rubric)

Declarazion de el
Cavo Lorenzo Trujillo
En la Villa de Santa Fee en veynte y quatro dias del mes de Octubre de mil setezientos y treynta y un años yo dicho Theniente General en virtud del auto antezedente por mi proveydo hize parezer ante mi al Cavo Lorenzo Trujillo al qual estando presente le resevi juramento que hizo por Dios Nuestro Señor y una senal de Cruz de bajo de cuyo cargo prometio de dezir verdad en todo lo que supiere y le fuere preguntado y haviendo salido a campana de orden de dicho Señor Governador estando en el Ojo de Juan Lujan estando ya para salir dijo Isidro Sanchez que hurtaran la comida y no le hurtaran la munizion a lo qual respondio este declarante que quien se la havia de aver hurtado por que todos los soldados de esta Villa llebaban muniziones de sobra, y el dicho Isidro vino a caballo a donde estaba este declarante apie y le dijo que dezia mucha verdad y que quando las tenian les cojian otra cosas y este declarante respondio que no la tenia con ningun y este declarante suvio acavallo y aranco la espada para darle y al suvir acavallo arranco el arcabuz y entonzes le tiro un golpe con la espada y quieso sacar el arcabuz y no pudo por estar con una vuelta de pano en buelto y amarado con una correa y visto que no pudo le tiro un palo con el dicho arcabuz y este declarante lo reparo y selo quito de las manos y entonzes yamando a los soldados que lo cojieran y no pudieron por que estaban a pie por haver arrancado a huir, y gano la derezera de Abo y haviendo ydo en su seguimiento con Balthazar de Abeytia y Joachin de Anaya lo alcanzaron y le dijo este declarante que si savia el delito que havia cometido; respondio que vien savia lo que hazia; y este declarante le tiro con tres cuchilladas para castigarlo y que se acabara, a lo cual arranco a cavallo y se vino ala Ysleta por cuyo motibo lo dejo y se vino a cuydar del Real, y que esto es lo que passo y save so cargo del juramento que fecho tiene en que se afirmo y ratifico siendole leyda esta su declarazion y que es de edad de treynta y ocho años, no firmo por no saver, firmelo yo dicho Theniente con los testigos de mi assistensia.
      Antonio Perez Velarde (rubric)
      Alphonso de Aguilar (rubric)
      Felipe Tafoya (rubric)

Auto que pide al
dicho Isidro Sanchez
Reo

En esta Villa de Santa Fee en veynte y sinco dias del mes de Octubre de mill setezientos treynta y un años yo dicho Theniente General digo que haviendo visto la declarazion fecha por el Cavo Lorenzo Trujillo y por ella consta el haver echado mano al arcabuz el dicho Isidro Sanchez y lo demas que expressa en dicha su declarazion y para prozeder contra el dicho Isidro Sanchez, reo en esta causa devia de mandar y mando sele reziva su confession y fecha seguir las demas deligencias que combengan, asi lo provey, mande y firme con los testigos de mi asistensia actuando por Receptoria a falta de Escribano Publico y Real.

      Antonio Perez Velarde (rubric)
    Felipe Tafoya (rubric) Alphonso de Aguilar (rubric)

Confession de
Isidro Sanchez
Reo en esta caussa

  En la Villa de Santa Fee en dicho dia, mes y año yo dicho Theniente General en virtud del auto de susso por mi proveydo hize parezer por esta caussa al qual estando presente le rezevi juramento que hizo en forma de derecho de bajo de cuyo cargo prometio de dezir verdad en todo lo que supiere y le fuere preguntado y haviendo sido como se llama que edad y ofizio tiene de donde es natural y que estado tiene. Dijo, que se llama Isidro Sanchez, que es de edad de treynta y un año y que su ofizio es servir al Rey Nuestro Señor en este Real Presido y es natural de la Ciudad de Zacatecas y que su estado es ser casado y responde. ____

  Preguntado si save la caussa de su prision? Dijo, que hasta aora no a cometido ningun delicto por donde pueda ser preso, y esto responde. ____ Preguntado diga y declare la verdad por que consta en estos autos, el haver tenido razones con el Cavo Lorenzo Trujillo estando en campana en el Paraje del Ojo de Juan Lujan sobre aver dicho este confesante que le havian hurtado las muniziones y que el dicho Cavo Lorenzo Trujillo. Respondio que quien selas havia de haver hurtado y otras rasones que pasaron sobre que este confesante arranco el arcabus y quizo cusarlo y no pudo por estar enbuelto con una muestra de pano y amarrado con una correa; dijo que es falso, y supuesto que no arranco arcabuz por que lo que passo fue que este confesante dijo que le havian hurtado la polvora y que el dicho Cavo respondio que no la trayia que era un embustero y que esto lo repitio muchas veses; y que subio acavallo y se vino para este confesante dandoles dizintarazos con un chafalote y temeroso este confesante arranco a hujir y lo fue siguiendo como tres leguas y haviendo visto que se paro el dicho Cavo se paro tambien a donde vino Balthazar de Abeytia y le dijo que se bolviera, alo qual respondio que buelto estaba y benia huyendo del dicho Cavo y dije que le dijera que se acabara aquello supuesto que no havia ningunos motivos y el dicho Balthazar fue y estubo con dicho Cavo quien vino a donde estaba este confesante y le dijo que se diesse por presso a lo qual obedezio zeguramente y le entrege las riendas del cavallo y cruzado los brazos lo llebo de diestra donde estaba dicho Abeytia a quien le entrego las riendas para que llebara a este confesante y entonzes de bajo de esta obedienzia le dio muchos golpes y maltrato que estubo adolorido muchos dias y viendo esta cruelldad echo mano a las riendas y echo a huyir, visto que lo que le avia pasado de bajo de engano arranco a huyir y se vino a efujar al sagrado dela Santa Yglesia con el conozimiento de que siempre havia de acriminar que havia cometido grave delicto de donde con justarizia y palabras enganossas le dijo que ya se havia acabado y asi que vien podra con seguro valer de el sagrado de la yglesia que no faltaria en nada delo que le dezia que fuera hazer su obligazion al Real de la cavallada lo qual executo de donde lo sacaron para traerlo presso, que esto es la verdad y lo que paso por el juramento que fecho tiene en que se afirmo y ratifico siendole leyda esta su confession y lo firmo con migo y los testigos de mi assistencia actuando por rezeptoria a falta de escribano Publico y Real, ut supra.

    Antonio Perez Velarde (reubric)
    Isidro Sanchez Banales (rubric)
  Felipe Tafoya (rubric) Alphonso de Aguilar (rubric)

Auto

En la Villa de Santa Fee en veynte y seis dias del mes de Octubre de mill setezientos treynta y un años yo dicho Theniente General digo que haviendo visto la confession que ante me tiene fecha Isidro Sanchez reo y preso por esta caussa y la negativa de la calumnia que sele haze de haver zacado el arcabuz y solisitando el casailo como obsta dela declarazion del Cavo Lorenzo Trujillo y para saver y aberiguar la verdad devia de mandar y mando sele resiva las declaraziones a Joachin de Anaya y a Balthazar de Abeytia soldados de este Castillo Presidial a quienes zita en su declarazion dicho Cavo para que digan y declaren si el dicho Isidro Sanchez arranco el arcabuz y proviso el cazarlo y lo demas que en dicha declarazion consta y resulta contra el dicho reo y para que conste asi lo provey mande y firme con los testigos de mi assistenzia actuando por Resecptoria a falta de escribano, ut supra.

    Antonio Perez Velarde (rubric)
  Felipe Tafoya (rubric) Alphonso de Aguilar (rubric)

Declarazion de
Joachin de Anaya

En la Villa de Santa Fee en dicho dia mes y año yo dicho Theniente General en virtud del auto antezedente por mi probeydo hize parecer ante mi a Joachin de Anaya soldado de este Presidio al qual estando presente le rezevi juramento que hizo por Dios Nuestro Señor y una Señal de Cruz de bajo de cuyo cargo prometio dezir verdad en todo lo que supiere y le fuere preguntado y haviendole sido al tenor del referido auto dijo que estando en el Ojo de Juan Lujan estaba este declarante de bajo de un savino retirado de donde estaba dicho Cavo y no vido ni oyo el rruydo y marmolle que tubieron que solamente pudo perzevir quando dijo dicho Cavo aqui del Rey y entonzes monto este declarante a cavallo y el dicho Isidro arranco a huyr y el dicho Cavo tras de el y este declarante lo fue siguiendo como legua y media de donde dicho Cavo le cojio el cavallo a este declarante y le dio el suyo y se bolvio al Real con orden que le despachesse cinco soldados que fueran a alcanzar a dicho Cavo: y que esto es lo que vido y no otra cosa por ser la verdad por el juramento que fecho tiene en que se afirmo y ratifico siendole leyda esta su declarazion y que es de edad de treynta y zinco años, no firmo por no saber firmelo yo dicho Theniente con los testigos de mi assistenzia actuando por Rezeptoria a falta de Escribano Publico y Real, ut supra.

    Antonio Perez Velarde (rubric)
 Felipe Tafoya (rubric) Alphonso de Aguilar (rubric)

Declarazion de
Balthazar de Beytia

 En la Villa de Santa Fee en dicho dia mes y año yo el Theniente General para la prosocuzion de esta caussa y en virtud del auto por mi prebeydo hize parezer ante mi a Balthazar de Beytia soldado deste Castillo Presidial al qual estando presente le rezevi juramento que hizo por Dios Nuestro Señor y una Señal de Cruz de bajo de cuyo cargo prometio de dezir verdad en todo lo que supiere y le fuere preguntado y haviendolo sido al thenor del referido auto dijo; que lo que save y vido es que tubieron question, el Cavo Lorenzo Trujillo y Isidro Sanchez sobre que a este le havian hurtado la polvora y que el dicho Cavo le dio dezintaros y le dijo que no hera bastante caussa para que le diera; y entonzes aranco huyendo el dicho Isidro y el dicho Cavo le pedio el cavallo a este declarante y se lo dio y fue siguiendo dicho Cavo a dicho Isidro y lo mismo hize este declarante y lo alcanzo, y prosiguio en alcanzar a dicho Isidro y haviendolo alcanzado le dijo que a donde yba que este declarante lo compondria con dicho Cavo y bolvio donde estaba y le suplico que compusiera aquel negocio y que se acabara: y el dicho Cavo respondio que no, y se vino donde estaba el dicho Isidro y le bajo las riendas del cavallo llebandolo de diestro a dicho Cavo y asi que llego donde estaba este declarante le dijo que llebase aquel soldado y siempre con los brazos cruzados el dicho Isidro a quien el dicho Cavo lo bolvio Segunda vez a a dar de cuchilladas con el espadin y le dijo el dicho Isidro be Usted como es pasion la que Usted me tiene, y entonzes arranco a huir temeroso de que no lo baldava usandolo tan sumamente colerico y enojado y se vino a efujar al Sagrado de la Yglesia de la Ysleta y responde._____

 Preguntado se vido que el dicho Isidro Sanchez echo mano del arcabuz y lo saco para tirarle a dicho Cavo? Dijo que no lo vido por que con la muestra de pano que tenia enbuelto en la llave, lo vido que lo llebaba un companero. Y que esto es la verdad so cargo del juramento que fecho tiene en que se afirmo y ratifico siendole leyda esta su declarazion y dijo ser de edad de veynte y dos años y lo firmo con migo dicho Theniente y los testigos de mi assistenzia.

      Antonio Perez Velarde (rubric)
      Baltazar de Abeita (rubric)
   Felipe Tafoya (rubric) Alphonso de Aguilar (rubric)

Auto

En la Villa de Santa Fee en veynte de Octubre de mill setezientos y treynta y un años yo dicho Theniente General haviendo hecho sus declaraziones Joachin de Anaya y Balthazar de Abeytia aquienes zita el Cavo Lorenzo Trujillo en su declarazion y para que este se ratifique en ella mandaba y mande comparesca ante me y sele lea para que la reconozca si es suya y si tiene que anadir o que quitar cossa alguna lo haga assi lo provey mande y firme con los testigos de mi assistenzia.

      Antonio Perez Velarde (rubric)
   Felipe Tafoya (rubric) Alphonso de Aguilar (rubric)

Ratificazion de
Lorenzo Trujillo

En la dicha Villa de Santa Fee en dicho dia mes y año yo dicho Theniente General en virtud del auto antezedente por mi proveyido hize pareser ante mi al Cavo Lorenzo Trujillo al qual estando presente le resevi juramento que hizo en forma de derecho de bajo de cuyo cargo prometio de dezir verdad en todo lo que supiere y le fuere preguntado y haviendole leydo una declarazion que tiene en estos autos fecho dijo que la reconoze por suya y que en ella se afirma y ratifica una, dos y tres vezes y las demas que nezesario fuesen y que no tiene que anadir ni que quitar cosa alguna mas que lo que tiene dicho y declarado por que es la verdad so cargo del juramento que tiene fecho y que es de la hedad que consta en su declarazion, no firmo por no saver firmelo yo dicho Theniente con los testigos de mi assistenzia actuando por Reseptoria a falta de escribano.

      Antonio Perez Velarde (rubric)
   Felipe Tafoya (rubric) Alphonso de Aguilar (rubric)

Auto

En la Villa de Santa Fee en veynte y ocho dias del mes de Octubre de mill setezientos y treynta y un años yo dicho Theniente General para la prosecuzion de esta caussa mandaba y mande que se ratifique en su confession Isidro Sanchez y lo mismo hagan los testigos que en esta caussa an declarado zitados por el Cavo Lorenzo Trujillo asi lo provey mande y firme con los testigos de mi assistenzia auctuando por Rezeptoria a falta de escribano.

Antonio Perez Velarde (rubric)
Felipe Tafoya (rubric) Alphonso de Aguilar (rubric)

Ratificazion de
Isidro Sanchez
En la Villa de Santa Fee en dicho dia mes y año yo dicho Theniente General en virtud delo mandado por el auto de arriba hize parecer ante mi a Isidro Sanchez presso por esta caussa al qual estando presente le resevi juramento que hizo en forma de derecho de bajo de cuyo cargo prometio de dezir verdad en todo quanto le fuese preguntado y haviendole leydo la confession que tiene fecha en estos autos dijo que la reconoze por suya y que no tiene que quitar cosa alguna mas que tan solamente que al arrancar a huyr sele cayo el arcabuz sobre todo lo qual se afirma y ratifica una, dos y tres vezes y las demas que nezesario fuesen por que es la verdad y lo que passo por el juramento que fecho tiene y que es de la edad que consta en su confesion y lo firmo con migo y los testigos de mi assistenzia actuando por Rezeptoria.

Antonio Perez Velarde (rubric)
Isidro Sanchez Banales (rubric)
Felipe Tafoya (rubric) Alphonso de Aguilar (rubric)

Rataficazion de
Joachin de Anaya
En la Villa de Santa Fee en dicho dia mes y ano yo dicho Theniente General en virtud del referido auto hize parezer ante mi a Joachin de Anaya al qual le rezevi juramento que hizo en forma de derecho de bajo de cuyo cargo prometio de dezir verdad y haviendole leydo una declarazion que tiene fecha en estos autos dijo que es suya y que en ella se afirma y ratifica y que no tiene que anadir ni que quitar mas que lo que tiene dicho que es la verdad por el juramento que tiene fecho es de la hedad que consta en su declarazion, no firmo por no saver, firmelo yo dicho Theniente con los testigos de mi assistenzia.

Antonio Perez Velarde (rubric)
Felipe Tafoya (rubric) Alphonso de Aguilar (rubric)

Ratificazion de
Balthazar de Abeytia
Luego yncontinenti yo dicho Theniente General hize parezer ante mi a Balthazar de Abeytia al qual le rezevi juramento que hizo en forma de derecho de bajo de cuyo cargo prometio dezir verdad en todo lo que supiere y le fuere preguntado y haviendole leydo

una declarazion que tiene fecha en estos autos dijo que la reconoze y ratifica y que no tiene que anadir ni que quitar cossa alguna mas que la que tiene dicha que es la verdad por juramento que fecho tiene y que es de la edad que tiene dicho en su declarazion y lo firmo con migo dicho Theniente General y los testigos de mi assistenzia.
    Antonio Perez Velarde (rubric)
    Balthazar de Abeitia (rubric)
Felipe Tafoya (rubric) Alphonso de Aguilar (rubric)

Auto de
Culpa y Cargo
En la Villa de Santa Fee en veynte y nueve dias del mes de Octubre de mill setezientos y treynta un años yo dicho Theniente General digo que haviendo seguido esta caussa criminal contra Isidro Sanchez soldado de este Castillo Presidial al qual en embargo dela negativa que haze en su confession le hago el cargo dela culpa de haver amarrado la escopeta y quisso cargarlo el arcabuz para tirarle al Cavo Lorenzo Trujillo lo qual no executo por estar con una envuelta de pano enbuelto y amarrado de lo qual y de lo demas que de la caussa resulta le hago el cargo como dicho es para que de su descargo y responda dentro del termino de tres dias para lo qual sele notifique este dicho auto y sele de traslado de todos ellos y para que conste lo firme con los testigos de mi assistenzia actuando por Rezeptoria a falta de escribano. Testado el arcabuz no viene.
    Antonio Perez Velarde (rubric)
Felipe Tafoya (rubric) Alphonso de Aguilar (rubric)

Notificazion
Luego yncontinenti yo dicho Theniente General en virtud delo mandado por el auto de arriba para que sele notifique a Isidro Sanchez reo en esta caussa al qual sele lei y notifique en su persona y le di traslado de los autos y caussa criminal y estando entendido de su thenor dijo que lo oye y lo firmo con migo dicho Theniente y los testigos de mi assistenzia actuando por Rezeptoria a falta de Escribano Publico y Real.
    Antonio Perez Velarde (rubric)
    Isidro Sanchez Bañales (rubric)
Felipe Tafoya (rubric) Alphonso de Aguilar (rubric)

Señor Theniente General
Isidro Sanchez Banales soldado de este Castillo Presidial y preso en este Real Cuerpo de Guardia por la ocusasion que contra mi tiene hecha el Cabo Lorenzo Trujillo su thenor presupuesto y alo nesesario satisfaciendo afirmandome enla confession y ratificazion que tengo hecha en esta caussa en lo que ase a mi fabor, digo que justizia

mediante, Vmd. deve absolverme a dar por libre de la prizion en que estoy por lo general, y siguiente lo primero por que no he dado ni cometido ninguna caussa para que se me aya puesto en prizion: por que lo que dize el dicho Cavo de que saque la escopeta y procure cazarla y no pude por estar enbuelta con una muestra de pano y amarrada con una correa: es yrrita, falso y supuesta su caluniosa acusazion por que ni por la ymajinacion me paso semejante hecho, por que de haverlo yntentado hubiera prebenido el arcabuz quitandole la dicha muestra para ejecutar sin enbaraso, lo que yntentaba: con que es bisto que el dicho Cavo con temeridad asi puesto contra mi semejante calunia, manifestando su enconosa enemigo, como desde los principios de la question lo hizo, asi de palabras ofensibas como de obras por que no tan solamente fazio su benenosa pasion en darme de cuchilladas una vez, sino es lo volvio aser por Segunda que fue quando de su rigor aranque a huyr yme fue siguiendo y asi que se paro lo yse yo tambien deseando siempre su amistad y que se templara de su enojo para cullo efecto espere a Balthazar de Beytia quando me dijo que lo compondria con dicho Cavo y abiendo buelto donde estava estubieron ablando y de alli se vino dicho Cavo para donde yo estaba deciendome me diese por preso y desde luego me di; y quite las riendas de mi cavallo y selas entregue bolbiendome con furiosos golpes y a todo con los brazos cruzados como lo testifican los testigos que en su declarazion zita el dicho Cavo y reconosiendo que no se podia contener de colerica y enconada pasion volvi a huyrme de temor y medio que es el que cambiaron constante y me esufuje en el Sagrado de la Yglesia de la Ysleta por reconoser havia acriminar esta materia y que abia de padeser lo que al presente estoy experimentando: sacandome dicho Cavo de dicho Sagrado debajo del seguro de que por ningun dano ni perjuicio; pues aora Señor Theniente General pongo en la alta considerasion de Vmd. este punto por que caso que yo ubiera cometido el delicto que se me ymputa dicho Cavo, quando me saco de la Yglesia de bajo del seguro de que no seme aria ningun agrabio luego es bisto que por todas maneras me allo libre mayormente abiendo cometido el delicto que dicho me calunia por todo lo qual a Vmd. pido y suplico sea muy serbido demandar darme por libre ya suelto dela prizion en que estoy que en ello administrara zela justizia la qual pido y juro en forma de derecho no ser de malizia protesto costas y en lo nesesario, ut supra.

      Isidro Sanchez Banales (rubric)

En la Villa de Santa Fee en treynta dias del mes de Octubre de mill setezientos y treynta y un años ante mi Dn. Antonio Perez Velarde Theniente General de este Reyno la presento el contenido en ella; y por mi visto la hube por presentada y mandaba y mande se acomule alos autos asi le probey, mande y firme con los testigos de mi asistenzia actuando por Rezeptoria a falta de Escribano Publico y Real.

      Antonio Perez Velarde (rubric)
  Felipe Tafoya (rubric) Alphonso de Aguilar (rubric)

Auto de
Remission

En la Villa de Santa Fee en dicho dia mes y año yo dicho Theniente General digo que haviendo finalizado esta caussa que contra Isidro Sanchez he seguido en virtud de comission del Señor Coronel Dn. Gervasio Cruzat y Cruzat y Gongora Governador y Capitan General de este Reyno por Su Majestad la qual doy por conclussa, y estar en estado de sentenzia, y para su pronunzazion hazia y hize remission a Su Señoria para que en su vista y segun los meritos de esta caussa determine y desponga lo que mas viene visto le fuere que sera como siempre lo mejor, asi lo provey mande y firme con los testigos de mi asistenzia actuando por Reseptoria a falta de Escribano Publico y Real.

     Antonio Perez Velarde (rubric)
  Felipe Tafoya (rubric) Alphonso de Aguilar (rubric)

En la Villa de Santa Fee en diez y siette dias del mes de Noviembre yo el Coronel Dn. Gervasio Cruzat y Cruzat y Gongora Governador y Capitan General de este Reino dela Nueva Mexico por Su Majestad. En vista dela remission que estos auttos me haze mi Theniente General Dn. Antonio Perez Velarde y nesesitar esta caussa demas prueba para su maior justificazion devia mandar y mande que Dn. Diego Arias de Quiros quien en el ha subcedido en el dicho empleo de Theniente General la prosiga y reciva nuevas informaciones examinando en forma juridica a los soldados Francisco Belasques, Joseph Jaramillo, Joachin Sanchez, Miguel de Ribera y Geronimo de Ortega que se hallaron presentes en el caso que expresa en su declarazion Lorenzo Trujillo. Asi lo provei mande y firme con los testigos de mi asistenzia actuando por Receptoria a falta de Escribano Publico y Real que no lo ay en este Reino.

   Dn. Gervasio Cruzat y Cruzat y Gongora (rubric)
  Gaspar Bitton (rubric) Juan Antonio de Unanue (rubric)

En esta Capital Villa de Santa Fee en beinte y seis dias de el mes de Noviembre de mill zetezientos y treynta y un años yo el Capitan Diego Arias de Quiros Theniente General, en cumplimiento de el auto de arriva espedido por el Señor Coronel Dn. Gervacio Cruzat y Cruzat y Gongora Governador y Capitan General de este Reyno passe a hazer ynformasiones de la caussa criminal que se prosigue contra Isidro Sanchez soldado de este Real Presidio por haverle perdido el respecto a su Cavo Lorenzo Trujillo segun consta de su declarazion en la foja primera buelta y para que asi conste lo firme con los testigos de mi asistensia actuando ante mi por Reseptoria a falta de Escribano Publico y Real que no lo ai en este Reino.

     Diego Arias de Quiros (rubric)
  Juan Manuel Chirinos (rubric) Juan Joseph Lovato (rubric)

Declarazion de
Miguel de Rivera

Yncontinenti en dicho dia mes y año para proseguir en este negocio yo el Capitan Diego Arias de Quiros, Theniente General, hize pareser ante mi a Miguel de Rivera soldado de este Real Presidio al cual estando presente le recevi juramento que hizo por Dios Nuestro Señor y la Señal de la Santa Cruz so cargo del cual prometio de decir verdad en todo lo que supiere y le fuere preguntado.

Preguntado si se allo presente en el Paraje que llaman de el Ojo de Juan Luxan en donde dize el Cavo Lorenzo Trujillo arranco el arcabuz para tirarle con el, el dicho Isidro Sanchez, diga. Dixo que no se hallo presente por razon de haverse vajado a el aguaje a llenar una guaje de agua y luego que llego a donde estavan los companeros llego orden de el Cavo dicho Lorenzo Trujillo de que apartaran cavallos una escuadra para ir en seguimiento de dicho Isidro Sanchez yllendo en ella dicho declarante no lo pudieron alcansar y se bolvieron a el Real; y haviendole preguntado y repreguntado diferentes preguntas dixo este declarante que no save otra cosa mas que lo que lleva dicho de vajo del juramento que fecho tiene en que se afirmo y ratifico, dijo ser de edad de treinta y cuatro años poco mas o menos, no firmo por no saver, firmelo yo con los testigos ynfrascriptos de mi asistencia actuando por Reseptoria por falta de Escribano Publico y Real que no lo ai en este Reino.

        Diego Arias de Quiros (rubric)
Juan Manuel Chirinos (rubric) Juan Joseph Lovato (rubric)

Declarazion de
Joseph de Xaramillo

Yncontinenti en dicho dia mes y añno yo dicho Theniente General en prosecuzion de estas diligencias hize parecer ante mi a Joseph Jaramillo soldado de este Real Presidio a quien estando presente le resevi juramento que hizo por Dios Nuestro Señor y la Señal de la Cruz devajo de el cual prometio de decir verdad en lo que supiere y le fuere preguntado

Preguntandole si se hallo presente en el Paraje del Ojo de Juan Luxan en donde dize dicho Cavo Lorenzo Trujillo que el dicho Isidro Sanchez arranco el arcabuz para tirarle con el? Dixo, que oyo que el dicho Isidro Sanchez dixo que le havian hurtado las municiones ala cual razon le replico dicho Cavo diciendole que quien se las havia de hurtar que no las llevaria y que era un embustero que no vido mas por quanto se puso dicho declarante a cargar una carga de tras de un sabino y que haviendo acavado oyo el alboroto y salio de alli y vido a Francisco Velasques con la escopeta de Isidro Sanchez dicho en la mano y que dicho Cavo y otros yvan corriendo en pos de dicho Isidro Sanchez; y preguntandole si ha visto o oyo dezir otra cosa alguna perteneciente a este negocio; dijo que no y que es la verdad por que lo vido y que no save otra cosa so cargo del juramento que fecho tiene, en que se afirmo y ratifico y dixo ser de edad de veinte y dos años poco mas o menos. No firmo por no saver, firmelo yo con los testigos de asistenzia actuando ante mi por Reseptoria por falta de Escribano Publico y Real que no lo ay en este Reino.

       Diego Arias de Quiros (rubric)
   Juan Manuel Chirinos (rubric) Juan Joseph Lovato (rubric)

Declarazion de
Joachin Sanchez
Luego yncontinenti yo dicho Theniente General en prosecuzion de estas diligencias hize parecer ante mi a Joachin Sanchez aquien estando presente le resebi juramento que hizo por Dios Nuestro Señor y la Señal de la Cruz de bajo de cuio cargo prometio de desir verdad en lo que supiere y le fuere preguntado

Preguntado si se hallo presente en el Paraje de El Ojo de Juan Luxan en donde dise el Cavo dicho Lorenzo Trujillo que el dicho Isidro Sanchez aranco la escopeta para tirarle diga; dixo que no vido ni supo nada por que estava distante de el Real en el aguaje y que quando salio de dicho aguaje vido que ivan corriendo en seguimiento de dicho Isidro Sanchez a onde fue tambien el dicho declarante y no pudieron darle alcanse. Esto es lo que sabe de vajo de el juramento que fecho tiene y que en ello se afirma y ratifica; dijo ser de edad de treinta y ocho años poco mas o menos y lo firmo con migo y los testigos infrascriptos de mi asistenzia actuando ante mi por Receptoria a falta de Escribano Publico y Real que no lo ai en este Reino.

       Diego Arias de Quiros (rubric)
       Joachin Sanchez (rubric)
   Juan Manuel Chirinos (rubric) Juan Joseph Lovato (rubric)

Declarazion de
Francisco Belasques
En esta Capital Villa de Santa Fee, Capital de este Reino dela Nueva Mexico en seis dias de el mes de Diciembre de mill zetezientos y treynta y un años yo el Capitan Diego Arias de Quiros Theniente General de dicho Reino para proseguir en las diligencias que se siguen contra Isidro Sanchez soldado de este Real Presidio por haverle perdido el respecto al Cavo de Escuadra Lorenzo Trujillo segun consta a su declarazion que comiensa a foxa primera buelta hise parecer ante mi a Francisco Belasques soldado de dicho Real Presidio al cual estando presente le resevi juramento que hizo por Dios Nuestro Señor y la Señal de la Cruz de vajo de cullo cargo prometio decir verdad en todo lo que supiere y le fuere preguntado._____

Preguntado que si se hallo presente en el Paraje que llaman El Ojo de Juan Luxan en donde dise dicho Cavo Lorenzo Trujillo aranco el arcabuz para darle con el dicho Isidro Sanchez, diga y declare: lo que vido dijo este declarante que estando cargando su carga con dicho reo ya para salir a su viaje le dijo dicho Isidro Sanchez que le avian hurtado la polvora y que de alli fue el dicho Isidro y se lo dixo al Cavo, el qual le respondio que quien se la havia de hurtar que nunca la cargavan a lo cual le respondio dicho Isidro que por lo mismo queria que luego que salieran ala correduria les pasaran muestra y replico el dicho Cavo que ya savia que nunca la cargava y fue arrancando la espada y le tiro unos sintarasos de los cuales hullo el reo y al arancar se le yva a caer la escopeta de la funda y le corrio a cojerla y la puso en defensa de los golpes que le dava dicho Cavo quien de un sintaraso se la tumbo al suelo y que dicho declarante allo dicha escopeta y que la vido enbuelta en dos muestras yliada con un mecate fuerte y que assi que cojieron al dicho reo segunda ves comenso a tirarle otros golpes y que entonses bolvio a arrancar dicho Isidro y no lo pudieron alcansar y que desde que salieron para la correduria vido que el dicho Isidro llevava lleno el frasco de polvora; preguntado que si save o oyo decir quando el dicho reo se efugio dela Yglesia si vido o oyo decir los motivos que tuvo para salir de dicha Yglesia; dixo este declarante que fue dicho Cavo a caso de dicho Isidro Sanchez y que dicho Cavo le dixo que se saliera de la Yglesia a cumplir con su obligazion que ya a todo lo suso dicho no se sabria nada que saliera con toda seguridad y que esta es la verdad de todo lo que save y vido de vajo de el juramento que fecho tiene en que se afirmo y ratifico; dijo ser de edad de cuarenta años poco mas o menos; no firmo por no saver firmelo yo dicho Theniente General con los testigos ynfrascriptos de mi assistenzia actuando por Reseptoria por falta de Escribano Publico y Real que no lo ai en este Reino.

    Diego Arias de Quiros (rubric)
  Juan Manuel Chirinos (rubric) Juan Joseph Lovato (rubric)

Declarazion de
Geronimo de Ortega
En esta Capital y Villa de Santa Fee deste Reino dela Nueva Mexico en beinte y nuebe dias de el mes de Diciembre de mil setezientos y treinta y un años yo el Capitan Diego Arias de Quiros Theniente General de dicho Reino para la prosecuzion de esta caussa contra Isidro Sanchez soldado de este Real Presidio, hize parecer ante mi a Geronimo Ortega soldado de dicho Presidio al cual estando presente le recevi juramento que hizo por Dios Nuestro Señor y la Señal de la Santa Cruz de bajo de cuio cargo prometio de decir verdad en todo lo que supiere y le fuere preguntado que si se hallo presente en el Paraje que llaman el Ojo de Juan Luxan cuando yva el Cavo de Escuadra Lorenzo Trujillo a recorrer la tierra; Dixo este declarante que estando ensillado ya para salir de dicho Paraje oyo que el dicho Isidro Sanchez le dixo al Cavo dicho que sele havian hurtado la polvora y dicho Cavo le replico que todos los soldados yevavan suficientes municiones que quien sela havia de hurtar que no la yevaria y que respondio Isidro que el que sela havia hurtado bien podia sino la yebaba darle una poca y quedarse con la demas y que bolvio dicho Cavo a replicarle que quien sela havia de hurtar que todos heran hombres de bien y que hedad tenia el dicho Isidro Sanchez para mentir y que luego dicho Cavo subio a cavallo y le dixo dicho Isidro, Señor Cavo de Escuadra

esto que usa Uste estema y que aranco dicho Cavo la espada y fue corriendo en pos de dicho Isidro Sanchez y que despues de haver ensillado dicho declarante oyo que dixo dicho Cavo aqui del Rey y que luego algun lo monto a cavallo y vido que Francisco Belasques traia en la mano la escopeta de dicho Isidro Sanchez enbuelto en la muestra que de continuo le usa y que salieron en pos de dicho Isidro Sanchez y no lo pudieron dar alcanze y se bolvieron al Real; y haviendole preguntado otras preguntas dijo que no save nada mas de lo que lleva referido y que es la verdad so cargo de el juramento que fecho tiene en que se afirmo y ratifico, dixo ser de edad de cuarenta años no firmo por que dixo no saver firmelo yo dicho Theniente General con los testigos de mi asistenzia actuando ante mi por Reseptoria a falta de Escribano Publico y Real que no lo ai en este Reino.

    Diego Arias de Quiros (rubric)
  Juan Manuel Chirinos (rubric) Juan Joseph Lovato (rubric)

Auto

En esta Villa de Santa Fee Capital de este dicho Reino en dicho dia mes y año yo dicho Theniente General para la presecuzion de esta caussa mandava y mande que se ratifiquen los testigos que en esta caussa an declarado sitados en el auto expedido por el Señor Coronel Dn. Gervasio Cruzat y Cruzat y Gongora Governador y Capitan General de dicho Reyno por Su Magestad, assi lo provei mande y firme con los testigos de mi assistenzia actuando por Reseptoria a falta de Escribano Publico y Real que no lo ai en este Reino.

    Diego Arias de Quiros (rubric)
  Juan Manuel Chirinos (rubric) Juan Joseph Lovato (rubric)

Ratificazion de
Miguel de Rivera

En la Villa de Santa Fee en dicho dia mes y año yo dicho Theniente General en virtud de el referido auto hize parecer ante mi a Miguel de Rivera al cual estando presente le resevi juramento que hizo en forma de derecho de vajo de cullo cargo prometio de decir verdad y haviendole leido una declarazion que tiene fecha en estos autos dixo que era sulla y que en ella se afirma y ratifica y que no tiene que anadir ni que quitar mas que la que tiene fecho y es de la edad que const en su declarazion, no firmo por no saver firmelo yo dicho Theniente con los testigos de mi asistensia.

    Diego Arias de Quiros (rubric)
  Juan Manuel Chirinos (rubric) Juan Joseph Lovato (rubric)

Ratificazion de
Joseph Xaramillo
Luego yncontinenti yo dicho Theniente General hize parecer ante mi a Joseph Xaramillo al cual le resivi juramento que hizo en forma de derecho devaxo de cullo cargo prometio de dezir verdad en todo lo que supiere y le fuere preguntado y haviendole leido una declarazion que tiene fecha en estos autos, dixo que la reconose por sulla y que en ella se afirma y ratifica y que no tiene que anadir ni quitar cosa alguna mas que lo que tiene dicho que es la verdad por el juramento que fecho tiene y que es de edad que tiene dicho en su declarazion, no firmo por no saver firmelo yo dicho Theniente General con los testigos de mi asistensia.
    Diego Arias de Quiros (rubric)
  Juan Manuel Chirinos (rubric) Juan Joseph Lovato (rubric)

Ratificazion de
Joachin Sanchez
Luego yncontinenti yo dicho Capitan Diego Arias de Quiros Theniente General hize parecer ante mi a Joachin Sanchez al cual le recefi juramento que hizo en forma de derecho de vajo de cullo cargo prometio dezir verdad en todo lo que supiere y le fuere preguntado y haviendo leido una declarazion que tiene fecha en estos autos dixo que la reconose por sulla y que en ella se afirma y ratifica y que no tiene que anadir ni que quitar cosa alguna mas que lo que tiene dicho en su declarazion y lo firmo con migo dicho Theniente General y los testigos ynfrascriptos de mi asistensia.
    Diego Arias de Quiros (rubric)
    Joachin Sanchez (rubric)
  Juan Manuel Chirinos (rubric) Juan Joseph Lovato (rubric)

Ratificazion de
Francisco Belasques
Yncontinenti yo dicho Theniente General hize parecer ante mi a Francisco Belasques al cual le recevi juramento que hizo en forma de derecho de vajo de cullo cargo prometio de dezir verdad en todo lo que supiere y le fuere preguntado y haviendole leido una declarazion que tiene fecha en estos autos dixo que la reconose por sulla y que en ella se afirma y ratifica que no tiene que anadir ni quitar cosa alguna mas que lo que tiene dicho que es la verdad por el juramento que tiene fecho y que es de la edad que tiene dicho en su declarazion y no firmo por no saver firmelo yo dicho Theniente General con los testigos de mi asistenzia.
    Diego Arias de Quiros (rubric)
  Juan Manuel Chirinos (rubric) Juan Joseph Lovato (rubric)

Ratificazion de
Geronimo de Ortega
Luego incontinenti yo dicho Theniente General hise parecer anate mi a Geronimo de Ortega al cual le recevi juramento que hizo en forma de derecho de vajo de cuyo cargo prometio de dezir verdad en todo lo que supiere y le fuere preguntado y haviendole leido una declarazion que tiene fecha en estos autos dixo que la reconose por suya y que en ella se afirma y ratifica que no tiene que anadir ni que quitar cosa alguna mas que lo que tiene fecha y que es de la edad que tiene dicho en su declarazion, y no firmo por no saver firmelo yo dicho Theniente General y los testigos de mi asistenzia.
     Diego Arias de Quiros (rubric)
  Juan Manuel Chirinos (rubric) Juan Joseph Lovato (rubric)

Auto de
Remizion
En esta Capital Villa de Santa Fee de este Reino de la Nueva Mexico en siete dias de el mes de Henero de mill setezientos y treinta y dos años yo el Capitan Diego Arias de Quiros Theniente General de dicho Reino, digo que haviendo examinado en forma jurica los testigos sitados en el auto expedido por el Señor Coronel Dn. Gervasio Cruzat y Cruzat y Gongora Governador y Capitan General de dicho Reyno por Su Magestad para finalizar esta caussa que se ha seguido contra Isidro Sanchez la cual doi por conclusa y estar en estado de sentenzia y para su pronunciazion hacia y hize remizion a Su Señoria para que en su vista y segun los meritos de esta dicha caussa determine y disponga lo que mas bien vista le fuere que sera como siempre lo mejor, asi lo provei, mande y firme con los testigos de mi asistensia actuando por Receptoria a falta de Escribano Publico y Real.
     Diego Arias de Quiros (rubric)
  Juan Manuel Chirinos (rubric) Juan Joseph Lovato (rubric)

Sentencia
En el pleito y caussa criminal que se ha seguido contra Isidro Sanchez, soldado de la Compañia de Cavallos deste Real Presidio de la Villa de Santa Fee sobre la fuga que cometio desamparando el Real de campana y sobre la accion que hiso de tomar la escopeta contra el Cavo Lorenzo Trujillo segun expone en su declarazion y haviendose conprovado dicha fuga y examinado los motivos que para ella tubo y bisto los autos y lo demas que ver combino, hallo atento los hauctos y meritos del proceso que atendiendo a haver salido del sagrado de la Yglesia del Pueblo de la Ysleta bajo la palabra del Cavo Lorenzo Trujillo y de la prision que a padesido devia mandar y mande sele borre la plaza de soldado y se saque testimonio desta mi sentencia para que en su bista se execute. Asi lo jusgo, pronuncio y mando: y lo firme con los testigos infrascriptos de

mi assistencia a falta de Escribano Publico y Real que no lo ay en este Reino, y va en papel comun por no correr aqui el sellado.

        Dn. Gervasio Cruzat y Cruzat y Gongora (rubric)

        Gaspar Bitton (rubric) Juan Antonio de Unanue (rubric)

Pronunciazion

Dada y pronunciada fue la sentencia sobre escripto por me el Coronel Dn. Gervacio Crusat y Cruzat y Gongora Governador y Capitan General deste de la Nueva Mexico haciendo audienzia publica en mi tribunal en esta Villa de Santa Fee en dies y seis del mes de Henero de mil setesientos y treinta y dos años y lo firme con los testigos ynfrascriptos de mi asistencia a falta de Escribano Publico y Real que no lo ay en este Reino.

        Dn. Gervasio Cruzat y Cruzat y Gongora (rubric)

        Gaspar Bitton (rubric) Juan Antonio de Unanue (rubric)

Notes

1. Lorenzo Trujillo was a New Mexico native with the El Paso presidio in 1681. He is listed as selling property at Santa Cruz in 1724. In 1738 Lorenzo married Juana Maese, the marriage document stating that Lorenzo was originally from El Paso (Chávez, *Origins*: 298; NMGS, *Aquí*: 131; SANM I #1034).
2. In 1680 Sandía was the largest of the existing Tiwa Pueblos, which also included Alameda, Puaray, and Isleta. The pueblo was abandoned after the Spanish return in 1692. The residents left to live with the Hopis did not return until 1747. The pueblo served as a bulwark against the depredations of the Apaches (Kessell and Hendricks, *RCR*: 126 n19; Hackett, *Historical Documents*: 389-90).
3. [Juan]Antonio Pérez Velarde was a native of Asturias, Spain, and was in El Paso in 1725 as alguacil mayor, or sheriff, of the Holy Office of the Inquisition. By 1725, still in El Paso, he was married to Doña Juana de Valverde y Cosio, the daughter of former governor Antonio Valverde y Cosio. He was lieutenant governor of Santa Fe in 1728 (Chávez, *Origins*: 304, 308; SANM II #354).
4. The specific location of the Ojo or Paraje of Juan Luján is unknown, though this document shows that it was in the vicinity of the Sandía Mountains. It could have been named for the prerevolt settler Juan Luján, though he had land in the Taos area, being an alcalde mayor of that district, and was dead by 1663. Perhaps he or some of his relations owned land in the Río Abajo (Barrett, *Settlement*: 113, 122).
5. That is, toward the east. The Abo pueblo and mission were abandoned in the 1672–1679 period because of Indian attacks (Hackett, *Historical Documents*: 298).
6. Baltazar Abeytia was probably the son of Diego de Vectia (aka Beitia, Abeitia), who came from Zacatecas. Baltazar lived in Río Arriba around 1728. In 1741 he married Antonia Durán de Chávez, possibly the daughter of Nicolás de Chávez, and in the same year he is listed as a presidio solider. He was a brother of Paulín Abeytia (Chávez, *Origins*: 119; Christmas, *Military Records*: 54).
7. Joachín Rojas de Anaya was born in 1697, the son of Francisco de Anaya Almazán and his third wife, Felipa Sedillo Rico de Rojas. Francisco was a native New Mexican and encomendero, most of whose family was killed in 1680. He returned in 1692 and was dead by 1716. Joachín was present at the presidio muster of March 29, 1723. He married Margarita de Ortega in 1716 and Josefa Martín in 1719 (Chávez, *Origins*: 125; Christmas and Rau, "Una Lista": 52; Barrett, *Settlement*: 106, 199; Christmas and Rau, *La Cienega*: 12).
8. The mission was composed of the Tiwa Indians that left with the Spanish in 1680 and returned in 1706. In 1744 it had eighty families as well as some Hopi families (Hackett, *Historical Documents*: 377, 405).
9. That is, the church at Isleta, as mentioned above. For a discussion of the right of sanctuary, see Doc. 18.
10. See Doc. 1.
11. See Doc 10.
12. Joseph Jaramillo could be the son of Gerónimo and grandson of Cristóbal Varela Jaramillo, a native New

Mexican who served with the El Paso presidio in 1680s and returned to New Mexico by 1701 (Chávez, *Origins*: 199).

13. Chávez suggests that Joachín Sánchez is the son of Jacinto Sánchez, a native New Mexican and a short-term alcalde of Santa Cruz. Joachín was born around 1693–1695 and married Manuela Montoya in Santa Fe in 1719. Her father, Andrés Montoya, was a native New Mexican. Joachín was a survivor of the 1720 Villasur expedition (Chávez, *Origins*: 280; Thomas Chávez, *Moment*: 306; Christmas and Rau, *La Cienega*: 30, 43).
14. According to Chávez, Miguel Rivera was a son of Juan Felipe de Rivera, from Zacatecas. He was listed on the June 18, 1723, muster with all his weapons, four horses, and no stirrups (Chávez, *Origins*: 267; Christmas, *Military Records*: 50).
15. Gerónimo Ortega was in Santa Fe by 1715 and married Sebastiana González, an adopted daughter of Sebastián Gonzales Bas, an uncle of Juan Gonzalez Bas. Gerónimo is listed on the June 18, 1723, muster with all his weapons, four horses, and a macho or a male mule (Chávez, *Origins*: 189; Christmas, *Military Records*: 49).
16. *Guaje* is a gourd for carrying water.
17. The Spanish here is "*de edad tenía*," which in context probably means something like, "How old are you to be saying this?" or "You are talking like a child."
18. The Spanish is "Aquí del Rey," literally, "Here for the king."
19. This has been interpreted to mean that because he had come out of sanctuary voluntarily and had served time in prison while his case was being discussed, (September 28 to January 16, 1731) the sentence would be reduced to dismissal from the military service only (West, "Asylum": 134).

23

ALBUQUERQUE DISPUTE OVER NEW ACEQUIA; INJURIES FEARED FOR FAMILY
August 1–November 9, 1732. Source: SANM II #372.

Synopsis and editor's notes: This document is one of several cases in the Spanish Colonial archives that address disagreements over water rights. In this case, Cristóbal García wanted to dig an acequia take-out from the Río Grande with the acequia running through the property of Joseph Montaño before it got to his. There was an existing acequia nearby, but García wanted to dig another one close to Montaño's house. Montaño quibbled, citing difficult access to his fields for himself and his livestock and danger to his house and family because of the proximity of the ditch. Alcalde Juan Gonzales Bas ordered the two men to meet. After some arguing and finger-pointing, they agreed in writing that García could dig the acequia and would build a bridge over it for Montaño, with maintenance by both parties. García was not to be liable for any damages to Montaño's property. The governor, Cruzat y Góngora, added to the agreement that if there was any additional dissension, each would be fined fifty pesos.

The basis for the decision of the governor and the alcalde seems to be a determination that, if a settler wanted an additional take-out of water, then the water from that source was to be shared with the owners of the property through which it ran (see also Doc. 52). In this document, as in others, the alcalde and the governor act as arbitrators, pushing for a compromise that would benefit both parties. Note that Montaño is careful about the final determination, asking the governor for a *juridical*, or formal legal statement. This statement is provided by the governor with a list of written conditions.

Villa of Alburquerque
August 19, 1732
and I rubricated it

Alcalde mayor and war captain (rubric)

[I] Cristóbal García,[1] resident of this villa of San Francisco Xavier of Alburquerque, present myself before the Christian judgment of your honor in the best form which there is and in which I come forth and say that, I find myself below a piece of land belonging to Joseph Montaño,[2] and it being most necessary to take out an acequia for the maintenance of my family, which was denied by the said Joseph Montaño, telling me that he does not want to leave any possible damages to his sons, by my causing damages to his entrances and exits. For this reason, I petition your honor to attend to my request through which I shall receive mercy, and I swear according to my proper form not to be of any malice but for what is necessary, etc.

Cristóbal García (rubric)

It [the petition] herein contained was presented to me, and upon my review, and according to his [García's] rights, I ordered him and Joseph Montaño to get together at the home of Juan Griego[3] so that verbally they can hear his petition, and according to their individual arguments they can in justice determine what is most convenient. I thus decreed, ordered, and signed it acting as presiding judge along with my assisting witnesses in the present month of August of the year of 1732.

Juan Gonzales Bas[4] (rubric)

Witness:
Francisco Antonio Gonzales (rubric)
Ysidro Sánchez (rubric)

In this villa of San Felipe de Alburquerque on the fourth day of the month of September of 1732, I, Captain Juan Gonzales Bas, alcalde mayor and war captain of the said villa and of its jurisdiction, ordered Joseph Montaño and Cristóbal García to appear at the home of Juan Griego so that they can verbally agree to the petition presented by the said individual. Because Joseph Montaño did not want to agree to the take-out [*saca de agua*] of the acequia through his lands, I ordered that a copy of the juridical[5] proceedings be sent to the superior government [the governor] for the continuation of the arguments. For this purpose, I ordered that a copy be sent to Joseph Montaño so that he can respond to it within the three days following, so that he can answer to his rights in whichever way he wants. I thus approved, ordered, and signed it with my two assisting witnesses due to the lack of a public or royal scribe because there is none in this kingdom, on the said day, month, and year, etc.

before me as presiding judge
Juan Gonzales Bas (rubric)

Witness:
Francisco Antonio Gonzales (rubric)
Ysidro Sánchez (rubric)

[I] Joseph Montaño, resident of this Villa of San Felipe de Alburquerque, appear before your honor in the best form and manner in which I have a right and say that, having seen the document of Cristóbal García and it being my obligation to respond to it, he asking to take out an acequia through my lands, for which I gave him my permission to do so, with the agreement that I could have access to it, agreeing to help with the work to maintain it, but he did not want to agree to this. I [then] objected to it because I recognized the great damage that could be caused by the acequia, where some of my sheep, chickens, calves, or even one of my sons through an accident, could fall into the acequia and drown, since the acequia which he plans to take out is so near my home. Cristóbal García did not want to be obligated to compensate me if any of the above accidents or damages occurred. I also was to partake in the use of the said acequia by irrigating whatever it was that I planted, being obligated to assist in the cleaning of the acequia, but not to the actual taking-out of the said, all of which was to be juridically agreed to according to both parties. Under these conditions, I agreed that he could take out the acequia without any issues arising during the coming time period and without questions being asked, but agreeing to live in accord and compliance.

For all of this, I petition and ask that your honor be pleased to approve what I have asked for, as it is just that I should receive the mercy and benefit to which I swear in the proper form that this document is not done in malice, protesting the costs, but for what is necessary, etc.

José Montaño (rubric)

In this villa of San Felipe de Alburquerque on the 7th day of September, 1732, I, Captain Juan Gonzales Bas, alcalde mayor and war captain of the said villa and its jurisdiction, reviewed what was presented and contained within it, and ordered that a copy be given to Cristóbal García, resident of this villa, so that he, upon reviewing the response of Joseph Montaño, can respond to it within the time allowed by law, according to his right and in the manner that would be more convenient and favorable to him. I thus approved, ordered, and signed it with my assisting witnesses, acting as presiding judge, on the said day, month, and year, etc.

Juan Gonzales Bas (rubric)

Witness:
Joseph Gonzales Bas (rubric)
Ysidro Sánchez (rubric)

Alcalde mayor

[I] Cristóbal García, resident of the this villa of San Felipe de Alburquerque, one of its original founders, appear before your honor in the best form according to my rights and say that, upon having read the response and charges that Joseph Montaño makes against me regarding that which I have justifiably asked for, and in response to the various clauses answer as follows.

Regarding what he says about me seeing him in order to take out an acequia, I say that I, with proper respect, did ask him for permission to do so, indicating to him his right to use the said acequia and that he should benefit from its use. It is not as he says, that I had denied him the aforesaid. This is totally wrong, void, and false, and I prove it by what I stated before your honor at the house of Juan Griego on the 19th of the past August, when I told him that I would not disallow him to irrigate all of the lands which the acequia would cover. In addition, I told him that he did not need to assist in the taking-out of the acequia, but he would be obligated to assist in the cleanings which were required of the acequia, which is only right. The said Joseph Montaño is confused by saying that I denied him that right, when I was the one who brought up the issue; and not by saying that I denied him that right.

Regarding the charges in which he talks about the grave damages that can come about by me taking out the acequia, I responded that the most damage that can result is that he cannot make use of his lands by not consenting to its taking-out. It is not good to disallow this, as it is seen that others have taken out acequias through other person's lands, and there have not ever been any impediments, as I can offer evidence to prove this. As far as the charges regarding the calves, sheep, and chickens, which can be drowned, I say that the said Joseph Montaño is to give me the evidence that a chicken, sheep, or calf was drowned, leaving the said in the water, and to let me see how it was drowned (because due to his malice he will state that it so happened, in order to avoid my taking out the acequia), at which time I will judiciously pay him whatever he seeks for these and the other grave damages which occurred, excepting those which could happen to his children, as I do not know what they would be worth and thus would be left up to his mercy, if he can place a value on them. As such, I hope that he does not lose any children by being drowned. But why, I ask, should I be obligated to pay him for such, when others are not obligated to do so, as I have stated, when others have taken out acequias in other person's lands and neither they nor the owners are charged for anything. It is up to each one to care for what they have, hoping to avoid accidents, as nothing which they own is immortal.

This, señor alcalde, is what I have to respond, and as I have stated, I obligate myself (if it is consented by the said Joseph Montaño) to allow him to irrigate from the said acequia, assisting in the cleanings, but not in the taking-out, and not to have to pay him any damages as he asks. For all of this, I ask and petition your honor to do as I have asked, which is all within reason, and I swear in my proper form that it is not done in malice, but only to maintain, with much desire, my family which is large, protesting the charges, but for what is necessary, etc.
Cristóbal García (rubric)

In this villa of San Felipe de Alburquerque on the 20th of September of 1732, I, Captain Juan Gonzales Bas, alcalde mayor and war captain of the said villa and its jurisdiction, reviewed that which was contained in what was presented and argued, and I ordered that a copy be given to Joseph Montaño, resident of the said villa, so that upon him seeing the response and the charges made by Cristóbal García, he can within three days respond to that which is convenient and in his favor. I thus approved, ordered, and signed it, acting as presiding judge with my two assisting witnesses due to the lack of a public or royal scribe, which there is none in this kingdom, on the said day, month, and year, etc.

Juan Gonzales Bas (rubric)

Witness:
Joseph Gonzales Bas (rubric)
Ysidro Sánchez (rubric)

Alcalde mayor and war captain

[I] Joseph Montaño, resident of this villa of San Felipe de Alburquerque, one of its original founders, appear before your honor in the best form which I have through my right and say that upon having seen the response of Cristóbal García say, first of all, that I am not confused in what I have stated, as the first time that he went to see me in order to take out the said acequia, he did not allow what I was planning to do with it. As from the very beginning, he agreed with my having conceded to it being taken out, but because he had denied me the use, I did not consent. If he had not denied me the use, I would have consented to having him take it out. But as he had denied me the use, as he had, I did not consent. Then later at the home of Juan Griego he agreed for me to have access to the acequia and would not agree to what he stated in the presence of the said Juan Griego, adding that in the coming summer he and his sons would do the work required for the said acequia. But I was not very confident in what was said.

Secondly, upon being assured by the said Cristóbal García that from this time on they [we?] would live in agreement and accord with the said acequia, I allowed it to be taken out. In regard to what he states, that I maliciously was apt to put in the water anything that died, saying that it had drowned, afterwards charging him for what had died, I do not have such a bad conscience that I could do such a thing. As is already seen, as through his heart he accuses mine, particularly through the example of the acequias as stated, he already has another acequia which runs through my lands and to which I did not deny him the right. It should be noted that the one which he wants to take out is very close to my home, thus the reason for the damages to be considered. There are other reasons which I have not to allow him to take out the acequia, one being that his son has had a disagreement with Juan Griego.

For the above reasons, I have been reluctant to allow him the right to take out the acequia, but if we can live agreeably and conform, sharing equally from the acequia, I will allow him to do so, juridically allowing him permission. As such, I ask and petition your honor to approve it as agreed, and I swear that this, my petition, is not done in malice but for what is necessary, etc.

Joseph Montaño (rubric)

In this villa of San Felipe of Alburquerque on the 30th of September, 1732, I, Captain Juan Gonzales Bas, alcalde mayor and war captain of the said puesto[6] and its jurisdiction, say that I took it as it was presented and in the manner that it was argued in their rights, and sent a copy to Cristóbal García so that he can respond to the charges which are made by the said Joseph Montaño in this said document, compelling him to complete his argument, so that upon it being finalized, I can submit it to the superior government, or to sentence the case as required. I thus approved, ordered, and signed it acting as presiding judge with my two assisting witnesses due to the lack of a public or royal scribe, which there is none in these parts, on this said day, month, and year, etc.

     Juan Gonzales Bas (rubric)

Witness:
Bernardo Vallejo (rubric)
Ysidro Sánchez (rubric)

Alcalde mayor and war captain

[I] Cristóbal García, resident and founder of this said villa of San Felipe de Alburquerque, appear before the Christian and upright judgment of our majesty in the best and most proper form with which I come forth. And [I] say, that understanding everything, *verbo ad verbum* [word for word], that was spoken against me by Joseph Montaño, and not being charged with everything as was stated, I see that in the third point or clause, he allows me full power to proceed and begin the work of taking out the acequia, applying what the law orders that no one can do anything without the consent of the owner, which I have, as he has given me the permission to proceed with the work.

Your honor can proceed to make final the argument as is consented to by José Montaño in his response and to prepare a juridical sentence as is asked for by the said; and I will agree to it as he asks (as long as he does not put a stop to the permission). I will obligate myself to do the work of taking out the acequia, and will not require him to assist in any way. I will also take it upon myself to build a bridge so that his animals can go across it. This is not done by any obligation or custom, but only to live in agreement and conform and to avoid problems. I also obligate myself to the cleaning with his assistance, as he is a participant in the acequia, which obligation should be noted down juridically as the said wishes and as justice requires and is promised with full rigor to fulfill. For all of this, I ask and petition your honor to do as I ask so that everything is done right. I swear in my proper form that it is not done in malice but for what is necessary, etc.

     Cristóbal García (rubric)

Order of remission

In this villa of San Felipe de Alburquerque on the 9th of November, 1732, I, Captain Juan Gonzales Bas, alcalde mayor and war captain of the said villa and its jurisdiction, upon seeing the request of Cristóbal García and the oppositions of Joseph Montaño, both residents of this villa and settlers of this kingdom, and the conclusions of both of their arguments being placed in the act of sentencing, with Joseph Montaño consenting to allow the said Cristóbal García to take out the said acequia, with the stipulation that Cristóbal García does not accept the damages, which could result from any accident that could be caused to Joseph Montaño, I submit the proceedings to the superior government, so that upon that review, the proper judgment will be made. I thus approved, ordered, and signed it, acting as presiding judge with my two assisting witnesses due to the lack of a public or royal scribe, there being none in these parts, on the said day, month, and year, etc.

Juan Gonzales Bas (rubric)

Witness:
Joseph Gonzales Bas (rubric)
Ysidro Sánchez (rubric)

In this villa of Santa Fe, on the 12th of November, 1732, I, Colonel don Gervasio Cruzat y Góngora, governor and captain general of this kingdom of New Mexico and of its provinces, say that Captain Juan Gonzales Bas, alcalde mayor of the villa of Alburquerque and of its jurisdiction, has submitted to me the proceedings which he has completed in the case of Cristóbal García, resident of the said villa, against Joseph Montaño, also a resident of the same villa, requesting to take out an acequia through the lands of the said Joseph Montaño so that he can benefit from the irrigation of his lands. After going through a number of delays and opposition on the part of Joseph Montaño, he finally, after careful consideration, voluntarily consented to allow the said Cristóbal García to take out the acequia which he requested under the condition that they remain in agreement and comply equally by sharing the said acequia.

He [Montaño] also desires a juridical agreement for the purpose of complying with certain conditions, for which reason and for the conclusion of these proceedings, I declare the following: that the said Cristóbal García is to take out the said acequia at his expense as agreed to by both parties and is also to build the bridge which he offers in his document, and as such both Cristóbal García and the mentioned Joseph Montaño are to benefit from the use of the said acequia. Both parties are in agreement to clean out the acequia without any dissensions or problems, with the proviso that whoever might cause a problem I will fine them in the sum of fifty pesos in reales, of which one-half will be immediately applied to the royal treasury of his majesty and the rest to the expenses of the judge. As to that which reflects upon the said Cristóbal García and his obligation of paying the damages which said acequia could cause to the stated Joseph Montaño, I declare and state that he is not obligated to pay them, as they are considered remote accidents that as such are not considered by executive justice.

  I thus determined, declared, and signed it with my assisting witnesses due to the lack of a public or royal scribe, which there is none in this kingdom. Santa Fe, November 12, 1732.

        Don Gervasio Cruzat y Góngora (rubric)

Gaspar Bitton (rubric)
Juan Antonio Unanue (rubric)

ORIGINAL DOCUMENT

Villa de Alburquerque
Agosto 19 de 1732
Y lo rubrique.

Señor Alcalde Mayor y Capitan Aguerra

Xptobal Garcia vesino de esta Villa de San Francisco Xavier de Alburquerque paresco ante la Xptiana justificacion de Vmd. en la mejor forma que aya lugar y al mio combengo y digo que allandome de bajo del sitio de Joseph Montaño y ser muy necesario abrir una acequia para el mantenimiento de mi familia la qual me enbarasa dicho Joseph Montaño, disiendome que no quiere dejarla perjuicio a sus hijos siendo hasi que yo no le embarasare sus entradas ni salidas; por tanto a Vmd. pido y suplico se sirva de atender mi peticion en que resiviere merced y juro en devida forma no ser de malicia y en lo nesesario, ut supra.

        Xptobal Garcia (rubric)

La presento el contenido en ella y por mi bista la ube por presentada y en quanto a lugar y derecho mando al contenido en ella y a Joseph Montaño se allen juntos en la casa de Juan Griego para berbalmente oyer su pedimento y segun su alegata de cada parte determinar en justicia lo mas combeniente asi lo decrete, mande y firme autuando como Jues Receptor con dos testigos de mi asistencia en el presente mes de Agosto del año de mil setecientos y treynta y dos.

        Juan Gonzales Bas (rubric)

testigo testigo
Francisco Antonio Gonzales (rubric) Ysidro Sanchez (rubric)

En esta Villa de San Phelipe de Alburquerque en quatro dias del mes de Septiembre de mil setesientos y treynta y dos yo el Capitan Juan Gonzales Bas Alcalde Mayor y Capitan Aguerra de dicha Villa y su jurisdiccion, por cuanto mande compariesen en la casa de Juan Griego, Joseph Montaño y Xptobal Garcia para que verbalmente se conformaran al pedimento de esta suso dicha parte; y no abiendose querido conformar Joseph Montaño ala saca del sequia por sus tierras mando coran traslados juridicos de una parte y otra para que sigan su alegata aser remicion al Superior Govierno; por lo qual devo mandar y mando se de traslado ala parte de dicho Joseph Montaño para que responda en tiempo de tres dias perentorios que dispone el derecho lo que mas le combenga, asi lo provey, mande, firme con dos testigos de mi asistencia a falta de escribano publico y real que no lo ay en este Reyno, en dicho dia, mes y año, ut supra.

    Ante mi como Jues Receptor
    Juan Gonzales Bas (rubric)

testigo testigo
Francisco Antonio Gonzales (rubric) Ysidro Sanchez (rubric)

Joseph Montaño besino de esta Villa de San Felipe de Alburquerque paresco ante Vm. en la mejor bia y forma que ayga lugar en derecho y al mio combengo y digo que abiendo bisto el escrito de Xptobal Garcia y asiendo mi cargo de su contesta digo que abiendome bisto el dicho Xptobal Garcia para el efecto de sacar la sequia por mis tierras le consedi que la sacara con tal de tener probecho de la dicha sequia y el dando con mi trabajo a su mantension a esto no se quiso conformar el dicho y conosiendo yo el grabe dano que en ella se me sige pues pueden en la dicha sequia aogarse algunos boregos, gallinas o beseros que por asidente pueden caer en la dicha sequia o irva hijo mio pues tan inmediata a mi casa pretende sacarla y asi digo que no lo obligándose jurídicamente el dicho Xptobal Garcia a pagarme todos los atrasos, danos y bejasiones que se me siguieren en lo adelante obtener yo parte en la dicha sequia y sembrar de bajo de ella lo que me paresiere obligandomen ayudar en las limpias menos en sacarla y esta obligacion se aga jurídica asi de su parte como de la mia y con estas condisiones le consedo con que la saque sin que en el tiempo benidero se nos ofrezcan questiones sino es vivir animes y conformes; y por tanto a Vm. pido y suplico se sirba de probier como yo boi pedido pues es justicia en que resibire bien y merced y juro en debida forma este mi escrito no es de malasia protesto costas y lo necesario, ut supra.

    Jose Montaño (rubric)

En esta Villa de San Phelipe de Alburquerque in siete dias del mes de Septiembre de el año de mil setesientos y treynta y dos yo el Capitan Juan Gonzales Bas Alcalde Mayor y Capitan Aguerra de dicha Villa y su jurisdiccion la presento el contenido en ella y por mi bista, mando sele de traslado a Xptobal Garcia vesino de esta dicha Villa para que bista la respuesta de Joseph Montaño, responda en el tiempo de la ley del derecho lo que fuere mas combeniente a su fabor, hasi lo provey, mande y firme con los testigos de mi asistencia, autuando como Jues Receptor en dicho dia, mes y año, ut supra.

    Juan Gonzales Bas (rubric)

Señor Alcalde Mayor

Xptobal Garcia vesino de esta Villa de San Phelipe de Alburquerque y uno de sus originarios fundadores de ella paresco ante Vmd. en la mejor forma que a luger en derecho y digo; que abiendo leydo la respuesta y cargos que Joseph Montaño me ase sobre lo que tengo pedido justamente y asiendome cargo de todas sus claseulos, digo, que por lo que dise aberlo bisto para la saca de la asequia digo quien perefue pidiendole lisencia para ello pero obligandome a que participara de la dicha acequia y que gosara de ellas como proprios; no como el dicho dise que le ynpedi dicho fuero, que eso es ylito, nulo y falso y lo pruebo con aberselo dicho ante Vmd. en casa de Juan Griego el dia dies y nuebe del pasado mes de Agosto, que le dije que yo no le ynpedia el que regase todo lo que banase de sus tierras la dicha asequia y mas que no alludara ala saca de ella, si obligado alas limpias que se ofresieran en dicha asequia, con que es ligitima consequencia el que se cumplica el dicho Joseph Montaño diciendo que yo selo ympedi quando quando yo fui el que le saque el partido, y no que dise que no selo consenti; al cargo que dise del grave dano que sele sigue con que saque la dicha asequia digo; que el mas dano que sele ase es el que venga en parte de sus tierras y que no quiera consentirlo, no por que ami besino sele ase otro, fuere de que no es exemplar el que lo ympidan pues esta visto que otros an sacado asequias por tierras ajenas y no an tenido ningun ympedimento como ofresco ynformacion en su lugar, por lo que mira al cargo de los beserros, borregos y gallinas que sele pueden aogar digo; que el dicho Joseph Montaño es el que me a de dar el seguro primero de que muriendosele una gallina, borrego o besero de otro asidente las deje en la agua y me la trayga con que se aogo (porque de su malicia se espresa lo aga onde no me permite sacar dicha asequia) y entonses selo dare yo juridicamente como lo pide de pagarselos esos y otros graves danos que sele ofrescan, menos el de sus hijos por que esos yo no se lo que balen y su mersed si, pues les puede poner el presio, y dado y no consedido que no sele aogen hijos y lo que lleba dicho porque de estar yo obligado apagarselo quando otros no estan obligados a ello siendo como llebo dicho aber exemplar de asequias por tierras ajenas y estos ni los duenos de dichas asequias pagan los danos ni los danos de las tierras les cobran sino que cada uno cuida lo que tiene como propio sin esperar asidentes para haser ynmortal lo que tienen, esto es Señor Alcalde lo que tengo que responder y como llebo dicho me obligo (consintiendo el dicho Joseph Montaño) a que riege por dicha asequia y que me allude alas limpias menos ala saca y no a pagarle los danos como pide, por tanto, a Vmd. pido y suplico aga como llevo pedido que es rason y juro en debida forma no ser de malicia sino por mantener con mas desoyo mi familia que es larga portesto costas y en lo nesesario, ut supra.

Xptobal Garcia (rubric)

En esta Villa de San Phelipe de Alburquerque en beynte dias del mes de Septiembre de mill setesientos y treynta y dos yo el Capitan Juan Gonzales Bas Alcalde Mayor y Capitan Aguerra de dicha Villa y su jurisdiccion, la presento el contenido en ella y por mi bista la ube por presentada y en quanto alegar en derecho devo mandar y mande se le de traslado a Joseph Montaño vesino de dicha Villa para que vista la respuesta y cargos que le ase Xptobal Garcia, responda en el tiempo de tres dias que el derecho le consede lo que mas combeniente le fuere a su fabor; asi lo provey, mande y firme autuando como Jues Reseptor con dos testigos de mi asistencia a falta de escribano Publico y Real que no lo ay en este Reyno en dicho dia, mes y año, ut supra.
     Juan Gonzales Bas (rubric)
testigo testigo
Joseph Gonzales Bas (rubric) Ysidro Sanchez (rubric)

Alcalde Mayor y Capitan Aguerra

Joseph Montaño vesino de esta Villa de San Phelipe de Alburquerque uno de sus primeros fundadores paresco ante Vm. en la mejor bia y forma que aiga en derecho y al mio combenga y digo que abiendo onve la respuesta de Xptobal Garcia digo lo primero que no me conplico en lo que tengo dicho pues la primer bes que me fue a necesario para sacar la dicha sequia me negó lo ausion ausion que yo pretendia tener en ella si desde luego se ubiera conformado le ubiera concedido con que la sacara y por aberse negado el me nego y que después en casa de Juan Griego se conformo a que necesario yo parte en la asequia desconfie de su palabra presumiendo que quien no ser conformado con la sequia en coompania de Juan Griego tiene aunque no el sino sus hijos pues este berano hisieran trabajo cuenta sobre la dicha asequia y este motibo me ase desconfiar y digo lo segundo que asegurandome el dicho Xptobal Garcia que en lo adelante no tendremos desinsion si no es que posemos unanimes y conformes de la dicha sequia le consedo con que la saquen cuanto a lo que dice que malisiosamente pudiera yo mojar en el agua lo que seme muriera y después irselo a cobrar a el no coresponden mis obligaciones a las suyas para que yo y si era semejante cosa pues no tengo tan mala consiencia que tal abia de aser pues esta visto que por su corazón jusga el mio mayormente pues en el ejemplar de las acequias que dice tambien el dicho tiene sacada otra sequia por mis tierras y no sele inpedi y conocer que la quiere sacar tan inmediata a mi casa y conosiendo los danos que yebo expresados, que se me pueden seguir es el motibo que tenia yo para inpedirselo y los sin sabores que a tenido el dicho su hijo con Juan Griego y esos son los motibios que he tenido para inpedirselo y asi buelbo a desir que le consedo con que la saque con tal que menos de necesario onvenga y conformes gosando ygualmente la asequia y que esta conformidad conste juridicamente, y por tanto a Vm. pido y suplico se sirba de prober lo que mas convenga y juro en debida forma este mi escrito no es de malisia y en lo necesario, ut supra.
     Joseph Montaño (rubric)

En esta Villa de San Phelipe de Alburquerque en treynta de Septiembre de mill setecientos y treynta y dos años yo el Capitan Juan Gonzales Bas, Alcalde Mayor y Capitan Aguerra de dicho Puesto y su jurisdiccion, digo que la ube por presentada y en quanto alegar en derecho devo mandar y mando sele de traslado a Xptobal Garcia para que responda a los cargos que dicho Joseph Montaño le ase en este sobre dicho escrito y le conpelo a que la parte sea llana para que con la respuesta y en lo que mas combenga se abiniere aser remision al Superior Gobierno o sentenciar loque mas al caso se requiere asi lo probey, mande y firme actuando como Jues Receptor con dos testigos de mi asistencia a falta de escribano publico y real que no lo ay en estas partes en dicho dia, mes y año, ut supra.

      Juan Gonzales Bas (rubric)

testigo testigo
Bernardo Vallejo (rubric) Ysidro Sanchez (rubric)

     Señor Alcalde Mayor y Capitan Aguerra

Xptobal Garcia vecino y fundador de esta Villa de San Felipe de Alburquerque paresco ante la Xptiana y recta justificacion de Vmd. en la mejor via y forma que ala parte de derecho y ami combenga y digo: que abiendome enterado de verbo adverbum delo que responde contra mi Joseph Montaño y no siendome a cargo delo que me dijo en ella pues beo el por tres punto o clausula en que me consede plena y bastante facultad para que ponga por obra la saca dela asequia y asta garandome dela ley que ordena que ninguno pone la cosa sin voluntad de su dueño tengo por mia pues como lleba dicho me concede licencia para cullo efecto y poder obrarse a de servir Vmd. de sentenciar como el dicho Jose Montaño promete en su escrito presente ala conposision jurídica que dicho pide y yo me abengo se aga que en todo sera como pide (no poniendo reparo en la licencia) pues yo me obligo con mi trabajo a sacarla y que el dicho no ponga mano para ello como tambien a poner puente en el paso de su ganado y esto no por obligacion ni costumbre sino por vivir unanimes y conformes y bensar disturbias; como tambien me obligo alas limpias allundando el dicho como partisipante en la dicha asequia, y esta obligacion la consedo jurídicamente como el dicho la pide y que la justicia me compela y apromise con todo rigo al cumplimiento por todo lo cual a Vmd. pido y suplico se sirva de aser como pido que en ello resevire bien y juro en debida forma y no ser de malicia y en lo nesasario, ut supra.

      Xptobal Garcia (rubric)

Auto de remicion

En esta Villa de San Phelipe de Alburquerque en nuebe dias del mes de Nobiembre de mil setesientos y treynta y dos años yo el Capitan Juan Gonzales Bas Alcalde Mayor y Capitan Aguerra de dicha Villa y su jurisdiccion en bista del pedimento de Xptobal Garcia y contradicion de Joseph Montaño vesinos de esta Villa y pobladores deste Reyno conclusas sus alegatas de una parte y otra y puestos en estado de sentencia conformandose Joseph Montaño ala saca de la dicha asequia y dicho Xptobal Garcia no aseta alos danos que le puede asidental causar a Joseph Montaño por lo cual ago remision al Superior Gobierno para que en vista de los auctos ariba espresos sentencie lo mas combeniente, asi lo provey mande y firme auctuando como Jues Receptor con dos testigos de mi asistencia a falta de escribano publico y real que no lo ay en eastas partes, en dicho dia, mes y año, ut supra.
      Juan Gonzales Bas (rubric)
testigo testigo
Joseph Gonzales Bas (rubric) Ysidro Sanchez (rubric)

En la Villa de Santa Fee en dose dias del mes de 9bre (Noviembre) del mil setecientos treinta y dos años yo el Coronel don Gervasio Cruzat y Gongora Governador y Capitan General de este Reyno dela Nueva Mexico y sus Provincias digo que por quanto el Capitan Juan Gonzales Bas, Alcalde Mayor de la jurisdiccion y Villa de Alburquerque me ha hecho remision de estos havidos que ha seguido por instancia de Xptobal Garcia vecino de dicha Villa ha presentado contra Joseph Montaño vesino tambien de la misma Villa solisitando abrir zequia por las tierras de dicho Joseph Montaño para lograr el beneficio del riego para las suias; y despues de haver prosedido algunos reparos de embaraso y oposision de parte del referido Joseph Montaño viene ultimamente de su grado y voluntad a conseder a dicho Xptobal Garcia zaque la asequia que solisita con la condision que aga de hacer unanimes y conformes gosando ygualmente de la expresada asequia; y que desea conformidad conste juridicamente para la seguridad de esta su condision que por todo lo qual y por lo que ministra los hautos devia desir y declarar como digo y declaro que dicho Xptobal Garcia aura la dicha zequia a sus expensas y no el para que en que estan combenidos ambas partes y ponga el puente que ofrese en su escripto, y gosar asi dicho Xptobal Garcia como el mensionado Joseph Montaño del beneficio de dicha asequia concoriendo una y otra parte a limpiarla sin que aya disensiones ni disturbios con y porsivimiento de que al que les causare le multe en la canatidad de sinquenta pesos en reales los que desde luego aplico por mitad para la Real Camara de Su Magestad y gastos de justicia y por lo que mira a que dicho Xptobal Garcia este ala obligacion de repartir los danos que por rason de dicha zequia podrian sobrevenir al expresado Joseph Montaño devia declarar y declaro no estar obligado a ellos asi por sere acsidentes remotos como por no reconoserse al presente por juisio executivo asi lo determine, declare y firme con los testigos de mi asistencia a falta de escribano publico y real que no lo ay en este Reyno. Santa Fee, y 9bre (Noviembre) 12 de 1732.

      Dn. Gervasio Cruzate y Gongora (rubric)
      Juan Antonio Unanue (rubric)
      Gaspar Bitton (rubric)

Notes

1. See Doc. 5. There was also a Cristóbal García II, though he was born in 1703, making it unlikely that he was a first founder as this Cristóbal García claims to be. In 1733 a Cristóbal García was once again part of a complaint when two Albuquerque residents, Felipe Gallegos and Antonio Gurulé, charged him with opening an acequia and conducting it through their lands (SANM II #379). In 1737 Cristóbal García and Diego García were accused of assaulting a certain Juan Montaño (who may have been José Montaño's twin), but they were acquitted (SANM II #416).
2. This José Montaño is likely to be the person whose mother-in-law had been the wife of Tomás García. According to Chávez, this José Montaño was twenty years old in Santa Fe in 1695, when he married María de Cuellar. He then went to live in the Río Abajo area, where he later wounded a man. In 1750 he was fined for trespassing on Indian land at Alameda Pueblo. Chávez suggests he may have been the José Montaño who died a *muerte violente* in 1756 (SANM II #215; Chávez, *Origins*: 234).
3. This is probably the Juan Griego listed in the El Paso muster of 1692–1693 and who was named in a 1718 Albuquerque document regarding lands for which he had a 1708 deed. His wife was Juliana Saiz. Juan was also listed in a presidio document of 1713, when he was replaced because he could no longer serve. He is possibly a descendant of the Juan Griego and Pascuala Bernal who owned land on the Río del Norte south of Bernalillo before the revolt (Kessell and Hendricks, *RCR*: 90 n77; SANM I #716; Barrett, *Settlement*: 137, 176, 212).
4. See Doc. 21.
5. This term appears to mean that the proceedings were as set forth in the law.
6. This seems an odd word to use, given that Albuquerque was a chartered villa and a puesto was an outpost. Albuquerque was spread along the river, much of it not included in a compact urban area, and the place of the argument may have had the appearance of an outpost.

24

SOLDIER WOUNDED WHEN BULLET FROM PRESIDIO SALVO RICOCHETS OFF CEMETERY MONUMENT
September 9–11, 1732. Source: SANM II #375.

Synopsis and editor's notes: When a bullet from a presidio salvo hit Juan de Santistevan in the face while he was sitting near a stone cross in a Santa Fe cemetery, the four soldiers involved claimed it ricocheted off the cross. Nevertheless, Governor Cruzat y Góngora, known for being careful about procedures, carried out an investigation. Perhaps he wondered why, if the soldiers were shooting a salvo, presumably into the air, a bullet would hit a monument not far off the ground. He appears to be looking for some grievance against Santistevan, though none was found in the testimony. The location of the cemetery is not specified, but in an earlier document (Doc. 20), translated above, it is noted that in June of 1727, the presidio company performed their royal salvos at the cemetery adjacent to the parochial church where the cathedral is now located.

Year of 1732

Criminal case against Pedro Guillen,[1] Cayetano Tenorio,[2] Cristóbal Luján,[3] and Andrés Trujillo,[4] soldiers of the royal presidio, for the wounding of Juan de Santistevan[5] at the time that they fired their arquebuses during the salvo, which they made in honor of the Nativity of Our Lady.[6]

In the villa of Santa Fe on the 9th day of the month of September of the year 1732, I, Colonel don Gervasio Cruzat y Góngora, governor and captain general of this kingdom of New Mexico and their provinces, say that I have been informed that Juan de Santistevan, a soldier in the company of this royal presidio, was wounded when a salute was fired on the afternoon of the 7th day of this month during the celebration of the vespers which were sung in the parish church of this said villa in honor of the Nativity of the Blessed Mary, Our Lady. For this reason, I have ordered Captain Antonio de Urribarí,[7] alcalde mayor of this villa, to make the required investigation in order to find out and determine how the wounding occurred, and to take the necessary declarations from Pedro Guillen, Cayetano Tenorio, Cristóbal Luján, and

Andrés Trujillo, all soldiers of the said company of this presidio and who were the ones who fired the salvo at that time. The master barber, Antonio Durán de Armijo,[8] was ordered to appear in order to get his opinion according to the knowledge which he has, determining what caused the wound. I thus ordered this to be done, and I signed it with my assisting witnesses due to the lack of a public or royal scribe, which there are none in this kingdom.

      don Gervasio Cruzat y Góngora (rubric)
      Gaspar Bitton (rubric)
      Juan Antonio de Unanue (rubric)

Order

In the villa of Santa Fe on the 9th day of the month of September of 1732, I, Captain Antonio de Urribarí, alcalde mayor and war captain of this said villa, in order to fulfill the order given to me by Colonel Gervasio Cruzat y Góngora, governor and captain general of this kingdom of New Mexico, made to appear before me the master barber, Antonio Durán de Armijo, so that he, in a sworn statement, can give his expert opinion, according to his knowledge, as to the type of wound that Juan de Santistevan has incurred. I thus ordered, approved, and signed this with my assisting witnesses due to the lack of a public and royal scribe.

      Antonio de Urribarí (rubric)
      Felipe Tamaris (rubric)
      Dimas Girón (rubric)

Statement of Antonio Durán de Armijo

In this villa of Santa Fe on the said day, month, and year, before me, Captain Antonio de Urribarí, alcalde mayor of this said villa, appeared the master barber, Antonio Durán de Armijo, from whom I received his sworn statement which he made before God and the sign of the Cross in which he promised to say the truth as to what he knew, and was asked if he knew that Juan de Santistevan was hurt. He answered that he did know that Juan de Santistevan was hurt from a wound which he has in his face from a bullet, which he says was the cause of the wound. He was asked if he knew how the wound came about. He answered that according to what he can see, and according to what he knows, the bullet ricocheted from somewhere. This was his answer according to his sworn statement which he made, and he affirmed and ratified it as his statement was read back to him, and thus he signed it along with me and my assisting witnesses due to the lack of a public and royal scribe.

      Antonio de Urribarí (rubric)
      Dimas Girón (rubric)
      Antonio Durán de Armijo (rubric)
      Felipe Tamaris (rubric)

[Statement of Juan de Santistevan]

In the villa of Santa Fe on the 10th day of the month of September of 1732, I, Captain Antonio de Urribarí, alcalde mayor of this said villa, accompanied by my assisting witnesses, proceeded to the house and dwelling [*casa y morada*] of Juan de Santistevan and, being in his presence, received his sworn statement which he gave to God, Our Lord, and the sign of the Cross, under which he promised to tell the truth in whatever he was asked.

He was asked what type of accident or what type of hurt he has. He answered that he has a bullet wound. On the 20th of this present month, in the afternoon at the time of the vespers, he found himself seated next to the cemetery cross when the salvo was made, but he did not see who it could have been who fired the bullet because everyone fired at the same time; that he felt the hit, but could not tell where it came from. He was asked if he had any arguments or disagreements with any of the ones who fired the shots. He answered that he did not have any disagreements, or problems, or bad feelings with any of them at any time. This he said is the truth regarding his sworn statement which he has made, and affirmed it and ratified it. He did not sign because he did not know how. I, the said alcalde mayor, signed it along with my assisting witnesses due to the lack of a public or royal scribe.

     Antonio de Urribarí (rubric)
     Felipe Tamaris (rubric)
     Dimas Girón (rubric)

Order

In the villa of Santa Fe on the 10th day of the month of September, 1732, I, Captain Antonio de Urribarí, alcalde mayor and war captain of this said villa, in fulfillment of the order of the Colonel don Gervasio Crusat y Góngora, governor and captain general of this kingdom, proceeded to the royal guard house of this castellan presidio, along with my assisting witnesses, where I found Pedro Guillen, Andrés Trujillo, Cristóbal Luján, and Cayetano Tenorio, all soldiers of this royal presidio, in jail [*zepo*],[9] and from whom I begin to take their sworn statements. So that it is valid, I signed it with my assisting witnesses due to the lack of a public or royal scribe, which there are none in this kingdom.

     Antonio de Urribarí (rubric)
     Felipe Tamaris (rubric)
     Dimas Girón (rubric)

Statement of Pedro Guillen

In the villa of Santa Fe on the said day, month, and year, I, the said alcalde mayor, in fulfillment of the order, made appear before me and my assisting witnesses Pedro Guillen, soldier of this royal presidio, and upon being present received his sworn statement which he made to God, Our Lord, and to the sign of the Cross, under which he swore to tell the truth in what knew and the reason for finding himself a prisoner.

He answered that on the 7th of the present month he was ordered to give the salvo at the vespers of Our Lady, and that at the time that the salute was fired by Cristóbal Luján, Cayetano Tenorio, and Andrés Trujillo. Francisco Mascareñas[10] was also to have fired, but he had forgotten his arquebus, so that he, Guillen, fired his weapon instead, pointing the barrel of his arquebus towards the road that goes to Galisteo,[11] as was seen by Sergeant Antonio Tafoya and corporal of the squadron, Cayetano Lobato. He was asked if he knew who had fired towards where Juan de Santistevan was seated. He answered that he had not seen anything. This is all he knows regarding the sworn statement which he has made, and he affirmed it and ratified it. He did not sign because he did not know how; I, the alcalde mayor, signed it with my assisting witnesses due to the lack of a public and royal scribe, which there is none in this kingdom.

Antonio de Urribarí (rubric)
Felipe Tamaris (rubric)
Dimas Girón (rubric)

Statement of Cristóbal Luján

In the villa of Santa Fe on the said day, month, and year before me, Antonio de Urribarí, alcalde mayor of this said villa, made appear before me Cristóbal Luján, soldier in this royal presidio from whom, upon being present, I received his sworn statement which he made to God, Our Lord, and to the sign of the Cross, under which he promised to tell the truth in what he knew and he was asked if he knew why he was a prisoner.

He says that he is a prisoner because on the 7th of the present month while being at the vespers for the Nativity of Our Lady, Juan de Santistevan was hit by a bullet. He also says that while at the guard house before going to the vespers, in the presence of Sergeant Antonio Tafoya and Corporal Juan Felipe, he discharged his arquebus and then removed the two bullets which he had. He says that he knows nothing else other than that the said Juan de Santistevan had been hit by a bullet but does not know by whom. This is what he responds regarding the statement which he has made and he affirmed and ratified it. He did not sign because he did not know how. I, the alcalde mayor, signed it with my assisting witnesses due to the lack of a public or royal scribe, which there is none in this kingdom.

Antonio de Urribarí (rubric)
Felipe Tamaris (rubric)
Dimas Girón (rubric)

Statement of Andrés Trujillo

In the villa of Santa Fe on the 10th day of September, 1732, before me, Captain Antonio de Urribarí, alcalde mayor of this said villa, made appear before me Andrés Trujillo, soldier in this presidio, from whom upon being present took his sworn statement which he made to God, Our Lord, and to the sign of the Cross, under which sworn statement he promised to tell the truth in what he was asked.

He was asked if he knew the reason for being a prisoner. He answered it was because of a bullet wound that Juan de Santistevan received during the time of the vespers of the Nativity of Our Lady. He stated that he was one of the ones that fired the salute, but that he did not see who it was that fired at him [Santistevan]. This is what he stated under the oath that he has made and which he affirmed and ratified. He did not sign because he did not know how. I, the said alcalde mayor, signed it along with my assisting witnesses due to the lack of a public or royal scribe, which there are none in this kingdom.

Antonio de Urribarí (rubric)
Felipe Tamaris (rubric)
Dimas Girón (rubric)

Statement of Cayetano Tenorio

In the villa of Santa Fe on the said day, month, and year, I, Captain Antonio de Urribarí, alcalde mayor and war captain of this said villa, made appear before me Cayetano Tenorio, soldier of this presidio and from whom, upon being present, took his sworn statement which he made to God, Our Lord, and to the sign of the Cross, under which he promised to tell the truth in what he knew. He was asked if he knew the reason for being a prisoner.

He answered that the reason for being a prisoner was because he was one of the four who did the salvo during the vespers for the Nativity of Our Lady, and it was known that Juan de Santistevan had been hit by a bullet, but he does not know how or by whom the shot was fired. This is what he knows and what he declares regarding his sworn statement which he has made, and he affirmed and ratified it; he did not sign it because he did not know how. I, the alcalde mayor, signed it along with my assisting witnesses due to the lack of a public or royal scribe, which there are none in this kingdom.

Antonio de Urribarí (rubric)
Felipe Tamaris (rubric)
Dimas Girón (rubric)

Order of Remission

In the villa of Santa Fe, on the 10th day of the month of September, 1732, having terminated these proceedings as ordered by Colonel Gervasio Crusat y Góngora, governor and captain general of this kingdom for our majesty, I submit them so that upon review, your honor will determine as he decides, which is always done for the best. I thus ordered and signed it with my assisting witnesses, acting as presiding judge due to the lack of a public or royal scribe, which there is not one in this kingdom.

Antonio de Urribarí (rubric)
Felipe Tamaris (rubric)
Dimas Girón (rubric)

[Sentence]

In the villa of Santa Fe on the 11th day of September, 1732, these proceedings having been reviewed by me, Colonel don Gervasio Crusat y Góngora, governor and captain general of this kingdom of New Mexico and its provinces, it was determined that they were not guilty, and it was undecided who was to blame for the wound which Juan de Santistevan, soldier in this royal presidio, incurred. It was not done in malice, nor as a result of the salvo performed on the 7th day of the present month at the Nativity of Our Lady by the four soldiers, who are found in jail in the royal guard house. I thus order that they be released from jail, and they are to be warned that in similar functions they are not to bear their arms with bullets or anything which could cause a wound.[12] I feel that they have already been punished enough in what happened, but if this happens again, the sentence which will be imposed will be that which is prescribed according to the laws due to the gravity of the matter and its effects. I thus ordered, approved, and signed it with my assisting witnesses due to the lack of a public or royal scribe which there is none in this kingdom.

don Gervasio Cruzar y Góngora (rubric)
Gaspar Bitton (rubric)
Juan Antonio de Unanue (rubric)

ORIGINAL DOCUMENT

Año de 1732

Causa criminal contra Pedro Guillen, Caietano Thenorio, Xptobal Luxan y Andrés Truxillo, soldados de este Real Presidio sobre la herida que resivio el soldado Juan de Santistevan a tiempo que dispararon los quatro referidos en la salva que se hiso en honor de la Natividad de Nuestra Señora Villa de Santa Fee en nueve dias del mes de Septiembre de mil setecientos trienta y dos años yo el Coronel Don Gervasio Cruzat y Gongora, Governador y Capitan General de este Reyno de la Nueba Mexico y sus Provincias; digo que por quanto se me a dado parte de haver herido a Juan de Santistevan soldado dea Compania de este Real Presidio al tiempo que se executo la salva y disparo el dia siete del corriente por la tarde en solemnidad de las visperas que se cantaron en la Yglesia Parroquial de esta dicha Villa en honor y obsequio dela Natividad de Maria Santissima, Nuestra Señra; Por tanto de via mandar y mande que el Capitan Antonio de Urribari, Alcalde Mayor de esta Villa haga las diligencias que competen para saver y averiguar la forma en que se ha executado dicha herrida y tome las declaraciones combenientes a Pedro Guillen, Galetano Thenorio, Xptobal Luxan y Andres Truxillo, soldados todos de la dicha Compania Presidial, que fueron los que dispararon al tiempo que se ocasiono la referida herida de la que deve declarar el Maestro Barbero Antonio Duran de Armijo con que instrumento pudo ser causada en conformidad del reconocimiento que de dicha hiso. Asi lo probey mande y firme con los testigos de mi assistencia, a falta de escribano publico y Real que no lo ay en este Reyno.

   Don Gervasio Cruzat y Gongora (rubric)
 Gaspar Bitton (rubric) Juan Antonio de Unanue (rubric)

Auto
En la Villa de Santa Fee en nuebe dias de el mes de Septiembre de mil setesientos y treinta y dos años yo el Capitan Antonio de Urribari, Alcalde Mayor y Capitan Aguerra de dicha Villa en cumplimiento de lo mandado por el Señor Coronel Don Gerbasio Cruzat y Gongora, Gobernador y Capitan General deste Reino dela Nueba Mexico yse comparecer ante mi a el Maestro Barbero Antonio Duran de Armijo para que debajo de juramento diga y declare segun su saber y por el reconocimiento que yso de la calidad de la herida que tiene Juan de Santistevan, asi lo probei mande y firme con los testigos ynfrascriptos de mi assistencia a falta de escribano publico y Real.
   Antonio de Urribari (rubric)
    Dimas Giron (rubric)
    Phelipe Tamaris (rubric)

Declarasion de Antonio Duran de Armijo
En la Villa de Santa Fe en dicho dia mes y año yo el Capitan Antonio de Urribari Alcalde Mayor de esta dicha Villa paresio ante mi Antonio Duran de Armijo Maestro Barbero a quien estando presente le resevi juramento que yso por Dios Nuestro Señor y la señal de Cruz debajo de cuio cargo prometio de deseñor verdad en lo que supiere y fuera preguntado y siendolo a este tenor si sabe que Juan de Santistevan esta malo. Responde que si sabe que el dicho Juan de Santistevan esta malo de una erida que tiene en la cara de una bala la qual le bido este declarante salir de dicha herida. Preguntado si sabe como fue dicha herida? Responde que asu pareser y segun su conosimiento la dicha bala fue rechasada de alguna parte y esto responde so cargo de el juramento que fecho tiene en que se afirmo y ratifico siendole leida esta su declaracion y lo firmo con migo y los testigos de mi assistencia a falta de escribano publico y Real.
    Antonio de Uribarri (rubric)

Antonio Duran de Armijo (rubric)
Dimas Giron (rubric)
Phelipe Tamaris (rubric)

En la Villa de Santa Fe en dies dias del mes de Septiembre de mil setesientos y treinta y dos años yo el Capitan Antonio de Urribari Alcalde Mayor desta dicha Villa pase en compania de los testigos de mi assistencia ala casa y morada de Juan de Santisteban aquien estando presente le resivi juramento que yso por Dios Nuestro Señor y la señal de Cruz debajo de cuio cargo prometio de deseñor berdad en lo que fuera preguntado y siendole preguntado que que adzidente tiene o que enfermedad a esto responde que se alla herido de un balaso que estando el dia veinte de este presente mes en la tarde en bisperas se allaba este declarante sentado junto ala cruz del simenterio quando dispararon y que no bido quien pudiera ser quien disparo con bala porque a un tiempo dispararon todos que el golpe sintio pero que no bido por donde le bino el dano. Preguntado si abia tenido con alguno delos que dispararon algun desgusto o rasones en algun tiempo? A esto respondio que con ninguno a tenido aora ni en ningun tiempo disgusto ni plieto ni mala boluntad y que esto es la berdad so cargo del juramento que fecho tiene en que se afirmo y ratifico, no firmo por no saber, firmelo yo dicho Alcalde Mayor y los testigos de mi asistencia a falta de escribano publico y real.

Antonio de Urribari (rubric)
Dimas Giron (rubric)
Phelipe Tamaris (rubric)

Auto
En la Villa de Santa Fee en dies dias de el mes de Septiembre de mil setesientos y treinta y dos años yo el Capitan Antonio de Urribari Alcalde Mayor y Capitan Aguerra de esta dicha Villa en cumplimiento delo mandado por el Señor Coronel Don Gerbasio Crusat y Gongora, Governador y Capitan General de este Reino pase con los testigos de mi assistencia a el Real Cuerpo de Guardia de este Castillo Presidial en donde alle presente y el el sepo a Pedro Guillen, Andres Truxillo y Xptobal Luxan y Caietano Tenorio soldados de este Real a quienes les fui tomando sus declaraciones y para que conste lo firme con los testigos de mi assistencia a falta de escribano Publico y Real que no lo ai en este Reino.

Antonio de Urribari (rubric)
Dimas Giron (rubric)
Phelipe Tamaris (rubric)

Declaracion de Pedro Guillen
En la Villa de Santa Fee en dicho dia, mes y año yo dicho Alcalde Mayor en

cumplimiento de lo mandado yse pareser ante mi y los testigos de mi asistencia a Pedro Guillen soldado de este Real Presidio a quien estando presente le resevi juramento que yso por Dios Nuestro Señor y la Señal de Cruz debajo de cuio cargo prometio de deseñor berdad en lo que supiere y siendolo si sabe la causa por que esta preso. Dixo y responde, sabe que el dia siete de el corriente les mandaron disparar en las visperas de Nuestra Señora y dise este declarante que al tiempo que dispararon Xptobal Luxan, Caietano Tenorio, Andres Truxillo abia de aber disparado Francisco Mascareñas y a este le falto el alcabus y este declarante disparo su alcabus y que puso la renteria para el camino de Galisteo y que esto lo bieron el Sargento Antonio Tafoia y el Cabo de Escuadra Caietano Lobato; preguntado si bido quien disparo para donde estaba Juan de Santisteban; responde que no bido nada, esto es lo que sabe y no otra cosa so cargo del juramento que fecho tiene en que se afirmo y ratifico, no firmo por no saber, firmelo yo dicho Alcalde Maior y los testigos de mi asistencia a falta de escribano Publico y Real que no lo ai en este Reino.
      Antonio de Urribari (rubric)
      Dimas Giron (rubric)
      Phelipe Tamaris (rubric)

Declaracion de Xptobal Luxan
En la Villa de Santa Fe en dicho dia mes y año ante mi Antonio de Urribari Alcalde Maior de esta dicha Villa yse parecer ante mi a Xptobal Luxan soldado de este Real Presidio aquien estando presente le resevi juramento que yso por Dios Nuestro Señor y la señal de Cruz de bajo de cuio cargo prometio de decir verdad en lo que supiere y siendolo si sabe la causa de su prision dixo; que sabe que esta preso por que el dia siete del corriente estando en las bisperas de la Natibidad de Nuestra Señora le dieron un pelotaso a Juan de Santisteban y dise este declarante que en este Cuerpo de Guardia antes de yr a bisperas en presencia del Sargento Antonio Tafoia y el Cabo Juan Felipe descargo este declarante su alcabuz y le saco las dos balas que tenia y que no sabe mas que a el dicho Juan de Santisteban le dieron un pelotaso pero que no bido quien, esto responde so cargo de el juramento que fecho tiene en que se afirmo y ratifico no firmo por no saber firmelo yo dicho Alcalde Maior y los testigos de mi asistencia a falta de escribano publico y real que no lo ai en este Reino.
      Antonio de Uribarri (rubric)
      Dimas Giron (rubric)
      Phelipe Tamaris (rubric)

Declarasion de Andres Truxillo
En la Villa de Santa Fe en dies dias del mes de Septiembre de mil setesientos [treinta] y dos años ante mi el Capitan Antonio de Urribari Alcalde Maior de esta dicha Villa comparecio Andres Truxillo soldado de este Presidio a quien estando presente le resevi juramento que yso por Dios Nuestro Sñnor y la señal de la Cruz debajo de cuio

cargo premetio de deseñor verdad en lo que le fuere preguntado y siendo lo si sabe por que causa estaba preso dixo y responde que por un balaso que le dieron a Juan de Santisteban la vispera de la Natividad de Nuestra Señora estando en las visperas y que este declarante fue uno de los que dispararon a este tiempo pero que no bido quien le tiro y esto declara so cargo de el juramento que fecho tiene en que se afirmo y ratifico no firmo por no saber firmelo yo dicho Alcalde Mayor y los testigos de mi asistencia a falta de escribano Publico y Real que no lo ai en este Reino.
Antonio de Urribari (rubric)
Dimas Giron (rubric)
Phelipe Tamaris (rubric)

Declarasion de Caietano Tenorio

En la Villa de Santa Fe en dicho dia mes y año yo el Capitan Antonio de Uribarri Alcalde Mayor y Capitan Aguerra desta dicha Villa paresio ante mi Caitano Tenorio soldado de este Presidio a quien estando presente le resevi juramento que yso por Dios Nuestro Señor y la Señal de la Cruz de bajo de cuio cargo prometio deseñor verdad en lo que supiere y siendo lo sabe la causa de su prision, a esto responde que la causa de su prision es por ser uno de los quatro que dispararon en las visperas de la Natividad de Nuestra Señora y aber bisto que a Juan de Santisteban le abian dado un balaso pero que no sabe ni bido quien le tiro y que esto es lo que sabe y declara so cargo de el juramento que fecho tiene en que se afirmo y ratifico no firmo por no saber firmelo yo dicho Alcalde Maior y los testigos ynfrascriptos de mi asistencia a falta de escribano Publico y real que no ai en este Reino.
Antonio de Urribari (rubric)
Dimas Giron (rubric)
Phelipe Tamaris (rubric)

Auto de Remision

En la Villa de Santa Fee en dies dias de el mes de Septiembre de mil setesientos y treinta y dos años digo que abiendo fenesido estas diligencias echas por orden del Señor Coronel Gerbasio Crusat y Gongora Gobernador y Capitan General de este Reino por Su Magestad ago remision para que en su bista determine Su Señoria lo que fuere serbido que sera como siempre lo mejor asi lo probei mande y firme con los testigos infrascriptos de mi asistencia autuando como Juez receptor a falta de escribano Publico y Real que no lo ai en este Reino.
Antonio de Urribari (rubric)
Dimas Giron (rubric)
Phelipe Tamaris (rubric)

En la Villa de Santa Fee en onse dias del mes de Septiembre de mil setesientos treinta y dos años vistas estos hautos por mi el Coronel Don Gervasio Crusat y Gongora Governador y Capitan General de este Reyno de la Nueva Mexico y Sus Provincias y no resultando de ellos culpa ni indisio de que la herida de Juan de Santistevan soldado de este Real Presidio que se mensiona en ellos, no ha sido de malisia ni de caso acordado por los quatro soldados que dispararon el dia siete del corriente a tiempo de la Natividad de Nuestra Señora que hallarse presos en el Real Cuerpo de Guardia devia mandar y mande sean sueltos de la prision y se les apersiva de que en semejantes funsiones no cargen las armas con bala ni pesta ni otra cosa con que pueda causar herida por que senti rigorosamente castigados en su contravesion y se les impondran las penas que imponen las leyes con lo damas que pidiere la gravedad de la materia en sus efectos. Asi lo provei y mande y firme con los testigos de mi asistencia a falta de escribano Publico y Real que no lo ay en este Reyno.
    Don Gervasio Cruzat y Gongora (rubric)
Gaspar Bitton (rubric) Juan Antonio de Unanue (rubric)

Notes

1. Pedro Guillen was a presidio soldier in Santa Fe by 1716 and is listed in a muster of 1723 as having all his weapons and five horses (Chávez, *Origins*: 193; Christmas, *Military Records*: 50; SANM I #957).
2. Cayetano Tenorio is not listed in the June 18, 1723, presidio muster, but was listed in the 1741 list of soldiers signing a power of attorney to the governor for collection of their salaries. A 1737 deed shows him as the recipient of a Santa Fe property sale. He was a survivor of the 1720 Villasur expedition (Christmas, *Military Records*: 49-51, 79; Thomas Chávez, *Moment*: 306).
3. Cristóbal Luján was the son of Juan Luján, who was a corporal with the presidio and a grandson of Domingo Luján, arriving in New Mexico by 1693. By 1762 he was listed as the alcalde of Santa Cruz and possibly of Galisteo (Chávez, *Origins*: 212; Doc. 4).
4. Andrés Trujillo was the son of Pascual Trujillo, a native of New Mexico who returned in 1694. The father was killed in Nuevo Viscaya when returning to New Mexico as part of an escort (see Doc. 13).
5. Juan de Santistevan was in New Mexico in 1716. In the June 18, 1723, presidio muster, he is listed as having all his weapons and seven horses (Chávez, *Origins*: 284; Christmas, *Military Records*: 49).
6. As shown below in the statement of Cayetano Tenorio, there were only four presidio soldiers performing the salvo.
7. See Doc. 6.
8. Antonio Durán de Armijo is here cited as a master barber. Among other duties, master barbers were called in cases where an alcalde or governor needed an inspection of a wound for purposes of a court record (see Docs. 13 and 34; and Cutter, *Legal Culture*: 115).
9. The word zepo, or cepo, means stocks. In this case, unless the city of Santa Fe had stocks accommodating four people, it is likely to mean jail or some other kind of restraint to prevent escape. In Doc. 32, a Pawnee Indian boy called "el coyote" was taken from the stocks for questioning. It may have been that the stocks were for legs rather than the arms and head.
10. Francisco Mascareñas was the son of Juan Mascareñas, who came from Mexico City with his family in 1693.
11. This suggests that the idea of the salvo was not necessarily to shoot up into the air, but to shoot off in the distance—a risky business as it turns out.
12. The governor's intention seems to be that the soldiers could add powder to their guns, but not the bullet.

25

PEDRO GARCÍA JURADO DISCIPLINED BY ALBUQUERQUE PRIEST FOR BRAIDED HAIR
April 20, 1733. Source: SANM II #382a.

Synopsis and editor's notes: At some time before April 30, 1733, Fray Joseph Antonio Guerrero received a complaint from Reverendo Padre Fray Pedro Montaño in Albuquerque about the disrespectful behavior of Pedro García [Jurado]. Earlier, in 1729, Montaño had admonished members of his congregation to enter the church properly and decently clothed with their hair unbraided. However, in 1733, when Montaño was dressed in his vestments and conducting a mass for the dead, Pedro García entered the church with his hair braided and without a cloak, ignoring the earlier instrustions. Montaño then asked García three times to undo his braid, and García refused. When Montaño said he would report this in a letter to Governor Cruzat y Góngora, Martín Hurtado, García's grandfather, a first founder of Albuquerque and formerly a captain of the military squadron who was also attending the mass, said that he would take any such letter to the governor himself.

Padre Montaño did write the letter regarding García's behavior, and Governor Cruzat y Góngora asked Albuquerque alcalde mayor Juan Gonzales Bas to investigate the complaints and send the proceedings back to him. Gonzales Bas did so, in the mean time placing García and Hurtado in prison. Testimony was then taken from eight witnesses and from García and Hurtado. According to witnesses, García told the priest that he did not want to unbraid his hair because he was on his way to Bernalillo, and he did not have any money to pay someone to comb it out. Montaño then said he would excommunicate him, but later, when García begged forgiveness, Montaño pardoned him and absolved him in case the excommunication had taken effect.

Hurtado testified that after talking back to Montaño about carrying the letter to the governor, he had been sorry he said those words and had prostrated himself at the feet of the priest and asked forgiveness. Montaño refused, so Hurtado went back to the church the next day and, he said, again threw himself at the feet of Montaño, asking forgiveness. This time the priest pardoned him. Hurtado then announced his faults to the congregation and Montaño took his hand and gave a lengthy sermon on forgiving.

As stated, before the proceedings began, García and Hurtado had been placed in the Albuquerque prison. Hurtado, saying that he was unwell, asked the governor that he be placed elsewhere, which the governor did. Then Montaño wrote to governor insisting that Hurtado be placed back in prison under lock and key in the stocks so he would be secure. He said that he originally asked that Hurtado be placed in leg irons, but later decided that was not necessary. The document ends with written proceedings being sent to the governor and Fray Guerrero. Historian Jim Norris states that García was kept in jail, but that Hurtado was not, perhaps because of his age and illness. Hurtado died on October 17, 1734, less than eighteen months after Montaño's complaint (Norris, *Year Eighty*: 91).

It is possible that the paragraphs in the document as we have it are in some way out of order. Was Montaño really spiteful enough to tell the governor that Hurtado should be placed in prison, in stocks and with leg irons, after Hurtado had begged forgiveness and Montaño pardoned him?

The action of Montaño and, to some extent, Guerrero, again shows the importance of ritual and symbolic behavior as an indicator of power, as has been seen before in these documents (Docs. 16 and 20). Another example is an accusation made in 1729 by Fray Montaño, who accused Pedro Gómez y Chávez of Albuquerque, the youngest child of don Fernando Durán y Chávez, of scandalous behavior for saying things that were close to heresy and for general disrespect, including refusing to take off his hat while attending mass. Montaño did not seem to get along with his religious peers any better than he did with the civil officials. For example, in 1751 he was involved in charges and countercharges between him and Frailes Iniesta and Iregoyen that resulted in his being removed from New Mexico (Greenleaf, "Inquisition": 43-45; Doc. 39).

What may seem to modern minds a small-minded insistence on ritual could reflect the response of the Franciscans to their declining influence in the colony. The Franciscan superiors in Mexico City insisted on tightening discipline after the scandal of a 1733 witchcraft trial in Isleta. In addition, it may have had to do with negative comments about the Franciscans by Bishop Crespo of Durango in 1730. The Fransicans may have responded by trying to exert more control over the settlers, including their behavior and dress. That is, appearing at a mass for the dead without the proper attire and with the hair braided, as Indians wore it, may have seemed an unacceptable act of defiance (Norris, *Year Eighty*: 39, 45).

Governor and captain general

Fray Joseph Antonio Guerrero, Predicador Substito, Ex-Visitado of this Holy Custody, current Ministro of the villa of Santa Fe, Comisario[1] of the Holy Office of this Holy House, Vice-Custodian of this Holy Custody of the Conversion of San Pablo of New Mexico, etc.

I appear before your honor [Governor Gervasio Cruzat y Góngora] in the best form that I am allowed and say that having received notice from the minister of the villa of Alburquerque, who is the Reverendo Padre Fray Pedro Montaño,[2] about the excesses committed by a resident of the said villa by the name of Pedro García [Jurado],[3] whom, while the said Padre Ministro was dressed in his holy garments and singing a vigil, the said Pedro García entered the said church without a cloak and with his hair braided [*capote y con a tensa amarada*] and placed himself in front of the ministro, who, with all dignity and love, tried to make him understand the reverence, respect, and composure that is due to our Divine Majesty and to his home, asking him to undo his braid, telling him this three times. All of the times that he asked him to do this, the said Pedro García replied by saying that he would not do it. Due to his obnoxious replies, the said Padre Ministro told him that he would inform your honor so that he would punish him. Upon hearing this, his grandfather, Martín Hurtado,[4] stood up from where he was and in a high tone of voice asked the Padre Ministro, "What is the governor going to do to him? I will act as a witness and will take the letters." All of which caused a great deal of scandal, interruption of the divine services, the lack of respect to God, Our Lord, to his house, and to the minister. All of this I offer for the justification of your honor so that upon being informed and arguing the cause, he will seek the most convenient answer for refraining and stopping the insults committed by the said. Of your honor I ask and petition that you be pleased to do and justify the above, protesting as I protest, but it is through my love that the said not be executed with the loss of blood, or mutilation of their joints, etc. All of the above can be substantiated through the witnesses who were present. This is done because it is necessary, etc.

      Joseph Antonio Guerrero (rubric)

[Decree by Governor Cruzat y Góngora]

 At the villa of Santa Fe on the 30th of April, 1733, upon being seen by me, Colonel don Gervasio Cruzat y Góngora, governor and captain general of this kingdom of New Mexico and of its provinces for his majesty, took it as it was presented according to its proper right and paying attention to that which was presented by the Reverendo Padre Vicario Fray Joseph Antonio Guerrero, I was justified to send it and ordered the captain Juan Gonzales Bas, alcalde mayor of the jurisdiction of the villa of Alburquerque, to proceed with the arguments of everything that is contained in the said written document and continue with all of the arguments which are brought forth until the case is placed in the state of sentencing, at which point it is to be submitted to this supreme government for final determination. I thus approved it, ordered, and signed it along with my assisting witnesses due to the lack of a public or royal scribe, there being none in this kingdom. It is done on plain paper because the sealed type is not found in these parts.

      Don Gervasio Cruzat y Góngora (rubric)

witness witness

Gaspar Bitton (rubric) Juan Antonio de Unanue (rubric)

Decree of Commission

At this villa of San Felipe de Alburquerque on the 4th of May, 1733, I, Captain Juan Gonzales Bas, alcalde mayor and captain of war of the said villa and of its jurisdiction, in fulfillment of the decree above provided by the colonel don Gervasio Cruzat y Góngora, governor and captain general of this kingdom of New Mexico and of its provinces, proceeded with the argument of what is contained in the written document which appears at the head of these proceedings, placing in prison the said two, Martín Hurtado and Pedro García Jurado. So that it is valid I signed it as presiding judge along with my assisting witnesses due to the lack of a public or royal scribe, there not being one in this kingdom.

       Juan Gonzales Bas (rubric)

witness
Isidro Sánchez (rubric)

Statement of
Salvador Cristóbal Gómez[5]

At this said villa on the said day, month, and year, I, the said alcalde mayor, in order to proceed with the argument of these proceedings, made appear before me Salvador Cristóbal Gómez, from whom upon being present took his sworn statement which he made before God and the sign of the Holy Cross, under which he promised to tell the truth about everything that he knew and what he was asked. He was asked if he knew or has heard that the Reverendo Padre Minister has preached, admonished, and instructed that no Christian be allowed into the Holy Church without being properly clothed, without any indecency, and with their hair braided. He stated that he did know it and has heard it. He was asked if he knows and saw Pedro García when he entered the church without a cloak and with his hair braided and approached the priest, standing before him, while the priest was dressed in the vestments of the dead [*revestido con todo oficio de difuntas*], and if he knows that the priest called upon the said Pedro and ordered him to remove his braid. He stated that he did know it and had heard it. He said that two or three times he [Pedro] answered the Reverendo Padre that he did not want to remove his braid because he was on his way to Bernalillo, and that he did not have anyone to comb him [rebraid his hair?].

He was asked if he knew the motives that Martín Hurtado had for arguing in a loud voice in the said Holy Church with the said Reverendo Padre. The said declarant stated that the motives were that Martín Hurtado had ordered his grandson Pedro García to get out of the church and that upon attempting to leave the Reverendo Padre turned around and told him (Pedro) not to leave but to remove his braid. At which time the said Pedro García said that he did not want to, and proceeded to leave the church. The said Reverendo Padre then told him, go ahead and leave, you will see that I will write to the governor and to this the said Martín Hurtado responded, "What is the governor going to do to him?" The priest then answered, "I shall write and see that he does." To this the said Martín said, "Go ahead and write Father, I shall be a witness and shall carry the letter." Once this was finished the Reverendo Padre continued with his divine services. He was asked if he knew anything else about what had happened. He said that all he knows is that the following day, at the proper place, the said Martín had asked the said Reverendo Padre to forgive him for what he had said the previous day and that the priest had forgiven him, and that as an example of all that happened the priest had gone on to give a very lengthy sermon.

He stated that he did not know anything else and that it was the truth regarding the sworn statement that he had made, and that he is in no way related [to anyone involved]. He stated that he was one hundred and three years of age. When his statement was read back to him, the said declarant said that he had nothing to add or delete, and he did not sign it because he did not know how; I signed it as presiding judge along with my assisting witnesses due to the lack of a public or royal scribe, which there is none in these parts.

Juan Gonzales Bas (rubric)

witness witness
Joseph de Apodaca (rubric) Isidro Sánchez (rubric)

Statement of
Antonio Varela[6]

Continuing on the said day, month, and year, I, the said alcalde mayor in prosecution of this proceedings, made appear before me Antonio Varela, from whom, upon being present, I received his sworn statement which he made to God, Our Lord, and to the sign of the Cross, under which he promised to tell the truth in whatever he knew and what he was asked. He was asked if he knew or has heard that the Reverendo Padre Ministro has admonished and instructed that the parishioners enter the church properly dressed and with their braid undone. He stated that he does know it and has heard it. He was asked if he knows or has heard that Pedro García Jurado entered the Holy Church without a cloak and with his hair braided and had approached the Reverendo Padre, who was dressed in his vestments and singing a religious song for the dead; and if he knows that the Reverendo Padre ordered the said Pedro to undo his braid. He stated that he did know it and had heard it, and that the said Pedro had stated that he was on his way to Bernalillo and that he did not have anyone to comb his hair. He stated that the Reverend Guardian had told him (García), "Son, undo your braid even if you are going to Bernalillo." The said García then said that he did not want to, and continued on his way out of the church.

He was asked if he knew what Martín Hurtado had said after the Father had stated that he would inform the governor about this embarrassment. He stated that he did not because he was situated too far in the back of the church, but that he did hear the Father say that all who were present were witnesses to what had occurred. He was asked if he knew anything else. He stated that he did not, other than on the following day at the same place Martín Hurtado asked the Reverendo Padre to forgive him, and that the Father had done so. He then stated that he did not know anything else regarding the sworn statement that he had made and that he was not related in any way]. He said that he was twenty-six years of age, and upon his statement being read back to him he said that he did not have anything to add or to delete, and he affirmed and ratified it, but did not sign it because he did not know how. I, the said alcalde mayor, signed it acting as presiding judge along with my assisting witnesses due to the lack of a public or royal scribe which there is none in this kingdom.

Juan Gonzales Bas (rubric)

witness witness
Joseph de Apodaca (rubric) Isidro Sánchez (rubric)

Statement of
Lorenzo Carvajal[7]

Continuing on the said day, month, and year, I, the said alcalde mayor in prosecution of these proceedings, made to appear before me Lorenzo de Caravajal, whom upon being present received his sworn statement which he made to God, Our Lord, and to the sign of the Cross, under which he promised to tell the truth in what he knew and what he was asked. He was asked if he knows or has heard the Reverendo Padre Ministro of this villa admonish all of his parishioners to enter the church with all the reverence and decency due the Holy Church. He stated that he knows it and has heard it. He was asked if he knows or saw Pedro García Jurado enter the Holy Church without a cloak and with his hair braided and approach the Reverendo Padre, who was dressed in his vestments and was singing religious prayers for the dead; and if he knows that the Reverendo Padre called upon him and asked him to undo his braid. He stated that he did know it and saw him do it, and also that two or three times he [García] answered the Reverendo Padre that he did not want to do it, saying that he would not do it because he was going to Bernalillo and he did not have anyone to comb him. He was asked if he knew the motives that Martín Hurtado had for speaking out in the said Holy Church to the said Reverendo Padre. He said that he had seen it, and that it came about after the said Martín had ordered Pedro García to leave the church, and that as he [García] was leaving the Reverendo Padre approached him and told him not to leave, to enter and undo his braid, and when he (García) did not do this, the priest told him to go on, that he would write to the governor so that he could castigate this inattention and embarrassment, and that it was at this time that Martín Hurtado, in a raised voice, asked, "And what is the Governor going to do"? The Reverendo Padre then said, "His Honor is not a Christian if he does not castigate this," and turning to all of those who were present, he said, "Everyone of us who is here present are witnesses." To which the said Martín Hurtado responded, "Write, Father, I will carry the letter and will be a witness."

After all of this was over, the Father continued with his divine prayers, and the witness said that he did not hear anything else. He was asked if he knew anything else. He stated that he did not and that this was the truth regarding his sworn statement that he has made. He was asked if he was related to anyone. He said that he was not, and said that he was seventy years of age, more or less, and upon his statement being read back to him, he did not have anything to add or to delete, and he affirmed and ratified it, but did not sign because he did not know how; I, the said alcalde mayor, signed it acting as presiding judge along with my assisting witnesses due to the lack of a public or royal scribe, which there is none in this kingdom.

Juan Gonzales Bas (rubric)

witness witness
Joseph de Apodaca (rubric) Isidro Sánchez (rubric)

Statement of
Bartolomé Olguín[8]

Continuing on the said day, month, and year, I the said alcalde mayor in prosecution of these proceedings, made to appear before me Bartolomé Olguín, from whom upon being present, received his sworn statement which he made to God, Our Lord, and to the sign of a Cross, under which he promised to tell the truth in whatever he knew and in what he was asked. He was asked if he knows that the Reverendo Padre Minister has preached and taught his parishioners to enter into the Holy Church with the proper dress and the braid of their hair undone. He stated that he does know it and has heard it. He was asked if he knew the motive that Pedro García Jurado had for having argued with the Reverendo Padre. He stated that upon the Reverendo Padre being dressed in his vestments and singing a vigil for the dead [*vigilia de difuntos*], Pedro García entered without a cloak and with his hair braided and stood before the Reverendo Padre, who silently told him, "Son, undo your braid." To this the said Pedro told him that he could not, that he was on his way to Bernalillo. The Reverendo Padre then told him, "Son, remove your braid, as there are some in here who are ignorant of the law of God, and who will say that it is fine if you do not remove it." The said Pedro García then responded by saying that he did not want to remove it and then proceeded to leave the church. The Reverendo Padre, upon seeing this, then told him not to leave, but when he did not pay attention to this, the Reverendo Padre then told him to go ahead and leave, but that he would inform the governor. At this time Martín Hurtado answered by saying in a loud voice, "What is the governor going to do to him?" The priest then said, "What is he going to do? The governor is no Christian if he does not castigate these disturbances." To this Martín Hurtado answered, "Go ahead and write, Father, I will be the carrier [of the letter], as well as a witness." At the conclusion of this, this witness states, the Reverendo Padre continued with his divine services (having stopped during this interruption). He was asked if he knew anything else. He stated that the only thing was that this was the truth regarding the sworn statement that he had made. He was asked if he was related in any way. He stated that he was not and that he was twenty-four years of age. His statement having been read back to him, he said that he did not have anything to add or delete, and he then affirmed and ratified it, but did not sign because he did not know how. I, the said alcalde mayor acting as presiding judge, signed it along with my assisting witnesses due to the lack of a public or royal scribe, there being none in the Kingdom.

Juan Gonzales Bas (rubric)

witness witness
Joseph de Apodaca (rubric) Isidro Sánchez (rubric)

Statement of
Francisco Antonio Gonzales[9]

Continuing on the said day, month, and year, I, the said alcalde mayor in prosecution of these proceedings, made appear before me Francisco Antonio Gonzales, who upon being present received his sworn statement which he made to God, Our Lord, and to the sign of a Cross, under which he promised to tell the truth as to what he knew and what he was asked. He was asked if knows or has heard that the Reverendo Padre Ministro has preached, admonished, and taught that all of the Christians are to enter into the Holy Church with divine reverence and properly dressed. He stated that he did know it and has heard it. He was asked if he knew the motives and if he saw Pedro García Jurado enter the Holy Church without a cloak and his hair braided and place himself before the said Reverendo Padre, with the Reverendo Padre dressed in his vestments and singing a vigil to the dead. Also, if he knows if the Reverendo Padre called the said Pedro García aside and told him to remove his braid. He stated that he does know it and did see it, and that two or three times the said Pedro García responded to the said Reverendo Padre saying that he did not want to remove his braid because he was going to Bernalillo and that he did not have anyone to comb him.

He was asked if he knew the motives that Martín Hurtado had for speaking out in the Holy Church against the Reverendo Padre. He stated that he did see it and that it was because he, Martín, had told the said Pedro García to leave from the church, and upon his attempting to leave the said Reverend went back and told him not to leave, but to go back in and to remove his braid. However, when the said Pedro García did not mind him, the said Priest then said for him to leave, but that he would write to the governor so that he could castigate such inattentions and disturbances. At this the said Martín Hurtado said in a high tone of voice, "What is the governor going to do to him"? The Reverendo Padre then answered, "What is he going to do? The governor is not a Christian if he does not castigate this." The said Reverendo Padre then turned towards those who were present and in a high tone of voice said that they were all witnesses to what had been said. The said Martín then responded by saying, "Go right ahead, Father, you write, and I will be a witness as well as the carrier of the letter." After this the said Father proceeded with his divine services, and nothing else occurred. He was asked if he had seen anything else. He said that he did not and that this was the truth regarding his sworn statement that he had made. He was asked his age, and he responded by saying that he was twenty-five and that he was not related in any way. His statement being read back to him, he said that he did not have anything to add or to delete, and he affirmed, ratified, and signed it [signature not on document], along with my assisting witnesses due to the lack of a public or royal scribe, there being none in this kingdom.

Juan Gonzales Bas (rubric)

witness witness
Joseph de Apodaca (rubric) Isidro Sánchez (rubric)

Statement of
Matías Romero[10]

    Continuing on the said day, month, and year, I, said alcalde mayor in prosecution of these proceedings, made to appear before me Matías Romero, who upon being present received his sworn statement which he made to God, Our Lord, and to the sign of a Cross, under which he promised to tell the truth in what he knew and what he was asked, and he was asked if he knows and has heard that the Reverendo Padre Minister has admonished, taught, and preached that no Christian parishioner is to enter the Holy Church without being properly dressed and with the hair braided. He stated that he does know it and has heard it. He was asked if he knows or saw that Pedro García entered the Holy Church without a cloak and with his hair braided and placed himself before the Reverendo Padre, and if he saw that he was taken aside by the Father and secretly told to undo his braid. He stated that he did see it and that the said Pedro García once, twice, and three times answered him telling him that he did want to do it, and that then the said Pedro García attempted to leave. This witness states that the Reverendo Padre, upon seeing this, called him to come back and not to leave, and for that motive, and because he would not pay heed to what he, the priest, was saying, the priest told him that he would write to the governor so that he would punish this embarrassment, and that at this Martín Hurtado responded, saying in a high tone, "What is the governor going to do?" To this the said Reverendo Padre answered, "The governor is not a Christian if he does not castigate this inattention." Martín Hurtado then answered, "Then go ahead and write, and I will be the carrier of the letter and will also be a witness." The Father then answered, "You will not do that." After this the Father continued with his divine prayers. He was asked if he knew anything else other than what has been stated. He said that on the following day, Martín Hurtado, at the door of the church, asked the Father to forgive him, and that the Reverendo Padre did forgive him, and [he] does not know anything else. He stated that this was the truth regarding the sworn statement that he has made, and that he is forty-five years of age, more or less. He was asked if he was related in any way. He stated that he was, that Martín Hurtado was his uncle, and Pedro García was his nephew. His statement being read back to him, he did not have anything to add or delete, and he affirmed and ratified it, but did not sign because he did not know how. I signed it acting as presiding judge with my assisting witnesses due to the lack of public or royal scribe, because there is not one in this kingdom.

Juan Gonzales Bas (rubric)

witness witness
Joseph de Apodaca (rubric) Isidro Sánchez (rubric)

Statement of
Lugardo Vallejo[11]

At this villa of San Felipe de Alburquerque on the 5th day of May, 1733, I, Captain Juan Gonzales Bas, alcalde mayor and war captain of the said villa and of its jurisdiction, in prosecution of these proceedings made to appear before me Lugardo Vallejo, who, being present, received his sworn statement which he made to God, Our Lord, and to the sign of a Cross, under which he promised to tell the truth as to what he knew and what he was asked. He was asked if he knows or has heard the Reverendo Padre preach, teach, and admonish that none of his Christian parishioners are to enter the Holy Church without being properly dressed, as it is owed to such a Holy place. He stated that he knows it and has heard it. He was asked if knows and saw that Pedro García Jurado entered the said church without his cloak and with his hair braided. He stated that he did see him, and also saw that the Reverendo Padre called him aside and secretly told him, "Pedro, son, undo your braid." Pedro responded by saying once and twice that he did want to, and proceeded to begin to leave the church. Upon seeing this, the Reverendo Padre told him, "Why don't you take off your braid?" Not paying heed, he [Pedro] proceeded to leave. Seeing this, the Father told him to go ahead and leave, but that this embarrassment is to be known by the governor. To this Martín Hurtado asked in a loud voice, "What is the governor going to do?" The said Reverendo Padre then said, "The governor is not a Christian if he does not punish this embarrassment." The said Martín Hurtado then said, "Then write, Your Reverence, as I will be the carrier as well as a witness."

He was then asked if he knew anything else regarding what happened in the Holy Church. He stated that he did not, except that he does know that on the following day, at the proper place, the said Martín Hurtado asked to be forgiven. All of this he stated is what he knows and does not know anything else regarding his sworn statement that he has made. He was asked if was related in any way. He stated that Martín was his uncle and Pedro his nephew, and that he was twenty-six years of age, more or less. Upon this being read back to him, he did not have anything to add or to delete, and he affirmed and ratified it, but did not sign because he did not know how; I, the said alcalde mayor, signed it acting as presiding judge along with my assisting witnesses due to the lack of a public or royal scribe, as there is not one in this kingdom.

Juan Gonzales Bas (rubric)

witness witness
Joseph de Apodaca (rubric) Isidro Sánchez (rubric)

Statement of
Lázaro García[12]

Continuing on the said day, month, and year, I, the said alcalde mayor in prosecution of these proceedings, made to appear before me Lázaro García, from whom I received his sworn statement which he made to God, Our Lord, and to the sign of a Cross, under which he promised to tell the truth as to what he knew and what he was asked. He was asked if he knows and has heard if the Reverendo Padre Minister has preached, taught, and admonished that none of the parishioners are to enter the Holy Church without being properly dressed and with their hair braided. He stated that he does know it and has heard it been said by the Reverendo Padre. He was asked if he knows and saw that Pedro García entered the Holy Church without a cloak and with his hair braided. He stated that he did see it, and he saw that the said Father called him aside and asked him to remove his braid. He stated that he did not hear anything that was said, but he did see that the Reverendo Padre called him over to where he was dressed in his vestments. He was asked if he saw that the said Pedro García left from the church and heard what he told the Reverendo Padre as he was leaving. He stated that when the Reverendo Padre saw him leave, he told him not to leave, calling him back and asking his reason for leaving and why he would not remove his braid. "Yes, I am leaving," responded the said Pedro García. Then the Father asked him, "And you will not remove your braid?" The said Pedro then said, "No, because I am leaving."

The witness was then asked what the said Martín Hurtado had stated, or what words he had exchanged with the Reverendo Padre. He stated that what happened was that the Father stated that everyone present in the church were going to be witnesses to what had occurred, at which time Martín Hurtado responded in a loud voice, "Father, I will be a witness, and if you write, Your Reverence, I will be the one to carry your letter." But, as to what else the said Martín said, he did not hear because he was at a distance. He was then asked if he knew anything else as to what happened. He stated that he did not hear anything else and that this was the truth regarding the sworn statement that he had made. He was asked if he was related to anyone. He stated that he was not, and that he was thirty-four years of age. His statement being read back to him, he said that he had nothing else to add or to delete, and he affirmed and ratified it but did not sign because he did not know how. I, the said alcalde mayor, signed it acting as presiding judge along with my assisting witnesses due to the lack of a public or royal scribe, there being none in this kingdom.

       Juan Gonzales Bas (rubric)

witness witness
Joseph de Apodaca (rubric) Isidro Sánchez (rubric)

Statement of
Pedro García [Jurado]

  At this villa of San Felipe de Alburquerque on the 6th of May, 1733, I, Captain Juan Gonzales Bas, alcalde mayor and War Captain of this said villa and of its jurisdiction, in order to continue with the prosecution made to appear before me Pedro García Jurado, a prisoner, from whom I received his sworn statement according to his proper right which he made to God, Our Lord, and to the sign of the Holy Cross, under which he promised to tell the truth as to what he was asked. He was asked if he knows that the Reverendo Padre Guardian has preached, admonished, and taught his parishioners to enter the Holy Church with the proper dress and decency. He stated that he did know it from having seen it and heard it. He was asked if he had entered the Holy Church with his hair braided and without a cloak. He stated that he had, and when the Reverendo Padre saw him, he was told, "Son, undo your braid." The declarant stated that he remained quiet and that the Reverendo Padre told him once again (having called him aside) to come to him and undo his braid. At this point the declarant answered him, telling the said Reverendo Padre that he would not do it because he was going to Bernalillo in a hurry, but being that the mass was in the vicinity, he went inside. He was then asked, "What does it cost you to undo it?" He then answered the priest, telling him, "Since we are so poor, I do not have anyone to comb me and thus will not untie it." Because of this the grandfather of this declarant told him to leave the church and untie his braid and return to mass; at this point he left the church, but the priest told him to stop, asking why he was leaving and not removing his braid. At that point, this witness states that he, García, did not answer but only continued with what he was doing and continued on his way. After all of this commotion was over, he went back into the mass. He was asked what his grandfather, Martín Hurtado, answered when the Reverendo Padre said that he was going to write to the governor. He stated that he did not hear anything because he left [the church] at the order of his grandfather. He stated that this was the truth and had nothing else to say regarding his sworn statement that he had made, and he said that he was twenty-three years of age, more or less. His statement being read back to him, he did not have anything to add or to delete, and said that what is in the margin and between lines is valid. He then affirmed and ratified it, but did not sign because he did not know how; I, the said alcalde mayor, signed it along with my assisting witnesses acting as presiding judge due to the lack of a public or royal scribe, as there is none in this kingdom. Also, in addition, something that is stated by this declarant is that after all of this had happened, he was told that the Father had said that he was excommunicated; however, because he finally did enter to hear the mass after all the commotion was over, it was ignored, and he asked to be pardoned as well as given absolution and that the Reverendo Padre absolved him, in case he had been [excommunicated] and pardoned him. All of this was done according to what he has to say, and that they both remained content, and that he then left for his home satisfied. This is valid.

      Juan Gonzales Bas (rubric)

witness witness
Joseph de Apodaca (rubric) Isidro Sánchez (rubric)

Statement of Martín Hurtado

  At this villa of San Felipe de Alburquerque on the 7th of May, 1733, I, Captain Juan Gonzales Bas, alcalde mayor and War Captain of the said villa and of its jurisdiction, in order to better argue this cause made to appear before me Martín Hurtado, from whom I received his sworn statement which he made to God, Our Lord, and to the sign of the Cross, under which he promised to tell the truth as to what he knew and what he was asked. He was asked if he knows, has seen, and has heard what Pedro García did when he entered [the church] without a cloak and with his hair braided. He stated that he did see him enter without a cloak but that he did have an overcoat [gaban]; and that the Reverendo Padre called upon the said Pedro García to remove his braid. At this, the declarant told him, "Come on, son, take the braid off and return to the mass," at which time he [García] left the church, and then the Father reentered the Holy Church. The Reverendo Padre then went to the pulpit and stated that he would write to the villa [Santa Fe] so that this embarrassment would be castigated.

At this, this witness stated that he would be a witness of having seen the said Pedro with his hair braided. Then the Reverendo Padre repeated that he would write about the crazy happening or lack of understanding and said, "Write, Reverendo Padre, and if there is no one who can carry the letter, I will take it." However, he says that he stated all of this in a low voice and not otherwise, and that at that point the Reverendo Padre continued with his services. This witness says that he was left rather confused and felt sorry for having said what he did. Because of this he could hardly wait for the Padre Ministro to finish with his divine services so that the Padre Ministro would leave the church and so that he could prostrate himself at his feet asking him for forgiveness, which he did do once he [the priest] left the church, asking him for forgiveness; however, the said Reverendo Padre would not do it, and he became so confused that he left for his home, where he remained until the next day, when the mass was to begin, and he then went and waited until the Reverendo Padre entered the church, and before the Reverendo Padre went into his prayers, this witness stood up from where he was and threw himself at the feet of the Reverendo Padre and asked him for his forgiveness, and then he was ordered to stand up, as he was forgiven. Hurtado then asked the Reverendo Padre for permission to publicly announce his faults, something that the Reverendo Padre very graciously did, and standing up from where he was, he spoke to those who were present [in the church], saying as follows, "Ladies and gentlemen, those of you who were present yesterday in this Holy Church know what I told the priest, and I admit that I did a terrible thing, something that I should have never done in such a Holy place, being that we must always enter this place without any particular bother and with humility to ask God for his blessings and forgiveness, and I ask everyone for forgiveness for the bad example that I showed."

After this was done, the Reverendo Padre took his hand and then delivered a lengthy spiritual talk, the theme being the forgiveness that everyone as Christians should have, including the example shown by this witness. He confessed his fault, and once again asked for forgiveness, for the love of God and for the wounds inflicted upon our Seraphic Father San Francisco. He was then asked if he had anything else to say. He answered that he did not, and that this is the truth regarding the sworn statement that he has made, and stated that he was sixty-three years old, more or less. His sworn statement having been read back to him, he said that he did not have anything to add or delete, and he ratified and affirmed it before me and my assisting witnesses, being that there is no royal or public scribe in this kingdom.

Martín Hurtado (rubric)
Juan Gonzales Bas (rubric)
witness witness
Joseph de Apodaca (rubric) Isidro Sánchez (rubric)

[Submission to Governor Cruzat y Góngora]
At this villa of San Felipe de Alburquerque on the 7th of May, 1733, I, Captain Juan Gonzales Bas, alcalde mayor and war captain of this said villa and of its jurisdiction, having concluded these proceedings and placing them in the state of sentencing, declare that those who are mentioned within these are to be kept in jail until the final determination by the supreme government, and they are to obey this order and are to comply with it, and they are to have nothing to argue in their favor without his honor being informed. Because of all of this, I submit them to the supreme government, and they consist of fourteen pages, one being blank, with the approval of a petition that is included with them. So that it is valid I signed it as presiding judge along with my assisting witnesses because of the lack of a public or royal scribe, there not being one in this kingdom.
Juan Gonzales Bas (rubric)
witness witness
Joseph de Apodaca (rubric) Isidro Sánchez (rubric)

Alcalde mayor and war captain
Juan Gonzales

[Complaint by Fray Pedro Montaño]
Fray Pedro Montaño, retired preacher and present minister of the villa of San Felipe de Alburquerque, appear before your honor in my best and proper form which I am granted and say that because I have presented a complaint as Your honor knows before the governor and Captain of this kingdom against Martín Hurtado and his grandson, Pedro García, for disrespect and desecration which they both committed within the temple of God, Our Lord, and due to this, your majesty was pleased to send an order to your honor so that he would place them in jail and to continue with the cause until it was finalized, which has been done by your honor. At this time I am awaiting the final results as his honor has now taken them into his home, where he has them under guard, even though not in the rigorous manner that they should be for what they committed. His honor has recently taken them to a home in the proximity of the home of Martín Hurtado and is without the proper guards and what is required for keeping him under security. As such the said Martín Hurtado is as free as if he had committed miracles, and as if he had been faultless in the grave deed that he had committed, and needs to be placed in a dungeon where he cannot see the sun or the moon.

He is more at fault then his grandson, and because he is so delinquent he needs to be in shackles and locked up in a strong stock where he cannot communicate with any person. More so, he should not be at any place where he can cause problems. All of this is due to the proof that I have offered due to his abuses and his daring actions against the respect that is due to God, Our Lord, and to his Holy home. I ask and petition your honor that you be pleased to take these said delinquents and return them to where they were previously, where they should be in the stocks, not necessarily in shackles, but under lock and key with competent guards to keep them secure for whenever the governor calls them and sees that they are criminals with a grave crime, and so that it does not appear that the said Martín Hurtado is a saint.

I sincerely await that for the good of justice your honor will attend to this my just petition, transporting or taking the said once more to the jail where they had been. All of this is not necessarily done in a bad way for now, and I swear in due form that my petition is not done in malice, but for the stated motive and for what is necessary, etc.

Fray Pedro Montaño (rubric)

[Submission by Juan Gonzales Bas][13]

At this villa of San Felipe de Alburquerque on the 3rd of May, 1733, I, Captain Juan Gonzales Bas, alcalde mayor and war captain of this said villa and of its jurisdiction, in attention to what Martín Hurtado, a prisoner, has presented to me, that he is in bad health, and so that his afflictions are cared for, I placed him within a home belonging to this villa, which was made available to him and in which he is found in the same manner as where he was being held as a prisoner. As such, the contrary party has argued that he be returned to his old prison, and I have ordered and did order that the lieutenant of this villa, Gerónimo Jaramillo,[14] once he receives this decree, to return him to the place where he was in prison along with Pedro García. I thus approved, ordered, and signed this along with my two assisting witnesses due to the lack of a public or royal scribe, being that there is not one in this kingdom.

Juan Gonzales Bas (rubric)

witness witness
Manuel Carillo (rubric) Isidro Sánchez (rubric)

[Transmittal by Governor Cruzat y Góngora]

At the villa of Santa Fe on the 9th of May, 1733, I, Colonel don Gervasio Cruzat y Góngora, governor and captain general of this kingdom of New Mexico, after having reviewed the proceedings that were submitted to me by the alcalde Juan Gonzales Bas, order and did order that a copy of them be given to the Most Reverendo Padre Fray Joseph Antonio Guerrero. I thus approved, ordered, and signed this along with my assisting witnesses due to the lack of a public or royal scribe because there is not one in this kingdom.

Don Gervasio Crusat y Góngora (rubric)

Gaspar Bitton (rubric) Juan Antonio de Unanue (rubric)

[Transmittal by Fray Guerrero]

Having been reviewed by me, Fray Joseph Antonio Guerrero, Retired Priest and Commissary of the Holy Office of this kingdom and of the Holy House, Ex-Visitor of the Holy Court of the Conversion of San Pablo of New Mexico, and actual Vice-Custodian of it, after having reviewed the proceedings that the Colonel don Gervasio Cruzat y Góngora, governor and captain general of this kingdom, and castellan of the forces and presidios for his majesty, order that a copy be given to me and upon having reviewed them, conclude them and approve them in my favor, and will then return them to the superior government of his honor so that he can execute what he thinks is for the best, which is always done for the better, and so that it is valid I signed it at this villa of Santa Fe on the 11th of May, 1733.

Fray Joseph Antonio Guerrero (rubric)

ORIGINAL DOCUMENT

Señor Governador y Capitan General

Fray Joseph Antonio Guerrero Predicador Substito, Ex-Visitador de Esta Santa Custodia, Ministro presente de la Villa de Santa Fee, Comisario del Santo Oficio y de la Casa Santa, Vice Custodio de esta Santa Custodia dela Conversion de San Pablo de la Nueva Mexico, ut supra.

Paresco ante Vuestra Senoria en la forma que el derecho me permite y digo; que aviendome noticiado por el ministro de la Villa de Alburquerque que lo es el Reverendo Padre Fray Pedro Montano del exceso cometido por un vezino de dicha Villa llamado Pedro Garcia, qual es, que allandose dicho Padre Ministro revestido cantando una vigilia, el dicho Pedro Garcia entro en la dicha yglesia sin capote y con la trensa amarada y se puso delante el ministro el qual con gran venignidad y carino le dio a entender la reverencia, molestia y conpostura que ala Magestad Divina y asu cassa se deve; y que assi se diastase la trensa lo qual executo por tres veses, y a todas ellas le respondio el dicho Pedro Garcia que no queria, y viendo su osada respuesta el dicho Padre Ministro le dixo daria quanta a Vuesta Senoria para que le castigara, y a esto se levanto su abuelo Martin Hurtado y con vos alterada y discompuesta dixo al Padre Ministro, que le a de aser el governador; yo sere testigo y llevare las cartas; aviendo causado los dichos el gravissimo escandalo interrumpiendo los Divinos oficios, faltando al devido respecto a Dios Nuestro Senor, a su cassa, y a su ministro. Todo lo cual pongo en la justificacion de Vuestra Senoria para que informado y averiguado del caso sea muy servido de azer lo que ayare por conveniente para atajar y refrenar los insultos cometidos por los dichos =

    A Vuestra Senoria pido y suplico se sirva de aser y justificar lo referido protestando como protesto no ser mi amistad de que alos dichos sele siga ejucion de sangre, mutilacion de miembros, ut supra y de todo lo referido ofresco informacion con los testigos que se ayaran presentes y en lo necesario, ut supra =
                      Joseph Antonio Guerrero (rubric)

En la Villa de Santa Fee en treinta dias del mes de Abril de mill setesientos y treynta y tres anos, visto por mi el Coronel Don Gervasio Cruzat y Gongora, Governador y Capitan General de este Reyno de la Nueva Mexico y sus provincias por Su Magestad, la huve por presentada en lo que ha lugar en derecho y en atension a lo que en ella presenta el Reverendo Padre Vicario Fray Joseph Antonio Guerrero devia mandar y mande que el Capitan Juan Gonzales Bas, alcalde mayor de la jurisdicion de la Villa de Alburquerque haga la averiguasion de todo lo que se contiene en este dicho escripto y corra todas las diligencias que condusen para dicha averiguasion asta poner la causa en estado de sentencia en cuio caso la remitira a este Superior Govierno para su determinasion. Asi lo provey, mande y firme con los testigos infraescriptos de asistencia a falta de Escribano Publico y Real que no lo ay en este Reyno, y va en el presente papel hordinario por no corer en estas partes el sellado =
                      Don Gervasio Cruzat y Gongora (rubric)
testigo testigo
Gaspar Bitton (rubric) Juan Antonio de Unanues (rubric)

Auto de Comision
En esta Villa de San Felipe de Alburquerque en quatro dias de el mes de Mayo de mil setesientos y treynta y tres, yo el Capitan Juan Gonzales Bas, alcalde mayor y Capitan Aguerra de dicha Villa y su jurisdicion en cumplimiento del auto ariva prevuydo por el Senor Coronel Don Gervasio Cruzat y Gongora, Governador y Capitan General de este Reyno dela Nueba Mexico y sus probincias, pase ala aberiguacion delo que contiene el escrito que consta por cabesa de estos autos, poniendo en prision alos suso dichos Martin Hurtado y Pedro Garcia Jurado, y para que conste lo firme autuando por Reseptoria con testigos ynfraescritos de mi asistencia a falta de Escribano Publico y Real que no lo ay en este Reyno =
                      Juan Gonzales Bas (rubric)
testigo
Isidro Sanchez (rubric)

Declaracion de
Salvador Xptobal Gomes

En esta sobre dicha Villa en dicho dia, mes y ano, yo dicho Alcalde mayor para la aberiguacion de estas diligencias yse compareser a Salvador Xptobal Gomes y que en estando presente le resebi juramento que yso por Dios Nuestro Senor y la señal de la Santa Cruz de bajo de cuyo cargo prometio de dezir berdad en quanto supiere y fuese preguntado y serle preguntado si save o a oydo desir que el Reverendo Padre Ministro tiene predicado amonestado y en senal, no entre ningun Xptiano ala Santa Yglesia con descompostura e yndesencia y con la trenza echa; dixo que si lo save y a oydo; preguntado si save e bido entrar a Pedro Garcia ala yglesia sin capote y con la trenza echa y ponersele a este Padre delante y estando dicho Padre revestido con todo oficio de difuntos, y si save que llamo dicho Padre a dicho Pedro y le mando se quitase la trensa; dixo que si lo save y a oydo, y que tambien por dos y tres veses le respondio a dicho Reverendo Padre que no queria quitarsela por que se yba a Bernalillo y que no tenia quien lo peynase; y preguntado los motives que tubo Martin Hurtado para tener voses en dicha Santa Yglesia con dicho Reverendo Padre; dixo dicho declarante que los motives fueron aber dicho Martin Hurtado mandadole a su nieto Pedro Garcia se saliera de la yglesia, y que allandose saliendo boltio el dicho Reverendo Padre y le dixo ombre no te salgas sino quitarte la trensa y que a estas rasones respondio dicho Pedro Garcia que no queria y prosiguio saliendose dela yglesia y bisto esto por el Reverendo Padre le dixo pues anda bellas que yo escrivire al Senor Governador y que a esto respondio Martin Hurtado pues que le a de aser el governador, a que respondio el Padre que yo escribire y beran si le ase; a que respondio dicho Martin pues escriva Padre, que yo sere testigo y llebare la carta; y que acabado esto prosiguio el dicho Reverendo Padre sus divinos oficios; y preguntado si save otra cosa a serca de este suseso; dixo que lo que save es que luego al otro dia en el proprio lugar le abia dicho Martin pedido perdon a dicho Reverendo Padre desdisiendose delo que el dia antes abia susedicho y que el Padre le abia perdonado y que a exemplo de esta acion abia el Padre echado una platica muy larga; y que no sabe mas y que esta es la verdad so cargo del juramento que fecho tiene, y que no le toca en las generales y que es de edad de siento y tres anos y leyda la declaracion dixo dicho declarante no tener que anadir ni quitar y no firmo por no saber, firmelo yo dicho Reseptor con los testigos ynfraescriptos de mi asistencia a falta de Escribano Publico y Real que no lo ay en estas partes =

Juan Gonzales Bas (rubric)

testigo testigo
Joseph de Apodaca (rubric) Isidro Sanchez (rubric)

Declaracion de
Antonio Barela

Luego yncontinenti en dicho dia, mes y ano yo dicho Alcalde mayor en prosecusion destas diligencias yse comparecer a Antonio Barela aquien estando presente le resevi juramento que yso por Dios Nuestro Senor y la Senal de una Cruz debajo de cuyo cargo prometio desir verdad en quanto supiere y fuere preguntado; y siendo preguntado si saveo a oydo desir que el Reverendo Padre Ministro tiene amonestado y ensenado entren ala Santa Yglesia sus feligreses con divida conpostura y trensa desbaratada; dixo que si lo sabe y a oydo; preguntado si save o a oydo desir que Pedro Garcia Jurado entro a la Santa Yglesia sin capote y con la trensa del pelo echa y ponerselo al Reverendo Padre delante estando dicho Padre revestido cantando oficio de difuntos, y si sabe que llamo dicho Reverendo Padre a dicho Pedro y le mando quitara la trensa; dixo, que si lo sabe y a oydo y que respondio dicho Pedro que se yba a Bernalillo y no tenia quien lo peynara y que a esto replico el Padre Guardian pues quitatela trensa hijo aunque te bayas a Bernalillo; a culla respondio dicho Pedro Garcia que no queria, y se fue saliendo; preguntado, si save lo que respondio Martin Hurtado; respondio sobre de desir el Padre que sabria el Senor Governador esta desberguensa; dixo, que no lo save ni oyo por estar muy abajo dela yglecia solo se que oyo quando el Padre sito a todos por testigos pero por que no lo oyo; y preguntado si sabe otra cosa serva de lo suso dicho; dixo que no sabe mas sino que Martin Hurtado le pidio perdon a dicho Reverando Padre otro dia en el mesmo lugar y que dicho Padre le perdono; y que no sabe otra cosa so cargo del juramento que fecho tiene y que no les toca en las generales y ser de edad de beynte y seys anos y leyda su declarasion dixo no tener que anadir ni quitar si no que esta es la verdad en que se afirmo y ratifico y no firmo por no saber, firmelo yo dicho Alcalde mayor autuando como Jues Reseptor con los testigos ynfraescriptos de mi asistencia a falta de Escribano Publico y Real que no lo ay en este Reyno =

                    Juan Gonzales Bas (rubric)

testigo testigo
Joseph de Apodaca (rubric) Isidro Sanchez (rubric)

Declaracion de
Lorenso Carabajal

Luego yncontinente en dicho dia, mes y ano yo dicho Alcalde mayor en prosecusion de esta diligencias yse compareser a Lorenso de Caravajal a quien estando presente le resevi juramento que yso a Dios Nuestro Senor y la Senal de una Cruz de bajo de cuyo cargo prometio desir verdad en quanto supiere y fuere preguntado y siendo preguntado si save o a oydo desir que el Reverendo Padre Ministro de esta Villa tiene amonestado a todos los fieles entren con reverencia compostura y toda disencia ala Santa Yglesia; dixo que si lo sabe y a oydo; preguntado si sabe o bido entrar a Pedro Garcia Jurado entrar ala Santa Yglesia sin capote y con la trensa echa y ponersele al Reverendo Padre delante, estando el dicho revestido cantando oficio de difuntos, y si sabe que llamo dicho Reverendo Padre a dicho Pedro Garcia y le mando se quita la trensa; dixo que si lo sabe y bido y que tambien por dos y tres veses le respondio a dicho Reverendo Padre que no queria, que no queria quitarsela por que se yba a Bernalillo y que no tenia quien lo peynara; preguntado que si bido los motivos que tubo Martin Hurtado para tener boses en dicha Santa Yglesia con dicho Reverendo Padre; dixo que si lo bido y que fueron aber dicho Martin mandado a Pedro Garcia se saliera dela Yglecia; y que llendose saliendo bolvio el dicho Reverendo Padre y lo dijo no se saliera que entrara y que se quitara la trensa y que asiendo caso dise este declarante dicho Pedro Garcia le respondio dicho pues anda que yo escrivire al Senor Governador para que castigue esta desatencion y desberguensa y que entonses respondio Martin Hurtado con alterada voz pues que le a de aser el Governador que le a de aser? No sera Xptiano Su Senoria si aque esto no castiga y bolteando a todos los presentes dicho Reverendo Padre, Senores seamos todos testigos a que respondio dicho Martin Hurtado, escriva Padre, que yo llebare la carta y soy testigo y cabado esto prosiguio el Padre las divinas oficios y que no oyo mas dise dicho declarante; y preguntado si save otra cosa; dixo que no y que esta es la verdad so cargo del juramento que fecho tiene; y preguntado si le toca alas generales; dixo que no y que es de la edad de setenta anos poco mas o menos, y leyda su declaracion no tubo que anadir ni quitar en que se afirmo y ratifico y no firmo por no saber, firmelo yo dicho Alcalde mayor autuando como Jues Reseptor con los testigos ynfraescriptos de mi asistencia a falta de Escribano Publico y Real que no lo ay en este Reyno =

     Juan Gonzales Bas (rubric)

testigo testigo
Joseph de Apodaca (rubric) Isidro Sanchez (rubric)

Declaracion de
Bartolome Olguin
Luego yncontinente en dicho dia, mes y ano yo dicho Alcalde mayor en prosecusion de estas diligensias yse comparecer ante mi a Bartholome Olguin aquien estando presente le resivi juramento que yso por Dios Nuestro Senor y la Senal de una Cruz debajo de cuyo cargo prometio desir verdad en cuanto supiere y fuere preguntado; y siendo preguntado si save que el Reverendo Padre Ministro tiene predicado y ensenado entren sus feligreses ala Santa Yglesia con devida compostura y la trensa del pelo desbarata; dixo que si lo save y a oydo; y preguntado si save el motivo que tubo Pedro Garcia Jurado para tener boses con dicho Reverendo Padre; dixo que estando el dicho Reverendo Padre revestido cantando vigilia de difuntos entro Pedro Garcia sin capote y con la trensa echa y sele puso delante a dicho Reverendo Padre y que llandolo en secreto le dixo, hijo quitate la trensa; aque respondio dicho Pedro que no podia, que yba a Bernalillo; y que a esto le replico el dicho Reverendo Padre pues hijo quitate la trensa por que aqui abra algunos ygnorantes de la ley de Dios y diran que esto es bueno con que no tela quites; a esto le respondio dicho Pedro Garcia que no queria quitarsela y que luego se fue saliendo y bisto por el dicho Reverendo Padre lo bolbio a llamar y no asiendo caso de su llamado le dixo entonses dicho Reverendo Padre pues anda que lo sabra el Senor Governador y que a esto respondio Martin Hurtado con bos aclarada pues que le a de aser el Governador; y que a esto respondio el Padre que le a de aser, no fuera Xptiano el Senor Governador si estas desberguensas no castigara; y a esto respondio Martin Hurtado, pues Padre escriba Usted, que yo sere el protador y

tambien sere testigo; y concluido esto dise este declarante prosiguio dicho Reverendo Padre sus divinos oficios (abiendo parado ynter estas boses); y preguntado si save otra cosa; dixo, que no mas que esta es la verdad so cargo del juramento que fecho tiene, y si le toca en las generales; dixo que no y que es de edad de beynte y quator anos; y leyda su declaracion no tubo que anadir ni quitar en que se afirmo y ratifico y no firmo por no saber firmelo yo dicho Alcalde mayor autuando como Jues Reseptor con los testigos ynfraescriptos de mi asistencia a falta de Escribano publico y Real que no lo ay en este Reyno =

       Juan Gonzales Bas (rubric)

testigo testigo
Joseph de Apodaca (rubric) Isidro Sanchez (rubric)

Declaracion de
Francisco Antonio Gonzales

Luego yncontinente en dicho dia, mes y ano, yo dicho Alcalde mayor en prosecusion de estas diligencias yse compareser a Francisco Antonio Gonzales a quien estando presente resevi juramento que yso por Dios Nuestro Senor y la Senal de una Cruz debajo de cuyo cargo prometio desir berdad en quanto supiere y fuere preguntado; y siendo preguntado si sabe o a oydo desir que el Reverendo Padre Ministro tiene predicado, amonestado y ensenado entren todos los Xptianos ala Santa Yglesia con devida reverencia y compostura; dixo que si lo save y a oydo; preguntado si save los motives que tubo y si bido entrar a Pedro Garcia Jurado ala Santa Yglesia sin capote y la trensa del pelo echa y ponersele al dicho Reverendo Padre delante estando el dicho Reverendo Padre revestido cantando oficio de difuntos; y si save que llamo a solas dicho Reverendo Padre a dicho Pedro Garcia y le mando se quitase la trensa; dixo que si lo sabe y bido y que tambien por dos y tres veses le respondio Pedro Garcia a dicho Reverendo Padre que no queria quitarse la trensa por que se yba a Bernalillo y que no tenia quien lo peynara; preguntado que si bido los motivos que tubo Martin Hurtado para tener voses en la Santa Yglesia con dicho Reverendo Padre; dixo que si lo bido y que fue por aber dicho a Pedro Garcia dicho Martin que se saliera dela yglesia y que llendose saliendo bolvio el dicho Reverendo Padre y le dijo no se saliera, que entrara y se quitara la trensa y que no asiendo caso dicho Pedro Garcia le bolvio a desir el dicho Padre pues anda que yo escrivire al Senor Governador para que castigue esta desberguensa y desatencion y que entonses respondio Martin Hurtado con alterada vos pues que le a de aser el Governador, que le a de aser; replico el Reverendo Padre que le a de aser, no sera Xptiano el Senor Governador si a que esto no castiga y bolteando a todos los presentes dicho Reverendo Padre en altas boses dixo le fueran testigos delo que abian oydo, a que respondio dicho Martin, pues Padre escriva Usted, a que yo soy testigo y tambien sere el portador; y que acabado esto prosiguio sus oficios divinos el dicho Padre y no paso mas; preguntado si bido otra cosa; dixo que no y que es la verdad so cargo del juramento que fecho tiene; y preguntado que edad tiene; dixo ser de beynte y cinco anos y que no le toca en los generales; y leyda su declaracion dixo no tener que anadir ni quitar en que se afirmo y ratifico y lo firmo con migo y los testigos ynfraescriptos de mi asistensia a falta de Escribano Publico y Real que no lo ay en este Reyno =

Juan Gonzales Bas (rubric)

testigo testigo
Joseph de Apodaca (rubric) Isidro Sanchez (rubric)

Declaracion de
Matias Romero

Luego yncontinenti en dicho dia, mes y ano, yo dicho Alcalde mayor en presecucion de estas diligencias yse comparecer a Matias Romero aquien estando presente le recivi juramento que yso por Dios Nuestro Senor y la Senal de una Cruz debajo de cuyo cargo prometio de desir verdad en quanto supiere y fuere preguntado; y siendo preguntado si save y a oydo desir que el Reverendo Padre Ministro tiene amonestado, ensenado y predicado que ningun fiel Xptiano entre en la Santa Ygelsia con desconpostura yndesencia y con la trensa del pelo echa; dixo que si lo sabe y a oydo; preguntado si save o bido que Pedro Garcia Jurado entro en la Santa Yglesia sin capote y con trensa echa y se puso delante del dicho Reverendo Padre y si bido que bisto por el dicho Padre lo llamo y en secreto le dixo que se quietase el la trensa; dixo que si lo bido y que dicho Pedro Garcia por una, dos y tres beses le respondio que no queria quitarse la trensa y que dicho Pedro Garcia se fue saliendo y bisto por dicho Reverendo Padre dise este declarante lo bolvio a llamar disiendo que no se saliera y que por ese motivo y por que no yso caso de la llamada le dixo dicho Reverendo Padre pues anda que llo escrivire al Senor Governador para que castigue esta desberguensa y que a esta rason respondio Martin Hurtado pues que le a de aser el Governador, esto con bos alterada; y que a esto replico el Reverendo Padre no sera Xptiano el Senor Governador si esta desatencion no castiga; y a esto respondio Martin Hurtado pues escriva Usted que yo sere el portador y llebare la carta y tambien soy testigo; y que a esto respondio el Padre no sera menester y que luego dise este declarante presiguio dicho Reverendo Padre su dibinos oficios abiendo echo mancion ynterin pasaron estas boses; y preguntado si save otra cosa acerca delo que alli prendi; dixo solo bido que al otro dia le pidio perdon en dicha puerta al dicho Reverendo Padre Martin Hurtado, y que el Padre le perdono y que no sabe otra cosa, y que esta es verdad so cargo de su juramento que fecho tiene y que es de edad de quarenta y cinco anos poco mas o menos; y preguntado si le toca en las generales; dixo que si, que Martin es su tio y Pedro Garcia su sobrino; y leyda su declaracion no tubo que anadir ni quitar en que se afirmo y ratifico y no firmo por no saber, firmelo yo autuando como Jues Reseptor con los testigos de mi asistencia a falta de Escribano Publico y Real que no lo ay en este Reyno =

Juan Gonzales Bas (rubric)

testigo testigo
Joseph de Apodaca (rubric) Isidro Sanches (rubric)

Declaracion de
Lugardo Ballejos
En esta Villa de San Felipe de Alburquerque en cinco írm del mes de Mayo de mil setecientos y treynta y tres anos, yo el Capitan Juan Gonzales Bas, alcalde mayor y Capitan Aguerra de dicha Villa y su jurisdicion en prosecusion de estas diligencias yse compareser a Leogardo Ballejos, aquien estando presente le resevi juramento que yso por Dios Nuestro Senor y la Senal de una Cruz debajo de cuyo cargo prometio de desir verdad en quanto supiere y fuere preguntado; y siendo preguntado si save o a oydo desir que el Reverendo Padre Ministro tiene predicado, ensenado y amonestado que ningun fiel Xptiano entre en la Santa Yglesia sin la devida conpostura que se devia a tan Santo lugar; dixo que si lo save y a oydo; preguntado si save y bido entrar ala dicha Yglesia a Pedro Garcia Jurado sin capote y con la trensa echa; respondio que si lo bido y que tambien bido a dicho Reverendo Padre que llamo en secreto a dicho Pedro y le dixo; hijo quitate la trensa, a que respondio dicho Pedro que no queria por una y dos beses y en esto se fue saliendo dicho Pedro y bist por el dicho Reverendo Padre le dixo, con que no te quitas la trensa; y no asiendo caso prosiguio su camino; y bisto esto por el Padre le dixo, pues anda que esta desberguensa la sabra el Senor Governador y que a esto respondio Martin Hurtado con bos alterada, pues que le a de aser el Senor Governador y que a esto respondio dicho Reverendo Padre que no sera el Senor Governador Xptiano si esta desberguensa no castiga, y que a esto respondio dicho Martin Hurtado pues Padre escriva Vuestro Reverendo, que yo sere portador y tambien soy testigo; y preguntado si sabe otra cosa a serca de esto que paso en la Santa Yglesia; dixo que no solo si lo que sabe que otro dia en el propio lugar pidió perdon dicho Martin Hurtado y que esto es lo que save y no otra cosa y que esta es la verdad so cargo del juramento que fecho tiene; y preguntado si les toca alas generales; dixo que si que Martin es su tio y Pedro su sobrino y que es de edad de beynte y siete anos poco mas o menos y leyda su declaracion no tubo que anadir ni quitar en que se afirmo y ratifico y no firmo por no saber fírmelo yo dicho Alcalde Maior autuando como Jues Reseptor con los testigos de mi asistencia a falta de escribano publico y Real que no lo ay en este Reyno =

                Juan Gonzales Bas (rubric)

testigo testigo
Joseph de Apodaca (rubric) Isidro Sanchez (rubric)

Declarasion de
Lasaro Garcia
Luego yncontinenti en dicho dia, mes y ano yo dicho Alcalde mayor en prosecusion de estas diligencias yse conparecer a Lasaro Garcia a quien le resevi juramento que yso por Dios Nuestro Senor y la Senal de una Cruz debajo de cuyo cargo prometio desir verdad en quanto supiere y fuere preguntado; y siendo preguntado si sabe y a oydo tiene predicado, ensenado y amonestado que el Reverendo Padre Ministro que ningun

feligres entre con desconpostura yndesencia ala Santa Yglesia; dixo que si lo save y a oydo a dicho Reverendo Padre; preguntado si save y bido entrar a Pedro Garcia Jurado a la Santa Yglesia sin capote y con la trensa del pelo echa; dixo que si bido que lo llamo el dicho Padre y le mando que se quitase la trensa; dixo que no le oyo que le dixese nada pero que si bido que lo llamo a solas a onde estava dicho Reverendo Padre revestido; preguntado si bido que dicho Pedro Garcia se salio dela Yglesia y lo que le dixo al dicho Reverendo Padre llendose saliendo; dixo que abiendolo bisto el dicho Reverendo Padre salir lo yso no se saliera y lo llamo y dixo con que te sales; si respondio dicho Pedro Garcia, y no te quitas la trensa respondio el Padre; y dixo el dicho Pedro, no, por que me boy; y preguntadolo que respondio Martin Hurtado o las boses que tubo con el Reverendo Padre; dixo que lo paso es que abiendo el Padre sitado por testigos a todo el auditorio respondio Martin Hurtado con bos alta Padre yo soy testigo y tambien escriva Vuestro Reverendo, que yo sere el portador, pero que por lo que lo desia el dicho Martin, que no lo oyo por estar retirado; y preguntado si save otra cosa delo que alli paso; dixo que no oyo mas y que esta es la verdad so cargo del juramento que fecho tiene; preguntado si le toca en las generales; dixo que no, y que es de edad de treynta y quatro anos; y leyda su declarasion no tubo que anadir ni quitar en que se afirmo y ratifico y no firmo por no saber, firmelo yo dicho Alcalde mayor autuando como Jues Receptor con los testigos ynfraescriptos de mi asistencia a falta de escribano Publico y Real que no lo ay en este Reyno =

Juan Gonzales Bas (rubric)

testigo testigo
Joseph de Apodaca (rubric) Isidro Sanchez (rubric)

Declaracion de
Pedro Garcia
En esta Villa de San Felipe de Alburquerque en seys dias del mes de Mayo de mil setesientos y treynta y tres anos yo el Capitan Juan Gonzales Bas, alcalde mayor y Capitan Aguerra de dicha Villa y su jurisdicion para la aberiguacion de esta causa yse comparecer a Pedro Garcia Jurado prisionero a quien resevi juramento en forma de derecho que yso por Dios Nuestro Senor y la Senal dela Santa Cruz debajo de cuyo cargo prometio desir verdad en cuanto fuere preguntado y siendo preguntado si save que el Reverendo Padre Guardian tiene predicado, amonestado y ensenado que entren ala Santa Yglesia con la debida conpostura y desencia; dixo que si lo save de oyda y bista; preguntado si entro ala Santa Yglesia (el dia de fiesta) con trensa y sin capote; respondio que si y que bisto por el Reverendo Padre, le dixo muchacho quitate la trensa; y dise este declarante que se estubo callado y que el dicho Reverendo Padre bolbio a desirle (abiendolo llamado y le dixo ben aca) con que hijo ben aca, quitate la trensa, y entonses dise este declarante le respondio a dicho Reverendo Padre por que yba para Bernalillo de prisa y con la ocacion de estar la misa proxima entro a ella; pues desatatela hijo que no cuesta muy poco; le respondio este declarante Padre como somos pobres y no tengo quien me peyne no mela desato, y que a esta rason le dixo

el abuelo de este declarante al muchacho salte alla fuera y desatate esa trensa y buelbe a missa como lo executo luego y que llendose salido le grito el Padre opa, con que te sales y no te quitas la trensa; entonses dise este declarante no le respondio nada sino que prosiguio su camino y entro oyer misa; preguntadolo que respondio su abuelo Martin Hurtado quando dixo que escribiria al Senor Governador el Reverendo Padre; dixo que no oyo nada por que se salio por mandado de su abuelo y que esta es la verdad y no otra so cargo de juramento que fecho tiene y que es de edad de beynte y tres anos poco mas, y leyda su declarasion no tubo que quitar ni anadir mas que lo que iba a la margen y entre dos renglones, en que se afirmo y la ratifico y no firmo por no saber, firmelo yo dicho Alcalde mayor autuando como Jues Reseptor con los testigos de mi asistensia a falta de Escribano Publico y Real que no lo ay en este Reyno = = = Otro que dise este declarante que despues delo dicho y que salio de misa tubo noticia como el Padre abia dicho que este declarante estava descomulgado y que como dicho abia entrado a misa despues del ruydo lo ynorava y que le pidio perdon junto con que lo absolbiera y que el dicho Reverendo Padre absolio por si acaso lo estubiera y le perdono dise este declarante y quedaron contentos y se fue a su casa muy descuydado = Vale =

Juan Gonzales Bas (rubric)

testigo testigo
Joseph de Apodaca (rubric) Isidro Sanchez (rubric)

Declaracion de
Martin Hurtado
En esta Villa de San Felipe de Alburquerque en siete dias del mes de Mayo de mil setesientos y treynta y tres anos yo el Capitan Juan Gonzales Bas, alcalde mayor y Capitan Aguerra de dicha Villa y su jurisdicion para mayor aberiguacion de esta causa yse compareser a Martin Hurtado aquien le resevi juramento que yso por Dios Nuestro Senor y la Senal de la Cruz debajo de cuyo cargo prometio de desir verdad en quanto supiere y fuere preguntado; y siendo preguntado si save, bido y oyo lo que yso Pedro Garcia quando entro con la trensa echa y sin capote; dixo que si lo bido que entro sin capote pero con gaban; y que abiendo el dicho Reverendo Padre llamado al dicho Pedro Garcia le mando se quitase la trensa, entonses abiendoselo mandado bolbio este declarante y le dixo, anda muchacho quitate esa trensa y buelbe a entrar a misa y que se salio luego y bolbio a entrar dicho Padre ala Santa Yglesia; y que bolbio dicho Reverendo Padre al puebo dixo que escribiria ala Villa para que se castigara semejante desberguensa y que entonses respondio este dicho declarante, Padre yo sere testigo de aber bisto a dicho Pedro trensado y que bolbio a repetir dicho Reverendo Padre que escriviera sierto loco o fuera de entendimiento escriba Reverendo Padre que si no ay quien llebe la carta yo la llebare y que esto le dixo dijo este declarante con bos baja y no alterada, de que no paso a otra y de ay prosiguio el dicho Reverendo Padre sus oficios; y dise este tal confesante que quedo confuso y arepentido de aber dicho tales rasones por cuyo motivo estubo deseando el que el Padre Ministro acabare sus debinos oficios para que su paternidad saliera para echarse a sus pies y pedir misericordia como asi lo

executo luego que salio dicho echandose a sus pies y pidiendole perdon y no estando con la misericordia que dicho Reverendo Padre yso con este declarante dise quedo tan confuso que se fue a su casa a onde estubo asta otro dia por la manana tocaran a missa y paso este declarante y espero asta que el Reverendo Padre entro ala yglesia y que abiendo entrado en el respuesto antes de entrar el dicho Reverendo Padre en oracion se lebanto este confesante y arodillandose alos pies de dicho Reverendo Padre le pidio renderas perdon y abiendo mando sele lebantara de sus pies y perdonandole, le suplico le diese licensia para dar satisfacion de su culpa a los circumstantes de su culpa la qual dise este declarante sela consedio dicho Reverendo Padre con gran caridad y dise se puso en pie en el mesmo lugar y bolbien alos que estaban presentes les dixo con estas palabras, Senores y Senoras, los que ayer se allaron en esta Santa Yglesia sepan y albiertan que lo que le respondi aller al Padre en ello yse muy mal y que no debia en tan Santo lugar abler una palabra pues que solo devemos entrar con la debida molestia y umildad a pedir a Dios misericordia y si le pido perdon a todos del mal exemplo que les abia dado; y que despues a deber presedido esto tomo el Reverendo Padre la mano dise este declarante y que el dio una platica esperitual tomando por tema el arepentimiento que debemos todos los Xptianos tener de tan exemplar acion como la que abian bisto en este confesante; dise este declarante que confesa su culpa, nuebamente arepentido pide perdon por amor de Dios y por las llagas de nuestro serafico padre San Francisco; y preguntado si tiene otra cosa; dixo que no tiene y que esta es la verdad so cargo del juramento que fecho tiene y que es de edad de sesenta y tres poco mas o menos y leyda su declaracion dixo no tener que anadir ni quitar en que se afirmo y ratifico y lo firmo con migo y los testigos ynfraescriptos de mi asistencia a falta de Escribano publico ni Real que no lo ay en este Reyno =
      Martin Hurtado (rubric)
      Juan Gonzales Bas (rubric)
testigo testigo
Joseph de Apodaca (rubric) Isidro Sanchez (rubric)

En esta Villa de San Felipe de Alburquerque en siete dias del mes de Mayo de mil setesientos y treynta y tres anos yo el Capitan Juan Gonzales Bas, alcalde mayor y Capitan Aguerra de dicho Villa y su jurisdiccion concluydas estas diligencias puestas en estado de sentenciales ago cargo alos mensionados en ellas que se mantengan en la prision asta la determinacion del Superior Govierno quienes lo obedesieron y cumplieron y no tener que alegar a su favor sin que se aga en ellos lo que fuere Su Senoria serbido, en cuya atencion ago remicion de estos al Superior Govierno los quales constan de catorse fojas con una blanca sin una peticion probeyda que ba al fin ynclusa en ellos y para que conste lo firme autuando como Jues Reseptor con los testigos ynfraescriptos de mi asistencia a falta de escribano publico y Real que no lo ay en este Reyno =
      Juan Gonzales Bas (rubric)
testigo testigo
Joseph de Apodaca (rubric) Isidro Sanchez (rubric)

Senor Alcalde Mallor y Capitan Aguerra
Juan Gonzales

Fray Pedro Montano Predicador Jubilario y Ministro presente dela Villa de San Felipe de Alburquerque, paresco ante Vuestra Magestad en la mejor forma que mejor combenga y digo, que por quanto tengo presentado querella como Vuestra Majestad sabe, ante el Senor Governador y Capitan de este Reino contra Martin Hurtado y su nieto Pedro Garcia, por las irreberencias y desacator que los dichos cometieron en el templo de Dios Nuestro Senor, y sobre esto se sirbio Su Senoria de despachar orden a Vuestra Magestad para que los pusiere en prision y siguiesse la causa en fin de lo qual lo executo Vuestra Majestad, assi espero resulta a ora, el que haviendolos llebado Vuestra Majestad a su casa, en donde los tenia asegurados aunque no con el rigor debido a su delicto los ha trasportado Vuestra Majestad a una casa mui proxima ala del dicho Martin Hurtado sin las guardias debidas y combenientes a su seguro en donde dicho Martin Hurtado esta tan suelto como si hubiera hecho milagros, y no tubiera sobre si una culpa tan grave que meresia estar en una bartholina, en donde no viera sol ni luna, pues mas culpa tiene el que su nieto, y como tal delinquente debe estar a demas de con grillos en un fuerte cepo y enserrado, en donde no comunique con persona alguna; y mas grande el dicho puede ocasionar alguna inquietud; por todo lo qual y para la prueba que tengo ofresido de su osadia y atrebimiento contra el respecto debido a Dios Nuestro Senor y a su mui santa casa; pido y suplico a Vuestra Majestad se sirba de quitar de ai a dichos delinquentes y volverlos ala parte donde antes estaban en donde estando los dos en el cepo y aunque no ai grillos, y debajo de llabe con guardias competentes esten seguros para quando el Senor Governador los pida y se conosca y vea que son reos y con delicto grabe, y no quede la suerte que esta dicho Martin Hurtado no parese sino un santo =
Y por que espero dela buena justicia de Vuestra Magestad atendera a este mi justo pedimento, transportando o llebando a los dichos otra ves ala carcel en donde estaban, pues assi combiene no digo mal por a ora, y juro en debida forma esta mi peticion no ser de malicia, sino por el motibo dicho y en lo nesesario, ut supra =
      Fray Pedro Montano (rubric)

En esta Villa de San Felipe de Alburquerque en tres dias del mes de Mayo de mil setesientos y treynta y tres yo el Capitan Juan Gonzales Bas, alcalde mayor y Capitan Aguerra de dicha Villa y su jurisdiccion por quanto Martin Hurtado, preso, me represento allarse falto de salud y para curar las dolencias lo traspaso a una casa de las de esta Villa, lo qual le fue consedido a las casas de mi morada en dicha Villa en donde se alla en la mesma forma que a onde estava prisionero; y por quanto se me tiene representado por la parte contraria se debuelba a su antigua pricion devo mandar y

mando al Teniente de esta Villa Geronimo Jaramillo lo debuelba luego que resiva este decreto ala prision a onde estava juntamente con Pedro Garcia; asi lo provey, mande y firme con dos testigos ynfraescriptos de mi asistencia a falta de escribano publico y Real que no lo ay en este Reyno =
      Juan Gonzales Bas (rubric)
testigo testigo
Manuel Carillo (rubric) Isidro Sanchez (rubric)

En la Villa de Santa Fee en nueve dias del mes de Mayo de mil setesientos treynta y tres anos visto por mi el Coronel Don Gervasio Cruzate y Gongora, Governador y Capitan General de este Reyno de la Nueva Mexico estas hautos de que me ha hecho remission el Alcalde Juan Gonzales Bas devia mandar y mande se de traslado de estos hautos al Muy Reverendo Padre Fray Joseph Antonio Guerrero; asi lo provey, mande y firme con los testigos infraescriptos de mi asistensia a falta de Escrivano Publico y Real que no lo ay en este Reyno =
      Don Gervasio Cruzat y Gongora (rubric)
Gaspar Bitton (rubric) Juan Antonio de Unuanuez (rubric)

Bisto por mi Fray Joseph Antonio Guerrero Padre Jubilario Commissario del Santo Oficio de este Reino y de la Cassa Santa ex-Visitador de la Santa Corte de la Combercion de San Pablo de la Nueba Mexico actual Vice-Custodio de ella, visto estos autos que el Senor Coronel Don Gervasio Cruzate y Gongora, Governador y Capitan General de este Reino y Castellano de Sus Fuerzas y Presidios por Su Magestad, mando se me diese traslado, y aviendolos reconosidos y bisto estar conclusos y probado como de ellos consta lo que en mi fabor hasia los debuelba el Superior Govierno de Su Senoria para que haga y execute lo que mejor le pareciere que sera como siempre lo mejor y para que conste lo firme en esta Villa de Santa Fee en onze dias de el mes de Mayo de mill setesientos y treinta y tres anos =
      Fray Joseph Antonio Guerrero (rubric)

Notes

1. "Predicador Substito, Ex-Visitado, and Comisario" meant that Guerrero was a substitute preacher, had formerly been a kind of inspector, and had formerly been given authority for the New Mexico province. See also Doc. 15.
2. Fray Pedro Montaño was in New Mexico around 1728, though he spent much of his time at El Paso. In 1743 he was made a representative of the Holy Tribunal of the Inquisition for the Custodio of St. Paul, which included New Mexico. According to this document, he was the comisario of the custodio (Greenleaf, "Inquisition": 29; see Docs. 15 and 39).
3. Pedro [Alcantara] García y Jurado was the son of Ramón García y Jurado and Bernardina Hurtado, sister of Martín. They were married in 1710, and Pedro was married to Manuela Quintana in 1732 (Chávez, *Origins*:

183-84; see also Doc. 8).
4. See Doc. 9.
5. Based on this document, Salvador Cristóbal Gómez was 103 in 1733. If that is correct, he was born in 1630. To date, no information has been found about him. He may have been part of the Gómez de Castillo or the Gómez Robledo family.
6. Based on this document, Antonio Varela [de Losada] was born in 1707. He could be the son of Cristóbal Varela and Clementa de Ortega, a founding family of Albuquerque. In 1754 he was mentioned as a petitioner for a grant in Fuenclara (SANM I #1051).
7. Lorenzo Carabajal was born in Río Abajo and was twenty-six when he returned with the Reconquest in 1692. By 1699 he was living in Bernalillo, and in 1706 he had land in Albuquerque. He married Luisa de Hinojos (NMGS, *Aquí*: 204; SANM II #1560).
8. Based on this document, Bartolomé Olguín was born in 1709. He married María Romero, and in 1730 a son was born in Chama. In 1761 he was a petitioner for a land grant at Guelites, bordering the Tomé settlement. He was one of the settlers that abandoned a grant on the Río Puerco because of Indian raids. He may have been a relation of Tomás López Olguín (Chávez, *Origins*; 245; SANM I #649; Doc. 9; NMGS, *Aquí*: 519).
9. According to this document, Francisco Antonio Gonzales was born in 1708. This could be the Francisco Antonio Gonzales who acted as a church notary in Albuquerque in 1727. His wife may have been María Chávez (Chávez, *Origins*: 190; NMGS, *Aquí*: 166).
10. In this document Matías Romero stated that he was born in 1688. His parents were Bartolomé Romero and Luisa Varela, sister of Catalina Varela, wife of Martín Hurtado. The wife of Matías was Ángela Vallejo. His daughter, Rosa or Rosalia Romero, married Lugardo Vallejo, mentioned below, who appears to have been a half brother to Ángela. In 1736 Matías purchased land from Cristóbal Jaramillo (Chávez, *Origins*: 271; SANM I #751).
11. Based on this document, Lugardo Vallejo was born in 1707, the son of Manuel Gonzales Vallego, a blacksmith, and Mariana Hurtado, who came to New Mexico with the Farfán-Velasco expedition. His grandparents were Bernardina de Salas Orozco y Trujillo and Andrés Hurtado, the parents of Martín Hurtado. Lugardo married Rosa Romero, the daughter of Matías Romero. His half-sister was Ángela Teresa Vallejo Romero, mentioned above. He died in 1769 in Albuquerque (Chávez, *Origins*: 271, 303; NMGS, *Aquí*: 79; Esquibel, "Mexico City": 68; see also Doc. 30).
12. Lázaro García stated that he was born in 1699. He was probably the son of Francisco García de Noriega (see Doc. 9). In 1720 he married Nicolosa López, and in 1728, Francisca Varela. In 1739 he was buying land in Santa Fe (Chávez, *Origins*: 358; SANM I #328, #844).
13. This document appears to be out of order, if the date is correct.
14. See Doc. 5.

26

SILK SKIRTS TRADED AND RETURNED AS FALSE; TRADER COMPLAINS
January 19 to April 6, 1734. Source: SANM II #397.

Synopsis and editor's notes: In this Bernalillo case, Miguel Carrillo sent a petition to Governor Cruzat y Góngora, claiming that Nicolás de Aragón had not complied with a contract for purchase of some silk skirts. Carrillo, who was lodged next to Aragón's house, initiated the trade when he showed Aragón's wife, Margarita, some silk skirts. She said that she wanted to buy them, but needed to talk to her husband, and as a pledge gave Carrillo a box of powder, probably face powder. Carrillo claimed it was of no use to him, since his wife did not use powder. Nevertheless, a contract was made between Carrillo and Aragón, with Aragón offering a mule for the skirts. Aragón said that the mule was at Jémez Pueblo and that he, Aragón, would have to go and get it. However, after five days, Aragón sent Carrillo a written note, saying that the skirts were not of silk, and there was no agreement. Carrillo argued that the agreement was still in force. Aragón went to Governor Cruzat y Góngora, stating that there was no contract. The governor agreed with Aragón, determining that the contract was not valid because it had never been made final, by which he probably meant that the contract had not been renegotiated after it was determined that the skirts were not made of silk. The governor further stated that Carrillo was to pay the expenses for the proceedings. The status of the box of powder was not mentioned. Note that the cost of the silk garment was equal to that of one mule.

Year of 1734

Manuel Carrillo,[1] resident of Alburquerque, complaint against Nicolás de Aragón,[2] resident of the puesto of Bernalillo, over a contract involving long silk skirts.[3]
Governor and captain general
1734

[I] Nicolás Aragón, born in this kingdom and a resident of the puesto of San Francisco de Bernalillo, appear before the greatness of your honor in my best and proper form which I have been given and say, sir, that in obedience to the mandate of your honor and at the order of the alcalde mayor of the said jurisdiction, which specified that I appear before your honor within the period of three days which has to do with the following complaint of Manuel Carrillo in which he says that I had a contract with him which I had not completed. He says that I should have complied with a contract, which he says that I did not fulfill and should have been paid with hard money [*plata*][4] for something that his wife was interested in, which [contract] I gave to him for some long skirts,[5] which the said Carrillo told me were made of silk. I, not knowing anything about the skirts, called upon some persons who were knowledgeable about the material because they dealt in such things and who would know if it was silk or not, and they told me that it was not. Those persons were Felipe de Ramírez,[6] Captain Borrego,[7] and Juan Durán de Armijo.[8] For this reason, I say that the contract which was supposedly consummated according to Carrillo was not fulfilled, and is the reason that I have not given him the remainder of what I should have given him, which included a macho and two goats. It has been more than three months since the so-called contract was made, and for which I do not feel obligated to comply with, being that his end was not completed, and which I will not fulfill until I am ordered to do so by your honor. I swear that this document is not done in malice, but for what is necessary.

       Nicolás de Aragón (rubric)

At the Villa of Santa Fe on the 19th of January, 1734, upon being reviewed by me, Colonel don Gervasio Cruzat y Góngora, governor and captain general of this kingdom of New Mexico, took it as it was presented according to all rights and should order and did order that the contracting parties appear before Captain Joseph Gonzales Bas, alcalde mayor of the jurisdiction of the puesto of Bernalillo, and present their information, so that upon his review he can determine according to justice. I thus approved, ordered, and signed it with my assisting witnesses due to the lack of a public or royal scribe, which there are none in this kingdom.

      don Gervasio Cruzat y Góngora (rubric)

Gaspar Bitton (rubric)
Juan Antonio de Unanue (rubric)

At this puesto of San Francisco de Bernalillo, on the 13th of February, 1734, I, Captain Jose Gonzales Bas, alcalde mayor and war captain of the said puesto and of the three pueblos within my jurisdiction, by virtue of the above which was approved by the colonel don Gerbasio Cruzat y Góngora, governor and captain general of this kingdom, should order and did order, that a copy of these proceedings be given to Manuel Carrillo so that he will respond to it within the term of three days and so that he can present the argument which is in his favor. I thus approved, ordered, and signed it with my two assisting witnesses.

       Joseph Gonzales Bas (rubric)

Witness:
Antonio Gurulé (rubric)
Felipe Romero (rubric)

Alcalde mayor

[I] Manuel Carrillo, native of this kingdom and resident of the villa of Alburquerque, appear before your honor as best as I can, and say that upon being informed of the proceedings that have been filed against me by Nicolás de Aragón before the superior government, and in obedience to the proceedings which have been approved by your honor, which state that I have to respond within the term of three days with whatever I have to argue in my favor, I have the following to state: I say that the said demand is false and imagined, because what happened is as follows (as I have verbally stated to the governor), that having been lodged immediately next to the house of the said Aragón, and having some items to show that I had for sale, without intention of selling some long skirts to them, it so happened that the spouse of the said Nicolás Aragón came to my house, or rather the house where I was lodged. It being that her said husband was not at home at the time, and as it is, women always being fond of pretty things which they can use, she happened to like the long skirts, trying them on a number of times. She asked me how much I was asking for them. I told her, I intend on selling them, but it appears to me that you may not have what I am asking for them, that being a fat cow and a number of other items. The woman answered me telling me that although her husband did not have any cows, he had other things which he could pay me with. She added that her husband was not at home at the moment, but that upon his arrival he would see to it that something could be agreed upon. Meanwhile, so that I would not sell them, she told me to hold onto them, and gave me a small box of powder[9] for which her uncle Antonio Montoya[10] had promised to give her a cow along with a calf. Agreeing to do this, I told the lady that I would gladly wait for her husband to return home, but nevertheless I would to try to sell the long skirts, whether he [Nicolás] would come looking for me or not, to try to make a deal.

When the said Nicolás Aragón returned, he went to where I was staying to see what deal could be made. Proposing to make a deal for himself and his wife, he offered to give me a macho that he said had excellent qualities, saying that within a few days he would go to the pueblo of Jémez, where he had the macho, to bring the animal back. Feeling good about what Nicolás had proposed, I said I would gladly wait for the delivery of the macho, which I could use as my transportation, but I would not complete the deal until I was given what I was promised, and told them that they could keep my item [the skirts], feeling that the trade would be completed. Nevertheless, at the insistence of the said Aragón and his wife, I kept the box [of powder], and the trade was considered done. Due to the fact that I had lost my mare, I remained at the place of my lodging for five days, during which time, alcalde mayor, it appeared that they decided against the deal, and at the end of the promised time I left for my home, and on the following day I found that the said Aragón had left me a written note saying that the deal would not be completed.

    Your honor, could you see to it that through some manner it [the deal] goes through and let me know what is to happen? He [Aragón] says that I misled him, which is the reason why he did not go through with the deal. To this I say that if I did, it was justifiable, because if I told him that they were made of silk, I told him so because I had received them as such, along with a number of other items. I was not the one trying to deceive him, as I did not know that it was not silk, as the governor surmises, being that I took it as such, and as such I had shown them to some soldiers. Given but not considered is the fundamental fact that he [Aragón] fell back on his deal, and as I have stated there is enough reason to believe that your honor will rigorously go against him for failing to complete it. He stated that he was not obligated to see that the deal was completed, as it was under his control, since the macho and the two goats were his. To this I say, that if he had given them to me, his obligation would have been met, but he did not come forth on the said day that he was to turn them over to me. Instead, Aragón wrote to me declining to go through with it [the purchase], but yet holding onto something that belonged to me. If the macho was intended to be in good faith of his word, under the circumstances which he gave me, and not because he was short of time and did not give it to me, but if it [the mule] had died or any accident occurred, he would have always been responsible for it and would still be owing to me.[11]

    Because of this, alcalde mayor, your honor should understand my argument and compel him rigorously to complete the said deal, it being through justice, now that he has done it in this manner by placing it in litigation. For all of this I ask and petition your honor that you be pleased to see to it that it is done as I have asked, which is through justice and reason, and I swear in due form that this presentation is not done in malice, but in what I seek, etc.

                      Manuel Carrillo (rubric)

    At this puesto de San Francisco de Bernalillo on the 18th of February, 1734, I, the said Captain Joseph Gonzales Bas, alcalde mayor and war captain of the said puesto and of the three pueblos under my jurisdiction, having reviewed it as was presented and having understood what is contained within it, by virtue of which I should order and did order that a copy of the proceedings be given to Nicolás de Aragón, who is to respond within the time of three days, so that he can argue whatever he can according to his right, giving his account of what he believes. I thus ordered and signed it with my two assisting witnesses due to the lack of a public or royal scribe, which there is none in this kingdom.

                      Joseph Gonzales Bas (rubric)

Witness:
Antonio Gurulé (rubric)
Felipe Romero (rubric)

Alcalde mayor

[I] Nicolás de Aragón, resident of this puesto de Bernalillo, involved in proceedings with Manuel Carrillo, continuing in my favor, received the copy which was given to me by your honor on the 18th of the present month and respond to the argument given by the said Carrillo, who being dressed in very poor clothes,[12] which neither aids him nor are held against him, and so that the issue is continued by your honor, it should be followed and understood solely on the proofs of the witness who was present when the deal was done, and [in regard] to the circumstances which each one of us refers to in this written document. It is my obligation that if my witness (who is Juan Antonio Gallegos)[13] is disallowed, I shall return that which I have, and if he is [allowed], the deal should not be consummated, being that I shall renounce the documents that have been introduced regarding the matter. I thus petition your honor to receive the sworn statement from the said, for which I petition and request of your honor to please do as I request. I swear in due form for what is necessary, etc.

Nicolás de Aragón (rubric)

At this puesto de San Francisco de Bernalillo on the 25th of February, 1734, I, the said Captain Joseph Gonzales Bas, alcalde mayor and war captain of this said puesto and of its jurisdiction, took the petition as it was presented within its context, and I ordered that it be passed on to the said Manuel Carrillo. As to that which the contrary party seeks, I say that this is not the place to allow a witness, which cannot be done until the copies are passed from one party to the other, which is the major justification of these proceedings. I thus decreed, ordered, and signed it with my assisting witnesses due to the lack of a public or royal scribe, which there is none in this kingdom.

José Gonzales Bas (rubric)

Witness:
Joseph Pacheco (rubric)
Juan Julián Gonzales Bas (rubric)

Alcalde mayor

[I] Manuel Carrillo, involved in these proceedings against Nicolás Aragón, appear before your honor in my best and proper form and say that in responding to the copy that was given to me at the order of your honor, dated the 25th of February, and understanding the response of the said Aragón, in which I see little, if anything, which he argues in his favor, only correcting your honor, and not arguing for his behalf, he says that it was not right to allow the written documents, but only to allow that which the witness has to say that he brings forth, who is Juan Antonio Gallegos. I do not allow this witness because of numerous circumstances, being that he cannot be a witness for one part and not the other, but particularly on his behalf because he lives alone with the said Aragón, and who is his brother-in-law. He [Aragón] says that he renounces the documents which were introduced regarding the matter, to that I say that your honor is satisfied with them, and that I [should] be paid the rest of what is owed to me for the deal which we concluded. To continue with other proceedings I will never agree, and above all, if your honor should continue with these proceedings, he will understand the reasoning for them. Violence should not be part of this, because the said Aragón out of his own free will gave me the box of powders, and I of my own, left my item, along with the contract that we had, and the said [Aragón] did not get violent, but as it was, it was done according to his free will.

    That this is fulfilled is what I seek, and if there is a law that does not allow me to execute the deal, I will allow it according to its right; but it says that your honor will allow it as information of the witness. Your honor shall do what is according to justice. The witness which is offered lives in the house of the said Aragón, notwithstanding everything else, and if his qualities and circumstances over his sworn statement are brought up, he will not reveal them per se, and will be against me. Of your honor I petition and request that he be pleased to look at this cause in justice, as it should be, and that I be allowed to comply with the contract. I swear in my proper form that this is not done in malice, but for what is necessary, etc.

    Manuel Carrillo (rubric)

    At this puesto de San Francisco de Bernalillo on the 10th of March, 1734, I, Captain Joseph Gonzales Bas, alcalde mayor and war captain of the said puesto and of its jurisdicition, took it as was presented and as to its content I order that a copy be given to Nicolás Aragón and that he respond to it within three days arguing that which is in his favor. As such I ordered, decreed, and signed it with two assisting witnesses due to the lack of a public or royal scribe, which there is none in this kingdom.

    Joseph Gonzales Bas (rubric)

Witness:
Joseph Pacheco (rubric)
Juan Julián Gonzales Bas (rubric)

Alcalde mayor

[I] Nicolás de Aragón, resident of this puesto of Bernalillo involved in proceedings with Manuel Carrillo, appear before your honor in my best form and say that even though I have renounced the copies, in obedience to the decree of your honor, dated the 10th of the present month, my answer to that in which he says that I corrected your honor, is that it is false, as the parties cannot bring forth other issues but are restricted to that which can be proven. As for that where I offer three considerations, they are, first of all that Juan Antonio Gallegos lives in the home with me, that is wrong, as is proven by the document. Secondly, that he is not capable of providing a sworn statement because he does not know the circumstances about similar propositions; those who say that should be punished because it discredits men in good standing. What needs to be done is to question him about the said circumstances, and if he is not aware of them, disallow his testimony. What I know about him is that the witness is Spanish, Catholic, and is under obligation to know the law of God, and he should not be afraid of doing it [testifying] because it is a sin. The said Carrillo upon seeing everything that is stated is afraid of the proof and refuses the issue of having other witnesses to be brought in by me, which I have presented as such. Of your honor I petition and ask that you be pleased to prove through justice whatever needs to be done, to which I swear in due form, etc.

Nicolás de Aragón (rubric)

At this puesto of San Francisco de Bernalillo on the 17th of March, 1734, I, Captain Joseph Gonzales Bas, alcalde mayor and war captain of the said puesto and of my jurisdiction, took it as it was presented according what is right, and the charges having been presented by the said Nicolás Aragón, I should order and did order that a copy be given to other party, because according to his response or argument the proceedings are to go into the final justification by presenting the witnesses which they have for the issue. I thus approved, ordered, and signed it with my two assisting witnesses due to the lack of a public or royal scribe, which there is none in this kingdom.

Joseph Gonzales Bas (rubric)

Witness:
Juan Julián Gonzales Bas (rubric)
Alexandro Gonzales Bas (rubric)

Alcalde mayor

[I] Manuel Carrillo, involved in these proceedings with Nicolás Aragón, appear before your honor and say that, according to the copy which at the order of your honor was given to me on the 17th of the present month, and having read the ridiculous response which was given to your honor by the said Nicolás Aragón, in which he has nothing fruitful to argue in his favor, saying that the proof should be according to the testimony given by the witnesses (which is right), but if the contract which was agreed to was done person to person, without any other testimony other than that of Aragón's wife and a brother of the wife, given as a brother who lives so close by, on a ranch as neighbors, how favorable can they be to me? In addition, more so when all the laws say that the witnesses who are so close or they know each other and who are related should be disallowed. What I have argued are congruent reasons why they should not be witnesses. In addition to these circumstances, it so happens that the said Juan Antonio Gallegos was a third party, along with the wife of the said Aragón, when I made the deal.

After it was completed, it was easily understood that his brother-in-law, Aragón, was fortunate that I waited in order to execute the said deal (because as I have stated, Aragón was not at home) until he arrived, and he, Juan Antonio, became involved in trying to convince me by telling me about the excellent qualities of the macho, which I believed that which the three of them, husband, wife, and brother-in-law, told me, and thus I left the item with them and took the box of powders. Suddenly, without being totally aware of it, the said Juan Antonio was wanting to deal with me over the box, promising to give me a horse for it. I told him that I would see if I liked it [horse], and if I liked it I would give the box back to him, as I did not need it, nor did my wife, as she did not use powder. Upon having returned back to my home, the said Juan Antonio arrived, bringing the horse, which upon my seeing it I did not like, nor was it worth the price of the box that I had received. Not pleased with this, the said Juan Antonio went back to his home and then on the following day he returned with the paper that said that he would refuse the deal. With such grave circumstances, how can it be that he would make a favorable witness? Your honor can see and understand the circumstance for the just reason that I bring forth. It is said that those who are not capable of being proper witnesses can be punished according to the subject. To this I say that the proof of such should be questioned by your honor, who should ask the three circumstances which are in my favor of the witnesses who are to know and not state to the contrary of what occurred. It says that I, on my behalf, should present those witnesses whom I might have. To which I say that I have no witnesses to present, as among those stated, I was the only one there. I also say that they should be examined as to what they state, and if they contradict themselves, I should be held to everything that I have argued, which are contrary to the statements that the said Aragón has given.

Of your honor I request and petition that you be well served to look at this cause as I have asked, which is just and reasonable, and I swear in due form to the sign of the Holy Cross, that what I have argued is the truth and not in malice but for what is necessary, etc.

Manuel Carrillo (rubric)

At this puesto de San Francisco de Bernalillo on the 27th of March, 1734, I, Captain Joseph Gonzales Bas, alcalde mayor and war captain of the said puesto and for the three pueblos within my jurisdiction, took it as it was presented according to their right, and having reviewed that which was submitted by Manuel Carrillo, justified the proceedings and ordered that the witnesses whom they have offered for their evidence be brought forth. I also ordered that Juan Antonio Gallegos, who is offered by both parties, appear before me. I thus approved, ordered, and signed it with my two assisting witnesses due to the lack of public or royal scribe, which there is none in this kingdom.

Joseph Gonzales Bas (rubric)

Witness:
Alexandro Gonzales Bas (rubric)
Juan Julián Gonzales Bas (rubric)

At this said puesto on the said day, month, and year, I, said alcalde mayor, upon the continuation of these proceedings made to appear before me Juan Antonio Gallegos, who upon being present at the request of both parties was asked about the circumstances of his sworn statement. Upon being capable of taking his sworn statement, he was sworn in before God, Our Lord, and the sign of the Holy Cross, under which he promised to tell the truth in whatever he knew and in what he was asked. He was asked if he knew or was present when Manuel Carrillo made a trade with Nicolás Aragón for some long skirts, and how it occurred. He answered that he was present and that what he knows is that the deal was never made. He was asked if the said Aragón was forced or persuaded into it. He said that they both tried to make the deal, but only if Aragón's wife wanted to do it. He was asked how it was that Carrillo took the box of powders. He said that Manuel Carrillo asked for it so that his wife could see it and see if she liked it, and if she did not like it he would return it. He was asked if he knew anything else. He said that when trying to make the deal Carrillo wanted to see the macho. He was asked why it was not brought forth. He said that it was not brought forth because the macho was at Jémez, and they both agreed that on the day of Santiago, they would both go to Jémez to look at the macho to see if he liked it so that he could take it, and if he did not like it they would not make the deal. It was taken as such, saying that nothing was lost and the items were to be returned. He was asked if he knew anything else. He said that he did not, and he ratified and affirmed what he had stated regarding the sworn statement that he had made, and upon his statement being read back to him, he said he had nothing to add or to delete. He was asked if he was related to anyone. He said that he was, to Nicolás, because he was married to his sister. He did not sign because he did not know how; I, the said alcalde mayor, signed it along with my two witnesses.

Joseph Gonzales Bas (rubric)

Witness:
Alexandro Gonzales Bas (rubric)
Juan Julián Gonzales Bas (rubric)

At this puesto de San Francisco de Bernalillo on the 27th of March, 1734, I,

Captain Joseph Gonzales Bas, alcalde mayor and war captain of the said puesto and of its jurisdiction, having finalized and concluded these proceedings, consisting of ten pages, submit them to the superior government. So that they are valid, I signed them acting as presiding judge with my two assisting witnesses due to the lack of a public or royal scribe, which there is none in this kingdom.

Joseph Gonzales Bas (rubric)

Witness:
Alexandro Gonzales Bas (rubric)
Juan Julián Gonzales Bas (rubric)

At this villa of Santa Fe, on the 6th of April, 1734, after having reviewed the complaint by Manuel Carrillo, resident of the Villa of Alburquerque, against Nicolás de Aragón, who says that a contract was completed and consummated for some silk skirts, I, Colonel don Gervasio Cruzat y Góngora, governor and captain general of this kingdom of New Mexico, find that it is not valid according to these said proceedings, because it was not formally made final, and due to this, I should declare and did declare that with respect to the said skirts, they are to be returned to the said Carrillo, and both parties are to be freed from the so-called contract. Also, I should order and did order that the said Manuel Carrillo is to pay the expenses for these proceedings. I thus approved, ordered, and signed it with my assisting witnesses due to the lack of a public or royal scribe, which there is none in this kingdom.

Don Gervasio Cruzat y Góngora (rubric)

Gaspar Bitton (rubric)
Juan Antonio de Unanue (rubric)

ORIGINAL DOCUMENT

Año de 1734

Demanda puesta por Manuel Carrillo vesino de la Villa de Alburquerque contra Nicolas Aragon vesino del Puesto de Bernalillo sobre la contrata de unas faldillas caprichola.

Señor Governador y Capitan General
1734

Nicolas Aragon originario deste Reyno y vesino del Puesto de San Francisco de Bernalillo paresco ante la grandesa de Su Señoria en la mas bastante forma que ayga lugar y el derecho me concede y digo Señor que obedesiendo el mandato de Vmd. Y orden del Señor Alcalde Mayor de dicha jurisdision el que en termino de tres dias me

pusiere ante la grandesa de Vmd. Alas ya que disiera esto; por demanda que Manuel Cariyo pues dice tubo yo con el dicho Cariyo en que pide le de yo cumplimento a dicho trato no abiendo selebrasion a el pues se afiansa el dicho Cariyo el desir que yebo por señal de dicho trato una la que a de ser de plata siendo asi que la que la yebo para que la biese es su esposa supiera una de las prendas que yo le dava por un tapapiés que el dicho Cariyo me dijo es por de caprichola y no entendiendo yo de generos yame a personas de enterro consimiento tratando en contratantes para que conosieran si era caprichola o no me dijeeran el no serla y fueron estas sircumstancias que me lo dijeron Felipe de Ramires y el Capitan Borrego, Juan Durán de Armijo quienes digan o no ser caprichola si no trajeron mas, asi digo si el trato que es celebrado como dise el dicho Cariyo como no a yebado lo restante que es un macho y dos cabras aviendo el tiempo de tres meses que a que se yebo la propuesta de dicho trato no estando yo obligado a cuidar lo que era que no yso y no le e entregado asta guardar la gran justificasion de Vmd. Que es la que yo me conformo = y por todo lo qual a Vmd. Me la justifique necesario el derecho me asistiere y juro en devida forma no ser de malicia este mi escrito = en lo n
ecesario =
     Nicolas Aragon (rubric)

En la Villa de Santa Fee en dies y nueve dias del mes de Henero de mil setesientos treinta y quatro años vista po mi el Coronel Dn. Gervasio Cruzat y Góngora Governador y Capitan General de este Reyno de la Nueva Mexico la huve por presentada en lo que era lugar en derecho y devia mandar y mande que las partes contrayentes recuran ante el Capitan Joseph Gonzales Bas, Alcalde Mayor dela jurisdizion del Puesto de Bernalillo y presenten su informasion para en vista de ella determinar lo que fuese de justicia. Asi lo provey, mande y firme con los testigos de mi sistencia a falta de Escribano publico y Real que no lo ay en este Reyno =
    Dn. Gervasio Cruzat y Góngora (rubric)
  Gaspar Bitton (rubric) Juan Anttonio de Unanue (rubric)

En este Puesto de San Francisco de Bernalillo en trese dias del mes de Febrero del año de mil setesientos y treinta y quatro años yo el Capitan Jose Gonsales Bas, Alcalde Mayor y Capitan Aguerra de dicho puesto y los tres Pueblos de mi jurisdicion en birtud de la arriva probido por el Señor Coronel don Gerbasio Cruzat y Gongora, Gobernador y Capitan General de este Reyno debia mandar y mande para mayor aberiguasion de estas diligensias hube traslado a la parte de Manuel Cariyo y que responda dentro de tres dias y lo que a su fabor pueda alegar. Asi lo probey, mande y firme con dos testigos de mi asistensia =
    Joseph Gonsales Bas (rubric)
Testigo Testigo
Antonio Gurule (rubric) Phelipe Romero (rubric)

Señor Alcalde Mayor

Manuel Carrillo natural de este Reyno y vecino dela Villa de Alburquerque paresco ante Vmd. como major proseda y digo que abiendome enterado dela representasion que contra mi yso Nicolas de Aragon ante el Superior Govierno y obedeciendo el auto que Vmd. prove en que me manda responda dentro de tres dias lo que ami favor puedo alegar; digo que la dicha demanda es falsa y supuesta, por que lo que paso es de esta manera (como mas berbal lo tengo representado al Señor Governador) que abiendo ospedado ynmediato ala casa de dicho Aragon, llevando yo otra senda y no a benderle al dicho tal tapapies, susedio que como tan proximo bino ami casa o casa de ospedaje la esposa de dicho Nicolas Aragon no estando ay su marido, y como las mugeres siempre son afisinadas a cosas bonitas y de su uso, cuadrole a la tal el tapapies poniendoselo una y muchas veses; y con la aficion que le cobro me trato de cobrarlo y ystando le disiera que queria por el; alo que le respondi, Señora y abenderlo boy, pero Uste me parese no tiene lo que yo busco que es una baca gorda y lo restante en otras cosas; a que respondio dicha muger pues mi marido aunque no tiene bacas, tiene otras cosas con que selo pagara y asi me ara fabor Uste de esperarlo que no esta en casa que biniendo no se dejaran de componer y yo enterado que se conchabaran le dare una cajuela de polvos que mi tio Antonio Montoya dio una baca con su cria por ella; a culla proposion respondi; respondili yo pues Señora lla me aguardo mas por aserle el gusto que por otra cosa que aunque boi a bender el tapapies, fuera cosa que con si o no bolbiera breve a mi casa; bino el dicho Nicolas Aragon quien me fue a buscar ami posada tratome el cambalache y despues de abermelo rogado por si y su muger quedarme a dar un macho que tenia futuro ynsinandome las exelencias de tal macho, el que pasado algunos dias abiade yr a resebir al Pueblo de Xemes que (era donde lo tenia) contentome con que en su palabra no me faltaria alo que dicho macho me abia portado quede contento y digne la casuela la que yo por ningun modo queria resevir asta resevir todo junto y que sus Mercedos quedaran con mi prenda en su poder con apersevimento que lla el cambalache estava echo; mas despues a ynstancia de dicho Aragon y de su esposa hube de resebir la caja; quedose en ese estado dicho cambalache y yo por asidente de aberseme perdido una llegua, me estube en dicha mi posada cinco dias que tiempo fue Señor Alcalde Mayor para que se ubieran arepentido yno lo ysieron, sino que al cabo de dicho tiempo que me fui para mi casa al siguiente dia alle que me escribe dicho Aragon que no pasaba por tal cambalache. Vuestra Merced bea si a rason para que la cosa suseda y aga refleja en todo mi relativo; dise que yo lo engane motivo por donde se arepiente alo qual digo: que siendo asi era muy justo por que si yo le dixe que era capichola dixe bien por que por tal la resevi yo y la resebieron otros y no abia de ser yo quien por estenso la conosia para que yo lo enganara que si es asi que no es capichola el primer enganado sera el Señor Governador que por tal la resive y por tal la destrivuella en los soldados, y dado y no consedido que ensea el fundamento que tenga para repentirse con lo que llevo dicho ay bastante para que con todo rigor le compela Vmd. al cumplimento de dicho trato. Dise que no esta obligado a cuidarlo que es ageno quando esta en su poder el macho y las dos cabras alo qual digo que si Vmd. melo ubiera entregado no ay duda que no estaba obligado, pero sin aber llegado el dia sitado que lo abia de entregar me escrive dicho Aragon esta arepentido como es dable ni rason que cuyde cosa mia, que si es mio el macho es en fee de su palabra con las sircumstancias que de el me pinto, no por que siento de tiempo no melo entrega y sele muere u otro asidente le susede siempre esta obligado y muy obligado a entregarlo o pagarlo asi Señor Alcalde Mayor, Vmd. puede enterado de mi alegata compelarlo rigorosamente me cumpla dicho trato, por ser de justisia lla que el dicho lo a puesto en litis; por todo lo qual a Vmd. pido y suplico sea muy serbido de aser como llevo pedido que es de justisia y rason y juro en debida forma no ser de malicia esta mi representasion sin por conseguir lo que pido, ut supra.

     Manuel Carrillo (rubric)

En este Puesto de San Francisco de Bernalillo en dies y ocho dias del mes de Febrero del año de mil setesientos y treinta y quatro yo el Capitan Joseph Gonsales Bas, Alcalde Mayor y Capitan Aguerra de dicho Puesto y los tres pueblos de mi jurisdision la ve por presentada y echo cargo delo que en eya se contiene en virtud delo cual devia mandar y mande se de traslado al parte de Nicolas de Aragon y que responda dentro de tres dias de su derecho lo que alegar puede y pase a dar la ynformasion de su alegata. Asi lo mande y firme con dos testigos de mi asistensia a falta de Escribano publico y Real que no lo ay en este Reino.

     Joseph Gonsales Bas (rubric)

Testigo testigo
Antonio Gurule (rubric) Phelipe Romero (rubric)

     Señor Alcalde Maior

Nicolas de Aragon vesino deste Puesto de Bernalillo en los autos con Manuel Carrillo, como major combenga ami favor, supuesto el traslado que seme notifico por Vmd. el dia diesiocho del corriente digo que haviendo reconosido lo alegado por el tal Carrillo, bestido de menudensias ynfructiferas, que estas ni agravan el hecho ni lo desminullen, y que para un negosio también
Vmd. deve seguirse y redusirse a solo la prueba del testigo que se hallo presente quando se trato este cambio, y de las sircumstancias que uno y otro referimos en los escriptos, y asi me hobligo a que si me condena dicho testigo (que es Juan Antonio Gallegos) entregar lo que en mi poder para, y de no, que no pase el trato referido, por lo qual renunsio los escriptos que se ofresieron sobre esta material, y solo suplico a Vmd. que se resiva juramento en forma del dicho por tanto a Vmd. pido y suplico se sirva haser como lo pido, juro en forma y en lo nessesario, ut supra.

     Nicolas de Aragon (rubric)

En este Puesto de San Francisco de Bernalillo en beynte y sinco dias del mes de Febrero del año de mil setesientos y treinta y cuatro yo el Capitan Joseph Gonsales Bas Alcalde Mayor y Capitan Aguerra de dicho Puesto y su jurisdision la ube por presentada y en cuanto a su contenido debo mandar a su contenido ala parte de Manuel Cariyo, y en cuanto ala ynformasion que el contrayente pide digo que no ay lugar asta que coran los traslados de una parte a otra para la mayor justivicacion destas diligensias; asi lo decrete, mande y firme con dos testigos de mi asistensia a falta de Escribano publico y Real que no lo ay en este Reino.

     Jose Gonsales Bas (rubric)

testigo testigo
Joseph Pacheco (rubric) Juan Julian Gonsales Bas (rubric)

     Señor Alcalde Mayor

Manuel Carrillo comprendido en estos autos contra Nicolas Aragon paresco ante Vmd. como mejor prosida ami fabor y digo: que respuesta el traslado que se me yntimo por mandado de Vmd. su fecha beynte y cinco de Febrero, y enterado dela respuesta de el tal Aragon y en ella beo lo poco o nada que a su fabor alega pues ba solo a corregir a Vmd. y no alegar de su derecho pues dise que para una parbedad no era menester escriptos sino solo ala que el testigo que ofrese que es Juan Antonio Gallegos (disiere) este por muchas circumstancias lo repudio y recuso por que no puede ser testigo de una y otra parte y por la sulla menos por que bive solo con dicho Aragon de quien es cunado; dise que renuncia los escritos que se ofresieren tocantes a esta material alo qual digo, que por ese motivo puede Vmd. estar satisfecho y que seme pague lo restante que me deve en el trato que ysimos y de pasar a otras dilixensias nunca consierto y sobre todo, aga Vmd. juesio eyendo estos autos y conosera la mucha rason que me asiste, y no seme arguyra en ellos ninguna biolensia, por que dicho Aragon de su boluntad me dio la caja de polvos, y yo dela mia le dexe me prenda, contrato que asentado teniamos, y su puesto que el dicho no fue biolentado sino es que de su boluntad quedo a ello, que seme cumpla que es lo que pido y si ubiere ley que ami me compela a que no sea executado dicho cambalache me resino a que se obre segun derecho; dise que pase Vmd. ala ynformasion de el testigo; Vmd. aga lo que fuere de justicia, el testigo que ofrese bive en casa de dicho Aragon ynobstante eso, si le preguntan las calidades y sircumstancias de el juramento no las dira por tanto, y lo que a mi fabor puede aber; a Vmd. pido y suplico sea muy servido de mirar en justicia esta causa pues de ella es, que seme cumpla el trato, y juro en debida forma no ser de malisia lo que pido, y en lo nesesario, ut supra.

     Manuel Carrillo (rubric)

En este Puesto de San Francisco de Bernalillo en dies dias del mes de Marso del año de mil setesietos y treinta y cuatro años yo el Capitan Joseph Gonsales Bas, Alcalde Mayor y Capitan Aguerra de dicho Puesto y su jurisdision, la ube por presentada y en cuanto a su contenido debo mandar se de traslado ala parte de Nicolas Aragon y que responda dentro de tres dias lo que alega pedir a su fabor, asi lo mande y decrete y firme con dos testigos de mi asistensia a falta de Escribano publico y Real que no lo ay en este Reino.

      Joseph Gonsales Bas (rubric)
testigo testigo
Joseph Pacheco (rubric) Juan Julian Gonsales Bas (rubric)

      Señor Alcalde Maior

Nicolas de Aragon vesino de este Puesto de Bernalillo en los autos con Manuel Carrillo paresco ante Vmd. En la forma mas combeniente y digo que aunque tengo renunciados los traslados por usticia el auto de Vmd. Su fecho dies del corriente digo que que lo que lleva alegado y alego es que el trato no puedo asentado como dise la parte, y en lo que dise que yo corrijo a Vmd. Es falso pues las partes pueden por no multiplicar entidades reducirse las pruebas. Y aunque en la que ofresco poner tres reparos, el uno que bive Juan Antonio Gallegos en una casa con migo es surreptisio, como esta patente la ustic = El Segundo que no es capaz de juramento por que no ust sus sircumstancias que semexantes proposiciones deven ser castigados por que es llegar a el ustici de hombres de bien y lo que en este caso se debe hazer es preguntarle dichas sircumstancias y de no saverlas repudiarlo, por que lo que yo se es que dicho testigo es Español y Catholico, y tiene hobligasion de saber la ley de Dios, y no havia de querer por ni miedades como ser un pecado, y viendo dicho Carrillo todo lo referido y que a de quedar bencido en la ustic la recusa y en caso de que tenga otros testigos son admitidos por mi que los presente por tal; a Vmd. Pido y suplico se sirva de proveer en justicia lo que fuere, juro en forma, ut supra.

      Nicolas de Aragon (rubric)

En este Puesto de San Francisco de Bernalillo en dies y siete dias del mes de Marso del año de mil setesientos y treinta y cuatro años, yo el Capitan Joseph Gonsales Bas, Alcalde Mayor y Capitan Aguerra de dicho Puesto y mi jurisdision la ube por presentada y en cuanto aya lugar en derecho, y echo cargo de la representasion del suso dicho Nicolas Aragon debia mandar y mande se de traslado al parte por que segun su respuesta o alegata se pase ala ultima justificasion presentando los testigos que para dicho efecto tubiere, asi lo probei, mande y firme con dos testigos de mi asistensia a falta de Escribano publico y Real que no lo ai en esta Reino =

Joseph Gonsales Bas (rubric)

testigo testigo
Juan Julian Gonsales Bas (rubric) Alexandro Gonsales Bas (rubric)

Alcalde Mayor

Manuel Carrillo en los autos con Nicolas Aragon paresco ante Vmd. y digo que supuesto el traslado que de orden de Vmd. seme yntimo dies y siete del corriente y abiendome enterado dela sindestia respuesta que dicho Nicolas Aragon ase ante Vmd. pues echo de el caso no alega cosa que le sea frutuosa, disiendo que ala prueba se a de estar de lo que disen los testigos (lo qual es sierto) pero si este trato que ysimos fue de persona a persona sin que lo testificara mas de la muger de dicho Aragon y un ermano de dicha muger y este como ermano y que biven tan proximos, pues en un rancho viven abesindados, que faborables me pueden ser, y mas quando por todas leyes los testigos apacionados, o que se conosca, que en parte son parte alo que se ventila; son repudeados esto supuesto, y lo que alegado llevo son congruentes rasones para que por ningun modo sea testigo; y pasando estas mas circumstancias; que son dicho Juan Antonio Gallegos fue tercero con su ermana y muger de dicho Aragon para que yo ysiese tal cambalache y despues de aberme fasilitado que su cunado, Aragon tendria afortuna el que yo me detubiese para que se ejecutase dicho trato (por que como llevo dicho no estava en casa dicho Aragon) y abiendo benido tambien se metio para que se consiguiera pintandome dicho Juan Antonio las excelensias del macho por que no estava presente los que yo cuyo en fee de lo que los tres me pintaron; esto es marido, muger y cunado, ay abido yo resebido la caxa de polvos que a ystancias de los dichos resevi, y quedando por sulla mi prenda y por mia la caxa, luego aun descuydo trato dicho Juan Antonio de comprarmela dicha caxa prometiendome por ella un caballo, a que respondi que lo beria si me quadrava y que de quadrarme sela daria pues yo no la nesesitaba ni mi esposa pues no usaba tomar polvos; y abiedome benido para mi casa, luego atras, me bino dicho Juan Antonio a traer el caballo, el que bisto por mi no me quadro ni llegava al costo delo que yo resevia dicha caxa, desgustado por esto dicho Juan Antonio se fue luego a su casa y luego otro dia bolvio con el papel en que se arepentia; con esta sircumstancia tan grabante como podra ser que me sea faborable testigos? Bealo Vmd. y considerelo y sacara consecuencia ala justa rason que me asiste; dise que es digno de castigo quien propone la yncapasidad de el juramento en el dicho sujeto; alo qual digo, que ala prueba pues tambien dise que sele pregunte Vmd., le pregunte las tres circumstancias que aun me faborese el que las sepa, pues sabiendolas no dira lo contrario de lo que paso; dise que yo de mi parte presente los testigos que tubiere, alo qual digo; que yo no tengo que presentar ninguno pues entre los dichos solos con migo paso el trato; mas digo que esaminen, por que de su parte ofresen, y que de disir lo contrario me cometo alo que yo en toda forma llevo alegado y poco contradesido en las respuestas que dicho Aragon a dado; Vmd. aga lo que fuera de justicia y no lo que le pareciere como en la representacion alega dicho Aragon, por tanto a Vmd. pido y suplico sea muy servido de mirar esta causa como que en ella pido muy justa rason y juro en toda forma ala Señal dela Santa Cruz ser asi verdad lo que llevo alegado y no de malicia y en lo nesesario, ut supra.

Manuel Carrillo (rubric)

En este Puesto de San Francisco de Bernalillo en beinte y siete dias del mes de Marso del año de mill setecientos y treinta y cuatro años yo el Capitan Joseph Gonsales Bas, Alcalde Maior y Capitan Aguerra de dicho puesto y los tres Pueblos de mi jurisdision la ube por presentada y en cuanto a lugar en derecho y echo cargo dela representasion de Manuel Carrillo pone mayor justificasion destas diligencias mande presentasen los testigos que tiene ofresidos por la prueba como tambien comparesca ante mi Juan Antonio Gallegos ofresido por ambas partes, asi lo probei, mande y firme con dos testigos de mi asistensia a falta de Escribano publico ni Real que no lo ai en este Reino =

Joseph Gonsales Bas (rubric)

testigo testigo
Alexandro Gonsales Bas (rubric) Juan Julian Gonsales Bas (rubric)

En este sobre dicho Puesto en dicho dia, mes y año yo dicho Alcalde Mayor en prosecusion destas diligencias yse compareser ante mi a Juan Antonio Gallegos a quien estando presente por petision de las partes le fue preguntado las sircumstancias del juramento y ayandolo capas le fue resebido y asiendole juramento que yso por Dios Nuestro Señor y la Señal de la Santa Cruz, de bajo de cuyo cargo prometio dezir verdad en quanto supiere y fuere preguntado y siendo preguntado si save o se allo presente quando Manuel Carrillo yso con Nicolas Aragon canbalache de un tapapies y de como paso, aque respondio dicho declarante que si estaba presente y que lo que sabe es que no quedo echo tal trato. Y preguntado si fue forsado dicho Aragon o rogado? Dise que entre los dos lo trataron y que y que solo si sabe que su muger de Aragon queria; y preguntado si sabe como yebo Carrillo la cajuela de polbos? Dise dicho declarante que Manuel Carrillo la pidio por que la biera su muger aber si le cuadraba y de no cuadrarle la bolberia; y preguntado save otra cosa? Dise que estandolo asiendo, queria Carrillo traer el macho; y preguntado que por que no lo trujo? Dise dicho declarante que no trujo por que el macho estaba en Xemes, y que quedaron sitados para el dia de Santiago que abian seles ir a Jemes donde abian de ver el macho aber si le cuadraba para resibirlo, y sino le caudrabase queda cada uno con lo que era cuyo, y que en eso quedaron que dixieron que poco se perdia en traer las prendas. Y preguntado si sabe otras cosas? Dijo que no, en que se afirmo y ratifico so cargo del juramento que fecho tiene y leida su declarasion no tubo que anadir ni que quitar. Preguntado si le tocan en las generales? Dijo que aquien le benia a tocar era Nicolas por estar casado con su ermana; y no firmo por que dixo no saber firmar, firmelo yo dicho Alcalde Mayor con dos testigos.

      Joseph Gonsales Bas (rubric)

testigo testigo
Alexandro Gonsales Bas (rubric) Juan Julian Gonsales Bas (rubric)

En este Puesto de San Francisco de Bernalillo en beinte y siete dias del mes de Marso del año de mill setesientos y treinta y cuatro años yo el Capitan Joseph Gonsales Bas, Alcalde Maior y Capitan Aguerra de dicho puesto y su jurisdision finalisadas y concluydas estas diligencias ago remission al Superior Govierno las quales costan de dies foxas y para que conste lo firme autuando como Jues Reseptor con dos testigos de mi asistencia a falta de Escribano publico y Real que no lo ay en este Reino =

      Joseph Gonsales Bas (rubric)

testigo testigo
Alexandro Gonsales Bas (rubric) Juan Julian Gonsales Bas (rubric)

En la Villa de Santa Fee en seys dias del mes de Abril de mill setesientos treynta y quatro años vistos estos autos por mi el Coronel Dn. Gervasio Cruzat y Gongora, Governador y Capitan General de este Reyno dela Nueva Mexico sobre la demanda puesta por Manuel Carrillo vesino dela Villa de Alburquerque contra Nicolas de Aragon vesino del Puesto de Bernalillo disiendo haverse echo y selebrado contrato sobre unas faldillas de caprichola y no costando por lo que prodiese dichos hautos no haverse concluido ni finalisado formalmente el contrato devia declarar y declaro que respecto a ello se debuelban las dichas faldillas al referido Manuel Carrillo y queden ambas partes libres del referido contrato y devia mandar y mande que el referido Manuel Carrillo pague las costas prosesales. Asi lo provey, mande y firme con los testigos de mi asistensia a falta de Escribano Publico y Real que no lo ay en este Reyno.

      Dn. Gervasio Cruzat y Gongora (rubric)

Gaspar Bitton (rubric) Juan Antonio de Unanue (rubric)

Notes

1. Manuel Carrillo was the son of María de Mondragón and Miguel Carrillo, who was in New Mexico by 1694. Miguel was a native of New Galicia, and his name is included in the 1697 presidio muster. Manuel was married to María Varela in 1727. By1739, he is listed as one of the original petitioners of the Tomé Land Grant (Chávez, *Origins*: 157; Kessell and Hendricks, *RCR*: 956 n50; *TDC*: 128, Alexander, *Cottonwoods*: 286).
2. Nicolás de Aragón may have been the son of Ignacio Aragón, who was in New Mexico by 1705 and Bernalillo by 1710. Ignacio, a weaver, came to New Mexico with the Farfán-Velasco colonists in 1793. Nicolás's wife was Margareta Gallegos. In 1744 Nicolás was named in a complaint by the lieutenant alcalde de Jémez and asked to be allowed to move to Valencia (NMGS, *Aquí*: 65, 440: Chávez, *Origins*: 127-28; Kessell et al., *TDC*: 284, 337 n188; SANM II #459).

3. The Spanish, *unas faldillas caprichola*, can mean petticoat or skirt of silk or ribbed silk. The terminology varies throughout the document.
4. Literally, *plata* means silver.
5. The literal meaning of *tapapiés* is "cover the feet." It could also mean a long skirt or overskirt.
6. To date no information has been found on Felipe de Ramírez.
7. Diego Vásquez Borrego was in New Mexico by 1733, buying the Joaquín Sedillo grant south of the Isleta Pueblo and west of the Río Grande. Borrego was mention in a 1768 petition for land near Cochiti. The land was identified as once belonging to Diego Vásquez Borrego, who lived near a spring called Ojo de Borrego (SANM I #178; NMGS, *Aquí*: 150-51; Christmas, "Nerio Antonio Montoya": 3).
8. Juan Durán y Armijo was a brother of the militia sergeant and barber Antonio Durán de Armijo, who appeared in Docs. 12 and 24, and of Vicente Durán de Armijo (Doc. 19), who prepared a written contract for his son's apprenticeship (Chávez, *Origins*: 136).
9. *Cajuela de polvos*, or powder box—probably a fancy box for face powder.
10. Antonio Montoya's sister, María de la Rosa, was married to Antonio Gallegos. They were the parents of Margarita, the wife of Nicolás Aragón. That is, Antonio Montoya was Margarita's uncle. María and Antonio Montoya were the children of Diego Montoya and María Josefa de Hinojos. The family returned to New Mexico with Vargas in 1692 (NMGS, *Aquí*: 59, 65; Chávez, *Origins*: 235-236; Doc. 1).
11. This argument is muddled, but Carrillo seems to be saying that Aragón agreed to buy the skirts, and the fact that they were not silk is not relevant.
12. *Bestido menudensias ynfructiferas* can be translated as "dressed in rags."
13. Juan Antonio Gallegos was the son of Rosa Montoya and Antonio Gallegos II, who was living in Bernalillo in 1699 and was known as a sheep rancher. Juan Antonio's grandfather, Antonio Gallegos I, was in New Mexico prior to 1680 and was part of the 1680 muster at La Salineta by Otermín. Juan Antonio was married to Juana Varela in 1722. He appears not to have been the Juan de Gallegos who was in New Mexico by 1694 and the husband of Catarina Palomino Rendón (Chávez, *Origins*: 179; Hackett, *Historical Documents*: 140, Kessell et al., *BOB*: 960 n68; Baxter, *Las Carneradas*: 21).

27

ACCUSATIONS OF ILLEGAL TRADING EXCHANGED BY NORTHERN NEW MEXICO OFFICIALS; GOVERNOR PUNISHES BOTH
April 2–May 1735. Source: SANM II #402.

Synopsis and editor's notes: This case shows Juan García de la Mora, a presiding judge and possibly an alcalde, and Diego de Torres, a lieutenant alcalde, both trading illegally with the Indians outside an authorized trade fair. A trade fair had been officially approved for the first of April but was postponed for Easter. When informed of the postponement, the Utes and Comanches, who had already arrived ready to trade, threatened violence. Because of this, and because apparently neither García de la Mora nor Torres wanted to pass up the chance to trade, they traded some goods with the Indians. For some reason, maybe some former disagreement, García de la Mora immediately rode to Santa Fe with an accusation that Torres had illegally traded some knives for skins. Torres then tried to cover up his trading by saying that the knives belonged to other persons. This defense fell apart when these persons were interviewed by the officials and both said the knives belonged to Torres. After lengthy and sometimes rambling testimony, in which Torres also accused García de la Mora of trading illegally, both García de la Mora and Torres agreed that they had bought and sold goods outside an authorized trade fair. Governor Cruzat y Góngora punished both by fining de la Mora and confiscating Torres's trade merchandise. The funds from the sale of those goods were to go for the new church at Santa Cruz. Torres was also required to pay court costs. By 1739 Diego Torres was in the Río Abajo, where in 1740 he led the settlement in the Belén area (SANM I #113).

As background, at the time this complaint was made, there were at least five governors' mandates prohibiting trade with the infidel Indians except at trade fairs opened by the governor or his official. One such mandate from 1705 is discussed in Document 2. The second and third were in 1712, when Governor Flores Mogollón prohibited settlers from visiting the Indian *rancherías* for barter and trade without the governor's permission. Governor Bustamante ordered much the same for the settlers from Taos and Pecos in 1725 (SANM II #185 and #339). A fourth mandate was ordered in 1737 by Governor Olavide y Micheleña and widely published in areas where the trading occurred or where the traders lived: Santa Cruz, Ojo Caliente, Albuquerque, Isleta, Laguna, Zuni, Acoma, Bernalillo, Zia, Santa Rosa, Jémez, San Felipe, Cochiti, Santo Domingo, Taos, and Pecos (SANM II #414). Nearly twenty-seven years later, in 1754, Governor Marín del Valle prohibited trading of certain goods and set limits on prices. This order was likely based on an earlier edict of Governor Cachupín (Doc. 43). The multitude of prohibitions suggest that the laws were ignored and illegal trading continued, the financial reward for trading outside the law being greater that the cost incurred if apprehended (also see Thomas, *Plains Indians*: 130; Foote, "Spanish-Indian Trade").

Year of 1735
Criminal case against Diego de Torres,[1] lieutenant to the alcalde mayor of the jurisdiction of Chama, for having committed acts which are prohibited during a ransom or trade fair [*rescate*]. Lieutenant Torres having been denounced by don Juan García de la Mora.[2]

Lieutenant governor and captain general

[I] Juan García de la Mora, resident of the puesto de Río Arriba,[3] jurisdiction of the new villa of Santa Cruz, appear before your honor in the best form which is possible according to my right and say that having gotten notice that five *ranchos* of Comanches had arrived at Ojo Caliente[4] on the first day of the present month of April, I went to that said place and upon arriving there I found out that the officials of that jurisdiction had not gotten there to open the trade or ransom fair as is the custom. Upon having waited there all day long until four in the afternoon, at which time two Comanches approached the houses and stated that two of their Ute enemies were in the area and that they wanted to leave that night in order to save their lives, and that the Spanish officials were too slow [in opening the fair], and that no one would come to them to buy what they had for sale. For this reason, and because they did not want to wait, they told those who were there to accompany them if they wished. We consulted with each other and no one wanted to go. We told them that we had officials to respect and for this reason they should not get mad. They then left and stated that they would burn everything that they had with them because the Spanish were not on good terms with them and that they only cared for the Utes.

They then left to return to their ranchos, which were set up next to the houses, and I, in order to set a good example due to the circumstances and the experiences which I have in the kingdom and knowing well that in such cases everyone wants to buy whatever they can by circumventing the officials, left in a stealthy way through the back of the houses with some large knives [*belduques*].[5] Upon arriving at the ranches of the said Comanches I found out that a servant of the lieutenant Diego Torres had already purchased a large number of hides and a grayish-colored horse and was trying to purchase other items with some of the knives which he had left. Upon seeing this and knowing as I did that he [the servant] belonged to the said lieutenant of the alcalde mayor, because I knew that he had sent him. I, thus, with more determination and more effort, wanted to find out if it [the trade fair] had been accomplished, or if it had been ordered to be opened by the superiors according to law, and if not, they should not be breaking the law, as was the case by the said lieutenant. If he, the lieutenant, did this and broke the law according to human and divine justice, he should pay for it, and not those who followed him due to his example. In case he, the lieutenant, should deny that the Comanche carrier was sent by him, I will prove it with the information which I offer through competent witnesses, and through myself, by swearing to God and to the sign of the Cross, if necessary. All of this I ask of your honor and request that you agree to receive the said information and punish the guilty one with the sentence that he warrants due to his wrongdoing, and I swear in all form that this my written document is not done in malice but for what is necessary, etc.

Juan García de Mora (rubric)

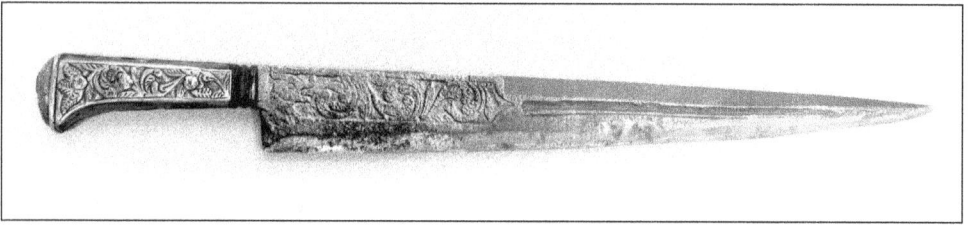

Belduque, eighteenth century, hand-forged steel, silver, and wood. Padilla, *Conexiones*: 100. #1974.15. Image courtesy of the Museum of Spanish Colonial Art, Collections of the Spanish Colonial Arts Society, Inc., Santa Fe.

At the villa of Santa Fe of New Mexico on the 13th of April, 1735, [I], the general Juan Páez Hurtado, lieutenant governor and captain general of this kingdom, was presented with that which was stated above, and upon being reviewed by me, I accepted it as presented in its property right and wished to order, and did order, that the witnesses offered by the petitioner be brought before me to present the information which they have to offer. I thus approved and signed it as juez receptor with my assisting witness on the said day.[6]

Juan Páez Hurtado (rubric)
Witness Joseph Terrus (rubric) Witness Domingo Páez Hurtado (rubric)

Statement of an *infidel* [heathen]
Comanche Indian who was brought
forth as a witness by don Juan
García de Mora

At the villa of Santa Fe on the 14th of April, 1735, I, the lieutenant general, made appear before me an infidel Indian of the Comanche Nation, who having become a Christian Indian, has learned the Castillean language and knows the language of the Comanches, [who] was asked if it is true that he had been sent by the lieutenant Diego Torres to Ojo Caliente with some knives to trade for hides at the camp of the Comanches who were at the said paraje [of Ojo Caliente], and how many hides he had purchased for the said lieutenant. He stated that it was true that he had taken some knives belonging to the said lieutenant Diego Torres with which he purchased ten buffalo hides, and that when he arrived at Ojo Caliente he saw at the houses of those residents some hides which they had purchased, for which reason he purchased the hides which he has declared, assuming that the trade fair had been opened. He said that what he has said is the truth, and that he did not purchase anything else for the lieutenant. So that it is valid he signed it acting as presiding judge on the said day with my assisting witnesses.

      Juan Páez Hurtado (rubric)
Witness Joseph Terrus (rubric) Witness Antonio Montoya (rubric)

Statement of
Joachín Sánchez presented by
don Juan García de Mora

 Continuing, on the said day, I, the said lieutenant general in prosecution of these proceedings made to appear before me and my assisting witnesses Joachín Sánchez,[7] who was presented as a witness by don Juan García de Mora, and upon being present, I received his sworn statement which he made before God according to his right and in which he promised to tell the truth as to what he knew and to what he was asked.

 The petition which was presented by the said don Juan having been read, and understanding what was stated, he [Joachín Sánchez] said that everything that was presented was true and was the way it happened. He has heard that the Comanche purchased for the lieutenant Diego Torres ten buffalo hides with the knives that were given to him by the lieutenant Torres. He does not know if he purchased anything else. So that it is valid I signed it as presiding judge with my assisting witnesses. He said that he was forty years of age and that he is not related in any way. He did not sign because he did not know how. I, the said lieutenant general, signed it along with my assisting witnesses on the said day.

      Juan Páez Hurtado (rubric)
Witness Joseph Terrus (rubric) Witness Antonio Montoya (rubric)

 At Santa Fe on the 18th of April, 1735, I, General don Juan Páez Hurtado, examined the witnesses in this *sumaria*[8] as presented by don Juan García de la Mora and ordered a copy be given to Lieutenant Diego de Torres so that he can respond to it within the period of three days.

      Juan Páez Hurtado (rubric)
Witness Diego de Ugartte (rubric) Witness Francisco Guerrero (rubric)

Lieutenant General

[I] Diego de Torres resident of the puesto de Chama,[9] jurisdiction of the new villa of Santa Cruz, and lieutenant to the alcalde mayor of that jurisdiction, appear before your honor in my best form and say that having been presented with a copy of a petition which don Juan García de la Mora presented against me, and upon reviewing it say that the charges are wrong, false, and void, as is everything that he is trying to prove with a witness, and everything that he says is unfounded.

He [García de la Mora] says that through a notice that he received that five ranchos of Comanches had arrived, he immediately left to be able to trade with the same upon not finding the justice who by custom opens the trade or ransom fairs. To which I argue that as such he proved his intended malice, saying that he had waited for them until three o'clock in the afternoon, during which time the alcalde mayor did not arrive to open the trade or ransom fair and during which time the said don Juan purchased, and was among the most liberal in purchasing items, without respect to the justices, saying that he had been waiting the entire day. As such the said don Juan was the one who was delinquent. Being informed by what an infidel and incapable Indian told him, that I had given him ten knives so that he could sell them for as many buffalo hides as he could get. This is only hearsay, as it was said by an infidel, who had understood that the ransom or trade fair was opened, and whose example was followed by a number of others, causing much confusion, by which reason he, along with a number of others, purchased items. Besides, it was Antonio Trujillo,[10] who, when at my house, gave the knives to the Comanche as I shall prove through the same person when asked and under oath shall tell the truth as shall be proven.

He [García de la Mora] continued by saying that the said Comanches had stated that because the Spanish were waiting so long in making any purchases, they were going to burn everything which they had with them, saying that their enemies, the Utes, were awaiting them [the Comanches] at a distance. To this I answer that he received, or those who were there received, a piece of paper with a note[11] which was written by the alcalde in which he ordered me to hold them until Easter [*Pasqua*] was over as it was a Holy time, and they [the Comanches] were not to leave, which paper with the note I will reveal when I am asked for it. The person who delivered the paper with the note was Paulín de Abeytia[12] and was seen by the said don Juan, and who out of his own free will opened the ransom fair. As can be seen, he was the one who purchased the most, and was the one responsible for opening the trade fair, and I shall prove that without the fear of God and without attention to what is dictated by the laws. He [García de la Mora] was selling two small short swords [*espadines*] (on which your honor can reflect in regard to what he is blamed for in this said matter) along with some knives, which he confesses to in his own written statement. He continues by saying that he has presented information [for his case] by competent witnesses who have appeared before your honor, and that it is not as is stated. For one, it [the testimony] was not seen, but rather hearsay; and second, it was given by an infidel, who is without the fear of God, and whom I at once disregarded and who I say is not one to say the truth due to the few or no obligations that he has. I do not argue that he is my servant, because the said don Juan will interject if I argue that, but he could say that he is his [servant], because he has him in his home, and as such he has him convinced, advised, and persuaded, and the said Indian has accepted this for all the things that have been given to him and for which reason he will not do otherwise.

Also, so that it is annulled, and not justified according to what the said don Juan is trying to prove. Therefore, your honor, upon reading my arguments, shall be able to determine through justice who is at fault and who should be punished as is merited. Your honor shall be able to determine this. Upon receiving the information which I have given and which I am going to prove in this cause according to what don Juan has presented against me before your honor, and which will be seen by the delegates which the governor has in that jurisdiction, who are vigilant to what is ordered by your honor, and in particular to matters concerning trade or ransom fairs. All of this will be seen, and it is known that everyone can benefit whatever they can from the ransom fairs when they are opened by the said justices and regulated by them as is accepted by everyone. Fundamentally the said don Juan argues against this, which is proven by the fact that he opened the trade or ransom fair on his own without waiting for a justice to open it, lacking the proper respect as is meant to be shown to the ministers of the King, Our Lord. A reason can be seen that charges should be imposed for not being obedient, along with not being honest, and voiding everything that he states.

To your honor I plead and ask very respectfully that you be best served to prove in justice that which you think is just, which as such, I shall accept as justice and swear in the best form that this is not done in malice, but for what is necessary, etc.

Diego Torres (rubric)

[At Santa Fe on the 19th of April, 1735, I, General don Juan Páez Hurtado reviewed and accepted the above document and ordered that it be made part of the proceedings, and also ordered that Diego Torres present the witnesses he has to offer.]
Juan Páez Hurtado (rubric)
Witness Juan Domingo Páez Hurtado (rubric) Witness Diego de Ugartte (rubric)

Statement of Paulín de Abeytia presented
as a witness by Diego de Torres.

At this villa of Santa Fe, on the 22nd of April, 1735, before me, General don Juan Páez Hurtado, lieutenant governor and captain general of this kingdom, in prosecution of these proceedings, the lieutenant Diego Torres presented as a witness to provide the information which he has to offer Paulín de Abeytia, from whom upon being present I received his sworn statement which he made to God and the sign of the Cross, under which oath he promised to tell the truth about what he knew and what he was asked.

He was asked if he saw or heard that the knives that were sold at Ojo Caliente by an infidel Comanche belonged to the lieutenant and to Antonio Trujillo. He stated that he did not know if they belonged to one or the other, but what he does know is that the Comanche told him that the knives that he sold belonged to Manuel Martín.[13] He was asked if it is true that he took a paper with a note to Ojo Caliente from the alcalde mayor that ordered the said lieutenant Torres not to consider opening the ransom or trade fair until the Pasqua, as it was a Holy time. He stated that it was true that he took the paper with the note in question and that it was read at Ojo Caliente by don Juan García de Mora before all who were present at the said paraje. He was asked if he knew if the justice of that jurisdiction proceeded to open the ransom or trade fair as was customary. He stated that it was not opened, and the only one who bought anything was the Comanche [servant] who purchased some hides. He was asked if he knew if the said don Juan García had sold two short swords to the infidel Comanche. He said that he only saw him sell one, and that a brother-in-law of said don Juan, named Pedro,[14] told him that he had sold another one. He also knows that he had sold two horses for hides, and that the said don Juan had been among the first to purchase from the Comanches, and at his example others followed. It was said that the said don Juan upon hearing that the Comanches wanted to leave and burn their goods because the Spanish would not purchase anything, stated that it was a shame that they were going to burn them, and that it would be better if they [the Spanish] purchased what they could, and that was what he did. In addition, this witness stated that it was evident that the Comanches had no alternative but to say this, as they were angry.

Although he was asked other questions regarding the case, he stated that he did not know anything else other than what he has said. His statement being read back to him, he said that it was as such, and as he has stated it, and that he affirmed and ratified it; and he added that he was nineteen years of age, more or less, and that he is not related to anyone. He did not sign because he did not know how. I, the said lieutenant general, signed as presiding judge along with my assisting witnesses, on the said day.

       Juan Páez Hurtado (rubric)
Witness Diego de Ugartte (rubric)

Statement of
Antonio Trujillo
presented as a witness
by Diego de Torres

  At this villa of Santa Fe on the 25th of April, 1735, before me, General don Juan Páez Hurtado, lieutenant governor and captain general of this kingdom of New Mexico, Diego de Torres presented as his witness, Antonio Trujillo, a resident of Chama, so that he could offer the information which he had. At which [point], upon being present he was placed under oath which he made before God, Our Lord, and the sign of the Cross, under which he promised to tell the truth about what he knew and what he was asked.

He [Antonio Trujillo] was asked if he knew or had heard that some knives that were used for trade, and that were traded by an infidel Comanche at Ojo Caliente for some buffalo hides, belonged to him [Trujillo] as has been stated in his initial writing by the said Lieutenant Torres. He stated that by the sworn statement that he has made as a Catholic Christian, what he knows is that upon being sent by Lieutenant Torres to see the alcalde mayor of Santa Cruz to ask how it was that five or six ranchos of Comanches had arrived at the house of the said lieutenant and to see what he could do for them. This is what he [Trujillo] told the said alcalde, who told him that he had already been informed by the said lieutenant general through a letter, requesting that he carefully examine the proceedings whether his lieutenant had usurped the ransom or trade fair through contraband, which was against that which he had ordered and for him [Torres] to be punished accordingly if he was in the wrong. He [Trujillo] had received information that don Juan García de la Mora had gone to the said villa [of Santa Fe] to present a written complaint against the alcalde mayor and his lieutenant.

Returning with this information to relate it to the said lieutenant Torres, he [Trujillo] told him [Torres] that he was wrong in sending some knives to Ojo Caliente with the infidel Comanche. Responding hastily, he told the lieutenant that his honor [Torres] could say that they belonged to someone else. To this the lieutenant answered, why could we not say that they were yours? Without hesitation he answered, tell his honor that they were mine, at which time he showed him the written note, which had been given to him. Upon the lieutenant's return from the villa, he once more went to see this witness [Trujillo], and he told him that he, the lieutenant general, called upon him to state if the said knives were indeed his. He [Trujillo] said that under oath he had to tell the truth. How could he say the truth and say that the knives that the Comanche took belonged to him [Trujillo], which he knew from his own statement? Trujillo then told him, then why did you go to the villa? To this the witness stated, how could I not go, being that I was ordered to go by my superior?

Seeing that through this method he could not convince him, he referred him to Antonio de Abeytia so that he could contact that witness to see if he could convince him to say that the knives were his, and so that he would not say anything that was proposed by the said Antonio de Abeytia that would be convincing. Later on, the said lieutenant Torres went to see his alcalde mayor accompanied by the said Antonio de Abeytia to see if he could convince him [the alcalde] not to accompany the witness to the villa and also to see if he [the alcalde] could accomplish that which Antonio de Abeytia would not do. The said alcalde mayor then told his lieutenant that he was his worst enemy by having been delinquent in breaking the order.

Having been asked other questions regarding the case, he said that he did not know anything else other than what he has stated. His statement having been read back to him, he said that he is thirty years of age, and that he is not related in any way. He affirmed and ratified his statement, and he signed it with my assisting witnesses acting as presiding judge on said day.

Juan Páez Hurtado (rubric)

Antonio Trujillo (rubric)
Witness Diego de Ugartte (rubric)
Witness Juan Domingo Páez Hurtado (rubric)

Statement of
Pedro Gomes de Chaves
witness presented by Don
Juan García de Mora

At this villa of Santa Fe on the 20th of April, 1735, before me, General don Juan Páez Hurtado, lieutenant general and captain general of this kingdom, don Juan García de Mora presented as his witness for the information that he could offer, Pedro Gomes de Chaves, resident of Ojo Caliente, from whom, upon being present received his sworn statement which he made to God and the sign of the Cross, under which he promised to tell the truth about what he knew and was asked.

He was asked if he knew, saw, or had heard that the lieutenant Diego Torres had sent an infidel Comanche to Ojo Caliente to purchase from some Indians of his nation, who had arrived to trade buffalo hides for knives belonging to the said lieutenant before the justice, as is customary, could open the ransom or trade fair. He said that what he saw was that the infidel Comanche Indian went to their *ranchería* and purchased some buffalo hides which he carried upon a horse. Also, that don Juan García had gone to trade some [hides] for some knives which he wanted to give to the said Comanche, but who told him that they did not belong to him, that he had purchased them [the hides] with some knives that the lieutenant Diego Torres had given to him, and that they belonged to him. He stated that the purchase had taken place before the justice had opened the ransom or trade fair. He was asked if he knew if the Comanche had purchased anything else for the said lieutenant. He stated that he did not know anything else other than what he has declared. He affirmed and ratified it, saying that he was thirty-two years of age, more or less, and that he is not related to anyone. He did not sign because he did not know how. I signed it as presiding judge along with my assisting witnesses on said day, etc.

Juan Páez Hurtado (rubric)
Witness Diego de Ugarte (rubric) Witness Juan Domingo Páez Hurtado (rubric)

Statement of
Antonio Martín
witness presented by
Juan García de Mora

At the villa of Santa Fe on the 23rd of April, 1735, before me, General don Juan Páez Hurtado, lieutenant governor and captain general of this kingdom, don Juan García presented as his witness for the information which he could offer, the captain

Antonio Martin,[15] resident of Ojo Caliente, whom upon being present received his sworn statement which he made to God, Our Lord, and to the sign of the Holy Cross, under which he promised to tell the truth about what he knew and what he was asked.

He was asked if he knew, saw, or has heard say that an infidel Indian of the Comanche nation had traded some knives which belonged to the lieutenant of the alcalde mayor, Diego de Torres, and that if when they were purchased, the ransom or trade fair had been opened as is the custom by a royal justice. He [Martin] said that what he knows is that when five rancherías of Comanches arrived at his home with hides to trade along with some other items, on the second day after their arrival, don Juan García de Mora, from Río Arriba, along with some other Spanish residents, also arrived, and the Comanches told them to go and purchase what they had to offer, being that they had to leave because the Utes were spying on them. The Spanish told them that they could not go because their captains had not arrived to officially open the ransom or trade fair. The Comanches then left, saying that the Spanish were no good and that they were going to burn everything which they had with them. Don Juan García then told this witness and the other persons who were there that it was a shame that they would burn the goods; saying that they [the Spanish] could go to purchase what they [Comanches] had, if they wished. In the meantime, Paulín de Abeytia arrived with a note from the alcalde mayor written to Lieutenant Diego Torres in which he ordered him not to open the ransom or trade fair until the Pasqua, being that it was a Holy time, and if the Comanches did not wish to wait, they could leave. The said note was read by don Juan García, and after being read, they went to the ranchos and ransomed some hides and other items, and for this witness they brought to his home three items, which he did not want to purchase, having witnesses that he returned them to the owner. Among those who purchased hides, there was a Comanche who told this witness that the hides that he had bought belonged to the Lieutenant Diego Torres. This is what he answered. He was asked if he knew that the said don Juan García had sold two short swords to the infidel Comanches. He said that he did not know, and does not know anything else other than what he has stated; and that he is forty years of age, and that even though he is related to both parties, he is not faulting his religion by the sworn statement. His statement having been read to him, he affirmed and ratified it. He did not sign because he did not know how; I, the lieutenant general, signed it as presiding judge along with my assisting witnesses, who signed it with me, on said day.

Juan Páez Hurtado (rubric)

Witness Diego de Ugartte (rubric) Witness Juan Domingo Páez Hurtado (rubric)

Lieutenant General

[I] Diego de Torres, resident of the jurisdiction of Chama, appear before your honor in my best form possible and in my proper right and say that in response to what has been said that I had sent a number of knives with an infidel, and it having reached me because it was told to me by the captain Juan Esteban García, and shortly after he told me this, I met up with Antonio Trujillo, and upon me telling him about it, he said that he had not pursued it because the knives belonged to him. I then answered him, saying that don Juan should then prove what he is saying, being that he has accused me and reported it to my justice. Trujillo then told me that I should go to the villa of Santa Fe and ask for a copy, and in his response should say that the knives were his. I then proceeded to go to the said villa and upon asking for a copy, it was given to me. Responding to it, I did as Trujillo told me, and I stated that he would confirm what I stated. Returning from the said villa of Santa Fe to my jurisdiction, he asked me how things had gone, and I responded by telling him that everything went fine, that things could not go bad for me by you saying that the knives belonged to you.

After a few days had gone by, I went to his house and place where he lived so that he could give me the same statement, and he then told me that he was going to be a witness in the case. Knowing that my written statement should then be against the said Trujillo for him having first told me that the knives were his, and now he would be saying that they were mine. At this time, your honor should understand his argument and the intent which the said Trujillo now has, and I should have never done what I did, as it would have been found against me, but I was not certain if the knives were mine. Now is the time that it is known if I was really the one who gave the said knives to the Comanche in front of the said Antonio Trujillo, as he has been called as a witness so that he can now do the harm that he wanted to do, without any reason. If the said Trujillo now does this, it will show that the said Trujillo had told me that the said knives were his, or that he said that because he was afraid or through the influence which he has had that they would have said, or he would have had, if he would say that the said knives were his and the punishment would be made against him, but as it is the charges will be made against Torres. However, for the best proof that the said knives really belonged to Trujillo, Baltazar de Abeytia[16] should be called as a witness to see if the said Trujillo told the said Baltazar de Abeytia, without asking him, that the said knives were his and did not belong to Torres. What I have stated is the truth and I swear in my best form that this written document is not done in malice, the costs are not mine, but for what is necessary, etc. Of your honor I ask and humbly petition that he approve this written document as it is done for justice and that your honor will do as is accustomed and execute it as accustomed.

Diego Torres (rubric)

[At Santa Fe on the 25th of April, 1735, the above was presented to me, the general don Juan Páez Hurtado, who reviewed and accepted it as was presented, and ordered that the statement of Baltazar de Abeytia be taken and including in the proceedings.]

Juan Páez Hurtado (rubric)
Witness Diego de Ugartte (rubric) Witness Juan Domingo Páez Hurtado (rubric)

Statement of
Baltazar de Abeytia
witness presented by Diego
de Torres

Continuing, I the said lieutenant general, in prosecution of the these proceedings, made appear before me the soldier of this royal presidio, Baltazar de Abeytia, who upon being present I received his sworn statement which he made before God, Our Lord, and the sign of the Holy Cross, under which he promised to tell the truth about what he knew and what he was asked.

He was asked if it is true that Antonio Trujillo, resident of Chama, told him that the knives that the infidel Comanche sold at Ojo Caliente belonged to the said Antonio Trujillo and not to the Lieutenant Diego Torres. He said, that on Friday, the 22nd of the present month, the said Trujillo told him at Río Arriba that at the pueblo of San Juan, the said Antonio Trujillo had told a Comanche to take fourteen knives to sell for him to Ojo Caliente, and that for doing this he could keep two, from which he returned two, selling ten for buffalo hides which he brought to Trujillo. How could this be done if they were not his? [The lieutenant general said] that it has been heard said that the knives belonged to the lieutenant Diego Torres and not to him, Trujillo. He [Abeytia] insisted that they belonged to Trujillo and not to the lieutenant. He said that this was the truth regarding the charges of the oath which he has taken and which he affirmed and ratified upon it being read back to him. He said that he was twenty-five years of age, and that he was not related to anyone. He signed it along with me, the said lieutenant general and my assisting witnesses, acting as presiding judge, on said day.

      Juan Páez Hurtado (rubric)
      Baltazar de Abeytia (rubric)
Witness Diego de Ugarte (rubric)

Statement of
Antonio de Abeytia

At the villa of Santa Fe on the 28th of April, 1735, I, the said lieutenant general in prosecution of these proceedings and for his satisfaction, made appear before me the militia alférez Antonio de Abeytia, who was cited for his statement by Antonio Trujillo, and being present I received his oath which he made to God, Our Lord, and to the sign of the Cross, to which he promised to tell the truth as to what he knew and what he was asked.

He was asked if it is true that the lieutenant Diego de Torres called this witness so that he would go to the house of Antonio Trujillo to tell him to say that some knives which had been sold by a Comanche at Ojo Caliente, before the ransom or trade fair was opened by a justice, as is the custom, belonged to the said Antonio Trujillo, and under his own free will would make his statement before him. He [Abeytia] said that it was true that this witness [Abeytia] was called to come to his home [that of Torres] on a certain night by the lieutenant Diego Torres, who pleaded with him to go to the home of Antonio Trujillo and tell him that some knives which had been sold by a Comanche at Ojo Caliente, and which belonged to him [Torres], really belonged to Trujillo, telling him that he had a lost cause. This witness, in order to please him, went to see him and to tell him. The said Trujillo told him [Abeytia] that in no way would he do that, and that he had already made a sworn statement.

This answer was taken back to the said lieutenant Torres, who then pleaded with him to go with him to see the alcalde mayor, at whose advice he had told him to have this said witness to go to see the said Antonio Trujillo. This witness and the lieutenant then went to the home of the alcalde mayor to see how the whole issue could be fixed, being that the said Trujillo would not go along with the idea, and he was the one who had told him to try and convince the said Trujillo. The lieutenant then told the alcalde mayor Juan Esteban [García de Noriega][17] that if he had not advised him to say that the knives that had been sold belonged to Antonio Trujillo this would not have happened. To this the alcalde mayor answered by asking why he had done this in writing, telling him that if he had done it to make an argument of the case because it was an issue of his honor, he should have kept his opinions to himself and that he who has fallen, has fallen.

Seeing that this had not worked, the lieutenant then pleaded with this witness to go to this villa [of Santa Fe] to see his said lieutenant to see if he would have compassion and that he would give him a cloak upon it being done. However, it did not work because the case had been so highly publicized and because the damage done was so commonly known. This is the truth regarding the charges of the oath which he has made and which upon his statement being read back to him, he affirmed and ratified it. He said that he was thirty-seven years of age and that he was not related to anyone. He signed it along with me and my assisting witnesses acting as presiding judge on the said day.

Juan Páez Hurtado (rubric)
Antonio de Abeytia (rubric)

Witness Diego de Ugartte (rubric) Witness Juan Domingo Páez Hurtado (rubric)

At Santa Fe on the 28th of April, I, the lieutenant general don Juan Páez Hurtado, having examined the witnesses in this sumaria as presented by the accused, and in order to finalize the proceedings and submit them to the colonel Gervasio Cruzat y Góngora, my governor and captain general, I ordered a copy be given to don Juan García de la Mora so that he can respond to it within the period of three days.

Juan Páez Hurtado (rubric)

Witness Diego de Ugartte (rubric) Witness Juan Domingo Páez Hurtado (rubric)

Lieutenant governor and captain general

[I] Juan García de Mora, resident of Río Arriba, jurisdiction of the new villa of Santa Cruz, appear before his honor in my best form possible and for the better, I say that being given a copy of the proceedings which his honor has been following concerning the litigation between myself and lieutenant Diego Torres over the ransom and trade fair, and being made aware of the what the other party has presented, I say that in the copy that was given to me of the action taken by his honor against the said lieutenant, including the statement of Joachín Sánchez, he [responded] by denials and giving falsehoods to that which I presented, and it [his response] is not true. I have proven it through the competent witnesses whom I have presented including the ones who he presented, as well as the one who was presented by Antonio Trujillo, who all find him guilty and condemn him due to all of the fraud which he went about doing and what he attempted to do by going through numerous routes, which I, in telling the truth, have proven through the information which has been offered and given.

Another thing, even though the said lieutenant says that it is not sufficient that I have seen and know that the knives which the Comanche used to purchase what he did were his, though there is no doubt that they were. This is what happens when certain terms and slander, which are used by men when they want to criminate [distort] the case when they have a bad case, but it is not true and should not be of any value, not even in doing me wrong. In legalities it is not right to argue without justification, and much less in allegations that require proof. So that I am convinced by the slander which was given under my authority, he needs to give information that says that I told those who were present that they could go ahead and purchase what they wished, and it was through my authority or absolute power, which I wish I had. It is my ultimate intention to charge what is merited and [to take responsibility for] that which I merit, thus I would say that and which is also that understood by the said lieutenant and is comprehended to follow, that without fear of God, I sold the short swords and [if for] that I deserve to be excommunicated, then I do not know what laws give that order. The certainty is that the said lieutenant should have studied more of what he talks about regarding publications of certain laws, which if there are any, and he knows them, they should be published as bandos so that they are known by everyone and so that he as a justice can punish by law anyone who breaks the laws. They should be made known to foreigners and those newly arrived in the area, as I am one of them.[18] They should be reviewed every year so that no one can argue their ignorance and being in the fear of God to care for and safeguard them, so that no one can be at fault [for misunderstanding] what is meant, and not being done through a bando and through ignorance which has occurred up to the present, I find myself sufficiently secure with God and for his honor.

I say that I cannot argue that which I could not and justify myself through the censure which has cost me so much, but I trust that these proceedings will bring about a definitive sentence and have not caused a bother to his honor, so that through the whole matter he shall be totally convinced and that the said lieutenant be punished and placed under his care and custody and his job is to be cared for so that the orders are carried out as his superiors deem them to be performed. As it is, he is the one who broke them and gave a bad example as he has given to me and to those who also purchased items, and as such your honor should find it right to set us free of any wrongdoing, and that he be given everything that is justified in whatever he should merit for his wrongdoing, either punishing him or pardoning him or whatever your honor deems is correct. For everything else which the said lieutenant Diego Torres argues in his defense, I do not wish to mention anything else about it for being implicated for it as such and condemned for the malice which has occurred and the truth being confessed by those on his behalf as presented for everything which has happened and has been argued. Of your honor, I ask and petition that he be pleased to approve that which is done through justice, through which I shall mercifully receive and I swear in proper form that it is not done in any malice but for what is necessary, etc.

     Juan García de Mora (rubric)

  At Santa Fe on the 28th of April, I the lieutenant general don Juan Páez Hurtado, having examined the witnesses in this sumaria as presented by the accused, and in order to finalize the proceedings and submit them to the colonel Gervasio Cruzat y Góngora, my governor and captain general, I ordered a copy be given to the lieutenant Diego Torres so that he can respond to it within the period of three days.

     Juan Páez Hurtado (rubric)
Witness Diego de Ugarte (rubric) Witness Nicolás Ortiz (rubric)

     Lieutenant general

[I] Diego de Torres, resident of the puesto of Chama, jurisdiction of the new villa of Santa Cruz, say that upon your honor having given me a copy of the petition on the 2nd day of May regarding the charges which I am being accused of, in the second document presented by don Juan García de Mora, I answer what is the truth and is certain, that in the past month of April, on the first, which was Holy Friday [*viernes de Dolores*], being at the new villa of Santa Cruz in the company of Captain Juan Esteban García, alcalde mayor of the said jurisdiction, we received notice from the alcalde mayor of the pueblo of San Juan that five rancherías of Comanches had arrived at Ojo Caliente. The message was sent by the Indian Santiago,[19] who knows the Spanish language as well as the language of the Comanches, and who knew the reason for their coming to that place. A notice was then sent back with the same Indian to find out why they had come and what they were looking for, which was all done on that same Friday. He returned later that night, about eleven o'clock, saying that five ranchos had gone into Ojo Caliente, and that the Comanches told him that they could not go to the pueblo of San Juan, which was what the Indian had told them, because their horses were very tired and they were on the lookout for the Utes, who were following them. I know that the Spanish, on the following day, it being a Saturday, went to Ojo Caliente, where they were to hold a trade fair for the goods that they [Comanches] brought with them. For this same reason I sent the same Indian to see the said alcalde mayor and await the response of the alcalde mayor at the home of the said Diego Torres. On this same Saturday, in the morning, the infidel Comanche, who lived at Río Arriba, arrived on a very tired mare and asked me if he could borrow a horse so that he could go to Ojo Caliente. I tried to hold him back for a while until I got word from the alcalde mayor, but he told me that he would proceed at a slow pace. By virtue of this whole thing, it is true that I gave him some of my knives so that at the arrival of the said alcalde mayor, who was to open the trade fair, he would sell them for me, and I told him that I would give him two knives for doing this for me.

However, the alcalde mayor did not go there, but instead sent a written order, as is known by his note, which is within these proceedings between pages three and four [see the end of this document], which was sent by my order with Paulín de Abeytia, as was seen in his statement, to Ojo Caliente, and was read at that place by don Juan García de Mora, who was the one who had the most interest that it be opened and who stated that it could have very easily been opened. Due to this it is possible that the infidel Comanche could have done what he did, without a direct order from me. It is clear that I was to have gone there in the company of the said alcalde mayor. In response to that which he says that the knives belonged to me, it was due to the agreement that was made with me by the said Antonio Trujillo as can be seen in his statement, where your honor can understand my very small malice. It was best that I negate a truth that was so certain. As for what is stated by don Juan García de Mora, in which he ignores that he sold some swords [*espadas*] and some short swords to the infidels, I say, sir, that I cannot ignore that. Also, he is not recently arrived here as he says. In all of the occasions where trade fairs have occurred, there was initially a bando by the said governor as well as others which were done by his predecessors, which specified that arms were not to be sold, as it was against the royal laws to do so, from which I have the full understanding that it is not right to sell them. For all of this I ask and petition your honor that he be pleased to serve to grant to me his accustomed charity, being that my malice was small. All of this I await the Christian zeal of your honor and swear in all form that my writing is in certainty and truth and for what is necessary, etc.
      Diego Torres (rubric)

At the villa of Santa Fe on the 4th of May, 1735, I, the general don Juan Páez Hurtado, lieutenant governor and captain general of this kingdom, having followed these proceedings until placing them in the state of obtaining a sentence, I submit them to the commandant don Gervasio Cruzat y Góngora so that his honor, upon his review, can make a final decision. So that it is valid I signed it acting as jues receptor along with my assisting witnesses, on said day.
      Juan Páez Hurtado (rubric)
Witness Joseph Torres (rubric) Witness Diego de Ugarte (rubric)

Sentence

This dispute and criminal cause has been reviewed by me after having been heard by the lieutenant general don Juan Páez Hurtado, due to my absence, on account of a denunciation made by don Juan García de la Mora, resident of Río Arriba, against Diego de Torres, resident of Chama and lieutenant to the alcalde mayor of the jurisdiction of the new villa of Santa Cruz, over some knives that were sent by the said Diego de Torres with a Comanche Indian so that he could purchase some hides before the ransom and trade fair was opened by a competent official. In the same manner, I have reviewed that which resulted against the said don Juan García de la Mora, denouncer, along with what is found in the proceedings and which for now are combined, etc.

Lacking attendance at the proceedings and merits of the proceedings to which I refer, and through which I am to condemn and do condemn the said Diego de Torres so that he loses the ten buffalo hides which are referred to in the proceedings as having been purchased before the ransom or trade fair was opened in the accustomed manner, and which I apply for the construction of the new church which is being built in the said new villa of Santa Cruz, and I also condemn him so that he has to pay the expenses which were incurred. I also have seen that which resulted against the said don Juan García de la Mora, and I condemn the said don Juan García in the amount of ten pesos of the current money of the country, which I apply for the [purchase] of *luminarias*[20] for the Holy Sacrament of the altar at the church of the said new villa of Santa Cruz, being that the proceedings reveal that he purchased some hides before the said ransom or trade fair was opened. I exonerate and absolve him from everything else that the hides could possibly bring as to a specific amount as well as for the said denunciation which he brought forth against the said lieutenant Diego de Torres as can be seen through these proceedings. In the future the said lieutenant Diego de Torres and the said don Juan García de la Mora are warned that they will lose, without any doubt, everything that they purchase at any ransom or trade fair without the ransom or trade fair being opened by the royal justice, and in addition they will be fined in the amount that is convenient along with any other arbitrary punishment.

For this, my definitive sentence which has resulted, is hereby pronounced, ordered, and signed at this villa of Santa Fe on the 7th of May, 1735, along with my assisting witnesses due to lack of a royal or public scribe, which there is none in this kingdom and which appears on common paper because the sealed type is not found in these parts.

don Gervasio Cruzat y Góngora (rubric)
Witness Gaspar de Bitton (rubric) Witness Juan Antonio de Unanue (rubric)

Act of Pronouncement

At Santa Fe on the 7th of May, 1735, being that the closing of that which was

argued is finished, and the sentence above given and pronounced by me, Colonel don Gervasio Cruzat y Góngora, governor and captain general of this kingdom of New Mexico, I signed it along with my assisting witnesses, to which I certify.
     don Gervasio Cruzat y Góngora (rubric)
Witness Gaspar Bitton (rubric) Witness Juan Antonio de Unanue (rubric)

Order
  At the villa of Santa Fe on the said day, month, and year, I, the colonel Gervasio Cruzat y Góngora, governor and captain general of the kingdom of New Mexico, should say and do say to notify the herein contained Diego de Torres and don Juan García de la Mora of the aforesaid sentence, and I approved, ordered, and signed it with my assisting witnesses due to the lack of a public or royal scribe, which there is none in this kingdom.
     don Gervasio Cruzat y Góngora (rubric)
Witness: Gaspar Bitton (rubric) Witness Juan Antonio de Unanue (rubric)

Notification
  At the villa of Santa Fe on 16th of May, 1735, I, Colonel don Gervasio Cruzat y Góngora, governor and captain general of this kingdom of New Mexico, in compliance with the order of the previous proceedings, made it known and personally notified the persons involved, the lieutenant Diego de Torres and don Juan García de Mora, verbally, of everything contained in the said sentence. They stated that they heard it, consent to it, and obey everything that is stated in the sentence and they will comply with what it says. This is what they answered and I signed it along with my assisting witnesses due to the lack of a public or royal scribe, which there is none in this kingdom.
     don Gervasio Cruzat y Góngora (rubric)
      Diego Torres (rubric)
     Juan García de Mora (rubric)

[Paper with notes. The following is the written note sent to Captain Diego de Torres from alcalde mayor Juan Esteban García denying the opening of the ransom or trade fair.]

Captain Diego Torres
  My dear sir. Santiago has arrived to tell me the reason that the ranchos of the Comanches have arrived, [which is to] bring meat and hides. Your honor, do not allow any person of any class to go to them now because we find ourselves at a Holy time.

If they [the Comanches] wish to wait until the Passover, they can wait, and if they do not, they can leave. Your honor should find out if anyone has purchased anything before the lieutenant gave the approval. I also inform you that Santiago told me that the Comanches might come down to your home. You should send word to them that they should not do so until the Sunday of the Pasqua. This is all that I ask of you. God guard your honor for many years. La Cañada, April 2, 1735.

    I kiss the hand of your honor. Your friend who esteems you.
    Juan Estevan García (rubric)

ORIGINAL DOCUMENT

Año de 1735

Causa criminal fulminada contra Diego de Torres Theniente de Alcalde Mayor dela jurisdizion de Chama sobre haver contravenido a lo providido en los Resgates. Por denuncia que hiso Dn. Juan Garcia de la Mora contra dicho Theniente Diego de Torres.

Señor Theniente de Governador y Capitan General

Juan Garcia de Mora vezino del Puesto del Rio Arriba jurisdizion dela Villa Nueba de Santa Cruz paresco ante Vuestra Señoria en la mejor forma que aya lugar en derecho y a el mio combenga y digo que habiendo tenido notizia de que entraron zinco Ranchos de Cumanches en el Ojo Caliente el dia primero del corriente mes de Abril pase a dicho Puesto de Ojo Caliente y llegado halle no haver benido las justizias de dicha jurisdizion para que como se acostumbra se habriese la feria o rescatte y estaba esperando todo el dia asta las cuatro de la tarde que binieron para las casas dos Cumanches quien dijeron hallarse zerca dos de sus enemigos los Yuttas y que querian yrse ala noche para livertar sus bidas y que los Capitanes Españoles estaba mui despazio y no benian a comprarles lo que train a bender por cuya razon y la de no querer espararse nos dijeron alos que alli nos hallabamos que fueramos acompanarlos lo que cada uno pudiera por que no podian aguardarse consultamos los Españoles sobre esto y ninguno se determino; dijimosles que nosotros teniamos justizia a quien respectar por cuya razon no podianse enojarse y salieron diziendo se yban a quemar lo que train por que ya los Españoles estaban mui mal con ellos y que solo querian alos Yutas y con esto se fueron yendo para sus Ranchos que estaban ynmediatos a dichas casas yo por no dar mal exemplo alos zircumstantes con la esperienza que del Reyno tengo y saber que en tales casos todos porcuran hazer diligenzia de comprar con solo recatarse de la justizia me fui saliendo a espaldas de la casa con el recato posible con unos belduques y llegando alos dichos Ranchos de dichos Cumanches halle que ya tenia comprado (un criado del Theniente Diego

Torres) una carga de pieles, un caballo tordillo y prosiguiendo ha bender una porzion de cuchillos que le quedaban. Yo biendo y sabiendo como supe ser del Theniente de Alcalde Mayor dicho criado (pues a la razon lo hera pues hera su embiado); hize con mas resoluzion mi dilixensia attenido a que los que establezen o por sus superiores sello manda establezer una ley, no pueden ser derogadores de la ley, y si el dicho Theniente lo fue, derogandola si acaso sobre lo dicho la ubiere sera Justizia Divina y humana que dicho Theniente lo pague, y no los que despues de el, y a el exemplo del hizimos nuestra diligenzia, y si acaso dicho Theniente negase ser el Cumanche a quien embio; embiado suyo yo lo probare con ynformazion que ofresco por testigos competentes y por mi, que con, juramento a Dios y la Senal de la Santa Cruz la dare si nesesario fuere por todo lo cual, a Vuestra Merzed pido y suplico se sirba dar por bueno lo hecho o de resibirme dicha ynformazion castigando a el culpado con la pena que mereziere su culpa, y juro en toda forma que este mi escripto no es de maldad alguna y en lo nezesario, ut supra.
       Juan Garcia de la Mora

En la Villa de Santa Fee de la Nueba Mexico en trese dias del mes de Abril de mill setecientos treinta y sinco años, ante mi el General Juan Paez Hurtado Theniente de Governador y Capitan General deste Reyno, la presento el contenido y vista por mi la ube por presentada en quanto a lugar en derecho y devia mandar y mande presente los testigos del suplicante para la ynformasion que ofrese, asi lo provei y firme actuando como Juez receptor con testigos de asistensia en dicho dia.
    Juan Paez Hurtado (rubric)
Testigo Joseph Terrus (rubric) Testigo Domingo Paez Hurtado (rubric)

Declarazion de un Yndio
Cumanche infiel presentado
Por Dn. Juan Garcia de Mora

En la Villa de Santa Fee en catorze dias del mes de Abril de mil setecientos treinta y sinco años yo dicho Teniente General yse pareser ante mi a un Yndio infiel de Nacion Cumanche a el qual mediante un Yndio Xptiano llamado inteligente en la lengua Castellana y en el idioma de los Cumanches, le pregunta si es verdad lo havia embiado el Theniente Diego Torres a el Ojo Caliente con unos cuchillos a rescatar pieles a las tiendas de los Cumanches que se hallaban en dicho Paraje y quantas pieles compro para dicho Theniente. Dijo que es verdad que llebo unos cuchillos de dicho Teniente Diego Torres y que con ellos le compro diez queros de Sibolo, y que quando llego a el Ojo Caliente bido en las casas de aquella vezindad algunos pieles que abian comprado, por cuya causa compro el las pieles que lleva declaradas presumiendo estar abierto el rescate, y que es verdad lo que lleva dicho, y que no compro otra cosa para dicho

Teniente y para que consta lo firmo actuando como Juez receptor con los testigos ynfrascriptos de mi asistencia en dicho dia.

      Juan Paez Hurtado (rubric)

Testigo Joseph Terrus (rubric)
Testigo Antonio Montoya (rubric)

Declarasion de
Joachin Sanchez presentado
por Dn. Juan Garcia de Mora

Yncontinente en dicho dia yo dicho Teniente General en prosecusion de estas diligencias yse parecer ante mi y los testigos de mi asistencia a Juachin Sanchez, presentado por testigo dela informazion que ofreze Dn. Juan Garcia de Mora a el qual estando presente le resebi juramento que iso por Dios Nuestro Señor en forma de derecho debajo de cuio cargo prometio desir verdad delo que supiere y le fuese preguntado y habiendo leido la peticion presentada por dicho Dn. Juan y enterado de su contesto dijo, que es verdad todo lo que en ella refiere haver pasado asi, y que le oio decir a dicho Cumanche haverle comprado a el Theniente Diego Torres diez queros de Sibolo con los cuchillos que le dio a bender dicho Theniente Torres y que no sabe ubiese comprado otra cossa, y para que conste lo firme como Juez receptor con testigos de asistenzia. Dijo ser de edad de quarenta años y que no le tocan las generales, no firmo por no saber, firmelo yo dicho Theniente General y los testigos de mi asistenzia en dicho dia.

      Juan Paez Hurtado (rubric)

Testigo Joseph Terrus (rubric) Testigo Antonio Montoya (rubric)

En la Villa de Santa Fee, en diez y ochoc dias del mes de Abril de mil setesientos treinta y sinco años yo el General Dn. Juan Paez Hurtado, Theniente y Capitan General de este Reino dela Nueba Mexico haviendo examinado los testigos de esta sumaria presentados por Dn. Juan Garcia de la Mora mando seles de traslado al Theniente Diego de Torres y que responda dentro del termino de tres dias, asi lo probey firme actuando como Juez receptor con testigos de asistenzia en dicho dia.

      Juan Paez Hurtado (rubric)

Testigo Diego de Ugartte (rubric) Testigo Francisco Guerrero (rubric)

      Señor Theniente General

Diego de Thorres vesino de la poblazon de Chama jurisdizion de la Villa Nueba de Santa Cruz y Teniente de Alcalde Mayor en ella paresco ante Vmd. como mejor proseda y digo: que abiendoseme dado traslado de una petizion que contra mi presento Dn. Juan García de la Mora la que bisto por mi y echo cargo de lo que me ymponga allo ser ylita, falso y nulo por nada de lo que con testigo y lites ba aprobar aserlo y lo que en ella alega es cosa de fundamento por que dise el dicho Dn. Juan que por noticia que tubo de que entreban cinco ranchos de Cumanches se puso en camino para tener feria con los dichos y que por no allar a las justizias como es costumbre para que se abriesen dicha feria o rescate alo que digo que solo en eso se le puede conoser su deprobada malicia pues dise estubo aguardando asta las tres de la tarde y siendo asi que en ese tiempo ni llego el Alcalde Mayor ni yo para que abriesemos dicha feria o rescate como dicho Dn. Juan compro y fue uno de los mejores librados en la compra, faltando a respecto de justicia que dise aguardo todo el dia, luego el dicho Dn. Juan es el que dilenquio; pues llebado delo que un Yndio Gentil y yncapas y como rustico le dixera yo le abia dado dies cuchillos para que los bendiese por otros tantos cueros de Sibolo, y esa es la que di por causal sin mas que lo dijo un ynfiel motibo bastante que tubo el dicho para abrir la feria y dado y no consedido que fuera como melo calunia no es bastante para que poder absoluto comprase el dicho y otros que en su exemplo compraron fuera de que los cuchillos los entrego Antonio Truxillo en mi casa a dicho Comanche como dare ynformazion con el mismo que zele pregunte de bajo de juramento y dira la verdad por donde quedara bastantemente probado; delante esto prosigue disiendo que por que los dichos Cumanches avia dicho tardando los Españoles en comprarles que se yban a prender fuego a lo que trayan, por que estaban con sus enemigos los Yutas ala bista amenasandoles alo qual digo que en estos del caso supuesto que resibio o resibieron los que alla estaban un papel que escribe el Alcalde en que me dise los mande detener asta pasado Pasqua por ser tiempo Santo y de no que se ballan el cual mostrare quando seme pida y el que llevo dicho papel fue Paulin de Abeytia el que bisto por dicho Dn. Juan y lo que su voluntad le dicto abrio la feria o rescate y en bista de ella fue el que mas compro pues con mucho trayde, delo yngano se yso cabesa para abrir dicha feria y le probare como sin temor de Dios pues esta yncurso en una descomunio sin las leyes que el derecho dispone bendio dos espadines (en donde Vmd. puede aser reflexa delo culpado que en dicha materia se alla) amas de algunos cuchillos que en su mesmo escrito confiesa; prosigue disiendo dara ynformasion con testigos competentes la qual tomo Vmd. y no son como los promete por uno no es ocular, sino es de oydo, y otro ynfiel sin temor de Dios el que desde luego anulo, y pongo por yncapas de desir verdad por las pocas o ningunas obligaciones que le asisten, no alego no ser mi criado por que el dicho Dn. Juan lo antepone si le arguyo que suyo lo es, porque lo tiene en su casa, y como tal lo tendra bien alusinado, aconsejado y eyndusido, y dicho Yndio aber aseptado por tener los gratos no le echen de su combenencia motivo uno y otro para que y lo anule, y no lo consienta se justifique con el lo que el dicho Dn. Juan ba aprobar por donde Vmd. leydo mi alegato podra ser juicio de quien es el culpado y que se de debajo pena meresida resevida la ynformazion de la que boi a probar esto supuesto doy esta causal para que el dicho Dn. Juan alla ante Vmd. presentado contra mi; y es el ser los delegados que el Señor Governador tiene en aquella jurisdizion vexilios alo que por Su Señria seles ordena y mas en particular en esta materia de feria o rescate que miren los dichos sea con apersibimento de que todos gosen de ellos lo que pudiesen siendo abiertos por dichas Justicias este cuydandoles es amargo a muchos y con mayor fundamento sele deve arguir al dicho Dn. Juan pues quede probado abrio el rescate de motu proprio sin esperar Justicia que lo abriera faltando al devido respecto que como a ministros del Rey Nuestro Sñeor se les deve motivo por donde Vmd. le puede aser cargo de ynobediente amas de ser falso y nulo lo que le dispone. Por todo lo qual y lo que alegar puede resebida que sea la ynformasion. A Vmd. pido y suplico muy rendidamente sea muy serbido de probar en justicia lo que le paresiere ser justo que en ello resevire justicia y juro en debida forma no ser de malicia y en lo nesesario, ut supra.

Diego Torres (rubric)

En la Villa de Santa Fee en dies y nuebe dias del mes de Abril de mil setesientos treintna y sinco años, ante mi el General Dn. Juan Paez Hurtado, Theniente de Governador y Capitan General de este Reino la presento el contenido y por mi bisto la ube por presentada y debia mandar y mande se acumule a los autos de esta materia y que el Theniente Diego Torres presente los testigos que ofreze para determinar en Justicia asi lo probey, y firme actuando como Juez receptor, con testigos de asistensia, en dicho dia, ut supra.

Juan Paez Hurtado (rubric)

Testigo Juan Domingo Paez Hurtado (rubric) Testigo Diego de Ugartte (rubric)

Declarazion de
Paulin de Abeytia presentado
por Diego de Torres

En la Villa de Santa Fee en veinte y dos dias del mes de Abril de mill setesientos treinta y sinco años ante mi el General Dn. Juan Paez Hurtado, Theniente de Governador y Capitan General de este Reino en prosecusion de estas diligencias el Theniente Diego Torres presento por testigo para la informasion que tiene ofrezida a Paulin de Abeytia a el qual estando presente le resebi juramento que iso por Dios Nuestro Señor y la Señal dela Cruz de vaxo de cuio cargo prometio dezir verdad delo que supiere y le fuere preguntado, si sele vido o oido desir que los cuchillos que bendio en el Ojo Caliente un Cumanche infiel eran del Theniente y de Antonio Truxillo; dijo, que no sabe si eran del uno o del otro, que lo que sabe es por haverselo dicho el Cumanche que los cuchillos que bendia eran de Manuel Martin, y responde. Preguntado si es berdad que llevo un papel a el Ojo Caliente del Alcalde Mayor en que ordenaba a dicho Theniente Torres no consintiese abrir dicho resgate asta la Pasqua, por ser tiempo Santo. Dijo que es verdad que llebo el papel que la pregunta contiene y que en dicho Ojo Caliente lo leiyo Dn. Juan Garcia de Mora delante de todos los que se allaban en dicho Paraje y responde. Preguntado si sabe que la Justicia de aquella jurisdizion prosedio abierto el rescate como es costumbre. Dijo, que no estaba abierto sino por el Cumanche que huviera comprado unos cueros, y responde. Preguntado si sabe que dicho Dn. Juan Garcia ubiese vendido dos espadines a los infieles Cumanches. Dijo, que solo uno bido bender este declarante y que el otro le dixo un cunado de dicho Dn. Juan, llamado Pedro, que lo avia bendido tambien, y que asi mismo sabe haber bendido dos cavallos por pieles, y que el dicho Dn. Juan fue el primero en comprar alos Cumanches y a su exemplo otros y que dicho Dn. Juan oiendo que los Cumanches se querian ir, y quemar la ropa, por que no sela compraban los Españoles, dise dicho Dn. Juan Garcia no es lastima que se lleben o quemen la ropa, mas a comprarsela como con efecto asi lo executo, y anade este declarante que adbirtio en el senblante de dichos Cumanches no tener alterazion alguna ni estar enojados y aunque sele isieron otras preguntas a el caso tocantes, dixo no saber mas delo que lleba declarado, y siendole leida su declarasion dijo estar segun y como lo tiene dicho y que en ella se afirma y ratifica, y que es de edad de diez y nuebe años poco mas o menos y que no le tocan las generales con ninguna delas partes, no firmo por no saber, firmelo yo dicho Theniente General como Juez receptor actuando con testigos de asistensia que lo firmaron con migo en dicho dia.

                      Juan Paez Hurtado (rubric)

Testigo Diego de Ugarte (rubric)

Declarasion de
Antonio Truxillo
Presentado por
Diego de Torres

En la Villa de Santa Fee en veinte y cinco dias del mes de Abril de mil setecientos treinta y sinco años ante mi el General Dn. Juan Paez Hurtado, Theniente de Governador y Capitan General de este Reino dela Nueba Mexico el Theniente Diego de Torres presento por testigo para la informasion que dicho ofresia Antonio Truxillo vezino de Chama a el qual estando presente le resevi juramento que yso por Dios Nuestro Señor y la Señal de la Cruz debajo de cuio cargo prometio desir verdad delo que supiere y le fuere preguntado. Preguntado si sabe o a oido desir que unos cuchillos de resgatte que un Cumanche infiel bendio en el Ojo Caliente por unos pieles de Sibolo eran deste declarante como lo sita en su primer escripto dicho Theniente Torres. Dijo, que por el juramento que fecho tiene como Catolico Xptiano, lo que sabe es que haviendolo enbiado dicho Theniente Torres a ber a el Alcalde Maior ala Villa de Santa Cruz a dar razon de como habian llegado a casa de dicho Theniente sinco o seis ranchos de Cumanches haver que disponia de ellos como con efecto asi selo dixo a dicho Alcalde quien le dijo a este declarante que ya me abia dado quenta ami dicho Theniente General por carta, pidiendome ysiese esquisitas diligencias sobre si el su Theniente ubiesen usurpado el rescate en contrabension delo por mi mandado los castigase con la pena correspondiente ala culpa por haver llegado a su notizia que Dn. Juan Garcia de la Mora pasaba a esta dicha Villa a presentar escripto contra dicho Alcalde Mayor y su Theniente Torres; y bolviendo con esta razon este declarante a darsela a dicho Theniente Torres le dise que estaba perdido por haver enbiado unos cuchillos a el Ojo

Caliente con el Cumanche infiel, yntiendolo apurado este declarante le dixo a dicho Theniente pues no puede Vmd. desir que eran de otro; a cuia rason respondio dicho Theniente, pues dise que eran de Vmd. y sin adbertir en lo que ofresia, le dixo diga Vmd. que son mios, en cuya su posesion metio el escripto ofreziendolo por testigo de su informazion y debuelta que fue dicho Theniente dela Villa, bolvio haver este declarante y le dijo como yo dicho Theniente General lo llamaba para que declarase si dichos cuchillos eran suyos; a que le respondio, pues llegado haser juramento he de desir la verdad, de como los cuchillos que llebo el Cumanche eran de Vmd., y esto lo supe de su misma boca; y entonses le dijo pues no vaya Vmd. ala Villa, a que este declarante le respondio como puedo dejar de yr siendo llamado de mi superior yiendo que por este camino no pudo conseguir nada se balio de Antonio de Abeytia para que biese a este declarante a que lo reduxese a desir que los cuchillos son suios o que no biniese ha declarar que nada delo propuesto por dicho Antonio de Abeytia puede conseguir; y despues dicho Theniente Thorres paso a ber a su Alcalde Mayor acompanado del dicho Antonio de Abeytia haver si podia alcansar con el que no biniese este declarante ala Villa y juntamente haver si podia alcanzar, lo que no havia podido, Antonio de Abeytia; y el dicho Alcalde Mayor le dijo a su Theniente que el habia de ser su peor cuchillo habia deliquido en quebrantar el orden y responde; y aunque se le isieron otras preguntas al caso tocante, dijo no saber mas de lo que lleva declarado, y siendole leida su declarazion dijo que es de edad de treinta y ocho años y que las generales no le tocan y que en su declarazion se afirma y ratifica y lo firmo con migo y los testigos de mi asistencia actuando como Jues Receptor, en dicho dia.
      Juan Paez Hurtado (rubric)
      Antonio Truxillo (rubric)
Testigo Diego de Ugartte (rubric) Testigo Juan Domingo Paez Hurtado (rubric)

Declarazion de
Pedro Gomes de Chaves
Presentado por Dn.
Juan Garcia de Mora
En la Villa de Santa Fee en veinte dias del mes de Abril de mil setecientos treinta y sinco anos, ante mi el General Dn. Juan Paez Hurtado, Theniente General y Capitan General de este Reyno, Dn. Juan Garcia de Mora presento por testigo para la informazion que tiene ofresida, a Pedro Gomes de Chaves, vesino del Ojo Caliente, el qual estando present le resebi juramento que iso por Dios Nuestro Señor y la Señal dela Cruz, de bajo de cuyo cargo prometio de dezir berdad delo que supiere y le fuere preguntado. Preguntado si sabe, bido, oio desir, que el Theniente Diego Thorres enbio un Cumanche ynfiel a dicho Ojo Caliente a comprar a unos Yndios de su Nasion que abian entrado con rescate, pieles de Sibolo, con cuchillos de dicho Theniente antes que por la Justicia como es costumbre se abriese dicho rescate. Dijo que lo que bido este declarante fue que el Yndio Cumanche infiel entro en la rancheria y compro unos pieles de Sibolo que traia en un cavallo yllendo a cojerle algunas dicho Dn. Juan Garcia, por unos cuchillos

que le abia dado a bender a dicho Cumanche, esto le dijo que no eran sullos aquellos cueros, que los havia comprado con cuchillos del Theniente Diego Torres, cuios eran; y que esta compra se iso antes que por la Justicia se abriese el rescate. Preguntado si sabe que dicho Cumanche ubiese comprado otra cosa para dicho Theniente. Dijo, no sabe mas delo que lleba declarado por ser la verdad, y lo que bido; y dijo siendole leida su declarazion que es como lo lleba declarado, y que en ella se afirme y ratifico, y que es de edad de treinta y dos anos poco mas o menos y que las generales no le tocan; no firmo por no saber, firmelo yo dicho Theniente General actuando como Jues Receptor con los infrascriptos testigosde mi asistencia en dicho dia ut supra.

    Juan Paez Hurtado (rubric)

Testigo Diego de Ugartte (rubric) Testigo Juan Domingo Paez Hurtado (rubric)

Declarazion de
Antonio Martin
Presentado por Dn.
Juan Garcia de Mora

En la Villa de Santa Fee en veinte y tres dias del mes de Abril de mil setesientos treinta y sinco anos ante mi el General Dn. Juan Paez Hurtado, Theniente de Governador y Capitan General de esta Reino, Dn. Juan Garcia de Mora presento por testigo para la informazion que tiene ofresida a el Capitan Antonio Martin, vezino del Ojo Caliente, a el qual estando presente le rezevi juramento que iso por Dios Nuestro Señor y la Señal de la Santa Cruz debajo de cuio cargo prometio desir berdad de lo que supiere y le fuese preguntado. Preguntado si sabe, bido o a oido desir que un Yndio infiel de Nasion Cumanche ubiese vendido unos cuchillos del Theniente de Alcalde Mayor Diego de Thorres, y si quando los compro, estaba abierto el rescate como es costumbre, por la Real Justicia. Dijo, que lo que sabe es que haviendo llegado ala casa de este declarante sinco ranchos de Cumanches con rescate de pieles y algunas piezas al segundo dia de haver llegado, llego del Rio Arriba Dn. Juan Garcia de Mora y otros Españoles, binieron los Cumanches a desirles fueran a comprarles lo que traian por que se querian ir por andar los Yutas ispandolos y disiendoles dichos Españoles no podian ir por no haver benido sus Capitanes abrir el rescate y entonses dichos Cumanches se fueron entendidos disiendo no estaban buenos los Españoles que ellos yban a quemar lo que tenian, a estas rasones dixo dicho Dn. Juan Garcia a este declarante y los demas Señores no es lastima que estos quemen la ropa, bamos a comprarsela a que fueran ellos si querian y estando en esto llego Paulin de Abeytia con un papel del Alcalde Mayor escrito a su Theniente Diego Torres en que le mandaba no abriese el rescate asta la Pasqua, por ser Semana Santa, y que si no querian esperarse los Cumanches que se fueran, cuyo papel leiyo dicho Dn. Juan Garcia y despues de leido bajaron a los ranchos y rescataron algunas pieles y piezas, y a este declarante le trageron a su casa tres piezas, las quales no quiso comprar asiendo testigos de como las bolvio a su dueno; y entre los que resgataron pieles fue uno el Cumanche quien le dijo a este declarante ser las pieles que havia comprado del Theniente Diego Torres, y responde.

Preguntado, si sabe que dicho Dn. Juan Garcia ubiese bendido dos espadines a los infieles Cumanches. Dixo, no saberlo y que no sabe mas delo que lleba declarado y que es de edad de quarenta anos y que aunque le tocan las generales con ambas partes, no por eso a faltado a la religion del juramento y siendole leida su declarazion dijo estar segun y como la tiene declarada y que en ella se afirmo y ratifica, no firmo por no saber, firmelo yo dicho Theniente General actuando como Jues Receptor con testigos de asistencia, que lo firmaron con migo dicho dia.

      Juan Paez Hurtado (rubric)

Testigo Diego de Ugartte (rubric) Testigo Juan Domingo Paez Hurtado (rubric)

      Señor Theniente General Dn. Juan Paez

Diego de Torres vezino y morador dela jurisdizion de Chama paresco ante Vmd. en la mejor forma que ayga lugar y a mi derecho conbenga y digo: que en atenzion aver presentado de que yo havia enbiado una punta de cuchillos con un ynfiel y haviendo llegado a mi notizia por havermelo dicho el Capitan Juan Esteban Garcia y despues de haverme dicho esto me encontre con Antonio Truxillo y dandole yo la rason zitada arriba me dijo pues no a presentado en su lugar por que los dichos cuchillos son mios; y a esto le respondi pues yo con dezir que me diera la prueba dicho Dn. Juan delo que hubiera presentado contra mi Juez volvio dicho Truxillo y me dijo Vmd., passe ala Villa de Santa Fee y pida traslado, y en su escripto diga Vmd., que los cuchillos son mios; y passe ala dicha Villa y pidiendo el traslado luego seme dio; y respondiendo a el hize lo que dicho Truxillo me dijo zitandolo para mi ynformazion y volviendo de dicha Villa de Santa Fee para mi jurisdizion me pregunto que como me havia ydo y le respondi que bien, que ami nunca me pudiera ir mal mayormente diziendome Vmd. que eran suyos los cuchillos. Haviendo pasado unos dias ya le fui aver a su casa y morada para que volviera a dar dicha declarazion y me respondio que el venia a declarar en contra causa y notorio que de nuebamente este mi escripto contra dicho Truxillo por haverme dicho que siendo suyos dichos cuchillos venia a dezir que eran mios, aqui acavara de conozer Vmd. su mucho su aleguada y depravada yntenzion, con que obra de sus prenzipios dicho Truxillo, que yo poca nesesidad tenia de haverlo presentado el suio seme hubiera descubierto ami, que yo no savia de zierto si eran suyos los cuchillos o no; aqui se acava de conoser mi mucha rason pues si yo hubiera dado dichos cuchillos al Cumanche delante de dicho Antonio Truxillo lo avia de haver zitado de testigo para que me hiziesse el dano que el me pretende aser aora sin ninguna razon; pues teniendola que hiziera dicho Truxillo, pues el haver rretratadose dicho Truxillo delo que me avia dicho de que eran dichos cuchillos suyos lo a echo por miedo o por ynflusiones que aya tenido de que le avieran dicho o el lo abra alcanzado si digo que son mios dichos cuchillos me caia la pena enzima pues como saldre esto echandole la carga a Torres. Pero para mayor prueba de que dichos cuchillos son de dicho Truxillo llamase a Baltazar de AAbeytia a juramento que le dijo el dicho Truxillo al dicho Baltazar Abeita sin preguntarle los dichos cuchillos son mios y no de Torres y

lo dicho es la verdad y juro en devida forma no ser este mi escripto de malicai, costas, y en lo nesesario, ut supra. A Vmd. pido y suplico rendidamente se sirva de probeir este dicho escrito como es de justizia y Vmd. los acostumbrado y acostumbre executarlo.
      Diego Torres (rubric)

En la Villa de Santa Fee en veinte y sinco dias del mes de Abril de mil setecientos treinte y sinco anos, ante me el General Dn. Juan Paez Hurtado, Theniente de Governador y Capitan General deste Reino la presento el contenido y bista por mi la ube por presentada en lo que a lugar en derecho y debia mandar y mando se resiba declaracion a Baltazar de Abeytia y fecha que se acumule alos auctos desta materia y asi lo probey y firme actuando como Juez receptor con testigos de asistencia en dicho dia.
      Juan Paez Hurtado (rubric)
Testigo Diego de Ugarte (rubric) Testigo Juan Domingo Paez Hurtado (rubric)

Declarazion de
Baltazar de Abeytia
Presentado por Diego
de Torres
Luego incontinenti yo dicho Theniente General en prosecusion de estas diligencias yse pareser ante mi a Baltazar de Abeytia soldado de este Real Presidio a el qual estando presente le recevi juramento que yso por Dios Nuestro Señor y la Señal de la Cruz de vajo de cuio cargo prometio desir verdad delo que supiere y le fuese preguntado. Preguntado si es berdad que Antonio Truxillo, vesino de Chama le dijo que los cuchillos que un Cumanche ynfiel havia bendido en el Ojo Caliente eran de dicho Antonio Truxillo y no del Theniente Diego Torres. Dijo, que el Viernes, veinte y dos del coriente le dijo el dicho Truxillo a este declarante en el Rio Arriba que en el Pueblo de San Juan havia bisto dicho Antonio Truxillo a un Cumanche para que le llevara ha bender a el Ojo Caliente catorze cuchillos y que de ellos le dio dos por su trabajo y otros dos le bolbio, y diez que le bendio, cuios cueros de Sibolo le trajo a dicho Truxillo, y para que fuera a el Ojo Caliente el dicho Cumanche le presto un caballo tordillo el Theniente Diego Torres; y recombiniendole este declarante a el dicho Truxillo que como desia ser suios los cuchillos quando corrian bozes ser del Theniente Diego Torres y no suios; y se afirmo ser de dicho Truxillo y no del Theniente, y esto es la verdad so cargo del juramento que fecho tiene en que se afirmo y ratifico siendole leida su declarasion. Dijo ser de edad de veinte y cinco anos; y que las generales no le tocan, y lo firmo con migo dicho Theniente General y los testigos de mi asistensia actuando como Juez receptor, en dicho dia.
      Juan Paez Hurtado (rubric)
      Baltazar de Abeytia (rubric)
Testigo Diego de Ugartte (rubric)

Declarazion de
Antonio de Abeytia

En la Villa de Santa Fee en veinte y ocho dias del mes de Abril de mil setecientos treinta y sinco anos yo dicho Theniente General en presecuzion de estas diligencias y para su maior justificazion yse pareser ante mi a el Alferez de Milizia Antonio de Abeytia a quien zita en su declarazion Antonio Truxillo, el qual estando presente le resevi juramento que yso por Dios Nuestro Señor y la Señal de la Cruz devajo de esta causa prometio desir verdad delo que supiere y le fuese preguntado. Preguntado si es verdad que el Theniente Diego de Torres enbio a llamar a este declarante para que fuese de ir a Antonio Truxillo a su casa afin de que digase que unos cuchillos que havia bendido un Cumanche en el Ojo Caliente antes que se habriera el resgate por la Justicia como es costumbre, eran de dicho Antonio Truxillo, y que de su poder consiguir este que biniese a declarar ante mi. Dijo, que es verdad que fue llamado este declarante por el Theniente Diego Torres una noche a su casa y le rogo pasase ala de Antonio Truxillo le dijese que unos cuchillos que havia bendido un Cumanche en el Ojo Caliente de dicho Theniente, diguese eran de dicho Truxillo por desirle se allava perdido; y que este declarante por haserle el gusto pase haverlo y haviendoselo propuesto. Respondio dicho Truxillo que de ninguna manera la haria, llegandole aser juramento y que esta respuesta sela trajo a dicho Theniente Torres quien le rogo a este declarante pasaze en su compania haver a el Alcalde Mayor de cuio consexo havia mandado el recado a este declarante para que pazase a ber a dicho Antonio Truxillo; y haviendo pasado ha ber a el Alcalde Mayor a su casa este declarante y dicho Theniente para ber como se podia componer al que el dicho Truxillo no biniese ha declarar ante mi como lo havia consegido dicho Alcalde Mayor el que no biniese y este declarante le haconsejo no digase de benir a desir la verdad y recombiniendole dicho Theniente a su Alcalde Mayor Juan Esteban que sino lo havia aconsexado le cargase Antonio Truxillo en que los cuchillos bendidos eran suios que como a esa lo deconpasaba; a que le respondio dicho Alcalde Mayor que por que me havia dado quenta por carta y en ella me pedia ysiese aberiguacion del caso por que le padisiese su credito o quedase en opiniones y que el caido, caido, y biendo que por el camino no zurtia efecto, rogo dicho Theniente a este declarante pasaze a esta Villa ha berme a mi dicho Theniente por si pudiese tener composision y sele diese capote alo edetuado como derecho me lo bino a proponer lo que no tubo efecto por la publisidad del casso y ser su perjuicio del comun, y que esta es la verdad so cargo del juramento que fecho tiene en que se afirmo y ratifico siendole leida su su declarasion; dijo ser de edad de treinta y siete anos, y que las generales no le tocan, y lo firmo con migo y los testigos de mi asistencia actuando como Juez receptor en dicho dia.

       Juan Paez Hurtado (rubric)
       Antonio de Abeytia (rubric)
Testigo Diego de Ugartte (rubric) Testigo Juan Domingo Paez Hurtado (rubric)

En la Villa de Santa Fee en dicho dia veinte y ocho de Abril yo el Theniente General Dn. Juan Paez Hurtado haviendo esaminado los testigos de esta sumaria presentados por las partes para finalizarlas y haser remision de ellos a el Señor Coronel Dn. Gervasio Cruzat y Góngora mi Governador y Capitan General mando sele de traslado a Dn. Juan Garcia de Mora para que responda dentro del termino de tres dias, asi lo probei y firme como Juez receptor con los testigos de mi asistencia en dicho dia.

        Juan Paez Hurtado (rubric)

Testigo Diego de Ugartte (rubric) Testigo Juan Domingo Paez Hurtado (rubric)

        Señor Theniente de Governador y Capitan General

Juan Garcia de Mora, vezino del Rio Arriba, jurisdizion dela Villa Nueba de Santa Cruz paresco ante Su Merzed en la mejor forma que aya lugar y como mejor prozeda y digo que habiendoseme por Su Merzed traslado de los autos que se estan siguiendo por mi y el Theniente Diego Torres sobre el litis del rescate y hecho capaz de todo lo que por parte dela parte contraria seme ympugna devo decir y digo que en el traslado que sele dio de lo actuado por Su Merzed a el dicho Theniente asta la declarazion de Juachin Sanchez responde negando y dando por falso y de ningun fundamento lo presentado por mi y no lo es pues, lo tengo probado con testigos competentes como ofrezi y como los propios que el presento y el que zita Antonio Truxillo presentado por el lo damnifican y condenan con los muchos fraudes que andubo haziendo y trataba de hazer solapando por mill caminos lo que yo con mi berdad le tengo probado por la ynformazion ofresida y dada; otro si dize dicho Theniente que no es sufiziente el que yo biese y supiese que heran suyos los cuchillos con que el Cumanche habia comprado aqueyo de poder absoluto comprase; alo qual digo no tengo ningun poder ni absoluto ni particular para ello y que eso espenderazion de terminos y calumnias que usan los hombres para querer acriminar la causa cuando mal pleito tienen pero no le es ni deve ser de ningun balor; ni ami de dano; por que en lo juridico no sirbe alegar sin justificar y mas en los alegatos que nesesitan de prueba y para que yo me halle compreendido en esa calumnia que da a entender de autoridad mia nezesita dar ynformazion de que yo les dijese a los que presentes hallaron que bien podran comprar que yo tenia autoridad para ello o poder absoluto que dado que sea quiero, y es mi ultima voluntad cargar no solo a para que merezia y merezia quien tal dijera y tambien la que en el dicho Theniente esta comprendida prosigue y dize que sin temor a Dios bendi asi espadines y que estoy yncurso en descomunion y no se que leyes del derecho; lo zierto es que el dicho Theniente debe de haber estudiado mucho que sabe de zensuras y tales leyes las que si las ay y las sabe debieran publicarse por bando para que llegar a notizia de todos y pudiera como Justicia a el que le quebrantara echarle las leyes enzima y mas para los foroneos y nuebos en la tierra como yo lo soy renobarlos todos los anos para que ninguno pudiera alegar la ygnorandola y como tan temorozo de Dios zelar, cuidar y guardar el que ninguno yncurriera en la zensura que dise y por que con la falta de bando y ygnorancia que padezia asta la presente me hallo bastantemente salbo para Dios y para Su Merzed no digo y alego lo que pudiera alegar y justificar sobre dicha zensura en que muchos me consta an yncurrido pero trato de que se den y pongan dishoc autos en parajes de sentenzia yno de molestar a Su Merzed pues con lo actuado se halla bastantemente conbenzido y culpado dicho Theniente y ageno de poderse azer a su cuidado y custudio el empleo que aserze pues no solo no sela cuida y guarda las hordenes que por sus superiores le son dadas, sino es que el es el que las quebranta dando mal exemplo como nos le dio a mi y alos que a su exemplo compraron de que se ha de servir Su Merzed darnos por libres de toda culpa y a el que en virtud de todo lo justificado lo estubiere para que la pena que mereziere su delito castigando o perdonando o como a Su Merzed le pareziere combeniente y para todo lo demas que el dicho Theniente Diego Torres alega en su defensa no quiero hazer menzion de ello por estar ymplicado el propio y condenado por la malizia con que ha obrado y la berdad confesada por los de su parte presentados por todo lo cual y que alegar puedo; a Su Merzed pido y suplico sea mui servido probeir lo que fuese de justizia que en ello rezivire merzed y juro en debida forma no ser de malizia alguno y en lo nezesario, ut supra.

Juan Garcia de Mora (rubric)

En la Villa de Santa Fee en dos dias del mes de Mayo de mill setezientos treinta y sinco anos ante mi el General Juan Paez Hurtado, Theniente de Governador y Capitan General de este Reyno se presento esta petision por el contenido en ella y por mi vista mande sele de traslado a el Theniente Diego Torres quien respondera dentro del termino de tres dias, asi lo probei y firme como Juez receptor con testigos de assistensia en dicho dia.

Juan Paez Hurtado (rubric)
Testigo Diego de Ugartte (rubric) Testigo Nicolas Ortiz (rubric)

Señor Theniente General

Diego de Torres besino del Puesto de Chama jurisdizion de la Villa Nueba de Santa Cruz digo que haviendome Vm. dado traslado el dia dos del presente mes de Mayo de los cargos que contra mi resultan en el escripto segundo presentado por Dn. Juan Garcia de Mora respondo lo sierto y berdadero que el pasado mes de Abril el dia primero Viernes de Dolores estando en la Villa Nueva de Santa Cruz en compania del Capitan Juan Esteban Garcia Alcalde Mayor de dicha jurisdizion tubimos noticia de aber llegado a el Ojo Caliente sinco Cumanches por cuyas noticias me enbio el dicho Alcalde Mayor del Pueblo de San Juan y enbiase de el a el Yndio Santiago, ladino y que entiende el ydioma de los Cumanches, a que trujese rason sierta que a que benian o que buscaban con esta noticia fue el dicho Yndio a el Ojo Caliente en aquel dia Viernes y bolbio aquella noche come alas onse y dijo que a el llegar a el Ojo Caliente yban entrando seis tiendas y que los Cumanches le dijeron que no podian bajar a el Pueblo de San Juan como les desia el dicho Yndio por allarse con sus bestias mui fatigadas y estar con el reselo de que los Yutas andaban en seguimiento, se que fuesen los Españoles por el dia siguiente Sabado a el Ojo Caliente en donde tendrian feria delos generos que trayen y que esta mesma rason le enbio con el mismo Yndio a el Alcalde Mayor el dicho Teniente Diego Torres aguardando la rason del dicho Alcalde Mayor en la casa del referido Diego Torres, a este tiempo Sabado por la manana llego a su casa el Cumanche ynfiel que bibia en el Rio Arriba en una llegua cansada y me pidio le prestara un cavallo para pasar a el Ojo Caliente a el qual detenia yo que yriamos juntos por estar aguardando a el Alcalde Mayor, y me dijo se yria poco a poco. En cuya birtud es berdad haberle dado unos cuchillos mios para que llegado el dicho Alcalde Mayor abrir la feria me los bendiese dandole de ellos dos. Y no haviendo benido el referido Alcalde Mayor sino solo aber enbiado orden por escripto como costa por su papel que esta en estos autos a ojas entre quatro y sinco, y con dicho orden paso por orden mio Paulin de Abeytia como costa por su declarazion asta el Ojo Caliente y costar en ella aberla leydo Dn. Juan Garcia de Mora y ser el mas ynteresado en dicho rescate que bien pudieran haverlo echo y a su semejanza les dicemos pues el Cumanche ynfiel lo havia echo fue por su dictamen y no por orden mio, como es sierto que esperaba yo el yr en compania del dicho Alcalde Mayor y por lo que mira del haver llegado ser los cuchillos mios fue por el pacto que con migo yso Antonio Truxillo como costa por su declarazion en donde puede Vmd. entrar en el conosimiento de mi poca malicia pues fue lo mejor de que yo negase una berdad tan sierta. Y por lo que dise Dn. Juan Garcia de Mora que ynora el que estaba dado el bender espadas y espadines a los ynfieles, digo Señor que no puede ynorarlo pues no esta resien benido como dize y en todas las ocasiones que se an ofrecido en rescates sele yso primero bando por los Señores Gobernadores asi el autual como sus antesesores que no se bendan las dichas armas por ser contra las leyes reales el benderlas de donde tengo el conosimiento no ser bueno el benderlas por todo lo qual, a Vmd. pido y suplico sea mui serbido de aplicarme su acostumbrada caridad mirandome poca malisia asi lo espero del Cristiano selo de Vmd. y juro en forma este mi escrito ser sierto y berdadero y en lo nesesario, ut supra.

Diego Torres (rubric)

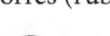

En la Villa de Santa Fee en quatro dias del mes de Mayo de mil setesientos treinta y sinco anos yo el General Dn. Juan Paez Hurtado Theniente de Governador y Capitan General de este Reino haviendo seguido estas diligencias asta ponerlas en estado de sentenzia ago remision de ellas al Señor Comandante Dn. Gervasio Cruzat y Gongora Governador y Capitan General de dicho Reino para que Su Señoria en su vista las determine, y para que conste lo firme actuando como Jues Receptor con testigos de asistencia en dicho dia.

Juan Paez Hurtado (rubric)
Testigo Joseph Terruz (rubric) Testigo Diego de Ugartte (rubric)

Sentencia

Visto por me el pleyto y causa criminal que ha seguido por ausencia mia el Theniente General Dn. Juan Paes Hurtado por denunsia que Dn. Juan Garcia de la Mora vesino del Rio Arriba hiso contra Diego de Torres vesino de Chama y Theniente de Alcalde Mayor de la jurisdizion de la Villa Nueva de Santa Cruz sobre unos cuchillos que enbio dicho Diego de Torres con un Yndio Cumanche para que le comprase unos cueros antes que se avriese el resgate por ministro competente. Y asi mismo visto lo que resulta contra dicho Dn. Juan Garcia de la Mora denunsiante con lo demas que en dichos autos consta y por agora ver cumbinio, ut supra. Falto atentos los autos y meritos del proseso a que me refiero que deve condenar y condeno al dicho Diego de Torres a que pierda los dies cueeros de Sivolo que consta en los autos haverse comprado antes que se avriese el resgate en la forma acostumbrada los que aplico para la fabrica de la Yglesia nueva que se esta asiendo en dicha Villa Nueva de Santa Cruz y asi mismo le condeno a que pague las costas prosesales, visto tambien lo que resulta contra el referido Dn. Juan Garcia de la Mora desir condenar y condeno a dicho Dn. Juan Garcia en dies pesos al corriente del pais las que aplico para la luminaria del Santisimo Sacramento de la Yglesia de dicha Villa Nueba de Santa Cruz por constar los dichos autos aver comprado algunos cueros antes de abrirse dicho resgate y le exonero y absuelvo de lo demas que pudiesen importar los cueros que superasen a dicha cantidad, en atension a la referida denunsia que hiso contra dicho Theniente Diego de Torres como parese por estos autos; y para en adelante queden apersevidos dicho Theniente Diego de Torres y el referido Dn. Juan Garcia de la Mora de que perderan sin remision alguna todo quanto resgatasen sin abrirse dicho resgate por la Real Justicia y a mas seran multado en la cantidad que paresiese combeniente y otras penas arbitrarias. Y por esta mi sentencia definitibamente jusgando hasi lo pronuncio, mando y firmo en esta Villa de Santa Fee a siete de Mayo de mil setecientos y treinta y sinco anos y con los testigos de mi asistencia a falta de Escribano Publico y Real que no lo ay en este Reyno y va en el presente papel comun por no correr en estas partes el sellado.

Dn. Gervasio Cruzat y Gongora (rubric)
Testigo Gaspar Bitton (rubric) Testigo Juan Antonio de Unanue (rubric)

Auto de
Pronunsiamiento
En al Villa de Santa Fee en siete dias del mes de Mayo de mil setesientos treinta y sinco anos estando en los estrados de mi alegado fue dada, pronunsiada y firmada por mi

el Coronel Dn. Gervasio Cruzat y Gongora, Governador y Capitan General de este Reyno de la Nueva Mexico la sentensia que antesede siendo testigos los infrascriptos de que doi fee.

     Dn. Gervasio Cruzat y Gongora (rubric)
Testigo Gaspar Bitton (rubric) Testigo Juan Antonio de Unanue (rubric)

Auto
En la Villa de Santa Fee en dicho dia mes y ano yo el Coronel Dn. Gervasio Cruzat y Gongora Governador y Capitan General de este Reyno de la Nueva Mexico devia desir y dije se notifique a los contenidos Diego de Torres y Dn. Juan Garcia de la Mora la sentensia que antesede asi lo probey, mande y firme con los testigos infrascriptos de mi assistansia a falta de Escrbano Publico y Real que no lo ay en este Reyno.

     Dn. Gervasio Cruzat y Gongora (rubric)
Testigo Gaspar Bitton (rubric) Testigo Juan Antonio de Unanue (rubric)

Notificasion
En la Villa de Santa Fee en dies y seis dias del mes de Mayo de mil setesientos treinta y sinco anos yo el Coronel Dn. Gervasio Cruzat y Gongora, Governador y Capitan General de este Reyno de la Nueva Mexico en cumplimento de lo mandado en el auto antesedente hise saber y notifique en sus personas de verbo adverbum a los referidos Theniente Diego de Torres y a Dn. Juan Garcia de Mora todo lo contenido en dicha sentensia quienes entendidos de ella dijeron que la oyen, consienten y obedesen todo lo que en dicha sentensia se expresa y daran cumplimento conforme a su tener y esto respondieron y lo firmaron con migo y los testigos de mi asistensia a falta de escribano Publico y Real que no lo ayan en este Reyno.

     Dn. Gervasio Cruzat y Gongora (rubric)
       Diego Torres (rubric)
      Juan Garcia de Mora (rubric)

[The following is the paper sent to Captain Diego de Torres from Alcalde Mayor Juan Esteban García denying the opening of the trade fair. This paper was found out of sequence.]

Señor Capitan Diego Torres

Mui Señor mio, a benido Santiago a darme la rason de que abian benido ranchos de Cumanches con cueros y carne; Vmd., no consienta que balla ninguna persona de ninguna calidad no se diga que por hallarmos en tiempo Santo que si ellos quisieran esperar asta la Pasqua que se esperen y si no que se ballan; si Vmd., procure saber si alguna persona compre algo para executar lo mandado por el Teniente y el que yo le dare notisia de lo que me dijo Santiago puede ser que se bajen los Cumanches a su casa de Vmd., enbiandoles desir que no se pueden pasar asta el Domingo de Pasqua es quanto se ofrese pidira. Dios Guarde a Vmd. muchos anos. La Cañada y Abril 2 de 1735 anos.

 Beso la mano de Vmd., su amigo que lo estima.
Juan Estevan Garcia (rubric)

Notes

1. Diego de Torres was the son of a prerevolt settler, Cristóbal de Torres, and Ángela de Leyba. Cristóbal had been the alférez for Albuquerque. Torres petitioned the governor in 1713, asking that because of his many ailments, he be replaced at the presidio by Nicolás Torres. In 1731 Diego petitioned Governor Cruzat y Góngora for a revalidation of a Chama grant made to his father, but the petition was rejected. By 1739 he was in the Río Abajo, where in 1740 he led the founding of the settlement at Belén (SANM I #113, #950; Chávez, *Origins*: 294-95).
2. Juan García de la Mora did not come to New Mexico until 1725. According to Chávez, he left Spain after killing his wife because of suspected adultery. In 1735 he married Josefa Martín of La Soledad in Río Arriba. She was the granddaughter of well-known Indian fighter Sebastián Martín Serrano. In a document from 1740, he said that he was the alcalde for the jurisdiction in which Chama is located, probably Santa Clara, but signed himself as the presiding judge, probably considering himself to be acting in that capacity. In 1743 Juan was the presiding judge for Santa Cruz in a case relating to property of Vicente García de Armijo. In 1752 he was involved in a lawsuit over a contract for iron work with the Indians. In this case, Alcalde Juan Joseph Lovato of La Soledad del Río Arriba named Garcia de la Mora as a "captain," perhaps referring to a position in the militia (Chávez, *Origins*: 184; Christmas and Rau, "Una Lista": 199; Jenkins, "Tewa": 100; SANM I #26; Docs. 31 and 40).
3. See Doc. 15.
4. In 1744 Fray Miguel de Menchero found sixteen families living in the puesto of Ojo Caliente (Jones, *Los Paisanos*: 123).
5. Note that in September 17, 1735, a few months after this complaint was filed, Governor Cruzat y Góngora ordered that settlers were not to sell offensive or defensive weapons or arms to the Indians (SANM II #403).
6. Hereafter this section is abbreviated when similar language is used. The language to be deleted is shown in brackets. The complete document is found in the transcription.
7. See Doc. 22.
8. A *sumaria* was a fact-finding inquiry carried out by a magistrate. In this case, the information was provided by García de la Mora and the infidel Indian testifying before Juan Páez Hurtado. The next step was to hear from Diego Torres (Cutter, *Legal Culture*: 114).
9. See Map 5, Appendix, for the location of Puesto de Chama, located some distance south of today's town of Chama near the present town of Hernández. Bishop Crespo mentioned it in his visitation of 1730, and Menchero notes that there were eleven families at the Rancho de Chama and Río del Oso in 1744 (Adams, *Tamarón*: 96; Jones, *Los Paisanos*: 123).
10. Antonio Trujillo was a resident of Chama. He may be the son of the soldier Pasqual Trujillo, killed in 1715 (Doc. 13; Chávez, *Origins*: 298).
11. The note is shown at the end of this document.
12. Paulín de Abeytia was an alférez in New Mexico by 1704. He was a brother of Baltazar Abeytia (Doc. 22) and a son of Diego Vectia (Abeytia). Paulín married Ángela Martín, a daughter of Francisco Martín Serrano (Doc. 44; Chávez, *Origins*: 119).
13. Manuel Martín [Serrano] was a son of Francisco Martín Serrano and a grandson of Luis Martín Serrano, a prerevolt settler. (The original colonist was Hernán Martín Serrano I, arriving there in 1598.) That is, Manuel was part of the Martín Serrano family that lived in the Chama area. Manual is mentioned in several land transactions in Río Arriba, La Soledad, and Chama (Chávez, *Origins*: 224; Barrett, *Settlement*: 111; SANM I #33, #369, #464). For more on the prerevolt Martín Serrano family, see Esquibel, "Descendants": 159-71.
14. This is probably Pedro Gómez de Chávez, from the Ojo Caliente area, who was married to Petrona Martín [Serrano], a sister of the wife of Juan García de la Mora. Pedro was the youngest child of don Fernando

Durán de Chávez and the only member of the clan to settle outside the Río Abajo. In 1729 in Albuquerque, Fray Pedro Montaño denounced Gómez de Chávez for scandalous conduct and blasphemies bordering on heresy. When the case was sent to the Holy Tribunal of the Inquisition in Mexico City, they determined that a severe reprimand was adequate. It may be that his presence in northern New Mexico was a response to the reprimand (Chávez, *Origins*: 161-63, 222; Greenleaf, "Inquisition": 35-38).

15. Antonio Martín Serrano, another member of the Martín Serrano family, may have been a son of Luis Martín Serrano, the original settler, and thus uncle to the Manuel Martín mentioned above. He is mentioned in several lawsuits and transactions in Ojo Caliente and Chimayó, though he was dead by 1753 (Chávez, *Origins*: 222-24, SANM I #20, #32, #534, #686).
16. See Doc. 22.
17. Juan Esteban [García de Noriega] was the alcalde for the area including Santa Cruz, San Juan, and Abiquiu for the period around 1736. When he married Luisa Gómez Luján or Gómez del Castillo in 1721, Governor Valverde was their sponsor. His name appears in land-transaction documents for Santa Cruz and Abiquiu (Chávez, *Origins*: 181-82; SANM I #320, #322, and #347).
18. García de la Mora was in Spain in 1725 and appears in New Mexico in 1733, when he was married to Juana Martín at La Soledad (Chávez, *Origins*: 184).
19. To date, nothing is known about this person.
20. The *luminarias* could have been the perpetual lamps or candles that were used at the altar, or the wood fires used to light the pathway for processions of the Holy Sacrament.

28

ALBUQUERQUE RANCHERS REFUSE GOVERNOR'S ORDERS TO PULL LIVESTOCK BACK TO SETTLEMENT
January 30, 1736. Source: SANM II #408.

ynopsis and editor's note: In this document, five Albuquerque settlers petitioned Alcalde Juan Gonzales Bas for a reprieve from the mandate of Governor Cruzat y Góngora ordering them to keep themselves and their livestock near their houses (see SANM II #401). They pointed out that there was little pasturage near their houses, that their young men were diligently riding guard on the herds night and day, and that they had a tower from which to watch. The governor agreed to rescind his order.

Finding adequate feed for their animals without losing them to Indian raiders was an ongoing problem for the settlers. Over thirty years later, Governor Marín de Valle, confronting the same problem, ordered the settlers to keep track of their animals, stating, "I find that . . . the residents of the jurisdiction of the villa of Albuquerque, even though they have been brought before the alcalde mayor of this villa and his lieutenants, find themselves with increased reluctance to care for their animals, leaving them loose, resulting in grave damages, some animals being killed by the enemies. Seeing that said reluctance causes such bad consequences and [seeing the] increasing cunning of the Apache enemies, I order and mandate that the alcalde mayor and his lieutenants order that no resident shall lose [fail to keep] either horse herds or cattle. The punishment for not complying shall be for a citizen of Spanish extraction a fine of 20 pesos and two months of imprisonment, and if it shall be a mestizo, twenty lashes and three months of imprisonment, and the said fine of 20 pesos I apply from now for the repair of the palace of his majesty" (SANM II #534).

Note that most if not all of the persons signing the document were related to each other directly or by marriage.

Alcalde mayor and captain of war

The citizens signing below in this letter, who are Pedro Varela,[1] Joseph Sánchez,[2] Antonio Lucero,[3] Juan García,[4] Jacinto Varela,[5] each one for themselves, all united and in solidarity, appear before your excellency in the best conduct, and we say:

Your excellency having made known and sent out an order from the governor and captain general of this kingdom, the tenth day of the last month of December in which your excellency's order stated that you being notified about finding us to be outside of this villa with our livestock, that you ordered us to return to our houses, which order we submissively obeyed. But no one being is denied by any of the laws the right to appeal for his greater protection and well-being, for which we say one and all together, that we incur great damage by returning and moving ourselves, for these causes:

There is the little pasturage that we have near our houses, and if there is any it is at a great distance, where there is more risk that the enemies will take the livestock, being confident that we are near our houses. So the great loss of livestock that originates for us from having the grazing and pasturage being far from the houses is among the great difficulties that they present to us. Only through much adversity, it has come to pass that in the place where we are, we are very vigilant, for that reason referred to, the young men staying close together with arms and horses and in the saddle day and night, riding over the land, and every morning reconnoitering the land immediately next to the pueblo of Isleta, and keeping the animals in sight and close to the towers [*torreones*] and houses that we have made for our protection in order to keep great watchfulness.

This being understood, and which we will assert if it can be allowed, we beg that your excellency could be better served by making it so that we can continue in the location in which we are, for by bringing our livestock to our houses, there will be many damages that will occur of which we anticipate having to make mention.

For all of which reasons, we ask and supplicate very reverently your excellency to decree with reason and justice what we ask, and we swear in the correct form that this is not being done through malice and in the necessary way etc.

      Pedro Varela (rubric)
At the request of Juan García, Antonio Lucero, Joseph Sánchez, and Jacinto Varela [Signed by] Isidro Sánchez[6] (rubric)

  In the villa of Santa Fe on the 30th day of the month of January of 1736, I, the colonel don Gervasio Cruzat y Góngora, governor and captain general of this kingdom of New Mexico, upon seeing the letter presented to Captain Juan Gonzales Baz, alcalde mayor of the jurisdiction of the Villa of San Felipe of Alburquerque from the residents who signed it. I should say and I do say that in consideration of the owners of the livestock being careful and vigilant, as was expressed in said letter, and likewise there not being pasturage enough to maintain them, for this cause, seeing they are obliged to keep said livestock there now, said owners can continue doing this so that they achieve the preservation of said livestock in the place they find themselves now or in others areas that could be convenient.

Thus I approve, mandate, and sign with my assisting witnesses for lack of a public or royal notary, of which there are none in this kingdom.
      don Gervasio Cruzat y Góngora (rubric)
      Gaspar Bitton (rubric)
      Juan Antonio de Inanue (rubric)

ORIGINAL DOCUMENT

No. 630
Señor alcalde mayor y capitan aguerra

Los vesinos ynfra escritos en este escrito como son Pedro Varela, Joseph Sanchez, Antonio Lucero, Juan Garcia, Jazinto Varela todos juntos y cada uno de por si por el todo yn solidum paresemos ante Vuestro Merced, como mejor proseda y desimos que abiendonos Vuestro Merced, yntimado, y notificado un orden del Señor Governador y Capitan General de este Reyno, el dia dies del proximo mes de Diziembre, en que ordena su señoria, que por notisioso que se alla estar fuera de esta Villa con nuestros ganados mandanos retiremos a nuestras casas, lo qual orden obedesemos pecho por tierra; pero no siendo negado a ninguno por todas leyes el recurrir a su mayor recurso y bien estar; por lo qual desimos uno y todos juntos el gravisimo daño que resevimos con retirarnos y mudarnos por otros causales que son el poco pasto que tenemos cerca de nuestras casas, y si lo ay es muy lejos, mas riesgo para que los enemigos se lo lleben por la confianza de que sta serca de casa, como la mucha perdida de ganado que se nos origen a por estar el comedero y pasto lejos de las casas a mas de tras estorsiones que se ofrecen y en la parte que estamos (solo a mucha desgracia podra suseder) por estar muy bigilosos a mas de los referidos, mosos arimados con armas y caballos consillados de dia y de noche recorriendo la tierra todos las mañanas immediatos al Pueblo de la Isleta, y como tierra empastada el ganado a la vista; y serca de los torreones y casas que tenemos echas a si para nuestros abrigos como para estar con ajor cuydado, esto supuesto y lo que alegar podemos si se ofrese suplica mas a Vuestro Merced sea muy servido de aser que nos continuemos en el paraje en que estamos por ser muchos los daños que esperemos mantenermos y que de traer nuestros ganados a nuestras casas se nos morirá todo = por todo lo qual=
A Vuestro Merced pidimos, y suplicamos muy rendidamente provea en razon y justicia lo que pedimos y juramos en debida forma no ser de malicia y en los nesesaria et cetera

Pedro Varela (rubric)

Aruego de Juan Garcia, de Antonio Luzero, de Joseph Sanches, y de Jazinto Varela = Isidro Sanchez (rubric)

En la villa de Santa Fee en trenta (sic) dias de la mes de henero de mil setecientos trenta (sic) y seis años yo el Coronel don Gervasio Cruzat y Gongora Governador y Capitan General de este Reyno de la Nueva Mexico en vista de el escripto presentado al Capitan Juan Gonsales Baz Alcalde Mayor de la jurisdicion de la Villa de San Phelipe de Alburquerque por los vesinos que en el [escripto] van firmados devia desir y dije que en atension a estar quidadosos, y vigilantas los dueños de los ganado como en dicho esripto se expresa, y asi mismo no haver pastos para mantenerlos y por este motivo verse presisados a tener dichos ganados en el para de que oy se halla podran dichos dueños mantenerse para que logren la conservasion de dichos ganados en el que oy se hallan, o en otro que le sea combeniente asi lo provey y mande y firme con los testigos de mi asistensia a falta de escribano publico y Real que no lo ay en este Reyno=

don Gervasio Cruzat y Gongora (rubric)
Gaspar Bitton (rubric)
Juan Antonio de Unanue (rubric)

Transcribed and translated by Gerald Gonzales and Linda Tigges

Notes

1. Pedro Varela [Jaramillo] was a son of Juan Varela Jaramillo and a grandson of Pedro Varela Jaramillo, a native New Mexican, who did not return from El Paso. The younger Pedro married Juana Gonzáles Bas, a daughter of Juan González Bas, a relationship that may explain why Pedro's name is first on the list. Juan Varela Jaramillo was listed by Juan Candelaria as a first founder of Albuquerque (NMGS, *Aquí*: 17, 20, 39, 462, 487-89; Chávez, *Origins*: 108, 305; see also Docs. 5 and 22).
2. Joseph Sánchez was the son of Jacinto Sánchez de Iñigo and Isabel Telles Jirón. He married Teresa Jaramillo, who was a daughter of Cristóbal, a brother of Juan, and was listed by Juan Candelaria as a first founder. Jacinto, the father, was listed in a 1681 El Paso muster roll, suggesting that he was originally from New Mexico (NMGS, *Aquí*: 17, 464; Hackett, *Historical Documents* 2: 84).
3. Antonio Lucero II [de Godoy] was the son of Antonio Lucero de Godoy I, who returned to New Mexico in 1694. Antonio II was also the nephew of Nicolás Lucero de Godoy, named as one of Albuquerque's first founders. He married Francisca Varela Jaramillo, sister of Teresa, named above, and a daughter of Cristóbal Varela Jaramillo. For Antonio Lucero de Godoy I, see Doc. 1 (NMGS, *Aquí*: 17, 464, 466). This Juan García cannot be identified by the information on the document. It is likely that he is related to the Varela and Lucero families.
5. Jacinto Varela [Jaramillo] was a brother of Pedro Varela, listed above. He married Valentina Gonzalez Bas, a sister of Juana, named above (NMGS, *Aquí*: 20, 39, 462, 487-89; Chávez, *Origins*: 189, 305).
6. See Doc. 22. Note that Isidro was married to Teresa Varela Jaramillo, a sister to Jacinto and Pedro. Here Isidro is signing for four of the petitioners (Chávez, *Origins*: 487).

29

MEETING OF ALBUQUERQUE RESIDENTS HELD; GOVERNOR PROHIBITS EXPORTS OF GOODS
May 15–June 5, 1736. Source: SANM II #410.

Synopsis and editor's notes: In 1735 Governor Cruzat y Góngora published a bando prohibiting the sale of grain, sheep, cattle, and wool outside New Mexico because of the lack of reserves of those goods in the colony. Subsequently, he called a meeting of citizens to discuss the matter further, whereupon, according to him, the group decided that the ban on sales should continue, at least on cattle, sheep, and wool. It is not stated where the meeting was held. The governor then ordered that goods could be sold between the Spanish and the Indians living within the province, but not to owners of herds, muleteers, or others that would sell the goods outside the province.

This document is one of several orders for embargos, two of which are translated in this book. The embargos were on outside exports of sheep, cattle, and wool, and intended to ensure that enough goods stayed in the province to provide reserves of food and clothing for the residents at times of unexpected conditions and for emergencies. John Baxter points out that at that time the cattle industry and the growing sheep industry were not strong enough to provide excess goods for trade outside the colony. In 1737, after the next governor, Olavide y Micheleña, published a similar embargo, a larger number of settlers approached him asking for it to be lifted, as shown in the following document (Baxter, *Las Carneradas*: 26-28; Docs. 23 and 30).

Don Gervasio Cruzat y Góngora, colonel in his majesty's forces, governor and captain general of this kingdom of New Mexico, castellan of the forces and presidios for his majesty, etc.

In the past year of 1735, a bando was published which prohibited bales of grains , sheep, cattle, and wool from being taken out of the kingdom. This was ordered because of the problems that are affecting the public good and the conservation of this kingdom, due to the shortages of food supplies and of clothing, as is now well known.[1] This [shortage] is brought about because these items have been leaving this kingdom for the past two years. Due to this, the kingdom has found itself in a situation unfavorable for a prompt response to the emergencies that cannot be avoided due to unexpected conditions and other incidents, being that the distances from the places of remedy [where additional food and clothing are available] are so great. In any case, in this adversity, I had to immediately bring together a group of practical and intelligent people and those who have the largest holdings of the said goods, so that attention could be brought to all of the circumstances of a problem so important and so worthy of being considered for the public good. This was the matter of the amount of the [above] mentioned goods that could assure the maintenance of this kingdom and of provision of everyday clothes [comun vestar] which the poor people wear about them. This [meeting] was held on the 15th of the present month of May, and the best part of those who attended the meeting agreed that none of the mentioned goods were to leave or to be brought outside this kingdom due to the well-known problem that it has caused to the public good, maintenance, and conservation of our kingdom.

Because of this, I order and mandate that no person, of any condition or quality, be allowed to take outside, nor shall take out of the kingdom any number of cattle or sheep, or wool, under the penalty to the Spanish of two hundred pesos in silver or in reales, which are to be paid in the usual way. They will be stopped from taking anything, and will lose their said goods as well as their mares and other animals that were used for the transportation of goods outside the kingdom. This penalty I will apply immediately, half to his majesty's royal treasury and the other half to the expenses of the justice. The Indians I will penalize with two hundred lashes, the loss of their goods, as well as the animals on which the goods are taken. This penalty I will also apply in the same manner to the royal treasury and for the expenses of the justice. I also prohibit in a like manner to the Spanish and the Indians respectively that no one is to sell nor is allowed to sell the said prohibited goods to owners of herds of animals, muleteers, or outsiders. They can be sold only between the Spanish and to Indians who live within the jurisdictions and districts of the villas of the Spanish and the Indian pueblos of this kingdom, as has been practiced forever and which has been observed since the time of settlement and, at the expense of the king, the establishment in this area of the raising of cattle and sheep, resulting in the increased number of sheep, rams, cattle, and mares, for which reason his majesty (whom God may guard) sent them so that the kingdom would abound in food and clothing.

For the attention of the Spanish and Indians, and complete fulfillment, I order the alcaldes mayores, and in their absence, their lieutenants, to publish this bando in their respective jurisdictions so that it is known by everyone and so that no one can argue their ignorance. They are then to place at the foot of the document the date of publication and to take the copies that are necessary to place them at the accustomed places. Once this is done, they are to return the original to this superior government. The said alcaldes mayors, lieutenants, and other officials of justice shall see to it and observe that they are complied with and observed by this message under penalty that they are responsible for any omissions which are allowed. I thus determined, ordered, and signed it with my assisting witnesses due to the lack of a public or royal scribe, which there is none in this kingdom. Santa Fe, May 24, 1736.[2]

don Gervasio Cruzat y Góngora (rubric)

Witnesses
Gaspar Bitton (rubric)
Joseph Trujillo (rubric)

At this villa of Santa Fe, headquarters of this kingdom and provinces of New Mexico, on the first day of the month of June, 1736, I, Captain Antonio de Uribarrí,[3] alcalde mayor and war captain of the said villa, say that in fulfillment of the order given in this royal bando by the captain Cruzat y Góngora, governor and captain general of this kingdom, made known to all the residents of this villa the order given by his honor in a clear and intelligible voice at the sound of the drum at this plaza of this capital, and attached it, in testimony to this, at the doors of the casas reales so that no one can be ignorant of it, and so that it is valid I signed it at this said villa on the said day, month, and year.
    Antonio de Uribarrí (rubric)

At the new villa of Santa Cruz on the 3rd of June, 1736, I, Captain Juan Esteban García de Noriega,[4] alcalde mayor of this said villa, in fulfillment of that which is provided in this royal bando by Colonel don Gervasio Cruzat y Góngora, governor and captain general of this kingdom, publicized it in a clear and intelligible voice to the residents of this jurisdiction and to the natives of these pueblos who heard it and who are to observe it; and so that it is valid I signed it with two assisting witnesses on the said day, month, and year.
    Juan García de Noriega (rubric)
Witnesses
Miguel de Quintana (rubric)
Joseph García de Noriega (rubric)

At this Pueblo de San Gerónimo de los Taos on the 5th of June, 1736, I, Captain Francisco Guerrero,[5] alcalde mayor and war captain of it and of its jurisdiction, in fulfillment of what is ordered in this royal bando given by Colonel Don Gervasio Cruzat y Góngora, governor and captain general of this kingdom, made to gather together all of the residents and Indians to whom in a high and clear voice made known to them everything that was contained in the said bando issued by his honor, and having heard and understood it, they all said that they observe it and comply with it, and they gave their testimony together in the manner accustomed. So that it is valid I signed it at the said Pueblo de San Gerónimo de los Taos on the said day, month, and year.
    Francisco Guerrero (rubric)

ORIGINAL DOCUMENT

Don Gervasio Cruzat y Gongora, Coronel de los Exercitos de Su Magestad, Governador y Capitan General de este Reyno dela Nueva Mexico, Castellano de Sus Fuerzas y Presidios por Su Magestad, ut supra.

Por el ano proximo pasado de mill setesientos treinta y sinco se publico Bando prohiviendo la extracsion y saca de granos, ganados mayors y menores y de lanas por lo graves y notenas perjuicios que se siguen al bien publico y conservasion de este Reyno como actualmente se reconosen asi en el comestible, como en el vestuario con los Yndios por las extracsiones y sacas que de dos años a esta parte se han hecho de este Reyno por tierra fuera; y hallandose dicho Reyno una situasion tampoco favorable para sus promptos recursos en las urgencies que no se pueden ofreser asi por las esporlidades de los tiempos, como otros acsidentes que pueden sobrevenir siendo las distancias muy dilatada para el logro de su remedio en qualquier caso que fuese adverso, tube por obediente haser una junta de personas practices y entelligentes y de las mas hasendades en los referidos generos para que atentas todas las sobrecumstancias en una material tan importante y tan digna de considerarse como es el bien publico y de que abunden los mencionados generos para la seguridad de la manutension de este Reyno y el comun bestuario, expusieron los paresores sobre ello; lo que executaron el dia quinse del corriente mes de Mayo, siendo de pareser la mayor parte dela que compusieron dicha junta, de que no se saquen ni se permita el que extraygen del Reyno los mensionados generos, por ser en conosido perjuisio del bien publico, manutension y conservasion de nuestro Reyno = Por tanto ordeno y mando que ninguna persona de qualesquiera condision y calidad que sea pueda sacar, ni saque, para tierra fuera grandes ganados, asi mayors y menores, ni lanas; so pena a los Espanoles de dosientos pesos en plata, o en reales cobrados por la via executada, lo major parado de sus bienes, y con perdimiento de los generos referidos, y de las lleguas y bestias en que dichos generos se transportasen para tierra fuera; la qual pena aplico desde luego por mitad para la Real Camara de Su Magestad y gastos de Justisia; y a los Yndios so pena de dosientos asotes y perdimiento de los generos y de las bestias en que los condujesen; cuia pena aplico tambien en la misma forma para la Real Camara y gastos de justisia prohibiendose asi mismo a los Espanoles y Yndios debajo de las mismas penas respectivamente asignadas, que ninguno venda ni pueda vender a duenos de requas, arrieros ni forasteros los expresados generos prohibidos; y solo se puedan vender entre los Espanoles a Yndios estantes en las jurisdisiones y districtos de las Villas de Espanoles y Pueblos de Yndios de este Reyno como se ha practicado incumsuremente, y lo han obserbado todo mas antes a ora, desde que se poblo este y se establecio en el a expensas de la piedad del Rey la cria de ganados mayors y menores con el cresido numero de obejas, carneros, vacas y yeguas que para este efecto embio Su Magestad (que Dios guarde) a fin de que abandose el Reyno de lo comertillo y del

vestuario; en cuia atension y devido cumplimiento mando a los Alcaldes Mayores y en su defecto a sus Thenientes hagan publicar en sus respectivas jurisdisiones este Bando para que llegue a notisias de todos y ninguno pueda alegar ygnoransia poniendo al pie de el la fee de su publicasion y saquen las copias que fuesen nesesarias para ponerlas en los parajes acostumbrados; y fecho que sea debelvasen el original a este Superior Govierno: y dichos Alcaldes Mayores, Thenientes y demas ministros de Justisia cuidaran y zelaran del pontual complimiento y observansia de este recaudo, pena de ser responsables de la omission que en ello tubiesen. Asi lo determine, mande y firme con los testigos de mi asistensia a falta de Escribano Publico y Real que no lo ay en este Reyno. Santa Fee a veinte y quatro de Mayo de mil setesientos treinta y seis anos.
     Don Gervasio Cruzat y Gongora (rubric)
testigo testigo
Gaspar Bitton (rubric) Joseph Truxillo (rubric)

En la Villa de Santa Fee, Cavesera deste Reyno y Provinsias dela Nueva Mexico en primer dia del mes de Junio de mill setesientos treinta y seis anos yo el Capitan Antonio de Uribarri Alcalde Maior y Capitan Aguerra de dicha Villa digo que en cumplimiento delo mandado en este Real Bando por el Senor Capitan Cruzat y Gongora, Governador y Capitan General deste Reyno yse notorio a todos los vesinos desta Villa lo mandado por Su Senoria en bos clara yntellegible a son de caxa en esta Plasa desta capital, Villa, figando un testimonio de esto dejando en las puertas de las Casas Reales para que ninguno tenga ygnorancia y para que conste lo firme en esta referida Villa en dicho dia mes y ano.
     Antonio de Urribarri (rubric)

En la Villa Nueba de Santa Cruz en tres dias del mes de Junio de mill setezientos treinta y seis anos yo el Capitan Juan Estevan Garcia de Noriega Alcalde Maior desta dicha Villa en cumplimiento delo procuido en este Real Vando por el Coronel Don Gervasio Gruzat y Gongora, Governador y Capitan General deste Reino, lo hize publicar en vos clara y yntelligible a los vezinos desta jurisdicion y naturales destos Pueblos quienes lo oyeron y quedaron a su observancia y para que conste lo firme con dos testigos de mi asistencia en dicho dia mes y ano.
     Juan Garcia de Noriega (rubric)
testigo testigo
Miguel de Quintana (rubric) Joseph Garcia de Noriega (rubric)

En este Pueblo de San Geronimo de los Thaos en cinco dias del mes de Junio de mill setesientos treynta y seis anos, yo el Capitan Francisco Guerrero, Alcalde Mayor y

Capitan Aguerra en el y su jurisdision en cumplimiento de lo mandado en este Real Bando por el Senor Coronel Don Gervasio Cruzat y Gongora, Governador y Capitan General de este Reyno hise juntar en estas Casas Reales a todos los vesinos y Yndios a quienes en vos alta y clara hise notorio todo lo contenido en dicho Bando dipuesto por Su Senoria y aviendolo oydo y entendido dijieron todos lo obserbaban y davan a su observansia y dan los testimonios agrados en la manera acostumbrada y para que conste lo firme en dicho Pueblo de San Geronimo de los Thaos en dicho dia, mes y ano =

                    Francisco Guerrero (rubric)

Notes

1. A bando was published in 1735 prohibiting the sale of defensive or offensive arms to the Indians (SANM II #403). However, this bando did not address the sale of grains, cattle, sheep, or cattle. The document to which Cruzat was referring has not been located at this time (see Docs. 23 and 24).
2. Note that Governor Cruzat y Góngora, whose term began in 1731, was about to leave New Mexico in 1736. The new governor, Enrique de Olavide y Micheleña, took office by January 7, 1737, and subsequently mandated the same prohibitions. A large group of residents of Albuquerque then sent him a petition asking that the mandate be repealed, which he categorically denied (see Doc. 30).
3. See Doc. 24.
4. See Doc. 27.
5. See Doc. 29.

30

FORTY-TWO ALBUQUERQUE SETTLERS REQUEST REPEAL OF TRADE PROHIBITIONS
August 24–September 23, 1737. Source: SANM II #421.

Synopsis and editor's notes: Upon his arrival in New Mexico, the new governor, Enrique de Olavide y Micheleña, reimposed Governor Cruzat's ban on the sale of sheep and wool outside the colony. However, he added an amendment providing that sheep and wool given as tithes for the bishop of Durango could be sold outside the kingdom by the tithe collectors. This so enraged Albuquerque settlers that on August 24, 1737, forty-two Albuquerque residents[1] joined together to ask again for a repeal of the embargo on wool, stating that the trading of wool was how they sustained themselves and that there was not any place within New Mexico where they could sell it. The governor stood firm, stating, among other reasons, that none of the persons signing the petition had any kind of ranch [*hacienda*].

The subject of tithe rentals is discussed in the introduction under the section on the governor's responsibilities on trade. It should be noted here that Olavide y Micheleña had a hard choice to make. The bishop of Durango insisted on the tithe rentals, which in New Mexico were provided in goods, there being little cash in the province. To convert the collected goods into cash, the collectors had to be allowed to take the goods outside of the province to sell. It is also possible that Governor Micheleña understood that the sheep herds in New Mexico were not large enough to accommodate outside trading of wool by both the tithe collectors and the residents.

However, just seven years later, Governor Codallos y Rabal lifted the ban on the sale of wool, apparently believing that by that date, with the increased size of the herds, outside sales could be made without endangering the colony (Baxter, *Las Carneradas*: 2; Ritch Collection, Roll 3, #58, August 17, 1737, Zimmerman Library, University of New Mexico; see also Doc. 36).

Governor and Captain General

The residents of the villa of Alburquerque who have herein signed below each one for himself, and all under one voice, placed before the feet of your honor, in order to achieve a favorable response without prejudicing anyone's right which is due to us, say, that on the 24th of the present month there was promulgated a decree[2] at this said villa, at the order of your honor, which prohibited us from selling wool and sheep [*carneros*]. This is something that we have honored and obeyed since the time of the colonel, who was the predecessor of your honor, as is well known, and for which reason we have lost the wool that we have sheared. Also, another reason for losing it is that there is no place within this kingdom that we can sell it or find any beneficial use for it, and as such is the reason for doing what we have to do. The said wool and rams are commodities with which we sustain ourselves for clothing for ourselves as well as for the women and children along with using them for other things that we need, and as such is the only commerce found in this villa. If this is prohibited we have no other recourse, particularly because when we sell the said wool and sheep, it is beneficial to the royal treasury, as taxes are paid in the cities where they are required, and along with that, they produce such things as woolen clothes [*paños*] and blankets [*vayetas*]. Sir, we have been obedient to the decree promulgated by your honor, and to the one ordered by your predecessor, the colonel, even though we held a meeting with the residents of this villa in order to put an end to the selling of the items [see Doc. 29]. As such we have seen the grave damage that has resulted, and as we have stated, we have without due recourse lost everything being that we have absolutely no other goods in this country other than the above items. For all of these reasons, your honor should be pleased to abolish the said mandate, and as such we will receive it with mercy and goodness. For all of this we petition your honor, to have mercy upon us and do as we ask, all for the sake of justice, and we swear in due form that this petition is not done in malice, avoiding costs, and only for what is necessary, etc.

Antonio Durán y Chaves (rubric)[3]

Francisco Chaves[4] (rubric)

At the request of Francisco Sanches[5]

[Signed by] Salvador Martines[6] (rubric)

Baltasar Romero[7] (rubric)

Diego Padilla[8] (rubric) Antonio Baca[9] (rubric)

Miguel Lusero[10] (rubric) Joseph Baca[11] (rubric)

Francisco Padilla[12] (rubric)

Domingo Baca[13] (rubric) Eusebio Rael de Aguilar[14] (rubric)

Francisco Guadalupe Chaves[15] (rubric)

Pedro Romero[16] (rubric)

Nicolás de Chaves[17] (rubric)

At the request of Jacinto Varela[18]

[Signed by] Isidro Sánchez[19] (rubric)

at the request of Juan Vallejos[20]

[Signed by] Isidro Sánchez (rubric)

Salvador Martínez (rubric)

Antonio Gurulé[21] (rubric)

Andrés Aragón[22] (rubric) Joseph Sánchez[23] (rubric)

Francisco García[24] (rubric) Antonio Samora[25] (rubric)

Juan Montaño[26] (rubric) Cayetano Lucero[27] (rubric)

Matías Romero[28] (rubric) Francisco Silva[29] (rubric)

Gregorio Jaramillo[30] (rubric)
Visente García[31] (rubric)
Francisco Perea[32] (rubric) Martín Montoya[33] (rubric)
Joseph Garsia[34] (rubric) Andrés Martin[35] (rubric)
Salvador Durán[36] (rubric)
Antonio Lucero[37] (rubric)
Lugardo Vallejos[38] (rubric)
Xptobal García[39] (rubric) Salvador García[40] (rubric)
Javier Miranda[41] (rubric)
Bernardo Vallejos[42] (rubric)
Manuel Carillo[43] (rubric)
Juan Antonio Zamora[44] (rubric)
Salvador García (rubric) Ramón García Jurado (rubric)

At the villa of Santa Fe, headquarters of this kingdom of New Mexico, on the 3rd of [August crossed out] September, 1737, after I, Governor and Captain General of this kingdom, don Enrique de Olavide y Micheleña, have seen the above written document that was submitted in common by the residents of the villa of San Felipe de Alburquerque regarding the abolishment of the order in the promulgated decree that no muleteers, nor anyone who enters or leaves this said kingdom, is allowed to take grains, animals [cattle or sheep], or wool outside of the kingdom, at the expense of losing everything that they have. They [the petitioners] have not established a fundamental reason to allow their petition, being that none of those who have signed have any type of a ranch [*hacienda*]. I thus order that everything that I have mentioned in the said decree be complied with and executed totally, observing everything as written. Anyone who does not comply will be prosecuted. No one is to be allowed to go against it in any manner whatsoever. I thus order, approve, and sign it acting as presiding judge with my assisting witnesses due to the lack of a royal or public scribe, being that there is none in this kingdom. That which is dated as August is not valid.
Enrique de Olavide y Micheleña (rubric)
Juan Felipe Rivera (rubric) Pedro Joseph de León (rubric)

ORIGINAL DOCUMENT

Señor Governador y Capitan General
Los vecinos de la Villa de Alburquerque que aqui bamos firmados todos a vos de uno y cada uno de por si ynsolidum, puestos a los pies de Vuestra Señoria por el recurso mas favorable sin perjudicar derecho alguno delo que nos asisten, desimos, que por cuanto el dia beinte y cuatro del corriente se promulgo un bando en esta dicha Villa por mandado de Vuestra Señoria en que se nos proibe la benta de lanas y carneros,

a lo cual hemos obedesido desde el tiempo del Señor Coronel, antesesor de Vuestra Senoria, pues es patente, el que los lanas, los que emos tresquilado, senos an perdido; y los que no lo emos echo tambien, a causa de no aber en este Reyno espendio de estos efectos ni onde benefisiarlas; y siendo como es sierto el que los esqudemos; de las susa dichas lanas y carneros son generos con que nos manteniamos de vestuarios asi nosotros como nuestras mujeres e yjos, y otras cosas nesesarias de nuestro uso, que es el unico comersio de que se compone esta Villa, y que prohibido no tenemos otro recurso, mayormente, cuando en vender las dichas lanas y carneros es benefisiada la Real Hacienda, pues se pagan sus alcabalas en las cuidades donde son reconosidas y despues de la uradas, de la misma suerte, como son paños, vayetas, lo emos obedecido Senor el bando promulgado por Vuestra Señoria; y el de el Señor Coronel, su antesesor, aunque se yso junta en esa Villa, de los vesinos para el fin de que no se bendiese; emos reconsido el grabisimo perjuicio que se nos sigue, pues como llevamos dicho senos perdio sin recurso ninguno, y no tener ausolute otros bienes en este pais mas que los referidos; por estas rasones se a de serbir Vuestra Señoria de derogar el referido mandato que en lo resibiremos bien y merse; por tanto a Vuestra Señoria pedimos y suplicamos rendidamente se sirba de haser como pedimos, que asi es justisia, juramos en forma no ser malisioso nuestro pedimento; costas, y en lo nesesario, ut supra =

      Antonio Duran y Chabes (rubric)
       Francisco Chabes (rubric)
     A ruego de Francisco Sanches
      Salvador Martines (rubric)
      Baltasar Romero (rubric)
       Diego Padilla (rubric)
       Antonio Baca (rubric)
   Miguel Lusero (rubric) Joseph Baca (rubric)
      Francisco Padilla (rubric)
       Domingo Baca (rubric)
     Eusevio Rael de Aguilar (rubric)
    Francisco Guadalupe Chaves (rubric)
       Pedro Romero (rubric)
      Nicolas de Chabes (rubric)
      A ruego de Jacinto Barela
       Ysidro Sanches (rubric)
      a ruego de Juan Ballejos
       Ysidro Sanches (rubric)
      Salbador Martines (rubric)
       Antonio Gorole (rubric)
   Andres Aragon (rubric) Joseph Sanches (rubric)
   Francisco Garsia (rubric) Antonio Samora (rubric)
   Juan Montano (rubric) Cayetano Lusero (rubric)
   Matias Romero (rubric) Francisco Silba (rubric)
   Gregorio Jaramillo (rubric) Jasinto Sanches (rubric)
       Bisente Garsia (rubric)

Francisco Perea (rubric) Martin Montoya (rubric)
Joseph Garsia (rubric) Andres Martin (rubric)
Salavador Duran (rubric)
Antonio Lusero (rubric)
Lugardo Ballejos (rubric)
Xptobal Garsia (rubric) Salvador Garcia (rubric)
Jabier Miranda (rubric)
Bernardo Ballejos (rubric)
Manuel Carillo (rubric)
Juan Antonio Samora (rubric)
Salvador Garsia (rubric) Ramon Garcia Jurado (rubric)

En la Villa de Santa Fee capital de este Reyno de la Nueva Mexico en tres dias de el mes de (Agosto crossed out) Septiembre de mil setecientos treinta y siete aviendo visto yo el Governador y Capitan General de este dicho Reyno Dn. Henrique de Olavide y Michelena este escrito remitido a este Superior Govierno por el comun y vesindad de la Villa de San Phelipe de Alburquerque serca de que se desague lo mandado en el Vando promulgado para que ningun arriero ni entrante y saliente en este dicho Reyno saque granos, ganados ni lanas, por sedar todo en su beneficio = Visto asi mismo el ningun fundamento que ministra su pedimento como tambien el que los mas firmados no tienen hasienda alguna = Devia mandar y mande se guarde, cumpla y execute lo por mi mandado en el mensionado Vando, observando su contexto en todo, y por todo, so la pena de que el que en ello contraviniese, sera inculto en las que se imponen; y no seles admita en orden a este particular escrito alguno por no aver lugar en derecho lo que se pide, y ser contra el su ocurso. Asi lo provei, mande y firme actuando por Receptoria con testigos de asistencia a falta de Escribano Real y Publico que no se aya en este Reyno.
Fechado Agosto no vale.

Henrique de Olavide
Y Micheleña (rubric)
Pedro Joseph de Leon (rubric)
Juan Phelipe Rivera (rubric)

Notes

1. Note that of the forty settlers signing the petition, thirty-two signed their own names, a respectable number.
2. This is the decree written on August 17, 1737, for which they may have received notice on August 24. In this decree, Governor Olavide y Micheleña prohibited the sale of goods by the settlers to those outside the province but exempted traders selling goods collected for church tithes, called the *renta decimal*. The language of the decree is as follows: "I also order that the Spanish residents and Indians of this kingdom, under the same penalties [as in the previous decrees, for the Spanish two hundred pesos in silver or hard money and loss of all goods, and for the Indians two hundred lashes along with the loss of everything], are not to sell to the

owners of pack trains or drivers those goods that are prohibited, *with the exception of those goods that remain inside the kingdom and those goods that are for the tithes of the Holy Church of Durango. The outside traders are to inform me, first of all if the goods are for the said* renta decimal, *acquiring for this a license from the superior government so that they can travel freely*" (editor's emphasis; Ritch Collection, Roll 3, #58, August 17, 1737, Zimmerman Library, University of New Mexico).

3. This is likely to be the Antonio Durán y Chávez, who was a son of don Fernando Durán y Chávez, a native New Mexican. He married Magdalena Montaño and then Antonia Baca. He died in 1738 (Chávez, *Origins*: 162).
4. A Francisco de Chávez was part of a military muster in Bernalillo in 1705. He married Juana Baca the younger in 1713 (Chávez, *Origins*: 162; NMGS, *Aquí*: 68).
5. See Doc. 33.
6. See Doc. 37.
7. Baltasar Romero was a native New Mexican, returning by 1694. He and his family lived in Bernalillo and moved to Albuquerque as one of the first founding families. A soldier, he was included in the 1705 muster. In 1716 Captain Romero was an alcalde for Laguna Pueblo. Later he acquired landholdings near Isleta and Taos. He appears to have died around 1745 (NMGS, *Aquí*: 387-90).
8. Diego Padilla I came to New Mexico from El Paso by 1706, marrying Catalina Gutiérrez de Salazar, and then María Vásquez Baca (or de Lara). He lived in the Isleta jurisdiction. This person could be his son, Diego II, who married María Luisa Chávez in 1741 in Albuquerque. Diego I was involved in several legal cases, including a complaint against Jacinto Sánchez for slander (Chávez, *Origins*: 253; NMGS, *Aquí*: 188, 390; SANM II #460, #681, #684).
9. There were several Antonio Bacas at this time. This one may be one of the sons of Manuel Baca, who came to New Mexico in 1693 and married María de Salazar. He could also be one of the four sons of Josefa Baca, a sister to Manuel (Chávez, *Origins*: 141-44).
10. Miguel II Lucero was the son of Miguel I Lucero de Godoy, who died from wounds sustained at El Morro in 1710. Miguel II was an alcalde of Albuquerque in the 1750s and 1760s. He married Rosa Baca and then Antonia Durán y Chaves. By 1746 he was in Tomé/Fuenclara (Chávez, *Origins*: 211; NMGS, *Aquí*: 68, 330, 331; SANM I #29, #586).
11. Captain Joseph Baca was one of the original petitioners for the Tomé grant in 1739-1750. In 1745 he was alcalde of Fuenclara and also alcalde and war captain of Albuquerque. A Captain Joseph Baca is named as the wife of Josefa Gallegos in 1746 in Albuquerque. A will for a Joseph Baca appears in 1770 at Pueblo Quemado in the Santa Fe jurisdiction, but it is not known if this is the same person (SANM I #117, WPA translation; SANM II #463; NMGS, *Aquí*: 243; Alexander, *Cottonwoods*: 328).
12. Francisco Padilla was a son of Diego I Padilla and María Vásquez Baca, and a brother to Diego II. In 1732 Francisco married Isabel Baca, one of the natural children of Josefa Baca. By 1769 he was involved in the sale of the Diego Padilla grant (NMGS, *Aquí*: 72, 195, 196, 207; SANM I #695).
13. Domingo Baca appears to have been one of the natural children of Josefa Baca (Chávez, *Origins*: 144).
14. See Doc. 8.
15. There were several persons named Francisco Chávez, but to date, no information has been found on Francisco Guadalupe Chávez.
16. Pedro Romero was the son of Baltazar Romero and Francisca Góngora. The family lived in Bernalillo. Pedro's siblings were Gregorio, María Gregoria, Felipe, another Pedro, José, and maybe Ventura. He married Gregoria Baca Luna in 1728 in Isleta and María Josepha Jaramillo in 1751 in Albuquerque (Chávez, *Origins*: 271; NMGS, *Aquí*: 68,155, 388).
17. See Doc. 21.
18. See Doc. 28.
19. See Doc. 33.
20. See Doc. 5.
21. Antonio Gurulé was the son or grandson of Santiago Grolé, or Grolet, who had been a member of the La Salle expedition with Juan Archibeque. He was from the area of Sandía and married Antonia Quintana. In 1733 he made a complaint against Cristóbal García for opening an acequia through his land in Albuquerque, and in 1746 was a witness in a case regarding the heirs of Luis García (Chávez, *Origins*: 421; SANM II #340, #379).
22. At this time, little is known about Andrés Aragón, though in 1773 he and Elena Durán y Chaves were godparents of María Gregoria Sena (NMGS, *Aquí*: 258).
23. See Doc. 28.
24. See Doc.5.
25. Antonio Zamora [Martín] could be the Diego Antonio Zamora Martín from Tomé, son of Tomás Martín and Bárbara Rivera, who married Catarina Bazilia Benavides at Albuquerque in 1775. Or he could be the Antonio Zamora Martínez who married Margarita Vallejo in Albuquerque in 1774 and had a household at Tomé (NMGS, *Aquí*: 94, 236).
26. Juan Montaño is most likely the son of Juan Montaño Sotomayor and Isabel Jorge de Vera, who returned to

New Mexico with Vargas in 1693, living in Santa Fe. Isabel moved to the Río Abajo after her husband died. In 1737 Juan Montaño was part of a criminal prosecution in Albuquerque against Diego and Cristóbal García for having assaulted him (Chávez, *Origins*: 233-34; SANM II #416a).

27. Cayetano Lucero was married to María Salas. In 1734 he held lands in Albuquerque adjacent to those of Lugardo Vallejo (NMGS, *Aquí*: 66, 79, SANM I #1040).
28. Matías Romero was the son of Bartolomé Romero III and Luisa Varela, who returned to New Mexico in 1693. His wife was Ángela Teresa Vallejo, a widow of Miguel Lucero. He purchased property in Albuquerque in 1733 from Cristóbal Jaramillo. Bartolomé Romero I came with Oñate in 1598, and Bartolomé Romero II was mentioned as an encomendero of Picuris Pueblo in the early 1660s (Chávez, *Origins*: 271; NMGS, *Aquí*: 462; Barrett, *Settlement*: 123-24).
29. Francisco Silva was the son of Antonio de Silva and Gregoria Ruiz, and a brother of Felipe and María Silva, mentioned elsewhere in these documents. He married Rosa Gertrudis Durán y Chaves in 1729. In 1733 he was involved in a case against Nicolás Chávez regarding a dowry (NMGS, *Aquí*: 424, 426; Chávez, *Origins*: 70, 288-89; SANM I #234).
30. See Doc. 33.
31. Vicente García was the son of Alonso García de Noriega and was born in El Paso. He lived in Alameda in the 1730s and was married to Catalina González Bas, a daughter of Juan I González Bas. He was also a soldier at the Santa Fe presidio. In 1733 he was part of a witchcraft trial in which he accused the Indians of Isleta of bewitching him (Chávez, *Origins*: 182; NMGS, *Aquí*: 321-22; SANM II #381).
32. This could be Francisco Perea, who was the son of Juan de Perea, a native New Mexican who came from El Paso by 1694. Francisco married María Varela some time before 1709. This could also be his son, also named Francisco, who married Rosa de Torres before 1731. One of these people, perhaps the latter, was named in the 1743 will of Vicente Armijo, who stated that he owed him a mule and "transportation of the same" (Chávez, *Origins*: 256; NMGS, *Aquí*: 490; SANM I #26, Twitchell translation).
33. To date, little is known about Martín Montoya except that he married María Bárbara Viviana Varela, a daughter of Jacinto Varela Jaramillo in 1738 in Albuquerque. He is apparently not the son of Francisco Xavier Montoya and Juan Baca (NMGS, *Aquí*: 255, 346, 348,409, 490; Chávez, *Origins*: 271; SANM II #303, #307).
34. Joseph García was a son of Vicente García, born in 1715. In 1739 his name was listed as selling land in Santa Fe. He may be Captain José García, listed with Ana de Luna in 1761 as marriage witnesses (NMGS, *Aquí*: 80, 310; SANM I #330, #331).
35. Andrés Martín [Serrano] was a brother of Mateo. In the 1730s, he moved from Santa Cruz to Alameda. His name appears in proceedings against Eusebio Chávez (Chávez, *Origins*: 225; SANM II #242).
36. Salvador Durán could have been the Salvador Durán who was a godparent, with Tomasa Durán, of Fulgencia Candelaria in Albuquerque in 1734. He could also have been the Salvador Durán who served with the El Paso presidio from 1693 to 1701 and was living in Santa Cruz by 1709—or maybe these two are the same person (NMGS, *Aquí*: 132; Kessell et al., *TDC*: 180 n13).
37. This could be the Antonio Lucero II, who was the son of the alférez, Antonio Lucero de Godoy I, who came to New Mexico around 1695 with Antonia Varela de Perea or de Losada. Antonio II married Francisca Jaramillo in Albuquerque in 1712 (Chávez, *Origins*, 209).
38. See Doc. 25.
39. See Doc. 5.
40. See Doc. 40.
41. Javier Miranda was in New Mexico by 1711, when he married Catalina Durán y Chávez. He may have been a brother or relation to the Fray Antonio Miranda who performed the wedding ceremony, and may have been a brother of Matías Miranda. Javier is listed in 1735 as conveying land in Atrisco (Chávez, *Origins*: 232; SANM I #321; Kessell et al., *TDC*: 422 n29).
42. Bernardo Vallejo was the natural son of Pedro Durán y Chávez and grandson of don Fernando Durán y Chávez. He married Francisca Silva, a sister of Felipe Francisco. In the 1760s, he was involved with the Los Quelites grant near Tomé (Chávez, *Origins*: 288, 303, 425; NMGS, *Aquí*: 79, 151).
43. See SANM II #397.
44. Juan Antonio Zamora may be the son of Juan de Zamora, who was a New Mexico native, passing muster in El Paso in 1681 and living in Santa Cruz in 1696. Juan Antonio was listed as one of the petitioners for the Tomé grant (Alexander, *Cottonwoods*: 329; Chávez, *Origins*: 314).

31

PAWNEE BOY, SON OF FAMILY SERVANT, IDENTIFIED IN ANIMAL THEFT
July 11–13, 1740. Source: SANM II #432.

Synopsis and editor's notes: This 1740 document from Chama finds Pablo Trujillo traveling from the house of the Santa Cruz alcalde, Juan García de la Mora, having collected a mule previously stolen from him by Francisco, also called El Coyote. Governor Gaspar Domingo de Mendoza had ordered that the mule be returned to Trujillo. Francisco was the son of a Pawnee servant of Trujillo's mother-in-law, doña Juana Márquez. On his way home, he was attacked by Francisco, who wanted the mule back and who pulled Trujillo from his horse. Apparently fed up with Francisco's unrepentant behavior, Trujillo complained to the alcalde about the attack and Francisco's earlier thefts. When the alcalde went to get Francisco from the stocks in Santa Cruz and questioned him, Francisco freely admitted that earlier he had taken a cow and a one-year-old heifer and sold them. He said that when he was caught, the woman for whom his mother was a servant, doña Juana Márquez, paid the owners of the animals for them. The presiding judge, Juan García de la Mora, had the owners of these animals and doña Márquez testify. The case was referred to the governor and then ends without determination, possibly because doña Márquez or others once again made restitution for Francisco's behavior, the alcalde arrived at some other solution, or the governor's sentence has been lost.

This case may speak to the Pawnee culture, where theft of loose livestock may have been accepted, or it may be that Francisco was raised as a kind of "pet" in the household of doña Márquez, with all of his transgressions forgiven and made right. It is likely that the Pawnee mother was purchased at one of the trade fairs through the ransoming process.

Alcalde mayor and war captain

[Marginal note]
Proceedings by the
alcalde mayor of La Cañada at
the request of Pablo Trujillo[1]

I, Pablo Trujillo, resident of Chama,[2] appear before your honor in my best form and manner which there is and according to my right and say that I am filing a complaint, on my own behalf, against Francisco, *El Coyote*,[3] who lives in the house of Juana Márquez,[4] for having attacked me on the road when I left the house of your honor, and demanded my macho that your honor ordered him [El Coyote] to pay to me, for which reason he apparently felt angry. He is a coyote, the son of a Pawnee [Panana] Indian woman, who had the cunning to come out to challenge me and was armed with a knife [*cuchillo*] on his belt on a sheath [*cuchillo de sinta procuse sosegarle*]. I had no weapons on me and tried to calm him down by trying to reason with him. But it was of no avail to try and control his temper, and he raised his hand to punch me, which I was able to avoid. He then grabbed me by the arm and threw me off the horse that I was on, tearing my sleeves off my jacket and my shirt, as I have shown to you.

Because of this, I ask and petition your honor that you be well served not to leave him without being punished. I also inform your honor, as a leader of this republic [*padre de republica*], that this servant is a vagabond [*vago*], who cannot be reformed, and even though he is within the household of doña Juana Márquez, who is the one who brought him up due to the fact that he was born in that house, he will not listen to what that lady orders him to do. He lives a carefree life, drinking a lot, smoking, and many other wasteful things that bring him to thieving and doing other bad deeds and cause him to bring about other problems which he thinks are justifiable. I offer witnesses who can support this because they know who has helped him by purchasing items which he has stolen. It can also be proven by my own mother-in-law, [doña Márquez], who has paid for one of the cows that was stolen by the said coyote, who was the one who profited. I know all of this because I am part of that household, and I do not wish for these similar problems to continue without his being properly punished and stopped along with others of the same character. Because of this, I ask and petition that your honor admit this document, reserving the information which I offer, so that you can determine what is best for justice, and I swear in my proper form that this document can be of some value, and is not done in malice, but for what is necessary, etc.

                     Pablo Trujillo (rubric)

On the 11th of July of 1740, he, the above, presented that which is contained before me, Juan García de Mora,[5] alcalde mayor and war captain of this jurisdiction, and admitted it as presented. In attending to what is requested I went to get Francisco, El Coyote, offender in this complaint or case and prisoner in the stocks [*zepos* or *cepos*] of this jurisdiction in order to take his sworn statement according to that which is contained in this matter, receiving his sworn statement, which he promised to make to God and the sign of the Holy Cross. When he was asked regarding the complaint, he said that it was true that he stole a cow which he sold at the pueblo of San Juan to an Indian named Pichule, and that the owner turned out to be Gerónimo Martín,[6] who demanded payment from his keeper, Juana Márquez, who paid for it, and the said Gerónimo Martín was satisfied. He, Francisco, also said that from Ignacio Martín[7] he had stolen a one-year-old heifer, about to turn two, which he sold to Nicolás Quintana[8] and for which he [Martín] was paid with a horse and some hides so that it would not go before a justice, if it could possibly be avoided, and Martín was satisfied. He, Francisco, said that this was all, and that he is not indebted to them in any way. He said that this was the truth regarding his sworn statement which he has made, and it being read back to him, he affirmed and ratified it, saying that he was twenty-four years of age, more or less. He did not sign it because he did not know how. I, the said justice, signed it with my assisting witnesses with whom I act as presiding judge due to the lack of a public or royal scribe, which there is none in this kingdom and on the present paper, as there is none of the sealed kind in the kingdom, to which I certify.

      Juan García de Mora (rubric)
      Presiding judge

Assisting Witnesses
Juan Antonio Luján (rubric)
Diego García (rubric)

  On the said day, month, and year, in reference to the information which has been given by Pablo Trujillo, complainant, he presented as a witness Ignacio Martín, resident of Chama, from whom, I, the said judge, received his sworn statement which he made to God and to the sign of the Holy Cross, under which he promised to tell the truth as to what he knew and to what he was asked. He was asked if he knew about the document which has been presented by Pablo Trujillo. He said that it was true that in the past year of 1739, he recognized at the house of the Quintanas a cow that belonged to him. Upon asking them where or how it was that they had that certain cow, they responded by saying that they had purchased it from Francisco, El Coyote, who is in the home of Juana Márquez. Upon learning this, I approached Francisco and asked him if he had done this wrong, and he, Francisco, agreed to pay him, which he did, by giving him a horse and five hides, by virtue of which he [Martín] was fully paid for the cow and was satisfied. He said that this was the truth regarding the sworn statement which he has made, and he does not know anything else. He said that he was twenty-four years old, more or less, and because he did not know how to sign, I, the said judge, signed it along with my assisting witnesses due to the lack of a public or royal scribe, which there is none in this kingdom, acting as presiding judge, as is stated, and on the present common paper, as the sealed kind is not available in these parts, to which I certify.

      Juan García de Mora (rubric)
      Presiding judge
Assisting witness Juan Antonio Luján (rubric)

On the 12th of the said month and year, the said Pablo Trujillo presented Juana Márquez as a witness for the information which he has presented and from whom I, the said judge, received a sworn statement which was made to God and to the sign of the Holy Cross, under which she promised to tell the truth regarding what she knew and what she was asked about the document that is found at the beginning of these proceedings. She said that it was true that she had paid Gerónimo Martín for a cow for her said servant, for which she felt sorry that it had gotten to that point. When the said Gerónimo Martín told her about the bad thing which had been committed by the said offender [Francisco], he knelt down before her and asked for her pardon, and he asked her if she could help him get out of what he had done before it got to a judge. She says that she did as he requested by paying, as she did pay Gerónimo Martín for the said cow. However, being placed in the position that she is now under the sworn statement that she has made, she cannot dismiss the truth, feeling so bad that she brought him up in her house. As for what happened between him and Pablo when he attacked him, she does not know any more than [that] before Francisco went to the house of the declarant, she asked him how things had gone with the judge regarding the demand of the macho. He told her that it was neither good nor bad, but that at this time Pablo would have reason to complain, and that he, Pablo, had already gone to the home of the alcalde to file a complaint. This she says is what she has heard, but does not know if he beat him up or what happened between them. This she says is the truth regarding the sworn statement which she has made and said that she is fifty years of age, more or less. She did not sign because she did not know how. I, the said judge, signed it along with my assistants as is the custom and as is done, to which I certify. Having read this back to her, she affirmed and ratified it, saying that she did not have anything to add or delete, to which I certify.

Juan García de Mora (rubric)
Presiding judge

Assisting witnesses
Juan Antonio Luján (rubric)
Diego García (rubric)

On the 13th of the said month and year there appeared before me Gerónimo Martín, witness, who was presented for the information that has been offered by Pablo Trujillo against Francisco, El Coyote, offender in this complaint, from whom I received his sworn statement which he made to God and the Holy Cross, by which he promised to tell the truth about what he knew and what he was asked regarding the contents of the document at the beginning of these proceedings. He was asked to tell what he knew about the particular problem. He said that it is true that when he went to look for and inquire about a cow which he was missing, he found out that it had been slaughtered at the pueblo of San Juan at the house of an Indian named Pichule, and this Indian told him that he had bought it from the said Francisco, El Coyote, who had gone to see him. At that time, my sister, Juana Márquez, the mistress [*ama*] of the Indian woman who is the mother of el coyote, agreed to pay me for it so that it would not go before a judge. He said that he did not know anything else about the complaint against the said el coyote. He said that this was the truth regarding the sworn statement which he has made, and it being read back to him he affirmed and ratified it, and said that he was thirty-eight years of age, more or less, and he signed it along with myself and my assistants with whom I act as presiding judge due to the lack of a public or royal scribe, which there is none in this kingdom, and on the present paper because the sealed kind is not available in these parts, to which I certify.

      Juan García de Mora (rubric)
      Presiding judge
      Gerónimo Martín (rubric)

Assisting witnesses
Antonio de Abeytia (rubric)
Diego García (rubric)

On the said day, month, and year, I, said judge, recalled Francisco, El Coyote, to see if he had anything else to add or delete from the statement which has made. He said that it was as it is and as he has stated. He was asked if he had approached Pablo Trujillo to assault him. He said that for several days Pablo Trujillo had been after him in a bad way, and when he [Trujillo] went to a justice to claim his macho, he saw that he [Trujillo] had started bad-mouthing him, which is shown by what he has done in his document. That is the reason that he approached him on the road and told him that this was where men are found to be men,[9] and grabbed him by the arm and threw him from his mule to the ground, but that he did not attack him, nor pulled a knife on him. This he says is the truth regarding the sworn statement which he has made and which he affirms and ratifies saying that he is of the referred to age of twenty-four. He did not sign because he did not know how. I, the said judge, signed it along with my assistants, acting as presiding judge due to the lack of a public or royal scribe which there is none in this kingdom, and on the present paper as has been said, to which I certify.

      Juan García de Mora (rubric)
      Presiding judge

Assisting witnesses
Antonio de Abeytia (rubric)
Diego García (rubric)

On the said day, month, and year, I, the said judge, having concluded these proceedings, am about to submit them, and I do submit them, with Gerónimo Martín, in four fully written pages, to Lieutenant Colonel don Gaspar Domingo de Mendoza,[10]

captain of the Spanish infantry, adjutant major of the plaza of the city of Rodrigo, in the kingdoms of Castile, governor and captain general of this kingdom, his castles and frontiers, etc., so that upon his review, his honor shall determine that which he finds convenient, and I signed it with my assisting witnesses as has been stated, to which I certify.

Juan García de Mora (rubric)
Presiding judge

Assisting witnesses
Diego García (rubric)
Antonio de Abeytia (rubric)

ORIGINAL DOCUMENT

Señor Alcalde Mayor y Capitan Aguerra

Unas diligencias que se ysieron por
el Alcalde Mayor de La Cañada a
pedimento de Pablo Trujillo

Pablo Trujillo vezino de Chama paresco ante Vmd. en la mejor bia y forma que aya lugar e en derecho y mejor proseda y digo que me querello en toda forma de Francisco, el coyote, de casa de Juana Marques por aberme salido al camino desafiandome quando Sali de casa de Su Mersed a demandarle mi macho que Usted se sirvio de mandar pagar a dicho coyote y parese se sintio de esta demanda y siendo un coyote hijo de una Yndia Panana tubo el abilantes de salirme desafiando y yo biendome sin armas y qual el los traya que era un cuchillo de sinta procure sosegarlo con buenas rasones y nada desto fue sufisiente a sosegar abilantes pues also la mano a tirarme un bojeton y librandome del me agaro del braso y me tiro de la bestia en que benia de cuyo tiron me rompio las mangas de almilla y camisa como a Vmd. manifiesto cuyo abilantes pido y suplico a Vmd. sea muy serbido no dexar sin castigo como asi mismo pongo en notisia de Vmd. como a padre de republica que este moso es bago y sin suxesion alguna por que aunque esta arimado ami dona Juana Marques que es quien lo a criado por aber nasido en casa no quiere sujetarse alo que mi Señora le ordena y manda y bibe lisensiosamente manteniendose en beber, chupar y de todos los demas gastos que sele ofresen de urtar y maldades y por que quien calumia es fuerza que justifique ofresco justificasion con los testigos aquienes les auxilado con los que compran la cosa hurtada. Y con mi propia suegra quien pago una de las bacas hurtadas por el dicho coyote atendiendo aque lo ozio en cosa y como yo soy sabedor destas maldades por estar dentro de casa no quiero que semejantes ynfamias queden solapados sin que lleguen a tener el debido castigo por que sirba de freno a este y a otros desta calidad y por tanto a Vmd. pido y suplico se sirba de admitir este mi escripto resibiendome la

ynformasion que ofresco y aser y determinar lo que allare de justizia y juro en debida forma serbir doi este me escripto y nada de malisia y en lo necesario, ut supra.
Pablo Trujillo (rubric)

En onse dias del mes de Jullio deste ano de mill setezientos y quarenta la presento el contenido en ella ante mi Juan Garcia de Mora, Alcalde Mayor y Capitan Aguerra desta y la de por presentada y en atenzion a su pedimento pase a prender a Francisco, el coyote, reo en esta calumnia, o causa, y preso en el zepo de esta jurisdizion lo pase a tomar su declarazion por el thenor desta querella con los testigos de mi asistenzia aquien rezivi juramento que hizo por Dios y la Señal de la Santa Cruz bajo el cual prometio dezir berdad en lo que supiere y le fuere preguntado, y siendolo por el thenor desta querella dijo; que es berdad que cojio una baca y la bendio en el Pueblo de San Juan a un Yndio llamado Pichule, y que a esto le salio por dueno a Geronimo Martin, quien la demando a mi Señora Juana Marquez quien la pago por mi, y se quedo assi contento dicho Geronimo Martin, y ha Ygnacio Martin, coyote, le coji otra becerra de ano que yba a dos, la cual bendi a Nicolas Quintana, pero sela tengo pagada con un caballo y algunas pieles, dejandolo contento para que no llegase a quejarse silo pudiera hazer; y que no le es a ninguno encargo de otra cosa ni a estos les debia nada, y que esta es la verdad so cargo del juramento que fecho tiene, el que siendole leyda en el se afirmo y ratifico y dijo ser de edad de veinte y cuatro anos poco mas o menos; no firmo por no saber firmelo yo dicho Juez con los de mi asistenzia con quienes actuo por Reseptoria a falta de Escribano Publico ni Real que no lo ay en este Reyno, en el presente papel por no correr en este Reyno del sellado de que doi fee.
Juan Garcia de Mora (rubric)
Juez receptor

De asistenzia De asistenzia
Juan Antonio Lujan (rubric) Diego Garcia (rubric)

En dicho dia mes y ano para la ynformazion que tiene ofrezida Pablo Trujillo querellante, presento por testigo a Ygnacio Martin vezino de Chama aquien yo dicho Juez le rezivi juramento que hizo por Dios y la Señal de la Santa Cruz bajo del cual prometio dezir verdan en lo que supiere y le fuere preguntado y siendolo saber el escripto que tiene presentado Pablo Trujillo dijo: que es berdad que el ano pasado de treinta y nuebe conozi en casa de los Quintanas una baca mia; y preguntandoles que como o de donde les habia venido aquella baca le respondieron haverla comprado a Francisco, el coyote, que esta en casa de Juana Marquez y que con esta razon que tubo le recombino desta maldad a dicho Francisco y se havino a pagarsela; y que le dio por ella un caballo y zinco pieles en cuya virtud quedo pagado y satisfecho de dicha baca; que esta es la berdad so cargo del juramento que fecho tiene y que no sabe mas. Dijo, ser de edad de veinte y cuatro anos poco mas o menos y por no saber firmar lo firme yo dicho Juez con los testigos de assistenzia a falta de Scribano Publico ni Real que no lo ay en este Reyno actuando por Reseptoria como dicho es, y en el presente papel comun por no correr en estas partes del sellado de que doi fee=

      Juan Garcia de Mora (rubric)
      Juez receptor

De assistenzia
Juan Antonio Lujan (rubric)

En doze dias de dicho mes y ano presento por testigo a Juana Marquez el dicho Pablo Trujillo para la ynformazion que tiene ofrezida a quien yo dicho Juez rezivi juramento que hizo por Dios y la Señal de la Santa Cruz bajo del cual prometio dezir verdad en lo que supiera y le fuera preguntado, y siendolo, por el thenor del escripto que esta por cavesa destas diligencias dijo: que es berdad que pago a Geronimo Martin una baca por dicho mozo, que siento mucho que aya llegado a esto. Pues cuando dicho Geronimo Martin le recombino dela maldad a el dicho reo, sele ynco de rodillas y le pidio perdon y me suplico ami le sacase deste empeno por que llegase a terminos de justizia, y yo le hize por lo mismo pagandole como le pague dicha baca a Geronimo Martin pero puesta ya en la pregunta de debajo de juramento no puede faltar ala berdad aunque lo siento mucho por averlo criado en casa; y que delo que tubo con Pablo de desafio no save mas que el que dicho Francisco fue a su casa dela declarante y preguntandole que como le havia ydo en mi jusgado sobre el demando del macho; que respondio que entre bien y mal, que aora si se quejaria con razon dicho Pablo; que ya abia buelto a casa del Alcalde a quejarse que esto le oyo mas que no sabe si le dio golpes o tirones o lo que subsedio entre ellos; que esta es la verdad so cargo del juramento que tiene fecho y que es de edad de zinquenta anos poco mas o menos y no firmo por no saber, firmelo yo dicho Juez con los de mi asistenzia como acostumbro y dicho es, de que doy fee = Y siendolo leydo este su dicho en el se afirmo y ratifico y dijo not tener que anadir ni quitar de todo doy fee =

      Juan Garcia de Mora (rubric)
      Juez receptor

De assistenzia de assistenzia
Juan Antonio Lujan (rubric) Diego Garcia (rubric)

En treze dias del dicho mes y año parezio ante mi Geronimo Martin testigo que presento para la ynformazion que tiene ofrezida Pablo Trujillo contra Francisco, el coyote, reo en esta querella, a quien le resivi juramento que hizo por Dios y la Santa Cruz bajo del cual prometio dezir verdad en lo que supiere y le fuere preguntado; y siendole por el thenor del escripto que se halla por caveza destos autos; y que sobre ello diga lo que sabe en este particular, dijo: que es berdad que andando solizitando e ynquiriendo de una baca que le falto, supo haberse matado en el Pueblo de San Juan en casa de un Yndio llamado Pichule, y que este Yndio le dijo haversela comprado a dicho Francisco, coyote, que fue aberlo y que luego se halla a no a pagarmela, mi hermana Juana Marquez, ama de la Yndia, su madre de este coyote; atento a que no se llegara a poner entre la de justizia, que no sabe delo demas dela querella otra cosa contra dicho coyote, que esta es la verdad so cargo del juramento que fecho tiene el que siendole leydo en el se afirmo y ratifico y dijo estar segun y como su declarazion y dijo ser de edad de treinta y ocho anos poco mas o menos y lo firmo con migo y los de mi assistenzia con quienes actuo por Receptoria a falta de Scribano Publico ni Real que no lo ay en este Reyno y en el presente papel comun por no correr en estas partes el sellado de que doi fee =

       Juan Garcia de Mora (rubric)
         Juez receptor

Geronimo Martin (rubric)
De assistenzia de assistenzia
Antonio de Abeytia (rubric) Diego Garcia (rubric)

En dicho dia mes y año yo dicho Juez bolbi a llamar a Francisco, el coyote, que dijese si tenia otra cosa que declarar o anadir o quitar de la declarazion hecha, y dijo estar segun y como lo que tenia declarado y preguntadole sobre el haverle salido a Pablo Trujillo a desafiar, dijo: que habia dias ya que dicho Pablo Trujillo andava con el de malas y que haviendo venido ante la justizia a demandar su macho, bio el dicho declarante que comenso a soltarse con razones prenadas y aun claras de lo que a ora a echo por escrito tocante a su credito y por esa rason salio al camino y le dijo aqui se an de ber los hombres y le fue asiendo de un brazo y lo tiro dela mula a el suelo pero que no le desafio, ni saco cuchillo por el; y que esta es la verdad so cargo del juramento qu fecho tiene en el que se afirma y ratifica y que es de la edad referida de veinte y cuatro anos, no firmo por no saber, firmelo yo dicho Juez con los testigos de mi asistenzia actuando como Juez receptor a falta de Scribano Publico ni Real que no lo ay en este Reyno y en el presente papel como dicho es de que doi fee =

       Juan Garcia de Mora (rubric)
         Juez receptor

De assistenzia de assistenzia
Antonio de Abeytia (rubric) Diego Garcia (rubric)

En dicho dia mes y año yo dicho Juez estando ya concluidas estas diligencias debia de hazer remission de hellas como lo hago con Geronimo Martin en que ban concluidas en quatro fojas todas utiles, a el Señor Theniente Coronel Dn. Gaspar Domingo de Mendoza, Capitan de Ynfanteria Española, Ayudante Mayor de la Plaza de Ziudad Rodrigo en los Reynos de Castilla, Governador y Capitan General deste Reyno, Sus

Castillos y Fronteras, ut supra, para que en su bista Su Señoria determine lo que hallara por combeniente y lo firme con los testigos de mi assistenzia como dicho es de todo doy fee =

Juan Garcia de Mora (rubric)
Juez receptor

De assistenzia de assistenzia
Diego Garcia (rubric) Antonio de Abeytia (rubric)

Notes

1. Pablo [Manuel] Trujillo may have been the son of Bartolo Trujillo, a resident of the Pojoaque area (see Doc. 4). Pablo married Francisca Márquez, daughter of Diego Márquez and Juana Martín Serrano, in Pojoaque in 1728. In 1766 he was in another lawsuit having to do with a mule (Chávez, *Origins*: 297; SANM II #602).
2. The document is probably referring to the settlement of Puesto de Chama, located south of the current town of Chama. Alfred Barnaby Thomas states that the word *chama* can be translated as "exchange" (Thomas, *Forgotten Frontiers*: 386 n125).
3. Here the term *coyote* seems to serve as a racial designation—a person of Indian and mestizo parents. No mention is made of Francisco's father.
4. Doña Juana Márquez may be the Juana Martín Serrano who married Diego Márquez of Santa Cruz, and possibly the mother-in-law of Pablo Trujillo. Diego Márquez was dead by 1729 (Chávez, *Origins*: 221).
5. See Doc. 27.
6. Gerónimo Martín appears to have been part of the large Martín Serrano family in northern New Mexico (see Doc. 42). He and Ignacio Martín, mentioned below, received a grant in the Abiquiu area around 1735, though it was later revoked by Governor Cruzat y Góngora. However, in the 1760s, he was still dealing with land in Abiquiu (SANM I #154 and #160; SANM II #233).
7. Ygnacio Martín, also a part of the Martín Serrano family, may have been the son of Diego Martín II and Rosa de Atienza. As stated above, he, along with Gerónimo Martín, was one of the recipients of the Abiquiu land grant, which was later revoked. In 1730 he married Mariana Giltomey (Chávez, *Origins*: 225; SANM I #154).
8. Nicolás [Miguel] Quintana was the son of Miguel Quintana, who came to New Mexico in 1693 from Mexico City. Nicolás lived in Santa Cruz. His wife was María Antonia de Herrera. In 1697 he is shown as a scribe-elect of the cabildo (Chávez, *Origins*: 261-62; Kessell et al., *TDC*: 34).
9. The Spanish reads, "*le dijo aquí se an ber los hombres.*"
10. Mendoza was governor from 1739 to 1743. He is known for entertaining Mallet and his party from New Orleans in 1749–1750 (Kessell, *Kiva*: 389).

32

ATTACK ON ALCALDE MAYOR OF LAGUNA; WOUNDED WITH OWN SWORD
October 19–23, 1743. Source: SANM II #449.

Synopsis and editor's notes: In this document, Juan Miguel Álvarez del Castillo, the alcalde of Zuni, Laguna, and Acoma, also called the lieutenant of Fuenclara, walked from his house to go to the puesto of Nuestra Señora de Belén, one of the plazas in the newly approved land grant of Tomé. Bernardo de Chaves rode by and stopped to talk to Castillo, insulting him. Chaves then dismounted, grabbed Castillo's sword, and hit him on the shoulder with it. Castillo then made a formal complaint to Captain Diego Torres. Torres placed Chaves in prison, looked at Castillo's shoulder, and referred the case to Governor Domingo de Mendoza in Santa Fe. Mendoza ordered Chaves imprisoned, fining him 20 pesos. Unusually, there was no testimony by either Chaves or any bystanders or other settlers, nor was Chaves given a chance to respond to Castillo's accusation. Note that Castillo apparently lived in Fuenclara even though he was alcalde of the Zuni/Laguna/Acoma jurisdiction. This agreed with the official policy that alcaldes were not to live and own property in their assigned jurisdiction, but were to be located within a day's ride (Simmons, *Spanish Government*: 175).

In the late 1730s, Governor Gaspar de Mendoza gave settlers permission to settle on the Tomé grant, which was then located on both sides of the Río Grande. In 1740 Captain Diego de Torres and Antonio Salazar led twenty-seven men, five women, and twenty Genízaro Indians to the grant, which eventually included six plazas or hamlets, including Sausal, Belén (originally Bethlehem), Plaza de las Genízaros, Los Trujillos, Los Jarles or Los Jarales, and Sabinal. Whatever the original composition of the settlers, the 1750 census showed that the population of the plaza of Belén was 41 percent Genízaros. Genízaros were a mixed group of Plains Indians that had been captives, reared in a Hispanic environment, and lost their tribal identity. They were settled in several areas, but concentrations were at Abiquiu, San Miguel de Vado, Belén, and the Barrio de Analco. Generally their settlements were located so as to provide bulwarks against the hostile Indians such as the Apaches and Comanches (Horvath, "Genízaros": 62-64).

The puesto of Fuenclara, mentioned later in this document, was a settlement located just outside of the Tomé grant on the north and is sometimes shown on maps as "Fuenclara/Tomé. This later name was an early designation for a hill mentioned by Vargas as belonging to Tomé Domínguez de Mendoza prior to the 1680 revolt. When the area was resettled in the 1740s it took the name of Fuenclara and is shown as such by Menchero on his 1746 map, though located on the west side of the river. Neither settlement is mentioned in the 1750 census. The 1759 Miera y Pacheco map shows a "Fonclara" on the east side of the river south of Valencia, but without Tomé. However, on the 1779 Miera y Pacheco map (Map 2, Appendix), Tomé (but not Fuenclara) is shown. Fuenclara appears to have been named after Viceroy Pedro Cebrián y Agustín, count of Fuenclara (1742–1746). Fuenclara was not one of the Tomé plazas (Horvath, "Genízaros": 62-64; Jones, "Rescue": 132-33; Wheat, *Mapping* 1: 84, 119; Olmstead, "Enlistment," unnumbered first page; Kessell and Hendricks, *BFA*: 375; Kessell, *Kiva*: 509).

[Marginal note]
Criminal case
Of Captain of War
Joseph Álvarez de
Castillo against
Bernardo Chaves

Alcalde mayor and captain general

 I, Juan Miguel Álvarez del Castillo,[1] alcalde mayor and war captain of Zuni, the pueblo of Laguna, and of San Esteban de Acoma, appear before the greatness of your majesty in the best manner that I have. And I say that upon my leaving from my house on the 18th of the present month of October to go to the puesto of Nuestra Señora de Belén, I met up with Bernardo de Chaves,[2] who stopped to chat with me, and as we talked alone, he only brought up things that he wanted to talk about that were touchy and insulting, saying that we were in a good spot to do just that. Continuing with this issue, he got down from his horse, and [I], not realizing what his intentions were, [found that] all of a sudden he went for the small short sword [*espadin*] that I had strapped on the lower part of my leg. Having used this trick and being assured that I had no other weapon, he attacked me with it, hitting me quite forcefully on my back, as can be seen by the mark that was left on me. For all of this, your honor, I ask and petition that he be punished for this bold affront, although I do not know of any law that will be favorable to me even though I am officially a justice, even if from another jurisdiction. I swear in due form that this written request is not done in malice, but only to ask and petition the greatness of your majesty to attend to this in justice and to accept it as it is most necessary, etc.
Juan Miguel Álvarez del Castillo (rubric)

Puesto de Fonclara [Fuenclara]
October 19, 1743

The above was presented before me, Captain Diego Torres, and I, upon reviewing it, took it as it was presented and, attending to this just request, ordered and did order that the said Bernardo de Chaves be placed in prison for the reason of having done what he did, and this is what the petitioner seeks. Having seen what the lieutenant [Castillo] of Fuenclara showed me regarding the blow that he was given with the small sword [*espaldilla*] as indicated by the width of the blow of the sword on the left side of the shoulder blade, and as it was, it indicated that it was a hard blow that was given over the clothes that were worn and it showed that the area was swollen and the skin cut and bruised the width of the sword. Being charged with this assault, I submitted it to the tribunal of this superior government of this Villa, the capital, so that a decision can be handed down. I thus approved and signed it, acting as presiding judge along with my assisting witnesses.

Diego Torres (rubric)
Presiding judge

witness witness
Isidro Sánchez (rubric) Joseph Gallegos (rubric)

Fifth count of Fuenclara, Pedro Cebrián y Agustín, viceroy from 1742 to 1746.
Image from *Los governantes de México*, by Manuel Rivera, Vol. 1 (México, 1872).

Decree

At this villa of Santa Fe, capital of this kingdom of New Mexico, on the 23rd of October, 1743, I, the lieutenant colonel don Gaspar Domingo de Mendoza, governor and captain general of this said kingdom, was to say and did say, that upon the review of this document and the complaint of the alcalde mayor of La Laguna, Juan Miguel Álvarez del Castillo, against Bernardo de Chaves, resident of the jurisdiction of Alburquerque, I ordered the alcalde mayor Diego de Torres to imprison the said Bernardo de Chaves in order to punish him for the assault and additionally to follow up with a fine of twenty pesos of the land, half to be paid to the injured party and the other ten for the proceedings handled by the alcalde mayor and the assistants. I thus approved, ordered, and signed it along with my assisting witnesses due to the lack of a royal or public scribe, which there is none; also it is done on regular paper, being that the sealed type is not available, to which I certify.

    don Gaspar Domingo de Mendoza (rubric)
  Joseph de Terrus (rubric) Juan Felipe de Rivera (rubric)

ORIGINAL DOCUMENT

    Señor Alcalde Mayor y Capitan General

Yo Juan Miguel Albares del Castillo, Alcalde Mayor y Capitan Aguerra de Suni, Pueblo de la Laguna y San Esteban de Acoma paresco ante la grandesa de Vuestra Majestad en la mejor forma que alla lugar y al mio combengo y digo que abiendo yo salido de mi casa el dia diez ocho del presente de Octubre para el Puesto de Nuestra Señora de Belen me encontre con Bernardo de Chabes el cual se puso a parlar con migo y entre barias cosas que parlamos solo procuro introducir platica a su intento de donde su pudiera seguir disturbio como dicho se segia asi desafiandome y disiendo que en buen paraje justicia y abiendo presidido estas rasones se apio y no entendiendo yo fuese con malisia necesario echo mano de mi mismo espadin el qu llebaba yo de bajo de una pierna y abiendo usado esa traysion y biendo no trae yo otra arma alguna alebosamente me dio un sintaraso en las espaldas como costara por la senal que tengo y asi Vuestra Magestad pido y suplico se sirba de castigar a dicha osadia no reconosiendo ninguna lei de las que me favorescan respecto de ser ministro de Justicia que como a tal aunque me estrana jurisdision debiendo respetarme y juro en la debida forma no ser este me escrito de malisia, por lo que pido y suplico ala grandesa de Vuestra Majestad me atienda en justisia y lo reciba en lo necesario, ut supra.
    Juan Miguel Albares del Castillo (rubric)

[Marginal note]
Puesto de Fonclara
8bre [Octubre] 19 de 1743

Ante me el Capitan Diego Torres la presento el contenido y por mi bista la hube por presentada y atendiendo alo justo de su pedimiento debia mandar y mande se pusiera en prision dicho Bernardo de Chaves comprexendido por atrebiendo en la que pide el suplicante, abiendo dado fee por me y el Theniente de Fonclara del golpe que dise resivio el dicho, allo aberle dado con el espadin de ancho ariva dela espaldilla del lado ysquierdo, y por lo bisto recio golpe pues a un abido recevido ensima dela comun ropa que le bestia le llego arollar el pellejo enchinado a la punta, y en lo demas quedo un berdugon del anchor dela dicha espadin; y asiendole cargo de su desberguenza diga daria su satisfacion y descargo en la Villa capital ante el superior govierno en culla sele ago remicion a dicho tribunal. Asi lo provey y firme auctuando por reseptoria con testigos de asistensia.

     Diego Torres (rubric)
     Jues Reseptor

testigo testigo
Ysidro Sanchez (rubric) Joseph Gallegos (rubric)

Auto
En la Villa de Santa Fee capital deste Reyno dela Nueba Mexico en beynte y tres dias del mes de Octubre del año de mill setesientos quarenta y tres, yo el Theniente Coronel Dn. Gaspar Domingo de Mendoza, Governador y Capitan General de dicho Reyno devia desir y digo que en bista de escrito y querella del Alcalde Mayor de la Laguna, Juan Miguel Albares del Castillo contra Bernardo de Chaves vecino de la jurisdiccion de Alburquerque por lo que mande a el Alcalde Mayor Diego de Torres pusiera en prision al dicho Bernardo de Chaves para castigarle su atrebimiento y por la primera bes sele apersibe con la multa de beynte pesos del pais, por mitad a el agrabido y los dies para las deligensias del Alcalde Mayor y el amanuente. Asi lo probey, mande y firme con los ynfrascritos de mi asistensia por la falta de Escribano Real y Publico que no le ay; y en el papel comun por no correr el sellado, de que doy fee =

    Dn. Gaspar Domingo de Mendoza (rubric)
     Joseph de Terrus (rubric)
     Juan Phelipe de Rivera (rubric)

Notes

1. Juan Miguel Álvarez del Castillo was married first to Bárbara Baca, then Gertrudis Montoya, and then Rosalia García. He died in 1765 in El Paso. We know that in 1747 his house in San Clemente was robbed by two Genízaro Indians from the paraje of Belén. (San Clemente is in the present county of Valencia). He was a trader in Chihuahua and El Paso and an alcalde of the Acoma, Laguna, and Zuni jurisdiction. He died suddenly at the house of his son-in-law at Fuenclara in 1765. John Baxter states that when he died, his debtors ranged from Ojo Caliente to Belén, and that most of the debts were for sheep. After his death, his descendants became some of the biggest sheep merchants in New Mexico. Perhaps his occupation as a merchant was related to the attack by Chaves (Baxter, *Las Carneradas*: 46-47; SANM II #480; Scurlock, "Camino Real": 234; Chávez, *Origins*: 158-59).
2. Bernardo Chaves was the son of Nicolás Durán de Chaves, who had a residence in Atrisco and large landholdings in the Isleta area. He would have been the grandson of don Fernando Durán y Chaves, one of the few of his family who returned to New Mexico in 1693 as part of the Reconquest (Chávez, *Origins*: 160-63).

33

FUENCLARA NEIGHBORS TRADE INSULTS IN ACEQUIA DISPUTE
MAY 16–27, 1744. SANM II #453.

Synopsis and editor's notes: The situation described in this document occurred shortly after settlers had arrived in the Fuenclara[1] area. José Salas and Francisca and Gregorio Jaramillo dug an acequia running from the Río Grande, and María Silva tried to use some of the water for her garden. Francisca Salas Jaramillo complained to Alcalde Joseph Baca that María was impeding the flow of water so that her family did not have enough for their garden. In the process of hearing the claim, Lieutenant Alcalde Francisco Sánchez stated that the use of water from an irrigation ditch was not limited to those who dug the ditch, a statement that, seen from our current perspective, is an important principal of Spanish Colonial water use. This position of Sánchez caused José Salas and his son-in-law, Gregorio Jaramillo, to become so angry that voices were raised and obscenities said, leading to the arrest and imprisonment of both by Alcalde Joseph Baca. Though Salas and Jaramillo offered to put up goods as a kind of guarantee, the alcalde would not release them until the case was investigated and heard by Governor Codallos y Rabal. The case ended with the governor supporting the alcalde and fining Salas and the Jaramillos, with the money to go toward the remodeling of the palace in Santa Fe.

Apparently the conflict between the Salas family and María Silva continued into 1745, when Salas again petitioned the governor, this time to have María Silva removed from his land at Fuenclara. He said that his wife had given María permission to build a house on his land, but with the condition that she would move as soon as the Río Grande was lower and she was able to cross it. She did not do this; instead, according to Salas, she planted a garden and used the water he needed for his crops. At the same time, an Albuquerque resident, Gregorio Gutiérrez, also submitted a petition to have María Silva removed from his land in Fuenclara (SANM I #338; #845; Chávez, *Origins*: 228, 303; NMGS, *Aquí*: 65, 257, 421-22, 425).

Year of 1744

Demand by Francisca Salas,[2] wife of Gregorio Jaramillo,[3] resident of the puesto of Fuenclara, against Captain Joseph Baca,[4] alcalde mayor of the said place, for having insulted her verbally. The alcalde presented his argument as seen in these proceedings which are found at the end of this *cuaderno*,[5] etc.

Governor and captain general

Francisca de Salas, wife of Gregorio Jaramillo, resident of this puesto of Fuenclara, placing herself at the feet of your honor, as best as can be done, appears and says: Sir, asking for justice, I say that on the very day that Captain José Baca was given his title [captain], he treated my mother as a crazy person in front of my father for having stood up for a lady by the name of Albenedisa[6] for a number of other reasons, one of them being because the flow of the water to a garden was impeded, which myself, my father, my mother, and my husband, as well as the said Albenedisa, have, and for the grave damage which that caused to us, having cost us our sweat and our work.

The said alcalde mayor is now holding my father and my husband prisoners by his lieutenant Francisco Sánchez,[7] waiting for them to go before your honor to present their case for all of the damage which has been caused to us by the alcalde mayor and for which he has requested that a fine be imposed by your honor. My father and my husband have not been released, even though they have promised to put up their goods, but he will not release them without a notice from your honor. I have gone personally before the said alcalde mayor to see about the release of my father and my husband, as well as about the great damage which was done to us and our planted garden and about the injustice which has been done to me by telling me publicly that I was a crazy whore and for which I can provide witnesses at the time that this case is brought forth, along with other points which I can argue in my favor. I thus request justice from your honor for such disreputable remarks.

My husband has been told all of this, and he has gotten so mad that he has told me that he does not want to see me. Because of this, I request a good investigation by your honor to remedy this, otherwise it can result in a fatal ruin of me personally, as well as my children, being that there are many, some of them being very young. If I am granted permission to present my case, I will verbally inform the grandness [*grandesa*] of your honor of everything, all of which I request as a favor along with any others which I may receive. From your honor I ask and petition that I be granted the right to prove and determine that which is done for justice, and I swear in my right that it is not done in malice, protesting costs, but for what is necessary, etc.

Francisca de Salas (rubric)

Santa Fe, May 16, 1744

You are to inform this alcalde mayor of that which is contained in this request. He is to continue with this.

(rubric of Governor Joachín y Rabal)

At this puesto of Nuestra Señora de la Concepcion de Fuenclara, on the 13th of May, 1744, I, Joseph Baca, alcalde mayor and war captain of the villa of San Felipe de Alburquerque, pueblo of Isleta, the said settlement of Fuenclara, and the other districts, having received a note from Isidro Sánchez,[8] my secretary, which is found at the head of these proceedings in which I am insinuated, that I have in prison, being held by my lieutenant Francisco Sánchez, one Gregorio Jaramillo and a Joseph de Salas,[9] for the reason that they lacked respect by not doing what I had ordered them to do, which is allowing a certain married woman[10] to water her garden (in the same order which my predecessor had given them), and all along being mean and not cooperating in ever allowing her to irrigate.

With that notice I, said alcalde mayor, proceeded to go to the said puesto de Fuenclara, and I found everything as had been stated in the note. I then proceeded to the house, where they were found as prisoners (being that there is no public jail at this puesto), where I asked them about the motives they had for not obeying my orders, nor those of my lieutenant, those being the reasons for being held prisoners. They, Gregorio and Joseph Salas, were asked to respond.

They said that their motives were that the acequia was theirs, and because it was theirs no one else could irrigate from it. *I responded to this by saying that their supposing that the only ones who could irrigate were those who had assisted in taking out the acequia was not a sufficient reason.*[11] I then added that they should appear before me so that I could hear what they had to say and hear their argument. They denied that, saying that they would go before a higher justice, which I denied unless they could justify it, and I left it as part of the sentence. I ordered to appear before me those witnesses which my lieutenant had brought forth so that they could be ordered to irrigate. So that it is valid I signed it with my assisting witnesses due to lack of a public or royal scribe, which there is none in this kingdom, as was done, etc.

Joseph Baca (rubric)

Witnesses
Bernardo Vallejo (rubric)
Ysidro Sánchez (rubric)

Continuing, on the said day, month, and year, I, the said alcalde mayor, in order to argue this cause, made to appear before me Juan Vallejo,[12] whom I certify that I know, and from whom, upon being present, I received his sworn statement which he made to God, Our Lord, and to the sign of a Holy Cross, under which he promised to tell the truth in whatever he knew and was asked.

He was asked if he was present at the time that my lieutenant went to ask what the reasons were for not allowing María Silva[13] to irrigate her garden, and if the lieutenant had ordered it with full rigor and without any bother. He said that, upon the said lieutenant arriving at the house of Salas, he asked, "Señor Salas, did you allow María de Silva to irrigate?" He answered that she had not attempted to do it a second time, saying that under no pretense could she do so. For this reason, the said lieutenant went to call Ramón, the son-in-law of the said Silva, and he told him to go get the water and irrigate, ordering him to do so.

Upon this happening, the said Joseph Salas went to stop the water, and an Indian woman went to block the water and fill in the acequia with dirt. Due to all this, the said Gregorio said that there were going to be blows, but he did not state with whom or by whom. This is all that is stated by this declarant and nothing else because he could not come up with anything else. He said that this was the truth regarding his sworn statement which he has made, and that he did not have anything to add or delete. He affirmed and ratified it, once, twice, and three times, and said that he was not related to anyone, only that Gregorio was his nephew through affinity, that he [Gregorio] was a nephew to his wife, and that he was forty-eight years of age. He did not sign because he did not know how; I, said alcalde mayor, signed it with my assisting witnesses as has been said.

Joseph Baca (rubric)

Witnesses
Bernardo Vallejo (rubric)
Ysidro Sánchez (rubric)

Continuing, I, the said alcalde mayor, on the said day, month, and year, in prosecution of this cause made appear before me Lugardo Vallejo,[14] resident of this jurisdiction, whom I certify that I know and from whom upon being present I took his sworn statement which he made to God, Our Lord, and to the sign of a Cross, under which he promised to tell the truth in what he knew and was asked.

He was asked if he was present when the lieutenant Francisco Sánchez went to order María de Silva to irrigate her garden, and what happened. He said that, upon the lieutenant having arrived at their home [of Salas and Jaramillo], being most courteous, with his hat in his hand, he asked them if they recognized him as their lieutenant. They answered him saying that they did. He then told them that as such they should let María Silva irrigate her garden. The said Joseph Salas and Gregorio then answered him, saying that they would not consent to it. He then asked them the same thing a second and third time, and each time they told him the same thing, that they would not consent to it. The lieutenant then ordered the son-in-law of the said Silva to go and irrigate. At that instant Salas and the said Gregorio left, one to stop the water and the other to fill in the acequia with dirt. An Indian woman also went along to fill in the acequia. He [Vallejo] also said that he heard Gregorio say that there were going to be blows on that day, but he did not know for whom that was meant. That, he said, was the reason for him [Sánchez] to place them in jail. This he says is the truth of what he saw and heard and is the truth as to what he knows and the truth regarding the sworn statement which he has made. His statement having been read back to him, he said that he did not have anything to add or to delete, and he ratified it once, twice, and three times, saying that he was thirty-six years of age and that they are related through affinity and sanguinity, and he signed along with me and my assisting witnesses as it is, etc.

Joseph Baca (rubric)
Lugardo Vallejo (rubric)

Witnesses
Bernardo Vallejo (rubric)
Ysidro Sánchez (rubric)

Continuing on the said day, month, and year, I, the said alcalde mayor, in order to continue with the investigation of the above, made appear before me Francisco Sánchez, my lieutenant. From whom upon being present, I received his sworn statement in which he promised to tell the truth in whatever he was asked and in what he knew.

He was asked under what circumstances and what motive he had for placing Joseph de Salas and Gregorio Jaramillo in jail. He answered that the motives which he had and has were that their alcalde mayor had gone to the home of Salas to plead for them to let María Silva irrigate a garden. Besides that, the said Silva had complained to the said declarant that they, along with their wives, would not let her irrigate her garden. That was the motive for him having gone the night before with all courtesy, requesting that they allow the water to flow through so the poor lady could irrigate. He, however, was not able to convince them, they giving numerous indecent reasons for not allowing her to do so, saying that if the said Silva wanted to irrigate she could bring the water from the mouth of river, and then she could have all the water she wanted, even enough to wet her vagina,[15] and that she could not irrigate even if ordered by the lieutenant, the alcalde, and the governor, telling the declarant to leave from there.

The following morning, the lieutenant went directly to order the said Silva to irrigate, taking with him two witnesses, imposing a fine of twelve pesos upon Salas and Jaramillo to see if they would consent to let her irrigate, but they would not allow it. He then asked them if they recognized him as their lieutenant. They answered once, twice, and three times that they did. He then very politely told them to allow her to irrigate. They answered that they would not, repeating it a number of times. This declarant then, with his authority, ordered the son-in-law of the said Silva to go and irrigate, to go and let the water through, saying that he ordered him to do it. At this order they together stated in one voice that they would not allow it, at which time the said Salas went to stop the water, and the said Gregorio, along with an Indian woman, went to fill in the acequia with dirt, at which time the said Gregorio said that it would be a time for blows, bad-mouthing the king. The lieutenant then took them as prisoners.

This declarant also says that, while being held as prisoner, the said Gregorio left orders to have the entire acequia filled in with dirt. He said that these were the motives which he had for having taken them prisoners. He complained about the disrespect which they had shown for him, even though they considered him as their lieutenant, disregarding other bad things which they had brought up and which would be brought up at the proper time. He said that this was the truth regarding his sworn statement which he has made. His statement having been read back to him, he said that he did not have anything to add or to delete, which he affirmed and ratified once, twice, and three times, saying that he was thirty-six years of age, more or less, and that there was no relationship. He did not sign because he did not know how. I, the said alcalde mayor, signed it, along with my two assisting witnesses due to the lack of a royal or public scribe, which there is none in this kingdom, etc.

Joseph Baca (rubric)
Presiding judge

Witnesses
Bernardo Vallejo (rubric)
Ysidro Sánchez (rubric)

Proceedings

At the villa of Santa Fe on the 20th of May, 1744, I, Sergeant Major don Joachín Codallos y Rabal, governor and captain general of this kingdom, reviewed the aforesaid proceedings which were carried out by Joseph Baca, the alcalde mayor of the villa of Alburquerque and its jurisdiction, in which were set forth the various improper motives and the disobedience which was shown against the said alcalde and his lieutenant, Francisco Sánchez, at the pueblo of Fuenclara, by Gregorio Jaramillo, his wife Francisca Salas, and Joseph Salas, residents of said pueblo, regarding the irrigation of a garden and other circumstances which are shown in these proceedings.

For these reasons, I order that the mentioned alcalde notify through these proceedings Gregorio Jaramillo and his wife, Francisca Salas, that I fine them in the amount of thirty pesos, which they are both to pay immediately. Also, I fine Joseph Salas in the amount of twenty pesos. The total amounts I apply to the remodeling of the palace, which is being done at this time. All of this is done with the understanding that if, in the future they are disobedient to the said alcalde mayor and his lieutenant, or any other minister of justice, with improper words and by being disrespectful, I will proceed against the said with full rigor according to my right. I thus determined this and signed it acting as presiding judge due to the lack of royal or public scribe, which there is none in this kingdom, and with my assisting witnesses. Done, etc.

Joachín Codallos y Rabal (rubric)

Witnesses
don Francisco de Roa y Carrillo (rubric)
Antonio de Aramburu (rubric)

At this puesto of Fuenclara on the 27th of May, 1744, I, the above said alcalde mayor and war captain, Joseph Baca, in order to comply with the above decree approved by Sergeant Major don Joachín Codallos y Rabal, governor and captain general of this kingdom, went and notified the said Joseph de Salas, and Gregorio Jaramillo and his wife, about all which is contained herein, who obeyed and submitted the above fine as imposed. So that it is valid, I submit the results of these proceedings to the superior government. I signed it with my assisting witnesses as above stated in eight sheets of paper, one which is blank, on the said day, etc.

        Joseph Baca
        Presiding judge

Witnesses
Bernardo Vallejo (rubric)
Ysidro Sánchez (witness)

ORIGINAL DOCUMENT

Año de 1744

Demanda de Francisca Salas muger de Gregorio Jaramillo vecina de la poblazon de Fuenclara contra el Capitan Joseph Baca, Alcalde Mayor de dicho partido sobre decir haverla injuriada de palabras a que dio satisfacion dicho Alcalde en cuia vista se probeio el auto que esta al fin de este quaderno, ut supra.

Señor Gobernador y Capitan General

Francisca de Salas hesposa de Gregorio Jaramillo vesina deste Puesto de Fuenclara puesta a los pies de Vuestra Señoria como mejor proseda paresco y digo Señor pidiendo justizia y digo que el propio dia que sele lello su titulo al Capitan Jose Baca trato a mi madre de loca delante de mi padre por defender a una Señora Albenedisa y sobre diferentes consecuensias que se a ofrecido sobre no dejar pasar el agua por una ortalisa que tenemos, mi padre, mi madre, mi espose y llo, ala dicha Albenedisa por el grabe perjuicio que senos sige y abernos costado nuestro sudor y trabajo. Dicho Señor Alcalde Mayor tiene preso a mi padre, a mi esposo por mano de Su Teniente Francisco Sanchez escusandoles el ponerse a los pies de Vuestra Señoria a representar su justisia, esto es sin aber faltado a respecto alguno sin mas motibo que no dejar crusar el agua, por onde tanto daño senos sige hechado el Señor Alcalde Mallor bos de que Vuestra Señoria a enbiado multa sobre este particular no se an escusado mi padre ni mi esposo sobre entregarla en lo mejor de los bienes solo si pediendo testimonio de dicho orden de Vuestra Señoria y pasado llo aber a dicho Alcalde Mallor sobre la prision de mi padre y mi esposo y el grabe perjuicio que senos sige pues a medio sembra se nos an quedado indignazion que me quitara delante de en bista que era una loca publica raniera delante de testigos que ofresco para quando llege el caso sobre este particular y lo demas que alegar puedo ami fabor, a Vuestra Señoria pido justizia sobre rasones tan infamatorias pues a llegado a notisias de mi esposo quien colerico se puso a de Señor no me pusiera a su bista ocura a la gran justificasion de Vuestra Señoria en que lo remedie pues de aquien se puede originar una fatal ruina en mi persona y mis hijos que son muchos y menorsitos y porque a boca le dire al grandesa de Vuestra Señoria dandome lisensia representare mi justisia por todo lo cual y demas que a mi fabor ago otro pedimento que me conbenga. A Vuestra Señoria pido y suplico de prober y determinar que es de justisia y juro en forma de derecho no ser de malisia, protesto costas y en lo nesesario, ut supra.

    Francisca de Salas (rubric)

    Santa Fee y Mayo 16 de 1744

Ynforme este Alcalde Mayor sobre el contenido de este pedimento = lo que hara a su continuacion.
    [Rubric of Governor Joachín y Rabal]

En este Puesto de Nuestra Señora de la Concepcion de Fonclara en treze dias de Mayo de mill setecientos y quarenta y quatro, yo Joseph Baca, Alcalde Mayor y Capitan Aguerra de la Villa de San Phelipe de Alburquerque, Pueblo de la Ysleta, dicha poblazon de Fonclara y demas distritos abiendo resevido un papel de Ysidro Sanchez mi Secretario el qual ba por cabesa de estos autos en el que me ynsinua tener en prision mi Theniente Francisco Sanchez a Gregorio Jaramillo y a Joseph de Salas por aberle faltado al respecto devido de no obedeser lo que les abia mandado en orden a que regara una muger casada una huerta (y abiendo por mi antesedido el mismo mandato) y amas de muchas veses malas y descompuestas nunca dejaron regar, con esta notizia pase yo dicho Alcalde Mayor a dicho Puesto de Fonclara, y allo ser como lo dise el papel, y abiendo pasado a la casa en donde estan presos (por no aber en este Puesto carcel publica) les yse cargo de los motivos que abian tenido para no obedeser asi mis ordenes, como las de mi Teniente motivos con dignos para que estubiesen en pricion. Respondieron los dichos Gregorio y Joseph Salas. Respondieron que los motivos que tenian ser sulla la sequia y que como suia no abian de regar la dicha ni ninguno. A lo qual les respondi no ser bastante lo supuesto que los otros o los que abian de regar abian alludado a sacar la sequia y asiendoles ystancia para que representaran ante mi para darles oydo y ver en rason su justisia se negaron disiendo querian pasar a mayor tribunal lo que no admito ni a lugar asta justificarlo y ponerlo en estado de sentencia asi lo puse por diligensia y mande compareser ante mi a los testigos que llebo con sigo mi Theniente para yr a mandar consentiesen regar y para que conste lo firme con testigos de asistensia por falta de Escribano Real y publico que no lo ay en este Reyno, fecho, ut supra =

Joseph Baca (rubric)

testigo testigo
Bernardo Vallejo (rubric) Ysidro Sanchez (rubric)

Luego yncontinenti en dicho dia, mes y año yo dicho Alcalde Mayor para la aberiguacion de esta causa yse compareser ante mi a Juan Vallejo a quien doy fee conosco a quien estando presente le resevi juramento que yso por Dios Nuestro Señor y la Señal de una Santa Cruz debajo de cuyo cargo prometio de Señor verdad en quanto supiere y fuere preguntado y siendolo dise se allo presente quando fue mi Teniente a preguntar los motivos que tenia para no dexar regar a María Silva su huerta y si el Theniente abia lo mandado con rigor y sin ninguna molestia? Dijo que abiendo llegado dicho Teniente a casa de dicho Salas, Señor Salas dixa Usted regar su huerta a Marid Silva? Respondio que no le bolvio asar ystancia segunda ves. Respondio dicho Salas que no que por ningun pretesto. A esta rason se fue el dicho Teniente y llamo a Ramon yerno de dicho Silva y le dixo be y echa la agua y riega que yo telo mando, y a esta rason fue Joseph Salas a tapar el agua y una Yndia a telaplenar el agua y la sequia y que a esta rason abia dicho Gregorio a ora a de aber aqui muchos palos, pero que no sabe a quien selos abia de dar y esto responde este declarante y no otra cosa porque no apersivio mas y que esta es la verdad so cargo del juramento que fecho tiene y le da su declaracion no tubo que anadir ni quitar en que se afirmo y ratifico por una, dos y tres vezes y que no les toca en las generales que solo Gregorio es su sobrino por afinidad, que es sobrino de su muger y que es de edad de quarenta y ocho años, y no firmo porque dixo no saber firmar, firmelo yo dicho Alcalde Mayor con testigos de asistensia como dicho es.

Joseph Baca (rubric)
Jues Receptor

testigo testigo
Bernardo Vallejo (rubric) Ysidro Sanchez (rubric)

Yncontinenti yo el sobre dicho Alcalde Mayor en dicho dia mes y año en prosecusion de esta causa yse comparecer ante mi a Lugardo Vallejo vezino de esta jurisdicion a quien doi fee conosco y estando presente le resevi juramento que yso por Dios Nuestro Señor y la Señal de una Cruz de bajo de cullo cargo prometio de Señor verdad en quanto supiere y fuere preguntado y siendolo disese abia allado presente quando el Teniente Francisco Sanchez fue a mandar regar la huerta de Maria Silva y que presidio en este particular? Dixo que abiendo llegado dicho Teniente a casa de Salas y dichole muchas cortecias con el sombrero en la mano Señores ustedes me reconosen por su Teniente. Respondieron que si, pues con ese es supuesto dejar regar la huerta a Maria Silva. Le respondieron dicho Joseph Salas y Gregorio, no Señor no lo consentimos, y lo yso por segunda y tercera ves les respondieron lo mismo y que en ese entonses dicho Teniente mando al yerno de dicho Silva anda y riega que yo telo mando alo qual en ese entonses fue Salas y dicho Gregorio uno a telaplenar la sequia y otro a tapar el agua y tanbien una yndia fue a telaplenar dicha sequia y que tambien oyo como abia dicho dicho Gregorio oy a de aber aqui muchos palos, pero que no sabe para quien y que por eso los puso en pricion dicho Teniente y que esta es la verdad delo que sabe y bido y que esta es la verdad de lo que save y que esta es la berdad so cargo del juramento que fecho tiene y leida su declaracion no tubo que anadir ni quitar en que se afirmo y ratifico por una, dos y tres vezes y es de edad de treynta y seis años y que les toca en las generales por afinidad y sanguinida y lo firmo con migo y los testigos de mi asistenzia como dicho es, ut supra.

       Joseph Baca (rubric)
       Jues Receptor

Lugardo Vallejo (rubric)
testigo testigo
Bernardo Vallejo (rubric)
Ysidro Sanchez (rubric)

Yncontinenti en dicho dia mes y año yo dicho Alcalde Mayor para la aberiguacion de esta cavesa yse compareser ante mi a Francisco Sanchez mi Theniente a quien estando presente le resevi juramento en forma de derecho que yso por Dios Nuestro Señor y la Señal de una Santa Cruz debajo de cullo cargo prometio de Señor veredad en quanto supiere y fuere preguntado y siendolo de que motivo y Señor cumstancias abia tenido para poner en pricion a Joseph de Salas y a Gregorio Xaramillo? Dixo que los motivos que tuvo y a tenido son aberle mandado su Alcalde Mayor les amonestara ala casa de Salas dejase regar a Maria Silva una huerta y amas de eso abia querellado la dicha Silva a dicho declarante como no la consentian regar asi los dichos como sus mugeres y que por ese motivo abia ydo aquella noche antes con cortes comedimiento disiendoles a todos juntos dejaran pasar el agua para que regase aquella pobre lo que no consiguio antes si muy muchas malas rasones yndecorosas como fueron no querer por ningun protesto dejar que regara, y que se queria que regara la dicha Silva su huerta que fuera y la traxera el agua en la boca del rio y que se la echara asta mojarle el culo, y que no abian de regar aunque lo mandara el Teniente, el Alcalde y el Governador con este supuesto dise este declarante que se quite de alli, y fue otro dia por la manana rectamente a mandar que regara la dicha Silva llebando con sigo dos testigos y que abiendoles ynpuesto multa de dose pesos por ber si por eso consentian regar, no quisieron y que entonses les abia dicho Ustedes me reconosen por su Theniente? Respondieron que si por una y dos vezes y por otras tres con cortecia les dijo pues dejen Ustedes regar a esa muger. Respondieron que no, que no muy repetidamente entonses dise este declarante que de su poder mando al yerno de dicha Silva anda riega y echa la agua que yo telo mando a cullo mandato respondieron todos a una voz que no lo consentian antes se fue Salas a tapar la sequia, y dicho Gregorio a telaplenarla junto con una yndia y que llendo para esto abia dicho dicho Gregorio aya de aber aqui muchos palos y que entonses apellido al Rey, y los prendio, y dise mas este declarante que estando lla presos despacho dicho Gregorio a mandar teraplenar toda la sequia; con que esos fueron los motivos que tubo y a tenido para prenderlos, y que se querella dela desatencion que le tubieron a un reconosiendolo por su Teniente y que no se ase a cargo de otras muchas malas rasones que se an dejado de ser que si se ofresese querellara asu tiempo y que esta es la verdad so cargo del juramento que fecho tiene y leyda su declarasion no tubo que anadir ni quitar en que se afirmo y ratifico por una, dos y tres veses, declara ser de treynta y siete años poco mas o menos y que no les toca en las generales de la ley y no firmo porque dixo no saber firmelo yo dicho Alcalde Mayor, de que doi fee con dos testigos de mi asistensia por falta de Escribano Real y Publico que no lo ay en este Reyno fecho, ut supra.

Joseph Baca (rubric)
Jues Receptor

Testigo testigo
Bernardo Vallejo (rubric) Ysidro Sanchez (rubric)

Auto
En la Villa de Santa Fee a 20 de Mayo de 1744 años yo el Sargento Mayor Don Joachin Codallos y Rabal, Gobernador y Capitan General de este Reyno, en vista delos autos antecedentes seguidos por el Alcalde Mayor de la Villa de Alburquerque y Su Jurisdiccion, que lo es Joseph Baca, en los que resulta haberse propasado con rasones impropias, y desobedecimiento contra dicho Alcalde y su Teniente Francisco Sanchez en el Pueblo de Fuenclara, Gregorio Xaramillo, su muger Francisca Salas y Joseph Salas, vecinos de dicho Pueblo, sobre regar una huerta y demas circumstancias que en dichos autos se expesan. Por lo que mando a el mencionado Alcalde notifique este auto a Gregorio Xaramillo, y su muger Francisca Salas, a quienes multo en treinta pesos que ambos pagaran irremisiblemente: y a Joseph Salas en veinte pesos: cuyas cantidades aplico a la obra de el reedifisio de este Palacio, que actualmente se esta haciendo: con apercibimiento que si en adelante fuesen desobedientes a dicho Alcalde Mayor y su Theniente, o qualesquiera ministros de justisia con palabras impropias y desvergonzados, procedere contra los dichos con todo rigor de derecho. Assi lo determine y firme actuando por Receptoria a falta de Escribano Real y Publico, que no lo hai en este Reyno, y con los testigos de mi asistencia. Fecho, ut supra.

Joachin Codallos y Rabal (rubric)

Testigo
Don Francisco de Roa y Carrillo (rubric)
Testigo
Antonio de Aramburu (rubric)

En este Puesto de Fonclara en veynte y siete de Mayo de mil setesientos y quarenta y quatro años yo el sobre dicho Alcalde Mayor y Capitan Aguerra Joseph Baca para el cumplimiento del auto arriva proveydo por el Sargento Mayor Don Joachin Codallos y Rabal, Governador y Capitan General de este Reyno pase y notifique lo que en el se contiene a Joseph de Salas, a Gregorio Xaramillo y su esposa quien obedesieron y exivieron la multa ariva expresada, y para que conste hago denuncion de estos auctos al superior govierno y firme con testigos de assistenzia como dicho es en ocho fojas una en blanca y dicho dia, ut supra.

Joseph Baca (rubric)
Presiding judge

Testigo testigo
Bernardo Vallejo (rubric) Ysidro Sanchez Vanares (rubric)

Notes

1. See Doc. 32.
2. Francisca Salas was the daughter of José Salas and Bernardina Hurtado, daughter of a first founder of Albuquerque, Martín Hurtado. Francisca married Gregorio Varela Jaramillo in 1721, son of Cristóbal Varela Jaramillo, another Albuquerque first founder (NMGS, *Aquí*: 17, 403-5; Chávez, *Origins*: 197; SANM II #476).
3. Gregorio Jaramillo was the son of Cristóbal Jaramillo and his second wife, Francisca Salas y Hurtado. He was a stepbrother of Gerónimo Jaramillo (Chávez, *Origins*: 199; see Docs. 5 and 25).
4. See Doc. 30.
5. *Cuaderno* in this case probably means a book of memorandum.
6. To date, no further information has been found about this woman.
7. Francisco Sánchez was the son of Jacinto Sánchez de Iñigo, a native New Mexican who returned by 1696. Francisco married Josefa de Chávez, daughter of Pedro Durán y Chávez. In 1737 a Francisco Sánchez signed a petition to Governor Olavide y Micheleña asking for a repeal of trade restrictions. His name is listed as an original petitioner for the Tomé land grant by 1739. He was a lieutenant of the militia under Governor Thomas Vélez Cachupín in 1763-1764 (Docs. 50 and 30; Chávez, *Origins*: 280-81; NMGS, *Aquí*: 187-91; Alexander, *Cottonwood*: 328).
8. This appears to be the same Isidro Sánchez who was in such trouble for robbing the casas reales in 1720 and for disrespect to an officer in 1731. In 1744 he was accused by the alcalde, Joseph Baca, of "inciting poor citizens to file lawsuits," but apparently he was quickly forgiven since he was shown as a witness for Alcalde Baca in later documents (SANM II #307; Docs. 22 and 35; Ebright, "Advocates": 318).
9. José de Salas is listed as a first founder of Albuquerque. He married Bernardina Hurtado, daughter of another first founder, Martín Hurtado, and had a daughter, Francisca, born around 1710. By 1713 Salas was with the Santa Fe presidio in the Albuquerque garrison, also appearing on the 1715 and 1717 Santa Fe presidio muster. In 1721 he was a witness at Bernalillo for a marriage investigation for José Gallegos and María Silva. By the 1739-1750 period, he had married Bárbara Aragón and was one of the first petitioners for the Tomé land grant. In 1747 José de Salas was accused of wounding a Tadeo Romero, both residents of Fuenclara. He died in 1781 at Tomé (NMGS, *Aquí*: 17, 403-5; Chávez, *Origins*: 197; SANM II #476; Alexander, *Cottonwoods*: 328).
10. That is, María Silva, as named below. She was apparently taking water from a ditch that the Salas family had dug from the river, leaving the Salas family with less water than they needed.
11. This sentence could be considered a summary of the policy of the Spanish toward water rights in New Mexico.
12. Juan Vallejo was married to Angelina Varela Jaramillo, an aunt of Gregorio Varela Jaramillo. It is likely that he was a brother or at least related to Lugardo Vallejo, named below (Chávez, *Origins*: 303).
13. María Silva was a daughter of Antonio de Silva, a blacksmith from Zacatecas. He lived in Santa Cruz in 1695 but then moved his family to the Río Abajo, where he purchased land, served in the military, and acted as a notary. María was married to José Gallegos in 1721. A María Silva married Juan Velasco Armijo in 1732, but it is not known whether this is the same person. María's sister, Micaela Silva, was married to Antonio Vallejo, brother of Lugardo Vallejo and probably of Juan (SANM I #338; #845; Chávez, *Origins*: 228, 303; NMGS, *Aquí*: 65, 257, 421-22, 425).
14. See Doc. 30.
15. Obscenity. See the Spanish transcription.

34

PARENTS APPLY FOR PRIESTHOOD FOR SON
AND ARE INVESTIGATED FOR PURITY OF BLOOD
March 7–June 7, 1745. Source: SANM II #464.

Synopsis and editor's notes: When don Joseph Romo de Vera and doña Ángela Valdez made a request for testimonials to be used in an application for priesthood for their seven-month-old son, Joseph Manuel, testimony was provided by four men swearing as to the *limpiesa*, or purity of blood, of Romo de Vera and his wife. All of these men had come to New Mexico as part of the Reconquest. Note that the testimonials were not to be presented to the Franciscan representative of the Holy Tribunal of the Inquisition, as one might expect, but to a secular authority, don Antonio de Ulibarrí, the alcalde mayor of Santa Fe. In this case, he was serving in a lay position as the head of the Ecclesiastical Tribune and stated that he would pass the information along to another secular authority, the governor, don Joachín Codallos y Rabal. Perhaps the Franciscan representative from El Paso was not available, or maybe this was the regular procedure. The repetition of the language of the testimonials suggests that the three men gave their information on the same day, each repeating what the other said.

In regard to the requirement of purity of blood, Helen Rawlings states that the term comes from statutes enacted in fifteenth- and sixteenth-century Spain. The intent was to restrict access to the church to those able to prove purity of blood, that is, proof of non-Jewish, non-Muslim, or non-Lutheran ancestry over four generations. As well as applying to priests, it also applied to public offices, notary publics, and other officials (Rawlings, *Spanish Inquisition*: 50-53, 158).

Year of 1745

Investigation of don Joseph Romo de Vera[1] and doña Ángela Valdez in the manner which follows.

I, don Joseph Romo de Vera, resident of this villa within my proper right and without confusing or without causing problems for anyone with whom I use or to their competent reputation or to any tribunal that might be opposed to me, appear before your majesty and say that having contracted marriage, according to Our Holy Mother Church, with doña Ángela Francisca

Valdez,[2] legitimate daughter of Domingo Valdez[3] and doña Ana María Márquez,[4] residents and natives of this said villa, we have procreated and brought forth into this world our legitimate son, Joseph Manuel,[5] who today is seven months old. And being that his mother and I have made the decision to deliver him into the state of becoming a priest, until he attains priesthood, state that our son does not have any defects that could impede him from the said sacred orders.

We ask of your majesty that he be pleased to order that the necessary testimonies be obtained and state that my said wife is the legitimate daughter of Domingo Valdez and doña Ana María Marques, and that their parents were don Joseph Valdez,[6] deceased, native of the kingdom of Castile in the mountains of Oviedo;[7] and of doña María de Cabrera, native of the city of Puebla; and of Mateo Marques[8] and Agustina Romero.[9] All of the above stated that they have always been and are old Spanish Christians, descendants of the same, free of any bad race such as Moors, Jews, nor coming from those newly converted into the light of Our Holy Mother Church, nor have ever been castigated or punished by the Holy Tribunal of the Inquisition nor by any other ecclesiastic or secular, and that they are not, nor have been, blacks, mulattos, nor of any other inferior race, but as such have always been and continue to be and have always been reputed to be, without being to the contrary. The said information continues in the same tenor as is written and as decreed in this document and in one or more written testimonies authorized publicly, and the originals are to be placed into the archives of this government, which is done in justice, and [I] swear to God and to the Cross that it is not done in malice, but for what is necessary, etc.

Joseph de Vera (rubric)

Order

In the villa of Santa Fe, in the kingdom of New Mexico, the capitol of said, on the 7th day of March, 1745, before me, don Antonio de Ulibarrí, alcalde mayor and war captain of this said villa and its jurisdiction, the said petition was presented by the person contained within it. Being seen by me as presented, I ordered that the information which he has presented be admitted, along with the information which he has to present, and the testimony of the witnesses who are to be publically examined, swearing to tell the truth, and the originals are then to be placed into the archives of the government of this kingdom, for which reason they are to be turned over to the sargento mayor, don Joachín Codallos y Rabal, governor and captain general of this said kingdom. I thus approved, ordered, and signed it, acting as presiding judge along with my assisting witnesses, due to the lack of public or royal scribe, which there is none in this kingdom, to which I certify.

Antonio de Ulibarrí (rubric)

Witnesses
Antonio Felix Sánchez (rubric)
Gregorio Garduño (rubric)

Declaration of Antonio Durán de Armijo

In the villa of Santa Fe, capitol of this kingdom of New Mexico, on the 24th of May, 1745, before me Captain don Antonio de Ulibarrí, alcalde mayor and war captain of this said villa and its jurisdiction, appeared don Joseph Romo de Vera, as forementioned in the preceding document. So that the information which he has offered and can be taken regarding the pureness of his legitimate wife, doña Ángela Francisca de Valdez, he presented as his witness Antonio Durán de Armijo, resident of this said villa at the public oratory of this ecclesiastical tribune of this said kingdom, where I, the said alcalde mayor, received his testimony, which he gave according to God, Our Lord, and to the sign of the Holy Cross, and in its proper form was questioned in the tenor of the aforesaid document. He stated that he has known the said doña Ángela Valdez since she was born, seeing her raise a family, and knows that she is married and veiled [*velada*][10] according to the order of Our Holy Mother Church to don Joseph Romo, being that they lived in the immediate vicinity, and the witness was the person, as a notary public, who provided the proofs for her marriage. He also knows that they have a son, named Joseph, who is in the state of infancy, and whom he has seen numerous times and knows that he is healthy and sane. He knows that she [Ángela Valdez] is the legitimate daughter of Domingo Valdez and of doña Ana María Marques, residents of this said villa; and that he [Domingo] was the legitimate son of Joseph Valdez and doña María Cabrera, both deceased. He knows from having heard it from them, that the said don Joseph Valdez was originally from the kingdom of Castile, in the mountains of Hubiedo [Oviedo], and the said doña María Cabrera was from the city of Puebla de los Ángeles. Ana María was the daughter of Mateo Marques and Agustina Romero, deceased, whom he knew personally from dealing with them and from speaking to them, and he also knows that they were and have always been old Spanish Christians, descendants of them who were pure of all bad [*mala*] races of Moors, Jews, or from those newly converted to the light of Our Holy Mother Church, and that they have not been ecclesiastics or seculars and that they were not black, mulattos, or of any other bad race, but in whose opinion they have always been, have held and have commonly been reputed to be such [Christians]. He states that everything he has said concerning his testimony is the truth, and he affirmed and ratified it, adding that everything is public and publically known. He declared that he was seventy-four years of age and he signed it with me and my assisting witnesses with whom I act due to the lack of a scribe which there is none in this kingdom, to which I certify.

       Antonio de Ulibarrí (rubric)
       Antonio Durán de Armijo (rubric)

Witness
Gregorio Garduño (rubric)
Antonio Felix Sánchez (rubric)

Declaration of Juan Manuel Chirinos[11]
Español[12]

In the villa of Santa Fe, on the 25th of May, 1745, before me, Captain don Antonio de Ulibarrí, alcalde mayor and war captain of this said villa, don Joseph Romo de Vera presented as his witness Juan Manuel Chirinos, Spanish and a resident of this said villa of Santa Fe, whom I certify that I know, and being in my presence I received his testimony which he gave before God, Our Lord, and the sign of the Holy Cross, under which he promised to state the truth in whatever he was asked, in the same tenor as was done previously as follows.

He was asked if he knew don Joseph Luis de Valdez and doña María Cabrera. He said he that he knew them since the year of 1695, and that he knew them from casual contact and that they entered together as settlers, coming from the city of México to the kingdom of New Mexico. He knows that he was a native of the kingdom of Castile, from the mountains of Oviedo, and that doña María Cabrera was originally from the city of Puebla de los Ángeles, and that from this marriage was born Domingo Valdez, the father of doña Ángela Francisca Valdez, and that they were old Spanish Christians, descendants of the same. He says that he knew and knows Mateo Marques and Agustina Romero, who were married and veiled as is ordered by the Holy Mother Church, and that from this legitimate marriage was born doña Ana María Marques, the legitimate wife of the said Domingo Valdez, whose daughter is the said doña Ángela Valdez, natives of this said kingdom, old Spanish Christians, which they have been and still are. He knows that they have not been castigated or sentenced by the Holy Tribunal of the Inquisition, nor by any ecclesiastic or secular and that they are not black, mulatto, or of any other inferior race and that they are pure of any bad race, and have been and are commonly reputed of not having anything to the contrary. This, he says, is the truth as to his testimony which he has made, and he held firm to it, ratified it once, twice, and three times, and he states that he is sixty-four years of age. He signed it with me and my assisting witnesses, acting as presiding judge, because of the known lack of a public or royal scribe, which there is none in this kingdom, to which I certify.

Antonio de Ulibarrí (rubric)
Presiding judge
Juan Manuel Chirinos (rubric)

Witness
Gregorio Garduño (rubric)
Antonio Felix Sánchez (rubric)

In addition, this individual declares that he knows Joseph Manuel, the legitimate son of don Joseph Romo and Ángela Francisca de Valdez, and that he is six or seven months old, and he knows that he is healthy and sane, and so that it is valid he signed it.

Juan Manuel Chirinos (rubric)
Antonio de Ulibarrí (rubric)

Declaration of Miguel de Sandoval Martínez[13]
Español

In the villa of Santa Fe on the 4th day of January, 1745, before me Captain don Antonio de Ulibarrí, alcalde mayor and war captain of this said villa and its jurisdiction in order to obtain the information which has been offered by don Joseph Romo de Vera, resident of this said villa, he brought forth as his witness Captain Miguel de Sandoval Martínez, Spanish and one of the conquistadors of this kingdom, whom upon being present I took his sworn statement which he made before God, Our Lord, and the sign of the Holy Cross, under which he swore to tell the truth as to what he knew and what he was asked.

He was asked if he knew don Joseph Luis de Valdez and doña María Cabrera. He said that he [Valdez] was Spanish, from the other side of the kingdom of Castile, from the mountains of Oviedo, and that his wife, doña María Cabrera, was Spanish, born at Puebla de Los Ángeles; and that from these was born Domingo Valdez, who is married and veiled with Ana María Marques, the legitimate daughter of Mateo Marques and Agustina Romero, natives of this kingdom; and from these was born doña Ángela Francisca de Valdez, who contracted marriage with don Joseph Romo de Vera, both Spanish, well opinioned of not having or ever had any blemish or have ever been sentenced by the Holy Tribunal of the Inquisition. He knows that they were old Christians, descendants of the same, pure of any bad race of Moors, Jews, or from those newly converted into the light of Our Holy Mother Church, and that they are not blacks, mulattos, or from any other bad race, but of the good opinion that they have been and have held and commonly been reputed as being such. From don Joseph Romo de Vera and doña Ángela Francisca de Valdez, his legitimate wife, was born Joseph Manuel de Romo, who at the present time is alive, in good health, and sane, and is six or seven months old, and he knows him because they are all residents of this capital of the villa of Santa Fe. This is what he knows and what he has seen in favor of his sworn statement which he has made and which he affirmed and ratified, saying that he was seventy years of age. This he declared before the said alcalde mayor, don Antonio de Ulibarrí, who stated that he knew him, and he signed it along with my assisting witnesses, acting as presiding judge, due to the known lack of a royal or public scribe, which there is none in this kingdom, on the this said day, month, and year, to which I certify, etc.

Antonio de Ulibarrí (rubric)
Presiding judge

Miguel Sandoval Martínez (rubric)
Gregorio Garduño (rubric)
Antonio Felix Sánchez (rubric)

Declaration of Sebastián de Vargas[14]
Español

In the said Villa of Santa Fe on the 7th of June, 1745, I, the said alcalde mayor of the said villa and its jurisdiction, in order to obtain the information which is offered by Joseph Romo de Vera, made appear before me Captain Sebastián de Vargas, Spanish and resident of this said villa, whom upon being present, I received his sworn statement which he made for God, Our Lord, and the sign of the Holy Cross, under which he promised to tell the truth as to what he knew and what he was asked. He was asked if he knew don Joseph Luis de Valdez and doña María Cabrera. He said that he did know him, and that he knows that he was a native of the kingdom of Castile, from the mountains of Obiedo, and doña María Cabrera was a native of the city of Los Ángeles, and he knows that they were married and veiled according to the order of Our Holy Mother Church, from which marriage they procreated and had Domingo Valdez. He says that he also knew María Marques and Agustina Romero, who were also married and veiled as I have stated. [Something was left out of the Spanish document here.] From this marriage [omission] was born doña Ana María Marques, the legitimate wife of Domingo Valdez, from whom was born doña Ángela Francisca de Valdez, the legitimate daughter of the said Domingo Valdez and of doña Ana María Marques. He also knows from seeing them that don Joseph Romo de Vera was married to doña Ángela Francisca de Valdez, from which marriage was born Joseph Manuel de Romo, whom he knows is about six or seven months old, and he also knows that he is healthy and sane.

He says that he knew all of the above mentioned and knows that they were all old Spanish Christians, descended from such, free from all the bad race of Moors, Jews, and not coming from the newly converted to the light of Our Holy Mother Church, and he knows that they have not been castigated or sentenced by the Holy Tribunal of the Inquisition or by any other ecclesiastical or secular and that they are not blacks or mulattos, but it is the good opinion that they have held and hold and are commonly reputed to be such. He says that this is the truth regarding the sworn statement which he has made and he affirmed and ratified it, and [says] that everything is public and well known by voice and fame. He declared that he was seventy years of age, and signed it with me and my assisting witnesses, acting as presiding judge because of the well-known fact that there is no royal or public scribe in this kingdom, and on this paper because there is none with any seal in these parts, to which I certify.

      Antonio de Ulibarrí (rubric)
      Presiding judge
      Sebastián de Vargas (rubric)

Witness
Gregorio Garduño (rubric)
Antonio Felix Sánchez (rubric)

ORIGINAL DOCUMENT

Año de 1745

Informacion de Dn. Joseph Romo de Vera y de doña Angela Baldes en la forma que adentro se expresa.

Dn. Joseph Romo de Vera vecino de esta Villa como mejor procesa de derecho y sin confusir ni bulnerar los que me sean competentes que protesto y le soi para usar de ellos quando y en el tribunal que me combenga paresco ante Vuestra Magestad y digo que aviendo contraido matrimonio segun orden de Nuestra Santa Madre Yglesia con doña Angela Francisca Baldes, hija lexitima de Domingo Valdes y de doña Ana Maria Marques vecinos y originarios desta dicha Villa, emos havido y procreado por nuestro hijo lexitimo a Joseph Manuel que oy es de hedad de siete meses, y por que su madre y yo tenemos deliveraso inclinarlo a el estado Ecclesiastico hasta el sacro orden de Presbyterio, para que en todo tiempo conste no tener, como no tiene, dicho nuestro hijo ningun defecto que le pueda impedir dichos sagrados ordenes.

A Vuestra Majestad suplico se sirva de mandar se resiva informacion de como dicha mi muger es hija lexitima de los dichos Domingo de Valdes y donñ Ana Maria Marques, y que los suso dichos lo fueron de don Joseph Valdes, difunto, natural de los Reynos de Castilla en las montanas de Obiedo, y de doña Maria de Cabrera, originaria de la Ciudad de la Puebla; y de Mateo Marques y Agustina Romero; y todos los referidos han sido y son Españoles Christianos viejos desendientes de tales, limpios de toda mala rasa de Moros, Judios ni de los nuevamente conbertidos al gremio de Nuestra Santa Madre Yglesia, ni han sido castigados ni penitenciados por el Santo Tribunal dela Inquisicion ni otro eclesiastico ni cecular, y que no son ni fueron Negros, mulattos, ni de otra naturalesa inferior y que por tales han sido havidos y tenidos y comunmente reputados sin haver cosa en contrario y quedada dicha informacion al thenor de tal escripto se saquen de ella y de los decretos de el, uno o mas testimonios ala letra autorisados en publica forma que hagan fee poniendo los originales en el archivo desta Gobernacion, que es de Justicia y juro a Dios y a la Cruz la no malicia y en lo necesario, ut supra.

Joseph de Vera (rubric)

Auto

En la Villa de Santa Fee de el Reino de la Nueva Mexico, capital de el, en siete dias del mes de Marso de mil setecientos y quarenta y sinco años ante mi don Antonio

de Ulibarri, Alcalde Maior y Capitan Aguerra de esta dicha Villa y su jurisdiccion se presenta esta peticion por el contenido en ella. Que por mi bista la vi e por presentada y mande se resiba a esta parte la ynformasion que ofrese y los testigos que presentare se examinen a el tenor de este escripto y dada dicha ynformasion se saque de ella los testimonios que pidiere autorisados en publica forma y manera que agan fee, y los originales se pongan en el Archibo de el Superior Gobierno de este Reino y para ello se presenten ante el Señor Sargento Maior don Joaquin Codallos y Rabal, Gobernador y Capitan General de este dicho Reyno y asi lo probei, mande y firme autuando ante mi como Juez receptor con los testigos de mi asistencia a falta de Escribano Publico y Real que no los ai en este Reyno de ello doi fee.
    Antonio de Ulibarri (rubric)
Testigo
Antonio Felix Sanchez (rubric)
Gregorio Garduño (rubric)

Declarasion de Antonio Duran de Armijo
En la Villa de Santa Fee, capital de este Reino de la Nueva Mexico en beinte y quatro dias del mes de Maio de mill setecientos quarenta y sinco años ante mi el Capitan don Antonio de Ulibarri, Alcalde Maior y Capitan Aguerra de esta dicha Villa y su jurisdision comparesio don Joseph Romo de Vera contenido en el escripto antesedente y para la ynformasion que tiene ofresida y le esta mandada resebir de legitimidad y limpiesa de doña Angela Francisca de Baldes su muger lexitima presento por testigo a Antonio Duran de Armijo vecino tambien de la sitada Villa y orotario publico de el jusgado eclesiastico de este dicho Reino de quien yo dicho Alcalde Maior resevi juramento que yso por Dios Nuestro Señor y la señal de la Santa Crus en forma de derecho y siendo preguntado a el tenor del enunciado escripto. Dijo que conose ala dicha doña Angela Baldes desde que nasio por aberla visto criar casa en frente de el testigo y sabe que es casada y velada segun orden de Nuestra Santa Madre Yglesia con el dicho don Joseph Romo por la ynmediasion de vesindad y haber corido el testigo como notorio publico con las pruebas para su casamiento y save que tienen un hijo nombrado Joseph quien esta en mantillas y lo ha visto muchas veses y actualmente visto bueno y sano y save que la suso dicha es hija lexitima de Domingo Baldes y de doña Ana Maria Marques vesinos de esta Villa y los suso dichos fueron hijos lexitimos de don Joseph de Baldes y de doña Maria Cabrera, difuntos, y sabe de oidos a los referidos que el dicho don Joseph Baldes fue originario de los Reinos de Castilla en las montanas de Hubiedo y la dicha doña Maria Cabrera de la ciudad de la Puebla de los Angeles; y [Ana Maria Marques] de Mateo Marques y Agustina Romero, difuntos, y los conocio y conose el testigo de vista, trato y comunicacion por lo que sabe son y fueron Españoles Christianos viejos desendientes de tales limpios de toda mala rasa de Moros Judios ni de los nuevamente conbertidos a el gremio de Nuestra Santa Madre Yglesia y que no an sido eclesiastico ni seqular y que no son ni fueron Negros, mulatos ni de otra mala rasa en quia buena opinion an sido abidos y tenidos y comunmente reputados y que lo que lleba dicho es

la verdad so cargo de su juramento que fecho tiene en que se afirmo y ratifico y que todo es publico y notorio publica bos y fama declaro ser de edad setenta y quatro años y lo firmo con migo y testigos de mi asistencia con quienes autuo a falta de escribano que no lo ai en este Reyno de todo doi fee.

Antonio de Ulibarri (rubric)

Testigo
Antonio Duran de Armijo
Gregorio Garduño (rubric)
Antonio Felix Sanchez (rubric)

Declarasion de Juan Manuel Chirinos Español
En la Villa de Santa Fee en beinte y sinco dias del mes de Maio de mill cetesientos quarenta y sinco años, ante mi el Capitan don Antonio de Ulibarri Alcalde Mayor y Capitan Aguerra de esta dicha Villa presento por testigo el dicho don Joseph Romo de Vera a Juan Manuel Chirinos, Español y vecino de la dicha Villa de Santa Fee aquien doy fee conosco y estando en mi presencia le resevi juramento que hizo porp Dios Nuestro Señor y la Señal de la Santa Cruz devajo de cuio cargo prometio el desir verdad en lo que supiere y le fuere preguntado y siendolo a el tenor del primer escrito que ba por cabesa y siendolo; si conosio a don Joseph Luis de Valdes y a doña Maria Cabrera; dijo que desde el año de mill seiscientos y noventa y cinco los conosio de comun trato y entraron juntos por pobladores desde la Ciudad de Mexico a este Reyno de la Nueva Mexico y que save fue natural de los Reynos de Castilla en las montanas de Obiedo y doña Maria Cabrera originaria de la Ciudad de la Puebla de los Angeles y que de estos nasio Domingo Valdes padre de doña Angela Francisca de Valdes y que estos fueron Españoles Christianos biejos desendientes de tales y conose y conosio a Mateo Marques y Agustina Romero casados y belados como lo manda la Santa Madre Yglesia y que de estos nasio de legitimo matrimonio doña Ana Maria Marques muger legitima del dicho Domingo Valdes de quienes es hija doña Angela Valdes naturales de este dicho Reyno, Españoles Christianos biejos y por tales se an tenido y tienen y que save no an sido castigados ni penitensiados por el Santo Tribunal de la Ynquisicion ni otro eclesiastico ni secular y que no son ni fueron Negro, mulato ni de otra naturalesa ynferior y limpios de toda mala rasa y tenedor y comunmente reputados sin aver cosa en contrario y que esta es la verdad por el juramento que fecho tiene en que se afirmo y ratifico una, dos, y tres veses y dise ser de edad de sesenta y quatro años y lo firmo con migo y los testigos ynfrascriptos de mi asistencia autuando por reseptoria por la notoria falta de escribano publico ni real que no lo ay en este Reyno que de todo doy fee.

Antonio de Ulibarri (rubric)
Juez receptor

Gregorio Garduño (rubric)
Juan Manuel Chirinos (rubric)
Antonio Felix Sanchez (rubric)

Otro, si dise este declarante que conose a Joseph Manuel hijo lexitimo de don Joseph de Romo y de doña Angela Francisca de Valdes y que es de edad de seis a siete meses y que le consta estar bueno y sano y para que conste lo firme.

      Juan Manuel Chirinos (rubric)
      Antonio de Ulibarri (rubric)

Declarasion de Miguel de Sandoval Martinez Español
En la Villa de Santa Fee en quatro dias del mes de Henero de mill setecientos quarenta y sinco años ante mi el Capitan don Antonio de Ulibarri, Alcalde Mayor y Capitan Aguerra de esta dicha Villa y su jurisdiccion para la ynformacion que tiene ofresida don Joseph Romo de Vera vesino de dicha Villa presento por testigo a el Capitan Miguel de Sandoval Martinez, Español y uno de los Conquistadores de este Reyno quien estando presente le resivi juramento que hiso por Dios Nuestro Señor y la señal de la Santa Crus devajo de cuio cargo prometio desir berdad en lo que supiere y le fuere preguntado y siendolo si save y conosio a don Joseph Luis de Valdes y a doña Maria Cabrera, dijo que conosio ser Español de la otra banda de los Reynos de Castilla de las montanas de Obiedo y su esposa doña Maria Cabrera Española nasida en la Puebla de los Angeles y que de estos nacio Domingo Valdes quien asi mesmo es casado y belado con Ana Maria Marques hija legitima de Mateo Marques y de Agustina Romero naturales de este Reyno y de estos nacio doña Angela Francisca de Valdes con quien contrato matrimonio don Joseph Romo de Veras todos Españoles y bien opinados y que no tienen ni an tenido macula ninguna y no an sido penitenciados por el Santo Tribunal de la Ynquisicion y que sabe fueron Christianos biejos desendientes de tales limpios de toda mala rasa de Moros, Judios ni de los nuebamente conbertidos al gremio de Nuestra Santa Madre Yglesia y que no son ni fueron Negros, mulattos ni de otra mala rasa, en cuia buena opinion an sido avidos y tenidos y comunmente reputados y que de los dichos don Joseph Romo de Vera y de doña Angela Francisca de Valdes su lexitima esposa nasio Joseph Manuel de Romo que en el presente esta vivo, bueno y sano y es de edad de seis a siete meses y que lo conose por ser vesinos todos de esta Capital Villa de Santa Fee y que esto es lo que sabe y a bisto por el juramento que fecho tiene en que se afirmo y ratifico dise ser de edad de setenta añnos y asi lo declaro por ante mi dicho Alcalde Maior don Antonio de Ulibarri a quien doy fee conosco y lo firmo con migo y los testigos ynfrascritos de mi asistencia autuando por receptoria por la notoria falta de escribano real ni publico que no lo ay en este Reyno, en dicho dia, mes y año doy fee ut supra.

      Antonio de Ulibarri (rubric)
      Juez receptor

Gregorio Garduño (rubric)
Miguel Sandobal Martines (rubric)
Antonio Felix Sanchez (rubric)

Declarasion de Sebastian de Bargas
Español
En dicha Villa de Santa Fee en siete dias del mes de Junio de mill setecientos quarenta y sinco años yo dicho Alcalde Maior de dicha Villa y su jurisdision para la ynformasion que ofrese don Joseph Romo de Vera yse pareser ante mi a el Capitan Sebastian de Bargas, Español y vecino de esta Villa aquien estando presente le recivi juramento que hiso por Dios Nuestros Señor y la Señal de la Santa Crus devajo de cuio cargo prometio desir verdad en lo que supiere y le fuere preguntado y siendolo de que si conosio a don Joseph Luis de Valdes y doña Maria de Cabrera dixo que lo conosio y que sabe hera natural de los Reynos de Castilla en las montanas de Obiedo y doñ a Maria de Cabrera era natural de la Ciudad de los Angeles y que sabe fueron casados y belados segun orden de Nuestra Santa Madre Yglesia de cuio matrimonio ubieron y proquearon a Domingo Valdes; y que asi mesmo conosio a Maria Marques y a Agustina Romero que tambien fueron casados y belados como dicho llevo y que de estos nacio doña Ana Maria Marques muger legitima del dicho Domingo Valdes de cuio matrimonio nasio doñ Angela Francisca de Valdes hija legitima del mensionado Domingo Valdes y de la dicha doña Ana Maria Marques; y que tambien le consta de vista como don Joseph Romo de Vera caso con la doña Angela Francisca de Valdes de cuio legitimo matrimonio nasio Joseph Manuel de Romo y que sabe ser de edad de seis a siete meses y que esta bueno y sano y que a todos los referidos los conosio y sabe eran Españoles Christianos biejos desendientes de tales limpios de toda mala rasa de Moros, Judios ni de los nuebamente conbertidos al gremio de nuestra Santa Madre Yglesia y que no an sido castigados ni penitensiados por el Santo Tribunal de la Ynquisicion ni otro eclesiastico ni secular y que no son ni fueron Negros ni mulattos en cuia buena opinion an sido avidos y tenidos y comunmente reputados y que esta es la verdad so cargo del juramento que fecho tiene en que se afirmo y ratifico y que todo es publico y nottorio publica vos y fama, declaro ser de edad de setenta años y lo firmo con migo y los testigos de mi assistencia actuando por reseptoria por la notoria falta de escribano real ni publico que no lo ay en este Reyno y en el presente papel por no correr de ningun sello en estas partes que de todo doy fee.

       Antonio de Ulibarri (rubric)
       Juez receptor
       Sebastian de Bargas (rubric)
Testigo
Gregorio Garduño (rubric)
Antonio Felix Sanchez (rubric)

Notes

1. Joseph Romo de Vera was in New Mexico by 1731, coming from Mexico City. His first wife was doña María Maldonado y Sais, with whom he had nineteen children, all dying by 1750. His second wife was doña Ángela Francisca Valdez. As shown in his will of 1753, he was a Santa Fe merchant and stockraiser, dying in 1754 (Chávez, *Origins*: 273; Baxter, *Las Carneradas*: 23; SANM I #1052, WPA translation; see Esquibel, "Romo de Vera," Parts 1 and 2: 20-28, 41-45).
2. Doña Ángela Francisca Valdez died in 1749 in Santa Fe (Christmas et al., *New Mexico Burials*: 39).
3. In 1720 Domingo Valdez and his wife, Ana María Márquez, sold their house in Santa Fe to Arias de Quiros. In 1742 Valdez was granted land by Governor Domingo de Mendoza (SANM I #171; SANM I #1043).
4. According to Chávez, Ana María Márquez was the granddaughter of Ana María Pacheco (Chávez, *Origins*: 303).
5. In 1774 José Manuel was married to Marta de la Luz Martín, with whom he had thirteen children. He enlisted as a presidio soldier in 1783. There is no evidence that he became a priest (Chávez, *Origins*: 273; Rau, "Romo de Vera": 42-43).
6. José Luis Valdez arrived in New Mexico in 1693 and was a sergeant at Santa Cruz in 1696. He was killed in 1703 in the Zuni mission after attending church (Chávez, *Origins*: 301; Kessell and Hendricks, *RCR*: 319 n32).
7. Internet information on Oviedo shows that it is the capital city of the principality of Asturias, in northern Spain somewhat south of the coast and on the pilgrimage route to Santiago de Compostela. It is also the name of a mountain (Wikipedia, "Oviedo," accessed March 12, 2013; Kessell and Hendricks, *RCR*: 246).
8. Chávez states that Mateo Márques may have been the son of Nicolás Márques and Ana María Montoya, and the grandson of Carolina Márques and Nicolás de Aguilar, who lived in New Mexico in the seventeenth century. Aguilar was an alcalde of the Salinas jurisdiction. He was accused of being a partisan of Governor Mendizábal and of persecuting the missionaries He was found guilty by the Inquisition and banished from New Mexico (Chávez, *Origins*: 1).
9. Agustina Romero was a daughter of Salvador Romero, a native New Mexican who returned with the Reconquest in 1693. They were descendants of Bartolomé Romero I, who signed on with Oñate in 1598 (Chávez, *Origins*: 272; Barrett, *Settlement*: 204).
10. According to the *New Velázquez Spanish and English Dictionary* (2007), the term *velada* comes from the verb *velar*, which can mean to throw a piece of white gauze over a married couple after the marriage benediction has been given.
11. Juan Manuel Chirinos, also known as Martínez de Cervantes, came to New Mexico from Mexico City in 1693. In 1695 he was a resident of Santa Cruz and in 1705, a presidio soldier. He worked on the reconstruction of San Miguel Chapel in 1710 and in 1715 asked for a transfer to the presidio of Janos in New Spain (Chávez, *Origins*: 159; Kessell et al., *BOB*: 644, 670 n14).
12. Note that Chirinos, Sandoval Martínez, and Vargas all stated that they were "Españoles." According to State Historian Rick Hendricks, this could have meant that they were born in Spain, or simply that they were claiming to be a part of the Español casta (personal communication, June 26, 2012).
13. See Doc. 21.
14. Sebastián de Vargas came from Guadalajara to New Mexico with the Reconquest and was listed in the 1697 military muster, becoming a presidio captain by 1708 (Chávez, *Origins*: 307; Kessell et al., *BOB*: 129).

35

SANTA FE ACEQUIAS TO BE CLEANED AS MANDATED BY GOVERNOR
March 18–19, 1745. Source: SANM II #495.

Synopsis and editor's notes: In a group of orders from Governor Joachín Codallos y Rabal from 1745, one item referred to problems with blocked acequias, with Codallos stating that they were so winding that the water did not have a direct course. The governor mandated that all residents join together to clean and repair the acequias, with a penalty of ten pesos if a resident did not appear to do the work.

The problems with construction of ditches for irrigation, then and now, is that water flows best if there is a constant gradient, neither too level nor too steep. If the natural grade is too steep, curves are necessary to slow down the water, but if there are too many corners or curves, then the water is slowed or stops altogether. The problem of keeping the acequias clean and running was an ongoing one then, as now. In 1833 the Santa Fe ayuntamiento, or town council, ordered that "acequias and streams must be kept clean and persons prevented from polluting or befouling them with garbage, dead animals or whatever else" (Ebright, "Shortages": 15).

Sergeant Major don Joachín Codallos y Rabal
Governor and captain general of this kingdom of New Mexico, etc.[1]

Being that the time for preparing and planting the lands of this villa and the surrounding areas has arrived, and it being known that in the previous years some disorders were noticed (as I have been informed) in the irrigation of the said lands, and because of these excesses and little cooperation among the residents, the water has been lacking when it is needed the most. Due to this, much of what had been planted was lost. The reason for this is that the *acequias madres* and the laterals were blindly constructed without a direct course for the water to flow through. I thus order that this be corrected, being that they are too winding, for which reason they cause much damage. I order that all of the residents of the said villa and surrounding areas, of all qualities, state, and condition, whatever it may be, are to join together and in unison tomorrow, Monday (which is the 26th of the present month), with their *cavadores* and their *coas*,[2] to clean the said acequias. If any of the residents are unable to attend, they are to send their servants, under penalty of a ten pesos fine, which is to be paid without exception by those who do not show up and which I will apply immediately to the cleaning and repair of the acequias.³

Done at this villa, and headquarters of Santa Fe on the 18th of March, 1745. I thus signed it acting with my assisting witnesses due to the lack of a royal or public scribe, which there is none in this kingdom.

to which I certify
Joachín Codallos y Rabal (rubric)

Witnesses
don Francisco de Roa y Carrillo (rubric)
Felipe Jacobo de Unanue (rubric)

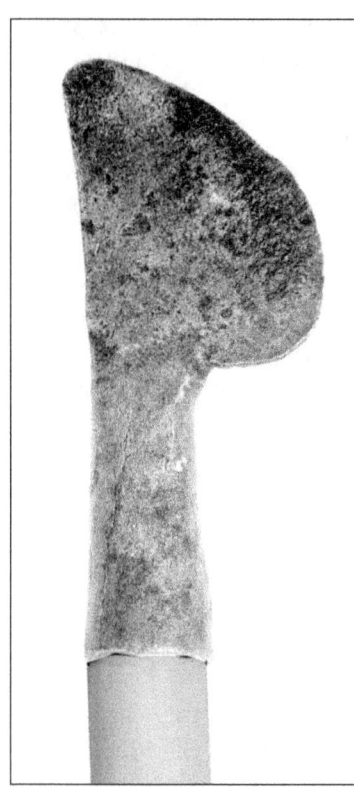

The *cavador* was a digging hoe made of wood or hand-forged iron. Nineteenth century. Photo by Robin Farwell Gavin. Pierce and Weigle, *Spanish New Mexico* 1: 127. #426. Image courtesy of the Museum of Spanish Colonial Arts, Collections of the Spanish Colonial Arts Society, Inc., Santa Fe.

At the villa of Santa Fe on the 19th of March, 1745, I, don Antonio de Ulibarrí,⁴ alcalde mayor and war captain of the said villa and of its jurisdiction, promulgate at its public plaza, before a large gathering of the residents, the foregoing bando expedited by Sergeant Major don Joachín Codallos y Rabal, governor and captain general of this kingdom of New Mexico. So that it is valid I signed it with my assisting witnesses, due to the lack of a royal or public scribe, which there is none in this kingdom.
to which I certify

Antonio de Ulibarrí (rubric)

ORIGINAL DOCUMENT

Año de 1745

Diferentes ordenes politicos y militares de Bandos y otras providencias de esta Governacion que se contiene en este quaderno para los efectos que en ellos se expresan y dentro se perciben, ut supra.

El Sargento Maior Don Joachin Codallos y Rabal, Governador y Capitan General de este Reino dela Nueva Mexico, ut supra.

Por quanto es llegado el tiempo de labrar y sembrar las tierras de esta Villa y sus arrabales; y haviendose reconosido que en los años antecedents se experimentaban algunos desordenes (segun me an ynformado) en los riegos de dichas tierras, y que por estos exsesos y poca union delos vezinos falta el agua al major tiempo que se nezesita, motibo a que se pierde mucha parte de lo sembrado causando tambien este atrazo el estar ciegas y mal aderesadas las acequias madres y otras por las que se conduce la agua, nesesitando de reparar tan permisiosos ynosibos danos por el torsentes, mando a todos los vesinos de dicha Villa y sus arrabales de qual quiera calidad, estado y condicion que sean, que compromisados y unidos todos se junten desde manana Lunes (que se contara veinte y un dias de el corriente) con cavadores y coas para limpiar dichas acequias y de no poder yr alguno devlos vezinos embiaran a sus criados o señorbientes, pena de dies pesos, que se le sacaran yrremisiblemente al que faltare, los que desde luego aplico para dicha limpia y composision de las acequias. Fecho en esta Villa capital de Santa Fee en diez y ocho del mes de Marso de mill setesientos y quarenta y sinco anos; y lo firme actuando con los testigos de mi asistensia a falta de Escribano Real y Publico que no lo ay en dicho Reyno. Doy fee.
                    Joachin Codallos y Rabal (rubric)
testigo
Don Francisco de Roa y Carrillo (rubric)
Phelipe Jacobo de Unanue (rubric)

En la Villa de Santa Fee a diez y nuebe dias del mes de Marzo de mill setesientos quarenta y cinco años: Yo Don Antonio de Ulibarri, Alcalde Maior y Capitan Aguerra de dicha Villa y su jurisdicion promulga en la Plaza publica de ella en concurso de mucho besindario el Bando antesedente expedido por el Señor Sarjento Maior Don Joachin Codallos y Rabal, Governador y Capitan General deste Reyno de la Nueva

Mexico; y para que coste lo firme ut supra con los testigos de mi asistencia, por la falta de Escribano Publico ni Real que no lo ay en este Reyno: Doy fee.

       Antonio de Ulibarri (rubric)

Notes

1. This document is one of several orders from Governor Joachín Codallos y Rabal for the years 1744 to 1848.
2. *Cavadores* are hoelike tools; *coas* are shovel-like tools (J. Richard Salazar, personal communication, August 11, 3011). *Cavadores* can sometimes, although not here, refer to the people that use the hoes in cleaning the acequias.
3. The document, like that on the flooding of the plaza in 1767 (Doc. 53), shows the role played by the governor in administering matters in the villa of Santa Fe.
4. See Doc. 24.

36

SETTLERS FEAR MOTHS, PLEAD FOR SALE OF WOOL
June 16, 1745. Source: SANM II #465a

Synopsis and editor's notes: In 1744 the Albuquerque settlers petitioned the new governor, Joachín Codallos y Rabal, for removal of the wool embargo on goods sold outside the province imposed earlier (see Docs. 29 and 30). They had found a buyer for the wool, and they feared that if they did not sell it, the moths would destroy it. Their petition was successful, with the governor allowing them to sell the wool to a trader from Mexico City. In 1745, as shown in this document, fifteen Albuquerque residents again petitioned the governor for permission to sell their surplus wool, this time to trader don Juan de la Garrida. They repeated that if they did not sell this surplus, it would be lost to the moths, decay, and other things. They pointed out that persons manufacturing blankets and cloth in New Mexico already had enough wool. The governor again granted permission to sell the wool, although apparently the sale of cattle and sheep was still restricted, not being named by the governor in the document.

During the following decades, New Mexicans traded sheep on a large scale, with some of the ranchers accused of attempting to control the market. Because of this and because of the increasing Indians raids, decreasing the supply of sheep, in 1777 Governor Mendiñueta outlawed the export of sheep cattle and raw wool outside the province (Baxter, *Las Carneradas*: 28, 29, 50-52; see also SANM II #410 and #421).

Year of 1745

A petition by the residents of the villa of San Felipe de Alburquerque requesting permission to sell the wool that has been sheared due to the problem which might arise from moths [*polillas*], etc.

Governor and captain general

The persons who sign below do it with all their solemnity according to their right and appear before your honor and say that, because of the circumstance in which they find themselves, having some amounts of wool, they have jointly made a deal to sell it for as much as they can get to don Juan de la Garrida,[1] who is the owner of numerous items [*dueño de requa*], in exchange for some goods which correspond to the value of the said wool. Due to which and so that it is valid and so that the said don Juan is able to take that which he purchases [out of the kingdom], we humbly petition your honor to grant us permission to allow us to sell the said wool. Upon obtaining the superior consideration of your honor, we can trade for the items that we are interested in getting. If we do not get rid of the wool within a certain time, it will be lost to moths, decay, and other things that will cause it to be ruined. Also, there is no way that it can be put to use in this kingdom, being that there are no businesses which can do anything with it except for those who produce blankets [*mantas*] and coarse cloth [*sallal*].

They, with only a small amount of wool, have enough of a supply to make these things and as such are left with an excess. In addition, we also say that we can acquire the necessary items to provide for our families, and if this is not done they will be left unclothed, being that there is no other commerce or goods which are available. Due to this, we bring it to the attention of your honor and ask for and petition that you order that this is done and allow us to do what we have asked for, granting us your mercy for what is necessary, etc.

Nicolas Aragón[2] (rubric)

Felipe de Silva[3] (rubric)

Pedro García Jurado[4] (rubric)

Antonio Baca[5] (rubric)

At the request of

Francisco Gutiérrez[6] signed by Antonio Baca (rubric)

Salvador Martínez[7] (rubric)

Luis García[8] (rubric)

Pedro Varela[9] (rubric)

Gerónimo Jaramillo[10] (rubric)

Ventura de la Candelaria[11] (rubric)

At the request of

Joseph Sánchez[12] signed by Juan Moya[13] (rubric)

Joseph Baca[14] (rubric)

Nicolás de Chávez[15] (rubric)

Juan Miguel Álbares del Castillo[16] (rubric)

Bernabé Baca[17] (rubric)

Decree

At the villa of Santa Fe on the 16th of June, 1745, before me, Sergeant Major don Joachín Codallos y Rabal, the governor and captain general of this kingdom of New Mexico, according to the petition that was presented to me by those who are listed in it, and upon being reviewed by me, I grant permission to the above said, allowing them to make the sale as stated. To don Juan de la Garrida, owner of the numerous goods, I grant him the permission that allows him to purchase it [the wool], and to take it out of this kingdom to the places and parts wherever he wishes, without anyone complaining about what he is doing. I thus approve and sign it, acting with my assisting witnesses due to the lack of a public or royal scribe, which there is none in this kingdom. To which I certify.

Joachín Codallos y Rabal (rubric)
Joseph Romo de Vera (rubric)
Antonio de Aramburu (rubric)

ORIGINAL DOCUMENT

Año de 1745

Una peticion de los vezinos de la Villa de San Phelipe de Alburquerque sobre que se les permita vender los esquilinos de sus lanas por el mucho atrazo que tienen de yntruducirse en ella polilla, ut supra.

Señor Governador y Capitan General

Las personas que aqui firmamos premisas las solenidades en derecho nesesarias paresemos ante Vuestra Señoria y desimos: que con el motivo de allarnos con algunos pegusales de lana, tenemos tratado de benderla cada uno segun su posible a Don Juan de la Garrida dueño de requa a cambio de algunos generos correspondiente su balor al de dichas lanas, para lo qual, y que tenga efecto, y el dicho Don Juan pueda sacar la que asi comprase, suplicamos a Vuestra Señoria rendidamente se señorva de consedernos licencia para dicha venta de la lana referida, con lo qual consiguiremos las utilidades que se dejan conoser, y ponemos en la superior consideracion de Vuestra Señoria y son que si no se sacara dicha lana en la ocacion se perdiera por polilla, mengua y otros acidentes que en esta tierra siempre se padesen, demas del qual no ay consumo de ella en este Reyno por no haver obrajes mas que algunas mantas y sallal que se fabrican para lo qual con corta cantidad de lana ay bastante, y lla los que hasen dicha fabrica tienen y aun les sobra = A que se agrega la rason de que con dichos generos se socoren nuestras familias y que si no fuera asi se padesieran desnudeses por no ofreserse otro comercio ni trafico, en culla atencion a Vuestra Señoria pedimos y suplicamos se señorva de mandar hazer y determinar como llebamos pedido en que rresibiremos merced, y en lo nesesario, ut supra.

Nicolas de Aragon (rubric)
Felipe de Silva (rubric)
Pedro Garcia Jurado (rubric)

Antonio Baca (rubric)
A ruego de Francisco Gutierres X Antonio Baca (rubric)
Salvador Martinez (rubric)
Luis Garcia (rubric)
Pedro Barela (rubric)
Geronimo Jaramillo (rubric)
Bentura de la Candelaria (rubric)
A ruego de Joseph Sanchez, Juan Moya (rubric)
Joseph Baca (rubric)
Nicolas de Chabes (rubric)
Juan Miguel Albares del Castillo (rubric)
Bernabe Baca (rubric)

Autto

En la Villa de Santa Fee en dies y seis dias del mes de Junio de mill setecientos y quarenta y cinco años ante mi el Sargento Maior Don Joachin Codallos y Rabal, Governador y Capitan General de este Reyno de la Nueva Mexico se presento esta peticion por los contenidos en ella; que por mi vista por este auto consedo lizencia a los suso dichos para la venta de lana que refieren y a Don Juan de la Garrida dueño de requas para que las pueda comprar y sacar de este Reyno para alas partes y lugares que sele ofresieren sin que a unos ni otros se les ponga embaraso para lo que pretenden; y assi lo probei y firme actuando con los testigos de mi asistencia por falta de Escribano que no lo hay Publico ni Real en este Reyno = Doy fee.

    Joachin Codallos y Rabal (rubric)
    Joseph Romo de Vera (rubric)
    Antonio de Aramburu (rubric)

Notes

1. To date, no information has been found on this person. Apparently he was a trader from New Spain.
2. See Doc. 26.
3. Felipe de Silva's parents were Antonio de Silva and Gregoria Ruiz. He was a brother of Francisco and Maria Silva, named in Doc. 33. Felipe married Juana Gallegos in 1732 in Albuquerque. In 1734 he was involved in a lawsuit over the delivery to a Mexico City merchant of a load of dirty wool fleeces (NMGS, *Aquí*: 65, 422; SANM II #399; Baxter, *Las Carneradas*: 26).
4. Pedro [del Canta or Alcantara] García Jurado was the son of Ramón García Jurado and Bernardina Hurtado. His grandfather was Martín Hurtado, an Albuquerque first founder. He married Manuela Quintana in 1732 in Albuquerque (NMGS, *Aquí*: 290).
5. See Doc. 30.
6. See Doc. 43.
7. See Doc. 37.
8. See Doc. 5.
9. See Doc. 28.
10. See Doc. 33.

11. Ventura de la Candelaria was born in El Paso, the youngest son of Francisco Candelaria, a native New Mexican and a first founder of Albuquerque. Ventura lived on the family property, at time sharing a house and land with Baltazar Romero and later with Juan Alejo Gutiérrez. Juan Alejo was his father-in-law when he married Inés Gutiérrez in 1717 in Albuquerque. Ventura's name also appears with that of Pedro Lucero and Cristóbal García in a document from1722 regarding the sale of land in Albuquerque (NMGS, *Aquí*: 78, 123-28; SANM I #172).
12. See Doc. 28.
13. The Juan Moya who signed this document for Joseph Sánchez was the lieutenant alcalde mayor of Albuquerque in 1746. In 1758 a Juan Francisco Moya sold a house and land in Santa Fe, and in 1763 a Juan Moya was imprisoned and in the stocks for stealing a cow, but this may not be the same person (NMGS, *Aquí*: 128; SANM I #554 and SANM II #567).
14. See Doc. 33.
15. See Doc. 21.
16. See Doc. 21.
17. Bernabé Baca and Margaret de Mata are shown as the parents of Baltazar Baca, who in 1762 married Rafaela Baca, the widow of Diego Torres. Baltazar was an alcalde of Acoma and Laguna. There are several cases regarding the two Bacas, including complaints by the Indians at Zuni and an accusation of disobeying the alcalde at Albuquerque regarding the use of Indians as shepherds (NMGS, *Aquí*: 64, 67, 74, 116, 156; Chávez, *Origins*: 145; SANM II #394, #523).

37

SALVADOR MARTÍNEZ, SON OF FORMER GOVERNOR FELIX MARTÍNEZ, ASKS VICEROY FOR APPOINTMENT AS ALBUQUERQUE SQUADRON LEADER
February 13–June 7, 1748. Source: SANM II #484.

Year of 1748

Synopsis and editor's notes: In an effort to be appointed corporal of the ten-soldier Albuquerque squadron, Salvador Martínez traveled to Mexico City with a petition that he be rewarded for his military accomplishments by being appointed as the corporal of the Albuquerque squadron. He stated that he wanted the position held by Martín Hurtado, including the same exemptions and privileges. Hurtado had been appointed leader of the squadron in 1706 and died in 1734. Martínez also asked that his sons, Joachín and Antonio, be admitted to the Albuquerque squadron. Included with his petition were credentials stating that he served at the Santa Fe presidio as a paid soldier for seven years and in El Paso for five years and with the Albuquerque militia without pay for twenty-two years. He also had documentation stating that he was the son of the former governor, Felix Martínez. The viceroy approved the appointment. The next problem, then, for Salvador and the men that went to Mexico City with him was how to afford the trip back to New Mexico, as addressed in the following document.

Regarding Salvador's claim that Felix Martínez was his father, Fray Angélico Chávez has stated that there was no record that Felix Martínez had children. In 1722, when he married Rosalia García de Noriega, he himself stated that his parents were unknown. This was, however, during the time (1717–1725) when Felix Martínez was under house arrest in Mexico City for complaints about his actions as governor of New Mexico, and Salvador may not have wished to admit his connection (Chávez, *Roots*: 1168; Warner, "Felix Martinez": 143).

The squadron in question is the same one that was originally granted to Albuquerque by Governor Cuervo y Valdez in 1706, subsequently removed by Governor Peñuela, and then reinstated in 1712 by Governor Mogollón. Apparently the squadron had remained in Albuquerque since that time (Simmons, *Albuquerque*: 88; Doc. 5).

A copy of a legal document that was presented by don Salvador

Martínez[1] to his excellency, the viceroy of New Spain, so that he could be rewarded for his accomplishments and for whatever else is contained within.

Excellency

I, the alférez don Salvador Martínez, resident of the villa of San Felipe de Alburquerque in the kingdom of New Mexico, proceeding in the proper way according to my right, along with the necessary protests and competencies, say that from the documents which I present under my sworn statement and the warranted solemnity, [I] state the following as presented.

First of all, Captain Juan Gonzales Bas,[2] alcalde mayor and war captain of the villa of San Felipe de Alburquerque and of San Agustín de la Isleta, certifies that I have served his majesty for seven years in this kingdom and at the presidio of El Paso del Río del Norte for five years, both terms with a salary. However, in addition to this, I have served without a salary and at my expense the lengthy period of twenty-two years with my arms, horses, and other equipment, always willing to sacrifice myself, as I have done, in order to forever save those dominions for his majesty, and to liberate them from the interference and assaults which are continuously threatened by the Indians from the barbaric nations of the Faraones, Gilenos, and Apaches. Don Juan Gonzales [Bas] states in his certification that for the period of fifteen years during which he was alcalde mayor of the stated villa, he saw me wounded from specific pursuits and campaigns in which I assisted in his company, spilling much blood in them, losing my weapons, the horses, and the equipment which I took with me. Nevertheless, such was the defense which we accomplished for his majesty, and as such we were able to gain the victory, triumphing over the enemy, and forcing them to retreat back to their distant lands.

Second is the certification given at my request by Ignacio Cayetano Briseño, royal scribe and resident of the villa of San Felipe el Real de Chihuahua, who was informed by don Francisco Vigil,[3] don Pedro Lucero,[4] and don Blas Martín,[5] Spaniards, who were soldiers of the above stated kingdom, who knew my father, who held the title of captain-for-life [*capitan vitalicio*] in that kingdom [of New Mexico], and who served his majesty as governor of the same from the year 1696 until 1717, whose name was don Felix Martínez,[6] and my mother was doña Catarina de Esparze. They are also aware that I have served his majesty during the times and in the manner which I have stated in the preceding paragraph. In addition, it is well known that in the last campaign and war which we had with the Apache and Ute nations, which was headed by Governor don Joachín Codallos y Rabal, I assisted not only personally but also with my weapons, gunpowder, horses, and other necessary items at my expense and without anything from the royal treasury. I also made one of my sons, named Joachín Martínez,[7] assist with other necessary weapons, and he enlisted without being ordered to serve his majesty on that occasion. Therefore, Excellency, who is to protest the multiple certifications and information as offered in this sincere testimony?

Also I thereby apply and endeavor to show what I have accomplished while serving his majesty to the best that I can, without showing the ignorance which in this particular case is held by the residents of these remote dominions. As such, this can serve as a basis regarding that which is stated along with the sincerity which is shown by that which I have presented, which qualifies the truth about my representation. I do not doubt that you will esteem it as is justified before the greatness of your excellency, in which conformity I have tried to serve you. During my lifetime I have not done anything else other than on a daily basis dedicate myself to the service of his majesty in the augmentation and conservation of your royal dominions. As far as I have been able to do so, I have expended joyfully in providing weapons, balls for muskets, horses, and other items to go on campaigns, and not even my sons have I left behind, sacrificing them joyfully and with dedication, being that I have nothing other than to serve his majesty in consideration of everything which has been expressed.

The superior judgment of your excellency should be pleased to order the remuneration of my said services by conferring upon me the military employment of corporal of the squadron of ten soldiers who are permanently stationed under the order of his majesty in the said referred-to villa of San Felipe de Alburquerque, acquiring it with all the exemptions and privileges which had been given to Captain Martín Hurtado.[8] No one will be prejudiced by you granting me this position as no one is presently in that employment. I will be grateful to you if you offer me the salary which was given to the stated Captain Martín Hurtado. In addition, your excellency, I would be grateful if you admitted into the service of your majesty my two sons, Joachín Martínez and Antonio Martínez,[9] employing them as soldiers with the regular salary which your majesty gives to those stationed at the villa of San Felipe de Alburquerque, with which equivalencies and the generous zeal which your excellency has, he will see to it that it is done. Also, he will be able to aid me due to my advanced age, and at the same time it will be of benefit to those residents so that with similar hope they will sacrifice their valuables or their few belongings as I have done in the kingdom's defense and large expansion, for all of which I am hopeful that I will be granted that which I ask for. Of your excellency, I ask that having presented that which I have, you will be kind to order that which I have asked for, for which I will be grateful and what is necessary, etc.

Salvador Martínez

México, February 13, 1748. Sent to the auditor, designated by a rubric.

Excellency

According to the order of this day, the auditor consults with your excellency, so that the decree is submitted to the resident of the villa of Santa Fe as a dispatch which seeks an amount in excess and restitution from the lieutenant of the company who resides in that villa and so that it be proposed to the governor so that he can

attend to the recommended merit of the petitioner for the [position] of corporal of the squadron of ten soldiers,[10] who reside in the villa of Alburquerque in the government of New Mexico. It is also so that this person can relate it to the said governor as has been ordered by your excellency according to the decree as dictated and approved by this dispatch, which has as its ending that it be merited to the petitioner for the said employment, and that it be returned to him as his copy, or for what his excellency sees best.
   Mexico City, February 19, 1748.

   Sent to the auditor general of war, designated by a rubric. As ordered by his excellency, don Juan Manuel Soria [Martínez].

   At this villa of Santa Fe on the 6th of June, 1748, I, Sergeant Major don Joachín Codallos y Rabal, governor and captain general of this kingdom of New Mexico, upon reviewing on this said day, the superior decree of his excellency, the viceroy of this New Spain, which was presented to me by the party upon whom it was conferred on this said day, stating that it would be safeguarded, complied with, and executed to the letter according to what is stated in the said superior decree. I am to inform his excellency the viceroy within reason of its reception that the petitioner has been informed of his appointment as corporal of the squadron of ten soldiers who are permanently stationed at the villa of San Felipe de Alburquerque. His excellency is to be informed of this at the first possible instance. I thus approved and signed it with my assisting witnesses acting as I do due to the lack of public or royal scribe, which there is none in this kingdom, to which certify.
      Don Joachín Codallos y Rabal
Witnesses
Felipe Jacobo de Unanue
Miguel Alire

   This copy agrees in full with the original, which was returned to its owner on the 7th of June, 1748, and is fully corrected and complete. Seeing that this was done were the witnesses, don Joseph Romo de Vera, Gregorio Garduño, and Sebastián de Apodaca, residents of the villa of Santa Fe, and which I signed on the said day and year, acting with my assisting witnesses due to the lack of a public or royal scribe, which there is none in this kingdom, to which I certify.
in testimony of the truth, I signed it
      Joachín Codallos y Rabal (rubric)
Witnesses
Felipe Jacobo de Unanue (rubric)
Miguel de Alire (rubric)

ORIGINAL DOCUMENT

Año de 1748

Un testimonio de escrito original que Don Salvador Martinez presento al Excellentisimo Señor Virrey de esta Nueva España en orden a que se le atienda por sus meritos y lo demas que en el se contiene, ut supra.

Excellentisimo Señor

El Alferez Don Salvador Martinez vecino de la Villa de San Felipe de Alburquerque en el Reyno del Nuevo Mexico como mejor proceda por derecho y con las protestas nesesarias y competentes digo que de los ynstrumentos que presento con el juramento y solemnidad nezesaria consta y se persibe lo siguiente = Lo primero que el Capitan Don Juan Gonzales Bas, Alcalde Maior y Capitan Aguerra de la Villa de San Felipe de Alburquerque y San Agustin de la Ysleta certifico haver servido a Su Magestad en dicho Reyno siete años; en el Presidio del Passo de el Río del Norte sinco y con sueldo en ambas ocasiones. Pero que amas destas he servido sin sueldo y ami costa el dilitado tiempo de veinte y dos anos con mis armas, cavallos y demas equipajes estando siempre prompto a sacrificarme como lo e echo por conserbar indemnes aquellos Dominios de Su Magestad y libertarlos de las yntroduciones y asaltos con que diariamente los ostilizan y persiguen los Yndios barbaros de las naciones Faraones, Gileños y Apaches asegurando Don Juan Gonzales en la enunciada certificazion que en el tiempo de quinze anos que fue Alcalde Maior en la enunciada Villa me vio alli herido en distintas correrias y campanas en que asisti en su compañía derramando en ellas mucha sangre y perdiendo las armas, los cavallos y demas equipajes que llevava; pero sin embargo desto hera tal el esfuerso con que en defensa de Su Magestad me porte que obtuvimos el logro de la vitoria triunfando de los enemigos y haciendolos retirar alo mas dilatado de su abitazion = Lo segundo consta por la certificazion dada en mi pedimento por Ygnacio Caietano Briseño, Escribano Real y vecino de la Villa de San Felipe el Real de Chiguagua haver expresado en su presencia Don Francisco Vigil, Don Pedro Luzero y Don Blas Martin, Españoles y soldados que han sido en el supra mencionado Reyno, que conosieron ami padre que fue Capitan Vitalico en el y governador y que señorvio a Su Majestad desde el ano de seiscientos noventa y seis hasta el de setezientos diez y siete cuio nombre hera Don Phelix Martinez y mi madre Dona Catharina de Esparze; y que asi mismo le consta haver yo servido a Su Magestad en los tiempos y en la forma que tengo ya expresado en el antecedente parrafo: amas de ser notoriamente constante que en la ultima campana y guerra que tubimos con la nacion Apache y Yuta en que concurrio el Governador Don Joachin Codallos y Rabal asisti no solo con mi persona aprontando armas, polbora, cavallos y demas nesesarias a mi costa y sin grabamen alguno del Real herario, sino que tambien hize que saliera un hijo mio nombrado Joachin Martinez ministrandole tambien a este los armamientos presisos y ofreciendolo sin ser nombrado a que señorviese a Su Magestad en aquella ocasion = De manera Señor Excellentisimo que el no protestar multiplicadas ynformaziones y certificaziones en verdadero testimonio del maior. Desbelo aplicazion y esmero con que me he destinado a servir a Su Magestad en quanto ha sido de mi parte ha estado dela ygnoranzia con que este particular nos manijamos los vezinos de aquellos remotos Dominios = A si esto puede servir de dispense sobre lo expresado tambien la misma sencilles que se verifica, en los que llevo presentados califica la verdad de mi representazion y no dudo que se estime por justificado ante la grandeza de Vuestra Excellenzia en cuia conformidad y en la de servirlo que toda mi vida no ha sido otro mi exercizio que salid y la batalla contra los Yndios ynfieles que mi ocupacion diaria ha sido dedicarme al servicio de Su Magestad en augmento y conserbazion de sus Reales Domicilios que quanto he podido adquirir todo lo expendido gustoso en armas, balas, cavallos y demas para salir alas campanas, y que ni aun amis hijos he reservado por que lo he sacrificado gustoso y dedicado, a que no tengan otra cosa por hefecto que el servizio de Su Magestad con considerazion a todo lo expresado, se ha de servir la superiorida de Vuestra Excellenzia de mandar que en remunerazion de dichos mis servicios seme confiera la plaza militar de Cavo de la Escuadra de dies soldados que continuamente estan de orden de Su Magestad en referida Villa de San Felipe de Alburquerque gozandola con los privilegios y exempciones con que la goso el Capitan Martin Urtado, con cuya gracia no se perjudica ninguno por no estar conferido este empleo ni servirlo ala presente determinada persona ministrandoseme el sueldo que se le ministraba a el enunciado Capitan Martin Urtado, señorviendose ygualmente Vuestra Excellenzia de mandar se admitan el servicio de Su Magestad a mis dos hijos nombrados Joachin Martinez y Antonio Martinez asentando plazas de soldados con el regular sueldo que Su Magestad da en dicha Villa de San Felipe de Alburquerque con cuias equitativas providencias y proprias del venigno celo con que la grandeza de Vuestra Excellenzia atienda a los que se destinan a el augmento delos estados de Su Magestad conseguire el tener algun alibio en lo abansado de mi edad y servira ygualmente de aliento a aquellos vecinos para que con esta misma esperanza sacrifiquen sus candales o cortos averes, como yo lo he practicado en su defensa y maior extenzion para todo lo qual seme libren los correspondientes despachos = A Vuestra Excellenzia suplico que haviendo por presentados dichos ynstrumentos se señorva de mandar hazer como llevo pedido en que recevire merzed y en lo nezesario ut supra. Salvador Martinez

Mexico y Febrero 13 de 1748. Al Señor Auditor señalado con una rubrica

Excellentisimo Señor. En dictamen de este dia consulta el Auditor a Vuestra Excellencia se libre a la parte del vecino de la Villa de Santa Fee darle el despacho que pide exseso y refaziones del Theniente de la Compañía que reside en dicha Villa y que se prevenga al Governador que atienda al recomendable merito del suplicante para Cavo de Escuadra de diez soldados que reside en la Villa de Alburquerque de la Governazion del Nuevo Mexico y para que esta parte pueda por si ynterpetar a dicho Governador sobre lo mandado se señorva Vuestra Excellenzia que el Decreto que a este dictamen se previere señorva de despacho dirijido al fin de quese atienda el merito del suplicante para dicho empleo; y que se le devuelba para sus ynstrumentos o lo que Vuestra Excellenzia mejor estimare. Mexico y Febrero 19 de 1748. Comparece al Señor Auditor General dela Guerra, señalado con una rubrica _____

Por mando de Su Excellenzia Don Juan Manuel Soria _____

En la Villa de Santa Fee a seis dias del mes de Junio de mil setezientos quarenta y ocho años yo el Sargento Maior Don Joachin Codallos y Rabal Governador y Capitan General de este Reino dela Nueva Mexico; en vista del superior Decreto de el Excellentisimo Señor Virrey de esta Nueva Espana que seme demonstro por la parte conferida en su escripto dicho dia. Dixe que se guarde, cumpla y ejecute ala letra como en dicho Superior Decreto se expresa con arreglamento alo que seme previene en el citado Decreto; y tengo que ynformar a dicho Señor Excellentizimo Virrey en razon de su pretenzion del suplicante sobre que se le confiera el nombramento de Cavo dela Esquadra de diez soldados que continuamente estan en la Villa de San Felipe de Alburquerque y dar quenta a Su Excellenzia de todo en la primera occasion que aya. Y asi lo provei y firme con los testigos de mi asistenzia con quienes actuo a falta de Escribano Publico y Real que no lo ay en este Reyno, doy fee. Don Joachin Codallos y Rabal = testigo Felipe Jacobo de Unanue = testigo Miguel Alire_____

Concuerda este traslado con su original que se volvio a la parte el dia siete de Junio de mil setezientos quarenta y ocho anos con el que va verdadero correjido y consertado, y al verlo sacar fueron testigos Don Joseph Romo de Vera, Gregorio Garduño y Sevastian de Apodaca vezinos dela Villa de Santa Fee, en la que lo firme dicho dia mes y ano actuando con los testigos de mi asistenzia a falta de Escribano Publico o Real que no lo ay en este Reyno, Doy fee _____

En testimonio de la verdad lo firme _____
Joachin Codallos y Rabal (rubric)
testigo
Felipe Jacobo de Unanues (rubric) testigo

Notes

1. Salvador Martínez, in addition to the biographical information that he provides about himself in this document, was married to Rosalia García de Noriega of Albuquerque, the daughter of Luis García. Documents in the Spanish Colonial archives show him attempting to acquire his wife's inheritance after the death of her father, Luis, and mother, Josepha Valverde, and also attempting to reclaim land allegedly lost to him in the resettlement of Sandía Pueblo (Chávez, *Origins*: 227; SANM I #1221, SANM II #414, #473, SANM I #532).
2. See Doc. 21 for biographical information on Juan Gonzales Bas I. However, since he died in 1743, there is a possibility that the reference is to his son, Juan Gonzales Bas II, who was born in 1710 and built the church at Alameda (Chávez, *Origins*: 189-90).
3. See Doc. 9.
4. Pedro Lucero [de Godoy] was the son of Antonio Lucero de Godoy and grandson of Juan, who had returned to New Mexico in 1693. He is listed as a soldier in the master of June 18, 1723, without stirrups and lance and with seven horses (Christmas, *Military Records*: 50).
5. Blas Martín [Serrano] was the son of Domingo Martín, who returned to New Mexico after the Reconquest. Blas was a presidio soldier who, in 1714, presented a petition to the governor stating that because of his many ailments, he could not continue (Kessell et al., *BOB*: 959 n 64; Christmas and Rau, "Una Lista": 200; see also Doc. 22).
6. For biographical information on Felix Martínez, see Doc. 13.
7. A Joaquín Martínez married Teresa Tenorio de Alba, the daughter of Captain Manuel Tenorio de Alba, in 1749. Joaquín is shown as a presidio soldier in 1761, listed with seven horses and otherwise fully equipped. In 1752 he sold a house and land in Santa Fe to Francisco García (Chávez, *Origins*: 293; Hadley et al., *Presidio*: 302; SANM I #350).
8. See Doc. 8.
9. Antonio [Facundo] Martínez was born in 1731. Information on two persons of this name is available: one with Andrea Jaramillo as a witness in Albuquerque in 1765, and another with Rita Salazar at a wedding of their son, Felipe José, in Sandía in 1788 (Chávez, *Origins*: 227; NMGS, *Aquí*: 315, 500).
10. See Docs. 1 and 5.

38

SALVADOR MARTÍNEZ AND SOLDIERS, STUCK IN MEXICO CITY WITHOUT FUNDS, ASK VICEROY FOR HELP
February 27–June 7, 1748. SANM II #487.

Synopsis and editor's notes: Having arrived in Mexico City, and with his petition to be corporal of the Albuquerque squadron approved by the viceroy (see Doc. 37), Salvador Martínez and the five presidio soldiers that went with him found themselves without money to return to Santa Fe. It seems that they expected to have their back pay provided to them from the Mexico City paymaster rather than receiving it along with the other soldiers at the presidio at Santa Fe, an expectation that was not borne out. Martínez again went to the viceroy, this time with a petition for funds, and his petition was again approved. It appears, however, that the soldiers had to wait five months for a message to be sent to and returned from New Mexico's governor, Codallos y Rabal, agreeing to the pay transfer and their return to the Santa Fe presidio.

Year of 1748

[This is] a copy of a legal document regarding the original petition which don Salvador Martínez, Tomás Madrid,[1] and Pedro Vigil[2] presented to the most excellent viceroy[3] requesting that don Jazinto Martínez[4] give them four hundred pesos from the account of the governor of New Mexico so that they can return to this kingdom [of New Mexico].

Your most excellent sir

[We] don Salvador Martínez, Thomas Madrid, and alférez Pedro Vigil, soldiers from New Mexico, in their best form present themselves before your excellency and ask that, by the great wisdom of your excellency, being aware of the great distance in which we find ourselves in order to return to our presidio in order to serve his majesty, you be pleased to order that don Jacinto Martínez, under the power-of-attorney from the governor of that province and with regard to our salaries, give four hundred pesos to each one of us. This is because we are five individuals who find ourselves before this tribunal, being under the power-of-attorney by the said governor, and were only given four hundred pesos for all of us. For which reason and so that the governor does not cause us any problem, your excellency should be pleased to order that we are not shorted of the said amount, wanting as it is not to give up our goods but to be paid the wages that we are owed for the service that we are committed to perform at the said presidio. In the case that any one of our employment is about to be terminated and something is still owed, his successor is to resume being paid, being certain that everything is done for justice. For this, the superior decree of your excellency will serve as a necessary warrant, during which time we ask that your excellency will be pleased to order that which we ask for, and by which we will receive his mercy with justice, etc.

Salvador Martínez

He signed for his companions who did not know how to write.

First count of Revillagigedo, Juan Francisco de Güemes y Horcasitas, viceroy from 1746 to 1755. Image from *Los governantes de México*, by Manuel Rivera, Vol. 1 (México, 1872).

Mexico, February 29, 1748. That which is asked for is granted as is provided by the decree which is being sent.

By order of his excellency, don Juan [Manuel] Martínez Soria[5]

At the villa of Santa Fe on the 6th of June, 1748, I, Sergeant Major don Joachín Codallos y Rabal, governor and captain general of this kingdom of New Mexico, upon reviewing the superior decree before me from his excellency, viceroy of this New Spain, which on this day was presented to me by Salvador Martínez and Thomas Madrid, and which is to be held as presented in order to inform the said his excellency in the manner which is directed by the petitioners in their written document, which is to be carried out at the first possible instance. I signed it with my assisting witnesses with whom I act due to the lack of a public or royal scribe, which there is none in this kingdom, to which I certify.

      don Joachín Codallos y Rabal

Witnesses
Felipe Jacobo de Unanue
Miguel de Alire

This copy is in agreement with the original, which was returned to the parties on this 7th of June, 1748, and which is properly corrected as concluded. Those who saw this done as witnesses were don Joseph Romo de Vera,[6] Gregorio Garduño,[7] and Sebastián de Apodaca,[8] residents of the Villa of Santa Fe, on this 7th day of the said month and year, which is when I signed it with my assisting witnesses with whom I act due to the lack of a public or royal scribe, which there is none in this kingdom, which I certify.

      In testimony to the truth I signed it
      Joachín Codallos y Rabal (rubric)

Witnesses
Felipe Jacobo de Unanue (rubric)
Miguel de Alire (rubric)

ORIGINAL DOCUMENT

Año de 1748

Un testimonio de la original petizion que Don Salvador Martinez, Thomas Madrid y Pedro Begil presentaron al Excellentisimo Señor Virrey en orden a que Don Jazinto Martinez les diese de quenta del Governador de la Nueva Mexico quatrocientos pesos para su regreso a este Reyno, ut supra.

Excellentisimo Señor= Don Salvador Martinez, Thomas Madrid y Pedro Vigil, Alferez y soldados de la Nueva Mexico como mas aya lugar paresco ante Vuestra Excellenzia y digo que la gran justificazion de Vuestra Excellencia atendiendo a la gran distanzia en que nos hallamos y para podernos restituir a nuestro Presidio al servizio de Su Magestad que servido mandar que Don Jazinto Martinez apoderado del Governador de aquella Provincia y por quenta de nuestros sueldos nos diese a rason de quatrozientos pesos a cada uno de los cinco indibiduos que nos hallamos en esta corte y respecto a la representazion que nos hizo dicho apoderado por dicho Governador nos dio solamente quatrozientos pesos para todos. Por lo qual y para que dicho Governador no nos quiere perjudicar por esta razon, se ha de servir Vuestra Excellencia mandarle que no nos pretenda exsivir dicha cantidad executibamente queriendo quitarnos por ello nuestros vienes sino que presisamente lo debenguemos con el servicio que hemos de hazer en dicho Presidio y que si acaso por estar ya para terminar su empleo sele quedare a dever algo lo libre en su subcesor por ser asi todo de Justizia y que para ello el Superior Decreto de Vuestra Excellencia señorva el despacho por la presicion en cuios terminos a Vuestra Excellencia suplico se señorva mandar como pedimos y en que reciviremos bien y merzed con Justizia ut supra. Salvador Martinez. Por mis companeros que no saven firmar.

Mexico y Febrero 29 de 1748, como lo piden y sirva el decreto de despacho. Por mando de Su Excellenzia, Don Juan Martinez Soria.

En la Villa de Santa Fee a seis dias del mes de Junio de mil setezientos quarenta y ocho años. Yo el Sargento Maior Don Joachin Codallos y Rabal Governador y Capitan General de este Reino dela Nueva Mexico. Visto el Superior Decreto antecedente del Excellentisimo Señor Virrey de esta Nueva Espana que en dicho dia me demonstraron Salvador Martinez y Thomas Madrid. Dixe que se tendra presente para ynformar a dicho Señor Excellentisimo en orden alo que se dirije la pretenzion delos suplicantes en su escripto lo que se ejecutara en la primera occasion que aya y asi lo provei y firme con los testigos de mi asistenzia con quienes actuo a falta de Escribano Publico o Real que no ay en este Reyno, doi fee. Don Joachin Codallos y Rabal = testigo Phelipe Jacobo de Unanue = testigo Miguel de Alire =

Concuerda este traslado con su original que se devolvio a las partes el dia siete de Junio de mil setezientos quarenta y ocho años, con el que va verdadero correjido y consertado y al verlo sacar fueron testigos Don Joseph Romo de Vera, Gregorio Garduno y Sevastian de Apodaca vezinos dela Villa de Santa Fee, en la que lo firme el dia siete de dicho dia mes y ano con los testigos de mi asistenzia con quienes actuo a falta de Escribano Publico o Real que no ay en este Reyno. Doy fee.
En testimonio de la verdad, lo firme
Joachin Codallos y Rabal (rubric)
testigo testigo
Phelipe Jacobo de Unanue (rubric) Miguel de Alire (rubric)

Notes

1. Tomás Madrid was a presidio soldier living in Pojoaque in 1750. By 1954 he was the commander of the militia. According to Governor Vélez Cachupín, he was "the subject of much valor and honor, and that his robust appearance commanded respect, which is also necessary." In 1780 Madrid sent a petition to Mexico City stating that he could not continue due to his advanced age of seventy-seven (Thomas, *Plains Indians*: 140; Christmas, *Military Records*: 8; SANM I #295).
2. Pedro [Montes] Vigil could have been the person who worked on the restoration of San Miguel chapel in 1710. In the will of cabildo member Salvador Montoya, Salvador stated that he bought a ranch at Tesuque from Pedro Montes Vigil, a resident of La Cañada (Santa Cruz). Vigil was the son of Francisco Montes Vigil I and María Jiménez de Ancizo, from Zacatecas, and a brother of Francisco Montes Vigil II. He was married to Juan Trujillo (Chávez, *Origins*: 312; SANM I #512, WPA translation).
3. The viceroy was the First Count of Revillagigedo.
4. Jacinto Martínez was apparently the paymaster.
5. Don Juan Manuel Martínez Soria appears to be a secretary or other official for the viceroy, perhaps associated with the auditor's office. The viceroy at this time was Juan Francisco de Güemes y Horcasitas, Conde de Revilla Gigedo.
6. See Doc. 34.
7. See Doc. 19.
8. Sebastián de Apodaca was a New Mexico native, marrying Juana Hernández de la Trinidad in 1707. He was in Santa Fe from 1716 to the 1740s, his name frequently appearing as a witness on various documents (Chávez, *Origins*: 127; Kessell et al., *BOB*: 636 n2; SANM I #334, #648).

39

MEXICAN INQUISITION INVESTIGATES BÁRBARA GARCÍA FOR CASTING A SPELL ON HER LOVER; REFERENCE MADE TO SCANDALOUS PRIESTS
October 29, 1751. Source: AGN Inq. L1049 Parte f 89-90.

Synopsis and editor's notes: Bárbara García,[1] a Spanish widow from Sandía, was reported by a neighbor, María Gertrudes Sánchez, also a widow, to be using magic recommended by Catalina Gutiérrez, a third widow. The magic was intended to increase the ardor of her lover, the husband of a woman also from Sandía. García did not deny the allegations, stating that the magic did what it was supposed to, but said that she did not think what she had done was a sin. She said that after her lover's wife complained to her about her husband's decreasing interest, she burned the love potion and told her lover to go back to his wife. The accusation was heard by Fray Pedro Montaño, a representative of the Holy Tribunal of the Inquisition in New Mexico. The names of the husband and wife were not given, following Inquisition procedures for victims.

This example of sexual witchcraft is one of many cases that occurred in New Spain, as cited in witchcraft studies of the seventeenth and eighteenth centuries.[2] These studies point out that while the Inquisition frequently investigated such cases, the inquisitors were likely to attribute the behavior to ignorance, illusion, or superstition. The persons investigated were often treated leniently as long as the accused were penitent. According to Rawlings, the same was true of the Inquisition in Spain (Rawlings, *Spanish Inquisition*: 128-34).

The background to this document, as reflected in the few lines about two other denunciations with which the document begins, was the political rivalry among several Franciscan officials, including Pedro Montaño, Juan Agustín Iniesta, Juan Sáenz de Lezaún, and José de Irigoyen. The situation seems to have been that, while Montaño had argued with governors and community leaders in earlier years (see Doc. 25), he did not support proceedings against Governor Cachupín in the 1750s, when the governor insisted that only he could legitimatize Franciscan mail before it left New Mexico. The effort to denounce Cachupín was supported by the three *frailes* named in this document: Fray Juan Sáenz de Lezaún, Fray José de Irigoyen, and Fray Juan Agustín de Iniesta. Because of Montaño's stand on Cachupín or for other reasons, these three asked for the recall of Montaño. Montaño then countered by accusing Iniesta and Irigoyen of having sexual relations with several women and of fathering their children. In turn Irigoyen accused Montaño himself of living with several different women. The fracas seems to have ended when Montaño was recalled from New Mexico in 1752, the Holy Tribunal of the Inquisition having decided that he had overstepped his authority. It may be that the two denunciations listed at the beginning of this document (but for which no detail was given) were those made against Iniesta and Irigoyen by Montaño. Note that Montaño is the same priest that denounced Pedro García Jurado for wearing his hair in a braid in Document 25. In his notes on colonial burial documents, Fray Angélico Chávez stated that by 1752 the handwriting of Montaño was extremely shaky, his age perhaps another reason for his later recall to Mexico City (Chávez, *Archives*: 239, 252; Greenleaf, "Inquisition": 43-45; Norris, *Year Eighty*: 91, 126-27).

New Mexico ~ Year of 1752

Proceedings brought forth by the Comisario of this Holy Office, Fray Pedro Montaño,[3] regarding a denunciation.

Second Time

against the priest Fray Agustín de Yniesta,[4] of the order of San Francisco in these missions.

Another one
Second Time

The priest Fray Joseph de Irigoyen[5] of the same order,

Also, a denunciation against Bárbara García, of little substance, over superstitions which are included in these proceedings, for which reason the first denunciation was brought forth against Yniesta.
This is no lie, and it was brought before me,
(rubric)

Not knowing how to sign, it was signed by the Reverend Father Comisario before me, the said notary, to which I certify, etc.

Fray Pedro Montaño (rubric)   Before me
Comisario of the Holy Office   Fray Juan Sáenz de Lezaún[6] (rubric)
                                  notary

[Marginal note]
This denunciation is against
Bárbara García and is of little substance.

At this mission of Nuestra Señora de los Dolores y San Antonio de Sandía[7] on the 29th of October, 1751. There appeared before me, the Reverend Father Comisario of the Holy Office of this kingdom, without being called, doña María Gertrudes Sánchez,[8] Spanish, widow and resident of this jurisdiction. She stated that upon examining her conscience, she denounced Bárbara García, who she had heard say that because she was badly in a state of love with a certain man,[9] another woman, her friend, asked her if the said married man loved her a lot, which she [Bárbara] said it appeared that he did according to the feelings that she experienced with him. Notwithstanding, her friend told her that if she wanted him to show more love and affection for her, she should do the following:

When she combed him, she was to take a few hairs from him, tie them in her sash or belt [*faja*], and she would experience how much more he would love her.[10] The said Bárbara García, to see if what her friend had told her would work, did as her friend had said. From all of this she experienced that what her friend had told her was true, finding that her male friend showed her much more love than he had shown before, to the point that he showed little emotion for his wife, not even making love to her. His legitimate wife complained to the said Bárbara García about the lack of love that her husband was showing to her, asking her what her reason was for having his hairs in her belt. Because of this and upon seeing the type of life that his legitimate wife was leading, Bárbara García determined to take the hairs from her belt and burn them in the fire, and she indeed did burn them. When the man went to see her, she told him to go back to his wife. He then did that immediately in order to show his wife the love that he had for her before, which he did in a very distinct manner, and from then on they were once again very much in love.

This is what she heard from the said Bárbara García and was what she denounced, ratifying the sworn statement which she had made. She did not sign it because she did not know how, and it was signed by the said Reverend Father Comisario on the said day, month, and year, etc.

      Fray Pedro Montaño (rubric)
      Comisario of the Holy Office

Done before me, Fray Juan Miguel Menchero (rubric), assigned notary

At this mission of Nuestra Señora de los Dolores y San Antonio de Sandía on the 31st of October, 1751, there appeared, upon being summoned, Bárbara García,

Spanish, widow and a resident of this jurisdiction, before the Reverend Father Comisario of this kingdom. She was asked if she knew why she had been summoned. She responded that she did not. She was then asked if she remembered ever having told anyone during a conversation that she was madly in love with a married man, and another woman, her friend, had asked her if the man loved her very much, and she, Bárbara, told her that he did love her very much. In spite of this, the other person then told her, if you want him to love you more, do the following and he will love you more. The said Bárbara then asked her what it was that she had to do. Her friend told her, when you comb his hair, take a few hairs from him and tie them in your sash and you will see that he will love you even more. The said Bárbara then asked her if this was done as an evil act.[11] Her friend responded that it was not, that it was only to unite them closer. The said Bárbara then took the hairs and tied them in her sash, and it indeed worked according to what her friend had told her. From this point on, the said married man totally abandoned his legitimate wife. The wife then complained to the said Bárbara, being that they were friends, about what had happened with her husband. The said Bárbara then realized that what had happened was due to what she had done with the hairs, and she then and there decided to burn them and return to believing in God. After that she never did that again and proposed never again to do anything like this, which was in opposition to the true doctrine of God. After she had burned the hair, the said married man returned to his wife and repented for what he had done, and stopped being the person that he was with her before the hairs were burned. Bárbara García was then asked who it was who had given her the said remedy. She responded that it was Catarina Gutiérrez,[12] widow, Spanish and a resident of this jurisdiction. She was then asked if she had anything to add or delete. She responded that she did not. She was asked if she would ratify what she had said. She said that she did, regarding the sworn statement that she had given. She did not sign because she did not know how. The said Reverend Father Comisario signed it along with me on the said day, month, and year, etc.

      Fray Pedro Montaño (rubric)
      Comisario of the Holy Office
    Fray Juan Miguel Menchero (rubric)[13]
       assigned notary

[Marginal note]
This Catalina [Gutiérrez] appears to be the same person who denounced Fray Agustín de Yniesta, and as such is credited with having done it.

ORIGINAL DOCUMENT

AGN, Inquisition, Legajo 1049

Nuevo Mexico ~ Año de 1752

Autos formados por el Comisario de este Santo Oficio Fray Pedro Montano sobre denuncia

2a

El Padre Fray Agustin de Yniesta del Orden de San Francisco en aquellas missiones

Otra
2a

El Padre Fray Joseph de Yrigoyen del mismo Orden

Y una denuncia contra Barbara Garcia de poca substancia sobre supesticiones que se inserta en estos autos, por lo que conduce a la primera denuncia contra Yniesta

No es embuste
Ponga en mi lugar
(rubric)

Por no saber firmar lo firmo el Reverendo Padre Comisario ante mi el ynfrascripto Notorio de que doi fee, ut supra.
Fray Pedro Montaño (rubric)
Comisario del Santo Oficio

Ante mi
Fray Juan Saenz De Lazaún (rubric)
Notorio

Esta denuncia es contra
Barbara Garcia de poca
substancia

En esta Mission de Nuestra Senora de los Dolores y San Antonio de Zandia en veinte y nueve dias del mes de Otubre de mil setezientos y cincuenta y un anos parezio Da. Maria Gertrudes Sanchez, Espanola, viuda y bezina de esta jurisdizion sin ser llamada ante el Reverendo Padre Comisario del Santo Ofizio deste Reino y dixo: que extimulada de su conzienzia hazia denunzia de aberle oido dezir a Barbara Garcia que estando la dicha en mala amistad con un ombre, le dixo otra muger su camarada que zi la queria mucho el tal casado aque le respondio que si le parezia la queria segun las finezes que experimintava no obstante le volbio a dezir la dicha camarada si quieres que radique mas su amor y finizar, has esta deligensia. Cuando lo peines toma algunas de sus cavellos y amarrate los en el zendor o faja y esperentaras quanto mucho mas te quiera. Y la dicha Barbara Garcia por ver si era verdad lo que la otra camarada le avia propuesto lo executo segun y como se lo dixo su camarada. Y de los efectos experimento salirle zierto lo que la otra su camarada le avia dicho; pues enzendiendose en mucho mas amor que el que antes le tenia el tal su amigo; llego asta mirar mal a su lexitama muger, perdiendole la voluntad de suerte que no le pagava el devito. Y quexandose la dicha lexitima muger con la dicha Barbara Garcia del desamor con que su marido la tratava, avirtio para si sola, que seria el motivo, la deligenzia que tenia, echaba guardar los cavellos de el dicho en su faja. Por lo que con el o bida dela que la dicha lexitima muger sele quejo determino el sacar dichos cavellos de su faja y quemarlos en la lumber, como defacto los quemo. Y biniendo dicho su amigo a verla le dixo: anda a ver a tu muger, lo que ejecuto el dicho prontamente y la que queria mas antes y le parezia mal experimento de distinto modo y reziprocamente se amaron en adelante. Esto es lo que le oio dezir a dicha Barbara Garcia y lo denunzia ratificandose en ello so cargo del juramento que fecho tiene. No firmo por no saber, frimelo con migo dicho Reverendo Padre Comisario en dicho dia, mes y ano, ut supra.

Fray Pedro Montano (rubric)
Comisario del Santo Officio

Paso ante mi
Fray Juan Miguel Menchero (rubric)
Notario Nombrado

En esta Mision de Nuestra Senora de los Dolores y San Antonio de Zandia en treinta y un dias del mes de Octubre de mill setezientos y cincuenta y un anos parezio siendo llamada Barbara Garcia, Espanola, viuda y bezina de esta jurisdizion ante el Reverendo Padre Comisario de este Reino. Y siedo preguntada si savia para que ere llamada? Respondio que no. Y repreguntada si se acuerda aver dicho a alguna persona en conversacion, que estando en mala amistad con un hombre casado, otra muger camarada le dixo que si la queria mucho dicho su amigo, a que respondio si me quiere, si la otra entonzes le dixo: no obstante haz esta deligenzia y con eso te queria mas; a que le dixo la dicha Barbara que e de hazer? As de tomar los cabellos de este tu amigo quando lo peinares y amarrateis en el zeindor, y versa mas tu quiere. Y entonzes la dicha Barbara le pregunto, si esto es por arte malo? Respondio la camarada que no, y solo si era para que se unieran las voluntades. Y entonzes la dicha Barbara cojio los cabellos y selos amarro en el zeindor. Y que defacto provo ser cierto lo que la camarada le abia dicho; de aqui se siguio el que el dicho hombre casado totalmente ubiese abandonado a su lexitima muger, la que quejandose a dicha Barbara (por tener amistad) de lo que padecia con su marido, advirtio la dicha Barbara, seria efecto de la deligenzia echa de los cabellos; por lo que luego se resolbio a quemarlos, diciendo creo en Dios, y nunca mas volvio a hazerlo y propuesto de detestar qualquiera de esta cosa que se opone a el verdadero culto de Dios. Y luego que quemo dichos cabellos y entonzes el dicho hombre casado abiendo buelto con su muger le paga el devito, sin aquel imposible que antes tenia antes de quemar dichos cabellos. Y preguntada para que dixera quien fue la que le dio el dicho remedio, respondio que Catarina Gutierrez, biuda, Espanola y vezina de esta jurisdizio. Y siendo preguntada si tenia que anadir o quitar? Respondio que no. Y que si se ratificava en lo dicho? Dijo que si, so cargo del juramento que fecho tiene. No firmo por no saber, firmelo el dicho Reverendo Padre Comisario con migo en dicho dia, mes y ano, ut supra.

      Fray Pedro Montaño (rubric)
      Comisario del Santo Oficio

      Paso ante mi
    Fray Juan Miguel Menchero (rubric)
      Notario nombrado

[Marginal note]
Esta Catalina [Gutierez] parece ser la misma que denuncio a Fray Agustin de Yniesta y por consequente paso credito de ver asserlo.

Translated by J. Richard Salazar, Gerald Gonzales, Rob Martinez, and Linda Tigges

Notes

1. While Bárbara García lived at Sandía, a pueblo reestablished for resettlement of the Tiwa Indians by Fray Menchero in 1746, she is described as Spanish. Though she has not been specifically identified, we know that her husband was dead by 1752, the date of this document. She may have been the wife of a Ramón García, with whom she was listed as a godparent in Albuquerque in 1750. More likely, she was the Bárbara García Hurtado who was the second wife of the well-to-do Luis García de Noriega from Albuquerque, who died in 1747 (NMGS, *Aquí*: 193, 476; Chávez, *Origins*: 181-82; Olmstead, *Censuses*: 81).
2. See Tibo Chávez, "Witchcraft": 7-9; Greenleaf, "Inquisition": 31-32; Gutiérrez, "Women": 378-80; McDonald, "Intimacy": 37-38; and Simmons, *Witchcraft*: 20-35. Regarding Abiquiu, see Martinez, "Toledo"; and Ebright and Hendricks, *Witches*. See also the 1708 witchcraft trial of Catarina Luján at San Juan Pueblo, where the defendants were acquitted, and the investigations of accusations of witchcraft at San Ildefonso in 1725, Isleta in 1730, and Santa Ana in 1715 (SANM II #137b, #338, #357, and 364a). Examples of witchcraft in Mexico are cited in Behar, "Sexual Witchcraft": 179-206.
3. See Doc. 25.
4. Fray Agustín de Iniesta professed his faith in Pueblo in 1733, coming to New Mexico in the 1740s. He was appointed notary of the Holy Tribunal of the Inquisition in 1744. He remained in New Mexico and was at San Felipe in 1754 and Santa Ana in 1756 (Chávez, *Origins*: 36; Norris, *Year Eighty*: 20).

5. Fray José de Irigoyen came to New Mexico sometime between 1719 and 1725. He is known as being fluent in the various Tano language subgroups. In 1744 and 1745 he accompanied Fray Delgado on expeditions to the Hopis and Navajos. In 1750, perhaps because of the controversy described above, he was removed from his post in Albuquerque. By 1760 Governor Cachupín reported that Irigoyen was sixty-three years old (Norris, *Year Eighty*: 92, 99, 105-6, 126, 140).
6. Fray Juan Sáenz de Lezaún was also appointed a notary of the Holy Tribunal in 1744, coming to New Mexico in the 1704s. He wrote a negative account of New Mexico in 1760, but it is not known whether he was living there at the time (Greenleaf, "Inquisition": 43; Norris, *Year Eighty*: 108; Hackett, *Historical Documents*: 468).
7. Sandía Pueblo was reestablished in 1746 by Fray Menchero as a mission for the Tiwa. It was also to serve as a bulwark for residents living on the Río Grande against the Faraón Apaches. In 1680, at the time of the revolt, Sandía was one of the largest of the southern Tiwa pueblos, which included Alameda, Puaray, and Isleta. In the mid-eighteenth century, there were Spanish settlers in the area, as shown by the documents about inheritance and about complaints of encroachment on their land by the new pueblo (Norris, *Year Eighty*: 106, 116; Hackett, *Historical Documents*: 472; Kessell and Hendricks, *RCR*: 126 n19; SANM I #414, #532; SANM II, #486).
8. María Gertrudes Sánchez may have been the daughter of José Sánchez and Teresa Jaramillo, born in 1731. If so, her grandfather was Jacinto Sánchez de Iñigo, a presidio soldier and native New Mexican who returned to New Mexico by 1696. In 1713 he was the alcalde of Santa Cruz, later settling in the Río Abajo area (Chávez, *Origins*: 280; Kessell et al., *BOB*: 565 n33).
9. The document does not provide the name of the man or his wife. According to Stanley Hordes, standard practice for the Inquisition was not to name the persons that were the target of the magic (personal communication, June 12, 2012).
10. Behar cites a related but more complicated case from Querétaro, México, where a woman was told that to change her husband's behavior she should wrap one of his hairs around the neck of a frog and run a thorn from its head to its feet, causing the man to waste away (Behar, "Sexual Witchcraft": 190).
11. García appears to be asking whether her act was considered a mortal sin, and therefore worthy of investigation by the Inquisition's courts.
12. Catarina Gutiérrez was a cook for the household of Pedro Varela, a resident of Sandía. It is of interest that in 1751–1752, Fray Montaño used an accusation of a certain Jacinto Gutiérrez of Sandía Pueblo to slander Fray Iniesta. Jacinto had accused Fray Iniesta of trying to recruit him to poison the stew of a certain Pedro de Varela so that Iniesta could continue a liaison with Pedro's wife, Casilda Gonzáles, a sorceress and Iniesta's mistress. A poisonous plant was to be added to the stew by Varela's cook, Catarina Gutiérrez, also a mistress of Iniesta. Catarina Gutiérrez swore that she had refused to use the plant in the stew. She also said that Fray Iniesta was her confessor and that she had conceived children by him. It is not known if she was related to Jacinto Gutiérrez (Greenleaf, "Inquisition": 43-44).
13. Fray Juan Miguel Menchero was named notary for Fray Montaño after Montaño complained that Frailes Iniesta and Sáenz de Lezaún were working against him. Menchero was born in Castile, professing in 1714. Members of his family were merchants from Mexico City. He was in New Mexico by 1729, carrying out an inspection. He headed a successful mission to the Navajos in 1746 and a second mission to the Gilas in 1748. The well-known 1746 Menchero map was prepared as a result of his travels (Norris, *Year Eighty*: 190-93, 99-100, 107, 117; Wheat, *Mapping*, 84).

40

DEAL MADE BETWEEN TRADERS FALLS APART; BLACKSMITH PETITIONS GOVERNOR VÉLEZ CACHUPÍN
May 24–November 3, 1752. Source: SANM II #520.

*ynopsis and editor's notes*: This document includes much information on trading in New Mexico but is so complicated that a detailed synopsis is provided.

Salvador García, a blacksmith and trader, said that earlier in 1752, he and don Juan García de la Mora ratified a contract in Albuquerque to divide the profits from trade with the Indians at Zuni, with Salvador contributing three *arrobas* (seventy-five pounds) of iron and his blacksmithing work. De la Mora was to provide six arrobas of iron. Salvador said that de la Mora then advanced him 100 pesos in goods (*lienza*, or canvaslike cloth*)* as a loan which Salvador would pay back from the profits from the ironwork at Zuni. The deal was that the trading could start when de la Mora returned to Albuquerque by May of 1752, presumably with his share of the iron. Then Salvador and de la Mora would go together to Zuni. According to Salvador, the agreement was that if de la Mora did not return, then he would lose the value of 100 pesos worth of goods in addition to any profits Salvador had made on these goods. Salvador seemed to consider the loan of 100 pesos in goods evidence of the contract. Then de la Mora sent a note to Salvador saying that he would be delayed because of illness. He never did show up, so Salvador petitioned the governor for what amounted to a lawsuit for a breach of contract. Salvador claimed that de la Mora owed 250 pesos, of which Salvador said he would credit de la Mora for the 100 pesos for the goods that were advanced to him.

De la Mora had a different version of what happened. He said that at the time he had been interested in such a deal, but there never was any written agreement. He had given Salvador 100 pesos worth of goods, but they were for some sheep that Salvador sold him and were not to be paid back by the profits from the blacksmithing trip to Zuni. De la Mora also said that he had promised some iron and his own blacksmithing equipment to a certain Juan de Leyba, who also wanted to go to the Indians and make and sell iron goods, and that there never was any written agreement with Salvador. De la Mora agreed that he said he would return in May or early June, barring any illness, but he did become ill for three months, during which time he wrote Salvador a letter explaining this. (The letter is attached at the end of the document.)

Salvador continued to argue that there had been an agreement, and that the 100 pesos of goods were not given to him for the sheep, but were a loan to be paid for by the profits from the iron work. In addition to the arrobas of iron, Salvador said that he was to take along three servants when going to trade, and that de la Mora would provide one servant. Salvador also stated that while he was waiting for de la Mora and did not trade with the Indians, he lost a profitable contract with don Bernardo Miera y Pacheco, and that, illness or not, the contract still stood. This section of the document is especially rambling and convoluted, perhaps reflecting Salvador's frustration about the missed opportunity to sell his goods and the loss of revenue.

Eventually, both men seem to more or less agree on what was discussed at their meeting in Albuquerque, but they did not agree about a final contract. The testimony by one and then the other went on. De la Mora said that no final contract was made and that Salvador's story kept changing. He added that he was a guest at the house of Salvador, that they were just talking, and that Salvador owed him 100 pesos for the goods. Salvador disagreed with the notion that they were just talking.

In the end, Governor Cachupín, apparently tired of hearing the two testify against each other, ordered that there be perpetual silence between the two traders. He also ordered that de la Mora owed Salvador nothing, and that Salvador owed de la Mora 100 pesos for the goods. Cachupín concluded by stating that there was no written agreement and that, besides, neither one had a license to trade with the Indians.

Among other things, this case shows the risk of making deals with a fellow traveler, or at least of assuming that deals were made. It also shows the entrepreneurial attitude of Salvador García, and probably others like him, in taking his equipment and raw materials to the Indians rather than waiting for the Indians to come to him. This apparently was not uncommon, since de la Mora also said that he had blacksmithing equipment that could also be used by Juan de Leyba to work iron for the Indians. While the document has repetitive and sometimes difficult and even incoherent sections, it shows how the traders of the time worked, and how precarious the business could be for either party.

Year of 1752

Case: Salvador García [de Noriega][1] vs. don Juan García de la Mora[2]

[I] Salvador García, resident of the villa of Alburquerque, in my best and proper form for which there is a reason, appear before your honor and say that having concluded a contract of agreement with don Juan García de la Mora, resident of the jurisdiction of La Cañada [Santa Cruz], to divide equally the profits which are produced by my personal work in the profession of a blacksmith, along with three arrobas[3] of iron, and the said don Juan de la Mora, with six arrobas, of the same [iron], which deal we entered into when we returned, along with a number of residents who had gone out of this kingdom. Upon the return to the said villa of Alburquerque, where I remained, he, García de la Mora, proceeded to my house in the said jurisdiction; and at the time of his departure we ratified a contract, with the understanding that he, the said Mora, would return to Albuquerque from La Cañada by the middle of May of this same year [1752], and if he did not return, he would lose the quantity of one hundred pesos, which in effects of the land [goods] he advanced to me, along with half of the profits which were gained [on the goods], and anything else that we made.

As it was, he did not return during the month of May, nor at any time thereafter, as I awaited his arrival. Therefore, I sent him a notice with Antonio Martín,[4] a resident from the same area, but he has never shown up. Because I wanted to fulfill my end of the contract, I did not want to enter into another one with don Bernardo de Miera [y Pacheco],[5] resident of this Kingdom, now residing in El Paso, in which I would have gained considerably at Zuni, as I annually make up to five hundred pesos during the time that I seasonally do work in that area, as is well known by all of the residents of Alburquerque. All of this I made known to him, García de la Mora, so that he should pay me the amount of two hundred and fifty pesos, which is half of what I would have made by doing the work as usual, and is what I state in my formal and juridical petition as is necessary.

Of your honor I ask and seek that you demand that the said don Juan García de la Mora, according to what he has sworn, comply with the law and agree with the intent of this written [agreement] and agree to pay me the said two hundred and fifty pesos, of which I agreed to promptly credit him the one hundred pesos which is due to him, and if he has to borrow the same, he should do it before your honor as conveniently as he can, so that his majesty is aware of it, until something else is ordered. All of which I ask is done in justice and I swear to God and to the Cross that it is not done in malice, but for what is necessary, etc.

Salvador García Noriega (rubric)

Santa Fe, September 24, 1752

The alcalde mayor of the villa of Santa Cruz de la Cañada, don Juan Joseph Lovato,[6] is to receive the declaration which is asked for according to this written document, and having done so, he will report to me. I thus approved, ordered it, and [it] was signed by me, don Thomas Vélez Cachupín, governor of this kingdom, acting with my two assisting witnesses due to the lack of a scribe, which there is none in this kingdom, to which I certify.

Vélez Cachupín (rubric)

Thomas de Alvear y Collado (rubric) Nicolás de Ortiz (rubric)

At this puesto of Nuestra Señora de la Soledad del Río Arriba,[7] on the 27th day of September, 1752, I, Juan Joseph Lovato, alcalde mayor and war captain of all this jurisdiction attending to the order expressed by don Thomas Vélez Cachupín, governor and captain general of this kingdom, made appear before me the captain don Juan García de la Mora, whom I certify that I know. Upon being present I received his sworn statement which he made according to his right, and by which he promised to tell the truth in what he knew and what he was asked, as was stated and presented by Salvador García.

I, García de la Mora, said that having stayed at the house of the complainant, after arriving from being out of the kingdom, and my occupation being that of a merchant and more specifically for over seven years having sold my merchandise in the villa of Alburquerque, the complainant asked if I could supply him with some goods. Which, as I have done on other occasions, when I provided him with one hundred pesos for fifty sheep, which he gave me in the form of large rams from Zuni, telling me how he acquired them, by taking his blacksmith equipment and three *arrobas* of iron which he had in his possession. To this I answered that I would not be in the wrong by not supplying him with what I had, as I already had promised to deal what I had to the blacksmith Juan de Leyba,[8] so that he [Juan de Leyba] would take my blacksmith equipment and the iron which I had left over from mining so that he could make the same trip. If this was necessary to prove, I would prove the truth with the said Leyba and the servants belonging to Gabaldón.

I then told the complainant that I was not totally contracted with Leyba and stated that if he was interested I could give him three arrobas of iron and some other blacksmith equipment, and that we could be partners and divide that which God promised, if he would do his best to get it, and that he could pay me from the profits which were made. He asked me when I could return. I told him sometime in May or at the beginning of June, barring any illnesses or obligations. I state that he falsely argues that the obligation was to follow the written agreement or some other instrument of compromise so that we would have to agree one with the other. But it is not like that at all, [since] we agreed that it would be according to the time, and barring any illnesses that God can give to his beings. And it being public knowledge, like it is in this jurisdiction, that Our Lord inflicted me with an illness that kept me for over three months without leaving my house, as is known by you, sir alcalde mayor. I have complied by writing to the complainant telling him about my illness so that he would not think that I had neglected him, which letter he confessed to our majesty that he had received. This letter I request be attached to these proceedings, so that the governor and captain general can see the falseness of what the complainant seeks, and so that it is not incumbent upon me to justify if he should have or not have the two hundred and fifty pesos which he asks for, as I am not at fault of said charge by the said letter.[9] I do not ask for the justification of the profits that I should have on my part. This is what I declare *verbo ad verbum* [word for word] according to what I state.

Upon having read this statement back to him, García de la Mora declared that it was his, and he affirmed and ratified it as many times as is required according to his right. He said that he was fifty years of age, and he signed along with me, the alcalde mayor, and the assisting witnesses with whom I act due to the lack of a royal and public scribe, which there is none within the limits over which he has the right, it is thus done, etc., to which I certify.

Juan Joseph Lovato (rubric)
Presiding judge

Juan García de la Mora (rubric) Witness
Juan Domingo Lovato (rubric) Witness
Francisco Sisneros (rubric) Witness

Continuing, I, the said alcalde mayor, submitted these proceedings to don Thomas Vélez Cachupín, governor and captain general of this kingdom, so that upon his review your honor can determine what is required, which as usual he will decide for the best, and so that it is valid I signed it as I am authorized to do so, etc., to which I certify.

Juan Joseph Lovato (rubric)
Presiding judge
Juan Domingo Lovato (rubric) Francisco Sisneros (rubric)

On the 3rd day of October, 1752, I ordered that it be sent to the other party, and I thus approved it and rubricated it, don Thomas Vélez Cachupín, governor of this kingdom of New Mexico.

Vélez Cachupín (rubric)

Governor and captain general

[I] Salvador García de Noriega, resident of the villa of Alburquerque in my best form and right and protesting to that which pertains to me so that I can use it whenever and however it is necessary, appear before your honor due to the document which your honor sent to me regarding the declaration made by don Juan García de la Mora involving the request made by me before the alcalde mayor of that villa. I state that I do not accept that statement due to the fact that it is not favorable to me because of my age and the lack of the truth as is seen in the form and in the following manner.

In the first place, that which he states that I asked him for some goods for which I supplied him with fifty sheep is not true, because the goods that he provided for me which amounted to one hundred pesos in the value of land were not given to me but were advanced to me as is the practice in this area among those who are occupied in their business or other ministers, to other persons, and which is currently and primarily carried out in this kingdom; and more so when they have to leave their homes to go to other places, and this type of payment is not done so with sheep. The payment is carried out by paying half of what was due according to what my personal work would produce with the six arrobas of iron which he had, and the three that I had, along with the two *mosos* [servants or young persons] which I would take with me, and another one which Mora was to provide on his behalf.

Also, the time that he was supposed to have come [to Albuquerque] so that we could go to Zuni was to have been the middle of May, during which time I waited for him, and because he did not show up within the required time, nor has he done so up to now, as is known through the paper which is included, I did not go to Zuni. It was agreed that I would wait for him to come to Alburquerque, which is the place where we agreed to meet for the said trip, and to secure the contract. For this reason I did not confirm with don Bernardo de Miera a contract which he wanted to make, which would have been very profitable, and could have been done at the time.

No written contract was ever made because it was not determined what part would be performed by whom. To this day it bothers me a lot, because it was decided that I was to be the consenter as it would have made it easier to bring everything together and would not have to provide the witnesses which I should have had at the time. That which he argues about having been inflicted with an illness for the period of three months does not provide an argument, as not even death does away with honorable contracts which can be complied with by the administrators, as in this case anyone could have been named by him to go to Zuni and thus benefit from what was gained, and I the half which was due to me.

I ask of the other party if he had not fulfilled the contract because of his illness or other accident or because he was a bad correspondent, and as such what was required would not be an obligation to be fulfilled, which is the reason for persons to go into contracts, as if one person does not comply, the rights of the contract go into effect.

He also states that he had complied by having written me a note informing me about his illness, so that it was not considered to be a wrongdoing, and which was attached to the proceedings. To this I respond that the note was dated the 9th of July, and I received it on August 5th, as has been noted and signed by me in the margin, to which in fulfillment I swear to God, Our Lord, and to the Holy Cross to be the truth. It is plausible that the date could have been written to accommodate him so as to set forth an excuse for his failure to comply with his obligation to show up as promised [in May], and as such not be compelled to pay by right and to be attentive to what is expressed in a formal and juridical petition which cannot be judiciously neglected.

To your honor I ask and petition that you determine and order as I seek, which is in justice. I swear to what is required and it is certainly not [done] in malice, etc.

 Salvador García de Noriega (rubric)

Santa Fe, October 26, 1752

It [the proceedings] is included with the part that goes to don Juan García de la Mora, so that within the term of his right, he will respond to it, and be placed with the order of the document and will serve to present it to me, and he shall be informed to appear before me at this villa, or to represented by an attorney in fulfillment of this proceeding. I thus approved and signed it, don Thomas Vélez Cachupín, governor of this kingdom of New Mexico.

 Vélez Cachupín (rubric)

Governor and captain general

Juan García de la Mora, native of the kingdom of Castile,[10] and resident of this kingdom, as one who complies with justice without having my rights denied or lacking in its defense, and in complying with my rights, I present myself before your honor and say this: That your honor, having given me a copy of the demand which Salvador García, which, not having said the truth in the demand which he made some twenty-three days after your honor gave him a copy of my statement, appears to me to be in expiration of the time period and thus a delay in the time which he has to pay me for my linens,[11] in spite of the false circumstances which are alleged.

I will now respond to his allegations point by point. First, he denies that the said linens[12] were given to him on a promissory basis; however, this is the way that business is practiced in this area among those who are in the business, etc. He says that this is due to the fact that I was consistently absent and [did not respond], but with this outrageous [statement], with all due respect, who is to say that this is a truth which cannot be doubted? To this, sir, I answer that it is totally false; as to all of what is stated in any instance and argument there are no such creditors, or lenders in this kingdom, as everyone knows. No similar deal has been practiced [for example] for a sword, it being done only to confuse with the knowledge that your honor has to realize in the reasoning and justice which you give to everyone in order to have justice within your administration, seeking within your knowledge to come up with the truth from all of the allegations which are made.[13] If your honor attends to that that is brought up in this first point by Salvador, and also to what is demanded of me in his first complaint, your honor shall find in the first point that he was only to perform his personal work [blacksmithing] and come up with three arrobas of iron. Then, in the following instance, he states that he was to take two additional servants, a variance and deviation from the said deal, [and] he lets his malice be known by proceeding with what follows in his [conveniently] short memory so that he can benefit from his lies, and as if it was necessary that I was to admit to the two servants so that he can prove what he states.

In regard to the second point that he brings up which deals with my note, which is attached to these proceedings and which gives the reasons for my not having gone [to meet him], what I have stated is the truth, and which I now bring forth. I decline to respond to the charge of having gone or not having gone, and I only respond as to the time. To this I say that in all of his statements there is not lacking such a thing as a lie; as he states that I was to have gone [to Albuquerque] by the middle of May. This not the way it was, as I told him it would be sometime during the entire month of May or the beginning of June, barring any illness. In any case everything else concerning the deal is false, including the obligation which was supposed to have occurred, and everything which he states is in his favor. The reason for my not going can be verified by my illness.

As for not concluding the deal with don Bernardo de Miera y Pacheco, it was not up to me, nor do I know if it was true or not that the deal was not finalized or even brought forth. As he claims in his first complaint, he looks forward to any contingencies or for Indian volunteers to purchase or not purchase anything from them, which is something I ignore totally. As for what he says why no written contract was made, it was because I did not want one and did not want to say who would be the purchaser [*habiador*] and who would be the tenderer [*habiado*], and that it would require too much from such an arrangement. I say, sir, that it is not true that within the instance of such a deal there has not been named a purchaser or a tenderer but only that simple agreement as I have stated and that neither he nor I would be responsible in case of any contingencies or any other incidental thing for which we would be responsible, but which would only be according to a compromise, and not anything that I would do on my own. I did not ask of the other party what security and interest I would be assured of by him, or what I would assure for him. If it was clear (which it is not) where we would get the amount of two hundred and fifty pesos, and I was to take (as it is also supposed) six arrobas of iron along with a servant, which is the truth, and which as such it would be more expensive for me to make the trip, because six arrobas of iron put to use at home would make me three hundred knives, and as a result would give me three hundred pesos of the land, and by including the salary of a servant, it would be more than that which I would realize and more than I would have to come forth with, and difficult to figure why I would want to do something as to obligate me to be so foolish. I do not think that I am such a fool. Even if I was such a fool, I would not let him have my goods so that he can continue to carry on with his accusations.

As for what he says concerning what I can gain from complaining about my illnesses, stating that not even death can do away with contracts, as administrators can see to it that they are complied with, and to what he adds that another person could have gone in my absence. To this I answer, in the first place this contract was never made, nor should it be given the name of a contract but merely a proposition of agreement to do something together, or trying to find something, and this was what we decided as a guest of the said complainant and which we did on that particular night as a way of conversation and a way of letting me know how much I owed him, and which the following morning I gave to him, but not as he says, as a way of owing to him, which should never be done. So that as he says that my administrators (in case of death) would be obligated to the said contract, and that he would be honored to proceed (as I have stated in my declaration) with a juridical instrument of witnesses on both parts in which case we would call it an honorable contract and all of those circumstances that he wants from our simple conversation which we had concerning the said badly planned trip.

As for having sent a person in my place, I say that I am so scared of sending any person to care for any of my businesses that I would never do that because I could not confide in them in what would be required of the trip. There are some goods that cannot be given an instant price, unless it would be something such as an Indian wanting a knife [*cuchillo*], another one wanting a hatchet [*hachita*], another one a [*coa*], etc., and credit for any other items would be allowed only to reliable persons. This cannot be done with everyone, and the ones that it can be done with have to be men of honor. Anyone who would do this would have to do this the same as if they were doing it for themselves at home, and these types of persons would not want to work for me for a salary. Anyone wanting to complain about any of this would look for me to do so, and they would not deal with anyone whom I would send as a replacement, and as I was not forced to do any such thing, I did not do it, or even think of doing it.

Regarding the question which he brings up concerning the issue of being absent due to an illness, I say that I would not have allowed it if it was done through a written contract, which is the reason that contracts are written, to obligate the person and the goods. I say, sir, that I would have never done it, as I would never scrupulously stoop so low as to place such an unjust demand in order to gain fame or notoriety for the lack of a conscience. I also state that if he had taken another course in order to avoid paying me for the reason that I presented in my note, and the reason of my illness, the trip would have been belated but it could have still been done. At this point he will not receive anything, as I ask your honor, that upon the case being decided (as I believe it will according to my honesty and justice) in my favor, he will submit to me, for the commercial goods, one hundred [pesos] in the value of the land.[14]

In response to the reference to my note, in which he questions the date of the 9th of July, and he not having received it until the 5th of August, I will totally ignore it. I say sir, that I have sent a representative to the Río Abajo along with three other documents including yours, which the same carrier is taking to various subjects regarding other business dealing with wool which I have there, and there being no suspicion other than what is made by him, he will be left out along with his unproven malice and my note left ignored. It could be possible that his notation, which I also protest, but which could have been possible, was found with his notation. I am persuaded that his notation is made with the most fundamental ones, as he swears it is certain; I also swear unequivocally that it is as I see it annotated. I will also swear that I received the said note on the date that it was annotated. As for what he says that the note will not be favorable to me because I did not deliver it on time, and that from that day forth it constitutes the belief for that which is demanded, I say sir, that he is not the judge, nor can he be for that specific cause which is placed into force, nor can he deny my right so strongly, nor suppose that his lies, which are to be seen by your honor; and your honor having seen as is expressed, the recognition of the malice which was brought forth against me in that which is my possession in the most formal and juridical petition, as is necessary.

To your honor I ask and seek that you be pleased to do the justice which I ask for with this, and I swear that this document is not in malice but in protest, and for what is necessary, etc.

Juan García de la Mora (rubric)

Definitive Order

In the villa of Santa Fe, on the 3rd day of the month of November, 1752. Having seen this document and everything which is herein contained in this summarized article, I say that having permitted the many inconveniences which resulted from the proceedings in this instance because it was such a prolific investigation, and because of the need for the large amount of time for the arguments, and because it could never be conveniently agreed since there was no document that was relative to what was argued, and being the complaint is founded in the most reasonable considerations which are interpreted by the complainant regarding the contingencies which can be proven, and because of the lack of a license and a permit from this government for the entry, which is prohibited without my knowing it, along with the other defects which are contained in the procedure, I order and do order that perpetual silence be placed on this matter and that no other document be brought forth nor any other recourse be placed on it [the case]. In relation to the one hundred pesos for the goods, which the said Salvador García confesses to have received, he will return to don Juan García de la Mora within five months, which are to be counted forth from this date, and I say that the two parties are to make do and agree to things, as they see best. This order is to be made known to the *teniente* of the alcalde mayor of this villa. I thus ordered it, don Thomas Vélez Cachupín, governor of this kingdom of New Mexico, acting with my two assisting witnesses, to which I certify.

Thomas Vélez Cachupín (rubric)

Witnesses
Nicolás de Ortiz (rubric) Thomas de Alvear y Collado (rubric)

[Note from de la Mora to Salvador García, July 9, 1752]

Señor, Salvador García. Friend and gentleman of mine, I have been so ill with pain since I arrived at my home that I have not felt well for at least one day. Twice I have escaped death, but always in continual pain, with the hope that eventually I will be fine, so that I can go to the Río Abajo. Now that I see that I cannot, I inform your excellency so that you can proceed with your work and your travel and so that you can do otherwise. I remain as such to serve our majesty and pray to God to guard him for many years. Río Arriba, July 9, 1752. I kiss the hand of our majesty. Your friend and servant.

Juan García de la Mora (rubric)

[Marginal note]
On this the fifth day of August, 1752, I received this note and I signed it.
Salvador García (rubric)

ORIGINAL DOCUMENT

Año de 1752

Ordinario: Salvador Garcia contra Dn. Juan Garcia de la Mora
Salvador Garcia vecino de la Villa de Alburquerque en la mejor forma via y forma que aia lugar en derecho paresco ante Vuestra Señoria y digo que abiendo selebrado pacto y combenio con don Juan Garcia de la Mora vecino de la jurisdiccion de la Cañada a partir ygualmente de ganancias de las que produjen mi travajo personal en el oficio de herrero juntamente con tres arrobas de hierro y el dicho don Juan de la Mora seis arrobas de dicho genero cuia ajuste tubimos viniendo entre la becindad que sale deste Reyno para tierra afuera y habiendo llegado de torna biaje a dicha Villa de Alburquerque me quede en ella y el suso dicho paso para su casa en la dicha jurisdiccion y al tiempo de su propartida se ratifico el contracto poniendo por condicion que el dicho Mora habia de benir ha Alburquerque ha mediado del mes de Mayo del mismo ano y que sino benia habia de perder la cantidad de cien pesos que a precios de la tierra me adelanto en cuenta de dicha mitad de ganancias con mas lo que se regulara tocarme del monton de ellas y es asi que no solo no bino por el mes de Mayo pero ni por otros despues estando yo esperandolo y enbiandole a rrequeria por recado que le enbie con Antonio Martin su becino y que lo es de aquella jurisdiccion siempre esperandolo: por cumplir mi palabra y con el pacto que assi teniamos otorgado en fuersa del cual no quise ajustar otro con Dn. Bernardo de Miera residente en este Reyno y vecino de El Paso en que hubiera tenido mucho logro en Suni [Zuni] como annualmente lo tengo de quinientos pesos en la temporada que halli me ocupo en mi oficio como es publico y notorio a todos los vecinos de Alburquerque de todo lo cual sale por concecuencia que lo doi acredor y me devera pagar la cantidad de docientos y cincuenta pesos que es la mitad de lo que me hubiere logrado en cuya atencion y abiendo por el esprecio el mas formal y juridico pedimento que necesario sea =

A Vuestra Señoria pido y suplico se sirva demandar que el dicho Dn. Juan Garcia de la Mora con juramento que aga conforme ala Ley declare al tenor de este escrito y confesando llanamente sele requiera me pagere luego dichos docientos y cincuenta pesos que estoy pronto a abonarle los dichos cien pesos que me anticipo y que si tubiere que pedir lo aga ante Vuestra Señoria como le conbenga Su Magestad ynorar asta que por Vuestra Señoria otra cosa se mande que todo es de justicia que pido y juro a Dios y a la Cruz no ser de malicia y en lo necesario, ut supra.

Salvador Garcia Noriega (rubric)

Santa Fee 24 de Septiembre de 1752
Cometiese al Alcalde Mayor de la Villa de la Cañada Dn. Juan Joseph Lovato reciva la declarasion que se pide al tenor de este escripto y fecho me de cuenta con ello. Asi

lo probehi, mande y firme yo Dn. Thomas Velez Cachupin Governador de este Reyno actuando con dos testigos de asistencia por la notoria falta de escribano que no lo ay en el Reyno, doi fee =

Velez Cachupin (rubric)

Thomas de Alvear y Collado (rubric) Nicolas de Ortiz (rubric)

En este Puesto de Nuestra Señora de la Soledad de el Rio Arriba en beinte y siete dias del mes de Septiembre de mill sietezientos y sinquenta y dos años, yo Juan Joseph Lobato Alcalde Mayor y Capitan Aguerra de toda esta jurisdiccion atento a el auto del suso expresado por el Señor Dn. Thomas Velez Cachupin, Governador y Capitan General de este Reyno Dn. Thomas Velez Cachupin Governador y Capitan General de este Reyno hize comparezer por ante mi al Capitan Dn. Juan Garcia de la Mora aquien doy fee conosco; y presente le recevi juramento que hizo en toda forma de derecho y por el prometio de dezir verdad en lo que supiera y fuera preguntado; y siendolo al thenor de el escrito que antesede presentado por Salvador Garcia, dixo: que haviendo llegado a hospedarse a casa de el querellante biniendo de tierra afuera y siendo mi tratado el de mercader y mui en particular haver mas de siete años que fio mis mercansias en la Villa de Alburquerque me pidio dicho querellante le supliesse unos generos; los que (como otras vezes he hecho) le supli sien pesos para sinquenta carneros, facilitandome su paga con carneros grandes de Suni [Zuni] platicandome el modo que tenia de conseguirlos llendo a Suni [Zuni] con su fragua y tres arrobas de fierro que tenia que llevar; aculla propuesta le respondi que estaba por no suplirselos por que no me fuera a hazer mala obra en la que ya havia pasado y medio tratado con el herrero Juan de Leyba, de pasar con mi fragua y el fierro que teni que me havia quedado de la mineria para hazer el mismo viaje, como si nesessario fuera probare esta verdad con el mismo Leyba y los mozos de Gabaldon; y que a causa de no haver quedado asentado en el todo el trato con dicho Leyba, le dixe al querellante que si le parecia que pusiera yo otras tres arrobas de fierro y fragua y que yriamos a medias como el dise de las buscas que Dios fuera servido de darnos y que de su mitad podria pagarme la expresada cantidad, lo que ase puesto diciendome que para quando podria benir, a que le respondi que en todo Mayo o principios de Junio, salvo accidentes, y sin la obligacion que hablando con el devido respecto falzamente alega pues en tal caso que assi fuera tan creida obligacion haria de preceder escriptura o otra algun ynstrumento de compromiso para que el uno al otro nos pudiermos compeler, pero como no es assi no lo hizimos si no es que (como dicho es) quedamos en el trato que contingencias del tiempo y de los accidentes que Dios puede embiar a las criatures; y siendo publico como lo es en esta jurisdiccion haverme embiado Su Magestad el de un dolor que me tubo mas de tres meses sin salir de casa como a Usted le consta (Señor Alcalde Mayor) cumpli con haverle escrito a dicho querellante un papel dandole parte de mi accidente para que no sele siguiera mala obra caso que no pudiera esperar mi mejoria cullo papel confesso haver recevido delante de Vuestra Majestad el que pido se acumule a estas dilixencias, para con el ser ci orar al Señor Governador y Capitan General lo falzo de el pedimento de el dicho querellante y por que no me yncumbe el justificar si tiene o no pudiera tener los dozientos y sinquenta pesos de logro por quedar desvanecido el dicho cargo con el expresado papel no pido sobre el particular justificazion de ganancias que tengo por dudosas por ser contingentes esto es lo que declara de verbo adberbum desde la palabra dixo. Y siendole leyda esta su declarazion la conosio por sulla y en ella se afirma y ratifica quantas vezes se nesesitare segun derecho dixo ser de edad de sinquenta años y la firmo con migo el expressado Alcalde Mayor y los testigos de mi asistencia con quienes actuo por falta de escribano Real y Publico que no los ay en las distancias que prebiene el derecho y es fecho ut supra que de todo doi fee.

      Juan Jose Lovato (rubric)
      Juez receptor
      Juan Garcia deLa Mora (rubric)

Testigo
Juan Domingo Lovato (rubric)
Testigo
Francisco Zisneros (rubric)

Yncontinenti yo el expresado Alcalde Mayor hize remizion de estas dilixencias al Señor Dn. Thomas Velez Cachupin Governador y Capitan General de este Reyno para que en su vista determine Su Señoria lo que combenga que sera como siempre lo mejor y para que conste lo firme con la actuazion sobre dicha, fecha ut supra, de que doi fee.

      Juan Joseph Lovato (rubric)
      Juez receptor
    Juan Domingo Lovato (rubric) Francisco Zisneros (rubric)

En tres dias del mes de Octubre de mil setecientos y cincuenta y dos años mande corra traslado con la otra parte y asi lo probehi y rubrique yo Dn. Thomas Velez Cachupin Governador de este Reyno de la Nueva Mexico.
      Velez Cachupin (rubric)

Señor Salvador Garcia. Amigo y Señor mio an sido tantos los dolores que me an perseguido desde que bine a mi casa que no ha tenido un dia de descanso, dos beses me ebute a la muerte y siempre de continuo mi dolor pegado con la esperanza de mas oy y mas manana seme quitara para poder yr a el Rio Abajo = Y aora que ya estoy biendo que no puedo abiso a Vuestra Magestad para que no se le siga mala obra en su biaje y tome otra determinazion. Ya quedo para servir a Vuestra Magestad y rogando a Dios mele guarde muchos años. Rio Arriva y Julio 9 de 1752. Beso la mano de Vuestra Magestad. Su seguro amigo y servidor.

       Juan Garcia de la Mora (rubric)

[Marginal note]
Oy sinco de Agosto de 1752 años recevi este papel y lo firme.
Salvador Garcia (rubric)

Señor Governador y Capital General
  Salvador Garcia de Noriega vecino de la Villa de Alburquerque como mejor aia lugar en derecho y portestando a salvo las que me combengan para usar de ellas como y quando me sea nesserarios paresco ante Vuestra Señoria supuesto el traslado que Vuestra Señria se sirvio mandarme dar dela declarasion fecha por Dn. Juan Garcia de la Mora de mi pedimento por ante el Alcalde Mayor de aquella Villa. Digo que no acepto dicha declarazion mas que en lo que me fuere favorable por ser de los años y contra berdad como se expendera en la forma y manera siguiente.
  Lo primero por que lo que acienta de que yo le pedi unos generos que me supliese por cinquenta carneros es falso, por que los generos que me dio que ympartaron cien pesos a precios de la tierra no fueron fiados sino por modo de abio como se practica en esta tierra entre los que ocupan en sus oficios y demas ministerios a otras personas y este es corriente y principio a centadissimo en este Reyno y mas cuando an de salir de sus casas para otros lugares y para dicha paga no ai tales carneros, sino que la refenda cantidad se habia de pagar de la mitad que me tocava en lo que prodiojese mi trabajo personal sus seis arrobas de hierro y las tres mias y dos mosos que yo tambien llebaba y otro que el dicho Mora habia de poner por su parte.
  Lo otro por que el tiempo en que habia de haber benido para que fuesemos a Suni [Zuni] habia de aber cido amediado de Mayo y estube esperandolo y no bino como costa de su papel que con la solemnidad nesesaria presento, no bino no solo en el tiempo oportuno pero ni asta ora lo a echo, y no me fui a Suni [Zuni] solo por esperarlo en Alburquerque donde capitulamos juntarnos para dicho biaje por que no biniera y dixera que yo le habia faltado a el trato: por cuia razon no me ajuste con Dn. Bernardo de Miera en el partido que me assia que me tenia mucha quenta y me hubiera sido mui util quien le declarara ha su tiempo.
  Y sino se hizo escritura fue por que el no lo ordeno hassi que era aquien tocaba como actor y abiador en el contracto y a el precente me olgara yo mucho de tal otorgamiento por que me fuera mas facil la reconbencion y seme escusara la prueba de testigos que aora ofresco para su tiempo.
  Lo que alega de que la contingencia de haber padecido una enfermedad tiempo de tres meses nole aprobecha por que ni aun la muerte desbarata los contratos onorosos que pueden cumplir sus alvaceas como en este caso qualquiera personero podia

yr en nombre del contratante a Suni [Zuni] y lograra el aprobechamiento y yo la parte que me tocaze por la mitad.

Y pregunto ala parte contraria si ya hubiera faltado al trato por enfermedad o otro hasidente o por mal correspondiente; no me habia de obligar al cumplimiento que es la razon por que en los contratos se obliga persona y bienes por si faltara la persona que lo reporten los bienes y aunque no se expresse se supone en todos derechos.

Dise tambien que complia con haberme escrito un papel dandome parte de su hasidente para que no seme siguiese la mala obra el que pide se acomule ha estas diligencias; haque respondo con el mismo papel en el qual se haze la fecha de nueve de Julio y yo la recebi a cinco de Agosto como esta hanotada y firmado por mi en su margen cuia nota ha maior habeunamiento juro a Dios Nuestro Señor y ala Santa Cruz ser sierta: con que es persuadible que la fecha la puso el ha cautela para que le quedase la disculpa que aora propone no por que le habrovecha por que luego que falto al tiempo en que se obligo a benir me costituyo ha creder alo que haora le demanda, y aquia paga sele deve compeler por todo rigor de derecho en cuia atencion y habiendo por expresso el mas formal y juridico pedimento que nesesario sea negandolo por judicial.

A Vuestra Señoria pido y suplico se sirva de mandar haser y determinar como llebo pedido que es de justicia, juro lo necesario y ser cierto y no de malicia, ut supra.
Salvador Garcia de Noriega (rubric)

Santa Fee 26 de Octubre de 1752
Corra traslado con la parte de Dn. Juan Garcia de la Mora para que dentro del termino del derecho responda a el; y pongase con los autos el papel y me sirva que se presenta y se le notifique al suso dicho comparesca en esta Villa por si o su apoderado al seguimiento de esta ynstancia. Asi lo probeni y firme yo Dn. Thomas Velez Cachupin Governador de este Reyno dela Nueva Mexico.
Velez Cachupin (rubric)

Señor Governador y Capitan General
Juan Garcia de la Mora, natural de los Reinos de Castilla y vezino de este Reyno como mejor proxeda en justicia sin que me sean confundidas ni buneradas las defensas en conformidad de mi derecho parezco ante Vuestra Señoria y digo: que habiendose Vuestra Señoria servido de darme traslado de la ynstancia que hase Salvador Garcia en la falsedad de su primera demanda y esta hazerlo despues de veinte y tres dias del traslado que Vuestra Señoria le dio de mi declarazion pareze tira al entretener el tiempo, y desta suerte dilatar la paga que me deve hazer en el presente mes de mis lienzos en que esta confeso. No obstante de las zircumstancias falsas que supone para su paga a cuyas ynstancias. Y respondiendo punto por punto a todas ellas. La primera niega que los dichos lienzos requiso fiados sino es por modo de haverlo como se

practica en esta tierra entre los que ocupan en sus ofizios ut supra. Y dise ser corriente asentadissimo con este superlativo en carezimiento quien no dira que esta sea una berdad que no se pueda dudar? Pues Señor a esto responda que es la mayor falsedad; de todas las que usa en su ynstancia y querella por que sino ay en este Reyno tales havios ni habiadores, ni habiados, como es publico a todos; ni se a practicado trato semejante para que es espada; sono solo para confundir con ella el juizio que Vuestra Señoria deve hazer de la razon y justicia que a cada uno le asiste y que deseoso Vuestra Señoria de hazertar en la administrazion de justizia se calienta la cabeza para entre sacar el grano de la verdad de entre las pajas sofisticas y retoricas cabilasidas de sus alegatos. Y si Vuestra Señoria atiende ala expedizion que haze en este primer punto de su ynstanzia y asi mismo a el trato que me demanda le cumpla en primera querella hallara Vuestra Señoria que en su primera querella exponiendo la forma de nuestro trato dize que solo habia de poner su trabajo personal, y tres arrobas de fierro. Y a ora en esta ynstanzia dize havia de llebar dos mozos mas en cuya bariedad e ymplicanzia de dicho trato se deja conozer la malizia con que prozede y poca memoria para usar de sus mentiras: y por si nezessario fuere admito los dos mozos para lo que me pueda ymportar a su tiempo: y en quanto a el segundo punto de su ynstancia digo que por tener respondio por mi papel que se halla unido a estas dilixencias la causa de no haver ydo y esta ser zierta como tengo dicho en mi declarazion que a ora reproduzco; omito responder a este cargo de haver ydo, o no haver ydo; y solo respondo en quanto a el tiempo y digo que porque en ninguno de sus capitulos no falte una falsedad dize que quede a mediado de Mayo debajar y no es assi sino es que le dije que en todo Mayo, o principios de Junio salvo azidente; a demas que si la zircumstanzia del trato es falso en quanto a la obligazion que supone, que le favoreze; el tiempo de mi bajada caso que no se berificara mi enfermedad; ni que le favoreze el no ajuste con Dn. Bernardo de Miera y Pacheco ni ami ni a mi punto contrario nos puede constar si le hubiera o no sido de mucha o poca validad; como ello asegura en su primera querella asignandose busca zierto de lo que prende de contijenzias y voluntades ajenas de yndios de comprar obras o no comprarles cosa por zierto digna de ygnorar della. =

Y en lo que dize de que sino se izo escriptura fue por que yo no le ordene siendo a quien tocaba como actor y habiador y que se olgara mucho de tal otorgamiento. Digo Señor que como es falso la dicha ynstanzia de dicho trato y no ay puesto actora ni habiador ni habiado si solo aquien el simple trato que dejo dicho en mi declarazion a que ni el ni yo heramos en caso de contigencias o otra causa alguna azidental y obligados por esta razon no hubo de su parte ni dela mia que pedimos obligazion alguna y sino la hubieramos de haver pedido dever haber de compromiso y no que yo solo sela hiziera a el; y si no pregunto yo ala parte contraria que seguridad de ynteres me aseguraba el a mi, pues que yo le debiera asegurar a el lo que supone? Porque aun siendo zierto (que no lo es) la buzca que dize hubieramos tenido de dozientos y zinquenta pesos cada uno, debiendo yo llevar (como tambien supone) seis arrobas de fierro y un mozo oficial que este si es berdad con todo me seria mas el costo del biaje que la busca, porque seis arrobas de fierro benefiziadas en mi casa son tresientos cuchillos, y por el consiquente trezientos pesos de la tierra, y anadiendole el salario del mozo serian mas delo que yo habia de tocar, lo que habia de poner; y es caso duro que quiera mi parte contraria acreditarme para con Vuestra Señoria y todos los que supieran semejantes obligazion de tan tonto; pues no me reconosco por tanto; aunque si soy nego en fiarle a el mis generos para que me corresponda buscandome estas ynquietadus.= Y en lo que dize de que no me aprobecha la contijencia de mi enfermedad por que ni aun la muerte desbarata los contratos honorosos que pueden cumplir los albazeas, y que en este caso cualquiera personero pudiera haber ydo en mi nombre; Digo Señor alo primero que este contrato no solo nolo es; ni sele deve dar nombre de contrato sino solo una propalazion de hazemos o practicaremos estos, aquellos, o los otros medios de buscar, y este fue el que como tratante y guespede del dicho querellante tubimos aquella noche por modo de combersazion y en el modo que tenia para solizitar mi paga delo que ya me tenia pedido; y que a otro dia mui demanana le entregue no como dize por modo de habio, que no ay tal; y para que mis albazeas (caso de muerte) estubieren como dize obligados al dicho contrato, y que merezera el nombre de onoroso habia de prezeder (como tengo dicho en mi declarazion) ynstrumento juridico de testigos de ambas partes y en tal caso le dariamos el nombre de contrato onoroso y todas esas zircumstanzias que quiere que tenga la simple combersazion que tubimos de que habiamos de hazer el zitado y mal demandado biaje. Y en quanto a que podia ymbiar personero digo qu estoy tan escaramentado de ymbiar personero a negozio mio de ninguna calidad que no lo haria nunca por que no los ay dela confianza que el caso y biaje requiera; por no ser generos que se pueden dar precios ni pedirles cuentas de cosa zierta sino es que este yndio pediria cuchillo, el otro hachita, el otro coa, ut supra, y hera necesario estar a la confianza; y esta no la tengo yo ni es dable hazerla de cualquiera y de las que un hombre lo pudiera hazer son hombres de onrra, y que hazeres en sus casas y ninguno destos havia de querer serbirme ami de peon, a salario; y asi ami me busca estos pleitos y casilosidades que borucs no le metiera a el personero; a demas que como no estaba obligado forsosamental; no yze ni pense hazer tal dilixensia.= Y en quanto a la pregunta que me hase de que si hubiera faltado por el por algun azidente, que sino le habia de obligar yo al cumplimiento que es la razon por que en los contratos se obliga persona y bienes; digo Señor que no le hiziera yo nunca; por que me sonrrojara mucho y escruplizara mucho mas de poner demanda tan ynjusta por no adquirir fama o nota de cabiloso y falto de conzienza.= Y tambien digo que si hubiera mi ynquilino tomado otro camino por ebadirse de pagarme por aora pretextando por causal mi papel y la causa de mi azidente por cuyo motivo, sele habia hecho tarde para por si hazer su biaje lo hubiera conseguido con migo; lo que a ora no consiguira sino es que pido a Vuestra Señoria que dezidido el juicio saliendo (como assi lo espero de mi verdad y justicia) ami favor; se sirva de mandar seme de satisfazion de mis zientos en los generos que la tierra ofreze comerziables.= Y en quanto a el rejuro de mi papel que dize espersadible que sobre la fecha de nuebe de Julio, y haverlo el resivido a cinco de Agosto, la pusiese yo con cautela. Digo Señor que tengo ymbiado personero a el Rio Abajo a recaudar otros tres papeles que juntos con el suyo llevo el mismo portador a barios sujetos sobre otras dependienzias de lana que halla tenia; y espero que sino todos algunos ayan quedado para que contestando aquellas fechas con este suyo, y no debiendo en aquellos caver la sospecha que del suyo haze quedara sin ella; su deprabada malizia y mi papel sin cautela; Y sera posible que su anotazion que tambien protexto practicar las que me fueron posibles para ber si sela hallo a su anotazion. Y devo yo persuadirme a que su anotazion la tenga con mas fundamentales por que aunque jura ser zierta; Yo tambien amphiboloficamente lo jurase que lo es; por que lo beo anotado; Mas no jurare ser rezivido dicho papel el dia de su anotazion. Y en lo que dize no me aprobechaba mi papel por haver faltado a el tiempo y que desde ese dia se constituye a creedor alo que aora me demanda. Digo Señor que como el no es el Juez ni puede serlo de su propria causa no me haze fuerza que el ni niegue con cabilosidades mi derecho ni suponga falsedades que an de ser vistas por Vuestra Señoria por lo cual y haviendo Vuestra Señoria por expresado, el conozimiento dela malizia con que prozede mi ynquilino con lo mas del formal y juridico pedimento que me fuere nezessario.=

A Vuestra Señoria pido y suplico sea mui servido de hazer que se me quede justizia; esta ymploro y juro este mi escripto en forma con la no malizia costas protexto y en los nexesario, ut supra.

Juan Garcia de la Mora (rubric)

Auto difinitibo
En la Villa de Santa Fee en tres dias del mes de Noviembre de mil setecientos y cincuenta y dos años. Haviendo visto este escripto y demas de que se compone este articulo sumario; digo que haviendo premitado los muchos yncombenientes que resultaran del seguimiento de esta ynstancia por ser de mui profija ymbestigacion y necesitar del mucho tiempo su averiguacion y que esta nunca pudiere ser combiniente por no haver ynstrumento expreso ni relatibo que la contenga; y que la demanda se funda en piadosas consideraciones que a su favor ynterpreta el demandante de vajo de las contingencias, que son probables y en falta de licencia y permiso deste Governacion donde esta prohivida la entrada sin noticia mia, con los demas defectos que conbiene el processo= Mandava y mande poner perpetuo silencio en esta materia, en que no se admita otro escripto ni recurso en ella: Y en cuanto alos cien pesos delos generos, que el mismo Salvador Garcia confiesa haver recivido; este los dara y bolvera a Dn. Juan Garcia de la Mora dentro de cinco meses que se cuenten desde oy dia dela fecha: salbo que entre las dos partes ayga composicion y combenzo como les combenga: Y este auto notificara a Theniente de Alcalde Mayor de esta Villa: Y asi lo probehi, yo Dn. Thomas Velez Cachupin, Governador de este Reyno dela Nueba Mexico attuando con los testigos de mi assistencia, doi fee. =

Thomas Velez Cachupin (rubric)

Testigos
Nicolas de Ortiz (rubric)
Thomas de Alvear Y Collado (rubric)

Notes

1. Salvador García [de Noriega] was probably the Salvador Mateo García listed as the son of Tomás García de Noriega, a soldier at the Santa Fe presidio in 1725. Salvador's grandfather was Alonso García de Noriega, who returned to New Mexico from El Paso in 1693 and was a presidio captain. In 1770 Salvador was the alcalde of Santa Cruz (Chávez, *Origins*: 181-82; SANM I #876).
2. See Doc. 27.
3. An *arroba* is a common eight or measure of about 25 pounds (Hadley et al., *Presidio*: 527).
4. Antonio Martín is most likely José Antonio Martín Serrano, the son of Sebastián Martín Serrano. Sebastián was at one time an alcalde of Santa Cruz. He received a large grant at La Soledad and built the chapel there. It is unlikely that the Antonio Martín mentioned in Doc. 11 (1715) was alive in 1752 (Chávez, *Origins*: 223-24).
5. See Doc. 45.
6. Juan Joseph Lobato was in New Mexico by 1731, when he was a witness to a military investigation. According to Chávez, he was the son of either Bartolomé or Matías Lobato. Juan Joseph was an alcalde from at least 1751 to 1753 of the jurisdiction Santa Cruz, Taos, and Río Arriba. In the 1751 Las Trampas grant document, he was called the chief justice and war captain. In 1754, in a letter to Governor Marín de Valle, Governor Cachupín stated, "In La Cañada, Juan Joseph Lobato is one of the most capable, a man of much zeal in the fulfillment of his obligations and greatly esteemed by the Utes. He is one whose opinion may be considered judicial and of substance. In my opinion, your grace should continue him in his office, as there is no one else to look for" (SANM I #33, #95, #975; Doc. 21; Chávez, *Origins*: 206; Thomas, *Plains Indians*: 140).
7. See Doc. 16.
8. This Juan de Leyba may be Juan Ángel Leyba, a descendant of the Juan de Leyba who was killed in New Mexico in 1680. Juan Ángel was the great grandson of José de Leyba, who was granted land near La Cienega in 1728 (Kessell, *Kiva*: 236; SANM I #441; and Chávez, *Origins*: 205).
9. See the letter at the end of the document.
10. More specifically, Chávez states that García de la Mora came from La Villa de Pozuelo de Almagro, in the archbishopric of Toledo (Chávez, *Origins*: 184).
11. *Lienzas* could refer to fabric, sometimes canvas, made from flax or hemp. The reference is probably to the goods worth 100 pesos that de la Mora gave to him.
12. That is, Salvador denies that the goods were provided to him as a kind of loan to see if he could sell them.
13. This confusing language, probably intended to flatter the governor, may reflect García's Spanish origins and pretensions: he had arrived from Castile in the 1730s.
14. The Spanish is *los géneros de la tierra*, or barter—goods for goods.

41

SANTA CRUZ RANCHER REGISTERS A BRAND AND VENTA FOR LIVESTOCK
November 8, 1752. Source: Twitchell Collection, File 113.

Synopsis and editor's notes: Livestock branding in New Spain seems to have had a long history, carried out at least by the time of Hernán Cortés, who was said to have had a brand with three Latin crosses. Thus it is not surprising that branding of open-range livestock and the registration of brands was an accepted practice in eighteenth-century New Mexico. To date, the earliest known registration in the post-Reconquest period is the 1716 request from Diego Márquez of Santa Cruz for a brand that had been registered by his father, implying that there was a brand registration system in place. It is not known whether his father's request was before or after 1680. In 1719 Governor Valverde, acting on a request from the viceroy, ordered that all presidial livestock be branded and that those animals not be sold or transported outside the province. In 1751 Governor Cachupín ordered a registry of land titles and a registry of livestock brands. The following document may be a remnant of Cachupín's registry. Over thirty years later, in 1784, Governor Anza ordered a registration of brands. The brands and *ventas* (or *marcas*) for the Santa Fe area were shown on the document (SANM II #275, #287a; Tigges, "Brand Registrations": 123-25; Hendricks, "Livestock Brands": 108).

Reference is made to brands and branding irons in several wills, including that of cabildo member Salvador Montoya, who in his will of 1727 claimed "delivery of a young sorrel-colored male mule with the brand of Juan de Archibeque." In 1739 the probate documents for Cristóbal Baca listed a branding iron with the value of ten pesos, compared to the value of a cart listed at 15 pesos and a three-year-old colt at 12 pesos. In her 1747 will, Josepha Baca declared as a possession, "70 head of cattle with my brand thereon, and if there should be any increase, they shall be known by my brand and mark." In 1756 Captain Juan José Moreno, native of Seville, declared that he owned "the cattle that may be found with my brand at said pueblo of Taos." In 1764 Francisco Martín humbly declared "one branding iron" in his will (SANM I #40; SANM I #88; SANM I #505; SANM I #512; SANM I #552, WPA translation).

Alcalde mayor and war captain

[Marginal note]
Río Arriba and November 8,
1752, this registration was
presented before Captain
Juan Joseph Lovato,[1]
alcalde mayor and war
captain, of this jurisdiction.

[I] Francisco Valdés y Bustos,[2] resident of the new villa of Santa Cruz in this kingdom of New Mexico, appear before your excellency, and I say that, finding myself with a small number of cattle, horses, mules, and livestock, and not have a branding iron or mark to use, a proper brand is drawn in the margin[3] conforming to and according to royal decrees so that your excellency will be enabled to authorize it (since by these means I register it); and I ask that your excellency will place it in the archives or wherever else is appropriate.

This, I ask in the name of the king, our lord, may God guard him, so that I, as well as my children and heirs, will be able to have the rights to said branding iron now as well as in the future as we brand that which God would be served to give us and that no other person will be able to use. For all of which I ask and beg that your majesty will be pleased to do this as I have said, so that in doing this, I will receive favor and justice, and I swear in the required form that this is not being done in malice and as is needful, ut supra.

Francisco Valdés y Bustos (rubric)

Through my review and consideration, I registered the brand and mark as in the margin so the supplicant, his children and heirs and successors, can mark their cattle, horses, mules, and livestock using it honestly and legally and in order that it is evident wherever suitable, I sign and authorize it with the following written witnesses for my assistance with whom I act as the investigating officer for lack of royal and public scribes, there being none in this kingdom, and this is dated ut supra.

Juan Joseph Lovato (rubric)
Assisting presiding judge

Assisted by
Juan Joseph Lovato (rubric)
Witness Antonio Martín
María and José Joaquín and Ana[4]

This copy of the petition for brand registration shows the brand and *marca* (or *venta*) in the margin as well as the signatures and rubrics of the officials. Twitchell Collection, #113, New Mexico State Records Center and Archives, Santa Fe.

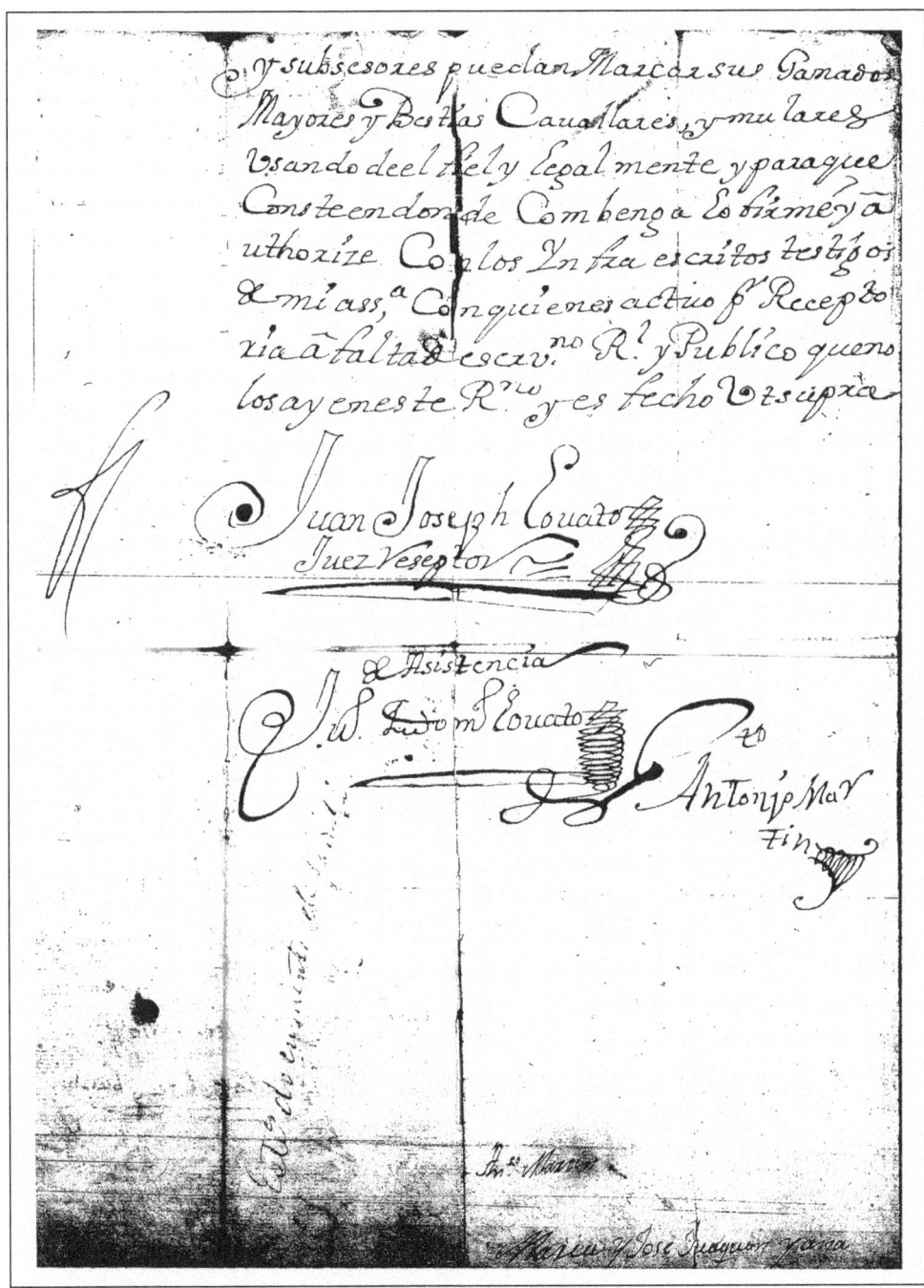

y subsesores puedan Marcar sus Ganados Mayores y Bestias Cauallares, y mulares Vsando deel fiel y legalmente y paraque Conste endonde Combenga lo firme, y ã uthorize Con los Ynfra escritos testigos de mi assa Con quienes actuo p.r Recep.to ria ã falta d.e escriv.no R.l y Publico que no los ay en este R.no y es fecho Vt supra

Juan Joseph Lovato
Juez Reseptor

de Asistencia
J.s Lud.co m.l Lovato

Antonio Mar
tin

ORIGINAL DOCUMENT

Señor Alcalde Mayor y Capitan Aguerra
Rio Arriba y
Novembre 9 de 1752
Se presento este
Registro Ante el Capitan
Juan Joseph Lovato
Alcalde Mayor y Capitan
Aguerra de esta
Jurisdizion,=

Francisco Valdes y Bustos, vesino de la villa Nueba de Santa Cruz en ese Reyno de la Nueba Mexico [yo] paresco ante V[uestra] M[erced] y dygo que allando me con un poco de ganado mayor unas bestias caballares y mulares y no tener xierro ni señal, con que poder tener aucion a ellas y acordado, segun hordenes Reales a ser xiero el que a lo margen ba pintado para que VM se sirva de autorisarlo ni serlo (como por este lo registro) y que VM lo ponga en su archivo o donde conbenga pues lo pido en nombre del Rey N[uestra] S[eñor] quien Dios le G[uarde] y que asi yo como mis hijos y herederos podemos tener derecho dicho que xiero para que asi aora como adelante eremos lo que D[ios] fuere serbido de darnos y que no otra persona puede usar del; por todo lo qual=
a V[uestra] M[agestad] pido y suplico sea mui serbido de aser como llebo dicho que en ello resebire mersed y justicia y juro en debido forma no ser de malisia y en lo nesesario ut supra

Francisco Valdes y Bustos

y por mi visto y reconsido doi por Registrado el hierro y marca de el margen para que el suplicante sus hijos herederos [blank space] y subsesores puedan marcar sus ganados mayores y bestias cavallares y mulares usando de el fiel y legalmente y para que conste en donde conbenga lo firme y autorize con los infraescrito testigos de mi assistencia con quienes actuo pora receptoría a falta de escribano Real y Publico que no los ay en este Reyno y es fecho ut supra.

Juan Joseph Lovato (rubric)
Juez Reseptor

De Assistencia
Testigo
Juan Joseph Lovato (rubric)
Antonio Martin
Maria y Jose Joaquin y Ana

Notes

1. See Doc. 40.
2. According to Chávez, Francisco Valdés y Bustos was a natural son of José Valdez and Josepha de Ontiveros of Santa Cruz. Josepha later married a Bustos. José Valdez was the son of Don José Luis Valdés, a native of Spain, who in 1696 was a sergeant major at Santa Cruz. He was killed in 1703. Francisco married Lugarda Martín in 1723 and then Thomasa de Benavides (Chávez, *Origins*: 301-2; Kessell and Hendricks, *BFA*: 319 n32; for José Luis Valdés, see Doc. 34).
3. The brand is shown in the margin as well as the *marca* (also called a *venta*), followed by the words *en al pesqueso* [*pescuezo*], or "on the neck." The marca was used over the original brand when the animal was sold to show that the original brand was no longer valid (Tigges, "Brand Registrations": 122).
4. These names were written by a different hand. Perhaps they were his wife and children.

42

TAOS SETTLERS STALL BUILDING FENCES ORDERED BY GOVERNOR CACHUPÍN
March 2–April 16, 1753.[1] Source: SANM I #1248.

Synopsis and editor's notes: In 1753 Governor Cachupín ordered the Taos Valley settlers to fence their properties in order to prevent their animals from causing damage to Indian crops, and not to obstruct the passageways used by the Indians as access to their fields. He sent the alcalde of the jurisdiction, Jacinto Martín, to give notice to the settlers, who asked for a time extension because it was planting time. Cachupín gave the extension, and Jacinto Martín once again visited the settlers to tell them this, writing down each of their responses. The settlers agreed to abide by the order for fencing but stated that it might not get done immediately since there was a lack of laborers and little money to hire them, and much other work to be done, and the distance to the forests made it difficult for them to go for wood for the fences. Even with the agreed-upon extension, their responses could not have been encouraging to Cachupín.

When Cachupín made the order to fence the property, he stated that the behavior of the colonists was "contrary to the laws," probably referring to a section of the 1550 law of Emperor don Carlos as recompiled in 1681, *Recopilación de leyes de los reynos de las Indias* (Laws of the Indies). The relevant law, found in Book IV, Title 12, Law 2, stated: "Farms of cattle, mares, hogs and other large and small livestock cause great damage to the cornfields of the Indians, and especially when they wander apart and without being watched. We command that no such farms shall be granted in parts or places where damage may result; and as this may not be possible to avoid, such farms shall be far from Indian towns and their planted fields. We command that the justices shall see to it that the owners of livestock and those who are interested in the public welfare shall employ as many herders and keeps as may be necessary to avoid damage; and in case of damage, they shall make recompense" (Tyler, *Indian Cause*: 161-62; Tyler, *Spanish Laws*: 52; Jenkins, "Taos": 95).

Cachupín's order is similar to other prohibitions made in response to complaints by the Indians about encroachment on their land that blocked passages. In 1718 Lieutenant Governor Villasur prohibited the setters of San Juan from allowing their cattle to trespass on lands of the Indians. In 1733 the settlers were prohibited from encroaching on Indian lands at Isleta, and a similar situation occurred in 1750 at Sandía. Then in 1731 the Taos Indians complained about encroachment by Sebastián Martín and Baltazar Romero. In both of these latter cases, the Taos Indians were supported by governors

Bustamante and Cruzat y Góngora (Baxter, *Las Carneradas*: 23, 24; Jenkins, "Taos": 93-95; SANM I #29, #684; SANM II #290, #361, #368, #534).

The problem, typical of situations with free-range livestock, planted fields, and an increasing number of settlers, continued through the next century. For example, the 1865-66 Legislative Assembly adopted an ordinance for Taos County, stating "that the inhabitants of the Trampas valley and of Vallecito, of the Chimisal [sic] precinct are hereby required to enclose their tillable lands with a good pole fence, six feet high, and which will prevent animals from damaging their lands" (*Laws of the Territory of New Mexico, Session 1865-1866*, Paragraph 32).

In regard to the Taos Valley settlers, it is disheartening to learn that many of the New Mexicans named in this document were killed in the August 4, 1760, Comanche raid on the Pablo Villalpando house, where settlers of the area had fled for safety. All the men were killed, and women and children were carried off. Any not present at the time of the raid, like Pablo Villalpando, may have been part of the defense of Taos against the Apaches by interim governor Portillo Urrisola in 1761. By 1776, when Fray Domínguez visited the area, he noted that Spanish families were living in the pueblo for protection, with the consent of the Indians (Jenkins, "Taos": 98; Adams, *Tamarón*: 58-59).

Year of 1753

[Marginal note]
Mandate that the residents
of the ranchos of the pueblo
of Taos shall fence their
fields for the freedom of the
herds of the Indians.

Don Tomás Vélez Cachupín, governor and captain general of the kingdom of New Mexico, castellan of the royal garrison in the capitol villa of Santa Fe

Whereas the native Indians of the pueblo of Taos of this government have made known to me the damages resulting to their community by some of the Spanish residents settled on the boundaries of said pueblo, with crops and fields that obstruct, impede, and render impassable the roads and passages used to take their cattle, sheep, and horses out to pasture, so that the said residents make the Indians go a greater distance and cause them great damage. They also verbally mistreat the Indian herders who legitimately pasture their livestock within the territory belonging to them.

In order to avoid such damages and the displeasure of the Indians, which is contrary to law,[2] so that the Indians may freely take their livestock out to pasture, and so that damages may not be caused to their crops, I order and command all the residents of the Taos Valley, near and far from the pueblo, to fence their planted fields and gardens with a sufficient and secure fence so that the livestock cannot enter and to leave the roads open and free for the livestock of the Indians. The resident who does not do this will be penalized by a fifty-pesos fine and three months in jail, and their fields will be laid waste by the livestock of the Indians. I advise them to fence before the first weeding of the cornfields. In the meantime, the ingress and the egress shall likewise remain free and open for the livestock of the Indians, without any resident daring to hinder or mistreat by word of mouth any Indian herder, under the existing penalties.

The lieutenant of the alcalde mayor of the said pueblo of Taos shall publish this mandate with all the residents of the aforesaid valley being present, so that they may not allege ignorance. He will annotate the publication and public knowledge and the reason of their being present, and the date; and he will personally bring these proceedings and published decrees to this villa and capital within ten days. The alcalde mayor and lieutenant shall observe the most prompt, dutiful fulfillment of this mandate, under the penalty of one hundred pesos fine and removal from office.

Issued in the villa of Santa Fe on the 29th day of March in the year 1753, and personally signed by me and two assisting witnesses. I certify.

Tomás Vélez Cachupín (rubric)
Juan Felipe Rivera (rubric)
Tomás de Alvear y Collado (rubric)

In the pueblo of San Jerónimo de Taos on the 4th day of the month of April, in the year 1753, I, Jacinto Martín,[3] lieutenant of the alcalde mayor and captain of war of same and its jurisdiction, giving due compliance to the preceding order issued by the governor and captain general of the kingdom, Thomas Cachupín, summoned to appear before me all the residents of the jurisdiction, to whom I made known this preceding decree. Understanding all together and each one for himself, they said that they obey and are ready to put into practice the order issued by his excellency, and that they humbly request his excellency to deign to prolong the time assigned because it is impossible to comply with it in that time, on account of the planting, as well as the lack of day laborers and the distance to the forests. But they will begin at once and will do all they possibly can in order to attain the desired end.

In evidence thereof, I signed in said pueblo on said day, month, and year, acting as presiding judge with the assisting witnesses. I certify.

Jacinto Martín (rubric)

Witnesses
Pablo Francisco de Villalpando (rubric)
Julian Padilla (rubric)

In the villa of Santa Fe on the 12th day of the month of April, in the year 1753, I, the said governor, after viewing the answer given by the residents of the pueblo of San Gerónimo de Taos, and their affability [*allanmiento*, sic] and acceptance of the contents of the order of the preceding page, with the request for the extension of the time assigned for the reasons set forth, I said that I would extend and did extend the said time until the last day of June of the present year so they can build their fences on their farms, in accordance with that which was ordered. If it is not so done within the time specified, no petition shall be accepted, nor will they have any recourse in the damage caused by the livestock of the natives, and the penalties shall be increased, which shall be adjudged by this government. The settlers shall be advised of this decree by Lieutenant Jacinto Martín. These proceedings having been executed, he shall return them to the government, in order that they may be evident at all times, without omitting any proceeding. Under the penalty designated in the said mandate, he shall list the names of the settlers who will be notified in order to place the damage which may be permitted according to law. I so provided and signed, acting as aforesaid, I certify.

    Thomas Vélez Cachupín (rubric)
    Thomas de Alvear (rubric)
    Juan Felipe Rivera (rubric)

In this pueblo of San Jerónimo de Taos, on the 16th day of the month of April, in the year 1753, I, Jacinto Martín, lieutenant of the alcalde mayor and captain of war of said pueblo and its jurisdiction, made known the preceding order to don Carlos Fernández,[4] Pablo Francisco de Villalpando,[5] Francisco Romero,[6] Diego Antonio Gallegos, Pedro de Chávez,[7] Francisco Martín,[8] Joseph Delgado, Antonio Romero, Julian Padilla,[9] Pablo Romero, Antonio Atensio,[10] Andrés Romero, Javier Gonzales, and Juan Romero, who, understanding the aforementioned superior decree, said in common that they would obey. Diego Gallegos in particular said that, although he had only one boy, nevertheless he would fence to the extent that his strength would permit. Francisco Romero, speaking for himself and for Pablo Romero, said that they had been fencing for two years, and the rest would be complied with. Pablo Francisco de Villalpando said that he would comply with the order, that he would get day laborers according to his means, and that if he could not obtain the help, he requested his excellency to deign to give him an order for the Indian laborers needed, paying them as customary in the kingdom by rations, bulls, and cows, that being what he has. Pedro de Chaves said that he is so poor that he has nothing with which he can pay the day laborers, but that he would personally fence as much as he could, and if he could not fence all, that his Excellency may do whatever he sees fit. Francisco Martín said that he would continue fencing and would be looking for laborers to help. If he could not find help, [he requested] that his excellency would deign give him an order for Indians, paying them for their labor with whatever he owned. Don Carlos Fernández spoke for himself and Julian Padilla and said that they had only two boys, the eldest being twelve years old, and day laborers not being available, he requests his excellency to deign to order Indians, paying them for their labor, as customary, with whatever they had. Antonio Atencio, Joseph Delgado, and Juan Romero said that they are only three, and that they would fence as much as possible. Andrés Romero with his three married sons, Antonio Romero, Javier Gonzales, and Miguel Romero, said that they would finish fencing what they lack.

This is what each said for himself, and all together again answered that they would give due compliance to the order of his excellency, as it is for their own convenience. They will not refuse to pay nor fail to do the work within the time specified, insofar as it may be possible for them in order to attain the desired end.

In evidence thereof, I, the said lieutenant, signed it in said pueblo on said day, month, and year, acting as presiding judge with assisting witnesses. I certify.

Jacinto Martín (rubric)

Witnesses
Julián Padilla (rubric)
Pablo Francisco de Villalpando (rubric)

ORIGINAL DOCUMENT

Año de 1753
Mandamiento para que los vecinos de los ranchos del Pueblo de Taos cerquen sus labores para la libertad de los ganados de los Yndios.

Don Thomas Velez Cachupin Governador y Capitan General del Reyno dela Nueba Mexico y Castellano de Su Real Presidio en la Villa Capital de Santa Fee

Por quanto los naturales Yndios del Pueblo de San Geronimo de Taos de esta governacion me an echo presente los perjuicios queles resultan a su comunidad de estar poblados algunos vecinos Españoles en los linderos de dicho Pueblo con sementeras y labores que ymposibilitan e ympiden los caminos y transitos de sus ganados maiores y menores y causilidades para sacarlos y pastearlos de modo que dichos vecinos selo ympiden y alegan con grave perjuicio y mal tratan de palabras los pastores Yndios que lexitimamente pastean el ganado en el territorio de su pertenencia y para obiar semejantes perjuicios y de razon de los naturales contra derecho; ordeno y mando a todos los vecinos del Valle de Taos cercanos y distantes del Pueblo que para que los Yndios puedan sacar libremente a pastear sus ganados y no ver las ocasiones perjuicios

en sus sementeras cerquen todas sus labores y huertas con cercas suficientes de modo que los ganados no puedan penetrarlas y dejen los caminos libres para los ganados de los Yndios; previniendose se an de cercar antes de dar la primera escarda alas milpas y en ynterin queda igualmente libre el paso de los ganados delos Yndios sin que ningun vecino sea osado a embarazarselo ni a maltratar de palabras a ningun Yndio pastor vajo la pena al que se arvitraren y el Theniente de Alcalde Mayor de dicho Pueblo de Taos presentes todos los vecinos del expresado Valle publicara este mandamiento de modo que no alegen ygnorancia y asentara la publicacion y notorio las declararan de estar presentes, y fecho el mismo en persona traera estas diligencias y mandamiento publicado a esta Villa su Capitan en termino de diez dias; y Alcalde Mayor y Theniente celaran el mas puntual devido cumplimiento de este mandamiento vajo de pena de cien pesos de multa y privacion de empleo. Dado en la Villa de Santa Fee en veinte y nuebe dias del mes de Marzo de mil setecientos cincuenta y tres años firmado de mi mano y de dos testigos de mi asistencia, doy fee =
    Thomas Velez Cachupin (rubric)
    Thomas de Alvear y Collado (rubric)
    Juan Phelipe Rivera (rubric)

En este Pueblo de San Geronimo de los Taos en cuatro dias del mes de Abril del año de mil setecientos y sincuenta y tres yo Jasinto Martin Theniente de Alcalde Mayor y Capitan General de el y su jurisdision dando el devido cumplimento al antesedente mandato de el Señor Don Thomas Veles Cachupin Governador y Capitan General de este Reyno yse pareser ante mi a los besinos desta jurisdizion a quienes yse notorio el refuerso del mandato y bien entendidos de el todos juntos y cada uno de por si dijeron que lo obedesen y estan prontos a poner en practica lo mandado por Su Señoria y que suplican rendidamente a Vuestra Señoria sea muy servido prologarles el termino designado pues es ymposible poderlo cumplir asi a por la siembra como por la ynopia de peones y distancia de los montes pero que luego dara principio y pondran en todos los medios posibles para consegir el fin y para que conste lo firme en dicho Pueblo en dicho dia mes y año autuando como Juez receptor con testigos de asistensia de que doi fee.
    Jacinto Martin (rubric)
testigo
Julian Padilla (rubric)
testigo
Pablo Francisco de Villalpando (rubric)

En la Villa de Santa Fee en doce dias del mes de Abril de mil setecientos cinquenta y tres años yo dicho Governador vista la respuesta dada por los circumbesinos del Pueblo de San Geronimo de Taos yso allanmiento en el contenido del mandamiento de la foja antecedente con la calidad de que seles prorrogue el termino en el senalado por las rasones en que representan; dige que les prorrogaba y prorrogue dicho termino hasta el dia fin de Junio de este presente año para que agan las cercas de sus labores con arreglamento alo un mandado, pena de que asi no lo haciendo dentro de dicho termino no seles admitira recurso ni tendran accion por los danos que seles causazen los ganados de los naturales pena de que seles agrabaran las que viese arbitraren por esta governacion y este auto lo notificara a los enunciados vecinos el Theniente Jacinto Martin y fechas dichas diligencias las pasare a este govierno para que en todo tiempo conste sin omitir diligencia de bajo la pena que esta senalada en dicho mandamiento nominando las personas delos vecinos a quienes notificare para que les pare el perjuicio y firme actuando como dicho es, doy fee.

      Thomas Velez Cachupin (rubric)

testigo

Thomas de Alvear (rubric)

testigo

Joseph Phelipe de Bera (rubric)

En este Pueblo de San Geronimo de los Taos en diez y seis dias de el mes de Abril de el año de mil setesientos y sincuenta y tres yo Jasinto Martin, Theniente de Alcalde Mayor y Capitan Aguerra de dicho Pueblo y su jurisdizion yse notorio el antesedente superior mandato a Don Carlos Fernandez, a Pablo Francisco Villalpando, Francisco Romero, Digo Antonio Gallego, Pedro de Chabes, Francisco Martin, Joseph Delgado, Antonio Romero, Julian Padilla, Pablo Romero, Antonio Atensio, Andres Romero, Xabier Gonsales, Juan Romero, quienes entendidos del referido superior mandato dijeron en comun que lo obedesian y en particular dijo Diego Gallegos que se alla solo con un muchacho pero que no obstante que sercara asta onde alcansaran sus fuersas. Francisco Romero por si y por Pablo Romero dijo a dos años que esta sercando y que alo que le falta dara cumplimiento. Pablo Francisco de Villalpando dijo que pondra en ejecusion lo mandado y que solisitara peones segun alcansaren sus fuersas y si no los allare suplica a Vuestra Señoria sea servido de mandar darle un bale de los Yndios que nesisitare pagandoles segun que es costumbre en el Reyno en bastimento, toros y bacas que es lo que tiene. Pedro de Chabes dijo que es tan pobre que no tiene con que pagar a peones pero que personalmente sercara asta donde pudiere y que sino pudiere todo aga Su Señoria lo que sea servido. Francisco Martin dijo que yra sercando ynterin busca mosos y sino que se sirba Su Señoria de darle un bale de Yndios pagandoles su trabajo en lo que tubiere. Don Carlos Fernandez dijo por si y Julian Padilla que se allan con solos dos muchachos el mallor de dose años y que por no aber peones que se puedan acomodar sea serbido Su Señoria de mandar seles den Yndios pagandoles su trabajo segun que es constumbre en lo que tubieren. Antonio Atensio con Joseph Delgado y Juan Romero dijeron que son solos los tres y que yran sercando asta donde sus fuersas alcansaren. Antonio Romero con sus hijos casados que son Antonio Romero, Xabier Gonsales y Miguel Romero dijeron que acabaran de sercar lo que les falta. Esto dijeron cada uno de porsi por su respuesta y todos juntos bolbieron a desir que asen por dar el debido cumplimiento al mandato de Vuestra Señoria como por ser combeniensia propia no resiviran paga ni omitiran trabajo en cuanto les sea posible para consegir el fin dentro del termino senalado; y para que conste lo firme yo dicho Theniente en dicho Pueblo dicho dia, mes y año autuando como Juez receptor con testigos de asistensia de que doi fee.

Jacinto Martin (rubric)

testigo de asistensia
Julian Padilla (rubric) Pablo Francisco de Villalpando (rubric)

Notes

1. This document was transcribed by J. Richard Salazar and translated by Clara Fischer Walker. One section of the document was also translated by Myra Ellen Jenkins (Jenkins, "Taos": 96-97).
2. See the editor's notes.
3. Jacinto Martín may be the Nicolás Jacinto Martín who married Catalina de la Serna at Santa Cruz in 1712. The father was Alejandro Martín, probably a brother of the more famous Sebastián Martín. The 1739 will of Cristóbal Baca states that Jacinto Martín owed the estate of the deceased a fine horse worth 15 pesos (Chávez, *Origins*: 225; SANM I #88, WPA translation).
4. Carlos Fernández was born in Zamora, Spain, and married Juana Padilla, the daughter of Juan Padilla and Margarita Martín, who was the daughter of Sebastián Martín Serrano. Through Margarita, Carlos owned land in Taos. He was alcalde of Taos in the 1740s and lieutenant of the Santa Fe presidio from at least 1757 to 1761. From 1762 to 1763, he was alcalde of Santa Cruz. In 1778 he was alcalde of Santa Fe. In 1779 he, along with Bernardo Miera y Pacheco, was named a distinguished solider of the presidio. For specific cases, he acted as an attorney for the Indians (Cutter, *Legal Culture*: 75, 76, 86, 87; Hadley et al., *Presidio*: 200; Chávez, *Origins*: 176-77; Christmas, *Military Records*: 60).
5. Pablo Francisco de Villalpando was a native of León, Spain, and a nephew of Diego Romero. His sister was Catalina Villalpando, who married Antonio Martín of Embudo, who appears to have been a nephew of Sebastián Martín Serrano, named above. Pablo owned a large, fortified residence in the Las Trampas area that was used as a last defense against a Comanche attack in 1761. The Spanish were defeated, the men killed, and women and children taken captive (Jenkins, "Taos": 97, 98; Chávez, *Origins*: 312; see also Martinez and Esquibel, "Villalpando Family": 182-91).
6. Francisco Romero was one of many Romeros named in this document who were in some way related to, descendants of, or married to descendants of Diego Romero. Andrés was a nephew, and Antonio and Miguel Romero were sons of Andrés, and Javier Gonzales was a son-in-law. Diego Romero was in Taos by 1714. In 1724 the heirs of Cristóbal Serna (Serna had been killed in the Villasur expedition of 1720) sold Romero land near Taos and Picuris. By 1743, when he died, his land was described as being in the Río de la Trampas area. According to Jenkins, he described himself as "a coyote, the son of a Spaniard and a coyote" (Jenkins, "Taos": 91-97).
7. See Doc. 27.
8. Another family group well represented in the area were the settlers related in some way to Indian fighter Sebastián Martín Serrano, founder of the settlement of La Soledad de Río Arriba, near San Juan. Francisco Martín could have been the youngest son of Sebastián, or perhaps a brother (Chávez, *Origins*: 312; SANM I #501).
9. Julián Padilla was the son of Juana Antonio Padilla, who was in New Mexico by 1720, and Margarita Martín, the daughter of Sebastián Martín. Julian's sister, Juana, married Carlos Fernández (Chávez, *Origins*: 176).
10. Antonio Atensio (aka Atienza) married Ana Romero and was the son-in-law of Diego Romero. He was probably the son of José de Atienza Sevillano and grandson of José de Atienza de Alcala de Escobar of Toledo, Spain, who came with the Farfán-Velasco immigrants in 1694 (Chávez, *Origins*: 139; Jenkins, "Taos": 97).

43

GOVERNOR MARÍN DEL VALLE TIGHTENS REGULATION OF TRADE FAIRS; RETALIATION BY INDIANS FEARED
November 2–December 26, 1754. Source: SANM II #530.

Synopsis and editor's notes: While Governor Cachupín brought peace among the hostile tribes and the Spanish and Pueblos, he was well aware that it was an uneasy one, aggravated by the trade fairs where the various groups came together. Before Cachupín left office for the first time in 1754, he mandated trade restrictions for trade fairs and left recommendations about them to his successor, Francisco Antonio Marín del Valle, stating that the regulations were intended to stop the extortion of the Indians by the settlers. Governor Valle repeated Cachupín's trade restrictions on entering office, as translated below. Among other things, Valle ordered that settlers were not to sell defensive weapons to the hostile Indians, nor were they to sell stallions, mares, or mules that could be used for breeding. He also set prices for the animals, captives, and skins, stating that this was done to prevent the dealing that caused so many disagreements. The settlers were once again prohibited from trading outside a licensed trade fair and from entering the Indian rancherías until the fairs were officially opened. Valle concluded the document by stating that the hostile Indians were not to be told about this prohibition for fear of retaliation.

Governor Valle's efforts to control an unstable situation were not a success, with disagreements and fights at the trade fairs continuing to occur, and raids on the settlers and pueblos increasing. In 1760, as discussed in Document 42, the Comanches attacked Taos Pueblo and nearby Spanish ranches, killing many settlers and taking thirty-six captives. In 1766 Blas Martín of the large Martín Serrano family asked permission to abandon his ranch near Ojo Caliente because of Indian raids. Permission was denied (Thomas, *Plains Indians*: 129-43; John, *Storms*: 329-30; see also Foote, "Spanish-Indian Trade"; and Works, "Trading Places"; as well as Frank, *Settler to Citizen*: 15-45; Hämäläinen, *Comanche Empire*: 40-57; and Kessell, *Kiva*: 359-86).

It may be that the mandates of Governors Cachupín and Valle were in part a response to the 1749 report of Fray Sáenz Lezaún, notary of the Holy Office of the Inquisition in New Mexico. In the report sent to the Holy Tribunal in Mexico City, he charged the settlers with carrying out illicit trade with the heathen Indians with the knowledge of the governors. He stated that this trade led to Indian raids, in particular those of the Comanches at Pecos and Galisteo. He pointed out that the trade violated church policy, which prohibited trade with the enemies of the faith (Greenleaf, "Inquisition": 41).

The specific prohibition against sale of breeding animals shows that the Spanish were aware that the Comanches and other tribes were breeding horses and mules as well as raiding for them. Hämäläinen states that during the early stages of their horse acquisition, the Comanches relied primarily on raiding; they later became very skillful horse breeders (Hämäläinen, *Comanche Empire*: 245).

Year of 1754

Order which prohibits the sale of mares, stallions, mules, donkeys, and arms used for defense, at the trade fairs held with the gentiles under the penalties which are herein stated.

Don Francisco Antonio Marín del Valle
Political and military governor and castellan of the royal forces and presidios for his majesty

Whereas, repeated orders have been published in the various jurisdictions of this province during the terms of the past and present governors that have treated with trying to contain the excesses by the residents of this province in their conduct, and in what they provide at the trade and ransom fairs for their barter with the barbaric heathen nations who are from within this province. The orders also dealt with the manner in which they [the Indians] show themselves to the various [Spanish] residents and their political rules, with the greatest precautions taken for the benefit of the residents, in particular and in general, and for the conservation and protection of these dominions of the king while maintaining good, rational relations with the barbaric gentile nations. This is being done with the good faith of the agreements and the commerce [commercial regulations] in which they [the Indians] are instructed and which they ought to have, familiarizing themselves and learning good customs and the rules of piety from the frequent trades with the Catholics by whom they are to be instructed.

But, having observed through the same experience that nothing has been lacking in the manner by which some residents have very rudely and stupidly done malicious things during the trade and ransom fairs in which they have participated, thus the reason for all of the aforesaid published orders. These orders state with just and specific prohibitions that they are not to sell arms used for defense to the barbaric nations, which consist of lances, swords, daggers, daggers with triangular blades, large knives [*lanzas, espadas, puñales, almaradas, cuchillas grandes*], or anything else which can be used for assaults; nor [are they to sell] tame or unbroken mares, nor stallions, jacks, mules, and male or female donkeys. [Sales of these is restricted] in order to prevent the breeding of horse herds by these nations with which they can terrorize the dominions of the king, coming from great distances [on horses] to commit the insults and dissolutions which have been and continue to be experienced.

Also, the orders are so that the citizens cannot trade horses to other more distant nations who do not know the use of the horse, and who can then possibly come to this province, [the lack of horses] thus keeping them a good distance away. This [the trade of horses] is done by the European nations that are established and settled to the east and north and that have commercial trade with the barbaric Indians and who can invade and terrorize the province. In this manner, our horses can be passed on and become established in the foreign dominions, which can then ally themselves to invade these of the king. For this reason you should not sell a horse that is of good health and good appearance for a price less then fifteen skins, [or sell] one of lesser appearance because it is thin or any other reason for twelve [skins]. For an Indian who is over the age of ten years, you can give two old, worn-out horses without adding a bridle, or a knife, or a piece of cloth, a hat, or without adding anything else. For a younger one, you can give a horse and add a bridle or something equivalent. For each skin you can give a knife that contains no brass and is not sharpened, or a small shield.[1]

Also, at the time that these exchanges or trade fairs are held, the citizens and the Pueblo Indians are not to incite the Comanches, Utes, and Carlane Apaches with whom they are dealing by robbing, [or] violence of any type. Nor are they to do other acts of unfaithfulness or bad communication by which they [the Indians] can be offended for which, in turn, they can show vengeance and hatred for the Spanish, so that, because of this, they can never establish their friendliness [and will] not be faithful to them [the Spanish] nor to the province, with the possibility being lost of them ever being reduced,[2] converted into the Catholic church, and becoming vassals of the king. Thus, the following circumstance is to be the object of primary concern: To be able to rescue from the control of these barbaric nations persons of both sexes who are enslaved by others of the same class [*arreglo*, that is, other Indians] in their frequent and cruel wars. This is so that we can indoctrinate them into the faith and Christian ways without them being slaves or some other such thing as being in the personal service of someone, but in placing them so as to be treated like their own sons until they can be on their own, and on finding themselves on their own, they can sustain themselves through their own personal work.

For this reason, other previous orders have come forth like the present order with the same penalties being imposed so that in their failing they can be reapplied in what follows and is newly added and mandated of all the residents in this kingdom who are here, those who are to follow, and those who leave. The orders are so that they who attend the trade and ransom fairs and who sell their goods do not cause problems among themselves by making adjustments to their prearranged or set price over the purchase of an item, by arguing with each other and offering to the unsettled Indians more items than are to be allowed. In this way they cause a problem to the other residents who had made the first offer for the purchase of the item, allowing the Indians to reevaluate the item so that the price which they ask becomes more excessive by observing the competition among the same Spanish who are dealing for the item.[3] Because of this, the trade fairs become more difficult to control by having the purchase price increased for the skins, which will reflect on the purchase price for a horse, which amounts to six or eight skins, thus making it more difficult to place a higher or lower value as set on the goods of the barbaric nations. They [the Indians] observe very closely the estimates [or values] which the Spanish give to them so that they can ask for a higher price, understanding the need which is shown for their goods and the value of their commerce and the depreciation of ours. They tolerate the abuse and the unfaithful friendship, responding with hostilities to the residents by their increased robberies and killings and other barbaric atrocities which they continue to carry on in this kingdom, and which are brought on by the specific behavior that the same residents show them in the trade fairs, provoking the enemy by their sour, indiscreet ways.

The penalty of seventy pesos of the value of the land and one month in jail [*carcel*][4] shall be imposed on a citizen or citizens who exceed the assigned prices or who prevents another citizen from purchasing the item by cutting in and adjusting the price. Half of the amount [of the penalty] will be applied to our majesty's royal treasury and the other half to the individual who denounced the person. I also order [punished] any person of any class, race, or other caste, whoever they be, who purchases anything, be they skins or Indians, or sells any kind of goods which are prohibited, including the sale of arms, for lower prices, causing problems with the Comanches, Utes, and Apaches before the trade fairs are opened or after they are closed or suspended. [I also ordered punished those] who go to deal with the Comanches during the night, or during the day, in places such as the *bosques* [wooded or well-watered areas] or arroyos, where in numerous instances these excesses are carried out without the knowledge of the justices and other persons who are in charge of looking out for this type of thing, including the governor. The penalty for this is that the items that were purchased, including any Indians or skins or anything else, will be taken from the persons who purchased the items. The fine will be applied to our majesty's royal treasury and the other half to the person or persons who denounced the person or persons, along with a sentence of three months in jail for those individuals.

I also order that no Spanish resident, mulatto, coyote, or Pueblo Indian is to enter, either in the night or the day, into a Comanche, Ute, or Apache ranchería[5] under any pretext until the trade fairs are ordered to be open, and the justices are to see that this is not done, and if anyone does so, they will be sentenced to two months in jail. Any coyote, mulatto, or Indian who does this will receive fifty lashes at the pillory [*picotta*]. This [order] is being made to avoid the damages and extortions which are caused to the rancherías, the residents of which continuously make these complaints. It is best for the service of both our majesty and the public cause to avoid them [complaints] in order to establish a more perfect friendship and good relations with these said nations and to give them the example and to instruct them in our good customs.

It is prohibited to all types of persons to sell mules at the trade fairs, not only because they are so scarce in this kingdom, but also because they are needed for their use in pack trains and for the commercial traffic. By keeping the mules away from those nations, they are forced to use their horses in doing the work of moving their camps continuously, which will keep them [the horses] tired, and [they, the nations, will] not be able to use them in their wars within the Catholic communities. Also, they will be more concerned about the growth of their horse herds and their consumption at home, for which reason they will need to maintain good faith with this kingdom. In addition to this, it will require them to continue their trade for provisions. The other thing is to prohibit the sale of stallions to these nations, so that they cannot have an abundance of horses, thus avoiding the attacks upon these dominions of the king. Any resident or Indian who is involved in the sale of mules during the trade fairs will lose the amount which he received for the mule, and the amount received will be given one half to our majesty's royal treasury and the other half to the denouncer.

I also order all of the residents and inhabitants of this kingdom not to declare or announce to the said nations with whom these trade or ransom fairs are held, particularly to the Comanches, who are not to be told anything regarding the rules prohibiting the sale of arms, mares, stallions, and male and female mules [*machos y mulas*], or the going prices. Under no circumstances are they to be told anything because of the consequent results to the public good of their resentments and other prejudices, which up to now have been spread by the malice and rudeness of many persons who notify these gentiles of our announced precautions. If it is known that anyone has given them this information, they will be castigated with all rigor and severity.

This order is to be published and made public in all of the three villas of this province and in the jurisdiction of San Gerónimo of Taos by their alcaldes mayores, who are to be instructed that everyone is to know about this so that they cannot claim their ignorance. In order to be certain that everyone knows about it, because of the dispersion of the jurisdictions, the alcaldes will publicize it every fifteen days, on Sundays, when the residents gather at the parishes, [and] during the sermon they can inform everyone for its compliance and observation. The alcalde mayor of the jurisdiction of Taos will do so every time fairs are licensed and at the beginning of the fair, gathering together to inform every resident and person within a place who might get involved, making sure that the ranchería that is in the proximity of the pueblo does not know what is told the citizens. All of the alcaldes within their proper jurisdiction, or any other in which they are present where a trade fair is to be held, shall hold, practice, and execute what is herein ordered. Anyone who consents tolerates or allows excesses will be punished severely.

Done in the villa of Santa Fe, on the 26th of November, 1754. Acting with me are my two witnesses, to whom I certify.

    Francisco Antonio Marín del Valle (rubric)

Witness
Felipe Tafoya (rubric)
Assisting
Juan Francisco Arróniz (rubric)

In the villa of Santa Fe on the 2nd of December, 1754, I, don Francisco Guerrero, the alcalde mayor of the villa and of its jurisdiction, in fulfillment and in obedience to that which was ordered by the governor and captain general of this kingdom, certify and state that the said bando was publicized at that this said villa at the gates of the guard house of this royal presidio, and upon being summoned, all of the residents appeared and were made to understand the meaning of it [the bando], to which they stated that they would obey everything as ordered by the señor governor. And so that it is valid, I certified it and signed it in the said villa of Santa Fe, acting as presiding judge with my assisting witnesses, to which I certify.

       Francisco Guerrero[6] (rubric)

Witness
Lucas Moya (rubric)
Diego Antonio de la Peña (rubric)

In the villa of Alburquerque on the 8th of December, 1754, I, don Joseph Baca,[7] alcalde mayor and war captain of this said villa, in compliance and obedience of that which was ordered by the governor and captain general of this kingdom, certify and faithfully see to it that the referred to bando be publicized in this villa and its jurisdiction, and for its publication all of the settlers were present, and all understanding the order stated that they would all obey everything that was stated by the said governor. So that it is valid, I rubricated and signed it at this villa of Alburquerque, acting as presiding judge with my assisting witnesses, to which I certify.

       Joseph Baca (rubric)

Witness
Miguel Montoya (rubric)
Juan Miguel Álbares del Castillo (rubric)

In this Pueblo of Zia on the 20th of December, 1754, I, Antonio Baca,[8] alcalde mayor and war captain of this said jurisdiction, in fulfillment and obedience to what is ordered by this bando as ordered by the governor and captain general of this kingdom, ordered the Indians from the three pueblos of Zia, Santa Ana, and Jémez, to appear before me, and being present, I made them understand, through their interpreters, the order mandated by the governor, and they stated that they understood and obeyed everything that was stated by the governor. So that it is valid, I certified it and signed it at the pueblo of Zia, acting as presiding judge with my assisting witnesses, which I certify.

       Antonio Baca (rubric)

Witness
Diego Antonio Baca (rubric)

In this pueblo of La Laguna on the 26th of December, 1754, I, Manuel Baca,[9] alcalde mayor and war captain of the said jurisdiction, in fulfillment and obedience of what is ordered by this bando as ordered by the governor and captain general of this kingdom, ordered the Indians from the pueblo of Acoma to appear before me, and being all together in the community house, and through their interpreter I made them understand what was ordered in this bando; to which they stated that they understood and would obey everything that is stated by the governor. So that it is valid, I certified and signed it in this pueblo of Laguna, acting as presiding judge with my assisting witnesses, to which I certify.

Manuel Baca (rubric)

Witness
Joseph Chávez (rubric)

ORIGINAL DOCUMENT

Año de 1754

Bando en que se prohive la benta de yeguas, caballos padres, bestias mulares, burros y armas ofensibas en los resgates de xentiles baxo las peñas que dentro se expresan.

Don Francisco Antonio Marin del Valle, Governador Politico y Militario y Castellano de Sus Reales Fuerzas y Presidios por Su Magestad, et supra.

Por quanto por repetidos vandos publicados en las jurisdiciones de esta Provincia en los timpos de los Governadores pasados y presente; con que se ha procurado contener el exceso con que las vecindades de esta dicha Probincia se manejan y prozeden en las ferias o rescattes que se tienen y hazen con las naciones barbaras, gentiles del continente de esta Provincia y con que se han manifestado alas dichas vecindades regalas politica, pias y dela mayor precauzion en beneficio de las mismas en particular y general y conserbazion y fomento de estos dominios del Rey y amantener la mas buena solida racional correspondencia con las dichas naciones barbaras gentiles con la Buena fee de los contrattos y comercios que los ynstruyen en la que deven tener, familiarizen y aprenden con el frequente trato delos Catholicos las buenas constumbres y reglas de piedad con que por los mismos deven ser ensenados; pero observante por la misma experiencia que nada ha bastado para que se exerciten por algunos vezinos las mas torpes desareglados y maliciosas obras en los acttos de las ferias y rescattes contrabiniendo a todos los ante dichos bandos publicados con desprecio de las justas y areglladas prohibiziones de que no se vendan armas ofensibas a las barbaras naziones, como son lanzas, espadas punales temaradas, cuchillos grandes ni ottra con que se puedan ofender ni tan poco yeguas mansas ni regegas, ni caballos enteros padres, machos, mulas ni burros y burras por ebitar el fomento y crias de cavalladas, a estas referidas nazions con que ostilizan los Dominios del Rey, viniendo de grandes distancias a cometer los ynsultos y desolaziones que se han experimentado y esperimentan; y a que no trasciendan las caballadas a otras naziones mas distantes con que posibilitten la venida a esta Probincia que fuera impracticable a no comprender el uso del caballo y tener abundante oria la que justamente se deve tener en las naciones Europeas establecidas y pobladas a el oriente y norte de esta Probincia las que tienen comercio con las delos Yndios barbaros que pueden ostilizarce, y ynbadirce; y por estas manos pasan nuestras caballadas a formentarse en los Dominios estranjeros y con que pueden perjudicar sus alianzas a estos del Rey, y asi mismo que no se excedan en bender un caballo de buenas carnes y presencia por menos precio que el de quinze pieles y el de menos presencia por flaco o alguna otra circumstancia que mas lo desestima por doze, y una pieza de Yndia que pase de dies años por dos caballos matalottes sin que sele anada otra cosa de freno, cuchillo, pedazos de pano, sombrero, ni otra alaja y la pieza mas pequena de un caballo con algun agregado de freno o otra alaja equibalente. Y por cada piel, un cuchillo de resgatte sin azero ni filo o veldeque pequeño. Como que a el tiempo de celebrarze este comercio de cambios y rescattes no perjudiquen los concurrientes vezinos e yndios delos Pueblos a las naciones de Cumanches, Yutas y Apaches Carlanes con quienes se tiene el referido comercio con robos, violencia y otros ultraxes de mala fee con que indisponen, odian y alteran a estas naciones, fomentandoles el animo a la mala correspondencia y a que exzitten su benganza y odio a los Españoles, y que nunca se establezca el amor y fiel amistad entre ellas y esta Probincia y se ymposibilita su reduccion al gremio de la Catholica yglesia y vasallage del Rey. Cuyas circumstancias es y deve ser el objecto de primera ynstancia; y rescatar del poder de las barbaras naciones las piezas de personas de ambos sexos que esclavizan a otras de la misma clase en sus frequentes y crueles guerras para doctrinarlas y ynstruirlas en la fee y Christianas costumbres sin la tirana malicia de la esclavitud ni otra de codizia ni de arreglo en el personal servicio en que se destinan debiendose tratar como a hijos, hasta que por si mismos se hallen en perfecto estado de libre albeldrio y sustenttazion con la aplicazion de su personal trabaxo. Por tanto se reputen y conmemoran dichos antezedentes vandos en el presente mandamiento con las mismas penas ympuestas las que en su defecto se reagrabaran a el contraviniere y nuebamente mando a todos los vezinos de este Reyno estates, entrantes y salientes que concurren a las ferias y rescattes que al tiempo de estar en ellas y hazer la de sus generos no se perjudiquen los unos a los otros en el de estar ajustando a el arreglado a rancelado precio la compra de las piezas, atravesandose otro en el ajuste, ofreziendo a el gentil mas alajas delas prebenidas; y perturbandole a el otro vezino que primero tenia echo el ajuste la compra dela pieza, fomenttando a los genitiles la estimazion del valor de ellas para que sea excesivo el prezio que pida en observazion de la codiziosa competencia que los mismos Españoles entre si tienen de hadelantarle el prezio perjudicialissimo y norivo a el comun de este comercio y dificultad del rescatte como subzede en la compra de pieles que con relafazion de lo mandado venden un caballo por seis o ocho pieles con lo que dificultan costearse mayor valor y fomento a los generos de las naciones barbaras que obserban sagarmente la estimazion que los Españoles les dan para pedir excesibo valor y comprehender la nezesidad que se tiene de su comercio para la desestimazion del nuestro y que sean tolerados a el abuso y ynfiel amistad en los robos y muertes con que han ostilizado a esta vezindad y a otras barbaras atrozidades con que han pretendido ha solar este Reyno a que no poco conspira los particulares motibos que los mismos vezinos les dan en los rescattes, probocando la enemiga con sus desabridos yndiscretos modos; vajo la pena de sesenta pesos a costos de la tierra y un mes de carcel del vezino o vezinos que se excedieren de los prezios senalados y que perturbaren a otro vezino la compra atravesandosele en el ajuste. Cuya cantidad se aplica por mitad ala Real Camara de Su Magestad y a el que denunciara la contravenzion, y asi mismo mando que ninguna persona de qualesquiera estado, calidad o condizion que sea compre fuera del tiempo en que se manda abrir el rescatte, ninguna pieza ni pieles, ni despues en que se manda zerrar o suspender la referida feria ni llevar ni zitar a los Comanches de noche ni de dia a las casas ni parajes ocultos de bosques o arroyos para comprarles o venderles algunor de estos generos, pues en estos casos se practican y experimentan los excesos de venderles armas prohibivas bulnesarlos arreglados aranzelados precios y perjudicar al Comanche, Yuta o Apache como distante y suelto a el exsamen y zelo dela justicias y otras personas encargadas de este cuidado y la del mismo Governador pena ala que contrabinieze de perdimiento delo que en tal caso comprase sea pieza de yndia o pieles y tanto valor mas en que sele graba aplicado todo por mittad al Real Camara de Su Majestic y ala persona o personas que lo denuncieren con mas tres meses de carcel. Tambien mando que ningun vezino Español, mulatto, coyote, ni yndio de Pueblo entre de noche ni de dia en la rancheria de Comanches, Yutas o Apaches con preteste alguno hasta tanto no seles permita y mande habrir la feria y que asistan en ella las justicias y a el que se cojiere o supiere posibilidad, y al que no la tubiere en dos meses de carcel; y al coyote, mulatto o yndio en zincuenta azotes en una picotta, para evitar por este medio los perjuicios y estersiones que les infieren alas rancherias de las que son repetidas las quexas; y combiene a el servicio de ambas magestades y causa publica evitarlas para conciliar la mas perfecta amistad y buena correspondencia de estas referidas naziones y darles el exemplo e ynstruzion de buenas constumbres ygualmente se prohibe a todo genero de persona la benta en los rescattes de bestias mulares asi por la escasez que ay en el Reyno como por lo que se nesezitan par regues y trafico del comercio debiendose escasear esta especie todo lo possible alas naziones para que consuman los caballos en el empleo de sus cargas y fatiguen en el ynzesante mobimiento de sus bagas republica y continua frequente casa con lo que no podran economizar ni reservar el caballo para hazer la guerra en los paises Catolicos y por la carenzia de su cria y gran consumo en casa y carga les estimulara la nesesidad a mantener fiel amistad con este Reyno para que no seles escasese su comercio y probision y la que no es posible sin grave mas fatales consequencias prohibir en el todo la venta a los gentiles de las caballadas caponas se hace preziso evitar su habundancia y fomento para que no sea perjudicarlissimo a estos dominios del Rey; y el vezino o

yndio que yncurriere en la venta de bestias mulares en los rescattes sele condena en el valor de la mula o macho aplicado ala Real Camara de Su Magestad y denunciador y lo hubiere por mitad; tambien mando a todos los vezinos y havitantes de este Reyno que no declaren ni hagan saber alas dichas naziones con quienes se selebran ferias y rescattes y especialmente ala Comancheria estas politicas y combenientes reglas de prohibicion de venta de armas, yeguas, caballos padres, vestias mulares y prebenidos aranzelados presios; pues por ningun motibo combiene sean sabedores de ellas por las consequentes resultas de sus resentimientos y otras perjudicialisimas al bien publico pues asta tanto se ha estendido la malizia y rudeza de muchas personas que han ynstruido y notiziado a los gentiles de nuestras arregladas precauziones y a el que se supiere fuera osado ha dar semejantes notizias sele castigara con todo rigor y severidad; y este mandamiento se publicara y hara publicar en todas las tres Villas de esta provincia y jurisdiccion de San Geronimo de Taos, por sus Alcaldes Mayores quien seles remitira testimonio para que llegue a noticia de todos y ninguno alegue ygnorancia y para que mejor sea comprendido por lo disperso delas jurisdicciones lo publicaran dichos Alcaldes de quinze en quinze dias quando los Domingos concurren las vezindades en las Parroquias al precepto de la Missa, alas que procuraran ynstruir para su observancia y cumplimiento: Y el Alcalde Mayor dela jurisdiccion de Taos lo hara siempre que se berifiquen rescattes hantes de empezarse la feria haziendo concurrir a todos los vezinos y demas personas en paraje donde seles pueda hazer notorio y que no lo comprenda la rancheria que se hallase situada en la zercania del Pueblo, y dichos Alcaldes todos y cada uno de por si bien sea en su propia jurisdiccion o en otra en que se hallaran a rescatte con sus vezindarios celeran la practica y ejecuzion de lo aqui mandado; sin consentir, tolerar ni disimular los excesos de que les resultara el mas severo castigo. Dado en la Villa de Santa Fee en veinte y seis dias del mes de Nobiembre de mill setezientos zinquenta y quattro años, actuando ante mi con los testigos de mi assistancia de que doy fee.
      Francisco Antonio Marin del Valle (rubric)
Testigo Assistencia
Phelipe Tafoya (rubric) Juan Francisco Arroniz (rubric)

En la Villa de Santa Fee en dos dias de el mes de Disiembre de mill setesientos sinquenta y quatro años yo Dn. Francisco Guerrero Alcalde Mayor en ella y su jurisdiccion en cumplimiento y obedicimiento de lo mandado por el Señor Governador y Capitan General de este Reyno certifico y doy fee que el expresado bando se publico en estta dicha Villa en las puertas del Cuerpo de Guardia deste Real Presidio y a suplicacion concurieron todos los vezinos que presentes se allaban y entendidos de su efecto dixeron que obedecian todo lo mandado por dicho Señor Governador y para que asi conste lo certifique y firme en la expresada Villa de Santa Fee actuando por Receptoria con los testigos de assistencia, de que doy fee.
      Francisco Guerrero (rubric)
Testigo
Lucas Moya (rubric) Diego Antonio dela Pena (rubric)

En la Billa de Alburquerque en ocho dias del mes de Diciembre de mil setecientos y sinquenta y cuatro años yo Dn. Joseph Baca, Alcalde Mayor y Capitan Aguerra de dicha Billa en cumplimiento y obedecimiento delo mandado por el Señor Governador y Capitan General de este Reyno certifico y doi fee que el referido bando se publico en esta Billa y su jurisdiccion y a su publicacion concurieron todos sus moradores los que y entendidos de su mandamiento dijeron que obedecian todos y todo lo expresado y mandado por dicho Señor Governador y para que conste lo rubrique y firme en esta Billa de Alburquerque que atuando por Receptoria con testigos de mi asistencia de que doi fee.
      Joseph Baca (rubric)
Testigo Juan Miguel Albares del Castillo (rubric)
Miguel Montoya (rubric)

En este Pueblo de Zia en beynte dias del mes de Disiembre de este año de mil setesientos sincuenta y cuatro años yo Antonio Baca, Alcalde Mayor y Capitan Aguerra de dicha jurisdiccion en cumplimiento y obedecimiento de lo en este bando mandado por el Señor Governador y Capitan General de este Reyno yse comparecer a los yndios de los tres Pueblos de Zia, Santa Ana y Xemes y estando juntos por ynterpretes les yse saber lo en este bando mandado de que disen lo an entendido y obedesido todo lo espresado por el Señor Governador y para que conste lo certifique y firme en este Pueblo de Zia autuando por Resetoria con testigos de asistencia de que doy fee.
      Antonio Baca (rubric)
Testigo
Diego Antonio Baca (rubric)

En este Pueblo de La Laguna en beinte y seis dias de el mes de Diciembre de este año de mil setesientos y cincuenta y cuatro años yo Manuel Baca Alcalde Mayor y Capitan Aguerra de dicha jurisdiccion en cumplimiento y obedecimiento de lo en este bando mandado por el Señor Governador y Capitan General de este Reyno yse comparecer a los yndios de el Pueblo de Acoma y estando juntos en esta casa de comunidad y con ynterprete les ysse saber lo en este bando mandado de que disen lo an entendido y obedesido todo lo espresado por el Señor Governador y para que conste lo certifico y firme en este Pueblo de la Laguna autuando por Receptoria con testigo de assistencia de que doy fee.
      Manuel Baca (rubric)
Testigo
Joseph Chavez (rubric)

Notes

1. The price for Indian captives varied. In 1704 Lieutenant Governor Páez Hurtado warned settlers against giving more than one horse for two Apaches, though he did not specify their age (see Doc. 2). In 1723 a Pecos Indian leader claimed that Governor Martínez owed him two horses for an Indian boy. Note that Marín de Valle's prices were provided entirely in "good of the land," or barter. No pesos or other monetary values are mentioned.
2. *Reducción* generally meant placing the roving Indians in a settled environment.
3. Valle seems to be saying that because Indian trade goods, that is, skins and hides, were in such demand, that when there was competition among the settlers, the Indians would keep raising their prices, and the settlers ended up undercutting each other. Also note that when the price of the skins increased, the price of the horses increased correspondingly.
4. Charles Cutter has stated that incarceration was not used as a punishment in the earlier days of the colony, but that by the mid-eighteenth century, the threat of imprisonment was beginning to be used as a deterrent to crime (Cutter, *Legal Culture*: 122).
5. *Ranchería*, or *rancho*, is a name given to an Indian camp, a collection of temporary or easily removable dwellings.
6. See Doc. 29.
7. See Doc. 33.
8. Antonio Baca's siblings included Diego Manuel, María Magdalén, Juan Antonio, Juana, Josefa, and Cristóbal Baca. Their father was Manuel Baca, and their grandfather was Cristóbal II, who lived in New Mexico before the revolt, served in the El Paso presidio, and returned to New Mexico by 1693. Cristóbal I was in New Mexico by 1603. Around that time, the family owned an estancia in the Santa Fe River Valley at El Alamo. Based on Antonio Baca's will, he was a trader with the Janos presidio, Sevilleta, and other areas to the south. When Antonio was an alcalde of Zia Pueblo, both he and his father were accused of mistreating the Indians. However, in Governor Cachupín's evaluation in 1754, he stated that Baca was a suitable alcalde for the pueblos of Zia, Santa Ana, and Jemez: "He is an accommodating man and, with his charity, attends to the building of the church at Zia. He has well-known valor and merit in the service (Thomas, *Plains Indians*: 141; Kessell and Hendricks, *RCR*: 88 n 69; Kessell et al., *BOB*: 1178 n108; Chávez, *Origins*: 144-45; Barrett, *Settlement*: 43; SANM I #83, WPA translation; NMGS, *Aquí*: 60-61,74-75).
9. There were several persons named Manuel Baca. This was probably the son of Josefa Baca, making him a nephew of the Antonio Baca named above. Manuel married Feliciana Chávez in 1746 (Chávez, *Origins*: 44-145).

44

ROYAL ROADS IN SANTA FE TO BE UNBLOCKED; OFFENDING PROPERTY OWNERS LISTED
April 5–20, 1756. Source: Chávez Collection, file 15.

Synopsis and editor's notes: In 1756 Governor Valle, referencing earlier documents in the presidio archives,[1] stated that the width of the main street in Santa Fe, known as San Francisco, should be eight varas—wide enough for carts and other business. He described this street as going on the west side of the Palace of the Governors north to an arroyo called *seco* (dry). On this street, as well as one that runs from the "cienega" to a swampy area to the west, he ordered that the fences and other obstructions were to be removed, leaving the road "as it was before," as described in the earlier documents. He named the people who had placed obstructions in the roads and ordered them to clear the street to the required width.

To those of us used to the later maps and the current alignment of the streets, the description of the two roads and their relationship to the fort and the Palace is not familiar, with San Francisco going east–west in front of the Palace and then turning a corner and going north to the "arroyo seco." In other words, San Francisco Street had both east–west and north–south sections. The 1767 Urrutia map (Map 1, Appendix) is of some help in following Valle's description, though that map does not provide street names.

In establishing towns in the Spanish colonies, the 1681 *Recopilación de leyes de los reynos de las Indias* (Laws of the Indies) provided guidelines for streets, as follows: "Book IV, Title 7, Law 10: Plan of the Streets. Madrid 1681. Don Felipe II. In cold towns, the streets shall be wide, and in hot towns they shall be narrow. Where there are horses, it will be necessary for defense in times of danger that the street be wide, and that they be enlarged in the way prescribed, making sure that they do not create any difficult situation that might lead to deformation in rebuilding of the town, and that might be prejudicial to its defense and comfort." The width of the wide and narrow streets was apparently left up the town founders and later administrators.

Year of 1756

Proceedings regarding the opening of the roads

Don Francisco Antonio Marín del Valle, governor and captain general of this kingdom of New Mexico and castellan of the royal forces and presidios for his majesty, etc.

Whereas the royal roads of this villa are found to have been blocked, as can be seen by the proceedings which are found in the archives and which was followed up on by the colonel don Gerbasio Cruzat y Góngora, governor and captain general, who was formerly of this kingdom of New Mexico [1731–1736], and through which it can been seen that there was left for the width of the road eight *varas*,[2] beginning from the fort which is on the west side of this palace, and going in a straight line to the north up to the arroyo which is commonly known as the *seco*, and which at the present time is blocked by residents who are as follows: Luis Jaramillo,[3] don Juan Joseph Moreno,[4] and Juan de Alari.[5] Thus I should order and did order that the lieutenant of this royal presidio, don Vicente Ginzo Ron y Thobar,[6] whom I commission to attend to this and to see that this is done, summon the said parties, carrying with him the stated proceedings, and summon the witnesses who are still found alive so that they can clarify where it [the road] ran. Once this is done he shall order those stated above, Luis Jaramillo, don Joseph Moreno, and Juan Alari, that they should immediately and without hesitation provide that which is stated and in the way which it is ordered.

With respect to knowing that the fence for the gardens of this palace and that of the said don Juan Joseph Moreno have blocked another ancient road which comes west from the cienega to this villa, which is to be left open by both parties, I order the said lieutenant to see that the fences are taken down in order to leave sufficient width so that the carts and other business which is common to this villa can move through, as this is ordered through royal laws. Those who are in this same alignment one after another, Juan de Alari, Luis Jaramillo, and the others who follow are to do the same up to where it meets the other royal road, which is to the west of the cienega of this villa. The said lieutenant is to order that this be executed immediately, giving them the time of twelve days, which are to be counted from the time of notification of my order, and, in case of renouncement by anyone, he is to notify me so that I can proceed with the punishment, which power is given to me in case of disobedience.

I thus approved, ordered, and signed it, acting as it is with my assisting witnesses due to the lack of a public or royal scribe, which there is none, and is done at the Villa of Santa Fe on the 5th of April, 1756.
    Francisco Antonio Marín del Valle (rubric)
Witnesses
Juan Antonio de Arróniz (rubric)
Thoribio Ortiz (rubric)

At this villa of Santa Fe on the 10th of April, 1756, I, don Vicente Ginzo Ron y Thobar, lieutenant in this royal presidio, by virtue of the decree issued by the don

Francisco Antonio Marín del Valle, governor and captain general of this kingdom, and by the commission given to me by the said governor, and in order to carry it out as ordered, I summoned the following persons to appear before me: don Joseph Moreno, Juan de Alari, Luis Jaramillo, Juan Gabaldón,[7] María and Juan de Ledesma,[8] Antonio Morán,[9] Joseph Luján,[10] the alférez Francisco Esquibel,[11] and the retired lieutenant general don Manuel Sanz de Garbizu,[12] all residents with encroachment on the road which according to royal ordinances was to be left as it was before; and everyone being present, along with my assisting witnesses, made them know and notified them of the decree which was issued by said governor and captain general, and everyone understanding what was ordered they said that they would obey and are ready to leave the royal road in the form and manner which is ordered. This they all gave as their response, and they signed it with me and my assisting witnesses due to the lack of a public or royal scribe, which there is none in this kingdom, to which I certify.

Luis Jaramillo Sáenz
Vicente Ginzo Ron y Thobar (rubric)
Juez comisario
Joseph Miguel de la Peña (rubric) Francisco Esquibel (rubric)
Juan de Gabaldón (rubric) Juan Joseph Moreno (rubric)
Manuel Sanz de Garbizu (rubric) Thoribio Ortiz (rubric)
Juan de Alari (rubric)

On the 11th of the said month and year, I, the said lieutenant, having concluded with that which was ordered by the governor and captain general don Francisco Antonio Marín del Valle, and finding myself about to submit this to his honor, respectfully leaving the roads in this villa in the manner which was ordered of me, and so that his honor is in full recognition of this and for those who come later and who are to follow them in the future, whoever they may be, and so that no resident along the roads will impede them with their fences. One of the roads is the one which comes from in front of the west side [on the opposite side] of the palace and goes in front of the lodging of the corporal of this royal presidio, Luis Jaramillo, which lodging is in the middle of said fort[13] along the said road [which goes] in a direct straight line to the north up to the arroyo seco. It is bounded by the fence of the palace and that of the said corporal Jaramillo, followed by that of retired lieutenant don Joseph Moreno, followed by his lands, and in front of the lands of Juan de Alari, until it meets the mentioned arroyo. The name of the said road is San Francisco.

The other road comes from east of the cienega of this villa in a straight line to the west until it meets the royal road which goes to Tesuque. It is bounded by the fence [*zerca* or *cerca*] of the palace and in front of [opposite] the road, that fence of the said don Joseph Moreno, and following the said street that [fence] of Luis Jaramillo, and in front of [opposite] that one is that [fence] of Juan de Alari, then the wall [*tapia*] of don Juan Gabaldón, the house of Ledesma, that of Antonio Morán and the lands of don Manuel Sanz de Garbizu, and in front of that one, the back of the house of the alférez of this royal presidio, Francisco Esquibel, along with his corral until it meets the said royal road, which goes to Tesuque. This road is named San Antonio.

So that is valid, I signed it acting as presiding judge along with my assisting witnesses as has been said, to which I certify.

Vizente Ginzo Ron y Thobar (rubric)
commissioned judge
Thoribio Ortiz (rubric)

Witness
Joseph Miguel de la Peña (rubric)

At the villa of Santa Fe on the 20th of April, 1756.

Having seen the proceedings which were carried out at my order by the lieutenant of this royal presidio, don Vicente Ginzo Ron y Thobar, regarding the opening of the roads as is ordered, and this having been executed by the said lieutenant, and it having been concluded, I order that this be placed in the archive of this government under my command so that those who succeed me are cognizant of what has been done. I, don Francisco Antonio Marín del Valle, governor and captain general of this kingdom, thus decreed, ordered, and signed it along with my assisting witnesses, which I certify.

Marín (rubric)
Thoribio Ortiz (rubric) Juan Francisco de Arróniz (rubric)

ORIGINAL DOCUMENT

Año de 1756

Diligencias seguidas sobre que se habran los caminos

En 3 foxas

Don Francisco Antonio Marin del Valle, Governador y Capitan General de este Reyno de la Nueba Mexico y Castellano de Sus Reales Fuerzas y Presidios por Su Magestad, ut supra.

Por quanto resulta hallarsen perjudicos los caminos reales de esta Villa como

claramente consta por dilixencias que se hallan en este Archibo que sobre ello siguio el Señor Coronel Don Gerbasio Cruzat y Gongora Governador y Capitan General que fue de este Reyno de la Nueba Mexico por las quales se biene en conosimiento se dexo el camino de ancho de ocho varas desde el fuerte que esta al poniente de este Palazio en linia recta al norte asta el arroyo que bulgarmente llaman seco y hallandose en la presente occasion ataxado por los vezinos a el como son Luis Jaramillo, Don Juan Joseph Moreno y Juan de Alari, devia de mandar y mando que el Theniente de este Real Presidio Don Vizente Ginzo Ron y Thobar aquien le confiero comision pase al reconosimiento de ello zitando alas partes expresadas y llevando para su govierno las expresadas dilixensias y zitando a los testigos que se hallaran bibos para que estos aclaren por la parte donde era y fecho que sea les mandara a los expresados Luis Jaramillo, Don Joseph Moreno y Juan de Alari que luego y sin la menor dilazion amplien el expresado en la manera que se mando. Otro si mando a dicho Theniente que respectto de ser sabedor que la zerca de las huertas de este Palazio y la del dicho Don Juan Joseph Moreno que tienen perjudicado otro camino antiguo que sale de la zienega de esta Villa al viento poniente se dexe libre de una y otra parte por lo que mandara se retiren las zercas dexandole la anchura sufiziente para el transito de carretas y demas negocios al comun de esta Villa por estar asi mandado por Leyes Reales y alinia recta Juan de Alari, Luis Jaramillo y demas que se siguieren executaran lo mismo asta salir al otro Camino Real que esta al poniente de la zienega de esta Villa, lo que mandara dicho Theniente se execute puntualmente consediendole el termino de dose dias que se contaran desde el de la notificazion de esta mi probedenzia y en caso de renunzia por alguno me dara quenta para prozeder al castigo que dexo a mi reservado por la ynobedienzia, hasi lo provey mande y firme actuando auna con los testigos de mi asistenzia a falta de Escribano Publico ni Real que no lo ay y es fecho en esta Villa de Santa Fee en zinco dias del mes de Abril de mill setezientos zinquenta y seys años.
                Francisco Antonio Marin del Valle (rubric)

Testigos
Juan Antonio de Arroniz (rubric)
Thoribio Ortiz (rubric)

En esta Villa de Santa Fee en diez dias del mes de Abril del año de mil setezientos y cinquenta y seis años yo Don Bizente Ginzo Ron y Thobar Theniente de este Real Presidio en birtud del aucto que antezede del Señor Don Francisco Antonio Marin del Valle, Governador y Capitan General de este Reino y comision en el ynserto ami cometida por dicho Señor para su cumplimento de mi obedezimiento ylo mandado zite ala persona de Don Joseph Moreno, Juan de Alari, Luis Jaramillo, Juan Gabaldon, María Ledesma y Juan de Ledesma, Antonio Moran, Joseph Lujan, el Alferez Francisco Esquibel, y el Theniente General reformado Don Manuel Sanz de Garbizu, todos circumbezinos al camino que segun ordenanzas reales se mando dejar alos quales estando todos presentes les hize saver y notifique el aucto que antezede de dicho Señor Governador y Capitan General en presenzia de los testigos de mi assistenzia quienes entendidos de todo lo contenido dijeron que le obedezen y que estan prontos a dejar el Camino Real en la forma y manera que seles manda esto dieron por su respuesta y lo firmaron con migo y testigos de asistenzia a falta de Scribano Publico ni Real que no lo ai en este Reino, doi fee = Entre renglones vale = Luis Xaramillo =

            Vizente Ginzo Ron y Thobar (rubric)
            Juez Comisario
Joseph Miguel de la Pena (rubric) Francisco Esquibel (rubric)
    Juan de Gabaldon (rubric) Juan Joseph Moreno (rubric)
  Manuel Sanz de Garbizu (rubric) Thoribio Ortiz (rubric)
              Juan de Alari (rubric)

En onze dias de dicho mes y año yo el expresado Theniente haviendo concluido con lo mandado en la providenzia del Señor Governador y Capitan General Don Francisco Antonio Marin del Valle, y allarme para azer la remision a Su Señoria de ello respecto de dejar yo puestos los caminos en esta Villa en la forma que seme ordena para que Su Señoria venga en pleno conozimiento de ello y los Señores subsesores quele subsedieren enlo adelante de quales son y que ningun vezino confinante a ellos lo ataje con sus zercas; es el uno que sale del frente que esta al lado del poniente del Palazio a la frente de la casa del Cavo de este Real Presidio Luis Jaramillo; en cuio medio de dicho fuerte y casa entre dicho camino en derechura a linia recta al norte asta el arroyo seco siendo lindantes a la zerca del Palacio, la de dicho Cavo Xaramillo, y sigue la del Theniente reformado Don Joseph Moreno prosiguiendo tierras del dicho, y a su frente tierras de Juan de Alari asta salir al menzionado arroio, y a dicho camino se le pone nombre de San Francisco. Y el otro es del oriente de la zienega de esta Villa en derechura al poniente asta salir al Camino Real que ba para Techuque y los lindantes a el son la zerca del Palacio y a su frente la del dicho Don Joseph Moreno siguiendo dicha calle la de Luis Xaramillo y a su frente la de Juan de Alari la tapia de Don Juan Gabaldon, la casa de Ledesma, la de Antonio Moran y tierras de Don Manuel Sanz de Garbizu y a su frente la espalda de la casa del Alferez de este Real Presidio Francisco Esquibel y corral de el dicho asta salir a dicho Camino Real que ba para Techuque al qual sele pone nombre de San Antonio. Y para que conste lo firme autuando como Juez receptor con los testigos de mi asistenzia como dicho es doi fee =

            Vizente Ginzo Ron y Thobar (rubric)
            Juez Comisario
            Thoribio Ortiz (rubric)

Testigo
Joseph Miguel de la Pena (rubric)

En la Villa de Santa Fee en veynte dias del mes de Abril de mill setezientos zincuenta y seys años = Haviendo bisto estas dilixencias que de orden mio siguio el Theniente de este Real Presidio Don Vizente Ginzo Ron y Thobar sobre abrir los caminos como consta por mi probidenzia y estar ya executado por dicho Theniente y concluydo por lo que mando se archiben en el Archibo de esta governazion de mi cargo para los Señores subsesores que me subrediesen vengan en conosimiento de ello; hasi lo decrete, mande y firme yo Don Francisco Antonio Marin del Valle, Governador y Capitan General de este Reyno con los testigos de asistenzia doy fee =

Marin (rubric)

Juan Francisco de Arroniz (rubric)

Thoribio Ortiz (rubric)

Translated by J. Richard Salazar, with the assistance of Cordelia Thomas Snow and Rick Hendricks

Notes

1. To date, no copies of these earlier documents have been found.
2. A *vara* is a linear measurement of approximately 33 inches (Hadley et al., *Presidio*: 534).
3. The 1764 will of Corporal Luis Jaramillo states that he was the son of Cristóbal Jaramillo and Leonora Luján Domínguez, and the husband of doña María Antonia Lucero de Godoy, the daughter of Juan Lucero. She was also the granddaughter of Juan Lucero de Godoy, who returned to New Mexico with the Reconquest. Luis's will lists his possessions, including his house, "composed of 17 rooms, six above and the rest below, with a patio," and "a piece of land adjoining said house half of which is made into a garden." In the muster of 1761, Luis is listed as a corporal with "seven horses and otherwise fully equipped" (SANM I #418, WPA translation; Hadley et al., *Presidio*: 300; Chávez, *Origins*: 198).
4. In Juan José Moreno's will of 1756, he states that he was born in Seville, Spain, and was married to doña Juana Roybal, the daughter of don Ignacio de Roybal (see Doc. 15) and doña Francisca Gómez. In 1737 he was an alférez and sergeant of the presidio. From 1744 to 1748, he was the alcalde at Pecos. Between 1748 and 1750, he was the collector of church tithes for the bishop of Durango. In 1754 Governor Vélez Cachupín stated that he was not in service because of an illness, "though he is a man of merit." His will shows that by the 1750s or earlier, he became a rancher, with a large numbers of horses and cattle in northern New Mexico, and a Chihuahua trader, with hides and goods on hand. He states that in Santa Fe, his residence contained "a hall, three rooms, kitchen, corrals, stables and two other rooms with cultivated land contiguous to the house, said lands running as far as the river" (Thomas, *Plains Indians*: 141; Frank, "Settler to Citizen": 447; SANM I #552, Tigges, "Pastures": 261; Pinart Collection, P-E 46: 1; SANM I #552, WPA translation; Kessell, *Kiva*: 505; Doc. 16).
5. Juan [Antonio] de Alari was the son of Juan Bautista Alari (Jean de Alay), a Frenchman who came to Taos around 1740. Juan Antonio was included in a 1761 presidio muster, with "seven horses and otherwise fully equipped." In 1864 he married Dominga Roybal, who had been raised by doña Juana Roybal, the wife of Juan José Moreno (Chávez, *Origins*: 122-23; Hadley et al., *Presidio*: 301).
6. Vicente Ginzo Ron y Thobar was the lieutenant of the Santa Fe presidio in 1755. After he petitioned the presidio in 1757 for resignation, his position was taken by Carlos Fernández. Vicente had previously married Prudencia Gonzales Bas, the daughter of Juan Gonzales Bas, an alcalde of Albuquerque (SANM II #533 and #537; Chávez, *Origins*: 186).
7. Juan [Manuel] Gabaldón was in New Mexico by 1731. In 1735 he was acting as an attorney for the widow of Tomé Domínguez de Mendoza, whose family had lived in New Mexico before 1680, but who had remained in Chihuahua. In 1735 Juan married Antonia Juliana Archibeque, a granddaughter of Juan Archibeque, and in 1739 he purchased a house in Santa Fe. He prepared a will in 1745, though he lived after that. The will stated that he was a native of Los Ángeles [Puebla, México], and that he had bought land formerly owned by Joseph Garzía, the tailor. In addition he had a large number of cattle, mules, an oxen and a cart, as well as saddles, lassos, and carpenter's tools. Finally he added that he owed money for 45 fanegas of tomatoes in twenty-seven sacks (Chávez, *Origins*: 129, 177; SANM I #331, #339, WPA translation).

8. It is likely that Juan de Ledesma was a descendant of Francisco de Ledesma, who came to New Mexico in 1662. Juan was in New Mexico as a soldier at least by June 18, 1723, with all his weapons and five horses. He was a survivor of the Villasur expedition. His first wife was Juana de la Cruz, who died in 1726. In 1767 Juan sold his house and land in Santa Fe (Christmas, *Military Records*: 46-47; Chávez, *Origins*: 204; SANM I #785; Barrett, *Settlement*: 151; Thomas Chávez, *Moment*: 306).
9. According to Chávez, Antonio Morán was the son of Miguel Morán, who returned to New Mexico in 1693. Miguel was listed in a 1680 muster called by Otermín. He and Antonio may have been descendants of Gerónimo Morán, who was in New Mexico in 1642 and 1662, or perhaps even Juan Morán, who came to New Mexico with Oñate. Antonio was married to Juana Dorotea del Gil in 1728 (Chávez, *Origins*: 239; Kessell et al., *BOB*: 1161 n13; Barrett, *Settlement*: 98, 101; Hackett, *Historical Documents*: 148).
10. A Joseph Luján is mentioned in a June 18, 1723, muster as a presidio soldier, and also in Doc. 18, describing the arrest of Alonso Real de Aguilar, though it is not known whether this is same person (Christmas, *Military Records*: 50).
11. In 1732 Francisco Esquibel was the son of Juan Antonio Esquibel, who settled in Santa Cruz by 1695. Francisco married Clara Gonzales Bas, a daughter of Antonio Gonzales Bas and granddaughter or great-granddaughter of Juan Gonzales Bas. He is shown in a presidio power-of-attorney for 1741 as having "six horses and fully equipped." Francisco is noted as an alférez in 1766 (Kessell et al., *BOB*: 644 n 25; SANM I #275; NMGS, *Aquí*: 312; Chávez, *Origins*: 189-90).
12. According to Chávez, Manuel Sanz (aka Sáenz) de Garvizu was a native of Spain and a lieutenant at the presidio in 1745. In 1738 he purchased the Diego Arias de Quiros property "next to the tower of the palace" (Chávez, *Origins*: 277; SANM I #846).
13. The Urrutia map does not indicate a fort, but it does shows a structure with an interior courtyard directly west of the palace. This courtyard, which could have been part of a residence, may have had access through the middle of the east wall of the fort onto the north–south street.

45

BERNARDO MIERA Y PACHECO PETITIONS GOVERNOR TO REPAIR CANNON; VILLAGES ELDERS EXPRESS DOUBT; BLACKSMITH TOMÁS DE SENA SUBMITS BID
February 15, 1757. Source: Pinart Collection, P-E 50: 2.

Synopsis and editor's notes: Having come to New Mexico in 1754 at the same time as Governor Marín de Valle, the enterprising don Bernardo Miera y Pacheco petitioned the governor for permission to repair the decrepit cannon he found at the Santa Fe presidio. The governor responded by asking three long-time presidio soldiers their opinion of the feasibility of the project. After consideration, they tactfully said that they could not condone it, but that nothing would be lost if he tried to make the repairs, which Miera y Pacheco did, but unsuccessfully. At this point Tomás Sena, blacksmith, made himself known and gave the governor a bid for the repair of the presidio cannon and for fifty lances made from the leftover material. To date there is no record of whether Sena's bid was approved or if his efforts at cannon repair were any more successful than Miera y Pacheco's.

Several cannons are mentioned in other documents. Much earlier, in 1692, don Diego de Vargas stated that he brought "gun carriages with the bronze cannon" to Santa Fe as part of the Reconquest. It is not known whether these cannons were those referred to sixty-five years later in this document, though Miera y Pacheco does refer to cannons of the "old type." The 1762 presidio inventory carried out by Governor Cachupín at the beginning of his second term, as translated in Document 47, listed five cannons. In a document from 1763, Cachupín referred to some old, useless cannons he wished to replace, very likely the same ones discussed here. Finally, much later, in 1810, the commandant general of the Interior Provinces of New Spain, Nemisio Salcedo, wrote to Governor Manrique about two artillery cannons in New Mexico with gun carriages found to be defective and gave instructions for making new ones (AGN PI Leg. 102, f 34; SANM II #2283; Kessell and Hendricks, *BFA*: 386).

Miera y Pacheco was a person of many accomplishments: military officer, alcalde mayor, trader, maker of paintings and religious images, cartographer, and member of the well-known Escalante expedition from Santa Fe to the Utah Basin in 1776 (Kessell, *Kiva*: 385; Chávez, *Origins*: 229-23; Bolton, *Pageant*, especially 243-50). Of particular interest is his own review of his military career, written to the viceroy to secure a military post in New Mexico (Miera y Pacheco, Newberry Library, Ayer Ms. 1, no date).

St. Raphael, by Miera y Pacheco, 1780. Oil and gesso painting on pine. The inscription states that it was commissioned by Doña Apolonia de Sandoval, wife of Salvador García de Noriega. Photo by Jack Parsons. Pierce and Weigle, *Spanish New Mexico* 1: 31. #83. Image courtesy of the Museum of Spanish Colonial Arts, Collections of the Spanish Colonial Arts Society, Inc., Santa Fe.

Governor and captain general

I, Bernardo Miera y Pacheco, alcalde mayor and war captain of the pueblos of Pecos and Galisteo, before your honor appear in the best form which I have as my right and say that this kingdom is found to be surrounded by enemies, especially by the nations of the north and northeast, which ought to be curtailed from their cruelties, which besides being so bellicose are being supplied with numerous firearms. There is not within this kingdom any more resistance than that supplied by the eighty mounted soldiers from this presidio, although there are numerous residents, but which are found, as your honor well knows, to lack offensive or defensive arms because they are so terribly poor.[1] Because of this, I wish to inform your honor that within the guard house there are found some metals from burst cannons of the old type with the firing chambers [*recameras*] also broken and totally useless. I feel that I can put them to some use and wish to see if I can somehow salvage one cannon, by doing everything I possibly can, as I have some working knowledge of how to do this (even though this has not been my profession). By applying myself to them, it is possible that one cannon can be made useful. With respect to these arms, and with their knowing about them, these large nations could be subjugated. For this I ask of your honor to order that these metals be given to me as I desire to use for fabrication and to provide this service to the King, my lord (whom God may guard). I swear in all form of my right that this document is not done in malice, but only for that which I have expressed, and for what is necessary, etc.

Bernardo de Miera y Pacheco (rubric)

Santa Fe, September 13th, 1756.

This petition is hereby presented and admitted as it has in all its proper right, as is that contained in it, and with the intent to that which was presented by this party, I should order and did order that the officials be asked if this subject is capable of doing what he has promised in his document so that by my seeing it I can make my determination. I thus decreed it, ordered it, and signed it, don Francisco Antonio Marín del Valle, governor and captain general of this kingdom.

Marín (rubric)

Sir, upon seeing that which was ordered by your honor in regard to the document presented by don Bernardo Miera y Pacheco, and by which your honor ordered the officials to inform him if the said don Bernardo could accomplish what he promised, we cannot affirm that he can accomplish what he promised (as he stated that it was not his profession), for which reason we are not certain of his zeal, although he does it for the service of our lord and king. With respect to what we understand, it will be interesting to see if the said don Bernardo can accomplish what was promised, as nothing can be lost by giving him the metals and firing chambers which he asks for, as they are of no value to this royal presidio and are totally useless. By not complying with what he asks for, the metals will remain in the same state as they are, which is of no value. By complying with it, they could be fabricated into something that can be used against the numerous nations of the north, which are being provided with firearms by the French, along with munitions and good gunpowder.

All of these metals are of value, being that we are lacking arms of all kinds. What arms we have are of bad quality, as your honor well knows, as after being fired twice, they are incapable of again firing rapidly because of the sediment which remains on the hammer and pan of the musket. There are times when they remain on fire without firing properly, causing the aim to be faulty and injury to our men. There is no other defense to this kingdom other than the eighty men in the presidio, nor other means of defense than that which is stated in order to repel the large Comanche nation, which is the one which attacks the northern part of the frontiers of this said kingdom. Taking advantage of what don Bernardo intends will aid the eighty presidial soldiers in such a way that they can contain the Comanches, even though they may come united, as they now are with the Jumana nation. Hopefully, as it appears it may be quite useful, said metals will be given to him, since by not giving them to him they will remain as we have stated. Your honor shall determine as he will, for his convenience, as is always the best. villa of Santa Fe, September 14, 1756

    Vicente Ginzo Ron y Thobar[2] (rubric)
    Francisco Esquibel[3] (rubric)
    Antonio Sedillo[4] (rubric)
    At the request of Sergeant Bartolomé Maese[5]
    Thomas Casillas[6] (rubric)

Santa Fe, September 15, 1756

 By virtue of the information given to me by the officials of this royal presidio in which they state that it appears to them to be proper to give the metals found in the guard house, which are of no value along with the firing chambers, to don Bernardo de Miera y Pacheco so that he can see if they can be used to create a cannon as he states in his document. Agreeing with information given, I order that the metals be given to the said don Bernardo as a result of his effort to do it in service to his majesty; and if the order is not carried out, everything will remain as it now is. I thus also order my administrator, who is to carry out the order in favor of the said don Bernardo to provide whatever is necessary, of [illegible] and wire and anything else that he may need. Once it is completed, he will present it to me so that what he promised is proven accordingly. As such I decreed it, ordered it, and signed it, don Francisco Antonio Marín del Valle, governor and captain general of this kingdom of New Mexico, acting with my assisting witness, to which I certify.

    Marín (rubric)

Witnesses:
Joseph Maldonado (rubric)
Francisco de Arróniz (rubric)

 At the villa of Santa Fe on the 20th day of the month of October of 1756, before me, don Francisco Antonio Marín del Valle, governor and captain general of this kingdom of New Mexico, appeared don Bernardo de Miera y Pacheco, saying that after having done everything possible that he desired and hoped could be done, it is not possible to accomplish what was promised in his petition. But hoping to see that the cannons are placed in working order, along with redoing the firing chambers as they need to be tapped and redone, it has come to light that the master blacksmith, Thomas de Sena,[7] is capable of doing this due to his ingenuity. I ordered that he appear before me and present himself. The cannons and firing chambers being within his presence, he stated that he would do everything he could to repair the firing chambers, redo the cannons, and reinforce them. As such, I ordered that everything be turned over to him as it was, so that, as he understands the idea of how to do it, he can perform the work. At the same time he was ordered that, from the excess iron he did not use on the cannons, he was to make thirty lances for the royal service. All of which he agreed to do. And so that it was carried out, I did it as a proceeding which was signed with me and assisting witnesses, to which I certify.

Francisco Marín del Valle (rubric)

Tomás Antonio de Sena (rubric)

Witnesses
Joseph Maldonado (rubric)
Juan Francisco de Arróniz (rubric)

In this villa of Santa Fe on the 15th day of the month of February, 1757, before me, don Francisco Antonio Marín del Valle, governor and captain general of this kingdom of New Mexico, appeared the master blacksmith, Thomas de Sena, who stated that he would make and did make an exhibition of five cannons, four which he made from iron and the other one which he made out of bronze, all of which he had made. He made three from iron and one from bronze, and the other one of iron was already there. He also made five firing chambers and thirty lances, which he was ordered to provide and which he was able to make serviceable from that which was of no value. I asked Sena how much his work was worth, and he stated that for the four cannons which he made and tapped, it would be twenty-five pesos of the current money of the land; for the one that was already made but which he reinforced, it would be eighteen pesos; for the five firing chambers which he tapped and drilled, it would be five pesos for each one; for the thirty lances which he made, it would be fifty pesos; and that everything totaled to the amount of one hundred ninety-three pesos currently of the land, stating that was his charge for his work. At the same time, he provided the iron which had been left over, and which, upon weighing, came to seven arrobas, eighteen and one-half pounds. I asked him if he wanted it for his work, to which he stated that he did, at which time I ordered that it be given to him. He took it as received and as paid for his work, to which I made a proceeding, and he signed it along with me and my assisting witnesses, to which I certify.

Francisco Antonio Marín del Valle (rubric)

Thomas Antonio de Sena (rubric)

Witnesses
Joseph Maldonado (rubric)
Juan Francisco de Arróniz (rubric)

This four-pounder Spanish light swivel cannon is the type used on the walls of presidios in the eighteenth century. It was found at a Spanish fort in the Philippines.
Brinkerhoff and Faulk, *Lancers*: 76, Plate 12. File #4023a.
Image courtesy of the Arizona State Museum, University of Arizona, Tucson.

ORIGINAL DOCUMENT

Señor Governador y Capitan General
Dn. Bernardo Miera y Pacheco Alcalde Mayor y Capitan Aguerra de los Pueblos de Pecos y Galisteo ante Vuestra Señoria paresco en la mejor forma que aya en derecho y digo, que hallandose este Reyno circumbalado de enemigos de que se deve recelar de sus crutelas y especialmente de las Naciones del Norte y nordeste que fuera de ser tan velicosas se ban fomentando con muchas armas de fuego y no aviendo en todo este Reyno mas resistencia que de los ochenta soldados montados de este Presidio pues aunque ay vezindario este se halla como a Vuestra Señoria Ie consta lo mas de el sin armas ofensitas ni defensibas por su suma pobresa. Por tanto devo exponer a Vuestra Señoria que en el Cuerpo de Guardia se hallan unos metales de canones rebentados de la moda antigua can las recamaras yndependientes tambien desfogonados totalmente enserbible se echo mano para fundirlo, respecto de hallarme con alguna mediana ynteligencia de hacerlo y ber de este modo si puedo sacar algun canon poniendo todos los medios posibles para dicho fm (aunque no asido mi profesion) que consiguiendo se podran ynfabricando otro para que sirban de util y respecto a estas armas y sujecion a el orgullo de estas crecidas Naciones por todo lo qual, a Vuestra Señoria supplico mande se me entriegen dichos metales pues mi deseo es de azertar en la fabrica y hacer este servizio al Rey mi Señor (que Dios Guarde) y juro en toda forma de derecho este mi escripto no ser de malizia solo si al fin que expressado llevo y en lo necessario, ut supra.

Bernardo de Miera y Pacheco (rubric)

Santa Fee Septiembre 13 de 1756 años

Por presentada y admitada esta pettision en quanto ha lugar en derecho, por el contenido en ella y atento a lo que esta parte biene expresando devia de mandar y mando ynformen los ofiziales si este suxecto hara lo que promete en su escrito para en su bista determinar lo que hubiere lugar. Asi lo decrette mande y firme yo Dn. Francisco Antonio Marín del Valle, Governador y Capitan General de este Reyno.

Marín (rubric)

Señor en vista de lo providenziado por Vuestra Señoria en el excripto presentado por Dn. Bernardo de Miera y Pacheco en que nos manda Vuestra Señoria a los ofiziales informemos si el expresado Dn Bernardo ara lo que promete, tenemos que en quanto a que aga lo que promete no podemos afirmar (mas expresando el dicho no ser su profesion) por lo que tenimos inconozimiento sumo zelo el que en el dicho reside al servizio de Nuestro Rey y Señor y respecto de ver nosotros que el poner los medios dicho Dn. Bernardo aver si sale con ello y no viniendose a perder nada, por quanto los metales que pide y camaras no son de ningun util a este Real Presidio por estar totalmente inservibles; pues no saliendo con ello quedan los mesmos mettales en la forma de inservibles como estan, y saliendo con ello se pondran fabricados algunos los que serviran de mucho respecto a estas armas para contra las numerosas Naziones del Norte, por quanto se allan abastezidas por los Franzeses de fuzilerra muniziones y polvera buena pues esta despues de ser las armas cortas es talla calidad de ella como a Vuestra Señoria Ie consta que a los dos turos ya quedala lla incapaz de bolver prontamente a dar fuego por el mucho sarro que de en el rastrillo y cazuleja; pues ai lomas de las ocaziones que se esta gran ratto ardiendo sin dar fuego biolento causa de perderse la punteria y que suseda desgrazia en los nuestros y no teniendo este Reyno defensa alguna mas que la de los ochenta ombres Presidiales ni otra mas fortaleza (illegible) que lo expresado para poder reparar ala crezida Nacion Cumanchi que es la que mas obstiliza por la parte del Norte a las fronteras de este dicho Reyno lograndose el intento que el dicho Dn. Bernardo expone servira con los ochenta Presidiales en algun modo contenerlos aunque esta benga coligados como lo estan con la Nazion Jumana y oxa por lo que nos pareze ser mui combeniente sele subministren dichos metales pues de no salir con ello quedaran como llevamos expresado. Vuestra Señoria en todo determinara lo que tubiere por mas de combeniente que sera como siempre lo mexor. Villa de Santa Fee y Septiembre catorze de mil setezientos y cinquenta y seis años.

Vizente Ginzo Ron y Thobar (rubric)
Francisco Esquibel (rubric) Antonio Sediyo (rubric)
Aruego del Sargento Bartolome Maese
Thomas Casillas (rubric)

Santa Fee Septiembre 15 de 1756 años.

En vista del ynforme que antezede echo por los ofiziales de este Real Presidio en que dizen parese ser combeniente sele suministren los metales que se hallan en el Real Cuerpo de Guardia ynservibles de las recamaras a Dn. Bernardo de Miera y Pacheco para ber se logra el fm de sacar el canon que en su escripto expone; conformandome con dicho ynoforme mando sele entreguen dichos metales del expresado Dn. Bernardo por resultar en consiguiendose el fin en servizio de Su Magestad y de no conseguirse la obra quedar tan ynservibles como estan; y hasi mismo mando ami administrador que ami costa suministre a el dicho Dn. Bernardo todo lo nezesarion de seb(illegible) y alambre y demas que para la obra nesisitara y concluyda me hara presentazion de ella para que se haga la prueba que corresponde. Asi lo decrete mande y fume yo Dn. Francisco Antonio Marin del Valle Governador y Capitan General de este Reyno de la Nueba Mexico autuando con testigos de assistencia de que doy fee.

     Marin (rubric)

Testigo Joseph Maldonado (rubric)
Testigo Francisco de Arroniz (rubric)

En la de Santa Fee en veinte dias del mes de Octubre de mill setezientos y zinquenta y seis años ante mi Dn. Francisco Antonio Marin del Valle Govemador y Capitan General de este Reyno de la Nueba Mexico comparesio Dn. Bernardo de Miera y Pacheco diziendo que haviendo puesto todos los medios para conseguir lo que en su escripto tiene ofrezido no Ie ha sido dable poder salir con ello por lo que deseando yo el ber si se puede conseguir poner los canones en corriente y las recamaras taparles los oydos para haserselo de nuebo y teniendo algunas luses para este fin de que el Maestro Herrero Thomas de Sena puede executarlo por su ynxenio mando conparesca ante mi y sele haga presente y estandolo y los conones y recamaras a la vista dixo que pondra todo su esmero en tapar los oydos alas recamaras recortar los canones taparlos y reforzarlos en cuya vista mande sele entregara todo defacto sele entrego para que segun su ydea lo execute y sedio por entregado y asi mismo sele mando que del xierro que sobrase delo que recortase a los canones hisiese treynta lanzas para el Real Servizio todo lo qual quedo en executar y para que conste lo puse por dilixenzia que fIrmo con migo y testigos de assistencia de que doy fee.

    Francisco Antonio Marin del Valle (rubric)

Testigo Joseph Maldonado (rubric)
    Tomas Antonio de Sena (rubric)
Testigo Juan Francisco de Arroniz (rubric)

En la Villa de Santa Fee en quinze dias del mes de Febrero de mill setezientos zinquenta y siete años ante mi Dn. Francisco Antonio Marin del Valle Govemador y Capitan

General de este Reyno de la Nueba Mexico comparezio el Maestro Herrero Thomas de Sena quien dixo que me hazia y hizo exsivision de zinco canones los quatro de fierro y el uno de bronze los quales havia conpuesto cortando los tres de fierro y el de bronze y el otro de fierro ya lo estaba y asi mismo zinco recamaras y treinta lanzas lo qual mandese probasen y se hallo poder servir lo que estaba yservible en cuya vista Ie mande dixeselo que era su trabaxo y dixo que por los quatro canones que recorto y tapo a veinte y zinco pesos cada uno a el corriente de la tierra que por el que estaba recortado que reforso diez y ocho pesos que por las zinco recamaras que tapo y taladreo a zinco pesos cada una y que por las treynta lanzas que hizo zinquenta pesos que todo monta Ie cantidad de ziento nobenta y tres pesos del corriente de la tierra que es lo que halla por costa por su trabajo y asi mismo hizo exibizion del xierro que havia sobrado el que haviendo mandado pesar tubo siete arrobas diez y ocho y media libras el que Ie dixe si queria por su trabajo y dixo que si en cuya vista mande se le entregase y se le entrego y se dio por rezevido y pagado de su trabajo y para que conste lo asiento por diligenzia que firmo con migo y testigos de assistencia a que doy fee.
                      Francisco Antonio Marin del Valle (rubric)
                      Thomas Antonio de Sena (rubric)
Testigo Joseph Maldonado (rubric)
Testigo Juan Francisco de Arroniz (rubric)

Notes

1. Miera y Pacheco's 1758 map of New Mexico includes notes stating that in the province there were 1,360 Spanish men between fifteen and sixty capable of bearing arms, and they had 531 muskets, 266 pistols, 367 lances, and 248 swords. The Pueblos Indians had 2,800 men capable of bearing arms, 48 muskets, 17 pistols, 85,520 arrows, 602 lances, and 103 swords. The Genízaros numbered 63 men, with 3 muskets, 11 lances, and 2,056 arrows. Of interest is that the Spanish had 2,543 horses, Pueblo Indians 4,813, and the Genízaros none. It is not known how he acquired this data or if it included the soldiers, arms, and horses of the presidio. It did not include the Spanish at El Paso (Kessell, *Kiva*: 512).
2. See Doc. 44.
3. Francisco Esquibel is listed as an alférez in the 1766 will of Francisco Xavier Fragoso. A Francisco Esquibel and María Clara Gonzales are listed as having a son, Ventura, who was a soldier at the presidio. In his recommendations to Governor Valle, Governor Cachupín stated, "The first sergeant, Francisco Esquibel, is a man of honor and known valor. I have seen him perform with gallantry and to my satisfaction against the enemy, and at the same time with thought and astuteness in this kind of war. He is the one who frequently instructs the soldiers in the management of arms" (SANM I #3275, WPA translation; Thomas, *Plains Indians*: 140; Christmas, *Military Records*: 57; Chávez, *Origins*: 172).
4. Antonio Sedillo [Rico y Rojas] was the son of Joaquín Sedillo Rico y Rojas and María Varela. Joaquín was a New Mexico notary. Antonio was in New Mexico in 1704 and married Gregoria Gonzales. In 1769 he was the alcalde for Laguna Pueblo (Chávez, *Origins*: 285; Doc. 1).
5. Chávez states that Bartolomé or Bartolo Maese was the grandson of Miguel Maese, a prerevolt settler who returned to New Mexico after the Reconquest but was killed in 1701 by an Apache arrow. Bartolomé may have been related to Juan Maese, who was in New Mexico in 1632, and to Luis, also a prerevolt settler. In a 1741 power-of-attorney presidio list, Bartolomé Maese was shown as a sergeant, as he was in a 1761 presidio muster, where he was listed as a first sergeant with seven horses. In 1779 he was at Tomé, and in September 1, 1785, was at the Santa Fe presidio with the horse herd (Chávez, *Origins*: 58; Barrett, *Conquest*: 101, 210; Christmas, *Military Records*: 54, 62, 154; Hadley et al., *Presidio*: 300).
6. Tomás Casillos, along with Bartolomé Maese, was included on the 1741 presidio power-of-attorney list. A 1753 document shows him purchasing land in Santa Fe. His father was Bernabé Casillos, an alférez with the presidio, who was in New Mexico by 1703 (Christmas, *Military Records*: 53; SANM I #192; Chávez, *Origins*: 158).

7. Tomás Sena was the son of Bernardino de Sena, a blacksmith, who came to New Mexico in 1693 with his parents. The senior Sena purchased property near the Santa Fe Plaza, which is still known by the family name, Sena Plaza. Tomás Sena was a blacksmith and armorer, and also an alcalde mayor of Galisteo and Pecos before Miera held that position. In 1954 Governor Cachupín stated, "as an alcalde, he is greatly loved because of his kindness: and [for] that he would be hard to replace" (Thomas, *Plains Indians*: 141; SANM I #511; Chávez, *Origins*: 236-37; Kessell, *Kiva*: 385).

46

PRESIDIO DRUMMER ESTEBAN RODRÍGUEZ REINSTATED AS REQUESTED BY SOLDIERS
May 1757. Source: SANM II #538.

Synopsis and editor's notes: In 1757 the officers and soldiers of the Santa Fe presidio wrote a petition to Governor don Francisco Antonio Marín de Valle asking that he reinstate Esteban Rodríguez as the presidio drummer. They pointed out that a drummer is a necessity in that "he instills valor in the soldier and fear in the enemy." Rodríguez, who had resigned after an accident, was reinstated with the condition that every morning and night he would instruct a person of his choice in drumming. He was the son of Sebastián Rodríguez, a previous presidio drummer and town crier. Esteban Rodríguez was the presidio drummer by at least 1716, and town crier by 1732 (Chávez, *Origins*: 270; Doc. 2).

The importance of the sound of the drum was made clear in a 1771 decree by Governor Pedro Mendiñueta. In the decree, the governor began by scolding the militia for not responding to the sound of the drum, stating that they were "compelled to give assistance to the Pueblo frontiers without having been given repeated verbal orders," and pointed out that they had been disobedient to the higher mandates of the royal service, which was "indubitably" to assist at the frontiers and to assist the presidio corps by responding to the call of the drum. He went on to state that "because the aggressiveness of the enemy [the Indians] is continued and one must fear them being armed on the frontier . . . I mandate a bando that all resident militia being and living in Santa Fe and in Royal Guard's Corps [the presidio soldiers] shall promptly respond to the playing of the drum, on foot or horse, with their offensive and defensive weapons." The penalty for disobedience was 25 pesos and eight days in prison for the first offense; the second offense was considered rebellion (SANM II #663).

The next we hear of the presidio drummer is in 1781, when the position was again vacant, due to the death of José Manuel Fragosa, the son of Francisco Xavier Fragosa. José Manuel died at the age of nineteen of smallpox (Chávez, *Origins*: 177; Christmas, *Military Records*: 87).

Year of 1757

Petition by the officials and soldiers of this royal presidio so that the position

of drummer [*tambor*] be reinstated for the reasons given below.
Governor and captain general

The officials, lieutenants, alférez, and first sergeant of this company who garrison this royal presidio [appear] on our behalf and in the name of the other corporals and soldiers appear before your honor with our divided attention and kindness, and we state that there is no person in this entire kingdom who knows how to beat the drum [*caja de guerra*] other than Esteban Rodríguez, who has been employed to do this for many years, and that your honor has not appointed anyone even though it has been requested, not finding anyone to do it as well as the said Esteban, who does not want to do it, saying that his conscience will not allow him to do it for the salary. With respect to his [Esteban's] having ceased to do it, due to the accident which has prevented him, your honor should at this time order that the said Esteban Rodríguez be reinstated, and if necessary, he should be ordered to instruct someone how to do it. This is so that the royal presidio is not left without a thing so necessary as the individual who is instructed in this precious instrument, which instills valor upon the soldiers and fear upon the enemy and is the most competent voice that there is to assemble all the military personal for all events, and for a number of other reasons, which we leave up the prudent consideration of your honor. For this reason we petition him in the said form being that is the accustomed manner of our petition that we swear in the proper form that it is not done in malice but rather in the most exact compliment of the royal service.

Carlos Fernández[1] (rubric)
Lieutenant
Toribio Ortiz (rubric) alférez
Bartolomé Fernández (rubric) first sergeant

Santa Fe, May 1757
Having reviewed the petition of the two officials and of the first sergeant, in which they ask me on their behalf, and on behalf of the corporals and soldiers of this company, that the position of the retired soldier, due to the illness which has been made known to me, is as of now reinstated, because he so well knows the drum to which the company is accustomed. Because there no one else in the entire kingdom who knows how to beat the drum, I attend to their petition, granting that he be allowed to serve as such for this company, so that he is employed in his former position. I will concede to this and as such order that he, Esteban Rodríguez, present himself at the time of first vacancy, and upon entering the royal service, he will every morning and every evening instruct a person of his satisfaction on how to play the drum well, so that the lieutenant and other officials are satisfied with that person, or with anyone who is capable of doing so, and who upon being able to do it, can be employed to serve

his majesty. I thus decreed and ordered his service, etc., don Francisco Antonio Marín del Valle, governor and captain general of this kingdom of New Mexico, along with the assisting witnesses.

Marín (rubric)
Miguel de Alirid (rubric)
Juan Francisco de Arróniz (rubric)

ORIGINAL DOCUMENT

Año de 1757

Petizion de los ofisiales y soldados de este Real Presidio para que se debuelba a la plaza de tambor por los motibos que en el constan.

Señor Gobernador y Capitan General
año
Los oficiales, Thenientes, Alferez y Sargento Primero de esta Compañía que guarnece este Real Presidio por nosotros y en nombre delos demas cabos y soldados parecemos ante Vuestra Señoria con la mas devida submission y rendimiento y decimos: que por quanto no ai en todo este Reino persona alguna que sepa tocar el tambor sino es Estevan Rodriguez que con plaza lo a practicado muchos años, no obstante el aver sido Vuestra sirvia servido de apuntarsela atendiendo a el pedido en forma que hiso el dicho Estevan diciendo que no podia en conciensia ganar el sueldo; que respecto a haver cesado el accidente que dio motibo a el expresado pedido, se a de servir Vuestra Señoria de mandar que el ya zitado Estevan Rodriguez buelba a asentar plaza y si nezesario fuere compelerle asta tanto que ensene a otra alguna persona para que este Real Presidio no caresca de una cosa tan nesesaria asi por que el marcial estruendo del velico ynstrumento ynfon de valor en los soldados y fabor en los enemigos como por ser la mas conpetente vos para congregar a los militares en qual quier evento y por otras muchas rasones que dejamos ala prudente consideracion de Vuestra Señoria a quien suplicamos en la forma dicha aviendo con la venignidad que acostumbre a esta nuestra suplica que juramos en devida forma no ser de malicia sino para el mas exacto cumplimiento del Real servizio =

Carlos Fernandez (rubric)
Teniente
Alferes Bartolome Fernandez (rubric)
Toribio Ortis (rubric)
Sargento Primero

Santa Fee y Maio de 1757

Haviendo visto el pedido delos dos ofisiales y el Primer Sargento en que me representan por si y los cavos y soldados de esta Compañía que el soldado reformado por enfermedad que me represento esta ya restablecido de ella y que por saver traer la caja de guerra a que la Compañía esta ya acostumbrada y no haver otro que la sepa tocar en todo el Reyno me Señorva de atender ala suplica concediendo el que buelba a servir asi de en esta Compañía para que se empleo en el exercio que antes; bengo en concederselo y asi mando se presente en la primera vacante el menzionado Estevan Rodriguez y entrado que sea al Real Servicio de exercite en que todos los dias a tarde y mañana ensene a persona de su satisfacion a tocar vien la caja, con toda aplicazion lo que zele ara al Theniente y demas oficiales para que se adiestre otra persona o las mas que nasca de inclinazion para que quando sea nesesario se exerciten en servir a Su Majestad. Asi lo decreto y mando su sentenzia, ut supra. Don Francisco Antonio Marin del Valle, Governador y Capitan General deste Reyno dela Nueba Mexico con los testigos de asistenzia.

      Marin (rubric)
    Juan Francisco de Arroniz (rubric)
     Miguel de Aliri (rubric)

Notes

1. See Doc. 42.

47

DRUMS, LEG IRONS, GUNS, CANNONS, AND OTHER WEAPONS INVENTORIED BY GOVERNOR CACHUPÍN
February 4, 1762. Source: AGN PI Leg 102, Parte II, f172.

Synopsis and editor's notes: When Governor Vélez Cachupín returned to New Mexico for his second term in 1762, one of his first acts was to order an inventory of the military equipment, although his predecessor, Governor Portillo y Urrisola, had made an inventory the previous year.[1] Knowledge of available weapons was important because the Plains Indians, particularly the Comanches, had returned to the raiding and violence that preceded Cachupín's first term as governor (1749–1754). The increase in Indian depredations may have come about partly because of lack of Spanish military leadership, but also because of the increasing presence of French traders who were selling guns to the Indians. Some of the French guns were listed in the inventory, perhaps captured by the soldiers or acquired at one of the trade fairs from the Indians. The fact that the area to the east, known as Louisiana, was secretly ceded to Spain in 1762 by the Treaty of Fontainbleu and later by the official Peace of Paris in 1763 may not have been known to Cachupín at this time, and anyway, may not have affected his position toward the Indians and French weapons (Weber, *Spanish Frontier*: 198-99).

The inventory consisted of everything from bells and a branding iron to war drums, cannons, guns, and gunpowder. It also included equipment used by squadrons outside of Santa Fe at Santa Cruz, Galisteo, Picuris, and Taos. The presidio cannon listed here is likely to be one of the old cannons discussed in the 1757 document, translated in Document 45.

Information about gunpowder and powder cartridges is discussed by Brinkerhoff and Faulk, who state that prior to 1772, there was a chronic shortage of gunpowder on the frontier and that few presidio soldiers were trained to use their firearms since there was little powder available for practice. In an apparent attempt to remedy this, the 1772 revised military regulations required that the amount of gunpowder to be held in reserve at each presidio was to be eight pounds per soldier. Individual soldiers were to have three pounds each, with an extra three pounds for each recruit. Whether or not this amount was ever available to soldiers at the Santa Fe presidio is unknown, though records from 1790 show that 986 pounds were available at the presidio, including 373 pounds in use. Of the available gun cartridges, 44 percent were kept to replace defective cartridges, 29 percent were for combat, 19 were for target practice, and 7 percent were for salvos on feast days (Blyth, "Los Vaqueros": 53; Brinkerhoff and Faulk, *Lancers*: 27).

Inventory of those arms of war that were found existing in the royal guard house and armory and the delivery that I have made of them to don Thomas Vélez Cachupín, governor and captain general of this new kingdom of Mexico, today, February 4 of the year 1762.

1 royal standard with the cross of the plaza banner of the royal presidio
1 banner of the citizen militia
2 war drums
8 pairs of leg irons
1 branding iron and 1 marca for branding the horses of the King
1 bell in the guard house
6 French *fusil*[2] in the armory, serviceable
1 *escopeta* in current use in the armory
1 fusil and 17 escopetas, not serviceable, only the barrels are good
1 sword with a ¾ blade
33 lances
10 good leather jackets
1 large club
5 copper chambers [for a gun]
1 copper mold [for bullets]
1 small cannon in the guard house with the caliber of the ball an *alibra* of old material[3]
    2 *arrobas*[4] (50 kg) of powder and 4 arrobas of lead for the availability of the citizen militia

Colonial lance, tang type. Photo by Blair Clark.
Courtesy Palace of the Governors Photo Archives, Neg. No. 147838.

The *escopeta* was an eighteenth-century smoothbore, muzzle-loading musket or carbine.
Brinkerhoff and Faulk, *Lancers*: 73, Plate 13. #4023a.
Image courtesy of the Arizona State Historical Society, Tempe.

In the villa de Santa Cruz de la Cañada

6 escopetas in good current use in the possession of the alcalde mayor, don Antonio Martín in the pueblo of Pecos
1 field cannon, 3 *libras*[5] of powder, and 250 fusil balls at the post of alcalde mayor don Cayetano Tenorio[6]
In the pueblo of Galisteo
1 field cannon, 2½ libras of powder, and 250 fusil balls at the post of alcalde mayor Cayetano Tenorio
In the pueblo of Picuris
1 field cannon, 400 fusil balls, and 6 libras of power in the post of the alcalde mayor of Taos, don Francisco Romero[7]
In the pueblo of Taos
1 field cannon,[8] 3 *muestras*[9] balls, and 7 libras of powder and 334 fusil balls at the post of the said don Francisco Romero
In the capital villa
1 fusil that the Genízaro Indian Diego de Sena has in the horse herd of the royal presidio
60 broken-in horses of the King
15 mares

           Thomas Vélez Cachupín (rubric)
           Manuel Costillo Yrrisola (rubric)

ORIGINAL DOCUMENT

Razon de los pelttrechos de guerra se hallon existentes en el real cuerpo de guardia y armero y enttrega que hago de ellas al Señor Don Thomas Vélez Cachupín, Governador y Capitan General de este Nuevo Reyno de Mexico oy 4 de febrero de 1762 años

el real estandante con su cruz de plaza
la vandera del real presidio
la vandera de los vecinos milicianos
2 . . . caxas de guerra
8 . . . pares de grillos
1 . . . fierro y una marca para herrar los cavallos de Rey
1 . . . campanita en el cuerpo de guardia
6 . . . fusiles Franzeses en el armero, serbibles
1 . . . escopetas en corriente en el armero
1 . . . fusil y 17 escopetas inserbibles solo los cañones estan buenos

1 . . . espada de ¾ de oja
22 . . . lanzas
10 . . . cueras buenas
1 . . . macana club
5 . . . recamaras de cobre
1 . . . balero de cobre
1 . . . cañoncito en el cuerpo de guardia de calibre de bala de alibra fabrica antigua
2 . . . arrobas de polbora y . . . 4 . . . arrobas de plomo para la havilitazion de los vecinos milicianos.

En la Villa de Santa Cruz de la Cañada
6 . . . escopetas en corriente buenas en poder de Alcalde Maior don Pedro Marttin en el Pueblo de Pecos
1 . . . cañoncito de campaña 3 libras de polbora y 250 balas de fusil al cargo del Alcalde Mayor don Cayettiano Thenorio
En el Pueblo de Galisteo
1 . . . cañoncito de campañas 2 ½ libras de polbora y 250 balas de fusil al cargo de dicho Alcalde Maior Don Cayetano Thenorio
En el Pueblo Pecuries
1 . . . Cañoncito de campaña 400 balas de fusil y 6 libras de polbora al cargo del Alcalde Maior de Taos don Francisco Romero
En el Pueblo de Thaos
cañoncito de campaña 3 balas muestras y 7 libras de polbora y 334 balas de fusil al cargo de dicho don Francisco Romero
En esta Villa capittal
1 . . . fusil que tiene el yndio genizaro Diego de Sena en la caballada de real presidio
60 . . . caballos mansos del Rey
15 . . . yeguas

                Thomas Velez Cachupin (rubric)
                Manuel Costillo Yrrisola (rubric)

Transcribed and translated by Linda Tigges and Rick Hendricks

Notes

1. For comparison, see the transcribed and translated inventory for the 1761 Santa Fe presidio in Hadley et al. (*Presidio*: 298-302).
2. According to State Historian Rick Hendricks, the terms *fusil* and *escopeta* have various meanings depending on the time and place. Generally, a fusil was a kind of musket. It fired a ball and had a long barrel with a smooth or rifled bore. The escopeta fired shot and had a shorter barrel, like a shotgun. It had a smooth bore and could have a belled barrel, like a blunderbuss (Rick Hendricks, email communication, September 16, 2011).

3. The meaning of *alibra* is not known. It could be a misspelling of *libra*.
4. One *arroba* is a common weight or measure of about 25 pounds (Hadley et al., *Presidio*: 527).
5. A *libra* is a little more than one pound (Hadley et al., *Presidio*: 527).
6. Note that Cayetano Tenorio also appears in Doc. 24, being investigated for the accidental shooting of Juan de Santisteban.
7. See Doc. 42.
8. This may have been the field cannon used by the interim governor, don Manuel Portillo Urrisola, in his December 1761 defense of Taos against the Comanches. The battle was described in a letter from Urrisola to Bishop Tamarón, stating, "And now that I found myself obliged to do so, invoking the Queen of Angels and men, I fired a small field cannon loaded with cartridges, and also a close volley of shotguns" (Adams, *Tamarón*: 61).
9. The meaning of the term *muestras* is unknown. Literally, it would mean a master ball or demonstration ball.

48

DEAD MULE AND HORSES CAUSE DISPUTE BETWEEN SANTA CRUZ TRADER AND SAN JUAN INDIAN; WHY MONEY IS BETTER THAN BARTER
August 4–September 13, 1762. Source: SANM II #558.

Synopsis and editor's notes: In this complicated document from 1762, we find Pedro Atienza, a trader from Santa Cruz, sending Juan de Dios, the servant of his sister, Francisca Atienza, on a mule of Francisca's to look for oxen or cows. For some reason, the mule was located near San Juan Pueblo, and Juan de Dios was sent to get it from there. On his way to pick up the mule, Juan went to the house of the Indian Miguel Ventura in the pueblo, telling Ventura that he knew where there was a mule. Ventura and Juan went and found the mule and loaded it up with trade goods, which included knives, lances, bridles, and corn. The trade goods came from an Indian, Juan Tafoya, who had gotten them from Ignacio Cornelia Figueroa, a trader, probably from El Paso. Then Juan de Dios went to look for oxen, and Ventura went to the Utes to trade, where the mule died or was killed. While there, he traded his goods for eight skins, of which three were withered. Later, Ventura said that he was "lashed" by the pueblo officials when he returned to San Juan, apparently for trading with the Utes without a license, or at least without the officials knowing about it.

At some point, Pedro Atienza returned to San Juan, where Juan Tafoya told him that his mule was dead. When Atienza confronted Ventura, Ventura said that he would pay him for it, whereupon, he, Ventura, traded one or two horses and some hides for a red mule from Fray Juan Mirabal at San Juan Pueblo. He gave this mule to the son of Francisca Atienza, the owner of the dead mule. On the way back to Santa Cruz, the son saw Antonio Domínguez on the road with a pack of trade goods. He lent him the mule to carry the goods, and Domínguez kept the mule for six days before returning it to Francisca Atienza.

Chico, a servant of Juan Tafoya, then went to Francisca's house and forcibly took the mule from her, returning it to Fray Mirabal. When Pedro Atienza went to see Ventura at San Juan to complain, Ventura said that he would pay for the mule, but to wait. As they argued about this, Fray Juan Mirabel arrived and said that the sale was no good. He apparently was referring to Ventura's claim that he, Fray Mirabel, had sold the red mule to Ventura.

Then Atienza talked to several people to prove that Ventura had bought the mule from Fray Mirabel, and also to prove that the trade goods handled by Ventura were not his. He seems to have done this to prove that he had not violated the prohibition of trading with the Indians without a license. Finally, seeing no other way to get his mule, Atienza took the case to the Santa Cruz alcalde, Carlos Fernández, claiming that Ventura owed him a mule and some other trade items. Fernández heard all the witnesses that he could find in his jurisdiction and turned the case over Governor Cachupín.

Upon hearing the case, Cachupín ordered that Ventura pay Atienza for the mule, giving him three months in which to do so. The other items that Atienza claimed Ventura owed to him were not mentioned.

Once again, this document shows the complications of barter commerce. It also shows the peripatetic tendencies of the Spanish and Puebloans. In this case, the main characters seem to be continually traveling around the countryside—going off to find a mule, doing a little illegal trading, meeting someone on the road, and going back and forth to San Juan, among other expeditions.

Proceedings between Pedro de Atienza[1] and Miguel Ventura,[2] Genízaro Indian from the Pueblo of San Juan, before don Carlos Fernández, alcalde mayor of La Cañada.

Year of 1762

Santa Fe, August 4, 1762

The alcalde mayor of the villa of La Cañada, don Carlos Fernández,[3] shall summon to appear before him Pedro Atienza, resident of La Cañada, who is to be informed about a note [see below] which is included from the missionary priest of the pueblo of San Juan concerning an Indian from his mission, Miguel Ventura, who argues against the debt brought forth by Pedro de Atienza for a macho. The alcalde mayor is to take testimony to ascertain his demands, being that the said Indian denies the debt. Upon this being done, it shall be submitted to me so that I can decide for the sake of justice. I thus approved, ordered, and signed it, don Thomas Vélez Cachupín, governor and captain general of this kingdom of New Mexico.

Vélez Cachupín (rubric)

[note from the priest]

Governor and captain general don Thomas Vélez Cachupín

My dear sir, the carrier of this [note] is an Indian [Miguel Ventura] from this pueblo against whom Pedro Atienza makes a demand for a mule for which the said

Indian is not to pay him, because it is as I tell you, your honor, that Pedro Atienza sent him to a trade fair [on a macho] with some lances, knives, and awls, and he [Ventura] purchased eight hides for him. The carrier states that he [Atienza] told him that if the macho became lost or died he would not be charged for it. Upon his return from his trip, he returned the macho to the son [actually the nephew] of the said Atienza, and on the following day the macho died. The carrier has proof that if the macho was to die, he did not have to pay for it, as he had been told that if the macho died he was not to worry about it.

    I am happy to see that your honor is in good health, and whom I, as always, am glad to serve. I ask that God guard you for many years.
San Juan, August 3, 1762.

                  I kiss the hand of your honor
                  Your chaplain and friend,
                  Fray Juan Mirabal[4] (rubric)

    At this puesto of Nuestra Señora de la Soledad del Río Arriba, on the 7th of August of 1762, I, don Carlos Fernández, alcalde mayor and war captain of this villa of Santa Cruz de la Cañada, in order to proceed with that which was ordered, I made to appear before me Pedro Atienza in order to obtain his sworn statement, so that he can make his claim, summoning witnesses for it so that they can be examined regarding those demands. I thus approved, ordered, and signed it with my witnesses, acting as has been said, due to the lack of a scribe, which there is none in this kingdom, to which I certify.

                  Carlos Fernández (rubric)

Witnesses
Miguel de Abeytia (rubric)
Francisco Sánchez (rubric)

    At this puesto on the said day, month, and year, there appeared before me the said alcalde mayor, Pedro Atienza, from whom I took his sworn statement in its proper form, which he made to God, Our Lord, and the Holy Cross, and to which he promised to tell the truth as to what he knew and about which he asked, which was done after he was read the above note, and for the reasons which he makes his demands against the Indian Miguel Ventura over a macho. He said that the reason was for the sake of justice, his having asked the Indian Miguel Ventura for a macho that he sent with an Indian servant [*criado*] who was brought up by my sister, Francisca Atienza. He [the servant] was given the macho so that he could look for some oxen. Arriving at the home of the Indian Miguel Ventura, he [the servant] told him where he could find a macho which belonged to the sister. The criado, whose name is Juan de Dios, went and showed him where it [the macho] was. They then took the macho to San

Juan and loaded it with corn, flour, bridles, and knives. Then they both left San Juan and, arriving at Abiquiu, the Indian Juan de Dios left him to go look for the oxen, and Miguel Ventura went to trade with the Utes. A few days having gone by, the declarant [Atienza] went to San Juan and met up with Juan Tafoya,[5] who told him that his macho was dead. He, the declarant, asked him who had killed it, and Juan Tafoya answered, telling him that the Indian Miguel Ventura had taken it to the Utes. The declarant then went to see the said Ventura and asked him why he had taken the macho and killed it. The Indian then told him how he had taken it, but he would not tell him about killing it, simply saying that it had been loaned to him and that he would pay him for it. Then he, the Indian Miguel, went and purchased from Joseph Mirabal[6] a red macho, having paid for it with a gray horse, and the two of them, Joseph and Miguel, then turned the red macho over to the son of the owner, who then took the macho as the owner to La Cañada. On his way, he met up with Antonio Domínguez,[7] who was afoot loaded with some items on his back, which they then loaded upon the macho, which he had for a period of six days [then returned the mule]. At the end of the sixth day, when the declarant [Atienza] was not at home, a servant of Juan Tafoya, named Chico, went and took possession of the red macho. Atienza's sister, Francisca, would not let him take it, but he with his powerful hand forcefully took it from her. He [Atienza] then proceeded to go to San Juan and told the said Ventura that they had taken his macho. The said Indian then told him that he would pay him for it, to just wait. The declarant then went to argue with Joseph Mirabal with reference to the sale, which [he said] he had not completed and which he had withdrawn from the Indian Miguel.

As they were arguing about this within the entryway of the convent at San Juan, Reverendo Padre Fray Juan Mirabal yelled at them that the sale was no good, and for him [Atienza] to go to the Devil. Atienza then quit arguing and returned to San Juan to try to get paid however he could by the Indian Miguel. In order to prove that the Indian Miguel Ventura had paid him with a macho, he summoned Antonio Domínguez, Joseph Padilla,[8] and don Joachín del Pino[9] to prove that he, Miguel, had purchased it [the replacement for the macho] from the same priest, Juan Mirabal. To prove that the knives and bridles which he [Miguel] took to the Utes were not his [Atienza's], he summoned the Indian, Juan de Dios, and Juan Diego Trujillo. In addition, so that it is known who [owned] the bridles and knives which Juan Tafoya submitted, he summoned Francisco Sánchez, as well as the note of Reverendo Padre Juan Mirabal.

In addition to the macho which he [Atienza] demanded from the Indian, Miguel Ventura, he also demanded fourteen knives that three years ago, now, he gave to the said Indian to sell, two for the owner of the knives, who was don Joachim del Pino, and one for him; all of which he [Ventura] still owed him, and his excuse for not paying was that he said that they were stolen. In addition he [Ventura] owed him for the work he [Atienza] did planting for him four corn fields with his oxen, plows, and workers as well as three cartloads of wood, all of which he owed him for and for which he has paid nothing. He [Atienza] says that everything that he has stated is the truth and is what he knows regarding his sworn statement, which he has made, and it having been read back to him, he affirmed and ratified it, and said that he was fifty years of age. He did not sign because he did not know how. I, the said alcalde mayor, signed it, acting as has been said, to which I certify.

Carlos Fernández (rubric)

Witnesses:
Miguel de Abeytia (rubric)
Francisco Sánchez (rubric)

At this puesto of La Soledad del Río Arriba, on the 16th of August, of the current year, I, said alcalde mayor, made appear before me Antonio Domínguez so that he can state what he knows about that for which he was summoned, and being present I took his sworn statement which he made in his proper right and promised to tell the truth about what he knew and what he is asked. He was asked if he knew that the Indian Miguel Ventura of the pueblo of San Juan paid Pedro Atienza for a macho. He said that what he knows is that upon this declarant [Domínguez] going to La Cañada afoot with a load of corn, he was met by Juan Miguel, son of Francisca Atienza, on a macho which appeared to him to be swallow colored, and that the said young man invited him to climb upon the macho, and he would take him and his load. The declarant then asked him where he was taking the macho, to which he answered that the macho was paid to him by an Indian from San Juan for one which had died on him, and that the Indian had purchased it from Joseph Mirabal for a horse and some hides. He stated that this was the truth and is what he knows regarding the sworn statement which he has made, which he affirmed and ratified. He said he was fifty years of age, and he signed it with me and my witnesses, acting as has been said, to which I certify that the [amendments] are valid.

Carlos Fernández (rubric)

Witnesses
Francisco Antonio Sisneros (rubric)
Juan Domingo Lovato (rubric)

At the said puesto on the said day, month, and year, before me, the said alcalde mayor in the presentation of this information, Juan de Dios, Genízaro Indian, [the servant of Francisca], presented himself to give his sworn statement which he made to God, Our Lord, and to the Holy Cross, and he promised to tell the truth about what he knew regarding the charges, and he was told about the gravity of the sworn statement and the obligation which he had in telling the truth.

He was asked if he knew how the Indian Miguel Ventura had acquired the macho which he took to trade with the Utes. He said that he was sent by his keeper [*ama*], Francisca Atienza, to look for some cows, and that he arrived at the home of the Indian Miguel Ventura about noon, who asked him where the macho that belonged to his keeper was at. He answered that it was at the cañada of San Juan. He [Ventura] also said that his *compadre*[10] Pedro Atienza had loaned the macho to him, and then they both went together to get the macho, and then early the next morning the said Ventura saddled the macho and loaded him with corn, flour, and tortillas and sent the Indian whom he mentioned to go ahead of him and wait for him at the *bosque* [a watered and woody place].

He was then asked what else he knew and saw. He said that on that same night he entered the home of the aforesaid named Indian Juan Tafoya, who gave to the Indian Miguel fifteen large heavy knives and six bridles, which he placed into a leather bag, and was told by Juan Tafoya to sell them as if they were his own. The said Indian accompanied him [Miguel] to Abiquiu, where they parted company, Miguel going to the Utes and he to look for the cows. He was asked if he knew if Pedro Atienza had loaned the macho to Miguel. He said that he did not know. He was asked if the Indian Miguel took with him any awls, lances, bridles, or knives which belonged to Pedro Atienza. He said that he did not know that he was taking anything that belonged to Pedro Atienza.

He was then asked if he had talked to anyone about this matter. He said the only person he had talked to about what has been said was Juan Diego Martín,[11] whom he told that the Indian Ventura was taking the macho and that he was also taking with him knives and bridles, and he said that he did not tell him anything else. He said that what he has stated is the truth and all that he knows regarding the charges of the sworn statement which he has made, and his statement having been read back to him, he affirmed and ratified it. He appears to be about eighteen years of age. He did not sign because he did not know how. I, the said alcalde mayor, signed it along with my witnesses, acting as has been said, to which I certify.

Carlos Fernández (rubric)

Witnesses
Francisco Antonio Sisneros (rubric)
Juan Domingo Lovato (rubric)

At this puesto de La Soledad del Río Arriba, on the 25th of August, there appeared before me, the said alcalde mayor, Juan Diego Martín, who was summoned and from whom I took his sworn statement which he made according to his right regarding these charges, and he promised to tell the truth as to what he knew and what he was asked. He was asked if he knew that the Indian from San Juan, Miguel Ventura, had gone to the Utes, if so, on what, and what he took with him. He answered, what he knows is that the Indian Juan de Dios, servant of Atienza's [sister], told him that the Indian Miguel had gone to the Utes on a macho which belonged to his keeper, and that he took bridles, knives, and lances. He said that he did not know [this] for sure, that what he has said was told him by the said Indian Juan de Dios, and that he does not know anything else. Upon this, his statement, he held firm and ratified it. He said he was thirty years of age. He did not sign because he did not know how. I, the said alcalde mayor, signed it with my witnesses, acting as has been said, to which I certify.

Carlos Fernández (rubric)

Witnesses
Francisco Antonio Sisneros (rubric)
Juan Domingo Lovato (rubric)

At the said puesto on the 2nd of September, 1762, before me, the said alcalde mayor, appeared as a witness Francisco Sánchez,[12] from whom I took his sworn statement which he made to God, Our Lord, and the Holy Cross, about which charges he promised to tell the truth about what he knew and was asked. He was asked if he knew if the Indian Miguel Ventura from San Juan had gone to the Utes, what he went on, and what he took.

He [Sánchez] stated that when Ygnacio Cornelio Figueroa[13] was at the house of the declarant [Sánchez] in the month of April selling some of his goods, he brought with him from his house two dozen large knives and nine bridles, and he told me that he was going to give them to Juan Tafoya, being that he [Tafoya] had told him that some Indians from San Juan were going to the Utes, and that he would give the items to them and they would take them and sell them. Some days later the said Cornelio told him [Sánchez] that the Indian Miguelillo [Ventura] had brought him back eight hides, but that he [Ventura] had not given them to him because the pueblo officials had lashed him for going to the Utes and for the death of the macho on which he had gone. He [Ventura] said he had told him [Figueroa] to go see him [at San Juan] on a certain night, which in fact he did, and brought back five hides, and that the other three had gotten withered. He told him [Figueroa] that at the time that he was going to El Paso he was to charge Juan Tafoya for the other three hides. He [Sánchez] was asked if he knew the owner of the dead macho. He said that he had gotten it from Atienza. He was asked if he knew how the Indian Miguel had acquired the said macho. He said that he did not. He said that what he has stated is the truth and what he knows, and [he] does not know anything else. Upon his statement being read back to him, he affirmed and ratified it, stating that he was forty years of age, and he signed it along with me and my witnesses acting as has been said, to which I certify.

      Carlos Fernández (rubric)
      Francisco Sánchez (rubric)

Witnesses
Juan Domingo Lovato (rubric)
Francisco Antonio Sisneros (rubric)

These proceedings having been concluded in the form which they are found, being that two witnesses who were summoned are not found in this jurisdiction, I submit them to his honor so that upon his review he will order whatever he decides. So that it is valid I signed it on the 6th of September, 1762.

      Carlos Fernández (rubric)

Santa Fe, September 13, 1762

    Having reviewed the proceedings which the alcalde mayor, don Carlos Fernández, has concluded, I ordered and did order, being that there is a legitimate debt, the Indian Miguel Ventura pay for the macho, or its value, according to the going price in this kingdom, to Pedro de Atienza, giving him the term of three months to pay for the said macho. I, don Thomas Vélez Cachupín, governor and captain general of this kingdom, thus approved and signed it, acting with my two assisting witnesses due to the lack of a scribe.

                      Thomas Vélez Cachupín (rubric)

Witnesses
Manuel Antonio Lorenz (rubric)
Mateo de Peñarredonda (rubric)

ORIGINAL DOCUMENT

Autos seguidos entre Pedro de Atienza y Miguel Yndio genizaro del Pueblo de San Juan por don Carlos Fernandez Alcalde Mayor de La Cañada

                      Año de 1762

Santa Fe 4 de Agosto de 1762

    El Alcalde Mayor de la Villa de La Cañada don Carlos Fernandez hara comparecer ante si a Pedro Atienza vezino de La Cañada y le hara saber el contenido del papel que se inserta del Ministro Misionero del Pueblo de San Juan a fabor del Yndio de su Mission Miguel Ventura alegando contra la demanda de Pedro de Atienza sobre la deuda de un macho aquien recivira dicho Alcalde Maior informacion de ser cierta su demanda por de negarla el referido Yndio y fecha mela remitira para proveer en Justizia lo que combenga.

    Asi lo probei, mande y firme yo don Thomas Velez Cachupin, Governador y Capitan General de este Reino del Nuebo Mexico.

                      Velez Cachupin (rubric)

                      (Papel del Ministro)
Señor Governador y Capitan Genereal don Thomas Velez Cachupin

Mi Señor el portador de este es un Yndio de este Pueblo a quien Pedro Atenzio le aze cargo de una bestia mular la que dicho Yndio no deve pagar por que fue assi como le dise a Vuestra Señoria que Pedro Atenzio lo imbio a rescatar con unas lanzas, cuchillos y alesna y le compro ocho gamuzas disiendole el portador que si el macho se perdia o se moria no le hiziera cargo de el. Vino de biaje y luego selo entrego a su muchacho del dicho y aquel dia despues se murio dicho macho; y previniendole el portador que si se moria el macho que no lo pagaba y le dijo el tal que si se moria el macho no le diera cuidado que no avia quien le cobrara; yo me alegrace este Vuestra Señoria bueno a cuio servicio quedo como siempre para servirle aquien pido a Dios Guarde Muchos Años. San Juan, Agosto 3 de 1762.

      Beso la mano de Vuestra Señoria
       Su Capellan y amigo
       Fray Juan Mirabal (rubric)

En este Puesto de Nuestra Señora de la Soledad del Rio Arriba en siete dias del mes de Agosto de mil setecientos sesenta y dos años yo don Carlos Fernandez, Alcalde Mayor y Capitan Aguerra de esta Villa de Santa Cruz de la Cañada para proceder alo mandado comparesca ante mi Pedro Atensio a fin de tomarle declarasion bajo la solemnidad del juramento que para que de la demanda citando testigos para ello los que se examinaran al tenor delo demandado asi lo porbehi, mande y firme autuando con testigos a falta de escribano que no lo ai en este Reino doi fee.

       Carlos Fernandez (rubric)
testigo testigo
Miguel de Abeytia (rubric) Francisco Sanchez (rubric)

En dicho Puesto dicho dia, mes y año parecio ante mi dicho Alcalde Mayor Pedro Atienza aquien tome juramento en forma que le hise por Dios Nuestro Señor y la Santa Cruz so cuio cargo prometio dezir verdad en lo que supiese y fuere preguntado y siendolo despues de averle leido el papel de enfrente por que razon demando contra el Yndio Miguel Ventura un macho; dixo, que la razon y justicia que tiene para pedir un macho a el Yndio Miguel Ventura es que embiando el declarante a un Yndio criado de su hermana Francisca Atensio a buscar unos bueyes llego en casa del Yndio Miguel Ventura y este lo ynquieto para que le fuera a ensenar a donde estaba un macho de la dicha su hermana y el mencionado criado que se llama Juan de Dios fue y selo enseno y los dos lo trajeron a San Juan y cargado con maiz, arina, frenos y cuchillos se fueron los dos asta Abiquiú de donde el Yndio Juan de Dios se fue a buscar los bueyes, y Miguel Ventura para los Yutas y que pasados algunos dias vino el declarante a San Juan y topo con Juan Tafoya quien le dijo que su macho estaba muerto, y preguntado el que declara que quien lo avia muerto le respondio Juan Tafoya que el Yndio Miguel Ventura lo abia llebado a los Yutas y pasando el citado declarante aver a el ya citado Ventura y haciendo cargo que porque abia cojido y muerto el macho; le respondio el Yndio el modo que abia tenido para cojerlo y le rogo mucho no lo disiese, sino que disese que se lo abia prestado, que el selo pagaria; y con efecto compro el dicho Miguel un macho colorado a Joseph Mirabal con un caballo tordillo y seis gamusas y los dos Joseph y Miguel le entregaron a el que demanda el referido macho, y llebandolo como suio para La Cañada lo encontro Antonio Dominguez y hallandolo apie y con un carguita en el lomo le cargo la carguita en el macho el que tubo en su poder seis dias, al cabo de los cuales, no estando el demandante en su casa, vino a ella un moso de Juan Tafoya que comunmente llaman Chico para quitar el ya referido macho, y aunque su hermana lo repugno, de mano poderosa lo cojio de la persoNa y selo llevo por lo qual paso el que a San Juan y reconbiniendole al dicho Ventura que le abian quitado el macho, le respondio el mencionado Yndio que el selo pagaria que lo esperase; y que estando el declarante alegando con Joseph Mirabal sobre aberse arrepentido del trato hecho con el Yndio Miguel en la porteria del combento de San Juan, grito desde adentro el Reverendo Padre Frai Juan Mirabal y dijo que el no pasaba por el trato, que me fuese a un cuerno; por lo qual dejo la alegazion, y bolbio a solicitar la paga del medio con el Yndio Miguel, y que para probar que el Yndio Miguel Ventura le pago el macho y lo tubo en su poder, cita a Antonio Dominguez, a Joseph Padilla y a don Joachin del Pino, aquien selo bendio en aquella occasion el mismo Padre y Juan Mirabal; y para probar que los cuchillos y frenos que llebo alos Yutas no eran del declarante cita al Yndio Juan de Dios y Juan Diego Trujillo; y a mayor abundamiento para que se sepa de quien eran los frenos y cuchillos que embio Juan Tafoya, cita a Francisco Sanches y en orden al papel del Reverendo Padre Mirabal; responde que el Padre esta mal informado pues las ocho gamusas que dice me trajeron ami no es asi, sino que selas trajeron al dicho Juan Tafoya familiar de dicho Reverendo Padre; y que ademas del macho demanda contra dicho Yndio Miguel Ventura catorce cuchillos que a ora tres años le dio al dicho Yndio para que los vendiese dos para el dueño de los cuchillos que era don Joachin del Pino y uno para el, y que todos los deve y se a escusado ala paga diciendo que selos hurtaron; con mas el trabajo de sembrarle quatro milpas con mis bueyes, arados y peones y tres carretadas de lena que todo a quedado a pagarme y nada me a pagado y que lo que lleba dicho es la verdad y lo que sabe so cargo del juramento que fecho tiene y siendole leida su declarazion en ella se afirmo y ratifico y dijo ser de edad de cinquenta años, no firmo por no saber firmelo yo dicho Alcalde Mayor autuando como dicho es de que doi fee.

                    Carlos Fernandez (rubric)
testigo testigo
Miguel de Abeytia (rubric) Francisco Sanches (rubric)

En este Puesto de La Soledad del Rio Arriba en diez y seis dias del mes de Agosto del corriente yo dicho Alcalde Mayor hize parecer ante mi a Antonio Dominguez para que declare lo que supiere para lo que es citado y estando presente le tome juramento que lo hizo en toda forma de derecho y prometio decir verdad en lo que supiere y fuere preguntadoy siendolo que si sabe que el Yndio Miguel Ventura del Pueblo de San Juan pagase a Pedro Atiensa un macho dixo: que lo que sabe es que yendo el declarante para La Cañada apie y con una carguita de maiz lo alcanzo Juan Miguel hijo de Francisca Atensio en un macho que le parecia golondrino y que el dicho muchacho lo convido a subir a caballo y llevarle la carguita y que el declarante le pregunto que de donde llevava aquel macho y que le respondio que aquel macho le pagaba un Yndio de San Juan por otro que el Yndio le abia muerto y que el Yndio selo compro a Joseph Mirabal por un caballo y unas gamuzas y que esto es la verdad y lo que sabe so cargo del juramento que fecho tiene en el que se afirmo y ratifico y dijo ser de edad de cinquenta años y lo firmo con migo y los testigos autuando como dicho es de que doi fee = del corriente = entre renglones vale.

    Carlos Fernandez (rubric)
Antonio Dominguez (rubric)
testigo testigo
Francisco Antonio Zisneros (rubric) Juan Domingo Lovato (rubric)

En dicho Puesto dicho dia, mes y año ante mi dicho Alcalde Mayor en presentacion de esta ynformacion se presento Juan de Dios Yndio genizaro aquien tome juramento que lo hizo por Dios Nuestro Señor y la Santa Cruz so cuio cargo prometio decir verdad en lo que supiere y fuere preguntado y abiendole la grabedad del juramento y la obligacion que tiene de decir verdad y siendole de que si sabe como adquirio el Yndio Miguel Ventura en macho que llevo a los Yutas. Dixo, que lo embio su ama Francisca Atiensa a buscar unas bacas y que llego despues de medio dia ala casa del Yndio Miguel Ventura y que este le dixo que a donde estaba el macho que era de su ama y que le respondio que en la Cañada de San Juan y que le dixo el dicho Miguel que su compadre Pedro Atiensa selo abia prestado que fuese con el a buscarlo y que los dos fueron y lo trajeron y que ala madrugada lo ensillo el dicho Ventura y cargo en el maiz, arina y tortillas y despacho el mencionado Yndio al que declara que se fuese delante y que lo esperara en el bosque. Y preguntado que fue lo mas que vio y supo. Dixo, que aquella misma noche entro en casa del predicho Yndio Juan Tafoya y le entrego al Yndio Miguel una docena y tres cuchillos de velduque y seis frenos los que metio en una bota y le dijo Juan Tafoya vendelos como tuios y que acompano al dicho Yndio asta Abiquiú desde donde se aparto Miguel para los Yutas y el a buscar las bacas; y preguntado si sabe que Pedro Atensio le avia prestado el macho a Miguel. Dixo que no sabe y preguntado si el Yndio Miguel llevo algunas alesnas, lanzas, frenos o cuchillos de Pedro Atensio. Dixo que no sabe que llevase cosa alguna de Pedro Atensio; y preguntado si a platicado este con alguno. Dixo, que con quien platico esto que lleva dicho fue con Juan Diego Martin aquien le dijo que el Yndio Ventura llevava el macho y que llevava cuchillos y frenos y que no sabe otra cosa y que lo que lleva dicho es la verdad y lo que sabe so cargo del juramento que fecho tiene y siendole leida esta su declarazion en ella se afirmo y ratificoy segun el aspecto tendra diez y ocho años, no firmo por no saber firmelo yo dicho Alcalde Mayor con los testigos autuando como dicho es de que doi fee.

      Carlos Fernandez (rubric)

testigo testigo

Francisco Antonio Zisneros (rubric) Juan Domingo Lovato (rubric)

En este Puesto de La Soledad del Rio Arriba en veinte y cinco dias del corriente Agosto se presento ante mi dicho Alcalde Mayor, Juan Diego Martin zitado aquien tome juramento que lo hizo en toda forma de derecho so cuio cargo prometio decir verdad en lo que supiere y fuere preguntado y siendolo de si sabe que el Yndio Miguel Ventura de San Juan aiga ydo a los Yutas en que y que aiga llevado. Dixo, que lo que sabe es que el Yndio Juan de Dios criado de la Atensia le dijo que el Yndio Miguel avia ydo a los Yutas en un macho de su ama y que llebaba frenos, cuchillos y lanzas. Dixo que no sabe y que lo que lleba dicho lo sabe por que selo dijo el dicho Yndio Juan de Dios; y que no sabe otra cosa mas delo que lleba dicho y en esta su declarazion se afirmo y ratifico y dijo ser de edad de treinta años, no firmo por no saber firmelo yo dicho Alcalde Mayor con los testigos autuando como dicho es de que doi fee.

      Carlos Fernandez (rubric)

testigo testigo

Francisco Antonio Zisneros (rubric) Juan Domingo Lovato (rubric)

En dicho Puesto en dos dias del mes de Septiembre de mil setecientos sesenta y dos años ante mi dicho Alcalde Mayor se presento por testigo Francisco Sanchez aquien tome juramento que lo hizo por Dios Nuestro Señor y la Santa Cruz so cuio cargo prometio decir verdad en lo que supiere y fuere preguntado y siendolo de si sabe que el Yndio Miguel Ventura de San Juan aiga ydo a los Yutas en que y que llevo. Dixo, que estando Ygnacio Cornelio Figueroa por el mes de Abril en casa del que declara comersiando generos saco el dicho Cornelio de su casa dos dozenas de balduques y nuebe frenos y que le dijo que los yba a entregar a Juan Tafoya por que este le avia dicho que yban unos Yndios de San Juan a los Yutas que por su mano los llevarian y venderian y despues de algunos dias le bolbio a decir el dicho Cornelio que el Yndio Miguelillo le abia traido ocho gamuzas y que no sela abia entregado por que los oficiales del Pueblo lo avian azotado por la ida a los Yutas y muerte del macho en que avia ydo y que lo abia zitado para la noche y que defacto fue a San Juan el dicho Cornelio y trajo cinco gamuzas y le dixo al que declara que Juan Tafoya le abia entregado cinco gamuzas y que las otras tres selas abia buelto boruca encargandole al tiempo que se fue para El Paso cobrase a Juan Tafoya las tres gamuzas y preguntado si sabe de quien era el macho que se murio. Dixo, que oyo de arquira de la Atensia. Y preguntado si sabe como adquirio el Yndio Miguel el referido macho. Dixo, que no sabe, y que lo que lleva dicho es la verdad y lo que sabe y no otra cosa y siendole leida esta su declarazion en ella se afirmo y ratifico y dijo ser de edad de quarenta años y lo firmo con migo y los testigos autuando como dicho es de que doi fee.

      Carlos Fernandez (rubric)
      Francisco Sanchez (rubric)

testigo testigo
Juan Domingo Lovato (rubric) Francisco Antonio Zisneros (rubric)

Concluidas estas diligencias en la forma que de ello constan no obstante faltar dos testigos de los zitados por no hallarse en esta jurizdizion, hago remision de ella a Su Señoria a su vista mande lo que mas estimare y para que conste lo firme en seis dias del mes de Septiembre de mil setecientos sesenta y dos años.

      Carlos Fernandez (rubric)

Santa Fe 13 de Septiembre de 1762

Vistas las diligencias que anteceden hechas por el Alcalde Maior don Carlos Fernandez debia mandar y mande que el Yndio Miguel Ventura pague el macho o su valor, segun el precio acostumbrado en este Reino, a Pedro de Atienza por resultar ser lexitima la deuda, dandole el termino de tres meses para la paga del referido macho. Asi lo provei y firme yo don Thomas Velez Cachupin, Governador y Capitan General deste Reino del Nuebo Mexico autuando con dos testigos de mi asistencia a falta de escrivano.

      Thomas Velez Cachupin (rubric)

testigo testigo
Manuel Antonio Lorenz (rubric) Matheo de Penarredonda (rubric)

Notes

1. A Pedro Atienza and María de Ortega were godparents for a baptism in 1705 at San Ildefonso, though this may not be the same person. In 1733 a Pedro Atienza and Estefania Trujillo were godparents for a baptism in Santa Cruz. Pedro may have been a part of the Atienza Servillano family, who were in Santa Cruz and Ojo Caliente, and perhaps was related to Lázaro or José de Atienza who were in Río Arriba in 1735 (Chávez, *Origins*: 139-44; SANM I #20; NMGS, *Aquí*: 27, 234).
2. To date, there is no information on Miguel Ventura from San Juan Pueblo. A Genízaro Indian named Ventura was in the Taos area around this time. His first name was not recorded, and he may not be the same person (Ebright and Hendricks, *Witches*: 32; SANM II #494).
3. See Doc. 42.
4. Fray Juan [José Pérez] Mirabal, a Franciscan friar, was in New Mexico from 1722 to 1757. Following the Franciscan practice of rotation, he served at Taos, Santa Cruz, San Ildefonso, Pecos, Picuris, San Juan, and Santa Clara. He also served as vice-custos and custos of the New Mexico custody, called the Custody of Saint Paul (Chávez, *Archives*: 234, 276; Norris, *Year Eighty*: 10).
5. Juan [Antonio] Tafoya was the son of Cristóbal de Tafoya Altamarino and Isabel Herrera. Cristóbal, a soldier, left El Paso in 1695 and married Isabel in 1698. Juan and his brother Antonio were named in a grant at Santa Clara in 1724. They were also named with Cristóbal in a 1727 document regarding complaints about

pastures in 1727 and water in 1734, both in Santa Clara. In 1763 Juan Antonio and his father, Cristóbal, were named in disputes with the Santa Clara Indians (Chávez, *Origins*: 290; SANM I #174, #949).
6. No information was found on a Joseph Mirabal, who seems to be a different person than the priest. There was a Carlos José Pérez Mirabal, who lived in the Santa Clara area, who Chávez suggests was the brother of Fray Juan Mirabel. Fray Juan might also have been, or was related to, the Joseph Mirabel mentioned here (Chávez, *Origins*: 231).
7. Antonio Domínguez was mentioned in the 1756 will of Juan José Moreno, where Moreno stated that he had given Antonio one load of buckskins on his account. If this is the same person, he may have been a trader (SANM I #552, WPA translation).
8. Joseph Padilla could be the person of that name who was born in El Paso and came to New Mexico by 1711, though he would have been in the seventies at the time of this document. A Joseph Padilla and Antonia Martín appear as godparents in Santa Cruz in 1752, though in 1758, a Joseph Padilla appears with Pasquala Martín as parents, and in 1761, Joseph Padilla and María Padilla are godparents (Chávez, *Origins*: 253; NMGS, *Aquí*: 10, 64, 75, 82, 102, 112).
9. Joachín [José] Pino was born in Mexico City and lived in Tomé. A trader in New Mexican products, in 1763 he complained that such products had been stolen from him in Santa Clara. He charged Juan de Dios before Alcalde Carlos Fernández, and Juan was sentenced to work for Pino. Pino also had a son named Joachín Mariano, who could also be the person mentioned here (Chávez, *Origins*: 230; SANM II #562).
10. While the word *compadre* often means "friend," it can also mean "godfather."
11. Juan Diego Martín is probably the person born in 1731 who was a son of Diego Martín and Rosa de Atienza and a member of the Martín Serrano clan. A Diego Martín Moraga was mentioned in the inventory of the estate for Pedro Durán y Chávez in 1735 regarding the purchase of an Indian servant from Picuris Pueblo, but it is not known if this is the same person (Chávez, *Origins*: 225-26; SANM I #177; Payne, "Lessons": 403).
12. See Doc. 33.
13. Ygnacio Cornelio Figueroa was named, along with Carlos Fernández, in a 1765 petition before Governor Cachupín regarding land in Belén. He appears to have been an El Paso trader (SANM I #362).

49

RETURN OF CHINESE COLCHA WITH SILK BORDER DISPUTED BY SANTA FE RESIDENTS
July 19–20, 1764. Source: SANM II #577.

Synopsis and editor's notes: Sometime around 1758, Juan Joseph Moreno borrowed a *colcha*, a kind of bedspread or drape, from Felipe Tafoya. At the end of two years, when Tafoya wanted it returned, he found that it had been damaged. Tafoya asked for 100 pesos in goods as compensation, but Moreno only offered goods that Tafoya said were old and of no value to him. Moreno offered four cows, but they were in a faraway place and therefore not acceptable to Tafoya. Tafoya, who was a *procurado*, someone who gave legal advice, then complained to Governor Cachupín, who ordered Moreno to pay him fifty sheep, but Moreno refused. He said that the colcha had been used as a cover for the statue of Our Lady when he took it with him to collect fees for the *cofradía*, a religious brotherhood, and that the corners did get damaged, adding that it should be the Cofradía of Our Lady that should pay for it. Moreno then said he would bring a colcha of the same kind or one like it from México. Tafoya agreed, but nothing happened, so he complained to the governor again. The governor ordered Moreno to have the colcha repaired and the costs to be paid from the funds of the cofradía, and Moreno agreed. Moreno was a charter member of the Confraternity of Our Lady of Light and one of the founders of La Castrense, a military chapel in Santa Fe dedicated to her (Chávez, *Origins*: 239).

In regard to Moreno's claim of taking along the statue of Our Lady when soliciting for funds, such a claim is supported by a 1710 reference to solicitation of funds for the rebuilding of San Miguel. In this instance, the alférez, don Agustín Flores, asked permission to "go about in this city and in the other territories of this kingdom with the holy image to make a collection of alms which will be for assistance in the erection of the chapel in which the image would be located" (Kubler, *San Miguel*: 21).

The term *colcha* can mean a bedspread or a coverlet, though in this context it probably was an embroidered, fringed fabric that was also used as a drape for the statue of Our Lady. Inventories from La Castrense and a church in Santa Cruz both use the term *colcha* to refer to a wall hanging, a curtain for a portrait of a saint, and a covering for altar steps. The term may have evolved from the word *colchón*, or mattress. It is characterized by the colcha stitch, a special kind of embroidery like crewelwork. It has been suggested that the colcha stitch came from the Orient on embroidered silks that look like Manila shawls from the Philippines, and that the colcha referred to here was in fact a "mantón de Manila" (Montaño, *Tradiciones*: 126-30; Cordelia Thomas Snow, personal communication, November 1, 2012; Robin Farwell Gavin, curator, Spanish Colonial Arts Society Museum, personal communication, November 5, 2012).

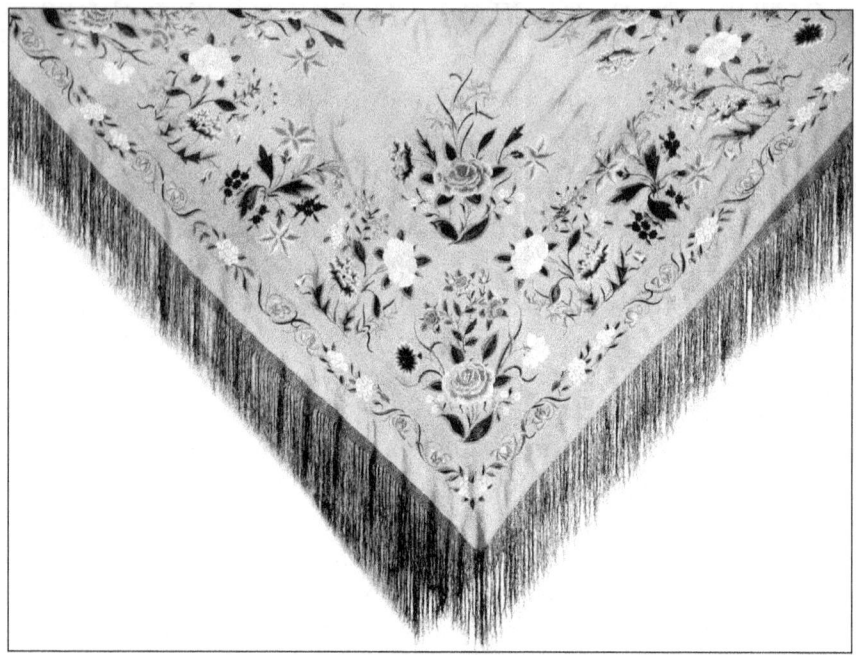

This late eighteenth- or early nineteenth-century *mantón de Manila*, or embroidered silk shawl, was from China or the Philippines and may be similar to the colcha described in this document. Photo by Jack Parsons. Padilla, *Conexiones*: 100. #1963.15. Image courtesy of the Museum of Spanish Colonial Art, Collections of the Spanish Colonial Arts Society, Inc., Santa Fe.

Year of 1764

Petition filed against don Juan Joseph Moreno[1]
by Felipe Tafoya,[2] a known attorney

Governor and Captain General

[1] Felipe Tafoya, resident of this Villa of Santa Fe, appear before Your Honor in my best possible form and right, and say that it is going on six years since don Juan Joseph Moreno, a resident of the said Villa, sent a message to my wife with Manuel Ortiz,[3] a soldier of this royal presidio, asking if he could borrow a colcha made in China, with a silk border and a fringe of the same material. This was something that my wife had, without ever having used it, with the thought of selling it for goods that are most needed by poor people. At the end of two years, having found out that the said colcha had been ill cared for, to the point that the four corners had been mended,

and having been ordered that it be washed, which was something that needed to be done before it was returned to us so that it could be sold, so that whoever purchased it could have it as such. For this reason, I requested that the said don Joseph Moreno pay me the sum of one hundred pesos of the land, which is something that he has not agreed to do because it does not belong to him. Instead, he offered to pay me with goods that were old and which he valued at a very high price, but which to me were of no value and served no purpose. In addition he offered to pay me with four cows, which I did not take because they were cared for in a faraway place, and which as such I would have been very likely to lose and thus would not be of any use to me. As can be seen the said don Joseph Moreno then looked for other means with which to pay me and which suited him best, and not to my liking.

I then went to see don Francisco Antonio Marín del Valle, the predecessor to your honor in the previous government, who then proceeded to call me in the presence of the said don Joseph Moreno, and upon seeing the issue which was being argued, he, the said Marín del Valle, ordered that I be given fifty sheep, which was the equal amount that I placed upon my said colcha, which he would bring immediately and have them within the patio of his home, which he did. But it seemed too much for him to give me, and he thus told me that he would order a colcha similar to mine from Chihuahua, and if he could not find one to my liking, he would give me goods of the value of the one hundred pesos. I consented to doing this and informed the said governor of our agreement. However, because to this day he has not complied with the just payment that he is supposed to give me, I was forced to bother your honor, it being quite clear that don Joseph was not going to comply with the order. As such, I thus placed this before your honor, even though it is a difficult problem, being that it has already been presented, justified, and a sentence pronounced by a competent judge, which was done by your honor, and the said don Joseph has protested this through some frivolous acts which he has argued in order to not pay me, and as such I ask and petition of your Honor that he be pleased to order the said don Joseph to fulfill the last agreement that we agreed to, being that so many years have gone by, and if done as has been ordered and determined as I have asked, I shall receive the justice with mercy, and I swear in due form that this is not done in malice, but for what is necessary, etc.

    Felipe Tafoya (rubric)

Santa Fe, [July] 19th, 1764

By virtue of what is represented by this party, the alcalde mayor of this villa, don Francisco Guerrero,[4] shall notify the said don Juan Joseph Moreno, involved in this complaint, about that which was ordered as the definitive sentence given by my predecessor of this government, don Francisco Antonio Marín del Valle, as is herein stated by the fifty sheep, or in other goods which are satisfactory to the said party. In order to comply with this order, don Juan Joseph Moreno is given eight days, beginning from the day of his notification, and if it is not complied with within the time period, the alcalde mayor will seize goods that are sufficient and accepted by the other party. The said Moreno is to pay the expenses brought about by these proceedings. I thus approved, ordered, and signed it along with my witnesses due to the lack of a scribe, which there is none in this kingdom.

                Vélez Cachupín (rubric)
                Carlos Fernández (rubric)
                Domingo Labadia (rubric)

Santa Fe, July 20, 1764

In fulfillment of that which was ordered by the governor and captain general of this kingdom according to the above decree, I proceeded to the house which belongs to don Juan Joseph Moreno, and he being present and laid up in bed, notified him of the order given by his honor. Fully understanding the order, he responded that it is true that he asked Felipe Tafoya for the colcha which was to be used as a cover for Our Lady [*Nuestra Señora*] when he took her with him to collect the fees [*limosna*]. Also, that it is true that it [the colcha] was somewhat mistreated in the corners, and I, as the *mayordomo* [of the *cofradía*]⁵ am obligated to pay for it, but from the funds of the cofradía, and with the colcha forever to remain in the service of Our Divine Lady.

As to what he [Tafoya] says that the governor ordered him to pay one hundred pesos, that is not true. What the said governor ordered was to have it repaired as if it was new, and to pay for that from the funds of Our Lady, and once that was done it was to be given back. He [Moreno] swears that everything that he [Tafoya] argues is not true. There were numerous times when he [Tafoya] went to his home, and the colcha was upon his bed, and he could have asked him for it. Where he states that I was willing to pay him with old goods, that is totally false. He said that he has everything that don Marín [de Valle] ordered to be done, which was to repair the colcha and not to give him [Tafoya] what he asked for, and that as *hermano mayor*⁶ says, that was the order given and determined. Accordingly, he notified your honor that it should be ordered that the said colcha be repaired by persons who are intelligent in doing this, and once it is done he would pay for it and report back to your honor that it had been done. He states that he knows of no law that he is to pay for it out of his pocket, but that he as the mayordomo that he was of Our Lady is obligated to pay for it, but not what he is asking. This is what he gave as his response, which he did not sign because he was disabled. I, the said alcalde mayor, signed it at the stated villa on the said day, to which I certify.

                Francisco Guerrero (rubric)

Santa Fe, dated the twenty-sixth. In attention to that which was ordered by the governor and captain general of this kingdom, and without paying attention to that which was argued by don Joseph Moreno, he was obligated to satisfy and pay to Felipe Tafoya in lieu of the one hundred pesos, fifty sheep, and he [Tafoya] being in agreement, received them as paid and was satisfied. So that is valid, the said alcalde mayor and the witnesses signed it along with me, to which I certify.

                Francisco Guerrero (rubric)
                Felipe Tafoya (rubric)
Joseph Miguel de la Peña (rubric) Estevan Rodrigues (rubric)

ORIGINAL DOCUMENT

Año de 1764
Peticion contra Dn. Juan Joseph Moreno echa
por el notorio procurador Felipe Tafoya.

                Señor Governador y Capitan General

Felipe Tafoya vesino desta Villa de Santa Fee, paresco ante Vuestra Señoria en toda forma de derecho y digo Señor que por cuanto ba para seis años que Dn. Juan Joseph Moreno vesino de dicha Villa mando un recaudo ha mi esposa con Manuel Ortis soldado deste Real Presidio, a pedir prestar una colcha fabrica de China bordada de seda y con el fleco delo mismo, la que tenia dicha mi esposa sin haver usado de ella para benderla por algunas otras cosas que son mas necesarias para los pobres y al cavo de dos anos que supimos que dicha colcha estaba tan maltratada que hasta le havian remendado las cuatro esquinas y mandado la lavar con lo que le merecio en el todo dela estimacion que para con nosotros y el que la comprara podia tener por cullo motibo ocurri a dicho Dn. Joseph Moreno a que mela pagara por sien pesos de la tierra lo que siempre le ha paresido mucho por no ser sulla, pues aunque en aquel entonses me ofrecia dichos sien pesos en algunas alajas biejas por mui subido precio y estas ami no me servian de ningun util como tambien me ofrecio quatro bacas las que no recevi por que eran cuidadas en distintas partes y estavan mas dispuesto a perderlas que a tener ningun util de ellas asta que dicho Dn. Joseph Moreno buscando modo para pagarme a su gusto y no al mio bido a el Señor Dn. Francisco Antonio Marin del Valle susesor de Vuestra Señoria en el anterior govierno quien me mando yamar en presencia de dicho Dn. Joseph Moreno y en bista delo alegado mando dicho Señor se me dieran sinquenta obejas que era lo mismo en que llo estimaba dicha colcha y las traia de pronto que las tenia en el patio de su casa y me trajo con sigo y aviendo pagado sele hiso pesado el entregarlas y me dijo que aquel mesmo ano me mandaria traer de Chiguagua otra colcha como la mia y de no encontrarla me daria cien pesos en generos alo que consenti dando aviso a dicho Señor Governador de nuestra compostura y biendo que hasta la presente no se ha verificado la justa paga que deve haserme me presisa molestar el juicio de Vuestra Señoria pues es claro que esto es nasido dela omision de dicho Dn. Joseph, pues pongo en la halta comprencion de Vuestra Señoria que es cosa dura que lo que esta pasado jusgado y sentenciado por Jues competente como lo era el Señor y quiera dicho Dn. Joseph derogarlo con protestos tan frigalos como son los que hasta aqui ha alegado por no pagarme por lo que a Vuestra Señoria pido y suplico sea mu servido de mandar a dicho Dn. Joseph me de cumplimiento a la ultima composision que tubimos puesto que tiene de que y que e casesido tantos años de ello, que en mandar haser y determinar como yevo pedido resevire mersed con justicia y juro en toda forma no ser de malicia y en lo nesesario, ut supra.

      Felipe Tafoya (rubric)

Santa Fee 19 de 1764

En vista delo que esta parte representa el Alcalde Mayor de esta Villa Dn. Francisco Guerrero notificara a Dn. Juan Joseph Moreno contenido en esta ynstancia cumpla con lo mandado por la difinitiba sentencia de mi antecessor en este govierno Dn. Francisco Antonio Marin del Valle, como aqui se expresa bien en las cinquenta obejas o en otros efectos que sean de la satisfaccion de esta parte para cuio cumplimiento se le da a dicho Dn. Juan Joseph Moreno el termino de ocho dias desde el dia de la notificacion y pasado no lo hacienda procedera dicho Alcalde Mayor por todo rigor de justicia a embargarle efectos equibalentes ala satisfaccion con que quede la parte a su dora satisfecha y que pague dicho Moreno las costas que se causaren en estas dilijensias; asi lo probehi, mande y firme autuado con testigos a falta de Escribanos que no las ai en este Reino.

      Velez Cachupin (rubric)
      Carlos Fernandez (rubric)
      Domingo Labadia (rubric)

Santa Fee y Julio 20 de 1764

En cumplimiento de lo mandado por el Señor Governador y Capitan General de este Reyno por el auto que antesede pase a la casa que prozada de Dn. Juan Joseph Moreno y estando presente y en cama le notifique lo mandado por Su Señoria, que entendido de su efecto responde que es cierto que le pidio a Felipe Tafoya la colcha para que sirviese de patio a la Divina Señora quando la saco a recoger la limosna, y que es verdad que se maltrato un poco en las esquinas y como mayordomo me obligue a pagarla pero siempre de la masa de la Cofradia, y que la colcha quedara siempre en zervicio de Nuestra Señora y que en quanto alo que dize de que el Señor Governador mando le diese cien pesos es falzo, por que lo que mando dicho Señor fue que se tratase como nueva y sele pagase de la limosna de la Señora y que en acabandose de juntarse le pagase, y jura que en todo lo que alega es falzo y que muchas veses que fue a su casa estaba la colcha en su cama en donde se la pudiera el pedirla y que a ver que dise que la pagaba en cosas viejas es falso todo lo que representa, y que tiene presente lo que el Señor Marin mando y es que setasas la colcha que no se le avia de dar lo que el pedia y que como hermano mayor dicho senos asi lo mando y determino, y que suplica a Su Señoria se zirva de mandar se tase la dicha colcha y que sea con personas yntelixentes y que luego pagara y dara cumplimiento alo mandado por Su Señoria, pero que le parece que no ay ley para que de su bolsa se pague la colcha que como mayordomo de la Divina Señora que lo era se obliga a pagarla, como la pagara, pero no por lo que el pide. Y esto dio por su respuesta la que no firmo por estar impedido. Firmelo yo dicho Alcalde Mayor en la expresada Villa en dicho dia de que doy fee.

      Francisco Guerrero (rubric)

Santa Fee fecha veinte y seis. En atencion de lo mandado por el Señor Governador y Capitan General de este Reyno y sin embargo delo alegado por Dn. Joseph Moreno dio entera satisfacion y paga a Felipe Tafoya y de los cien pesos en cinquenta obejas que a su contento se le entregaron y quedo satisfecho y pagado y para que conste lo firmo con migo dicho Alcalde Mayor y los testigos de que doi fee.

      Francisco Guerrero (rubric)
      Felipe Tafoya (rubric)
      Joseph Miguel de la Pena (rubric)
      Estevan Rodrigues (rubric)

Notes

1. See Doc. 44.
2. Felipe Tafoya was the son of Antonio Tafoya Altamirano, who came to New Mexico in 1695. Felipe was an alcalde of Santa Fe around 1770 and lieutenant general of the kingdom. In 1747 he was appointed church notary, even though he was a layman, and was instructed to see that the friars "strictly adhered" to the diocese's *arancel*, or fee schedule. He also acted as a procurado or a legal representative for the villa of Santa Fe, and was a legal defender for San Ildefonso (Kessell et al., *BOB*: 1169 n87; Chávez, *Origins*: 291-92; SANM I #995; Norris, *Year Eighty*: 117; Cutter, *Legal Culture*: 75-76).
3. Manuel Ortiz was a brother of Miguel Ortiz, half-brother of Domingo Romero, who together were granted the Mesita de Juan López in Cieneguilla, near Santa Fe. He may have been the son of Francisco or Luis, and therefore a nephew of Nicolás Ortiz (NMGS, *Aquí*: 350; Chávez, *Origins*: 250).
4. See Doc. 29.
5. A *cofradía* is a Catholic lay ecclesiastical brotherhood responsible for paying for specific religious services and the maintenance of an attached church or endowed chapel (Frank, *Settler to Citizen*: 466).
6. Moreno seems to be referring to himself as *hermano mayor*, or a senior fellow member of the cofradía. Later he refers to himself at the *mayordomo* of the cofradía of Our Divine Lady, which may mean the same thing.

50

CHIHUAHUA/SANTA FE MERCHANT TORIBIO ORTIZ SUES FOR SEVEN HIDES FROM CHAMA TRADER
November 9, 1763–November 12, 1764. Source: SANM II #581.

Synopsis and editor's notes: The events in this lengthy case between two traders began sometime before 1763 at Santa Clara Pueblo when Juan Ignacio Mestas announced that he would pay twenty-five hides to anyone who would give them to Domingo Baca, to whom he owed a debt. It seemed that Mestas was originally planning to give seventeen hides to Baca, with Joseph Antonio Naranjo giving Baca eight in lieu of a debt he owed to Mestas, for a total of twenty-five. Then, Toribio Ortiz, who was at Santa Clara, agreed to put up all twenty-five hides to Baca, with Mestas stating that he would pay Ortiz in goods later. But Mestas did not pay him, so Ortiz complained to Governor Cachupín, who ordered the debt paid.

Mestas then paid Ortiz two mules, which were not enough to cover the debt as far as Ortiz was concerned. This transaction took place at Santa Clara Pueblo, where, according to Ortiz, Mestas then announced that if anyone would give Ortiz ten additional hides to complete the deal, that person could choose from among his [Mestas's] horses, mares, or mules. Someone gave Ortiz three hides, but seven were still owed. Mestas said that he should have had the eight hides that were still owed to him by Naranjo, but he never got the hides from Naranjo. Ortiz kept repeating that this was irrelevant, as it seemed to be, since Mestas also said that he did not owe Ortiz anything.

In this document, Ortiz petitioned Governor Cachupín for the final seven hides. The governor referred his petition to Lieutenant Nicolás Ortiz, who heard the case. Mestas refused to pay and said that Ortiz had been paid in full with the two mules and three hides, and that Governor Cachupín had supported this, although Mestas had no receipt to prove it. Ortiz countered by submitting a receipt that said that Mestas had paid in full, with a statement written at the bottom of the receipt stating seven hides were still owed. Mestas said he never got a copy of that receipt, and that, anyway, the receipt was not correct. When Antonio Naranjo from Santa Clara supported the testimony of Ortiz, Mestas said that Naranjo's words should be discounted because he was an Indian, and Indians did not "recognize the gravity of their sworn statements."

Ortiz additionally claimed that the two mules that he did get from Mestas were not tame enough to use as pack animals and therefore not worth much. He also said that in the years trying to get paid what Mestas owed him, the price of hides had changed, so that the amount owed to him was greater than it had been. The twenty-five hides he was owed, Ortiz said, would have been worth 50 pesos, with which he could have bought thirty woven blankets, worth about 240 pesos when sold. Mestas countered by saying that the two mules plus three hides were worth 76 pesos, more than enough to cover the twenty-five-hide debt. At some point, Ortiz also said that he would return the mules in return for the original number of hides, thus canceling the entire transaction. But this does not appear to have been done, or at least it was not by the end of the proceedings.

Because of the upcoming departure date of the caravan to the south, the lieutenant governor set a time limit on the proceedings. But the two parties continued to argue, with Mestas saying that his witnesses had not been called. Finally Ortiz asked that the case be sent to Governor Cachupín. The lieutenant governor did so, explaining to the governor that the two parties had been allowed two terms to prove their cases but had not done so. Here the document ends without any judgment from the governor, either because the judgment has been lost, the parties compromised, or Ortiz gave up and left with the caravan.

Note that this 1763–1764 case took place in the relatively peaceful years of Governor Cachupín's second administration, which may have allowed the case to drag on longer than it would have in more difficult times. Cachupín's term was over in 1767. His successor, Governor Mendiñueta, was much less able at keeping the peace.

[The following two paragraphs were written in 1763, prior to the Ortiz-Mestas case, and are cited below in the third paragraph.]

Governor and captain general

[I] Toribio Ortiz,[1] the alférez of the militia cavalry, appear before your honor in my best possible form and say that Pablo Villapando,[2] resident of La Soledad,[3] Javier de Herrera[4] of La Cañada, and Juan Tafoya[5] of the puesto of Chama are indebted to me in the amounts that are entered in my book of accounts, along with the militia sergeant, Juan Ignacio Mestas,[6] who also is indebted and who has already had proceedings made against him in order to collect but has not done so, for all of which I petition and ask that your honor our majesty attend to this matter, as my credit is pending in Chihuahua, for which I ask that you order them, under the full rigor of justice, that they pay that which is so justly owed.

Toribio Ortiz (rubric)

Villa of Santa Fe, November 9, 1763.

In attention to that which is expressed by this party, I commission the lieutenant of the militia, Francisco Sánchez,[7] so that he may notify the indebted parties listed in this document so that they pay, immediately after they are notified through this proceeding, and upon failing to do so they are to be imprisoned in the royal guardhouse at their own expense.

I thus ordered, approved, and signed this, don Thomas Vélez Cachupín, governor and captain general of this kingdom.

Governor and captain general

[I] the lieutenant of militia, don Toribio Ortiz, resident of this villa of Santa Fe, appear before your honor in the best and proper form and say that by virtue of the decree issued by your honor, which he did as a favor to me, stating that the few subjects who are indebted to me for various amounts should come forth and pay me, one of them being Juan Ignacio Mestas, resident of Chama, who owes me seven hides. Upon asking him [Mestas] for them, he tells me that don Thomas Vélez [Cachupín], the predecessor of your honor, had ordered that the said Mestas did not have to pay me. But this was contrary to what happened. Proceedings were carried out as per my demand and are found in the archives [see the two paragraphs at the beginning of the document], which I request that your honor order to be reopened, and upon being reviewed they will show my just demand. If it is necessary, I will offer new proof that the said Mestas owes me the seven hides, fully owed to me, and I request that your honor order that they be promptly, without hesitation, paid to me. For all of this I ask that your honor be willing to order, approve, and determine as I have asked, which is for justice, to which I swear that it is not done in malice, etc.

Toribio Ortiz (rubric)

Toribio Ortiz and Juan Ignacio Mestas

Lieutenant governor

[I] Toribio Ortiz, resident of this kingdom, appear before your honor and say that Domingo Baca, resident of the Río Abajo, showed me a written bill, signed by Juan Ignacio Mestas, which I personally have, which proves that he was obligated to pay me twenty-five tanned hides, asking that anyone who could give them to the said Domingo Baca,[8] and he would give to me the twenty-five tanned hides in full payment. Confronting Mestas at a later date with the said bill [an IOU], he admitted that it was his and that he would pay me the twenty-five hides, which I have asked him for on various occasions. Seeing that he has been deceitful about it, and because they were so valuable to me, and in order to bring about the payment, I agreed to accept in lieu of them a mule and a macho that was not gelded and [both] broken for their work, along with the said Mestas agreeing to also owe me ten additional hides, of which I have received three, which were delivered to me by Julián Sánchez.[9] However, upon billing him for the remaining seven, not only has he not sent them to me, but has answered me verbally that he owes me nothing, and that I am trying to steal from him. Because of this, I petition your honor to be pleased to have him [Mestas] appear before you so that he will be compelled to pay the rest of what he owes me. In this way, I can prove that I am not a thief as he states, and as such I will receive mercy through justice, which is what I ask, and swear in due form that this request is not done in malice. I protest the costs for what is necessary, etc.

Toribio Ortiz (rubric)

Santa Fe, October 20, 1764[10]

As presented according to his right, and accepting what this individual is asking for, I order and did order that Juan Ignacio Mestas is to come to this capital. I thus approved, ordered, and signed it.

Nicolás Ortiz[11] (rubric)

Lieutenant General

[I] Juan Ignacio Mestas, resident of the puesto of Chama, appear before your honor in my best form and right and say, sir, that in response to the copy that your honor has been pleased to give to me and understanding what it says, I state that it is true that two years ago, I became indebted to Domingo Baca, resident of Belén, for seventeen hides, which I had promised to pay[12] to him. However, as I was away from my home, being in the Río Abajo, I gave him my bill, which was for the twenty-five hides, among them were eight which were to be given to him by Joseph Antonio Naranjo,[13] and which were owed to the said Domingo Baca. This has come to the attention of your honor, due to the fact that we have appeared before your honor, and during the past year being that don Toribio Ortiz has brought charges against me for the same bill for the full amount of the said twenty-five hides, and it had been agreed by the said individual that he would accept the two mules along with three hides, which would be the amount paid in full, with the eight hides that Naranjo owes being mine even though he has not yet given them to me. And I inform your honor that one [mule], according to the information which I have, is broken, and was one of the ones that I gave him, [and] is valued at 40 pesos, and the macho, which is also broken, is worth 36 pesos. These along with the three hides total up to 76 pesos of the land, all of which he was content with, and I was not to owe him anything else. The reason that I do not have a copy of the paid bill is because he never sent it to me, though he should have given it to me the same day that it was paid.

Regarding the charge which he raises that I called him a thief, I say that there is no one who should make that statement being that on a number of other occasions it has been denied, as I will deny that at the present time I owe him seven hides, for if I knew that I owed him those, I would have already paid him, as I have previously told him and which I would have done in order to get out of what was owed.

All of this I ask and petition your honor which in order to get clear of these charges, that he bring forth before him the said Domingo Baca and upon realizing what has occurred he will determine whatever he finds for the sake of justice, and with this I will receive the mercy that is due me, etc.

Juan Ignacio Mestas (rubric)

Santa Fe, October 29, 1764

A copy of each of these is given to Toribio Ortiz so that he can respond, and during the interim Juan Ignacio Mestas is to remain in this villa.

Nicolás Ortiz (rubric)

Lieutenant general

[I] Toribio Ortiz, resident of this villa, appear before your honor responding to that which is argued by Juan Ignacio Mestas about whether Domingo Baca had received or not received the eight hides which Naranjo should have given to him, and also asking if he had ever charged him for them. This is not the issue, and is not what I am demanding. It is the litigation which pertains to three of them [hides], and not to him in particular [to which he shows agreement] when he admits to the fact that it has nothing to do with what he brings forth. Regarding his allegation that the truth was lacking, it is not as he says it is, but as I have explained it in my petition. Neither the mule nor the macho which he gave to me was tame and broken, as he states, but they were merely broken; and as for the value in pesos, it is what he imagines. If he provides for your consideration the value of the mule and the macho, I will provide the value of the twenty-five hides at the time that I was idle [that is, not trading], as I am a merchant, and due to the differences that there are among the prices of various goods when I was trying to get him to pay the twenty-five.[14] I will also set forth statements about the mule and the macho, as I will prove in due time, and as for what is seen as being negative, as in the case of the scandalous words which he called me which I should not dare repeat, I shall provide the proof when your honor orders that the proceedings be concluded.[15] For all of this I swear that this is not done in malice, protesting the costs, but [that] which is necessary.

Toribio Ortiz (rubric)

Santa Fe, October 30, 1764

A copy is to be given to Juan Ignacio Mestas so that he can present the witnesses in order to prove what he has stated.

Nicolás Ortiz (rubric)

Lieutenant general

[I] Juan Ignacio Mestas resident of the puesto of Chama, appear before your honor in my best form and say that in answer to the copy that your honor was pleased to give me which came from don Toribio Ortiz, I say that at my request it is necessary that Domingo Baca appear before your Honor so that he can clear up the problem that resulted from the deal that was made and to verify if Naranjo does indeed owe the hides. As for the false statement that he [Ortiz] makes against me saying that the mules were not tame, I have plenty of proof to say that they were. For the [first] mule, the witnesses which I offer are Domingo Anselmo Santisteban,[16] Domingo Romero,[17] and Miguel Romero,[18] all residents of the puesto of Cieneguilla, which is where the said mule was broken. If necessary all of the residents from there can also be witnesses. As for the macho, I can present Juan Francisco Quintana,[19] who is the one who broke the macho, along with Julián Sánchez and Miguel Sánchez,[20] who saw him do it and saw that the macho was tame. The best proof that the macho was tame was the round trip that it made to Chihuahua as a working mule, which would not be made by any mule that is wild. Above all, if he [Ortiz] did not like them, he could have returned them to me with the same person who took them to him.

I am not in agreement with the charges which he made against me, because all of the account was paid with that which he has received, and I do not owe him anything else, as I have stated in my initial document. What is wrongly stated, sir, is that he [Naranjo] gave his goods to Domingo Baca, as what had been asked for were the twenty-five hides and no other goods. In my bill, I did not request that he [Naranjo] give me anything else, because if the said person [Naranjo] did not have the tanned hides, he should not have promised them to him, and as such I would have remained free of the charge which he makes against me [of having hides that he could pay to Ortiz]. If at the present time he [Ortiz] is not content with what he has received, he should return to me the mula and the macho along with the cargo from the past year, as is customary, and I will promptly give him the twenty-two tanned hides in fulfillment of the twenty-five, being that he has received three.

As far as the person who has gained from the twenty-five hides, it is not my fault, as I have stated, because in the first place he [Ortiz] was content, as was proven by the fact that he was pleased with receiving the mule and the macho instead of the hides, and secondly, because it was during the past year when he should have taken them. It appears to me that the delay has been his problem, and it [the exchange] should have been done during the appropriate time, although the contrary occurred, as is proven due to the delay in sending the mule and macho back, and when I was presented with the decree from the governor as was requested by the said don Toribio. In this decree [from the governor] I was ordered to come up with the remainder, exclusive of the mula and the macho, which I shall leave out for now. It is known and evident that no one takes only half, or part, of what is owed, but the whole amount.[21] Responding to this last point and the evidence that is offered, where he has stated that I am a thief, I do not know of anyone who can say that, and I do not agree with it, as one witness is no proof [is not enough].

Because of all of this, I request that our majesty, upon review of that which is argued by myself and by the other party, don Toribio Ortiz, and the proof that we have brought forth, you will determine whatever you find, as if this is not cleared up in favor of one of the corresponding parties, it will cause me great losses due to my being absent from my home, and upon it being done, I will receive mercy and justice; and I swear that this is not done in malice but for what is necessary, etc.

Juan Ignacio Mestas (rubric)

Santa Fe, October 31, 1764

As presented in his proper right, and on the part of Toribio Ortiz, I will admit the payment of the animals which were brought forth by Juan Ignacio Mestas. A copy of the proceedings are given to Ortiz, and if he is not in agreement, I will notify the two litigating parties so that they can further express the proof which they have within the period of eight days [until November 6, 1764], which shall be counted from this day of this date, with the understanding that if not done within the said time period it shall not be carried out, as it is necessary to attend to it due to the short period of time which is left before the residents leave on their customary commercial trip to outside lands. I thus approved, ordered, and signed it acting with my assisting witnesses, to which I certify.

Nicolás Ortiz (rubric)

Witness

Nicolás Ortiz (rubric) Antonio Joseph Ortiz (rubric)

Lieutenant general

[I] don Toribio Ortiz, understanding that which was ordered by your honor, say that I am in agreement with returning the mula and macho along with their two cargos as they were not good for carrying loads, not denying that they did serve me on the road for a few days, using them as saddle animals, it being that Juan Ignacio Mestas had given them to me in lieu of the twenty-five hides, which, if sold in Chihuahua at their regular price, would have been worth 50 pesos. With this, I could have bought at least thirty woven blankets, which at the current price of the land would have brought me about 240 pesos, saying that they were a species of skin that I handle that are taken from this land. I only agreed so as not to break the pact which we have made with them due to the proposition which has been accepted. He, Mestas, does not respond to the rest of the allegations because they are unjustifiable and are not opposed to my demands. With respect to the other [issue], I acknowledge the principal of the bill and [the other] absurdities as he has confessed, that the amount of the bill has been paid, excepting only the rest of the six [seven?] hides, which would be the total of what is owed to me.

If my demand is not met, as is proven, your honor should be pleased to have him pay what is owed me. As proof, he should bring before him the retired don Carlos Fernández,[22] who was the alcalde mayor for the jurisdiction of La Cañada at the time that I instigated my original demand against the said Juan Ignacio regarding the trade for the twenty-five hides as stated. This is so that he [Fernández] can testify as to what he knows, and so that I can prove that the deal which we had where Juan Ignacio did not have on hand all the [promised] hides, and to show the truth that he remained owing me the seven. Your honor should also take the sworn statement of Julián Sánchez, who was the one who delivered to me the animals and the three hides. Juan Ignacio refers, in his latest statement, to a decree of the governor [referred to above], which was brought forth, but which I have not been given, nor been notified of. As such it would be just to bring it forth or to state what was stated in it [about that which] was to be brought forth [in payment], or not to be brought forth, as evidence of the truth and [in response] to his frivolous accusations made so as not to pay. Regarding the last point, there is nothing that can be proven by taking the declaration of an individual without there being proof or of ever having seen the declaration [decree] of which I state. Also, your honor should be pleased to take a declaration, whenever your honor should find it convenient, from Francisco, Indian from Santa Clara, and ask him if there were other persons present when he heard the words which I have expressed in my original document, so that in case he knows, they should be examined regarding this particular point. I swear in due form not to be in malice, protesting costs, but for what is necessary.

Toribio Ortiz (rubric)

Santa Fe, November 3, 1764

A copy [of the testimony] should be given to Juan Ignacio Mestas so that he can see if it was, as Toribio Ortiz says, of witnesses not being examined. I thus approved it and signed, to which I certify.

Nicolás Ortiz (rubric)

I, Francisco Sánchez, certify that upon receiving an order[23] expedited by the governor and captain general don Thomas Vélez Cachupín during the past year, dated the 9th of November [of 1763], in which your honor ordered me to notify and make those who were indebted to don Toribio Ortiz to pay him. I responded that one of those who was indebted to him was Juan Ignacio Mestas, who stated that one day prior to the notification he had sent him a macho, a mula, and three hides, which would satisfy the twenty-five hides that he owed him.

Francisco Sánchez (rubric)

I, Miguel Sánchez, certify that it is true that a mule and a macho which Juan Ignacio Mestas gave to don Toribio Ortiz, which were bred by and carried the branding iron of Captain Pedro Sánchez, were recently broken and are so tame that they can be taken with just the bridle at any time, any place. I thus give this information and due to an accident, I could not appear at the indicated place.

Miguel Sánchez (rubric)
Lásaro Sánchez (rubric)

Lieutenant governor

[I] Juan Ignacio Mestas, resident of the puesto of Chama, appear before your honor in this litigation in my best and proper form which there is and comply in all form of right and say, sir, as I understand that in this litigation which I am involved with along with don Toribio Ortiz concerning twenty-five hides for which I have been billed by the said don Toribio, which I have paid to his satisfaction and contentment with a mule and a macho, which are tame, along with three hides, but he says that the mules are not tame, to which I offer to your honor the information that this is not correct. The expressed mules are tame and capable of serving him on his trip out of the country, but he says that this is not so. However, this is what I have paid and with which I remain in agreement. It appears to me that he must be fine with this, as I have not received a document or any other proof to indicate that I still owe him seven hides.

Also, he says that there is no way that I was notified by the lieutenant of militia, Francisco Sánchez, about that which he [Sánchez] presented to your honor, along with this so that it can come to the knowledge of the truth which I have up till now expressed, and which states that I do not owe the said seven hides. This is so, even though I was informed by don Carlos Fernández on three occasions, to whom I showed all of my goods, not hiding even one hide by which I could have satisfied the said account, which can be the only way that the said don Carlos, who was alcalde in that jurisdiction, could be satisfied. It cannot be understood how he [Ortiz] can certify that I still owed him the said hides as I made the payment through the person of Julian Sánchez, who was the one who turned over [the payment] to don Toribio Ortiz. I have [so] stated, and thus I remain without owing the bare minimum of the said amount. Also, if I can ask your honor to have appear before him the said Indian named Francisco, who should state how it was, when I was not even at home, when he brought the paper belonging to don Toribio. For all of this I ask and petition your honor that he be well pleased to conclude this litigation if he finds it according to justice and in which I will

receive mercy and which I swear is not done in malice but for what is necessary, etc.
      Juan Ignacio Mestas (rubric)

Santa Fe, November 9, 1764
 Being presented so that it can be argued according to their rights and attending to the fact that the litigating parties are not in agreement among themselves, I again order that because the time allowed for proving their case is almost gone, they are to present the witnesses which they have cited in their responses within the next twenty-four hours so that they can be examined on the corresponding points. The two parties shall be notified of this, and Juan Ignacio Mestas is to be prepared with his proceedings. I thus approved, ordered, and signed it, acting with assisting witnesses as there is no notary in the entire kingdom, to which I certify.
      Nicolás Ortiz (rubric)
Witness Joseph Miguel de la Peña (rubric)
Nicolás Ortiz (rubric)

 In this villa of Santa Fe on the 9th of November of 1764, I, don Nicolás Ortiz, lieutenant governor of this kingdom, had appear before me Julián Sánchez, resident of the new villa of Santa Cruz de la Cañada, as a witness brought forth by Toribio Ortiz to offer the information which he gives about the seven hides that were to be paid by Juan Ignacio Mestas from the twenty-five which the said Mestas owed to the said Toribio Ortiz. I took his sworn statement which he made before God and the sign of the Holy Cross, under which he swore to tell the truth as to what he knew and to what he was asked. Beginning, he said that it was true that it was with him that his brother-in-law, Juan Ignacio Mestas, sent a mule that was tame and could be ridden and a macho that was not gelded and could be ridden, as well as three hides, to Toribio Ortiz in payment for twenty-five hides which were owed according to a bill presented by the said Ortiz that was owed by Juan Ignacio Mestas. The said Mestas told him [Sánchez] to tell Ortiz that the rest of the hides that he still owed him would be paid at a later time, not to worry. This he stated was the truth about what he knew regarding the issue and is what he can say under the oath which he has taken. He said he was twenty-two years of age, and he signed it along with me the said lieutenant governor acting with assisting witnesses due to the lack of a notary, which there are none in this kingdom, to which I certify.
      Nicolás Ortiz (rubric) Julián Sánchez (rubric)
Witness Joseph Miguel de la Peña (rubric)
Witness Agustín Lobato (rubric)

At the said villa on the said day, month, and year, I, the said lieutenant governor, had appeared before me Antonio Naranjo, native of the pueblo of Santa Clara, as a witness presented by Toribio Ortiz in order to prove what he says about the hides which Juan Ignacio Mestas still owed him. He said that it was true that in front of him and the governor of his pueblo and the Indian, Sente Asencio Ydala, and a number of other Indians from his pueblo, Juan Ignacio Mestas asked the referred to Toribio Ortiz if he could pay him with a mule which was tame and could be ridden and a macho, which was not gelded, and could be ridden, and that he would still owe him ten hides. The said Ortiz hesitated to take the said mule and macho, wanting to get only the twenty-five hides. The said Mestas had to persuade him to take the mule and the macho, and remained owing him ten hides, to which he asked the Indians of the pueblo that if anyone would pay Toribio Ortiz the ten hides he would let whoever paid choose from among his animals, horses, mares, or mules. This, he says, is the truth and is what he knows about the issue, and says that he is thirty years of age, more or less. He did not sign because he did not know how. I, the lieutenant governor, signed it with my assisting witnesses due to the lack of a public or royal notary which there is none in this kingdom, to which I certify.

Nicolás Ortiz (rubric)

Nicolás Ortiz (rubric) Nicolás Rael (rubric)

Santa Fe, November 9, 1764

The retired lieutenant don Carlos Fernandez is to certify at the foot of this [page] what his thoughts are regarding this issue so that he can be cited as the last witness for Toribio Ortiz.

Nicolás Ortiz (rubric)

[I] Carlos Fernandez, retired lieutenant of this royal presidio, under my right I can say and will say that in the past year of 63, appeared before me the alcalde mayor of La Cañada, who was at the time don Toribio Ortiz, with a bill made and signed by Juan Ignacio Mestas under which he obligated himself to pay twenty-five hides to any person who would give them to Domingo Baca; and upon showing the said bill to Juan Ignacio Mestas, he acknowledged that it was his and that he was obligated to pay the said twenty-five hides. But because he did not have them at the time because he had not been home, he stated that he would pay the amount with other goods, but that the said Ortiz never concluded the business, so I do not know if it was ever paid. All of what I have said is what I know.

Carlos Fernández (rubric)

Santa Fe, November 10, 1764

A copy of this shall be given to Toribio Ortiz so that he can argue what he can prove. I thus signed and approved it.

Nicolás Ortiz (rubric)

Lieutenant general

[I] Toribio Ortiz appear before your honor and say that the information given by Juan Ignacio Mestas in the two papers which have been included with these proceedings in no way prejudice my demand. This is because in only one does he recognize the accusation which was made against him after he gave me the mule and the macho, to which I will swear he has denied it, and on the other one he says that they were tame, but which I say were wild and not broken nor able to be ridden. The same was verified in the statement by Julián Sánchez, the brother-in-law of Juan Ignacio Mestas, and which is seen in the little faith shown in the said papers because they belong to two in-laws, who are contrary to me. But I will put it aside because I have proven through [the testimony of] two witnesses who were present at the last agreement that we had the agreement with the remainder of the last seven hides, which I can prove with the receipt which I gave when I received the mules, and which should be with the person who turned them over to me with everything else. He will deny this so as not to pay, though, as can be seen, it is without any substance. The final issue is whether he owes me the seven hides or nothing. For all of this, your honor should be pleased to order him to pay me the seven hides if there is to be any justice, which is what I ask for, and swear that it is not done in malice.

Toribio Ortiz (rubric)

Santa Fe, November 10, 1764

A copy is to be given to Juan Ignacio Mestas so that he can argue what he has to prove, and I approved it and signed it.

Nicolás Ortiz (rubric)

Lieutenant governor

Juan Ignacio Mestas, resident of the puesto of Chama, appears before your honor in the best form and says that in responding to the copy which your honor has sent to me from don Toribio Ortiz and having seen it and recognized the summary of the proceedings and not finding among them any of the statements of the witnesses which

I have presented on my behalf except for one of them, that of Julián Sánchez, whose statement I find in my favor. This proves the great malice which is brought forth by the opposing party without [it] being cited by him and allows something which is malicious which he has had in his power, which is, the receipt which don Toribio Ortiz gave to him [Sánchez] at Tomé after he had received the mules in this villa. I am not in agreement with his statement, and the said receipt clearly proves that he has been paid as it reads: "I, Toribio Ortiz received from Julián Sánchez one mule and one macho which are tame enough to be ridden along with three hides for the amount which was owed to me by Juan Ignacio Mestas, and the said Juan Ignacio owes me seven hides on the account that is due." Then, through the same receipt, he says that, "In consideration for the demand that is due from him, nothing more is due."

Because of this, your honor, I say that all of this is proved to show that they are seven hides, as I have never had the receipt until now when it was brought forth before your honor. It appears to me to be very free to say on the receipt that in order to fulfill everything with the twenty-five hides, seven are still lacking. Regarding the declaration of the Indian Antonio Naranjo and the others, I say that it has no value, being that the document which was introduced by don Toribio did not include them, and even if they were included, they cannot be witnesses because he is an Indian very recently brought into the faith and does not recognize, along with the other Indians from the pueblo, the gravity of their sworn statements, and more so when the distance that there is from the pueblo of San Juan, which is where I had the dealings with don Toribio, and during which time he did not have with him any of the said Indians from the pueblo of Santa Clara. In no way can I agree.

On my behalf I have asked that Domingo Baca be brought forth, but he has not been called to do so. This does not surprise me, as on my behalf none of the witnesses which I have cited have been allowed to give their statements in the proceedings, and in reality even those who have been certified on my behalf [have not been called], except Francisco Sánchez, lieutenant of the militia of the jurisdiction of Río Arriba, which was approved by the same decree of the governor and captain general of this kingdom, which was done at the request of don Toribio, dated November 9th, 1763, which together with all of these proceedings were presented to your honor. All together, I ask that your honor be well pleased to see that these proceedings get to the hands of the governor and captain general of this kingdom so that upon his review, his honor will clarify the justice to the party that deserves it, though it has caused me a great deal of hardship by being away from my home, and upon doing it I shall receive justice, and I swear not to be in malice but for what is necessary, etc.

       Juan Ignacio Mestas

In this villa of Santa Fe on the 12th day of the month of November of the present year of 64, [I], don Nicolás Ortiz, lieutenant governor of this kingdom, submit these proceedings to the governor and captain general, as was requested by Juan Ignacio Mestas in his last response and in accordance with what I think is proper. I inform your honor that during the two terms which have been allowed to the two litigating parties so that they can prove what they argue in their documents and are brought forth in these proceedings, they have not brought forth any other witnesses or other documents other than those which are herein included.

[Editor's note: The governor's final decision is not included with these proceedings.]

ORIGINAL DOCUMENT

Señor Governador y Capitan General

Thoribio Ortis Alferes de Caballeria Milisiana paresco ante Vsia. en la mas debida forma y digo que Pablo de Villalpando besino de La Soledad, Jabiel de Herrera de La Cañada, Juan Tafolla del Partido de Chama, me son deudores de las cantidades que costan en mi libro de caja y el Sargento Miliciano Juan Ygnasio Mestas de la que por junto bale se manifiesta lla biendo practicado cuantas diligencias me son posibles para la cobranza ninguna a sido bastante por lo que pido y suplico a Vuestra Majestad que atendiendo a que mi credito esta pendiente en Chiguagua sea servido de mandar por todo rigor de justicia me pagen lo que tan justamente deben.
Thoribio Ortiz (rubric)

Villa de Santa Fee 9 de Noviembre de 1763
En atencion a lo que esta parte representa; doi comision al Theniente de Milicias Francisco Sanches para que notifique alas partes deudoras contenidas en esta ynstancia la satisfagan yncontinenti en el mismo auto de la notificazion y no lo haciendo los conduciera presos a este Real Cuerpo de Guardia a su costa y mencion. Asi lo probei, mande y firme, Dn. Thomas Velez Cachupin, Governador y Capitan General deste Reino.
Velez Cachupin (rubric)

Señor Governador y Capitan General

El Theniente Miliciano Dn. Thoribio Ortis vesino de esta Villa paresco ante Vssa. en toda forma de derecho y digo que en virtud del decreto que fue Vuestra Señoria servido librar ami favor para que varios sujetos que me son deudores de cantidades capases me dieren satisfacion y siendo uno de ellos Juan Ygnacio Mestas vecino de Chama que me resta siete gamusas y reconvenidole por ellas me responde que el Señor Dn. Thomas Velez antecesor de Vssa. mando que el citado Mestas no me pagara, haviendo precedido lo contrario, pues se corrieron diligencias ami pedimento las que paran en el Archibo las que suplico a Vssa. se sirva mandar reconocer y vistas se bendra en conocimiento de mi justa demanda, y en caso necesario ofresco nuebamente probar que el referido Mestas me deve las siete gamusas vien devidas y suplico a Vuestra Señoria mande me las pague prontamente sin demora alguna por tanto a Vssa.suplico ser mui servido de mandar provier y determinar como llebo pedido que es justicia, juro en forma no de malicia, ut supra.

Thoribio Ortis (rubric)

Señor Teniente de Governador

Torivio Ortis y
Juan Ygnacio Mestas
Toribio Hortis vezino deste Reyno parezco ante Vm. y digo; que Domingo Baca vezino del Rio Abajo me manifesto un vale de letra y firma de Juan Ygnacio Mestas que para en mi poder por el qual se obliga a pagar beinte y cinco gamusas ala persona que las diere o su ymporte a el dicho Domingo Baca en virtud de cuio vale entrege a el dicho Domingo Baca el ymporte delos beinte y cinco gamusas a toda su satisfacion y recombiniendo despues a dicho Mestas con el mencionado vale confesso ser suio y quedo a entregarme las beinte y sinco mencionadas gamusas las que le cobre en muchas ocasiones, y viendo sus muchos engaños y la mucha falta que me hazian para mi correspondencia por facilitarle la paga ube de admitir en quenta de ellas una mula y un macho entero en pecados adomar quedando el dicho Mestas a entregarme diez gamuzas de las quales recevi tres que me ynbio por mano de Julian Sanches y ynbiandole a cobrar aora las siete restantes no solo no melas embia pero me responde de palabra que nada me deve y que si no estoy arto de robar; por lo que suplico a Vm. sea serbido de mandar comparesca en su juzgado el dicho Mestas asi para que sea compelido alo resto delo que me deve como para que pruebe los robos que me ynputa que en hacerlo asi recibire merced con juzticia que pido y juro en devida forma no ser de malizia este pedimento, costas protesto, y en lo necesario, ut supra.

Thoribio Ortis (rubric)

Santa Fee 8re (Octubre) 20 de 1764
Por presentado en quanto a lugar en derecho y asento alo que esta parte biene pidiendo debia de mandar y mande paresca Juan Ygnacio Mestas en esta Capital, asi lo probei, mande y firme.

Nicolas Ortiz (rubric)

Señor Theniente General

Juan Ygnacio Mestas vecino del Puesto de Chama paresco ante Vmd. en toda forma a derecho y digo Señor que respondiendo al traslado que Vmd. fue servido de darme y entendido de el digo; que es verdad que haora dos años se balio de mi Domingo Baca vesino del Puesto de Belen para que le prestara diez y siete gamusas y estando como estaba fuera de mi casa en el Rio Abajo le di mi bale en que constan las veinte y sinco de que seme hase cargo con ocho que quedo ha dar Joseph Antonio Naranjo que este se las debia ha dicho Domingo Baca como a Vmd. le costara en comparesiendo ante Vmd. y el año pasado habiendome echo el cargo Dn. Thoribio Ortis por el mismo vale del todo de dicho veinte y sinco gamusas tubimos comportara mas ida de dicho Señor que me pidio dos vestias mulares y tres gamusas por el todo de la dependencia quedando a mi fabor las ocho gamusas de Naranjo que aun todabia no melas a entregado y pongo en la consideracion de Vmd. que una mansa como dare ynformacion lo hera la que entregue vale quarenta pesos y el macho manso vale treinta y seis de las tres gamusas que hasen la cantidad de setenta y seis pesos al corriente de la tierra con lo que dicho Señor quedo contento y no quede a deverle otra cosa ninguna que el no tener yo en mi poder dicho vale es por no habermelo enbiado como quedo con migo el dia que quedo pagado y tocante a el cargo que me hase de haberlo ynputado de ladron digo que no ai tal que no ha de haber quien pueda desirlo pues lo que a presedido de mi al Señor an sido otras veses negandome como me niego alo presente de dever dichas siete gamusas que si yo conosiera haver quedado debiendolas ya le pagado pues como yebo dicho a pedimento de dicho Señor y por salir de la dependensia hube de dar lo que llebo dicho con lo que a Vmd. pido y suplico sea mui servido en vista del cargo y de mi descargo haser compareser antes si a dicho Domingo Baca y en vista de su rason determinara lo que hallase por de justicia que en ello resibire mersed y juro no ser de malicia, ut supra.

      Juan Ygnacio Mestas (rubric)

Santa Fee 8re (Octubre) 29 de 1764
Corasele traslado a Toribio Ortis para que responda y en el ynter mantengase Juan Ygnacio Mestas en esta Villa.
      Nicolas Ortiz (rubric)

Señor Theniente General

Thoribio Ortis besino de esta Villa paresco ante Vm. y respondiendo alo alegado por Juan Ygnacio Mestas dijo que Naranjo daba o no daba a Domingo Baca las ocho gamusas que espresa que las aia cobrado o no, no es deste asunto no se opone ami demanda pues es el litis que pertenese a los tres y no a mi mallormente quando confiesa si que en el se espresa ser gustancia alguna de las que a ora pone; y en quanto ala conpostura que dise tubimos falta ala berdad, pues no fue como el dise, sino como llo lo tengo esplicado en mi pedimento ni la mula y macho que me entrego eran mansas como dise sino solo quebrantadas y asi el aguste de pesos que ase delas dichas bestias es un agenario y si el pone en la consideracion de Usted el balor dela mula y macho llo pongo el delas beinte y sinco gamusas que a del año que caresio desinutil pues soi comersiante y la diferencia que ai de genero a genero y en quanto a que llo solisitase que la paga de la beinte y sinco gamusas puse en la mula y el macho tambien falta ala berdad como a su tiempo probare, y por lo que mira ala negatiba que ase de las palabras afrentosas con que me la dijo faltare a el mismo onbre que las allo y me las dijo ami que las pruebas ofresco dar quando Vm. mandare estando los autos en positura para ello juro no ser de malisia costos protesto y en lo necesario.

Thoribio Ortis (rubric)

Santa Fee 8re 30 de 1764
Corasele traslado a Juan Ygnacio Mestas y que presente los testigos para la prueba de lo que tiene dicho.

Nicolas Ortiz (rubric)

Señor Theniente General

Juan Ygnacio Mestas vesino del Puesto de Chama paresco ante Vmd. en toda forma y digo que respondiendo al traslado que Vmd. se sirvio darme de Dn. Thoribio Ortis digo que ami derecho conviene que paresca ante Vmd. Domingo Baca para que se aclare el modo que hurto en este trato y si Naranjo deve o no las gamusas. Pues para la falsedad que me imputa de no ser mansas las vestias mulares ofresco plena prueba deserlo; pues para la mula podran ser testigos Domingo Anselmo Santisteban, Domingo Romero y Miguel Romero todos vesinos del Puesto de la Sieneguilla que es donde se amanzo dicha mula y si es necesario fuere los demas de alli como tambien del macho podra serlo Juan Francisco Quintana que lo domo Julian Sanchez y Miguel Sanchez que vieron y conocieron el macho manzo y la mayor prueba de serlo es el haver echo el viaje a Chiguagua de ida y buelta travajando que no lo haze ninguna vestia mular serrera y sobre todo sino le gustavan pudo havermelas buelto con el mismo que selas vino a entregar, y haverme echo el cargo que me haze con el que no me conformo por que quedo pagado del todo de la dependencia con lo que tiene resevido pues no quede a dever cosa ninguna como tengo expresado en mi primer escripto e hira mal dicho Señor de dar sus generos a Domingo Baca pues yo en mi vale lo que pido son las veinte y cinco gamusas y no generos pues en mi vale no consta que yo diesa facultad para que me vendiera por que si dicho Señor no tenia las gamusas cumplia con no prestarselas que en esso quedava libre del cargo que me hase y si al presente no esta contento con

lo que tiene resevido que me debuelba la mula y macho con sus flete del año pasado como es costumbre que estoi prompto luega a entregar las veinte y dos gamusas para el complimiento delas veinte y cinco pues tiene resevidas tres: y el que haya caresido del util delas veinte y cinco gamusas no tengo la culpa lo primero por su contenta como tengo expresado y lo segundo por que el año pasado era quando las havia de haver llevado pues segun me parese esse atraso lo ha tenido por si pues no me reconvino en su tiempo pues lo contrario es provado pues haviendome tardado en embiar la mula y macho se me recombino con decreto del Señor Governador apedido de dicho Dn. Thoribio con lo que queda provado ser mas gustoso en resevir la mula y macho que las gamusas y esta mas hasedero que en el dicho decreto seme ordenara la exevision de la resta aparte dela mula y el macho que no que lo dexara para ha ora. Pues es savido y evidente que ninguno cobra la mitad, ni parte de lo que se deve sino es el todo. Y respondiendo al ultimo que lo he imputado de ladron y la prueba que ofrese digo quedando y no consedido que haiga sujeto que pueda decirlo no me conformo por que un testigo no haze prueva. Por lo que a Vuestra Merced suplico que en vista de lo alegado por mi y la otra parte de Dn. Thoribio Ortis y las pruevas que tenemos ofresidas haser y determinar lo que hallare por denuncia pues de no aclararse ala parte que le corresponde seme sigue mucho atraso con la ausiencia de mi casa que en hacerlo asi resevire merced y justicia y juro no es de malicia y en lo necesario et supra.
     Juan Ygnacio Mestas (rubric)

Santa Fee 8re 31 de 1764
Por presentada en quanto a lugar en derecho y por si la parte de Thoribio Ortis admitiere la debolucion delas bestias que propone Juan Ygnacio Mestas corasele traslado a dicho Ortis y de no ser conforme notifiquesele alas dos partes litigantes que califiquen las preubas que tienen ofresidas dentro de el termino de ocho dias perenterios que se contaran desde oi dia de la fecha con apersebimiento de que dentro de dicho termino no lo ejecutare a que sera la rebeldia atendiendo a el corto tiempo que falta para que salga el besindario ala tierra fuera a sus acostumbrados comersios asi lo probei mande y firme autuando con testigos de asistencia de que doi fee.
     Nicolas Ortiz (rubric)
Testigo
Nicolas Ortiz (rubric) Antonio Joseph Ortiz (rubric)

     Señor Theniente General

Thoribio Ortis entendido delo por Vmd. mandado digo que soi conforme con debolber la mula y macho con sus dos fletes nos constante que solo me sirbieron en el camino algunos dias ala silla por no estar proposito para cargas con tal que Juan Ynasio Mestas me trage el producto delas beinte sinco gamusas que bendidas en Chiguagua a su regular precio ymportan sinquenta pesos con los que ubiere yo comprado alo menos treinta mantas de paños que al precio coriente desta tierra ynportan dosientos y quarenta pesos quando espesie de pieles delas que se secan deste Reino a comerciar lo ago no por disbaratar el pacto que tenemos echo suio por la proposicion que ase. No respondo alas demas alegatas por ser ynjustiansiables y no haver oposicion ami demanda respecto al otro confeso en lo principal que es el bale y mayor abundamiento tener confesado que el todo de el bale lo tiene pagado negando solo el resto de las seis gamusas que es el fin de mi demanda y pues sea de redusir a prueba en caso de no almitir mi propuesta sea de serbir Vmd. justicia mediante demandar que el dicho reformado Dn. Carlos Fernandez que era Alcalde Mayor de la jurisdiccion de La Cañada al tiempo que yo puse la primera demanda contra el dicho Juan Ygnacio sobre la cobranza delas beinte y cinco gamusas contenidas en el bale certifique lo que sobre este particular ubo y para probar que el trato o composicion que tubimos atendiendo a que Juan Ynasio aseguraba no tener prontas las gamusas y ser berda que me quedo debiendo las siete sea de serbir Vmd. de tomar declarasion jurada a Julian Sanchez que fue quien me entrego las bestias y las tres gamusas y abla Juan Ygnacio en esta su ultima respuesta de un decreto de el Señnor Governador lo que me ase notable fuersa pues ni llo e sacado ninguno ni menos selo e notificado y asi sera justo que lo manifeste o diga que en selo notifico lo que no ara y asi se lo ara en conocimiento de la berda de sus fribulas escusas para no pagar y en quanto al ultimo punto a un no ai en poder derecho a uno dar por bastante la declaracion de un onbre sin que no aiga no pruebo lo ni menos aiga bisto su declarasion delo que selo dije que despues le hise seguro antes de reciverla y pues llego el tiempo de prueba sea de serbir Vmd. de tomar declarasion en la mejor forma que Vmd. tubiere por combeniente a Francisco Yndio de Santa Clara y preguntarle a este si abia otras personas presentes quando el oyo las palabras que tengo referidas en mi primer escrito para sila supo sean esaminadas sobre este particular y juro en debida forma no ser de malisia, costos portesto, y en lo necesario.

    Thoribio Ortis (rubric)

Santa Fee y Noviembre 3 de 1764
Cora el traslado a Juan Ygnacio Mestas para que bea si asi era lo que dice Toribio Ortiz y de no esaminese testigos asi lo probei y firme, doi fee.
    Nicolas Ortiz (rubric)

Zertifico yo Francisco Sanches que haviendo resebido un auto expedido por el Señor Governador y Capitan General Dn. Thomas Veles Cachupin el año pasado fecha 9 de Noviembre en que me ordeno Su Señoria les notifique y compelar ala paga a las partes deudoras de Dn. Thoribio Ortis alo que respondio uno delos deudores que es Juan Ygnacio Mestas que un dia antes de la notificacion le tenia remitido un macho, una mula y tres gamusas para la satisfazion de 25 gamusas que eran las que debia. Y por ser berdad doi esta zertificacion firmada de mi mano.

Francisco Sanches (rubric)

Zertifico llo Miguel Sanches ser berdad que una mula y un macho que dio Juan Ygnacio Mestas a Dn. Thoribio Hortis criollas del fiero del Capitan Pedro Sanches eran mansas y nuebas como lo dise Lasaro Truxillo quien lo acabo de arendar que asta con el freno solo se cogia a onde quiera y por ser berdad doi esta informasion por allarme asidentado y no poder ir alla.

Lasaro Sanches (rubric)
Miguel Sanches (rubric)

Señor Theniente de Governador

Juan Ygnacio Mestas besino del Puesto de Chama paresco ante Vmd. en este litis en la mejor forma que ayaga lugar y al mio combengo en toda forma de derecho y digo Señor que por cuanto estar entendido en este litis que yo, y Dn. Thoribio Ortis tenemos en orden a beinte y sinco gamusas que de ellas selebre bale a el espresado Dn. Thoribio, los que tengo pagado a su satifacion y contento en una mula y un macho mansos con mas tres gamusas por que aun que dice el dicho Señor que dichas bestias mulares no eran mansas ofresco con este a Vmd. la ynformacion de que no es asi, pues que las espresadas bestias fueron mansas y capases de poder servirle a su viaje fuera de que aunque no fuera assi, una bes que yo page y quedo conforme. Me parese esta quedado el bien pues no consta por escripto ni de ninguna prueba a que yo quedara restando dichas siete gamusas. Como tambien dise que no abra por onde conste que se me notifico por el Teniente de Milicia Francisco Sanches la que presento a Vmd. junto con este para que benga en conosimiento dela berdad que tengo ya espresada y dicha de no dever las mensionadas siete gamusas solo si que fui recombenido por el Señor Dn. Carlos Fernandez por tres ocasiones aquien le manifieste todos mis bienes no reservando ni aun mi cuera para la satisfacion de dicha dependencia ques en los que solo puede decir dicho Señor Dn. Carlos que se allava en esa jurisdiccion de Alcalde Mayor como puede sertificar que llo quede deviendo las gamusas que espresan si llo la paga que hise fue por mano de Julian Sanches quien fue quien entrego a Dn. Thoribio Ortis lo que yevo dicho sin que yo quedara a dever lo mas minimo ala espresada cantidad. Otro, si pido a Vmd. comparesca el mencionado Yndio yamado Francisco quien dira de como yo ni aun en mi casa estava quando el yevo papel del Señor Dn. Torivio por lo que a Vmd. pido y suplico sea mui servido este litis lo de por concluido si lo aya por de justicia que en ello resivire merced y juro no ser de malicia en lo necesario, ut supra. (entre renglones pues, y como no bale.)

Juan Ygnacio Mestas (rubric)

Santa Fee 9 de Noviembre de 1764
Por presentado en quanto alegar en derecho y atendiendo a que las partes litigantes no se conforman entre si buelbo a mandar no estante aber pasado el termino de prueba presenten los testigos sitados en sus respuestas dentro de beinte y cuatro oras para ser examinados en los puntos correspondientes lo que sele notificara a las dos partes y ala de Juan Ygnacio Mestas acomularlo a estos autos, asi lo probei, mande y firme autuando con testigos de asistencia a falta de escribanos que no los ay en este Reyno doi fee.

      Nicolas Ortiz (rubric)
Testigo Joseph Miguel de la Pena (rubric)
Nicolas Ortiz (rubric)

En esta Villa de Santa Fee en nuebe dias del mes de Nobiembre de mil setesientos y sesenta y quatro años yo Dn. Nicolas Ortiz, Theniente de Governador deste Reino paresio ante mi Julian Sanches vesino de la Villa Nueba de Santa Cruz de la Cañada, testigo presentado por Toribio Ortis para la ynformasion que ofrese de siete gamusas que le quedo a deber Juan Ynasio Mestas de beinte y sinco que dicho Mestas debia a dicho Toribio Ortis al que tome juramento que hiso por Dios y la Señal de la Santa Cruz bajo del qual prometio desir berdad en lo que supiere y fuere preguntado y siendolo dijo que es berdad que con el embio su cunado JuanYgnacio Mestas una mula de dos riendas y un macho entero tambien de dos riendas y tres gamusas a Toribio Ortis en quenta de beinte y sinco gamusas que le restaba como costa por un bale que el dicho Ortis presenta a su fabor echo de Juan Ynasio Mestas y que le dijo dicho Mestas que le dijera al dicho Ortis que las otras gamusas que le quedaba restando selas traeria quanto antes que no tubiera quidado y que esta es la berdad y lo que sabe sobre el particular y lo que puede desir bajo del juramento que fecho tiene y que es de edad de beinte y dos años y lo firmo con migo dicho Theniente de Gobernador autuando con testigos de asistencia a falta de escribano que no los ai en este Reino de que doi fee.
      Nicolas Ortiz (rubric) Julian Sanches (rubric)
Testigo Joseph Miguel de la Pena (rubric)
Testigo Agustin Lobato (rubric)

En dicha Villa dicho dia mes y año yo dicho Theniente de Governador parescio ante mi Antonio Naranjo natural del Pueblo de Santa Clara testigo que presento Toribio Ortis para la prueba que ofrese delas gamusas que le quedo restando Juan Ygnacio Mestas dijo que es berda que delante del y el gobernadorcillo de su Pueblo y el Yndio Sente Asencio Ydala y otros barios Yndios de Su Pueblo le consta que fue Juan Ygnacio

Mestas a rogarle al referido Toribio Ortis con la pago de una mula de dos riendas y un macho entero de dos reindas y que le quedo a deber dies gamusas y que al dicho Ortis reso el cojer dicha mula y macho que solo le pedia las beinte y sinco gamusas y que tantas fueron las apersuassiones de dicho Mestas que le yso cojer la mula y macho quedandole a deber dies por la quales nos ofresio a todos los del Pueblo que al que diera dichas dies gamusas a Toribio Ortis le daria a escojer entre todas sus bestias, caballos, lleguas o bestias mulares y que esto es la berdad y lo que sabe sobre este particular y que es de edad de treinta años poco mas o menos. No firmo por no saber firmelo yo dicho Theniente de Governador y testigos de assistencia a falta de escribanos publico ni real que no los ai en ese Reino de ninguna clase de que doi fee.

                Nicolas Ortiz (rubric)

Nicolas Ortiz (rubric) Nicolas Real (rubric)

Samta Fee y Noviembre 9 de 1764
El Theniente reformado Dn. Carlos Fernandez sertificara al pie deste lo que le costare sobre el punto para que es sitado en la ultima respuesta de Toribio Ortis.
                Nicolas Ortiz (rubric)

Dn. Carlos Fernandez Theniente Reformado desta Real Presidio en dicho puedo y devo a el derecho permite como el año pasado de 63 se presento ante mi siendo Alcalde Mayor de La Cañada Dn. Toribio Ortis con un vale hecho y firmado por Juan Ygnacio Mestas por el que se obligo a pagar veinte y sinco gamusas a qual quiera persona que selas diese a Domingo Baca y manifestandole dicho vale a Juan Ygnacio Mestas confeso ser suio y que estaba obligado a pagar las dichas veinte y cinco gamusas pero que por no tenerlas prontas suplicaba sele no averse a dicho fuese a su casa y lo pagaria la cantidad en otros efectos lo que executo por no aber buelto a ocurrir el mencionado Ortis, ygnoro si pago o no pago, todo lo dicho es lo que me consta.
                Carlos Fernandez (rubric)

Santa Fe Noviembre 10 de 1764
Corrasele traslado a Toribio Ortis para que alege de bien probado asi lo probei y firme.
                Nicolas Ortiz (rubric)

                Señor Theniente General

Thoribio Ortis paresco ante Vmd. y digo que la ynformacion dada por Juan Ygnacio

Mestas en los dos papeles que estan acomulados a estos autos en nada perjudica ami demanda por que el uno solo asegura la notificasion que sele yso despues de aber entregado la mula y el macho lo que yo juro la e negado y el otro que eran mansas y yo jamas e dicho que eran serreras y no quebrantadas o de dos riendas que es lo mismo lo que se berifica en la declaracion de Julian Sanches, qunado de Juan Ygnacio Mestas pudiera recutar la poca fee que asen los dichos papeles por ser de dos cunados de mi parte contraria pero lo omito pues tengo probado con dos testigos contestes el trato ultimo que tubimos que fue el del resto de las siete gamusas en biendo para conprobarlo el resibo que yo di quando recibi las mulas el que aun paraban en poder de quien me las entrego las demas ramas de que se agara para no pagar ellas por si mismas se estan manifestando sin

sustancia y al fin principal que es si me debe o no las siete gamusas o nada prueciba por lo que se a de sirbir Vmd. de mandar me page dichas siete gamusas si lo hallare por de justicia que pido y juro no ser de malicia.

     Thoribio Ortis (rubric)

Santa Fee y Noviembre 10 del 1764
Corasele traslado a Juan Ygnacio Mestas para que alegue de bien probado asi lo probei y firme.

     Nicolas Ortiz (rubric)

     Señor Theniente General

Juan Ygnacio Mestas vecino del Puesto de Chama paresco ante Vmd. en toda forma y digo que respondiendo al traslado que Vmd. se ha servido darme de Dn. Thoribio Ortis y haviendo visto y reconosido el sumario de los autos y no hallar en ellos declaracion alguna delos testigos que por mi parte tengo estados antes si uno de ellos que es Julian Sanches hallo su declaracion a favor el que prueva la mucha malicia con que declara por la parte contrario sin ser citado por el y que es para permitir haigan tenido alguna composicion pues maliciosamente se ha tenido en su poder el resivo que Dn. Thoribio Ortis le dio en Thome despues de haver resivido en esta Villa las mulas por lo que no me conformo con dicha declaracion y el dicho resivo prueba claramente el estar pagado pues dise en el: digo yo Thoribio Ortis que resevi de Julian Sanches una mula y un macho de dos riendas con mas tres gamusas por dependencia que me devia Juan Ygnacio Mestas; y el dicho Juan Ygnacio me resta siete gamusas de dependencia atrasada. Luego por el mismo resivo se viene en conocimiento de que de la demanda puesta no quede a dever nada por lo que a Vmd. suplico se sirva de que se berifique de que son estas siete gamusas pues como en mi poder no havia estado dicho resivo hasta la presente que ante Vmd. parese que era mui libre en poner en dicho resivo que para el completo del todo delas veinte y sinco gamusas le faltavan las siete; y tocante ala declaracion del Yndio Antonio Naranjo y los demas que esta los doi por de ningun valor respecto aque desde el escripto que sito aprueva dicho Dn. Thoribio, no los sita en su escripto y este aunque fuera sitado no puede ser testigo respecto que es Yndio mui resien nacido en la fee, y mui lexos de saber ni conocer ni el ni los demas Yndios del Pueblo la gravidad del juramento y mas quando es manifiesta la distancia que hai del Pueblo de San Juan en donde tuve el ajuste yo con dicho Dn. Thorivio y no haver estado presente ninguno de dichos Yndios por ser del Pueblo de Santa Clara pues de ninguna manera me conformo pues de mi parte tengo suplicado comparesca Domingo Baca y no se verifica pero no me espanto quando de mi parte no se ha berificado que se haiga tomado declaracion a ninguno de los testigos que cito como consta en el todo de los autos y la realidad de la certificacion a mi favor dada de Francisco Sanches, Theniente de Milicia de la jurisdiccion del Rio Arriba asta provada con el mismo decreto del Señor Governador y Capitan General deste Reyno dado a pedimento de dicho Dn. Thoribio su fecha nueve de Noviembre de mil setesientos sesenta y tres el que junto con estos autos a Vmd. presento y juntamente suplico a Vmd. sea mui servido de que estos autos pasen a manos del Señor Governador y Capitan General de este Reyno para que en vista de ellos Su Señoria se sirva de aclarar la justicia por la parte que le corresponda pues delo contrario y me siguen muchos atrasos por estar fuera de mi casa que en haserlo assi resivira justicia y juro no ser de malicia y en lo necessario, ut supra. Quera. No vale.

      Juan Ygnacio Mestas (rubric)

En esta Villa de Santa Fee en dose dias del mes de Noviembre de el corriente año de sesenta y quatro Dn. Nicolas Ortiz Theniente de Governador de este Reyno ago remision de estos autos al Señor Governador y Capitan General respecto el pedimento de Juan Ygnasio Mestas en esta ultima respuesta por lo cual se conose me requea; poniendo en la ynteligencia de Vuestra Señoria que en los dos terminos que sele an dado alas partes litigantes para que prueben lo que no sus escritos alegan y constan en estos autos no an presentado mas testigos ni otros ynstrumentos mas que los que ban yncluidos en ellos.

      Nicolas Ortiz (rubric)

Notes

1. Toribio [Alejandro] Ortiz was the son of Nicolás Ortiz II and Juana Baca. His brother was Nicolás Ortiz III, the lieutenant general who presides in this case. Toribio was married to Leonarda de la Vega y Cosa in 1735. Her father had owned a part of the Cienega grant. Toribio was a sargento mayor of the Santa Fe presidio in 1756 and militia alférez in 1766. In addition to being a trader, he was a sheep rancher and owned lands in La Cienega and Santa Fe (Chávez, Origins: 249-50; Christmas and Rau, *Cienega*: 59, 100; Baxter, *Las Carneradas*: 45, 47).
2. See Doc. 42.

3. See the earlier reference to La Soledad in the Edict of Anathema (Doc. 16).
4. This could be the Francisco Xavier de Herrera who married Francisca Mestas, a granddaughter of Juan Mestas Peralta, around 1748. Their children were born in Santa Cruz. Herrera may have been a member of the Juan de Herrera prerevolt family or that of Tomás de Herrera Sandoval, both of whom came to New Mexico in 1693 (Chávez, *Origins*: 196-97; Christmas and Rau, *Pojoaque*: 50).
5. See Doc. 48.
6. Juan Ygnacio Mestas [y Peralta], also spelled Maestas, was the son of Ventura Mestas and Catalina Jurado, and the grandson of Juan de Mestas y Peralta, whose name was included on the 1697 presidio list of soldiers. Juan de Mestas y Peralta was born in Santa Fe and returned after the revolt. He lived in Pojoaque and was the recipient of a land grant that is there to this day. The name of Juan Ygnacio Mestas appears in lawsuits regarding property in 1772 and 1784 (Kessell et al., *BOB*: 129; SANM II #664, #845; Chávez, *Origins*: 218).
7. See Doc. 33.
8. Domingo Baca was probably the third son of Josefa Baca, who had six natural children. She was the daughter of Manuel Baca and María de Salazar, who are mentioned in Doc. 30. Domingo would have been the nephew of Antonio and Diego Manuel Baca. His first marriage was with Juana Chaves, a daughter of, or at least raised by, Pedro Duran y Chávez, who lived in northern New Mexico. His second wife was María Antonia de la Luz Montoya, whom he married in 1764 in Albuquerque (Chávez, *Origins*: 141-42; NMGS, *Aquí*: 67, 314, 438).
9. Julián Sánchez was married to María Antonia Sánchez; their son was José Lázaro. In 1773 Julián is listed as a notary for a marriage. He was dead by 1782. His first wife was Antonia Mestas, who died in 1767 (NMGS, *Aquí*: 477, 504; Chávez, *Origins*: 218).
10. Note the time lag here: the previous action took place on November 9, 1763.
11. Nicolás Ortiz III was lieutenant governor of the Santa Fe presidio. He was also the son of Nicolás Ortiz II and Juana Baca, and a brother of Toribio Ortiz. Nicolás III married Gertrudis Páez Hurtado, daughter of Juan Páez Hurtado. In 1754 Governor Cachupín stated that he was "an officer in whom the confidence of your grace can well be placed to command any expedition because of his experience, valor, and good conduct. He has great strength for the demands of war, is a moderate soul and without vanity. At the moment there is no other subject in the whole province suitable for this office who will give equal satisfaction and success in the royal service." Five years after this case, in 1769, Nicolás Ortiz III was killed by Indians during a campaign. A witness in this case, also named Nicolás Ortiz, appears to have been a first cousin, the son of Luis Ortiz, who was a brother of Nicolás Ortiz II. The other witness was Antonio Joseph Ortiz, a son of Nicolás Ortiz III (Chávez, *Origins*: 247-50; Thomas, *Plains Indians*: 139; Christmas and Rau, *Cienega*: 54-56).
12. In other words, Mestas owned Baca seventeen hides, and Naranjo owed eight to Baca. For some reason, Mestas agreed to pay Baca twenty-five hides, including the eight hides from Naranjo. According to Mestas, Baca never paid him the eight hides.
13. Joseph Antonio Naranjo II was the grandson of José López Naranjo, an Indian from Santa Clara, who supported Vargas and was killed with the Villasur expedition. José was alcalde of Zuni in 1702 and captain of the Indian scouts in 1704. He carved his name on Inscription Rock at El Morro. Joseph Antonio killed a man in 1731and fled the kingdom. He is also named in a 1752 dispute with Diego Torres over land at San Juan. According to Chávez, he was named captain *de gente de guerra*, but the title was withdrawn and changed to captain for Indian troops only. Because of rustling and other activities, the second title was also withdrawn (Chávez, *Origins*: 241-42; SANM II #643).
14. Here, Ortiz seems to saying that by being forced to wait, the value of the hides changed. That is, the two mules and three hides were no longer enough.
15. As far as we know, the proceedings were never concluded, or the conclusion has been lost.
16. Domingo Anselmo Santistevan was the son of José Santistevan, a survivor of the Villasur massacre, and Josefa Montoya. José was teniente of justice of Pecos and El Vado and one of the fifty-two owners of the San Miguel del Vado land grant (NMGS, *Aquí*: 347, 355).
17. Domingo and Miguel Romero were both sons of Antonio Romero de Pedreza and perhaps grandsons of Francisco Romero de Pedreza, a native New Mexican and alcalde of Santa Fe in 1693. Domingo married Lugarda Montoya in 1781; a son was killed or stolen by Comanches, along with a son of Alejandro Ortega. One of the boys was rescued, and both Alexandro and Domingo claimed the boy was theirs (Chávez, *Origins*: 271; SANM II #303, 307; NMGS, *Aquí*: 255, 346, 348).
18. Miguel Romero was married to Rosa Montoya. He is mentioned in a will of Francisco Xavier Fragoso of 1766, which states that Fragoso owed Miguel Romero for two pairs of shoes, suggesting that Miguel was a cobbler, or perhaps just had shoes to trade (SANM I #275, WPA translation; SANM #1352; NMGS, *Aquí*: 472).
19. Juan Francisco Quintana was married to Rosalia or Rosa Trujillo in 1745 in Santa Cruz. He is probably the son or grandson of Miguel de Quintana, who came to New Mexico in 1693 from Mexico City. Miguel lived in Santa Cruz, where he gained fame as a poet. A Francisco Quintana was involved in a land grant near Abiquiu in 1735, but this may not be the same person (NMGS, *Aquí*: 471; Chávez, *Origins*: 261-62; SANM I #322).

20. Miguel Sánchez may have been the son of María Rodarte de Castro Xabalera and Jacinto Sanchez de Iñigo, a New Mexico native who returned in 1693. Miguel was married to a Margarita Romero by 1753 (NMGS, *Aquí:* 102, 377, 477, 504; Chávez, *Origins:* 280-81).
21. Mestas may be saying that because the governor's decree did not refer to the seven hides, they were not owed. That is, if he wanted three hides plus seven more hides, he should have made a claim for them all at one time.
22. See Doc. 46.
23. This is the order of November 9, 1763, shown on the first page of this document.

51

RELICARIO STOLEN OR LOST ON RETURN FROM EL PASO; OWNER ACCUSES SOLDIER
May 2–August 12, 1767. SANM II #616a.

Synopsis and editor's notes: In this document, Manuel Benítez petitioned Governor Pedro Fermín de Mendiñueta for return or replacement of a *relicario* that he had sent to El Paso. He accused the retired soldier, Francisco Xavier Fragoso, whom he had hired to carry the relicario, of stealing and selling it. Fragoso claims that he lost it on the return journey to Santa Fe.

The testimony shows that Fragoso traveled with a squadron of soldiers from Santa Fe to El Paso, which was going to meet a presidio supply caravan carrying clothes and other goods for the soldiers. Fragoso said that he was wearing the relicario inside his coat in a special bag inside another bag. While traveling to El Paso, he admitted that he did show the relicario to some other persons. He also stated that when he was on the return journey from El Paso, at the paraje of El Brazito, he discovered that he did not have it. He asked his sergeant permission to ride back and look for it, but he was not allowed to go until the next morning, when he searched back south to Los Alamitos but found nothing. He did meet some travelers coming from El Paso and hinted that they may have found the relicario and kept it.

After extensive testimony by both parties in the presence of Governor Mendiñueta about whether or not Fragoso sold the relicario or just lost it, the two agreed that Fragoso would deliver another relicario to Benítez, or if the original relicario was found, then Fragoso would give that one to Benítez. The original relicario is described as having crosses and gilded filigree inside a knitted bag, inside another bag, and tied by a string of white silk. The replacement was to be made of silver with a wax representation of the Lamb of God (Agnus Dei) and have a piece of the true cross.

In *Relicarios: Devotional Miniatures from the Americas*, Martha Egan defines an *agnus*, or *agnus dei*, as a wax medallion made in Rome from Paschal candles as early as the fourth century. These medallions were commissioned by a pope in the first year of his papacy, and thereafter, every seven years. They were made in circular or oval shapes in various sizes. On one side of the medallion was the image of the Lamb of God holding a crucifix in its crossed legs, and posed on the book of Seven Seals—a symbol of Christ and the Redemption. A legend encircled the lamb, stating the name of the pope who commissioned the agnus. On the reverse side of the medallion was the image of a favorite saint of the pope's, with a legend in Latin identifying that holy personage.

Generally, the agnus was encased in a frame of brass, silver, wood, gold, or other material, with glass or rock crystal covering each side of the medallion. A ring at the top of the case allowed the locket to be worn around the neck on a ribbon or chain, or hung on the wall of a church or chapel. Especially during the Spanish Colonial era, these relicarios, as they were often called, were a popular form of devotional jewelry, distributed by clergy worldwide and prized as relics that might protect the wearer from harm. They also served as trade goods and important gifts. In 1588 Juan de Oñate carried thirty-three agni dei of tin and gold, among other items (Egan, *Relicarios*: 68-70; Hammond and Rey, *Oñate*: 135).

It is possible, but unlikely, that this relicario was one of Oñate's and survived into the time of Benítez and Fragos. In regard to the filigree on the case, it is known that a filigree maker, Juan Fernández, came to New Mexican with the Farfán-Velasco expedition in 1694 (Kessell and Hendricks, *RCR*: 247).

Year of 1767

Complaint by Manuel Benítez[1] against the soldier Francisco Xavier Fragoso[2] over a relicario.

Governor and captain general

[I] Manuel Benítez, resident of this villa, appear before your honor in my best and proper form which I have and state that on the 25th of the past May, a squadron of soldiers was dispatched by your honor to the presidio of El Paso del Norte to meet the supply train [*recua*] which carried clothes [*la ropa*] and other goods for the use of the soldiers. The said squadron was under the command of Sergeant Bartolo Maese.[3] One of the members was the soldier Xavier Fragoso, to whom I gave a relicario which had crosses and was gilded in gold and was carried in a small knitted bag which was carried within another lined bag tied by a drawstring of white silk. The relicario was given to him so that he could take it to show it to an individual at El Paso, and upon being seen by the individual it was to be returned to the owner. Until now, Fragoso, who has returned to this capitol from El Paso, has not returned it to me. Upon proceeding to his house to ask for it, he informed me that upon crossing the river he had given it to a cart driver [*arriero*] so that it would not get wet when crossing, telling him to safeguard it, and that the cart driver had held on to it, placing it in his box, for four days, until the corporal of the drivers returned it to the said Fragoso, and he now informs me that it has been lost, and as such he wants to pay me.

Eighteenth-century Agnus Dei relicario medallion in gold frame.
Photo by Anthony Richardson. Image courtesy of Papalote Press, Albuquerque.

Taken to understand this, I cannot state anything else but to tell your honor that the said Fragoso has either hidden or sold it. When he was on his way to El Paso, at the paraje known as Las Nutrias,[4] it was known that he was trying to sell it, but because he could not find anyone who would buy it, did not sell it. There was only one individual, named Manuel Vigil,[5] who offered to give him a plow mule, but he would not take it. This was told to me by Sergeant Maese, who said that he was doing this. I am left without a doubt that the said Fragoso sold the said relicario or that he has it hidden, particularly when I very secretly gave it to him so that he would do as I told him. But he was very disloyal, failing to do everything legally and faithfully. Instead, he went around showing the said relicario to all of the soldiers to see if anyone would buy it; all of which I say to your honor that it was well known that the said Fragoso has used me to commit fraud and other illegal acts. Because of this, I ask and petition your honor to ask that he return my relicario back to me or an equivalent with which I am satisfied. All of this I petition your honor to humbly see to it that it is done and to determine as I have requested, so that I might receive my favor and I swear in due form that my document is not done in malice, protesting all costs, but for what is necessary, ut supra.

Manuel Benítez (rubric)

Villa of Santa Fe, July 11, 1767

    I took the petition as was presented and in attention to what was stated by the said party, I ordered that the soldier Francisco Xavier Fragoso appear before me so that I could take his declaration, under the religious oath, to which it was to be done. I thus approved and ordered it, I, don Pedro Fermín de Mendiñueta of the Order of Santiago, and colonel of the royal forces, governor and captain general of this kingdom of New Mexico, acting with my two assisting witnesses due to the lack of a scribe, as there is not one of any type within this government.

                  Pedro Fermín de Mendiñueta (rubric)

Witnesses
Mateo de Peñarredonda (rubric)
Antonio Moreta (rubric)

    In the said villa on the said day, month, and year, before me, the said governor and captain general, appeared the soldier Francisco Xavier Fragoso, from whom I took his sworn statement according to his right, which he made to God, Our Lord, and to the Holy Cross, under which he promised to tell the truth as to what he knew and in what he was asked, and according to that tenor he stated the following:

    He stated that it is true that he received a relicario as was described by the said Benítez in his petition and that he was to show it to a person at El Paso and then return it to the said Benítez. He was asked why upon his return Benítez had to approach him to return his relicario, which until now he had not done. He stated that he had not returned it because he had lost it at the Paraje de Los Alamitos.[6] He was asked if he always had possession of the relicario since Manuel Benítez gave it to him until he lost it at Los Alamitos. He stated that no, when they were returning from El Paso, after passing the Río del Norte, he turned it over to a pack-train driver named Vicente, one of the workers on the pack train, so that he would safeguard it so as not to get it wet on recrossing the Río del Norte once more, and that it remained in his possession for five or six days, until they reached the paraje de Los Alamitos, where the driver returned it to him shortly after the hour of prayer; and that on the following day, upon reaching the paraje that is known as El Brazito,[7] he realized that it was missing.

    He was asked how or in what manner he carried the relicario. He stated that he had it slung over his left shoulder and under his right arm, and the reason that he found out it was missing about one o'clock in afternoon was that he removed his leather jacket [*el cuera*], as it was very hot. He immediately asked Sergeant Bartolomé Maese for permission to go back as far as the place where the Reverendo Padre Custodio had taken breakfast, but he was denied it. On the following morning he once again asked for permission to go back to look for the relicario, and he was allowed to go back accompanied by the alférez of the militia, Juan Antonio Luján,[8] and they proceeded to go back as far as the paraje de Los Alamitos, following the tracks which they had made on their route the previous day, but they did not find it. He was asked what motive he had when he told the said Manuel Benítez, when he went to get his relicario, by telling him that he had not lost it and that it was not lost. He stated that the motive which he had was that on the day they left the paraje de Los Alamitos on the same march, near some small hills which are where the river makes its turn, they met up with the residents of El Paso who were returning from within this kingdom, and he asked them if by chance they had found it, and it was because of this that he had the confidence to tell him that God knew it was not lost. He was asked if he had tried to sell the relicario to anyone at the Paraje de las Nutrias when they were on their way to El Paso. He said that he had not tried to sell the said relicario at Las Nutrias, but upon approaching Sevilleta,[9] three residents from Las Nutrias arrived at that place, and because he was unbuttoned due to the heat, he took the relicario from the bag and showed it to a person named Juan Domingo, asking him how much he would give him for the relicario. Juan Domingo answered him saying that he did not have the means to pay him for the item, and upon hearing his response he put it away.

He was asked if he had shown the said relicario to Manuel Vigil, and if the said had offered him a plow mule for the item. He stated that it was true that he showed the relicario to the soldier Manuel Vigil, and it is true that the said Vigil did offer him a mule, but that he did not want to sell it to him. He was asked if all the soldiers had seen the relicario and if he had tried to sell it when he got to El Paso to others besides those already mentioned. He stated that all of the soldiers had seen the relicario but that none of them were interested in buying it.

Having read the declaration back to him and understanding what it said, he said that he did not have anything to add or delete, and he affirmed and ratified it, saying that it was the truth according to the sworn statements which he has made, and he said that he was forty years of age, more or less, and he signed it along with me and my assisting witnesses with whom I act as is stated.

      Pedro Fermín de Mendiñueta (rubric)
      Francisco Xavier Fragoso (rubric)
testigo Matheo de Penarredonda (rubric)
testigo Antonio Moreto (rubric)

At the said villa on the said day, month, and year, I, the said governor and captain general of this kingdom, made appear before me the sergeant of this said company, Bartolomé Maese, and upon being present I took his sworn statement which he made to God, Our Lord, and to the sign of the Holy Cross, promising to tell the truth about whatever he knew. He was asked regarding the charges and he was asked if when he left to escort the pack train he knew that Francisco Xavier Fragoso, one of the soldiers on the squad, had with him a gilded filigree [*feligrana sobredorado*] relicario. He answered that he did see it, two different times. He was asked if he knew that the said Fragoso tried to sell the said relicario. He stated that what he knows is that the soldier Manuel Vigil offered to give him a mule or a macho, but Fragoso answered him by telling him that he would not sell it. He was asked if when they were on their return trip he, Fragoso, at the paraje of Brazito, asked him for permission to backtrack to look for the relicario which he had lost, and at what hour the permission was requested. He stated that he had asked for permission to go back to look for it, but that he did not grant it because it was already sundown, and the site or place where the declarant and the Reverendo Padre Custodio, who came with the vanguard, had stopped to reunite themselves with the convoy was very far. But that on the following day, early in the morning, the said Fragoso once more asked for permission for the same purpose, adding that he had a resident who would accompany him to help him, and he then granted him permission to go as far as the said paraje where they had stopped, but he later found out that they had gone as far as Los Alamitos.

He was asked if he had anything else to add regarding these charges. He stated that he does not know nor has he heard anything else regarding this and that what he has stated is the truth about the charges of the sworn statement which he has made. His declaration having been read back to him, he affirmed and ratified it. He said that he was sixty-five years of age and did not sign it because he did not know how, so I, the said governor and captain general, signed it with my assisting witnesses, acting as said.

Pedro Fermín de Mendiñueta (rubric)

Witnesses
Mateo de Peñarredonda (rubric)
Antonio Moreto (witness)

In this said villa on the 13th of the said month and year, I, the said governor and captain general, made appear before me the soldier Manuel Vigil from whom I took his sworn statement which he made according to his right and regarding the charges, promising to tell the truth as to what he knew and what he was asked.

He was asked if when he left to perform the escort he saw that the soldier Francisco Xavier Fragoso had a relicario that was filigreed and gilded and which was carried within two bags, one of silk and the other one lined and were held together by a string of white silk. He said that when he was resting in front of the house of Mateo Lente[10] at the time of leaving for El Paso to perform the escort of the pack train, he saw in the possession of the soldier Fragoso a relicario as above described. He was asked if the said Fragoso attempted to sell the relicario to him. He said, what happened at this time was that Fragoso showed him the relicario saying that it was his, and he asked him if he was willing to sell it, to which Fragoso asked how much he would give him for it, to which he answered that he would give him a mule. Fragoso then stated that he would not sell it even if he was offered one hundred pesos. He then said that it was all that happened. He was asked if he knew that during their trip the said Fragoso attempted to sell the said relicario to any other person. He said that he does not know, that he never saw him again.

He continued saying that everything he has stated is the truth regarding his testimony, and his statement having been read back to him, he affirmed and ratified it, and stated that he was thirty-one years of age, and he signed it with me and my assisting witnesses with whom I act due to the lack of a scribe, which there are none of any type within this government.

Pedro Fermín de Mendiñueta (rubric)
Manuel Vigil (rubric)

Witnesses
Mateo de Peñarredonda (rubric)
Antonio Moreto (rubric)

Villa of Santa Fe, July 14, 1767

Manuel Benítez is to be given these proceedings so that, as the one who makes the demands, he can review them and present his argument in his favor, which is done according to his right.

Mendiñueta (rubric)

Governor and captain general

In accordance with the proceedings that your honor has been pleased to give to me for my review so that I can argue in my favor with the evidence that I gave to the soldier Francisco Xavier Fragoso the same relicario which I have demanded and which the said soldier was given and took to El Paso. Upon his return to the Paraje de Alamitos, [that he had it] is once again evidenced by the fact that he showed it to all of the soldiers and residents who were all gathered together at Sevilleta. Of all of the times that he showed it and times that he tried to sell it, although it cannot be verified, it can be assumed that he did not sell it because he was not offered what he wanted. If he did not attempt to sell it, why did he show it?

The said soldier confesses that at the Paraje de Los Alamitos he was given the relicario by one of the drivers, who had carried it with him from the edge of the Río del Norte and at which time he placed over his left shoulder and below his right arm, in which position it was impossible to lose it over his head even if he slept without clothes. For it to come loose it had to be that the silk string which was holding it had to be cut, or the eye of the relicario had to break, but none of the above could have occurred because the string was new and strong; and besides, the string passed through the eye of the relicario. It also went in through four looped holes of the two bags which carried it. In case the string broke, the string could not get loose from the eye of the relicario to get lost, which would then remain under the lapel, where it would be retained. For these reasons it could not have been lost but it is more likely that he has hidden it in order to keep it for himself.

It can be understood that in order to avoid suspicions, he asked for permission

from the sergeant to go back to look for it, which he did so as not to look guilty. He was also fortunate that he encountered the residents of El Paso between Los Alamitos and El Brazito so he could say that he did not find it, but that it was found [and taken] by those residents. As it turned out everything happened on the same day and appears to have happened in his favor. Because of all of this, I petition and ask that your honor be pleased to ask that the soldier Fragoso be ordered to pay me for the said relicario as according to my right it should have been returned to me as I had given it to him. This I ask to receive in the mercy of justice which I ask for and I swear it is not done in malice but for what is necessary, etc.
      Manuel Benítez (rubric)

Villa of Santa Fe, July 20, 1767
  In attention to what is argued by Manuel Benítez as a result of the review of the proceedings taken by virtue of his first document, I should order and did order that Francisco Xavier Fragoso appear before me so that I can charge him according to the evidence that is argued against him by the other party. I thus approved, ordered, and signed it, acting as such.
      Pedro Fermín de Mendiñueta (rubric)

  In this villa of Santa Fe on the 24th of July of 1767, by virtue of the above decree, there appeared before me Francisco Xavier Fragoso, from whom I took his sworn statement which he made before God, Our Lord, and the sign of the Holy Cross, to which charges he promised to tell the truth in everything that he knew and what he was asked as to what happened to the relicario belonging to Manuel Benítez and which he showed to the soldiers and the residents who were gathered together at Sevilleta.
  He said that because he removed his leather jacket due to the extreme heat, one of the residents asked him what relicario he had and asked that he show it to him. He was then asked what he told the resident, and to respond to what the end result was when he showed it to the soldiers. He answered that he had no other intention but to show them, so that they could see the item which he carried. He was then asked what intent he had when he asked the resident how much he would give him for the relic. He answered that he merely wanted to see what he would say, being that he had no idea how much it could be worth. He was asked if the relicario was lost along with the string. He said that he had lost both, the string and the relicario. He was asked how he could have lost the relicario held by the string which was new and made of silk, very strong, which passed through four loop holes and through the eye of the same relicario and hung over the left shoulder and under the right arm. He said that the string was thin and worn out at the place from where the relicario hung, and that the string where it passed through two loops of the two bags on one part and going through the eye of the relicario and the two loops of the other part was held together

by a gold-threaded button which came down and held the two strings up to the eye of the relicario. Because the eye of the relicario was broken and was very thin, it finished wearing out the string, and because of all of this it was lost. [He was asked] if the string wore out due because the eye of the relicario was broken or if the breaking of the eye could have been the reason that the relicario was lost without the string, though if this was the case, would it not have remained under the lapel and the leather jacket? He said that the string was broken only on one side, but because of the weight, when the relicario fell the string went along with it.

He was asked if the morning when they left Los Alamitos he was running his horse. He said that he was at the head of the column, and that at a short distance from the paraje he was ordered by the sergeant to go to the back and march at the head of the pack train, for which reason he had to trot his horse to get to his assigned place. Further on, upon encountering the residents of El Paso who were returning from this said villa [of Santa Fe], he stopped to talk with them for a while, and from there he ran his horse until he met up with the train, which was at Estero Largo.[11] He was asked if during the time that he was talking with the residents of El Paso and when he trotted his horse to catch up with the train there were some whom he spoke with and who they were. He said that at that time that he was talking with the residents of El Paso he said that in his presence was Cayetano Góngora[12] and another person, whose name he does not remember, but although they left together to join up with the train, he left them behind, and he caught up to it before they did. He was asked if he had lost it after they encountered the residents of El Paso, would he not have found it the following day when he turned back to look for it, being that it was such a short distance from Los Alamitos to where they encountered the residents. If so, how could he have lost it in such a short distance? He said that it is true that if he had lost it from where he encountered the residents of El Paso at El Brazito, which is where he noticed that it was missing, he would have found it; but, even though it is a short distance, it could have been lost as he has said.

He said that what he has stated is the truth and all that he knows regarding what he has been asked over the charges of his sworn statement which he has made and his statement being read back to him, he affirmed and ratified it. He was asked if he had anything to add or to delete. He said that he did not have anything to add or delete and said that he was forty years of age more or less and he signed it along with me and my assisting witnesses acting as it is.

Pedro Fermín de Mendiñueta (rubric)
Francisco Xavier Fragoso (rubric)
Witness: Mateo de Peñarredonda (rubric)
Witness: Antonio Moreto (rubric)

Villa of Santa Fe, July 24, 1767
A copy is to be given to Manuel Benítez.
Mendiñueta (rubric)

Governor and captain general

[I] Manuel Benítez, resident of this villa, in response to the copy which your honor was pleased to give me, say that even though I could prove that the string which held the relicario and which Fragoso says was thin and worn out is not true, it is not so; it was to the contrary thick and new. But as such I will omit this, as in the same statement given by Fragoso, he proves that it was not lost. Fragoso says that the eye of the relicario was broken and gave way, but this cannot be so; even if it was broken and gotten loose from the string, the relicario could not be lost out of the two bags which were held by the string, nor could the relicario be lost out of the bags, because as Fragoso confesses the string was doubled up to where it met the gold-threaded button, and even if the string did break, the relicario could not be lost. If it was cut, the relicario would still remain attached to one of the two sides or the extremes of the string because the gold-threaded button attached both sides. He also confesses that if it was lost from the place where he stopped to talk to the residents of El Paso up to El Brazito, he would have found it the following day, which he did not do. If it was not lost where he says that he was running his horse, which was quite a distance, much less could it have been lost when he trotted his horse only for a short distance. All of this proves that he did not lose the relicario, but rather has it hidden. I thus petition and ask your honor to be served to order and do whatever he feels is done according to justice, and I swear that this is not done in malice, etc.
      Manuel Benítez (rubric)

Santa Fe, August 3, 1767
 A copy is given to Francisco Xavier Fragoso.

      Mendiñueta (rubric)

Governor and captain general

[I] Francisco Xavier Fragoso, resident of this villa and retired soldier, appear before your honor with all of the right which I have and responding to the copy which your honor was pleased to give me from the opposing party. Upon seeing and understanding it, [I say that it] is entirely malicious as it relates to the litigation over the relicario, as these proceedings claim that it was given to me so that I could show it to an individual, which he claims I did not do, and which I have testified to your honor and have given my declaration which I have ratified and affirmed and in which I have nothing to add or delete other than the truth as I have stated, that the said relicario was lost. The said opposing party responds with increasing malice, as he states in the original document about my declaration where I stated that I hoped that God would not let it be lost, and to which Benítez stated that I assured him that it would not happen; and he confesses against me in malicious writings and suspicions, with nothing certain proofing any truth, the only truth being that in all of his responses he says that he gave me the relicario so that I would show it to an individual and return it to him, which I have not denied. But nevertheless, not knowing what the future would bring, he did not assure me how long he had the relicario, and I did not know anything about it, as he states in his third declaration where he says that he had enough proof through my statements that I did not lose the relicario.

Here I shall prove that Benítez is wrong with my own statements which are entered to the point where I have said that I did not lose the relicario, even though I have said that it was lost somewhere close to where I encountered the Pasoeños up to El Brazito, if so, I would have found it the follow day. I did not discount nor is it contrary to him saying that it was contingent upon finding it, with all the attentions with which I looked for it, particularly when I was not aware of what would happen and could happen with my officer for not obeying his orders when he did not grant me permission which I asked him for, but which he in fact did grant me even though I almost broke his order, but which was rather risky for me and for the resident who accompanied me, being that we could have both lost our lives. As of now, sir governor, I do not know what better proof there could be even though the contrary party does not accept it, saying that I have hidden the relicario. I prove all of the malice which his documents contain, saying that he has only presumptions and suspicions, and it is not dignified for my opposing party to say differently, but it is dignity which only God has. In various places he says that if the string had cut the relicario would have remained in place held by the two ends, but to what extremes has he gone by saying that I could not have lost my life by looking for the relicario, when I have lost my good standing.

Overall, I will prove to the contrary by affirming things against his maliciousness that states that the relicario was not lost, but that I have it hidden. He should give me the proof and be truthful about it, because I will not be conforming to his malicious suspicion, for which I ask your honor to be pleased to do and determine as I ask according to justice and I swear that I do not do this in malice, but in my defense and for what is necessary, etc.

      Francisco Xavier Fragoso (rubric)

Santa Fe, August 4, 1767
  Give a copy to Manuel Benítez so that if he has any proof, he should come forth with it
according to justice.
      Mendiñueta (rubric)

[I] Manuel Benítez, resident of this villa, in response to the copy which your honor has served to give to me, say that the statements of Francisco Xavier Fragoso, my opposing party, and those of the soldier Manuel Vigil, to whom the said Fragoso offered to sell the relicario, clearly show that he attempted to sell it to him when he asked him how much he would give him for it, and it does not satisfy that he asked him only to hear what he would offer him. It is not known that anyone would do it solely to hear what the offer would be without the intent. For such reason, whoever attempts to sell something that is not his would be better off hiding it himself, as by selling it would be easy to prove by witnesses or by the same purchaser, and by hiding it, it would be difficult for me to prove it through a witness. I cannot but think by thoughts, but also by actions, a man, due to his avarice, will not do something unless he gets something out of it; and this is the reason that Fragoso speaks with such individual audacity using indecent and negative words, treating me as being depraved and malicious so as to be blamed in any litigation. I ask, what depraved malice does he include in what I ask for when I ask only that he return to me the relic that I gave him, which he affirms he received, he not having any proof that he lost it? He only has uncertainties which prove his maliciousness.

I ask that Fragoso return to me a relic which I gave to him and which he received, not having anything relevant to prove that he lost it, but which proves that he maliciously has hidden it, as he has stated himself that it is not lost. I prove my demand through convincing reasons taken from his statements that the relicario had a broken eyelet. But in which case it would have remained within the two bags, not being able to drop out of the bags unless the four loops were torn, in which case the relicario would have fallen along with the two bags, but leaving the string which fastened them and which was assured by the button sewn with gold thread. It could happen if the string was cut, but in order to cut the string it had to be by force. Fragoso says that it was worn out at the spot from where the relicario hung, which for no reason could it have been worn out; in such case the relicario and the bags would have fallen, but not the string. All of these unlikely things would have been impossible to happen because of the button which fastened everything.

From all of this can be inferred that in order to lose the relicario and the string, they had to have been taken out by the feet or over the head, according to the position which he was in at the time, it being almost impossible to lose, and more likely that he has it hidden. As the said Fragoso does not have the proof that is required to prove what he says and by me argued, it is difficult to mistakenly say that the ends of the string are the cause of what I argue regarding my relic. I ask and petition your honor that Fragoso replace it the relicario with another one of the same type and same condition as the one which I had and to practically show the way in which it could have been lost as it can be visually seen that the reasons argued by me prove my just demand in which I insist, being conforming with whatever our honor determines, and I swear it is not done in malice.

       Manuel Benítez (rubric)

Santa Fe, August 8, 1767

These proceedings are to be given to Francisco Xavier Fragoso so that he can argue, prove, and respond to the charges which are made by his opposing party, so that upon seeing them, I can determine according to justice.

      Mendiñueta (rubric)

Governor and captain general

[I] Francisco Xavier Fragoso, resident of this villa and retired soldier, in compliance with and in obedience to what was ordered by your honor in the proceedings which were presented in order for me to respond and argue whatever I have on my behalf, and in my proper right, I say, sir, that which is argued by my opposing party regarding the charges which he has filed against me concerning the opinion which he has about the said relic which he placed in my charge, I have proven, sir, that I did not sell or much less have I hidden it as he says in his irrational judgment. It is by the word of God, from heaven to earth, that I have nothing hidden. What he says is all false, and I humbly beg of your honor that he prove the false charges and demands that the said Benítez places against me, as what he says is not sufficient. The statement made by Vigil does not bother me, as it cannot be proven that I sold the relic to him or to anyone else, nor that I have it hidden, as is presumed by the my opposing party. I will be quite conforming with whatever your honor decides, determines, and orders regarding this matter. This is what I give as my answer, and I sign it in this Villa of Santa Fe on the 8th of August, 1767.

      Francisco Xavier Fragoso (rubric)

In this villa of Santa Fe on the 12th of the present month of August, there appeared before me, the said governor and captain general, at my order, the two litigating parties in which Manuel Benítez asks that a relicario similar to and of the same type and same condition be given to him and in which Fragoso counters the request saying that the eye of the relicario and the loopholes of the bags which were firmly held together by a button and the string broken, as if cut with scissors, stating that it was worn at the place where the relicario hung from the eye and the relicario fell, and the bags and the string remained in place held by the button. Due to all of this Francisco Xavier Fragoso promised to deliver to Manuel Benítez a relicario made of silver with *agnus cera* and *dignum cruces*, with which the said Benítez agreeing, with the stipulation that if his first relicario was found and returned at any time by any person it would be returned to him. Fragoso executed what was ordered of him in my presence, and

I finished and concluded these proceedings definitively; and the two parties signed it along with my assisting witnesses due to the lack of a scribe, which there is none of any type in this government.

                    Pedro Fermín de Mendiñueta (rubric)
                    Francisco Xavier Fragoso (rubric)
                    Manuel Benítez (rubric)

Witnesses
Mateo de Peñarredonda (rubric)
Antonio Moreto (rubric)

ORIGINAL DOCUMENT

Año de 1767
Demanda puesta por don Manuel Benitez contra el soldado Francisco Xavier Fragoso sobre un relicario.

                    Señor Governador y Capitan General

Manuel Venitez residente en esta Villa paresco ante Vuestra Señoria en la mejor forma que haya lugar y al mio conbenga y digo que el dia veinte de Mayo del mes prosimo pasado salio de esta Villa una escuadra de soldados despachada por Vuestra Señoria al Presidio del Passo del Rio del Norte a conduzir la recua que conducio la ropa y demas generos para el huaso delos dichos señores soldados, y dicha escuadra fue al cargo del Sargento Bartolo Maese y en ella fue el soldado Xaviel Fragoso a quien se entrego un relicario alinie en curzes de feligrano sobredorado en oro dentro de una bolsa de teja y otra de terzio pelo con su cordon de seda blanca; y encarnada, y este dicho relicario selo de para que lo llevera y selo ensenara a un yndibiduo del dicho pueblo del Passo, y visto por dicho yndibiduo que seme debolbiesse; y este no se me ha devuelto por dicho Fragoso pues haviendo llegado a esta capital a vuelta del Passo yo fui a su cassa ha visitarlo y que me entregase el relicario y pidiendoselo yo me respondio que pasando el rio selo dio a un arriero por que no selo mojasse que selo guardase y dicho arriero lo guardo en su caxa quatro dias y su Cavo de ellos el dicho arriero selo entrego al dicho Fragoso y aora me dise que sele perdio y con esto me quiere haser pago, pero me aseguro por dos otras ocasiones que no se perdiera que no estaba perdido y ahassi lo entiendo y no puedo menos de dezir a Vuestra Señoria el que dicho Fragoso lo tiene oculto o lo vendio respecto de que quando yba de aqui para El Passo, en el Paraje que llaman Las Nutritas lo handava vendiendo y por no hallar sujeto que selo comprasse no lo vendio; solo uno de los señores soldados llamado Manuel Vegil le dava una mula de dos riendas y no lo quiso dar: esto quien melo dijo fue el Sargento Maese con que quien andaba hasiendo esto. No me queda duda que dicho Fragoso vendiese dicho

relicario o lo tenga oculto; y mayormente quando yo devajo de todo sijilo y secreto selo doy para lo ya referido, andubo este desleal, faltando ala legalidad, y fialidad, que me devia de tener, y no que andubo hasiendo plaza con dicho relicario entre todos los soldados haver quien selo compraba con que de vajo delo ya referido puede Vuestra Señoria benir en conocimiento a que este dicho Fragoso ha usado con migo de todo fraude y ninguna legalidad; por lo que pido y suplico a Vuestra Señoria se sirva de mandar que me debuelba dicho mi relicario o su hequibalente ami satisfazion, por todo lo qual a Vuestra Señoria pido y suplico rendidamente se sirva de mandar hase y determinar como llevo pedido que en este rezivire favor y mersed y juro en devida forma no ser de malicia este mi escrito costado protesto y en lo necesario, ut supra.
      Manuel Benitez (rubric)

Villa de Santa Fee 11 de Julio de 1767
Por presentada la antecedente peticion y en atencion alo que esta parte expresa mando comparesca ante mi el soldado Francisco Xavier Fragoso a fin de tomarle su declarasion bajo la religion del juramento que para ello sele tomara y por este asi lo probehi y mande yo Dn. Pedro Fermin de Mendinueta del Orden de Santiago y Coronel de los Reales Exercitos, Governador y Capitan General de este Reyno del Nuebo Mexico auctuando con dos testigos de mi asistencia a falta de escribano que no lo hai en esta governacion de ninguna clase.
    Pedro Fermin de Mendinueta (rubric)
testigo
Matheo de Penarredonda (rubric)
testigo
Antonio Moreta (rubric)

En dicha Villa, dicho dia, mes y año ante mi el expresado Governador y Capitan General parecio el soldado Francisco Xavier Fragoso a quien tome juramento en forma de derecho que hizo por Dios Nuestro Señor y la Señnal de la Santa Cruz so cuio cargo prometio decir verdad en todo lo que supiere y le fuere preguntado y siendolo al tenor de la demanda dijo: que es verdad que recivio de Manuel Benetiz un relicario con las mismas senas y circumstancias que expresa el dicho Benitez en su pedimento y manifestarlo a una persona del Passo y devolverselo al ya dicho Benitez; y preguntado que por que en su regreso haviendo Manuel Benitez recombenido de que le entregase el relicario no lo ha ejecutado; dijo, que por que se le perdio en el Paraje de Los Alamitos; y preguntado si siempre tuvo en su poder el relicario desde que se lo entrego Manuel Benitez hasta que se le perdio en Los Alamitos; dijo, que no por que quando venian de regreso del Passo despues de pasado el Rio del Norte se lo entrego a un arriero llamado Vicente uno de los abiadores dela recua para que selo guardase por mojarlo en el repaso que tenia que hacer del Rio del Norte otra vez para el Passo en cuyo poder se mantuvo el relicario cinco o seis dias hasta que en el Paraje de Los Alamitos se lo volvio a entregar dicho arriero a el declarante poco despues dela oracion; y que el siguiente dia al llegar al Paraje que lllaman del Brazito lo hecho menos; y preguntado que en que modo o forma traia el mencionado relicario puesto; dijo, que terciado desde el hombro ysquierdo por debajo el brazo derecho, y que como ala una del dia seria quando lo hecho menos al tiempo de quitarse la cuera y que imediatamente pidio licensia al Sargento Bartholome Maese para bolver a buscarle hasta un paraje en que havia almorsado el Reverendo Padre Custodio lo que no ejecuto por haversela dado y el dia siguiente por la mañana bolvio el declarante a evestar al dicho Sargento le diese la licensia para ir a buscar su relicario despacho a acompanarlo el Alferez Miliciano Juan Antonio Lujan y haviendosela concedida bolvieron los dos hasta el Paraje de Los Alamitos por el mismo rastro que el dia antecedente havia venido pero que no pudo hallarlo; y preguntado que que motivo tuvo para responderle al mencionado Manuel Benitez al tiempo del cobro de su relicario que no perderia y que no estava perdido; dijo, que el motivo que tuvo fuese el dia que salieron del Paraje de Los Alamitos en la misma marcha y en unos meganitos que estan a la buelta del Rio encontraron a los vecinos del Paso que se regresavan delo interno de este Reyno y se persuadio a que estos lo havrian hallado, en cuia confianza le dijo que esperava en Dios no se perderia; y preguntado si trato de vender en el Paraje de Las Nutrias quando ivan para el Paso el mismo relicario a alguna persona; dijo, que no trato de vender dicho relicario en Las Nutrias, pero que llegando a Sevilleta llegaron a el mismo Paraje tres vecinos de Las Nutrias, y estando desabrochado el que declara por el mucho calor saco el relicario dela bolsa y se lo enseno a uno de ellos llamado Juan Domingo diciendole que quanto se atrevia a darle por aquel relicario, a lo que respondio Juan Domingo que de donde havia de cojer el con que pagar aquella alaja, y oida su respuesta lo volvio a guardar; y preguntado si a Manuel Vegil le manifesto el expresado relicario y si este le ofrecio una mula de dos riendas por la alaja; dijo, que es berdad que manifesto el relicario al soldado Manuel Vegil y que tambien lo es que el dicho Vegil le ofrecio una mula por el, pero que el que declara no lo quiso dar; y preguntado que si todos los soldados vieron el relicario y si trato de de su venta a la ida para el Paso con otros fuera de los dos ya declarados; dijo, que todos los soldados vieron el relicario pero que ninguno de ellos tuvo trato alguno de venta. Y haviendole leida esta su declaracion y entendido de ella dijo que no tiene que anadir ni que quitar y que en ella se afirma y ratifica por ser la verdad bajo del juramento que fecho tiene y dijo ser de edad de quarenta añnos poco mas o menos y lo firmo con migo y los de mi asistencia con quienes auctuo como dicho es.

    Pedro Fermin de Mendinueta (rubric)
    Francisco Xavier Fragoso (rubric)
testigo Matheo de Penarredonda (rubric)
testigo Antonio Moreto (rubric)

En dicha Villa dicho dia, mes y año yo dicho Governor General de este Reyno hize

parecer ante mi a Bartholome Maese Sargento de esta Compania y estando presente le tome su juramento que hizo por Dios Nuestro Señor y la Señal de la Santa Cruz so cuio cargo prometio decir verdad en todo quanto supiere y le fuere preguntado y siendole si quando salio a escoltar la requa vio en poder de Francisco Xavier Fragoso uno delos soldados de la esquadra un relicario feligrana sovredorado; responde, que si lo vio dos vezes; y preguntado, si supo que dicho Fragoso tratase de vender el mencionado relicario; dijo, que lo que save es que el soldado Manuel Vegil le ofrecio por el una mula o un macho y que Fragoso respondio que no lo vendia; y preguntado si quando venia se regreso en el Paraje del Brazito le pedio licensia el expresado Fragoso para ir a buscar el relicario que sele havia perdido y a que ora; responde, que si le pidio la licensia para ir a buscarlo y que no sela dio por ser ya al meterse el sol y estar distante el sitio o lugar en donde el declarante con el Reverendo Padre Custodio que venian en la manguardia hizieron alto para esperar se reuniese el comboi, y que a otro dia por la mañana volvio el mismo Fragoso a pedirle licensia para el mismo fin, facilitando tener un vecino que le acompanase en alio supuesto se la dio hasta el citado Paraje donde hicieron alto, pero que despues supo que havian llegado hasta Los Alamitos; y preguntado si tiene alguna otra cosa que desir en orden a este punto; dijo, que no save ni ha oido decir cosa alguna y que lo que llevo dicho es la verdad so cargo del juramento que fecho tiene y siendole leyda esta su declaracion en ella se afirma y ratifica; y dijo ser de edad de sesenta y cinco años; no firmo por no saver, firmelo yo dicho Governador General con los de mi asistencia actuando como dicho es.
    Pedro Fermin de Mendinueta (rubric)
testigo Matheo de Penarredonda (rubric)
testigo Antonio Moreto (rubric)

En esta dicha Villa en treze dias de dicho mes y año yo dicho Governador y Capitan General hize parecer ante mi el soldado Manuel Vegil aquien tome juramento que hizo segun derecho so cuio cargo prometio desir verdad en lo que supiere y le fuere preguntado; y siendole desir quando salio a executar la requa bio en poder del soldado Francisco Xavier Fragoso un relicario de feligrana sobredorado metido en dos bolsas una de tela y otra de terciopelo y pendiente de un cordon de seda blanca y encarnada; dijo, que estando sesteando quando salian pare El Paso a escoltar la reque enfrente de la casa de Matheo Lente vio en poder del soldado Fragoso un relicario con todas las senas que le han preguntado; y preguntado si el mencionado Fragoso trato de venderle el relicario; dijo, que lo que en este caso paso fue que manifestando Fragoso el relicario diciendo ser suio le pregunto el declarante si lo vendia a lo que respondio Fragoso quanto le daria por el a lo que respondio el que declara que daria una mula; y dijo Fragoso que no lo daria aunque le diesen cien pesos; y que no paso otra cosa; y preguntado si supo que en la ida o buelta tratase el ya dicho Fragoso vender el mencionado relicario a otra alguna persona; dice, que no save ni lo bolvio a ver; y que lo que lleva dicho es la verdad so cargo del juramento que fecho tiene y siendole leida esta su declaracion en ella se afirmo y ratifico y dijo ser de edad de treinta y un años y lo firmo con migo y los testigos de mi asistencia con quienes auctuo a falta de escribanos que no los hai en esta governacion de ninguna clase.

      Pedro Fermin de Mendinueta (rubric)
      Manuel Vigil (rubric)
testigo Matheo de Penarredonda (rubric)
testigo Antonio Moreto (rubric)

Villa de Santa Fee 14 de Julio de 1767
Desele vista de estas diligencias a Manuel Benitez actor demandante para que alegue a su favor lo que le combenga segun derecho.
      Mendinueta (rubric)

     Señor Governador y Capitan General

Delas diligencias que Vuestra Señoria fue servido darme vista para que alegase a mi favor so prueba con ebidencia que yo entregue a el soldado Francisco Xavier Fragoso el mismo relicario que tengo demandado y que dicho soldado le resivio y llebo al Paso y bolvio asta el Paraje del Alamitos tambien se porsibe delas declaraciones que lo manifesto a todos los soldados y vecinos que se incorporaron en Sebilleta. De cuias manifestaciones y tratos de ventas aunque no se verificaron se presume que fue por que no le ofrecieron cosa que le gustase que si le huviere gustado lo huviera bendido; y si no trataba de benderlo para que lo manifestaba; confiesa dicho soldado que en el Paraje de Los Alamitos recibio de mano de uno delos arrieros el dicho relicario en cuio poder estaba desde la orilla del Rio del Norte y que selo puso sobre el hombro yzquierdo y debajo del braso derecho en cuia positura era ymposible sele saliese por la cabesa aunque durmiese desnudo y para que sele cayese era preciso que el cordon de seda en que estaba pendiente se cortase o que el ojo del anillo del relicario se quebrase y no lo uno ni lo otro puede ser por que el cordon era nuebo y fuerte y ademas de entrar dicho cordon por el anillo del relicario entraba tambien por quatro presillas de las dos bolsas en que iba metido y caso que el cordon se cortase por donde podria juirlo el ojo del relicario perdeaxase este pero no el cordon que era preciso quedase de baxo de la solapa y de todo lo qual se coloje que no sela perdio sino que lo hizo perdediese para ocultarlo y quedarse con el y nada desminuye esta behemento sospecha la licensia que pidio a el Sargento para yr a buscarlo y la diligencia qu hiso pues esto fue solo para cubrir sudeprabado fin, baliendose dela ocacion de encontra alos vecinos del Paso entre Los Alamitos y El Brazito para protestar que no lo hallo y que los dichos vesinos lo hallarian y aviendo acaecido esto el mismo dia induce una conocida malicia por todo lo qual y demas ami derecho conforme a Vuestra Señoria pido y suplico ser servido de mandar me page el soldado Fragoso dicho relicario que donde yo como quedo a derecho de bolverle lo que recibiere en lo recibise merced con justicia que pido y juro no ser de malisia y en lo necesario, ut supra.
      Manuel Benitez (rubric)

Villa de Santa Fee 20 de Julio de 1767
En atencion a lo alegado por Manuel Benitez en consequencia ala vista que sele dio de las diligencias practicadas en virtud de su primer escripto devia mandar y mando comparecer ante mi Francisco Xavier Fragoso para hacerle los cargos que le resultan de lo alegado contra el por su parte contrario; asi lo probehi, mande y firme autuando como dicho es.
        Pedro Fermin de Mendinueta (rubric)

En esta Villa de Santa Fee en veinte y cuatro del mes de Julio de mill setecientos sesenta y siete en virtud del decreto de arriba parecio ante mi Francisco Xavier Fragoso aquien tome juramento que hizo por Dios Nuestro Señor y la Señal de la Santa Cruz so cuio cargo prometio decir verdad en todo quanto supiere y le fuere preguntado y siendolo que fin manifesto el relicario que llevava de Manuel Benitez a los soldados y al vecino que se las junto en Sevilleta; dijo, que con occasion de haverse quitado la cuera por el mucho calor que hacia y haverle preguntado uno delos vecinos que que reliquia era la que trahia puesta se la manifesto y bueltole a preguntar y hechole cargo que aunque tiene respondido en orden a el vecino, responda el fin que tuvo para manifestarselo a los soldados; y responde, que no tuvo otro fin mas que el que viesen la presca que llevava; y preguntado, que que fin le movio a preguntarle al vecino que quanto le daria por aquella alaja; responde, que que solo por oir su respuesta considerando que no tendria conocimiento de lo que podria valer; y preguntado si el relicario se le perdio junto con el cordon; dijo, que cordon y relicario juntos sele perdieron; y preguntado como pudo perdersele dicho relicario pendiente de un cordon de seda nuebo y fuerte pasado por cuatro presillas y el ojo del mismo relicario y puesto sobre el hombro yzquierdo y debajo del brazo derecho; dijo, que el cordon era delgado y rozado en el lugar que sostenia el relicario, y que dicho cordon entrando por las dos presillas de las dos bolsas de la una parte y pasando por el ojo del relicario, y las dos presillas de la otra parte se juntava con un boton de hilo de oro correduro que bajava uniendo los dos cordones hasta el ojo del relicario y que persuade que por estar reventado el ojo del relicario y ser mui delgado acavaria de rozar el cordon y que ese fue el motivo de haversele perdido; y haciendo cargo de que si se rozo el cordon con el ojo del relicario o se quebro dicho ojo perderiase solo el relicario pero no el cordon, que debia quedar debajo de la solapa y cuera; dijo, que se cortaria un solo lado del cordon y es mas moperso de relicario al caerse llevaria cordon y todo; y preguntado si la mañana que salieron de Los Alamitos anduvo corriendo a cavallo; dijo, que viniendo delante dela recua a corta distancia del Paraje le mando el Sargento bolbiese atras y marchase defrente dela recua para cuio fin y ponerse en el lugar señalado fue corriendo y que mas adelante encontrandose con los vecinos del Paso que se regresaban de esta Villa se paro un rato a hablar con ellos y desde alli volvio a correr hasta alcanzar la recua que fue en el Estero Largo; y preguntado si en tiempo que estuvo platicando con los vecinos del Passo y quando corrio para alcansar la recua huvo algunos sugetos de los que entraron en aquella conducta, que se hallasen presentes; dijo, que al tiempo de estar hablando con los vecinos del Paso estava presente Cayetano Gongora y otra persona, que no se acuerda quien es y que aunque salieron juntos a alcansar la recua los fue dejando atras y el llego primero a su lugar; y preguntado, que si se le huviera perdido despues de encontrar con los vecinos del Paso lo huviera hallado a el otro dia quando bolbio a buscarlo y haviendo tan corta distancia desde Los Alamitos a donde encontraron a los vecinos como pudo perdersele en tan poco trecho; dijo, que es cierto que sele huviera perdido desde donde encontro a los vecinos del Paso hasta el Brazito que fue en donde lo hecho menos lo huviera hallado; y que aunque sea corta la distancia pudo perdersele en a modo que tiene dicho; y que quanto lleva dicho es la verdad y todo lo que save sobre lo que sele ha preguntado so cargo de juramento que echo tiene y siendole leida esta su declaracion en ella se afirmo y ratifica; y preguntado si tiene algo que anadir o que quitar; dijo, que no tiene algo que anadir ni que quitar; y dijo ser de edad de quarenta años poco mas o menos y lo firmo con migo y los de mi asistencia autuando como dicho es.

     Pedro Fermin de Mendinuete (rubric)
     Francisco Xavier Fragoso (rubric)
testigo Matheo de Penarredonda (rubric)
testigo Antonio Moreto (rubric)

Villa de Santa Fee 24 de Julio de 1767
Corrasele traslado a Manuel Benitez.
     Mendinueta (rubric)

    Señor Governador y Capitan General

Manuel Benitez residente en esta Villa respondio al traslado que Vuestra Señoria fue servido de mandar se me diese, digo que aunque pudiera probar que el cordon que dice Fragoso que era delgado y rosado en el lugar que pendia el relicario es falso, pues no era sino grueso y nuebo, lo omito por hallar en la misma declarasion del mencionado Fragoso prueba bastante de que no sele perdio el relicario: dise Fragoso que el ojo del relicario estaba quebrado y dado y no concedido que asi fuese, aunque por la quebradura se saliese del cordon avia de quedar forsozamente dentro de las dos bolsas y pendientes estas del cordon ni pudiera saltar el relicario fuera de las bolsas, pues como el dicho Fragoso confiesa oprimia el boton de hilo de oro el cordon doblado asta topar con el ojo y presillas, con que sin cortarse el cordon no pudo perderse el relicario; y aunque se cortase quedase el relicario pendiente de uno delos dos lados o estremos del cordon por que el boton de hilo de oro apretaba los dos estremos. Tambien confiesa que si sele ubiera perdido desde el lugar en donde estubo hablando con los vesinos asta El Brazito lo hubiere hallado el dia siguiente pues no lo hallo so ser perdido en

donde hubo mas motibo por correr mucha tierra y no se perdio coriendo mas menos se perdiera corriendo poco y andando poca tierra de todo lo qual se prueba que no perdio el relicario sino que lo a ocultado por lo que pido y suplico a Vuestra Señoria sea servido de mandar lo que tubiere por de justicia y juro no ser de malicia, ut supra.
Manuel Benitez (rubric)

Santa Fee 3 de Agostode 1767
Corra traslado con Francisco Xavier Fragoso
Mendinueta (rubric)

Señor Governador y Capitan General

Francisco Xavier Fragoso besino de esta Villa y soldado reformado paresco ante Vuestra Señoria en cuanto a derecho y respondiendo al traslado que Vuestra Señria sea dignado darme de la parte contraria y bisto y entendido la depropada malisia con que me ba articulando sobre el litis del relicario que en estos autos consta me entrego para que se lo ensenase a un individuo como dize en su escrito lo cual llo me e negado la entrega que me iso como consta en mis declaraciones que a Vuestra Señoria tengo dadas vaxo la religion del juramento en las que me ratifico y afirmo y no tengo que quitar ni poner mas de que es berdad que seme perdio el referido relicario como dicho tengo. Y no contesta la cresida malisia de mi contrallente como dize en su primer escrito con mi declarasion en que dize llo le asegure no se perderia el relicario y ba mucho de que llo le dijera que esperaba en Dios no se perderia alo que dicho Benitez dize llo le asegure que me muestre el seguro por que su dicho no es bastante especialmente con la pasion que confiesa contra mi en sus escritos de malicias y sospechas y nada afirmatibo con prueba de berdad pues la unica berdad que allo en todos sus escritos es que me entrego el relicario para que lo ensenara a una individo y lo bolbiera esto llo no lo e negado pero tampoco no sabiendolo por benir de lo futuro menos me ise cargo de asegurar la reliquia si tenia algun contra tiempo en ella pues no soi capas de alcansarlo por benir assi mesmo en su terser escrito dela parte mia bersaria dize que alla prueba suficiente en mis declarasiones de que no seme perdio el relicario aqui pruevo llo su nulidad de Benitez con mis propias declarasiones las que se registraran hasta allarse donde aiga dicho llo no seme perdio el relicario por que aunque tengo dicho que si seme hubiera perdido desde a onde encontre a los Pasenos hasta El Brazito lo hubiera allado otro dia, no desminulle ni es contra ni el aberlo dicho pues era contingensia allarlo o no con el amor que lo buscaba especialmente no atendiendo en brebe rato alo por benir de lo que me pudiere acaeser con mi oficial por aberme pasado de la orden que me dio en la lisencia que le pedi como defacto dicho mi oficial me dio una correra por haber quebrantado su orden esto es por la menor no prebiniendoseme el riesgo tan grande en que me puse ajunto con el besino que me acompano no da menos que me puse en peligro de perder no una bida sino dos con tal de que mi credito no lo lastase como lo esta lastando y asi Señor Governador no se cual prueva sea mexor que esta por que aunque dize mi contrario que desecha para ocultar el relicario pruebo toda la malisia que en sus escriptos afirma solo de presumsiones y sospechas y no es digno mi contrallente de penetrar interiores pues esa dignidad solo Dios la tiene a pocos renglones dize si se ubiera cortado el cordon del relicario hubiera quedado pendiente de los dos estremos pero que mas estremos que los que a echo pues lla que no perdi mi bida por buscar dicho relicario quisa y sin quisa e perdido mi bien estar y al fin de todo prueba mi contrario por cosa afirmatiba con sus malisias no se perdio el relicario sino que lo tengo oculto que me de prueba sierta y berdadera por que llo no me conformo con su maldita sospecha por lo que a Vuestra Señoria pido y suplico sea mui servido de hazer o determinar como llebo pedido si se alla de por justicia y juro no ser de malisia esta mi defensa y en lo nesesario, ut supra.

   Francisco Xavier Fragoso (rubric)

Santa Fee y Agosto 4 de 1767
Desele traslado a Manuel Benitez para que si tiene prueba que dar la desale que lo que le combenga segun justicia.

   Mendinueta (rubric)

Manuel Benitez residente en esta Villa respondiendo al traslado que Vuestra Señoria se sirve de mandar seme corra digo: que las declaraciones de Francisco Xavier Fragoso mi parte contraria y la de el soldado Manuel Vegil consta que puso el referido Fragoso el relicario que demando en venta, respecto aber dicho que quanto le davan por el; cuyas palabras claramente lo manifestan y no satiface el decir que lo hizo por oir lo que le respondio por que las palabras se oyeron y la intencion con que las dijo, ni se oye ni se ve por lo que se deve estar a las palabras y no alas intenciones, por cuya razon quien tartaba de bender lo que no era suyo, mejor lo ocultaria pues de venderlo me seria facil provarlo con testigos o el mismo comprador, y de ocultarlo esta seguro de que yo lo pruebe con testigo, pues no lo puede haver delos pensimientos ni de las obras que el hombre a sus selos hace asta que el tiempo saca aluce algunas y este es el fundamento por que Fragoso habla con tan indevida audacia usando de palabras yndecorosas y denegratibas tratandome de deprabado y malicioso so que es reprensible en qualquiera litigante. Pregunto que depravada malicia incluye que yo pido que Fragoso me buelba una alaja que yo le entrege y el resibio, no teniendo por cierto que sele perdio con sobrado fundamentos, los que prueban su malicia incluye que yo pido que Fragoos me buelba una alaja que yo le entrege y el resibio, no teniendo por cierto que sele perdio con sobrado fundamentos, los que prueban su malicia en ocultarla y me justicia en pedirla; hallase Fragoso confiado por que no pruebo con testigos y pide que lo ejecute de donde se infiere no la perdida del relicario sino su ocultacion pues para esto no los puede haver por averlo dicho el solo ni para la perdida pues si los huviera no se huviera perdido; pero pruebo mi demanda con razones convinientes sacadas de sus declaraciones por que ose quebrado el ojo del relicario y en tal caso se quedo dentro de las dos bolsas, y no pudiendo salirse de ellas para perderse era nesesario se rompiesen los cuatro presillas y entonces cayerase el relicario con las bolsas, pero no el cordon que estaba oprimido y asegurado con el boton de hilo de oro; o se corto el cordon, y de cortarse avia de ser forsosamente por donde el mismo Fragoso dice que estaba rosado que era en el lugar de donde pendia el relicario y no por otra parte pues no avia motibo para rosarse, y en tal caso caeria relicario y bolsas pero no el cordon, cuyas estremos quedaban imposibilitados ocorrese por el boton que los unia, de todo lo qual se ynfiere que para perderse juntos, relicario y cordon avia de salirse todo por los pies o por la cabesa segun la positura en que lo traia ysiendo esto ymposible resulta que no sele perdio sino que lo oculto y como dicho Fragoso no puede desbanecer las fuerzas de estas razones ya por mi alegadas biese la dificultad con el equiboco de los estremos del cordon con los que yo hago por mi alaja. Pido y suplico a Vuestra Señoria sea servido de mandar sele ponga a Fragoso otro relicario en la misma forma y positura que estaba el mio y que practicamente manifeste el modo como pudo perdersele; por que ocularmente se vea que las razones por mi alegadas prueba mi justa demanda en la que insisto conformandome con lo que Vuestra Señoria fuere servido de determinar y juro no ser de malicia.

      Manuel Benitez (rubric)

Santa Fee y Agosto 8 de 1767
Entregensele estos autos a Francisco Xavier Fragoso para que alegue de bien probado y responda a los cargos que le hace su parte contraria para en su vista determinar conforme a justicia.

      Mendinueta (rubric)

      Señor Governador y Capitan General

Francisco Xavier Fragoso vesino desta Villa y soldado reformado y en cumplimiento y obedesimiento a lo mandado por Vuestra Señoria en el aucto que antesede para que responda y alege lo que ami derecho combenga en su cumplimiento digo Señor que lo que alega mi contraria parte sobre la caluguia que tanto tiene asegurado contra mi credito y opinion de que asegura y dize que la espresado alaxa que de ruego y encargo puso ami cuidado tengo probado Señor que ni la bendi ni menos la e ocultado como dize en su temorario juisio, y puesto que es palabra de Dios que del cielo ala tierra no a de haber nada oculto y siendo esto mui denegratibo aun credito buelbo a suplicar rendidamente a Vuestra Señoria que prueve la caluguia y demanda que contra mi pone el mensionado Benitez que por solo su dicho no es bastante siendo asi que ami no me danifica la declaracion de Begil pues no se prueva haver bendido al mensionado ni a otro ninguno dicha alaxa por lo que presume la parte contraria tenerla llo oculta por lo que en esta y en todo lo demas tocante a esta materia soi mui conforme con lo que Vuestra Señoria fuere serbido de mandar y determinar y esto doi por mi respuesta que firme en esta Billa de Santa Fee en ocho dias del mes de Agosto del presente año de sesenta y siete.

      Francisco Xavier Fragoso (rubric)

En esta Villa de Santa Fee en doce dias del corriente Agosto parecieron ante mi dicho Governador y Capitan General y de mi orden las dos partes litigantes y estando presentes se hizo practicamente la diligencia pedida por Manuel Benitez con otro relicario puesto en la misma forma y positura en que estava el que demanda dicho Benitez y declara Fragoso y dando por quebrado el ojo del relicario y presillas de las bolsas resulta que queda seguro con el votton que le oprima y cortado el cordon como defacto se corto con unas tixeras por la parte que Fragoso declara estaba rosado que es en el lugar donde pende el ojo del relicario ymediatamente caio relicario y bolsas y el cordon quedo firme con el voton, en vista delo qual prometio Francisco Xavier Fragoso entregar a Manuel Benitez otro relicario de plata con cera de agnus y dignam crucis lo que se conformo el mencionado Benitez quedando su derecho a salvo para recaudar su primer relicario en qualquier lugar y tiempo y de qualquiera persona que lo tuviere con la obligacion de devolver le que aora recive a el dicho Fragoso executado todo ante mi dava y doy por concluidas estas diligencias por este mi difinitivo auto, que firmaron con migo las partes y los de mi asistencia a falta de escribano, que no hai en esta Governacion de ninguna clase.

      Pedro Fermin de Mendinueta (rubric)
      Manuel Benitez (rubric)
      Francisco Xavier Fragoso (rubric)
testigo Matheo de Penarredonda (rubric)
testigo Antonio Moreto (rubric)

Notes

1. To date, no information has been found about Manuel Benítez.
2. Francisco Xavier Fragoso was the son of don Domingo Fragoso from Guadalajara. In a muster at the Santa Fe presidio in 1761, Francisco is listed as a corporal with seven horses. His name also occurs when he vouches for the supply inventory at Taos Pueblo. His only son, a presidio drummer, died of smallpox at the age of nineteen. Fragoso made his first will in 1766, a year before the adventure described in this document, but he did not die until 1790. In the will, he named Vicente Armijo and Toribio Ortiz as his compadres and stated that he owed a barrel to Ortiz. He must have been a small-time trader, since he also stated that he owed Joseph Rivera for two mules he had used for freighting to El Paso (Hadley et al., *Presidio*: 299 n8, 300; SANM I #275, WPA translation; SANM II #1096a).
3. See Doc. 45.
4. In 1760 it was noted in Bishop Tamarón's itinerary that the paraje of Las Nutrias was one day south of Tomé and five days north of Fray Cristóbal (Adams, *Tamarón*: 76).
5. To date there is no certain information on Manuel Vigil. In 1776 a Manuel Vigil was the alcalde of Taos County, married to Gertrudis Armijo, but this may not be the same person (Chávez, *Origins*: 311; SANM I #48).

6. The paraje of Los Alamitos was one day south of El Brazito, two days south of Robledo, and one day north of El Paso (Adams, *Tamarón*: 77).
7. The paraje of El Brazito was one day south of Robledo, one day north of Alamito, and two days north of El Paso (Adams, *Tamarón*: 77).
8. An Antonio Luján appears in the enlistment papers, stating that he enlisted in 1769 in place of his brother, Domingo Luján. Antonio Luján served until 1779. Domingo's name appears in a 1761 presidio muster. It may be that he started the substitution a little early or that there were two persons of this name (Olmstead, "Enlistment": 297; Hadley et al., *Presidio*: 301).
9. Sevilleta was on the east side of the Río Grande, north of Socorro and Alamillo and southeast of the mouth of the Río Puerco and Isleta (Kessell et al., *BOB*: 1070).
10. Mateo Lente is most likely Matías el Ente, a well-known resident of Isleta Pueblo, who purchased land from members of the Candelaria family near or at the San Clemente grant between 1744 and 1760. By the 1802 census, he and the other settlers had prospered, and the area was called La Plaza de los Lentes (Chávez, *Origins*: 205; Guggino: "Los Lentes": 1, 2).
11. Estero Largo was a marshy area about 75 km north of El Paso (Kessell and Hendricks, *RCR*: 544 n 5).
12. Caytano Góngora may have been a descendant of Juan de Góngora and Petronilla de la Cueva, who came to New Mexico in 1693 (Chávez, *Origins*: 188).

52

ATRISCO FAMILY MEMBERS DISPUTE ENTRANCES AND EXITS TO PROPERTY
July 8-27, 1767. SANM II #616b.

Synopsis and editor's notes: This petition to Governor Pedro Fermín Mendiñueta from an Atrisco settler, Joseph Sánchez, was made on behalf of his mother, doña Efigenia Sánchez, daughter of Pedro Durán y Chávez and sister of don Diego Antonio Chávez. Joseph claimed that the entrances and exits on their land were shared with those of don Diego Antonio until 1767, when don Diego built a house that blocked the access. The animals of Efigenia then had to cross an acequia to get to the pastures. When Efigenia complained in writing to the lieutenant alcalde, Bartolomé Griego, he sent a notice to don Diego stating that he should not impede the access. When nothing happened, Efigenia appeared three times before the alcalde, Juan Cristóbal Sánchez. He said her family could use the access, but not until completion of the harvest. This was not satisfactory, so Joseph Sánchez went to Tomé five times, apparently to visit the alcalde, or perhaps to see Felipe Tafoya, a procurador, who prepared the petition for the governor. The governor agreed that the entrances and exits should be for common use, stating that since the parties could not agree, he would appoint Nicolás de la Sierra, and in his absence, Alejandro Gonzales, to make known to don Diego that the entrances and exits were not to be blocked. Additionally, the appointees were to remind the alcalde and the lieutenant alcalde that this was not the first time that complaints had been made against them. When the governor's decree was signed, Sierra took it to don Diego, but upon being told that don Diego was at his ranch at the place of the Navajos, Sierra sent him a letter at his own expense.

The valley of Atrisco was the site of a seventeenth-century Spanish settlement on the west side of the Río Grande. It was reoccupied by Fernando Durán y Chávez and others after the Reconquest, and the settlement of Atrisco was officially named as such in 1703. At that time, the channel of the Río Grande was farther to the east side of the valley, leaving a much greater area for the colonists. (For information on the Atrisco land grant, see Greenleaf, "Atrisco"; Sanchez, *Atrisco Land Grant*; and Barrett, *Settlement*: 135-49.)

Year of 1767

Complaint by Joseph Sánchez[1] against Diego Antonio Chávez[2] over the crossing of an acequia by the animals belonging to the residents of Atrisco.

Governor and Captain General of this Kingdom

I, Joseph Sánchez, resident of the valley of Atrisco, jurisdiction of the villa of Alburquerque, appear before your honor in my best and proper form and on behalf of my mother, doña Efigenia Chávez, widow of my deceased father, don Jacinto Sánchez, and say that my said mother and myself, along with the rest of the heirs of our grandfathers and of our legitimate fathers, owners of the said valley, have through our inheritances, which are equally shared, without contradiction, have used the entrances and exits for our animals, until this present year, when don Diego Antonio Chávez, legitimate brother of my said mother, has totally forcefully disallowed the use of the entrances and exits on the south part [of the property] by constructing a house right in the middle of the said entrance and exit, which is also in front of our house. Because of this, the animals have to cross the acequia, which they must do, being that the said acequia goes across the area used for the entrances and exits, and which is used only to irrigate the garden close to the house. All of this could be solved without an argument on being presented to your honor, as it is proven that the said Diego Antonio Chávez and my mother have an equal right to the said entrance and exit because they are legitimate owners of the said site and rightful heirs of my deceased grandfather, don Pedro Chávez.[3] Due to this right they cannot and should not impede the right of the entrances and exits to the rest of the residents, being that it is an ancient custom that is beneficial for everyone.

Due to all of this, my mother sent a written complaint to the lieutenant alcalde mayor of that district, Baltazar Griego,[4] who did not provide much of anything in regard to the said document, merely sending a one-page notice so that the said Diego Antonio would not impede the said passage by the animals. She then went with the said paper to the house of the said lieutenant from where she returned with another document to the contrary, imposing upon me a fine of thirty pesos if I was to proceed to go through the said entrance and exit. Due to this, my said mother appeared before the alcalde mayor, don Juan Cristóbal Sánchez,[5] on her own behalf and on behalf of the rest of the heirs and residents who used the entrance and exit, not once, twice, but three times with documents, and what finally was provided by the said alcalde mayor was that the entrance and exit could be used, but not until the harvests were completed.

All of this favors only the values of don Diego Antonio, and not the just rights that we seek or the final dispositions of my ancestors, who did not designate a limited time for the use of the said entrance and exit, which until the present we have been using without any limitation. It is something that has never been seen, not even in places that have designated entrances and exits, that they are not limited to a specific time, but they have been upheld forever, without any exception. Sir, all of what has been executed in this matter is contrary to reason, right, and justice, and in all of the notices that have been given by the said alcalde mayor, he has caused and sustained the most grave damages, injustices, and illegalities upon my small hacienda, destroying my horses in the five trips that I have made to Tomé in order to acquire what we want approved and as such diminishing my animals, making me lose my corn fields, and not being able to fulfill the obligations of my home. The most sensitive thing, sir, is that the said alcalde mayor, in not giving me the justice that I so clearly ask for, has defamed my good opinion and honor with denigrating words.

For which just reasons, I seek the goodwill of your honor so that, as the father [padre] to the afflicted, he will honor my said mother with the right that will benefit her as well as me, declaring that the said entrances and exits are to be left for the use and passage of such, without limitation as to time and for the common good of all of the residents of the said valley. By such a superior mandate, the unjust demands shall be decided and finalized and presented to the said don Diego Antonio, who is the one who initiated everything, causing restlessness to all of us, disturbing the peace and prosperity, which we all shared, as well as causing dangerous escorted trips, all of which can only be justifiably rectified by your honor, restoring the peace, as only he can do by his pious acts, and by not having me appear before the said alcalde mayor, as I am afraid of the insulting words with which he treats me. For all of this, I hopefully ask and petition our honor that he order what he finds for the sake of justice and with what myself, my mother, and the others will be happy to receive. I swear that this is not done in malice, etc.

At the request of the petitioners
Felipe Tafoya (rubric)
Attorney

Villa of Santa Fe, July 18, 1767

In attention to the reasons and allegations, which in this document have been revealed by Joseph Sánchez on his behalf and on behalf of his mother, against don Diego Antonio Chávez, her brother, stating that the entrances and exits have been customarily accepted for the longest time for the common use for everyone, and in particular when they belong to the family tree with the same branches, and it should not be for the convenience and use of one individual, but should be shared by everyone with equal right. In regards to the damage done to them, as well as what was brought forth by the lieutenant, along with the alcalde mayor, as has been revealed, in their failure to fulfill their obligation by not providing a decision for the documents, which were being presented as a footnote so that the parties could deduce and argue their rights, but rather by submitting separate ones, or verbally giving their responses without completing or coming up with proceedings that could be used to qualify each one for the sake of justice. For which reason, the parties could not come up with some arrangement so that the Judge could avoid discord among them in what was to follow.

Because of this, I commission don Nicolás de la Sierra,[6] resident of the jurisdiction of Alburquerque, and in his absence, Alexandro Gonzales,[7] resident of Alameda,[8] so that they can make it known to Joseph Sánchez and all others who are interested in the entrances and exits for their animals, which are being impeded by don Diego Antonio Chávez, that they can use and use freely and in conformity with the way that they did it before, and they are not to be stopped. Diego Antonio Chávez is to be notified that he is not to impede either the party who initiated the action, or any other resident of Atrisco, from using the entrances and exits for their animals, or for any other reasons for which they are needed, under penalty brought forth by the royal sovereign laws against anyone who disobeys the superior mandates. If they have anything else to argue, it is to be brought forth before this government.

I also order the said delegated person to notify the alcalde mayor, don Juan Cristóbal Sánchez, and his lieutenant, Baltazar Griego, of the grave wrongdoing, which they have committed in their lack of administering justice by not approving the documents that this party has presented in the form that is allowed so that they can argue their rights according to justice. They are deemed deserving of corresponding charges for the grave damages, which were suffered by the parties for the lack of formal action taken by the said alcalde mayor, which is not the first time that a complaint has been lodged against him for the way he treats the litigating parties, which is something he should not do when an unjust demand is brought forth. For such reasons, there are corresponding penalties, and in no case should he use defamatory words. If the said alcalde or his lieutenant allows another complaint to happen, I will take appropriate action.

Once this notice is given to the proper persons, the said delegate shall see to it that a note is written in regards to this decree, and return it to me for final results. I, don Pedro Fermín de Mendiñueta, of the Order of Santiago, colonel of the royal forces, governor and captain general of this kingdom of New Mexico, thus approved, ordered, and signed it, along with my assisting witnesses, with whom I act due to the lack of a scribe, whom there are none of any type within this government.

        Pedro Fermín de Mendiñueta (rubric)
witness Mateo de Peñarredonda (rubric)
witness Antonio Moreto (rubric)

At the puesto of Alameda on the 20th of July 1767, I, said Nicolás Antonio de la Sierra, by virtue of the commission given to me by Sir Pedro Fermín de Mendiñueta, of the Order of Santiago, colonel of the royal infantry forces, governor and captain general of this kingdom, I promptly acted in obedience to what was asked of me and placed into execution that which was ordered; and so that it was valid, I started the proceedings, which I signed as presiding judge, appointed as a delegate judge, with two assisting witnesses, due to the known fact that there are no scribes, neither

public nor royal, in these parts, and on common paper, being that sealed paper is not found, and without prejudice to the royal crown, to which I certify.
      Nicolás Antonio de la Sierra (rubric)
        Presiding Judge
witness Alexandro Gonzales (rubric)
witness Joseph Gonzales Bernal (rubric)

  In the valley of Atrisco, on the 21st of July 1767, I, the said delegate, in order to proceed with that ordered by the said governor of this kingdom, was to order, and did order, that don Diego Antonio Chávez appear before me to inform him in person of the supreme decree of the 18th of the present month, and upon this being done, to continue with the rest of the proceedings. I thus determined, ordered, and signed it, as delegate judge with my assistants with whom I act, to which I certify.
      Nicolás Antonio de la Sierra (rubric)
witness Alonso García de Noriega (rubric)
witness Joseph Hurtado de Mendosa (rubric)

  Continuing, I, the said delegate, by virtue of what was ordered previously, in order to fulfill what was stated, received notice that don Diego Antonio Chávez is absent from here and is at his ranch in the province of Navajo, about twenty-five leagues distant from this valley. Because of this, I ordered that a letter be sent to him, at his expense, and, in the meantime, being that he has not appeared, these proceedings are suspended. So that it is valid, I placed it with the proceedings, which I signed, to which I certify.
      Nicolás Antonio de la Sierra (rubric)
witness Alonso García de Noriega (rubric)
witness Joseph Hurtado de Mendosa (rubric)

  At the puesto of Alameda on the 27th of July 1767, I, the said delegate by virtue of the specific order of the governor and captain general, dated the 24th of the present month, arranging for the demand of the suspension of the prosecution in this proceedings, and in the state in which they are, submit them so that upon your honor reviewing them, he shall do what is best according to justice. I so determined and signed, acting as I see best, to which I certify.
      Nicolás Antonio de la Sierra (rubric)
        Judge Delegate
witness Alonzo García de Noriega (rubric)
witness Alexandro Gonzales (rubric)

ORIGINAL DOCUMENT

Año de 1767

Demanda puesta por Joseph Sanchez contra Diego Antonio Chaves sobre el transito de los ganados de los vecinos de Atrisco por una zequia.

Señor Governador y Capitan General
deste Reyno

Joseph Sanchez vecino del Valle de Artisco jurisdiccion de la Villa de Alburquerque paresco ante Vuestra Señoria en toda forma de derecho por mi y en nombre de mi madre dona Efigenia Chabes, vuida de mi difunto padre don Jacinto Sanchez y digo Señor que aviendo la dicha mi madre y yo y los demas herederos de nuestros antepasados abuelos y padres legitimos duenos de dicho Valle emos gosado cada uno de la heredad que nos corresponde igualmente sin contradicion alguna de las entradas y salidas de nuestros ganados hasta que este presente año don Diego Antonio Chavez, legitimo hermano de dicha mi madre nos impide con el maior rigor el passo dela entrada y salida por la parte del sur, tan solo por que fabrico su cassa en medio de dicha entrada y salida y estar delante de las nuestras; y por que el ganao le pissa la asequia que es fuerza que la pise; pues dicha asequia atrabiesa dicha entrada y salida, la que solo le sirbe para regar la huerta que tiene en dicha su casa, lo que podia estar remediado sin llegar a bentilarlo ante Vuestra Señoria pues es probado que el dicho don Diego Antonio y mi madre tienen igual derecho a dicha entrada y salida por ser legitimos duenos de dicho sitio y forsosos herederos de mi difunto abuelo don Pedro Chabes, y con todo este derecho no pueden ni deben inpedirles alos demas vezinos dicha entrada y salida por aber sido anticuada costumbre por todos, para cuio efecto se presento dicha mi madre por escrito al Theniente de aquel partido Baltazar Griego, el que no probeio cosa alguna en dicho escrito, solo dio un papel suelto para que dicho don Diego Antonio no inpidiera el dicho passo; y dado por el referido con el sitado papel se fue ala cassa del dicho Theniente de donde trajo otro en contra imponiendome ami la multa de treinta pesos si proseguia a pasar por dicha entrada y salida, por cuio motibo se presento dicha mi madre ante el Alcalde Maior don Juan Xptobal Sanchez por si y por todos los demas herederos y vecinos comprendidos en dicha entrada y salida, por uno, dos y terzer escritos, y al ultimo lo que a proveido dicho Alcalde Mayor es que declara por tal entrada y salida la que ba referida, pero que no se usse de ella hasta que se alzen las cosechas, cuya providencia mira solo ala contemplazion del dicho don Diego Antonio, y no al justo derecho que nos asiste de rogando por este hecho la ultima disposizion de mis antepasados, pues estos no senalaron tiempo limitado para el usso de dicha entrada y salida como hasta aqui la emos estado gozando sin limitazion alguna, pues es cosa nunca vista, ni en ningun paraje que tiene entradas y salidas es su usso por tiempos, sino en todos tiempos sin ezepzion alguna; y siendo Señor todo lo que hasta aqui sea executado tan contrario a razon, derecho y justicia, y por las moratorias con que dicho Alcalde Mayor a hecho e experimentado gravisimos danos, perjuicios y menoscabos en mi corta hazienda, matando bestias en sinco viajes que he hecho a Thome solicitando lo proveido y por su caussa aniquilandoseme mi ganado, perdiendose mis milpas, faltando a las obligaciones de mi cassa, y lo mas sensible es Señor, que dicho Alcalde Mayor, ya que no me da la justicia tan clara que le pido, maltrato mi buena opinion y fama con palabras denigratibas y bochornosas por cuios justos motibos ocurro al amparo de Vuestra Señoria para que como padre de afilixidos ampare ami triste madre con el derecho que le asiste como ami igualmente, declarando por tal entrada y salida la referida, siguiendo dexe aora el usso y paso de ella sin limitazion de tiempo pues es bien comun de todo el vezindario de dicho Valle, con cuio superior mandato quedara disidido y finalizada la injusta demanda interpuesta por dicho don Diego Antonio, que es quien la a intentado, inquietandonos a todos, caresiendo de la paz, y sosiego en que antes estabamos y teniendo por esta cavilosidad otros peligrosos escoltos, los que solos la recta justificacion de Vuestra Señoria como el yris de la paz, puede remediar, sirbiendose la alta piedad de Vuestra Señoria el que sobre este particular no baia en presencia de dicho Alcalde Maior, temeroso de las malas palabras con que me trata; por todo lo qual a Vuestra Señoria redidamente pido y suplico sea mui servido de mandar lo que hallase ser de justicia que en ello reciviremos yo, dicha mi madre, y todos los demas, merced con justicia y juro en toda forma no ser de malicia, ut supra.

     A ruego de los suplicantes
     Felipe Tafoya (rubric)
     Procurador

Villa de Santa Fee 18 de Julio de 1767
En atencion a las rassones y alegatas que en este escrito expone la parte de Joseph Sanchez por si y en nombre de su madre contra don Diego Antonio Chavez, su hermano, y e que las entradas y salidas casuadas sin intermision por largo tiempo e imbaserdad costumbre deven permanecer para el comun uso y con especialidad quando son pertenecientes a las ramas de un mismo tronco y a que la combenencia y comodid de un individuo no se deve anteponer ala demuestra de igual derecho y en perjuicio de ellos y asi mismo a que asi en el Theniente, como en el Alcalde Maior se avierte (segun lo relacionado) una gravisima falta en el cumplimiento de su indispensable obligacion por no haver dado providencia a los escriptos presentados por esta parte al pie de ellos para que las partes deduzgan y aleguen sus derechos y no por papeles sueltos o de palabras y contraxiarse en los mandatos sin preceder diligencia que califique la justicia de cada uno en caso de que las partes no se combengan entre si en este deve ser autorizado por el Juez para obviar discordias en lo subcesivo por tanto

doy comision a don Nicolas de la Sierra residente en la jurisdicion de Alburquerque yen su ausencia a Alexandro Gonzales vecino de la Alameda para que haga saber a la parte de Joseph Sanchez y demas interesados en la salida y entrada de ganados que les impide don Diego Antonio Chaves que pueden ussar y usen de ella libremente y en la misma conformidad que lo hacien antes que se les pusiese empedimento y a don Diego Antonio Chavez notificara no impide ni a la parte demandante ni a otro vecino alguno de Atrisco la entrada y salida de ganados y otras qualesquiera casuas para que sea necesario, pena de incurrir en las impuestas por las Reales Soberanas Leyes alos inobedientes a los superiores mandatos, y si tuviere que alegar lo hagan en este mi jusgado de governacion y asi mismo mando a dicho comisario notifique a el Alcalde Maior don Juan Christobal Sanchez y su Theniente Baltazar Griego que por la grave culpa que han cometido en faltar ala devida administracion de justicia no probeyendo los escriptos que esta parte ha presentado en la devida forma para que las partes aleguen sus derechos y se juzgue conforme a justicia se han hecho dignos de correspondiente castigo por los graves perjuicios que se siguen a las partes por las indevidas demoras en sus formales providencias previniendo a dicho Alcalde Maior que no es esta la primera queja se me ha dado en orden a el ultraje con que trata a los litigantes lo que no deve practicar aun quando la demanda se verifique injusta; pues en tales casos hai castigos correspondientes y en ningun caso deve usar de palabras denigrativas y que si dicho Alcalde o su Theniente dieron lugar a nueba queja tomare la probidencia combeniente y fecha la notificacion en sus proprias personas pondra dicho comisario razon en forma que haga fee al pie de este decreto y de todo me hara remision para los efectos que combengan. Asi lo probehi, mande y firme yo don Pedro Fermin de Mendinueta del Orden de Santiago Coronel de los Reales Exercitos, Governador y Capitan General de este Reyno del Nuebo Mexico con dos testigos de mi asistencia con quienes actuo a falta de escribanos que no los hai en esta governacion de ninguna clase.

     Pedro Fermin de Mendinueta (rubric)
testigo Matheo de Penarredonda (rubric)
testigo Antonio Moreto (rubric)

En el Puesto de la Alameda en veinte dias del mes de Julio de mil setecientos sesenta y siete años yo dicho don Nicolas Antonio de la Sierra en virtud de la comision que antecede del Señor don Pedro Fermin de Mendinueta del Orden de Santiago, Coronel de los Reales Exercitos de Ynfanteria, Governador y Capitan General de este Reyno di pronto ovedicimiento hize admision de ella poniendo en execusion lo que se me manda y para que conste le puse por diligencia a que firme como Juez receptor autuando por receptoria con dos testigos de asistencia por la notoria falta de escribano publico ni real que no lo ay en estas partes ni en los terminos por derecho establecidos y en el presente papel comun por no correr en ellas de ningun sello sin perjuicio del real haver que de todo doy fee.

    Nicolas Antonio de la Sierra (rubric)

Juez Comisario
testigo Alexandro Gonzales (rubric)
testigo Joseph Gonzales Bernal (rubric)

En el Valle de Atrisco en veinte y un dias del mes de Julio de mil setecientos sesenta y siete años yo dicho comisario para el seguimiento delo mandado por el Señor Governador de este Reyno devia de mandar y mande comparezer ante mi don Diego Antonio Chavez aquien sele haga saver el superior decreto de diez ocho del corriente mes y notificazion en su persona y fecho se procede a las demas diligencias; asi lo determine, mande y firme yo dicho Juez Comisario con los de mi asistencia con quienes autuo como dicho es, doy fee.
     Nicolas Antonio de la Sierra (rubric)
       Juez Comisario
testigo Alonso Garcia de Noriega (rubric)
testigo Joseph Hurtado de Mendosa (rubric)

Yncontinenti yo dicho Comisario en virtud de lo mandado en el auto que antecede para efecto delo que en el se expresa se me condujo la noticia que don Diego Antonio Chavez se hallava ausente en su rancho de la Provincia de Navajo a distancia como de veinte y cinco leguas de este Valle por cuio motivo mande se libre carta misiva a su costa y en el ynterin no se certifica su conparezencia se suspendan estos autos y para que conste lo pusse por diligencia que firme autuando como dicho es doy fee.
     Nicolas Antonio de la Sierra (rubric)
testigo Alonzo Garcia Noriega (rubric)
testigo Joseph Hurtado de Mendosa (rubric)

En el Puesto dela Alameda en veinte y siete dias del mes de Julio de setezientos sesenta y siete años yo dicho Comisario en virtud la cierta horden del Señor Governador y Capitan General su fecha de veinte y quatro del que corre, areglado al demando se suspenda la prosecuzion de estas diligencias y en el estado en que se hallan se haga remision de ellas para que en su vista Su Señoria determine lo que jusgare en justicia. Asi lo determine y firme autuando como dicho es de que doi fee.
     Nicolas Antonio de la Sierra (rubric)
       Juez Comisario
testigo Alonzo Garcia Noriega (rubric)
testigo Alexandro Gonzales (rubric)

Notes

1. Joseph Sánchez was the son of don Jacinto Sánchez and doña Efigenia Chávez. Efigenia was the daughter of Pedro Durán de Chávez and Juana Montoya, granddaughter of Fernando Durán de Chávez. Both Fernando and Pedro were considered first founders of Albuquerque. Jacinto Sánchez (de Iñigo), a native New Mexican, was listed in 1697 as one of the 100 soldiers of the Reconquest, and in 1702 was listed as a sergeant (Chávez, *Origins*: 160-61; Kessell and Hendricks, *RCR*: 82-83 n41; Kessell et al., *TDC*: 128; Kessell et al., *ASA*: 145).
2. Diego Antonio Chávez was the brother of Efigenia, named above, and one of the younger sons of Pedro Durán y Chávez. He was twelve when his father died in 1735 (Chávez, *Origins*: 160-62)
3. This is Pedro Durán y Chávez (see Doc. 7).
4. Baltazar Griego, the lieutenant alcalde of Albuquerque, was also involved in the Canue settlement, near Albuquerque. It is not known if he was related to the prerevolt family of Griegos (Simmons, *Albuquerque*: 109).
5. Juan Cristóbal Sánchez was the son of Josefa Chávez, a daughter of Pedro Durán y Chávez and a sister of Efigenia and Diego Antonio; that is, he was their nephew and a first cousin on the Chávez side. His father was Francisco Sánchez, a nephew of Jacinto and the first cousin of Joseph Sánchez. So Juan Cristóbal was a second cousin of Joseph Sánchez, if this reading of the information, provided by Chávez, is correct (Chávez, *Origins*: 279-81). Also, Juan Cristóbal was married to Juana de Chávez, who appears to have been a granddaughter of Pedro Durán y Chávez (Chávez, *Origins*: 161-63). These complicated relationships reflect the comment, so often made about Spanish Colonial New Mexico, that "everyone is a cousin."
6. Nicolás [Antonio] de la Sierra, who does not appear to have been related to any of the above persons, came from Spain to El Paso in 1743 and was in Santa Fe in 1766 as a merchant (Chávez, *Origins*: 288; SANM II #619).
7. Alexandro Gonzales [Bas] was the son of Juan Gonzales Bas II, who lived and built the church in Alameda. Juan Gonzales Bas I was an early alcalde of Albuquerque in 1712. Alexandro is mentioned as a witness in a case before the governor in 1734, and in 1738 in an inventory for Joseph Gonzales, of Alameda, who died intestate (Chávez, *Origins*: 189-90; Doc. 26; SANM I #326).
8. Alameda was between Bernalillo and Albuquerque, in those days near the Río Grande. Over time, the river moved to the west.

53

FLOOD DAMAGES VISITED BY GOVERNOR AND LOCAL WORTHIES; EMERGENCY PROCEDURES INITIATED
November 7–9, 1767. Source: Pinart Collection, P-E 53-5.

Synopsis and editor's notes: In response to a November 1767 flood of the Santa Fe River and the Río Chiquito, a drainage channel adjacent to the river, Governor Pedro Fermín de Mendiñueta and various Santa Fe religious and lay worthies investigated the damage and gave orders to the residents for cleanup and repairs. The governor stated that one person per household would be assigned to a neighborhood crew. He also ordered that the presidio corporals were to have a list of persons and a schedule for alternating the work crews so that members of the crews could also attend to their own work. The quick response of the governor to the flood—the investigation, the bando, and orders to the presidio corporals—suggests that some kind of emergency response system for defending the villa and managing natural disasters may have been already in place, though it could have been invented by the governor and the officials for the occasion.

Though the Urrutia map (Map 1, Appendix) was drawn in 1767, the same year as the flood, the Río Chiquito is not shown. The next available map of Santa Fe, the 1846 Gilmore map, suggested that the Río Chiquito was to the north of the river channel. A 2009 study suggested that the Río Chiquito was a side channel, an oxbow, or a tributary to the Santa Fe River from a nearby spring at the cathedral (Plewa, "Trickle": 180-84).

A similar flood happened on August 5, 1910, as described in the *Santa Fe New Mexican* newspaper: "The rush of water down the Santa Fe canyon was like a raging torrent, black in color and troublesome in demeanor, big bounders crashing along unable to withstand the stream's momentum." On July 25, 1968, the *New Mexican* reported that downtown had again been inundated when the Santa Fe River and the Río Chiquito went over their banks, the floodwaters displacing alluvial soils and large rocks scarring the area. These floods have had consequences for archaeologists and other persons interested in Spanish Colonial history, in that very few Spanish Colonial artifacts have been found on the south side of the plaza, probably because they were washed away (Cordelia Thomas Snow, personal communication, September 25, 2012).

Don Pedro Fermín de Mendiñueta of the order of Santiago, colonel of the royal forces, governor and captain general of this kingdom of New

Mexico, castellan of these royal forces and of the presidio of his majesty. Whereas, it is timely and necessary to act with an appropriate and prompt remedy because of the evident risk by the river to the churches, royal houses, and rest of the center of the villa by the rising flood of the days of the sixteenth and seventeenth of the past month of October. The flood filled up the old channel with rocks and sand, for which reason the floodwaters were diverted to that called the Río Chiquito, causing considerable damage in the houses and fields.

For which reason, I was accompanied by the *bachiller*[1] don Santiago Roybal,[2] *vicario* and *juez eclesiástico*[3] of this villa, along with some informed residents who went along with me to do a visual inspection so as to order the suitable labor to prevent such certain danger. By virtue of which it was resolved that planks will be provided that are to be placed in the shallow water to serve as footpaths so they [the residents] can get to the rocks and sand, which is to be taken from the old channel of the said river so that it regains its natural course. So that the proposed and necessary work is executed and done quickly and divided effectively, I order a public bando that all the residents and soldiers of this said villa and presidio, without exception of person, shall comply with the above said work, which everyone is to answer to the list and allotment that has been made with the most equitable consideration and method, which is to be executed with exact promptness. Those who do not comply will be punished as being disobedient, according to these superior orders and judgments as they are ordered.

So that every one of the individual residents and soldiers knows what it will take to do said work to the end, I order that this coming Monday, which would be the ninth day of the coming November, at the beat of the drum, the residents are to be at the gate of the royal guard house, one person from each household, so they can be instructed as to which squad they belong and make themselves known to their respective corporal. The corporal shall have a list of those who are assigned to him, the order of which he is to keep in the alternating of the squads, who is to succeed one and the other in the work, so that they have time to attend to their own needs. The alcalde mayor of this villa shall be responsible to see that he has published this order and returned it to this *juzgado*[4] of the government.

Published on the seventh day of November 1767, signed by my hand and undersigned my two assisting witnesses due to the lack of a scribe, not one of which is found in this government.

                          Pedro Fermín Mendiñueta (rubric)

Witness Mateo Perrarredonda (rubric)

Witness Antonio Moreto (rubric)

In this Villa of Santa Fe on the 9th day of the month of November of this present year, I, the alcalde mayor of this villa, in compliance with that which was ordered by don Pedro Fermín de Mendiñueta, of the order of Santiago, governor and captain general of this kingdom, all the residents of this said villa and the soldiers from this royal presidio were gathered together, to the sound of the drum. To the voice of the

town crier, the bando's information was made public and made known to all of them as was ordered by said governor and captain general, just as it was contained herein they were made known, and so that his honor is certain that his order was complied with, to which I certify and sign in said villa on said day of that year.
                            Francisco Guerrero[5] (rubric)

ORIGINAL DOCUMENT

Pedro Fermin de Mendiñueta del Orden de Santiago Coronel de los Real Exercitos. Governador y Captain General de este Reyno del Nuevo Mexico y Castellano de Sus Fuerzas y Presidios por Su Magestad. Por quanto combiene y es necesario ocurir con pronto y oportuno Remedio al ebidente riesgo en que puso y aun amenaso el Rio de esta Villa a las yglesias, casas del Rey y de mas del centro de esta Villa la irregular creciente del dia diez y seis y diez y siete del proximo pasado mes de Octubre llenando su antigua caxa de piedra y arena por cuia razon tomo su corriente por el que llaman Rio Chiquito causando considerables danos en cassas y tierras de labor en cuia inteligencia acompanado del Senor Bachillor Don Santiago Roybal Vicario y Juez Eclesiastico de este Villa y de algunos vecinos de inteligencia se passo por mi a hacer vista de ojos para mandar las maniobras correspondientes a precaber tan indubitible peligro en virtud de la qual resolbi se condujesen maderos que puestos en las partes flacas sirvan de pie y arrima a la piedra y arena que devera salir de la antigua caxa de dicho Rio para que coja su natural corriente y para que la proyectada e indispensable obra se execute y lleve apuro y devido efecto; mando por este Publico Bando que todos los vecinos y soldados de esta dicha Villa y Presidio sin excepcion de personas concurran ala arriba dicha maniobra con lo que a cada uno corresponde segun la lista y distribucion que se ha hecho con la mas equitatiba consideracion y metodo lo que ejecutaran con esacta prontitud pena de que seran castigados los inobedientes con las prebenidas a los que no cumplen los superiores mandatos; y las arbitras las que combenga y para que cada uno de los indibiduos vecinos y soldados sepan lo que les corresponde para llevar la ya dicha obra a su fin mando que el Lunes primero venidero que contaremos nuebe del corriente Noviembre al toque de la Caja de Guerra concurra ala puerta del Real Cuerpo de Guardia una persona de cada casa para que sean instruidos de la quadrilla a que pertenecion de las que estan formadas y reconoscan a sus respectibos Cavos que estan nombrados y a estos se les contregaran sus listas de los que les estan asignados y el orden que deveran guardar en la altematiba de las quadrilles las que se sucedaran unas a otras en el trabajo por dar lugar a que atiendan a sus precisos negocios; y el Alcalde Maior de esta Villa pondra razon de haverlo publicado y lo debolberia a este Juzgado de Govenacion y es fecho en siete dias del mes de Nobiembre de mill setecientos sesenta y siete firmado de mi mano y de mis dos infrascritos testigos de asistencia a falta de Escribanos que no los hai en esta Govenacion de ninguna clase.
                          Pedro Fermin de Mendiñueta (rubric)
Testigo Matheo de Penarredonda (rubric)
Testigo Antonio Moreto (rubric)

En dicha Villa de Santa Fee in nuebe dia de el mes de Noviembre de el eso pres ado ano, Yo el alcalde mayor de esta Villa en cumplimiento de lo mandado por el Senor Dn. Pedro Fermin de Mendiñueta de el Orden de Santiago, Govenador y Captain General de este Reyno a el son de al Caja de Guerra se junto todo lo mas de el vecindario de esta dicha Villa y los soldados de este Real Presidio y a bos de pregonero y en forma de Vando se publico y a todos se les hizo saver lo mandado por dicho Senor Govenador y Captain General que segun y como en ello se contiene quedaron entendidos, y para que a Su Senoria Ie conste su devido cumplimenito, ha silo certifico y lo firme en dicho Villa y en dicho dia de que doy fee, ut supra
Francisco Guerrero (rubric)

Notes

1. *Bachiller* refers to a recipient of the lowest university degree (Hadley et al., *Presidio*: 534).
2. Bachiller de Santiago Roybal was appointed as the vicar and ecclesiastical judge in New Mexico for Bishop Crespo in 1730. It was a controversial appointment, since Roybal was a secular priest, not a Franciscan, the first to be so appointed. He was confirmed in his appointment in 1733 and served in El Paso from 1733 to 1736 before returning to New Mexico. His father was Ignacio Roybal de Torrado, from Galicia, Spain, a soldier and an alguacil mayor (sheriff) of the Inquisition. His sister, María Manuela, was the second wife of Juan de Archibeque. Upon his death, she married Bernardino de Sena. Another sister, Juana, married Juan José Moreno (Norris, *Year Eighty*: 78, 187 n37; Doc. 15; Chávez, *Origins*: 275).
3. *Vicario* is defined as one who transacts ecclesiastic affairs as a substitute for the bishop or archbishop. A *juez eclesiástico* is a person acting as an ecclesiastical judge.
4. *Juzgado* can mean jail or court, but in this case, it probably means the archives at the Palace of the Governors.
5. See Doc. 29.

54

CADAVER FOUND UNDER TREE BY YOUNG HERDER; RESULTS IN INQUEST
September 10–17, 1774. SANM II #682.

ynopsis and editor's notes: This document tells the story of a ten-year-old shepherd, Joseph María, who, when herding cows in the Cañada de los Ojitos, found a dried-out human body under a tree at Las Bocas, a pasture at the mouth of the Santa Fe River where it empties into the Río Grande. Afraid, the boy fled with his cows and told his mother, who told his aunt, who told her husband, Felipe Romero. Romero then sent his servant, Manuel de la Cruz, accompanied by Alejandro Ortega, to collect the body. They identified the body as Domingo Blea on the basis of his clothes. He was a former servant of doña Josepha de Bustamante, so they took the body to her house, after which the alcalde, Manuel García Pareja, held an inquest. Upon hearing testimony from the parties involved, the alcalde again identified the body as Domingo Blea. The inquest ended without a final determination by the alcalde, or else the determination was lost.

Though later than the other documents in this collection, this one was included because it is one of the few documents in the Spanish Archives that deals with children.

At this villa of Santa Fe on the 10th of September, 1774, before me the alcalde mayor and war captain of the said villa, don Manuel García Pareja,[1] appeared doña Josepha de Bustamante,[2] resident of the said villa, who stated and brought forth a cadaver, which had been taken to her house and which had been found at the paraje of Las Bocas, in the Cañada de Los Ojitos. Having recognized the body solely on the basis of the clothes, it was known to have been Domingo Blea,[3] former servant of the said Bustamante. In fulfillment of my duty, I, the said alcalde mayor, along with two assisting witnesses, went to her said house and identified the said cadaver, which was wrapped in a cloth, and which I ordered to be unwrapped. I saw the head, without hair or skin, which for the most part was already dry and separated from the body. Likewise, I saw that the body was dry, only the bones remained, without skin, and was dressed in pants and a jacket, all of which I saw and recognized. Because of this, I order that Manuel de la Cruz[4] appear before me, being that he was the one who brought in the body. I also order that the herder, who is said to have found the body, appear before me. They are to give their testimonies in order to continue with these proceedings before this royal justice. This, my determination, is to be placed at the head of the proceedings. I thus approved, ordered, and signed it acting with my assisting witnesses due to the lack of a scribe, which there is none of any type in this government. To which I certify.

       Manuel García Pareja (rubric)

witnesses
Felipe Sandoval (rubric)
at the request of Matías Sena
[signed by] Thomas de Sena (rubric)

  At this villa of Santa Fe on the 15th of September, 1774, upon continuation of these proceedings, I made appear before me don Manuel García Pareja, alcalde mayor and war captain of this said villa, [and] Manuel de la Cruz, servant of Felipe Romero,[5] from whom I took his sworn statement, which he made before God, Our Lord, and the sign of the Holy Cross, under which he promised to tell the truth as to what he knew and was asked. He was asked what his motive was to go for the body that was found dead. He answered that the herder at Las Bocas, who is the herder for his master, came to inform him that he had found a dead body at Las Bocas in the Cañada de Los Ojitos. Upon being advised of this by the young boy, his master sent him [de la Cruz] for the body at the said paraje. He located the body at the said puesto, under some oak trees, without a head, the head being separated from the body, without hair, or skin, except for a small piece of skin, and the body already dried, but it could be seen that the body was head down. The hands and lower arms were detached from below the elbows, and he was wearing leather pants and a woolen jacket. He was lacking his feet, which I looked for in the company of Alejandro Ortega,[6] but which we could not find. The rest of the body was in one piece, but without any skin. After that we wrapped the body, head, and arms in a cloth, loaded them on a burro, and brought them to my house, and from there I took it to the villa, to the house of doña Josepha de Bustamante.

  The boy was asked if he had anything else to state regarding this case. He answered that he did not, that this is what he saw and knows. His statement having been read back to him word by word, once, twice, and three times, he affirmed, ratified it, and said that he was twenty years of age, more or less. He did not sign because he did not know how. I, the said alcalde mayor, signed it along with my assisting witnesses, with whom I act due to the lack of a public or royal scribe, which there is none in this government, to which I certify.

       Manuel García Pareja (rubric)

witnesses
Simón de Armenta (rubric)
Joseph de Armenta (rubric)

Continuing, on the said day, month, and year, and in order to conclude these proceedings, I, don Manuel García Pareja, the alcalde mayor and war captain of this said villa, made appear before me the young boy of ten years of age, more or less, Joseph María, who because he was not of a legal age, I explained to him the obligations of his sworn statement, and understanding this, I swore [for him] before God, Our Lord, and the Holy Cross, that he would tell the truth as to what he knew and what he was asked. He was asked what he was doing when he saw the dead body. He answered that he was going to bring some cows to the Cañada de Los Ojitos, being that they had strayed away going to water, and having gathered them, he found the body under some oak trees. Being afraid, he fled, gathering his cows, and came to inform his mother. He said that his mother then informed his aunt, who was the wife of Felipe Romero. Upon finding the body, he saw that the head was not attached to the body. He was asked if he knew anything else. He answered that he did not.

His statement having been read back to him word by word, once, twice, and three times, he affirmed and ratified it. He did not sign because he said he did not know how. I, the said alcalde mayor, signed it along with my assisting witnesses with whom I act due to the lack of a public or royal scribe, which there is none in this government, to which I certify.

Manuel García Pareja (rubric)

witness
Joseph de Armenta (rubric)

At this villa of Santa Fe on the 17th of September, 1774, in continuation of these proceedings, I, the alcalde mayor and war captain, don Manuel García Pareja, made appear before me Alejandro Ortega, resident of this jurisdiction, and being in my presence took his sworn statement, which he made to God, Our Lord, and to the Holy Cross, regarding the charges, and he promised to tell the truth as to what he knew and was asked.

He was asked what his motive was in going for the cadaver that was found dead at Las Bocas in the company of Manuel de la Cruz. He said that the said Manuel had gone to his house and asked him to go with him for a dead body that had been found by a young boy from his home. Having gone with him, we found the body at the Cañada de Los Ojitos, under an oak tree, head down, headless, which was found a few feet away, without any hair or skin, except for a small area where he had skin. His hands were detached from below the elbows, detached from the bones, and away from the body, the bones dried. The feet were missing, and having looked for them, they could not find them. His pants, made of leather, still held his muscled bones, which were dry, wearing a wool jacket. He was asked if he knew who it was by what he was wearing. He answered that it was Domingo Blea.

[Editor's note: The document ends at this point without a formal determination or signatures.]

ORIGINAL DOCUMENT

En esta Villa de Santa Fee en diez dias del mes de Septiembre de mil setecientos setenta y quatro años ante mi el alcalde mayor y capitan aguerra de la expresada Villa, don Manuel Garcia Pareja se presento doña Josepha de Bustamante, vesina de dicha Villa, quien declaro y manifesto un cadaver que le trajeron a su casa, que hallaron en el Paraje de las Bocas, en la Cañada de Los Ojitos, que por haver reconocido por solo el bestuario ser Domingo Blea, sirbiente que era de la dicha Bustamante; en cumplimiento de mi obligasion pase yo dicho Alcalde Mayor a la expresada casa, con dos testigos de mi asistensia y reconoci el dicho cadaber; el que estaba embuelto en una manta; el que mande desembolber, y bi la calabera, sin cabello y sin pellejo, la qual podacito en algunas partes ya seca y dibidida del cuerpo; y asi mismo el cuerpo seco, solo los huesos sin piel y su vestuario calsones y cotton lo que vi y reconosi; en cuya consequencia mando conparesca en mi jusgado Manuel de la Cruz, el mismo que trajo el cuerpo y asi mismo el pastor que disen que lo hallo, para que a estos seles tome su declaracion y proceder a las deligencias que combengan de oficio de la Real Justisia, poniendo por cabesa de proceso esta mi determinacion y asi lo probehi mande y firme autuando con los testigos de asistencia a falta de Escribano que no lo ay en esta gobernacion de ninguna clase, de todo doy fee =

                    Manuel Garcia Pareja (rubric)

Testigo A ruego de Matias Sena
Phelipe Sandoval (rubric) Thomas de Sena (rubric)

En esta Villa de Santa Fee en quinze dias del mes de Septiembre de mil setecientos setenta y quatro añnos, en prosecucion de estas deligencias, hise compareser ante mi, Dn. Manuel Garcia Pareja, Alcalde Mayor y Capitan Aguerra de esta dicha Villa, a Manuel de la Cruz, sirbiente de Felipe Romero, a quien le tome juramento el que hiso por Dios Nuestro Señor y la Señal de la Santa Cruz, debajo del qual prometio desir verdad en lo que supiere y fuere preguntado; y siendolo, que motibo tubo para yr por el cuerpo que se hallo muerto? Responde que el pastorcito de Las Bocas del dicho mi amo, vino avisar que se habia hallado un cuerpo muerto en Las Bocas en la Canada de Los Ojitos; y con este aviso a el muchachito, el embio, su ama por el a el Paraje citado; el qual cuerpo lo encontro en el dicho Puesto de bajo de unos encinos, sin cabeza, y la cabeza tirada del cuerpo, sin cabello, ni cuero la cabeza tal qual pedacito tenia de cuero, y el cuerpo ya seco pero se conocia que el cuerpo estaba boca abajo, desprendidos los dos brazos, con las manos desde el codo para abajo, con sus calzones de gamuza y coton de lana faltandole los pies, los que andube buscando en compania de Alexandro Ortega, los que no pudimos hallar estando todo lo demas del cuerpo unido; pero sin carne; y en despues cargase el cuerpo, cabeza y brazos en un burro enbuelto

en una manta y lo truje ami casa, y desde mi casa lo conduci a la Villa en casa de Dna. Josepha de Bustamante: Fuele preguntado que si tiene otra cosa que declarar sobre este particular? Responde que no, que esto es lo que vido y sabe; y siendole leyda esta su declaracion de berbo ad berbum por una, dos y tres vezes en la que se afirmo, ratifico y dijo ser de edad de veinte anos poco mas o menos no firmo por que dijo no saber, firmelo yo dicho Alcalde Mayor con los testigos de mi asistenzia con quienes autuo a falta de Escribano Publico ni Real que no lo ay en esta Gobernacion de que doy fee =
                Manuel Garcia Pareja (rubric)

Testigo testigo
Simon de Armenta (rubric) Joseph de Armenta (rubric)

Yncontinenti en dicho dia mes y año, y para asi mismo fin de estas deligencias; hise comparezer ante mi el Alcalde Mayor y Capitan Aguerra de esta dicha Villa, Dn. Manuel Garcia Pareja, a Joseph María, muchachito de edad de diez a onze años poco mas o menos, a quien por faltarle la edad competente le hise los cargos del juramento y entendido a ellos, juro a Dios Nuestro Señor y la Santissima Cruz desir verdad en lo que supiere y fuere preguntado, y siendolo; que handaba haziendo quando vido el cuerpo muerto? Responde que yendo a traer unas bacas a la Cañada delos Ojitos, que sele habian bajado a el agua, y handandolas juntando, me encontre con el cuerpo debajo de unos encinos; y atemorizado, arranque y junte mis bacas y me bine a habisar a mi madre; y mi madre abiso ami tia, muger de mi tio Felipe Romero, pero al encontrarme con el cuerpo vide que tenia la cabeza desprendida del cuerpo; fuele preguntado que si sabe otra cosa? Responde que no; y siendole leyda esta su declarasion de verbo adberbum por una dos y tres veses en la que se afirmo, ratifico no firmo por que dijo no saber firmelo yo dicho Alcalde Mayor con los testigos de mi asistensia con quienes autuo a falta de Escribano Publico ni Real que no lo ay en esta gobernacion de que doy fee =
                Manuel Garcia Pareja (rubric)

testigo
Joseph de Armenta (rubric)

En esta Villa de Santa Fee en diez y siete dias del mes de Septiembre de mil setecientos y setenta y quatro años, en prosecucion de estas deligencias hize comparezer ante mi a Alexandro Ortega vezino de esta jurisdiccion, el Alcalde Mayor y Capitan Aguerra de esta dicha Villa Dn. Manuel Garcia Pareja, y estando en mi presencia le tome juramento el que hizo por Dios Nuestro Señor y la Santa Cruz so cuyo cargo prometio dezir verdad en lo que supiere y le fuere preguntado y siendole, que motibo tubo para hir por el cadaver que hallo muerto en Las Bocas en compania de Manuel de la Cruz? Responde, que el dicho Manuel le fue a llamar a su casa, que le acompanara que yba por un cuerpo que se havia hallado muerto un muchachito de su casa; y yendo en su compania hallamos el cuerpo en la Canada de Los Ojitos, devajo de un encino boca abajo, sin cabeza la que estaba retirada del cuerpo, y la cabeza sin cabello, ni pellejo en la cabeza; tal qual lunarito tenia de pellejo, y desde los codos para las manos desprendidos los huesos y retirados del cuerpo y secos los huesos; y sin pies, los que andubimos buscando y no los pudimos hallar; con calzones de gamuza dentro los huesos de los muslos pero secos y un coton de lana; fuele preguntado que si por el bestuario conosio quien era; responde ser Domingo Blea.

Notes

1. Manuel García Pareja was a Spaniard from a town near Toledo, who was in New Mexico by 1755 and later lived at La Soledad del Río Arriba (Chávez, *Origins*: 184).
2. Josepha de Bustamante appears to have been the adopted daughter of don Bernardo de Bustamante de Tagle, a lieutenant governor under Governor Juan Domingo de Bustamante. She was the second wife of Captain Nicolás Ortiz III, a large landowner and trader and a lieutenant alcalde of Santa Fe in the 1750s, who was killed by Indians in 1769. According to Chávez, Josepha was instrumental in reestablishing the fiesta and Confraternity of La Conquistadora, partly in his memory (Chávez, *Origins*: 249-50; Jenkins, "Women": 333-44).
3. It is not known if this person is a descendant or dependent of the Carlos Blea family that came to New Mexico from Puebla in 1694 (Chávez, *Origins*: 148-49).
4. It may be that Manuel de la Cruz was a descendant or dependent of Francisco de la Cruz, who returned to New Mexico after the revolt (Chávez, *Origins*: 167).
5. A Felipe Romero is listed as a witness at Pueblo Quemado in Río Arriba in 1751. He could also be the Felipe who was the son of Bartolomé Romero, though that name is usually associated with Taos or Bernalillo (Chávez, *Origins*: 271).
6. Alejandro Ortega was the son of Antonio Ortega and grandson of Gerónimo Ortega, from Zacatecas, an early settler who was in New Mexico by 1715. Alejandro Ortega enlisted at the presidio in Santa Fe in 1777, stating that he was a farmer (Kessell et al., *ASA*: 1169 n82; Olmsted, *Enlistments*: 301).

GLOSSARY

Acequia. Irrigation canal or ditch.
Alcalde mayor. In New Mexico, an official appointed by the governor with civil jurisdiction over one of the six to eight alcaldías.
Alcalde ordinario. A member of the cabildo, a leading magistrate; in some cases, chosen by the rest of the cabildo.
Alcaldía. Region of a province overseen by an alcalde mayor; includes both the Indian and Spanish population.
Alférez. Standard bearer, the lowest ranking commissioned officer in the Spanish military; also, the standard bearer for the cabildo.
Alguacil mayor. Chief constable or peace officer of a community or province.
Arquebus. Smoothbore matchlock or wheellock firearm with a stock resembling a rifle's; it had a range of about 650 feet, or 200 meters.
Arroba. A dry measure equal to about 25 pounds or a liquid measure equal to about 3½ to 4 gallons.
Audiencia real. Highest royal high court of appeals; council of state to the viceroy.
Auto. Judicial or administrative decree.
Ayudante. In military terms, loosely translated as "aide"; it did not carry the authority of a higher officer.
Bachiller. Recipient of the lowest university degree, often a parish priest.
Bando. Proclamation.
Belduque. Long knife.
Bosque. Wet and woody place.
Caballería. Military unit on horseback; cavalry.
Cabildo, justicia, regimiento. Municipal council with judicial and administrative powers; composed of regidores and alcaldes ordinarios.
Cabo. Corporal, squad leader. There could be cabos of different kinds, for example, a cabo of the horse herd.
Caja de guerra. War drum.
Canoa. Wooden flume to carry water in an acequia.
Capitán de compañía. Head of a military operation during a field campaign, a temporary position.
Capitán general. Chief military officer, often filled by the governor in frontier areas.
Capitán vitalicio. Captain-for-life.
Carneras. Sheep, sometimes rams.
Castellano. Commander of a castle or fortification.
Cavador. Hoelike tool.
Cédula. Decree from the king; a royal order.
Ciénaga. Marsh, swamp, bog. *Cienega* is the English spelling.
Coa. Shovel-like tool used for tilling in place of a hoe.
Cofradía. Catholic lay ecclesiatical brotherhood responsible for paying for specific religious services and the maintenance of a church or endowed chapel.
Colcha. In New Mexico, an embroidered weaving made using a distinctive couching, or "colcha," stitch; also a heavily embroidered shawl, bedcover, or covering.
Compadre. Godfather, or a special friend.

Convento. Community of religious men or women, including, but not only, a habitation.

Coyote. Racial category describing the product of Spanish or mestizo and Indian parents; sometimes used to refer to the offspring of Plains Indians born in a Spanish household as captives or servants, and sometimes to a person having mestizo and mulatto ancestry.

Criado. Servant.

Cuchillo. Generic term for knife.

Cuero. Jacket used by soldiers made up of many layers of leather.

Custodia. In the Fransican order, a transitional phase for a jurisdiction that has not yet attained the status of a province.

Custos. Head of a Franciscan custodia.

Encomienda. Grant of specified land and Indian labor made to a colonist by the king; in return, the grantee, an *encomendero*, agreed to provide for the Indians' welfare and instruct them in Christianity.

Escopeta. A gun that fired shot, like a shotgun.

Espada. General term for a sword.

Espadín. Small, short sword.

Español. Person born in Spain; person that claimed to be part of the Española caste.

Estancia. Grant of land for raising or cattle; a livestock ranch.

Fanega. Dry measure roughly equivalent to 1½ to 2½ bushels. There are two fanegas in a carga and twelve almudes in a fanega; the amount of grain that fills a bin of about eighteen inches by seven inches by nine inches.

Fray. Title preceding the name of a friar.

Fuerte. Military stronghold.

Fusil. Firearm smaller than but similar to a musket. It fired a ball and had a long barrel with a smooth or rifled bore; sometimes considered a later version of an arquebus.

Gamusa. Heavy buckskin used for clothing in New Mexico.

Genízaro. Captured and purchased or ransomed nomadic or their offspring, baptized and raised in or included as part of a Spanish family and then freed. Sometimes refers to captured Indians who have lost their tribal identity but have not quite acculturated as Spanish.

Gentiles. Indians who have not been converted to Christianty; also called infidels, heathens, or *Indios bárbaros*; or roving or unsettled Indians, usually Plains Indians.

Gobernador. Governor.

Hachita. Hatchet.

Indios bárbaros. See Gentiles.

Infidels. See Gentiles.

Juez comisario. Official given authority in judicial matters.

Juez eclesiástico. Ecclesiatical judge.

Juez receptor. Judge in charge of collecting evidence and payments, sometimes called "presiding judge."

Junta de guerra. War council or committee.

Junta de hacienda. Treasury council or committee.

Justicia. Justice or judge; magistrate.

Libra. Common unit of weight, equal to slightly less than one modern pound.

Lienza. Fabric woven from flax or hemp; sometimes a canvas.

Limpieza. Purity; in the case of the Holy Office of the Inquistion, it meant purity of blood, that is, not Jewish, Muslim, or Protestant. It sometimes took four generations for someone to attain limpieza.

Macho. General term for male mule; also a male donkey, or jack. A female mule is a *mula.*
Manta. General term for an item made of cotton, often referring to a blanket for a human or a horse.
Marca. Secondary brand used over the original brand when an animal was sold, showing that the original brand was no longer valid; also called a *venta.*
Mestizo. Offspring of European and Indian parents.
Moso. Male servant or young male.
Mulato. Person with a mixture of European and African ancestry.
Obraje. Work place; usually refers to a cotton or cloth factory.
Paraje. Place, campsite, and watering hole; sometimes called a *sitio* or *aguaje.*
Pieza. Piece or part of something, as in *pieza de oro* (piece of gold); sometimes refers to an Indian for sale.
Plaza de armas. Military parade ground, often in the central plaza or town square, used for musters for campaigns and drilling of troops.
Polilla. Moth.
Pólvora. Gunpowder.
Procurador. Solicitor or legal representative, usually in municipal cases.
Puesto. Small settlement or outpost.
Puñal. Dagger.
Ranchería. Cluster of temporary Indian dwellings; Indian encampment.
Real. Coin worth one-eighth of a silver peso; also a mining camp.
Real de mina. Camp or district specializing in mining.
Real de plata. Silver real.
Receptor. Collector of judicial fines, or treasurer or custodian of funds.
Reformado. Person in military reserves; often used to mean retired.
Regidor. Member of a cabildo.
Rescate. Literally, "ransom." In New Mexico it referred to ransoming of Indians or Hispanics captured by Indians and sold at trade fairs. Sometimes the trade fairs were called rescate fairs. *Indio de rescate* was an Indian made part of Spanish society by capture or ransom.
Residencia. Judicial review of an official's conduct held at the end of a term made by the incoming office holder.
Rubric. Unique mark or flourish added to a signature.
Sallal. Coarse woolen cloth.
Tambor. Drum.
Teniente. Lieutenant or sometimes assistant.
Vala. Ball or bullet.
Vara. Castilian yard, about 33 inches; or a staff of office.
Vecino. Householder or resident of a community or citizen, often used to indicate a property owner.
Venta. See *marca.*
Verbo ad verbum. Latin term meaning verbatim, or exactly as it happened; literally meaning "word for word."
Vicario. Person transacting ecclesiatical affairs as a substitute for the bishop or archhishop.
Villa. In New Mexico, a settlement with royally defined privileges, including the right to have a cabildo.
Virrey. Viceroy.

APPENDIX: MAPS

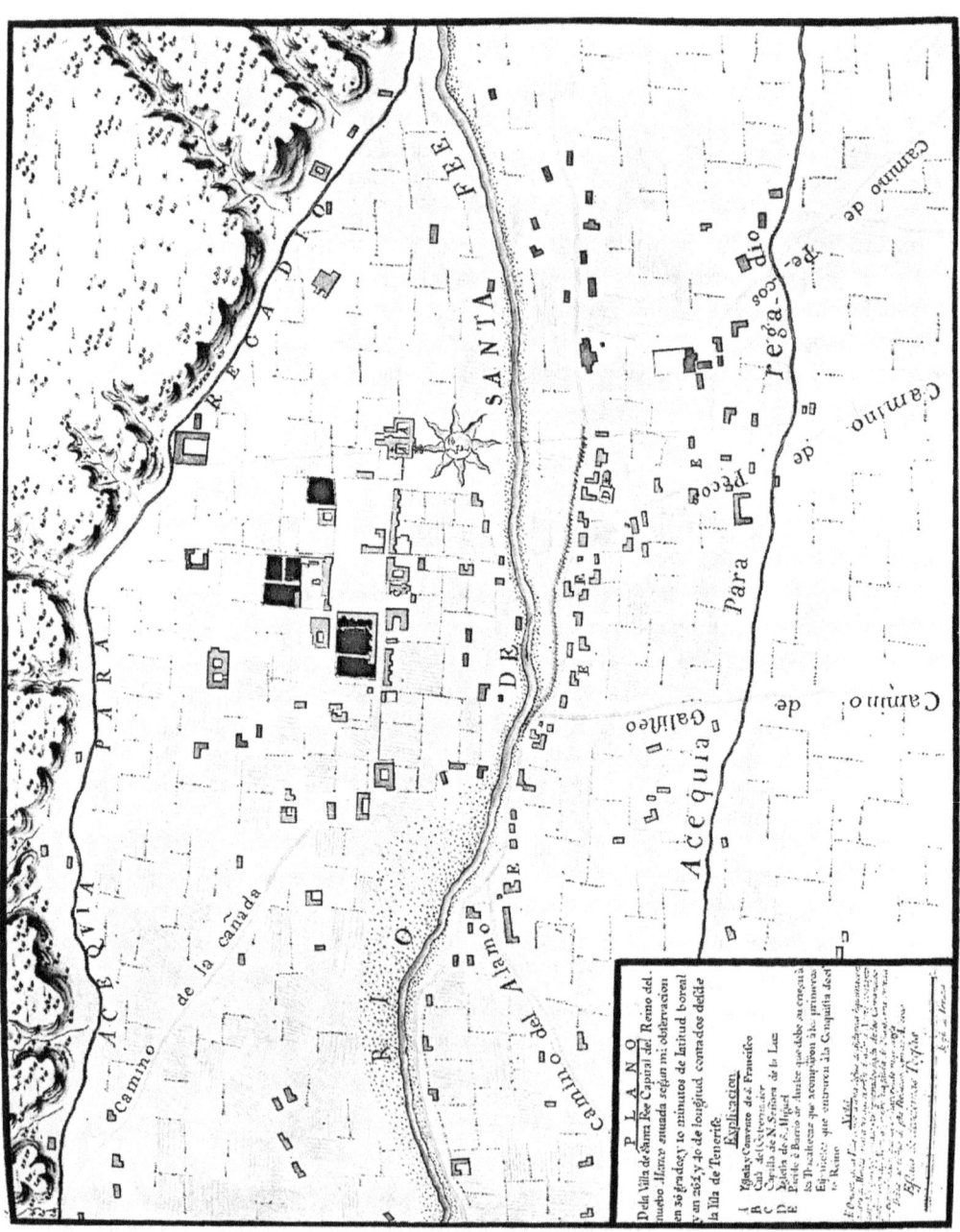

Map 1. 1767 Urrutia map. "Map of the villa of Santa Fe, capital of the kingdom of New Mexico, situated, according to my observation, at 36 degrees north latitude and 262 degrees 40' longitude measured from the island of Tenerife." Prepared by José Urrutia. Center for Southwest Studies, Zimmerman Library, University of New Mexico, Albuquerque; British Library, Add. Ms 17662, M.

Map 2. 1779 Miera y Pacheco map. "Plan of the internal province of New Mexico which is made by command of lieutenant colonel of the cavalry, governor, and commanding general of said province, don Juan Baptista de Ansa [sic], by don Bernardo de Miera y Pacheco, distinguished soldier of the royal presidio of Santa Fe." Center for Southwest Studies, Zimmerman Library, University of New Mexico, Albuquerque.

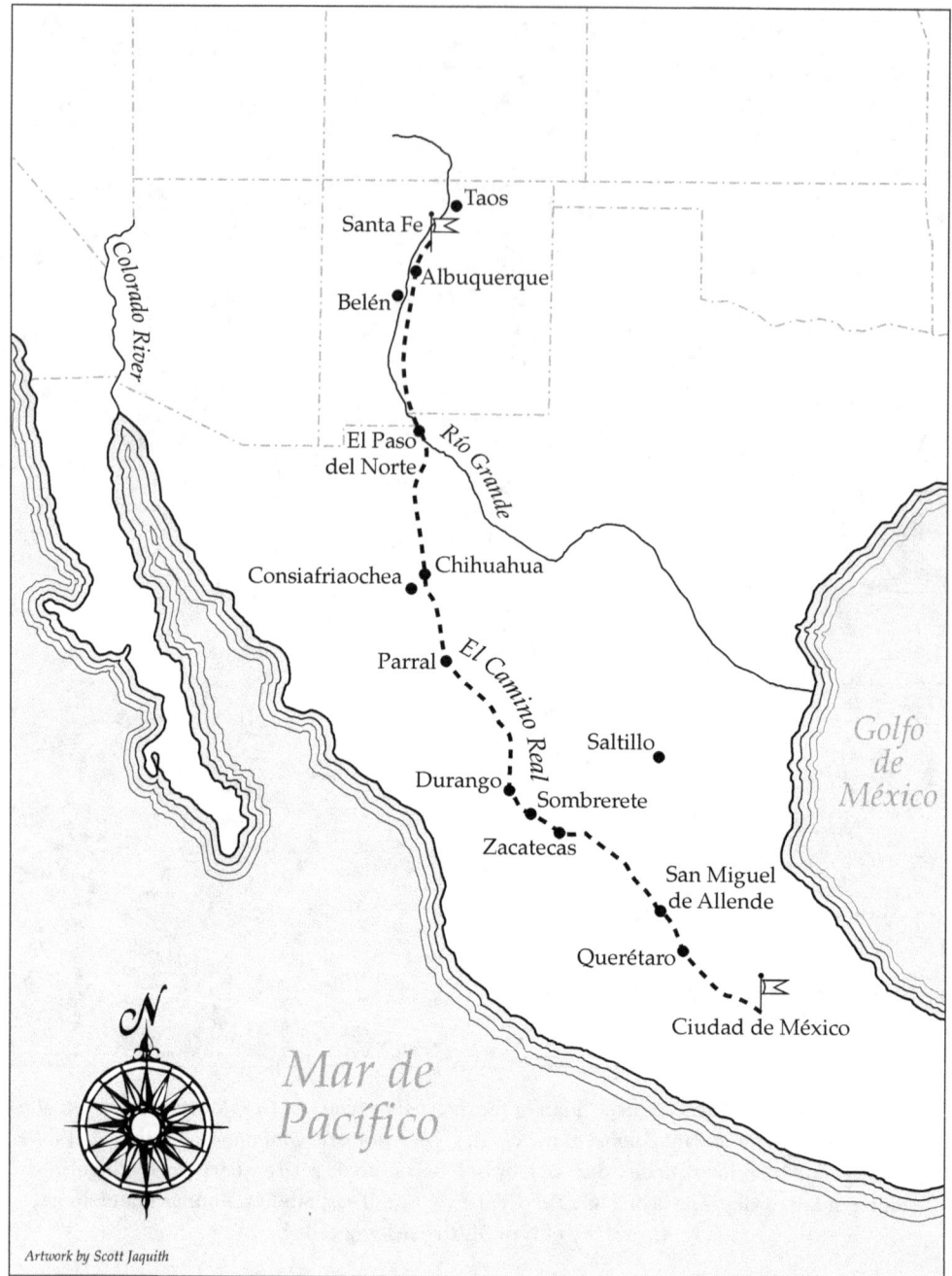

Map 3. Central and Northern New Spain in the Eighteenth Century. Prepared by Scott Jaquith.

Documents from the Spanish Colonial Archives of New Mexico, 1705–1774

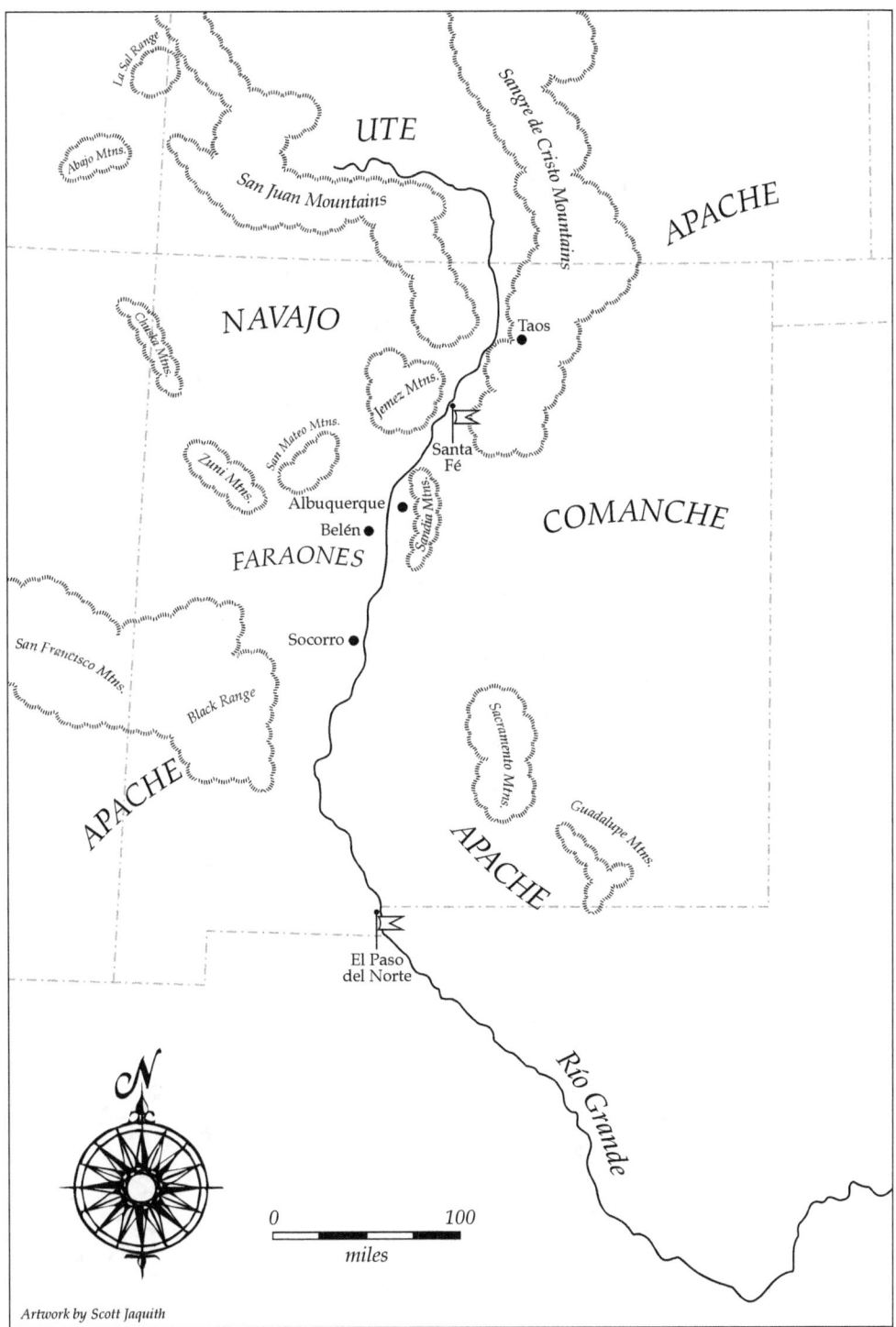

Map 4. General Locations of Roving Indian Tribes in the Early and Mid-Eighteenth Century. Prepared by Scott Jaquith.

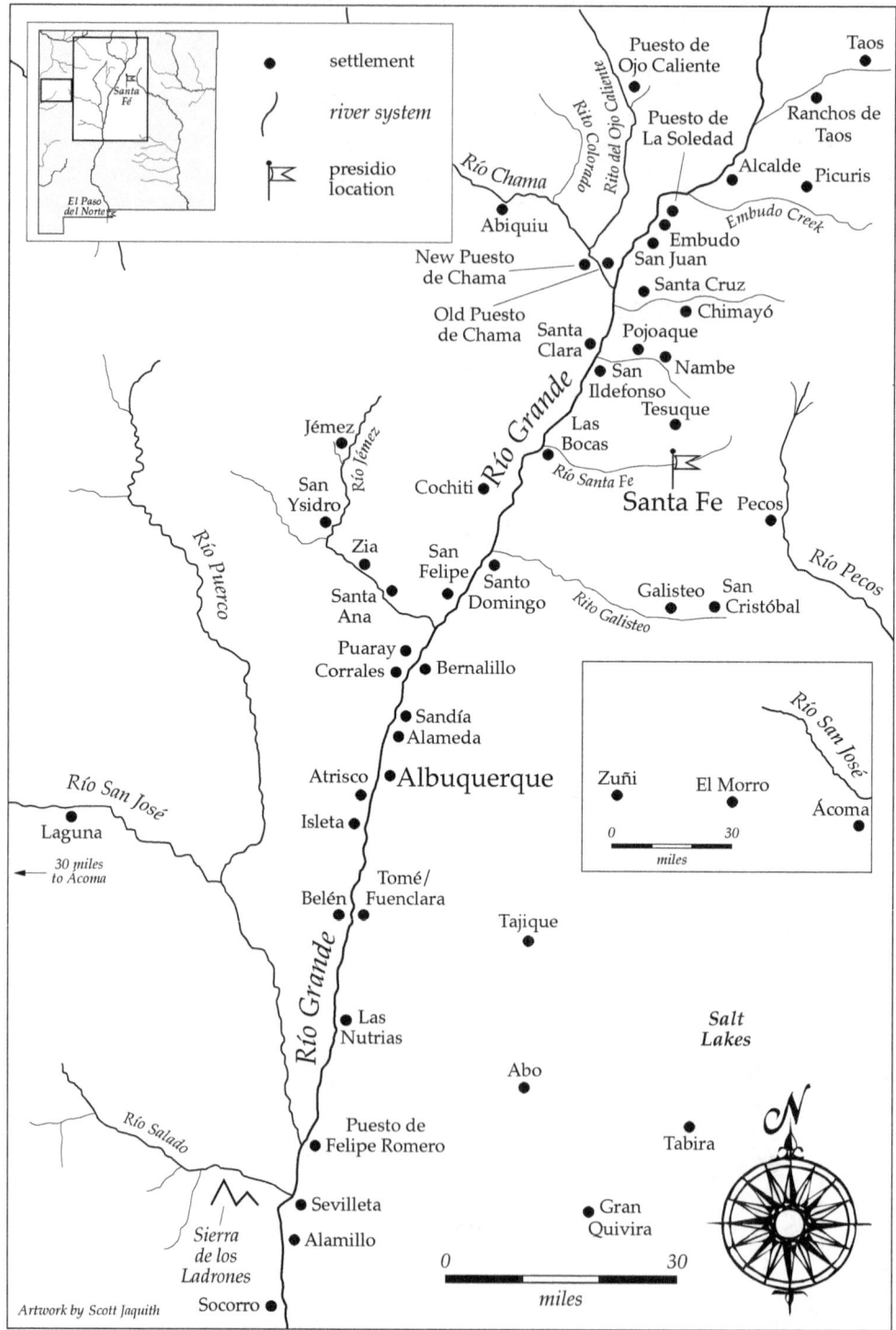

Map 5. New Mexico in the Early and Mid-Eighteenth Century, Upper Río Grande. Prepared by Scott Jaquith.

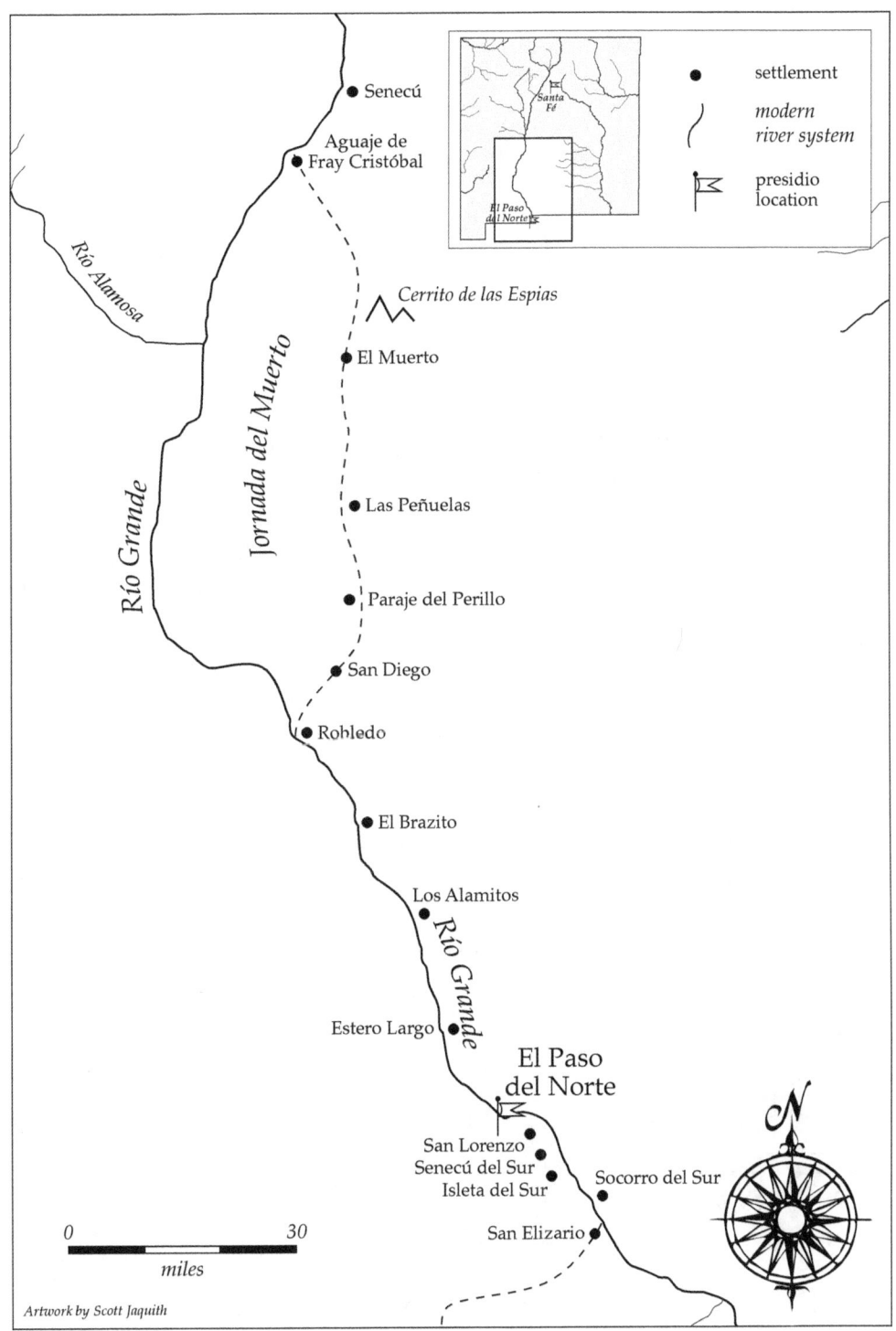

Map 6. New Mexico in the Early and Mid-Eighteenth Century, Lower Río Grande.
Prepared by Scott Jaquith.

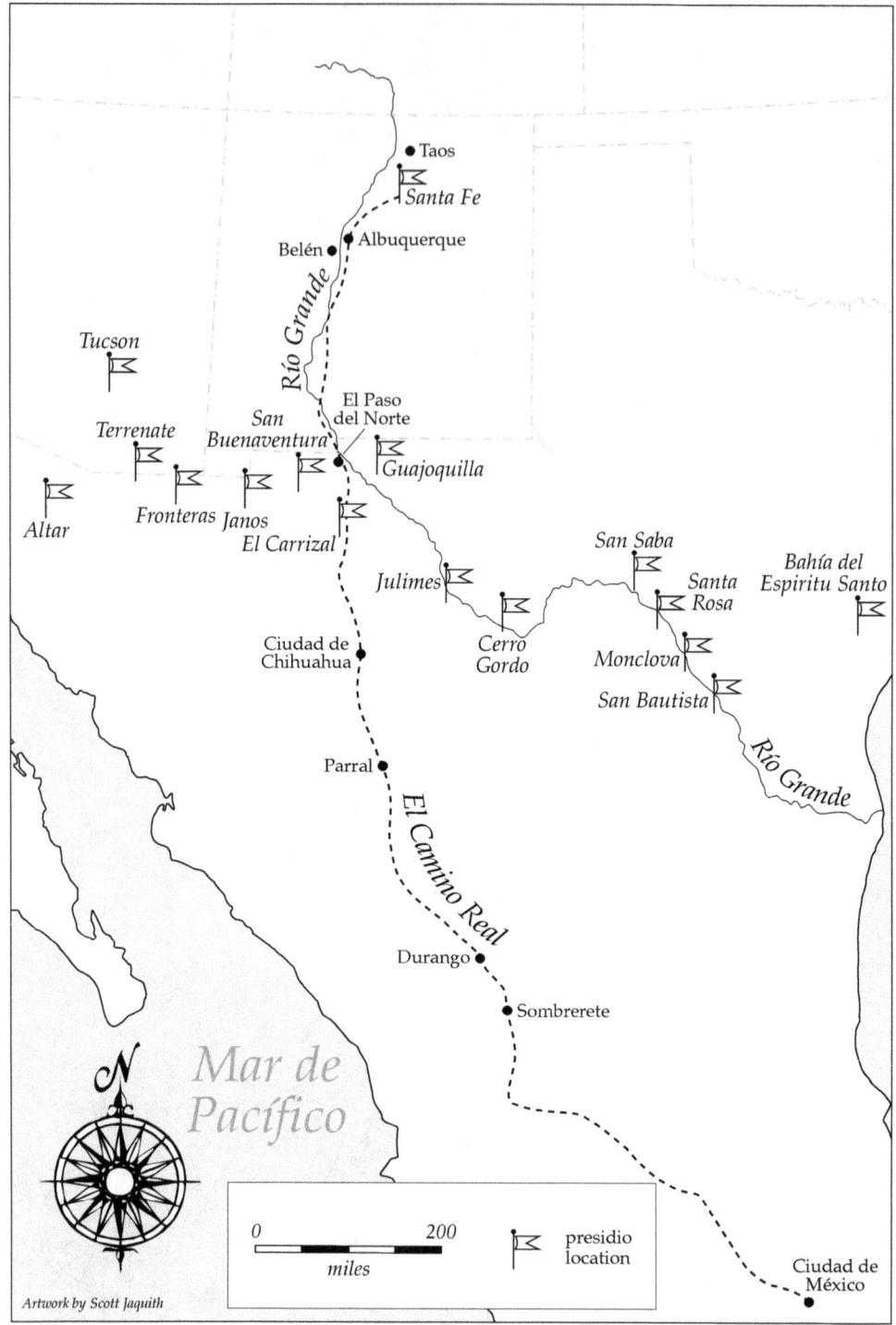

Map 7. Borderland Presidios in the Mid-Eighteenth Century. Prepared by Scott Jaquith.

BIBLIOGRAPHY

ARCHIVAL MATERIALS

Archivo General de la Nación, Mexico City, México. Documents at the Center for Southwest Research, University of New Mexico, Albuquerque, New Mexico.

Fray Angélico Chávez Collection, Archives and Historical Services Division, State Records Center and Archives, Santa Fe, New Mexico.

Law of the Territory of New Mexico, New Mexico Supreme Court Library, Santa Fe, New Mexico.

Pinart Collection, Bancroft Library, University of California, Berkeley. Schedule at the Center for Southwest Research, University of New Mexico, Albuquerque.

Ritch Collection, Henry E. Huntington Library, San Marino, California. Documents at the Center for Southwest Research, University of New Mexico, Albuquerque.

Spanish Archives of New Mexico I and II, Archives and Historical Services Division, State Records Center and Archives, Santa Fe, New Mexico.

Twitchell Collection, Center for Southwest Research, University of New Mexico, Albuquerque.

BOOKS, ARTICLES, AND MISCELLANEOUS MATERIALS

Adams, Eleanor, B., ed. "Bishop Tamarón's Visitation of New Mexico, 1760." *Historical Society of New Mexico* 15 (February 1954). Albuquerque: University of New Mexico.

Adams, Eleanor, B., and Fray Angélico Chávez, eds. and trans. *The Missions of New Mexico, 1776: A Description by Fray Francisco Atanasio Domínguez, with Other Contemporary Documents*. New Edition. Santa Fe: Sunstone Press, 2012.

Alexander, Francelle E. *Among the Cottonwoods: The Enduring Rio Abajo Villages of Peralta & Los Pinos, New Mexico before 1940*. Los Ranchos, New Mexico: Rio Grande Books, 2012.

Archer, Christon I. *The Army in Bourbon Mexico, 1760–1800*. Albuquerque: University of New Mexico Press, 1977.

Bandelier, Adolph F. A., and Fanny R. Bandelier. *Historical Documents relating to New Mexico, Nueva Vizcaya and Approaches Thereto*. Washington: Carnegie Institution of Washington, 1937.

Bannon, John Francis. *The Spanish Borderlands Frontier, 1512–1821*. Albuquerque: University of New Mexico Press, 1963.

Barrett, Elinore M. *Conquest and Catastrophe: Changing Rio Grande Pueblo Settlement Patterns in the Sixteenth and Seventeenth Centuries*. Albuquerque: University of New Mexico Press, 2002.

———. *The Spanish Colonial Settlement Landscapes of New Mexico, 1598–1680*. Albuquerque: University of New Mexico Press, 2012.

Baxter, John O. *Las Carneradas*. Albuquerque: University of New Mexico Press, 1987.

———. *Spanish Irrigation in the Pojoaque and Tesuque Valleys, during the Eighteenth and Early Nineteenth Centuries*. Santa Fe: Office of the State Engineer, 1984.

Behar, Ruth. "Sexual Witchcraft, Colonialism, and Women's Powers: Views from the Mexican Inquisition." In *Sexuality and Marriage in Colonial Latin America,* edited by Asunción Lavrin. Lincoln: University of Nebraska Press, 1989.

Blackhawk, Ned. "Violence over the Land: Colonial Encounters in the American Great Basin." PhD dissertation, University of Washington, 1999.

Bloom, Lansing B. "Alburquerque & Galisteo, Certificate of Their Founding." *New Mexico Historical Review* 10 (1, June 1935): 48-51.

———. "New Mexico under Mexican Administration, 1821–1846." *Old Santa Fe* 1 (1, July 1913): 16.

Blyth, Lance R. "Los Vaqueros Buenos: The Presidial Soldiers of Santa Fe, 1778–1805." Thesis, Colorado State University, Fort Collins, 1997.

Bolton, Herbert E. *Pageant in the Wilderness: The Story of the Escalante Expedition to the Interior Basin, 1776*. Salt Lake City: Utah State Historical Society, 1950.

Boyd-Bowman, Peter. "Spanish Soldier's Estate in Northern NM (1642)," *Hispanic American Historical Review* 53 (1, February 1973): 95-105.

Brand, Donald D. "The Early History of the Range Cattle Industry in Northern Mexico." *Agricultural History* 35 (3, July 1961): 132-39.

Brayer, Herbert O. *Pueblo Indian Land Grants of the "Rio Abajo," New Mexico*. Albuquerque: University of New Mexico Press, 1939.

Brinkerhoff, Sidney, and Odie B. Faulk. *Lancers of the King*. Phoenix: Arizona Historical Foundation, 1965.

Brooks, James F. "This Evil Extends Especially to the Feminine Sex, Negotiating Captivity in the New Mexico Borderlands." *Feminist Studies* 22 (2, summer 1996): 279-303.

Brugge, David M. "Captives and Slaves on the Camino Real." In *El Camino Real de Tierra Adentro*, Vol. 2, essays compiled by Gabrielle G. Palmer and Stephen L. Fosberg. Santa Fe: New Mexico State Office, Bureau of Land Management, 1999.

Burkholder, Mark A. "The Council of the Indies in the Late 18th Century: A New Perspective." *Hispanic American Historical Review* 56 (3): 404-23.

———. *From Impotence to Authority: The Spanish Crown and the American Audiencias, 1687–1808*. Columbia: University of Missouri Press, 1977.

Bustamante, Adrian. "The Matter Was Never Resolved: The *Casta* System in Colonial New Mexico, 1693–1823." *New Mexican Historical Review* 66 (2, April 1991): 143-63.

Calloway, Colin G. *One Vast Winter Count*. Lincoln: University of Nebraska Press, 2003.

Cámara, Luis Millet. "Logwood and Archaeology in Campeche." *Journal of Anthropological Research* 40 (2, summer 1984): 324-28.

Candelaria, Juan. "Information Communicated by Juan Candelaria, Resident of This Villa de San Francisco Xavior de Alburquerque." *New Mexico Historical Review* 4 (3, July 1939): 274-97.

Cañeque, Alejandro. *The King's Living Image*. New York: Routledge, 2004.

Carter, William B. *Indian Alliances and the Spanish in the Southwest, 750-1750*. Norman: University of Oklahoma Press, 2009.

Chávez, Fray Angélico. "De Vargas' Negro Drummer." *El Palacio* 56 (May 1949): 131-38.

———. *Archives of the Archdiocese of Santa Fe*. Washington: Academy of American Franciscan History, 1957.

———. *Origins of New Mexico Families*. Santa Fe: William Gannon, 1975.

———. "Genízaros." In *Handbook of North American Indians*, Vol. 9, *Southwest*, edited by Alfonzo Ortiz. Washington: Smithsonian Institution, 1979.

———. *New Mexico Roots, Ltd*. Santa Fe: Museum of New Mexico Press, 1982.

———. "Some Mission Records and Villasur." In *A Moment in Time: The Odyssey of New Mexico's Segesser Hide Paintings*, edited by Thomas E. Chávez. Los Ranchos, New Mexico: Rio Grande Press, 2012.

Chávez, Thomas E., ed. *A Moment in Time: The Odyssey of New Mexico's Segesser Hide Paintings*. Los Ranchos, New Mexico: Rio Grande Press, 2012.

Chávez, Tibo J. "Early Witchcraft in New Mexico." *El Palacio* 76 (3, 1969): 7-9.

Christmas, Henrietta. "Alcalde, Nerio Antonio Montoya." *Herencia* 20 (4, 2012): 2-23.

Christmas, Henrietta, extractor and compiler. *Military Records. Colonial New Mexico. Notas y Revistas*. Albuquerque: Hispanic Genealogical Research Center, 2004.

Christmas, Henrietta Martinez, compiler. *The Santa Fe Presidio Soldiers: Their Donation to the American Revolution*. Albuquerque: New Mexico Genealogical Society, 2006.

Christmas, Henrietta Martinez, and Patricia Sanchez Rau. "Una Lista de Soldados: Presidio de Santa Fe, 1712–1719." *New Mexico Genealogist* 42 (4, December 2003): 195, 201).

———. *The Early Pojoaque Valley: Labradores, Jornaleros y Artesanos*. Hispanic Genealogical Research Center of Albuquerque, 2004.

———. *Early Settlers of La Cienega: A Family History*. Revised edition. Hispanic Genealogical Research Center of Albuquerque, 2008.

Christmas, Henrietta Martinez, Jeanette Gallegos, and Patricia S. Rau. *New Mexico Burials, Santa Fe–St. Francis Parish and Military Chapel of Our Lady of Light (La Castrense), 1726-1834*. Albuquerque: New Mexico Genealogical Society, 1997.

Cisneros, Jose. *Riders across the Centuries: Horsemen of the Spanish Borderlands*. University of Texas Press at El Paso, 1984.

Colligan, John B. *The Juan Páes Hurtado Expedition of 1695*. Albuquerque: University of New Mexico Press, 1995.

Crouch, Dora P., Daniel J. Carr, and Alex I. Mendijo. *Spanish City Planning in North America*. Cambridge: MIT Press, 1982.

Cruz, Gilbert R. *Let There Be Towns: Spanish Municipal Origins in the American Southwest, 1610–1810*. College Station: Texas A&M University Press, 1988.

Curtin, Philip. *Cross-Cultural Trade in World History*. Cambridge University Press, 1984.

Cutter, Charles. *The Protector de Indios in Colonial New Mexico, 1659–1821*. Albuquerque: University of New Mexico Press, 1986.

———. *The Legal Culture of Northern New Spain, 1700–1810*. Albuquerque: University of New Mexico Press, 1995.

Cutter, Donald, and Iris Engstrand. *Quest for Empire: Spanish Settlement in the Southwest*. Golden, Colorado: Fulcrum Publishing, 1996.

Dean, Carolyn. *Inka Bodies and the Body of Christ: Corpus Christi on Colonila Cuzco, Peru*. Durham: Duke University Press, 1999.

De la Teja, Jesús, and Ross Frank, eds. *Choice, Persuasion, and Coercion: Social Control on Spain's North American Frontiers*. Albuquerque: University of New Mexico Press, 2005.

Dictionary of the English Language, Unabridged. Springfield, Massachusetts: Merriam Webster, 1986.

Don, Patricia Lopes. *Bonfires of Culture: Franciscans, Indigenous Leaders, and Inquisition in Early Mexico, 1524–1540*. Norman: University of Oklahoma Press, 2010.

Dory-Garduño, James E. "The 1766 Ojo del Espiritu Santo Grant: Authenticating a New Mexico Land Grant." *Colonial Latin American Historical Review* 16 (2, 2007): 157-96.

Dunmire, William W. "New Mexico's Spanish Livestock Heritage." In *Sunshine and Shadows in New Mexico's Past, the Spanish Colonial and Mexican Periods, 1540–1848*, edited by Richard Melzer. 2 vols. Los Ranchos, New Mexico: Rio Grande Books in collaboration with the Historical Society of New Mexico, 2010.

Dusenberry, William H. *The Mexican Mesta: The Administration of Ranching in Colonial Mexico*. Urbana: University of Illinois Press, 1963.

Ebright, Malcolm. *Land Grants and Lawsuits in Northern New Mexico*. Albuquerque: University of New Mexico Press, 1994.

———. "Advocates for the Oppressed: Indians, Genizaros & Their Spanish Advocates, 1700–1786." *New Mexico Historical Review* 71 (3, October 1996): 305-39.

———. "Sharing the Shortages: Water Litigation and Regulation in Hispanic New Mexico, 1600–1850." *New Mexico Historical Review* 75 (1, January 2001): 2-45.

Ebright, Malcolm, and Rick Hendricks. *The Witches of Abiquiu, the Governor, the Priest, the Genizaro Indians, and the Devil*. Albuquerque: University of New Mexico Press, 2006.

Ebright, Malcolm, Teresa Escudero, and Rick Hendricks. "Tomas Vélez Cachupín's Last Will and Testament, His Career in New Mexico, and His Sword with a Golden Hilt." *New Mexico Historical Review* 78 (3, 2003): 285-321.

Egan, Martha. *Relicarios: Devotional Miniatures from the Americas*. Santa Fe: Museum of New Mexico Press, 1993.

Eidenbach, Peter L. *An Atlas of Historic New Mexico Maps, 1550–1941*. Albuquerque: University of New Mexico Press, 2012.

Ellis, R. Stewart. "Santa Cruz: Authority and Community Response in the History of New Mexico Town." PhD dissertation, University of Oklahoma, 1980.

Encyclopedia Britannica. 15th edition. 2006.

———. Online article accessed February 16, 2013.

Espinosa, Carmine. *Shawls, Crinolines, Filagree: The Dress and Adornment of the Women of New Mexico, 1739–1900*. El Paso: Texas Western Press, 1970.

Esquibel, José Antonio. "Residents Traveling from New Mexico, 1712–1716." *New Mexico Genealogist* 35 (3, September 1996): 75-81.

———. "Mexico City to Santa Fe: Spanish Pioneers on the Camino Real, 1693–1694." In *El Camino Real de Tierra Adentro*, Vol. 2, essays compiled by Gabrielle G. Palmer and Stephen L. Fosberg. Santa Fe: New Mexico State Office, Bureau of Land Management, 1999.

———. "Descendants of Hernán Martín Serrano in New Mexico: Part I." *New Mexico Genealogist* 51 (4, 2012): 159-71.

———. "The Romo de Vera Ancestry: Part I," *Herencia* 20 (4, 2012): 41-45.

———. "The Romo de Vera Ancestry: Part II," *Herencia* 21 (1, 2013): 20-28.

Fehrenbach, T. R. *Comanches*. New York: Anchor Books, 1974.

Fisch, Olga. *Danzantes de Corpus Christi*. Donación de Olga Fisch al Museo del Banco Central del Ecuador, 1985.

Flagler, Edward K. "Governor Jose Chacón." *New Mexico Historical Review* 65 (4, October 1990): 455-75.

———. "Defensive Policy and Indian Relations in New Mexico during the Tenure of Governor Francisco Cuervo y Valdés, 1705–1707." *Revista Española de Antropología Americana* 22 (1992): 89-104.

Flint, Richard. "La Salina of the Estancia Valley, New Mexico." *New Mexico Historical Review* 83 (1, 2008): 39-55.

Foote, Cheryl. "Spanish-Indian Trade along New Mexico's Northern Frontier in the 18th Century." *Journal of the West* 24 (2, April 1985).

Franco, John Klingemann. "Blacks in Northern New Spain." *Journal of Big Bend Studies* 16 (2004): 47-58.

Frank, Ross. "From Settler to Citizen: Economic Development and the Cultural Change in Late Colonial New Mexico, 1750–1820." PhD dissertation, University of California Press, Berkeley, 1992.

———. *From Settler to Citizen: New Mexican Economic Development and the Creation of Vecino Society, 1750–1820*. Berkeley: University of California Press, 2000.

Gallegos, Albert, and Jose Antonio Esquibel. "Alcaldes and Mayors of Santa Fe, 1613–2008." In *All Trails Lead to Santa Fe*. Santa Fe: Sunstone Press, 2010.

Garate, Donald T. *Juan Bautista de Anza*. Reno: University of Nevada Press, 2003.

Gavin, Robin, Donna Pierce, and Alfonso Pleguezuelo, eds. *Cerámica y Cultura: The Story of Spanish and Mexican Mayolica*. Albuquerque: University of New Mexico Press, 2003.

Góngora, Mario. *Studies in the Colonial History of Spanish America*. Cambridge University Press, 1975.

Greenfield, Myrtle. *A History of Public Health in New Mexico*. Albuquerque: University of New Mexico Press, 1962.

Greenleaf, Richard E. "The Founding of Albuquerque, 1706." *New Mexico Historical Review* 39 (1, 1964): 1-15.

———. "Atrisco and Las Ciruelas, 1723–1769." *New Mexico Historical Review* 61 (1, 1987): 5-25.

———. "The Obraje in the Last Mexican Colony." *The Americas* 23 (3, 1967): 227-50.

———. "The Inquisition in Eighteenth Century New Mexico." *New Mexico Historical Review* 60 (1, 1985): 29-60.

Guggino, Patty. "Los Lentes." Written for the New Mexico Office of the State Historian. Internet article accessed October 2, 2012.

Gutiérrez, Rámon A. *When Jesus Came, the Corn Mothers Went Away: Marriage, Sexuality, and Power in New Mexico, 1500–1846.* Stanford: Stanford University Press, 1991.

———. "Women on Top: The Love Magic of the Indian Witches of New Mexico." *Journal of the History of Sexuality* 16 (3, 2007): 373-90.

Hackett, Charles Wilson. *Historical Documents relating to New Mexico, Nueva Vizcaya, and Approaches Thereto, to 1773.* 3 vols. Washington: Carnegie Institution of Washington, 1937.

Hadley, Diana, Thomas H. Naylor, and Mardith K. Schuetz-Miller. *The Presidio and Militia on the Northern Frontier of New Spain: A Documentary History.* Vol. 2, Part 2, *The Central Corridor and the Texas Corridor, 1700–1765.* Tucson: University of Arizona Press, 1997.

Haggard, J. Villasana. *Handbook for Translators of Spanish Colonial Documents.* Austin: University of Texas, 1941.

Hämäläinen, Pekka. *The Comanche Empire.* New Haven and London: Yale University Press, 2008.

Hammond, George P., and Agapito Rey. *Oñate, Colonizer of New Mexico, 1595–1628.* Albuquerque: University of New Mexico Press, 1953.

Hammond, George P., and Agapito Rey, eds. *The Rediscovery of New Mexico.* Albuquerque: University of New Mexico Press, 1995.

Hamnett, Brian R. *The Mexican Bureaucracy before the Bourbon Reforms,1700–1770: A Study in the Limitations of Absolutism.* Occasional Papers, No. 26. University of Glasgow Press, 1979.

———. *Politics and Trade in Southern Mexico, 1750–1821.* Cambridge University Press, 1971.

Hanke, Lewis. *Spanish Viceroys in America: The Smith History Lecture.* Houston: University of St. Thomas Press, 1972.

Hardwick, Michael R. "Arms and Armament: Presidios of California." Document available from the author. Revised January 20, 2010.

Hendricks, Rick. "The Last Years of Francisco Cuervo y Valdés, 1707–1714." In *Sunshine and Shadows in New Mexico's Past: The Spanish Colonial and Mexican Periods, 1540–1848*, edited by Richard Meltzer. Los Ranchos, New Mexico: Rio Grande Books, 2010.

———. "Early Livestock Brands in El Paso de Norte." *Password* 45 (3, 2000): 107-16.

———. "Antonio de Valverde Cosio." In *American National Bibliography* 22 (1999): 148-49.

———. "Pedro de Villasur." In *American National Bibliography* 22 (1999): 365-66.

Hendricks, Rick, and Gerald Mandell. "The Apache Slave Trade in Parral." *Journal of Big Bend Studies* 16 (2004): 59-82.

———. "Allegations of Extortion: New Mexico Residencias of the Mid-1600s." *New Mexico Historical Review* 80 (1, 2005): 1-18.

Hendricks, Rick, and John P. Wilson. *The Navajos in 1705: Roque Madrid's Campaign Journal*. Albuquerque: University of New Mexico Press, 1996.

Hodge, Frederick Webb, George P. Hammond, and Agapito Rey. *Alonso de Benavides' Revised Memorial of 1634*. Albuquerque: University of New Mexico Press, 1945; México: Archivo General de la Nación, *Inquisición*, Vol. 356.

Horvath, Steven. "The Social and Political Organization of the Genízaros of the Plaza de Nuestra Señora de los Dolores de Belén, New Mexico, 1740–1812." PhD dissertation, Brown University, 1979.

Hotz, Gottfried. *The Segesser Hide Paintings*. Santa Fe: Museum of New Mexico Press, 1970.

Humboldt, Alexander de. *Ensayo político sobre el Reino de la Nueva España, Tomo V: Atlas*. México: Editorial Pedro Robredo, 1941.

Jackson, Hal. *Following the Royal Road: A Guide to the Historic Camino Real de Tierra Adentro*. Albuquerque: University of New Mexico Press, 2005.

Jenkins, Myra Ellen. "Taos Pueblo & Its Neighbors, 1520–1847." *New Mexico Historical Review* 41 (1966): 85-114.

———. "Spanish Land Grants in the Tewa Area." *New Mexico Historical Review* 47 (1972): 113-34.

———. "Some 18th Century New Mexican Women of Property." In *Hispanic Arts & Ethnohistory in the Southwest*. Santa Fe: Ancient City Press, 1983.

John, Elizabeth A. H. *Storms Brewed in Other Men's Worlds*. Lincoln: University of Nebraska Press, 1975.

John, Elizabeth A. H., ed., and John Wheat, trans. *Views from the Apache Frontier: Report on the Northern Provinces of New Spain by Jose Cortés*. Norman: University of Oklahoma Press, 1989.

Jones, Kenneth Warren. "New Spain and the Viceregency of the Marqués de Casafuerte, 1922–1734." PhD dissertation. University of California, Santa Barbara, 1971.

Jones, Oakah, Jr. *Pueblo Warriors & Spanish Conquest*. Norman: University of Oklahoma Press, 1966.

———. *Los Paisanos: Spanish Settlers on the Northern Frontier of New Spain*. Norman: University of Oklahoma Press, 1979.

———. "Rescue and Ransom of Spanish Captives from the Indios Bárbaros on the Northern Frontier of New Spain." *Colonial Latin American Historical Review* 4 (2, 1995): 128-48.

Kagan, Richard L. *Urban Images of the Hispanic World, 1493–1793*. New Haven: Yale University Press, 2003.

Kamen, Henry. *Spain's Road to Empire: How Spain Became a World Power, 1492–1763*. New York: Harper Collins Press, 2003.

Kantor, Deborah E. *Hijos del Pueblo: Gender, Family, and Community in Rural Mexico, 1730–1850*. Austin: University of Texas Press, 2008.

Katzew, Ilona. *Contested Visions in the Spanish Colonial World*. New Haven: Yale University Press, 2012.

Kessell, John. *Kiva, Cross, and Crown*. Albuquerque: University of New Mexico Press, 1987.

———, ed. *Remote Beyond Compare*. Albuquerque: University of New Mexico Press, 1989.

———. *Spain in the Southwest.* Norman: University of Oklahoma Press, 2002.

———. *Pueblos, Spaniards, and the Kingdom of New Mexico.* Norman: University of Oklahoma Press, 2008.

———. "A Long Time Coming: The Seventeenth-Century Pueblo-Spanish War." *New Mexico Historical Review* 86 (2, 2011): 141-56.

Kessell, John, and Rick Hendricks, eds. *By Force of Arms: The Journals of don Diego de Vargas, New Mexico.* Albuquerque: University of New Mexico Press, 1992.

———. *To the Royal Crown Restored: The Journals of don Diego de Vargas, New Mexico, 1692–1694.* Albuquerque: University of New Mexico Press, 1995.

Kessell, John L., Rick Hendricks, and Meredith D. Dodge, eds. *Blood on the Boulders: The Journals of don Diego de Vargas, New Mexico, 1694–1697.* Books 1 and 2. Albuquerque: University of New Mexico Press, 1998.

Kessell, John L., Rick Hendricks, Meredith D. Dodge, and Larry Miller, eds. *That Disturbances Cease: The Journals of don Diego de Vargas, New Mexico, 1697–1700.* Albuquerque: University of New Mexico Press, 2000.

———. *A Settling of Accounts: The Journals of don Diego de Vargas, New Mexico, 1700–1704.* Albuquerque: University of New Mexico Press, 2003.

Kinnaird, Lawrence. "The Spanish Tobacco Monopoly in New Mexico, 1766–67." *New Mexico Historical Review* 21 (October 1946): 328-39.

Kraemer, Paul. "New Mexico's Ancient Salt Trade." *El Palacio* 82 (1, 1976).

Kubler, George. *The Rebuilding of San Miguel at Santa Fe in 1710.* Colorado Springs: Taylor Museum, 1939.

Lamadrid, Enrique, and J. Gurule. "The Threads of Memory: Kingdoms and Nations in Paper and Ink." *El Palacio* 115 (3, fall 2010): 40-45.

Lavrin, Asuncíon, ed. *Sexuality and Marriage in Colonial Latin America.* Lincoln: University of Nebraska. 1989.

Lavrin, Asuncíon, and Edith Couturier. "Dowries and Wills: A View of Women's Socioeconomic Role in Colonial Guadalajara and Puebla, 1640–1790." *Hispanic American Historical Review* 50 (5, 1979): 280-304.

Lea, Henry Charles. *A History of the Inquisition of Spain.* 2 vols. New York: Macmillan, 1906.

Marshall, Michael P., and Henry J. Walt. *Rio Abajo: Prehistory and History of a Rio Grande Province.* Santa Fe: New Mexico Historic Preservation Program, Historic Preservation Division, 1984.

Martinez, Robert D. "Fray Juan José Toledo and the Devil in Spanish New Mexico: A Story of Witchcraft and Cultural Conflict in Eighteenth Century Abiquiu." Master's thesis, University of New Mexico, Albuquerque, 1997.

Martinez, Robert D., and José Antonio Esquibel. "Villalpando Family Origins." *New Mexico Genealogist* 51 (4, 2012): 182-91.

Mather, Christine, ed. *Colonial Frontiers: Art and Life in Spanish New Mexico. The Fred Harvey Collection.* Santa Fe: Ancient City Press, New Mexico, 1986.

McAlister, Lyle N. *The Fuero Military in New Spain.* Gainesville: University of Florida Press, 1957.

McDonald, Dedra S. "Intimacy and Empire: Indian-African Interaction in Spanish Colonial New Mexico. In *Sunshine and Shadows in New Mexico's Past*, Vol. 1, *The Spanish Colonial and Mexican Periods, 1540–1848*, edited by Richard Melzer. Los Ranchos, New Mexico: Rio Grande Press, 2010.

Melzer, Richard, ed. *Sunshine and Shadows in New Mexico's Past*. Vol. 1, *The Spanish Colonial and Mexican Periods, 1540–1848*. Los Ranchos, New Mexico: Rio Grande Press, 2010.

Miera y Pacheco, Bernardo. "Memorial sobre mis servicios" in Ayer Manuscripts, No. 1165, Newberry Library, Chicago, no date.

Montaño, Mary. *Tradiciones Nuevomexicanas: Hispano Arts and Culture of New Mexico*. Albuquerque: University of New Mexico Press, 2001.

Moorhead, Max L. *New Mexico's Royal Road: Trade and Travel on the Chihuahua Trail*. Norman: University of Oklahoma Press, 1958.

———. *The Apache Frontier: Jacobo Ugarte and Spanish-Indian Relations in Northern New Spain, 1769–1791*. Norman: University of Oklahoma Press, 1968.

———. *The Presidio, Bastion of the Spanish Borderlands*. Norman: University of Oklahoma Press, 1975.

———. "The Soldado de Cueva: Stalwart of the Spanish Borderlands." *Journal of the West* 8 (1969): 38-55.

Morrissey, Richard J. "The Northward Expansion of Cattle Ranching in New Spain, 1550–1600." *Agricultural History* 25 (3, July 1951).

Muñoz y Rivero, D. Jesús. *Paleografía popular: Arte de leer. Los documentos antiguos*. Madrid: Librería de la Viuda de Hernando, 1886.

National Park Service, Long Distance Trails' Group. *El Camino Real de Tierra Adentro National Historic Trail. Draft, Comprehensive Management Plan/Environmental Impact Statement*. National Park Service, Bureau of Land Management, United States Department of the Interior, 2002.

Naylor, Thomas H., and Charles W. Polzer. *Pedro de Rivera and the Military Regulations of Northern New Spain, 1724–1729*. Tucson: University of Arizona Press, 1988.

New Velázquez Spanish and English Dictionary. El Monte, California: Velázquez Press, 2007.

NMGS (New Mexico Genealogical Society). *New Mexico Baptisms, Santa Cruz de la Cañada Church*. Vol. 1, *1710–1794*. Albuquerque, 1994.

———. *Aquí Se Comienza: A Genealogical History of the Founding of La Villa de San Felipe de Alburquerque*. Albuquerque: New Mexico Genealogical Society, 2007.

Noble, David Grant. *Santa Fe: History of an Ancient City*. Santa Fe: School of American Research Press, 1989.

Norris, Jim. *After "the Year Eighty": The Demise of Franciscan Power in Spanish New Mexico*. Albuquerque: University of New Mexico Press in cooperation with the Academy of American Franciscan History, 2000.

———. "Franciscans Eclipsed, Church in Spanish New Mexico, 1750–1780." *New Mexico Historical Review* 76 (2, 2001): 162-73.

Noyes, Stanley. *Los Comanches: The Horse People, 1751–1845*. Albuquerque: University of New Mexico Press, 1992.

Ocaranza, Fernando. *Establecimientos franciscanos en el misterioso reino de Nuevo Mexico*. México, 1934.

Olmstead, Virginia Langham, compiler. "Spanish Enlistment Papers of New Mexico, 1732–1820." *National Genealogical Society Quarterly* 67 (1979): 229-36, 294-301.

———. *Spanish and Mexican Censuses of New Mexico, 1750–1830*. Albuquerque: New Mexico Genealogical Society, 1981.

Owen, Carmalee Gallegos. "A Military Family: Miera y Pacheco." *New Mexico Genealogist* 42 (4, 2003): 209-15.

Owens, Sarah E. "Journey's to Dark Lands: Francisca de los Angeles' Bilocations to the Remote Provinces of Eighteenth-Century New Spain." *Colonial Latin American Historical Review* 12 (2, 2003): 151-71.

Pacheco, Jaime, and LeRoy Anthony Reaza. "The Municipal Origins of la Villa de San Felipe el Real de Chihuahua, 1718–1725: The Cabildo's Struggle for Jurisdictional Autonomy." *New Mexico Historical Review* 80 (1, 2005): 29-53.

Padilla, Carmella, ed. *Conexiones: Connections in Spanish Colonial Art*. Santa Fe: Museum of Spanish Colonial Art, 2002.

Pagden, Anthony. *Lords of All the World: Ideologies of Empire in Spain, Britain and France c. 1500–1800*. New Haven: Yale University Press, 1995.

———. *Spanish Imperialism and the Political Imagination*. New Haven: Yale University Press, 1990.

Palmer, Gabrielle, and Donna Pierce. *Cambios: The Spirit of Transformation in Spanish Colonial Art*. Albuquerque: Santa Barbara Museum of Art in cooperation with the University of New Mexico Press, 1992.

Palmer, Gabrielle G., project director. *El Camino Real de Tierra Adrentro I*. Santa Fe: New Mexico State Office, Bureau of Land Management, Department of Interior, 1993.

Palmer, Gabrielle G., and Stephen. L. Fosberg, compilers. *El Camino Real de Tierra Adrentro II*. Santa Fe: New Mexico State Office, Bureau of Land Management, Department of Interior, 1999.

Parry, J. H. *The Sale of Public Office in the Spanish Indies under the Hapsburgs*. Berkeley and Los Angeles: University of California Press, 1953.

Payne, Melissa. "Lessons from the Rio Abajo: A Colonial Patron's Contested Legacy." *New Mexico Historical Review* 80 (4, 2005): 397-416.

Pérez-González, María Luisa. "Royal Roads in the Old and the New World: The *Camino de Oñate* and Its Importance in the Spanish Settlement of New Mexico." *Colonial Latin American Historical Review* 7 (2, 1998): 191-218.

Pierce, Donna, and Cordelia Thomas Snow. "A Harp for Playing." In *El Camino Real de Tierra Adentro*, Vol. 2, essays compiled by Gabrielle G. Palmer and Stephen L. Fosberg. Santa Fe: New Mexico State Office, Bureau of Land Management, Department of Interior, 1999.

Pierce, Donna, and Marta Weigle, eds. *Spanish New Mexico*. Vol. 1, *The Arts of Spanish New Mexico*. Santa Fe: Spanish Colonial Arts Society Collection, Museum of New Mexico Press, 1996.

Pike, Ruth. "Penal Servitude in the Spanish Empire: Presidio Labor in the Eighteenth Century." *Hispanic American Historical Review* 58 (1, 1978): 21-40.

Plewa, Tara Marie. "A Trickle Runs through It: An Environmental History of the Santa Fe River, New Mexico." PhD dissertation, University of South Carolina, 2009.

Rau, Patricia Sanchez. "José Romo de Vera, Santa Fe Soldier and Grantee." *Herencia* 20 (3, 2012): 39-48.

Rawlings, Helen. *The Spanish Inquisition*. Oxford: Blackwell Publishing, 2006.

Reinhartz, Dennis, and Gerald D. Saxon. *Mapping and Empire: Soldier-Engineers on the Southwestern Frontier*. Austin: University of New Mexico Press, 2005.

Riley, Carroll L. "Blacks in the Early Southwest." *Ethnohistory* 19 (3, summer 1972): 247-60.

Riley, James D., ed. *The Inquisition in Colonial Latin America: The Selected Writings of Richard E. Greenleaf*. Berkeley: Academy of American Franciscan History, 2010.

Rock, Rosalind Z. "Pido y Suplico: Women and the Law in Spanish New Mexico, 1697-1763." *New Mexico Historical Review* 65 (2, 1990): 145-59.

Rose, Martin, Jeffrey S. Dean, and William Robinson. *The Past Climate of Arroyo Hondo, New Mexico, Reconstructed from Tree Rings*. Santa Fe: School of American Research, 1981.

Rosenmüller, Christoph. *Patrons, Partisans, and Palace Intrigues: The Court Society of Colonial Mexico, 1702-1710*. Calgary: Alberta Foundation for the Arts, University of Calgary Press, 2008.

Sanchez, Joseph P. *Between Two Rivers: The Atrisco Land Grant in Albuquerque History, 1692-1968*. Norman: University of Oklahoma Press, 2008.

Scholes, France V. "Civil Government and Society in New Mexico in the Seventeenth Century." *New Mexico Historical Review* 10 (2, 1935): 71-111.

———. "Church and State in New Mexico, 1610-1650. Chapter III, Governor Juan de Eulate vs Friar Esteban de Perea, 1618-1626." *New Mexico Historical Review* 11 (2, 1936): 145-78.

———. "Royal Treasury Records relating to the Province of New Mexico, 1596-1683." *New Mexico Historical Review* 50 (1, 1975): 5-164.

Scholes, France V., Marc Simmons, and José Antonio Esquibel, eds. *Juan Domínguez de Mendoza, Soldier and Frontiersman of the Spanish Southwest, 1727-1693*. Translated by Eleanor B. Adams. Albuquerque: University of New Mexico Press, 2012.

Scurlock, Dan. "The Camino Real at Cerro and Plaza Tomé. In *El Camino Real de Tierra Adentro*, Vol. 2, essays compiled by Gabrielle G. Palmer and Stephen L. Fosberg. Santa Fe: New Mexico State Office, Bureau of Land Management, Department of the Interior, 1999.

Secoy, Frank Raymond. *Changing Military Patterns of the Great Plains Indians*. Lincoln: University of Nebraska Press, 1953.

Simmons, Marc. *Spanish Government in New Mexico*. Albuquerque: University of New Mexico Press, 1968.

———. *Witchcraft in New Mexico: Spanish and Indian Supernaturalism on the Rio Grande*. Lincoln: University of Nebraska, 1974.

———. "Spanish Attempts to Open a New Mexico–Sonora Road." *Arizona and the West* 17 (1, 1975): 5-20.

———. *Albuquerque: A Narrative History*. Albuquerque: University of New Mexico Press, 1982.

———. *Southwestern Colonial Ironwork: The Spanish Blacksmithing Tradition*. Santa Fe: Sunstone Press, 2007.

Sisneros, Francisco. "Anna de Sandoval y Manzanares: A New Mexico Spanish Colonial Woman of Perseverance and Triumph." In *Sunshine and Shadows in New Mexico's Past: The Spanish Colonial and Mexican Periods, 1540–1848*, edited by Richard Melzer. Los Ranchos, New Mexico: Rio Grande Books in collaboration with the Historical Society of New Mexico, 2010.

Smith, Donald E. *The Viceroy of New Spain*. Berkeley: University of California Press, 1913.

Smith, Robert Sidney. "Sales Taxes in New Spain, 1575–1770." *Hispanic American Historical Review* 28 (1, February 1948).

Snow, Cordelia Thomas. "A Headdress of Pearls: Luxury Goods Imported over the Camino Real during the Seventeenth Century." In *El Camino Real de Tierra Adentro*, Vol. 1. Cultural Resources Series No. 11. Santa Fe: New Mexico Office, Bureau of Land Management, Department of Interior, 1993.

Snow, David H. "A Note on Encomienda Economics in Seventeenth Century New Mexico." In *Hispanic Arts and Ethnohistory in the Southwest*. Santa Fe: Ancient City Press, 1983.

———. "Purchased in Chihuahua for Feasts." In *El Camino Real de Tierra Adentro*, Vol. 1. Cultural Resources Series No. 11. Santa Fe: New Mexico Office, Bureau of Land Management, Department of Interior, 1993.

Snow, David H., compiler and arranger. *New Mexico's First Colonists: The 1597–1600 Enlistments for New Mexico under Juan de Oñate, Adelante & Gobernador*. Albuquerque: Hispanic Genealogical Research Center of New Mexico, 1996.

Steel, Thomas J., S.J. "Francisco Xavier Romero: A Hitherto Unknown Santero." In *A Moment in Time: The Odyssey of New Mexico's Segesser Hide Paintings*. Los Ranchos, New Mexico: Rio Grande Press, 2012.

Swann, Michael M. *Migrants in the Mexican North: Mobility, Economy, and Society in a Colonial World*. Boulder: Westview Press, 1989.

Sze, Corinne. "History of the Los Luceros Ranch, Rio Arriba County, New Mexico." Los Luceros Foundation Planning Report. Santa Fe: Los Luceros Foundation, 2000.

Taylor, Quintard. *In Search of the Racial Frontier: African-Americans in the American West*. New York: W. W. Norton, 1998.

Taylor, William B. *Drinking, Homicide and Rebellion in Colonial Mexican Villages*. Stanford University Press, 1979.

Thomas, Alfred Barnaby. "Governor Mendiñueta's Proposals for the Defense of New Mexico, 1772–1778." *New Mexico Historical Review* 5 (1931): 21-39.

———. *Forgotten Frontiers: A Study of the Spanish Indian Policy of Don Juan Bautista de Anza, Governor of New Mexico, 1777–1787*. Norman: University of Oklahoma Press, 1932.

———. *After Coronado*. Norman: University of Oklahoma, 1935.

———. *The Plains Indians and New Mexico, 1751–1778*. Albuquerque: University of New Mexico Press, 1940.

———. *Teodoro de Croix and the Northern Frontier of New Spain, 1776–1783*. Norman: University of Oklahoma, 1941.

Tigges, Linda A. "The Santa Fe Presidial Company, 1712." *New Mexico Genealogist* 50 (2, 2011): 71-76.

———. "Santa Fe Brand Registrations, 1785." *New Mexico Genealogist* 50 (3, 2011): 121-25.

———. "The Pastures of the Royal Horse Herd of the Santa Fe Presidio." In *All Trails Lead to Santa Fe*. Santa Fe: Sunstone Press, 2010.

Torok, George D. *From the Pass to the Pueblos: El Camino Real de Tierra Adentro National Historic Trail*. Santa Fe: Sunstone Press, 2012.

Tórrez, Robert J. "Crime & Punishment in Spanish Colonial New Mexico." New Mexico State Records Center and Archives, Santa Fe, May 20, 1990.

———. *UFOs over Galisteo and Other Stories of New Mexico's History*. Albuquerque: University of New Mexico, 2004.

———. "The Presidio of Santa Fe." In *Sunshine and Shadows in New Mexico's Past: The Spanish Colonial and Mexican Periods, 1540–1848*, edited by Richard Melzer. Los Ranchos: New Mexico Rio Grande Books in collaboration with the Historical Society of New Mexico, 2010.

Trigg, Heather. "Food Choice and Social Identity in Early Colonial New Mexico." *Journal of the Southwest* 46 (2, 2004): 223-52.

Twinam, Ann. *Public Lives, Private Secrets: Gender, Honor, Sexuality & Illegitimacy in Colonial Spanish America*. Stanford University Press, 1999.

Twitchell, Ralph Emerson. *The Spanish Archives of New Mexico*. 2 vols. Cedar Rapids, Iowa: Torch Press, 1914.

Tyler, Daniel. "Ejido Lands in New Mexico." In *Spanish and Mexican Land Grants and the Law*, edited by Malcolm Ebright. Manhattan, Kansas: Sunflower Press, 1987.

Tyler, S. Lyman, ed. and compiler. *The Indian Cause in the Spanish Laws of the Indies*. Salt Lake City: American West Center, University of Utah, 1980.

———. *Spanish Laws concerning Discoveries, Pacification, and Settlements among the Indians*. Salt Lake City: American West Center, University of Utah, 1980.

Vierra, Bradley J., ed. *Current Research on the Late Prehistory and Early History of New Mexico*. Albuquerque: New Mexico Archaeological Council, 1992.

Vinson, Ben, III. *Bearing Arms for His Majesty: The Free-Colored Militia in Colonial Mexico*. Stanford University Press, 2001.

———. *Black Mexico: Race and Society from Colonial to Modern Times*. Albuquerque: University of New Mexico Press, 2009.

Walz, Vina. "History of the El Paso Area, 1680–1692." PhD dissertation, University of New Mexico, 1961.

Warner, Ted J. "Don Felix Martinez and the Santa Fe Presidio." PhD dissertation, University of New Mexico, 1963.

Weber, David J. *The Spanish Frontier in North America*. New Haven: Yale University Press, 1992.

———. *Bárbaros: Spaniards and Their Savages in the Age of Enlightenment*. Yale University Press, New Haven. 2005.

Webster's New Collegiate Dictionary. Based on *Webster's New International Dictionary*, second edition. Springfield, Massachusetts: G. & C. Merriam, 1960.

Weigle, Marta, ed. *Hispanic Arts & Ethnohistory in the Southwest.* Santa Fe: Ancient City Press, 1983.

West, Eliza Howard. "The Right of Asylum in New Mexico in the Seventeenth and Eighteenth Centuries." *New Mexico Historical Review* 41 (2, 1966): 115-53.

West, Robert C. *The Mining Community in Northern New Spain: The Parral Mining District.* Berkeley and Los Angeles: University of California, 1949.

Wheat, Carl I. *Mapping the Transmississippi West.* Vol. 1, *The Spanish Entrada to the Louisiana Purchase, 1540–1861.* San Francisco: Institute of Historical Cartography, 1957.

Will de Chaparro, Martina E. "Treatment of the Dead." *New Mexico Historical Review* 79 (1, 2004): 1-29.

Wolfenstine, Manfred R. *The Manual of Brands and Marks.* Norman: University of Oklahoma Press, 1970.

Works, Martha A. "Creating Trading Places on the NM Frontier." *Geographical Review* 82 (3, July 1991): 268-81.

INDEX

Page numbers in bold refer to illustrations.

Abeytia, Antonio de, 375, 379–80, 425–26
Abeytia, Baltazar de, 264-68, 270, 293n6, 378–79, 402n12
Abeytia, Diego (vectia), 293n6, 402n12
Abeytia, Miguel de, 565, 567
Abeytia, Paulín de, 293n6, 372–74, 377, 383, 402n12
Abiquiu, 212n9; *alcaldes mayores* of, 403n17; Comanches raid on, 14; early landowners of, 403n17; and Genízaros, 27, 431; and land grants, 430n6–7, 608n19; and trade, 568; witchcraft trials in, 202
Abo Pueblo, 263, 293n5
acequias (irrigation ditches): disputes over, 23, 295–302, 308n1, 419n21, 437–43, 448n10; governor orders cleaning of, 461–62; and property access dispute, 635–36
Acoma Pueblo, 29, 104n10, 123n2, 368, 431–32, 436n1, 469n17, 530
Acuña, Juan de, **242**. *See also* Casa Fuerte, Marqués de (viceroy)
agnus dei (Lamb of God) medallion, 610–11, **612**
Aguaje de Fray Cristóbal, 132, 146n18
aguajes. See specific names
Aguilar, Nicolás de, 460n8
Aguilera Isasi, Antonio de, 36, 40n10, 44
Alameda Pueblo, 147n22, 293n2, 308n2, 420n31, 420n35, 477n2, 490n7, 638–39, 644n7–8
Alari, Juan Antonio de, 537–38, 542n5
Alari, Juan Bautista, 542n5
Alari, Miguel, 556
Albuquerque, 32n119, 33, 124n4, 159n8, 254–55, 308n6; and *acequia* dispute, 295–302, 308n1, 419n21, 420n26; as *alcaldía*, 21; Apaches in, 133–34; and attack on *alcaldes mayores*, 434; and church sanctuary, 221–23; early landowners of, 308n3, 348n7, 348n10, 420n27–28, 437, 469n11, 477n1; early settlers of, 13, 79–80, 83n9–10, 260n10, 261, 297, 299, 348n11, 419n8, 419n11, 419n16, 419n25, 420n33, 420n36–37, 468n3, 489n1, 608n8; and edicts of faith, 203; first *alcade* of, 40n7, 134, 198–99; first Franciscan friar of, 213n19; founders of, 79–80, 83n10, 134, 147n28, 195n1, 297, 308n1, 320, 348n6, 407n1–3, 419n7, 448n2, 448n9, 468n4, 469n11, 644n1; and fugitive soldiers, 91, 106–15; and García discipline case, 320–34; garrison of, 57, 448n9; and livestock, 57–58, 134, 261–62, 404–05; merchants of, 494; militia/military of, 19, 79–80, 147n28, 320, 419n7, 470–73, 478–80; and property dispute, 636, 638; protection of, 79–81; and silk clothes contract, 349, 351, 358; and textile weaving, 26; and trade, 19, 26, 368; and trade *bandos*, 408–10, 413n2, 414–16, 418n1, 529; and traders' contract, 491–500; and weapons *bando*, 198–99; and wool embargo, 465–67
Albuquerque, Duke (Viceroy) of, 16, 35–36, **37**, 58, 133
alcaldes mayores: in Albuquerque, 20–21, 42, 58, 82n6–7, 108–10, 113, 147n28, 255–56, 260n10, 261, 295–97, 300–301, 320, 322–34, 404–05, 419n10–11, 439, 442, 469n17, 471, 542n6, 644n7; and *alcaldías*, 56n6; and *bandos*, 46–48, 409–10, 528–30; and baptism of Apaches, 84–87; complaints/cases against, 437–43, 635–38; duties/roles of, 15–16, 19–23, 25, 33, 66, 295, 431, 529; and edicts of faith, 212n4; in El Paso, 40n8; on leaving the colony, 182; lieutenants of, 469n13, 644n4, 654n2; and Pedro López case, 150; of Río Arriba, 402n2, 509n6, 511; in Santa Cruz, 40n7, 42, 61–64, 66–70, 77n1, 77n7, 78n10, 90n5, 147n27, 147n33, 159n9, 166–68, 170–71, 181n3, 181n8, 197–98, 212n9, 222, 294n13, 319n12, 372, 375, 382, 403n17, 410, 421, 490n8, 493, 509n1, 509n4, 509n6, 523n4, 564, 591, 594; in Santa Fe, 40n9, 40n14, 55n1, 90n1, 90n10, 147n34, 235, 239n3, 244–46, 253–54, 260n9, 309–14, 410, 449, 462, 523n4, 529, 553n7, 579, 583n2, 608n17, 646–47, 649; in Taos, 46–48, 78n10, 90n1, 90n6, 147n23, 214, 293n4, 410, 509n6, 518, 523n4, 528, 560, 633n5; and trade, 22, 24–25, 42, 44. *See also* specific pueblos
alcaldes ordinarios (magistrates), 20, 40n9, 105n21, 133, 135, 147n33, 183, 186–89, 205
Alcalde (town of), 212n9
alcaldías (jurisdictions), 21, 56n6
alférez (ensign), 83n12, 147n26, 402n12, 420n37, 543n11, 585, 613; of Albuquerque, 159n9, 402n1, 471; at council of war, 133–34; in El Paso, 55n1, 126–29; in Moqui campaign, 124n4; as paid position, 15; of Santa Cruz, 167, 222–23; of Santa Fe, 40n9, 90n7, 124n8, 146n4, 151, 245, 379, 538, 542n4, 552n3, 552n6, 577, 607n1
alguacil mayor (chief constable), 40n10, 90n8, 124n4, 181n8, 183, 203, 210–11, 213n15, 293n3
Alire, Miguel de, 473, 480
Alirid, Miguel de. *See* Alari, Miguel
alms, 159n1, 577
Álvarez, Juan, 202
Alvear y Collado, Thomas de, 493, 500, 518–19
ammunition: bullet mold for, 559; cannon balls, 559–60; gunpowder, 33, 35, 263, 265, 267, 272, 274–75, 319n12, 471, 546, 558–60; musket balls, 253, 256, 472; powder cartridges, 558; of presidios, 558–60
amnesty, 221–28, 233n1
Anaya, Joachín de, 264, 266–68, 293n7
Anaya Almazán, Francisco de, 293n7
animal skins, 153, 239n2; buffalo, 24, 26–27, 42, 56n3, 56n5, 239n2, 371–72, 375–76, 379, 384; deer, 26, 56n3; and gambling debts, 61–66, 68; prices of, 524, 527, 535n3, 584–85, 587–88, 590, 608n14; as sign of peace, 131; trader sues for, 584–97, 608n12, 609n21; trading of, 24–26, 42, 56n3, 56n5, 56n8, 368–69, 371–72, 374–77, 384, 423, 524, 526–27, 535n3, 542n4, 563, 565, 567, 569, 576n7; wolf, 93, 104n5
Anza, Governor Juan Bautista de, 28, 510
Apaches, 13, 56n8; baptism of, 84–87; campaigns against, 14, 57, 84, 125, 471, 517; and the Comanches, 14; and council of war, 132–36; discouraged from ambushes, 214–15; and Genízaro settlements, 431; harass military escort, 125–36; keeping peace with, 131–35, 526–27; kill Pueblo Indians, 218; kill settlers, 82n6, 85, 125, 134, 552n5; raid settlers, 33–34, 79–80, 107, 149, 404, 471; and Sandía Pueblo, 293n2; settlers' trading/selling of, 84, 251–52, 255, 261, 535n1; steal horses/livestock, 57–58, 60n1, 80, 125, 127–30, 134; and trade, 23, 27, 42, 45, 526
Apodaca, Joseph de, 324–31, 333
Apodaca, María Gonzales, 104n2
Apodaca, Sebastián de, 473, 480, 482n8
apprenticeships, 235–37
Aragón, Andrés, 415, 419n22
Aragón, Bárbara, 448n9
Aragón, Ignacio, 366n2
Aragón, Juan de, 163
Aragón, Margarita, 349–51, 356–57, 367n10
Aragón, María de, 90n7
Aragón, Nicolás de, 349–58, 366n2, 367n10–11, 466
Aramburu, Antonio de, 442, 467
Archibeque, Antonia Juliana, 542n7
Archibeque, Juan de: and Apache attack, 127–29; biography of, 78n14; at council of war, 125, 133, 135–36; family of, 146n5, 184n3, 542n7, 648n2; and gambling case, 61, 66; and La Salle expedition, 78n14, 419n21; livestock brand of, 510
Archibeque, María de, 146n5, 184n3
Arellano, Cristóbal de, 91, 106–10, 112–14, 123n2, 126, 225, 234n14
Argüello, Juana de, 90n5
Arias de Quiros, Diego, 36, 40n9, 44, 237, 244–46, 253–54, 262, 271–76, 460n3, 543n12
Armenta, Joseph de, 650–51
Armenta, Simón de, 650
Armijo, Gertrudis, 633n5
Armijo, José de, 239n2, 239n6
Armijo, Vicente de, 235–37, 239n2, 239n5–6, 239n8, 367n8, 420n32, 633n2
armorers, 34, 39n2, 553n7
arms, 14, 22, 24, 405; ban on carrying of, 20, 196–98, 201n2; club, 559;

fired for *salvos*, 243–46, 314; French, 30n48; of Indians, 25, 30n48, 545–46, 552n1, 554; instruction in using, 552n3, 558; inventories of, 558–60; lack of, 107, 545–46; petition for, 33–35, 39n1–2; prohibited in trade, 383, 402n5, 413n1, 524–25, 527–28; of soldiers, 90n10, 146n4, 147n22, 149, 152, 226–28, 260n13, 294n14–15, 319n1, 319n5, 471–72, 543n8, 554; trading of, 25–26, 525; used to contain Indians, 134–35. *See also* specific types
arquebuses (guns), 18, 127–29, 146n8, 152, 163, 167, 245–46, 261–67, 269–70, 272–76, 309, 312. *See also* guns
Arróniz, Juan Antonio de, 537
Arróniz, Juan Francisco de, 528, 539, 547–48, 556
arrows, 58, 127, 131, 552n1, 552n5
Arroyo Hondo, 214
artifacts, 645
artillery, 210
Aspeitia Chávez, Inez de, 146n19
Atensio, Antonio, 519–20, 523n10
Atienza, Francisca, 563, 565–68
Atienza, José de, 181n8, 198, 575n1
Atienza, Juan de, 63–64, 66–67, 69, 161–68, 170–71, 181n8, 198, 222
Atienza, Juan Miguel, 567
Atienza, Lázaro, 575n1
Atienza, Pedro, 563–70, 575n1
Atienza, Rosa de, 430n7, 576n11
Atienza de Alcala de Escobar, José de, 523n10
Atienza Sevillano, José de, 523n10
Atrisco, 13, 26, 104n10, 124n5, 260n4–5, 420n41, 436n2, 635–39
attorneys, 124, 261–62, 496, 523n4, 542n7, 578, 637
audiencia (court of appeals), 33, 35, 40n5, 196, 213n18
autos (judicial/admin. decree), 21. *See also* bandos (orders)
ayudantes (aides-de-camp), 15, 30n53, 56n14, 90n4, 146n4, 147n26, 234n12
ayuntamiento (town council), 21, 196, 201n1, 214, 218, 227, 461. *See also* cabildo (town council)

Baca, Antonia, 419n3
Baca, Antonio, 86, 90n7, 415, 419n9, 466, 529, 535n8–9, 608n8
Baca, Baltazar, 469n17
Baca, Bárbara, 436n1
Baca, Bernabé, 466, 469n17
Baca, Bernarda, 147n34
Baca, Cristóbal I, 535n8
Baca, Cristóbal II, 510, 535n8
Baca, Diego Antonio, 529
Baca, Diego Manuel, 535n8, 608n8
Baca, Domingo, 415, 419n13, 584, 586–89, 594, 596, 608n8, 608n12
Baca, Isabel, 419n12
Baca, Josefa, 419n9, 419n12–13, 510, 535n8–9, 608n8
Baca, Joseph, 261–62, 415, 419n11, 437–43, 448n8, 466, 529
Baca, Juana, 419n4, 420n33, 535n8, 607n1, 608n11
Baca, Juan Antonio, 535n8
Baca, Manuel, 90n7, 419n9, 530, 535n8–9, 608n8
Baca, María Magdalén, 535n8
Baca, Rafaela, 469n17
Baca, Rosa, 419n10
Baca Luna, Gregoria, 419n16
bachiller, 646, 648n1–2
Bañales, Isdro Sánchez. *See* Sánchez, Isidro
bandos (orders), 16, 21; and church sanctuary, 221–28, 233n1; for cleaning *acequias*, 461–62; for cleanup after flood, 645–47; concerning trade, 41–49, 55n3, 56n15, 381, 383, 524–30; prohibiting carrying weapons, 196–98, 201n2, 201n4; prohibiting sale of arms, 413n1; 524–25, 527–30; prohibiting trade outside province, 408–10, 413n1, 414–16, 418n2; publishing/reading of, 197–98, 409–10, 462, 528–30, 646–47; for responding to drum call, 554; for trip to salt lakes, 218–19. *See also* decrees
banners, 210, 241, 559
baptism, 83n10, 84–87, 90n3, 181n6, 575n1
Barba, Esteban, 181n11
Barba, María, 104n2, 163–64, 181n11

Barrio de Analco, 431
Bazán y Albornoz, Francisco, 209
belduques (knives), 369, **370**. *See also* knives
Belén, 13, 27, 368, 402n1, 431–32, 436n1, 576n13, 587
bells, 558–59
Benavides, Catarina Bazilia, 419n25
Benavides, Fray Alonso de, 202, 208–11, 213n20
Benavides, Thomasa de, 515n2
Benítez, Manuel, 610–14, 616–23, 633n1
Berdugo, Martín. *See* Verdugo de Haro y Ávila, Martín
Bernal, Joseph Gonzales, 639
Bernal, Pascuala, 308n3
Bernalillo, 147n30, 159n8, 213n17, 448n9; *alcaldes mayores* of, 46, 82n7, 124n4, 350, 352–58; and clothing contract, 349–50, 352–58; early landowners of, 308n3; early settlers of, 82n2, 82n8, 104n10, 260n8, 260n10, 348n7, 366n2, 367n13, 419n7, 419n16, 654n5; and edicts of faith, 203; and García discipline case, 320, 323–27, 331; military of, 82n6, 419n4; and trade, 44–46, 368
Betanzos, Andrés de, 77n1
Bitton, Gaspar, 262, 271, 276–77, 302, 310, 314, 322, 335, 350, 358, 384–85, 405
blacks, 23, 43, 56n9, 84–85, 201n4, 450–54
blacksmiths, 78n10, 182, 235, 260n7, 348n11, 448n13, 491–92, 494–95, 497–98, 544, 547–48, 553n7
blankets, 26, 415, 465–66, 585, 590
blasphemy, 90n3
Blea, Carlos, 654n3
Blea, Domingo, 649–51, 654n3
blood purity testimony case, 449–54
blunderbuss, 152, 159n11, 561n2
Bohorques y Corcuera, Francisco Bueno de, 235–37, 239n3
Bosque Grande de doña Luisa Montoya de Trujillo, 146n14
Bosque Grande de Los Alamos, 131
branding: irons for, 510, 558–59, 592; licenses for, 16; registration of, 510–11, **512**, **513**, 515n3
brandy, 26, 40n8
bridles, 18, 26, 159n12, 163, 526, 563, 566, 568–69, 592
Briseño, Ignacio Cayetano, 471
buckskins. *See* animal skins
bugles, 210
burials, 62, 484
burros. *See* mules
Bustamante, Governor Juan Domingo de, 16, 654n2; biography of, 240; and the *cabildo*, 21, 31n91, 56n12; charges against, 15, 124n4; clashes with Fray Guerrero, 240–46; orders campaign against Moquis, 251, 253; supports Indians, 517; trade regulations of, 32n112, 368
Bustamante, Josepha de, 649–50, 654n2
Bustamante, Joseph de, 24
Bustamante de Tagle, Bernardo de, 654n2
buttons, 26, 109

cabildo (town council), 40n11–12, 430n8; and *bandos*, 48; demise of, 21, 31n91, 33; duties of, 20–21; of El Paso, 90n8, 146n15; and judicial process, 33; of Mexico City, 33; notaries for, 124n16; petitions of, 33–36; political power of, 19, 33, 56n12; *procurador general* (attorney) of, 124n4; *regidores* (members) of, 19–21, 124n16, 205, 214, 217n1, 218, 223, 227, 234n18, 482n2, 510; and religious processions, 203–05; of Santa Fe, 16, 19–21, 33–36, 40n10, 40n13, 41–46, 48, 56n3, 79–80, 90n8, 105n21, 124n4, 148n36, 197–98, 203–04, 209–10, 212n14; scribes for, 78n10
Cabrera, María de, 450–54
Callexas, Juan, 93
Camargo, Antonio, 205, 213n17
Camino Real, 24, 26, 124n11, 131, 146n1, 146n16, 214
campaigns, 28, 181n4; and *alcaldes mayores*, 22; against Apaches, 33; equipment needed for, 226–28; governors in charge of, 16; against Moqui (Hopi) pueblos, 221, 226–28, 251; most important of, 13–14; against Navajos, 33; and Pueblo auxiliaries, 18–19; as punishment, 149, 154; soldiers assigned to, 18, 149, 154; soldiers killed during, 608n11; soldiers wounded in, 471. *See also* specific names; specific tribes

Cañada de los Ojitos, 649–51
Candelaria, Feliciano de la, 80, 82n4, 195n1
Candelaria, Francisco de la, 80, 82n4, 195n1, 469n11
Candelaria, Fulgencia, 420n36
Candelaria, Juan, 407n1–2
Candelaria, Ventura de la, 466, 469n11
cannons, 544–48, **549**, 558–60, 562n8
Canoa, 212n9
Canseco, María, 195n6
Canue settlement, 644n4
capitán de guerra (war captain), 21, 79, 104n1, 509n6
captives, 526, 608n17; Apache, 56n8, 84, 251–52; baptism of, 84; conversion of, 27; and Genízaros, 431; prices of, 524, 535n1; raised in Hispanic home, 431; selling of, 27–28, 261; trading of, 24–28, 32n112, 56n4, 84, 251–52, 255, 524, 535n1
Capuchín, Thomas. *See* Vélez Cachupín, Governor Thomas
carbines, 196–97, 201n2, **559**, 560
Carillo, Manuel, 334
Carlane Apaches, 526–27
Carlos V (emperor, king of Spain), 516
carpenters, 542n7
carretas (carts), 84, 146n16, 181n2, 214, 536–37
Carrillo, Manuel, 349–58, 366n1, 367n11
Carrillo, Miguel, 366n1
Carrillo Terrazas, María, 234n12
cartographers, 544, 552n1. *See also* maps
carts. *See carretas* (carts)
Carvajal, Lorenzo, 325–26, 348n7
Casados, Francisco Joseph de, 146n5, 182–83, 184n3, 245–46, 250n11
Casados, Francisco Lorenzo de, 12, 127–30, 133, 135–36, 146n5, 182–83, 184n3, 203, 205
Casa Fuerte, Marqués de (viceroy), 15, **242**, 250n1. *See also* Acuña, Juan de
casa reales, 17, 21, 23, 48–49, 410, 448n8. *See also* Palace of the Governors
Casillos, Bernabé, 552n6
Casillos, Thomas, 547, 552n6
Cassidy, Gerald, 240–41
Castile, Spain, 426, 450–54, 490n13, 497, 509n13
Castilian language, 86–87, 370
Castillo, Juan Miguel Álvarez del, 431–34, 436n1, 466, 529
Castrillón, Antonio Álvarez, 126, 131–34, 136, 146n3
Catholic Church, 44; and Corpus Christi festival, 240–42, **243**, 244–46, 250n3, 250n5; and insistence on ritual, 321; lay brotherhood of, 577, 580, 583n5; *prelados* of, 245, 250n9; and the priesthood, 449; and trade policies, 524–25. *See also* baptism; Christianity; edicts of faith; feast days; Franciscans; religious processions; religious services
cattle. *See* livestock
cavadores (hoe), 461, **462**, 464n2
cédula (decree). *See* autos (judicial/admin. decree); bandos (orders); decrees
cemetery, 245, 309, 311
census records, 12–13, 212n9, 431–32
cessa magestatis, 223, 234n7
Chacón, José. *See* Peñuela, Marqués de la (governor)
Chama, 13, 26, 212n9, 220n1, 348n8, 402n9; *alcaldes mayores* of, 369; and animal theft case, 421–26; Comanche attack on, 14; early landowners of, 402n13; early settlers of, 402n9–10, 402n13; and illegal trading case, 369, 372, 374, 377, 379, 382, 384; and land grants, 159n9, 402n1; militia of, 585, 592; settlement of, 430n2; and trader dispute, 584–97
Chamita, 212n9
chapels, 90n5, 212n9; and *agnus dei* (Lamb of God) medallions, 611; and *colchas*, 577; construction/reconstruction of, 239n2, 460n11, 482n2, 577; inventory of, 577; in La Soledad, 509n4; and lay brotherhood, 577, 583n5; maintenance of, 583n5; military, 260n7, 577; in Santa Fe, 260n7, 460n11, 482n2, 577. *See also* La Castrense Chapel; San Miguel Chapel
Chávez, André, 251, 255–56
Chávez, Angélico, 470
Chávez, Bernardo de, 431–34, 436n2. *See also* Durán y Chávez, Bernardo

Chávez, Clara de, 90n6, 147n23
Chávez, Diego Antonio, 635–39, 644n2
Chávez, Efigenia, 644n1–2
Chávez, Eusebio, 420n35
Chávez, Feliciana, 535n9
Chávez, Francisco de, 415, 419n4
Chávez, Francisco Guadalupe, 415, 419n15
Chávez, Josefa de, 448n7, 644n5
Chávez, Joseph de, 251–54, 260n4, 530
Chávez, Juana de, 608n8, 644n5
Chávez, Juan de, 251–56, 260n6, 260n11
Chávez, María, 348n9. *See also* Durán y Chávez, María
Chávez, María Luisa, 419n8
Chávez, Nicolás de, 251–55, 260n4–6, 293n6, 415, 420n29, 466
Chávez, Pedro de, 87, 519. *See also* Durán y Chávez, Pedro
Chico (Indian servant), 563, 566
Chihuahua, Mexico, 184n3, 542n7; *colchas* in, 579; merchants/traders of, 24, 26, 436n1, 542n4, 584–85, 589–90; mines in, 12, 182–83, 184n1, 250n11; paymaster in, 30n58; royal scribe of, 471
Chimayó, 26, 160–71, 181n1, 181n6, 181n11, 203, 214, 403n15
Chirinos, Joseph Manuel, 237
Chirinos, Juan Manuel, 254, 271–76, 452–53, 460n11–12
Christianity, 370; conversion to, 27, 43, 84, 223, 526, 596; and priesthood application, 449–54; teaching of, 56n9, 84, 525; and trade relations, 525. *See also* Catholic Church; baptism; edicts of faith; religious processions; religious services
churches, 29, 61, 509n4, 583n2; and *agnus dei* (Lamb of God) medallions, 611; at Alameda, 477n2, 644n7; in Albuquerque, 320–34, 348n9; alms collected for, 159n1, 169–70; construction of, 61, 169–70, 197, 240, 368, 384; death records of, 29n7; inventory of, 577; at Isleta Pueblo, 261, 265, 267, 293n9; maintenance of, 583n5; at Nambe Pueblo, 240–41; and proper clothing/hair style, 320–32, 484; reconstruction of, 159n1, 239n2, 460n11, 482n2, 577; as sanctuaries for accused persons, 23, 124n3, 221–28, 233n1, 261, 265, 267, 270, 274, 276, 293n9, 294n19; in Santa Cruz, 368, 384, 577; in Santa Fe, 27, 56n9, 159n1, 170, 197, 202–06, 209–11, 221, 239n2, 240–46, 250n3, 309, 460n11, 577, 646; and tithes, 25–26; at Zia Pueblo, 535n8. *See also* specific names
Cieneguilla, 583n3, 589
cigarro, 160, 163
cirujano (surgeon). *See* medicine: practiced by surgeons
cloth. *See* fabric
clothing: and apprenticeships, 235–36; ban on sale of, 408–09; cloth pants, 251–52, 256; on corpse, 649–51; hats, 26, 152, 159n14, 321, 526; leather, 18, 559, 613, 617–18, 650–51; and legal cases, 106, 109, 111–12; listed in payroll document, 27; listed in wills, 159n14, 260n8, 608n18; petitions for, 33, 35; poor quality of, 353, 367n12; proper type for church, 320–32; of religious persons, 240, 243, 250n4, 320–27, 330; shoes, 608n18; shortages of, 408–09; silk shawls, 577, **578**; silk shirts, 251–52, 255; silk skirts, 349–52, 357–58, 367n3, 367n5, 367n11; silk stockings, 251–52, 256; for soldiers, 559, 610–11, 617–18; trading of, 25–26, 44–45, 251–52, 255–56, 349–52, 357–58, 367n11, 408–09, 466, 526, 608n18; of wool, 415, 650–51. *See also colcha*; tailors
coa (shovel), 160, 163, 165, 461, 464n2, 498
cobbler, 608n18
Coca, Mariana, 90n1
Coca, Miguel, 85, 90n1
Cochiti Pueblo, 86, 367n7, 368
Codallos y Rabal, Joachín: and *acequia* dispute, 437–38, 442–43; and blood purity testimonies, 449–50; collects tithe goods, 17; defends Pecos, 14; leads campaign against Utes/Apaches, 14, 471; orders cleaning of *acequias*, 461–62, 464n1; pays for soldiers' return, 478–80; repeals wool embargo, 414, 465–67; and Salvador Martínez appointment, 473
cofradía (religious brotherhood), 577, 580, 583n5–6. *See also* Confraternity of Our Lady of Light
colcha, 577, **578**, 579–80
Comanches: attack Pueblo Indians, 14; attack/raid settlers, 13–14, 517, 523n5, 547, 558; attack Taos, 524, 562n8; breed horses/mules, 525; campaigns against, 14, 147n21; defeat Apaches, 14; and Genízaro settlements, 431; keeping peace with, 526–27; kill settlers, 260n9, 517,

523n5, 524; raid Pecos, 14, 25, 524; steal horses, 525; take captives, 524, 608n17; and trade, 23, 25–26, 368–86, 526–28
comisarios, 202–06, 211n2, 212n11, 213n18, 321, 335, 347n1–2
Confraternity of La Conquistadora, 654n2
Confraternity of Our Lady of Light, 577, 580, 583n6
conquistadores, 453
contracts, 45; importance of, 25; for iron work, 402n2; for tailor apprenticeship, 235–37, 367n8; for trading, 43, 349–58, 491–500
convento, 202–06, 212n8
copper items, 26, 559
corn: and debts, 65; farming of, 516, 518, 566, 637; for feed, 253; listed in payroll document, 27; and tithes, 26; trading of, 563, 566–67; used for a drink, 146n17; used for court costs, 163
corpses, 649–51
Corpus Christi festival, 240–42, **243**, 244–46, 250n3, 250n5
Correa Falcón, Manuel, 210
corruption, 15, 17, 30n58, 66
Cortés, Hernán, 510
Cortés, Juan, 93
cotton mills. *See* obrajes (cotton mills)
Council of Trent, 241
council of war. *See* junta de guerra (council of war)
couriers, 18, 35, 104n6, 124n15, 159n9
court costs, 160–61, 163, 169–71, 181n1, 349, 358
cows, 68, 260n8, 351, 421–24, 469n13, 519, 567–68, 577, 579, 649–51
coyote, 430n3, 523n6, 527
Crespo, Bishop, 402n9, 648n2
criollo (servant), 250n2
Croix, Marqués de (viceroy), 77n6, 104n6, 221
crosses, 131, 309, 311, 510, 559, 610–11
Cruz, Francisco de la, 654n4
Cruz, Juana de la, 543n8
Cruz, Manuel de la, 649–51, 654n4
Cruzat y Góngora, Governor Gervasio, 14, 18, 62, 90n10, 517; and *acequia* dispute, 295, 301–02; calls council of war, 261; and clothing contract, 349–50, 358; and García discipline case, 320–23, 333–35; and illegal trading case, 368, 380, 383–85, 402n5; investigates Sánchez case, 261–62, 271, 276–77; investigates soldier case, 309–11, 313–14, 319n12; and land grants, 402n1, 430n6; and livestock mandate, 404–05; orders roads cleared, 537; prohibits trade outside province, 408–10, 413n1––2, 414–15; trade regulations of, 402n5
Cruz y Armijo, Salvador Manuel de la, 235–37, 239n5
cuaderno (notebook), 438, 448n5
Cubero, Governor Rodríguez, 55n3, 78n8, 212n15, 221
Cuellar, María de, 308n2
Cuera, Petronilla de la, 146n19
Cuervo y Valdés, Alfonso Luis, 92, 98
Cuervo y Valdés, Governor Francisco, 40n14, 93, 98, 148n36, 213n19; assigns soldiers to presidio, 79–80; and *bandos* limiting trade, 41, 45–48, 56n15; and *cabildo* petition for aid, 33–34, 36; establishes squadron in Albuquerque, 470; expeditions/campaigns of, 14; and land grants, 90n4; orders Christian instruction, 56n9, 84; resettles Santa Cruz, 56n7; *residencia* of, 91–92; selects first *alcade* of Albuquerque, 147n28
Cueva, Francisco Fernández de la, 37
Cueva, Petronilla de la, 634n12
Cusihuiriáchic, Mexico, 182–83, 184n3
custodia, 205, 212n13
Custody of Saint Paul, 575n4

daggers, 196–97, 201n2, 525
death, 29, 35, 41, 185–90, 218. *See also* diseases
decrees: and attack on *alcaldes mayores*, 434; to baptize Apaches, 84–87; concerning Apache attack, 132–36; for fencing property, 517–20; for García discipline case, 322–23; and Pedro López case, 149–50; prohibiting carrying of weapons, 196–99; publishing of, 518; for registering brands, 511; for repealing wool embargo, 466–67; for road clearing, 214–15, 536–39; and soldier Isidro Sánchez, 263, 266–69, 271, 275–76
Delgado, Carlos, 204–05, 212n11
Delgado, Joseph, 519–20

demographics, 12–13, 212n9, 552n1
diseases, 35, 43; deaths from, 12, 29, 40n4, 56n11, 201n4; dysentery, 43, 56n11; and epidemics, 29, 33; measles, 29, 29n7; smallpox, 29, 29n7, 554, 633n2
Domingo, Juan, 614
Domingo de Mendoza, Gaspar, 218, 421, 425–26, 430n10, 431, 434, 460n3
Domínguez, Antonio, 563, 566–67, 576n7
Domínguez, Joseph, 132, 134–35, 147n26
Domínguez de Mendoza, Antonio, 147n26
Domínguez de Mendoza, José, 14, 147n26, 542n7
Domínguez de Mendoza, Tomé, 14, 431–32
Domínguez de Mendoza, Tomé II, 147n26
dowry, 420n29
drought, 31n111, 43
drummers, 15, 43, 46, 56n9, 85, 198, 201n6, 554–56, 633n2, 646
drums, 20, 410, 554–55, 558–59, 646
Durán, Antonia, 185–90, 195n1
Durán, Catalina, 239n2
Durán, Catarina, 104n2
Durán, Lázaro, 133, 147n31, 227
Durán, Salvador, 416, 420n36
Durán, Tomasa, 420n36
Durán de Armijo, Antonio, 161, 168–69, 181n5, 183, 184n1–2, 188, 237, 310, 319n8, 451
Durán de Armijo, Juan, 182–83, 184n2
Durán de Armijo, Manuel, 239n5
Durán de Chávez, Antonia, 293n6
Durán de Chávez, Nicolás, 436n2
Durango, Bishop of, 17, 25, 240, 321, 414, 419n2, 542n4
Durán y Armijo, Antonio, 367n8
Durán y Armijo, Juan, 350, 367n8
Durán y Armijo, Vicente. *See* Armijo, Vicente de
Durán y Chaves, Antonia, 419n10
Durán y Chaves, Elena, 419n22
Durán y Cháves, Fernando, 147n23, 436n2
Durán y Cháves, Fernando II, 104n10
Durán y Chaves, Rosa Gertrudis, 420n29
Durán y Chávez, Antonio, 260n6, 415, 419n3
Durán y Chávez, Bernardo, 260n6. *See also* Chávez, Bernardo de
Durán y Chávez, Catalina, 420n41
Durán y Chávez, Fernando, 79, 260n4–6, 321, 403n14, 419n3, 420n42, 635, 644n1
Durán y Chávez, Isabel, 124n8
Durán y Chávez, María, 90n10. *See also* Chávez, María
Durán y Chávez, Pedro, 182, 576n11, 608n8, 635–36, 644n1–3, 644n5
Durán y Chávez, Pedro II, 91, 93–97, 104n10, 104n13, 124n8, 125, 130–31, 133, 136, 420n42
Durán y Chávez, Pedro III, 448n7

Earp, Wyatt, 196
Easter. *See* Pasqua (Easter)
economy, 25, 28, 201n4
edicts of faith, 202–06, 209–11
El Alamo, 535n8
El Brazito paraje, 610, 613, 615, 617–20, 634n6–7
El Coyote (Pawnee Indian), 421–25, 430n3
El Cuartelejo, 14
El Morro, 419n10. *See also* Inscription Rock (El Morro)
El Muerto paraje, 125–29, 131, 146n1, 146n16
El Paso, 20, 90n4, 181n11, 436n1; *alguacil mayor* of, 90n8, 293n3; and couriers, 18; early settlers of, 12–13, 146n5, 147n34, 407n1, 419n8, 420n31–32, 469n11, 493, 509n1, 576n8, 644n6; and Franciscan friars, 212n11, 347n2; freighting to, 633n2; merchants/traders of, 24, 26, 436n1, 563, 576n13; priests in, 648n2; refugees travel to, 82n6, 90n8; and *relicario* lawsuit, 610–20; and religious processions, 205; and tailor apprenticeship, 235–37, 239n5
El Paso presidio: captains of, 40n7–9, 40n12, 77n7, 133; commander of, 56n14; and council of war, 133–35; drummers of, 56n9; general of, 125–26; horses at, 189; and hostile Apaches, 125–31, 133–34; lieut.

governor of, 240; military escort to, 91, 93–96, 149–52; soldiers of, 40n11, 82n2, 104n2, 146n7, 146n15, 147n28, 148n35, 159n9, 181n13, 195n1, 293n1, 294n12, 308n3, 407n2, 420n36, 420n44, 470–71, 535n8, 575n5
El Perrillo paraje, 131, 146n16
el torderito (game), 62
El Torero/El Toreador (New Mexican gambler), 62
El Vado, 608n16
El Valle de San Bartolomé, 234n8
Embudo, 13, 28, 212n9, 523n5
encomenderos, 14, 147n28, 293n7, 420n28
encomienda / estancia system, 14, 28
Enríquez, Miguel, 246
Ente, Matías el, 634n10. *See also* Lente, Mateo
entertainment/games, 27, 61–62, 65, 77n5
entrada of 1692, 12
Escalante expedition, 544
escopeta. See muskets
espadines. See swords
Esparza, Catarina de, 471
Esquer, Pedro Antonio, 240
Esquibel, Francisco, 538–39, 543n10, 547, 552n3
Esquibel, Juan Antonio, 543n10
Esquibel, Ventura, 552n3
Estero Largo, 618, 634n11
Estremera, Alonso, 211
Eulate, Juan de, 213n20
excommunication, 320, 331, 381
expeditions. *See* campaigns

fabric: baize, 35; campeche, 35, 40n6; cotton, 26, 35, 40n6; dyes for, 40n6; flannel, 27; lack of, 65; *lienza* (canvas-like cloth), 491, 497, 509n11; prices of, 17; *sallal* (sailcloth), 65, 466; for San Juan Feast Day, 111; silk, 17, 26–27, 159n14; spun, 26; trading of, 26, 491, 497, 526; wool for, 465. *See also* clothing; colcha; textiles
face powder, 349, 351, 354, 356–57, 367n9
fanega, 25, 32n115, 64–65
Faraón Apaches, 14, 18, 261, 471, 490n7
Farfán, Francisco, 12, 221
Farfán-Velasco expedition: and filigree maker, 611; settlers arriving with, 40n10, 40n13, 77n1, 78n14, 124n18, 146n5, 181n8, 234n12, 260n3, 348n11, 366n2, 523n10; and tailors, 239n4; and weavers, 147n33
farming: and *acequias*, 437–41, 461–62; on Camino Real, 214; of chile, 26, 165; and court costs, 163; equipment for, 33, 35; and harvesting of crops, 161, 169, 635–36; near El Paso, 40n8; and presidio soldiers, 18, 654n6; of Pueblo Indians, 516–18, 566; of settlers, 13, 516–19
feast days, 107, 109–11, 240–42, 357, 558
Felipe Romero paraje, 127–28, 146n9
Felipe V (king of Spain), **34**, 196
fencing, 214, 516–20, 536–38
Fernández, Bartolomé, 555
Fernández, Bernardino, 91, 96, 105n19, 106–10, 112–14, 124n3
Fernández, Carlos, 542n6, 576n13; as *alcalde mayor*, 564–70, 576n9, 591–92, 594; biography of, 523n4; and *colcha* dispute, 580; family of, 523n9; ordered to build fences, 519–20; and presidio drummer petition, 555; and traders' disputes, 564–70, 591–92, 594
Fernandez, Joseph, 234n11
Fernández, Juan, 611
Figueroa, Ignacio Cornelia, 563, 569, 576n13
filigree work, 610–11, 614–15
fines, 23, 554, 636; for *acequia* disputes, 295, 301, 437–38, 441–43; for assaulting *alcalde mayor*, 431, 434; for carrying arms, 197; for illegal trading, 45, 48, 368, 384, 409, 418n2, 527–28; for loose livestock, 404, 518; for not cleaning *acequias*, 461–62; for selling captives, 261; for trespassing on Indian land, 308n2; used for church construction, 169–70, 384; used for remodeling palace, 437, 442
flood of 1767, 645–47
Flores, Agustín, 577
Flores, Antonia, 90n4
Flores Mogollón, Governor Juan Ignacio, 82n1, 90n2, 183, 220n2, 252;

abolishes *cabildo*, 21; and Albuquerque petition, 79; appoints Rael de Aguilar captain, 225–26, 234n13; calls council of war, 125, 132; and death benefits petition, 185, 187–89, 195n9; and dispute in Chimayó, 160–61, 165–70; and fugitive soldiers case, 107–08, 115, 124n20; investigates Apache attacks, 125–36; and mail delivery case, 91–98; orders baptism of Apaches, 84–87; oversees López criminal case, 149–54; reinstates Albuquerque squadron, 470; and Santa Fe presidio, 104n9; trade regulations of, 368
food: ban on sale of, 408; *biscochos* (biscuits), 131; chocolate, 17, 26, 239n2; flour, 566–67; meat, 26, 385; shortages of, 35, 408–09; sugar, 26; tallow, 26; and tithes, 26; tomatoes, 542n7; tortillas, 106, 112, 567; trading of, 25–26, 385, 408–09, 566–67
Fragoso, Domingo, 633n2
Fragoso, Francisco Xavier, 552n3, 554, 608n18, 610–23, 633n2
Fragoso, José Manuel, 554
Franciscans, 212n11, 250n2, 449, 583n2; accompany settlers to Santa Fe, 12; in Albuquerque, 213n19, 320–21, 347n1–2; *comisarios* of, 211n2, 347n1–2; and Corpus Christi festival, 240, 242–46; declining influence of, 321; and edicts of faith, 203–06, 209–11, 212n4; in El Paso, 90n8; and García discipline case, 320–21, 347n1–2; missions of, 490n5–6; political rivalry among, 483–84; practices of, 575n4; and preaching the gospel, 209; and religious processions, 203–06, 210, 240; scandalous behavior of, 483–84, 490n5, 490n12–13; and tithes, 17; and trade of captives, 27; and witchcraft accusation, 483–84. *See also* missions/missionaries; specific names
Francisco, Juan, 48
Francisco (Pawnee Indian). *See* El Coyote (Pawnee Indian)
Francisco (Santa Clara Indian), 591–92
French: explorers, 78n14; settlers, 542n5; traders, 25–26, 546, 558; weapons, 30n48. *See also* Archibeque, Juan de
Fuenclara: and *acequia* dispute, 437–43; *alcaldes mayores* of, 419n11, 439; and attack on *alcaldes mayores*, 431–34; early settlers of, 147n26, 262, 419n10, 432, 436n1, 437, 440, 448n9; and land grants, 348n6
Fuenclara, Count (Viceroy) of, 432, **433**

Gabaldón, Antonio, 32n112
Gabaldón, Juan, 538, 542n7
Galicia, Spain, 648n2
Galisteo, 13, 312; *alcaldes mayores* of, 319n3, 545, 553n7; attacked by Comanches, 14; and military equipment, 558, 560; raided by Comanches, 25, 524; and trade, 26; and trip to salt lakes, 218
Gallegos, Antonio I, 260n8, 367n13
Gallegos, Antonio II, 260n8, 367n10, 367n13
Gallegos, Diego Antonio, 519
Gallegos, Felipe, 308n1
Gallegos, José, 448n9, 448n13
Gallegos, Josefa, 419n11
Gallegos, Joseph, 433
Gallegos, Juan, 251, 254, 260n8
Gallegos, Juana, 468n3
Gallegos, Juan Antonio, 353–57, 367n13
Gallegos, Margareta, 366n2
gambling, 16, 19, 61–70, 77n5, 78n9, 78n11, 109, 124n12. *See also* rifara (raffle, gambling)
García, Alonso, 107–08, 146n18
García, Bárbara, 483–86, 489n1, 490n11
García, Cristóbal I, 80, 83n10, 295–302, 308n1, 416, 419n21, 420n26, 469n11
García, Cristóbal II, 83n10, 308n
García, Diego, 308n1, 420n26, 423–26
García, Francisco, 108, 110–11, 114, 133, 147n30, 415, 477n7
García, José, 420n34
García, Joseph, 416, 420n34
García, Juan, 404–05, 407n4
García, Juan Esteban, 378, 380, 382, 385–86, 403n17
García, Lázaro, 329–30, 348n12
García, Ramón, 489n1
García, Rosalia, 82n6, 436n1
García, Salvador, 416
García, Tomás, 308n2

García, Vicente, 416, 420n31, 420n34
García Carnero, Francisco, 228, 234n8. *See also* Tamaris, Francisco
García de Armijo, Vicente, 402n2
García de la Mora, Juan: and animal theft case, 421–26; biography of, 402n2, 403n18, 509n10; and contract with Salvador García, 491–500, 509n11; family of, 402n14; and illegal trading case, 368–78, 380–85; will of, 24
García de la Riva, Juan, 98, 170, 222; biography of, 105n21, 147n33; at council of war, 133, 135–36; family of, 212n14; as judge, 183; ordered to clear roads, 214–15; in religious procession, 203, 205
García de la Riva, Miguel, 105n21, 147n33
García de Luna, Ramón, 159n9
García de Mora, Juan, 402n8
García de Noriega, Alonso I, 82n6, 147n30
García de Noriega, Alonso II, 82n6, 124n7, 420n31, 639
García de Noriega, Alonso III, 124n7, 509n1
García de Noriega, Antonio, 147n32
García de Noriega, Francisco, 147n30, 348n12
García de Noriega, Joseph, 410
García de Noriega, Josepha, 40n14
García de Noriega, Juan Esteban, 410
García de Noriega, Lázaro, 147n30
García de Noriega, Luis, 40n14, 80, 82n6, 107–08, 113, 124n7, 419n21, 466, 477n1, 489n1
García de Noriega, Rosalia, 470, 477n1
García de Noriega, Salvador, 491–500, 509n1, 509n11–12, **545**
García de Noriega, Tomás Cristóbal, 83n10, 509n1
García Hurtado, Bárbara, 489n1
García Jurado, José, 124n4
García Jurado, Pedro, 320–34, 347n3, 466, 468n4, 484
García Jurado, Ramón: biography of, 124n4; criminal case against, 91, 106–11, 113–14, 124n15; family of, 124n14, 347n3, 468n4; leaves kingdom without permission, 91, 106; seeks repeal of wool embargo, 416; as witness, 154
García Pareja, Manuel, 649–51, 654n1
gardens/gardening, 214, 437–41, 448n10, 518, 537, 542n3–4, 636. *See also* farming
Garduño, Bartolomé, 123n2, 124n3, 159n3, 159n10; biography of, 104n1; criminal case against, 91–98, 104n5–6, 104n13, 106–14, 124n15, 124n20; family of, 239n8; flees the kingdom, 106–14, 234n14; travels to Mexico City, 91–98, 104n6, 105n19, 125, 130
Garduño, Gregorio, 237, 239n8, 450–54, 473, 480
Garrida, Juan de la, 465–67
garrisons. *See* presidios; specific towns
Garvizu, Manuel Sanz de, 14, 538, 543n12
Garzía, Joseph, 235–37, 239n1, 239n4, 542n7
Genízaro Indians, 27–28, 32n133, 431, 436n1, 552n1, 560, 564, 567, 575n2
Gil, Juana Dorotea del, 543n9
Gila Apaches, 14, 490n13
Giltomey, Joseph Manuel, 85, 90n4
Giltomey, Joseph María, 136
Giltomey, Juan, 90n4
Giltomey, Mariana, 430n7
Girón, Dimas. *See* Jirón, Dimas
Godines, Antonio, 213n15
Godines, María Luisa, 147n32
Gómez, Francisca, 542n4
Gómez, Francisco, 210
Gómez, Salvador Cristóbal, 323–24, 348n5
Gómez de Arellano, Luisa, 239n7
Gómez de Chávez, Pedro, 402n14
Gómez Luján, Luisa, 403n17
Gómez Robledo, Francisca, 212n15
Gómez Robledo, Francisco, 124n11
Gómez Robledo, Lucía, 260n3, 260n12
Gómez Robledo, María, 40n9
Gómez y Chávez, Pedro, 321, 376
Góngora, Bartolomé, 40n13
Góngora, Cayetano, 618, 634n12
Góngora, Cristóbal de, 36, 40n13, 44, 67–68, 132, 136, 146n19
Góngora, Francisca, 419n16
Góngora, Juan de, 146n19, 634n12
Gonzales, Alejandro, 635, 638–39
Gonzáles, Casilda, 490n12
Gonzales, Francisco Antonio, 296, 327–28, 348n9
Gonzales, Gregorio, 552n4
Gonzales, Javier, 519–20, 523n6
Gonzales, Joseph, 644n7
Gonzales, María Clara, 552n3
Gonzales, Sebastiana, 294n15
Gonzales Bas, Alexandro, 355, 357–58, 644n7
Gonzales Bas, Antonio, 543n11
Gonzales Bas, Catalina, 420n31
Gonzales Bas, Clara, 543n11
Gonzales Bas, Inés, 82n2
Gonzales Bas, Joseph, 301, 350, 352–58
Gonzales Bas, Juan, 294n15, 295–301, 320, 322–31, 333–34, 404–05, 407n1, 471, 542n6, 543n11
Gonzales Bas, Juana, 407n1, 407n5
Gonzales Bas, Juan I, 260n10, 420n31, 477n2, 644n7
Gonzales Bas, Juan II, 251, 255–56, 260n10, 477n2, 644n7
Gonzales Bas, Juan III, 260n10
Gonzales Bas, Juan Julián, 353–55, 357–58
Gonzales Bas, Prudencia, 542n6
Gonzales Bas, Valentina, 407n5
Gonzales Vallego, Manuel, 348n11
governors, 30n57, 40n8, 55n1, 56n5, 56n14, 181n12; and *cabildos*, 56n12; and church sanctuary, 221; corruption of, 15, 17, 30n58; and delivery of decrees, 215, 217n4; duties/roles of, 15–20, 33, 185, 295, 464n3; establish military squadrons, 470; and land grants, 28, 82n6, 90n4–5; and legal cases, 22–23, 90n10; and petitions, 19, 22, 25, 28; prohibit gambling, 61–62, 78n9, 124n12; prohibit trade outside province, 408–10, 413n2, 414–16; protests against, 124n4; in religious processions, 210; and ritual procedures, 240–46; schedule trips to salt lakes, 218–19; and settlers leaving province, 182–83; and soldiers' supplies, 30n58; and spiritual welfare of settlers, 84; trade regulations of, 22, 24–25, 27–28, 41–49, 56n15, 368–69, 373, 383, 414, 448n7, 524–30, 535n1; visit pueblos, 18. *See also* specific names
grain, 408, 413n1, 416. *See also* wheat
Griego, Baltazar, 635–38, 644n4
Griego, Juan, 296, 298–99, 308n3
Grolet, Jacques, 78n14
Grolet, Santiago, 419n21
Gruciaga, Antonio de, 244, 250n7
Guadalajara, 20, 47, 460n14, 633n2
guaje (gourd), 272, 294n15
Guelites, town of, 348n8
Guerrero, Francisco, 371, 410, 529, 579–81, 646–47
Guerrero, Fray Joseph Antonio, 203, 212n7, 240, 242–46, 250n2, 250n5, 320–22, 334–35, 347n1
Guillen, Pedro, 309, 311–12, 319n1
guns, 26, 33, 62, 146n8, 196, 240, 319n12, 544, 558–59, 561n2, 562n8. *See also* arms; arquebuses (guns); muskets
Gurulé, Antonio, 308n1, 351–52, 415, 419n21
Gutiérrez, Antonia, 78n14
Gutiérrez, Antonio, 223, 234n5
Gutiérrez, Francisco, 466
Gutiérrez, Gregorio, 437
Gutiérrez, Inés, 469n11
Gutiérrez, Jacinto, 490n12
Gutiérrez, Juan Alejo, 469n11
Gutiérrez de Salazar, Catalina, 419n8, 483, 486, 490n12
Gutiérrez Flores, Juan, 209

haciendas, 79, 212n9, 414, 416, 637
harquebuses, 146n8, 210. *See also* arquebuses (guns)
herders, 516–18, 649–51
heresy, 202, 211, 241, 321, 403n14
Hernández, town of, 402n9

Herrera, Francisco Xavier de, 251, 256, 260n13, 608n4
Herrera, Isabel, 575n5
Herrera, Javier de, 585, 608n4
Herrera, Juan de, 260n13, 608n4
Herrera, María Antonia de, 430n8
Herrera Sandoval, Tomás de, 608n4
hides. *See* animal skins
Hinojos, Luisa de, 348n7
Hinojos, María Josefa de, 367n10
Holy Office of the Inquisition. *See* Inquisition
Hopis, 12, 293n2; campaigns against, 14, 147n27, 147n29; Fray Delgado's work with, 212n11, 490n5; at Isleta Pueblo, 293n8; Jesuit control of, 240
horses, 43, 90n10, 159n13, 163, 542n4, 542n7, 552n1, 637; branding of, 189, 511; breeding of, 524–26; for campaigns, 226–28, 471–72; of *encomenderos*, 14; and fugitive soldiers case, 106–14; and gambling, 62; guarding of, 18, 106, 127–28, 149–52, 197; of Indians, 26, 28, 527–28; killed by Apaches, 125–31, 133; mentioned in will, 523n3; of militias, 19; ordered fenced in, 516; pastures for, 517–18; petition for, 33, 35; at presidios, 16–19, 24, 35, 46, 60n2, 146n4, 147n22, 149, 152, 227; price/value of, 60n2, 510, 526–27, 535n3; prohibited in trade, 41–46, 524–28; of Pueblo Indians, 517–18, 552n1; raising of, 409; of soldiers, 260n13, 294n14–15, 319n1, 319n5, 477n4, 477n7, 542n3, 542n5, 543n8, 543n11, 552n5, 633n2; and street width, 536; theft of, 26, 58, 60n1, 80, 107, 127–30, 525; trading of, 25–26, 48, 56n3, 149, 152, 251–56, 260n11, 356, 369, 374, 423, 524–27, 535n1, 535n3, 563, 566–67, 584, 594. *See also* bridles; royal horse herd; saddles; stirrups
Hortega, Fray Pedro de, 209, 211
houses: and *acequia* dispute, 295, 298, 437; building of, 437, 635–36; of *cabildo*, 203; damaged by flood, 646; descriptions of, 165, 542n3–4, 579; grants for, 212n15; and "house arrest," 23, 439, 470; Indian ranches near, 369; in Las Trampas area, 523n5; and livestock mandate, 404–05; and property access dispute, 635–36; protection of, 205, 405; raids on, 517; robbing of, 436n1; sale of, 460n3, 469n13, 477n7, 542n7, 543n8; in Santa Fe, 203, 241, 542n4, 542n7, 543n8, 543n13, 579, 646; shared by families, 189–90, 469n11; used for protection, 517
Hurtado, Andrés, 147n28, 348n11
Hurtado, Bernardina, 106, 111–12, 124n14, 347n3, 448n2, 448n9, 468n4
Hurtado, Juana, 40n7
Hurtado, María, 147n34
Hurtado, Mariana, 348n11
Hurtado, Martín: biography of, 147n28; as captain of Albuquerque squadron, 79, 147n28, 470, 472; at council of war, 133–34, 136; family of, 40n7, 124n14, 146n7, 147n28, 347n3, 348n10–11, 448n2, 448n9, 468n4; as first *alcade* of Albuquerque, 40n7, 134, 147n28; and fugitive soldiers case, 106, 109–10, 113; and grandson's discipline case, 320–34; and horse trade case, 255–56; prohibits carrying of weapons, 198–99
Hurtado de Mendoza, Joseph, 639

illness. *See* diseases
imprisonment. *See* jails; penalties/punishment; stocks
Indian scouts, 608n13
indigo, 26
inheritance, 477n1, 490n7, 636
Iniesta, Fray Juan Agustín, 321, 483–84, 486, 489n4, 490n12–13
Inquisition, 147n33; *alguacil mayor* (high sheriff) of, 78n14, 181n8, 183, 293n3, 648n2; and blood purity testimonies, 449–50, 452–54; *comisarios* of, 104n3, 202–03, 208–11, 212n3, 212n11, 321, 335, 347n2, 483–86; *custos*/vice-*custos* of, 104n3, 212n3, 212n7; and edicts of faith, 202–03, 205, 209, 212n4; and illicit trade in province, 524–25; in Mexico, 403n14, 483–84; notaries of, 203–06, 209–11, 489n4, 490n6, 490n13, 524; and punishment of settler, 460n8; recalls Pedro Montaño, 484; and witchcraft accusation, 483–86, 490n9, 490n11
Inscription Rock (El Morro), 147n27, 181n3, 608n13
intermarriage, 13, 147n26
interpreters, 86–87
inventories: of chapels/churches, 577; of estates, 576n11, 644n7; of goods, 32n119, 227; of military equipment, 558–59; of presidios, 104n1, 544; of Taos Pueblo supplies, 633n2
Irigoyen, José de, 483–84, 490n5

iron: for blacksmithing work, 491–92, 494–95, 497–98, 544–48; for cannons, 544–48, **549**; ingots of, 26; for lances, 544, 547; tools made of, 26, 163, **462**, 464n2; work, 402n2, 491–92, 498
irrigation, 110, 165, 297–98, 301, 437–42, 461–62, 636
Isleta Pueblo, 133, 234n5, 293n2, 367n7, 634n10; *alcaldes mayores* of, 439, 471; church of, 261, 265, 267, 270, 274, 276, 293n9; early landowners of, 82n3, 419n7, 436n2; early settlers of, 82n8, 195n1, 419n8, 419n16; Fray Delgado's work with, 212n11; home to Tiwas, 490n7; and livestock, 405, 516; mission of, 293n8; and soldier Isidro Sánchez, 261, 264–65, 267, 270, 274, 276, 293n9; and trade, 368; and witchcraft trial, 321, 420n31, 489n2

Jaehi, Miguel, 159n12
jails, 169, 527, 648n4; stocks; in Albuquerque, 320–21, 330–31, 333–34, 404; in Fuenclara, 433–34, 437–41; lack of, 166; local, 23, 61, 431; in royal guardhouse, 23, 94, 150–54, 160, 164, 166, 169–70, 262–71, 276, 294n19, 311–14, 586; in Taos, 518. *See also* penalties/punishment
Janos presidio, 460n11, 535n8
Jaramillo, Andrea, 477n9
Jaramillo, Cristóbal I, 80, 82n2, 109–10, 113, 348n10, 407n2–3. *See also* Varela Jaramillo, Cristóbal I
Jaramillo, Cristóbal II, 82n2, 420n28, 542n3. *See also* Varela Jaramillo, Cristóbal II
Jaramillo, Francisca, 82n2, 420n37. *See also* Varela Jaramillo, Francisca
Jaramillo, Gerónimo, 80, 82n2, 82n7, 293n12, 334, 448n3, 466
Jaramillo, Gregorio, 416, 437–43, 448n2–3, 448n12. *See also* Varela Jaramillo, Gregorio
Jaramillo, Joseph, 271–73, 275–76, 293n12
Jaramillo, Luis, 537–38, 542n3
Jaramillo, María de la Rosa, 82n2
Jaramillo, María Josepha, 419n16
Jaramillo, Teresa, 407n2–3, 490n8. *See also* Varela Jaramillo, Teresa
Jémez Pueblo, 366n2; *alcaldes mayores* of, 124n2, 535n8; attacked by Utes, 14; and baptism of Apaches, 86; Fray Delgado's work with, 212n11; smallpox epidemic at, 29; and trade, 349, 351, 357, 368; and trade *bando*, 529
Jesuits, 240
Jesús, Juan de, 235
jewelry, 26, 62, 610–11, **612**, 614–15. *See also* relicarios
Jews, 449–51, 453–54
Jicarilla Apaches, 14
Jiménez, Elvira Sánchez, 77n2, 77n4
Jiménez de Anciezo, María, 482n2
Jirón, Dimas, 150–51, 159n5, 310–14
Jirón, Isabel Telles, 407n2
Jirón, Tomás, 159n5
Jorge de Vera, Isabel, 419n26
Jornada del Muerto, 125, 146n1, 146n18
Juan de Dios, 563, 565–68, 576n9
judges, 638–39; *alcaldes mayores* as, 66, 235, 245, 368, 402n2, 494; ecclesiastical, 243, 646, 648n2–3; governors act as, 20; in Santa Cruz, 402n2
judicial system, 22–23. *See also* audiencia (court of appeals); penalties/punishment
jues receptor (presiding judge), 237
juez de comisión (magistrate), 40n14, 108–15, 124n9
Jumana, 547
junta de guerra (council of war), 14, 16, 40n3, 125–26, 132–36, 261
Jurado, Catalina, 608n6
juridicial agreements, 295, 299–301, 496, 498–99
justicias mayor, 55n1, 79, 213n15

Keres Pueblo, 86
knives, 152; making of, 498; prohibition of, 196–97, 201n2; trading of, 25–26, 239n2, 368–72, 374–81, 383–84, 525–26, 563, 565–66, 568–69; used for protection, 422; used in fight, 221, 224–25. *See also* belduques

Labadia, Domingo, 580
La Cañada. *See* Santa Cruz de la Cañada
La Castrense Chapel, 260n7, 577

La Cienega, 509n8, 607n1
Ladrón mountains, 14
Laguna Pueblo, 127; *alcaldes mayores* of, 90n10, 104n10, 419n7, 431–32, 434, 436n1, 469n17, 530, 552n4; as *alcaldía*, 21; protection of, 124n8; and trade, 368, 530
La Joya, town of, 212n9
Lamb of God medallion. *See* agnus dei (Lamb of God) medallion
lances, 18, 260n13, 477n4, 525, 544, 548, 552n1, **559**, 563, 565, 568
land: boundaries of, 21–23, 181n1; disputes over, 402n2, 608n6, 608n13, 635–39; titles for, 510; trading of, 28; trespassing on, 308n2; and water rights, 295–301
land grants, 82n2, 104n1, 147n22, 212n15, 460n3; in Abiquiu area, 430n6-7, 608n19; in Albuquerque area, 82n6; and *alcaldes mayores*, 21; authorized by governor, 20; in Belén, 576n13; and boundaries, 22; in Chama area, 159n9, 402n1; in Cochiti Pueblo area, 367n7; of Diego Padilla, 419n12; documents for, 28; in Fuenclara, 348n6; at Guelites, 348n8; in Isleta Pueblo area, 82n3, 367n7; of Joachín Sedillo, 367n7; in La Cienega area, 509n8, 607n1; at La Soledad, 509n4; Los Quelites, 420n42; near Santa Fe River, 90n4, 239n2; in Picuris area, 90n5; in Pojoaque, 77n8, 104n2, 608n6; of Río Arriba, 212n9; in Río Grande bosque, 147n30; in San Ildefonso area, 181n3; in Santa Clara area, 148n35, 575n5; in Santa Fe, 40n9; and Sitio de Gutiérrez, 234n5; soldiers ask for, 18. *See also* specific names
La Plaza de los Lentes, 634n10
La Salineta, 367n13
La Salle Expedition, 78n14, 419n21
Las Bocas paraje, 649–51
Las Espías hill, 128–29, 146n10
Las Nutrias paraje, 27, 612, 614, 633n4
La Soledad, 13, 402n2, 402n13, 403n18, 509n4, 523n8, 585, 654n1. *See also* Nuestra Señora de la Soledad of Río Arriba
Las Peñuelas paraje, 126, 128–29, 131, 146n1, 146n16
Las Trampas, 26, 184n2, 509n6, 523n5
laws: for Apache baptisms, 84; for captives, 27; concerning road width, 536–37; and livestock protection, 405; for pawned items, 62, 66; prohibiting slavery, 84; for trade, 24, 41–49, 368–69, 381, 383
Laws of the Indies, 16–17, 19, 27, 30n59, 61, 148n36, 516, 536
leather goods, 26, 559, 568, 613, 617–18, 650
Ledesma, Francisco de, 543n8
Ledesma, Inés de, 181n11
Ledesma, Juan de, 169
Ledesma, María and Juan de, 538, 543n8
leg irons, 321, 559
Legislative Assembly, 517
Lente, Mateo, 615, 634n10. *See also* Ente, Matías el
León, Pedro Joseph de, 416
León, Spain, 523n5
Leyba, Angela de, 159n9, 402n1
Leyba, José de, 509n8
Leyba, Juan Ángel, 509n8
Leyba, Juan de, 491–92, 494, 509n8
limpiesa (purity of blood), 449–54
Linares, Duke (Viceroy) of, 56n14, 96, **97**, 126, 135, 196, 220n2
livestock, 542n4, 542n7; ban on sale of, 408–09, 413n1, 414–16, 465; branding of, 510–11, **512**, **513**, 515n3; distribution of, 181n2; governor's mandate for, 404–05; lambs, 189; and legal cases, 23, 295, 297–98; near El Paso, 40n8; ordered fenced in, 516–20; pastures for, 13, 404–05, 517–18, 576n5; and presidio soldiers, 18, 510; prices of, 524–25; and property dispute, 635–38; protection needed for, 80; of Pueblo Indians, 517–18; raising of, 460n1; theft of, 13, 57–58, 80, 134, 404–05, 421–24, 469n13; and tithes, 17; trading of, 24–26, 350–52, 519, 524–25; trespass on Indian lands, 516–17; *ventas* for, 510, **512**, 515n3, 559. *See also* specific types
López, Antonio, 183
López, Carlos, 159n3; biography of, 104n2, 159n10; criminal case against, 91, 93–98, 104n5, 104n13, 105n19, 106–11, 113–14, 124n3, 124n20; and Pedro López case, 152, 159n10; travels to Mexico City, 91, 125
López, Juan, 104n2
López, Juana, 181n4
López, Nicolás, 104n2, 159n10
López, Nicolosa, 348n12
López, Pedro. *See* López Gallardo, Pedro
López de Castillo, Pedro, 80, 83n12
López del Castillo, María, 260n10
López de Mendizábal, Bernardo, 460n8
López Gallardo, Gerónimo, 159n1
López Gallardo, Pedro, 149–54, 159n1, 159n10
López Naranjo, José, 608n13
López Olguín, Juan I, 147n27
López Olguín, Juan II, 147n27
López Olguín, Thomas. *See* Olguín, Thomas
López Sambrano, Juana, 147n26
Lorenz, Manuel Antonio, 570
Los Alamitos paraje, 610, 613–18, 634n6
Los Esteros de San Pablo, 107–09, 124n5
Los Gómez paraje, 109, 124n11
Los Luceros, 212n9
Los Quelites grant, 420n42
Los Queres, 21
Louisiana area, 558
Lovato, Agustín, 593
Lovato, Bartolomé, 69, 509n6
Lovato, Cayetano, 312
Lovato, Juan Domingo, 495, 567–69
Lovato, Juan Joseph, 212n9, 271–76, 402n2, 493–95, 509n6, 511, **512**, **513**
Lovato, Matías, 186, 195n3, 509n6
Lucero, Cayetano, 415, 420n27
Lucero, Miguel I, 420n28
Lucero, Miguel II, 415, 419n10
Lucero, Pedro, 469n11, 471, 477n4. *See also* Lucero de Godoy, Pedro
Lucero, Santiago, 212n9
Lucero de Godoy, Antonio I, 36, 40n12, 407n3, 420n37, 477n4
Lucero de Godoy, Antonio II, 404–05, 407n3, 416, 420n37
Lucero de Godoy, Francisco, 39n2
Lucero de Godoy, Juan, 147n29, 477n4, 542n3
Lucero de Godoy, María, 146n15
Lucero de Godoy, Miguel I, 419n10
Lucero de Godoy, Nicolás, 182, 407n3
Lucero de Godoy, Pedro, 40n12, 477n4
Lucero de Godoy, Santiago, 212n9
Luján, Agustín, 127–28, 146n7
Luján, Ana, 104n2
Luján, Catarina, 489n2
Luján, Cristóbal, 309, 311–12, 319n3
Luján, Domingo, 234n9, 319n3, 634n8
Luján, José, 234n9
Luján, Joseph, 223, 234n9, 538, 543n10
Luján, Juan, 147n29, 234n9, 293n4, 319n3
Luján, Juan Antonio, 423–24, 613–14, 634n8
Luján, Juan Luis, 147n29
Luján, María, 90n5, 181n11
Luján, María Barba. *See* Barba, María
Luján, Miguel, 124n3
Luján, Pedro, 133, 147n29
Luján Domínguez, Lenora, 542n3
Luján Romero, Juan, 195n4
luminarias, 384, 403n20
Luna, Ana de, 420n34
Luz Martín, Marta de la, 460n5
Luz Montoya, Antonia de la, 608n8

macho (male mule), 260n1; and animal theft case, 422, 424–25; branding of, 592; breeding of, 592; and disputes among traders, 563–70, 586–90, 592–96; as pack animals, 586, 588–90, 592–93, 595–96; prices of, 587–88; of soldiers, 260n12, 294n15; trading of, 251–54, 351–52, 356–57, 528, 563–70. *See also* mules
Madrid, Francisco I de, 77n7
Madrid, Francisco II de, 77n7
Madrid, Josefa, 146n21

Madrid, Joseph, 161, 163, 181n4
Madrid, Roque, 14, 61, 63–64, 66–69, 77n7, 78n9, 134, 136, 146n21, 181n4
Madrid, Tomás, 478–80, 482n1
Maese, Bartolomé (or Bartolo), 547, 552n5, 552n6, 611–15
Maese, Juan, 552n5
Maese, Juana, 293n1
Maese, Luis, 552n5
Maese, María Luisa, 146n7
Maese, Miguel, 552n5
Magdalena mountains, 14
mail, 20, 91–98, 104n6, 108, 130, 135, 214, 483
maize. *See* corn
Maldonado, Joseph, 547–48
Maldonado y Sais, María, 460n1
Manrique, José, 544
mantas, 26, 35, 466. *See also* blankets
mantón de Manila (*colcha* shawl), **578**
Manzanares, María de, 181n3
maps: Arrowsmith, 212n9; Gilmore (1846), 645; Gregg (1844), 212n9; Menchero (1745), 13, 146n1, 432, 490n13; Miera y Pacheco (1758), 552n1; Miera y Pacheco (1759), 432; Miera y Pacheco (1779), 13, 21, 56n6, 146n1, 212n9, 220n1, 432, **659**; Urrutia (1767), 536, 543n13, 645, **658**. *See also* Appendix: Maps
Marcial Rael, Pedro, 251, 260n9
María, Joseph, 649–51
Marín del Valle, Governor Francisco Antonio: and *colcha* dispute, 579–80; collects tithe goods, 17; orders animals contained, 404; orders roads cleared, 214, 536–39; and petition for cannon repairs, 544–48; and presidio drummer petition, 554–56; sets trade price regulations, 524–25, 535n1, 535n3; tightens trade regulations, 368–69, 524–30; Vélez Cachupín's report to, 509n6, 552n3
Márques, Carolina, 460n8
Márques, Mateo, 450–54, 460n8
Márques, Nicolás, 460n8
Márquez, Ana María, 450–54, 460n3–4
Márquez, Diego, 430n1, 430n4, 510
Márquez, Francisca, 430n1
Márquez, Juana, 421–25, 430n4
marriage, 20, 56n9, 294n13, 451–54, 460n10, 608n9. *See also* intermarriage
Martín, Alejandro, 523n3
Martín, Andrés, 416, 420n35
Martín, Ángela, 402n12
Martín, Antonia, 576n8
Martín, Antonio, 163–64, 166–68, 181n11, 376–77, 403n15, 493, 509n4, 511, 523n5, 560
Martín, Barbara, 212n9
Martín, Blas, 471, 477n5, 524
Martín, Diego, 160–61, 163–71, 181n1, 181n10–11, 576n11
Martín, Diego II, 430n7
Martín, Domingo, 159n1, 477n5
Martín, Fernando, 164–65, 181n13
Martín, Francisco, 510, 519, 523n8. *See also* Martín Serrano, Francisco
Martín, Gerónimo, 422–25, 430n6–7
Martín, Ignacio, 423, 430n6–7
Martín, Jacinto, 518–20, 523n3
Martín, Josefa, 160, 163, 165, 293n7, 402n2
Martín, Juana, 403n18
Martín, Juan Diego, 568, 576n11
Martín, Lugarda, 515n2
Martín, Manuel, 374, 402n13, 403n15
Martín, Margarita, 523n4, 523n9
Martín, María, 234n9
Martín, Mateo, 420n35
Martín, Miguel, 165–68
Martín, Nicolás Jacinto, 523n3
Martín, Pasquala, 576n8
Martín, Petrona, 402n14
Martín, Sebastián, 86, 90n5, 212n9, 516, 523n3, 523n9

Martín, Sebastiana, 149–50, 152, 159n1
Martín, Tomás, 419n25
Martín de Salazar, Francisca, 147n29
Martínez, Antonio, 470, 472, 477n9
Martínez, Governor Felix, 47, 234n12, 535n1; and *bando* prohibiting carrying of weapons, 196–98, 201n1, 201n3–4; biography of, 56n14, 104n9; complaints against, 15, 56n14, 470; and Corpus Christi festival, 241; and death benefits petition, 185–89; and edicts of faith, 202–04, 212n4; family of, 470–71; gives amnesty for persons under church sanctuary, 221–28; as governor, 159n9, 195n6, 212n4, 220n2, 470; leads campaign against Apaches, 57; leads campaign against Moquis, 14; orders roads cleared, 214–15; re-establishes *cabildo*, 21; schedules trip to salt lakes, 218–19, 220n2; travels to Mexico City, 91, 93, 95–96, 125, 130, 159n3
Martínez, Jacinto, 478, 482n4
Martínez, Joachín, 470–72, 477n7
Martínez, Juan de Dios, 114, 124n19, 199
Martínez, Salvador, 82n6, 415, 466, 470–72, 477n1, 478–80
Martín Moraga, Diego, 576n11. *See also* Martín, Diego
Martín Serrano, Antonio, 403n15
Martín Serrano, Apolinario, 181n11
Martín Serrano, Cristóbal, 160, 163, 181n1, 181n10
Martín Serrano, Francisco, 402n12–13
Martín Serrano, Hernán I, 402n13
Martín Serrano, José Antonio, 509n4
Martín Serrano, Juana, 430n1, 430n4
Martín Serrano, Luis, 181n10, 402n13, 403n15
Martín Serrano, Luis II, 181n11, 181n13
Martín Serrano, Sebastián, 212n9, 402n2, 509n4, 523n4–5, 523n8
Mascareñes, Francisco, 312, 319n10
Mascareñes, Juan, 319n10
Mata, Margaret de, 469n17
Mecía Lobo, Gonzalo (licenciado), 209
medicine, 181n6; and *canser* (septic/infected), 162, 181n9; practiced by master barbers, 161, 168, 181n5, 184n2, 310, 319n8; practiced by surgeons, 160–62, 181n5, 211n1
Medina, Diego de, 104n16
Medina, Manuela, 90n1
Medina, Ramón de, 95–96, 104n16, 105n18
Menchero, Fray Miguel de, 26, 212n9, 402n14, 402n9
Menchero, Juan Miguel de, 485–86, 489n1, 490n7, 490n13
Mendiñueta, Governor Pedro Fermín de: campaigns of, 14; complains about clergy, 241; and keeping the peace, 585; orders cleanup after flood, 645–47; orders response to drumming, 554; settles property access dispute, 635, 637–39; settles *relicario* case, 610, 613–20, 622–23
Mendoza, Tomé Domínguez de, 542n7
merchants, 436n1; and contracts, 494; and Mexico, 468n3, 490n13, 584; outside province, 41; in Santa Cruz, 77n1; in Santa Fe, 460n1, 588, 644n6; of sheep, 436n1; and tithes, 17; and trade, 24–26
Mesita de Juan López grant, 583n3
Mestas, Antonia, 608n9
Mestas, Francisca, 608n4
Mestas, Juan Ignacio, 584–97, 608n6, 608n12, 609n21
Mestas, Ventura, 608n6
Mestas y Peralta, Juan de, 61, 65, 68, 77n4, 77n8, 608n4, 608n6
mestizos, 23, 404, 430n3
Mexico City, 15–16; *audiencia* in, 33, 196, 213n18; church officials of, 213n18; and civil suits, 250n2; Franciscan superiors in, 321; Inquisition in, 403n14; merchants in, 468n3, 490n13; New Mexico settlers from, 40n13, 124n19, 452, 576n9, 608n19; paymaster in, 30n58, 478, 482n4; and petitions, 33–36, 470–73, 478–80, 482n1; prisoners escorted to, 21, 33, 105n19, 124n3; *residencia*/mail delivered to, 20, 91–98, 104n6, 104n9, 130; and trade, 26, 465, 468n3
Miera y Pacheco, Bernardo de, 492–93, 496, 498, 523n4; campaigns against Comanches, 14; maps of, 13, 21, 56n6, 146n1, 212n9, 220n1, 432, 552n1; painting by, **545**; petitions to repair cannons, 544–48; professions of, 544, 553n7; will of, 24
military: of early settlers, 12–15; equipment for, 24, 90n10, 185; escorts, 91–98, 104n9, 125–34, 149–52, 159n3, 218–19; goods, 17, 26, 60n3; and Indian auxiliaries, 57; leaders of, 16, 28, 558; musters of, 82n2,

82n6, 234n15; parade grounds for, 234n15; and reading of *bandos*/decrees, 42–43, 46, 85, 197–98, 204, 222, 410, 646–47; regulations for, 60n2, 61–62, 558; and religious processions, 18, 240, 242–46; royal appointments in, 470–73. *See also* campaigns; presidios; soldiers
militias: aid presidio soldiers, 18–19; of Albuquerque, 57, 79, 470; and *alcaldes mayores*, 19, 21; *alférez* of, 585, 613; called by the drum, 554; campaigns of, 147n34; of Chama, 585, 592; leaders of, 104n10, 146n5, 183, 379, 402n2, 448n7, 482n1, 592, 596, 607n1; necessity of, 13; of Río Arriba, 596; of Santa Fe, 147n34, 183, 559, 585
mines, 26, 494; and captives, 27; in Mexico, 12, 78n14, 182–83, 184n1, 250n11; in New Spain, 201n4; in Parral, 58, 60n3, 182, 218; for salt, 218; sentences to work in, 23, 201n4; for silver, 182, 218
Mingues, Fray Juan, 205, 213n19
Miquelena, Martín de, 93
Mirabal, Fray Juan, 563–66, 575n4, 576n6
Mirabal, Joseph, 566–67, 576n6
Miranda, Antonia de, 181n13, 420n41
Miranda, Javier, 416, 420n41
Miranda, Juan, 125
Miranda, Matías, 420n41
mirrors, 26
missions/missionaries, 27, 29, 212n11, 221, 240–41, 293n5, 293n8, 460n8, 490n5–6, 490n13, 564. *See also* Franciscans
Mizquia, Domingo, 131, 146n15
Mizquia, Lázaro de, 146n15
Mogollón, Flores. *See* Flores Mogollón, Governor Juan Ignacio
Molleno (*santero*), **204**
Mondragón, María de, 366n1
money: gold coins, 56n8, 61; lack of, 252, 414, 478, 516; and *piezas*, 42, 56n8; *plata* (silver), 350, 367n4, 409, 418n2; and soldiers, 30n58; of Spanish settlers, 384; and tithes, 17; and trade, 25, 252. *See also* fines
Montaño, José, 295–302, 308n2
Montaño, Juan, 308n1, 415, 419n26
Montaño, Magdalena, 419n3
Montaño, María, 181n13
Montaño, Pedro, 320–34, 347n2, 403n14, 483–86, 490n12–13
Montaño Sotomayor, Juan, 419n26
Montes Vigil, Francisco I, 482n2
Montes Vigil, Francisco II, 482n2
Montoya, Ana María, 460n8
Montoya, Andrés, 294n13
Montoya, Antonio, 36, 40n11, 133, 135–36, 147n34, 351, 367n10, 371
Montoya, Bárbara, 184n2
Montoya, Diego, 147n34, 212n14, 367n10
Montoya, Francisco Xavier, 420n33
Montoya, Gertrudis, 436n1
Montoya, Josefa, 608n16
Montoya, Juana, 644n1
Montoya, Lugarda, 608n17
Montoya, Manuela, 294n13
Montoya, María, 90n1, 181n10, 367n10
Montoya, Martín, 416, 420n33
Montoya, Miguel, 529
Montoya, Rosa, 367n13, 608n18
Montoya, Salvador, 48, 205, 212n14, 214–15, 223, 482n2, 510
Moors, 450–51, 453–54
Moqui (Hopi) pueblos, 14, 124n4, 147n34, 221, 223–24, 226–28, 233n1, 251
Moraga, Antonia, 181n1, 181n10
Morán, Antonio, 538, 543n9
Morán, Gerónimo, 543n9
Morán, Juan, 543n9
Morán, Miguel, 543n9
Mora Pineda, Juan de la, 132, 134–35, 147n23, 150–52
Moreno, Juan José, 24, 510, 537–38, 542n4–5, 577–81, 583n6, 648n2
Moreto, Antonio, 613–16, 618, 623, 638, 646
Moya, Juan, 466, 469n13
Moya, Lucas, 529
mulattos, 56n9, 84, 450–54, 527
mules, 260n1, 542n7; branding of, 511, 592; breeding of, 524–26, 592; and disputes among traders, 563–70, 584–90, 592–96, 608n14; killed by Apaches, 125, 127–30; mentioned in wills, 420n32, 510; for military escort, 131; as pack animals, 527, 584, 586, 588–90, 592–93, 595–96; for plowing, 612, 614–15; of presidio soldiers, 58, 60n2, 294n15; prices of, 60n2, 585, 587–88; prohibited in trade, 524–28; scarcity of, 527; theft of, 125, 421–22, 430n1, 525; trading of, 26, 41–46, 56n3, 251–54, 349–52, 594–95, 633n2. *See also* macho (male mule)
muleteers, 408–09, 416
muskets, 17–18, 546, 552n1, **559**, 560, 561n2. *See also* arquebuses (guns)

Nambe Pueblo, 29, 213n17, 218, 240–41
Naranjo, Joseph Antonio II, 584, 587–89, 594, 596, 608n12–13
Narváez Valverde, Fray José, 202–06, 211n1
Nativity of Our Lady, 309, 312–14
Nava de Brazinas, Marqués de la. *See* Vargas, Governor Diego de
Navajos, 13, 635, 639; campaigns against, 14, 33, 147n21; missionaries work with, 212n11, 490n5, 490n13; raid settlers, 33–34, 60n1; and trade, 23
Negroes. *See* blacks
nomadic Indians, 12, 27, 608n11, 654n2; constant threat of, 205, 545–47, 554; containment of, 526, 535n2; extortion of, 524, 527; and firearms, 545–46, 554, 558; keeping peace with, 524–27; and Law of the Indies, 148n36; Spanish Crown's policy toward, 16; and trade, 17, 24–26, 28, 41, 524–28. *See also* rancherías (Indian camps); specific tribes
notaries, 184n2, 211n1, 484, 552n4; and blood purity requirement, 449; for *cabildo*, 124n16; for churches, 348n9, 583n2; in El Paso, 40n13, 90n8; of Inquisition, 203–06, 209–11, 489n4, 490n6, 490n13, 524; lack of, 235; and marriage, 451, 608n9; for pueblos, 213n15; in Río Abajo, 448n13; in Santa Cruz, 90n4, 213n15
Nuestra Padre San Francisco convento/parrochia, 202–06
Nuestra Señora de la Soledad (Molleno), **204**
Nuestra Señora de la Soledad of Río Arriba, 90n5, 203–05, 212n9. *See also* La Soledad
Nuestra Señora de Los Ángeles de Porciúncula, 48, 56n16. *See also* Pecos Pueblo
Nueva Viscaya, 15, 27, 185–86, 319n4
Nuevo León, 84, 90n2

obrajes (cotton mills), 23, 31n107, 201n4
Ojo Caliente, 436n1, 524; early settlers of, 26–28, 402n4, 402n14, 403n15, 575n1; and illegal trading case, 368–69, 371, 374–77, 379–80, 382–83
Ojo de Borrego, 367n7
Ojo de Juan Luján paraje, 263, 265–66, 272–75, 293n4
Olavide y Micheleña, Governor Enrique de, 218, 368, 408, 413n2, 414–16, 418n2, 448n7
Olguín, Barolomé, 326, 348n8
Olguín, Thomas, 133–36, 147n27, 348n8
Olivas, Isabel, 90n4
ollas, 112
Oñate, Juan de, 611
Oñate expedition, 146n16, 420n28, 460n9, 543n9
Ontiveros, Josepha de, 515n2
Orosco, Juan Felipe de, 93
Orozco y Trujillo, Bernardina de Salas, 348n11
Ortega, Alejandro, 608n17, 649–51, 654n6
Ortega, Antonio, 654n6
Ortega, Clementa, 348n6
Ortega, Gerónimo de, 159n1, 271, 274–75, 294n15
Ortega, Margarita de, 293n7
Ortega, María de, 575n1
Ortega, Tiburcio de, 86, 90n8
Ortiz, Antonio Joseph, 590, 608n11
Ortiz, Francisco, 583n3
Ortiz, Luis, 583n3, 608n11
Ortiz, Manuel, 578, 583n3
Ortiz, Miguel, 583n3
Ortiz, Nicolás de (witness), 382, 493, 500
Ortiz, Nicolás II, 583n3, 607n1, 608n11
Ortiz, Nicolás III, 584–85, 587–91, 593–97, 607n1, 608n11, 654n2
Ortiz, Toribio, 24, 537–39, 555, 584–97, 607n1, 608n11, 608n14, 633n2

Otermín, Antonio de, 146n18, 367n13, 543n9
Otón, Margaríta, 90n8
Our Lady statue, 577, 580
Oviedo (Spain), 450–54, 460n7
oxen, 66, 68, 189, 542n7, 563, 565–66

Pacheco, Ana María, 460n4
Pacheco, Antonio, 251, 253–54, 260n7
Pacheco, Joseph, 353–54
pack trains, 419n2, 527, 613–15, 618
Padilla, Diego I, 419n8, 419n12
Padilla, Diego II, 415, 419n8, 419n12
Padilla, Francisco, 415, 419n12
Padilla, Joseph, 566, 576n8
Padilla, Juan, 523n4
Padilla, Juana, 523n4, 523n9
Padilla, Julian, 518–20, 523n9
Padilla, María, 576n8
Padilla, Pasquala, 181n6
Páez, Francisco Antonio, 205, 212n12
Páez Hurtado, Gertrudis, 608n11
Páez Hurtado, Juan, 12, 56n5, 170, 402n8, 608n11; biography of, 55n1; and captives, 535n1; and church sanctuary, 221; and council of war, 132, 135; and death benefits petition, 187–89; and gambling case, 61, 67–70; and illegal trading case, 370–71, 373–80, 382–84; leads campaigns against Utes/Apaches, 14; and presidio supply prices, 17; and Rael de Aguilar, 221, 227; recruits settlers, 147n22; in religious procession, 205; sent to Mexico, 21; and trade *bandos*, 41–43, 45
Páez Hurtado, Juan Domingo, 370, 373, 376–78, 380
Palace of the Governors, 40n9, 543n12; archives of, 648n4; and edicts of faith, 203; Franciscan friar lives in, 213n19; goods stolen from, 159n7, 261, 448n8; and religious processions, 243–44; remodeling of, 437, 442; and road-clearing decree, 536–38, 543n13; staff of, 104n2, 147n26. *See also* casa reales
palo (cudgel/pole), 162
parajes, 109, 124n11, 125, 131, 146n1, 146n16, 265, 293n4. *See also* specific names
Parral, Mexico, 26, 58, 60n3, 93, 104n5, 182, 218
Pasqua (Easter), 368, 372, 374, 377, 386
pawned items, 62, 64–66, 68
Pawnees, 13–14, 23, 30n48, 319n9, 421–26
payroll documents, 26–27
peace: and Apaches, 126, 131–35; arms needed for, 135; expenses relating to, 57–58; in the frontier colony, 41, 160; with hostile tribes, 16, 30n59, 148n36; and Law of the Indies, 30n59; at trade fairs, 22; during Vélez Cachupín's term, 524, 585
Peace of Paris, 558
Pecos Pueblo, 32n112, 56n16, 159n12, 212n14; *alcaldes mayores* of, 42, 46–48, 181n3, 214, 239n7, 542n4, 545, 553n7, 560; *custodia* of, 205; deaths in, 29; Franciscan friars in, 575n4; Indian leader of, 535n1; and military equipment, 560; mission of, 240; raided by Comanches, 14, 25, 524; and road-clearing decree, 214; *teniente* of justice for, 608n16; and trade, 25–26, 42, 44–45, 47–48, 56n13, 56n15, 368
Peña, Baltazar de la, 212n5
Peña, Diego Antonio de la, 529
Peña, Joseph Miguel de la, 538–39, 581, 593
Peña, Juan de la, 212n5
Peña, Mateo de la, 203, 205, 212n5
penalties/punishment: banishment, 23, 42–44, 46, 149, 161, 169, 197, 321, 460n8; dismissal from military service, 261, 276, 294n19; excommunication, 320, 331, 381; to guard horse herds, 18, 46, 149–52, 265; imprisonment, 535n4, 554, 586; to join military campaigns, 149, 154, 221, 223, 233n1; loss of goods/livestock, 23, 45–46, 48, 56n5, 56n15, 368, 384, 409, 416, 418n2, 527–28; loss of Indian captives/ slaves, 85; loss of position/rank, 23, 42, 153, 518; pay court costs, 23, 160–61, 169–71, 349, 358, 368; repair buildings, 23, 61, 169–70; to serve as labor, 23, 201n4, 576n9; whipping, 23, 197, 261, 404, 409, 418n2, 527, 563, 569. *See also* fines; jails; stocks
Peñarredonda, Mateo de, 570, 613–16, 618, 623, 638, 646
Peñuela, Marqués de la (governor), 31n63, 56n14, 218; asks viceroy for guns/horses, 57–58; campaigns of, 14, 57–58; and gambling case, 61, 67, 69; and land grants, 82n6; and mail delivery, 104n6; prohibits gambling, 124n12; removes Albuquerque squadron, 470; removes presidio soldiers, 79–80
Peralta, Pedro, 221
Perea, Francisco, 416, 420n32
Perea, Juan de, 420n32
Pérez Mirabal, José, 576n6
petitions: and *acequia* dispute, 437; and animal theft case, 422; for arms/ammunition, 33–35, 39n1; for breach of contract, 491–500; for clothing, 33, 35; and *colcha* dispute, 577–81; for death benefits, 185–90, 195n1, 195n6; for debt payment, 584–90; explanation of, 13, 19–22; and gambling case, 62–70; and García discipline case, 321–22, 333–34; for horses, 33, 35; for land grants, 28, 82n2, 82n5, 83n11, 402n1; to leave the province, 182–83, 251–52; for military appointment, 470–73; for presidio soldiers, 79–81; and property disputes, 21, 576n13, 635–39; for reinstating drummer, 554–56; and *relicario* replacement, 611–23; for repairing cannons, 544–48; to repeal wool embargo, 465–67; of Santa Fe *cabildo*, 33–36; for silk clothes contract, 353–55; for soldiers' salaries, 478–80; and trade, 25, 43–44, 252–56, 496; and water rights, 21, 295–302
Philip V. *See* Felipe V (king of Spain)
Pichule (San Juan Indian), 422, 424–25
Picuris Pueblo, 220n1, 420n28; *alcaldes mayores* of, 47, 90n1; early landowners of, 523n6; Franciscan friars in, 575n4; Indian servant from, 576n11; and land grants, 90n5; and military equipment, 558, 560; and road-clearing decree, 214–15; and trade, 25–26, 56n13, 56n15
pieza, 27, 42, 56n8
Piñeda, Juan de, 86, 90n6
Pino, Joachín Mariano, 566, 576n9
Pino, Juan del, 29
piñole de mescale, 131, 146n17
piñon nuts, 26, 56n3, 93, 104n5, 239n2
Pinto, Roque de, 226; and Apache attack, 126–30; biography of, 104n11; and council of war, 132, 136; and death benefits petition, 187, 189–90; and dispute in Chimayó, 168–70; and fugitive soldiers case, 108; and gambling case, 70; and mail delivery case, 94–96; and soldiers' criminal case, 150–54
pistols, 196, **197**, 201n2, 552n1. *See also* arms; guns
Plains Indians, 27, 431, 558
plata (silver, money). *See* money: *plata* (silver)
Plaza de Jarales, 27
Plaza de Los Ángeles, 212n9
plazas, 23; description of, 13, 234n15; and reading of *bandos*, 46, 222, 462; and religious processions, 18, 240–46, 250n3; in Santa Fe, 18, 46, 197, 222, 226, 240–46, 410, 462, 464n3, 553n7, 645; of Tomé grant, 431–32
plazas de armas, 226, 234n15, 242–46
plowshare, 68
poet, 608n19
Pojoaque Pueblo, 63, 77n2, 77n4, 77n8, 104n2, 124n18, 213n15, 234n11, 430n1, 482n1, 608n6
police authority, 20–21, 33
political power, 19, 213n18, 241, 321
poor, the, 23, 34–35, 42, 253, 331, 409, 448n8, 519, 545, 578
Portillo y Urrisola, Governor Manuel del, 17, 517, 558, 562n8
pottery, 26, 106, 112
presidios, 12–13, 40n7, 40n12, 90n6; and armorers, 39n2; cannons for, 544–48, **549**; corruption at, 15; description of, 18; drummers of, 56n9; and gambling, 62; and Indian attacks, 30n48; inventories of, 558–60; prisoners held at, 18, 23, 94, 150–51, 153–54; protect settlers, 79–80; soldiers at, 16, 18, 35, 40n13, 57, 77n8, 82n9, 90n5, 104n10; supplies of, 15–17, 60n2; system of, 14–15
priests/priesthood, 212n3, 449–50, 460n5, 648n2
prisons. *See* jails
probate cases, 82n6
procurador (legal adviser), 577, 583n2, 635. *See also* attorneys
Propaganda Fide, 212n11
Protector of the Indians, 181n7–8
Puaray Pueblo, 293n2, 490n7

public ritual, 241. *See also* Corpus Christi festival; religious processions
Puebla, Mexico, 181, 450–54, 542n7, 654n3
Pueblo Indians: arms of, 552n1; attorneys for, 523n4; and conflict with Spanish, 25, 469n17; conversion of, 27; and Corpus Christi, 241; demographics of, 12–13, 29n7, 552n1; enslavement of, 27–28, 31n107; farming of, 516–18; and gambling, 62; and hostile tribes, 13, 490n7, 524, 526; and lawsuits, 22–23, 90n10, 181n7; legal rights/privileges of, 181n7; mistreatment of, 22, 90n8, 124n4, 517, 524, 535n8; protection of, 13, 16–18, 28, 40n14, 181n7; protect settlers, 517; settlers encroach on, 516–19; Spanish Crown's policy toward, 16; and trade, 22–28, 41–42, 44–45, 47–49, 56n4–5, 56n15, 106, 261, 408–10, 418n2, 491–93, 498, 526–28, 535n3, 563–70, 584; and trip to salt lakes, 218–19; used as labor, 214–15, 469n17, 519–20, 576n11
Pueblo of San Geronimo de Taos. *See* Taos
Pueblo Revolt of 1680, 12, 28, 44, 125, 181n4, 432, 490n7
Pueblos: abandonment of, 293n2, 293n5; and *alcaldías*, 21; governors' visits to, 18, 20; and hostile tribes, 13; land of, 28, 308n2; presidio soldiers flee to, 106, 110, 124n2; raids on, 25, 524
puesto, 13, 26, 308n6, 349. *See also* specific names
punche (tobacco), 26, 77n6. *See also* tobacco

Quantitlán, Mexico, 93, 104n5, 181n6
Quemado Pueblo, 26, 419n11, 654n5
Querétaro, Mexico, 104n1, 205, 490n10
Quintana, Antonia, 419n21
Quintana, Joseph de, 255–56
Quintana, Juan Francisco, 589, 608n19
Quintana, Manuela, 347n3, 468n4
Quintana, Miguel de, 63–64, 66–67, 410, 430n8, 608n19
Quintana, Nicolás, 423, 430n8
Quiros, José de, 182–83, 184n1
Quiros, María de, 12, 182–83, 184n1, 250n11

racial issues, 23, 449–54
Rael, Nicolás, 594
Rael, Pedro Marsial, 254
Rael de Aguilar, Alfonso I, 36, 40n4, 40n14, 43, 46–48, 108–15, 124n8, 132–34, 136, 169–70, 186, 196, 212n14, 221, 239n2
Rael de Aguilar, Alonso II, 195n1, 201n3, 221, 223–28, 234n13, 260n9, 263–64, 266–71, 543n10
Rael de Aguilar, Eusebio, 108–15, 124n8, 221, 223, 415
raids, 19, 21; of Apaches, 33–34, 79–80, 149, 261; of Comanches, 14; constant threat of, 13–14; and land grants, 28, 348n8; on livestock herds, 31n111, 404–05, 465; of Navajos, 14, 33–34; on Pueblos, 25, 524; on settlers, 517, 524, 527–28
Ramírez, Felipe de, 350, 367n6
Ramírez, Gregorio, 186, 188, 195n5
Ramos, Juan Antonio, 186, 188, 195n4, 195n6
rams, 169–70, 189, 409, 415, 494
rancherías (Indian camps), 26, 368–69, 376, 524, 527–28, 535n5
ranches/ranching, 15, 26–27, 212n9, 356, 367n13, 465, 482n2, 524, 542n4, 607n1, 635, 639
Rancho San Clemente, 82n3
ransom. *See* rescate (ransom)
reales cédulas (royal orders), 21. *See also* decrees
Reano, Joseph de, 254
receipts, 21–22, 25, 584, 596
regidores (*cabildo* members). *See* cabildo (town council): regidores (members) of
Reglamento de 1729, 15–19, 24, 30n52
relicarios, 610–11, **612**, 613–22
religious brotherhood, 577
religious processions, 18, 20, 202–06, 210, 240–42, **243**, 244–46, 250n3, 403n20
religious services, 384; baptisms, 83n10, 84–85, 86, 90n3, 181n6, 575n1; for Corpus Christi, 240–46, 250n5; and edicts of faith, 202, 205–06, 210–11; and lay brotherhood, 583n5; mass for the dead, 320–28, 331–32; for Our Lady of Nativity, 309, 311–14, 319n6; paying for, 580; and reading of *bandos*, 528; vespers, 250n10, 309, 311–14. *See also* luminarias

Rendón, Catarina Palomino, 367n13
Rendón, Francisco, 183
renta decimal (church tithes). *See* tithes: church
rescate (ransom), 27, 42, 48, 56n4, 252, 369, 525. *See also* trade; trade fairs
residencia (report on governor), 17, 19, 91–93, 98, 104n5
Revillagigedo, Count of, **479**, 482n3, 482n5
Rico de Rojas, Casilda Cedillo, 82n7
Rico de Rojas, Felipa Sedillo, 293n7
Rico de Rojas, Juan Sedillo, 239n8
Rico y Rojas, Joachín Sedillo, 552n4
rifara (raffle, gambling), 62–66, 77n5, 78n9. *See also* gambling
Río Abajo: early landowners of, 293n4; early settlers of, 82n4, 104n2, 159n10, 212n14, 308n2, 348n7, 368, 420n26, 448n13, 490n8, 586–87; and horse trade case, 251–54; and land grants, 402n1; lieut. governor of, 147n30; location of, 159n8; and Pedro López case, 149–50, 152; and traders' contract, 499; and traders' dispute, 586–87
Río Arriba, 654n5; and branded livestock, 511; and dispute among traders, 565, 567–68, 596; early history of, 212n9; early landowners of, 402n13; early settlers of, 293n6, 402n2, 523n8, 575n1, 654n1; and illegal trading case, 369, 379, 381, 383–84; militia of, 596; and traders' contract, 493–94, 500
Río Chiquito, 645–46
Río del Norte, 146n9, 613, 616. *See also* Río Grande
Río del Oso, 402n9
Río Grande: and *acequia* disputes, 295, 437; changing shape of, 635, 644n8; and land grants, 82n3, 234n5, 367n7, 431; settlers living near, 13, 146n1, 146n4, 147n26, 220n1, 490n7, 635, 644n8. *See also* Appendix: Maps
Río Puerco, 13, 28, 234n5, 260n4, 348n8
Río Trampas, 220n1, 523n6
Rivera, Bárbara, 419n25
Rivera, Francisco de, 61–66, 68–70, 77n1, 77n5, 78n9, 222
Rivera, Joseph, 633n2
Rivera, Juan Felipe de, 294n14, 416, 434, 518–19
Rivera, Miguel de, 271–72, 275–76, 294n14
Rivera, Pedro de, 15, 17, 19, 24, 31n91, 32n112
roads, 214–15, 536–39
Roa y Carrillo, Francisco, 442, 462
Rodarte de Castro Xabalera, María, 609n20
Rodríguez, Estevan, 56n9, 85, 198, 201n6, 554–56, 581
Rodríguez, Lorenzo, 95, 104n15, 105n18
Rodríguez, Sebastián, 43, 46, 56n9, 201n6, 554
Romero, Agustina, 78n10, 450–54, 460n9
Romero, Ana, 523n10
Romero, Andrés, 519–20, 523n6
Romero, Antonio, 519–20, 523n6
Romero, Baltazar, 79, 415, 419n7, 419n16, 469n11, 516
Romero, Bartolomé I, 460n9
Romero, Bartolomé III, 348n10, 420n28, 654n5
Romero, Diego, 184n2, 523n5–6, 523n10
Romero, Domingo, 27, 583n3, 589, 608n17
Romero, Felipa, 260n7
Romero, Felipe, 127–28, 351–52, 419n16, 649–51, 654n5
Romero, Francisco, 519, 523n6, 560
Romero, Francisco Xavier, 160–62, 169–70, 181n6
Romero, Graziana, 106, 109, 112, 124n16
Romero, Gregorio, 419n16
Romero, Isabel, 83n10
Romero, José, 419n16
Romero, Juan, 519–20
Romero, Margarita, 609n20
Romero, María, 348n8
Romero, María Gregorio, 419n16
Romero, Matías, 328, 348n10–11, 415, 420n28
Romero, Miguel, 520, 523n6, 589, 608n17–18
Romero, Pablo, 519
Romero, Pedro, 415, 419n16
Romero, Rosalia, 348n10–11
Romero, Salvador, 460n9

Romero, Tadeo, 448n9
Romero de Pedraza, Antonio, 608n17
Romero de Pedraza, Francisco, 124n16, 608n17
Romero de Salas, Francisca, 124n16
Romero Vallejo, Ángela Teresa, 348n11
Romo, José Manuel de, 449–54, 460n5
Romo de Vera, Joseph, 449–54, 460n1, 467, 473, 480
Ron y Thobar, Vicente Ginzo, 537–39, 542n6, 547
Rosa, María de la, 367n10
royal horse herd, 18, 106–08, 111, 113–14, 149–52, 197, 265, 552n5, 560. *See also* horses
royal *junta*, 35, 40n3
royal treasury, 24, 40n3, 47, 104n6, 301, 409, 415, 471, 527–28
Roybal, Dominga, 542n5
Roybal, Joseph de, 24
Roybal, Juana, 542n4–5
Roybal, Manuela de, 78n14
Roybal, María Manuela, 648n2
Roybal, Santiago, 78n14, 646, 648n2
Roybal, Ygnacio de, 154, 205, 212n15, 542n4
Roybal de Torrado, Ignacio, 648n2
rubric, 31n96, 40n7
Ruiz, Gregoria, 420n29, 468n3
Ruiz Cordero, Juan, 169, 183, 225, 234n12
rustling, 608n13

Sabinal, 27
saddles, 18, 61–66, 68, 77n3, 78n11, 107, 151, **153**, 163, 275, 405, 542n7, 567, 590
Sáenz, Luis Jaramillo, 538
Sáenz de Lezaún, Juan, 483–84, 490n6, 490n13, 524–25
Saint Paul, 209–10, 212n13
Saiz, Juliana, 308n3
Salas, Bernardina, 147n28
Salas, Francisca, 448n9
Salas, José de, 437, 439–43, 448n2, 448n9–10
Salas, María, 420n27
Salas, Sebastián de, 113–14, 124n18
Salas Jaramillo, Francisca de, 437–38, 440, 442–43, 448n2, 448n10. *See also* Jaramillo, Francisca
Salas y Hurtado, Francisca, 448n3
Salazar, Antonio, 431
Salazar, J. Richard, 241
Salazar, María de, 90n7, 419n9, 608n8
Salazar, Rita, 477n9
Salazar y López, Alfonso, 239n7
Salazar y Villaseñor, Joseph Chacon Medina. *See* Peñuela, Marqués de la (governor)
Salcedo, Nemisio, 544
Salinas, 20, 149–51, 218–19, 460n8
salvos (salutes), 210, 241–43, 245–46, 250n8, 309–14, 319n6, 319n11–12, 558
San Agustín de la Isleta, 87
San Antonio grant, 82n6
San Buenaventura, 77n8
Sánchez, Antonio Felix, 450–54
Sánchez, Bartolomé, 49
Sánchez, Efigenia, 635–37
Sánchez, Francisco, 415, 437–42, 448n7, 565–67, 569, 585–86, 591–92, 596, 644n5
Sánchez, Isidro: biography of, 261–62; criminal case against, 261–76, 294n19, 448n8; family of, 407n6; robs Palace of the Governors, 159n7, 261, 448n8; signs for petitioners, 405, 407n6, 415; as witness, 296–97, 299–301, 323–31, 333–34, 433, 439–43, 448n8
Sánchez, Joachín, 271, 273, 276, 294n13, 371, 381
Sánchez, José, 404–05, 407n2, 415, 466, 469n13, 490n8, 635–38, 644n1, 644n5
Sánchez, José Lázaro, 592, 608n9
Sánchez, Juan Cristóbal, 635–38, 644n5
Sánchez, Julián, 586, 589, 591–93, 595–96, 608n9

Sánchez, María Antonia, 608n9
Sánchez, María Gertrudes, 483, 485, 490n8
Sánchez, Miguel, 589, 592, 609n20
Sánchez, Pedro, 592
Sánchez de Iñigo, Jacinto, 70, 294n13, 407n2, 419n8, 448n7, 490n8, 609n20, 636, 644n1, 644n5
San Clemente, 436n1, 634n10
Sandía Mountains, 13–14, 18, 261–62, 293n4
Sandía Pueblo: abandonment of, 293n2; as *alcaldía*, 21; description of, 293n2, 490n7; early settlers of, 419n21, 477n1, 477n9, 490n7, 490n12; Franciscan friars in, 489n1, 490n7; Hopis and Tewas arrive at, 212n11; livestock trespass in, 516; resettlement of, 477n1, 489n1, 490n7; and witchcraft accusation, 483–86, 489n1
Sandoval, Andrés de, 256, 260n12
Sandoval, Apolonia de, **545**
Sandoval, Felipe, 650
Sandoval de Martínez, Juan de Dios, 124n19, 260n3
Sandoval de Martínez, Miguel, 251–56, 260n3, 453, 460n12
Sandoval y Manzanares, Ana de, 195n1
San Felipe de Albuquerque. *See* Albuquerque
San Felipe Pueblo, 86, 213n17, 368, 489n4
San Gerónimo de Taos Pueblo. *See* Taos
San Ildefonso Pueblo: *alcaldes mayores* of, 123n2; baptism at, 575n1; and edicts of faith, 202–03; Franciscan friars in, 92, 104n3, 212n3, 213n17, 575n4; *justicias mayor* of, 213n15; *procurador* (legal adviser) of, 583n2; and witchcraft accusations, 489n2
San Juan Feast Day, 107, 109–11
San Juan Pueblo: *alcaldes mayores* of, 382, 403n17; and animal theft case, 422, 424–25; early settlers of, 212n9; Franciscan friars in, 575n4; and illegal trading case, 379, 382; and land disputes, 608n13; and land grants, 90n5; livestock trespass in, 516; and traders' disputes, 563–70, 575n2, 596; and witchcraft trial, 489n2
San Miguel Chapel, 26–27, 159n1, 239n2, 460n11, 482n2, 577
San Miguel de Vado, 27, 431, 608n16
Santa Ana Pueblo, 29, 86, 124n2, 147n28, 489n2, 489n4, 529, 535n8
Santa Clara Pueblo, 576n9; *alcaldes mayores* of, 402n2; early settlers of, 576n6; Franciscan friars in, 104n3, 575n4; and hostile tribes, 13; and land grants, 148n35, 575n5; and traders' dispute, 584, 591–92, 594, 596, 608n13
Santa Cruz de la Cañada, 20, 33, 90n4, 147n31, 460n6; and 1696 Revolt, 41, 56n7; as *alcaldía*, 21, 220n1; and animal theft case, 421; baptisms in, 86, 181n6, 575n1; and Chimayó dispute, 161–68, 170–71; and church sanctuary, 221–23; deaths in, 29; early landowners of, 124n18, 147n22, 181n3, 195n1, 293n1, 403n17; early settlers of, 13, 77n1, 77n4, 78n10, 159n1, 159n5, 181n13, 195n3–4, 260n3, 420n35–36, 420n44, 430n4, 430n8, 448n13, 460n11, 482n2, 515n2, 523n3, 543n11, 575n1, 576n8, 585, 593, 608n4, 608n19; and edicts of faith, 203; founding of, 56n7; Franciscan friars in, 575n4; and gambling case, 61–70; and illegal trading case, 369, 372, 375, 381–82, 384, 386; and livestock branding, 510–11, **512**, **513**; military of, 181n3, 515n2, 558, 560; and Pedro López case, 149–50; and trade, 42, 44–46, 368, 410; and traders' contract, 492–93; and traders' disputes, 563–70, 593; and trip to salt lakes, 218–19; and weapons *bando*, 197–98
Santa Fe: and *acequia* disputes, 301, 442, 461–62; as *alcaldía*, 21; and Apache attack, 125–26, 131–36; and attack on *alcalde mayor*, 431, 434; *ayudantes* of, 146n4; *ayuntamiento* of, 196, 201n1, 214, 227, 461; Benavides reception in, 208–10; black residents of, 56n9; and blood purity testimonies, 449–54; and church sanctuary, 221–28; and *colcha* dispute, 577–81; and corpse inquest, 649–51; and death benefits petition, 186–90, 195n1, 195n6; deaths in, 29; and debt petitions, 585–88; and dispute in Chimayó, 160–61, 166, 168–71; early landowners of, 77n7, 90n6, 104n16, 148n35, 319n2, 348n12, 420n34, 469n13, 477n7, 538–39, 542n4, 543n8, 543n12, 552n6, 553n7, 607n1, 654n2; early settlers of, 13, 90n7, 146n5, 147n27, 294n15, 420n26, 460n3, 482n8, 608n6; and edicts of faith, 202–03, 209–11; fiesta of, 654n2; flooding in, 18, 464n3, 645–47; and gambling case, 67–69; and García discipline case, 322, 332, 334–35; and horse trading, 252–56; and illegal trading case, 368, 370–80, 382–85; and Isidro Sánchez case, 294n19; lieut. general of, 262–62, 373–74, 583n2, 607n1; and livestock, 405, 510; and mail delivery case, 91–98; and military appointments, 472–73; militia

of, 147n34; and petitions, 20, 62, 67–69, 183; and property dispute, 637; and reading of *bandos*, 46, 48, 197–98; and *relicario* lawsuit, 610–23; religious processions in, 202–06, 210, 240–42, **243**, 244–46, 250n3; and road-clearing decrees, 214–15, 536–39; San Francisco Street in, 536–38; Sena Plaza in, 553n7; and silk clothes contract, 350, 358; and tailor apprenticeship, 235–37; and Taos fences, 517–19; and trade *bando*, 410, 416; and trade restrictions, 528–29; and traders' contract, 500; and traders' disputes, 564, 590, 593–96; and trip to salt lakes, 218–19; and weapons *bando*, 196–99. *See also* cabildo (town council); casa reales; chapels; churches; militias; Nuestra Padre San Francisco convento/parrochia; Palace of the Governors; plazas

Santa Fe guardhouse, 18, 23, 149–51, 153–54, 159n7, 160, 166, 170, 198, 222–27, 261–63, 269–70, 311–12, 314, 529, 545, 547, 559, 586

Santa Fe New Mexican, 645

Santa Fe presidio: ammunition supplies of, 263, 274–75, 544–48, 558–59; auditor of, 187; campaigns of, 147n21; captains of, 56n14, 91, 104n1, 104n9, 146n21, 147n27, 187, 260n3; chaplain of, 213n19; consolidation of forces in, 79; and council of war, 132–36; description of, 15, 18; and edicts of faith, 203–04; and flood cleanup, 645–46; and fugitive soldiers case, 91, 93–94, 96, 108, 110, 114; inventory of, 544, 558–60; and Isidro Sánchez case, 261–77; lieutenants of, 523n4, 542n6, 543n12; number of soldiers at, 18, 104n2, 147n30, 195n6, 545–47; officers of, 319n3, 554–56, 608n11, 633n2, 645–46; and Pedro López case, 149–54; and reading of *bandos*, 646–47; and religious processions, 203–04; and retrieval of stolen livestock, 57–58; sergeants of, 146n15, 184n2, 186, 234n8, 552n5, 644n1; soldiers of, 104n15, 148n35, 159n12, 195n3, 195n5, 260n3, 261–76, 294n15, 319n1, 319n5, 379, 420n31, 448n9, 460n5, 470–71, 478–80, 509n1, 544–48, 552n3, 554, 578, 634n8, 654n6; and soldiers' salaries, 18, 319n2, 478–80; supply caravan of, 610–11, 613–15, 618; and trade *bando*, 529; and wounded soldier case, 309–14. *See also* drummers

Santa Fe River, 90n4, 535n8, 645, 649

Santa Rosa, 368

santero, 544, **545**

Santiago (Comanche Indian), 382, 386

Santistevan, Domingo Anselmo, 589, 608n16

Santistevan, José, 608n16

Santistevan, Juan de, 309–14, 319n5, 562n6

Santistevan, Salvador de, 126–29, 132, 134, 146n4, 244–46

Santo Domingo Pueblo, 86, 124n16, 208–09, 223, 368

scandals, 17, 242–44, 321–22, 483–84

scribes, 12–13, 23, 78n10, 90n8, 430n8, 471

Sedillo, Antonio, 547, 552n4

Sedillo, Casilda López, 82n2

Sedillo, Isabel López, 82n5

Sedillo, Joachín, 80, 82n2–3, 82n5, 104n2, 239n8, 367n7, 552n4

Sedillo, Juana de, 104n2, 239n8

Segura, Pedro, 95, 105n17–18

Sena, Bernardino de, 553n7, 648n2

Sena, Diego de, 560

Sena, Manuel, 235

Sena, María Gregoria, 419n22

Sena, Matías, 650

Sena, Tomás Antonio de, 544, 547–48, 553n7, 650

Serna, Catalina de la, 523n3

Serna, Cristóbal de la, 132, 134–35, 146n21, 523n6

Serna, Felipe de la, 146n21

Serrano de Salazar, Pedro Martín, 90n5

servants, 422, 424, 461, 490n12, 492, 494–95, 497, 563, 565–68, 576n11, 649–51

Seville, Spain, 55n1, 90n2, 124n18, 510, 542n4

Sevilleta, 26, 146n9, 535n8, 614, 616–17, 634n9

sheep, 189; ban on sale of, 408–09, 414–16, 465; and *colcha* dispute, 577, 579–80; early ranchers of, 367n13, 607n1; legal case concerning, 261, 297–98; pastures for, 517–18; of Pueblo Indians, 517–18; raiding of, 25, 31n111; and tithes, 414; trading of, 26, 31n111, 56n3, 436n1, 465, 491, 494–95

shields, 18, 163, 526

shoemaker, 181n6

Sierra, Nicolás de la, 635, 638–39, 644n6

Sierra de Los Ladrones, 58, 60n1

silla (seat), 205, 213n18

Silva, Antonio de, 420n29, 448n13, 468n3

Silva, Felipe de, 420n29, 466, 468n3

Silva, Francisca, 420n42

Silva, Francisco, 415, 420n29, 468n3

Silva, Gertrudis, 82n7

Silva, José de, 199

Silva, María, 420n29, 437, 439–41, 448n9–10, 448n13, 468n3

Silva, Micaela, 448n13

silver, 182, 218, 367n4, 370, 409, 418n2, 610–11, 622

Sisneros, Francisco Antonio, 495, 567–69

Sitio de Gutiérrez, 234n5

sitios, 146n1

slander, 181n1, 270, 381, 419n8, 490n12, 588

slavery, 13, 27, 84, 201n4, 526. *See also* captives; rescate (ransom)

smoke signals, 128–29, 132

smoking, 422

Socorro del Sur, 31n107

soldiers, 30n52, 77n4; additional petitioned for, 33; aided by militias, 18–19; cases/claims against, 106–15, 159n12, 261–77, 309–14; complaints of, 56n14; as couriers, 18, 104n6, 124n15, 159n9; and death benefits, 185–90, 195n6; desertion of, 149–54, 159n1; duties of, 15, 17–19, 35; equipment/uniforms of, 18, 30n58, 33, 57, 149, 152, 471–72, 477n4, 477n7; as escorts, 18, 79–80, 91–98, 104n6, 104n9–10, 105n19, 108, 124n3, 125–34, 610, 615, 618; flee the kingdom, 106–15, 234n14; and gambling, 61–62; and guarding of horse herds, 18–19, 46, 197; killed by Indians, 186; and lawsuits, 22–23; and mail delivery case, 91–98; poor pay of, 18–19, 30n58, 185, 188; at presidios, 13, 15–19, 24, 35, 40n13, 46, 57, 90n5, 96, 104n2, 104n15–16, 105n17–19, 149; protect settlers, 79–81, 149; pursue Apaches, 57–58, 149; and religious processions, 240, 242–46; and royal horse herd, 106–07, 149–52; and trade, 24; and weapons prohibition, 196–97

sombrero gordo (large hat), 152, 159n14

Soria, Juan Manuel, 473, 479, 482n5

Sotelo Osorio, Felipe, 209, 213n20

Spain, King of, **34**; appoints governors, 19; attitude toward Indians, 16; confidential letters of, 93; and council of war, 134; municipal charters of, 20; orders Apaches baptized, 84–85; privileges given by, 33; and weapon prohibition *bando*, 196. *See also* Carlos V (emperor, king of Spain); Felipe V (king of Spain)

Spanish Reconquest, 41, 644n1; changes resulting from, 14, 16, 19–20, 28; led by Vargas, 12–14, 33, 544; and returning settlers, 77n2, 82n6, 146n21, 147n26, 147n29, 348n7, 436n2, 449, 460n9, 460n14, 477n5, 542n3, 552n5, 635

Spanish settlements: and 1696 Revolt, 41; complicated relationships among, 644n5; conflicts between, 31n112; and conflicts with Indians, 25, 149, 517, 523n5; defense of, 13–15; demographics of, 12–13, 29n7, 552n1; encroach on Indian lands, 77n2, 516–19; financial viability of, 24, 35; Franciscans' control over, 321; and Indian depredations, 212n9; laws of, 27; and legal cases, 22–23; protection of, 17–18, 28, 34, 79–81, 107, 135, 149, 205, 525, 536, 545–47, 554; raids/attacks on, 524, 527; seek peace with hostile tribes, 524–26; spiritual welfare of, 84; and street width, 536; and traveling outside province, 20, 91–98, 106–15; and weapons *bando*, 196–99

stirrups, 62, **63**, 64–65, 77n3, 294n14, 477n4

stocks, 23, 319n9, 321, 334, 421–22, 469n13

stonemason, 77n1

St. Raphael (Miera y Pacheco painting), **545**

sumaria, 371, 402n8

supply caravans, 104n6, 209, 213n20, 610–11, 613–15, 618

swords, 17, **264**, 552n1; and López case, 152; prohibition of, 196–97, 201n2, 525; of Santa Fe presidio, 559; soldiers pay for, 18; trading of, 372, 374, 377, 381, 383, 497; use of, 223–24, 261, 263, 265, 267, 270, 274–75, 431–33

Tafoya, Antonio, 575n5

Tafoya, Felipe, 263–64, 266–71, 528, 577–81, 583n2, 635–37

Tafoya, Juan, 563, 566, 568–69, 575n5, 585

Tafoya Altamarino, Antonio, 133, 147n32, 312, 583n2

Tafoya Altamarino, Cristóbal de, 575n5
Tagle, Fray Juan de, 91–93, 98, 104n3, 203–06, 212n3
tailors, 235–37, 239n1, 239n4–5, 542n7
Tamaris, Felipe, 310–14
Tamaris, Francisco, 195n1, 196, 201n3, 221, 223–24, 228, 234n8
Tamarón, Bishop, 212n9, 562n8, 633n4
Tano language, 490n5
Taos, 31n112, 40n12, 575n2; as *alcaldía*, 21; attacked by Comanches, 517, 562n8; and baptism of Apaches, 86; blacksmiths in, 182; and branded livestock, 510; campaigns leave from, 14; early landowners of, 184n2, 293n4, 419n7, 523n4, 523n6; early settlers of, 13, 523n6, 523n8, 542n5, 654n5; Franciscan friars in, 212n11, 575n4; and Indian land, 77n2, 516–20; and land grants, 28; and military equipment, 558, 560; and order to fence property, 516–20; and pueblo supply inventory, 633n2; and road-clearing decree, 214–15; and trade, 25–26, 42, 44–45, 47–48, 56n13, 56n15, 368, 528; and trade *bandos*, 410, 529; and trip to salt lakes, 218–19
taxes, 16, 415
Tenorio de Alba, Cayetano, 78n10, 309, 311–13, 319n2, 319n6, 560, 562n6
Tenorio de Alba, Manuel, 32n112, 237, 239n7, 477n7
Tenorio de Alba, Miguel: biography of, 78n10; and church sanctuary *bando*, 222, 225, 227–28; and Corpus Christi, 245–46; family of, 78n10, 239n7; and gambling case, 61, 65–66, 68–69; land of, 77n2; and trip to salt lakes, 219; and weapons *bando*, 198; as witness, 188
Tenorio de Alba, Teresa, 477n7
Territorial Laws (1851), 235
Territorial Legislature, 214
Terrus, Joseph de, 370–71, 434
Tesuque Pueblo, 90n10, 213n17, 214–15, 220n1, 482n2, 538–39
Tewas, 147n22, 147n33, 212n11, 213n15, 218–19
Texas settlers, 25–26
textiles: brocade hangings, 245; looms for, 32n119; mills for, 201n4; prices of, 585; and tithes, 26; trading of, 26, 585; wall tapestries, 239n2; woven, 26, 32n119, 585, 590. *See also* blankets; colcha; fabric; wool
tithes: church, 25–26, 414, 418n2, 542n4; collection of, 17, 24–26, 414, 418n2, 542n4; records of, 24, 26; and trade goods, 414, 418n2
Tiwas, 293n2, 293n8, 489n1, 490n7
tobacco, 17, 26, 61, 63–66, 68, 77n6, 131
Toledo, Spain, 509n10, 523n10
Tomé, 146n14, 147n26, 262, 419n10, 419n25, 420n42, 552n5, 576n9, 596, 633n4, 635, 637
Tomé grant, 27, 82n2, 82n5, 83n11, 348n8, 366n1, 419n11, 420n44, 431–32, 448n7, 448n9
tools: awls, 26, 239n2, 565, 568; axes, 215, 241; for carpenters, 542n7; for farming/cleaning *acequias*, 461, **462**, 464n2; hatchet, 498; metal utensils, 26, 239n2; trading of, 26; used as weapons, 160, 163, 165. *See also* coa (shovel)
torreones (towers), 404–05, 543n12
Torres, Cristóbal de, 56n5, 133–34, 136, 151, 159n9, 222, 402n1
Torres, Diego de, 24, 82n2, 83n9, 159n9, 368–86, 402n1, 402n8, 431, 433–34, 469n17, 608n13
Torres, Francisca de, 181n2
Torres, Joseph, 383
Torres, Juan de, 80, 82n9
Torres, Nicolás, 402n1
Torres, Rosa de, 420n32
town criers, 20, 201n6, 554, 647
trabuco (blunderbuss), 152, 159n11
trade: by barter, 18, 25, 251–56, 368, 509n14, 525, 535n1, 564–65; of captives, 24–28, 32n112, 84, 527, 576n11; caravans of, 14–15, 18, 20, 24, 26, 585, 590, 592; centers of, 56n13; complaints about, 576n9; contracts for, 349–58, 491–500; disputes over, 563–70; embargos of, 408–10, 414, 465–67; of face powder, 349; and governors, 17; illegal, 12, 24, 27, 41, 56n5, 368–86, 524–25, 563–64; importance of, 25, 28, 45; licenses for, 16, 22, 24, 56n15, 492, 500, 564; and money, 252, 350, 414; and outsiders, 41–49, 56n15; of presidio items, 149; and prices, 20, 25, 41–46, 524–27, 535n1, 535n3; profession of, 239n2; and prohibited goods, 22, 383, 402n5, 527; prohibited outside province, 368–86, 408–10, 413n1, 414–16, 418n2, 465; prohibited outside trade fairs, 368–69, 527; for provisions, 528; regulations for, 19, 23–24, 28, 41–49, 56n15, 368–69, 402n5, 448n7, 524–30, 535n1; routes of, 15, 24–28; and tithes, 17, 414, 418n2; unlicensed, 19, 26
trade fairs: and Apaches, 42, 84; authorization/opening of, 368–77, 379, 383–86; and Comanches, 25, 558; disagreements at, 524, 526–27, 535n3, 565; licensed, 20, 22, 24, 27, 56n15, 524, 528; overseen by governors, 20; Pawnees purchased at, 421; and ransom, 48, 56n4, 421; and reading of *bandos*, 528; restrictions on, 27, 41–49, 381, 524–30; soldiers barter goods at, 18–19
traitors, 48
treason, 234n7
Treaty of Fontainbleu, 558
tribute, 14, 22
Trinidad, Juana Hernández de la, 482n8
Truchas, 26, 28
Trujillo, Andrés, 309–13, 319n4
Trujillo, Antonio, 372, 374–76, 378–81, 383, 402n10
Trujillo, Baltazar, 61–68, 70, 77n2, 77n4, 78n9
Trujillo, Bartolo, 430n1
Trujillo, Cristóbal, 181n3, 195n1
Trujillo, Estefania, 575n1
Trujillo, Joseph, 159n5, 160–68, 170–71, 181n3, 189, 195n9, 198
Trujillo, Juan, 61–65, 68, 77n2, 77n4, 189
Trujillo, Juan Diego, 566
Trujillo, Lorenzo, 261–76, 293n1
Trujillo, María, 77n4
Trujillo, Mateo, 133, 136, 148n35
Trujillo, Pablo, 421–25, 430n1, 430n4
Trujillo, Pasqual, 104n2, 185–90, 195n1, 319n4, 402n10
Trujillo, Rosalia, 608n19

Ugarte, Diego de, 371, 373–74, 376–80, 382–83
Ulibarrí, Antonio de, 87, 90n10, 260n7, 309–14, 410, 449–54, 462
Ulibarrí, Juan de, 36, 40n7, 44, 47–49, 90n10, 181n3
Ulibarrí expedition, 14, 181n3
Unanue, Felipe Jacobo de, 462, 473, 480
Unanue, Juan Antonio de: and *acequia* dispute, 302; collects tithe goods, 24; and García discipline case, 322, 335; and illegal trading case, 384–85; and Isidro Sánchez case, 262, 271, 276–77; and livestock mandate, 405; and silk clothes contract, 350, 358; and wounded soldier case, 310, 314
Uribarrí. *See* Ulibarrí
Urrisola, Manuel Costillo, 560
Utes, 13; attack Jemez, 14; campaigns against, 14, 19, 147n21, 471; and Juan Joseph Lobato, 509n6; keeping peace with, 526–27; threaten Comanches, 14, 368–69, 372, 377, 382; and trade, 23, 526–27, 563, 566–69

Valdés, Catalina de, 124n3
Valdés, José Luis, 515n2
Valdés y Bustos, Francisco, 511, 515n2
Valdez, Ángela Francisca de, 449–54, 460n1–2
Valdez, Domingo, 450–54, 460n3
Valdez, José, 515n2
Valdez, José Luis, 450–54, 460n6
Valencia, 366n2
Valenzuela, Inés, 234n11
Valenzuela, Martín de, 224, 234n11
Vallejo, Ángela Teresa, 348n10–11, 420n28
Vallejo, Antonio, 82n7, 159n14, 448n13
Vallejo, Bernardo, 300, 416, 420n42, 439–43
Vallejo, Juan, 80, 83n11, 415, 439–40, 448n12–13
Vallejo, Lugardo, 329, 348n10–11, 416, 420n27, 440–41, 448n12–13
Vallejo, Margarita, 419n25
Valverde, Josepha, 477n1
Valverde Cosío, Antonio de, 36, 240, 403n17; abolishes *cabildo*, 21; biography of, 40n8; campaigns of, 14; as captain of El Paso presidio, 40n8, 93, 96, 125–26, 133; charges against, 15, 124n4; and hostile Apaches, 125–26; and illegal trade, 56n5; leads military escort, 131; as lieutenant governor, 90n8; orders livestock branding, 510; sends

cabildo members to Mexico City, 21, 33; stock-raising operations of, 17, 40n8
Valverde y Cosio, Juana de, 293n3
vara (cane), 152
varas, 65, 78n13, 93, 536–37, 542n2
Varela, Antonio, 80, 324–25, 348n6
Varela, Catalina, 348n10
Varela, Cristóbal, 80, 82n5, 82n8, 348n6
Varela, Francisca, 348n12
Varela, Jacinto, 404–05, 407n5–6, 415
Varela, Juana, 367n13
Varela, Luisa, 348n10, 420n28
Varela, María, 366n1, 420n32, 552n4
Varela, María Bárbara Viviana, 420n33
Varela, Nicolosa, 147n30
Varela, Pedro, 404–05, 407n1, 407n5–6, 466, 490n12
Varela de Losada, Antonia, 420n37
Varela de Losada, Cristóbal, 82n8
Varela de Losada, Diego, 82n8
Varela Jaramillo, Angelina, 83n11, 448n12
Varela Jaramillo, Catalina, 124n14
Varela Jaramillo, Cristóbal I, 82n7, 293n12, 407n2–3, 448n2–3. *See also* Jaramillo, Cristóbal I
Varela Jaramillo, Cristóbal II, 82n8. *See also* Jaramillo, Cristóbal II
Varela Jaramillo, Francisca, 407n3. *See also* Jaramillo, Francisca
Varela Jaramillo, Gregorio, 448n2. *See also* Jaramillo, Gregorio
Varela Jaramillo, Jacinto, 420n33
Varela Jaramillo, Juan Francisco, 80, 82n2, 407n1–2
Varela Jaramillo, Pedro, 407n1
Varela Jaramillo, Teresa, 261, 407n6. *See also* Jaramillo, Teresa
Vargas, Governor Diego de, 12–13, 39n2, 40n8, 40n14, 56n7, 57, 608n13; campaign journal of, 234n9; and church sanctuary, 221–23; death of, 55n2, 56n11; and land grants, 90n5, 239n2, 431; leads Reconquest, 14, 33, 544; and list of *parajes*, 146n1; muster list of, 18; officers of, 56n14, 77n7, 147n34, 181n4, 240; and presidio supply price list, 17, 60n2; and prices of trade goods, 41–46; prohibits carrying of weapons, 196–97; prohibits gambling, 61, 124n12; settlers returning with, 367n10, 420n26; and trade restrictions, 41–46
Vargas, Manuela de, 181n1
Vargas, Sebastián de, 454, 460n12, 460n14
Vásquez, Antonio, 167
Vásquez, José, 181n2
Vásquez, Joseph, 160–70, 181n2
Vásquez Baca, María, 419n8, 419n12
Vásquez Borrego, Diego, 260n5, 350, 367n7
Vectia, Diego de. *See* Abeytia, Diego (vectia)
Vega, Cristóbal de la, 90n1
Vega y Coca, Francisca, 239n7
Vega y Cosa, Leonarda de la, 607n1
veiled, 451–54, 460n10
Velarde, Antonio Pérez, 262–71, 293n3
Velasco, Ana, 147n26
Velasco, Cristóbal, 12
Velasco, Diego, 40n4
Velasco Armijo, Juan, 448n13
Velásquez, Francisco, 152, 159n12, 271–76
Vélez Cachupín, Governor Thomas, 28, 212n9, 214, 369, 448n7, 490n5; campaigns of, 14; and *colcha* dispute, 577, 580; collects tithe goods, 17; and land grants, 576n13; mandates trade regulations, 524; orders fencing of Taos property, 516–19; orders military equipment inventory, 544, 558–60; orders registry of land titles/livestock brands, 510; orders settlers to defend themselves, 79; proceedings against, 483; settles traders' disputes, 491–93, 495–96, 500, 509n13, 564, 570, 584–86, 591, 597, 609n21; views on Antonio Baca, 535n8; views on Francisco Esquibel, 552n3; views on Juan José Moreno, 542n4; views on Juan Joseph Lobato, 509n6; views on Nicolás Ortiz III, 608n11; views on Tomás de Sena, 553n7; views on Tomás Madrid, 482n1
Ventura, Miguel, 563–70, 575n2
verbal insults, 77n2, 322, 431–32, 437–43, 448n14, 517, 637
Verdugo de Haro y Ávila, Martín, 93, 104n8

vicario, 646, 648n3
viceroy, 213n18, 250n1, 432; appointments of, 21, 104n9; approves funding, 30n58; and council of war, 133–35, 148n36; investigations of, 56n14; and lawsuits, 20; and livestock branding, 510; petitions to, 19, 33–37, 470–73, 478–80, 482n3, 482n5, 544; places duty on tobacco, 77n6; policies of, 16; portraits of, **242**, **433**, **479**; and sending mail, 104n6; and weapon prohibition *bando*, 196. *See also* specific names
Vigil, Francisco, 471
Vigil, Francisco Montes, 132, 134–35, 147n22, 149–50
Vigil, Manuel, 18, 147n22, 612, 614–16, 621–22, 633n5
Vigil, Pedro, 478–79, 482n2
Villalpando, Catalina, 523n5
Villalpando, Pablo Francisco de, 517–20, 523n5, 585
Villa Nueva de Santa Cruz, 44, 61–70. *See also* Santa Cruz de la Cañada
Villas (chartered towns), 20, 31n88, 33
Villasur, Pedro, 14–15, 30n48, 516
Villasur expedition: description of, 14–15, 30n48; Indians killed during, 608n13; soldiers killed during, 78n10, 78n14, 104n15–16, 105n17–18, 147n27, 213n19, 523n6; survivors of, 40n9, 294n13, 319n2, 543n8, 608n16

war, 28, 30n61, 36, 79, 552n3, 608n11; among hostile tribes, 526; with Apaches, 35, 132–36, 148n36; and capture of slaves, 27, 84; constant threat of, 13–14, 43, 527; councils of, 132–36; defensive, 148n36; drums, 558–59; expenses relating to, 45, 57–58; "just," 16, 84; petitions regarding, 35, 43. *See also* junta de guerra (council of war)
water, 21, 576n5; *guaje* (gourd) used for, 272, 294n15; holes for, 146n1, 146n16; rights, 22–23, 295–302, 308n1, 419n21, 420n26, 437–41, 448n11; Spanish policy towards, 437, 448n11. *See also* acequias (irrigation ditches)
wax candles, 245
weapons. *See* arms; specific types
weavers, 147n33, 366n2
wheat, 25–26, 64, 110, 163
wills, 21; of Antonio Pacheco, 260n7; of Antonio Vallejos, 159n14; of Baca family, 419n11, 510, 523n3, 535n8; brands/branding irons mentioned in, 510; clothing listed in, 159n14; contested, 82n6; of Francisco Xavier Fragoso, 552n3, 608n18, 633n2; hides mentioned in, 576n7; horses mentioned in, 523n3; of Juan Gabaldón, 542n7; of Juan Gallegos, 260n8; of Juan José Moreno, 542n4, 576n7; of Luis Jaramillo, 542n3; of Manuel Mares, 235; of Manuel Vigil, 18; of merchants/traders, 24; of Miguel Coca, 90n1; of Miguel Lucero, 32n119; of Salvador Montoya, 482n2, 510; of Vicente Armijo, 239n2, 239n8, 420n32
wine, 26, 40n8
witchcraft, 202, 211, 321, 420n31, 483–86, 489n2, 490n9–12
wood, 35, 40n6, **63**, 85, 131, **153**, 241, 370, 403n20, 462, 516, 566, 611
wool, 19, 26, 408–09, 414–16, 465–67, 468n3, 499

Ydala, Sente Asencio, 594

Zacatecas, Mexico, 82n9, 93, 104n5, 104n8, 104n15–16, 105n17, 147n22, 184n2, 195n5, 239n2, 261, 265, 293n6, 294n14, 448n13, 482n2, 654n6
Zaldivar Jorge, Nicolasa, 260n10
Zamora, Antonio, 415, 419n25, 420n44
Zamora, Juan Antonio, 416
Zamora, Juan de, 420n44
Zamora, Spain, 523n4
Zamora Martín, Diego Antonio, 419n25
Zamora Martínez, Antonio, 419n25
Zárate, Ascensio de, 210–11
Zia Pueblo: *alcaldes mayores* of, 106, 124n2, 535n8; and *bando* restricting trade, 529; and baptism of Apaches, 86; church of, 535n8; and trade, 368
Zuni Pueblo, 12–13, 84, 124n4, 469n17; *alcaldes mayores* of, 104n10, 431–32, 436n1, 608n13; deaths in, 29, 460n6; and ironwork, 491–92; revolt of, 14; sheep of, 494; and soldiers, 106, 123n2; and trade, 368, 491–93, 496

www.ingramcontent.com/pod-product-compliance
Lightning Source LLC
Chambersburg PA
CBHW080750300426
44114CB00020B/2688